The American Re[public] to 1877

Features and Benefits

Dynamic Instructional Structure

...presents a clear and comprehensive coverage of American history.
- Engaging section introductions include Reading Preview, Reading Strategy, and An American Story.
- Two Viewpoints, What If…, and Why It Matters features provide opportunities for discussion and in-depth examination of historical issues.
- The Primary Sources Library allows students to read and analyze primary source documents from throughout history.

A Strong Reading Strand

...encourages active reading and learning for students of all reading levels.
- Foldables help students organize key concepts as they read.
- The CRISS Pedagogy and CRISS Purpose for Reading in each chapter provide concrete methods for helping students read in the content area.
- Reading Checks in every section keep students on track as they read the narrative.
- Various activities throughout are identified as Reading Strategies.
- America's Literature enables students to share a wealth of literary experiences.

Differentiated Instruction

...makes *The American Republic to 1877* accessible to students of all learning levels.
- Differentiated Instruction activities are specifically designed and leveled for students of different abilities, according to Gardner's theory of Multiple Intelligences.
- Activities throughout the book are provided for varying levels of learners, including less proficient readers, English learners, and gifted and talented students.

Standardized Test Preparation

...gives students the opportunity to practice for state and national exams.
- Chapter assessments provide chapter-specific multiple choice practice questions.
- Test-Taking Tip helps students learn how to successfully approach test questions.

A Variety of Activities and Features

...are essential for student success and get students excited about history.
- Geographic Skills maps throughout the book give students the opportunity to interpret different types of maps and apply geography skills.
- Geography & History features draw students in with engaging narratives and opportunities for analyzing how geography impacts history.
- Skillbuilders emphasize skill development—from reading maps to analyzing primary and secondary sources.
- TIME Notebooks allow students to step into the past, learning about every day life in various periods.

Teacher Resources

...provide convenient strategies to help new and experienced teachers.
- Unit Resources provides background information to help you prepare for each unit.
- Fast File™ unit resources contain important reproducible masters.

Technology

...provides time-saving software products to help you creatively engage your students and reduce your prep time.
- *The American Republic to 1877* Video Program
- TeacherWorks™ All-in-One Planner and Resource Center
- A text-specific Web site provides Online study tools such as chapter overviews, student self-check quizzes, and textbook updates to ensure that your classroom presentation is current and accurate.

Improving Active Reading and Study Skills

Dinah Zike's FOLDABLES™

Foldables are easy-to-make, three-dimensional, interactive graphic organizers that students create out of plain sheets of paper. The Teacher Classroom Resources includes *Dinah Zike's Reading and Study Skills Foldables™*. This booklet provides you with step-by-step instructions for using Foldables in your classroom. Each Foldable is designed to be used as a study guide for the main ideas and key points presented in a chapter. Foldables can also be used for a more in-depth investigation of a concept, idea, opinion, event, or a person or place studied in a chapter. These unique hands-on tools for studying and reviewing were created exclusively for Glencoe by education specialist Dinah Zike.

Why Use Foldables in Social Studies?

Because they:

- organize, display, and arrange information, making it easier for students to grasp social studies concepts, theories, facts, opinions, questions, research, and ideas.

- are student-made study guides that are compiled as students listen for main ideas, read main ideas, or conduct research.

- integrate language arts, the sciences, and mathematics into the study of social studies.

- provide a multitude of creative formats in which students can present projects, research, interviews, and inquiry-based reports.

- replace teacher-generated writing or photocopied sheets with student-generated print.

- incorporate the use of such skills as comparing and contrasting, recognizing cause-and-effect, and finding similarities and differences.

- continue to immerse students in previously learned vocabulary, concepts, information, generalizations, ideas, and theories, providing them with a strong foundation that they can build upon with new observations, concepts, and knowledge.

- can be used by students or teachers to easily communicate data through graphs, tables, charts, models, and diagrams, including Venn diagrams.

- allow students to make their own journals for recording observations, research information, primary and secondary source data, surveys, and so on.

- can be used as alternative assessment tools by teachers to evaluate student progress or by students to evaluate their own progress.

- provide a sense of student ownership or investiture in the social studies curriculum.

Student Edition, p. 305 ▶

FOLDABLES™ Study Organizer

Cause-and-Effect Study Foldable Make this foldable to help you analyze the causes and effects of growth in the East and expansion into the West of the United States.

Step 1 Fold one sheet of paper in half from top to bottom.

Step 2 Fold it in half again, from side to side.

Step 3 Unfold the paper once. Sketch an outline of the United States across both tabs and label them as shown.

Step 4 Cut up the fold of the top flap only.

This cut will make two tabs.

Reading and Writing As you read the chapter, list causes and effects of eastern growth and western expansion under the appropriate tabs of your foldable.

The American Republic

To 1877

Joyce Appleby, Ph.D.

Alan Brinkley, Ph.D.

Albert S. Broussard, Ph.D.

James M. McPherson, Ph.D.

Donald A. Ritchie, Ph.D.

NATIONAL GEOGRAPHIC

 Glencoe

New York, New York   Columbus, Ohio   Chicago, Illinois   Peoria, Illinois   Woodland Hills, California

Authors

Joyce Appleby, Ph.D. is Professor of History at UCLA. Dr. Appleby's published works include *Inheriting the Revolution: The First Generation of Americans; Capitalism and a New Social Order: The Jeffersonian Vision of the 1790s;* and *Ideology and Economic Thought in Seventeenth-Century England,* which won the Berkshire Prize. She served as president of both the Organization of American Historians and the American Historical Association, and chaired the Council of the Institute of Early American History and Culture at Williamsburg. Dr. Appleby has been elected to the American Philosophical Society and the American Academy of Arts and Sciences, and is a Corresponding Fellow of the British Academy.

Alan Brinkley, Ph.D. is Allan Nevins Professor of American History at Columbia University. His published works include *Voices of Protest: Huey Long, Father Coughlin, and the Great Depression,* which won the 1983 National Book Award; *The End of Reform: New Deal Liberalism in Recession and War; The Unfinished Nation: A Concise History of the American People;* and *Liberalism and its Discontents.* He received the Levenson Memorial Teaching Prize at Harvard University.

Albert S. Broussard, Ph.D. is Professor of History and Graduate Coordinator at Texas A&M University. Before joining the Texas A&M faculty, Dr. Broussard was Assistant Professor of History and Director of the African American Studies Program at Southern Methodist University. Among his publications are the books *Black San Francisco: The Struggle for Racial Equality in the West, 1900–1954* and *African American Odyssey: The Stewarts, 1853–1963.* Dr. Broussard has also served as president of the Oral History Association.

James M. McPherson, Ph.D. is George Henry Davis Professor of American History at Princeton University. Dr. McPherson is the author of 11 books about the Civil War era. These include *Battle Cry of Freedom: The Civil War Era,* for which he won the Pulitzer Prize in 1989, and *For Cause and Comrades: Why Men Fought in the Civil War,* for which he won the 1998 Lincoln Prize. He is a member of many professional historical associations, including the the Civil War Preservation Trust.

Donald A. Ritchie, Ph.D. is Associate Historian of the United States Senate Historical Office. Dr. Ritchie received his doctorate in American history from the University of Maryland after service in the U.S. Marine Corps. He has taught American history at various levels, from high school to university. He edits the Historical Series of the Senate Foreign Relations Committee and is the author of several books, including *Doing Oral History; The Oxford Guide to the United States Government;* and *Press Gallery: Congress and the Washington Correspondents,* which received the Organization of American Historians Richard W. Leopold Prize. Dr. Ritchie has served as president of the Oral History Association and as a council member of the American Historical Association.

The National Geographic Society, founded in 1888 for the increase and diffusion of geographic knowledge, is the world's largest nonprofit scientific and educational organization. Since its earliest days, the Society has used sophisticated communication technologies, from color photography to holography, to convey knowledge to a worldwide membership. The School Publishing Division supports the Society's mission by developing innovative educational programs—ranging from traditional print materials to multimedia programs including CD-ROMs, videodiscs, and software. "National Geographic Geography & History," featured in each unit of this textbook, was designed and developed by the National Geographic Society's School Publishing Division.

About the Cover The background images on the cover show immigrants bound for the United States. The smaller images, from left to right, are: Native American of the Southwest, Abigail Adams, statue of Thomas Jefferson, pioneers traveling west, and Civil War soldier.

 Glencoe

The McGraw·Hill Companies

Send all inquiries to:
Glencoe/McGraw-Hill, 8787 Orion Place, Columbus, Ohio 43240–4027

ISBN 0-07-860983-6 (Student Edition) ISBN 0-07-860984-4 (Teacher Wraparound Edition)
Printed in the United States of America.
4 5 6 027/043 08 07 06 05

Academic Consultants

Richard G. Boehm, Ph.D.
Professor of Geography
Southwest Texas State University
San Marcos, Texas

Margo J. Byerly, Ph.D.
Assistant Professor of Social
    Studies Methods
Ball State University
Muncie, Indiana

Maureen D. Danner
Project CRISS
National Training Consultant
Kalispell, MT

Frank de Varona
Visiting Associate Professor
Department of Curriculum and
    Instruction
Florida International University
Miami, Florida

FOLDABLES **Dinah Zike**
Educational Consultant
Dinah–Might Activities, Inc.
San Antonio, Texas

William E. Nelson, Jr., Ph.D.
Research Professor of Black Studies and
    Professor of Political Science
The Ohio State University
Columbus, Ohio

Bernard Reich, Ph.D.
Professor of Political Science and
    International Affairs
George Washington University
Washington, D.C.

Carol Santa, Ph.D.
CRISS Project Developer
Kalispell, MT

Elmer Whitcraft
Project CRISS Master Trainer
Kalispell, MT

Teacher Reviewers

Barbara P. Barge
Teacher
Woodlake Hills Middle School
San Antonio, Texas

John R. Doyle
Director, Division of Social Sciences
Dade County Public Schools
Miami, Florida

Bette Gilmore
Campus Instructional Specialist
Killeen Independent School District
Killeen, Texas

Harry J. Hancock
Social Studies Teacher
Theodore Roosevelt Middle School
Kenner, Louisiana

Mary Lynn Johnson
Program Director for Social Studies
Spring Independent School District
Houston, Texas

Tony Murillo
Teacher
Socorro Middle School
El Paso, Texas

Ronald A. Murphy
Classroom Teacher
Grand Prairie High School
Grand Prairie, Texas

Elysa E. Toler Robinson, Ed.D.
Program Supervisor
Detroit Public Schools
Detroit, Michigan

Kay R. Selah
Social Studies Teacher
Landmark Middle School
Jacksonville, Florida

Deborah N. Smith
Social Studies Teacher
New Albany Middle School
New Albany, Ohio

Larry John Smith
United States History Teacher
Mt. Savage School
Mt. Savage, Maryland

Melissa Taylor
Teacher
Twin Creeks Middle School
Spring, Texas

Renée Marie Trufant
Social Studies and Communications
    Skills Teacher
Brevard Middle School
Brevard, North Carolina

Sonya Lou Weaver
Social Studies Teacher
Greencastle-Antrim Middle School
Greencastle, Pennsylvania

Glenda Gail Williams
Classroom Teacher
Webb Middle School
Garland, Texas

Carol Davenport Wood
Social Studies Teacher
Lusher Extension
New Orleans, Louisiana

Contents

UNIT 1

Different Worlds Meet   12
Beginnings to 1625

UNIT 2

Colonial Settlement   66
1587–1770

UNIT 3

Creating a Nation   128
1763–1791

Contents

Two ViewPoints

More About...

Technology & History

Linking Past & Present

What If...

You Decide

TIME NOTEBOOK

Why It Matters

Causes and Effects

Features

What *Life* Was Like...

America's LITERATURE

SKILLBUILDER

Critical Thinking

Social Studies

Study & Writing

Technology

People In History

Fact Fiction Folklore

Primary Source Quotes

A variety of quotations and excerpts throughout the text express the thoughts, feelings, and life experiences of people, past and present.

Abigail Adams

Primary Source Quotes

> *"They have driven us from the sea to the lakes— we can go no farther."*
>
> —*Tecumseh*

Frederick Douglass

Charts & Graphs

NATIONAL GEOGRAPHIC Maps

NATIONAL GEOGRAPHIC **Missions in New Spain by the 1800s**

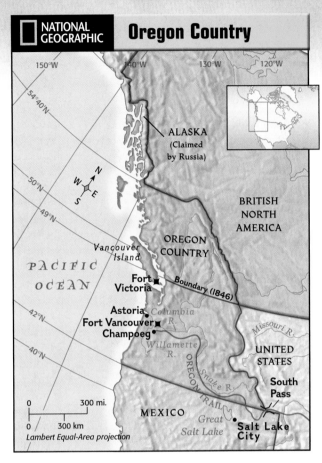

NATIONAL GEOGRAPHIC **Oregon Country**

Project CRISS

How Can I Teach My Students How to Learn Social Studies?

by Carol M. Santa, Ph.D

We all know that teaching social studies involves far more than teaching just course content. We understand that students need to become engaged, confident learners. Achieving that goal means helping them to understand, organize, and retain information.

Teaching Both Content and Skills

In other words, we want our students to have the skills and confidence to be life-long learners. With its rich content, social studies offers an ideal arena for teaching both content and skills.

✔ **A Dual Responsibility** Let's take a moment to consider why the dual responsibility of teaching both content and skills is so important. Think back to your own middle and high school years. What do you remember about the content

you learned? If I recall my experiences, I find I remember remarkably little content. What did I learn in biology or history? What did my textbooks look like? As the years go by, I don't even remember the names of most of my teachers.

✔ **An Inspiring Teacher** Yet I have vivid memories of my eighth-grade social studies teacher, who came out of retirement to fill in for a history teacher who left on maternity leave. I remember how fascinated I became with ancient history; I recall giving oral reports and how she helped me become comfortable speaking before a group. In fact, I remember more from her class than any other I took during high school.

✔ **Teach How to Learn** More important, I now understand that she taught me to learn how to learn. She showed me how to underline, how to organize information using different note-taking formats, and how to write coherent

answers on essay tests. She taught me the need to test myself on what I knew. And during that vulnerable, adolescent year, I went from being a mediocre student to being an excellent one.

This inspirational teacher did something else for me. At some point during that eighth-grade year, I decided to become a teacher. Later I realized that she had launched me on my professional mission—to spread her wisdom to others. Eventually this led to Project CRISS.

What is CRISS?

CRISS stands for **CR**eating **I**ndependence through **S**tudent-owned **S**trategies. It is a staff development program that I created in collaboration with middle and high school teachers in Kalispell, Montana.

✔ **Origin of CRISS** CRISS had its start 20 years ago in a lunchtime conversation in a teacher's lounge. One of the social studies teachers said, "My students aren't doing a good job of answering chapter questions. In fact, I don't think they even read my assignments. My reading assignments are becoming a waste of time!" His words struck a chord. "My students don't have a clue about how to study, and they don't write very well either," another teacher lamented.

✔ **Evolving Strategies** Supported by a state grant, we started working together to find practical ways to help students read, write, and learn content. We met in teams, read professional literature, and designed studies to test classroom strategies. From these efforts, we evolved a project to help students become better readers, writers, and

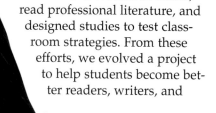

Tom & DeeAnn McCarthy/CORBIS STOCK MARKET

learners. Once the project took shape, we shared our discoveries with other teachers by offering a two- or three-day CRISS workshop to schools and districts in the state.

✔ **Constant Growth** Over the last two decades, Project CRISS has spread from teacher to teacher across this country, into Canada, and to several European countries. The project seems to sell itself. Teachers who use CRISS principles and strategies find that their students attain a deeper understanding of course content and become better readers, writers, and learners at the same time. In fact, data from numerous quantitative studies shows that using CRISS strategies improves student learning. (For the most recent data and for information on CRISS workshops, see www.projectcriss.com.)

CRISS Strategies in the Teacher Edition

When the editors of Glencoe/McGraw-Hill asked me and my colleagues to help them integrate CRISS strategies into their social studies texts, we welcomed the opportunity. In this teacher wraparound edition, we offer many references to CRISS strategies. We have packed the pages with strategies that help students gain a deeper understanding of specific content.

CRISS Training

We have one word of caution, however: the integration of CRISS strategies within this teacher wraparound edition does not take the place of a Project CRISS workshop, which provides an in-depth knowledge of CRISS. So, if you haven't yet participated in a CRISS workshop, we encourage you to do so. During a workshop, CRISS trainers take you step-by-step through the philosophy and instructional strategies. Participants are actively involved in all aspects of the program—practicing, adapting, and applying strategies to meet teaching needs.

Long-lasting change occurs when teachers and administrators work together to share, extend ideas, and problem solve. The most effective implementations occur when the initial workshop is supported by follow-up sessions, including a specific follow-up day. At this session, teachers bring examples of strategies they have used since the initial training. Part of this time may be spent in review and in learning new strategies. The rest of the time is for sharing applications. Additional on-going support can occur in teacher planning periods.

In any case, for those of you unfamiliar with Project CRISS, let's begin with a little background knowledge. In this way you will have some context for the various activities suggested throughout the teacher wraparound edition.

The CRISS Philosophy

The first thing to know is that Project CRISS is more than a collection of learning strategies. Its underlying power rests not on the individual strategies but on the teaching philosophy behind them. This philosophy integrates work from cognitive psychology, social learning theory, and neurological research about how the brain learns. It includes these overlapping principles:

✔ background knowledge and purposeful reading
✔ author's craft
✔ active involvement
✔ discussion
✔ organization
✔ writing
✔ teacher modeling

Let's look at each of these principles in more detail, along with examples of instructional strategies that illustrate them.

Background knowledge and purposeful reading are powerful determinants of reading comprehension.

Teachers involved in Project CRISS often talk about the importance of background knowledge. Readers are

(Continued on next page)

Using CRISS to Set a Purpose

Advice from Malla S. Kolhoff
Palm Harbor University High School
International Baccalaureate Program
Palm Harbor, Florida

As educators, it is our responsibility to set a purpose for historical reading. Students often must struggle to connect history with their own lives. To compare and contrast, establish cause and effect, and sequence events in chronological order presents a challenge for even the best reader. CRISS strategies allow students to move beyond words to the real significance for their society. With CRISS, my students are able to become engaged in the learning process through:

a. background knowledge
b. active reading, listening, and learning
c. discussion

d. metacognition
e. writing
f. organization
g. understanding

I have found that these strategies help my students attain a higher level of historical thinking and understanding.

Project CRISS

far more likely to learn new information when they have some previous knowledge and have a purpose in mind before they read or listen.

✔ **More Than Simply Reading** We warn students not to simply begin reading. We ask them, *"What might you already know about the topic? What questions do you have about the topic?"* We also remind them to preview the assignment and think about their goals for reading. We often have to be very explicit about the goals. For example, we might tell students, *"After reading this selection, you should be able to . . . ,"* or, *"After viewing the video, you should be able to identify. . . ."*

✔ **KWLH** In the teaching strategies included for each chapter in this book, we offer ideas for helping students tap into their background knowledge. For example, we suggest that students preview their reading assignment and consider what they already know about a topic. Or, we might develop a whole class **KWLH** chart (**K**now, **W**ant to learn, **L**earned, **H**ow to learn more), where students work on this task together. They can generate questions about what they want to learn, and then, after completing the assignment, they can list the new information they have learned and how they can learn more.

K	W	L	H
What I **Know**	What I **Want** to Find Out	What I **Learned**	**How** I Can Learn More

✔ **Reading Goals** We also suggest ways to make sure your students have clear goals for their reading. Each section opener lists reading strategies and main ideas that outline reading goals. Most students will skip over this material and simply start reading. Teachers need to help students understand that the reading goals are important tools for understanding. We tell students, *"Don't ignore your purposes for reading. Take time to think about them before delving into your reading."* Project CRISS also provides hints about how to get students to use these purpose statements to evaluate whether they have understood their reading.

Good readers have an intuitive understanding of the author's craft.

When students know how authors craft their writing, they can more readily understand and remember what they read.

✔ **Pay Attention** Good readers and writers know that paying attention to how text is organized—its headings and paragraphs, for example—makes it easier to comprehend its content. Good readers will analyze the author's style of presentation as they read. They might ask themselves, *"What is this author doing to help me learn key concepts? How does the writer lead me from one idea to the next?"* When students become aware of what the author is doing to impart content, they have a clearer idea of what the author is saying.

✔ **The Walk Through** In the sample lesson on pages T18–T19, we offer advice about "walking through" the text to discover the author's style of presentation. Our suggestions go beyond examining the surface structure (headings, bold print, color coding of topical headings, italicized words) to analyzing how the author elaborates on key topics.

Effective learners are actively involved when they listen and read.

We learn best when we act on the information presented. We can do this by using a variety of organizing activities that require us to write, talk, and transform the information we are absorbing. None of us learns much from reading alone—it's far too passive.

CRISS strategies encourage active engagement in learning. We might ask students to read a section and describe what they are learning to a partner, or we might be more elaborate and have students develop concept maps or write summaries.

Students need many opportunities to talk with one another about what they are learning.

Discussion is critical to learning. The discussions we advocate are different from those in which the teacher remains the authority figure, with students simply reciting answers to

(Continued on next page)

Jose L. Pelaez/CORBIS STOCK MARKET

questions. If discussion becomes mere recitation and there is little interaction among students, little learning occurs. Thus we focus on how to get students to lead their own discussions about a topic. We want them to understand that it is their discussing, their oral grappling with meaning—not ours—that leads to deeper understanding.

Competent readers know several ways to organize information for learning.

Learning depends on organization. We show students different ways to organize information. They can take notes, underline selectively, develop concept maps, and summarize ideas in charts. Once we have taught students these techniques, we tell them, *"You have to do more than just read this assignment. How are you going to organize the information from this assignment? You have to change it, to transform it so that it becomes your own."*

For each chapter of this text, we offer ideas for assisting students in organizing information. Once students have learned a variety of organizing systems, we suggest ways to help them apply these structures independently.

Students deserve opportunities to write about what they are learning.

Writing is an integral part of the CRISS project. Writing lets us figure out what we know and what we still need to know. We cannot write about something we do not understand. While we teach students how to write expository papers and essay exams, we also encourage students to write more informally by questioning, speculating, and writing explanations in learning logs. We make sure that students are writing continually about what they are learning.

For each chapter of this text, we offer ideas for assisting students in organizing information. Once students have learned a variety of organizing systems, we suggest ways to help them apply these structures independently.

Teaching involves explanation and modeling.

Our final principle has to do with our own teaching. Students learn to think strategically when we use these processes as part of our instruction. Our demonstrations are especially critical for struggling readers. Most have never been taught how to learn.

We have to show them how.
- ✔ **Take Center Stage** When you introduce a new strategy, you should take the center stage: showing, telling, modeling, demonstrating, and explaining not only the content but the process of active reading. As students learn, gradually release responsibility to them. Strategy instruction involves two overlapping steps. First we explain what the strategy is and why students should use it. If students do not know why they are performing an activity, they will rarely use the activity on their own. Next, we demonstrate and talk about procedures for carrying out the strategy. We discuss, demonstrate, and think aloud while modeling. Then, students practice under our guidance and feedback.
- ✔ **A Systematic Approach** Project CRISS is a valuable basis for instruction. It provides a systematic approach for using what we now know about teaching and learning. The following chart lists questions we need to continually ask ourselves while we are teaching. Use this chart to monitor your efforts to incorporate CRISS principles into your teaching.

CRISS Principles	The CRISS Philosophy	Yes	No	Somewhat
Background knowledge:	Did I assist students in thinking about what they already knew about the topic before beginning the unit? Did I develop necessary concepts before students read?			
Purpose setting:	Did my students have a clear purpose about what they were going to learn before beginning the lesson?			
Author's craft:	Can my students use the author's style of presentation to facilitate their understanding?			
Active involvement:	Were my students engaged in the topic? Did I help students become actively involved in their learning?			
Discussion:	Did my students have opportunities to talk about what they were learning?			
Organization:	Did my students organize information in a variety of ways?			
Writing:	Did my students write about what they were learning?			
Teacher modeling:	Did I do enough teacher modeling of learning strategies so that students could begin doing them on their own?			

Project CRISS

How Do I Use Project CRISS to Teach The American Republic to 1877?

When students know how authors structure their writing, they can better understand and remember what they read. For the first several chapters of this book, show students how to analyze the author's craft by "walking through" the chapter. Then show students how to use the author's organization to develop two-column notes.

To demonstrate these strategies, make transparencies of pages 14-19 of Chapter I *The First Americans.* Then organize students into small groups to complete the following activities.

Michael Zabe/Museo Templo Mayor

Introducing the Chapter

Place a transparency of pages 14-15 on the overhead and begin modeling.

Tell students: *"Before reading a text, I take time to figure out how the author has presented the information. The authors of this book have a consistent organization plan for presenting information. Let's discover what it is."*

Ask students to turn to page 14 and 15. Then say: *"In your small groups, read through these two pages and discuss the following questions:*

✔ *What type of information has the author included?*

✔ *How might you use this information* (Why It Matters, the Foldables, the Timeline) *to understand the content of this chapter?*

✔ *How do these pages help you gain an overview of what you will learn?*

✔ *How might you use the reference to History Online to expand your understanding of the chapter? Be prepared to share what you have discovered with the whole class."*

✔ Ask students to turn to page 15. *"Why do you think the chapter includes a Foldables Study Organizer?"* (as an organizing aid, to outline themes and important events covered in the chapter)

Introducing the Section

Guide to Reading

Direct students to page 16. *"Notice how this page is organized."* (It begins with a Guide to Reading that includes the Main Idea, Key Terms, Reading Strategy, Read to Learn, and Section Theme.) *"Let's take a moment and talk about how these features might help you."*

Main Ideas

"Why has the author included the main ideas at the beginning of the section?" (to let readers know what they will learn, help them think about what they already know about the topic, and help them set reading goals)

Key Terms

"Now look at the list of key terms (artifact, archaeology, etc.) *and skim the first several pages of the chapter. What do you notice about how the key terms are sequenced and highlighted in this chapter?"* (The key terms are highlighted in blue and presented in the same order as in the chapter.)

Reading Strategy

"Notice the reading strategy suggested for this section. How could you use it to organize the information for learning?"

Read to Learn

"Why has the author included these questions?" (to help readers set goals or purposes for reading the chapter) *"Keep these questions in mind as you read. After reading, see if you can answer them."*

Section Theme

"Read the information presented under the Section Theme. Why did the author include this?" (helps readers begin to think about what they know; links an important concept to the chapter content)

Timeline

"Why has the author included another timeline for this section? How might this timeline help you understand the content?" (to provide an overview of the time period for this section, and to organize information)

An American Story

Ask students to read this excerpt. *"Why has the author included this section at the beginning of each chapter?"* (providing background knowledge, generating interest in reading the selection)

Walking Through the Narrative

As you talk aloud, note features on chapter transparencies of pages 14–19. *"Now let's see how the authors have helped us figure out the main topics in this chapter. Notice the bold print heading. The main topics are printed in larger blue print and the subtopics are printed in smaller red print. This organization and color coding should help me figure out what is important.*

At the end of each subsection, I notice a Reading Check. There are also assessments at the end of each section (page 19). The Reading Check questions will help me know if I have understood each subsection. When I come to a reading check, I will stop and try to answer the question. If I can't, I will reread. I should read through these questions before I begin reading. In this way, I would know what I am supposed to get out of this section.

As I continue my walk-through of the chapter, I also notice the illustrations throughout this section, the visual depicting the Causes and Effects of Migration on page 17 and the map of Prehistoric Migration Through the Americas on page 18. I realize these illustrations contain important information for understanding the content. I should never just skip over them."

Reading the Chapter

Ask students to read the first section of the chapter (pages 16-19). Remind them to pay close attention to the bold print topics and vocabulary words. Prompt them to look for the reading check questions in the section.

Main Idea-Detail Notes

Ask students to divide their notebook paper into two columns to create a graphic organizer like the one on the right. Explain that they will record key points in the left column and details explaining the key points in the right column. Main points should be questions or key words. Students then use their notes as a study guide. They can use the key words or questions to quiz themselves.

✔ Demonstrate how to use the author's clues (headings, bold print vocabulary) to develop main idea-detail notes. On a blank transparency develop two-column notes over the first section of the chapter while students take notes at their desks. Model how to include main topics and the terms essential to understanding content in the left column. On the right record details that elaborate on the main points. Talk about being brief and using your own words. Explain why making the author's message your own insures better comprehension and retention.

✔ Continue modeling notes over the rest of this section. Then ask students to work in pairs or small groups to develop two-column notes for the rest of the chapter. Ask students to share their notes in a class discussion.

✔ Demonstrate how to use the note to test themselves. Show students how you cover the right column with a sheet of paper and recite what you can remember. Talk about why testing yourself is as important for learning. *"You are the only one who knows if you know. Self-testing is an excellent way to learn and to check your understanding."*

✔ Take time for reflection. After students have completed their notes, allow time for discussion about these strategies. Ask students to write and then to talk about how analyzing the author's craft and developing two-column notes helped them read and learn, and how they might use these strategies in the future.

N. Carter/North Wind Picture Archive

SAMPLE ORGANIZER

Main Ideas	Details
Archaeology	study ancient cultures using artifacts
Coming to America	1. land bridge created between Asia and America during Ice Age 2. nomads migrated across land bridge searching for food 3. wild animals were plentiful 4. early Americans became skilled hunters 5. many different groups lived in the Americas
Building communities	1. early Americans fished, hunted, and gathered 2. early Americans found ways to plant and grow their own food 3. many people gave up nomadic way of like to settle in one place 4. people built permanent homes and developed customs

Reading in the Content Areas

How Can I Use Jamestown Education Products to Help Struggling Readers?

For over 30 years, Jamestown Education has made its primary focus helping older readers become better readers. The Jamestown products shown on this page support the basic elements of reading cited by the National Reading Panel. Each of them can help your struggling readers become better readers.

Timed Readings Plus in Social Studies

✔ **Reading Levels:**   4-13+

✔ **Benefits:**

This ten-book series will help your students increase both reading rate and comprehension. The nonfiction passages cover current social studies topics and are similar to those found on both state and national tests. Each of the two-part lessons focuses on reading rate, factual recall, comprehension strategies, and higher-level critical thinking skills.

Reading in the Content Areas: Social Studies

✔ **Reading Levels:** 4-12+

✔ **Benefits:**

This book concentrates on six essential reading skills that will help your students better comprehend what they read. Seventy-five high-interest nonfiction passages written at increasing levels of difficulty, followed by consistent, targeted skills, teach the techniques needed to organize, understand, and apply information.

Reading Fluency

✔ **Reading Levels:**   1-10

✔ **Benefits:**

This seven-book series will help your students read smoothly, accurately and expressively. Students work in pairs to provide immediate feedback and self-assessment. Author Camille Blachowicz states that "the ability to read fluently is highly correlated with many other measures of reading competence."

Jamestown's Reading Improvement

✔ **Reading Levels**   4-10

✔ **Benefits:**

Authored by renowned reading expert Edward Fry, this eight-book series focuses on helping build your students' comprehension, vocabulary, and skimming and scanning skills. Repeated practice with targeted exercises ensures mastery of valuable reading skills.

Critical Reading Series
✔ **Reading Levels:** 2-8
✔ **Benefits:**

This twenty-four book high-interest series, written at three reading spans, encourages your reluctant readers to build a love for nonfiction while focusing on critical reading skills. Topics ranging from Fateful Journeys to Weird Science to Heroes draw students in, while giving students ample opportunities to master important skills found on both state and national tests.

To order Jamestown products, call 1-800-334-7344

In addition to the Project CRISS Reading Strategies, you may find it effective to implement some of the following instructional methods. They help *your* struggling students take increasing ownership of the reading process.

Reciprocal Teaching

Reciprocal teaching is characterized by a dialogue between you and your student, and ultimately among students in a group, in which students take the role of dialogue reader. Construction of meaning is built upon four reading strategies:

✔ **Summarizing** Readers identify the most important information in a segment of text and state that information in their own words. Summarizing involves students in recognizing and communicating the significant ideas in a text.

✔ **Questioning** Readers ask themselves questions about the text segment. Self-questioning aids comprehension by helping students identify where their understanding of the text has broken down and what they still need to know in order to understand what they have read.

✔ **Clarifying** Readers try to find answers to the question they have raised and to make sense of parts of the text that have caused confusion. They seek clarification by rereading, reading ahead or by seeking outside help, such as through a peer or a reference source.

✔ **Predicting** Readers tell what they think will happen next, basing their predictions on evidence from the text they have already read.

Modeling

An important element of strategic instruction is teacher modeling. As a part of the modeling process, think aloud as you apply a strategy to solve a reading problem, putting words to the inner voice that successful readers have with text and demonstrating the strategy used for understanding. To construct a "think-aloud," read aloud a passage, stopping at pertinent points to talk about what you are thinking. A think-aloud demonstrates the cognitive process and allows students to observe how a proficient reader approaches a problem with reading.

"Fix-Up" Strategies

Explain that readers perform certain tasks. Guide them through these following steps:

✔ **Stop** Tell students to stop and fix the problem when they do not understand.

✔ **Identify the Problem** Have students ask themselves when they stopped understanding and what they don't understand.

✔ **Apply a Fix-up Strategy** Encourage students to try these strategies:

✔ **Reread**

✔ **Read ahead**

✔ **Alter** the pace or voice

✔ **Ask** for help

CRISS and the Jamestown Reader

Advice from Dr. Sara Wartenberg
Palm Harbor University High School
International Baccalaureate Program
Palm Harbor, Florida

Help your students achieve testing success by combining CRISS strategies with the Jamestown Readers. The stories appeal to students of all reading levels. The stories are interesting and informative for students and teachers alike. Implementing CRISS strategies as students read the selections will help them respond with greater success to the questions that accompany each selection. Students will gain confidence and thus work for greater skill in reading comprehension and critical thinking.

Primary Source Strategies

How Do I Use Primary Sources in My Classroom?

A primary source is direct evidence of an event, idea, period, or development. It is an oral or written account obtained from actual participants in an event. Examples of primary sources include the following:

- ✔ official documents (records, statistics)
- ✔ political declarations, laws, and rules for governance
- ✔ speeches and interviews
- ✔ diaries, memoirs, and oral histories
- ✔ autobiographies
- ✔ recipes and cookbooks
- ✔ advertisements and posters
- ✔ letters

Physical objects, such as tools and dishes, can be primary sources; so can visual evidence in the form of fine art, photographs, maps, films, and videotapes. Primary sources can also include songs and audio recordings.

Why Use Primary Sources in Your Classroom?

Using primary sources to teach transforms the study of social studies from a passive process to an active one. Students become investigators—finding clues, formulating hypotheses and drawing inferences, making judgments, and reaching conclusions. Bringing primary sources into the classroom stimulates students to think critically about events, issues, and concepts rather than just memorizing dates, names, and generalizations reached by others.

Choosing Primary Sources

- ✔ Provide exposure to a variety of source types, including historic photographs, folk or popular music, financial records or household accounts, as well as letters, journals, and historic documents.
- ✔ When choosing print sources, consider the interests and reading levels of your students. Many texts contain challenging vocabulary and unfamiliar sentence structure. You may need to create a reader's guide that defines key vocabulary and paraphrases the main points of the reading.
- ✔ Some documents may be too long. Decide whether using an excerpt will provide enough information for students to draw conclusions.
- ✔ Depending upon the topic and your instructional objectives, you may need to provide several different primary sources to expose students to a variety of perspectives.
- ✔ Decide how students will access the primary sources: through the Internet, the library, a museum, or other print resources. Consider the possibility of an Internet virtual field trip for students. Moving from URL to URL, students can visit museum sites and other Web pages to view artifacts; interpret economic or census data; and read journals, letters, and official documents.

How Do I Introduce Students to Primary Sources?

Carefully explain the nature of primary sources when you introduce them to students. Although primary sources contain valuable clues, be sure to alert students that primary sources contain biases and prejudices, and must be approached with caution. Every primary source reflects the creator's point of view to some degree.

Using Primary Sources in the Classroom

Primary sources provide a rich source of inspiration for a variety of instructional strategies. They can be used to spark interest in a new topic, foster deeper exploration into a historical era, or assess students' understanding of social studies concepts and facts.

- ✔ **Pre-Reading Activities** Present a primary source for students to study at the beginning of a new chapter or topic. Have students analyze the source, using the questions and guidelines presented on the next page. Then have students make

Aaron Haupt

Anthony Redpath/CORBIS STOCK MARKET

Interpreting a Primary Source

Before students interpret a primary source, they need to know the context into which the source fits. Then they can use questions and guidelines, such as those below, to help them analyze and interpret the primary source.

Print Sources

- Who created the source, and what was the purpose for doing so?
- Did the writer personally experience or witness the event(s)?
- At what point did the writer record the information—as it happened or afterward? How long after?
- Who was the intended audience?
- Was the writer trying to record facts, express an opinion, or persuade others to take action?
- What is the author's main message?
- What values does the document convey?
- What bias does it reflect?
- What information about the topic can you gather from this document?
- Compare this document with what you know about the topic. Does it confirm those ideas or introduce a new perspective?
- How might other accounts about this topic support or modify the message this source delivers?

Visual Sources

- Who created the source, and what was the purpose for doing so?
- What does the image show?
- What mood does the image convey?
- Who or what dominates the image or catches your eye?
- How does the view impact the message?
- What details can you learn from the image?
- What is excluded from view?
- What bias does the visual reflect?
- What information about the topic can you gather from this visual?
- How might other visuals about this topic support or modify the message this one delivers?

Audio Sources

- Who created the source? What was the purpose for creating this source?
- What is the main idea of the audio?
- What mood does the recorder's voice convey?
- What bias does the audio text reflect?
- What information about the topic can you gather from this audio source?
- Compare the information in this source with what you already know about the topic. Does it confirm those ideas or introduce a new perspective?
- How might other sources about this topic support or modify the message that this one delivers?

predictions about what they might learn in the upcoming lessons.

✔ **Exploring Information** Provide a variety of primary sources related to a topic or time period. Have students compare and contrast the items, analyzing the information, making inferences, and drawing conclusions about the period.

✔ **Evaluation Activities** Have students evaluate a primary source and tell how it supports or refutes what they learned in the textbook or have students read a primary source document that provides one perspective on a topic, and have students write their own account, presenting another perspective or opinion.✦

Classroom Activity: Reading and Understanding Primary Sources

Advice from Leslie Espinosa
Humble Independent School District
Humble, Texas

1. Before class make a list of student reading partners. Make sure one of the two is a good reader.
2. Have students read a primary source document (or part of a primary source document), taking turns as they go. They should "mark" any words that they do not understand.
3. After each paragraph, the student pair should stop and paraphrase what it says in their own words.
4. Students should look up unfamiliar words they've marked and create an illustrated dictionary entry for each term (over the course of the year or semester).
5. Ask student pairs to present their paraphrased primary source to the rest of the class.

Addressing the Needs of Special Students

How Can I Help ALL My Students Learn Social Studies?

Today's classroom contains students from a variety of backgrounds and with a variety of learning styles, strengths, and challenges. With careful planning, you can address the needs of all students in the social studies classroom. The following tips for instruction can assist your efforts to help all students reach their maximum potential.

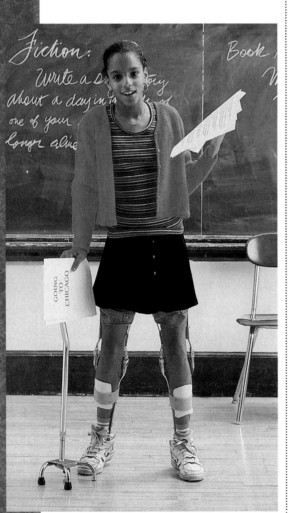

✔ Survey students to discover their individual differences. Use interest inventories of their unique talents so you can encourage contributions in the classroom.

✔ Model respect of others. Adolescents crave social acceptance. The student with learning differences is especially sensitive to correction and criticism—particularly when it comes from a teacher. Your behavior will set the tone for how students treat one another.

✔ Expand opportunities for success. Provide a variety of instructional activities that reinforce skills and concepts.

✔ Establish measurable objectives and decide how you can best help students meet them.

✔ Celebrate successes and praise "work in progress."

✔ Keep it simple. Point out problem areas—if doing so can help a student affect change. Avoid overwhelming students with too many goals at one time.

✔ Assign cooperative group projects that challenge all students to contribute to solving a problem or creating a product.

How Do I Reach Students with Learning Disabilities?

✔ Provide support and structure. Clearly specify rules, assignments, and responsibilities.

✔ Practice skills frequently. Use games and drills to help maintain student interest.

✔ Incorporate many modalities into the learning process. Provide opportunities to say, hear, write, read, and act out important concepts and information.

✔ Link new skills and concepts to those already mastered.

✔ Allow students to record answers on audiotape.

✔ Allow extra time to complete tests and assignments.

✔ Let students demonstrate proficiency with alternative presentations, including oral reports, role plays, art projects, and with music.

✔ Provide outlines, notes, or tape recordings of lecture material.

✔ Pair students with peer helpers, and provide class time for pair interaction.

How Do I Reach Students with Behavioral Disorders?

✔ Provide a structured environment with clear-cut schedules, rules, seat assignments, and safety procedures.

✔ Reinforce appropriate behavior and model it for students.

✔ Cue distracted students back to the task through verbal signals and teacher proximity.

✔ Set very small goals that can be achieved in the short term. Work for long-term improvement in the big areas.

How Do I Reach Students with Physical Challenges?

✔ Openly discuss with the student any uncertainties you have about when to offer aid.

✔ Ask parents or therapists and students what special devices or procedures are needed, and whether any special safety precautions need to be taken.

✔ Welcome students with physical challenges into all activities, including field trips, special events, and projects.

✔ Provide information to help able-bodied students and adults understand other students' physical challenges.

How Do I Reach Students with Visual Impairments?

✔ Facilitate independence. Modify assignments as needed.

✔ Teach classmates how and when to serve as guides.

✔ Limit unnecessary noise in the classroom, if it distracts the student with visual impairments.

✔ Provide tactile models whenever possible.

✔ Foster a spirit of inclusion. Describe people and events as they occur in the classroom. Remind classmates that students with visual impairments cannot interpret gestures and other forms of nonverbal communication.

✔ Provide taped lectures and reading assignments.

✔ Team the student with a sighted peer for written work.

How Do I Reach Students with Hearing Impairments?

✔ Seat students where they can see your lip movements easily and where they can avoid visual distractions.

✔ Avoid standing with your back to the window or light source.

✔ Use an overhead projector to maintain eye contact while writing.

✔ Seat students where they can see speakers.

✔ Write all assignments on the board, or hand out written instructions.

✔ If the student has a manual interpreter, allow both student and interpreter to select the most favorable seating arrangements.

✔ Teach students to look directly at each other when they speak.

How Do I Reach English Language Learners?

✔ Remember, students' ability to speak English does not reflect their academic abilities.

✔ Try to incorporate the students' cultural experience into your instruction. The help of a bilingual aide may be effective.

✔ Avoid cultural stereotypes.

✔ Pre-teach important vocabulary and concepts.

✔ Encourage students to preview text before they begin reading, noting headings, graphic organizers, photographs, and maps.

How Do I Reach Gifted Students?

✔ Make arrangements for students to take selected subjects early and to work on independent projects.

✔ Ask "what if" questions to develop high-level thinking skills. Establish an environment safe for risk taking.

✔ Emphasize concepts, theories, ideas, relationships, and generalizations.

✔ Promote interest in the past by inviting students to make connections to the present.

✔ Let students express themselves in alternate ways, such as creative writing, acting, debate, simulations, drawing, or music.

✔ Provide students with a catalog of helpful resources, listing such things as agencies that provide free and inexpensive materials, appropriate community services and programs, and community experts.

✔ Assign extension projects that allow students to solve real-life problems related to their communities. ✦

Customize Your Classroom!

**Advice from Marilyn Gerken
Pickerington Local Schools
Pickerington, Ohio**

Provide individualized activities and assignments for a variety of student ability levels. Develop learning packets for chapters and units of study with varying formats, levels, and types of assignments. Assign points and contract students based on their selection of activities to be completed. The activities in the Student Edition can be used for many of the learning activities and assignments.

NCSS Ten Thematic Strands

In *Curriculum Standards for Social Studies: Expectations of Excellence*, the National Council for the Social Studies (NCSS) identified 10 themes that serve as organizing strands for the social studies curriculum at every school level. These themes are interrelated and draw from all of the social science disciplines. Each theme provides student performance expectations in the areas of knowledge, processes, and attitudes. The 10 NCSS themes were the basis for the themes used in *The American Republic to 1877*.

Theme and Performance Expectation	Student Pages
I. *Culture* The study of culture helps students understand similarities and differences within groups of people. By studying a culture's beliefs, values, and traditions, students begin to gain a perspective that helps them relate to different groups. In the middle grades, students begin to examine aspects of culture and how culture influences human behavior. **Related Theme: Culture and Traditions**	
A. Compare similarities and differences in the ways groups, societies, and cultures meet human needs and concerns.	23–26, 29–33, 34, 74–75, 94, 370–371, 374, 402–407
B. Explain how information and experiences may be interpreted by people from diverse cultural perspectives and frames of reference.	34, 50, 295, 370–371, 373–374, 401–407, 409, 592–593
C. Explain and give examples of how language, literature, the arts, architecture, other artifacts, traditions, beliefs, values, and behaviors contribute to the development and transmission of culture.	14–15, 22–34, 39, 42, 295, 370–371, 402–405, 407–408, 552, 588–589
D. Explain why individuals and groups respond differently to their physical and social environments and/or changes to them on the basis of shared assumptions, values, and beliefs.	23–26, 30–31, 34, 36–37, 53–55, 295, 401–407, 552
E. Articulate the implications of cultural diversity, as well as cohesion, within and across groups.	34, 50, 369–374, 384–385, 401–407, 590–591
II. *Time, Continuity, and Change* Understanding time, continuity, and change involves being knowledgeable about what things were like in the past and how things change and develop over time. Knowing how to read and reconstruct the past helps students gain a historical perspective. In the middle grades, students will continue to increase their knowledge of the past and of historical concepts. Students will also begin to learn how individual experiences, social values, and cultural traditions influence interpretations of the past. **Related Theme: Continuity and Change**	
A. Demonstrate an understanding that different scholars may describe the same event or situation in different ways but must provide reasons or evidence for their views.	21, 118, 434–435, 440–444, 448, 510, 514, 516–517, 519–520
B. Identify and use key concepts such as chronology, causality, change, conflict, and complexity to explain, analyze, and show connections among patterns of historical change and continuity.	63–65, 108–113, 273, 335–337, 339, 441–448, 512–513, 518–520, 526–527, 554–555
C. Identify and describe selected historical periods and patterns of change within and across cultures, such as the rise of civilizations, the development of transportation systems, the growth and breakdown of colonial systems, and others.	35, 68–69, 109, 110–115, 116–119, 305, 336–337, 354–355, 396, 443–444, 512, 519–520, 524–525
D. Identify and use processes important to reconstructing and reinterpreting the past, such as using a variety of sources, providing, validating, and weighing evidence for claims, checking credibility of sources, and searching for causality.	20, 35, 114–115, 146, 339–340, 429, 448, 517, 520, 551, 587
E. Develop critical sensitivities such as empathy and skepticism regarding attitudes, values, and behaviors of people in different historical contexts.	107, 127, 140, 146, 312–313, 339–340, 379, 382–383, 409, 416–417, 429, 441–442, 444, 454–455, 465, 512, 519–521, 588–601

Theme and Performance Expectation	Student Pages
F. Use knowledge of facts and concepts drawn from history, along with methods of historical inquiry, to inform decision-making about and action-taking on public issues.	35, 409, 447–448, 514, 516, 518–520

III. People, Places, & Environments

The study of people, places, and environments will help students as they create their spatial views and geographic perspective of the world. Students begin to make informed and critical decisions about the relationship between humans and their environment. In the middle school years, students can relate their personal experiences to happenings in other environments. These experiences will help students increase their abstract thought when analyzing human behavior in relation to physical and cultural environments.

Related Theme: Geography and History

A. Elaborate mental maps of locales, regions, and the world that demonstrate understanding of relative location, direction, size, and shape.	16, 17, 20–21, 27, 34, 177–182, 282–285, 363, 367, 451–453, 466–472, 528–529, 531–532, 552
B. Create, interpret, use, and distinguish various representations of the earth such as maps, globes, and photographs.	3–5, 35, 48–49, 56–57, 65, 74–75, 95, 127, 152–153, 159, 169, 189, 215, 265–266, 275, 284–287, 301–303, 329, 346–347, 353, 361, 381, 409, 431, 452–453, 457, 470, 472, 492–493, 495, 523, 531, 533, 553, 587
C. Use appropriate resources, data sources, and geographic tools such as aerial photographs, satellite images, geographic information systems (GIS), map projections, and cartography to generate, manipulate, and interpret information such as atlases, databases, grid systems, charts, graphs, and maps.	4, 27, 56–57, 74–75, 346–347, 361, 381, 492–493
D. Estimate distance, calculate scale, and distinguish other geographic relationships such as population density and spatial distribution patterns.	21, 27, 35, 65, 95, 169, 215, 303, 394–395, 452–453, 523, 531, 533, 587
E. Locate and describe varying landforms and geographic features, such as mountains, plateaus, islands, rain forests, deserts, and oceans, and explain their relationship within the ecosystem.	3, 286–287, 530
F. Describe physical system changes such as seasons, climate and weather, and the water cycle and identify geographic patterns associated with them.	16–17, 19
G. Describe how people create places that reflect cultural values and ideals as they build neighborhoods, parks, shopping centers, and the like.	6, 34, 393, 395
H. Examine, interpret, and analyze physical and cultural patterns and their interactions, such as land use, settlement patterns, cultural transmission of customs and ideas, and ecosystem changes.	6–7, 17–19, 34–35, 74–75, 126, 264–266, 282–283, 285, 328, 363–364, 366, 368, 391, 393–395, 450–453, 468, 528–533
I. Describe ways that historical events have been influenced by, and have influenced, physical and human geographic factors in local, regional, national, and global settings.	6–7, 16–19, 21, 34, 44–49, 64, 152–153, 177–182, 263–266, 282–285, 362–368, 391–395, 450–453, 466–472, 528–533
J. Observe and speculate about social and economic effects of environmental changes and crises resulting from phenomena such as floods, storms, and drought.	7, 393
K. Propose, compare, and evaluate alternative uses of land and resources in communities, nations, and the world.	34, 64, 74–75, 126, 393, 468, 531

IV. *Individual Development & Identity*

People and culture influence a person's identity. Examining the different forms of human behavior improve one's understanding of social relationships and the development of personal identity. The study of human behavior helps students become aware of how social processes influence a person's identity. In the middle years, issues of personal identity become important as students begin to view themselves in relation to others.

Related Theme: Individual Action

A. Relate personal changes to social, cultural, and historical contexts.	82–85, 418–424, 485–491, 553
B. Describe personal connections to place—as associated with community, nation, and world.	158, 321–324, 418–419, 424, 485–491, 592–595

Theme and Performance Expectation	Student Pages
C. Describe the ways family, gender, ethnicity, nationality, and institutional affiliations contribute to personal identity.	82–85, 158, 409, 418–424, 485–491, 592–593
D. Relate such factors as physical endowment and capabilities, learning, motivation, personality, perception, and behavior to individual development.	85, 122–125, 420–421, 423–424, 485–491
E. Identify and describe ways regional, ethnic, and national cultures influence individuals' daily lives.	123–125, 409, 418–424, 485–491
F. Identify and describe the influence of perception, attitudes, values, and beliefs on personal identity.	189, 322–325, 327, 418–424, 485–491
G. Identify and interpret examples of stereotyping, conformity, and altruism.	419–420, 424, 491, 552
H. Work independently and cooperatively to accomplish goals.	35, 127, 159, 189, 215, 303, 329, 353, 381–383, 409, 457, 496–497, 523, 553, 587

V. Individuals, Groups, & Institutions

Institutions, such as schools, governments, and churches, influence people and often reflect a society's values. Because of the vital role that institutions play in people's lives, it is important that students know how institutions develop, what controls and influences them, and how humans react to them. Middle school students will gain experience by studying how institutions change over time. They should also be able to use their understanding to suggest ways how institutions can work for the common good.

Related Theme: Groups and Institutions

A. Demonstrate an understanding of concepts such as role, status, and social class in describing the interactions of individuals and social groups.	34–35, 87, 90–93, 343–344, 428, 475, 477, 503, 542–543, 545, 552
B. Analyze group and institutional influences on people, events, and elements of culture.	136–139, 141–145, 162–164, 167–168, 170, 173, 175–176, 183, 185, 187, 200–202, 205–206, 341–345, 375–378, 410–411, 425–428, 500–503, 522, 540–543, 545
C. Describe the various forms institutions take and the interactions of people with institutions.	87, 89, 91–93, 152–153, 376–377, 427–428, 502, 522, 540–545
D. Identify and analyze examples of tensions between expressions of individuality and group or institutional efforts to promote social conformity.	64, 94, 158, 175–176, 200, 205, 343–345, 375, 377–378, 425–428, 542–543
E. Identify and describe examples of tensions between belief systems and government policies and laws.	64, 94, 137–139, 158, 163, 168, 186–187, 200–203, 205, 343–345, 425–428, 474–477, 494, 500–503, 541–542
F. Describe the role of institutions in furthering both continuity and change.	34, 94, 141–142, 145, 152–153, 158, 185–187, 199–206, 343, 377–378, 410–411, 427–428, 430, 456, 473, 475–477, 500–503, 522, 540–543, 545, 552
G. Apply knowledge of how groups and institutions work to meet individual needs and promote the common good.	94, 141–142, 145, 158, 185–187, 201–206, 214, 375–378, 410–411, 427–428, 473, 475, 477, 502, 522, 544

VI. Power, Authority, & Governance

Studying structures of power, authority, and governance and their functions in the United States and around the world is important for developing a notion of civic responsibility. Students will identify the purpose and characteristics of various types of government and how people try to resolve conflicts. Students will also examine the relationship between individual rights and responsibilities. During the middle school years, students apply what they have learned about rights and responsibilities in more complex contexts.

Related Theme: Government and Democracy

A. Examine persistent issues involving the rights, roles, and status of the individual in relation to the general welfare.	159, 192–194, 197–198, 214, 217–218, 221, 228–231, 244–251, 260, 269, 271–272, 439, 463–464, 498–499, 522, 552

Theme and Performance Expectation	Student Pages
B. Describe the purpose of government and how its powers are acquired, used, and justified.	94, 147–151, 154–157, 190–198, 214, 217–231, 232–251, 256–262, 267–269, 271–272, 274, 278–281, 300, 302, 436–439, 460–464, 458–459, 495, 572–578
C. Analyze and explain ideas and governmental mechanisms to meet needs and wants of citizens, regulate territory, manage conflict, and establish order and security.	148, 150–151, 154–157, 193–198, 214, 217–231, 232–251, 267–272, 279–281, 296–300, 436–439, 460–464, 458–459, 495, 522, 552, 572–578, 586
D. Describe the ways nations and organizations respond to forces of unity and diversity affecting order and security.	94, 148, 150–151, 192–198, 217, 268–272, 300, 436–439, 460–464, 522, 575–576, 578
E. Identify and describe the basic features of the political system in the United States and identify representative leaders from various levels and branches of government.	214, 217–231, 232–251, 256–260, 262, 276–277
F. Explain conditions, actions, and motivations that contribute to conflict and cooperation within and among nations.	94, 147–151, 158, 160–161, 188, 259–262, 267–272, 274, 298, 300, 436–439, 458–459, 460–464, 572–578
G. Describe and analyze the role of technology in communications, transportation, information processing, weapons development, or other areas as it contributes to or helps resolve conflicts.	152–153
H. Explain and apply concepts such as power, role, status, justice, and influence to the examination of persistent issues and social problems.	259–260, 262, 270, 462, 574–576, 578
I. Give examples and explain how governments attempt to achieve their stated ideals at home and abroad.	147–151, 154–157, 160–161, 190–198, 214, 217, 259–260, 280–281, 437, 460–464, 572–578, 587

VII. Production, Distribution, & Consumption

Societies try to meet people's needs and wants by trying to answer the basic economic questions: What is to be produced? How should goods be produced? How should goods and services be distributed? How should land, labor, capital, and management be allocated? By studying how needs and wants are met, students learn how trade and government economic policies develop. In the middle grades, students increase their knowledge of economic concepts, principles, and reasoning.

Related Theme: Economic Factors

A. Give and explain examples of ways that economic systems structure choices about how goods and services are to be produced and distributed.	72–73, 101–106, 126, 306–311, 349–351, 386–387, 389–390, 409, 494
B. Describe the role that supply and demand, prices, incentives, and profits play in determining what is produced and distributed in a competitive market system.	306, 308, 310–311, 350, 357–358, 360, 389–390, 522–523, 552
C. Explain the difference between private and public goods and services.	348
D. Describe a range of examples of the various institutions that make up economic systems such as households, business firms, banks, government agencies, labor unions, and corporations.	126, 348–350, 480, 483
E. Describe the role of specialization and exchange in the economic process.	126, 357–358, 360, 389
F. Explain and illustrate how values and beliefs influence different economic decisions.	94, 126, 348–351, 480–481, 483, 553
G. Differentiate among various forms of exchange and money.	95, 357–358, 483, 552

Theme and Performance Expectation	Student Pages
H. Compare basic economic systems according to who determines what is produced, distributed, and consumed.	357–358, 386, 389–390, 408
I. Use economic concepts to help explain historical and current developments and issues in local, national, or global contexts.	74–75, 101–106, 120, 189, 214–215, 306–311, 352, 356–360, 386–390, 478–483, 553
J. Use economic reasoning to compare different proposals for dealing with a contemporary social issue such as unemployment, acid rain, or high quality education.	381, 483, 553

VIII. Science, Technology, & Society

The study of science, technology, and society is ever changing. It raises questions about who will benefit from it and how fundamental values and beliefs can be preserved in a technology-driven society. By the middle grades, students research the complex relationships among technology, human values, and behavior. Students will learn how technology and science have brought about change and how they have often challenged accepted societal beliefs.

Related Theme: Science and Technology

A. Examine and describe the influence of culture on scientific and technological choices and advancement, such as in transportation, medicine, and warfare.	96, 314–315, 319, 397–400, 408, 534–536
B. Show through specific examples how science and technology have changed people's perceptions of the social and natural world, such as in their relationship to the land, animal life, family life, and economic wants, needs, and security.	35, 65, 398–400, 408, 534–537, 539, 552
C. Describe examples in which values, beliefs, and attitudes have been influenced by new scientific and technological knowledge, such as the invention of the printing press, conceptions of the universe, applications of atomic energy, and genetic discoveries.	35, 57, 398–400, 408, 536, 552
D. Explain the need for laws and policies to govern scientific and technological applications, such as the safety and well-being of workers and consumers and the regulation of utilities, radio, and television.	329, 535–536
E. Seek reasonable and ethical solutions to problems that arise when scientific advancements and social norms or values come into conflict.	319, 328, 400, 408-409

IX. Global Connections

As countries grow more interdependent, understanding global connections among world societies becomes important. Students will analyze emerging global issues in many different fields. They will also investigate relationships among the different cultures of the world. In the middle years, students analyze the interactions among states and countries and respond to global events and changes.

Related Theme: Global Connections

A. Describe instances in which language, art, music, belief systems, and other cultural elements can facilitate global understanding or cause misunderstanding.	188, 580–582, 585
B. Analyze examples of conflict, cooperation, and interdependence among groups, societies, and nations.	34, 58–60, 62, 152–153, 158, 188, 288–294, 380, 546–550, 557–563, 580–586, 600–601
C. Describe and analyze the effects of changing technologies on the global community.	60, 561, 563, 583, 600–601

Theme and Performance Expectation	Student Pages
D. Explore the causes, consequences, and possible solutions to persistent, contemporary, and emerging global issues, such as health, security, resource allocation, economic development, and environmental quality.	59–62, 556–557, 579, 584–585
E. Describe and explain the relationships and tensions between national sovereignty and global interests, in such matters as territory, natural resources, trade, use of technology, and welfare of people.	59, 61, 288–291, 293–294, 380, 558, 585
F. Demonstrate understanding of concerns, standards, issues, and conflicts related to universal human rights.	120, 550
G. Identify and describe the roles of international and multinational organizations.	547, 550, 559–561, 563, 584

X. Civic Ideals & Practices

Understanding civic ideals and practices is crucial to complete participation in society and is the main purpose of social studies. Students will learn about civic participation and the role of the citizen within his or her community, country, and world. By the middle grades, students will broaden their understanding to analyze and evaluate relationships between civic ideals and practices.

Related Theme: Civic Rights and Responsibilities

Theme and Performance Expectation	Student Pages
A. Examine the origins and continuing influence of key ideals of the democratic republican form of government, such as individual human dignity, liberty, justice, equality, and the rule of law.	76–80, 94, 98–99, 130–131, 133–135, 154–158, 160–161, 207–213, 217–231, 232–251, 275, 332–333, 412, 415, 504–508, 522–523, 566–568, 570
B. Identify and interpret sources and examples of the rights and responsibilities of citizens.	95, 133–135, 154–158, 189, 218–221, 228–231, 244–251, 275, 332–333, 412, 415, 431, 504–508, 522–523, 564, 567–568, 570, 587
C. Locate, access, analyze, organize, and apply information about selected public issues—recognizing and explaining multiple points of view.	76–80, 133–135, 231, 413, 415, 495, 504–505, 507–508, 566–567, 569–571
D. Practice forms of civic discussion and participation consistent with the ideals of citizens in a democratic republic.	80, 159, 189, 215, 222, 231, 275, 495, 523, 587
E. Explain and analyze various forms of citizen action that influence public policy decisions.	412–415, 566–568, 570
F. Identify and explain the roles of formal and informal political actors in influencing and shaping public policy and decision-making.	154–157, 201–213, 412–415, 504–508, 566–568, 570–571, 586
G. Analyze the influence of diverse forms of public opinion on the development of public policy and decision-making.	94, 211–213, 412–415, 505–506, 566–567, 570
H. Analyze the effectiveness of selected public policies and citizen behaviors in realizing the stated ideals of a democratic republican form of government.	160–161, 189, 221, 504–508, 567–568, 570–571
I. Explain the relationship between policy statements and action plans used to address issues of public concern.	413, 415, 505–508, 565, 567, 569
J. Examine strategies designed to strengthen the "common good," which consider a range of options for citizen action.	217, 415, 505–508, 571

Scope and Sequence

Themes and Concepts

Each section of *The American Republic to 1877* focuses on one central theme, although related themes also appear in each section. The section numbers highlighted here in red indicate the central theme that is key to that section. Related themes are listed in black.

Chapter	1	2	3
Culture and Traditions	Section 1, 2, 3	Section 1, 3, 4	Section 4, 5
Continuity and Change	Section 3	Section 3	Section 1, 4
Geography and History	Section 1, 2, 3	Section 1, 2, 3, 4	Section 3
Individual Action	Section 2	Section 1, 2, 3, 4	Section 1, 2, 3, 4
Groups and Institutions	Section 3	Section 1, 2, 3, 4	Section 1, 3, 4
Government and Democracy			Section 1, 2
Economic Factors	Section 2	Section 1, 4	Section 1, 4
Science and Technology	Section 2	Section 1	
Global Connections		Section 1, 2, 3, 4	Section 4
Civic Rights and Responsibilities			Section 1, 2

Skills

These skills are taught in the Chapter SKILLBUILDERS and reinforced in the Chapter Assessment Activities, **Chapter Skills Activities** in the Unit Resource books, and **Glencoe's Skillbuilder Interactive Workbook CD-ROM**.

	1	2	3
Skill Category	*Social Studies Skill*	*Social Studies Skill*	*Social Studies Skill*
Specific Skill	Understanding the Parts of a Map	Reading a Time Line	Reading a Bar Graph

4	5	6	7	8	9
Section 1, 2		Section 1	Section 2		
Section 2, 3, 4	Section 1, 4	Section 1, 2	Section 2	Section 1	Section 3
Section 1, 3, 4	Section 1, 2	Section 3	Section 1	Section 2	Section 2
Section 1, 2, 3, 4	Section 1, 2, 3, 4	Section 1, 2, 3, 4	Section 1, 2, 3	Section 1, 2, 3	Section 1, 2, 3, 4
Section 3	Section 1, 2, 3	Section 1, 2, 3, 4	Section 2, 3	Section 2, 3	Section 2, 3, 4
	Section 4		Section 1, 2, 3	Section 1, 3	Section 1, 3, 4
Section 1, 2	Section 1	Section 2	Section 1, 2	Section 1, 3	Section 3
Section 2					Section 2, 3
Section 4	Section 1, 4	Section 2, 4		Section 2, 3	Section 2, 3
Section 2	Section 1, 3, 4	Section 2	Section 1, 2, 3	Section 2, 3	Section 1
Critical Thinking Skill	*Critical Thinking Skill*	*Social Studies Skill*	*Critical Thinking Skill*	*Social Studies Skill*	*Study and Writing Skill*
Understanding Cause and Effect	Distinguishing Fact from Opinion	Reading a Military Map	Making Comparisons	Reading a Flowchart	Writing a Journal

Chapter	10	11	12	13
Themes and Concepts				
Culture and Traditions	Section 2, 3		Section 2, **3**, 4	Section 2, **4**
Continuity and Change	Section 1, 2	Section **1**	Section 2	
Geography and History	Section 1, 2, 3		Section 1, **2**, 3, 4	Section 1, **2**, 3
Individual Action	Section 1, 2, **3**	Section 1, 2, 3	Section 1, 2, 3, 4	Section 1, 3, 4
Groups and Institutions	Section 3	Section 1, **2**, 3	Section 1, 4	Section 2, 4
Government and Democracy		Section 1		
Economic Factors	Section **1**, 2	Section 1, **3**	Section **1**, 4	Section 1, 3, 4
Science and Technology	Section 1, **2**			Section 1, **3**
Global Connections	Section 3		Section 3	Section 2
Civic Rights and Responsibilities		Section 1		Section 2, 4
Skills				
Skill Category	*Social Studies Skill*	*Study and Writing Skill*	*Social Studies Skill*	*Social Studies Skill*
Specific Skill	Reading a Diagram	Analyzing Primary Sources	Understanding Latitude and Longitude	Reading a Circle Graph

14	15	16	17	18	19
Section 1		Section 1		Section 1, 2	Section 4
Section 3	Section 2, 3, 4	Section 1, 2, 3, 4	Section 1, 3, 4	Section 1, 2, 4	Section 2, 3
	Section 2, 4	Section 1, 2, 5	Section 4	Section 1, 2, 3, 4	Section 1, 2, 4
Section 1, 2, 3	Section 1, 2, 3, 4	Section 2, 3, 4, 5	Section 1, 4	Section 3	Section 2, 3, 4
Section 1, 2, 3	Section 1, 3	Section 3, 4	Section 1, 2, 3, 4	Section 1, 2, 3	Section 2, 4
	Section 1, 3	Section 1	Section 2	Section 1, 3, 4	Section 1, 2, 3, 4
Section 2		Section 1, 4, 5	Section 4	Section 1, 2, 4	Section 1, 2, 3
		Section 4	Section 4	Section 2	Section 1, 3, 4
Section 2				Section 3, 4	Section 1, 2, 3, 4
Section 1, 3	Section 2, 3	Section 3	Section 1, 2, 3, 4	Section 3	Section 2, 4
Technology Skill	*Critical Thinking Skill*	*Study and Writing Skills*	*Critical Thinking Skill*	*Technology Skill*	*Critical Thinking Skill*
Evaluating a Web Site	Recognizing Bias	Taking Notes	Identifying the Main Idea	Building a Database	Problem Solving

Previewing Your Textbook

Your textbook has been organized to help you learn about the significant events and people that make up American history. Before you start reading, though, here is a road map to help you understand what you will encounter in the pages of this textbook. Follow this road map before you read so that you can understand how this textbook works.

Units

Your textbook is divided into 7 units. Each unit begins with two pages of information to help you begin your study of the topics.

WHY IT MATTERS

Each unit begins with *Why It Matters.* This is a short summary about what you will study in the unit and the important topics in the unit.

QUOTATION

A short quotation gives a glimpse of the idea of a key figure from the era.

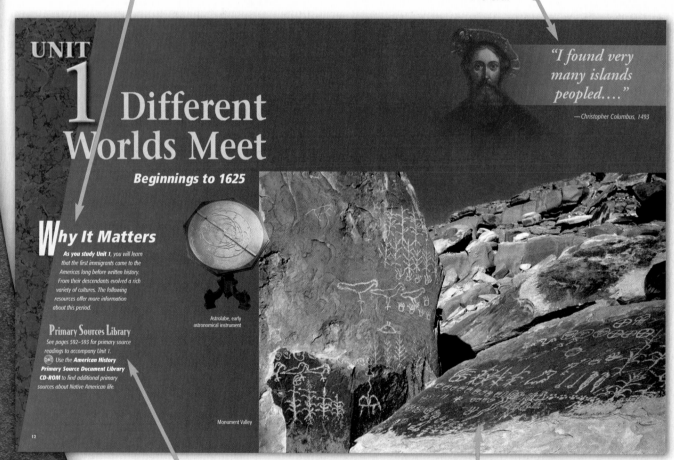

UNIT

1 Different Worlds Meet

Beginnings to 1625

Why It Matters

As you study Unit 1, you will learn that the first immigrants came to the Americas long before written history. From their descendants evolved a rich variety of cultures. The following resources offer more information about this period.

Primary Sources Library

See pages 592–593 for primary source readings to accompany Unit 1.

Use the **American History Primary Source Document Library CD-ROM** to find additional primary sources about Native American life.

Astrolabe, early astronomical instrument

Monument Valley

12

"I found very many islands peopled...."

—Christopher Columbus, 1493

PRIMARY SOURCE LIBRARY

This tells you where to find the *Primary Sources Library* readings that accompany the unit.

VISUALS

A photograph or painting shows you what life was like during the time period.

Chapters

Each unit in *The American Republic to 1877* is made up of chapters. Each chapter starts by providing you with background information to help you get the most out of the chapter.

CHAPTER TITLE
The chapter title tells you the main topic you will be reading about.

WHY IT MATTERS
Why It Matters tells you why events you will study are important.

THE IMPACT TODAY
The Impact Today explains how these events changed the way we live today.

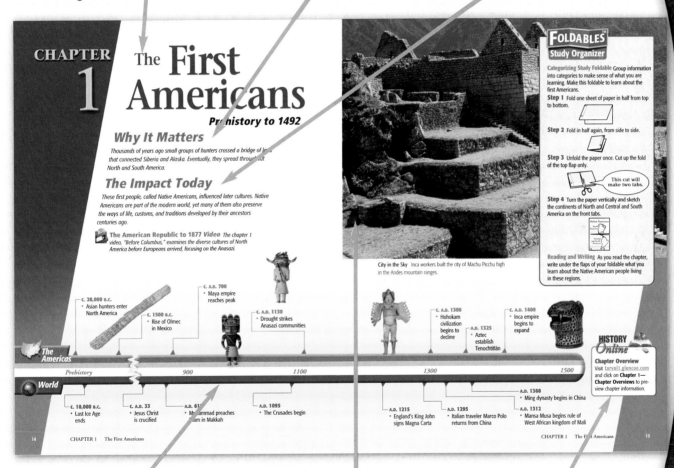

TIME LINE
The time line shows you when and where events happened during the period of time covered in the chapter.

VISUALS
A photograph or painting shows how people of the time lived.

WEB SITE
History Online directs you to the Internet where you can find more information, activities, and quizzes.

Previewing Your Textbook

Sections

A section is a division, or part, of the chapter. The first page of the section, the section opener, helps you set a purpose for reading.

READING STRATEGY

Completing the *Reading Strategy* activity will help you organize the information as you read the section.

READ TO LEARN

Keep the *Read to Learn* statements in mind as you read the section.

SECTION THEMES

Your textbook organizes the events of your nation's past and present around themes. You can read about the themes on pages xx-xxi.

MAIN IDEA

The *Main Idea* of this section is introduced here. Below it, are important terms you will encounter as you read the section.

TIME LINE

The time line identifies important events you will study in the section.

AN AMERICAN STORY

Think of *An American Story* as a moment in time. It introduces you to an important event that you will read about.

SECTION 1 Early Peoples

Guide to Reading

Main Idea
The first Americans spread throughout North, Central, and South America.

Key Terms
archaeology, artifact, Ice Age, nomad, migration, maize, carbon dating, culture

Reading Strategy
Determining Cause and Effect As you read Section 1, re-create the diagram below and explain why the first Americans came to the continent and the consequences of their arrival.

Migration to the Americas	
Causes	Effects

Read to Learn
- how the first people arrived in the Americas.
- which discovery changed the lives of the early Native Americans.

Section Theme
Geography and History The Ice Age made it possible for hunters to migrate to the Americas.

Preview of Events

♦30,000 B.C.	♦10,000 B.C.	♦5000 B.C.	♦1000 B.C.
c. 28,000 B.C. Asian hunters enter North America	c. 10,000 B.C. Last Ice Age ends	c. 7000 B.C. Farming develops in Mexico	c. 3000 B.C. Early villages established in Mexico

AN American Story

Arrowhead, hand-chipped stone

No one knows for sure how the first people arrived in America. They may have crossed a land bridge that many scientists think connected Asia and North America thousands of years ago. They may have come by boat from Asia or Europe. Why they came is also a mystery. Possibly they followed mammoths or other game animals or were hunting seals and whales along the coast. Over time these people settled in America, becoming the first "native Americans."

The Journey From Asia

These first Americans arrived thousands of years ago. As food supplies improved, the population of the Americas increased. By A.D. 1500, millions of Native Americans, belonging to more than 2,000 different groups, lived on the two continents of North America and South America.

When Europeans arrived in the Americas in the late 1400s, they found Native Americans living there. The Europeans wondered where these peoples had come from and how they happened to settle in the Americas. Some believed the Native Americans had come from Atlantis, an island that was supposed to have sunk beneath the waves of the Atlantic Ocean.

16   CHAPTER 1   The First Americans

Previewing Your Textbook

Reading Roadmap

You will get more out of your textbook if you recognize the different elements that help you to understand what you read.

MAPS

Easy-to-read maps provide a link between geography and history. Questions test your understanding of the map's information.

READING CHECKS

This *Reading Check* helps you check yourself. Did you understand the main ideas?

OUTLINE

Think of the headings as forming an outline. The blue titles are the main heading. The red titles that follow are the subsections.

VOCABULARY

The terms in blue are the key terms. The definition is also included here.

SECTION ASSESSMENT

The *Section Assessment* is the last item in every section. Completing the assessment can help evaluate how well you understand.

PHOTOGRAPHS

Photographs show you important people, places, and events of the time.

Special Features

A variety of special features will help you as you study *The American Republic to 1877.*

PEOPLE IN HISTORY

People In History tells you the story of individuals that influenced American history.

People In History

Benjamin Franklin 1706–1790

Ben Franklin learned the printer's trade as a young man. By the time he was 23, he owned his own newspaper in Philadelphia. Soon afterward he began publishing *Poor Richard's Almanack,* a calendar filled with advice, philosophy, and wise say-

man healthy, wealthy, and wise."

Franklin was deeply interested in science. He invented the lightning rod, bifocal eyeglasses, and the Franklin stove for heating. Energetic and open-minded, Franklin served in the Pennsylvania Assembly for many years. He founded a hos-

America's first lending library, and an academy of higher learning that later became the University of Pennsylvania.

Franklin's greatest services to his fellow Americans would come during the 1770s. As a statesman and patriot, Franklin would help guide the colonies toward

AMERICA'S LITERATURE

America's Literature analyzes excerpts from famous pieces of American fiction and describes its historical lessons.

SKILLBUILDERS

Skillbuilders teach valuable skills that will be useful throughout the book.

Social Studies
SKILLBUILDER

Understanding the Parts of a Map

Why Learn This Skill?

Maps can direct you down the street or around the world. There are as many different kinds of maps as there are uses for them. Being able to read a map begins with learning about its parts.

TWO VIEWPOINTS

Two Viewpoints compares the opposing viewpoints of two historic figures on a particular issue.

TWO VIEWPOINTS

Union or Secession?

President Abraham Lincoln and Jefferson Davis, president of the Confederacy, were inaugurated just several weeks apart. These excerpts from their Inaugural Addresses will help you understand differing points of view about secession from the United States in 1861.

Abraham Lincoln's Inaugural Address, March 4, 1861

One section of our country believes slavery is *right* and ought to be extended, while the other believes it is *wrong* and ought not to be extended. This is the only substantial dispute . . . .

Physically speaking, we can not separate. We can not remove our respective sections from each other nor build an impassable wall between them. A husband and wife may be divorced and go out of the presence and beyond the reach of each other; but the different parts of our country can not do this. . . .

In *your* hands, my dissatisfied fellow countrymen, and not in *mine,* is the momentous issue of civil war.

Abraham Lincoln

Jefferson Davis

Jefferson Davis's Inaugural Address, February 18, 1861

As a necessity, not a choice, we have resorted to the remedy of separation, and henceforth our energies must be directed to the conduct of our own affairs, and the [continuation] of the Confederacy which we have formed. If a just perception of mutual interest shall permit us peaceably to pursue our separate political career, my most earnest desire will have been fulfilled. But if this be denied to us . . . [we will be forced] to appeal to arms. . . .

Learning From History

1. According to Lincoln, what was the only substantial disagreement between the North and the South?
2. What did Lincoln compare the United States to?
3. Did Lincoln and Davis say anything in their inaugural addresses that was similar?

Douglas for ported pop ern Democ slavery—no inridge of the *Dred S* from both had form Union Part Tennessee. tion on sla

Lincoln N

The Rep ham Lin designed quarters, left undis that it sh territories however, would en

Lincoln

With t coln wor toral v received ular vo any oth second

The tional l even a Southe Northe the So states. Misso seven

In e had o for L howe to lea

Esther Forbes (1891–1967)

Esther Forbes wrote a number of books; among them is the prize-winning biography *Paul Revere and the World He Lived In.* As she researched Paul Revere's life, Forbes learned that many young apprentices played a role in the American Revolution. *Johnny Tremain,* a fictional work, tells the story of such an apprentice.

READ TO DISCOVER

In this passage from *Johnny Tremain,* 14-year-old Johnny and his friend Rab have disguised themselves as Mohawks. They join the crowd at Griffin's Wharf in Boston Harbor, where three English ships carrying tea are docked and are unable to leave or unload their cargo.

READER'S DICTIONARY

boatswain: officer on a ship
warped: roped
jargon: strange language
hold: place where cargo is stored on a ship
winch: machine for hauling

America's LITERATURE

Johnny Tremain

There was a **boatswain's** whistle, and in silence one group boarded the *Dartmouth.* The *Eleanor* and the *Beaver* had to be **warped** in to the wharf. Johnny was close to Mr. Revere's heels. He heard him calling for the captain, promising him, in the **jargon** everyone talked that night, that not one thing should be damaged on the ship except only the tea, but the captain and all his crew had best stay in the cabin until the work was over.

Captain Hall shrugged and did as he was told, leaving his cabin boy to hand over the keys to the **hold.** The boy was grinning with pleasure. The "tea party" was not unexpected. . . .

The **winches** rattled and the heavy chests began to appear—one hundred and fifty of them. As some men worked in the hold, others broke open the chests and flung the tea into the harbor. But one thing made them unexpected difficulty. The tea inside the chests was wrapped in heavy canvas. The axes went through the canvas easily enough—the canvas made endless trouble. Johnny had never worked so hard in his life.

Then Mr. Revere called the captain to come up and inspect. The tea was utterly gone, but Captain Hall agreed that beyond that there had not been the slightest damage.

It was close upon dawn when the work on all three ships was done. And yet the great, silent audience on the wharf, men, women, and children, had not gone home. As the three groups came off the ships, they formed in fours along the wharf, their axes on their shoulders. Then a hurrah went up and the fife began to play.

Paul Revere

ANALYZING LITERATURE

1. **Recall and Interpret** Why was the "tea party" expected?
2. **Evaluate and Connect** What does the conduct of the "tea party" participants suggest about the protest? Explain your answer.

Interdisciplinary Activity

Expository Writing Write a one-page paper about how you think you would react in Johnny's situation.

140

✓ Reading Check caused the split in the Democratic Party in 1860?

Jefferson Davis, a senator from their president.

They

Scavenger Hunt

The American Republic to 1877 contains a wealth of information. The trick is to know where to look to access all the information in the book. If you run through this scavenger hunt exercise with your teachers or parents, you will see how the textbook is organized, and how to get the most out of your reading and study time. Let's get started!

1. How many chapters and how many units are in the book?
   19 chapters, 7 units

2. What time period does Unit 2 cover? 1587–1770

3. How many chapters are there in Unit 3? What is this unit about?
   3; independence and forming a new nation

4. What is the title of Chapter 14, Section 3?
   The Women's Movement

5. On what page of Chapter 4 can you find the *Foldables* Activity? What does the Activity help you do?
   Page 99; analyze the French and Indian War

6. What is the skill you practice when you do the Chapter 8 Skillbuilder? Reading a Flowchart

7. There are 3 Web sites in Chapter 5. The first previews the chapter and the second summarizes it. What does the third one do?
   provides a link to a self-check chapter quiz

8. You want to quickly find all the maps in the book on the Civil War? Where do you look?
   see Unit 6 in the Maps section of the Table of Contents

9. Most sections of a chapter open with an excerpt from a primary source—a document or other testimony dating from the period. Where else can you find extended primary sources in the textbook? in the Primary Sources Library in the Appendix

10. Where can you learn the definition of a physical map, a political map, and a special-purpose map?
    in the section "How Do I Use Maps?"

How Do I Study History?

As you read *The American Republic to 1877*, you will be given help in sorting out all the information you encounter. This textbook organizes the events of your nation's past and present around 10 themes. A theme is a concept, or main idea that happens again and again throughout history. By recognizing these themes, you will better understand events of the past and how they affect you today.

Themes in *The American Republic to 1877*

Culture and Traditions
Being aware of cultural differences helps us understand ourselves and others. People from around the world for generations have sung of the "land of the Pilgrims' pride, land where our fathers died" even though their ancestors arrived on these shores long after these events occurred.

Continuity and Change
Recognizing our historic roots helps us understand why things are the way they are today. This theme includes political, social, religious, and economic changes that have influenced the way Americans think and act.

Geography and History
Understanding geography helps us understand how humans interact with their environment. The United States succeeded in part because of its rich natural resources and its vast open spaces. In many regions, the people changed the natural landscape to fulfill their wants and needs.

Individual Action

Responsible individuals have often stepped forward to help lead the nation. America's strong family values helped create such individuals. These values spring in part from earlier times when the home was the center of many activities, including work, education, and daily worship.

Groups and Institutions

Identifying how political and social groups and institutions work helps us work together. From the beginning, Americans formed groups and institutions to act in support of their economic, political, and religious beliefs.

Government and Democracy

Understanding the workings of government helps us become good citizens. Abraham Lincoln explained the meaning of democracy as "government of the people, by the people, for the people." Democracy, at its best, is "among" the people.

Science and Technology

Americans have always been quick to adopt innovations. The nation was settled and built by people who blended their old ways with new ways. Americans' lives are deeply influenced by technology, the use of science and machines. Perhaps no machine has so shaped modern life as the automobile. Understanding the roles of science and technology helps us see their impact on our society and the roles they will play in the future.

Economic Factors

The free enterprise economy of the United States is consistent with the nation's history of rights and freedoms. Freedom of choice in economic decisions supports other freedoms. Understanding the concept of free enterprise is basic to studying American history.

Global Connections

The world seems smaller than it did only 50 years ago. Modern transportation and communication have brought people around the globe closer together. As a result, countries today are more dependent on one another. As citizens of the United States and members of the global community, we have a responsibility to keep informed about developments in other nations and the world. Being aware of global interdependence helps us make decisions and deal with the difficult issues we will encounter.

Civic Rights and Responsibilities

For a democratic system to survive, its citizens must take an active role in government. The foundation of democracy is the right of every person to take part in government and to voice one's views on issues. An appreciation for the struggle to preserve these freedoms is vital to the understanding of democracy.

Using the Themes

You will find Section Themes at the beginning of every section of your text. You are asked questions that help you put it all together to better understand how ideas and themes are connected across time—and to see why history is important to you today.

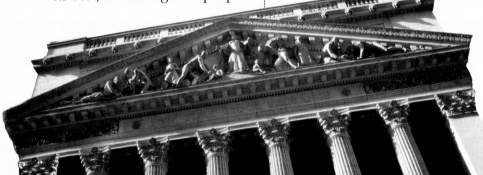

Reading Skills Handbook

Why Should I Teach Reading to My Social Studies Students?

For many social studies teachers, helping students develop reading skills is a low priority—nice to do if there's time, but not necessary. After all, there is scarcely time to meet many of the state-mandated subject-area learning objectives. Why add reading instruction to the list? The answer is that reading skills are essential to the learning of subjects. In the social studies, students must read to learn. Struggling readers risk learning less than those who are proficient in reading.

Teachers who infuse literacy strategies with social studies content actively engage students in learning. Once students internalize reading strategies such as visualizing, predicting, and making connections, they inevitably become better social studies students.

READING TO LEARN

This handbook focuses on skills and strategies that can help you understand the words you read. The strategies you use to understand whole texts depend on the kind of text you are reading. In other words, you don't read a textbook the way you read a novel. You read a textbook mainly for information; you read a novel mainly for fun. To get the most out of your reading, you need to choose the right strategy to fit the reason you're reading.

USE THIS HANDBOOK TO HELP YOU LEARN

- how to identify new words and build your vocabulary
- how to adjust the way you read to fit your reason for reading
- how to use specific reading strategies to better understand what you read
- how to use critical thinking strategies to think more deeply about what you read

You will also learn about

- text structures
- reading for research

TABLE OF CONTENTS

Professional Development: Teaching Reading

The following sources will help you teach reading skills:

- *Subjects Matter: Every Teacher's Guide to Content-Area Reading,* by Harvey Daniels and Steven Zemelman. Portsmouth, NH: Heineman, 2004.
- *When Kids Can't Read, What Teachers Can Do: A Guide for Teachers, 6–12,* by G. Kylene Beers. Portsmouth, NH: Heinemann, 2003.
- *I Read It But I Don't Get It: Comprehension Strategies for Adolescent Readers,* by Cris Tovani. Portland, ME: Stenhouse Publishers, 2000.
- *Teaching Reading in the Middle School,* by Laura Robb. New York, NY: Scholastic Professional Books, 2000.

Identifying Words and Building Vocabulary

What do you do when you come across a word you do not know as you read? Do you skip over the word and keep reading? If you are reading for fun or entertainment, you might. But if you are reading for information, an unfamiliar word may get in the way of your understanding. When that happens, try the following strategies to figure out how to say the word and what the word means.

Reading Unfamiliar Words

Sounding out the word One way to figure out how to say a new word is to sound it out, syllable by syllable. Look carefully at the word's beginning, middle, and ending. Inside the word, do you see a word you already know how to pronounce? What vowels are in the syllables? Use the following tips when sounding out new words.

- **Roots and base words** The main part of a word is called its root. When the root is a complete word, it may be called the base word. When you come across a new word, check whether you recognize its root or base word. It can help you pronounce the word and figure out the word's meaning.

ASK YOURSELF

- What letters make up the beginning sound or beginning syllable of the word?

  Example: In the word *coagulate, co* rhymes with *so.*

- What sounds do the letters in the middle part of the word make?

  Example: In the word *coagulate,* the syllable *ag* has the same sound as the

ag in *bag,* and the syllable *u* is pronounced like the letter *u.*

- What letters make up the ending sound or syllable?

  Example: In the word *coagulate, late* is a familiar word you already know how to pronounce.

- Now try pronouncing the whole word:

  co ag u late.

- **Prefixes** A prefix is a word part that can be added to the beginning of a root or base word. For example, the prefix *pre-* means "before," so *prehistory* means "before history." Prefixes can change, or even reverse, the meaning of a word. For example, *un-* means "not," so *unconstitutional* means "not constitutional."

- **Suffixes** A suffix is a word part that can be added to the end of a root or base word to change the word's meaning. Adding a suffix to a word can also change that word from one part of speech to another. For example, the word *joy,* which is a noun, becomes an adjective when the suffix *-ful* (meaning "full of") is added. *Joyful* means "full of joy."

Determining a Word's Meaning

Using syntax Like all languages, the English language has rules and patterns for the way words are arranged in sentences. The way a sentence is organized is called the **syntax** of the sentence. If English is your first language, you have known this pattern since you started talking in sentences. If you're learning English now, you may find the syntax is different from the patterns you know in your first language.

Identifying Words and Building Vocabulary

Why It's Important

Research documents the relationship between a strong vocabulary and the ability to read and write proficiently. Vocabulary may be the most important factor in comprehension, showing that ongoing, specific vocabulary instruction must be an integral part of every lesson.

Before Reading

Activating Prior Knowledge
Distribute index cards with a key word from the chapter written on each card. Organize students into groups of four, and give them time to discuss their words. After the group discussion, ask each group to write what they think the word means on the back of the card. Then have groups present the words to the class by writing their words and definitions on the board. Other students should help confirm or revise the definitions. Use pictures or graphs to enhance or correct the students' definitions.

Differentiated Instruction

Meeting Special Needs: Less-Proficient Readers One way to help students increase their vocabularies is to have them play word games before they read the chapter. Give students a word from the chapter that they do not know, and allow them to ask questions about its definition. When a student correctly guesses its meaning, he or she can then be "it," choosing a new word for the class to question. This type of game demonstrates that there are often many definitions for a word, and it allows students to learn from each other.

Reading Skills Handbook

During Reading

Learning Vocabulary Post a chart on the wall listing the steps for learning new vocabulary. Students may refer to the chart as they read. Steps include: sound out the word; look at prefixes, suffixes, and roots; look at how the word is used in the sentence; use context clues in surrounding sentences; use reference materials such as dictionaries and thesauruses; ask someone the meaning of the word. Encourage students to experiment with different steps to find the one that works best for them.

After Reading

Reinforcing Vocabulary

Students should use graphic organizers and web diagrams to explain the definition of a word. Have students write the word in the center of a sheet of notebook paper. Then have them write *What it is* at the top left of the page, *What it is like* at the top right, *Examples of its meaning* at the bottom left of the page, and *What it is not* at the bottom right. Have students write the appropriate information under each head.

In a simple sentence in English, someone or something (the *subject*) does something (the *predicate* or *verb*) to or with another person or thing (the *object*): The *soldiers attacked* the *enemy*.

Sometimes adjectives, adverbs, and phrases are added to add details to the sentence: *The courageous young* soldiers *fearlessly* attacked the *well-entrenched* enemy *shortly after dawn*.

CHECK IT OUT

Knowing about syntax can help you figure out the meaning of an unfamiliar word. Just look at how syntax can help you figure out the following nonsense sentence.

The blizzy kwarkles sminched the flerky fleans.

Your experience with English syntax tells you that the action word, or verb, in this sentence is *sminched*. Who did the *sminching?* The *kwarkles*. What kind of kwarkles were they? *Blizzy*. Whom did they *sminch?* The fleans. What kind of fleans were they? *Flerky*. Even though you don't know the meaning of the words in the nonsense sentence, you can make some sense of the entire sentence by studying its syntax.

Using context clues You can often figure out the meaning of an unfamiliar word by looking at its context, the words and sentences that surround it. To learn new words as you read, follow these steps for using context clues.

1. Look before and after the unfamiliar word for:
   • a definition or a synonym, another word that means the same as the unfamiliar word.
   • a general topic associated with the word.
   • a clue to what the word is similar to or different from.
   • an action or a description that has something to do with the word.
2. Connect what you already know with what the author has written.
3. Predict a possible meaning.
4. Use the meaning in the sentence.
5. Try again if your guess does not make sense.

Using reference materials Dictionaries and other reference sources can help you learn new words. Check out these reference sources:

• A **dictionary** gives the pronunciation and the meaning or meanings of words. Some dictionaries also give other forms of words, their parts of speech, and synonyms. You might also find the historical background of a word, such as its Greek, Latin, or Anglo-Saxon origins.

• A **glossary** is a word list that appears at the end—or Appendix—of a book or other written work and includes only words that are in that work. Like dictionaries, glossaries have the pronunciation and definitions of words.

• A **thesaurus** lists groups of words that have the same, or almost the same, meaning. Words with similar meanings are called *synonyms*. Seeing the synonyms of words can help you build your vocabulary.

More About the Reading Strategy

How can teachers help students understand word concepts instead of just learning simple definitions? One way is to use words often and in a variety of ways. Teams of teachers can choose common vocabulary words which they will present in various content area classes. Teachers should provide opportunities for integrating the words into meaningful contexts. The goal is for students to develop full knowledge of the words so that they become fixed parts of their vocabularies.

Recognizing Word Meanings Across Subjects

Have you ever learned a new word in one class and then noticed it in your reading for other subjects? The word probably will not mean exactly the same thing in each class. But you can use what you know about the word's meaning to help you understand what it means in a different subject area.

CHECK IT OUT

Look at the following example from three subjects:

Social studies: One major **product** manufactured in the South is cotton cloth.

Math: After you multiply those two numbers, explain how you arrived at the **product.**

Science: One **product** of photosynthesis is oxygen.

Reading for a Reason

Why are you reading that paperback mystery? What do you hope to get from your geography textbook? And are you going to read either of these books in the same way that you read a restaurant menu? The point is, you read for different reasons. The reason you are reading something helps you decide on the reading strategies you use with a text. In other words, how you read will depend on **why** you're reading.

Knowing Your Reason for Reading

In school and in life, you will have many reasons for reading, and those reasons will lead you to a wide range of materials. For example,

- **to learn and understand new information,** you might read news magazines, textbooks, news on the Internet, books about your favorite pastime, encyclopedia articles, primary and secondary sources for a school report, instructions on how to use a calling card, or directions for a standardized test.

- **to find specific information,** you might look at the sports section for the score of last night's game, a notice on where to register for a field trip, weather reports, bank statements, or television listings.

- **to be entertained,** you might read your favorite magazine, e-mails or letters from friends, the Sunday comics, or even novels, short stories, plays, or poems!

Adjusting How Fast You Read

How quickly or how carefully you should read a text depends on your purpose for reading it. Because there are many reasons and ways to read, think about your purpose and choose a strategy that works best. Try out these strategies:

- **Scanning** means quickly running your eyes over the material, looking for *key words or phrases* that point to the information you're looking for. Scan when you need to find a particular piece or type of information. For example, you might scan a newspaper for movie show times.

Reading Skills Handbook

Reading for a Reason

Why It's Important

When students have a reason or purpose for reading, the task becomes relevant and meaningful, both of which are necessary for comprehension. Good readers inherently set purposes for themselves, but less-proficient readers might need help finding a reason for reading.

Before Reading

Skimming Help students establish a reason for reading by skimming the text. Point out section headings, illustrations, and boldfaced words. Tell students that these text features can help establish a purpose for reading.

During Reading

Identifying a Reason for Reading Give students a specific task to perform while they read, such as looking for a specific piece of information, summarizing content, finding details to support a position, or writing a response to what they have read.

Differentiated Instruction

Meeting Special Needs: Less-Proficient Readers Students need practice with establishing a reason for reading. Encourage students to read news magazines, newspapers, historical novels, nonfiction books, or Internet articles. Before reading, have students write a rationale for why they have chosen that type of reading. Students should describe what they will do after they read, such as present an oral report.

After Reading

Paraphrasing When students finish reading, have them work with a partner to paraphrase what they have read. Encourage them to reread sections of text or share notes and answers to questions in order to clarify the reading.

Understanding What You Read

Why It's Important

Students who read but don't "get it" or who simply will not read at all cannot adequately master the content of their courses. Helping students learn to use a variety of reading strategies as tools for comprehension will lead to long-term benefits in school and everyday life.

Before Reading

Making Predictions On index cards, write important words from the chapter—one word per card. Place the cards on various desks around the room. Allow students to move from desk to desk until they find a word that they think they may know something about. Have students use the word to make predictions about what they will learn in the chapter.

- **Skimming** means quickly reading a piece of writing *to find its main idea* or to *get a general overview* of it. For example, you might skim the sports section of the daily newspaper to find out how your favorite teams are doing. Or you might skim a chapter in your textbook to prepare for a test.

- **Careful reading** involves *reading slowly and paying attention* with a purpose in mind. Read carefully when you're learning new concepts, following complicated directions, or preparing to explain information to someone else.

Understanding What You Read

Reading without understanding is like trying to drive a car on an empty gas tank. Fortunately, there are techniques you can use to help you concentrate on and understand what you read. Skilled readers adopt a number of strategies before, during, and after reading to make sure they understand what they read.

Previewing

If you were making a preview for a movie, you would want to let your audience know what the movie is like. When you preview a piece of writing, you are trying to get an idea about that piece of writing. If you know what to expect before reading, you will have an easier time understanding ideas and relationships. Follow these steps to preview your reading assignments.

DO IT!

1. Look at the title and any illustrations that are included.

2. Read the headings, subheadings, and anything in bold letters.

3. Skim over the passage to see how it is organized. Is it divided into many parts?

Is it a long poem or short story? Don't forget to look at the graphics—pictures, maps, or diagrams.

4. Set a purpose for your reading. Are you reading to learn something new? Are you reading to find specific information?

Using What You Know

Believe it or not, you already know quite a bit about what you are going to read. You bring knowledge and personal experience to a selection. Drawing on your own background is called *activating prior knowledge*, and it can help you create meaning in what you read. Ask yourself, *What do I already know about this topic?*

Predicting

You do not need any special knowledge to make *predictions* when you read. The predictions do not even have to be accurate. Take educated guesses before and during your reading about what might happen in the story or article you are reading.

Visualizing

Creating pictures in your mind as you read—called *visualizing*—is a powerful aid to understanding. As you read, set up a movie theater in your imagination. Picture the setting—city streets, the desert, or the surface of the moon. If you can visualize what you read, selections will be more vivid, and you will recall them better later on.

More About the Reading Strategy

What does it mean to read? What do we know about how the brain processes the written word? Consider forming a study group with other teachers interested in learning more about the process of reading. There are books available through several educational presses that focus on new research about the learning process and comprehension.

Identifying Sequence

When you discover the logical order of events or ideas, you are identifying *sequence*. Do you need to understand step-by-step directions? Are you reading a persuasive speech with the reasons listed in order of importance? Look for clues and signal words that will help you find the way information is organized.

Determining the Main Idea

When you look for the *main idea* of a selection, you look for the most important idea. The examples, reasons, and details that further explain the main idea are called *supporting details*. Some main ideas are clearly stated within a passage—often in the first sentence of a paragraph, or sometimes in the last sentence of a passage. Other times, an author does not directly state the main idea but provides details that help readers figure out what the main idea is.

ASK YOURSELF

- **What is each sentence about?**
- **Is there one sentence that tells about the whole passage or that is more important** than any of the other sentences?
- **What main idea do the supporting details point out?**

Questioning

Keep up a conversation with yourself as you read by *asking questions* about the text. Ask about the importance of the information you are reading. Ask how one event relates to another. Ask yourself if you understand what you just read. As you answer your questions, you are making sure that you understand what is going on.

Clarifying

Clear up, or *clarify,* confusing or difficult passages as you read. When you realize you do not understand something, try these techniques to help you clarify the ideas.
- *Reread* the confusing parts slowly and carefully.
- *Look up* unfamiliar words.
- Simply *"talk out"* the part to yourself.

Reread the passage. The second time is often easier and more informative.

Reviewing

You probably *review* in school what you learned the day before so the ideas are firm in your mind. Reviewing when you read does the same thing. Take time now and then to pause and review what you have read. Think about the main ideas and reorganize them for yourself so you can recall them later. Filling in study aids such as graphic organizers, notes, or outlines can help you review.

Monitoring Your Comprehension

As you read, check your understanding by using the following strategies.

- **Summarize** what you read by pausing from time to time and telling yourself the main ideas of what you have just read. Answer the questions *Who? What?*

During Reading

Engaging With the Text

Encourage students to write questions or mark confusing parts of the text with a sticky note as they read. Organize students into groups and allow them to discuss the comments they made on their notes. Have a member of the group record common difficulties. Discuss as a class the sections of the reading that were difficult or confusing, and help clarify the material for the students.

After Reading

Reviewing Remind students to use the following strategies after each section or chapter to ensure greater comprehension:

- Readers should summarize the most important parts of the text in their own words.
- Readers should clarify confusing content by rereading, asking questions, or seeking outside help.
- Readers should predict what might happen next.

Differentiated Instruction

Meeting Special Needs: Less-Proficient Readers Prediction guides (often called anticipation guides) are an effective way of setting a purpose for reading, engaging students during reading, and monitoring comprehension after reading. Create statements related to the upcoming section or chapter. Write some statements that are true, some that are false, and some that are outrageous or funny. Have students write *True* or *False* beside each statement. Students should then check and make corrections to their predictions as they read.

Thinking About Your Reading

Why It's Important

While many students are capable of reading the text and answering specific comprehension questions about what they have read, understanding subtleties of meaning or thinking critically may be more difficult. Students become better readers, writers, and thinkers when they know how to use critical thinking skills.

Before Reading

Modeling When teaching critical thinking skills, it is best to focus on teaching only one or two skills prior to reading. Explain the skill, and model how you, as a reader, use it to comprehend the reading.

During Reading

Thinking Critically Students who interact with the text will have a better chance of thinking more critically about it. Organize students into small groups, and assign a section of text for each group to read. Have students discuss questions such as, "Why did the stock market fall at this particular time?" or "Is the reason why this event occurred based on fact or opinion?" Encourage students to examine the questions from different perspectives. Have students share their discussions with the class.

Where? When? Why? and *How?* Summarizing tests your comprehension by encouraging you to clarify key points in your own words.

- **Paraphrase** Sometimes you read something that you "sort of" understand, but not quite. Use paraphrasing as a test to see whether you really got the point. *Paraphrasing* is retelling something in your own words. So shut the book and try putting what you have just read into your own words. If you cannot explain it clearly, you should probably have another look at the text.

Thinking About Your Reading

Sometimes it is important to think more deeply about what you have read so you can get the most out of what the author says. These critical thinking skills will help you go beyond what the words say and get at the important messages of your reading.

Interpreting

When you listen to your best friend talk, you do not just hear the words he or she says. You also watch your friend, listen to the tone of voice, and use what you already know about that person to put meaning to the words. In doing so, you are interpreting what your friend says. Readers do the same thing when they interpret as they read. *Interpreting* is asking yourself, *What is the writer really saying here?* and then using what you know about the world to help answer that question.

Inferring

You may not realize it, but you infer, or make inferences, every day. Here is an example: You run to the bus stop a little later than usual. There is no one there. "I have missed the bus," you say to yourself. You may be wrong, but that is the way our minds work. You look at the evidence (you are late; no one is there) and come to a conclusion (you have missed the bus).

When you read, you go though exactly the same process because writers don't always directly state what they want you to understand. By providing clues and interesting details, they suggest certain information. Whenever you combine those clues with your own background and knowledge, you are making an inference.

An *inference* involves using your thinking and experience to come up with an idea based on what an author implies or suggests. In reading, you *infer* when you use context clues and your own knowledge to figure out the author's meaning.

Drawing Conclusions

Skillful readers are always *drawing conclusions,* or figuring out much more than an author says directly. The process is like a detective solving a mystery. You combine information and evidence that the author provides to come up with a statement about the topic. Drawing conclusions helps you find connections between ideas and events and gives you a better understanding of what you are reading.

Analyzing

Analyzing, or looking at separate parts of something to understand the entire piece, is a way to think critically about written work.

- In analyzing persuasive *nonfiction,* you might look at the writer's reasons to see if they actually support the main point of the argument.

More About the Reading Strategy

Have students evaluate their proficiency with using different types of critical thinking skills. Draw a continuum on the board for each skill, with 0 representing great difficulty using the skill and 10 indicating mastery of it. Have students rate their abilities by answering questions such as: Am I usually able to infer and understand what the author is suggesting, even if it is not stated? Can I usually draw conclusions when I read? Can I easily tell facts from opinions?

- In analyzing *informational text,* you might look at how the ideas are organized to see what is most important.

Distinguishing Fact From Opinion

Distinguishing between fact and opinion is one of the most important reading skills you can learn. A *fact* is a statement that can be proved with supporting information. An *opinion,* on the other hand, is what a writer believes, on the basis of his or her personal viewpoint. Writers can support their opinions with facts, but an opinion is something that cannot be proved.

FOR EXAMPLE

Look at the following examples of fact and opinion.

Fact: George III was the British king during the American Revolution.

Opinion: King George III was an evil despot.

You could prove that George III was king during that period. It's a fact. However, not everyone might see that King George III was a despot. That's someone's opinion.

As you examine information, always ask yourself, "Is this a fact or an opinion?" Don't think that opinions are always bad. Very often they are just what you want. You read editorials and essays for their authors' opinions. Reviews of books, movies, plays, and CDs can help you decide whether to spend your time and money on something. It's when opinions are based on faulty reasoning or prejudice or when they are stated as facts that they become troublesome.

Evaluating

When you form an opinion or make a judgment about something you are reading, you are *evaluating.* If you are reading informational texts or something on the Internet, it is important to evaluate how qualified the author is to be writing about the topic and how reliable the information is that is presented. Ask yourself whether the author seems biased, whether the information is one-sided, and whether the argument presented is logical.

Synthesizing

When you *synthesize,* you combine ideas (maybe even from different sources) to come up with something new. It may be a new understanding of an important idea or a new way of combining and presenting information. For example, you might read a manual on coaching soccer, combine that information with your own experiences playing soccer, and come up with a winning plan for coaching your sister's team this spring.

Understanding Text Structure

Good writers do not just put together sentences and paragraphs in any order. They structure each piece of their writing in a specific way for a specific purpose. That pattern of organization is called *text structure.* When you know the text structure

After Reading

Writing Questions Tell students that after they read, they will write one question that reflects each type of the thinking skills described in the *Reading Skills Handbook.* For example, "What conclusion can you make about Rosa Parks' refusal to give up her seat on the bus?" Knowing that they will have to write questions about the text will help students think more about it as they read.

Understanding Text Structure

Why It's Important

Students who begin reading without understanding text structures may have difficulty with comprehension and retention. Students can categorize information better and make sense of the text more easily when they learn how authors organize the text.

Before Reading

Skimming Before students read the chapter, walk them through it. For each page, note photos, charts, diagrams, maps, headings, and boldfaced words. Ask students questions such as: Why did the author choose this particular photograph to illustrate this topic? How does this map relate to the topic described in the title? What do you think the author intends for you to learn in this section?

Differentiated Instruction

Meeting Special Needs: Less-Proficient Readers When students find connections to their own lives in the text, their ability to comprehend it improves. Offer projects that build upon these connections. Projects may include: debating issues presented in the text; writing articles for the school or local paper; conducting interviews with others who have knowledge of the subject; role playing; finding relevant poetry, art, or music to share with the class; and reading and reporting on books or magazine articles related to the subject.

Reading Skills Handbook

During Reading

Identifying Text Structure

Organize students into groups of four, and assign different sections of the text to each group. Have groups choose a facilitator, a reader, a recorder, and a reporter. As the reader reads a section aloud, have the recorder note all the signal words. The facilitator will help the group identify the section's text structure based on the categories listed in the *Reading Skills Handbook*. The reporter will describe to the class the signal words and the text structure that the group identified.

After Reading

Organizing Information

Graphic organizers help students organize and comprehend ideas and events. Have a variety of blank graphic organizers available for students to choose from to help them organize text information, including flow charts, time lines, and Venn diagrams.

Reading for Research

Why It's Important

There are vast amounts of information available to students today. It is important for students to know how to access, evaluate, and use it.

---

of a selection, you will find it easier to locate and recall an author's ideas. Here are four ways that writers organize text.

Comparison and Contrast

Comparison-and-contrast structure shows the similarities and differences between people, things, and ideas. Maybe you have overheard someone at school say something like "He is better at throwing the football, but I can run faster than he can." This student is using comparison-and-contrast structure. When writers use comparison-and-contrast structure, often they want to show you *how things that seem alike are different, or how things that seem different are alike.*

- **Signal words and phrases:** *similarly, on the one hand, on the other hand, in contrast to, but, however*

Cause and Effect

Just about everything that happens in life is the cause or the effect of some other event or action. Sometimes what happens is pretty minor: You do not look when you are pouring milk *(cause);* you spill milk on the table *(effect).* Sometimes it is a little more serious: You do not look at your math book before the big test *(cause);* you mess up on the test *(effect).*

Writers use cause-and-effect structure to explore the reasons for something happening and to examine the results of previous events. This structure helps answer the question that everybody is always asking: *Why?* A historian might tell us why an empire rose and fell. Cause-and-effect structure is all about explaining things.

- **Signal words and phrases:** *so, because, as a result, therefore, for the following reasons*

Problem and Solution

How did scientists overcome the difficulty of getting a person to the moon? How will I brush my teeth when I have forgotten my toothpaste? These questions may be very different in importance, but they have one thing in common: Each identifies a problem and asks how to solve it. *Problems* and *solutions* are part of what makes life interesting. Problems and solutions also occur in fiction and nonfiction writing.

- **Signal words and phrases:** *how, help, problem, obstruction, difficulty, need, attempt, have to, must*

Sequence

Take a look at three common forms of sequencing, *the order in which thoughts are arranged.*

- **Chronological order** refers to the order in which events take place. First you wake up; next you have breakfast; then you go to school. Those events don't make much sense in any other order.

    Signal words: *first, next, then, later,* and *finally.*

- **Spatial order** tells you the order in which to look at objects. For example, take a look at this description of an ice cream sundae: *At the bottom of the dish are two scoops of vanilla. The scoops are covered with fudge and topped with whipped cream and a cherry.* Your eyes follow the sundae from the bottom to the top. Spatial order is important in descriptive writing because it helps you as a reader to see an image the way the author does.

More About the Reading Strategy

Why should students understand the different types of text structure? Knowledge about the different types of text structure helps students remember content. It also helps students make sense out of unfamiliar text. Students who internalize the process of cause and effect or problem and solution are developing thinking processes that will serve them for the rest of their lives.

Signal words: *above, below, behind,* and *next to.*

- **Order of importance** is going from most important to least important or the other way around. For example, a typical news article has a most-to-least-important structure.

    Signal words: *principal, central, important,* and *fundamental.*

CHECK IT OUT

- **Tables of contents** Look at the table of contents first to see whether a resource offers information you need.
- **Indexes** An index is an alphabetical listing of significant topics covered in a book. It is found in the back of a book.
- **Headings and subheadings** Headings often tell you what information is

going to follow in the text you're reading. Subheadings allow you to narrow your search for information even further.

- **Graphic features** Photos, diagrams, maps, charts, graphs, and other graphic features can communicate large amounts of information at a glance.

Reading for Research

An important part of doing research is knowing how to get information from a wide variety of sources. The following skills will help you when you have a research assignment for a class or when you want information about a topic outside of school.

Reading Text Features

Researching a topic is not only about asking questions; it is about finding answers. Textbooks, references, magazines, and other sources provide a variety of text features to help you find those answers quickly and efficiently.

Organizing Information

When researching a topic, you have to make sense of that information, organize it, and put it all together in ways that will help you explain it to someone else. Here are some ways of doing just that.

- **Record** information from your research and keep track of your resources on note cards.

- **Interpret graphic aids** carefully. These could include charts, graphs, maps and photographs.

- **Summarize** information before you write it on a note card. That way you will have the main ideas in your own words.

- **Outline** ideas so you can see how subtopics and supporting information will fit under the main ideas.

- **Make a table or graph** to compare items or categories of information.

Before Reading

Writing a Research Plan
Help students create a research plan for organizing information. The plan should include: a topic question to research; a list of related subtopics; sources for finding information; forms that show how to cite bibliographic information; and a time line for the completion of the research project.

During Reading

Organizing Information
Have students divide a piece of notebook paper into three columns to help them organize research information. The first column should list the main ideas found in the source. The second column should identify supporting details, and the last column should include an exact quote from the article, book, or Web site that supports the research.

After Reading

Evaluating Sources Discuss as a class the Web sites that were the most helpful for researching topics. Students should identify Web sites and search engines that were easy to use, and they should share them with the class.

Differentiated Instruction

Meeting Special Needs: Less-Proficient Readers Remind students to evaluate the sources that they cite in their research before they use them. Evaluating requires making a judgment or forming an opinion. Students should remember that the author should be qualified to write about the topic. Students should also evaluate the information for biases or opinions.

REFERENCE ATLAS

NATIONAL GEOGRAPHIC

ATLAS KEY

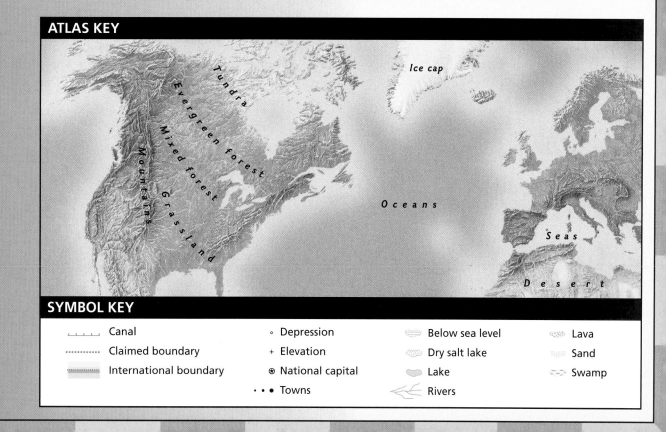

Tundra
Ice cap
Evergreen forest
Mixed forest
Mountains
Grassland
Oceans
Seas
Desert

SYMBOL KEY

⊥⊥⊥⊥ Canal	∘ Depression	Below sea level	Lava
·········· Claimed boundary	+ Elevation	Dry salt lake	Sand
International boundary	⊛ National capital	Lake	Swamp
	· · · Towns	Rivers	

UNITED STATES POLITICAL

0 mi — 600
0 km — 600

OBLIQUE AZIMUTHAL EQUIDISTANT PROJECTION

NATIONAL GEOGRAPHIC

GREENLAND
(KALAALLIT NUNAAT)
Den.

ARCTIC CIRCLE

C A N A D A

MONTANA
Helena
Billings

NORTH DAKOTA
Bismarck

MINNESOTA

Lake Superior

MICHIGAN

Lake Huron

MAINE
Augusta
Montpelier
Portland
Concord, N.H.
NEW YORK
VT.
Boston, MASS.
Albany
Providence, R.I.
Hartford, CONN.

SOUTH DAKOTA
Pierre

WISCONSIN
Minneapolis
St. Paul
Milwaukee
Madison
Lansing

L. Michigan

Lake Ontario
Buffalo
Detroit
L. Erie
Cleveland PA.
New York City
Trenton, N.J.
Philadelphia

WYOMING
Casper
Cheyenne

Sioux City
IOWA
Des Moines
Chicago
ILLINOIS
IND.
Toledo
Harrisburg
Pittsburgh
Columbus
OHIO
Baltimore
Dover, DEL.
Annapolis, MD.

NEBRASKA
Lincoln
Omaha
Indianapolis
Dayton W. VA.
Washington, D.C.
Cincinnati

Denver
COLORADO

Kansas City
MISSOURI
Springfield
Frankfort
Charleston
Richmond
Virginia Beach

Topeka
St. Louis
VIRGINIA

KANSAS
Jefferson City
Louisville
KENTUCKY

Santa Fe
Tulsa
Nashville
TENNESSEE
NORTH CAROLINA
Raleigh
Charlotte

Albuquerque
Oklahoma City
ARKANSAS
Memphis
SOUTH CAROLINA
Columbia

NEW MEXICO
OKLAHOMA
Little Rock
Atlanta
Charleston

Fort Worth
Birmingham
GEORGIA
Savannah

El Paso
Dallas
MISS.
ALABAMA
Montgomery
Jackson

TEXAS
LOUISIANA
Tallahassee
Jacksonville

Austin
Baton Rouge
FLORIDA

San Antonio
Houston
New Orleans
Tampa

M E X I C O

Gulf of Mexico

Miami

Straits of Florida

CUBA

BAHAMAS

ATLANTIC OCEAN

Bermuda Is.
U.K.

Caribbean Sea

JAMAICA

HAITI
DOMINICAN REPUBLIC

San Juan
PUERTO RICO
U.S.

ANTIGUA & BARBUDA
ST. KITTS & NEVIS

DOMINICA

A 1 130°W 2 125°W 3 50°N 120°W 4 115°W 5 110°W 6 105°W 7 100°W 8

Cape Flattery
Mt. Olympus
7,965 ft
2,428 m
Seattle

C A N A D A

45°N

B

CASCADE RANGE
COAST RANGE
Columbia
Columbia
Blue Mts.
Clearwater Mts.
COLUMBIA PLATEAU
Bitterroot Range
Salmon River Mts.
ROCKY
Absaroka Range
Bighorn Mts.
Missouri
Black Hills
Missouri

130°W
40°N
Cape Mendocino
Great Sandy Desert
Snake
Snake River Plain
Shoshone Falls
Wind River Range
Laramie Mts.
N. Platte
Sand Hills
Platte

C

SIERRA NEVADA
Great Salt Lake
Wasatch Range
Uinta Mts.
M O U N T A I N S
GREAT

D

PACIFIC
Lake Tahoe
Central Valley
GREAT BASIN
Colorado
14,433 ft
4,399 m
Mt. Elbert
Denver
P L A I N S
HIGH

35°N
OCEAN
San Francisco
Mt. Whitney
14,494 ft
4,418 m
Lake Powell
San Juan Mts.
Arkansas

E

Death Valley
-282 ft, -86 m
Lake Mead
Grand Canyon
Colorado Plateau
Sangre de Cristo Mts.
High
Red

Point Conception
Mojave Desert
Colorado

F

Channel Islands
Los Angeles
Salton Sea
Phoenix
Sonoran Desert
Colorado
Sacramento Mts.
Llano Estacado
Dallas
Brazos

San Diego
30°N
Rio Grande

125°W
120°W
115°W

G

68°N
Point Barrow
Beaufort Sea
Edwards Plateau
C O

ARCTIC OCEAN
180°
Chukchi Sea
North Slope
Brooks Range
68°N

RUSSIA
Bering Strait
ARCTIC CIRCLE
Seward Pen.
ALASKA
CANADA
110°W

H

St. Lawrence Island
Yukon
Kuskokwim
Tanana
Alaska Range
Mt. McKinley (Denali)
20,320 ft, 6,194 m
Anchorage
60°N
25°N
Rio Grande

172°W
60°N
Nunivak Island

J

Bering Sea
Bristol Bay
Gulf of Alaska
Alexander Archipelago
MEXICO

Alaska Peninsula
Kodiak I.
TROPIC OF CANCER

K

ALASKA
0 mi   300
0 km   300
PACIFIC OCEAN
52°N
52°N

164°W 156°W 148°W 140°W 132°W   105°W   100°W
1 2 3 4 5 6 7 8

UNITED STATES PHYSICAL

0 mi   300

0 km   300

ALBERS CONIC EQUAL-AREA PROJECTION

NATIONAL GEOGRAPHIC

CANADA

Lake of the Woods

Isle Royale
Lake Superior

Upper Peninsula

Minneapolis

Mississippi

Milwaukee

Lake Michigan

Lower Peninsula

Lake Huron

Detroit

Chicago

CENTRAL LOWLAND

Lake Erie

Cleveland

Pittsburgh

Indianapolis

Ohio

St. Louis

Wabash

Flint Hills

Ozark Plateau

Boston Mts.

Memphis

Ouachita Mts.

Tennessee

Black Belt

Mississippi

Red

New Orleans

Houston

Mississippi River Delta

Gulf of Mexico

Lake Champlain

Adirondack Mts.

Niagara Falls

Lake Ontario

Appalachian Plateau

Allegheny Mts.

Cumberland Plateau

Cumberland

Mt. Mitchell
6,684 ft
2,037 m

APPALACHIAN

Blue Ridge

Atlanta

Savannah

Piedmont

COASTAL

Jacksonville

Green Mts.

White Mts.

Connecticut

Hudson

Boston

Cape Cod

Gulf of Maine

Long Island

New York City

Philadelphia

Baltimore

Delaware Bay

Washington

Chesapeake Bay

ATLANTIC OCEAN

Cape Hatteras

APPALACHIAN MOUNTAINS

PLAIN

Cape Canaveral

Lake Okeechobee

The Everglades

Miami

Florida Keys

Straits of Florida

TROPIC OF CANCER

CUBA

PRINCIPAL HAWAIIAN ISLANDS

Niihau

Kauai

Oahu

Honolulu

Molokai

Lanai

Kahoolawe

Maui — 21°N

Hawaii

Mauna Kea
13,796 ft
4,205 m

PACIFIC OCEAN

0 mi   100

0 km   100

159°W   156°W

90°W

95°W

85°W   80°W   75°W

A New Nation, 1787

BRITISH NORTH AMERICA

Claimed by U.S. and Great Britain

Claimed by U.S. and Great Britain

Claimed by N.H. and N.Y.

Part of Mass.

NEW HAMPSHIRE

MASSACHUSETTS

RHODE ISLAND
CONNECTICUT

Awarded to Pa. from Conn. 1782

Ceded by Mass. to N.Y. 1786

Ceded by Mass. to U.S. 1785

NORTHWEST TERRITORY

Ceded by Va. to U.S. 1784

New York City (1787-1790)

PA.

NEW JERSEY

MD.

DELAWARE

Missouri

Mississippi

SPANISH

SPANISH LOUISIANA

NORTH

Ceded by Conn. to U.S. 1786 & 1800

Wabash

Ohio

UNITED

VIRGINIA

STATES

ALTA CALIFORNIA

Arkansas

Ceded by New York to U.S. 1782

Claimed by Virginia

NORTH CAROLINA

AMERICA

Claimed by North Carolina

Colorado

Gila

Claimed by Georgia

SOUTH CAROLINA

Ceded by S.C. to Ga. 1787

GEORGIA

Original 13 states

Land still claimed by states 1787

U.S. territory

British territory

Spanish territory

Disputed boundary

Rio Grande

BAJA CALIFORNIA

WESTERN INTERIOR PROVINCES

Claimed by Ga., Spain and U.S.

SPANISH FLORIDA

EASTERN INTERIOR PROVINCES

Coming of Age, 1821

Columbia

U.S.-British treaty line of 1818

BRITISH NORTH AMERICA

Claimed by U.S. and Great Britain

RED RIVER BASIN To U.S. 1818

MAINE 1820

OREGON COUNTRY

U.S.-British agreement to joint occupation in 1818

Snake

Adams-Onis Treaty line of 1819

UNORGANIZED

TERRITORY

Mississippi

MICHIGAN TERRITORY

Missouri

Ohio

Wabash

INDIANA 1816

Washington

ALTA CALIFORNIA

Arkansas

ILLINOIS 1818

MISSOURI 1821

M E X I C O

ARKANSAS TERRITORY

Red

MISSISSIPPI 1817

ALABAMA 1819

TEXAS

Rio Grande

LOUISIANA 1812

FLORIDA To U.S. 1819

UNITED STATES
TERRITORIAL GROWTH

NATIONAL GEOGRAPHIC

Expanding West of the Mississippi, 1803

BRITISH NORTH AMERICA

Claimed by U.S. and Great Britain

OREGON COUNTRY
Claimed by Great Britain, Russia, Spain, and United States

Claimed by U.S. and Great Britain

VERMONT 1791

Mississippi

Missouri

INDIANA

TERRITORY

Philadelphia (1790-1800)

Washington (new capital 1800)

OHIO 1803

Ohio

LOUISIANA PURCHASE
Purchased by U.S. in 1803 from France

Wabash

NEW SPAIN (SPANISH MEXICO)

Arkansas

KENTUCKY 1792

TENNESSEE 1796

Red

Ceded by Georgia to U.S. 1802

MISSISSIPPI TERR.

Rio Grande

Claimed by U.S. and Spain

BAJA CALIFORNIA

SPANISH FLORIDA

Claimed by U.S. and Spain

States previously in the Union
States newly admitted

Coast to Coast, 1850 and beyond

BRITISH NORTH AMERICA

Treaty line of 1846

Treaty line of 1842

Treaty line of 1842

WASHINGTON 1889

OREGON TERRITORY
Added to U.S. in 1846

MONTANA 1889

NORTH DAKOTA 1889

MINNESOTA 1858

MINNESOTA TERRITORY

MICHIGAN 1837

OREGON 1859

Snake

IDAHO 1890

WYOMING 1890

SOUTH DAKOTA 1889

WISCONSIN 1848

NEVADA 1864

UNORGANIZED

NEBRASKA 1867

IOWA 1846

Missouri

UTAH TERRITORY

TERRITORY

Washington

CALIFORNIA 1850

UTAH 1896

COLORADO 1876

KANSAS 1861

Wabash

Ohio

W. VA. 1863

Arkansas

Colorado

ARIZONA 1912

NEW MEXICO TERRITORY

OKLAHOMA 1907

ARKANSAS 1836

Red

Gila

GADSDEN PURCHASE
To U.S. 1853

NEW MEXICO 1912

Mississippi

Rio Grande

TEXAS 1845

RUSSIA

ALASKA 1959
Purchased by U.S. 1867

MEXICO

FLORIDA 1845

States admitted after 1850

HAWAII 1959
Annexed by U.S. 1898

MIDDLE AMERICA

PHYSICAL/POLITICAL

0 mi 400

0 km 400

AZIMUTHAL EQUIDISTANT PROJECTION

NATIONAL GEOGRAPHIC

UNITED STATES

Tijuana
Mexicali
Sonoran Desert

BAJA CALIFORNIA

Ciudad Juárez

SONORA

CHIHUAHUA
Chihuahua

COAHUILA

Rio Grande

Nuevo Laredo

BAJA CALIFORNIA SUR

La Paz

DURANGO

Monterrey

NUEVO LEON

Matamoros

Gulf of Mexico

False Cape

ZACATECAS

Mazatlan

SINALOA

SAN LUIS POTOSI

TAMAULIPAS

NAYARIT

AGUASCALIENTES

Ciudad Madero
Tampico

Guadalajara
San Luis Potosi
Leon

QUERETARO

VERACRUZ

JALISCO

Merida YUCATAN

Yucatan
Peninsula

GUANAJUATO
COLIMA

HIDALGO
TLAXCALA

Bay of Campeche

Mexico City
Orizaba
18,855 ft
+5,747 m

DISTRITO FEDERAL
MICHOACAN
Popocatepetl
17,802 ft
5,426 m

Veracruz

CAMPECHE

QUINTANA ROO

PUEBLA

MEXICO
Sierra Madre del Sur

TABASCO

Belize
City

MORELOS
Acapulco

GUERRERO

OAXACA

Belmopan
BELIZE

*Gulf of
Hondur*

Isthmus of
Tehuantepec

CHIAPAS

HO

Sierra Madre

*Gulf of
Tehuantepec*

GUATEMALA

Guatemala City
EL SALVADOR
San Salvador

Tegucigalpa

Leo

CENTRA

AMERICA

PACIFIC

OCEAN

Cocos Islan
C.R.

BAJA CALIFORNIA

Gulf of California

Baja California

Sierra Madre Occidental

Sierra Madre Oriental

MEXICO

Revillagigedo Islands
Mex.

110°W 100°W 90°W

30°N

20°N

10°N

0°

ATLANTIC
OCEAN

TROPIC OF CANCER

BAHAMAS

W E S T

• Freeport

⊛ Nassau

Straits of Florida

Andros
Island

Turks &
Caicos Islands
U.K.

I N D I E S

ST. KITTS & NEVIS

⊛ Havana

CUBA

• Camaguey

• Holguin

• Santiago
de Cuba

Santiago

HAITI

Hispaniola

Santo
Domingo

Port-au-
Prince ⊛

DOMINICAN
REPUBLIC

Isle of Youth

Cayman
Islands
U.K.

G r e a t e r   A n t i l l e s

San Juan

Puerto
Rico
U.S.

ANTIGUA &
BARBUDA

Virgin
Islands
U.S. & U.K.

Guadeloupe
Fr.

DOMINICA

Bird I.
Venez.

Martinique
Fr.

ST. LUCIA

BARBADOS

nel

Montego
Bay

JAMAICA

⊛ Kingston

C a r i b b e a n   S e a

ST. VINCENT &
THE GRENADINES

GRENADA

TRINIDAD & TOBAGO

Tobago

Port-of-Spain ⊛

Trinidad

60°W

Neth.
Curacao
Bonaire

Aruba
Neth.

Lesser Antilles

L e s s e r   S   A n t i l l e s

URAS

Coco

Mosquito Coast

NICARAGUA

⊛ Managua

Lake
Nicaragua

COSTA

Puerto
Limon

Gulf of
Mosquitos

Isthmus of Panama

• San Jose ⊛

RICA

PANAMA

⊛ Panama City

• David

Gulf of
Panama

SOUTH

AMERICA

EQUATOR

80°W

70°W

CANADA
PHYSICAL/POLITICAL

0 mi   400

0 km   400

AZIMUTHAL EQUIDISTANT PROJECTION

NATIONAL
GEOGRAPHIC

Ellesmere
Island

evon Island

GREENLAND
(KALAALLIT NUNAAT)
Den.

ICELAND

Baffin
Bay

Baffin Island

Davis Strait

Melville
Peninsula

Foxe
Basin

A V U T

Southampton
Island

Iqaluit

Hudson Strait

Labrador
Sea

Ungava
Bay

Hudson

Bay

Belcher
Islands

NEWFOUNDLAND
AND LABRADOR

Cartwright

Schefferville

Happy Valley-
Goose Bay

Smallwood
Reservoir

"Churchill Falls

Island of
Newfoundland

James Bay

QUEBEC

St. John's
Avalon
Peninsula

Manicouagan
Reservoir
Sept-Iles

Anticosti I.

St.-Pierre & Miquelon
Fr.

SHIELD

Gulf of
St. Lawrence

Gaspe
Pen.

PRINCE
EDWARD
ISLAND

Cape Breton I.

ATLANTIC

ONTARIO

Chicoutimi

Lake
Nipigon

Rouyn-Noranda

Charlottetown

NEW
BRUNSWICK

NOVA
SCOTIA

Thunder
Bay

Lake
Superior

Quebec
City

Fredericton

Saint John

Halifax

OCEAN

Sudbury

Montreal

St. Lawrence

Bay of Fundy

Ottawa

Lake
Huron

Toronto

Niagara Falls

L. Ontario

London

L. Erie

Lake Michigan

WORLD
POLITICAL

0 mi　　　　2000
0 km　　　　2000

WINKEL TRIPEL PROJECTION

NATIONAL GEOGRAPHIC

**Map labels:**

ARCTIC
150°W　120°W　90°W　60°W　30°W

Queen Elizabeth Islands

GREENLAND
(KALAALLIT NUNAAT)
Den.

Chukchi Sea
Beaufort Sea
RUSSIA
ALASKA U.S.
60°N
Bering Sea
Anchorage
Gulf of Alaska
Aleutian Islands

Great Bear Lake
Mackenzie
Great Slave Lake

Baffin Bay
Baffin Island

Greenland Se.

Nuuk

ARCTIC CIRCLE
Reykjavik
ICELAND

CANADA
Hudson Bay
Labrador Sea

UNITE KINGDO
Dublin
IRELAND
Londo

Vancouver
Seattle
Calgary

Great Lakes
Island of Newfoundland

NORTH

NORTH
PACIFIC

San Francisco
UNITED STATES
Missouri
Ohio
Chicago
Toronto
Ottawa
New York City
Washington

ATLANTIC

Madrid
PORTUGAL
SPA
Azores Port.

30°N
Los Angeles
Atlanta

OCEAN
TROPIC OF CANCER

Houston
Rio Grande
Gulf of Mexico
Bahamas

OCEAN

Madeira Is. Rabat
Port.
MOROCCO
Canary Is. Sp.
Morocco
WESTERN SAHARA

Hawaiian Islands U.S.

MEXICO
Havana
CUBA
DOMINICAN REP.
Santo Domingo
Puerto Rico U.S.

CAPE VERDE

MAURITANIA

Guadalajara
Mexico City
BELIZE
HAITI
JAMAICA
ST. KITTS & NEVIS
ANTIGUA & BARBUDA
DOMINICA
BARBADOS
ST. LUCIA
ST. VINCENT & THE GRENADINES
GRENADA
TRINIDAD & TOBAGO

SENEGAL
GAMBIA
GUINEA-BISSAU
GUINEA

MAI

GUATEMALA
Guatemala City
HONDURAS
EL SALVADOR
NICARAGUA
Caribbean Sea

BURKINA FASO
SIERRA LEONE
LIBERIA
CÔTE D'IVOIRE

COSTA RICA
PANAMA
Caracas
VENEZUELA
FRENCH GUIANA Fr.

Medellin
Bogota
COLOMBIA

GUYANA
SURINAME

Christmas Island
Kiribati

EQUATOR
0°
Galapagos Islands
Ecua.
Quito
ECUADOR
Manaus
Negro
Amazon

PERU
Madeira
BRAZIL
Recife

Marquesas Islands Fr.

Lima
Xingu
São Francisco
Salvador (Bahia)

SAMOA
AMERICAN SAMOA U.S.

La Paz
BOLIVIA
Brasilia

SOUTH

FRENCH POLYNESIA Fr.
TROPIC OF CAPRICORN
Sucre
Rio de Janeiro
Sao Paulo

ATLANTIC

TONGA
PARAGUAY
Asuncion

Paraná
Cordoba
Porto Alegre

OCEAN

30°S
Santiago
Buenos Aires
CHILE
URUGUAY
Montevideo

SOUTH

ARGENTINA

PACIFIC

OCEAN

Falkland Islands U.K.
Tierra del Fuego
South Georgia U.K.

Strait of Magellan

Drake Passage

60°S
ANTARCTIC CIRCLE
Antarctic Peninsula

Weddell Sea

Ross Sea
Berkner Island

ABBREVIATIONS

AUST.	AUSTRIA
B.&H.	BOSNIA & HERZEGOVINA
BELG.	BELGIUM
CROAT.	CROATIA
CZECH REP.	CZECH REPUBLIC
DEM. REP. OF THE CONGO	DEMOCRATIC REPUBLIC OF THE CONGO
EQ. GUINEA	EQUATORIAL GUINEA
EST.	ESTONIA
HUNG.	HUNGARY
LITH.	LITHUANIA
MACED.	MACEDONIA
MOLD.	MOLDOVA
NETH.	NETHERLANDS
SERB. AND MONT.	SERBIA AND MONTENEGRO
SLOV.	SLOVENIA
SWITZ.	SWITZERLAND
U.A.E.	UNITED ARAB EMIRATES

United States Facts

1 Delaware
Year Admitted: 1787
Population: 783,600
Land area: 1,955 sq. mi.
Representatives: 1
Dover

2 Pennsylvania
Year Admitted: 1787
Population: 12,281,054
Land area: 44,820 sq. mi.
Representatives: 19
Harrisburg

3 New Jersey
Year Admitted: 1787
Population: 8,414,350
Land area: 7,419 sq. mi.
Representatives: 13
Trenton

9 New Hampshire
Year Admitted: 1788
Population: 1,235,786
Land area: 8,969 sq. mi.
Representatives: 2
Concord

10 Virginia
Year Admitted: 1788
Population: 7,078,515
Land area: 39,598 sq. mi.
Representatives: 11
Richmond

11 New York
Year Admitted: 1788
Population: 18,976,457
Land area: 47,224 sq. mi.
Representatives: 29
★ Albany

17 Ohio
Year Admitted: 1803
Population: 11,353,140
Land area: 40,953 sq. mi.
Representatives: 18
★ Columbus

18 Louisiana
Year Admitted: 1812
Population: 4,468,976
Land area: 43,566 sq. mi.
Representatives: 7
Baton Rouge

19 Indiana
Year Admitted: 1816
Population: 6,080,485
Land area: 35,870 sq. mi.
Representatives: 9
Indianapolis

25 Arkansas
Year Admitted: 1836
Population: 2,673,400
Land area: 52,075 sq. mi.
Representatives: 4
Little Rock

26 Michigan
Year Admitted: 1837
Population: 9,938,444
Land area: 56,809 sq. mi.
Representatives: 15
Lansing

27 Florida
Year Admitted: 1845
Population: 15,982,378
Land area: 53,997 sq. mi.
Representatives: 25
★ Tallahassee

33 Oregon
Year Admitted: 1859
Population: 3,421,399
Land area: 96,003 sq. mi.
Representatives: 5
★ Salem

34 Kansas
Year Admitted: 1861
Population: 2,688,418
Land area: 81,823 sq. mi.
Representatives: 4
Topeka ★

35 West Virginia
Year Admitted: 1863
Population: 1,808,344
Land area: 24,087 sq. mi.
Representatives: 3
★ Charleston

36 Nevada
Year Admitted: 1864
Population: 1,998,257
Land area: 109,806 sq. mi.
Representatives: 3
★ Carson City

42 Washington
Year Admitted: 1889
Population: 5,894,121
Land area: 66,582 sq. mi.
Representatives: 9
★ Olympia

43 Idaho
Year Admitted: 1890
Population: 1,293,953
Land area: 82,751 sq. mi.
Representatives: 2
★ Boise

44 Wyoming
Year Admitted: 1890
Population: 493,782
Land area: 97,105 sq. mi.
Representatives: 1
Cheyenne ★

45 Utah
Year Admitted: 1896
Population: 2,233,169
Land area: 82,168 sq. mi.
Representatives: 3
Salt Lake City

Washington, D.C.
Population: 572,059
Land area: 61 sq. mi.

U.S. Territories

Puerto Rico
Population: 3,808,610
Land area: 3,425 sq. mi.

Guam
Population: 155,000 (est.)
Land area: 210 sq. mi.

U.S. Virgin Islands
Population: 121,000 (est.)
Land area: 134 sq. mi.

American Samoa
Population: 65,000 (est.)
Land area: 77 sq. mi.

The states are listed in the order they were admitted to the Union.

Population figures are based on U.S. Bureau of the Census for 2000. House of Representatives figures are from the Clerk of the House of Representatives. States are not drawn to scale.

4 Georgia
Year Admitted: 1788
Population: 8,186,453
Land area: 57,919 sq. mi.
Representatives: 13

★ Atlanta

5 Connecticut
Year Admitted: 1788
Population: 3,405,565
Land area: 4,845 sq. mi.
Representatives: 5

★ Hartford

6 Massachusetts
Year Admitted: 1788
Population: 6,349,097
Land area: 7,838 sq. mi.
Representatives: 10

Boston ★

7 Maryland
Year Admitted: 1788
Population: 5,296,486
Land area: 9,775 sq. mi.
Representatives: 8

Annapolis ★

8 South Carolina
Year Admitted: 1788
Population: 4,012,012
Land area: 30,111 sq. mi.
Representatives: 6

Columbia ★

12 North Carolina
Year Admitted: 1789
Population: 8,049,313
Land area: 48,718 sq. mi.
Representatives: 13

★ Raleigh

13 Rhode Island
Year Admitted: 1790
Population: 1,048,319
Land area: 1,045 sq. mi.
Representatives: 2

★ Providence

14 Vermont
Year Admitted: 1791
Population: 608,827
Land area: 9,249 sq. mi.
Representatives: 1

★ Montpelier

15 Kentucky
Year Admitted: 1792
Population: 4,041,769
Land area: 39,732 sq. mi.
Representatives: 6

Frankfort ★

16 Tennessee
Year Admitted: 1796
Population: 5,689,283
Land area: 41,220 sq. mi.
Representatives: 9

★ Nashville

20 Mississippi
Year Admitted: 1817
Population: 2,844,658
Land area: 46,914 sq. mi.
Representatives: 4

★ Jackson

21 Illinois
Year Admitted: 1818
Population: 12,419,293
Land area: 55,593 sq. mi.
Representatives: 19

★ Springfield

22 Alabama
Year Admitted: 1819
Population: 4,447,100
Land area: 50,750 sq. mi.
Representatives: 7

Montgomery ★

23 Maine
Year Admitted: 1820
Population: 1,274,923
Land area: 30,865 sq. mi.
Representatives: 2

★ Augusta

24 Missouri
Year Admitted: 1821
Population: 5,595,211
Land area: 68,898 sq. mi.
Representatives: 9

Jefferson City ★

28 Texas
Year Admitted: 1845
Population: 20,851,820
Land area: 261,914 sq. mi.
Representatives: 32

Austin ★

29 Iowa
Year Admitted: 1846
Population: 2,926,324
Land area: 55,875 sq. mi.
Representatives: 5

Des Moines ★

30 Wisconsin
Year Admitted: 1848
Population: 5,363,675
Land area: 54,314 sq. mi.
Representatives: 8

Madison ★

31 California
Year Admitted: 1850
Population: 33,871,648
Land area: 155,973 sq. mi.
Representatives: 53

Sacramento ★

32 Minnesota
Year Admitted: 1858
Population: 4,919,479
Land area: 79,617 sq. mi.
Representatives: 8

Saint Paul ★

37 Nebraska
Year Admitted: 1867
Population: 1,711,263
Land area: 76,878 sq. mi.
Representatives: 3

Lincoln ★

38 Colorado
Year Admitted: 1876
Population: 4,301,261
Land area: 103,730 sq. mi.
Representatives: 7

Denver ★

39 North Dakota
Year Admitted: 1889
Population: 642,200
Land area: 68,994 sq. mi.
Representatives: 1

Bismarck ★

40 South Dakota
Year Admitted: 1889
Population: 754,844
Land area: 75,898 sq. mi.
Representatives: 1

Pierre ★

41 Montana
Year Admitted: 1889
Population: 902,195
Land area: 145,556 sq. mi.
Representatives: 1

★ Helena

46 Oklahoma
Year Admitted: 1907
Population: 3,450,654
Land area: 68,679 sq. mi.
Representatives: 5

Oklahoma City ★

47 New Mexico
Year Admitted: 1912
Population: 1,819,046
Land area: 121,365 sq. mi.
Representatives: 3

★ Santa Fe

48 Arizona
Year Admitted: 1912
Population: 5,130,632
Land area: 113,642 sq. mi.
Representatives: 8

Phoenix ★

49 Alaska
Year Admitted: 1959
Population: 626,932
Land area: 570,374 sq. mi.
Representatives: 1

Juneau ★

50 Hawaii
Year Admitted: 1959
Population: 1,211,537
Land area: 6,423 sq. mi.
Representatives: 2

Honolulu ★

1 FOCUS

Did you know❓

The early Inuit labeled distances on their maps with the time it took to travel rather than with miles. A map would show the distance between what is now Nome and Point Barrow as 10 days rather than 525 miles (845 km).

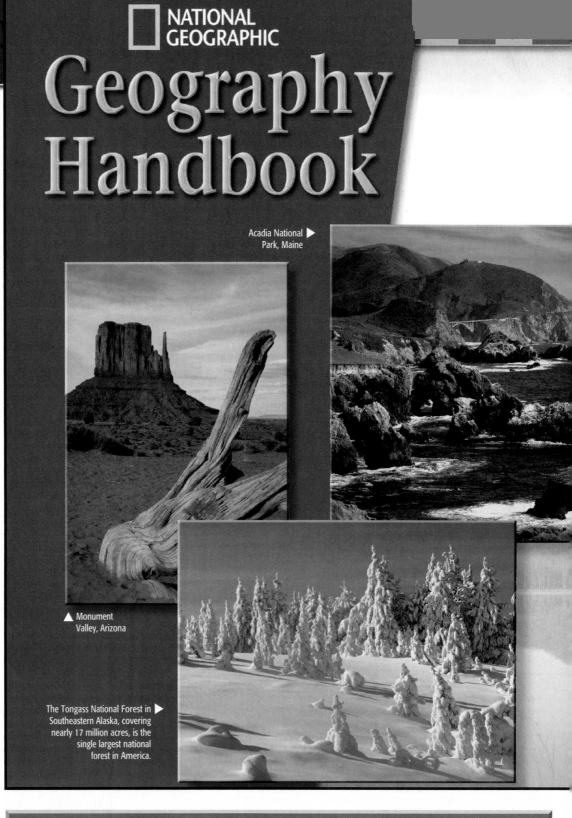

NATIONAL GEOGRAPHIC
Geography Handbook

Acadia National ▶
Park, Maine

▲ Monument Valley, Arizona

The Tongass National Forest in ▶ Southeastern Alaska, covering nearly 17 million acres, is the single largest national forest in America.

EXTENDING THE CONTENT

Careers in Geography Geographers work for the federal government in the Defense Mapping Agency, United States Geologic Survey, Central Intelligence Agency, Army Corps of Engineers, National Science Foundation, Smithsonian Institution, and Office of the Geographer in the Department of State. State environmental and transportation agencies hire geographers as analysts, planners, and cartographers. Some states even have an Office of the State Geographer. In the private sector, geographers work as professors, researchers, and cartographers.

What Is Geography?

The story of the United States begins with geography—the study of the earth in all of its variety. Geography describes the earth's land, water, and plant and animal life. It is the study of places and the complex relationships between people and their environments.

Geography of the United States

The United States is a land of startling physical differences. It is also a nation of diverse groups of people. A study of geography can help explain how the United States acquired its diversity.

The United States—with a total land area of 3,537,441 square miles (9,161,930 sq. km)—is the world's fourth-largest country in size.

The 50 States

Most of the United States—48 of the 50 states—spans the entire middle part of North America. This group of states touches three major bodies of water—the Atlantic Ocean, the Gulf of Mexico, and the Pacific Ocean. Two states—Alaska and Hawaii—lie apart from the 48 states.

Our Nation's Growth

Within the borders of the United States stretch a variety of landscapes—dense forests, hot deserts, rolling grasslands, and snow-capped mountains. Because of its large size and diverse regions, the United States throughout its history offered many opportunities. Over the centuries people from Europe, Africa, Asia, and other parts of the Americas have journeyed here. Today more than 281 million people make their homes in the United States.

2 TEACH

Using Geographic Terms
Survey students' knowledge of geographic terms. Create three columns on the chalkboard with the following headings: *Landforms*, *Bodies of Water*, and *Climates*. List one term that fits each column, such as *canyon*, *bay*, and *tropical*. Ask students to volunteer as many other terms for each column as they can. Have students turn to pages 8–9 and read the **Geographic Dictionary**. Then have them close their books and continue suggesting terms for each column on the chalkboard. **L2**

Where?When?Who?What?

National Boundaries National boundaries run to the center of the earth and to the top of the atmosphere. Airplanes need a country's permission to fly into its air space.

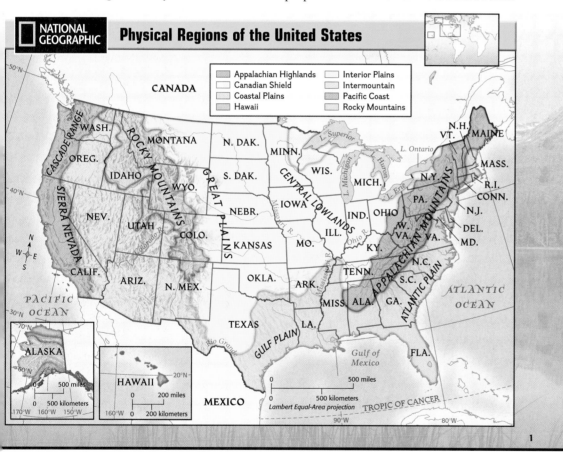

NATIONAL GEOGRAPHIC Physical Regions of the United States

- Appalachian Highlands
- Canadian Shield
- Coastal Plains
- Hawaii
- Interior Plains
- Intermountain
- Pacific Coast
- Rocky Mountains

COOPERATIVE LEARNING ACTIVITY

Identifying Place Organize students into groups of four. Have them draw a large outline map of their state on poster board. Then have them research the state's plants, animals, and major economic products, and list these items on the back of the poster. Distribute magazines (gardening, wildlife, and local) and tell students to find and cut out pictures of the items listed on the backs of their posters. Finally, direct students to glue the photos in the appropriate locations on the outline map, creating a montage of distinctive characteristics of the state. **L2**

Understanding the Six Essential Elements
Have students complete the following activities to learn more about the Six Essential Elements of geography.

Element 1: The World in Spatial Terms
Have students create a map that shows the route they travel from their home to school. Students should identify major roads and humanmade landmarks on their maps. Display the maps on the class bulletin board. **L2**

Element 2: Places and Regions
Explain that physical characteristics play a part in shaping human characteristics in a given place. For example, Native Americans in Alaska and Native Americans in Florida had widely differing clothing, economic pursuits, architecture, and lifestyles because of the physical characteristics of their regions. Ask students to describe a favorite city, state, or country. Ask them how the physical characteristics in the place might influence characteristics or customs of the inhabitants. **L1**

Element 3: Physical Systems
Ask students to think of ways that physical systems affect their lives and cultures. Have students explain how events such as hurricanes influence a region's population and economy. **L2**

I Study Geography?

To understand how our world is connected, some geographers have broken down the study of geography into five themes. The **Five Themes of Geography** are (1) location, (2) place, (3) human/environment interaction, (4) movement, and (5) regions. You will see these themes highlighted in the Geography Skills accompanying the maps of *The American Republic to 1877*.

Six Essential Elements

Recently, geographers have begun to look at geography in a different way. They break down the study of geography into **Six Essential Elements,** which are explained below. Being aware of these elements will help you sort out what you are learning about geography.

Element 1

The World in Spatial Terms
Geographers first take a look at where a place is located. **Location** serves as a starting point by asking "Where is it?" Knowing the location of places helps you develop an awareness of the world around you.

Element 2

Places and Regions
Place has a special meaning in geography. It means more than where a place is. It also describes what a place is like. These features may be physical characteristics such as landforms, climate, and plant or animal life. They may also be human characteristics, including language and way of life.

To help organize their study, geographers often group places or areas into regions. **Regions** are united by one or more common characteristics.

Element 3

Physical Systems
When studying places and regions, geographers analyze how **physical systems**—such as hurricanes, volcanoes, and glaciers—shape the earth's surface. They also look at communities of plants and animals that depend upon one another and their surroundings for survival.

DIFFERENTIATED INSTRUCTION

English Learners Students who have trouble understanding the material found on pages 2–3 should use graphic organizers to help them organize the information. Students should create three-column tables with the labels *Element*, *Theme*, and *Description*. As they read each element, they should complete their tables. **L1, ELL**

📁 Refer to *Inclusion for the Middle School Social Studies Classroom Strategies and Activities* in the TCR.

Element 4

Human Systems

Geographers also examine human systems, or how people have shaped our world. They look at how boundary lines are determined and analyze why people settle in certain places and not in others. A key theme in geography is the continual **movement** of people, ideas, and goods.

Element 5

Environment and Society

"How does the relationship between people and their natural surroundings influence the way people live?" This is one of the questions that the theme of **human/ environment interaction** answers. This theme also shows how people use the environment and how their actions affect the environment.

Element 6

The Uses of Geography

Knowledge of geography helps people understand the relationships among people, places, and environments over time. Understanding geography, and knowing how to use the tools and technology available to study it, prepares you for life in our modern society.

Geography Handbook   3

Element 4: Human Systems Call on volunteers to name places from which their family or ancestors moved. Students may describe a move within the United States or a migration from another country. Discuss the reasons that people move to different places. **L1,** ELL

Element 5: Environment and Society Give examples of ways that humans use and modify the environment in places they live. For example, people convert fields and forests into towns and irrigate arid land to support farming. Call on students to give examples of the ways people have modified the environment where they live in both positive and negative ways. **L2**

Element 6: The Uses of Geography Have students give examples of ways businesses use geography. Have students explain how geography influences where businesses such as gas stations and shopping malls are built. **L2**

EXTENDING THE CONTENT

Regions Geographers organize regions into three parts: formal regions, functional regions, and perceptual regions. Formal regions are characterized by the presence of a common human property (for example, language, religions, nationality, and political identity) or common physical property (for example, climate, landforms, and vegetation cover). Functional regions are organized around a node or focal point with surrounding areas linked to that node through transportation or communication systems or economic associations. Perceptual regions reflect human feelings or attitudes and are defined by subjective images of the area (for example, New England and the Corn Belt).

Geography Handbook

Demonstrating Ideas

Demonstrating Ideas Write the words *Distance* and *Direction* on the chalkboard. **Ask:** How do maps show distance and direction? *(scales and compass roses)* Then, give students practice in determining distance by showing them how to mark a map scale on the edge of a piece of paper. Have students practice measuring the distance between cities on the map on page 5. Give students practice in determining direction by having volunteers identify the direction from one city or state to another. **L2**

Did you know?

There is a place with no latitude and no longitude. The absolute location where the Prime Meridian and the Equator intersect is 0°N°S, 0°E°W.

CURRICULUM CONNECTION

History Until the 1700s, sailors seldom knew exactly where they were because they had only lines of latitude to guide them. John Harrison, an English instrument maker, invented a clock that could keep accurate time at sea. A navigator could determine longitude by figuring the difference between Greenwich Mean Time and the time at the ship's location.

I Use Maps?

Maps of many different kinds are used in *The American Republic to 1877* to help you see the connection between geography and the history of our nation.

Different Kinds of Maps

Physical Maps

A physical map shows the physical features of an area, such as its mountains and rivers. Physical maps use color and shadings to show **relief**—how flat or rugged the land surface is. Colors also may be used to show **elevation**—the height of an area above sea level.

Political Maps

Political maps generally show political, or human-made, divisions of countries or regions. The political map on pages RA2–RA3, for example, shows boundaries between the states that comprise the United States.

Special-Purpose Maps

Besides showing political or physical features, some maps have a special purpose. Human activities such as exploration routes, territorial expansion, or battle sites appear on special-purpose maps, also called **thematic maps.** The maps on pages RA6–RA7, for example, show territorial growth of the United States.

Latitude and Longitude

Maps have lines of latitude and longitude that form a grid. Lines of latitude circle the earth, either north or south of the Equator (0° latitude). Lines of longitude stretch from the North Pole to the South Pole, either east or west of the Prime Meridian (0° longitude). The distance between the lines is measured in degrees (°). Every place on the earth has a unique position or "address" on this grid.

Knowing this address makes it easier for you to locate cities and other places on a map. For example, the map on page RA5 shows you that the address of New Orleans is 30°N latitude, 90°W longitude.

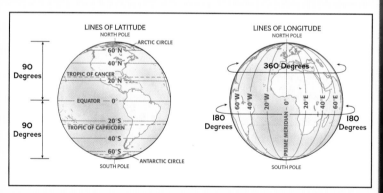

DIFFERENTIATED INSTRUCTION

Reading Support To help students remember the several different categories and examples of maps discussed in this section, guide them in creating a graphic organizer entitled "Types of Maps." Branching from this main head should be three boxes labeled "Political," "Physical," and "Special-Purpose." Have students complete the organizer by taking notes on each of the different types of maps. **L2**

Refer to ***Inclusion for the Middle School Social Studies Classroom Strategies and Activities*** in the TCR.

Parts of Maps

Map Key The map key explains the lines, symbols, and colors used on a map. For example, the map on this page shows the various climate regions of the United States. The key shows what climates the different colors represent. Map keys also may show structures created by people. Cities are usually symbolized by a solid circle (•). A star within a circle represents capitals (✪). On this map, you can see the capital of Texas and the cities of New Orleans, Los Angeles, and Chicago.

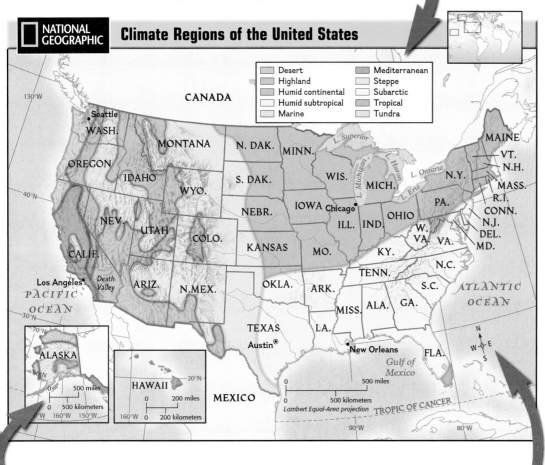

NATIONAL GEOGRAPHIC

Climate Regions of the United States

Key:
- Desert
- Highland
- Humid continental
- Humid subtropical
- Marine
- Mediterranean
- Steppe
- Subarctic
- Tropical
- Tundra

CANADA

Seattle, WASH., MONTANA, N. DAK., MINN., L. Superior, MAINE, VT., N.H.
OREGON, IDAHO, S. DAK., WIS., MICH., L. Huron, L. Ontario, N.Y., MASS., R.I.
WYO., IOWA, Chicago, ILL., IND., OHIO, PA., CONN., N.J., DEL.
NEV., UTAH, COLO., NEBR., MO., KY., W. VA., VA., MD.
CALIF., KANSAS, TENN., N.C.
Los Angeles, Death Valley, ARIZ., N.MEX., OKLA., ARK., S.C., ATLANTIC OCEAN
PACIFIC OCEAN, MISS., ALA., GA.
TEXAS, LA., New Orleans, FLA.
Austin, Gulf of Mexico
ALASKA, 500 miles, 500 kilometers
HAWAII, 200 miles, 200 kilometers, MEXICO
500 miles, 500 kilometers
Lambert Equal-Area projection, TROPIC OF CANCER
130°W, 40°N, 30°N, 70°N, 20°N, 160°W, 150°W, 90°W, 80°W

Scale A measuring line, often called a **scale bar,** helps you determine distance on the map. The map scale tells you what distance on the earth is represented by the measurement on the scale bar.

Compass Rose An important first step in reading any map is to find the direction marker. A map has a symbol that tells you where the **cardinal directions**—north, south, east, and west—are positioned.

Using a Map Key On slips of paper, write the page number of a map from the textbook and a question that requires the use of the map key. Ask volunteers to select slips and answer the questions. **L1**

Using Special-Purpose Maps Ask volunteers to bring to class special purpose maps. Special purpose subjects include bicycle trails, ocean currents, energy use, and bus routes. Even the treasure map that opens Robert Louis Stevenson's classic adventure story, *Treasure Island*, is a special-purpose map. Allow time for volunteers to show and explain their maps. Display selected maps on the wall. **L1, ELL**

Classifying Maps Have students work in groups to scan the textbook and classify the maps according to type: physical, political, or special purpose. Give each group the task of listing page numbers for maps of one type. **L1, ELL**

Reading Strategy   READING THE TEXT

Using Absolute Location Organize the class into teams. Have each team record the absolute location (in degrees of latitude and longitude) of 20 named places on the globe (cities, natural features, and so on). Then have teams challenge each other in a round-robin Absolute Location Tournament. In each round, one team will state the latitude and longitude of five places and time the other team as they locate the places on a globe. The teams will then switch roles. The team with the better time wins the round. **L2**

Geography Handbook

When? Who? What? Where?

Prehistory Many students probably believe that the North American environment remained untouched until the arrival of the Europeans. Native Americans, however, had been altering their environment for thousands of years. In the eastern woodlands, for example, Native Americans burned forested areas to make it easier to spot animals and to prepare the land for cultivation.

Cultural Diversity Discuss with students what is significant about the culture of the United States. If students do not mention it, point out the diversity of American culture. Have them look for some details in the Unit 1 and 2 summaries that may have contributed to the diversity of American culture. *(Native Americans occupied the land, then settlers from a variety of European nations arrived, bringing their cultures with them.)* **L1**

Did you know?

Efforts to preserve a healthy environment date back hundreds of years. In A.D. 1253 the English Parliament placed bans on burning coal. However, the increasing use of chemicals and fossil fuels, along with expanding populations, present new environmental challenges.

How Does Geography Influence History?

Geographic factors—landforms, waterways, natural resources—have shaped America's history. Here are some examples of geography's influences in history that are highlighted in *The American Republic to 1877*.

Unit 1 Different Worlds Meet As settlement spread, Native Americans created distinctive civilizations appropriate to their climates and resources. For example, Native Americans in the Great Plains depended on herds of buffalo for food, clothing, shelter, and tools.

Unit 2 Colonial Settlement Beginning in the 1500s, Europeans came to North America seeking land, riches, and freedom. Groups from Spain, France, Great Britain, and other countries established colonies. The British colonies along the Atlantic coast were hemmed in by the Appalachian Mountains—the first physical barrier to the West.

Unit 3 Creating a Nation The hardships of the land shaped the colonial settlers' cultural identities. The colonists were isolated from much of the world and became more independent. Eventually they broke away from Great Britain and won their independence.

6

EXTENDING THE CONTENT

Using Resources Early European settlers in North America were stunned by the abundance of trees. Vast tracts of European forest had been cleared to provide raw materials for various commercial activities. The shipbuilding industry was the largest consumer of forestland, for it took more than 2,500 trees to construct just one oceangoing ship. By the 1600s wood was in short supply in most European countries. No such shortage existed in North America. In fact, the harvesting of lumber became an important business for early settlers.

Unit 4 The New Republic When the United States was established, many doubted that the young government could control people over such great distances. New rivers, roads, and canals helped to open up the country. At the same time an Industrial Revolution had begun in New England.

Unit 5 The Growing Nation Through wars, treaties, and purchases, the United States gained control of the lands west of the Mississippi River. Settlers were drawn to Western territories by opportunities. Native Americans were forced onto reservations. Railroads enabled people to overcome geographic barriers.

Unit 6 Civil War and Reconstruction Demand for cotton by the textile industry increased the demand for labor provided by enslaved African Americans. In 1861 regional differences and a dispute over slavery sparked the Civil War between the North and South.

Unit 7 Modern America Emerges In the late 1800s and early 1900s, the United States became an urban industrial nation and took the leading role in international affairs. Americans entered the twenty-first century as a free nation committed to the truths expressed in the Declaration of Independence.

History and Geography Notebook Have students create a history and geography notebook. For pages 6–7 as well as for each chapter, tell students to divide a page into two columns and list in the first column any specific physical geography mentioned including landforms, waterways, climates, and so on. In the second column, students should write one or more historical events that were affected by the specific geography listed in the first column. **L2**

Where?When?Who?What?

The Appalachian Region A plateau called the Piedmont lies at the eastern edge of the Appalachians. The eastern edge of the Piedmont rises sharply from the low-lying Atlantic Coastal Plain. Where fast-moving rivers drop from the plateau to the plains, there are many rapids and waterfalls. The line formed where this drop takes place is called the fall line. Early European settlers were unable to travel beyond the fall line by boat. The waterfalls and rapids, however, later provided water power for industries. Thus, cities such as Macon, Georgia and Raleigh, North Carolina developed along the fall line.

EXTENDING THE CONTENT

Geographic Information Systems Like all scientists, geographers observe, hypothesize, and collect data to prove or disprove their theories. Aiding them in their tasks are advanced technological tools such as satellites, remote sensors, and computers. Satellites orbiting the earth carry remote sensors, or high-tech cameras and/or radar. These collect information and photographs about such topics as Earth's environment, weather, human settlement patterns, and vegetation. This information is then sent to computers on Earth. Computer programs known as Geographic Information Systems (GIS) process and organize the satellite images with other data collected through censuses, cartographers, and so on. The GIS technology is invaluable to urban planners, engineers, and geographers.

Constructing a Model Have students use clay to make a model landscape with the features mentioned on pages 8–9. Suggest that students paint the model after the clay dries to make it look more realistic. **L1**

The terms geographers use to describe the earth come from many different languages. To illustrate this, have students locate the term *mesa* on page 8. Point out that geographers use the Spanish word, which means "table," to describe flat-topped, steep-sided hills. Other foreign terms American geographers use include *tsunami*, a Japanese word meaning "overflowing wave," and *fjord*, a Norwegian word meaning "long, narrow bay."

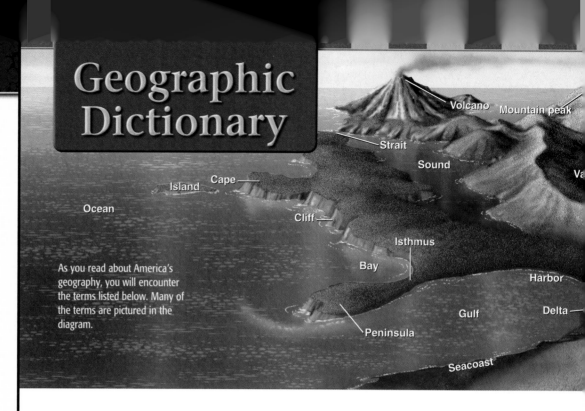

Geographic Dictionary

As you read about America's geography, you will encounter the terms listed below. Many of the terms are pictured in the diagram.

absolute location exact location of a place on the earth described by global coordinates

basin area of land drained by a given river and its branches; area of land surrounded by lands of higher elevations

bay part of a large body of water that extends into a shoreline, generally smaller than a gulf

canyon deep and narrow valley with steep walls

cape point of land that extends into a river, lake, or ocean

channel wide strait or waterway between two land-masses that lie close to each other; deep part of a river or other waterway

cliff steep, high wall of rock, earth, or ice

continent one of the seven large landmasses on the earth

cultural feature characteristic that humans have created in a place, such as language, religion, housing, and settlement pattern

delta flat, low-lying land built up from soil carried downstream by a river and deposited at its mouth

divide stretch of high land that separates river systems

downstream direction in which a river or stream flows from its source to its mouth

elevation height of land above sea level

Equator imaginary line that runs around the earth halfway between the North and South Poles; used as the starting point to measure degrees of north and south latitude

glacier large, thick body of slowly moving ice

gulf part of a large body of water that extends into a shoreline, generally larger and more deeply indented than a bay

harbor a sheltered place along a shoreline where ships can anchor safely

highland elevated land area such as a hill, mountain, or plateau

hill elevated land with sloping sides and rounded summit; generally smaller than a mountain

island land area, smaller than a continent, completely surrounded by water

isthmus narrow stretch of land connecting two larger land areas

lake a sizable inland body of water

latitude distance north or south of the Equator, measured in degrees

longitude distance east or west of the Prime Meridian, measured in degrees

lowland land, usually level, at a low elevation

map drawing of the earth shown on a flat surface

meridian one of many lines on the global grid running from the North Pole to the South Pole; used to measure degrees of longitude

mesa broad, flat-topped landform with steep sides; smaller than a plateau

COOPERATIVE LEARNING ACTIVITY

Map Quiz Organize the class into two teams. Provide one team with a United States map and the other team with a map of your state. Assign each team the following task: Locate every major body of water in your assigned area. Record your findings, including: (1) the name of each major body of water; (2) its relative and/or absolute location; and (3) the type of feature it is—lake, river, bay, and so on. When each team has completed its task, have them create a map quiz based on their work. The teams should then trade maps and challenge one another with their quizzes.

mountain land with steep sides that rises sharply (1,000 feet or more) from surrounding land; generally larger and more rugged than a hill

mountain peak pointed top of a mountain

mountain range a series of connected mountains

mouth (of a river) place where a stream or river flows into a larger body of water

ocean one of the four major bodies of salt water that surround the continents

ocean current stream of either cold or warm water that moves in a definite direction through an ocean

parallel one of many lines on the global grid that circle the earth north or south of the Equator; used to measure degrees of latitude

peninsula body of land jutting into a lake or ocean, surrounded on three sides by water

physical feature characteristic of a place occurring naturally, such as a landform, body of water, climate pattern, or resource

plain area of level land, usually a low elevation and often covered with grasses

plateau area of flat or rolling land at a high elevation, about 300–3,000 feet high

Prime Meridian line of the global grid running from the North Pole to the South Pole through Greenwich, England; starting point for measuring degrees of east and west longitude

relief changes in elevation over a given area of land

river large natural stream of water that runs through the land

sea large body of water completely or partly surrounded by land

seacoast land lying next to a sea or ocean

sea level position on land level with surface of nearby ocean or sea

sound body of water between a coastline and one or more islands off the coast

source (of a river) place where a river or stream begins, often in highlands

strait narrow stretch of water joining two larger bodies of water

tributary small river or stream that flows into a large river or stream; a branch of the river

upstream direction opposite the flow of a river; toward the source of a river or stream

valley area of low land between hills or mountains

volcano mountain created as liquid rock or ash erupts from inside the earth

3 ASSESS

Provide students with an outline map of the United States and colored pencils. Have students use a different color to label each of the following: Appalachian Mountains, Great Lakes, Mississippi River, Atlantic Ocean, Pacific Ocean, Rocky Mountains, Great Plains, and Gulf of Mexico. Have students think about how these features might affect European settlement patterns in North America.

4 CLOSE

Have students describe how a region's physical geography influences its economic development.

CRITICAL THINKING ACTIVITY

Analyzing Information Have students use atlases and other resources to plan a cross-country trip through the United States. Direct them to choose a definite starting point and destination and plot the route between the two points. Have them calculate the approximate distance of the journey, how long the journey might take, and to list points of interest along the way. Allow time for students to share their itineraries. **L2**

Reading Strategies

Helping students become active readers is only the first step in training students for success. The second step is helping students retain and use the knowledge they have gained through reading.

How Can You Help Students Retain What They Read?

The better students understand what they read, the more they will remember—so teaching students to use the reading strategies on these pages aids retention. In addition, you can help students use formal study systems such as working with graphic organizers.

Graphic Organizers That Help Students Read and Comprehend

Graphic organizers provide a visual format that requires students to restructure information as they analyze and interpret it. In addition, presenting information graphically helps students remember facts and concepts more easily, since they can "picture" it in their mind's eye. Students can productively use graphic organizers prior to reading to activate prior knowledge, during reading to process and analyze information, and after instruction to summarize and draw conclusions. Encourage students to use graphic organizers in the following ways (*see page 11*).

Reading for Information

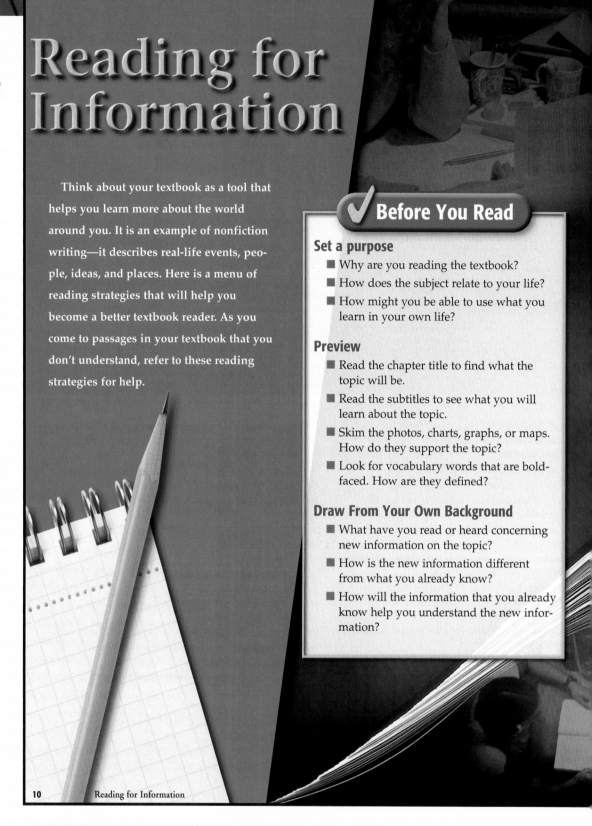

Think about your textbook as a tool that helps you learn more about the world around you. It is an example of nonfiction writing—it describes real-life events, people, ideas, and places. Here is a menu of reading strategies that will help you become a better textbook reader. As you come to passages in your textbook that you don't understand, refer to these reading strategies for help.

✓ Before You Read

Set a purpose
- Why are you reading the textbook?
- How does the subject relate to your life?
- How might you be able to use what you learn in your own life?

Preview
- Read the chapter title to find what the topic will be.
- Read the subtitles to see what you will learn about the topic.
- Skim the photos, charts, graphs, or maps. How do they support the topic?
- Look for vocabulary words that are bold-faced. How are they defined?

Draw From Your Own Background
- What have you read or heard concerning new information on the topic?
- How is the new information different from what you already know?
- How will the information that you already know help you understand the new information?

Good Study Habits for Successful Students

As you work with students on reading strategies, keep in mind and share the following tips for helping students retain what they read and prepare for all types of tests.

- **Keep Up:** Frequent review will help students build long-term memory and understanding.
- **Visualize and Recite Information:** Visual images are powerful ones. Students should try to associate a name, event, or idea with a picture. They can visualize the steps in a process or a sequence of events. Students should repeat important information aloud, whenever possible.

As You Read

Question
- What is the main idea?
- How do the photos, charts, graphs, and maps support the main idea?

Connect
- Think about people, places, and events in your own life. Are there any similarities with those in your textbook?
- Can you relate the textbook information to other areas of your life?

Predict
- Predict events or outcomes by using clues and information that you already know.
- Change your predictions as you read and gather new information.

Visualize
- Pay careful attention to details and descriptions.
- Create graphic organizers to show relationships that you find in the information.

Look For Clues As You Read

Comparison and Contrast Sentences
- Look for clue words and phrases that signal comparison, such as *similarly*, *just as*, *both*, *in common*, *also*, and *too*.
- Look for clue words and phrases that signal contrast, such as *on the other hand*, *in contrast to*, *however*, *different*, *instead of*, *rather than*, *but*, and *unlike*.

Cause-and-Effect Sentences
- Look for clue words and phrases such as *because*, *as a result*, *therefore*, *that is why*, *since*, *so*, *for this reason*, and *consequently*.

Chronological Sentences
- Look for clue words and phrases such as *after*, *before*, *first*, *next*, *last*, *during*, *finally*, *earlier*, *later*, *since*, and *then*.

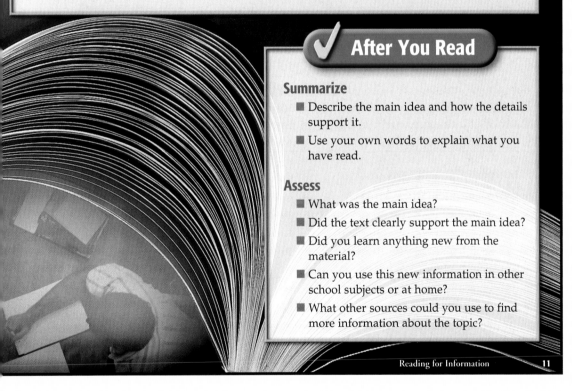

✔ After You Read

Summarize
- Describe the main idea and how the details support it.
- Use your own words to explain what you have read.

Assess
- What was the main idea?
- Did the text clearly support the main idea?
- Did you learn anything new from the material?
- Can you use this new information in other school subjects or at home?
- What other sources could you use to find more information about the topic?

- Use a web to show connections between related ideas, to describe the characteristics of a place or group, or to list examples.
- Use a tree to show a hierarchy of ideas or the structure of an organization or group.
- Use a flowchart to explain steps in a process. Use a time line or chain-of-events diagram to show a chronology or the order of events.
- Analyze causal relationships with a cause-and-effect chart or a problem-and-solution diagram.
- Use a Venn diagram to compare and contrast attributes or characteristics.

Use Writing to Help Students Understand What They Read
Writing provides a way for students to demonstrate what they have learned. More significantly, writing can facilitate greater understanding and richer learning by encouraging writers to transform knowledge into something new. Appropriate writing assignments can help students build social studies concepts in the following ways.

- Writing challenges students to analyze, evaluate, and interpret events.
- Writing invites students to synthesize information from a variety of sources, including students' own prior knowledge and experiences.
- Writing requires students to make connections, draw conclusions, and support their judgments with facts and details.
- The writing process promotes a systematic approach to content analysis by teaching students to focus their thoughts, expand and refine their ideas, and express their viewpoints precisely.

Good Study Habits for Successful Students

- **Use the Body:** Incorporate movement into study routines, if possible. Students can march in place or pace while reciting a sequence of events or saying a list of items.
- **Study Groups:** Encourage students to work with others to review for a test. They can discuss important topics and take turns asking and answering questions.
- **The Big Picture:** Essay tests often ask "big picture" questions. To help students get the big picture, have them identify main ideas in reading selections; develop summaries of important topics; and create webs, maps, or other graphic organizers to draw conclusions and analyze relationships.

Unit 1 Resources

SUGGESTED PACING CHART

Unit 1 (1 Day)	Chapter 1 (5 Days)	Chapter 2 (6 Days)	Unit 1 (2 Days)
Day 1 Introduction	**Day 1** Chapter 1 Intro, Section 1	**Day 1** Chapter 2 Intro, Section 1	**Day 1** Wrap-Up **Day 2** Unit 1 Assessment
	Day 2 Section 2	**Day 2** Section 2	
	Day 3 Section 3	**Day 3** Section 3	
	Day 4 Chapter 1 Review	**Day 4** Section 4	
	Day 5 Chapter 1 Assessment	**Day 5** Chapter 2 Review	
		Day 6 Chapter 2 Assessment	

Use the following tools to easily assess student learning in a variety of ways:

- Performance Assessment Activities and Rubrics
- Chapter and Unit Tests
- Section Quizzes
- Standardized Test Practice Workbook

- www.tarvol1.glencoe.com
- Interactive Tutor Self-Assessment CD-ROM
- MindJogger Videoquiz
- ExamView® Pro Testmaker CD-ROM

TEACHING TRANSPARENCIES

Unit 1 Map Overlay Transparencies L2

Cause-and-Effect Transparency 1 L2

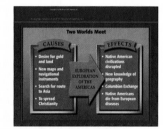

KEY TO ABILITY LEVELS

Teaching strategies have been coded.

L1 BASIC activities for all students

L2 AVERAGE activities for average to above-average students

L3 CHALLENGING activities for above-average students

ELL ENGLISH LANGUAGE LEARNER activities

READING SUPPORT FROM JAMESTOWN EDUCATION

- *Timed Readings Plus in Social Studies* help students increase their reading rate and fluency while maintaining comprehension. The 400-word passages are similar to those found on state and national assessments.

- *Reading in the Content Area: Social Studies* concentrates on six essential reading skills that help students better comprehend what they read. The book includes 75 high-interest nonfiction passages written at increasing levels of difficulty.

- *Reading Fluency* helps students read smoothly, accurately, and expressively.

- *Jamestown's Reading Improvement,* by renowned reading expert Edward Fry, focuses on helping build your students' comprehension, vocabulary, and skimming and scanning skills.

- *Critical Reading Series* provides high-interest books, each written at three reading levels.

For more information about these products, see the Jamestown Education materials in the Classroom Solutions in the front of this Teacher Wraparound Edition. To order these products, call Glencoe at 1-800-334-7344.

Unit 1 Resources

ASSESSMENT

Unit 1 Pretests L2

Unit 1 Posttests L2

INTERDISCIPLINARY ACTIVITIES

American Literature Reading 1 L2

Interdisciplinary Connection 1 L2

Economics and History Activity 1 L2

APPLICATION AND ENRICHMENT

Cooperative Learning Activity 1 L1, **ELL**

Citizenship Activity 1 L1

HANDS-ON ACTIVITIES

Hands-On History Activity 1 L1

History Simulations and Problem Solving 1 L1

Reading List Generator CD-ROM

GLENCOE BOOKLINK

The Glencoe BookLink CD-ROM is a database that allows you to search more than 15,000 titles to create a customized reading list for your students.

- Reading lists can be organized by students' reading level, author, genre, theme, or area of interest.

- The database provides Degrees of Reading Power™ (DRP) and Lexile™ readability scores for all selections.

- A brief summary of each selection is included.

Leveled reading suggestions for this unit:

For Students at a Grade 6 Reading Level:

- **The Iroquois Indians,** by Bill Lund

For Students at a Grade 7 Reading Level:

- **Ancient America,** by Marion Wood

For Students at a Grade 8 Reading Level:

- **The American Indian,** by Oliver La Farge

Extending the Content

Readings for the Teacher

- **Native Americans,** by Arlene Hirschfelder. Dorling Kindersley, 2000.

Multimedia Resources

- **Inca Secrets of the Ancestors.** VHS. TimeLife Video and Television, 1995.
- **Secrets of Lost Empires.** VHS. NOVA production by the WGBH/Boston Science Unit and BBC-TV, 1997.

Unit Overview

Unit 1 surveys the migrations and cultures of the first Americans. **Chapter 1** focuses on the contributions made by the native peoples living in the Americas. **Chapter 2** describes the impact made by the first Europeans who explored the Americas.

Unit Objectives

After studying this unit, students will be able to:

1. Explain how people arrived in the Americas.
2. Describe the cultural contributions of the Native Americans.
3. Classify the explorers and their areas of exploration.
4. Evaluate the impact of European exploration on Native American culture.

Why It Matters Activity

The explorers covered in this unit traveled to places that were previously unknown to Europeans. Brainstorm with students other places that have yet to be explored on the earth, such as the depths of the ocean floors. Have students identify reasons why these places should be explored and whether or not people would benefit from such exploration.

Glencoe Literature Library

As students study the unit, have them read *Bearstone* by Will Hobbs from the **Glencoe Literature Library.** The Glencoe Literature Library consists of novels and other readings for middle school students, along with study guides that offer instructional support and student activities.

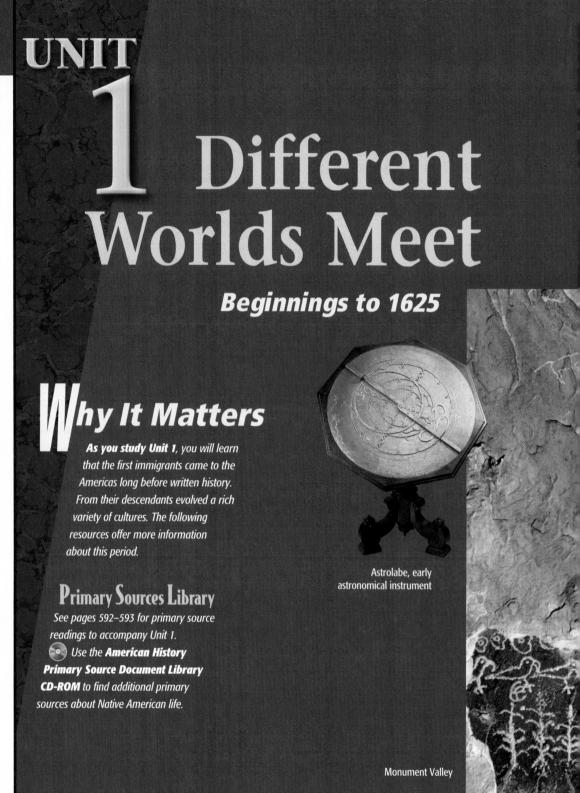

UNIT

1 Different Worlds Meet

Beginnings to 1625

Why It Matters

As you study Unit 1, you will learn that the first immigrants came to the Americas long before written history. From their descendants evolved a rich variety of cultures. The following resources offer more information about this period.

Primary Sources Library

See pages 592–593 for primary source readings to accompany Unit 1.

Use the **American History Primary Source Document Library CD-ROM** to find additional primary sources about Native American life.

Astrolabe, early astronomical instrument

Monument Valley

TEAM TEACHING ACTIVITY

Art Pacific Northwest Native Americans made totem poles from red cedar trees. Totem poles had many functions. They served as memorials, grave markers, and portals to homes, and they identified tribal territories. They also symbolized family lineage, power, and prestige. Display pictures of totem poles. With the Art teacher, organize the class into groups to create a totem. Hand out the following to each student: empty cylinder, colored paper, tape, scissors, glue, and markers. Instruct each student to draw a design on the colored paper to be glued onto the cylinder. As a group, students should stack and tape each cylinder together in order of importance to create a totem. Display totems and discuss the significance of each. **L2**

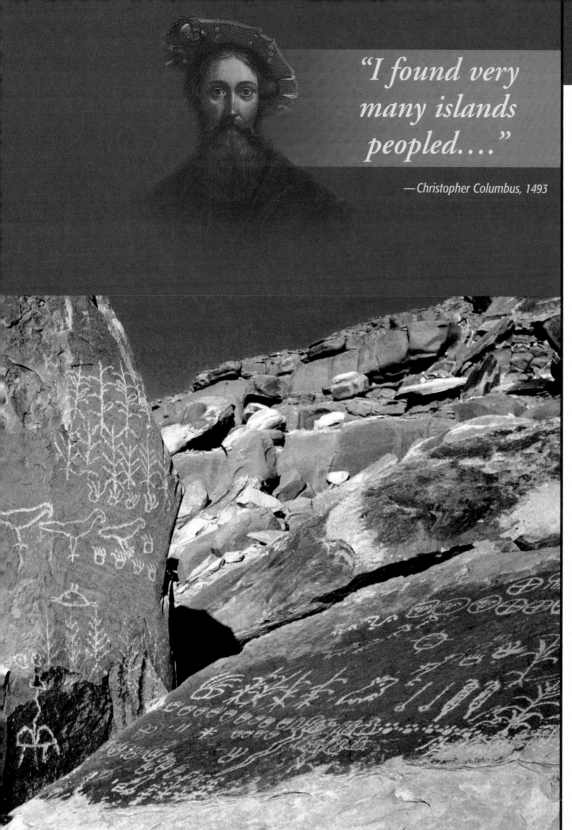

> "I found very
> many islands
> peopled...."
>
> —*Christopher Columbus, 1493*

GLENCOE TECHNOLOGY

CD-ROM
**American History
Primary Source
Document Library
CD-ROM**
Use the **American History Primary
Source Document Library CD-ROM**
to access primary source documents
related to the first Americans and
early explorers.

More About the Photo

Monument Valley is located along the
Utah and Arizona border towards the
southeast corner of Utah. It is an area
that contains freestanding sandstone
rock formations that rise from the
desert floor. The region has been heavily eroded, exposing very old strata in
the canyons. Found throughout the
world, petroglyphs were made by
scratching the stone with crude tools
such as sticks, rocks, or bone. Unlike
hieroglyphics, petroglyphs usually
were not language. With hieroglyphics,
each picture represented a particular
sound, word, action, or idea. Pictures
were assigned specific meanings that
did not necessarily relate to the image
depicted. Petroglyphs, however, did
not have specific meanings attributed
to each picture. Rather, meanings were
derived from the images presented in
the art itself. The meaning of petroglyphs came from the pictures in the
art, instead of from the sounds or
words the pictures represented. **Ask:**
**What do you think the petroglyphs
found at Monument Valley represent?** *(Possible answers may include:
animal life, plant life, a village, direction markers, or water.)*

SERVICE-LEARNING PROJECT

The land occupied by Native American tribes was valued for its benefit to the entire tribe. Have students brainstorm about the value of parks in your community. Have the class adopt a park. Discuss
your class's plans with your city's administration officials. Designate a day to pick up garbage at the
park, plant flowers, and perform other activities to beautify it. **L2**

Refer to ***Building Bridges: Connecting Classroom and Community through Service-Learning in
Social Studies*** from the National Council for the Social Studies for information about service-learning.

Timesaving Tools

TeacherWorks™ All-In-One Planner and Resource Center

- **Interactive Teacher Edition** Access your Teacher Wraparound Edition and your classroom resources with a few easy clicks.
- **Interactive Lesson Planner** Planning has never been easier! Organize your week, month, semester, or year with all the lesson helps you need to make teaching creative, timely, and relevant.

Use Glencoe's **Presentation Plus!** multimedia teacher tool to easily present dynamic lessons that visually excite your students. Using Microsoft PowerPoint® you can customize the presentations to create your own personalized lessons.

TEACHING TRANSPARENCIES

Graphic Organizer 6 L2

Why It Matters Chapter Transparency 1 L2

REVIEW AND REINFORCEMENT

Workbook Activity 1 L1

Time Line Activity 1 L2

Vocabulary Activity 1 L1

REVIEW AND REINFORCEMENT

Critical Thinking Skills Activity 1 L1

Take-Home Review Activity 1 L1

ENRICHMENT

Linking Past and Present Activity 1 L2

Primary Source Reading 1 L2

GEOGRAPHY

Geography and History Activity 1 L2

Meeting NCSS Standards

The following standards are highlighted in Chapter 1:

Section 1 III People, Places, and Environments: H, I

Section 2 I Culture: A, C, D

Section 3 I Culture: A, C, D

FOLDABLES™
Study Organizer

Dinah Zike's Foldables are three-dimensional, interactive graphic organizers that help students practice basic writing skills, review key vocabulary terms, and identify main ideas. Additional chapter activities can be found in the **Reading and Study Skills Foldables** booklet.

Chapter 1 Resources

Chapter 1 Test
Form A L2

Chapter 1 Test
Form B L2

Standardized Test Practice
Workbook Activity 1 L2

Performance Assessment
Activity 1 L1, ELL

ExamView® Pro
Testmaker CD-ROM

MULTIMEDIA

- Vocabulary PuzzleMaker CD-ROM
- Interactive Tutor Self-Assessment CD-ROM
- ExamView® Pro Testmaker CD-ROM
- Audio Program
- American History Primary Source Documents Library CD-ROM
- MindJogger Videoquiz
- Presentation Plus! CD-ROM
- TeacherWorks CD-ROM
- Interactive Student Edition CD-ROM
- Glencoe Skillbuilder Interactive Workbook CD-ROM, Level 1
- The American Republic to 1877 Video Program
- American Music: Hits Through History

SPANISH RESOURCES

The following Spanish language materials are available in the Spanish Resources Binder:

- Spanish Guided Reading Activities
- Spanish Reteaching Activities
- Spanish Quizzes and Tests
- Spanish Vocabulary Activity
- Spanish Take-Home Review Activity
- Spanish Summaries
- The Declaration of Independence and United States Constitution Spanish Translation

The following videotape programs are available from Glencoe as supplements to Chapter 1:

- **Leif Ericson: Voyages of a Viking** (ISBN 1-56501-673-4)
- **Ponce de Leon: The First Conquistador** (ISBN 1-56501-669-6)
- **The Maya** (ISBN 0-7670-0697-6)
- **The Mound Builder** (ISBN 0-7670-0822-7)

To order, call Glencoe at 1-800-334-7344. To find classroom resources to accompany many of these videos, check the following home pages:
A&E Television: www.aande.com
The History Channel: www.historychannel.com

HISTORY Online

Use our Web site for additional resources. All essential content is covered in the Student Edition.

You and your students can visit tarvol1.glencoe.com, the Web site companion to **The American Republic to 1877.** This innovative integration of electronic and print media offers your students a wealth of opportunities. The student text directs students to the Web site for the following options:

- **Chapter Overviews**
- **Self-Check Quizzes**
- **Student Web Activities**
- **Textbook Updates**

Answers to the student Web activities are provided for you in the **Web Activity Lesson Plans.** Additional Web resources and Interactive Tutor Puzzles are also available.

Chapter 1 Resources

SECTION RESOURCES

Daily Objectives	Reproducible Resources	Multimedia Resources
SECTION 1 **Early Peoples** 1. Understand how the first people arrived in the Americas. 2. Cite the discovery that changed the lives of the early Native Americans.	Reproducible Lesson Plan 1–1 Daily Lecture and Discussion Notes 1–1 Guided Reading Activity 1–1* Section Quiz 1–1* Reteaching Activity 1–1* Reading Essentials and Study Guide 1–1* Enrichment Activity 1–1	Daily Focus Skills Transparency 1–1 Interactive Tutor Self-Assessment CD-ROM ExamView® Pro Testmaker CD-ROM Presentation Plus! CD-ROM
SECTION 2 **Cities and Empires** 1. Describe why powerful empires arose in the Americas. 2. Investigate how the people of each empire adapted to their environment.	Reproducible Lesson Plan 1–2 Daily Lecture and Discussion Notes 1–2 Guided Reading Activity 1–2* Section Quiz 1–2* Reteaching Activity 1–2* Reading Essentials and Study Guide 1–2* Enrichment Activity 1–2	Daily Focus Skills Transparency 1–2 Interactive Tutor Self-Assessment CD-ROM ExamView® Pro Testmaker CD-ROM Presentation Plus! CD-ROM
SECTION 3 **North American Peoples** 1. Explore what early people lived in North America. 2. Examine how different Native American groups adapted to their environments.	Reproducible Lesson Plan 1–3 Daily Lecture and Discussion Notes 1–3 Guided Reading Activity 1–3* Section Quiz 1–3* Reteaching Activity 1–3* Reading Essentials and Study Guide 1–3* Enrichment Activity 1–3	Daily Focus Skills Transparency 1–3 American Art and Architecture, Transparency 1 American Music: Hits Through History ABCNews Interactive™ Historic America Electronic Field Trips Vocabulary PuzzleMaker CD-ROM Interactive Tutor Self-Assessment CD-ROM ExamView® Pro Testmaker CD-ROM Presentation Plus! CD-ROM

0:00 OUT OF TIME?
Assign the Chapter 1 **Reading Essentials and Study Guide.**

*Also Available in Spanish

 Blackline Master   Transparency   CD-ROM   DVD

Poster   Music Program   Audio Program   Videocassette

KEY TO ABILITY LEVELS

Teaching strategies have been coded.

L1   BASIC activities for all students
L2   AVERAGE activities for average to above-average students
L3   CHALLENGING activities for above-average students
ELL   ENGLISH LANGUAGE LEARNER activities

Chapter 1 Resources

 NATIONAL GEOGRAPHIC Teacher's Corner

INDEX TO NATIONAL GEOGRAPHIC MAGAZINE

The following articles relate to this chapter.

- "The Old Ones of the Southwest," by David Roberts, April 1996.
- "The Timeless Vision of Teotihuacan," by George E. Stuart, December 1995.
- "The Cherokee," by Geoffrey Norman, May 1995.
- "Maya Masterpiece Revealed at Bonampak," by Mark Miller, February 1995.
- "Powwow," by Michael Parfit, June 1994.

ADDITIONAL NATIONAL GEOGRAPHIC SOCIETY PRODUCTS

To order the following, call National Geographic at 1-800-368-2728:

- *Mystery of the Inca Mummy* (Video)
- *Mystery of the Maya* (Video)
- *Lost City of the Maya* (Video)
- *The Maya Way of Death* (Video)
- *The Mesoamericans/Ancient Mesoamerica* (Map)
- *National Geographic Desk Reference* (Book)
- *Lost Kingdoms of the Maya* (Book)
- *Indians of North America* (Map)
- *American Indians: A Brief History* (Video)

NGS ONLINE

Access National Geographic's Web site for current events, atlas updates, activities, links, interactive features, and archives.
www.nationalgeographic.com

MEETING SPECIAL NEEDS

In addition to the Differentiated Instruction strategies found in each section, the following resources are also suitable for your special needs students:

- *ExamView® Pro Testmaker CD-ROM* allows teachers to tailor tests by reducing answer choices.
- The *Audio Program* includes the entire narrative of the student edition so that less-proficient readers can listen to the words as they read them.
- The *Reading Essentials and Study Guide* provides the same content as the student edition but is written two grade levels below the textbook.
- *Guided Reading Activities* give less-proficient readers point-by-point instructions to increase comprehension as they read each textbook section.

From the Classroom of . . .

Lorraine O'Neil
MacKinnon Middle School
Wharton, NJ

Create a Disappearing Land Bridge

Organize students into groups of four or five. Using pie tins and modeling clay, have groups make a model of the Beringia land bridge inside the tins. Ask them to leave plenty of room for bodies of water, and allow them to use the map "Prehistoric Migrations Through the Americas" on p. 18 in their textbooks as a guide. After the model land bridges are complete, have students heap finely crushed ice around their bridges. (Make sure they use enough ice so that when it melts, the water covers the bridge.) Have students sprinkle a little cold water on top to help the ice form a sheet. Place the models in a freezer overnight to form the ice sheets. Remove the models from the freezer and allow them to return to room temperature. As students watch their land bridges submerge, explain that during Ice Ages, ocean levels were low because a large amount of water was frozen in the form of glaciers. As the glaciers melted, water levels rose again and covered the land bridge.

ADDITIONAL RESOURCES FROM GLENCOE

- American Music: Cultural Traditions
- American Art and Architecture
- Outline Map Resource Book
- U.S. Desk Map
- Building Geography Skills for Life
- Inclusion for the Middle School Social Studies Classroom Strategies and Activities
- Teaching Strategies for the American History Classroom (Including Block Scheduling Pacing Guides)
- American Crafts Hands-On Activities
- American Games Hands-On Activities
- American History Flash Cards

 Block Schedule

Activities that are suited to use within the block scheduling framework are identified by:

✓ Performance Assessment

Refer to Activity 1 in the Performance Assessment Activities and Rubrics booklet.

Why It Matters Activity

The native peoples of the Americas developed cultures with established social distinctions, art, traditions, and ways of life. Ask students to explain what the various aspects of a culture are. Have them evaluate their ideas as they complete the chapter.

GLENCOE
TECHNOLOGY

The American Republic to 1877 Video Program

To learn more about the Anasazi, have students view the Chapter 1 video "Before Columbus" from **The American Republic to 1877 Video Program.**

Available in DVD and VHS

MindJogger Videoquiz

Use **MindJogger Videoquiz** to preview the Chapter 1 content.

Available in VHS

The First Americans
Prehistory to 1492

Why It Matters

Thousands of years ago small groups of hunters crossed a bridge of land that connected Siberia and Alaska. Eventually, they spread throughout North and South America.

The Impact Today

These first people, called Native Americans, influenced later cultures. Native Americans are part of the modern world, yet many of them also preserve the ways of life, customs, and traditions developed by their ancestors centuries ago.

The American Republic to 1877 Video *The chapter 1 video, "Before Columbus," examines the diverse cultures of North America before Europeans arrived, focusing on the Anasazi.*

The Americas

- **c. 28,000 B.C.**
  - Asian hunters enter North America
- **c. 1500 B.C.**
  - Rise of Olmec in Mexico
- **C. A.D. 700**
  - Maya empire reaches peak
- **C. A.D. 1130**
  - Drought strikes Anasazi communities

Prehistory　　　　　900　　　　　1100

World

- **c. 10,000 B.C.**
  - Last Ice Age ends
- **C. A.D. 33**
  - Jesus Christ is crucified
- **A.D. 613**
  - Muhammad preaches Islam in Makkah
- **A.D. 1095**
  - The Crusades begin

14　　　CHAPTER 1　The First Americans

Graphic organizers help students examine their background knowledge before beginning a new chapter. A pre-reading organizer helps students connect prior information with new material. Organize students into groups of 3 or 4. Ask each group to create a two-column organizer with headings labeled "Environments" and "Characteristics." Ask the students to discuss types of environments found in North and South America. List at least five environments in the left hand column of the organizer. Then, have them complete the right side with what they know or think they know about characteristics of each environment. **L1**

FOLDABLES™
Study Organizer

Categorizing Study Foldable Group information into categories to make sense of what you are learning. Make this foldable to learn about the first Americans.

Step 1 Fold one sheet of paper in half from top to bottom.

Step 2 Fold in half again, from side to side.

Step 3 Unfold the paper once. Cut up the fold of the top flap only.

> This cut will make two tabs.

Step 4 Turn the paper vertically and sketch the continents of North and Central and South America on the front tabs.

Reading and Writing As you read the chapter, write under the flaps of your foldable what you learn about the Native American people living in these regions.

City in the Sky Inca workers built the city of Machu Picchu high in the Andes mountain ranges.

FOLDABLES™
Study Organizer **Dinah Zike's Foldables**

Purpose This foldable will help students organize information about the different groups of Native Americans who lived in the Americas before European colonization. When grouping information from the chapter into two categories–Native Americans of North America and Native Americans of Central and South America–students are required to determine what is relevant factual information and group this data into the appropriate categories.

📁 Have students complete **Reading and Study Skills Foldables** Activity 1. **L1**

HISTORY
Online

Introduce students to chapter content and key terms by having them access **Chapter Overview 1** at tarvol1.glencoe.com

TIME LINE
ACTIVITY

As students read the chapter, have them review the time line on pages 14–15. Using a world map, have students show where the events on the time line occurred.

C. A.D. 1300
• Hohokam civilization begins to decline

A.D. 1325
• Aztec establish Tenochtitlán

C. A.D. 1400
• Inca empire begins to expand

HISTORY
Online

Chapter Overview
Visit tarvol1.glencoe.com and click on **Chapter 1—Chapter Overviews** to preview chapter information.

1300   *1500*

A.D. 1368
• Ming dynasty begins in China

A.D. 1215
• England's King John signs Magna Carta

A.D. 1295
• Italian traveler Marco Polo returns from China

A.D. 1312
• Mansa Musa begins rule of West African kingdom of Mali

More About the Photo

Discovered in 1911, Machu Picchu was built between 1460 and 1470. Machu Picchu is found high in the Andes overlooking the Urubamba River Canyon. The city was most likely a religious center and the royal estate of Inca ruler Pachacuti Inca. Residents of the city included a crew of builders, planners, and other royal attendants. Some researchers believe that the city's water supply was unable to support the population, leading to its abandonment. The settlement and roadway leading to the once thriving city was destroyed in the 1536 Inca rebellion, eliminating discovery of the great city by Spanish conquistadors.

1 FOCUS

Section Overview

This section describes how the Ice Age made it possible for Asian hunters to migrate to the Americas.

BELLRINGER
Skillbuilder Activity

Project transparency and have students answer the question.

Daily Focus Skills Transparency 1–1

Reading Preview

Answers to Graphic: Causes: following herds in search of food, search for alternate sources of food when large animals began to die out; Effects: fishing communities established, development of farming techniques, stable communities established; more advanced cultures developed

Preteaching Vocabulary
Point out that the items under **Key Terms** are introduced and defined in this section. These terms are printed in blue type where they first appear.

Guide to Reading

Main Idea
The first Americans spread throughout North, Central, and South America.

Key Terms
archaeology, artifact, Ice Age, nomad, migration, maize, carbon dating, culture

Reading Strategy
Determining Cause and Effect As you read Section 1, re-create the diagram below and explain why the first Americans came to the continent and the consequences of their arrival.

Migration to the Americas	
Causes	Effects

Read to Learn
• how the first people arrived in the Americas.
• which discovery changed the lives of the early Native Americans.

Section Theme
Geography and History The Ice Age made it possible for hunters to migrate to the Americas.

Preview of Events

♦30,000 B.C.	♦10,000 B.C.	♦5000 B.C.	♦1000 B.C.

c. 28,000 B.C.
Asian hunters enter North America

c. 10,000 B.C.
Last Ice Age ends

c. 7000 B.C.
Farming develops in Mexico

c. 3000 B.C.
Early villages established in Mexico

AN American Story

Arrowhead, hand-chipped stone

No one knows for sure how the first people arrived in America. They may have crossed a land bridge that many scientists think connected Asia and North America thousands of years ago. They may have come by boat from Asia or Europe. Why they came is also a mystery. Possibly they followed mammoths or other game animals or were hunting seals and whales along the coast. Over time these people settled in America, becoming the first "native Americans."

The Journey From Asia

These first Americans arrived thousands of years ago. As food supplies improved, the population of the Americas increased. By A.D. 1500, millions of Native Americans, belonging to more than 2,000 different groups, lived on the two continents of North America and South America.

When Europeans arrived in the Americas in the late 1400s, they found Native Americans living there. The Europeans wondered where these peoples had come from and how they happened to settle in the Americas. Some believed the Native Americans had come from Atlantis, an island that was supposed to have sunk beneath the waves of the Atlantic Ocean.

SECTION RESOURCES

Reproducible Masters
• Reproducible Lesson Plan 1–1
• Daily Lecture and Discussion Notes 1–1
• Guided Reading Activity 1–1
• Section Quiz 1–1
• Reteaching Activity 1–1
• Reading Essentials and Study Guide 1–1
• Enrichment Activity 1–1

Transparencies
• Daily Focus Skills Transparency 1–1

Multimedia
• Interactive Tutor Self-Assessment CD-ROM
• ExamView® Pro Testmaker CD-ROM
• Presentation Plus! CD-ROM

Modern scientists are still trying to determine how the first people came to North and South America. The story of the first Americans is still being pieced together by experts in archaeology, the study of ancient peoples. Archaeologists learn about the past from artifacts, things left behind by early people, such as stone tools, weapons, baskets, and carvings. Their discoveries show that many early peoples may have come across a land that later sank into the sea. It was not the mythical Atlantis, however, but a strip of land called **Beringia** that once joined Asia and the Americas.

Crossing the Land Bridge

During its long history, the earth has passed through several Ice Ages. These are periods of very cold temperatures when part of the earth was covered with large ice sheets. Much of the water from the oceans was frozen into these sheets, or glaciers. For that reason the sea levels were much lower than they are today.

The most recent Ice Age began 100,000 years ago and ended about 12,000 years ago. During this period many scientists think the lower sea level exposed a wide strip of land between Asia and North America. This land bridge would have run from **Siberia** in northeastern Asia to present-day **Alaska,** the westernmost part of the Americas. The land bridge, Beringia, now lies under the **Bering Strait.**

One popular scientific theory states that the first Americans were people from Asia who crossed over Beringia during the last Ice Age. These early peoples reached the Americas thousands of years ago.

In Search of Hunting Grounds

The early Americans were nomads, people who moved from place to place. They gathered wild grains and fruits but depended on hunting for much of their food. While traveling in search of animals to hunt, they crossed Beringia into what is now Alaska and Canada.

The crossing of the land bridge was a migration, a movement of a large number of people into a new homeland. It did not happen in a single journey. As the centuries passed, many

groups of people traveled from Asia either on foot across the land bridge or in boats. From the north, the migrants gradually moved into new territory. They spread out across the Americas, going as far east as the Atlantic Ocean and as far south as the tip of South America.

Hunting for Food

Native American legends tell of giant beasts that roamed the earth in ancient times. When the first Americans arrived from Asia, they did indeed find huge mammals. There was the saber-toothed tiger, the woolly mammoth, and the mastodon. The mammoth and mastodon resembled modern elephants in size and shape but had shaggy fur and long tusks.

The early Americans were skilled at hunting these beasts. The hunters shaped pieces of stone and bone to make tools for chopping and scraping. They chipped rocks into extremely sharp points and fastened them on poles to make spears. Bands of hunters armed with these spears stalked herds of bison, mastodons, or

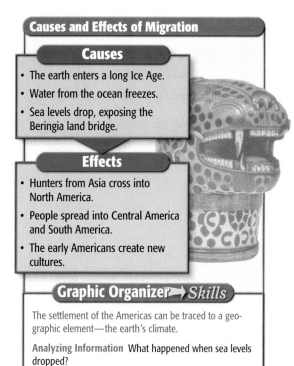

Causes and Effects of Migration

Causes
- The earth enters a long Ice Age.
- Water from the ocean freezes.
- Sea levels drop, exposing the Beringia land bridge.

Effects
- Hunters from Asia cross into North America.
- People spread into Central America and South America.
- The early Americans create new cultures.

Graphic Organizer → Skills

The settlement of the Americas can be traced to a geographic element—the earth's climate.

Analyzing Information What happened when sea levels dropped?

2 *TEACH*

Daily Lecture and Discussion Notes 1–1

Copyright © by The McGraw-Hill Companies, Inc.

Daily Lecture and Discussion Notes
Chapter 1, Section 1

Did You Know? Beringia, the ancient land bridge between Asia and North America, may have been around 937.5 miles wide. Early hunters who migrated across this land bridge to follow animals were not aware that they had crossed onto a new continent.

I.   The Journey From Asia *(Pages 16–18)*

A. The first people migrated from Asia to North, Central, and South America during the last Ice Age. They reached the Americas thousands of years ago.

B. This migration took centuries, and people spread out across the Americas as far east as the Atlantic Ocean and as far south as the tip of South America.

C. These early people crossed a land bridge from Siberia in northeastern Asia to present-day Alaska. This land bridge now lies under the waters of the Bering Strait.

Reporting Explain how news reports try to answer the basic questions *who, what, where, when, why,* and *how.* Ask each student to write a newspaper article describing the migrations across the Americas as outlined in this section. Have students read their articles aloud. **L1**

🗁 Use the rubric for writing a newspaper article on pages 35–36 in the *Performance Assessment Activities and Rubrics.*

Graphic Organizer → Skills

Answer: A land bridge was exposed that connected Asia to the Americas.

Graphic Organizer Skills Practice Ask: What happened after people spread into the Americas? *(They created new cultures.)*

Reading Strategy   **READING THE TEXT**

Summarizing Information Summarizing information teaches students to reduce information and to rethink what they have read. Have students read the information about the scientific theory of migration described in this section and then summarize what they have just read. Remind them that only the main ideas should be included in a summary but that all the main ideas should be included. Tell students that to determine whether they have included all the main ideas in the summary, they should ask themselves: Can my summary be easily understood by someone who has not read the selection? **L2**

L1, ELL

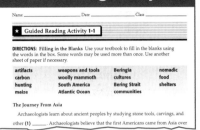

Guided Reading Activity 1–1

Name _____ Date _____ Class _____

★ Guided Reading Activity 1-1

DIRECTIONS: Filling in the Blanks Use your textbook to fill in the blanks using the words in the box. Some words may be used more than once. Use another sheet of paper if necessary.

artifacts	weapons and tools	Beringia	nomadic
carbon	woolly mammoth	cultures	food
hunting	South America	Bering Strait	shelters
maize	Atlantic Ocean	communities	

The Journey From Asia

Archaeologists learn about ancient peoples by studying stone tools, carvings, and other **(1)** _____. Archaeologists believe that the first Americans came from Asia over

Geography *Skills*

Answers:

1. Rocky Mountains and Andes

2. A land bridge was exposed that connected Asia to North America.

✔ **Reading Check**

Answer: They made points from rocks and attached them to poles and used them as spears.

3 ASSESS

Assign Section 1 Assessment as homework or as an in-class activity.

🕹 Have students use **Interactive Tutor Self-Assessment CD-ROM.**

L2

Section Quiz 1–1

Name _____ Date _____ Class _____

★ Chapter 1   Score ____

Section Quiz 1-1

DIRECTIONS: Matching Match the items in Column A with the items in Column B. Write the correct letters in the blanks. *(10 points each)*

Column A	Column B
___ 1. things left behind by early people	A. carbon dating
___ 2. people who move from place to place	B. artifacts
___ 3. movement of a group of people	C. maize
___ 4. an early form of corn	D. migration
___ 5. way to date artifacts	E. nomads

DIRECTIONS: Multiple Choice In the blank at the left, write the letter of the

---

NATIONAL GEOGRAPHIC

Prehistoric Migrations Through the Americas

Legend:
- Glaciers
- Land exposed during the Ice Age
- ← Possible migration routes
- • Known sites of prehistoric hunters

0   1,000 miles
0   1,000 kilometers
Azimuthal Equidistant projection

Geography *Skills*

Over thousands of years, prehistoric people migrated from other lands to the Americas.

1. **Movement** Along what major mountain ranges did the migration routes flow?

2. **Interpreting Information** How was it possible for prehistoric people to cross the Bering Strait?

---

mammoths and then charged at the animals, hurling their weapons.

A single mammoth provided tons of meat, enough to feed a group of people for months. The hunters and their families used every part of the animal. They made the skin into clothing, carved the bones into weapons and tools, and may have used the long ribs to build shelters.

About 15,000 years ago the earth's temperatures began to rise. The Ice Age was drawing to an end. As the great glaciers melted, the oceans rose, and Beringia was submerged again. The

Americas were cut off from Asia. At the same time, the hunters of America faced a new challenge. The mammoths and other large animals began to die out, either from being overhunted or because of changes in the environment. The early Americans had to find other sources of food.

✔ **Reading Check** **Describing** How did early American nomads hunt for food?

Settling Down

As the large animals disappeared, the early Americans found new sources of food. They hunted smaller game, such as deer, birds, and rodents. Those who lived along rivers or near the seacoast learned to catch fish with nets and traps. They continued to gather wild berries and grains.

DIFFERENTIATED INSTRUCTION

Reading Support Discuss with students the difference between "number of years ago" and "years B.C." Explain how to convert "number of years ago" to "years B.C." by subtracting 2,000 from the number of years. Have each student make a double time line listing the events in this section. On the top of the time line, use the heading *Number of Years Ago;* on the bottom, use the heading *Years B.C.* Have students use the conversion equation to complete the time line. **L1**

📁 Refer to *Inclusion for the Middle School Social Studies Classroom Strategies and Activities* in the TCR.

Planting Seeds

About 9,000 years ago, people living in present-day **Mexico** made a discovery that would shape the lives of Native Americans for thousands of years. They learned to plant and raise an early form of corn called maize. Their harvests of maize provided a steady, reliable source of food. No longer did they have to move from place to place in order to find food.

Early Americans in Mexico also experimented with other kinds of seeds. They planted pumpkins, beans, and squashes. They soon began producing more than enough food to feed themselves. The population grew along with the growing food supply.

Early Communities

With rising numbers of people and a dependable supply of food, early Americans in Mexico started to form stationary communities. Scientists have found traces of early villages that date from about 5,000 years ago. Scientists use a method called carbon dating to find out how old an artifact is. By measuring the amount of radioactive carbon that remains in something that was once alive—such as a bone or a piece of wood—they can tell approximately how long ago it lived. Carbon dating is imprecise and can only give a rough estimate of an artifact's age.

Sometime after the early settlements in Mexico, people began farming in what is now the southwestern United States. Not all the early peoples in the Americas farmed, however. Some remained nomadic hunters, and others relied on fishing or trading instead of agriculture.

The Growth of Cultures

Farming allowed people to spend time on activities other than finding food. Knowing that they would harvest an abundant supply of grains and vegetables, the people of ancient Mexico began to improve their lives in other ways. They built permanent shelters of clay, brick, stone, or wood. They made pottery and cloth and decorated these goods with dyes made from roots and herbs. They also began to develop more complex forms of government.

Agriculture changed the lives of these early people and led to a new culture, or way of life. Rather than move from place to place in search of food, the people who farmed were able to settle down. They formed communities and developed common customs, beliefs, and ways of protecting themselves. Over time, the many different groups of people living in the Americas developed their own cultures.

✓ **Reading Check** **Summarizing** What did farming mean for nomadic people?

SECTION 1 ASSESSMENT

Checking for Understanding

1. **Key Terms** Use each of the following terms in a complete sentence that will help explain its meaning: archaeology, artifact, Ice Age, migration, culture.

2. **Reviewing Facts** Why did the first people come to the Americas?

Reviewing Themes

3. **Geography and History** How did an Ice Age make it possible for Asian hunters to migrate to the Americas?

Critical Thinking

4. **Determining Cause and Effect** How do you think the first Americans discovered that they could grow their own plants?

5. **Organizing Information** Re-create the diagram below and explain how early Native Americans depended on their environment and natural resources.

Analyzing Visuals

6. **Geography Skills** Study the map on page 18. In which direction did the travelers migrate across the Bering Strait?

Interdisciplinary Activity

Geography Create a version of the map on page 18. Your version can be larger, if needed. Label all land masses and bodies of water. Illustrate the map to tell the story of how the first Americans migrated to North America.

SECTION 1 ASSESSMENT ANSWERS

1. Student work should reflect correct use of terms.

2. The first Americans were nomads searching for food by following animal herds.

3. Water froze, sea levels dropped, and large areas of land such as Beringia were exposed, allowing migration.

4. Answers may vary, but students should refer to the first Americans' observations and experimentation.

5. Any three: animals as food source, animal bones for weapons and tools, animal skins for clothing and shelter, stones shaped for tools, rocks shaped as spear points, and animal ribs as supports for shelter

6. east and southeast

Interdisciplinary Activity Maps should show migration patterns and include arrows, creative illustrations, and where possible, dates.

✓ **Reading Check**

Answer: It provided a steady food source, allowing Native Americans to establish permanent communities.

L1

Reteaching Activity 1–1

L1, ELL

Reading Essentials and Study Guide 1–1

L3

Enrichment Activity 1–1

4 CLOSE

Ask students to speculate what might have happened in the Americas if the Ice Age had never occurred.

19

TEACH

Analyzing Information

Have students read the information about Cactus Hill. **Ask**: **What is Cactus Hill?** *(an archaeological site discovered 45 miles south of Richmond, Virginia)* **Ask**: **What is the significance of the find at Cactus Hill?** *(It adds evidence that humans settled in North America earlier than previously thought.)* Discuss with students why such discoveries and archaeological evidence are important to an understanding of human migration patterns.

Have students mix plaster of Paris and water in a small aluminum pie pan. The mixture should be about 1.2 inches (3 cm) deep with a smooth, flat surface. Students should do the following: lay a leaf, twig, or other organic sample on the wet plaster of Paris; press down so that an imprint is made; carefully remove the sample and allow the plaster of Paris to dry. Lay out the students' casts and have students attempt to identify what was used to make the cast. Ask students how the casts represent how fossils are made. If possible, compare the casts with real fossils. **L2**

Visit the TIME Web site at www.time.com for up-to-date news, weekly magazine articles, editorials, online polls, and an archive of past magazine and Web articles.

TIME NOTEBOOK

New Ways to the New World

An old Virginia sandpit may change our views of the earliest Americans

IT HAS BEEN CALLED THE GREATEST STORY OF IMMIGRATION TO THE Americas. At the end of the last Ice Age, brave women and men from Siberia walked across the Bering Sea land bridge. This is a piece of land that once connected the Asian continent with North America. Within 500 years, their descendants had settled most of the hemisphere, from the Arctic Circle to the tip of South America. But it seems they may not have been first.

Cactus Hill

Well known archaeologist **JOSEPH McAVOY** and his team reported that they have located an ancient campsite that is about 18,000 years old. The place, known as Cactus Hill, is about 45 miles south of Richmond, Virginia (see map).

Scientists now believe the site may actually be thousands of years older than the land-bridge site. If that's true, then people were living in North America much earlier than once believed. "If the dates hold up, and I think they will," says archaeologist Dennis Stanford, "this is probably some of the oldest material in North America, if not the entire New World."

For decades, experts thought that 11,200-year-old stone spear points from a site in Clovis, New Mexico, were the earliest evidence of settlement in the hemisphere. But since the 1970s, older sites have been discovered on both sides of the North American continent. The most important finding has been a 17,000-year-old rock shelter in Meadowcroft, Pennsylvania.

More Proof

Now Cactus Hill presents still more proof that humans settled in North America earlier than anyone had thought. McAvoy's team has unearthed a variety of stone tools, probably used for hunting and butchering animals. The team also found burned bones of mud turtles, white-tailed deer, and other mammals, and bits of charcoal left over from hunters cooking the animals.

High-tech instruments were used to figure out how old the bones and objects are. The Meadowcroft rock shelter's chief archaeologist, James Adovasio, says: "This is another indication that people were running around North America earlier than 13,000 years ago."

McAvoy and wife, Lynn, working on what may be one of the oldest campsites in the Americas

GARRETT—NATL GEOGRAPHIC CACTUS HILL

EXTENDING THE CONTENT

Artifacts of Cactus Hill The soil chemistry of Cactus Hill contains larger than expected levels of phosphate, indicating human occupation. Much of the artifacts found are tools, such as blades used in butchering and hide processing. Archaeologist Michael F. Johnson speculates that the site was an ideal dry summer retreat above water-laden bogs for hunter-gatherers who stalked bison, elk, mastodon, and deer.

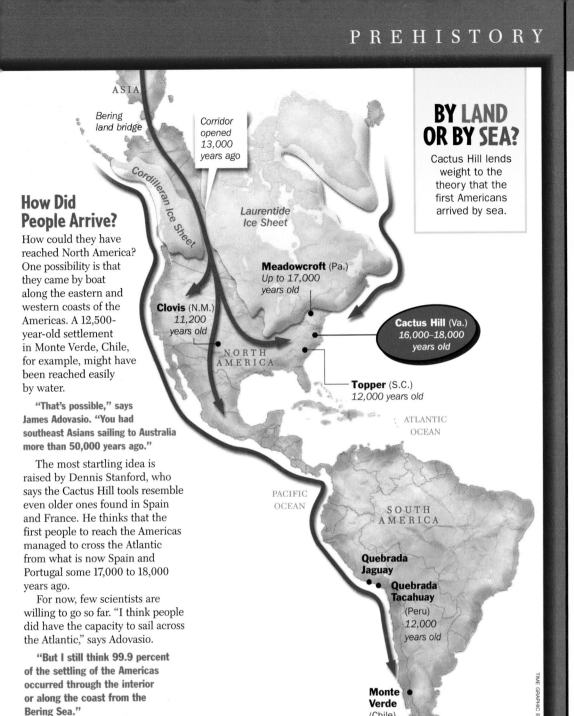

How Did People Arrive?

How could they have reached North America? One possibility is that they came by boat along the eastern and western coasts of the Americas. A 12,500-year-old settlement in Monte Verde, Chile, for example, might have been reached easily by water.

"That's possible," says James Adovasio. "You had southeast Asians sailing to Australia more than 50,000 years ago."

The most startling idea is raised by Dennis Stanford, who says the Cactus Hill tools resemble even older ones found in Spain and France. He thinks that the first people to reach the Americas managed to cross the Atlantic from what is now Spain and Portugal some 17,000 to 18,000 years ago.

For now, few scientists are willing to go so far. "I think people did have the capacity to sail across the Atlantic," says Adovasio.

"But I still think 99.9 percent of the settling of the Americas occurred through the interior or along the coast from the Bering Sea."

ASIA

Bering land bridge

Cordilleran Ice Sheet

Corridor opened 13,000 years ago

Laurentide Ice Sheet

Meadowcroft (Pa.)
Up to 17,000 years old

Clovis (N.M.)
11,200 years old

NORTH AMERICA

Cactus Hill (Va.)
16,000–18,000 years old

Topper (S.C.)
12,000 years old

ATLANTIC OCEAN

PACIFIC OCEAN

SOUTH AMERICA

Quebrada Jaguay

Quebrada Tacahuay
(Peru)
12,000 years old

Monte Verde
(Chile)
12,500 years old

BY LAND OR BY SEA?
Cactus Hill lends weight to the theory that the first Americans arrived by sea.

TIME GRAPHIC BY LON TWEETEN

Alternative Assessment

Have students review the map on page 21 and discuss the human migration patterns. Have students speculate as to the possibility that ancient people crossed the Atlantic Ocean to settle along the East Coast. **Ask:** What information on the map lends evidence to the possibility of a water migration route by ancient peoples? *(Sites such as Meadowcroft, Cactus Hill, and Topper are all similar in age and all close to coastal areas; tools found at the Cactus Hill site resemble those found in Spain and France.)* Have students study the work of archaeologists. Have them create a list that identifies what personality traits they think an archaeologist should have.

Did you know?

Radiocarbon dating is used to determine the age of artifacts by measuring its radiocarbon content. Radiocarbon is found in the tissues of all living organisms. It breaks down, or decays, at a uniform rate. Half of the radiocarbon disappears after about 5,700 years. This is known as the radiocarbon's *half-life*.

CLOSE

Have students research the extent of glacier movement in North America. Ask students to speculate on how glaciers affected human migration.

COOPERATIVE LEARNING ACTIVITY

Researching an Archaeological Site Have students form groups of three or four and choose an archaeological site from page 21 to study. Students should research the history of the site and the types of artifacts discovered. Each group should develop a map showing the location of the site and a time line showing the age of the chosen site in relation to other sites on page 21. Students also may want to create drawings of artifacts found at the site. Have each group present its research, explaining the significance of the discovery. **L2**

1 FOCUS

Section Overview

This section examines the complex cultures of the Maya, Aztec, and Inca civilizations that developed before the arrival of Europeans.

BELLRINGER
Skillbuilder Activity

 Project transparency and have students answer the question.

Daily Focus Skills Transparency 1–2

Reading Preview

Answers to Graphic: Maya: gods controlled everything on Earth and priests knew gods' wishes and made most decisions; Aztec: gods were all powerful and priests offered human sacrifices to them; Inca: emperor was a descendant of the sun god and special cities were built devoted to religious ceremonies

Preteaching Vocabulary
Ask students to define the word *civilization* using their own, made-up hieroglyphics.

SECTION 2 Cities and Empires

Guide to Reading

Main Idea
Several factors led to the rise and decline of great civilizations and empires in the Americas.

Key Terms
civilization, theocracy, hieroglyphics, terrace

Reading Strategy
Categorizing Information As you read the section, re-create the diagram below and describe the role religion played in each civilization.

Civilization	Religion
Maya	
Aztec	
Inca	

Read to Learn
- why powerful empires arose in the Americas.
- how the people of each empire adapted to their environment.

Section Theme
Culture and Traditions Civilizations such as the Maya, the Aztec, and the Inca arose in present-day Mexico and in Central and South America.

Preview of Events

1500 B.C.		B.C./A.D.		A.D.1200	A.D.1400

c. 1500 B.C.
Rise of the Olmec in Mexico

c. A.D. 700
Maya civilization at its height in Central America

c. A.D. 1325
Aztec establish Tenochtitlán in Mexico

c. A.D. 1400
Inca Empire begins to expand

Artifact, c. A.D. 900

AN American Story

Rumors of a lost city led American historian Hiram Bingham to the mountains of Peru in 1911. Bingham followed a steep mountain trail, pulling himself along by grabbing vines. After many hours of climbing, he reached a clearing. Suddenly he saw acres of huge, crumbling walls and pillars of white stone covered with vines and moss. "It fairly took my breath away," wrote Bingham. He knew that these temples and monuments were the remains of a very advanced people.

Early American Civilizations

Bingham had discovered the ruins of an early Inca city, Machu Picchu (MAH•choo PEE•choo). It is a small city—Machu Picchu covers only about five square miles (13 sq. km)—but it is an extraordinary place. Its structures, carved from the gray granite of the mountaintop, are wonders of design and craftsmanship and equal the achievements of the civilizations of Europe, Asia, and Africa.

Long before the arrival of Europeans in the early 1500s, several great civilizations, or highly developed societies, arose in present-day Mexico and in

22   CHAPTER 1   The First Americans

SECTION RESOURCES

📁 Reproducible Masters
- Reproducible Lesson Plan 1–2
- Daily Lecture and Discussion Notes 1–2
- Guided Reading Activity 1–2
- Section Quiz 1–2
- Reteaching Activity 1–2
- Reading Essentials and Study Guide 1–2
- Enrichment Activity 1–2

🛠 Transparencies
- Daily Focus Skills Transparency 1–2

Multimedia
- 💿 Interactive Tutor Self-Assessment CD-ROM
- 💿 ExamView® Pro Testmaker CD-ROM
- 💿 Presentation Plus! CD-ROM

Central and South America. These civilizations built enormous cities in thick jungles and on mountaintops that were hard to reach. They also developed complex systems for writing, counting, and tracking time.

Among the largest and most advanced of these early civilizations were the **Olmec,** the **Maya,** the **Aztec,** and the **Inca.** Each civilization spread out over hundreds of miles, included millions of people, and thrived for centuries.

The Olmec flourished between 1500 B.C. and 300 B.C. along the Gulf Coast of what are now Mexico, Guatemala, and Honduras. Olmec farmers produced enough food to sustain cities containing thousands of people. Olmec workers sculpted large stone monuments and built stone pavements and drainage systems. Their civilization strongly influenced their neighbors.

✔**Reading Check** **Identifying** What are civilizations?

The Maya

The Maya built their civilization in the steamy rain forests of present-day **Mexico, Guatemala, Honduras,** and **Belize.** They planted maize, beans, sweet potatoes, and other vegetables. They also pulled enormous stones from the earth to build monuments and pyramids that still stand today. Much of this labor was performed by enslaved people, usually prisoners of war.

Mayan Cities

By A.D. 300 the Maya had built many large cities. Each city had at least one stone pyramid. Some pyramids reached about 200 feet (60 m)—the height of a 20-story building. Steps ran up the pyramid sides to a temple on top. The largest Mayan city, **Tikal,** in present-day Guatemala, was surrounded by five pyramids.

The temples on top of the pyramids were religious and governmental centers. Wearing gold jewelry and detailed headdresses, the priests in the temples performed rituals dedicated to the Mayan gods. On special days, the city's people attended religious festivals.

The Maya believed the gods controlled everything that happened on earth. Because only priests knew the gods' wishes, the priests held great power in Mayan society and made most of the important decisions. The civilization of the Maya was a theocracy, a society ruled by religious leaders.

To keep accurate records for their religious festivals, the Maya became skilled astronomers. The Mayan priests believed that the gods were

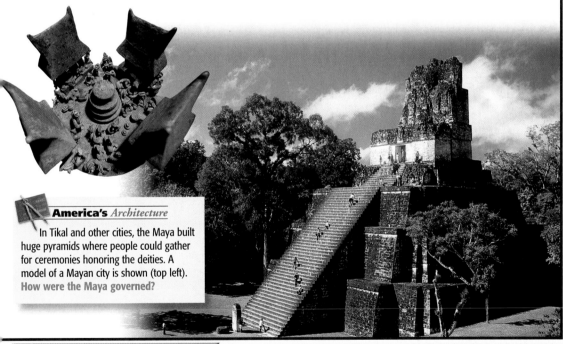

America's *Architecture*

In Tikal and other cities, the Maya built huge pyramids where people could gather for ceremonies honoring the deities. A model of a Mayan city is shown (top left). **How were the Maya governed?**

2 TEACH

Daily Lecture and Discussion Notes 1–2

Copyright © by The McGraw-Hill Companies, Inc.

Daily Lecture and Discussion Notes

Chapter 1, Section 2

Did You Know **?** The present-day metropolitan Mexico City area sits on the same site as the great Aztec capital, Tenochtitlán. Today the population is more than 20 million people.

I. Early American Civilizations *(Pages 22–23)*

A. Several great civilizations arose in present-day Mexico and in Central and South America. The most advanced were the Olmec, the Maya, the Aztec, and the Inca. Each thrived for centuries.

B. The Olmec people lived in what is now Mexico, Guatemala, and Honduras, between 1500 B.C. and 3000 B.C.

C. The Olmec built stone pavement and drainage systems and sculpted large stone monuments. Their civilization influenced their neighbors.

Discussion Question

Why do you think early American civilizations developed along large bodies of water? *(Answers will vary but should include the notion that early people settled near water as a means of transportation and a way to farm. If they needed to flee quickly, they could navigate along the waters.)*

II. The Maya *(Pages 23–24)*

A. The Mayan civilization flourished in present-day Mexico, Guatemala, Honduras, and Belize.

B. The people built large cities, each having at least one stone pyramid.

C. Tikal was the largest Mayan city and had six pyramids.

D. The Mayan civilization was a theocracy, or a society ruled by religious leaders.

E. The Maya believed the gods controlled all that happened on Earth. Atop the pyramids were religious and governmental centers.

F. The Maya became skilled astronomers and developed a writing system called hieroglyphics.

G. Mayan traders transported their goods such as maize, vegetables, jade, turquoise jewelry, and cacao beans on their backs and along the water.

H. No one knows what caused the decline of the Maya around A.D. 800, but descendants of the Maya still live in parts of Mexico and Central America.

turn

Creating a Game Organize the class into small groups to create a *Jeopardy!* style game about the Native American civilizations described in this section. Have students in each group first identify five categories, then write five answers with correct questions in each category. Pair groups to play the game. **L1**

✔**Reading Check**

Answer: highly developed societies

America's *Architecture*

Answer: by a theocracy, or religious leaders

Reading Strategy   READING THE TEXT

Brainstorming Use brainstorming to help engage students in a topic by allowing them to creatively explore the information. Use the ideas described in this section about the Maya, Aztec, and Inca communication systems to help students brainstorm a communication system of their own. Have each student create a calendar, an alphabet, or a way of counting. Then have students use their systems to create a message. Trade their message and system with another student and have the other student decode the message. **L2**

✓ **Reading Check**

Answer: A theocracy is a society ruled by religious leaders.

Why It Matters

Have students create a display showing the crops cultivated by the early Native American civilizations. Encourage students to create interesting and informative displays using agricultural products, poster board, and markers. **Ask:** Why was farming critical to the development of civilizations across the Americas? *(It allowed people to settle in one place and create unique cultures.)*

visible in the stars, sun, and moon. They used their knowledge of the sun and stars to predict eclipses and to develop a 365-day calendar. Their desire to measure time increased their knowledge of mathematics. The Maya also developed a form of writing called hieroglyphics. Hieroglyphics use symbols or pictures to represent things, ideas, and sounds.

🅢 Economics
Transport and Trade

The Maya did not have wheeled vehicles or horses, so everything they transported overland was carried on human backs. Mayan traders traveled on a network of roads that had been carved out of the jungle. Farmers brought maize and vegetables to outdoor markets in the cities. They exchanged their crops for cotton cloth, pottery, deer meat, and salt.

Mayan traders also transported goods by water. Mayan canoes traveled up and down Mexico's east coast. The canoes carried jade statues, turquoise jewelry, cacao beans for making chocolate, and other goods to traders throughout a large area.

Decline of a Civilization

Around A.D. 900 the Maya civilization in the lowlands began to decline. By A.D. 1100 the great cities were almost ghost towns. The jungle crept back across the plazas, roads, and fields. No one knows what caused the decline. Perhaps slaves and farmers revolted against their Mayan masters. Perhaps the soil became too exhausted by erosion and fire to produce enough food for the people. The Maya civilization collapsed, but descendants of the Maya still live in parts of Mexico and Central America.

✓ **Reading Check** **Explaining** What is a theocracy?

The Aztec

Centuries after the fall of the Maya, a group of hunters called the Aztec wandered through central Mexico, searching for a permanent home. In 1325 they came upon an island in Lake Texcoco, today part of Mexico City. There the

Why It Matters

Farming and the Growth of Civilization

Thousands of years ago, a quiet revolution took place. In scattered pockets of the Middle East, Asia, Africa, and the Americas, people learned to cultivate food-producing plants for the first time. As farming gradually spread, it encouraged the growth of permanent communities.

What, Where, and When

Once they had agriculture, people could settle in permanent communities.

c. 8000 B.C. ➝   **c. 7000 B.C.** ➝
Wheat (Syria)   Barley (Jordan)

Aztec saw a sign: an eagle sitting on a cactus, with a snake in its beak. That meant this island was to be their home.

Tenochtitlán

On this island emerged **Tenochtitlán** (tay•NAWCH•teet•LAHN), one of the greatest cities in the Americas. Its construction was a miracle of engineering and human labor. Directed by priests and nobles, workers toiled day and night. They pulled soil from the bottom of the lake to make causeways, or bridges of earth, linking the island and the shore. They filled parts of the lake with earth so they could grow crops.

In time the Aztec capital expanded to the mainland around the lake. At its height Tenochtitlán was the largest city in the Americas, and one of the largest in the world. Tenochtitlán also served as a center of trade, attracting thousands of merchants to its outdoor marketplaces.

DIFFERENTIATED INSTRUCTION

Gifted and Talented After reading Hiram Bingham's description on page 22 of seeing Machu Picchu for the first time, have each student write a first-person narrative describing how he or she would feel about finding remnants of the Aztec, Inca, or Maya civilizations. Have students read the account aloud to the class. Have the class name the civilization described. Record the number of correct responses for each description and award the student with the most correct responses the "Creative Writer of the Day Award." **L3**

📂 Refer to *Inclusion for the Middle School Social Studies Classroom Strategies and Activities* in the TCR.

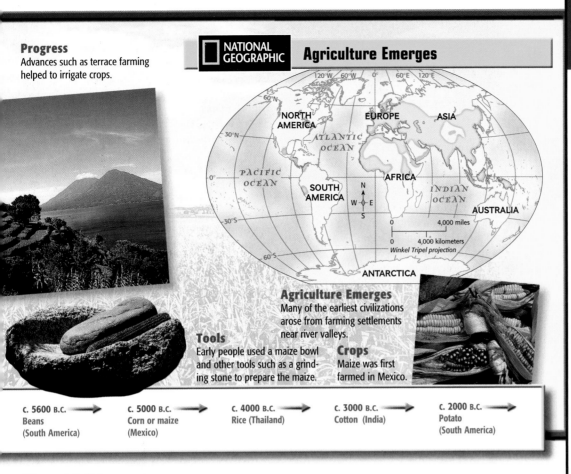

Progress Advances such as terrace farming helped to irrigate crops.

NATIONAL GEOGRAPHIC **Agriculture Emerges**

Agriculture Emerges
Many of the earliest civilizations arose from farming settlements near river valleys.

Tools
Early people used a maize bowl and other tools such as a grinding stone to prepare the maize.

Crops
Maize was first farmed in Mexico.

c. 5600 B.C. →	c. 5000 B.C. →	c. 4000 B.C. →	c. 3000 B.C. →	c. 2000 B.C. →
Beans (South America)	Corn or maize (Mexico)	Rice (Thailand)	Cotton (India)	Potato (South America)

War and Religion

The Aztec civilization grew into a military empire. In the 1400s the Aztec army marched through central and southern Mexico, conquering nearly all rival communities. Aztec warriors took everything they could carry from their victims, including maize, cotton cloth, copper, and weapons. Conquered people were forced to work as slaves in Aztec cities and villages.

Like the Maya, the Aztec organized their society around their religion. The Aztec believed that human sacrifices were necessary to keep the gods pleased and to ensure abundant harvests. Thousands of prisoners of war were sacrificed.

A Great City Remembered

The first Europeans to see the Aztec capital were awed by its splendor. In 1519, 550 Spanish soldiers entered Tenochtitlán, led by Hernán Cortés. He wrote:

    ❝There are forty towers at least, all of stout construction and very lofty. . . . The workmanship both in wood and stone could not be bettered anywhere.**❞**

Bernal Díaz del Castillo, one of the soldiers, marveled at the

    ❝great stone towers and temples and buildings that rose straight up out of the water.**❞**

Tenochtitlán, he explained, was a city of water, and many of the streets were waterways for canoes. Some of the Spanish soldiers thought that Tenochtitlán was more magnificent than Rome and the other great European capitals of the time.

✓**Reading Check** **Making Generalizations** Why was the Aztec city of Tenochtitlán a great city?

CHAPTER 1   The First Americans   **25**

✓**Reading Check**

Answer: The city was constructed when soil was pulled from the bottom of the lake to make causeways, and parts of the lake were filled with earth in order to grow crops.

CURRICULUM CONNECTION

Art Aztec art is highly detailed and colorful. Sculptures decorated temples and other important buildings. One surviving sculpture, the *Calendar Stone*, has carefully detailed carvings that represent the days of the month and religious symbols. It was used in ceremonies honoring the sun god Tonatiuh.

3 ASSESS

Assign Section 2 Assessment as homework or as an in-class activity.

💿 Have students use **Interactive Tutor Self-Assessment CD-ROM.**

L2

Section Quiz 1–2

Name _____ Date _____ Class _____

★ **Chapter 1**   Score ☐

Section Quiz 1-2

DIRECTIONS: Matching Match the items in Column A with the items in Column B. Write the correct letters in the blanks. *(10 points each)*

Column A	Column B
___ **1.** largest Mayan city	**A.** civilization
___ **2.** a highly developed society	**B.** Cuzco
___ **3.** builders of stone pyramids	**C.** Tikal
___ **4.** Incan capital city	**D.** Quechua
___ **5.** official Inca language	**E.** Maya

INTERDISCIPLINARY CONNECTIONS ACTIVITY

Music Have students create an Aztec *huehuetl* drum. Use an empty, clean can with one end or both ends removed. Place the open end of the can over heavy plastic or rubber sheeting and trace the outline of the rim. Then draw another circle three inches wider than the rim outline and cut around the wider circle. Tightly stretch this circle around the open end of the can and wrap with cord. Have students work in groups to create a rhythmic composition to play for the class. **L1,** **ELL**

4 CLOSE

Ask each student to choose one of the civilizations discussed in this section and write a short description of what life would be like if that civilization thrived today.

The Inca

Another great American civilization developed in the western highlands of South America. The empire of the Inca was the largest of the early American civilizations.

The Inca founded their capital city of **Cuzco** (KOOS•koh) around A.D. 1200. In 1438 an emperor named Pachacuti (PAH•chah•KOO•tee) came to the throne and began a campaign of conquest against the neighboring peoples. He and his son, Topa Inca, built an empire that stretched from north to south for more than 3,000 miles (4,800 km), from present-day Colombia to northern Argentina and Chile.

The Incan army was powerful. All men between 25 and 50 years old could be drafted to serve in the army for up to five years. Their weapons included clubs, spears, and spiked copper balls on ropes. Using slings of woven cloth, Incan soldiers could throw stones 30 yards (27 m).

Life in the Empire

At its height, the Inca Empire had a population of more than nine million, including many conquered peoples. To control this large empire, the Inca built at least 10,000 miles (16,000 km) of stone-paved roads that ran over mountains, across deserts, and through jungles. Rope bridges, made from grass, crossed canyons and rivers.

Runners carrying messages to and from the emperor linked remote outposts of the empire to Cuzco. The Inca language, Quechua (KEH•chuh•wuh), became the official language for the entire empire. Although the Inca did not have a system of writing, they developed a system of record keeping with string called *quipus* (KEE•poos). Using various lengths and colors of string, knotted in special patterns, the *quipus* carried information about resources such as grain supplies.

Although mountainous land is not well suited for farming, the Inca devised ways to produce a steady supply of food. They cut terraces, or broad platforms, into steep slopes so they could plant crops. They built stone walls on the terraces to hold the soil and plants in place. Incan farmers grew maize, squash, tomatoes, peanuts, chili peppers, melons, cotton, and potatoes.

All Inca land belonged to the emperor, who was believed to be a descendant of the sun god. Because the Inca thought that the sun god enjoyed displays of gold, they made magnificent gold jewelry and temple ornaments. The Inca also built special cities devoted to religious ceremonies. One of these cities was Machu Picchu, the mountaintop site described in "An American Story" on page 22.

✓**Reading Check** **Explaining** How did the Inca farm steep slopes?

SECTION 2 ASSESSMENT

Checking for Understanding

1. **Key Terms** Using standard grammar, write a short paragraph in which you use all of the following terms: **civilization, theocracy, hieroglyphics, terrace.**

2. **Reviewing Facts** Why did the Aztec choose the location of Tenochtitlán as their permanent home?

Reviewing Themes

3. **Culture and Traditions** Why did priests hold great power in Mayan society?

Critical Thinking

4. **Making Inferences** How does trade help to enrich a civilization? Provide examples in your answer.

5. **Analyzing Information** Re-create the diagram below and give three reasons the Maya, Aztec, and Inca are considered advanced civilizations.

Analyzing Visuals

6. **Picturing History** Study the photograph of the pyramid on page 23. Why do you think the Maya built such large pyramids?

Interdisciplinary Activity

Art Compile illustrations of some of the accomplishments of the Maya, Aztec, and Inca in the areas of communication, science, and math. Use your own drawings or use photographs from newspapers and magazines.

SECTION 2 ASSESSMENT ANSWERS

1. Student work should reflect correct use of terms.
2. They saw the eagle sitting on a cactus with a snake in its beak as a sign that it was their home.
3. The priests were considered to know the wishes of the gods.
4. Trade fosters the exchange of goods, ideas, technology, and culture.
5. Answers may include: organized civilization with distinct classes; created divisions of labor; established religion and government, and developed farming methods.
6. Answers will vary but should show a connection between religion and the building of great pyramids.

Interdisciplinary Activity
Student work should present an organized approach.

Understanding the Parts of a Map

Why Learn This Skill?

Maps can direct you down the street or around the world. There are as many different kinds of maps as there are uses for them. Being able to read a map begins with learning about its parts.

Learning the Skill

Maps usually include a key, a compass rose, and a scale bar. The map key explains the meaning of special colors, symbols, and lines used on the map.

After reading the map key, look for the compass rose. It is the direction marker that shows the cardinal directions of north, south, east, and west.

A measuring line, often called a scale bar, helps you estimate distance on a map. The map's scale tells you what distance on the earth is represented by the measurement on the scale bar. For example, 1 inch (2.54 cm) on the map may represent 100 miles (160.9 km) on the earth.

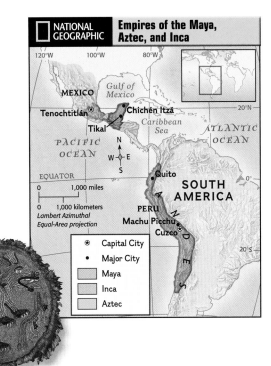

NATIONAL GEOGRAPHIC — Empires of the Maya, Aztec, and Inca

- ⊛ Capital City
- • Major City
- Maya
- Inca
- Aztec

Practicing the Skill

The map on this page shows where the ancient Maya, Aztec, and Inca built their empires in North America and South America. Look at the parts of this map, then answer the questions that follow.

1. What information is given in the key?
2. What color shows the Inca Empire?
3. What direction would you travel to go from Tenochtitlán to Chichén Itzá?
4. About how many miles long was the Inca Empire?
5. What was the capital of the Aztec Empire?

Applying the Skill

Drawing a Map Picture a mental image of your house or room. Draw a map showing the location of various areas. Include a map key explaining any symbols or colors you use. Also include a scale bar explaining the size of your map compared to the real area. Finally, add a compass rose and title to your map.

 Glencoe's **Skillbuilder Interactive Workbook CD-ROM, Level 1,** provides instruction and practice in key social studies skills.

27

TEACH

Understanding the Parts of a Map This skill demonstrates how to use the parts of a map, which could include a key, a compass rose, and a scale bar. By using the parts of a map, students will be able to read and understand the information provided on a map.

Invite students to practice using the scale bar. Ask them to first determine the scale on this map before measuring distances. Then have them use a string to measure distances that are not straight lines.

Additional Practice

L2

Chapter Skills Activity 1

Name _____ Date _____ Class _____

★ Chapter Skills Activity 1

Understanding the Parts of a Map

Whether you are looking at a city bus map or a world climate map, you will notice certain features to help you understand the information the map provides. The map key, or legend, explains the meanings of special symbols, colors, or lines. The scale bar enables you to determine actual distances between points on the map. A compass rose shows the directions north, south, east, and west.

DIRECTIONS: This map shows Native American pueblos as well as modern cities and towns in a portion of New Mexico. Use the map to answer the following questions on a separate sheet of paper.

North Central New Mexico

▲ Native American pueblo
• Modern town or city

GLENCOE
TECHNOLOGY

 CD-ROM
Glencoe Skillbuilder Interactive Workbook CD-ROM, Level 1

This interactive CD-ROM reinforces student mastery of essential social studies skills.

ANSWERS TO PRACTICING THE SKILL

1. capital city; major cities; location of Maya, Inca, and Aztec civilizations
2. green
3. east
4. about 3,000 miles (4,827 km) long
5. Tenochtitlán

Applying the Skill Students will draw a map of their home or room including a map key, scale bar, and compass rose on it.

1 FOCUS

Section Overview

This section reviews the many diverse early Native American cultures found in North America.

BELLRINGER
Skillbuilder Activity

 Project transparency and have students answer the question.

Daily Focus Skills Transparency 1–3

Reading Preview

Answers to Graphic: Anasazi: area of Four Corners; pueblos, cliff dwellings; Mound Builders: area from Pennsylvania to the Mississippi River valley; hunters and gatherers who built great mounds for burial and for temples; Inuit: along the Arctic Ocean; built igloos and hunted seal, whale, caribou, and walrus for food and clothing

Preteaching Vocabulary
Use the **Vocabulary PuzzleMaker CD-ROM** to create crossword and word search puzzles.

SECTION 3 North American Peoples

Guide to Reading

Main Idea
Many different cultures lived in North America before the arrival of the Europeans.

Key Terms
pueblo, drought, adobe, federation

Reading Strategy
Taking Notes As you read Section 3, re-create the diagram below and identify locations and ways of living for each culture.

Culture	Where they lived	How they lived
Anasazi		
Mound Builders		
Inuit		

Read to Learn
- what early people lived in North America.
- how different Native American groups adapted to their environments.

Section Theme
Culture and Traditions Early North Americans developed new societies.

Preview of Events

♦1000 B.C.	♦B.C./A.D.	♦A.D.1000	♦A.D.1300

C. 1000 B.C.
First ceremonial mounds built

C. A.D. 1000
Anasazi build pueblos in North America

C. A.D. 1100
Cahokia is built

C. A.D. 1300
Hohokam civilization begins to decline

Ancient jar, American Southwest

AN American Story

In the summer of 1991, a helicopter passenger made an amazing discovery in Arizona's Coconino National Forest. As the helicopter hovered among the sandstone cliffs, the sun shone into a cave 200 feet (61 m) below the rim of one cliff. Standing in the opening of the cave were three large pottery jars. The three jars had been sitting, untouched and unseen, for more than 700 years. The jars and other objects found in the cave were left there by the Sinagua. These people lived hundreds of years ago in what we now call Arizona. The Sinagua are just one of many Native American peoples who are now being studied by archaeologists and historians.

Early Native Americans

Many Native American cultures rose, flourished, and disappeared in North America long before Europeans arrived in the 1500s. Among the most advanced of these early cultures were the Hohokam and Anasazi of the Southwest and the Mound Builders of the Ohio River valley.

SECTION RESOURCES

Reproducible Masters
- Reproducible Lesson Plan 1–3
- Daily Lecture and Discussion Notes 1–3
- Guided Reading Activity 1–3
- Section Quiz 1–3
- Reteaching Activity 1–3
- Reading Essentials and Study Guide 1–3
- Enrichment Activity 1–3

Transparencies
- Daily Focus Skills Transparency 1–3
- American Art and Architecture, Transparency 1

Multimedia
- American Music: Hits Through History
- Vocabulary PuzzleMaker CD-ROM
- Interactive Tutor Self-Assessment CD-ROM
- ExamView® Pro Testmaker CD-ROM
- Presentation Plus! CD-ROM

The Hohokam

The dry, hot desert of present-day Arizona was home to the **Hohokam** people. They may have come from Mexico about 300 B.C. The Hohokam culture flourished from about A.D. 300 to A.D. 1300 in an area bordered by the Gila and Salt River valleys.

The Hohokam were experts at squeezing every drop of available water from the sun-baked soil. Their way of life depended on the irrigation channels they dug to carry river water into their fields. In addition to hundreds of miles of irrigation channels, the Hohokam left behind pottery, carved stone, and shells etched with acid. The shells came from trade with coastal peoples.

The Anasazi

The **Anasazi** lived around the same time as the Hohokam, roughly A.D. 1 to A.D. 1300, in the area known as the Four Corners (the meeting place of the present-day states of Utah, Colorado, Arizona, and New Mexico). There they built great stone dwellings that the Spanish explorers later called pueblos (PWEH•blohs), or villages. **Pueblo Bonito,** one of the most spectacular of the Anasazi pueblos, can still be seen in New Mexico. The huge semicircular structure of stone and sun-dried earth resembles an apartment building. It is four stories high and has hundreds of rooms. Archaeologists have found traces of a complex road system linking Pueblo Bonito with other villages. This suggests that Pueblo Bonito was an important trade or religious center for the Anasazi.

The Anasazi also built dwellings in the walls of steep cliffs. Cliff dwellings were easy to defend and offered protection from winter weather. **Mesa Verde** in Colorado, one of the largest and most elaborate cliff dwellings, held several thousand inhabitants.

In about 1300 the Anasazi began leaving the pueblos and cliff dwellings to settle in smaller communities. Their large villages may have been abandoned because of droughts, long periods of little rainfall, during which their crops dried up.

Kivas at Pueblo Bonito

Picturing History

Pueblo Bonito had more than 800 rooms and 32 kivas, or underground ceremonial chambers. Today, the ruins of Pueblo Bonito are part of Chaco Culture National Historical Park in northwestern New Mexico. **What other kind of dwellings were built by the Anasazi?**

2 TEACH

Daily Lecture and Discussion Notes 1–3

Copyright © by The McGraw-Hill Companies, Inc.

Daily Lecture and Discussion Notes

Chapter 1, Section 3

Did You Know Native Americans who hunted buffalo, such as the Apache and Navajo, relied on the animal for meat. The buffalo, however, served other uses such as hides for clothing, pouches, and dolls; hair for headdresses and pillow stuffing; tails for whips; hoofs for glue; and horns for cups and spoons.

I. Early Native Americans *(Pages 28–31)*

   A. Many Native American cultures existed in North America before Europeans arrived in the 1500s.

   B. The Hohokam lived in the desert of present-day Arizona. Their civilization flourished from about A.D. 300 to A.D. 1200. They built irrigation channels to bring water to the hot, dry land from the nearby Gila and Salt Rivers and left behind pottery, carved stone, and shells.

   C. The Anasazi lived in an area known as the Four Corners (or the meeting place) of present-day Utah, Colorado, Arizona, and New Mexico from A.D. 200 to A.D. 1300.

   D. The Anasazi built stone and cliff dwellings. A pueblo or stone dwelling looked like an apartment building. The cliff dwellings were built into the walls of steep cliffs. Pueblo Bonito and Mesa Verde are examples of each.

   E. In about 1300, the Anasazi left these dwellings to settle in smaller communities, perhaps due to droughts during which their crops dried up.

   F. The Mound Builders lived in central North America from present-day Pennsylvania to the Mississippi River valley. They built mounds of earth that looked like the Aztec stone pyramids.

   G. The Adena were hunters and gatherers and among the earliest Mound Builders living in the Ohio Valley around 800 B.C.

   H. The Hopewell people were farmers and traders who built large burial mounds shaped live birds, bears, and snakes. They left behind pearls, shells, cloth, and copper in the mounds to show their variety of trade.

   I. The Cahokia built the largest settlement in present-day Illinois. This city may have had 16,000 people. The highest mound, Monks Mound, rose nearly 100 feet and was probably the highest structure north of Mexico.

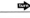

Reading Strategy

Charting Native American Groups Have students work in pairs to create a chart of all Native North American groups described in this section. Headings on the charts should include name of group, type of shelter, and unique cultural achievement. **L2,** ELL

Picturing History

To enter a kiva, people would climb down a ladder into the room, making sure they faced the rungs as they went. It was believed that to look down would shorten one's life. **Answer:** cliff dwellings

COOPERATIVE LEARNING ACTIVITY

Making a Diorama Have students choose a Native American group described in this section that interests them. Ask students to form groups based on this choice. Have each group create a diorama to show the unique characteristics of the Native American culture they selected. Allow each student in the group to choose one part of the culture, such as dwellings, clothing, environment, or crafts that they would like to create for the group's diorama. Ask students to present completed dioramas to the class, explaining each cultural characteristic shown. **L2,** ELL

Guided Reading Activity 1–3

Name _____ Date _____ Class _____

★ **Guided Reading Activity 1-3**

DIRECTIONS: Outlining Locate each heading in your textbook. Then use the information under the heading to help you write each answer. Use another sheet of paper if necessary.

I. Early Native Americans

A. The Hohokam—How did the Hohokam people help provide water for their fields?
_____

B. The Anasazi
  1. What kinds of dwellings did the Anasazi build? _____
  2. Why do archaeologists think Pueblo Bonito was an important center for the Anasazi? _____

C. The Mound Builders
  1. What was the purpose of some of the mounds built by the Mound Builders?
  _____
  2. What do the artifacts found in the mounds indicate? _____

D. Cahokia—Why is Cahokia a special place? _____

II. Other Native North Americans

A. Peoples of the North—How did the Inuit survive the cold Arctic climate?
_____

B. Peoples of the West
  1. How did the Tlingit, Haida, and Chinook adapt their way of life to the forest and sea environment of the West Coast? _____
  2. Where did the Nez Perce and Yakima settle? _____
  3. Why did the Ute and Shoshone travel to find food? _____

C. Peoples of the Southwest—How did the Apache and Navajo get most of their food? _____

D. Peoples of the Plains—What animal became important to the Plains peoples during hunting and warfare? _____

E. Peoples of the East and Southeast
  1. What five Iroquois nations joined to form the Iroquois League? _____
  2. What important activities did Iroquois women do? _____
  3. What are three of the Native American peoples who lived in present-day Georgia, Alabama, and Mississippi? _____
  4. What happened in the 1500s that changed the Native Americans' way of life?
  _____

Geography Skills

Answers:
1. the Southwest
2. the Plains cultures

History and the Humanities

♪ American Music: Hits Through History, "Iroquois Round Dance"

🖼 American Art and Architecture, Transparency 1, *Serpent Mound* **L3**

ABCNEWS INTERACTIVE™

 VIDEOCASSETTE
Historic America Electronic Field Trips

View **Chapter 3** to learn more about the Cahokia Mounds.

NATIONAL GEOGRAPHIC
Native American Cultures Before 1500

1 Tepees were used by the Plains cultures.
2 Cultures in the Northeast Woodlands built longhouses.
3 Southwest cultures built pueblos.

Culture Groups
- Arctic
- Subarctic
- Northwest Coast
- Plateau
- Great Basin
- California
- Southwest
- Great Plains
- Northeast Woodlands
- Southeast

Geography Skills

1. **Region** To which culture group did the Apache and Hopi belong?
2. **Making Inferences** Based on the description of the dwellings, which cultures were nomadic?

The Mound Builders

The early cultures of Mexico and Central America appear to have influenced people living in lands to the north. In central North America, prehistoric Native Americans built thousands of mounds of earth that look very much like the stone pyramids of the Maya and the Aztec. Some of the mounds contained burial chambers. Some were topped with temples, as in the Mayan and Aztec cultures.

The mounds are dotted across the landscape from present-day Pennsylvania to the Mississippi River valley. They have been found as far north as the Great Lakes and as far south as Florida. Archaeologists think that the first mounds were built about 1000 B.C. They were not the work of a single group but of many different peoples, who are referred to as the **Mound Builders.**

Among the earliest Mound Builders were the **Adena,** hunters and gatherers who flourished in the Ohio Valley by 800 B.C. They were followed by the **Hopewell** people, who lived between 200 B.C. and A.D. 500. Farmers and traders, the Hopewell built huge burial mounds in the shape of birds, bears, and snakes. One of them, the **Great Serpent Mound,** looks like a giant snake winding across the ground. Archaeologists have found freshwater pearls, shells, cloth, and copper in the mounds. The objects indicate a widespread pattern of trade.

Cahokia

The largest settlement of the Mound Builders was **Cahokia** (kuh•HOH•kee•uh) in present-day Illinois. This city, built after A.D. 900 by a

---

DIFFERENTIATED INSTRUCTION

Reading Support The Plains peoples used battle shields that expressed the personal characteristics of the carrier and reflected the Plains culture. Have each student cut out an 18-inch (46-cm) circle from stiff paper such as cardboard to use as the shield's base. Students should use paints, fabric, or colored paper to create a design on the front of the shield. Then have them tape or glue a strap of leather or stiff paper about 14 inches (36 cm) long to the back side of the shield. Pair students to interpret each other's shield. **L1**

📂 Refer to *Inclusion for the Middle School Social Studies Classroom Strategies and Activities* in the TCR.

Native American Population

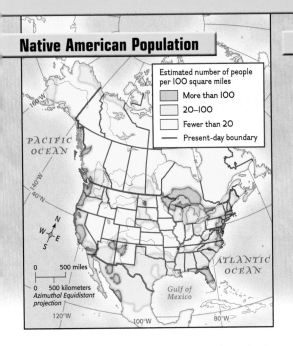

Estimated number of people per 100 square miles

- More than 100
- 20–100
- Fewer than 20
- — Present-day boundary

Hunters, Gatherers, and Fishers

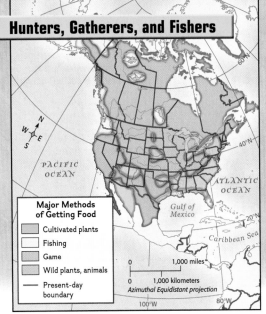

Major Methods of Getting Food

- Cultivated plants
- Fishing
- Game
- Wild plants, animals
- — Present-day boundary

people called the Mississippians, may have had 16,000 or more residents. The largest mound in Cahokia, the Monks Mound, rises nearly 100 feet (30 m). When it was built, it was probably the highest structure north of Mexico.

Cahokia resembled the great cities of Mexico, even though it was nearly 2,000 miles away. The city was dominated by the great pyramid-shaped mound. A temple crowned the summit—perhaps a place where priests studied the movements of the sun and stars or where the priest-ruler of Cahokia lived. A legend of the Natchez people, descendants of the Mississippians, hints of a direct link to Mexico:

> ❝Before we came into this land we lived yonder under the sun [the speaker pointed southwest toward Mexico]. . . . Our nation extended itself along the great water [the Gulf of Mexico] where this large river [the Mississippi] loses itself.❞

✓ **Reading Check** **Identifying** In what area did the Anasazi live?

Other Native North Americans

Although the civilizations of the Hohokam, the Anasazi, and the Mound Builders eventually faded away, other Native American cultures arose to take their place. Around the time that Europeans began arriving, North America was home to many different societies.

Peoples of the North

The people who settled in the northernmost part of North America, in the lands around the Arctic Ocean, are called the **Inuit.** Some scientists think the Inuit were the last migrants to cross the land bridge into North America.

The Inuit had many skills that helped them survive in the cold Arctic climate. They may have brought some of these skills from northern Siberia, probably their original home. In the winter the Inuit built igloos, low-lying structures of snow blocks, which protected them from severe weather. Their clothing of furs and sealskins was both warm and waterproof. The Inuit were hunters and fishers. In the coastal waters, they pursued whales, seals, and walruses in small,

CHAPTER 1   The First Americans   **31**

✓ **Reading Check**

Answer: The Anasazi lived around the area of the Four Corners (meeting place of the present-day states of Utah, Colorado, Arizona, and New Mexico).

Did you know?

Mound Builder settlements reached into the north. Aztalan near Madison, Wisconsin, was a 21-acre (9-ha) settlement surrounded by walls with towers. Inside the settlement walls were houses, pyramids, and cornfields. It is believed that the settlers of Aztalan migrated from Cahokia in southern Illinois. The name Aztalan comes from *alt,* a native term meaning "water" and *an,* meaning "near."

Potlatch The word *potlatch* means "to give away" or "a gift giving." The potlatch was an important and festive gathering of the peoples of the northwestern coast. The gatherings marked great events in the life of a leader, his family, and the village. All guests at a potlatch received gifts ranging from food, baskets, and jewelry to canoes and copper tablets. Those who attended a potlatch were expected to give away greater presents at their own potlatches, ensuring the distribution of wealth among the people.

INTERDISCIPLINARY CONNECTIONS ACTIVITY

Daily Life The moccasin game was a popular Native North American guessing game. Two teams of two players each sat in a circle and placed four moccasins in the center. One player from one team took four small stones, one of which was marked, and placed one stone in each moccasin, while the teammate distracted the other players by singing, making faces, or using hand tricks. Then the opposing team made one guess to find the marked stone. The team received a point for a correct guess. Teams rotated hiding and guessing until one team made four correct guesses to win. Explain these rules to students and have them play the game. **L1**

3 ASSESS

Assign Section 3 Assessment as homework or as an in-class activity.

ⓘ Have students use **Interactive Tutor Self-Assessment CD-ROM.**

L2

Section Quiz 1–3

Name _____ Date _____ Class _____

★ Chapter 1   Score ☐

Section Quiz 1-3

DIRECTIONS: Matching Match the items in Column A with the items in Column B. Write the correct letters in the blanks. *(10 points each)*

Column A	Column B
___ 1. cliff dwellers	A. Iroquois
___ 2. Mound Builders	B. Plains peoples
___ 3. lived in hogans	C. Hopewell
___ 4. nomads	D. Anasazi
___ 5. desired peace	E. Navajo

DIRECTIONS: Multiple Choice In the blank at the left, write the letter of the

L1

Reteaching Activity 1–3

Name _____ Date _____ Class _____

★ Reteaching Activity 1-3

DIRECTIONS: Completion In the space provided, write the word or words that best complete the sentence.

Present-day Arizona was home to the (1) _____ people.

Their way of life depended on the (2) _____ they dug to carry water to their fields. The (3) _____ lived in the area known as the Four Corners in great stone dwellings called (4) _____, or villages, as well as in cliff dwellings in the walls of steep cliffs.

Several different groups of peoples, known as (5) _____ built thousands of mounds of earth in central North America. One of these

Did you know?

Many states have Native American names. Kentucky is Iroquois for "meadowland"; Massachusetts means "at the big hill" in Algonquian; Mississippi is Chippewa for "big river"; and Utah means "higher up" in Navajo.

Iroquois Society

Powerful Iroquois Women did hold great power among the Iroquois people. Iroquois women owned houses, crops, and fields and chose the members of the Iroquois governing council.

---

skin-covered boats. On land they hunted caribou, large deerlike animals that lived in the far north. The Inuit made clothing from caribou skins and burned seal oil in lamps.

Peoples of the West

The mild climate and dependable food sources of the West Coast created a favorable environment for many different groups.

The peoples of the northwestern coast, such as the **Tlingit** (TLIHNG•kuht), **Haida,** and **Chinook,** developed a way of life that used the resources of the forest and the sea. They built wooden houses and made canoes, cloth, and baskets from tree bark. Using spears and traps, they fished for salmon along the coast and in rivers such as the Columbia. This large fish was the main food of the northwestern people. They preserved the salmon by smoking it over fires.

Salmon was also important for the people of the plateau region, the area between the Cascade Mountains and the Rocky Mountains. The **Nez Perce** (NEHZ PUHRS) and **Yakima** peoples fished the rivers, hunted deer in forests, and gathered roots and berries. The root of the camas plant, a relative of the lily, was an important part of their diet. The plateau peoples lived in earthen houses.

Present-day California was home to a great variety of cultures. Along the northern coast, Native Americans fished for their food. In the more barren environment of the southern deserts, nomadic groups wandered from place to place collecting roots and seeds. In the central valley, the **Pomo** gathered acorns and pounded them into flour. As in many Native American cultures, the women of the Pomo did most of the gathering and flour making.

In the Great Basin between the Sierra Nevada and the Rocky Mountains, Native Americans found ways to live in the dry climate. The soil was too hard and rocky for farming, so peoples such as the **Ute** (YOOT) and **Shoshone** (shuh•SHOHN) traveled in search of food. They ate small game, pine nuts, juniper berries, roots, and some insects. Instead of making permanent settlements, the Great Basin people created temporary shelters of branches and reeds.

Peoples of the Southwest

Descendants of the Anasazi formed the **Hopi,** the **Acoma,** and the **Zuni** peoples of the Southwest. They built their homes from a type of sun-dried mud brick called adobe. They raised corn or maize as their basic food. They also grew beans, squash, melons, pumpkins, and fruit. The people of the Southwest also took part in a sophisticated trade network that extended throughout the Southwest and into Mexico.

In the 1500s two new groups settled in the region—the **Apache** and the **Navajo.** Unlike the other peoples of the Southwest, the Apache and Navajo were hunters and gatherers. They hunted deer and other game. Eventually the Navajo settled into stationary communities and built square houses called hogans. In addition to hunting and gathering, they began to grow maize and beans. They also began raising sheep in the 1600s.

Peoples of the Plains

The peoples of the Great Plains were nomadic; villages were temporary, lasting only for a growing season or two. When the people moved from place to place, they dragged their homes—cone-shaped skin tents called tepees—behind them. The men hunted antelope, deer, and buffalo. The women tended plots of maize, squash, and beans.

When the Spanish brought horses to Mexico in the 1500s, some got loose. In time horses made their way north. Native Americans captured and tamed the wild horses, and the Comanche, the **Dakota,** and other Plains peoples became skilled riders. They learned to hunt on horseback and to use the horses in warfare, attacking their enemies with long spears, bows and arrows, clubs, and knives.

32   CHAPTER 1   The First Americans

Reading Strategy · READING THE TEXT

Reading Maps, Graphs, and Charts Have students review the physical map of North America in the Reference Atlas and the map of Native American cultures on page 30. Ask them to describe how geography affected the development of specific Native American cultures. Ask students to analyze the physical characteristics of each place to conclude how geography influenced these dwellings: forested areas in Eastern Woodlands—trees for longhouses; Plains with hot summers and cold winters—tepees were cool in summer and warm in winter; Southwest desert—adobe mud used for pueblos. **L3**

Citizenship

Peoples of the East and Southeast

The people who lived in the woodlands of eastern North America formed complex political systems to govern their nations. The **Iroquois** (IHR•uh•KWAWIH) and **Cherokee** had formal law codes and formed federations, governments that linked different groups.

The Iroquois lived near Canada in what is now northern New York State. There were five Iroquois groups or nations: the **Onondaga,** the **Seneca,** the **Mohawk,** the **Oneida,** and the **Cayuga.** These groups warred with each other until the late 1500s, when they joined to form the Iroquois League, also called the Iroquois Confederacy.

Iroquois women occupied positions of power in their communities. According to the constitution of the Iroquois League, women chose the 50 men who served on the league council.

The Iroquois constitution was written down after the Europeans came to North America. It describes the Iroquois peoples' desire for peace:

> ❝ I am Dekanawidah and with the Five Nations' Confederate Lords I plant the Tree of Great Peace. . . . Roots have spread out from the Tree of the Great Peace, one to the north, one to the east, one to the south and one to the west. ❞

The Southeast was also a woodlands area, but with a warmer climate than the eastern woodlands. The Creek, Chickasaw, and Cherokee were among the region's Native American peoples. Many Creek lived in loosely knit farming communities in present-day Georgia and Alabama. There they grew corn, tobacco, squash, and other crops. The Chickasaw, most of whom lived farther west in what is now Mississippi, farmed the river bottomlands. The Cherokee farmed in the mountains of Georgia and the Carolinas.

Wherever they lived in North America, the first Americans developed ways of life that were well suited to their environments. In the 1500s, however, the Native Americans met people whose cultures, beliefs, and ways of life were different from anything they had known or ever seen. These newcomers were the Europeans, and their arrival would change the Native Americans' world forever.

✓ **Reading Check** **Describing** How did the use of the horse change the lifestyle of Native Americans on the Great Plains?

HISTORY Online

Student Web Activity
Visit tarvol1.glencoe.com and click on **Chapter 1— Student Web Activities** for an activity on Native American cultures.

SECTION 3 ASSESSMENT

Checking for Understanding

1. **Key Terms** Use each of these terms in a complete sentence that will help explain its meaning: pueblo, drought, adobe, federation.

2. **Reviewing Facts** Identify clues that led archaeologists to believe that the Mound Builders were influenced by other cultures.

Reviewing Themes

3. **Culture and Traditions** What organization did the Iroquois form to promote peace among their people?

Critical Thinking

4. **Making Generalizations** Why was the environment of the West Coast favorable for settlement by so many groups of Native Americans?

5. **Comparing** Re-create the diagram below and explain how Native American cultures differed from one another by describing their locations and ways of living.

Culture	Region	Shelter
Tlingit		
Zuni		
Dakota		

Analyzing Visuals

6. **Geography Skills** Study the map on page 30. What groups lived in California? What groups lived in the Southeast?

Interdisciplinary Activity

Geography Create or sketch a model of a home that a Native American might have built. Use natural materials that exist in the area where you live and label the materials on your diagram. Consider the climate of your area in your design.

✓ **Reading Check**

Answer: They used the horses for hunting and warfare.

HISTORY Online

Objectives and answers to the student activity can be found in the **Web Activity Lesson Plan** feature at tarvol1.glencoe.com

L1, ELL

Reading Essentials and Study Guide 1–3

Name _____ Date _____ Class _____

Study Guide
Chapter 1, Section 3
For use with textbook pages 28–33

NORTH AMERICAN PEOPLES

KEY TERMS	
pueblo	Village of great stone or adobe houses *(page 29)*
drought	Long periods of little rainfall *(page 29)*
adobe	Building material made of clay and straw; sun-dried mud brick *(page 32)*
federation	Government that linked different groups *(page 33)*

DRAWING FROM EXPERIENCE
Have you ever wondered how different Native American groups lived? Have you ever wondered what role the environment played in their cultures? How does the environment in which you live affect your life today?

L3

Enrichment Activity 1–3

Name _____ Date _____ Class _____

★ **Enrichment Activity 1-3**

Native American Words
English settlers in America borrowed many words from the Native Americans. Over the centuries, many Native American words have become part of the English language. Find out more about some of these words below.

DIRECTIONS: Finding Definitions Use a dictionary to find out what each of the following words means. Write the definition to the left of the word. Then look at the list of Native American words in the box at the bottom of the page and write the Native American word from which the term was borrowed.

Definition   **Native American Word**

4 CLOSE

Discuss the ways in which Native American groups adapted to their environment.

SECTION 3 ASSESSMENT ANSWERS

1. Student work should reflect correct use of terms.
2. Some mounds had temples like Maya and Aztec cultures; artifacts indicate widespread trade.
3. the Iroquois League
4. mild climate; dependable food sources; plentiful forest resources
5. Tlingit: Northwest coast, wooden houses; Zuni: Southwest, adobe homes; Dakota: Great Plains, tepees
6. Pomo and Chumash; Yuchi, Cherokee, Choctaw, Creek, Seminole, Natchez, Chickasaw, Wichita

Interdisciplinary Activity Home designs should incorporate resources and climate found in the area where the student lives. Label materials. Challenge: Have students obtain samples of the products in their drawings and build an actual small-scale Native American home.

GLENCOE TECHNOLOGY

MindJogger Videoquiz
Use **MindJogger Videoquiz** to review the Chapter 1 content.

Available in VHS

Reviewing Key Terms

1. **Archaeology** is the study of ancient peoples.
2. An **artifact** is an item, such as a tool, left behind by a culture.
3. An **Ice Age** was a time period of cold temperatures when part of the earth was covered with ice sheets.
4. A **nomad** is a person who moves from place to place.
5. **Carbon dating** helps determine the age of an artifact.
6. **Culture** is a way of life for a particular group of people.
7. A **civilization** is a highly developed society.
8. **Hieroglyphics** use symbols or pictures to represent things, ideas, and sounds.
9. Each **pueblo,** or village, built by the Anasazi was carefully made from sun-dried earth and stone.
10. A **federation,** such as the one formed by the Iroquois, linked the governments of different groups.

Reviewing Key Facts

11. to follow herds of animals and find food
12. Asia and present-day Alaska
13. maize
14. the age of an artifact
15. an ancient form of writing using symbols and pictures to represent words, sounds, and concepts
16. the western highlands of South America
17. easy to defend; protection from weather

Chapter Summary
The First Americans

The first Americans begin to adapt to their surroundings.

Societies in South and Central America and in Mexico create powerful empires.

The Inca, Maya, and Aztec

- The **Inca** develop a complex political system. They also build a large network of paved roads.
- The **Maya** create a written language and develop new ways of farming.
- The **Aztec** build a large empire, stretching from north-central Mexico to the border of Guatemala, and from the Atlantic Ocean to the Pacific Ocean.

People of North America

- The people of North America do not develop empires as large as those of the Inca, Maya, and Aztec.
- Among the most advanced of the early cultures are the Hohokam and Anasazi of the Southwest and the Mound Builders of the Ohio River valley.
- People who settle in a particular region develop a common culture.
- In the **Southwest,** Native American peoples adapt to their harsh environment by improving techniques of irrigation to farm the land.
- Most of the people of the **Great Plains** were nomadic. They lived in tepees, and used horses, spears, and bows and arrows to hunt deer, antelope, and buffalo.
- Native Americans of the Northeast form the **Iroquois League** to solve disputes.

34

Reviewing Key Terms
On a sheet of paper, define the following terms.
1. archaeology
2. artifact
3. Ice Age
4. nomad
5. carbon dating
6. culture
7. civilization
8. hieroglyphics
9. pueblo
10. federation

Reviewing Key Facts
11. For what reasons did Asians cross the land bridge to the Americas?
12. What regions did the land bridge connect?
13. What was the first crop raised by Native Americans in Mexico?
14. What does carbon dating measure?
15. What are hieroglyphics?
16. What regions were under Inca control?
17. What were two advantages of living in dwellings built into the side of cliffs?
18. What type of dwelling was common among the people of the Southwest?
19. In what region did the Tlingit, Haida, and the Chinook peoples live?
20. What groups formed the Iroquois League?

Critical Thinking
21. **Comparing** Re-create the diagram below and explain how the environment of Native Americans who lived in the Northwest differed from the environment of those who lived in the Southwest.

Location	Environment
Northwest	
Southwest	

22. **Analyzing Themes: Culture and Traditions** Religion was an important part of life in many Native American civilizations. What role did priests play in Mayan society?
23. **Analyzing Information** In what ways did the Inca and Aztec use war to increase their power?

18. Hopi, Acoma, Zuni—adobe homes; Apache, Navajo—square houses called hogans
19. Northwest Coast
20. the Onondaga, Seneca, Mohawk, Oneida, and Cayuga

Critical Thinking
21. Northwest—forest, coastline, abundant rivers, mild climate, plentiful fish for food and wood for shelter; Southwest—dry climate, limited vegetation, dependence on farming and hunting for food

22. The priests held great power and made most of the important decisions.
23. They conquered others to increase population and land area.

NATIONAL GEOGRAPHIC Selected Sites of the Mound Builders

Adena sites
Hopewell sites
Mississippian sites

 Geography and History Activity

Study the map above and answer the questions that follow.

24. **Location** Along what two major rivers did many of the Mound Builders settle?

25. **Place** Near which river did the Adena build most of their settlements?

26. **Movement** Of the Adena, Hopewell, and Mississippian cultures, which settled the farthest east?

Practicing Skills

Understanding the Parts of a Map *Use the key, compass rose, and scale bar on the map of Native American cultures on page 30 to answer these questions.*

27. What does the map key highlight?

28. About how far from the Gulf of Mexico did the Omaha people live?

29. Which Native American peoples settled in the Southwest region?

30. Which people lived farthest west—the Pawnee or the Miami?

Online

Self-Check Quiz

Visit tarvol1.glencoe.com and click on **Chapter 1— Self-Check Quizzes** to prepare for the chapter test.

 Technology Activity

31. **Using the Internet** Search the Internet for a Web site created by a modern Native American group. Based on information you find at the site, explain the group's goals.

Citizenship Cooperative Activity

32. **Research** Work with a partner to investigate the early history of your community using primary and secondary sources. Find out when and why it was founded. Who were the first settlers and early leaders? How did the government change over the years? Prepare a report for your class about what you have discovered.

Economics Activity

33. Create a cause-and-effect chart. Write on your chart: *Cause: The development of farming changed the way early nomads lived.* Then, describe at least two effects.

 Alternative Assessment

34. **Portfolio Writing Activity** Research information about one aspect of Aztec or Iroquois life. Present your information in a report to the other students.

CHAPTER 1   The First Americans   35

Standardized Test Practice

Directions: Choose the *best* answer to the following question.

Because the Mayan civilization was a theocracy, the most powerful Maya were

A warriors.   C priests.

B craftsmen.   D enslaved people.

Test-Taking Tip:

This question asks you to draw an inference. What is the meaning of the word *theocracy?* Understanding the definition will help to answer the question.

Citizenship Cooperative Activity

32. Students should research their community at the local library, city hall, or historical center. Student reports may include time lines and illustrations.

Economics Activity

33. Answers may include that farming helped increase the population and establish permanent communities.

 Alternative Assessment

34. Students should research one aspect of Aztec or Iroquois life such as religion, government, or agriculture.

HISTORY Online

Have students visit the Web site at tarvol1.glencoe.com to review Chapter 1 and take the Self-Check Quiz.

Standardized Test Practice

Answer: C
Question Type: Culture/ Environment
Answer Explanation: According to page 23, Mayan priests held great power because they knew the gods' wishes.

Bonus Question ?

Ask: How can you summarize the development of Native American cultures in North America?
(Native American cultures developed advanced societies that adapted to their environments, maintaining a social order, division of labor, and government.)

 Geography and History Activity

24. the Mississippi and Ohio Rivers

25. the Ohio River

26. the Adena

Practicing Skills

27. Native American culture groups

28. about 1,000 miles

29. Zuni, Papago, Apache, Navajo, Hopi, Pueblo

30. Pawnee

 Technology Activity

31. Students should locate information on archaeological finds and should note how these finds changed scientists theories on the development of the earth.

Chapter 2 Resources

Timesaving Tools

TeacherWorks™ All-In-One Planner and Resource Center

- **Interactive Teacher Edition** Access your Teacher Wraparound Edition and your classroom resources with a few easy clicks.
- **Interactive Lesson Planner** Planning has never been easier! Organize your week, month, semester, or year with all the lesson helps you need to make teaching creative, timely, and relevant.

Use Glencoe's **Presentation Plus!** multimedia teacher tool to easily present dynamic lessons that visually excite your students. Using Microsoft PowerPoint® you can customize the presentations to create your own personalized lessons.

TEACHING TRANSPARENCIES

Graphic Organizer 4 L2

Why It Matters Chapter Transparency 2 L2

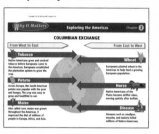

REVIEW AND REINFORCEMENT

Workbook Activity 2 L1

Time Line Activity 2 L2

Vocabulary Activity 2 L1

REVIEW AND REINFORCEMENT

Critical Thinking Skills Activity 2 L2

Take-Home Review Activity 2 L1

ENRICHMENT

Linking Past and Present Activity 2 L2

Primary Source Reading 2 L2

GEOGRAPHY

Geography and History Activity 2 L2

Meeting NCSS Standards

The following standards are highlighted in Chapter 2:

Section 1	I	Culture: C, D
Section 2	III	People, Places, and Environments: B, I
Section 3	I	Culture: B, C, D
Section 4	IX	Global Connections: B, C, D, E

FOLDABLES™

Study Organizer

Dinah Zike's Foldables are three-dimensional, interactive graphic organizers that help students practice basic writing skills, review key vocabulary terms, and identify main ideas. Additional chapter activities can be found in the *Reading and Study Skills Foldables* booklet.

Chapter 2 Resources

ASSESSMENT AND EVALUATION

Chapter 2 Test Form A L2

Chapter 2 Test Form B L2

Standardized Test Practice Workbook Activity 2 L2

Performance Assessment Activity 2 L1, ELL

ExamView® Pro Testmaker CD-ROM

MULTIMEDIA

- Vocabulary PuzzleMaker CD-ROM
- Interactive Tutor Self-Assessment CD-ROM
- ExamView® Pro Testmaker CD-ROM
- Audio Program
- American History Primary Source Documents Library CD-ROM
- MindJogger Videoquiz
- Presentation Plus! CD-ROM
- TeacherWorks CD-ROM
- Interactive Student Edition CD-ROM
- Glencoe Skillbuilder Interactive Workbook CD-ROM, Level 1
- The American Republic to 1877 Video Program
- American Music: Hits Through History

SPANISH RESOURCES

The following Spanish language materials are available in the Spanish Resources Binder:

- Spanish Guided Reading Activities
- Spanish Reteaching Activities
- Spanish Quizzes and Tests
- Spanish Vocabulary Activity
- Spanish Take-Home Review Activity
- Spanish Summaries
- The Declaration of Independence and United States Constitution Spanish Translation

---

THE HISTORY CHANNEL.

The following videotape programs are available from Glencoe as supplements to Chapter 2:

- **Leif Ericson: Voyages of a Viking** (ISBN 1-56501-673-4)
- **Ponce de Leon: The First Conquistador** (ISBN 1-56501-669-6)
- **Christopher Columbus: Explorer of the New World** (ISBN 1-56501-667-X)*
- **Viking Explorers** (ISBN 0-7670-0538-4)

To order, call Glencoe at 1-800-334-7344. To find classroom resources to accompany many of these videos, check the following home pages:
A&E Television: www.aande.com
The History Channel: www.historychannel.com

*Available individually or in *The American Republic to 1877 Video Library.*

Use our Web site for additional resources. All essential content is covered in the Student Edition.

You and your students can visit tarvol1.glencoe.com, the Web site companion to **The American Republic to 1877.** This innovative integration of electronic and print media offers your students a wealth of opportunities. The student text directs students to the Web site for the following options:

- **Chapter Overviews**
- **Self-Check Quizzes**
- **Student Web Activities**
- **Textbook Updates**

Answers to the student Web activities are provided for you in the **Web Activity Lesson Plans.** Additional Web resources and Interactive Tutor Puzzles are also available.

Chapter 2 Resources

SECTION RESOURCES

Daily Objectives	Reproducible Resources	Multimedia Resources
SECTION 1 **A Changing World** 1. Examine how technology made long sea voyages possible. 2. Explore the factors that allowed great civilizations in Africa to flourish.	Reproducible Lesson Plan 2–1 Daily Lecture and Discussion Notes 2–1 Guided Reading Activity 2–1* Section Quiz 2–1* Reteaching Activity 2–1* Reading Essentials and Study Guide 2–1* Enrichment Activity 2–1	Daily Focus Skills Transparency 2–1 Interactive Tutor Self-Assessment CD-ROM ExamView® Pro Testmaker CD-ROM Presentation Plus! CD-ROM
SECTION 2 **Early Exploration** 1. Explain Portugal's leadership roles in exploration. 2. Understand Columbus's plan for sailing to Asia.	Reproducible Lesson Plan 2–2 Daily Lecture and Discussion Notes 2–2 Guided Reading Activity 2–2* Section Quiz 2–2* Reteaching Activity 2–2* Reading Essentials and Study Guide 2–2* Enrichment Activity 2–2	Daily Focus Skills Transparency 2–2 Interactive Tutor Self-Assessment CD-ROM ExamView® Pro Testmaker CD-ROM Presentation Plus! CD-ROM
SECTION 3 **Spain in America** 1. Evaluate the decline of the Aztec and Inca Empires in the Americas. 2. Explore how Spain governed its empire in the Americas.	Reproducible Lesson Plan 2–3 Daily Lecture and Discussion Notes 2–3 Guided Reading Activity 2–3* Section Quiz 2–3* Reteaching Activity 2–3* Reading Essentials and Study Guide 2–3* Enrichment Activity 2–3	Daily Focus Skills Transparency 2–3 American Art and Architecture, Transparency 7 ABCNews Interactive™ Historic America Electronic Field Trips Interactive Tutor Self-Assessment CD-ROM ExamView® Pro Testmaker CD-ROM Presentation Plus! CD-ROM
SECTION 4 **Exploring North America** 1. Explain how the Protestant Reformation affected North America. 2. Evaluate why the activities of early traders encouraged exploration.	Reproducible Lesson Plan 2–4 Daily Lecture and Discussion Notes 2–4 Guided Reading Activity 2–4* Section Quiz 2–4* Reteaching Activity 2–4* Reading Essentials and Study Guide 2–4* Enrichment Activity 2–4	Daily Focus Skills Transparency 2–4 Vocabulary PuzzleMaker CD-ROM Interactive Tutor Self-Assessment CD-ROM ExamView® Pro Testmaker CD-ROM Presentation Plus! CD-ROM

0:00 OUT OF TIME?
Assign the Chapter 2 **Reading Essentials and Study Guide.**

*Also Available in Spanish

 Blackline Master   Transparency   CD-ROM   DVD

 Poster   Music Program   Audio Program   Videocassette

KEY TO ABILITY LEVELS

Teaching strategies have been coded.

L1   BASIC activities for all students

L2   AVERAGE activities for average to above-average students

L3   CHALLENGING activities for above-average students

ELL   ENGLISH LANGUAGE LEARNER activities

NATIONAL GEOGRAPHIC — Teacher's Corner

INDEX TO NATIONAL GEOGRAPHIC MAGAZINE

The following articles relate to this chapter.

- *The Millennium Series Exploration* (Special Edition), February 1998.
- "LaSalle's Last Voyage," by Lisa Moore LaRoe, May 1997.
- "The Old Ones of the Southwest," by David Roberts, April 1996.
- "New Face for a Desert Mission," by Alice J. Hall, December 1995.
- "The Timeless Vision of Teotihuacán," by George E. Stuart, December 1995.
- "The Cherokee," by Geoffrey Norman, May 1995.

ADDITIONAL NATIONAL GEOGRAPHIC SOCIETY PRODUCTS

To order the following, call National Geographic at 1-800-368-2728:
- *GeoKit: Colonial America* (Kit)
- *Spain in the Americas* (Map)
- *National Geographic Desk Reference* (Book)
- *American Indians: A Brief History* (Video)

NGS ONLINE

Access National Geographic's Web site for current events, atlas updates, activities, links, interactive features, and archives.
www.nationalgeographic.com

MEETING SPECIAL NEEDS

In addition to the Differentiated Instruction strategies found in each section, the following resources are also suitable for your special needs students:

- *ExamView® Pro Testmaker CD-ROM* allows teachers to tailor tests by reducing answer choices.
- The *Audio Program* includes the entire narrative of the student edition so that less-proficient readers can listen to the words as they read them.
- The *Reading Essentials and Study Guide* provides the same content as the student edition but is written two grade levels below the textbook.
- *Guided Reading Activities* give less-proficient readers point-by-point instructions to increase comprehension as they read each textbook section.
- *Enrichment Activities* includes a stimulating collection of readings and activities for gifted and talented students.

From the Classroom of . . .

Jane Spivey
J.N. Fries Middle School
Concord, NC

Play a Historical Memory Game

Begin with 50 to 60 large index cards. Number one side of each card consecutively from 1 to 50 or 60. Shuffle the cards thoroughly, and pull two at a time from the pile. On the reverse side of one card, write down a historical person's name, a date, a place, or an event. On the reverse side of the second card, write down something that links the two cards. For example, label the first card "Columbus's Ships," and label the second card "Niña, Pinta, and Santa María." Use all cards. If possible, illustrate the cards with pictures from old magazines or textbooks. Organize students into groups of five or six. Appoint a spokesperson, a recorder, and a card turner for each group. The cards should be turned numbered side up on the floor or a large table. Each group takes turns calling a number and trying to match that card's fact with its mate. Groups alternate until one group makes a match. Then the group recorder scores a point for the group, and the next group takes its turn. The group with the most points wins.

ADDITIONAL RESOURCES FROM GLENCOE

- American Music: Cultural Traditions
- American Art and Architecture
- Outline Map Resource Book
- U.S. Desk Map
- Building Geography Skills for Life
- Inclusion for the Middle School Social Studies Classroom Strategies and Activities
- Teaching Strategies for the American History Classroom (Including Block Scheduling Pacing Guides)
- American Crafts Hands-On Activities
- American Games Hands-On Activities
- American History Flash Cards

 ### Block Schedule

Activities that are suited to use within the block scheduling framework are identified by:

✓ Performance Assessment

Refer to Activity 2 in the Performance Assessment Activities and Rubrics booklet.

Why It Matters Activity

Ask students to identify how one culture can impact and influence another culture. Students should identify such factors as religion, traditions, language, art, and so on.

GLENCOE
TECHNOLOGY

The American Republic to 1877 Video Program

To learn more about the experiences of European explorers and the settlements that they established, have students view the Chapter 2 video "Exploring the Americas" from **The American Republic to 1877 Video Program.**

 Available in DVD and VHS

MindJogger Videoquiz

Use **MindJogger Videoquiz** to preview the Chapter 2 content.

 Available in VHS

CHAPTER 2

Exploring the Americas
1400–1625

Why It Matters

Although the English have been the major influence on United States history, they are only part of the story. Beginning with Native Americans and continuing through time, people from many cultures came to the Americas.

The Impact Today

The Americas today consist of people from cultures around the globe. Native Americans, Spanish, Africans, and others discussed in Chapter 2 have all played key roles in shaping the culture we now call American.

 The American Republic to 1877 Video *The chapter 2 video, "Exploring the Americas," presents the challenges faced by European explorers, and discusses the reasons they came to the Americas.*

The Americas

1492
- Christopher Columbus reaches America

1497
- John Cabot sails to Newfoundland

1513
- Balboa crosses the Isthmus of Panama

1400   *1450*   *1500*

World

1429
- Joan of Arc defeats the English at French town of Orléans

c. 1456
- Johannes Gutenberg uses movable metal type in printing

c. 1500
- Songhai Empire rises in Africa
- Rome becomes a major center of Renaissance culture

36   CHAPTER 2   Exploring the Americas

◖ Reading Strategy ◗ PURPOSE FOR READING

Seed discussions/stories are an effective way to help students lead their own discussion groups. Divide the class into groups of 5 or 6. Tell students that finding safer and more efficient routes to the treasures of East Asia motivated European governments to finance explorations westward. Assign each group to create a story. The first student in each group starts the story with the ship leaving a European port. Each student adds a "seed" to the story based on the adventures the ship and crew experienced sailing to North and South America. Tell the students their stories should include: dangers of the sea and obtaining water and food supplies. Students should remain focused on the topic. **L1**

Founding of Maryland by Emanuel Leutze Native Americans lived in North America long before the Europeans arrived.

FOLDABLES™
Study Organizer

Evaluating Information Study Foldable
Make this foldable to help you learn about European exploration of the Americas.

Step 1 Fold the paper from the top right corner down so the edges line up. Cut off the leftover piece.

> Fold a triangle. Cut off the extra edge.

Step 2 Fold the triangle in half. Unfold.

> The folds will form an X dividing four equal sections.

Step 3 Cut up one fold line and stop at the middle. Draw an X on one tab and label the other three.

Step 4 Fold the X flap under the other flap and glue together.

> This makes a three-sided pyramid.

Reading and Writing As you read, ask yourself why England, France, and Spain were exploring the Americas. Write your questions under each appropriate pyramid wall.

HISTORY Online

Introduce students to chapter content and key terms by having them access **Chapter Overview 2** at tarvol1.glencoe.com

TIME LINE ACTIVITY

Have students review the time line on pages 36–37. Ask students to identify whether specific events found on the time line occurred before or after other events listed.

1534
• Cartier claims Canada for France

c. 1570
• Iroquois form League of Five Nations

1607
• Jamestown settled

1620
• Pilgrims found Plymouth

1550   *1600*

HISTORY Online

Chapter Overview
Visit tarvol1.glencoe.com and click on **Chapter 2— Chapter Overviews** to preview chapter information.

1517
• Martin Luther promotes Church reform

1522
• Magellan's crew completes first world voyage

1588
• England defeats Spanish Armada

CHAPTER 2   Exploring the Americas   37

More About the Art

Paintings in the mid-1800s reflect a unique American style that romanticized the landing of Europeans in North America. Scenes were painted in soft tones, conveying a feeling of peace and tranquility. Europeans were shown as benevolent and in control, while Native Americans were often portrayed as showing respect and honor to the Europeans. Have students explain why they think American artists portrayed Europeans and Native Americans in this way.

SECTION 1 A Changing World

Guide to Reading

Main Idea
New knowledge and ideas led Europeans to explore overseas.

Key Terms
classical, Renaissance, technology, astrolabe, caravel, pilgrimage, mosque

Reading Strategy
Determining Cause and Effect As you read the section, re-create the diagram below and identify three reasons Europeans increased overseas exploration.

Causes of European exploration

Read to Learn
• how technology made long sea voyages possible.
• how great civilizations flourished in Africa.

Section Theme
Culture and Traditions The spirit of the Renaissance changed the way Europeans thought about the world.

Preview of Events

♦1200   ♦1300   ♦1400

1271
Marco Polo travels to China from Italy

1324
Mansa Musa makes a pilgrimage to Makkah

c. 1400
Renaissance spreads throughout Europe

Marco Polo

A European Story

In 1271 Marco Polo set off from the city of Venice on a great trek across Asia to China. Only 17 years old at the time, Polo journeyed with his father and uncle, both Venetian merchants. Traveling on camels for more than three years, the merchants crossed almost 7,000 miles (11,265 km) of mountains and deserts. Finally they reached the palace of Kublai Khan (KOO•bluh KAHN), the Mongol emperor of China. There Marco Polo spent 17 years working for the Khan and learning much about China's advanced culture.

Expanding Horizons

For centuries after the fall of the Roman Empire, the people of western Europe were isolated from the rest of the world. Their world, dominated by the Catholic Church, was divided into many small kingdoms and city-states.

Meanwhile, the religion known as Islam swept across the Middle East and Africa. The followers of Islam are known as Muslims. As Muslim power grew,

European Christians became fearful of losing access to the Holy Land, the birthplace of Christianity, in what is now Israel.

Beginning in 1095, the Europeans launched the first of nine expeditions, known as the Crusades, to regain control of their holy sites. The Crusades brought west Europeans into contact with the Middle East. Arab merchants sold spices, sugar, silk and other goods from China and India to the Europeans. As European interest in Asia grew, Marco Polo returned from China. In 1296, he began writing an account of his trip describing the marvels of Asia. Polo's *Travels* was widely read in Europe. Little did he realize that 200 years later his book about the East would inspire Christopher Columbus and others to sail in the opposite direction to reach the same destination.

$ Economics
The Growth of Trade

Merchants could make a fortune selling goods from the Orient. Wealthy Europeans clamored for cinnamon, pepper, cloves, and other spices. They also wanted perfumes, silks, and precious stones. Buying the goods from Arab traders in the Middle East, the merchants sent them overland by caravan to the **Mediterranean Sea** and then by ship to Italian ports. The cities of Venice, Genoa, and Pisa prospered and became centers of the growing East-West trade. The Arab merchants, however, charged very high prices. As demand for Asian goods increased, Europeans began looking for a route to the East that bypassed the Arab merchants.

The Growth of Ideas

In the 1300s a powerful new spirit emerged in the Italian city-states and spread throughout Europe. The development of banking and the expansion of trade with Asia made Italian merchants wealthy. These citizens were able to pursue an interest in the region's past and learn more about the glorious civilizations of ancient Rome and Greece.

Because they wanted to improve their knowledge of people and of the world, Italians studied the classical—ancient Greek and Roman—

works with new interest. Scholars translated Greek manuscripts on philosophy, poetry, and science. Many thinkers of this period began to take a more experimental approach to science; they tested new and old theories and evaluated the results.

Influenced by the classical texts, a great many authors began to write about the individual and the universe. Artists studied the sculpture and architecture of the classical world. They particularly admired the harmony and balance in Greek art, with its realistic way of portraying people.

The Renaissance

This period of intellectual and artistic creativity became known as the Renaissance (REH•nuh•SAHNTS). A French word meaning "rebirth," it refers to the renewed interest in classical Greek and Roman learning. Over the next two centuries, the Renaissance spread north, south, and west, reaching Spain and northern Europe in the 1400s.

The spirit of the Renaissance dramatically changed the way Europeans thought about themselves and the world. It encouraged them to pursue new ideas and set new goals; it paved the way for an age of exploration and discovery.

✓ **Reading Check** **Describing** What cultures influenced the Renaissance?

Powerful Nations Emerge

During the 1400s the population of western Europe began to increase. Merchants and bankers in the growing cities wanted to expand their businesses through foreign trade. If they could buy spices and silks from the East directly, without going through the Arab and Italian cities, they could earn huge profits. They looked for alternatives to the overland route through the Middle East.

The development of large nation-states in western Europe helped expand trade and interest in overseas exploration. For many years Europe had been a patchwork of small states. Political power was divided among local lords, and few people traveled outside their region.

CHAPTER 2   Exploring the Americas   **39**

2 TEACH

Daily Lecture and Discussion Notes 2–1

Copyright © by The McGraw-Hill Companies, Inc.

Daily Lecture and Discussion Notes

Chapter 2, Section 1

Did You Know? In the 1400s, the astrolabe was the explorer's most important tool to determine latitude at sea, although it had already existed for more than a thousand years. Islamic societies had been using the instrument beginning around A.D. 800. Today, the largest astrolabe collection in North America can be found at the Adler Planetarium in Chicago, Illinois.

I. Expanding Horizons *(Pages 38–39)*

   A. Marco Polo's book, *Travels*, written in 1296–97, described his travels to Asia. It inspired Columbus and other explorers to journey to these lands 200 years later.

   B. The cities of Venice, Genoa, and Pisa became centers of the growing trade in goods such as spices, silks, perfumes, and precious stones.

   C. The Renaissance, a period of renewed interest in classical Greek and Roman learning, spread throughout Europe in the 1400s. It encouraged Europeans to pursue new ideas and challenges and set the stage for exploration and discovery.

   Discussion Question
   Why do you think Western European explorers found Asia so interesting? *(Answers will vary but may include the ideas of becoming wealthy through foreign trade and learning about lifestyles in distant lands.)*

II. Powerful Nations Emerge *(Pages 39–41)*

   A. The development of large nation-states in Western Europe helped spark foreign trade and travel outside the region.

   B. The monarchies of Spain, Portugal, England, and France looked for ways to increase the power and wealth of their countries.

   Discussion Question
   Why was it necessary for monarchs to work at building powerful and wealthy countries? *(Answers will vary but may include the idea that countries wanted to appear powerful so they would not be invaded and overtaken by any other country. Wealth would allow the monarch to outfit a powerful army that could defend the country or invade another country.)*

turn

Reading Strategy

Categorizing Organize the class into small groups. Have each group review the section to find all the reasons for exploration. Each group should create a chart listing the reasons. To make the chart, have students categorize each reason under the following headings: *Cultural, Economic, Political,* and *Technological.* Encourage students to incorporate graphics into their charts. **L1**

✓ **Reading Check**

Answer: A renewed interest in classical Greek and Roman cultures inspired the Renaissance.

L1, ELL

Guided Reading Activity 2–1

Name _____ Date _____ Class _____

★ Guided Reading Activity **2-1**

DIRECTIONS: Filling in the Blanks Use your textbook to fill in the blanks using the words in the box. Some words may be used more than once. Use another sheet of paper if necessary.

magnetic compass	Africa	Arab traders	Asia
exploration and discovery	East	Italian	Mali
Marco Polo	maps	Muslims	caravels
Renaissance	stars	trade	

Expanding Horizons

More people became interested in India, China, and the rest of Asia as the story of **(1)** _____ spread and exotic goods from the East appeared in European marketplaces. The **(2)** _____, a period of great intellectual and artistic creativity, encouraged Europeans to pursue new ideas and paved the way for an age of **(3)** _____.

Powerful Nations Emerge

During the 1400s, merchants and bankers wanted to expand their businesses by buying goods from the **(4)** _____ directly, without going through the Arab and **(5)** _____ cities. Strong monarchs in Spain, Portugal, England, and France sought ways to increase **(6)** _____ and make their countries stronger.

Technology's Impact

Technological advances helped prepare the way for European voyages of exploration. They included navigational instruments, such as the **(7)** _____ and the astrolabe. These advances helped launch a new era of exploration as powerful countries began searching for sea routes to **(8)** _____.

African Kingdoms

Trade of such resources as gold, copper, iron ore, and ivory helped create wealthy, powerful kingdoms in **(9)** _____ south of the Sahara. Many West Africans in Ghana became **(10)** _____ as a result of their contacts with North African traders.

✓ Reading Check

Answer: Answers may include the establishment of national laws, courts, taxes, armies, and an interest in the expansion of trade.

Linking Past & Present

The first explorers used the astrolabe to determine latitude by suspending the astrolabe from a ring and moving the central rod until it aligned with the North Star or the sun.

By the 1400s, however, a new type of centralized state was emerging in western Europe. Strong monarchs came to power in Spain, Portugal, England, and France. They began to establish national laws, courts, taxes, and armies to replace those of local lords. These ambitious kings and queens sought ways to increase trade and make their countries stronger and wealthier.

✓ Reading Check **Explaining** What resulted from the emergence of large nation-states?

Linking Past & Present

Astrolabe to Satellite

"Land ho!" The tools that early explorers used to sail the uncharted seas were much different from the instruments used today. One early navigation tool was the astrolabe. A sailor held the astrolabe vertically, located a star through its sights, and measured the star's elevation above the horizon. A ship's approximate latitude could be identified this way.

Satellites transmit scientific data.

Sailors used the astrolabe for navigation.

Today navigation satellites do the work of an astrolabe—and more! The NAVSTAR Global Positioning System (GPS) satellites were launched by the United States in 1993. From space the GPS can track the location of a vehicle on the earth to within a few meters of its actual position.

Technology's Impact

Advances in technology—the use of scientific knowledge for practical purposes—paved the way for European voyages of exploration. In the 1450s the introduction of movable type and the printing press made it much easier to print books. Now more people could have access to books and to new information. After its publication in print form in 1477, many Europeans read Marco Polo's *Travels*.

★ Geography
Better Maps

Maps were a problem for early navigators. Most maps were inaccurate because they were drawn from the often-mistaken impressions of traders and travelers. Little by little, cartographers, or mapmakers, gradually improved their skills.

Using the reports of explorers and information from Arab geographers, mapmakers made more accurate land and sea maps. These maps showed the direction of ocean currents. They also showed lines of latitude, which measured the distance north and south of the Equator.

Better instruments were developed for navigating the seas. Sailors could determine their latitude while at sea with an astrolabe, an instrument that measured the position of stars. Europeans also acquired the magnetic compass, a Chinese invention that began to be widely used in Europe and the Middle East in the 1200s. The compass allowed sailors to determine their direction when they were far from land.

Better Ships

Advances in ship design allowed shipbuilders to build sailing vessels capable of long ocean voyages. The stern rudder and the triangular sail made it possible for ships to sail into the wind. Both of these new features came from the Arabs. In the late 1400s, the Portuguese developed the three-masted caravel. The caravel sailed faster than earlier ships and carried more cargo and food supplies. It also could float in shallow water, which allowed sailors to explore inlets and to sail their ships up to the beach to

---

DIFFERENTIATED INSTRUCTION

Reading Support Organize the class into small groups to create models of buildings typically found in a Renaissance village. The village could include these buildings: observatory, library, palace, theater, craftsperson's workshop, laboratory, home, monastery, chapel, and parliament. Have the groups make signs representing each building. Using the completed models, have other groups match the signs with the buildings. **L1**

📂 Refer to *Inclusion for the Middle School Social Studies Classroom Strategies and Activities* in the TCR.

make repairs. A Venetian sailor called the caravels "the best ships that sailed the seas."

By the mid-1400s the Italian ports faced increased competition for foreign trade. Powerful countries like Portugal and Spain began searching for sea routes to Asia, launching a new era of exploration. Portugal began its exploration by sending ships down the west coast of Africa, which Europeans had never visited before.

✓ **Reading Check** **Explaining** How did the caravel affect overseas exploration in the fifteenth and sixteenth centuries?

African Kingdoms

Powerful kingdoms flourished in Africa south of the Sahara between 400 and 1600. The region was rich with natural resources. Africans mined gold, copper, and iron ore. Trade with Islamic societies in North Africa brought both wealth and Islamic ideas and customs to the West African kingdoms.

City-states on the east coast of Africa also benefited from trade. There Arab traders from the Middle East brought cotton, silk, and porcelain from India and China to exchange for ivory and metals from the African interior.

As the Portuguese sailed south along the African coastline in the mid-1400s, they set up trading posts. From these, they traded for gold and for slaves.

Ghana—A Trading Empire

Between 400 and 1100, a vast trading empire called **Ghana** emerged in West Africa. Well located between the salt mines of the Sahara and the gold mines to the south, Ghana prospered from the taxes the leaders of the empire imposed on trade.

Caravans with gold, ivory, and slaves from Ghana crossed the Sahara to North Africa. Muslim traders from North Africa loaded caravans

with salt, cloth, and brass and headed back to Ghana. As a result of their trading contacts, many West Africans became Muslims.

In 1076 people from North Africa called Almoravids attacked Ghana and disrupted its trade routes. While Ghana fought the Almoravids, new trade routes and gold mines opened up to the east, bypassing Ghana. Ghana then began to decline, and new states emerged in the region.

Mali—A Powerful Kingdom

Mali, one of the new states, grew into a powerful kingdom. The people of Mali developed their own trade routes across the desert to North Africa. By the late 1200s, Mali's expanded terri-

CHAPTER 2 Exploring the Americas **41**

African Trading Kingdoms

NATIONAL GEOGRAPHIC

Ghana (c. 400–1200)
Mali (c. 1250–1500)
Songhai (c. 1500–1600)
← Trade route

Geography Skills

Wealthy African trading kingdoms existed before Europeans sailed west to find riches.
1. **Location** What direction is Ghat from Timbuktu?
2. **Comparing** What African kingdom covered the smallest area?

✓ **Reading Check**

Answer: The caravel traveled faster and allowed explorers to carry more cargo and food supplies than earlier ships did. It also could float in shallow water, making it possible to explore inlets.

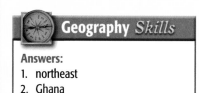

Geography Skills

Answers:
1. northeast
2. Ghana

3 ASSESS

Assign Section 1 Assessment as homework or as an in-class activity.

⏱ Have students use **Interactive Tutor Self-Assessment CD-ROM.**

L2

Section Quiz 2–1

Name _____ Date _____ Class _____

★ **Chapter 2** ___ Score ___

Section Quiz 2–1

DIRECTIONS: Matching Match the items in Column A with the items in Column B. Write the correct letters in the blanks. *(10 points each)*

Column A	Column B
___ 1. period of artistic creativity	**A.** classical
___ 2. ancient Greek and Roman works	**B.** ships
___ 3. early navigation tool	**C.** pilgrimage
___ 4. caravels	**D.** Renaissance
___ 5. journey to a holy place	**E.** astrolabe

L1

Reteaching Activity 2–1

Name _____ Date _____ Class _____

★ **Reteaching Activity 2-1**

DIRECTIONS: Recognizing Causes and Effects After each *Cause*, write the letter of its *Effect* from the Fact Bank.

1. Cause: Exotic goods from the East appeared in European marketplaces.
Effect: ___

2. Cause: Italians wanted to improve their knowledge of people and the world.
Effect: ___

3. Cause: The spirit of the Renaissance spread in Europe.

6. Cause: The astrolabe, which measured the position of the stars, was invented.
Effect: ___

7. Cause: The stern rudder and the triangular sail were invented.
Effect: ___

8. Cause: The kings of Ghana imposed taxes on trade.

📖 **Reading Strategy** **READING THE TEXT**

Writing a Paragraph Practice basic writing skills to help students synthesize information they have just learned. Ask students to jot down ideas about what they think would be an interesting scene for a show about European exploration. Have students then write a paragraph to describe the location of the scene: what it would look like and what characters would be in the scene. **L2, ELL**

✓ **Reading Check**

Answer: Ghana

L1, **ELL**

Reading Essentials and Study Guide 2–1

L3

Enrichment Activity 2–1

HISTORY
Online

Objectives and answers to the student activity can be found in the **Web Activity Lesson Plan** feature at tarvol1.glencoe.com

4 CLOSE

Ask students to identify the most compelling reason for exploration. They should support their choice with examples from the section.

---

tory included the former kingdom of Ghana. The country was mainly agricultural, but gold mines enriched the kingdom.

Mali's greatest king, **Mansa Musa,** ruled from 1312 to 1337. He was described at the time as "the most powerful, the richest, the most fortunate, the most feared by his enemies, and the most able to do good to those around him."

In 1324 Musa, a Muslim, made a grand pilgrimage to the Muslim holy city of **Makkah** (also spelled Mecca) in western Saudi Arabia. A pilgrimage is a journey to a holy place. Arab writers reported that Musa traveled with a huge military escort. Ahead of him marched 500 royal servants who carried gold to distribute along the way. Musa returned to Mali with an Arab architect who built great mosques, Muslim houses of worship, in the capital of **Timbuktu.** Under Mansa Musa, Timbuktu became an important center of Islamic art and learning.

The Songhai Empire

Some years later the Songhai (SAWNG•hy) people, who lived along the **Niger River,** rose up against Mali rule. They built a navy to control the Niger and in 1468 captured Timbuktu. In the late 1400s, **Askìya Muhammad** brought the Songhai

empire to the height of its power. Askìya strengthened his country and made it the largest in the history of West Africa. He built many schools and encouraged trade with Europe and Asia.

Plan of Government

Devoted to Islam, Askìya introduced laws based on the teachings of the holy book of Islam, the Quran. He appointed Muslim judges to uphold Islamic laws. Askìya also developed a sophisticated plan for his country's government. He divided Songhai into five provinces. For each province he appointed a governor, a tax collector, a court of judges, and a trade inspector. Everyone in Songhai used the same weights and measures and followed the same legal system.

In the late 1500s, the North African kingdom of Morocco sent an army across the Sahara to attack Songhai gold-trading centers. Armed with guns and cannons, the Moroccans easily defeated the Songhai.

✓ **Reading Check** **Identifying** Which African kingdom thrived between A.D. 400 and A.D. 1100?

HISTORY
Online

Student Web Activity
Visit tarvol1.glencoe.com and click on **Chapter 2— Student Web Activities** for an activity on African kingdoms.

SECTION 1 ASSESSMENT

Checking for Understanding

1. **Key Terms** Write sentences in which you use the following groups of terms: classical and Renaissance; technology, astrolabe, and caravel; pilgrimage and mosque.

2. **Reviewing Facts** Name three technological advances that furthered European exploration. Describe how these advances helped explorers.

Reviewing Themes

3. **Culture and Traditions** How did the Islamic religion spread to the early kingdoms of Africa? What is the name of the holy book of Islam?

Critical Thinking

4. **Drawing Conclusions** Why do you think the Renaissance began in Italy and not in another part of Europe?

5. **Comparing** Re-create the diagram below and compare three African kingdoms. In the outer spaces, describe each kingdom. In the shared space, identify similarities between them.

Analyzing Visuals

6. **Geography Skills** Review the map of the African trading kingdoms on page 41. Which of the trading kingdoms was established earliest? In which region of Africa did the three trading kingdoms develop?

Interdisciplinary Activity

Science Select a technological advance that has occurred during your lifetime. Compare its effects to the effects of one of the technological advances described in Section 1. Which has had the greater impact on society? Explain.

42   CHAPTER 2   Exploring the Americas

SECTION 1 ASSESSMENT ANSWERS

1. Student work should reflect correct use of terms.
2. Answers may include: mapmakers refined their methods and created more accurate maps; the astrolabe improved navigation; the three-masted caravel allowed ships to travel farther.
3. through trade between African kingdoms and Arab Muslims in

North Africa; the Quran
4. Answers should refer to Italy's prosperity, which enabled citizens to pursue an interest in the region's past.
5. Similarities include vast trading, Islamic religion, and powerful kingdoms. Contrasts include Songhai: largest empire ever in West Africa; Ghana: earliest African kingdom;

Mali: center of Islamic art and learning.
6. Ghana; West Africa

Interdisciplinary Activity Student answers should show a logical comparison between the two technologies, noting similarities and differences and their impact on society.

Guide to Reading

Main Idea
In search of trade routes, Portuguese explorers ushered in an era of overseas exploration.

Key Terms
line of demarcation, strait, circumnavigate

Reading Strategy
Organizing Information As you read the section, re-create the diagram below and identify explorers, when they traveled, and where they went.

Explorer	Date(s)	Region

Read to Learn
• how Portugal led the way in overseas exploration.
• about Columbus's plan for sailing to Asia.

Section Theme
Geography and History In 1400 Europeans had a limited knowledge of the geography of the world.

Preview of Events

♦1000   ♦1200   ♦1400   ♦1600

c. 1000
Leif Eriksson lands in present-day Newfoundland

1488
Bartholomeu Dias reaches the Indian Ocean

1492
Columbus lands in the Americas

1498
Vasco da Gama reaches India

1519
Magellan begins circumnavigation of the world

Compass

A European Story

More than 150 years after the death of Marco Polo, a young Italian sea captain—Christopher Columbus—sat down to read Polo's *Travels* with interest. Columbus read what Polo had to say about the islands of Cipangu, or present-day Japan. According to Polo, Cipangu lay some 1,500 miles (2,414 km) off the eastern shore of Asia. Because the earth is round, Columbus reasoned, a person sailing west from Europe should quickly reach Cipangu. It could be much closer than anyone thought.

Unfortunately, Marco Polo—and therefore Columbus—was wrong.

Seeking New Trade Routes

The maps that Columbus and the first European explorers used did not include America. They showed three continents—Europe, Asia, and Africa—merged together in a gigantic landmass, or large area of land. This landmass was bordered by oceans. Some explorers thought that the Western (Atlantic) and Eastern (Pacific) Oceans ran together to form what they called the **Ocean Sea.** At the time, no one realized that another huge landmass was missing from the maps. They also did not realize that the oceans were as large as they are.

CHAPTER 2   Exploring the Americas   **43**

2 TEACH

Creating a Chart Have students create an explorers' chart that chronologically orders the dates of expeditions, the countries the explorers sailed for, and where the explorers landed. Use the charts to help students summarize what countries supported exploration. **L2**

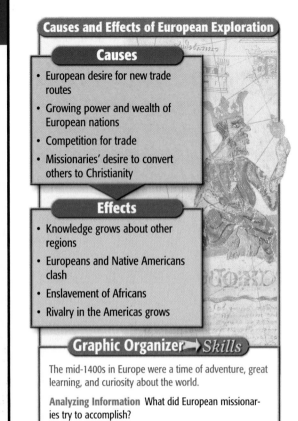

Causes and Effects of European Exploration

Causes

- European desire for new trade routes
- Growing power and wealth of European nations
- Competition for trade
- Missionaries' desire to convert others to Christianity

Effects

- Knowledge grows about other regions
- Europeans and Native Americans clash
- Enslavement of Africans
- Rivalry in the Americas grows

Graphic Organizer → Skills

The mid-1400s in Europe were a time of adventure, great learning, and curiosity about the world.

Analyzing Information What did European missionaries try to accomplish?

Portugal took the lead in exploring the boundaries of the known world. Because Portugal lacked a Mediterranean port, it could not be part of the profitable trade between Asia and Europe. The country's ambitious rulers wanted to find a new route to China and India.

The Portuguese also hoped to find a more direct way to get West African gold. The gold traveled by caravan across the desert to North Africa, then by ship across the Mediterranean. Portuguese traders needed a better route.

Early Portuguese Voyages

Prince Henry of Portugal laid the groundwork for a new era of exploration. He was fascinated by what lay beyond the known boundaries of the world. In about 1420 he set up a center for exploration on the southwestern tip of Portugal, "where endeth land and where

beginneth sea." Known as **Henry the Navigator,** the prince brought astronomers, geographers, and mathematicians to share their knowledge with Portuguese sailors and shipbuilders.

As Portuguese ships moved south along the coast of West Africa, they traded for gold and ivory and established trading posts. Because of its abundance of gold, the area came to be known as the **Gold Coast.** In the mid-1400s the Portuguese began buying slaves there as well.

King John II of Portugal launched new efforts to realize the Portuguese dream of a trading empire in Asia. If the Portuguese could find a sea route around Africa, they could trade directly with India and China. In the 1480s the king urged Portuguese sea captains to explore farther south along the African coast.

Bartholomeu Dias

In 1487 the king sent **Bartholomeu Dias** to explore the southernmost part of Africa. As Dias approached the area, he ran into a terrible storm that carried him off course and around the southern tip of Africa. Dias wrote that he had been around the "Cape of Storms." On learning of Dias's discovery, King John II renamed this southern tip of land the Cape of Good Hope—he hoped that the passage around Africa might lead to a new route to India.

Vasco da Gama

The first Portuguese voyages to India were made years later. In July 1497, after much preparation, **Vasco da Gama** set out from Portugal with four ships. Da Gama sailed down the coast of West Africa, rounded the Cape of Good Hope, and visited cities along the coast of East Africa. He engaged an Arab pilot who knew the Indian Ocean well. With the pilot's help, Da Gama sailed on to India. He reached the port of Calicut in 1498, completing the long-awaited eastern sea route to Asia.

The Portuguese Empire

Events moved quickly after that. Pedro Alvares Cabral, following Da Gama's route, swung so wide around Africa that he touched Brazil. By claiming the land for his king, he gave

COOPERATIVE LEARNING ACTIVITY

Describing Explorers' Routes Organize the class into groups of three. Assign each group one of the explorers mentioned in this section. Allow each group member to choose one of the following tasks: create a map of the explorer's voyage on poster board; write a newspaper-style report describing interesting facts about the voyage and the explorer; illustrate or cut out graphics of discoveries made on the explorer's voyage. Have each group mount the newspaper report and the graphics on the completed map. Display maps around the classroom. **L1**

Portugal a stake in the Americas. Meanwhile, Portuguese fleets began to make annual voyages to India returning with cargoes that made Lisbon the marketplace of Europe.

✔**Reading Check** *Analyzing* Why was Portugal interested in exploration?

Columbus Crosses the Atlantic

Christopher Columbus had a different plan for reaching Asia. He thought he could get there by sailing west. Born in Genoa, Italy, in 1451, Columbus became a sailor for Portugal. He had traveled as far north as the Arctic Circle and as far south as the Gold Coast.

In the 1400s most educated people believed the world was round. A more difficult matter was determining its size. Columbus was among those who based their estimates of the earth's size on the work of Ptolemy, an ancient Greek astronomer. Columbus believed Asia was about 2,760 miles (4,441 km) from Europe—a voyage of about two months by ship. Ptolemy, however, had underestimated the size of the world.

The Viking Voyages

Several centuries before Columbus, northern Europeans called **Vikings** had sailed west and reached North America. In the 800s and 900s, Viking ships visited Iceland and Greenland and established settlements. According to Norse

L1, ELL

Guided Reading Activity 2-2

Name _____ Date _____ Class _____

★ Guided Reading Activity 2-2

DIRECTIONS: Recalling the Facts Use the information in your textbook to answer the questions. Use another sheet of paper if necessary.

1. What country led exploration in the early 1400s? _____
2. Why was Prince Henry called Henry the Navigator?
3. Where was the Gold Coast? _____
4. What did the Portuguese trade and buy on the Gold Coast?
5. Who led the Portuguese expedition to India in 1497?

✔**Reading Check**

Answer: Portugal lacked a port along the Mediterranean Sea. The country wanted to find a route that would allow it trade access to China and India.

TECHNOLOGY & History

Spanish Galleon

In the late 1500s and early 1600s, Spanish galleons carried gold and silver from the West Indies to Spain. That's not all these ships carried, however. The threat of pirates prompted the Spanish galleons to carry weapons as part of their cargo. *What powered the Spanish galleons?*

The crow's nest served as a lookout.

1 Two or three sails on the **foremast** and **mainmast** allowed the ship to "catch the wind."

2 Elaborate living quarters for the captain were placed within the high **sterncastle**. The rest of the crew slept on deck.

3 Strong hands were needed to climb the rigging into the **crow's nest**, or lookout platform.

4 Stones and bricks provided **ballast** to keep the ship from tipping over. These stones would be replaced with cargo in the Americas. Many colonial streets and sidewalks were paved with ballast stones.

Spanish galleons were about 140 feet (43 meters) long.

1 mainmast
1 foremast
3 crow's nest
2 sterncastle
5 hold
4 ballast

5 Food and water were stored in the **hold**.

45

TECHNOLOGY & History

Spanish Galleons The word *galleon* is often used loosely to describe towering sailing ships of the fifteenth and sixteenth centuries, used for both commerce and war. Properly used, galleon refers to a specific type of sailing warship introduced in the mid-sixteenth century. Naval architects slimmed down top-heavy sailing ships of the time to produce the galleon, which had a "galley-like" look. The forecastle—upper deck—of this ship was reduced in size and set well back from the bow, which extended into a beak like a galley (a long, low, single-deck sailing ship). The first galleons were produced in England. By the early seventeenth century, the galleon had been replaced by a two-deck and a three-deck ship. Ask students to identify the forecastle and the part of the ship that looks like a galley. **Answer:** wind

DIFFERENTIATED INSTRUCTION

Reading Support Ask each student to choose an explorer mentioned in this section and write five personal quotations that the explorer might have said. Allow one student to read one quotation, then have the other students guess which explorer the student is portraying until all five quotations have been read. If no one guesses the correct explorer after the student has read the five quotations, the student should reveal the explorer's name. **L2**

📂 Refer to *Inclusion for the Middle School Social Studies Classroom Strategies and Activities* in the TCR.

Picturing **History**

Columbus made four trips to the Americas, each time bringing back to Europe plants and descriptions he claimed proved that the land he had found was part of Asia. Columbus brought back an inedible West Indian nut, *nogal de pais*, that he insisted must be the coconut that Marco Polo described in his accounts of Cathay.
Answer: the Bahamas

Did you know?

Christopher Columbus never referred to himself as Columbus, a name found today on cities and buildings across America. Later in life he preferred to be called Cristóbel Colón.

Who?What?Where?When?

Eric the Red The Vikings told long tales, or sagas, about their adventures. One of the most popular sagas is about Eric the Red, who lived in Iceland. He led a sailing expedition that found a rich and fertile land he called *Greenland*. Eric the Red settled there with his family. While there, his wife gave birth to a son they named Leif. Other Viking sagas call Eric the Red's son "Leif the Lucky" because Leif found a new land he called *Vinland*. Scholars believe Vinland was present-day Newfoundland.

Picturing **History**

Financed by Spain's Queen Isabella, the voyages of Columbus led to an exchange of goods between Europe and the Americas. **On what islands of the Americas did Columbus first set ashore?**

sagas, or traditional stories, a Viking sailor named Leif Eriksson explored a land west of Greenland—known as Vinland—about the year 1000. Other Norse sagas describe failed attempts by the Vikings to settle in Vinland. Historians think that Vinland was North America. Archaeologists have found the remains of a Viking settlement in Newfoundland. No one is sure what other parts of North America the Vikings explored.

The Viking voyages to other lands were not well known in the rest of Europe. Europeans did not "discover" the Americas until Columbus made his great voyage.

Spain Backs Columbus

For most of the 1400s, Spanish monarchs devoted their energy to driving the Muslims out of their country. With the fall of the last Muslim kingdom in southern Spain in 1492, **King Ferdinand** and **Queen Isabella** of Spain could focus on other goals. The Spanish had been watching the seafaring and trading successes of neighboring Portugal with envy. They, too, wanted to share in the riches of Asian trade. Columbus needed a sponsor to finance his ambitious project of a westward voyage to Asia. He visited many European courts looking for support. After years of frustration, he finally found a sponsor in Spain.

Queen Isabella, a devout Christian, was finally persuaded by her husband's minister of finance to support the expedition for two reasons. First, Columbus had promised to bring Christianity to any lands he found. Second, if he found a way to Asia, Spain would become very wealthy. She promised Columbus a share of any riches gained from lands he discovered on his way to Asia.

Columbus's First Voyage

On August 3, 1492, Columbus set out from Palos, Spain. He had two small ships, the *Niña* and the *Pinta,* and a larger one, the *Santa María,* carrying a total of about 90 sailors. The small fleet stopped at the Canary Islands for repairs and to stock up on supplies, then sailed westward into the unknown.

The ships had good winds, but after a month at sea the sailors began to worry. Columbus wrote that he was

> ❝having trouble with the crew . . . . I am told that if I persist in going onward, the best course of action will be to throw me into the sea.❞

Columbus, however, was determined. He told the men, "I made this voyage to go to the Indies, and [I] shall continue until I find them, with God's help." To convince the crew that they had not traveled too far from home, Columbus altered the distances in his ship's log. 📖 *(See page 593 of the Primary Sources Library for another log entry by Columbus.)*

"Tierra! Tierra!"

On October 12, 1492, at 2:00 in the morning, a lookout shouted, *"Tierra! Tierra!"*—"Land! Land!" He had spotted a small island, part of the group now called the Bahamas. Columbus went ashore, claimed the island for Spain, and named it San Salvador. Although he did not know it, Columbus had reached the Americas.

Reading Strategy — READING THE TEXT

Writing Free Writes Free writes are an important strategy to explore student background knowledge and engage the student using visual representations. After reading about Columbus's first voyage in this section, have students think about what it might have been like to be on one of his ships, searching for the Indies. Have each student write five diary entries from a crew member's viewpoint. Encourage students to describe their physical surroundings, feelings about traveling to strange places, feelings about Columbus as a leader, and so on.

Columbus explored the area for several months, convinced he had reached the East Indies, the islands off the coast of Asia. Today the **Caribbean Islands** are often referred to as the **West Indies.** Columbus called the local people Indians. He noted that they regarded the Europeans with wonder and often touched them to find out "if they were flesh and bones like themselves."

When Columbus returned to Spain in triumph, Queen Isabella and King Ferdinand received him with great honor and agreed to finance his future voyages. Columbus had earned the title of Admiral of the Ocean Sea.

Columbus's Later Voyages

Columbus made three more voyages from Spain in 1493, 1498, and 1502. He explored the Caribbean islands of Hispaniola (present-day Haiti and the Dominican Republic), Cuba, and Jamaica, and he sailed along the coasts of Central America and northern South America. He claimed the new lands for Spain and established settlements.

Columbus originally thought the lands he had found were in Asia. Later explorations made it clear that Columbus had not reached Asia at all. He had found a part of the globe unknown to Europeans, Asians, and Africans. In the following years, the Spanish explored most of the Caribbean region. In time their voyages led to the establishment of the Spanish Empire in the Americas.

Dividing the World

Both Spain and Portugal wanted to protect their claims, and they turned to Pope Alexander VI for help. In 1493 the pope drew a line of demarcation, an imaginary line running down the

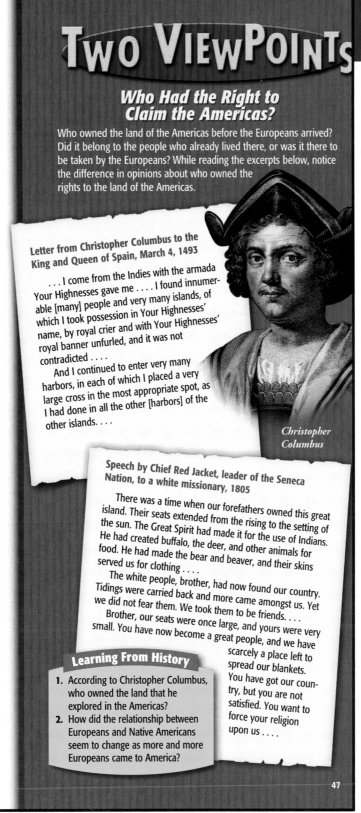

TWO VIEWPOINTS

Who Had the Right to Claim the Americas?

Who owned the land of the Americas before the Europeans arrived? Did it belong to the people who already lived there, or was it there to be taken by the Europeans? While reading the excerpts below, notice the difference in opinions about who owned the rights to the land of the Americas.

Letter from Christopher Columbus to the King and Queen of Spain, March 4, 1493

. . . I come from the Indies with the armada Your Highnesses gave me . . . . I found innumerable [many] people and very many islands, of which I took possession in Your Highnesses' name, by royal crier and with Your Highnesses' royal banner unfurled, and it was not contradicted . . . .

And I continued to enter very many harbors, in each of which I placed a very large cross in the most appropriate spot, as I had done in all the other [harbors] of the other islands. . . .

Christopher Columbus

Speech by Chief Red Jacket, leader of the Seneca Nation, to a white missionary, 1805

There was a time when our forefathers owned this great island. Their seats extended from the rising to the setting of the sun. The Great Spirit had made it for the use of Indians. He had created buffalo, the deer, and other animals for food. He had made the bear and beaver, and their skins served us for clothing . . . .

The white people, brother, had now found our country. Tidings were carried back and more came amongst us. Yet we did not fear them. We took them to be friends. . . . Brother, our seats were once large, and yours were very small. You have now become a great people, and we have scarcely a place left to spread our blankets. You have got our country, but you are not satisfied. You want to force your religion upon us . . . .

Learning From History

1. According to Christopher Columbus, who owned the land that he explored in the Americas?
2. How did the relationship between Europeans and Native Americans seem to change as more and more Europeans came to America?

47

TWO VIEWPOINTS

Answers:
1. Spain
2. The relationship became less friendly and more distrustful.

CURRICULUM CONNECTION

Geography Drawings of sea monsters appeared on many maps of this era. Tales of bizarre monsters enlivened the study of geography during Columbus's time. For many sailors, these monsters represented real threats and were more than flights of fancy. *Sciapodes* were monsters that had only one giant foot yet could walk amazingly fast. *Monoculars* were giants with a single eye in the middle of their forehead, and they ate only meat and raw fish. The *cynocephalus* were very intelligent and gifted with great intuition.

Did you know?

Columbus's largest ship, the Santa María, hit a reef off the coast of Haiti, destroying the ship. Columbus sailed home on the Niña, with the Pinta following behind. A storm west of the Azores separated the two boats. Later the Niña encountered another large storm, ripping off its sails and forcing the boat to dock in Lisbon. The Niña finally reached its home port of Palos on March 15, 1493. The Pinta arrived later that day.

CRITICAL THINKING ACTIVITY

Formulating Questions Discuss the difference between objective and subjective tests. An *objective test*, such as a multiple-choice text, is one that can be scored with a single answer key. No scorers can disagree as to whether responses are right or wrong. In contrast, a *subjective test*, such as an essay exam, can be scored differently by different scorers. Explain how to construct closed-ended, unambiguous questions from which respondents can choose only one correct answer. Ask individual students to create a 10-question, multiple-choice quiz covering the content in this section. Pair students to take each other's quiz. Have the student who created the quiz grade it and discuss wrong answers with the student who took the quiz. Allow each student to critique the other's questions. **L2**

Geography *Skills*

Answers:
1. John Cabot
2. The earth's greatest circumference is at the Equator, and sailing north or south of the Equator shortens the traveling distance.

Geography Skills Practice
Ask: Which explorer traveled along the coast of Brazil? For which country did he sail? *(Pedro Cabral; Portugal)*

3 ASSESS

Assign Section 2 Assessment as homework or as an in-class activity.

☉ Have students use **Interactive Tutor Self-Assessment CD-ROM.**

L2

Section Quiz 2–2

Name _____ Date _____ Class _____

★ Chapter 2   Score ☐

Section Quiz 2-2

DIRECTIONS: Matching Match the items in Column A with the items in Column B. Write the correct letters in the blanks. *(10 points each)*

Column A	Column B
___ **1.** Viking sailor	**A.** Pacific
___ **2.** Admiral of the Ocean Sea	**B.** circumnavigate
___ **3.** leading explorers in 1400s	**C.** Leif Eriksson
___ **4.** means "peaceful"	**D.** Christopher Columbus
___ **5.** to sail around the world	**E.** Portuguese

DIRECTIONS: Multiple Choice In the blank at the left, write the letter of the...

L1

Reteaching Activity 2–2

Name _____ Date _____ Class _____

★ Reteaching Activity 2-2

DIRECTIONS: Sequencing Events Number the events in the order in which they occurred.

___ **A.** The pope establishes the line of demarcation.
___ **B.** Ferdinand Magellan's crew circumnavigates the world.
___ **C.** Christopher Columbus claims San Salvador in the Caribbean for Spain.
___ **D.** Vasco da Gama completes the eastern sea route to Asia.
___ **E.** The Portuguese explore the Gold Coast of West Africa.

48

---

middle of the Atlantic from the North Pole to the South Pole. Spain was to control all the lands to the west of the line. Portugal was to have control of all lands to the east of the line. Portugal, however, protested that the division favored Spain. As a result, in 1494 the two countries signed the Treaty of Tordesillas (TOHR•day•SEE•yuhs), an agreement to move the line farther west. The treaty divided the entire unexplored world between Spain and Portugal.

✦Geography
Exploring America

In 1499 explorer Amerigo Vespucci began mapping South America's coastline. Vespucci concluded that South America was a continent, not part of Asia. By the early 1500s, European geographers had begun to call the continent America, in honor of Amerigo Vespucci. While European geographers discussed Vespucci's findings, others continued to explore America.

NATIONAL GEOGRAPHIC **European Voyages of Exploration**

John Cabot suggested that a voyage across the Atlantic could be quickened by sailing at a more northerly latitude than Columbus's route.

Verrazano explored the Atlantic coast from present-day Cape Fear, North Carolina, to perhaps as far north as Newfoundland.

Into the Unknown, 1492
September 6 Columbus's three ships set sail from the Canary Islands.
September 20–24 Variable winds force Columbus to change course.
October 10 Columbus promises to turn back if they do not sight land soon.
October 12 Land is sighted. Columbus names the land San Salvador.

0   1,000 miles
0   1,000 kilometers
Lambert Azimuthal Equal-Area projection

SPANISH
Christopher Columbus (1492–1504)
Amerigo Vespucci (1499–1500)

PORTUGUESE
Pedro Cabral (1500)

ENGLISH
John Cabot (1497–98)
Martin Frobisher (1576–78)

FRENCH
Giovanni da Verrazano (1524)
Jacques Cartier (1535)

DUTCH
Henry Hudson (1609)

Geography *Skills*

European sea captains explored North America, South America, and the islands of the Caribbean Sea.
1. **Movement** Who was the first English explorer to sail to the Americas?
2. **Evaluating Information** John Cabot's suggestion was true. Explain why.

48   CHAPTER 2   Exploring the Americas

EXTENDING THE CONTENT

Balboa The gold and pearls the Spaniards found along the coast of the Pacific Ocean, named the South Sea by Balboa, were received with great appreciation by the king and queen of Spain. Balboa was rewarded by being named governor of the area on the Pacific coast of Panama. There Balboa established the town of Acla. In order to build ships for further exploration and conquests, Balboa transported materials across the Isthmus of Panama. His success led to a rivalry with Pedrarias Dávila, the governor of nearby Darién. In 1518 Pedrarias falsely accused Balboa of treason. In 1519, six years after claiming the vast Pacific Ocean for Spain, Balboa was beheaded in a public square in Acla.

Vasco Núñez de Balboa (bal•BOH•uh), governor of a Spanish town in present-day Panama, had heard stories of the "great waters" beyond the mountains. In 1513 he formed an exploring party and hiked through the steaming jungles. After many days of difficult travel, the Spaniard climbed a hill and saw a vast body of water. When he reached the water's edge, Balboa waded in and claimed it and the adjoining lands for Spain. Balboa was the first European to see the Pacific Ocean from the Americas.

Sailing Around the World

The Spanish wanted to find a sea route through or around South America to Asia. In 1519 they hired **Ferdinand Magellan,** a Portuguese mariner, to lead an expedition of five ships. Sailing from Spain, Magellan headed west across the Atlantic Ocean and then south along the eastern coast of South America.

By late November 1520, Magellan had found and sailed through the narrow, twisting sea passage to the Pacific. This strait still bears his name. At the end of the strait, Magellan exclaimed: "We are about to stand [go] into an ocean where no ship has ever sailed before." He named the ocean the Pacific, which means "peaceful."

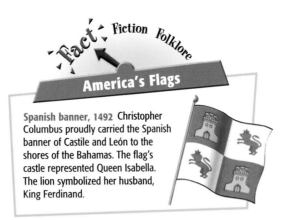

Fact Fiction Folklore

America's Flags

Spanish banner, 1492 Christopher Columbus proudly carried the Spanish banner of Castile and León to the shores of the Bahamas. The flag's castle represented Queen Isabella. The lion symbolized her husband, King Ferdinand.

Magellan expected to reach Asia in just a few weeks after rounding South America, but the voyage across the Pacific lasted four months. The crew ran out of food and ate sawdust, rats, and leather to stay alive. Magellan was killed in a skirmish in the Philippines, but some of his crew continued. Their trip had taken almost three years. Only one of the five original ships and 18 of the more than 200 crew members completed the difficult journey. These men were the first to circumnavigate, or sail around, the world.

✓ Reading Check **Describing** Why did Spain finance Columbus's voyage?

✓ Reading Check

Answer: so that he could find a trade route to Asia for Spain

L1, ELL

Reading Essentials and Study Guide 2–2

Name _____ Date _____ Class _____

Study Guide

Chapter 2, Section 2

For use with textbook pages 43–49

EARLY EXPLORATION

KEY TERMS	
line of demarcation	An imaginary line running down the middle of the Atlantic from the North Pole to the South Pole *(page 47)*
strait	Narrow sea passage *(page 49)*
circumnavigate	To sail around *(page 49)*

DRAWING FROM EXPERIENCE

Have you ever explored an area new to you? Why were you interested in learning about the new area? What did you learn from your explorations? Are there other places you might like to explore?

L3

Enrichment Activity 2–2

Name _____ Date _____ Class _____

★ **Enrichment Activity 2-2** ★

Old Views of the World

Until the Age of Exploration, some Europeans based their views of the world on a map made around A.D. 150 by an ancient geographer named Ptolemy. In 1490 a German mapmaker named Martellus made a new map of the world. Compare the maps of Ptolemy and Martellus below.

4 CLOSE

Ask students to debate who they think had the most valid claim to the lands described in this section—the Spaniards, the Portuguese, or the Native Americans. Ask them to debate first as a Spanish explorer, then as a Portuguese king or queen, and finally as a Native American.

SECTION 2 ASSESSMENT

Checking for Understanding

1. **Key Terms** Write a short paragraph in which you use the following terms: line of demarcation, strait, circumnavigate.
2. **Reviewing Facts** Who were the first Europeans to reach the Americas and when did they arrive?

Reviewing Themes

3. **Geography and History** What nations signed the Treaty of Tordesillas? What was the purpose of the line of demarcation? How did the treaty affect European exploration of the Americas?

Critical Thinking

4. **Making Inferences** For years, many history books have claimed that "Columbus discovered America." Why do you think Native Americans might disagree with the choice of the word "discovered" in this statement? What might be a better word?
5. **Organizing Information** Re-create the diagram below and identify the regions Columbus explored.

Regions Columbus explored

Analyzing Visuals

6. **Geography Skills** Review the map of European voyages of exploration on page 48; then answer the questions that follow. When did Verrazano make his voyage? For what country did he sail? How did Cabot's route to the Americas differ from that of Columbus?

Interdisciplinary Activity

Geography Draw a map of the world as you think Columbus might have seen it in 1492. Remember his error in calculating distance.

CHAPTER 2 Exploring the Americas **49**

SECTION 2 ASSESSMENT ANSWERS

1. Student work should reflect correct use of terms.
2. The first included: the Vikings (c.1000); Christopher Columbus (1492); and Vasco Núñez de Balboa (1513).
3. Spain and Portugal; it determined control of lands by Spain (all lands west of the line) and Portugal (all

lands east of the line).
4. Native Americans lived in the Americas before Columbus arrived. Answers will vary, but choices may include: *claimed, encountered, came upon,* or *reached*.
5. Caribbean islands of Hispaniola, Cuba, Jamaica, and the coasts of Central America and northern

South America.
6. 1524; France; He traveled farther north than Columbus.

Interdisciplinary Activity Students' maps should omit the Americas and the Pacific Ocean. Maps should show Asia about 2,400 miles (3,862 km) west of Europe.

Block Schedule

Team Teaching This selection from *Morning Girl* may be implemented in a team-teaching context, in conjunction with English/Language Arts.

Reinforcing Vocabulary

Review the **Reader's Dictionary** terms with students to be sure they understand any unfamiliar terms.

Historical Connection

In 1492 Columbus and his crew landed on an island in what is now called the Bahamas. He named it San Salvador, which is Spanish for "Holy Savior." He called the native Taino peoples who lived there *Indians* because he believed he had landed in the East Indies.

Background Information

Setting The excerpt takes place in the Bahamas during the landing of Columbus.

Characters The main character in this excerpt is Morning Girl, a young Native American woman.

Plot Morning Girl describes her initial encounter with Columbus and his crew.

HISTORY Online

Refer to tarvol1.glencoe.com for additional Glencoe Literature titles, lesson plans, and study guides related to this unit.

America's LITERATURE

Michael Dorris (1945–1997)

A Modoc Native American, Michael Dorris was an educator, a social activist, and an award-winning author. *Morning Girl,* his first book for young adults, portrays the lives of the Taino people of the Bahamas.

READ TO DISCOVER

Morning Girl is the fictional story of a young Native American woman who meets Columbus and his crew as they arrive in the Bahamas in 1492. While reading this passage, think about the ways that Morning Girl's life might change as a result of Columbus's visit.

READER'S DICTIONARY

backward: undeveloped
Morning Girl: a young Taino woman

Chief's chair, Taino people

Morning Girl

I swam closer to get a better look and had to stop myself from laughing. The strangers had wrapped every part of their bodies with colorful leaves and cotton. Some had decorated their faces with fur and wore shiny rocks on their heads. Compared to us, they were very round. Their canoe was short and square, and, in spite of all their dipping and pulling, it moved so slowly. What a **backward,** distant island they must have come from. But really, to laugh at guests, no matter how odd, would be impolite, especially since I was the first to meet them. If I was foolish, they would think they had arrived at a foolish place. . . .

I kicked toward the canoe and called out the simplest thing.

"Hello!". . .

The man stared at me as though he'd never seen a girl before, then shouted something to his relatives. They all stopped paddling and looked in my direction.

"Hello," I tried again. "Welcome to home. My name is **Morning Girl. . . .**"

All the fat people in the canoe began pointing at me and talking at once. In their excitement they almost turned themselves over, and I allowed my body to sink beneath the waves for a moment in order to hide my smile. . . .

When I came up they were still watching, the way babies do: wide eyed and with their mouths uncovered. They had much to learn about how to behave. . . . It was clear that they hadn't traveled much before.

From *Morning Girl* by Michael Dorris. Text © 1992 by Michael Dorris. Reprinted with permission from Hyperion Books for Children.

ANALYZING LITERATURE

1. **Recall and Interpret** How does Morning Girl describe the strangers' appearance?
2. **Evaluate and Connect** Are Morning Girl's impressions of the visitors positive or negative? Explain your reasoning.

Interdisciplinary Activity

Descriptive Writing Imagine that you are an explorer who arrived in America with Columbus. Describe the people and climate you encounter in America. Compare the way people live in America to your way of life in Europe.

50

ANSWERS TO ANALYZING LITERATURE

1. She describes them as being wrapped with colorful leaves and cotton, with their faces decorated with furs and shiny rocks on their heads. Morning Girl also describes the strangers as being round and fat.

2. Answers may include a variety of responses depending upon how students interpret Morning Girl's reaction to the visitors.

Interdisciplinary Activity
Students' descriptions should include information about Native Americans and the climate. Comparisons might include information about different farming methods or types of housing.

SECTION 3 Spain in America

Guide to Reading

Main Idea
In the sixteenth century, Spain established and governed a vast empire in the Americas.

Key Terms
conquistador, tribute, pueblo, mission, presidio, encomienda, plantation

Reading Strategy
Organizing Information As you read the section, re-create the diagram below and identify Spanish conquistadors, along with the regions they explored.

Conquistador	Region Explored

Read to Learn
- how the great Aztec and Inca Empires came to an end.
- how Spain governed its empire in the Americas.

Section Theme
Culture and Traditions The conquistadors conquered mighty empires in the Americas.

Preview of Events

♦1500	♦1530	♦1560

1519
Hernán Cortés lands in Mexico

1532
Francisco Pizarro captures Atahualpa

1541
De Soto crosses the Mississippi River

1565
Spain establishes fort at St. Augustine, Florida

AN
American Story

Would you like to visit a place described in the following way? "A river . . . [stretched] two leagues wide, in which there were fishes as big as horses. . . . The lord of the country took his afternoon nap under a great tree on which were hung a great number of little gold bells. . . . The jugs and bowls were [made] of gold."

"[It was] a land rich in gold, silver, and other wealth . . . great cities . . . and civilized people wearing woolen clothes."

Conquistador's armor

Spanish Conquistadors

Stories of gold, silver, and kingdoms wealthy beyond belief greeted the early Spanish explorers in the Americas. The reports led them far and wide in search of fabulous riches.

Known as conquistadors (kahn•KEES•tuh•dawrs), these explorers received grants from the Spanish rulers. They had the right to explore and establish settlements in the Americas. In exchange they agreed to give the Spanish crown one-fifth of any gold or treasure discovered. This arrangement allowed Spanish rulers to launch expeditions with little risk. If a conquistador failed, he lost his own fortune. If he succeeded, both he and Spain gained wealth and glory.

CHAPTER 2   Exploring the Americas   **51**

1 FOCUS

Section Overview

This section describes how the Spanish established settlements in the Americas.

BELLRINGER
Skillbuilder Activity

Project transparency and have students answer the question.

Daily Focus Skills Transparency 2–3

Reading Preview

Answers to Graphic: Answers may include: Hernán Cortés, Mexico; Francisco Pizarro, Peru; Juan Ponce de León, present-day Florida; and Hernando de Soto, present-day Florida west to Oklahoma.

Preteaching Vocabulary
Encourage students to describe Spain's American empire using the terms *pueblo, mission,* and *presidio.*

SECTION RESOURCES

📁 **Reproducible Masters**
- Reproducible Lesson Plan 2–3
- Daily Lecture and Discussion Notes 2–3
- Guided Reading Activity 2–3
- Section Quiz 2–3
- Reteaching Activity 2–3
- Reading Essentials and Study Guide 2–3
- Enrichment Activity 2–3

📖 **Transparencies**
- Daily Focus Skills Transparency 2–3
- American Art and Architecture, Transparency 7

Multimedia
- 📺 ABC News Interactive™ Historic America Electronic Field Trips
- 💿 Interactive Tutor Self-Assessment CD-ROM
- 💿 ExamView® Pro Testmaker CD-ROM
- 💿 Presentation Plus! CD-ROM

2 TEACH

Creating a Graphic Organizer

Suggest that students work in pairs to create a graphic organizer with the following information: conquistador's name, areas explored, motivation for exploration, and treatment of Native American groups. Ask students to categorize the motives as either "Gold," "Glory," or "God" and draw a conclusion about the primary motivation for exploration. **L1**

Answers:
1. De Soto
2. Cabeza de Vaca

Geography Skills Practice
Ask: Which explorer traveled the farthest north? *(Coronado)*

 American Art and Architecture, Transparency 7, *Mission San Xavier del Bac* **L3**

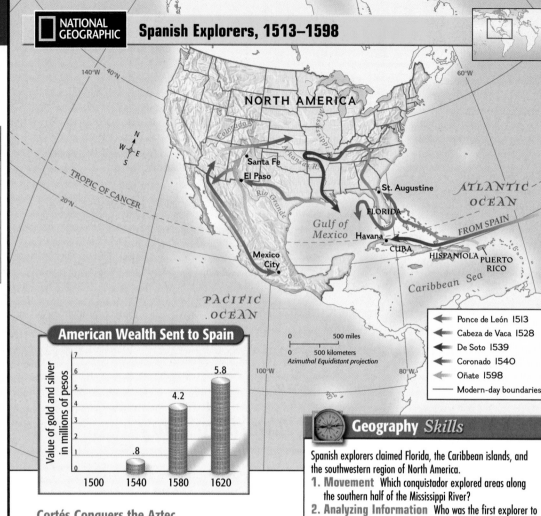

NATIONAL GEOGRAPHIC

Spanish Explorers, 1513–1598

←	Ponce de León 1513
←	Cabeza de Vaca 1528
←	De Soto 1539
←	Coronado 1540
←	Oñate 1598
—	Modern-day boundaries

American Wealth Sent to Spain

Value of gold and silver in millions of pesos

- 1500: —
- 1540: .8
- 1580: 4.2
- 1620: 5.8

Geography Skills

Spanish explorers claimed Florida, the Caribbean islands, and the southwestern region of North America.
1. **Movement** Which conquistador explored areas along the southern half of the Mississippi River?
2. **Analyzing Information** Who was the first explorer to cross the Rio Grande?

Cortés Conquers the Aztec

When **Hernán Cortés** landed on the east coast of what we now know as Mexico in 1519, he was looking for gold and glory. He came with about 500 soldiers, some horses, and a few cannons. Cortés soon learned about the great Aztec Empire and its capital of Tenochtitlán.

In building their empire, the Aztec had conquered many cities in Mexico. These cities were forced to give crops, clothing, gold, and precious stones to the Aztec as tribute. Cortés formed alliances with nearby cities against the Aztec.

Cortés marched into Tenochtitlán in November with his small army and his Native American allies. The Aztec emperor **Montezuma** (MAHN •tuh•ZOO•muh)—also spelled Moctezuma—

welcomed Cortés and his soldiers and provided them with food and a fine palace. However, Cortés took advantage of the Aztec's hospitality and made Montezuma his prisoner.

In the spring of 1520, the Aztec rebelled against the Spanish. During the fighting Montezuma was hit by stones and later died. The battle lasted for days. Eventually, the Spanish were forced to leave Tenochtitlán. Cortés, however, was determined to retake the city. He waited until more Spanish troops arrived, then attacked and destroyed the Aztec capital in 1521. An Aztec poem describes the awful scene:

52 CHAPTER 2 Exploring the Americas

COOPERATIVE LEARNING ACTIVITY

Creating a News Broadcast Organize the class into groups of four to create a news broadcast about an explorer or a Native American leader mentioned in this section. Assign the following roles: anchorperson to present background information; explorer or leader; reporter to interview the show's guest; art and sound technician to create graphs, maps, props, sound effects, and so on. (If camcorders are available, add a fifth role for a camera operator.) After each group has practiced the newscast, have the group either perform the newscast live or show the video to the class. **L3**

> 66Without roofs are the houses,
> And red are their walls with blood. . . .
> Weep, my friends,
> Know that with these disasters
> We have lost our Mexican nation.99

The Aztec Empire disintegrated, and Spain seized control of the region.

Pizarro Conquers Peru

The conquistador **Francisco Pizarro** sailed down the Pacific coast of South America with about 180 Spanish soldiers. Pizarro had heard tales of the incredibly wealthy Inca Empire in what is now Peru. In 1532 Pizarro captured the Inca ruler, **Atahualpa** (ah•tah•WAHL•pah), and destroyed much of the Incan army.

The following year, the Spanish falsely accused Atahualpa of crimes and executed him. The Inca were used to obeying commands from their rulers. Without leadership they were not able to fight effectively. Within a few years, Pizarro had gained control of most of the vast Inca Empire.

Why Spain Succeeded

The conquistadors' victories in Mexico and Peru were quick and lasting. How could Cortés and Pizarro, with only a few hundred Spanish soldiers, conquer such mighty empires?

First, the Spanish arrived with strange weapons—guns and cannons—and fearsome animals. They rode horses and had huge, ferocious dogs. To the Native Americans, the Spanish seemed almost like gods. Second, many Native Americans hated their Aztec overlords and assisted the conquistadors in overthrowing them.

Finally, disease played an extremely large role in the Spanish conquest. Native Americans had no immunity to the diseases the Europeans had, unknowingly, brought with them. Epidemics of smallpox and other diseases wiped out entire communities in the Americas and did much to weaken the resistance of the Aztec and Inca.

✓**Reading Check** **Analyzing** How were the Spanish able to defeat mighty Native American empires?

Spain in North America

Mexico and Peru were rich in silver and gold. Hoping to find similar wealth to the north, conquistadors explored the southeastern and southwestern parts of North America.

Juan Ponce de León made the first Spanish landing on the mainland of North America, arriving on the east coast of present-day Florida in 1513. According to legend, Ponce de León hoped to find not only gold, but the legendary fountain of youth, "a spring of running water of such marvelous virtue" that drinking it "makes old men young again." Ponce de León's exploration led to the first Spanish settlement in what is now the United States. In 1565 the Spanish established a fort at **St. Augustine**, Florida.

The Seven Cities of Cibola

Many other conquistadors searched for quick riches. None ever achieved this goal, and several lost their lives trying. **Álvar Núñez Cabeza de Vaca** (cah•BAY•sah day VAH•cah) was part of a Spanish expedition to Florida in 1528.

After encountering troubles in Florida, the expedition, led by **Pánfilo de Narváez,** sailed along the coast toward Mexico. However, in November 1528, three of the five boats were lost in a storm. The two boats that survived went aground on an island near present-day Texas. Within a few months, only a handful of the shipwrecked explorers were still alive.

The First Thanksgiving

Who celebrated the first Thanksgiving? We all know that the Pilgrims celebrated the first Thanksgiving. Or did they? On April 30, 1598, long before the Pilgrims came to North America, Spanish colonists held a thanksgiving feast near present-day El Paso, Texas. Juan de Oñate had led 400 men and their families across the desert from Mexico. After they reached the Rio Grande, Oñate told them to feast and give thanks for the abundance of the new land.

CHAPTER 2   Exploring the Americas   **53**

Reading Check

Answer: Answers may include: the use of guns, cannons, horses, and large dogs made the Spanish appear god-like; many Native Americans hated their Aztec overlords and helped the Spanish overthrow them; and Native Americans had no immunity to European diseases.

ABCNEWS
INTERACTIVE™

VIDEOCASSETTE
Historic America Electronic Field Trips

View **Chapter 4** to learn more about St. Augustine, a Spanish settlement in present-day Florida.

you don't say...

Florida's Flowers Ponce de León landed in present-day North America during Easter, which Spaniards also referred to as the Feast of Flowers. He called this land of luxuriant vegetation *Pascua Florida,* meaning Feast of Flowers. The name was later shortened to Florida.

DIFFERENTIATED INSTRUCTION

Gifted and Talented Have each student create a chart of explorers mentioned in this section. Have students include the following categories in the chart: *Explorer, Nationality, Country Sponsoring Explorer, Flag of Sponsoring Country* (illustration), *Dates of Exploration, Areas of Exploration,* and *Discoveries Made.* **L3**

☞ Refer to **Inclusion for the Middle School Social Studies Classroom Strategies and Activities** in the TCR.

People In History

Juana Inés de la Cruz was born into a prominent family. She learned to read when she was three years old and had read all the books in her grandfather's library by age six.

✓ Reading Check

Answer: An increased number of Spanish explorers traveled across vast and unknown areas in search of riches.

3 ASSESS

Assign Section 3 Assessment as homework or as an in-class activity.

🌐 Have students use **Interactive Tutor Self-Assessment CD-ROM.**

L2

Section Quiz 2–3

L1

Reteaching Activity 2–3

People In History

Juana Inés de la Cruz 1651–1695

A Mexican nun, Juana Inés de la Cruz, may have been the first woman in the Americas to write about women's rights. What is remarkable about Sor Juana ("Sister" Juana) is that she was a famous writer at a time when most women were not taught to read. Her poems and stories were well known in Mexico; her plays were performed in the royal palace of Mexico, and her books were popular in Spain.

An archbishop of the Church, however, did not approve of women freely expressing their opinions. He threatened to put her on trial for violating Church rules unless she followed a strict vow of poverty and sold her books and belongings.

Although she gave the appearance of obedience, an unfinished poem found in her belongings after her death showed that she continued to exercise her talent.

To survive, Cabeza de Vaca and an enslaved African named **Estevanico** became medicine men. Cabeza de Vaca later wrote that their method of healing was "to bless the sick, breathing on them" and to recite Latin prayers.

In 1533 the Spaniards set off on foot on a great 1,000-mile journey across the Southwest. Arriving in Mexico in 1536, Cabeza de Vaca related tales he had heard of seven cities with walls of emerald and streets of gold.

The stories inspired **Hernando de Soto,** who led an expedition to explore Florida and lands to the west. For three years De Soto and his troops wandered around the southeastern area of the present-day United States, following stories of gold. As the Spaniards traveled, they took advantage of the native peoples. Their usual method was to enter a village, take the chief hostage, and demand food and supplies.

De Soto crossed the **Mississippi River** in 1541, describing it as "swift, and very deep." After traveling as far west as present-day Oklahoma, De Soto died of fever. His men buried him in the waters of the Mississippi.

Francisco Vásquez de Coronado also wanted to find the legendary "Seven Cities of Cibola." After traveling through areas of northern Mexico and present-day Arizona and New Mexico, the expedition reached a town belonging to the Zuni people in early summer 1540. They realized at once that there was no gold. Members of the expedition traveled west to the Colorado River and east into what is now Kansas. They found nothing but "windswept plains" and strange "shaggy cows" (buffalo). Disappointed, Coronado returned to Mexico.

✓ Reading Check **Explaining** How did stories of the "Seven Cities of Cibola" affect Spanish exploration?

Spanish Rule

Spanish law called for three kinds of settlements in the Americas—pueblos, missions, and presidios. Pueblos, or towns, were established as centers of trade. Missions were religious communities that usually included a small town, surrounding farmland, and a church. A presidio, or fort, was usually built near a mission.

Juan de Oñate (day ohn • YAH • tay) was sent from Mexico to gain control over lands to the north and to convert the inhabitants. In 1598 Oñate founded the province of New Mexico and introduced cattle and horses to the Pueblo people.

Reading Strategy ⟩ READING THE TEXT

Evaluating Information When students form an opinion or make a judgment about something they are reading and evaluating. Direct students to the subsection titled *Why Spain Succeeded.* Ask them to analyze the information presented regarding the theories about why the Spaniards were able to conquer the mighty Native American empires. Ask students to write an essay explaining how they believed the empires were overcome. Students should make their own judgments about the fall of these empires, supporting their theories with information from the section. **L2, ELL**

Social Classes

A class system developed in Spain's empire. The upper class consisted of people who had been born in Spain, called *peninsulares*. The *peninsulares* owned the land, served in the Catholic Church, and ran the local government. Below them were the creoles, people born in the Americas to Spanish parents. Lower in the class structure were the mestizos (meh•STEE•zohs), people with Spanish and Native American parents. Still lower were the Native Americans, most of whom lived in great poverty. At the very bottom were enslaved Africans.

In the 1500s the Spanish government granted each conquistador who settled in the Americas an *encomienda,* the right to demand taxes or labor from Native Americans living on the land. This system turned the Native Americans into slaves. Grueling labor in the fields and in the gold and silver mines took its toll. Many Native Americans died from malnutrition and disease.

A Spanish priest, **Bartolomé de Las Casas,** condemned the cruel treatment of the Native Americans. He pleaded for laws to protect them. Las Casas claimed that millions had died because the Spanish "made gold their ultimate aim, seeking to load themselves with riches in the shortest possible time."

Because of Las Casas's reports, in 1542 the Spanish government passed the New Laws, which forbade making slaves of Native Americans. Although not always enforced, the laws did correct the worst abuses.

The Plantation System

Some Spanish settlers made large profits by exporting crops and raw materials back to Spain. In the West Indies, the main exports were tobacco and sugarcane. To raise these crops, the Spanish developed the plantation system. A plantation was a large estate. The Spanish used Native Americans to work their plantations.

Las Casas suggested replacing them with enslaved Africans—a suggestion he bitterly regretted later. He thought the Africans could endure the labor better than the Native Americans.

By the mid-1500s the Spanish were bringing thousands from West Africa to the Americas. The Portuguese did the same in Brazil. The Africans who survived the brutal ocean voyage were sold to plantation owners. By the late 1500s, plantation slave labor was an essential part of the economy of the colonies.

✓**Reading Check** **Describing** Whom did Las Casas try to protect?

✓**Reading Check**

Answer: Native Americans living on land that had been overtaken by the Spaniards

L1, ELL

Reading Essentials and Study Guide 2-3

L3

Enrichment Activity 2-3

4 CLOSE

Ask students to explain the organization of the social structure that developed in Spain's empire in the Americas. Have students create a graphic organizer showing how the classes were organized.

SECTION 3 ASSESSMENT

Checking for Understanding

1. **Key Terms** Write three true and three false statements using each of the following terms once: conquistador, tribute, pueblo, mission, presidio, plantation. Indicate which statements are false.

2. **Reviewing Facts** What three kinds of settlements did Spain establish in the Americas? How did they differ?

Reviewing Themes

3. **Culture and Traditions** What groups made up the class system in Spanish America?

Critical Thinking

4. **Analyzing Primary Sources** One conquistador explained, "We came to serve God and the king, and also to get rich." In what way do you think conquistadors planned to serve "God and the king"?

5. **Determining Cause and Effect** Re-create the diagram below and list causes of Spain's success in conquering Native American empires.

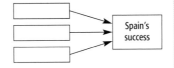

Analyzing Visuals

6. **Geography Skills** Review the map of Spanish exploration on page 52. What expedition traveled from Florida to the Mississippi River? Through what regions did the Coronado expedition travel?

Interdisciplinary Activity

Geography Using cookbooks as references, create an all-American dinner menu that features only foods introduced to Europeans by Native Americans.

CHAPTER 2 Exploring the Americas 55

SECTION 3 ASSESSMENT ANSWERS

1. Student work should reflect correct use of terms.
2. pueblos: centers for trade; missions: small religious communities; presidio: fort built near a mission
3. peninsulares, creoles, mestizos, Native Americans, enslaved Africans
4. by converting people to Christianity and claiming land and riches for the king
5. Answers may include: awe of the Spanish, weapons held by the Spanish, the native peoples' dislike of their Aztec overlords, and no immunity to European diseases.
6. De Soto; northern Mexico and present-day Arizona and New Mexico

Interdisciplinary Activity Menu items could include maize, sweet potatoes, beans, squash, avocados, peppers, and pineapple.

1 FOCUS

Have students brainstorm the changes brought to Native Americans by Spanish missionaries. Discuss and list the positive and negative aspects of the influence of missionaries among Native Americans. **Ask: Why did some Native Americans rebel against the work of missionaries?** (*Native Americans did not want changes brought to their culture, resented religious intrusion into their culture, were fearful of white settlement, and felt their traditions were threatened.*)

2 TEACH

Reading a Map Have students identify the area shown on the map and then locate the Nuestra Señora de los Delores mission. Have students note the location of other missions on the map. Have students identify the geographical features found where missions were located. Ask students to brainstorm reasons why missions were built in river valleys.

Draw students' attention to the mission inset. Have students describe the organizational layout of the mission. (*living quarters around outside of mission, area for grain storage, church as central point of mission, fields outside of mission walls, and large courtyard*)

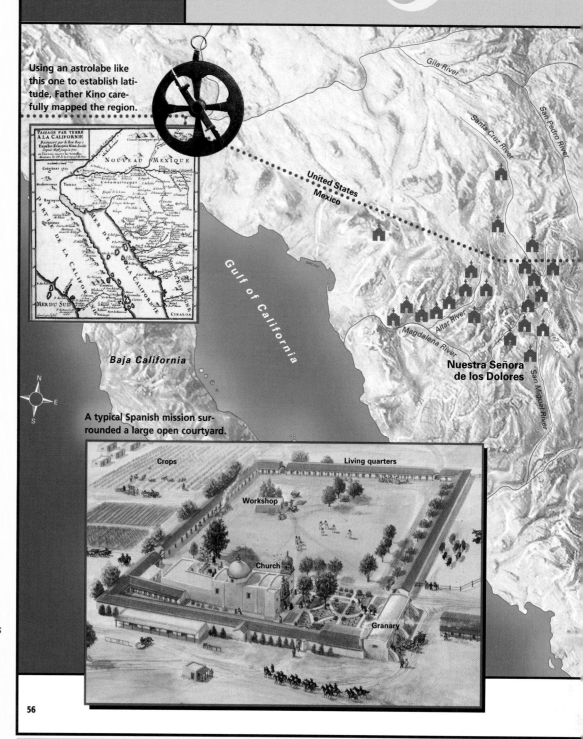

Using an astrolabe like this one to establish latitude, Father Kino carefully mapped the region.

Gila River

Santa Cruz River

San Pedro River

United States
Mexico

Gulf of California

Baja California

Altar River

Magdalena River

Nuestra Señora de los Dolores

San Miguel River

A typical Spanish mission surrounded a large open courtyard.

Crops

Living quarters

Workshop

Church

Granary

56

EXTENDING THE CONTENT

Pima Uprising In 1695 the Piman peoples of the Altar Valley region revolted, killed missionaries, burned public buildings, and drove off livestock. They were protesting the pressure and structure of the mission communities, the encroachment of Spain's frontier onto their lands, and the growing exploitation of Native American labor. Father Kino attempted to reassure the Pima by showing them a document written by the Spanish viceroy. The paper exempted the Pima from forced labor for at least 20 years. The Pima, however, revolted again in the early 1750s.

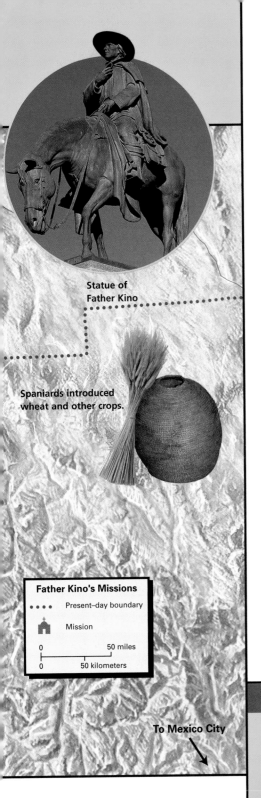

Statue of
Father Kino

Spaniards introduced
wheat and other crops.

Father Kino's Missions

•••• Present–day boundary

⛪ Mission

0   50 miles

0   50 kilometers

To Mexico City

PADRE ON HORSEBACK

MISSIONARY AND EXPLORER Eusebio Kino (yoo•SAY•be•oh KEE•no) was an Italian who studied astronomy, mapmaking, and mathematics before becoming a Jesuit priest. In 1681 he went to Mexico with the Spaniards to map the area and convert Native Americans to Catholicism.

MISSIONARY IN THE PIMERÍA ALTA

After several years in Mexico City and Baja California, Father Kino was sent to establish missions in the "Pimería Alta"—the Upper Pima Country—part of present-day Sonora, Mexico, and southern Arizona.

In March 1687 Father Kino established his first mission, Nuestra Señora de los Dolores at Cosari. He helped start more than 20 missions along the San Miguel, Magdalena, and Altar rivers.

Father Kino and other missionaries changed the face of Pimería Alta forever. The priests converted thousands of Native Americans to Christianity. By introducing livestock, wheat, European fruit, and other new crops, the missionaries altered the economy of the region.

EXPLORER AND MAPMAKER

Kino traveled so much he was known as the "padre on horseback." He covered thousands of miles tending to the needs of his converts and exploring and mapping the Sonoran Desert and California.

San Xavier del Bac, a mission started by Father Kino in 1700, still stands today outside of Tucson.

LEARNING *from* GEOGRAPHY

1. Where did Father Kino establish his missions? Why?

2. How did the introduction of food crops and domestic animals affect the development of the Southwest?

57

NATIONAL GEOGRAPHIC
GEOGRAPHY & HISTORY

3 ASSESS

Have students answer the **Learning from Geography** questions.

4 CLOSE

Have students design their own Spanish mission, determining which buildings would be needed, where they would be built, and where the fields would be located. Ask students to describe which feature they think is the most important one for the mission's survival.

History *and the* Humanities

💿 American Art and Architecture, Transparency 7, *Mission San Xavier del Bac* L3

NGS ONLINE

Access National Geographic's Web site for current events, atlas updates, activities, links, interactive features, and archives at www.nationalgeographic.com

Did you know?

The San Xavier del Bac mission held 3,000 Native Americans. With its fertile, irrigated farmland and pastures, however, it could support at least 30,000 people.

Answers to Learning *from* Geography

1. along rivers; to have a ready water supply for people and crops

2. They helped establish stable and permanent communities.

1 FOCUS

Section Overview

This section explains how mercantilism and religion fueled European nations to compete for territories in North America.

Reading Preview

Answers to Graphic: Protestant Reformation: Protestants sought religious freedom in North America; search for Northwest Passage: exploration of present-day Canada; early trading activities: French, Dutch, and English establish fur-trading posts

Preteaching Vocabulary
🖭 Use the **Vocabulary PuzzleMaker CD-ROM** to create crossword and word search puzzles.

SECTION 4 Exploring North America

Guide to Reading

Main Idea
Rivalries between countries, the search for a Northwest Passage to Asia, and early trading activities led to increased exploration of North America.

Key Terms
mercantilism, Columbian Exchange, Northwest Passage, coureur de bois

Reading Strategy
Determining Cause and Effect As you read the section, re-create the diagram below and provide an effect for each cause.

Exploration of North America	
Causes	Effects
Protestant Reformation	
Search for NW passage	
Early trading activities	

Read to Learn
• how the Protestant Reformation affected North America.
• why the activities of early traders encouraged exploration.

Section Theme
Global Connections European nations competed for overseas land and resources.

Preview of Events

◆1450	◆1500	◆1550	◆1600
1497 John Cabot lands in Newfoundland	**1517** Martin Luther starts the Protestant Reformation	**1535** Jacques Cartier sails up the St. Lawrence River to Montreal	**1609** Henry Hudson sails the Hudson River

Martin Luther

★ A European Story

In 1517 Martin Luther, a German priest, nailed a list of complaints about the Catholic Church on the door of a local church. Luther declared that the Bible was the only true guide for Christians. He rejected many Church practices—even the authority of the pope—because they were not mentioned in the Bible. Luther also believed that faith rather than good deeds was the way to salvation.

Church officials tried to get Luther to take back his statements. "I cannot go against my conscience," he replied. "Here I stand. I cannot do otherwise. God help me."

A Divided Church

Martin Luther's actions led to incredible changes in Europe. Before he voiced his beliefs, the countries of Europe had their differences, but they were bound together by a common church. For centuries, Catholicism had been the main religion of western Europe. In the 1500s, however, Luther's opposition to the policies of the Roman Catholic Church emerged.

58 CHAPTER 2 Exploring the Americas

SECTION RESOURCES

📂 **Reproducible Masters**
• Reproducible Lesson Plan 2–4
• Daily Lecture and Discussion Notes 2–4
• Guided Reading Activity 2–4
• Section Quiz 2–4
• Reteaching Activity 2–4
• Reading Essentials and Study Guide 2–4
• Enrichment Activity 2–4

📔 **Transparencies**
• Daily Focus Skills Transparency 2–4

Multimedia
🖭 Vocabulary PuzzleMaker CD-ROM
🖭 Interactive Tutor Self-Assessment CD-ROM
🖭 ExamView® Pro Testmaker CD-ROM
🖭 Presentation Plus! CD-ROM

Within a few years, Luther had many followers. They broke away from Catholicism to begin their own Christian churches. Martin Luther's protests were the start of a great religious and historical movement known as the **Protestant Reformation.**

Protestantism Spreads in Europe

From Germany Luther's ideas spread rapidly. **John Calvin,** a French religious thinker, also broke away from the Catholic Church. Like Luther, Calvin rejected the idea that good works would ensure a person's salvation. He believed that God had already chosen those who would be saved.

In England, King Henry VIII also left the Catholic Church, but not for religious reasons. Pope Clement VII had refused Henry's request to declare his first marriage invalid. In 1534 the English Parliament, working with the king,

denied the authority of the pope and recognized the king as the head of the Church of England. During the rule of Henry's daughter, Queen Elizabeth I, further reforms firmly established England as a Protestant nation.

Religious Rivalries in the Americas

Throughout western Europe, people and nations divided into Catholics and Protestants. When these Europeans crossed the Atlantic, they took along their religious differences.

Spanish and French Catholics worked to spread their faith to the Native Americans. The Spanish settled in the southwestern and southeastern regions of North America, and the French settled in the northeast. Dutch and English Protestants established colonies in lands along the Atlantic coast between the French and the Spanish settlements. Some of the English settlements were founded by Protestants who wanted to practice their beliefs in peace.

✔ **Reading Check** **Explaining** What role did religion play in the exploration of North America?

🅢 Economics

Economic Rivalry

Religion was only one of the factors that pushed European nations across the Atlantic Ocean. The promise of great wealth was equally strong, especially as other Europeans watched Spain gain riches from its colonies.

According to the economic theory of mercantilism, a nation's power was based on its wealth. Rulers tried to increase their nation's total wealth by acquiring gold and silver and by developing trade. Mercantilism provided great opportunities for individual merchants to make money. It also increased rivalry between nations.

Several countries in Europe competed for overseas territory that could produce wealth. They wanted to acquire colonies in the Americas that could provide valuable resources, such as gold and silver, or raw materials. The colonies would also serve as a place to sell European products.

Picturing History

In 1676 Kateri Tekakwitha, a 20-year-old Mohawk woman, accepted Christianity from French Catholic missionaries. **What region of North America was settled by the French?**

CHAPTER 2 Exploring the Americas   59

2 TEACH

Daily Lecture and Discussion Notes 2–4

Copyright © by The McGraw-Hill Companies, Inc.

Daily Lecture and Discussion Notes

Chapter 2, Section 4

Did You Know? French influence is still strong almost four centuries after the French explorer Samuel de Champlain established a settlement in present-day Quebec, Canada. Quebec is the only place in North or South America where French is the primary language spoken. French speakers are called *Francophones* and English speakers are called *Anglophones.*

I. A Divided Church (Pages 58–59)

   A. Martin Luther brought about changes in Europe in the 1500s with his opposition to Catholicism. His protests began the Protestant Reformation.

   B. In France, John Calvin, a Christian theologist, broke away from the Catholic Church.

   C. In England, King Henry VIII

Reading Strategy

Push and Pull Factors Explain to students the difference between push and pull factors. Push factors drive away and pull factors draw toward. Suggest that students work in small groups to review the section and list all factors that motivated explorers. Then label each factor as push or pull. As a class, discuss these factors and each group's interpretation of them. **L1**

Picturing History

Answer: Canada

✔ **Reading Check**

Answer: European settlers of different religions chose to establish new colonies in order to spread their faith or practice their beliefs.

COOPERATIVE LEARNING ACTIVITY

Creating a Marketing Campaign Organize the class into groups of five to develop a marketing campaign. Tell students that they are a team working for an advertising company and have been assigned to develop a marketing campaign to promote an exploration journey. Allow each group to choose the area of exploration, either historical or contemporary. Students in each group should choose from roles such as: copywriter for marketing brochure, layout artist to design brochure, writer of radio commercial, designer of a Web page on the Internet, and designer of a magazine advertisement. Then have each group sell the marketing campaign to the class. Have students vote on the most effective campaign. 📦 **L2**

Guided Reading Activity 2–4

Name _____ Date _____ Class _____

★ **Guided Reading Activity 2-4**

DIRECTIONS: Outlining Locate each heading in your textbook. Then use the information under the heading to help you write each answer. Use another sheet of paper if necessary.

I. A Divided Church

A. Introduction—Whose protests started the Protestant Reformation? _____

B. Protestantism Spreads in Europe
1. Who was John Calvin? _____
2. What did the English Parliament do in 1534 that helped establish England as a Protestant nation?
_____

C. Religious Rivalries in the Americas—How did the religious rivalries in western Europe affect the Americas?

Columbus's voyages marked the beginning of the Columbian Exchange, the movement of people, cultures, and ideas between two previously isolated worlds. This exchange grew into a worldwide movement in which whole populations expanded within their homelands or migrated to other lands. **Ask: Who do you think benefited the most from the Columbian Exchange?** *(Sample answer: Europeans reaped the benefits of free land, a cheap labor source, and new foods that helped to feed Europe's growing population.)*

CURRICULUM CONNECTION

Economics During the Age of Exploration, European nations believed that their power, and ultimately their survival, depended on their acquisition of wealth. This national economic purpose, known as mercantilism, fueled not only exploration but also colonization. European nations considered their colonies as sources of raw materials, which were used to manufacture goods.

MORE ABOUT... The Columbian Exchange

Trade between the continents, known as the Columbian Exchange, changed life on both sides of the Atlantic.

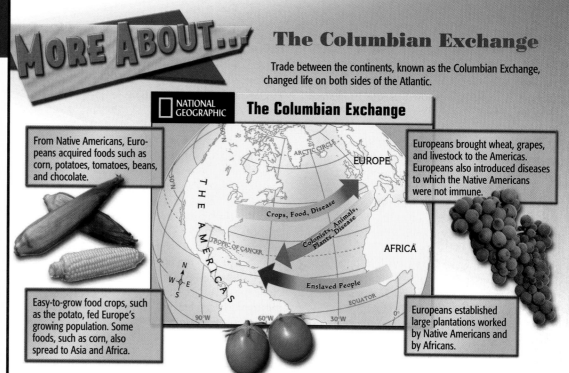

NATIONAL GEOGRAPHIC — The Columbian Exchange

From Native Americans, Europeans acquired foods such as corn, potatoes, tomatoes, beans, and chocolate.

Europeans brought wheat, grapes, and livestock to the Americas. Europeans also introduced diseases to which the Native Americans were not immune.

Easy-to-grow food crops, such as the potato, fed Europe's growing population. Some foods, such as corn, also spread to Asia and Africa.

Europeans established large plantations worked by Native Americans and by Africans.

Crops, Food, Disease
Colonists, Animals, Plants, Disease
Enslaved People

The Columbian Exchange

The voyages of Columbus and other explorers brought together two parts of the globe that previously had had no contact: the continents of Europe, Asia, and Africa in one hemisphere and the Americas in the other. The contact led to an exchange of plants, animals, and diseases that altered life on both sides of the Atlantic. Scholars refer to this as the Columbian Exchange.

A Northwest Passage

The Treaty of Tordesillas had divided the Americas between Spain and Portugal. It did not allow for claims by other nations—so England, France, and the Netherlands ignored the treaty. During the 1500s and early 1600s, these countries sent explorers to chart the coast of North America. They wanted to profit from trade and colonization as well. The voyage to Asia—either around the southern tip of Africa or around South America—was long and difficult. For this reason, the three countries hoped to discover a Northwest Passage to Asia—a more direct water route through the Americas.

In 1497 England sent **John Cabot,** an Italian, to look for a northern route to Asia. Cabot probably landed on the coast of present-day Newfoundland. England used Cabot's voyage as the basis for its claims to North America.

In 1524 France hired an Italian, **Giovanni da Verrazano,** to look for the northern sea route. Verrazano explored the coast of North America from present-day Nova Scotia down to the Carolinas.

In 1535 French explorer **Jacques Cartier** (KAR•tyay) sailed up the St. Lawrence River hoping it would lead to the Pacific. He got as far as the Huron village of Hochelaga. Cartier wrote that from the mountain next to the village, "one sees a very great distance." He named the peak Mont-Royal, which means "royal mountain." This is the site of the city now called **Montreal.** Cartier had heard stories about gold, but he found neither gold nor a sea route to Asia.

Hudson's Discoveries

The Netherlands, too, wanted to find a passage through the Americas. They hired **Henry Hudson,** an English sailor, to explore. In 1609 he discovered the river that now bears his name. In his ship, the *Half Moon,* Hudson sailed north on the Hudson River as far as the site of present-day Albany. Deciding that he had not found a passage

---

DIFFERENTIATED INSTRUCTION

At-Risk Students Organize the class into three groups, one representing the French, another the English, and the third the Dutch. Have students in each group choose a familiar melody and write words to accompany this melody that describe the cultural contributions brought to the Americas by the group they represent. Encourage students to include unique characteristics of that culture. Ask each group to sing the song. **L1**

📁 Refer to ***Inclusion for the Middle School Social Studies Classroom Strategies and Activities*** in the TCR.

to India, he turned back. The following year Hudson tried again, this time sent by England.

Sailing almost due west from northern England, Henry Hudson and his crew discovered a huge bay, now called **Hudson Bay.** Hudson thought he had reached the Pacific Ocean. After months of searching for an outlet from the bay, however, the crew rebelled. Hudson, his son John, and a few sailors were set adrift in a small boat—and never seen again.

French Open Trading Posts

France had shown little interest in building an empire in the Americas. Its rulers were preoccupied by political and religious conflicts at home. The French viewed North America as an opportunity for profits from fishing and fur trading rather than as a place to settle.

Furs were popular in Europe, and traders could make large profits from beaver pelts acquired in North America. A group of French

Geography *Skills*

Answers:
1. Cartier
2. It was English territory.

Geography Skills Practice
Ask: Who was able to trace the Mississippi River to its mouth?
(La Salle)

3 ASSESS

Assign Section 4 Assessment as homework or as an in-class activity.

◆ Have students use **Interactive Tutor Self-Assessment CD-ROM.**

L2

Section Quiz 2–4

L1

Reteaching Activity 2–4

NATIONAL GEOGRAPHIC — French Explorers, 1535–1682

① Cartier searched for a northwest passage to Asia. He explored the St. Lawrence waterways to Montreal. He discovered that Newfoundland was a single large island.

② La Salle became the first European to trace the Mississippi River to its mouth, the Gulf of Mexico. La Salle claimed the Mississippi River valley for France.

Cartier 1535–1536
Champlain 1609–1615
La Salle 1669–1671, 1679–1682
Marquette and Joliet 1673
French territory   • Settlement
English territory   ✖ Fort
Spanish territory

Geography *Skills*

Explorers from France followed rivers and lakes into the interior of North America.
1. **Movement** Which early French explorer traveled up the St. Lawrence River?
2. **Making Inferences** Why didn't the French explore east of the Appalachian Mountains?

INTERDISCIPLINARY CONNECTIONS ACTIVITY

Economics Northern Native Americans trapped beaver and traded beaver fur to European settlers in return for blankets and tools. Explain to students that this form of exchange is called bartering. Point out that beaver fur had value because beaver-fur hats were popular in Europe. Blankets and tools had value because Native Americans could use them. Brainstorm items in demand today that could easily be traded among students' peer groups. Consider why the items are popular. Decide what other item or items would be equal in value to trade for the original item. **L2**

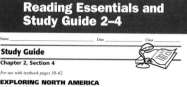

✓ Reading Check

Answer: Countries such as England and France wanted to find a more direct water route to Asia so that they could profit from trade and colonization.

L1, ELL

Reading Essentials and Study Guide 2–4

L3

Enrichment Activity 2–4

4 CLOSE

Ask students to debate which European country discussed in this chapter had the greatest impact on the development of American culture.

---

traders made an agreement with the Native Americans to trade fur. In 1608 the group sent **Samuel de Champlain** to establish a settlement in **Quebec** in what is now Canada. Champlain made several trips to the region and discovered Lake Champlain. He described the beautiful scenery and abundant wildlife and the Native Americans he met there.

From Quebec the French moved into other parts of Canada, where they built trading posts to collect furs gathered by Native Americans and French trappers. The trappers were called coureurs de bois (ku•RUHR duh BWAH), meaning "runners of the woods."

Dutch Settlements

Like other European countries, the Netherlands was also eager to claim its share of world trade. Until Hudson's voyage, there had been no Dutch exploration in North America. Hudson's voyage became the start for Dutch claims on the continent.

Although the Netherlands was a small country, its large fleet of trading ships sailed all over the world. In 1621 the Dutch West India Company set up a trading colony—New Netherland—in the area Hudson had explored. In 1624 the company sent 30 families to settle the area. They settled at Fort Orange (later

---

Fact · Fiction · Folklore

America's Flags

Flag of New France Settlers in New France often flew this flag of the French Royal Navy. They also flew the French Royal Banner, which was blue instead of white.

Albany) on the Hudson River and on Burlington Island in New Jersey. Shortly after that, Fort Nassau was established just opposite where Philadelphia stands today.

The center of the new colony was New Amsterdam, located on the tip of Manhattan Island where the Hudson River enters New York Harbor. In 1626 Peter Minuit, the governor of the colony, paid the Manhates people 60 Dutch guilders in goods for the island. The goods probably included cloth, and valuable tools such as axes, hoes, and awls. Like Portugal, Spain, and France, the Netherlands started colonies in the Americas.

✓ Reading Check **Analyzing** Why was the idea of a Northwest Passage important?

SECTION 4 ASSESSMENT

Checking for Understanding

1. **Key Terms** Write a sentence in which you correctly use each of the following terms: mercantilism, Columbian Exchange, Northwest Passage, coureur de bois
2. **Reviewing Facts** What were English, French, and Dutch explorers searching for while charting the coast of North America?

Reviewing Themes

3. **Global Connections** How did French goals in the Americas differ from the goals of other European nations?

Critical Thinking

4. **Identifying Central Issues** How did the economic theory of mercantilism influence the exploration and settlement of North America by Europeans?
5. **Determining Cause and Effect** Re-create the diagram below and explain how the Columbian Exchange affected both sides of the Atlantic Ocean.

Columbian Exchange	
Effects on the Americas	Effects on Europe

Analyzing Visuals

6. **Geography Skills** Review the map, *French Explorers, 1535–1682*, on page 61. Which of the French explorers traveled farthest south? Along what river did Marquette and Joliet travel?

Interdisciplinary Activity

Persuasive Writing Write a letter to one of the explorers who searched for a Northwest Passage. In the letter, explain why it is important for your nation to find a Northwest Passage.

SECTION 4 ASSESSMENT ANSWERS

1. Student work should reflect correct use of terms.
2. a more direct water route to Asia
3. The French wanted to make profits rather than settle land.
4. A nation's power was based on its wealth, which was increased by acquiring gold and silver and developing trade. Overseas territories were seen as potential sources of wealth.
5. Effects on the Americas: importation of wheat, grapes, and livestock; introduction of diseases; establishment of slavery; Effects on Europe: introduction of new foods and provided a cheap labor supply
6. La Salle; the Mississippi River

Interdisciplinary Activity Letters should include reasons for exploration.

Reading a Time Line

Why Learn this Skill?

Knowing the relationship of time to events is important in studying history. A time line is a visual way to show chronological order within a time period. Most time lines are divided into sections representing equal time intervals. For example, a time line showing 1,000 years might be divided into ten 100-year sections. Each event on a time line appears beside the date when the event took place.

Learning the Skill

To read a time line, follow these steps:
- Find the dates on the opposite ends of the time line to know the time span. Also note the intervals between dates on the time line.
- Study the order of events.
- Analyze relationships among events or look for trends.

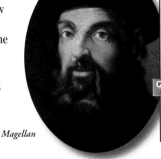

Magellan

Practicing the Skill

Analyze the time line of Magellan's voyage below. Use it to answer the questions that follow.

1. What time span is represented?

2. How many years do each of the sections represent?

3. Did Magellan's voyage to the Spice Islands occur before or after his voyage to the Philippines?

4. How long did Magellan's voyage around the world take?

Applying the Skill

Making a Time Line List 10 key events that have occurred in your life and the dates on which these events occurred. Write the events in chronological order on a time line.

 Glencoe's **Skillbuilder Interactive Workbook CD-ROM, Level 1,** provides instruction and practice in key social studies skills.

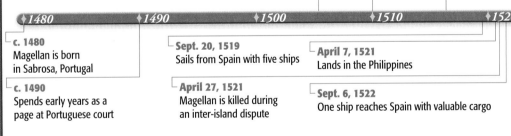

1517
Offers services to king of Spain

1510
Promoted to captain

c. 1506
Travels to Spice Islands on exploratory expeditions

◆1480   ◆1490   ◆1500   ◆1510   ◆1520

c. 1480
Magellan is born in Sabrosa, Portugal

c. 1490
Spends early years as a page at Portuguese court

Sept. 20, 1519
Sails from Spain with five ships

April 27, 1521
Magellan is killed during an inter-island dispute

April 7, 1521
Lands in the Philippines

Sept. 6, 1522
One ship reaches Spain with valuable cargo

63

TEACH

Reading a Time Line This skill demonstrates how to read a time line and relates the importance of time lines to the study of history. Explain to students that time lines are drawn to scale with each segment measuring a specific length of time and standing for the same number of years. For example, 1 inch (2.54 cm) equals 10 years. Ask students to find the scale on the time line on this page (1.5 inches [3.81 cm] equals 10 years). Invite students to find the scales used on the time lines at the beginning of this unit and each section.

Additional Practice
L2

Chapter Skills Activity 2

Name _____ Date _____ Class _____

★ **Chapter Skills Activity 2**

Reading a Time Line

A time line lists events that occurred over a period of time. The number of years covered is called a time span, and the segments are called time intervals. A time line can show events in more than one place.

The World Expands: 1000–1600

GLENCOE
TECHNOLOGY

CD-ROM
Glencoe Skillbuilder Interactive Workbook CD-ROM, Level 1

This interactive CD-ROM reinforces student mastery of essential social studies skills.

ANSWERS TO PRACTICING THE SKILL

1. 1480 to the 1520s

2. 10 years

3. before

4. 3 years

Applying the Skill Students should design time lines that plot 10 key events in their lives.

Assessment and Activities

GLENCOE
TECHNOLOGY

MindJogger Videoquiz
Use **MindJogger Videoquiz** to review the Chapter 2 content.

Available in VHS

Reviewing Key Terms

1. The **caravel** and the **astrolabe** were two advances in technology during the **Renaissance** that made exploration and the discovery of new lands possible.

2. Following the conquering of Native American land and peoples by a **conquistador,** settlements such as **missions** and **presidios** were built.

3. A search for the **Northwest Passage** across North America was motivated by the economic theory of **mercantilism.**

Reviewing Key Facts

4. for trade

5. Ghana, Mali, Songhai

6. Prince Henry

7. Dias: southernmost part of Africa; Vasco da Gama: around Africa to India

8. Spain

9. Vasco da Gama sailed around the southern tip of Africa; Ponce de León explored present-day Puerto Rico and Florida; John Cabot rediscovered Newfoundland.

10. for their riches, mainly gold

11. Conquistadors demanded taxes or labor from Native Americans; this turned them into slaves.

12. the Protestant Reformation

13. a Northwest Passage

Critical Thinking

14. the large area of land that Native Americans once occupied

Chapter Summary
Exploring the Americas

c. 1000
- Leif Eriksson lands in present-day Newfoundland

1488
- Bartholomeu Dias reaches Indian Ocean

1492
- Columbus lands in the Americas

1498
- Vasco da Gama reaches India

1519
- Magellan begins circumnavigation of the world
- Hernán Cortés lands in Mexico

1532
- Francisco Pizarro captures Atahualpa

1535
- Jacques Cartier sails up the St. Lawrence River to Montreal

1541
- De Soto crosses the Mississippi River

1565
- Spain establishes fort at St. Augustine, Florida

1609
- Henry Hudson sails the Hudson River

64

Reviewing Key Terms
Examine the groups of words below. Then write sentences explaining what each group has in common.

1. Renaissance, astrolabe, caravel
2. conquistador, mission, presidio
3. mercantilism, Northwest Passage

Reviewing Key Facts

4. Why were Europeans interested in Asia?

5. What three large African kingdoms south of the Sahara flourished between 300 and 1600?

6. What European leader set up a center for exploration in Portugal?

7. Where did the earliest Portuguese explorers sail?

8. Which country supported Columbus on his quest to find a water route to Asia?

9. List the major accomplishments of Vasco da Gama, Juan Ponce de León, and John Cabot.

10. What was the main reason the Spanish wanted to conquer the Aztec and the Inca?

11. How did the Spanish colonial system of *encomiendas* affect Native Americans?

12. What movement created religious rivalries in Europe that carried over into exploration of the Americas?

13. What were explorers searching for during their explorations of the North American coast?

Critical Thinking

14. **Analyzing Primary Sources** Read the Two Viewpoints on page 47. What does Red Jacket mean by "this great island"?

15. **Drawing Conclusions** Why do you think the Caribbean Islands are often referred to as the West Indies?

16. **Analyzing Information** Study the feature on the Columbian Exchange on page 60. What foods were shipped to Europe?

17. **Determining Cause and Effect** Re-create the diagram below and identify three reasons for voyages of exploration and three effects that resulted from the exploration.

15. Columbus originally believed he had landed in the East Indies near Asia. As a result, the islands were later named the West Indies.

16. corn, potatoes, tomatoes, beans, and chocolate

17. Answers may include any of the following three causes: new trade routes to the East, riches from spices, riches from gold and silver, religion, land acquisition, profits from fur and fish, and search for a Northwest Passage. Answers may include any of the

following three effects: colonization of the Americas, devastation of Native American empires, establishment of missions in North America, economic rivalry between European countries for control of wealth from colonies, and religious rivalry.

Geography and History Activity

18. Texas, New Mexico, Arizona, and California

19. San Francisco

20. northwest

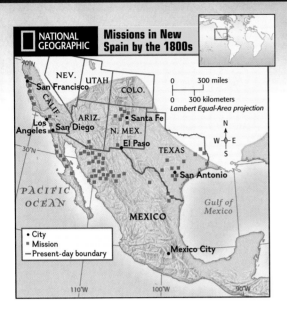

National Geographic

Missions in New Spain by the 1800s

0 300 miles
0 300 kilometers
Lambert Equal-Area projection

- City
- Mission
— Present-day boundary

 Geography and History Activity

Study the map above and answer the questions that follow.

18. **Place** In what present-day states were the Spanish missions located?

19. **Location** Near what city was the northernmost Spanish mission located?

20. **Location** In which direction would a traveler leaving Mexico City journey to reach San Diego?

Practicing Skills

Reading a Time Line *Study the time line on pages 36–37, then answer the following questions.*

21. What is the time span covered on this time line?

22. In which century does the greatest number of events take place on this time line?

23. What event occurred in 1522?

 Technology Activity

24. **Using Word Processing Software** Search the library for information on boats and sailing. Using word processing software, prepare a report about a navigational instrument that is in use today. Describe how it would have been helpful to an explorer such as Magellan.

Online

Self-Check Quiz

Visit tarvol1.glencoe.com and click on **Chapter 2— Self-Check Quizzes** to prepare for the chapter test.

Citizenship Cooperative Activity

25. **Interviewing** In a group of three, find out if any people in your community have come from Great Britain, Spain, France, or other countries. Try to interview these people and ask them about the political system of the country they came from. Prepare an oral report for the class.

Economics Activity

26. Ask family members and other adults about prices paid for common products in years past. Ask about grocery items, haircuts, cars, and so on. Compare these prices with current prices. Share your findings with the class.

Alternative Assessment

27. **Portfolio Writing Activity** Choose an explorer discussed in this chapter. Use library resources to research the explorer's life and achievements. Prepare an interview with that explorer. Plan the questions to ask and the answers you would expect the explorer to give. Write the interview as a magazine article.

Standardized Test Practice

Directions: Choose the *best* answer to the following question.

Juana Inés de la Cruz was an unusual woman because she was famous as a

A   writer.

B   prince.

C   farmer.

D   warrior.

Test-Taking Tip:

Eliminate answers that don't make sense. For instance, a woman could not be a prince, so **B** could not be the correct answer.

visual presentation of their findings. Drawings or pictures from magazines and newspapers could be added to their visual presentation to make them more informative and interesting.

Alternative Assessment

27. Student interviews should include biographical data, greatest moments of adventure, most difficult times, and greatest achievements. Interviews may be written in a dialogue style or as a summary of the interview.

HISTORY Online

Have students visit the Web site at tarvol1.glencoe.com to review Chapter 2 and take the Self-Check Quiz.

Standardized Test Practice

Answer: A
Question Type: History
Answer Explanation: According to page 54, Juana Inés de la Cruz was a well-known writer in Mexico during the 1600s.

Bonus Question ?

Ask: After what explorer is the Pacific end of the Panama Canal named? *(Vasco Núñez de Balboa)*

Practicing Skills

21. 1400–1620

22. the sixteenth century

23. Magellan's crew completes the first world voyage.

 Technology Activity

24. Students should describe a modern navigational instrument and explain how it could have aided an early explorer.

Citizenship Cooperative Activity

25. Students' oral reports should present an organized explanation of the political system of the person's country. Encourage students to use visual aids, such as charts and diagrams, to assist in their explanations.

Economics Activity

26. Students' findings should compare the previous prices of items with current prices. Students may create a

Unit 2 Resources

SUGGESTED PACING CHART

Unit 2 (1 Day)	Chapter 3 (6 Days)	Chapter 4 (6 Days)	Unit 2 (2 Days)
Day 1 Introduction	**Day 1** Chapter 3 Intro, Section 1	**Day 1** Chapter 4 Intro, Section 1	**Day 1** Wrap-Up/Project **Day 2** Unit 2 Assessment
	Day 2 Section 2	**Day 2** Section 2	
	Day 3 Section 3	**Day 3** Section 3	
	Day 4 Section 4	**Day 4** Section 4	
	Day 5 Chapter 3 Review	**Day 5** Chapter 4 Review	
	Day 6 Chapter 3 Assessment	**Day 6** Chapter 4 Assessment	

GLENCOE'S ASSESSMENT ADVANTAGE

Use the following tools to easily assess student learning in a variety of ways:

- Performance Assessment Activities and Rubrics
- Chapter and Unit Tests
- Section Quizzes
- Standardized Test Practice Workbook

- www.tarvol1.glencoe.com
- Interactive Tutor Self-Assessment CD-ROM
- MindJogger Videoquiz
- ExamView® Pro Testmaker CD-ROM

TEACHING TRANSPARENCIES

Unit 2 Map Overlay Transparencies
L2

Cause-and-Effect Transparency 2
L2

READING SUPPORT FROM
JAMESTOWN EDUCATION

- *Timed Readings Plus in Social Studies* help students increase their reading rate and fluency while maintaining comprehension. The 400-word passages are similar to those found on state and national assessments.

- *Reading in the Content Area: Social Studies* concentrates on six essential reading skills that help students better comprehend what they read. The book includes 75 high-interest nonfiction passages written at increasing levels of difficulty.

- *Reading Fluency* helps students read smoothly, accurately, and expressively.

- *Jamestown's Reading Improvement,* by renowned reading expert Edward Fry, focuses on helping build your students' comprehension, vocabulary, and skimming and scanning skills.

- *Critical Reading Series* provides high-interest books, each written at three reading levels.

For more information about these products, see the Jamestown Education materials in the Classroom Solutions in the front of this Teacher Wraparound Edition. To order these products, call Glencoe at 1-800-334-7344.

Unit 2 Resources

ASSESSMENT

Unit 2 Pretests L2

Unit 2 Posttests L2

INTERDISCIPLINARY ACTIVITIES

American Literature Reading 2 L2

Interdisciplinary Connection 2 L2

Economics and History Activity 2 L2

APPLICATION AND ENRICHMENT

Cooperative Learning Activity 2 L1, ELL

Citizenship Activity 2 L1

HANDS-ON ACTIVITIES

Hands-On History Activity 2 L1

History Simulations and Problem Solving 2 L1

Reading List Generator CD-ROM

GLENCOE BOOKLINK

The Glencoe BookLink CD-ROM is a database that allows you to search more than 15,000 titles to create a customized reading list for your students.

- Reading lists can be organized by students' reading level, author, genre, theme, or area of interest.

- The database provides Degrees of Reading Power™ (DRP) and Lexile™ readability scores for all selections.

- A brief summary of each selection is included.

Leveled reading suggestions for this unit:

For Students at a Grade 6 Reading Level:
- *The Landing of the Pilgrims,* by James Daugherty

For Students at a Grade 7 Reading Level:
- *Roanoke: The Story of the Lost Colony,* by Peter I. Bosco

For Students at a Grade 8 Reading Level:
- *The Devil in Salem Village: The Story of the Salem Witchcraft Trials,* by Laurel Van der Linde

Extending the Content

Readings for the Teacher
- *The Times Of Their Lives: Life, Love, and Death in Plymouth Colony,* by James Deetz and Patricia Scott. W.H. Freeman & Co., 2000.

Multimedia Links
- *The "Plymouth" Adventure: Voyage of the Mayflower.* Audiocassette. Colonial Theatre on the Air, 1999.

0:00 Out of Time?

If time does not permit teaching each chapter in this unit, you may want to use the **Reading Essentials and Study Guide** summaries.

Unit Overview

In the 1600s and 1700s, Europeans established colonies in North America, seeking profit as well as religious and political freedom. **Chapter 3** describes the people who established the American colonies and their objectives. **Chapter 4** focuses on what life was like in the colonies.

Unit Objectives

After studying this unit, students will be able to:
1. Describe the founding of the European colonies in America.
2. Discuss economic and cultural aspects of colonial life and explain the causes of the French and Indian War.

Why It Matters Activity

Explain that founding the American colonies eventually gave birth to a distinct new society and culture with representative government. Have students speculate about how their lives would be different today had the American colonies not been established or if they had been settled by different countries.

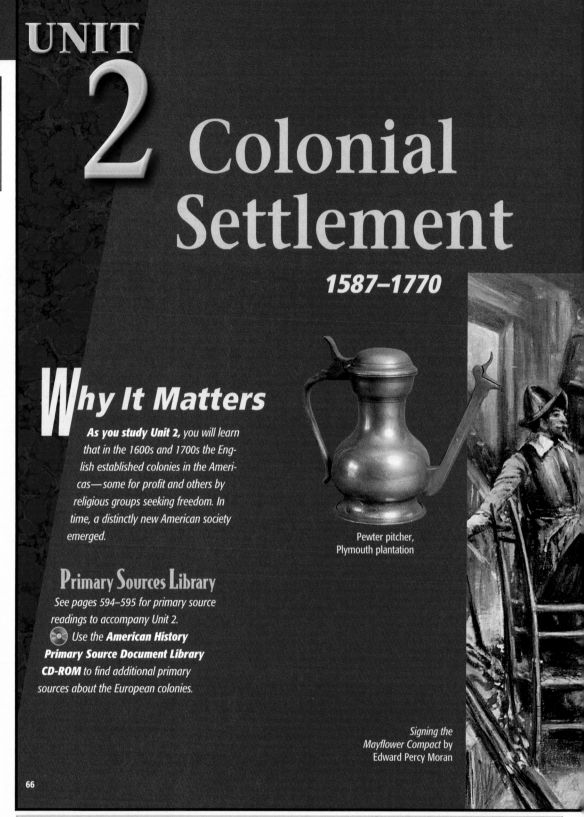

UNIT 2
Colonial Settlement
1587–1770

Why It Matters

As you study Unit 2, you will learn that in the 1600s and 1700s the English established colonies in the Americas—some for profit and others by religious groups seeking freedom. In time, a distinctly new American society emerged.

Pewter pitcher, Plymouth plantation

Primary Sources Library

See pages 594–595 for primary source readings to accompany Unit 2.

*Use the **American History Primary Source Document Library CD-ROM** to find additional primary sources about the European colonies.*

Signing the *Mayflower Compact* by Edward Percy Moran

66

TEAM TEACHING ACTIVITY

Language Arts In the mid-1600s, in an effort to build the population of New France, the French government sent about 4,000 people to the colony. Among these people were some 900 young, single women, many of whom came from orphanages or poor families and were sent at the king's expense. Have students work with a Language Arts teacher and write diary entries from the perspective of one of the single women sent to New France. **L1**

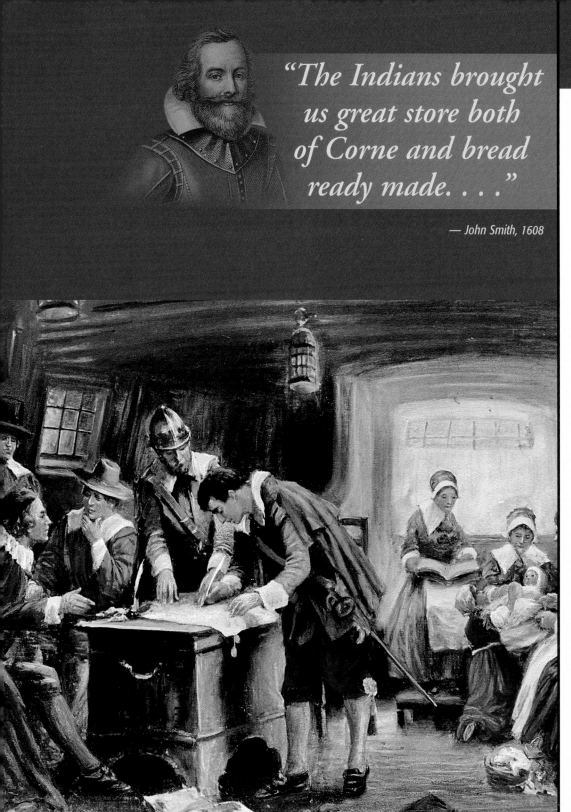

"*The Indians brought us great store both of Corne and bread ready made. . . .*"

— John Smith, 1608

GLENCOE TECHNOLOGY

CD-ROM
American History Primary Source Document Library CD-ROM

Use the **American History Primary Source Document Library CD-ROM** to access primary source documents related to the settlement and growth of the American colonies.

More About the Art

In this painting, Myles Standish aids William Bradford, who has his pen in his hand. Also at the table are John Carver, elected governor, and William Brewster. Moran, who specialized in colonial and historical subjects, came from an artistic family. His father was marine artist Edward Moran and his uncle, Thomas Moran, was one of America's great landscape painters. Have students describe how the artist focuses the viewer's attention to the Mayflower Compact signing. *(The artist positions it in the center of the painting.)* **Ask: Do you think the women signed the Mayflower Compact?** *(No, the women shown in the painting are not involved in the signing.)*

Glencoe Literature Library

As students study the unit, have them read *The Scarlet Letter* by Nathaniel Hawthorne from the **Glencoe Literature Library.** The Glencoe Literature Library consists of novels and other readings for middle school students, along with study guides that offer instructional support and student activities.

SERVICE-LEARNING PROJECT

Have students work in groups to conduct research about current bills or issues before the city, county, state, or federal government. Have each group choose an issue that might be of interest to classmates or the community. Tell the groups to provide information about where to address letters to representatives. Each class member should write a letter or an e-mail to the appropriate representative stating his or her opinion about the issue. **L3**

Refer to **Building Bridges: Connecting Classroom and Community through Service-Learning in Social Studies** from the National Council for the Social Studies for information about service-learning.

Chapter 3 Resources

Timesaving Tools

TeacherWorks™ All-In-One Planner and Resource Center

- **Interactive Teacher Edition** Access your Teacher Wraparound Edition and your classroom resources with a few easy clicks.
- **Interactive Lesson Planner** Planning has never been easier! Organize your week, month, semester, or year with all the lesson helps you need to make teaching creative, timely, and relevant.

Use Glencoe's **Presentation Plus!** multimedia teacher tool to easily present dynamic lessons that visually excite your students. Using Microsoft PowerPoint® you can customize the presentations to create your own personalized lessons.

TEACHING TRANSPARENCIES

Graphic Organizer 12 L2

Why It Matters Chapter Transparency 3 L2

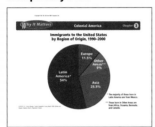

REVIEW AND REINFORCEMENT

Workbook Activity 3 L1

Time Line Activity 3 L2

Vocabulary Activity 3 L1

REVIEW AND REINFORCEMENT

Critical Thinking Skills Activity 3 L2

Take-Home Review Activity 3 L1

ENRICHMENT

Linking Past and Present Activity 3 L2

Primary Source Reading 3 L2

GEOGRAPHY

Geography and History Activity 3 L2

Meeting NCSS Standards

The following standards are highlighted in Chapter 3:

Section 1 VII Production, Distribution, & Consumption: A
Section 2 X Civic Ideals & Practices: A, C, D
Section 3 IV Individual Development & Identity: A, C, E
Section 4 V Individuals, Groups, & Institutions: A, C, D, F

FOLDABLES™ Study Organizer Dinah Zike's **Foldables** are three-dimensional, interactive graphic organizers that help students practice basic writing skills, review key vocabulary terms, and identify main ideas. Additional chapter activities can be found in the **Reading and Study Skills Foldables** booklet.

68A

Chapter 3 Resources

ASSESSMENT AND EVALUATION

Chapter 3 Test Form A L2

Chapter 3 Test Form B L2

Standardized Test Practice Workbook Activity 3 L2

Performance Assessment Activity 3 L1, ELL

ExamView® Pro Testmaker CD-ROM

MULTIMEDIA

- Vocabulary PuzzleMaker CD-ROM
- Interactive Tutor Self-Assessment CD-ROM
- ExamView® Pro Testmaker CD-ROM
- Audio Program
- American History Primary Source Document Library CD-ROM
- MindJogger Videoquiz
- Presentation Plus! CD-ROM
- TeacherWorks CD-ROM
- Interactive Student Edition CD-ROM
- Glencoe Skillbuilder Interactive Workbook CD-ROM, Level 1
- The American Republic to 1877 Video Program
- American Music: Hits Through History

SPANISH RESOURCES

The following Spanish language materials are available in the Spanish Resources Binder:

- Spanish Guided Reading Activities
- Spanish Reteaching Activities
- Spanish Quizzes and Tests
- Spanish Vocabulary Activity
- Spanish Take-Home Review Activity
- Spanish Summaries
- The Declaration of Independence and United States Constitution Spanish Translation

---

THE HISTORY CHANNEL.

The following videotape program is available from Glencoe as a supplement to Chapter 3:

- **Pocahontas: Her True Story** (ISBN 1-56501-555-X)

To order, call Glencoe at 1-800-334-7344. To find classroom resources to accompany many of these videos, check the following home pages:
A&E Television: www.aande.com
The History Channel: www.historychannel.com

HISTORY Online

Use our Web site for additional resources. All essential content is covered in the Student Edition.

You and your students can visit tarvol1.glencoe.com, the Web site companion to **The American Republic to 1877.** This innovative integration of electronic and print media offers your students a wealth of opportunities. The student text directs students to the Web site for the following options:

- **Chapter Overviews**
- **Self-Check Quizzes**
- **Student Web Activities**
- **Textbook Updates**

Answers to the student Web activities are provided for you in the **Web Activity Lesson Plans.** Additional Web resources and Interactive Tutor Puzzles are also available.

Chapter 3 Resources

SECTION RESOURCES

Daily Objectives	Reproducible Resources	Multimedia Resources
SECTION 1 **Early English Settlements** 1. Identify the crop that saved the people of Jamestown. 2. Explain how the colonists received political rights.	Reproducible Lesson Plan 3–1 Daily Lecture and Discussion Notes 3–1 Guided Reading Activity 3–1* Section Quiz 3–1* Reteaching Activity 3–1* Reading Essentials and Study Guide 3–1* Enrichment Activity 3–1	Daily Focus Skills Transparency 3–1 Interactive Tutor Self-Assessment CD-ROM ExamView® Pro Testmaker CD-ROM Presentation Plus! CD-ROM
SECTION 2 **New England Colonies** 1. Explain why the Pilgrims and the Puritans came to America. 2. Describe how the Connecticut, Rhode Island, and the New Hampshire colonies began.	Reproducible Lesson Plan 3–2 Daily Lecture and Discussion Notes 3–2 Guided Reading Activity 3–2* Section Quiz 3–2* Reteaching Activity 3–2* Reading Essentials and Study Guide 3–2* Enrichment Activity 3–2	Daily Focus Skills Transparency 3–2 Interactive Tutor Self-Assessment CD-ROM ExamView® Pro Testmaker CD-ROM Presentation Plus! CD-ROM
SECTION 3 **Middle Colonies** 1. Explain why the Middle Colonies had the most diverse populations in colonial America. 2. Identify America's first town planner.	Reproducible Lesson Plan 3–3 Daily Lecture and Discussion Notes 3–3 Guided Reading Activity 3–3* Section Quiz 3–3* Reteaching Activity 3–3* Reading Essentials and Study Guide 3–3* Enrichment Activity 3–3	Daily Focus Skills Transparency 3–3 Interactive Tutor Self-Assessment CD-ROM ExamView® Pro Testmaker CD-ROM Presentation Plus! CD-ROM
SECTION 4 **Southern Colonies** 1. Understand why the Southern Colonies were established. 2. Compare and contrast France's colony in North America with the English colonies.	Reproducible Lesson Plan 3–4 Daily Lecture and Discussion Notes 3–4 Guided Reading Activity 3–4* Section Quiz 3–4* Reteaching Activity 3–4* Reading Essentials and Study Guide 3–4* Enrichment Activity 3–4	Daily Focus Skills Transparency 3–4 Vocabulary PuzzleMaker CD-ROM Interactive Tutor Self-Assessment CD-ROM ExamView® Pro Testmaker CD-ROM Presentation Plus! CD-ROM

0:00 OUT OF TIME?
Assign the Chapter 3 **Reading Essentials and Study Guide.**

*Also Available in Spanish

 Blackline Master Transparency CD-ROM ● DVD

 Poster Music Program Audio Program Videocassette

KEY TO ABILITY LEVELS

Teaching strategies have been coded.

L1 BASIC activities for all students
L2 AVERAGE activities for average to above-average students
L3 CHALLENGING activities for above-average students
ELL ENGLISH LANGUAGE LEARNER activities

Block Schedule

Activities that are suited to use within the block scheduling framework are identified by:

NATIONAL GEOGRAPHIC Teacher's Corner

INDEX TO NATIONAL GEOGRAPHIC MAGAZINE

The following articles relate to this chapter.

- "Treasure from the Silver Bank," by Tracy Bowden, July 1996.
- "Portugal's Sea Road to the East," by Merle Severy, November 1992.

ADDITIONAL NATIONAL GEOGRAPHIC SOCIETY PRODUCTS

To order the following, call National Geographic at 1-800-368-2728:

- *GeoKit: Colonial America* (Kit)
- *Spain in the Americas* (Map)
- *Colonization and Trade in the Americas* (Map)
- *National Geographic Desk Reference* (Book)
- *Indians of North America* (Map)
- *American Indians: A Brief History* (Video)

NGS ONLINE

Access National Geographic's Web site for current events, atlas updates, activities, links, interactive features, and archives.

www.nationalgeographic.com

MEETING SPECIAL NEEDS

In addition to the Differentiated Instruction strategies found in each section, the following resources are also suitable for your special needs students:

- *ExamView® Pro Testmaker CD-ROM* allows teachers to tailor tests by reducing answer choices.
- The *Audio Program* includes the entire narrative of the student edition so that less-proficient readers can listen to the words as they read them.
- The *Reading Essentials and Study Guide* provides the same content as the student edition but is written two grade levels below the textbook.
- *Guided Reading Activities* give less-proficient readers point-by-point instructions to increase comprehension as they read each textbook section.
- *Enrichment Activities* includes a stimulating collection of readings and activities for gifted and talented students.

From the Classroom of...

Steve Burns
Colrain Middle School
Cincinnati, OH

Tracing Steps Toward Representative Government

Organize students into groups of four or five. Ask groups to use their textbooks to create an outline that will list chronologically places, events, individuals or groups, documents, and governing bodies linked to the development of representative types of government. Write the following partial outline on the board as an example:

I. Jamestown 1607
   A. Businesspeople
      1. Captain John Smith served as leader in beginning years.
      2. John Rolfe developed less bitter tobacco.
   B. The House of Burgesses
      1. First assembly of elected lawmakers in colonial America.
      2. People had a say in making their own laws.
II. Plymouth
III. Connecticut

Groups should take turns going to a map at the front of the room and pointing to key locations as they explain facts pertaining to that place.

ADDITIONAL RESOURCES FROM GLENCOE

- American Music: Cultural Traditions
- American Art and Architecture
- Outline Map Resource Book
- U.S. Desk Map
- Building Geography Skills for Life
- Inclusion for the Middle School Social Studies Classroom Strategies and Activities
- Teaching Strategies for the American History Classroom (Including Block Scheduling Pacing Guides)
- American Crafts Hands-On Activities
- American Games Hands-On Activities
- American History Flash Cards

✓ *Performance Assessment*

Refer to Activity 3 in the Performance Assessment Activities and Rubrics booklet. 📦

Why It Matters Activity

Encourage students to predict the consequences of establishing English colonies in North America. Do they think the colonists achieved their differing objectives? How do they think the new American society emerged? Students should verify or modify their predictions upon completion of the chapter.

GLENCOE
TECHNOLOGY

The American Republic to 1877 Video Program

To learn more about the settlements and lives of the first colonists, have students view the Chapter 3 video "The Lost Colony" from **The American Republic to 1877 Video Program.**

 Available in DVD and VHS

MindJogger Videoquiz

Use **MindJogger Videoquiz** to preview the Chapter 3 content.

 Available in VHS

CHAPTER
3
Colonial America
1587–1770

Why It Matters

The early North American colonies were a meeting place of cultures. The Europeans who settled these colonies included Protestants, Catholics, and Jews.

The Impact Today

The colonies influenced values and beliefs many Americans cherish today. For example:
• *Many people still come to the Americas in search of economic opportunity and religious freedom.*
• *Representative government remains an important part of the American political system.*

 The American Republic to 1877 *Video* The chapter 3 video, "The Lost Colony," examines the colony of Roanoke and how conditions were much harsher than settlers were led to believe.

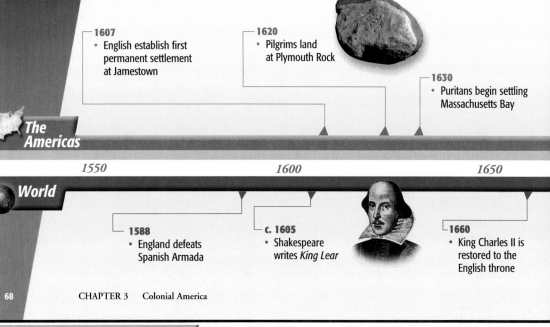

The Americas

1607
• English establish first permanent settlement at Jamestown

1620
• Pilgrims land at Plymouth Rock

1630
• Puritans begin settling Massachusetts Bay

1550   1600   1650

World

1588
• England defeats Spanish Armada

c. 1605
• Shakespeare writes *King Lear*

1660
• King Charles II is restored to the English throne

68   CHAPTER 3   Colonial America

📖 Reading Strategy **PURPOSE FOR READING**

Venn diagrams are a way for students to compare and/or contrast two or more items. Explain to the students that the overlapping circles in a Venn diagram are for recording similarities; information about differences belongs in the rest of the diagram. Colonists from Europe settled North America seeking profit and economic, religious, or political freedom. They brought African slaves and displaced Native Americans who were already on the land. Have each student make a Venn diagram comparing the values and beliefs of the colonists and Native Americans. **L1**

Pilgrims Going to Church by George Boughton George Boughton painted many scenes about American colonial life.

FOLDABLES™
Study Organizer

Comparison Study Foldable When you group facts into categories, it is easier to make comparisons. Make this foldable to compare and contrast the 13 colonies and their regions.

Step 1 Collect 7 sheets of paper and place them about ½ inch apart.

> Keep the edges straight.

Step 2 Fold up the bottom edges of the paper to form 14 tabs.

> This makes all tabs the same size.

Step 3 When all the tabs are the same size, crease the paper to hold the tabs in place and staple the sheets together. Label each tab with the name of a colony and color-code each region.

The Thirteen Colonies

Massachusetts	Northern
New Hampshire	
Rhode Island	
Connecticut	
New York	Middle
Delaware	
New Jersey	
Pennsylvania	
Virginia	Southern
Maryland	
North Carolina	
South Carolina	
Georgia	

> Staple together along the fold.

Reading and Writing As you read, write what you learn about each of the 13 colonies under each tab and compare the colonies.

FOLDABLES™
Study Organizer
Dinah Zike's Foldables

Purpose Students make and use a foldable to evaluate the similarities and differences among the thirteen American colonies. Students are asked to practice several social studies skills including categorizing the colonies into three groups (Northern, Middle, and Southern Colonies), identifying main ideas and facts found in the chapter, and comparing and contrasting the information they find.

📂 Have students complete **Reading and Study Skills Foldables** Activity 3. **L1**

HISTORY
Online

Introduce students to chapter content and key terms by having them access **Chapter Overview 3** at tarvol1.glencoe.com

TIME LINE
ACTIVITY

As students read the chapter, have them review the time line on pages 68–69. Have students offer one possible reason that a number of English colonies were established or attempted after the defeat of the Spanish Armada.

1675
• King Philip's War begins

1718
• French establish port of New Orleans

1763
• British tighten enforcement of Navigation Acts

1769
• Mission of San Diego founded

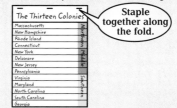

1700   *1750*

1670
• Alafin Ajagbo founds Oyo Empire in Nigeria

1702
• England and France go to war

HISTORY
Online

Chapter Overview
Visit tarvol1.glencoe.com and click on **Chapter 3— Chapter Overviews** to preview chapter information.

More About the Art

George Boughton was born in 1833 in England. His family moved to the United States in 1839 and made their home in Albany, New York. Boughton learned to paint and sketch and traveled to London and Paris to further his studies. When he returned to the United States, he became famous for his landscape paintings. Boughton's works are known for their simplicity and subdued colors. Many of Boughton's paintings focus on Puritan life in New England and peasant life in France.

1 FOCUS

Section Overview
This section examines why the Jamestown settlement was established and how it survived.

Reading Preview

Answers to Graphic: Economy: no profit from discovery of gold or silver; raised tobacco; Virginia Company encountered financial troubles in 1620s; Government: at first military-type rule, then representation by elected men called burgesses; in 1624 King James took control

Preteaching Vocabulary
Point out that the term *burgess* comes from an Old French word meaning "freeman of a town."

Guide to Reading

Main Idea
Jamestown became the first successfully established English colony in North America.

Key Terms
charter, joint-stock company, burgesses

Reading Strategy
Organizing Information As you read Section 1, re-create the diagram below and describe the economy and government of Jamestown.

Jamestown	Description
Economy	
Government	

Read to Learn
- what crop saved the people of Jamestown.
- how the colonists received political rights.

Section Theme
Economic Factors Many settlers journeyed to America with the hope of making a fortune.

Preview of Events

1580	1590	1600	1610	1620

1583
Sir Humphrey Gilbert claims Newfoundland for Queen Elizabeth

c. 1590
Settlers of Roanoke Island vanish

1607
Colonists settle at Jamestown

1619
House of Burgesses meets in Jamestown

English soldier's helmet, Jamestown

A European Story

In the summer of 1588, Spanish warships sailed toward the coast of England. King Philip II of Spain had sent the armada, or war fleet, of 132 ships to invade England. With 30,000 troops and 2,400 guns, the Spanish Armada was the mightiest naval force the world had ever seen. Yet the smaller, swifter English ships won the battle. The Spanish Armada fled north to Scotland, where violent storms destroyed and scattered the fleet. Only about one-half of the Spanish ships straggled home.

England in America

England and Spain had been heading toward war for years. Trading rivalry and religious differences divided the two countries. King Philip II, who ruled Spain from 1556 to 1598, was a powerful monarch and a strong defender of the Catholic faith. He wanted to put a Catholic ruler on the throne of England and bring the country back to the Catholic Church. King Philip did not consider Queen Elizabeth, a Protestant, the rightful ruler of England.

SECTION RESOURCES

Attacks on Spanish ships and ports by such English adventurers as **Sir Francis Drake** angered Philip. He thought that Queen Elizabeth should punish Drake for his raids. Instead, she honored Drake with a knighthood. Philip sent the Spanish Armada to conquer England— but it failed completely.

Although war between England and Spain continued until 1604, the defeat of the armada marked the end of Spanish control of the seas. Now the way was clear for England and other nations to start colonies in North America.

The Lost Colony of Roanoke

The English had made several attempts to establish a base on the other side of the Atlantic before their victory over Spain. In 1583 **Sir Humphrey Gilbert** claimed Newfoundland for Queen Elizabeth. Then he sailed south along the coast looking for a place to establish a colony. Before finding a site, he died at sea.

The following year, Queen Elizabeth gave **Sir Walter Raleigh** the right to claim land in North America. Raleigh sent an expedition to look for a good place to settle. His scouts returned with an enthusiastic report of **Roanoke Island,** off the coast of present-day North Carolina.

In 1585 Raleigh sent about 100 men to settle on Roanoke Island. After a difficult winter on the island, the unhappy colonists decided to return to England. In 1587 Raleigh tried again, sending 91 men, 17 women, and 9 children to Roanoke. **John White,** a mapmaker and artist, led the group. Shortly after arriving on the island, White's daughter gave birth. This baby, named Virginia Dare, was the first English child born in North America. White explored the area and drew pictures of what he saw. He and other explorers described the towns of the Native Americans who lived in the area:

❝Their towns are small and few . . . a village may contain but ten or twelve houses—some perhaps as many as twenty. . . . ❞

The new settlers began building a colony. They needed many supplies, however, and White sailed to England for the supplies and to recruit more settlers. Although he had hoped to be back within a few months, the war with Spain delayed his return for nearly three years.

When White finally returned to Roanoke, he found it deserted. The only clue to the fate of the settlers was the word *Croatoan* carved on a gatepost. White thought the colonists must have gone to Croatoan Island, about 50 miles to the south. Bad weather kept White from investigating. The Roanoke colonists were never seen again.

✓ Reading Check **Describing** Why did Raleigh choose Roanoke as the site for the colony?

Jamestown Settlement

Roanoke was Sir Walter Raleigh's last attempt to establish a colony. For a time his failure discouraged others from planning English colonies in North America. However, the idea emerged again in 1606. Several groups of merchants sought charters, the right to organize settlements in an area, from King James I.

The Virginia Company

One group of merchants, the Virginia Company of London, received a charter to "make habitation . . . into that part of America, commonly called Virginia." The Virginia Company was a joint-stock company. Investors bought stock, or part ownership, in the company in return for a share of its future profits.

The company acted quickly. In December 1606, it sent 144 settlers in 3 ships to build a new colony in North America. The settlers were supposed to look for gold and attempt to establish trade in fish and furs. Forty of them died during the voyage.

In April 1607, the ships entered **Chesapeake Bay** and then sailed up a river flowing into the bay. The colonists named the river the James and their new settlement **Jamestown** to honor their king. The settlers built Jamestown on a peninsula so they could defend it from attack. The site had major drawbacks, however. The swampy land swarmed with mosquitoes that carried disease. Jamestown also lacked good farmland.

CHAPTER 3   Colonial America   **71**

Identifying Contributions Have students name ways in which Jamestown left its mark on American society. *(Responses should include: established the English as colonists in America, introduced tobacco as a money-making activity, and established representative government.)* **L1**

✓ Reading Check

Answer: Scouts sent to the area by Sir Walter Raleigh returned with an enthusiastic report.

Reading Strategy ▶ **READING THE TEXT**

Brainstorming Organize students into several groups. Have students list what they know about the lost colony of Roanoke. Then, have students brainstorm possible outcomes to the colonists. Have each student write a paragraph explaining which outcome seems most likely to them. Students should include supporting evidence for their theory. **L2**

Guided Reading Activity 3–1

Name _____ Date _____ Class _____

★ **Guided Reading Activity 3-1**

DIRECTIONS: Outlining Locate the heading in your textbook. Then use the information under the heading to help you write each answer. Use another sheet of paper if necessary.

I. England in America
  A. Introduction
    1. What were the two major reasons for the conflict between England and Spain? _____
    2. What marked the end of the Spanish control of the seas? _____
  B. The Lost Colony of Roanoke—Who did Queen Elizabeth give the right to claim any land in North America not already owned by a Christian monarch? _____
  C. Roanoke Settlements—Why did both attempts to settle Roanoke fail? _____

Geography *Skills*

Answers:
1. Plymouth
2. Powhatan, Tuscarora

---

3 ASSESS

Assign Section 1 Assessment as homework or as an in-class activity.

🖱 Have students use **Interactive Tutor Self-Assessment CD-ROM.**

L2

Section Quiz 3–1

Name _____ Date _____ Class _____

★ **Chapter 3**   Score ☐

Section Quiz 3-1

DIRECTIONS: Matching Match the items in Column A with the items in Column B. Write the correct letters in the blanks. *(10 points each)*

Column A	Column B
___ 1. English raider of Spanish ships	**A.** Jamestown
___ 2. Sir Walter Raleigh's settlement	**B.** Captain John Smith
___ 3. settlement named after the king	**C.** Roanoke
___ 4. leader of Jamestown	**D.** John Rolfe
___ 5. husband of Pocahontas	**E.** Francis Drake

DIRECTIONS: Multiple Choice In the blank at the left, write the letter of the choice that best completes the statement or answers the question. *(10 points each)*

___ 6. What cleared the way for England to start colonies in North America?
  A. Drake's raids on Spain   C. defeat of the Spanish Armada
  B. Drake's knighthood   D. England declared war on Spain

___ 7. Which of the following is an example of a joint-stock company?
  A. the Roanoke Company   C. the Drake Company
  B. the England Company   D. the Virginia Company

___ 8. The Jamestown colonists called the winter of 1609-1610
  A. the lavish time.   C. the good time.
  B. the starving time.   D. the friendly time.

___ 9. Which crop saved Jamestown?
  A. tobacco   C. rice
  B. corn   D. indigo

___ 10. The first African American child born in the American colonies was
  A. James Yeardley.   C. William Tucker.
  B. John Rolfe.   D. John Smith.

NATIONAL GEOGRAPHIC

The First English Settlements

Plymouth, 1620
Adults 70%
Children 30%

MASSACHUSETTS
Plymouth • Cape Cod
Wampanoag
Narraganset

Susquehanna
Leni-Lenape

ATLANTIC OCEAN

Jamestown, 1607
Adults 96%
Children 4%

APPALACHIAN MOUNTAINS
Hudson River
Delaware River
Potomac R.
James R.
Roanoke R.

VIRGINIA
Nanticoke
Powhatan
Chesapeake Bay
Jamestown • 1607
1585, 1587
Tuscarora
Roanoke Island

0 100 miles
0 100 kilometers
Lambert Equal-Area projection

N E S W

Geography *Skills*

Many Native American groups lived near the first English settlements in the late 1500s and early 1600s.
1. **Location** Which colony was located farthest north?
2. **Location** Which Native American groups lived nearest to the Jamestown colonists?

The colonists faced more hardships over the next several months. Many of them were not accustomed to hard labor. Because the London investors expected a quick profit from their colony, the settlers searched for gold and silver when they should have been growing food. In addition, disease and hunger took a huge toll on the colonists. By spring 1608, when ships arrived with supplies and more settlers, only 38 of the Jamestown colonists remained alive.

Captain John Smith

Governing Jamestown was perhaps the biggest obstacle the colonists faced. The colony survived its first two years because of 27-year-old **Captain John Smith,** an experienced soldier and explorer. Smith forced the settlers to work,

---

explored the area, and managed to get corn from the local Native Americans led by Chief Powhatan. In August 1609, 400 new settlers arrived. Two months later, John Smith returned to England. Without strong leadership, the colony could not feed so many people. The winter of 1609–1610 became known as "the starving time." Fighting broke out with the Native Americans. When more settlers arrived in the spring they found only 60 survivors.

💲Economics

Farming the Land

Although the Virginia colonists did not find any gold or silver, they did discover another way to make money for the investors. One colonist, **John Rolfe,** learned to grow a type of tobacco using seeds from the West Indies. The first crop was sold in England in 1614. Soon planters all along the James River were raising tobacco, and the colony of Virginia began to prosper and grow. Relations with the Native Americans also improved after Rolfe married **Pocahontas,** the daughter of Chief Powhatan.

In 1614 some of the colonists were allowed to rent plots of land. Most of what they grew on their plots was their own. This move toward private ownership encouraged the colonists to grow food crops to sell—and work harder. One of the colonists explained that the colonists often avoided work when

❝our people were fed out of the common store, and labored jointly together.❞

Now that the colonists could farm their own land and operate for profit in a competitive system, they made greater efforts to succeed.

Pocahontas

DIFFERENTIATED INSTRUCTION

Reading Support Give students the following information:

Population of Jamestown, 1619–1624

Year	Number of People Arriving	Total Population
1619	–	1,000
1620	100 (est.)	866
1621	1,051	843
1624	4,000	1,277

Have students figure the number of deaths between 1619 and 1620, between 1620 and 1621, and so on. *(234; 1,074; 3,566)* **L1**

Private land ownership was expanded in 1618. All the colonists who had paid their own way to America were granted 100 acres of land. In order to attract more colonists, the company gave a land grant called a **headright** of 50 acres to those who paid their own way. A settler also received 50 acres for each family member over 15 years of age and for each servant brought to Virginia. This system convinced thousands of people to move to Virginia.

🏛 Citizenship
Representative Government

At first nearly all of Jamestown's settlers were men. They worked for the Virginia Company and lived under strict rules. As the colony grew, the settlers complained about taking orders from the Virginia Company in London. In 1619 the company agreed to let the colonists have some say in their government. Ten towns in the colony each sent two representatives called burgesses to an assembly. The assembly had the right to make local laws for the colony. On July 30, 1619, the **House of Burgesses** met for the first time in a church in Jamestown.

New Arrivals in Jamestown

In 1619 the Virginia Company sent 90 women to Jamestown. As a company report noted: "The plantation can never flourish till families be planted, and the respect of wives and children fix the people on the soil." Colonists who wanted to marry one of the women had to pay a fee of 120 pounds of tobacco. Men still outnumbered women in the colony, but marriage and children became a part of life in Virginia.

A Dutch ship brought another group of newcomers to Jamestown in 1619—twenty Africans who were sold to Virginia planters to labor in the tobacco fields. These first Africans may have come as servants—engaged to work for a set period of time—rather than as slaves.

Until about 1640 some African laborers in Jamestown were free and even owned property. William Tucker, the first African American born in the American colonies, was a free man. In the years to follow, however, many more shiploads of Africans would arrive in North America, and those unwilling passengers would be sold as slaves. Slavery was first recognized in Virginia law in the 1660s.

In the early 1620s, the Virginia Company faced financial troubles. The company had poured all its money into Jamestown, but little profit was returned. The colony also suffered an attack by the Native Americans. In 1624 King James canceled the company's charter and made Jamestown the first royal colony for England in America.

✓**Reading Check** **Analyzing** Why was the House of Burgesses important?

SECTION 1 ASSESSMENT

Checking for Understanding

1. **Key Terms** Write a short paragraph in which you use the following key terms: charter, burgesses, joint-stock company.

2. **Reviewing Facts** Why did the Virginia Company establish settlements in North America?

Reviewing Themes

3. **Economic Factors** What economic activity helped save the Jamestown settlement?

Critical Thinking

4. **Making Inferences** Why do you think the king of England was willing to let a group of merchants try to establish a colony in North America?

5. **Determining Cause and Effect** Re-create the diagram below and list two effects of Jamestown's growth.

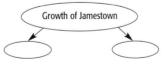

Growth of Jamestown

Analyzing Visuals

6. **Geography Skills** Study the map and graphs on page 72. What percentage of settlers in Plymouth were children?

Interdisciplinary Activity

Geography Create a poster that might have attracted early colonists to the area where you live. Focus on the location as well as natural features in your area such as good farmland, forests, waterways, and mineral resources.

✓**Reading Check**

Answer: The House of Burgesses gave Virginia settlers a voice in the government and allowed them to participate in making the laws.

L1

Reteaching Activity 3–1

L1, ELL

Reading Essentials and Study Guide 3–1

L3

Enrichment Activity 3–1

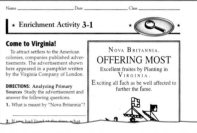

4 CLOSE

Have each student list five important facts from the section.

SECTION 1 ASSESSMENT ANSWERS

1. Student work should reflect correct use of terms.
2. Answers may include: originally they wanted to search for gold and trade in fish and furs.
3. growing tobacco
4. Answers should indicate that the king wanted both the political power of ruling overseas colonies and economic rewards, without risking his nation's resources on the venture.
5. Colonist demand created representative government; demand for labor led to slavery.
6. 30 percent

Interdisciplinary Activity Posters should show that students have an understanding of the geographic conditions in their area, including natural resources.

FOOTHOLD IN THE NEW WORLD

JAMESTOWN: THE FIRST PERMANENT ENGLISH COLONY In the spring of 1607, three ships carrying more than a hundred English settlers sailed into the Chesapeake Bay to establish a colony and find gold. The settlers built a fort on a marshy island in the James River and named it in honor of King James I.

THE EXPEDITIONS

Captain John Smith emerged as a leader of the group. An avid explorer, he led four expeditions in the area:

- Shortly after arriving, he and Captain Christopher Newport sailed up the James River to search for gold. Powhatan's followers made them turn back at the falls.

- In December 1607 Smith and a small band of settlers set out looking for gold and food along the Chickahominy River. According to Smith, he was captured and about to be clubbed to death by Powhatan's followers when Pocahontas (the chief's daughter) saved him.

- In 1608 Smith headed up two voyages to explore the northern reaches of Chesapeake Bay. He searched futilely for gold and an outlet to the Pacific Ocean.

THE SETTLEMENT

The colonists endured many terrible hardships. Bad water, disease, starvation, and conflict with the Native Americans took a heavy toll. By early 1608 only 38 hardy souls remained alive.

Settlers learned to grow crops in the new land. When tobacco from the West Indies was introduced, it became a commercial success and guaranteed Jamestown's future.

LEARNING from GEOGRAPHY

1. Compare the dwellings of the colonists and the Native Americans.

2. How did the introduction of tobacco affect the development of the colony?

74

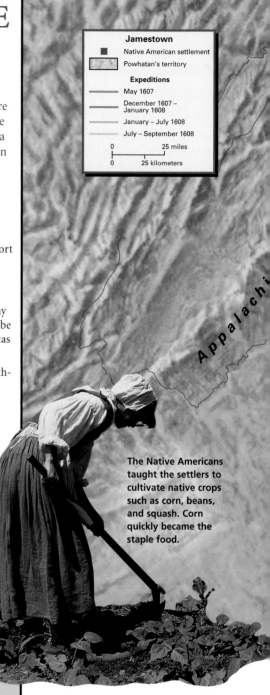

Jamestown
- Native American settlement
- Powhatan's territory

Expeditions
- May 1607
- December 1607 – January 1608
- January – July 1608
- July – September 1608

0   25 miles
0   25 kilometers

The Native Americans taught the settlers to cultivate native crops such as corn, beans, and squash. Corn quickly became the staple food.

EXTENDING THE CONTENT

Pocahontas The marriage of Pocahontas to John Rolfe in 1614 was followed by eight years of peace between the Native Americans and the English. When the Rolfes went to England, Pocahontas was received with royal honor by King James I and Queen Anne. When Pocahontas died of smallpox in 1617, Thomas Rolfe, her young son, was educated in England. Upon Thomas's return to Virginia, he became an important settler. Today many prominent Virginians claim to be his descendants.

The Native Americans lived in houses made of bent branches covered with woven reed mats.

The first English settlers constructed simple timber-frame houses with mud walls and thatched roofs.

■ Sasquesahannock

■ Tockwough

Delaware Bay

Mountains

Potomac River

Pamunkey River

Toppahannock ■

Wighcocomoco ■

Chickahominy River

Powhatan
May 1607

Arrohatoc ■

Waenoc ■

Werowocomo ■

Chickahominy
December 1607

Jamestown
May 1607

James River

Accomac ■

Chesapeake Bay

ATLANTIC OCEAN

Nansemond
September 1608

Albermarle Sound

NORTH
AMERICA

Area
enlarged

● Jamestown
May 1607

Atlantic
Ocean

England
December 1606

EUROPE

Canary
Islands

AFRICA

0   1000 miles
0   1000 kilometers

75

3 ASSESS

Have students answer the **Learning from Geography** questions.

4 CLOSE

Have students discuss the threats to Jamestown's survival and ultimately what helped it survive. Have students discuss how the Powhatans both threatened and aided the colonists' survival. Would students have expected the colonists to survive without Pocahontas's intervention? (*Powhatans turned Smith back on his first trip, captured him on his second, and would have clubbed him to death had Pocahontas not intervened. Later they taught the settlers to grow food. Students may speculate that had Pocahontas not prevented Smith's execution, the settlers would not have made friends with the Powhatans and would not have survived without their help.*)

NGS ONLINE

Answers to Learning from Geography

1. Both the settlers and the Native Americans had small, simple homes made from abundant natural materials. Settlers' homes had timber frames with mud walls and thatched roofs, whereas Native Americans constructed their homes of bent branches covered with reed mats.

2. It gave the colony a cash crop, made the colony commercially successful, and guaranteed its future.

1 FOCUS

Section Overview
This section describes why Puritan and Pilgrim colonists settled in New England.

BELLRINGER
Skillbuilder Activity

Project transparency and have students answer the question.

Daily Focus Skills Transparency 3–2

Reading Preview

Answers to Graphic: Massachusetts: religious freedom, better life; Connecticut: better farmland, dissatisfaction with Puritan leaders; Rhode Island: Roger Williams forced out of Massachusetts due to his belief in the separation of church and state

Preteaching Vocabulary
Introduce the terms *Puritan, Separatist,* and *Pilgrim* and ask students to use each term correctly in a sentence.

SECTION 2 New England Colonies

Guide to Reading

Main Idea
Settlers begin to form the New England Colonies.

Key Terms
dissent, persecute, Puritan, Separatist, Pilgrim, Mayflower Compact, toleration

Reading Strategy
Classifying Information As you read Section 2, re-create the diagram below and explain why different colonies in New England were settled.

Colony	Reasons the colony was settled
Massachusetts	
Connecticut	
Rhode Island	

Read to Learn
- why the Pilgrims and the Puritans came to America.
- how the Connecticut, Rhode Island, and New Hampshire colonies began.

Section Theme
Civic Rights and Responsibilities Puritan and Pilgrim colonists settled in America in search of religious freedom.

Preview of Events

♦ 1620	♦ 1630	♦ 1640

1620
Pilgrims land at Plymouth

1630
Puritans settle the Massachusetts Bay Colony

1636
Thomas Hooker founds Hartford

1638
Anne Hutchinson founds Portsmouth

Shoes, Plymouth Colony

★ AN ★ American Story

The young man looked around at the other passengers aboard the *Mayflower.* He and the other passengers sailed to the new world not knowing what they would find. They had muskets but knew little about shooting. They planned to fish but knew nothing about fishing. They had hoped to settle in Virginia but instead landed in New England without enough supplies to last the winter. The only thing these people had plenty of was courage. They would need it.

Religious Freedom

Unlike the Jamestown settlers, the next wave of colonists would arrive in search of religious freedom. England had been a Protestant country since 1534, when King Henry VIII broke away from the Roman Catholic Church and formed the Anglican Church. Not everyone in England was happy with the new church, however. Many people dissented—they disagreed with the beliefs or practices of the Anglicans. English Catholics, for example, still considered the pope the head of the church, and they were often persecuted, or treated harshly, for that reason.

76   CHAPTER 3   Colonial America

SECTION RESOURCES

📁 **Reproducible Masters**
- Reproducible Lesson Plan 3–2
- Daily Lecture and Discussion Notes 3–2
- Guided Reading Activity 3–2
- Section Quiz 3–2
- Reteaching Activity 3–2
- Reading Essentials and Study Guide 3–2
- Enrichment Activity 3–2

💧 **Transparencies**
- Daily Focus Skills Transparency 3–2

Multimedia
- 💿 Interactive Tutor Self-Assessment CD-ROM
- 💿 ExamView® Pro Testmaker CD-ROM
- 💿 Presentation Plus! CD-ROM

At the same time, some Protestants wanted to change—or reform—the Anglican Church, while others wanted to break away from it altogether. The Protestants who wanted to reform the Anglican Church were called Puritans. Those who wanted to leave and set up their own churches were known as Separatists.

The Separatists were persecuted in England, and some fled to the Netherlands. Though they found religious freedom there, the Separatists had difficulty finding work. They also worried that their children were losing their religious values and their English way of life.

The Pilgrims' Journey

Some Separatists in the Netherlands made an arrangement with the Virginia Company. The Separatists could settle in Virginia and practice their religion freely. In return they would give the company a share of any profits they made.

The Separatists considered themselves Pilgrims because their journey had a religious purpose. Only 35 of the 102 passengers who boarded the *Mayflower* in September 1620 were Pilgrims. The others were called "strangers." They were common people—servants, craftspeople, and poor farmers—who hoped to find a better life in America. Because Pilgrim beliefs shaped life in the Plymouth colony, however, all the early settlers are usually called Pilgrims.

The Mayflower Compact

The *Mayflower*'s passengers planned to settle in the Virginia colony. The first land they sighted was **Cape Cod,** well north of their target. Because it was November and winter was fast approaching, the colonists decided to drop anchor in Cape Cod Bay. They went ashore on a cold, bleak day in December at a place called Plymouth. **William Bradford,** their leader and historian, reported that "all things stared upon them with a weather-beaten face."

Plymouth was outside the territory of the Virginia Company and its laws. Before going ashore, the Pilgrims drew up a formal document called the Mayflower Compact. The compact pledged their loyalty to England and declared their intention of forming "a civil body politic, for our better

NATIONAL GEOGRAPHIC **The New England Colonies**

Area claimed by New York and New Hampshire

MAINE (part of Mass.)

Connecticut R.

NEW HAMPSHIRE • Portsmouth

MASSACHUSETTS • Salem
• Boston
• Plymouth

CONNECTICUT

• Newport

New Haven

RHODE ISLAND

ATLANTIC OCEAN

44°N

40°N

68°W

0   100 miles
0   100 kilometers
Lambert Equal-Area projection

Products

Grain	Fish	Ships
Cattle	Whales	Iron
Lumber	Furs	Rum

Geography *Skills*

The Atlantic waters and thick forests proved valuable for fishing and shipbuilding in New England.
1. **Region** What were the four New England Colonies?
2. **Analyzing Information** What did Connecticut produce?

ordering and preservation." The signers also promised to obey the laws passed "for the general good of the colony." The Mayflower Compact was a necessary step in the development of representative government in America.

📖 *(See page 612 of the Appendix for the entire text of the Mayflower Compact.)*

Help From the Native Americans

Their first winter in America, almost half the Pilgrims died of malnutrition, disease, and

2 TEACH

Daily Lecture and Discussion Notes 3–2

Copyright © by The McGraw-Hill Companies, Inc.

Daily Lecture and Discussion Notes

Chapter 3, Section 2

Did You Know Today in the city of Cape Cod, the Massachusetts House of Representatives deliberates under a giant carved wooden codfish whose head points at whichever party is in power—the Democratic or the Republican.

I. Religious Freedom *(Pages 76–78)*

A. There were two groups of Protestants in England. Those who wanted to reform the Anglican Church were Puritans. Those who wanted to leave and set up their own church were Separatists.

B. Some Separatists fled to the Netherlands for religious freedom. Some of these Separatists were given a guarantee by the Virginia Company to be able to practice their religion freely if they settled in Virginia. In return they had to share their profits

Reading Strategy

Identifying Steps to a Representative Government
Three important steps on the road to a representative government are discussed in the section. Have students identify them and briefly describe them. (*Mayflower Compact: agreement to form own government; creation of colonial legislature: gave Massachusetts Bay settlers a role in government; Fundamental Orders of Connecticut: first written constitution in America*) **L1,** ELL

Geography *Skills*

Answers:
1. Rhode Island, Connecticut, Massachusetts, New Hampshire
2. grain, cattle, ships, iron, rum

Geography Skills Practice
Ask: Which area that is now a state was a part of the colony of Massachusetts? *(Maine)*

Reading Strategy   **READING THE TEXT**

Reading Maps, Graphs, and Charts Have students work together to make a large map of the settlements in the New England Colonies. Some students should draw the map; others should make tags giving pertinent information about founders and reasons for settlement. Other students should use library resources to find the names of settlements not mentioned in the text. Save the map to use for comparing with the Middle and Southern Colonies. **L1** 📁

📂 Use the rubric for making a map on pages 44–45 in the ***Performance Assessment Activities and Rubrics.***

L1, ELL

Guided Reading Activity 3–2

Name _____ Date _____ Class _____

★ **Guided Reading Activity 3-2**

DIRECTIONS: Recalling the Facts Use the information in your textbook to answer the questions. Use another sheet of paper if necessary.

1. What were many of the settlers of New England seeking? _____
2. How did the Puritans differ from the Separatists? _____
3. Why were all the early settlers called Pilgrims? _____
4. What formal document was drawn up to maintain order in the Plymouth colony? _____
5. Who were Squanto and Samoset? _____
6. What lifesaving skills did Native Americans teach the Pilgrims? _____

✓ Reading Check

Answer: It was a necessary step in the establishment of a democracy as Pilgrims pledged to form a government and obey laws that were passed.

MORE ABOUT...

Sarah Josepha Hale, a magazine editor, wrote editorials in *Boston Ladies' Magazine* and *Godey's Lady Book,* supporting the movement to make Thanksgiving a national holiday. After 40 years of editorials and letters to governors and presidents, Hale's efforts were recognized. In 1863 President Abraham Lincoln proclaimed the last Thursday in November as a national day of Thanksgiving. In 1941 Congress officially approved Thanksgiving as a legal holiday on the fourth Thursday in November. **Ask: Why do you think the Pilgrims included Native American guests at their feast?** *(Without their help, the Pilgrims would have died.)*

MORE ABOUT...

The First Thanksgiving

In the autumn of 1621 the Pilgrims invited the Native Americans to celebrate the peace between them. After the struggle through the first winter, the Pilgrims also felt relieved to be raising food. During the feast the Pilgrims thanked God for the harvest and for their survival.

First Thanksgiving by Jennie A. Brownscombe

Who took part? About 50 men, women, and children colonists and 90 Wampanoag Native Americans took part in the three-day feast.

What did they do? Dancing, singing, and playing games were part of the celebration. The Wampanoag demonstrated their skills with the bow and arrow.

When was it held? Exactly when the festival took place is uncertain, but it is believed the celebration occurred sometime between September 21 and November 9.

What did they eat? They most likely ate wild fowl, duck, and turkey shot by the colonists and deer provided by the Wampanoag.

cold. In the spring a few Native Americans approached the settlement. Two of them, **Squanto** and **Samoset,** befriended the colonists. Squanto was a Pawtuxet who had been kidnapped to Europe and had learned English.

Squanto and Samoset showed the Pilgrims how to grow corn, beans, and pumpkins and where to hunt and fish. Without their help the Pilgrims might not have survived. Squanto and Samoset also helped the Pilgrims make a treaty with the Wampanoag people who lived in the area. **Massasoit,** a Wampanoag leader, signed a treaty with the Pilgrims in March 1621, and the two groups lived in harmony.

✓ Reading Check **Summarizing** Why was the Mayflower Compact an important step toward representative government?

New Settlements

In 1625 the English throne passed to Charles I. Charles objected to the Puritans' calls for reform in the Anglican Church, and persecution of Puritans increased again. Some Puritans looked for a way to leave England.

In 1629 a group of Puritans formed the Massachusetts Bay Company and received a royal charter to establish a colony north of Plymouth. This was the Puritans' chance to create a new society in America—a society based on the Bible.

The company chose a well-educated Puritan named **John Winthrop** to be the colony's governor. In 1630 Winthrop led about 900 men, women, and children to **Massachusetts Bay.** Most of them settled in a place they called Boston.

DIFFERENTIATED INSTRUCTION

Reading Support Have students use library resources to find out how to make a colonial craft of their choice. Possibilities include decorative work such as quilling and silhouette making; toys such as tops, whirligigs, kites, and rag or corn husk dolls; and items such as gourd rattles and bowls, corn husk hot pads, mats, and baskets. **L2, ELL**

📁 Refer to *Inclusion for the Middle School Social Studies Classroom Strategies and Activities* in the TCR.

Citizenship

Growth and Government

During the 1630s, more than 15,000 Puritans journeyed to Massachusetts to escape religious persecution and economic hard times in England. This movement of people became known as the **Great Migration.**

At first, John Winthrop and his assistants made the colony's laws. They were chosen by the General Court, which was made up of the colony's stockholders. In 1634, settlers demanded a larger role in the government. The General Court became an elected assembly. Adult male church members were allowed to vote for the governor and for their town's representatives to the General Court. In later years, they also had to own property to vote.

The Puritans came to America to put their religious beliefs into practice. The Puritans had little toleration—they criticized or persecuted people who held other religious views. This lack of toleration led to the creation of new colonies.

Connecticut and Rhode Island

The fertile Connecticut River valley, south of Massachusetts, was much better for farming than was the stony soil around Boston. In the 1630s colonists began to settle in this area.

A minister named Thomas Hooker became dissatisfied with Massachusetts. He did not like the way that Winthrop and the other Puritan leaders ran the colony. In 1636 Hooker led his congregation through the wilderness to Connecticut, where he founded the town of **Hartford.** Three years later Hartford and two other towns, Windsor and Wethersfield, agreed to form a colony. They adopted a plan of government called the **Fundamental Orders of Connecticut.** This was the first written constitution in America, and it described the organization of representative government in detail.

Good land drew colonists to Connecticut, but Rhode Island was settled by colonists who were forced out of Massachusetts. The first of these was **Roger Williams,** a minister. Williams felt that people should not be persecuted for their religious practices. In his view the government should not force people to worship in a certain way. Williams also believed it was wrong for settlers to take land away from the Native Americans.

The ideas of Roger Williams caused Massachusetts leaders to banish him in 1635. He took refuge with the Narraganset people, who later

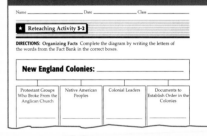

People In History

Anne Hutchinson organized meetings among Boston women, which community leaders later attended. She believed God could speak to people directly. This challenged the Puritan view that God spoke only through the Bible. **Ask:** Why was Hutchinson forced to leave Massachusetts? *(She questioned the religious authority of the colony's ministers.)*

3 ASSESS

Assign Section 2 Assessment as homework or as an in-class activity.

● Have students use **Interactive Tutor Self-Assessment CD-ROM.**

L2

Section Quiz 3–2

Reteaching Activity 3–2

People In History

Anne Hutchinson 1591–1643

Anne Hutchinson came to Massachusetts with her husband in 1634. She began questioning the religious authority of the colony's ministers.

As Hutchinson gained followers, she was seen as a danger to the colony's stability. In 1637 the Massachusetts leaders put her on trial for speaking false ideas.

Hutchinson defended herself well, but she claimed God spoke to her directly. This disagreed with Puritan beliefs that God spoke only through the Bible. Her accusers found her guilty and ordered her to leave the colony. With her family and some followers, Hutchinson moved to Rhode Island.

CHAPTER 3   Colonial America   **79**

INTERDISCIPLINARY CONNECTIONS ACTIVITY

Technology Organize the class into groups to make a bulletin board display comparing colonial and modern technology. Each group should work on a different category, such as kitchen implements, shop tools, cloth-making equipment, and farm tools. Students should research, then draw the equipment or cut pictures of tools from magazines or newspapers. Have students label their work. **L2**

📂 Use the rubric for creating a bulletin board display on pages 40–41 in the *Performance Assessment Activities and Rubrics.*

Objectives and answers to the student activity can be found in the **Web Activity Lesson Plan** feature at tarvol1.glencoe.com

✓ Reading Check

Answer: It was the first written constitution in America, describing representative government in detail.

L1, ELL

Reading Essentials and Study Guide 3–2

Study Guide

Chapter 3, Section 2
For use with textbook pages 76–80

NEW ENGLAND COLONIES

KEY TERMS	
dissent	To disagree *(page 76)*
persecute	To treat badly *(page 76)*
Puritan	Protestant who wanted to reform the Anglican Church *(page 77)*
Separatist	Person who wanted to leave the Anglican Church and form his or her own church *(page 77)*
Pilgrim	Person who makes a religious journey *(page 77)*
Mayflower Compact	Formal document in which the Pilgrims pledged their loyalty to England, promised to obey the laws, and declared their goal of forming a governing body *(page 77)*
toleration	

L3

Enrichment Activity 3–2

Name _____ Date _____ Class _____

★ Enrichment Activity 3-2 ★

A Colonial Household

Providence, Rhode Island, founded by Roger Williams, became a prosperous community. What was the household of an average citizen there like? Look at the partial inventory of the items in the estate, or property, for John Smith, a Providence miller who died in 1682.

An Inventory of the Estate of John Smith, Miller of Providence, Deceased

In the upper room of the dwelling house
• Two bedsteads with the beds and bedding
In the lower room of the dwelling house
• One bedstead with the bed and bedding
• A small piece of homemade cloth

• Two spinning wheels and old cards
• An old Bible, some lost and some of it torn
• Four old chairs
• Several wooden dishes
• Four old spoons

4 CLOSE

Reviewing Have students look back over the section and find examples of the role that civic rights played in the founding of the New England colonies.

---

sold Williams land where he founded the town of Providence. Williams received a charter in 1644 for a colony east of Connecticut called **Rhode Island and Providence Plantations.** With its policy of religious toleration, Rhode Island became a safe place for dissenters. It was the first place in America where people of all faiths—including Jews—could worship freely.

Others followed Williams's example, forming colonies where they could worship as they pleased. In 1638 **John Wheelwright** led a group of dissidents from Massachusetts to the north. They founded the town of Exeter in **New Hampshire.** The same year, a group of Puritans settled Hampton. The colony of New Hampshire became fully independent of Massachusetts in 1679.

Conflict With Native Americans

Native Americans traded with the settlers, exchanging furs for goods such as iron pots, blankets, and guns. In Virginia the colonists had frequent encounters with the many tribes of the Powhatan confederacy. In New England the settlers met the Wampanoags, Narragansets, and other groups.

Conflicts arose, however. Usually settlers moved onto Native American lands without permission or payment. Throughout the colonial period, English settlers and Native Americans competed fiercely for control of the land.

In 1636 war broke out between the settlers and the Pequot people. After two traders were killed in Pequot territory, Massachusetts sent troops to punish the Pequot. The Pequot then attacked a town in Connecticut killing nine people. In May 1637, troops from Connecticut attacked the main Pequot fort with the help of the Narraganset people. They burned the fort, killing hundreds.

In 1675 New England went to war against the Wampanoag people and their allies. Metacomet, the Wampanoag chief, was known to settlers as King Philip. He wanted to stop the settlers from moving onto Native American lands. The war began after settlers executed three Wampanoags for murder. Metacomet's forces attacked towns across the region, killing hundreds of people.

The settlers and their Native American allies fought back. King Philip's War, as the conflict was called, ended in defeat for the Wampanoag and their allies. The war destroyed the power of the Native Americans in New England, leaving the colonists free to expand their settlements.

✓ Reading Check **Evaluating** Describe the significance of the Fundamental Orders of Connecticut.

Student Web Activity
Visit tarvol1.glencoe.com and click on **Chapter 3— Student Web Activities** for an activity on King Philip's War.

SECTION 2 ASSESSMENT

Checking for Understanding

1. **Key Terms** Write a short paragraph in which you use the following terms: dissent, persecute, Puritan, Separatist, Pilgrim, Mayflower Compact, toleration.
2. **Reviewing Facts** Identify the reasons why the Separatists left Europe for the Americas.

Reviewing Themes

3. **Civic Rights and Responsibilities** What freedom did Rhode Island offer that other colonies did not?

Critical Thinking

4. **Comparing** What did the Mayflower Compact and the Fundamental Orders of Connecticut have in common?
5. **Determining Cause and Effect** Re-create the diagram below and describe the effects as colonists interacted with Native Americans.

The colonists interact with the Native Americans

Analyzing Maps

6. **Geography Skills** Study the map on page 77. What products came from New Hampshire?

Interdisciplinary Activity

Government Research and write a one-page paper about the life of Roger Williams. Explain why he left Massachusetts to found a new colony. Describe how his religious ideals contributed to the growth of the representative government in Rhode Island.

80   CHAPTER 3   Colonial America

SECTION 2 ASSESSMENT ANSWERS

1. Student work should reflect correct use of terms.
2. The Separatists had difficulty finding work in the Netherlands, and they were concerned that their children would not follow the English way of life.
3. religious freedom
4. Both documents provided for the organization of a government.
5. Effects may include: colonists survived by learning to grow corn, beans, and pumpkins; colonists survived by learning where to hunt and fish; and colonists negotiated a treaty with the Wampanoag.
6. furs, rum, and lumber

Interdisciplinary Activity Williams was banished. Students should note that Williams championed the ideals of religious freedom and democracy in the colonies.

Reading a Bar Graph

Population of Six English Colonies, 1700

Source: *Historical Statistics of the United States: Colonial Times to 1970.*

Why Learn This Skill?

A bar graph presents numerical information in a visual way. Bars of various lengths stand for different quantities. A bar graph lets you see a lot of information in an organized way. Bars may be drawn vertically—up and down—or horizontally—left to right. Labels along the left axis and the bottom axis explain what the bars represent.

Learning the Skill

To read a bar graph:
• Read the title to learn the subject of the graph.
• Look at the horizontal and vertical axes to find out what information the graph presents.
• Compare the lengths of the bars on the graph.

Practicing the Skill

Study the bar graph on this page and answer the following questions.

❶ Which colony had the largest total population in 1700? The smallest?

❷ Did Virginia or Maryland have a larger African American population?

Applying the Skill

Reading a Bar Graph Create a bar graph to represent the number of students in each American history class in your school.

 Glencoe's **Skillbuilder Interactive Workbook CD-ROM, Level 1,** provides instruction and practice in key social studies skills.

81

Social Studies
SKILLBUILDER

TEACH

Reading a Bar Graph Have students identify the various parts of the graph: title, horizontal axis, vertical axis, grid lines. **Ask:** What is the title of this bar graph? *(Population of Six English Colonies, 1700)*

Note that one has to estimate to find the approximate population when the top of a bar falls between grid lines. **Ask:** What was the total population of Connecticut? *(26,000)*

Additional Practice

L2

Chapter Skills Activity 3

Name _____ Date _____ Class _____

★ Chapter Skills Activity **3**

Reading a Bar Graph

A bar graph uses bars or columns of different lengths to show quantities. The horizontal axis along the bottom of the graph and the vertical axis along the side of the graph are labeled so you know what kind of information they show.

Population of the American Colonies

700,000
600,000
500,000
400,000

GLENCOE
TECHNOLOGY

 CD-ROM
Glencoe Skillbuilder Interactive Workbook CD-ROM, Level 1

This interactive CD-ROM reinforces student mastery of essential social studies skills.

ANSWERS TO PRACTICING THE SKILL

❶ Virginia; Pennsylvania

❷ Virginia

Applying the Skill Students' bar graphs should include accurately labeled horizontal and vertical axes, a title, a legend, and appropriate data.

1 FOCUS

Section Overview

This section describes who settled in the Middle Colonies.

BELLRINGER
Skillbuilder Activity

Project transparency and have students answer the question.

Daily Focus Skills Transparency 3–3

Analyzing Statistics

Directions: Answer the following question based on the chart.

Colonial Population Growth

State	Population in 1790	Population in 1860
Connecticut	238,000	746,000
Delaware	59,000	168,000
Georgia	83,000	1,057,000
Maryland	320,000	1,042,000
Massachusetts	379,000	2,239,000
New Hampshire	142,000	377,000
New Jersey	184,000	1,445,000
New York	340,000	6,093,000
North Carolina	394,000	1,618,000
Pennsylvania	434,000	5,258,000
Rhode Island	69,000	346,000
South Carolina	249,000	1,151,000
Virginia	692,000	1,856,000

Which state grew by the greatest rate from 1790 to 1860?

A Rhode Island B New York C Georgia D Virginia

Reading Preview

Answers to Graphic: New York Founder: Dutch West India Company, for land; New Jersey Founder: Lord John Berkeley and Sir George Carteret, for land, religious freedom, jury trials, and a representative assembly; Pennsylvania Founder: William Penn, for religious freedom and representative government

Preteaching Vocabulary
Point out that *pacifist* and *peace* come from the same Latin root, *pax*.

Guide to Reading

Main Idea
People from many different countries settled in the Middle Colonies for a variety of reasons, including religious freedom.

Key Terms
patroon, proprietary colony, pacifist

Reading Strategy
Classifying Information As you read the section, re-create the diagram below and describe how the Middle Colonies were founded.

Colony	Founder	Why settlers came
New York		
New Jersey		
Pennsylvania		

Read to Learn
- why the Middle Colonies had the most diverse populations in colonial America.
- who was America's first town planner.

Section Theme
Individual Action Leaders such as Peter Stuyvesant and William Penn helped the Middle Colonies grow.

Preview of Events

♦1600 — ♦1650 — ♦1700

1626 Manhattan Island purchased from the Manhates people

1664 New Amsterdam becomes New York

1681 William Penn founds Pennsylvania

1702 New Jersey becomes a royal colony

English royal plate

★ A European Story

In 1649, 17-year-old Philip Henry stood near the back of the crowd gathered around a public platform near Whitehall Palace in London. There he watched Charles I, the king of England, prepare to die. The king made a short speech, prayed silently, and then knelt with his head on the block.

With just one blow, the executioner severed the king's head from his body. At that moment, the crowd uttered "such a groan as I never heard before, and desire I may never hear again," Henry wrote in his diary.

England and the Colonies

In England the Puritans who controlled Parliament were engaged in a struggle for power against King Charles I. In 1642 a civil war began. Led by Oliver Cromwell, a Puritan, the Parliamentary forces defeated the king. Charles I was beheaded in 1649 after a parliamentary court declared him guilty of treason.

A new government was established with Cromwell as Protector. During these years of unrest, many Puritans left New England and returned to England to fight with Parliament's forces. After the war ended, English men and women loyal to the king went to royal colonies like Virginia.

SECTION RESOURCES

📁 Reproducible Masters
- Reproducible Lesson Plan 3–3
- Daily Lecture and Discussion Notes 3–3
- Guided Reading Activity 3–3
- Section Quiz 3–3
- Reteaching Activity 3–3
- Reading Essentials and Study Guide 3–3
- Enrichment Activity 3–3

🖼 Transparencies
- Daily Focus Skills Transparency 3–3

Multimedia
- 🖲 Interactive Tutor Self-Assessment CD-ROM
- 🖲 ExamView® Pro Testmaker CD-ROM
- 🖲 Presentation Plus! CD-ROM

After Cromwell died in 1658, Parliament brought back the monarchy, but placed new limits on the ruler's powers. Charles II, son of Charles I, became king in 1660. His reign is called the *Restoration* because the monarchy had been restored.

In 1660 England had two clusters of colonies in what is now the United States—Massachusetts, New Hampshire, Connecticut, and Rhode Island in the north and Maryland and Virginia in the south. Between the two groups of English colonies were lands that the Dutch controlled.

In 1621 a group of Dutch merchants had formed the Dutch West India Company to trade in the Americas. Their posts along the Hudson River grew into the colony of New Netherland. The main settlement of the colony was **New Amsterdam,** located on **Manhattan Island.** In 1626 the company bought Manhattan from the Manhates people for small quantities of beads and other goods. Blessed with a good seaport, the city of New Amsterdam soon became a center of shipping to and from the Americas.

To increase the number of permanent settlers in its colony, the Dutch West India Company sent over families from the Netherlands, Germany, Sweden, and Finland. The company gave a large estate to anyone who brought at least 50 settlers to work the land. The wealthy landowners who acquired these riverfront estates were called patroons. The patroons ruled like kings. They had their own courts and laws. Settlers owed the patroon labor and a share of their crops.

England Takes Over

New Netherland boasted an excellent harbor and thriving river trade. The English wanted to acquire the valuable Dutch colony that lay between England's New England and Southern Colonies. In 1664 the English sent a fleet to attack New Amsterdam.

At the time **Peter Stuyvesant** was governor of the colony. His strict rule and heavy taxes turned many of the people in New Netherland against him. When the English ships sailed into New Amsterdam's harbor, the governor was unprepared for a battle and surrendered the colony to the English forces.

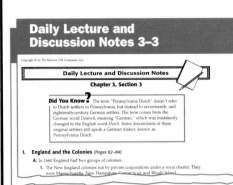

NATIONAL GEOGRAPHIC

The Middle Colonies

Area claimed by New York and New Hampshire

Albany

NEW YORK

New York City

PENNSYLVANIA   Perth Amboy

Wilmington   Philadelphia
NEW
JERSEY
Dover   *ATLANTIC*
DELAWARE   *OCEAN*

0   100 miles
0   100 kilometers
Lambert Equal-Area projection

72°W
40°N
76°W

Products

- Grain
- Cattle
- Fish
- Lumber
- Rum
- Iron

 Geography *Skills*

The Middle Colonies were settled by people from many different countries and ethnic backgrounds.

1. **Region** What were the four Middle Colonies and what were their main products?
2. **Drawing Conclusions** What geographic features made Philadelphia and New York City centers for trade?

King Charles II gave the colony to his brother, the **Duke of York,** who renamed it **New York.** New York was a proprietary colony, a colony in which the owner, or proprietor, owned all the land and controlled the government. It differed from the New England Colonies, where voters elected the governor and an assembly.

Most of New York's settlers lived in the Hudson River valley. The Duke of York promised the diverse colonists freedom of religion. In 1654, 23 Brazilian Jews had settled in New Amsterdam.

CHAPTER 3   Colonial America   **83**

2 TEACH

Daily Lecture and Discussion Notes 3–3

Copyright © by The McGraw-Hill Companies, Inc.

Daily Lecture and Discussion Notes

Chapter 3, Section 3

Did You Know? The term "Pennsylvania Dutch" doesn't refer to Dutch settlers in Pennsylvania, but instead to seventeenth- and eighteenth-century German settlers. The term comes from the German word *Deutsch,* meaning "German," which was mistakenly changed to the English word *Dutch.* Some descendants of these original settlers still speak a German dialect, known as Pennsylvania Dutch.

I.   **England and the Colonies** *(Pages 82–84)*

A.   In 1660 England had two groups of colonies:

1.   The New England colonies run by private corporations under a royal charter. They were Massachusetts, New Hampshire, Connecticut, and Rhode Island.

Identifying People Ask students questions about each of the following: Charles I, Oliver Cromwell, Charles II, Peter Stuyvesant, the Duke of York, Lord John Berkeley, Sir George Carteret, William Penn. Be sure the question can be answered with a yes or no or a name. For example, "Who founded Maryland?" or "Did William Penn found Pennsylvania?" **ELL**

Geography *Skills*

Answers:
1. New York: cattle, lumber, iron, grain, rum, fish; Pennsylvania: cattle, lumber, iron, grain, rum; New Jersey: cattle, iron, fish; Delaware: iron, fish
2. Philadelphia was on a river with an inlet to the Atlantic Ocean. New York City was on the Atlantic Coast with a good harbor. Both were about midway between the New England and Southern Colonies.

Reading Strategy   READING THE TEXT

Reading Maps, Graphs, and Charts Have students work together to make a large map of the Middle Colonies, as they did for the New England Colonies. (See the Reading Strategy: READING THE TEXT on page 77.) As with the New England map, some students should draw the map; others should create tags giving pertinent information about founders and reasons for settlement. Other students should use library resources to find the names of settlements not mentioned in the test. Have students compare the maps of the New England and Middle Colonies in terms of location of settlements and number of settlements. **L1**

L1, ELL

Guided Reading Activity 3–3

History *Through Art*

Answer: He saw the colony as a chance to put into practice Quaker ideals of toleration and equality.

✓**Reading Check**

Answer: New Jersey had no natural harbors.

3 ASSESS

Assign Section 3 Assessment as homework or as an in-class activity.

🌐 Have students use **Interactive Tutor Self-Assessment CD-ROM.**

L2

Section Quiz 3–3

Name _____ Date _____ Class _____

★ **Chapter 3**   Score

Section Quiz 3-3

DIRECTIONS: Matching Match the items in Column A with the items in Column B. Write the correct letters in the blanks. *(10 points each)*

Column A
_____ **1.** Charles II's brother
_____ **2.** colony of New Netherland
_____ **3.** wealthy landowners
_____ **4.** Society of Friends
_____ **5.** "city of brotherly love"

Column B
A. Quakers
B. Duke of York
C. New Amsterdam
D. Philadelphia
E. patroons

DIRECTIONS: Multiple...

History *Through Art*

Penn's Treaty with the Indians In 1682 William Penn made his first treaty with the Delaware people. **Why did Penn see Pennsylvania as a "holy experiment"?**

They were the first Jews to settle in North America. In 1664 New York had about 8,000 inhabitants. Most were Dutch, but Germans, Swedes, Native Americans, and Puritans from New England lived there as well. The population also included at least 300 enslaved Africans. New Amsterdam, which was later called New York City, was one of the fastest-growing locations in the colony.

By 1683 the colony's population had swelled to about 12,000 people. A governor and council appointed by the Duke of York directed the colony's affairs. The colonists demanded a representative government like the governments of the other English colonies. The duke resisted the idea, but the people of New York would not give up. Finally, in 1691, the English government allowed New York to elect a legislature.

New Jersey

The Duke of York gave the southern part of his colony, between the Hudson and Delaware Rivers, to **Lord John Berkeley** and **Sir George Carteret.** The proprietors named their colony New Jersey after the island of Jersey in the English Channel, where Carteret was born.

To attract settlers, the proprietors offered large tracts of land and generous terms. They also promised freedom of religion, trial by jury, and a representative assembly. The assembly would make local laws and set tax rates.

Like New York, New Jersey was a place of ethnic and religious diversity. Because New Jersey had no natural harbors, however, it did not develop a major port or city like New York.

The proprietors of New Jersey did not make the profits they had expected. Berkeley sold his share, West Jersey, in 1674. Carteret's share, East Jersey, was sold in 1682.

By 1702 New Jersey had passed back into the hands of the king, becoming a royal colony. The colonists still continued to make local laws.

✓**Reading Check** **Explaining** Why did no major port develop in New Jersey?

Pennsylvania

In 1680 **William Penn,** a wealthy English gentleman, presented a plan to King Charles. Penn's father had once lent the king a great deal of money. Penn had inherited the king's promise to

---

DIFFERENTIATED INSTRUCTION

Gifted and Talented Pose the following questions and have students answer it orally or in writing: Suppose you were a Quaker threatened with jail for your beliefs. Would you renounce your beliefs? After students have responded individually, discuss the issue as a class. Allow time for students to challenge the decisions of others, who may then defend their decisions. **L3**

📂 Refer to ***Inclusion for the Middle School Social Studies Classroom Strategies and Activities*** in the TCR.

repay the loan. Instead of money, however, Penn asked for land in America. Pleased to get rid of his debt so easily, the king gave Penn a tract of land stretching inland from the Delaware River. The new colony, named Pennsylvania, was nearly as large as England.

William Penn belonged to a Protestant group of dissenters called the Society of Friends, or **Quakers.** The Quakers believed that every individual had an "inner light" that could guide him or her to salvation. Each person could experience religious truth directly, which meant that church services and officials were unnecessary. Everyone was equal in God's sight. Though firm in their beliefs, the Quakers were tolerant of the views of others.

Many people in England found the Quakers' ideas a threat to established traditions. Quakers would not bow or take off their hats to lords and ladies because of their belief that everyone was equal. In addition they were pacifists, people who refuse to use force or to fight in wars. Quakers were fined, jailed, and even executed for their beliefs.

William Penn saw Pennsylvania as a "holy experiment," a chance to put the Quaker ideals of toleration and equality into practice. In 1682 he sailed to America to supervise the building of **Philadelphia,** the "city of brotherly love." Penn believed that

❝any government is free to the people under it . . . where the laws rule, and the people are a party to those laws.❞

Penn had designed the city himself, making him America's first town planner. Penn also wrote Pennsylvania's first constitution.

Penn believed that the land belonged to the Native Americans and that settlers should pay for it. In 1682 he negotiated the first of several treaties with local Native Americans.

To encourage European settlers to come to Pennsylvania, Penn advertised the colony throughout Europe with pamphlets in several languages. By 1683 more than 3,000 English, Welsh, Irish, Dutch, and German settlers had arrived. In 1701, in the Charter of Liberties, Penn granted the colonists the right to elect representatives to the legislative assembly.

The southernmost part of Pennsylvania was called the Three Lower Counties. Settled by Swedes in 1638, the area had been taken over by the Dutch and the English before becoming part of Pennsylvania. The Charter of Privileges allowed the lower counties to form their own legislature, which they did in 1704. Thereafter the counties functioned as a separate colony known as Delaware, supervised by Pennsylvania's governor.

✓**Reading Check** **Summarizing** How did William Penn encourage self-government?

SECTION 3 ASSESSMENT

Checking for Understanding

1. **Key Terms** Write a short paragraph in which you use the following key terms: **patroon, proprietary colony, pacifist**
2. **Reviewing Facts** What did the Charter of Liberties grant to Pennsylvania colonists?

Reviewing Themes

3. **Individual Action** How did William Penn earn the respect of Native Americans?

Critical Thinking

4. **Compare and Contrast** How was the Quaker religion different from that of the Puritans?
5. **Organizing Information** Re-create the diagram below and describe how each of the Middle Colonies was governed.

Colony	Type of government
New York	
New Jersey	
Pennsylvania	

Analyzing Visuals

6. **Geography Skills** Review the map on page 83. What is the title of the map? What items are shown in the key? What products were important to Pennsylvania?

Interdisciplinary Activity

Art Design a flag for one of the Middle Colonies. Decide what symbols and colors would be appropriate to represent that colony. Display your flags in class.

CHAPTER 3   Colonial America   **85**

SECTION 3 ASSESSMENT ANSWERS

1. Student work should reflect correct use of terms.
2. the right to elect representatives to the legislative assembly
3. He honored their claim to the land and believed settlers should pay for it.
4. Quakers had no formal church services or church officials, were tolerant of other religions, believed all people were equal, and were pacifists.
5. New York: owned by proprietor, then elected legislature; New Jersey: owned by proprietor, became royal colony, local laws still made by colonists; Pennsylvania: elected representatives
6. the Middle Colonies; grain, cattle, fish, lumber, rum, iron; grain, cattle, lumber, rum, iron

Interdisciplinary Activity Symbols and colors should have some relationship to the history or characteristics of the chosen colony.

✓**Reading Check**

Answer: In the Charter of Liberties, Penn granted European settlers the right to elect representatives to the legislative assembly.

L1

Reteaching Activity 3–3

Name _____ Date _____ Class _____

★ Reteaching Activity 3-3

DIRECTIONS: Organizing Facts The numbered items in the Fact Bank are related to each of the Middle Colonies. Complete the web diagram by writing the number of each item in the correct circle on the chart. Some items fit in more than one group.

New York   Middle Colonies   New Jersey

L1, ELL

Reading Essentials and Study Guide 3–3

Study Guide

Chapter 3, Section 3

For use with textbook pages 82–85

MIDDLE COLONIES

KEY TERMS	
patroon	Wealthy landowner in the New Netherlan colony who brought at least 50 settlers to work the land given to him by the Dutch West India Company (page 83)
proprietary colony	Colony in which the owner, or proprietor, owned all the land and controlled the government (page 83)
pacifist	Person who refuses to use force or to fight in wars (page 85)

DRAWING FROM EXPERIENCE

What are some of your beliefs? What if you were told that you had to change your beliefs? Would you move to another place you had never been to before in order to keep your beliefs?

L3

Enrichment Activity 3–3

Name _____ Date _____ Class _____

★ Enrichment Activity 3-3   ★

Across the Appalachians

Early settlers often followed Native American trails. The Mohawk, an eastern nation, used a path across the Appalachian Mountains in what is now New York. Many settlers from eastern settlements used the trail to reach western New York. The map below shows the Mohawk Trail.

The Mohawk Trail

4 CLOSE

Have students turn the **Read to Learn** phrases (page 82) from this section into questions and write answers to each.

1 FOCUS

Section Overview

This section explores how the Southern Colonies were established and describes how Spanish and French settlements were different from English settlements.

BELLRINGER
Skillbuilder Activity

Project transparency and have students answer the question.

Daily Focus Skills Transparency 3–4

Reading Preview

Answers to Graphic: Maryland: tobacco; North Carolina: tobacco; South Carolina: rice

Preteaching Vocabulary
Use the **Vocabulary PuzzleMaker CD-ROM** to create crossword and word search puzzles.

SECTION 4 Southern Colonies

Guide to Reading

Main Idea
The Southern Colonies relied on cash crops to survive, while the French and Spanish tried to establish their own settlements.

Key Terms
indentured servant, constitution, debtor, tenant farmer, mission

Reading Strategy
Classifying Information As you read the section, re-create the diagram below and identify the main crops of three of the Southern Colonies.

Colony	Main crop
Maryland	
North Carolina	
South Carolina	

Read to Learn
- how the Southern Colonies were established.
- how French and Spanish colonies differed from the English colonies.

Section Theme
Groups and Institutions Spanish and French settlements developed in different ways from English settlements.

Preview of Events

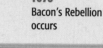

◆1600	◆1650	◆1700	◆1750

c. 1610
Spanish establish Santa Fe

1676
Bacon's Rebellion occurs

1718
French establish city of New Orleans

1733
First settlers arrive in Georgia

Slave drum, Virginia

AN American Story

How did it feel to be enslaved on the plantations of the South? In the 1930s, interviewers put this question to African Americans once under slavery. Many of them were approaching 100 years old, and some still carried deep scars on their backs from whippings. To be a slave meant to have no human rights. Elderly Roberta Mason remembered, "Once they whipped my father 'cause he looked at a slave they killed, and cried."

Coming to America

By 1660, while tobacco prices fell, large plantations continued to prosper because they were better able to maintain high profits than were small farms. Along with the growth of plantations, there was an increasing need for workers in the newly settled Southern Colonies.

Establishing colonies in North America involved a great deal of work. The settlers had to clear the land, construct homes and churches, plant crops, and tend the fields. As the colonies expanded, the demand for capable workers grew.

86   CHAPTER 3   Colonial America

SECTION RESOURCES

📂 Reproducible Masters
- Reproducible Lesson Plan 3–4
- Daily Lecture and Discussion Notes 3–4
- Guided Reading Activity 3–4
- Section Quiz 3–4
- Reteaching Activity 3–4
- Reading Essentials and Study Guide 3–4
- Enrichment Activity 3–4

📖 Transparencies
- Daily Focus Skills Transparency 3–4

Multimedia
- Vocabulary PuzzleMaker CD-ROM
- Interactive Tutor Self-Assessment CD-ROM
- ExamView® Pro Testmaker CD-ROM
- Presentation Plus! CD-ROM

Not all people came to work in the colonies of their own free will. English criminals and Scottish and Irish prisoners of war were also shipped to the colonies. They could earn their release by working for a period of time—often seven years. Some colonists complained that their settlements were dumping grounds for "His Majesty's seven-year passengers." African rulers took prisoners during wars and raids. They enslaved the captives and sold them to European slave traders who took them to the colonies. Many people came to the colonies as indentured servants. To pay for their passage to America, they agreed to work without pay for a certain period of time.

Establishing Maryland

Maryland arose from the dream of **Sir George Calvert, Lord Baltimore,** a Catholic. Calvert wanted to establish a safe place for his fellow Catholics, who were being persecuted in England. He also hoped that a colony would bring him a fortune.

Calvert's dream came true in 1632 when King Charles I gave him a proprietary colony north of Virginia. Calvert died before receiving the grant. His son Cecilius Calvert inherited the colony. It was named Maryland either after the English queen, Henrietta Maria, or after the Virgin Mary.

The younger Calvert—the new Lord Baltimore—never lived in Maryland. Instead, he sent two of his brothers to run the colony. They reached America in 1634 with two ships and more than 200 settlers. Entering the Chesapeake Bay, they sailed up the **Potomac River** through fertile countryside. A priest in the party described the Potomac as "the sweetest and greatest river I have ever seen." The colonists chose a site for their settlement, which they called St. Marys.

Knowing that tobacco had saved the Virginia colony, the Maryland colonists turned first to tobacco farming. To keep the colony from becoming too dependent on one crop, however, a Maryland law declared that "every person planting tobacco shall plant and tend two acres of corn." In addition to corn, most Maryland tobacco farmers produced wheat, fruit, vegetables, and livestock to feed their families and

their workers. **Baltimore,** founded in 1729, was Maryland's port. Before long Baltimore became the colony's largest settlement.

Aristocrats and Farmers

Lord Baltimore gave large estates to his relatives and other English aristocrats. By doing so he created a wealthy and powerful class of landowners in Maryland.

The colony needed people to work in the plantation fields. To bring settlers to the colony, Lord Baltimore promised land—100 acres to each

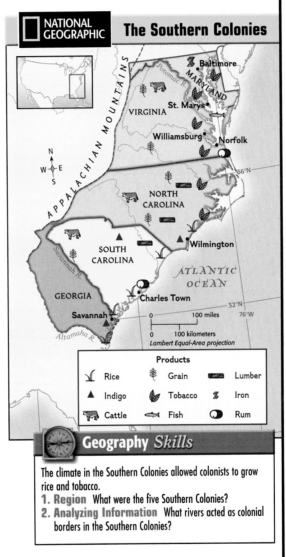

NATIONAL GEOGRAPHIC The Southern Colonies

Products

Rice		Grain		Lumber		
Indigo		Tobacco		Iron		
Cattle		Fish		Rum		

Geography *Skills*

The climate in the Southern Colonies allowed colonists to grow rice and tobacco.
1. **Region** What were the five Southern Colonies?
2. **Analyzing Information** What rivers acted as colonial borders in the Southern Colonies?

CHAPTER 3   Colonial America   **87**

2 TEACH

Choosing a Colony After students have read the section, have them choose the colony in which they would have preferred to live if they had been settlers. Have them explain their choice orally or in writing. To extend the activity, have students work in pairs, with each student presenting his or her choice and the other student challenging it. **L1, ELL**

Geography *Skills*

Answers:
1. Maryland, Virginia, North Carolina, South Carolina, Georgia
2. Potomac River, Savannah River, Altamaha River

Geography Skills Practice
Ask: In what three colonies was rice grown? *(North Carolina, South Carolina, Georgia)*

Reading Strategy   READING THE TEXT

Making a Map Have students work together to make a large map of the Southern Colonies, as they did for the New England and Middle Colonies. (See the Reading Strategy: READING THE TEXT activities on pages 77 and 83.) As with the other maps, some students should draw the map; others should create tags giving pertinent information about founders and reasons for settlement. Other students should use library resources to find the names of settlements not mentioned in the text. Have students compare the three maps in terms of location and number of settlements. **L2**

L1, ELL

Guided Reading Activity 3–4

Name _____ Date _____ Class _____

★ **Guided Reading Activity 3-4**

DIRECTIONS: Recalling the Facts Use the information in your textbook to answer the questions. Use another sheet of paper if necessary.

1. Why did Sir George Calvert want to establish a colony in America?

2. How was a wealthy and powerful class of Maryland landowners created?

3. What did the colony do to supply laborers for the plantation fields?

4. Why did Nathaniel Bacon and his followers attack Jamestown?

5. Why was the southern part of Carolina more prosperous than the northern part?

6. What was the "blue gold" of Carolina?

7. Why was the colony of Georgia established?

8. What two Frenchmen explored the Mississippi River by canoe in 1670?

9. What were these explorers looking for?

10. What did they discover about the Mississippi River?

11. What lands did the Spanish control in the early 1600s?

12. What are missions?

13. Who was the Franciscan monk who founded a mission at San Diego and eight other places in California?

People In History

Margaret Brent was a cousin of Cecilius Calvert, English proprietor of the Maryland colony. By 1639 her brothers Fulke and Giles were living in Maryland. Margaret joined them with her sister Mary. Calvert condemned her actions after she asked for a vote in the assembly. **Ask:** Why do you think Brent helped pay for Maryland's troops? *(Answers will vary, but students may note that she wanted to preserve her family's wealth.)*

✓ Reading Check

Answer: Calvert wanted a safe haven for persecuted Catholics and to make a fortune.

People In History

Margaret Brent c.1601—1671

Born in England, Margaret Brent moved to Maryland in 1638. She quickly accumulated several thousand acres of land and became one of the largest landowners. According to colonial records, she was also the first woman to own land in her own name.

Brave and forceful, Brent helped to put down a rebellion from neighboring Virginia, and she took charge of paying Maryland's troops. Refusing to follow the restricted life of most colonial women, she later served as attorney for Lord Baltimore, Maryland's proprietor.

In January 1648 Brent came into conflict with the colonial government when she appeared before the assembly. She demanded two votes, one for herself as a landowner and one as Lord Baltimore's legal representative. After the government denied her claim, she moved to a large plantation in Virginia. There, America's first woman lawyer lived the rest of her life.

---

male settler, another 100 for his wife, 100 for each servant, and 50 for each of his children. As the number of plantations increased and additional workers were needed, the colony imported indentured servants and enslaved Africans.

The Mason-Dixon Line

For years the Calvert family and the Penn family argued over the boundary between Maryland and Pennsylvania. In the 1760s they hired two British astronomers, Charles Mason and Jeremiah Dixon, to map the line dividing the colonies. It took the two scientists many years to lay out the boundary stones. Each stone had the crest of the Penn family on one side and the crest of the Calverts on the other.

Another conflict was even harder to resolve. The Calverts had welcomed Protestants as well as Catholics in Maryland. Protestant settlers outnumbered Catholics from the start.

Act of Toleration

To protect the Catholics from any attempt to make Maryland a Protestant colony, Baltimore passed a law called the **Act of Toleration** in 1649. The act granted Protestants and Catholics the right to worship freely but tensions continued between Protestants and Catholics. In 1692, with the support of the English government, the Protestant-controlled assembly made the Anglican Church the official church in Maryland, and imposed the same restrictions on Catholics that existed in England.

✓ **Reading Check** **Explaining** Why did George Calvert establish the colony of Maryland?

Virginia Expands

While other colonies were being founded, Virginia continued to grow. Wealthy tobacco planters held the best land near the coast, so new settlers pushed inland. As the settlers moved west, they found the lands inhabited by Native Americans. In the 1640s, to avoid conflicts, Virginia's governor William Berkeley worked out an arrangement with the Native Americans. In exchange for a large piece of land, he agreed to keep settlers from pushing farther into their lands.

Bacon's Rebellion

Nathaniel Bacon, a wealthy young planter, was a leader in the western part of Virginia. He and other westerners opposed the colonial

---

DIFFERENTIATED INSTRUCTION

Reading Support Have students use the figures in the text (pages 87–88) to calculate how much land the following male settlers would have received from Lord Baltimore. (Remind students to include the male settler's allotment.) Settler A has a wife, three children, and two servants *(550 acres)*. Settler B has a wife, six children, and five servants *(1,000 acres)*. Settler C is single, but has three servants *(400 acres)*. **L2**

📁 Refer to *Inclusion for the Middle School Social Studies Classroom Strategies and Activities* in the TCR.

government because it was dominated by easterners. Many of the westerners resented Governor Berkeley's pledge to stay out of Native American territory. Some of them settled in the forbidden lands and then blamed the government in Jamestown for not protecting them from Native American raids.

In 1676 Bacon led the angry westerners in attacks on Native American villages. Governor Berkeley declared Bacon "the greatest rebel that ever was in Virginia." Bacon's army marched to Jamestown, set fire to the capital, and drove Berkeley into exile. Only Bacon's sudden illness and death kept him from taking charge of Virginia. England then recalled Berkeley and sent troops to restore order.

Bacon's Rebellion had shown that the settlers were not willing to be restricted to the coast. The colonial government created a militia force to control the Native Americans and opened up more land to settlement.

Nathaniel Bacon

✓**Reading Check** **Analyzing** Why did Bacon oppose the colonial government?

Settling the Carolinas

In 1663 King Charles II created a large proprietary colony south of Virginia. The colony was called Carolina, which means "Charles's land" in Latin. The king gave the colony to a group of eight prominent members of his court who had helped him regain his throne.

The Carolina proprietors carved out large estates for themselves and hoped to make money by selling and renting land. The proprietors provided money to bring colonists over from England. Settlers began arriving in Carolina in 1670. By 1680 they had founded a city, which they called Charles Town after the

king. The name later became **Charleston.**

John Locke, an English political philosopher, wrote a constitution for the Carolina colony. This constitution, or plan of government, covered such subjects as land distribution and social ranking. Locke was concerned with principles and rights. He argued that

❝every man has a property in his own person. This nobody has any right to but himself. The labour of his body, and the work of his hands, we may say, are properly his. . . .❞

Carolina, however, did not develop according to plan. The people of northern and southern Carolina soon went their separate ways, creating two colonies.

⑤ Economics
Northern and Southern Carolina

The northern part of Carolina was settled mostly by farmers from Virginia's backcountry. They grew tobacco and sold forest products such as timber and tar. Because the northern Carolina coast did not have a good harbor, the farmers relied on Virginia's ports and merchants to conduct their trade.

The southern part of the Carolinas was more prosperous, thanks to fertile farmland and a good harbor at Charles Town. Settlements spread, and the trade in deerskin, lumber, and beef flourished. In the 1680s planters discovered that rice grew well in the wet coastal lowlands. Rice soon became the colony's leading crop.

In the 1740s a young Englishwoman named **Eliza Lucas** developed another important Carolina crop—indigo. Indigo, a blue flowering plant, was used to dye textiles. After experimenting with seeds from the West Indies, Lucas succeeded in growing and processing indigo, the "blue gold" of Carolina.

CHAPTER 3 Colonial America 89

✓**Reading Check**

Answer: Bacon thought the colonial government was dominated by easterners and resented the pledge to stay out of Native American territory.

Did you know?

Much colonial commerce took place without currency. Traders often relied on barter or money substitutes such as beaver skins.

CURRICULUM CONNECTION

Geography The coast of North Carolina is protected by long, narrow barrier islands. As one observer remarked, "The coast of North Carolina looks as if it was just coming unglued, with strips of land floating out to sea." These sandy islands shift and change when storms batter the coast. As a result, some of the bridges and roads built over the years have been rendered useless.

INTERDISCIPLINARY CONNECTIONS ACTIVITY

Health Have students work in groups to research the health effects of tobacco, economic effects on its users, statistics on modern tobacco usage, and deaths or disease from its use. Then have each group hold a panel discussion to decide whether the Southern colonists would have decided to grow tobacco and introduce it to other colonists and countries had they been able to see into the twenty-first century. Have them weigh such factors as the survival of the colonies and effects of that survival, as well as the health and economic effects of tobacco today. **L2**

✓ **Reading Check**

Answer: Locke was an English political philosopher. He wrote a constitution for the Carolina colony.

Picturing **History**

South Carolinians had experimented with growing rice very early in the colony's history. Success came only after 1690, however, when new channels for the supply of enslaved African labor were opened. South Carolina's heavy reliance on enslaved African labor coincided closely with the development of rice as a new and profitable staple.
Answer: Growing rice required much labor.

Did you know?

In 1770 about 62,000 tons of goods passed through South Carolina's harbors. Today Charleston alone handles about 9 million tons of goods yearly.

Slave Labor in the Carolinas

Most of the settlers in southern Carolina came from another English colony—the island of Barbados in the West Indies. In Barbados the colonists used enslaved Africans to produce sugar. The colonists brought these workers with them.

Many enslaved Africans who arrived in the Carolinas worked in the rice fields. Some of them knew a great deal about rice cultivation because they had come from the rice-growing areas of West Africa. Growing rice required much labor, so the demand for slaves increased. By 1708 more than half the people living in southern Carolina were enslaved Africans.

By the early 1700s, Carolina's settlers were angry at the proprietors. They wanted a greater role in the colony's government. In 1719 the settlers in southern Carolina seized control from its proprietors. In 1729 Carolina became two royal colonies—North and South Carolina.

✓ **Reading Check** **Explaining** Who was John Locke? What did he do for Carolina?

Picturing **History**

A rice plantation included the owner's large house surrounded by the small dwellings of enslaved Africans. **Why did rice cultivation increase the demand for enslaved labor?**

Georgia

Georgia, the last of the British colonies in America to be established, was founded in 1733. A group led by General **James Oglethorpe** received a charter to create a colony where English debtors and poor people could make a fresh start. In Great Britain, debtors—those who are unable to repay their debts—were generally thrown into prison.

The British government had another reason for creating Georgia. This colony could protect the other British colonies from Spanish attack. Great Britain and Spain had been at war in the early 1700s, and new conflicts over territory in North America were always breaking out. Located between Spanish Florida and South Carolina, Georgia could serve as a military barrier.

Oglethorpe's Town

Oglethorpe led the first group of "sober, industrial, and moral persons" to Georgia in 1733. They built a town called **Savannah,** as well as forts to defend themselves from the Spanish.

Oglethorpe wanted the people of Georgia to be hardworking, independent, and Protestant. He kept the size of farms small and banned slavery, Catholics, and rum.

CRITICAL THINKING ACTIVITY

Drawing Conclusions Lead a class discussion on why the Maryland law (mentioned on page 87) that required people to plant corn in addition to tobacco was a good idea. Solicit ideas from students and then add ideas as necessary. (*Possible responses include: soil on which only one crop is grown wears out quickly; if a disease attacked the crop, farmers could be wiped out; overproduction of tobacco could produce a glut on the market, prices would fall, and growers would suffer financially.*) **L2**

Founding the Thirteen Colonies

Colony	1st Permanent Settlement	Reasons Founded	Founders or Leaders
New England Colonies			
Massachusetts			
Plymouth	1620	Religious freedom	John Carver, William Bradford, John Winthrop
Mass. Bay Colony	1630	Religious freedom	
New Hampshire	c. 1620	Profit from trade and fishing	Ferdinando Gorges, John Mason
Rhode Island	1636	Religious freedom	Roger Williams
Connecticut	1635	Profit from fur trade, farming; religious and political freedom	Thomas Hooker
Middle Colonies			
New York	1624	Expand trade	Dutch settlers
Delaware	1638	Expand trade	Swedish settlers
New Jersey	1638	Profit from selling land	John Berkeley, George Carteret
Pennsylvania	1682	Profit from selling land; religious freedom	William Penn
Southern Colonies			
Virginia	1607	Expand trade	John Smith
Maryland	1634	To sell land; religious freedom	Cecil Calvert
North Carolina	c. 1660s	Profit from trade and selling land	Group of eight aristocrats
South Carolina	1670	Profit from trade and selling land	Group of eight aristocrats
Georgia	1733	Religious freedom; protection against Spanish Florida; safe home for debtors	James Oglethorpe

NOVA BRITANNIA OFFERING MOST Excellent fruites by Planting in VIRGINIA.

Chart Skills

The thirteen colonies were founded over a span of 125 years.

Sequencing What colony was the first to be settled? Which was the last?

Although Georgia had been planned as a debtors' colony, it actually received few debtors. Hundreds of poor people came from Great Britain. Religious refugees from Germany and Switzerland and a small group of Jews also settled there. Georgia soon had a higher percentage of non-British settlers than any other British colony in the Americas.

The Colony Changes

Many settlers complained about the limits on the size of landholdings and the law banning slave labor. They also objected to the many rules Oglethorpe made regulating their lives. The colonists referred to Oglethorpe as "our perpetual dictator."

Oglethorpe grew frustrated by the colonists' demands and the colony's slow growth. He agreed to let people have larger landholdings and lifted the bans against slavery and rum. In 1751 he gave up altogether and turned the colony back over to the king.

By that time British settlers had been in what is now the eastern United States for almost a century and a half. They had lined the Atlantic coast with colonies.

✓ **Reading Check** **Explaining** How did Georgia serve as protection for the English colonies?

CHAPTER 3 Colonial America **91**

✓ Reading Check

Answer: It was located between the British colonies and Spanish Florida.

Chart Skills

Answer: Virginia; Georgia

Chart Skills Practice
Ask: Which colony was originally settled by the Dutch? *(New York)*

Who? What? Where? When?

James Oglethorpe In 1734 James Oglethorpe returned to England with a group of Creek, among them his friend Chief Tomo-Chi-Chi. The Creek, who were formally received by the king and the Archbishop of Canterbury, created a huge sensation in London. Crowds followed them everywhere, even rioting in an attempt to catch a glimpse of the party. On their return, the group praised England so highly that both the Creek and the Cherokee made pacts of friendship with the Georgia colony.

EXTENDING THE CONTENT

Women in Colonial Georgia In colonial Georgia, women had few rights and usually stayed out of the public eye. Even so, a few were respected for outstanding achievements. When Oglethorpe arrived, Mary Musgrove ran a trading post near Savannah. Musgrove was half-Creek and half-English and a broker in the fur trade. She played a major role in maintaining peace between Native Americans and colonists, serving as an interpreter and negotiator, and recruiting Native American warriors for Oglethorpe's battles with the Spanish. She also gave supplies on credit to the colonists.

3 ASSESS

Assign Section 4 Assessment as homework or as an in-class activity.

⊕ Have students use **Interactive Tutor Self-Assessment CD-ROM.**

L2

Section Quiz 3–4

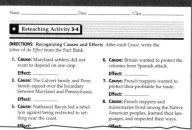

| Name | Date | Class |

⭐ Chapter 3 — Score

Section Quiz 3-4

DIRECTIONS: Matching Match the items in Column A with the items in Column B. Write the correct letters in the blanks. *(10 points each)*

Column A

_____ 1. means "Charles's land"
_____ 2. plan of government
_____ 3. led a rebellion
_____ 4. a French fur trader and explorer
_____ 5. religious settlements

Column B

A. Carolina
B. Louis Joliet
C. constitution
D. Nathaniel Bacon
E. missions

L1

Reteaching Activity 3–4

⭐ Reteaching Activity 3-4

| Name | Date | Class |

DIRECTIONS: Recognizing Causes and Effects After each *Cause,* write the letter of its *Effect* from the Fact Bank.

1. **Cause:** Maryland settlers did not want to depend on one crop.
Effect:

2. **Cause:** The Calvert family and Penn family argued over the boundary between Maryland and Pennsylvania.
Effect:

3. **Cause:** Nathaniel Bacon led a rebellion against being restricted to settling near the coast.
Effect:

6. **Cause:** Britain wanted to protect the colonies from Spanish attack.
Effect:

7. **Cause:** French trappers wanted to protect their profitable fur trade.
Effect:

8. **Cause:** French trappers and missionaries lived among the Native American peoples, learned their languages, and respected their ways.
Effect:

New France

The British were not the only Europeans who were colonizing North America, however. Elsewhere on the continent, the Spanish and the French had built settlements of their own.

The French had founded **Quebec** in 1608. At first they had little interest in large-scale settlement in North America. They were mainly concerned with fishing and trapping animals for their fur. French trappers and missionaries went far into the interior of North America. French fur companies built forts and trading posts to protect their profitable trade.

In 1663 **New France** became a royal colony. King Louis XIV limited the privileges of the fur companies. He appointed a royal governor who strongly supported new explorations.

Down the Mississippi River

In the 1670s two Frenchmen—a fur trader, **Louis Joliet,** and a priest, **Jacques Marquette**—explored the Mississippi River by canoe. Joliet and Marquette hoped to find gold, silver, or other precious metals. They were also looking for a water passage to the Pacific Ocean. The two explorers reached as far south as the junction of the Arkansas and Mississippi Rivers. When they realized that the Mississippi flowed south into the Gulf of Mexico rather than west into the Pacific, they turned around and headed back upriver.

A few years later, **René-Robert Cavelier, Sieur de La Salle,** followed the Mississippi River all the way to the Gulf of Mexico. La Salle claimed the region around the river for France. He called this territory Louisiana in honor of King Louis XIV. In 1718 the French governor founded the port of **New Orleans** near the mouth of the Mississippi River. Later French explorers, traders, and missionaries traveled west to the Rocky Mountains and southwest to the Rio Grande.

Growth of New France

French settlement in North America advanced very slowly. Settlement in New France consisted of a system of estates along the St. Lawrence River. The estate holders received land in exchange for bringing settlers

to the colony. Known as tenant farmers, the settlers paid their lord an annual rent and worked for him for a fixed number of days each year.

The French had better relations with the Native Americans than did other Europeans. French trappers and missionaries traveled deep into Indian lands. They lived among the Native American peoples, learned their languages, and respected their ways.

Although the missionaries had come to convert Native Americans to Catholicism, they did not try to change the Indians' customs. Most important, the French colony grew so slowly that Native Americans were not pushed off their lands.

✓ **Reading Check** **Describing** What region did La Salle explore?

New Spain

In the early 1600s, England, France, and the Netherlands began their colonization of North America. The Spanish, however, still controlled most of Mexico, the Caribbean, and Central and South America. They also expanded into the western and southern parts of what would one day be the United States.

Spain was determined to keep the other European powers from threatening its empire in America. To protect their claims, the Spanish sent soldiers, missionaries, and settlers north into present-day New Mexico.

In late 1609 or early 1610, Spanish missionaries, soldiers, and settlers founded **Santa Fe.** Another group of missionaries and settlers went to what is now Arizona in the late 1600s. When France began exploring and laying claim to lands around the Mississippi River, the Spanish moved into what is now Texas. Spain wanted to control the area between the French territory and their own colony in Mexico. In the early 1700s, Spain established San Antonio and seven other military posts in Texas.

Missions in California

Spanish priests built a string of missions along the Pacific coast. Missions are religious settlements established to convert people to a

92   CHAPTER 3   Colonial America

EXTENDING THE CONTENT

Jacques Marquette Born in France in 1637, Jacques Marquette became a Jesuit missionary and was sent to New France in 1666. He established a mission at Chequamegon Bay near Lake Superior where he worked among the Hurons. Marquette moved the mission to the northern shore of the Straits of Mackinac, between Lake Michigan and Lake Huron, after it was attacked by the Sioux. Marquette was chosen to be the missionary on the expedition to explore the Mississippi River. The missionary kept a comprehensive diary of the journey that described the tides of the lakes, topography, and the flowers and wildlife along the Mississippi River.

particular faith. The missions enabled the Spanish to lay claim to California.

The Spanish did more than convert Native Americans to Christianity. Spanish missionaries and soldiers also brought them to the missions—often by force—to serve as laborers in fields and workshops.

In 1769 **Junípero Serra,** a Franciscan monk, founded a mission at **San Diego.** Over the next 15 years, Father Serra set up eight more missions in California along a route called *El Camino Real* (The Royal Highway)—missions that would grow into such cities as Los Angeles and Monterey.

The distance from one mission to the next was usually a day's walk, and Serra traveled on foot to visit each one and advise the missionaries. Serra also championed the rights of the Native Americans. He worked to prevent Spanish army commanders in the region from mistreating them.

European Conflicts in North America

The rivalries between European nations carried over into the Americas. Britain and France fought several wars in the 1700s. When the two countries were at war in Europe, fighting often broke out between British colonists in America and French colonists in New France.

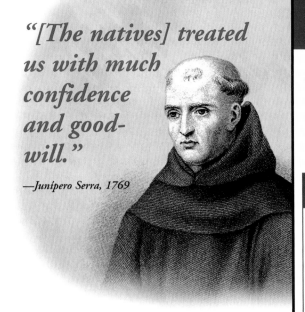

> "[The natives] treated us with much confidence and good-will."
>
> —Junípero Serra, 1769

France and Great Britain were the principal rivals of the colonial period. Both nations were expanding their settlements in North America. In the late 1700s and early 1800s, wars in Europe between the British and the French would shape events across the Atlantic even more decisively.

✓ **Reading Check** **Explaining** Why did Spain establish missions in California?

SECTION 4 ASSESSMENT

Checking for Understanding

1. **Key Terms** Write a short paragraph in which you use all of the following terms: indentured servant, constitution, debtor, tenant farmer, mission.
2. **Reviewing Facts** Explain why French settlement in North America was slower than in the English colonies.

Reviewing Themes

3. **Groups and Institutions** What role did Margaret Brent play in the government and economy of Maryland?

Critical Thinking

4. **Analyzing Information** Do you think uprisings such as Bacon's Rebellion were a sign of more unrest to come? Explain your answer.
5. **Organizing Information** Re-create the diagram below and describe the regions that these countries controlled in North America.

Country	Region
Spain	
France	

Analyzing Visuals

6. **Geography Skills** Review the map on page 87. Which of the Southern Colonies included the city of Norfolk? What were the main products in Georgia? What was the major city in South Carolina?

Interdisciplinary Activity

Art Work with a group to create a bulletin board display titled "The Southern Colonies." Include slogans and pictures to show the colonies' origins, climate, natural resources, and products.

4 CLOSE

Have students create web diagrams summarizing the section. The center oval should be labeled *The Southern Colonies,* with surrounding ovals labeled *Virginia, Maryland, North Carolina, South Carolina,* and *Georgia.* Students should note key facts about each colony in the appropriate web.

SECTION 4 ASSESSMENT ANSWERS

1. Student work should reflect correct use of terms.
2. The French concentrated on fishing and trading furs, not settlement.
3. Brent was a political adviser and landowner in Maryland.
4. Answers will vary, but students should recognize that a desire for land and representative government would be likely to continue to cause unrest.
5. Spain: Mexico and what is now Southwestern United States; France: area around Quebec in present-day Canada, Louisiana Territory (region around the Mississippi) in the present-day United States
6. Virginia; rice, indigo; Charles Town

Interdisciplinary Activity In addition to covering the stated topics accurately, displays should be visually attractive.

Reviewing Key Terms

1. A **charter** gave the **joint-stock company** the right to settle.

2. English Catholics were **persecuted** because they **dissented** with the beliefs of the Anglican Church.

3. A **patroon** ruled New Amsterdam before it became a **proprietary colony.**

4. **Debtors** and **indentured servants** traveled to the Southern Colonies.

5. The **Pilgrims** signed the **Mayflower Compact.**

Reviewing Key Facts

6. A peninsula would be easy to defend from attack.

7. Virginia settlers wanted a voice in the government, and the House of Burgesses allowed them to participate in making the laws.

8. Puritans wanted to reform the church from within. Pilgrims wanted to break away and establish their own church.

9. Native Americans showed the Pilgrims how to grow corn, beans, and pumpkins, and where to hunt and fish.

10. Jamestown, the first permanent English colony, was established.

11. Answers may include: offered large tracts of land, religious freedom, trial by jury, and the right to participate in government.

12. to establish a safe place for Catholics to practice their religion and make money

13. Labor-intensive crops were grown in the Carolinas.

Chapter Summary
Colonial America

1587–1650
- English settle Roanoke Island, 1587
- First permanent English colony at Jamestown, 1607
- Champlain founds Quebec, 1608
- Spanish settlers found Santa Fe, c. 1610
- House of Burgesses meets, 1619
- First Africans arrive at Jamestown, 1619

- Mayflower Compact signed, 1620
- Puritans settle Massachusetts Bay Colony, 1630
- Thomas Hooker founds Hartford, 1636
- Anne Hutchinson founds Portsmouth, 1638
- Maryland passes religious Toleration Act, 1649

1650–1700
- Marquette and Joliet explore Mississippi River, 1673
- King Philip's War, 1675
- Bacon's Rebellion, 1676
- William Penn receives charter for Pennsylvania, 1681

1700–1769
- French found city of New Orleans, 1718
- Carolina is divided into separate colonies, 1729
- Georgia settled, last of 13 English colonies, 1733
- Father Serra establishes mission at San Diego, 1769

94

Reviewing Key Terms

Examine the pairs of words below. Then write a sentence explaining what each of the pairs have in common.

1. charter, joint-stock company
2. dissent, persecute
3. patroon, proprietary colony
4. indentured servant, debtor
5. Pilgrim, Mayflower Compact

Reviewing Key Facts

6. Why did settlers choose a peninsula on which to build Jamestown?

7. Why did the Virginia Company create the House of Burgesses?

8. How did the Puritans' and the Pilgrims' view of the Anglican Church differ?

9. How did the Native Americans help the Pilgrims?

10. What is important about the year 1607?

11. Name two things that colonial leaders offered to attract settlers.

12. What were Sir George Calvert's two main reasons for establishing Maryland?

13. Why was there a high demand for slave labor in the Carolinas?

14. Describe the relationship between the French and the Native Americans.

15. Why did Spain send missionaries to the Pacific coast and the Southwest?

Critical Thinking

16. **Comparing** How did the economic activities of the French differ from those of the English in North America?

17. **Analyzing Themes: Civic Rights and Responsibilities** What role did religious freedom play in the founding of Rhode Island and Pennsylvania?

18. **Synthesizing Information** Re-create the diagram below. List three religious groups that left England and describe their beliefs.

14. The French respected Native Americans. They did not take their lands, but lived and traded with them.

15. to convert Native Americans to Christianity and to claim land for Spain

Critical Thinking

16. The French were mostly fishers, trappers, and traders. In addition to those activities, the English grew a variety of crops, raised animals, mined, harvested lumber, and built large settlements that gave rise to trade and industries.

17. Rhode Island was founded by Roger Williams after Puritans banished him from Massachusetts for his belief that government should be separate from religion. Pennsylvania was founded by William Penn to provide a haven for those who were persecuted in England.

18. Pilgrims: wanted to leave the Anglican Church and set up their own churches; Quakers: believed church was unnecessary since individuals could experience religious truth directly; Puritans: Protestants who wanted to reform the Anglican Church

Geography and History Activity

Study the map below and answer the questions that follow.

NATIONAL GEOGRAPHIC **Settlement of the British Colonies**

MAINE (Part of MASS.)

NEW YORK N.H.

MASS. • Boston

Hartford • • Providence
R.I.
CONN.
• New York City

PENNSYLVANIA

Philadelphia • N.J.

MD. — DEL.

ATLANTIC OCEAN

VIRGINIA

• Jamestown

0   200 miles
0   200 kilometers
Lambert Equal-Area projection

NORTH CAROLINA

SOUTH CAROLINA

GEORGIA • Charles Town
• Savannah

40°N

80°W

	Before 1660
	Between 1660 and 1700
	Between 1700 and 1760
•	Town or city

19. **Location** Which colonies had the largest areas of settlement before 1660?

20. **Place** During what time period was Boston settled?

Practicing Skills

Reading a Bar Graph *Study the bar graph on page 81; then answer these questions:*

21. Which colonies had passed 35,000 in population by 1700?

22. Which colony had the largest African American population?

 Technology Activity

23. **Using the Internet** Search the Internet for information about the Canadian cities of Quebec and Montreal. Find historical sites that show the French presence in these cities. Then, create a travel brochure.

Self-Check Quiz
Visit tarvol1.glencoe.com and click on **Chapter 3— Self-Check Quizzes** to prepare for the chapter test.

Citizenship Cooperative Activity

24. When you become 18 years old, you can begin to exercise one of your most important rights—the right to vote. First, however, you must register. Work with a partner to find out where you can obtain a voter registration card. Make a list of the information you will need for the card. Share your information with the class.

Economics Activity

25. Most societies use a medium of exchange—something accepted in return for goods and services. Money is one medium of exchange. In the colonies, however, the people never had a form of money that had the same value everywhere and was accepted by everyone. Since using money presented problems, colonists often traded goods without the use of money. This is called barter. Research to find out more about barter. Then answer: What are the advantages of barter?

 Alternative Assessment

26. **Portfolio Writing Activity** Examine the painting on page 84. What ideas is the artist presenting? Write a paragraph that answers the question.

Standardized Test Practice

Directions: Choose the *best* answer to the following question.

Which colony was founded to put Quaker ideas into practice?

A Plymouth   **C** Georgia

B Virginia   **D** Pennsylvania

Test-Taking Tip:
As you read the stem of each multiple-choice question, try to anticipate the answer before you look at the choices. If your answer is one of the choices, it is probably correct.

Economics Activity

25. Answers may include such advantages as the opportunity to exchange goods without a stable universal currency or any fears about its value, inflation, or deflation.

 Alternative Assessment

26. Students' may note that the painting reflects Penn's beliefs of equality and toleration and that Native Americans should be paid for any land taken from them.

HISTORY Online

Have students visit the Web site at tarvol1.glencoe.com to review Chapter 3 and take the Self-Check Quiz.

Standardized Test Practice

Answer: D
Question Type: History
Answer Explanation: According to page 85, William Penn considered Pennsylvania a place in which Quaker ideals could be practiced since many people in England did not accept or tolerate Quaker ways.

Bonus Question ?

Ask: How did the lack of religious toleration create new settlements? *(Students may note how people such as Thomas Hooker and Roger Williams founded Connecticut and Rhode Island as a result of the lack of toleration of religious beliefs.)*

Geography and History Activity

19. Massachusetts, Virginia

20. before 1660

Practicing Skills

21. Massachusetts, Virginia

22. Virginia

Technology Activity

23. Students' brochures should reflect information gathered on historical sites that show French influence in Quebec and Montreal.

Citizenship Cooperative Activity

24. Locations and information about voter registration should be complete and accurate.

THINKING CRITICALLY
You Decide

Navigate or Get Lost!

1 FOCUS

Ask students to think about the ways people find their way from place to place. **Ask:** If you were lost in a part of town you seldom visited, how would you find your way home? What might you use? (*Answers will vary but could include: use a street map, ask someone for directions, look for a familiar natural or human-made landmark, determine the general direction toward home and start walking that way until you see something familiar.*)

What?Where?When?Who?

Longitude Sailors could not determine longitude until a clock that could keep accurate time at sea was invented. Determining longitude at sea required knowing the time on board the ship and the time at some other place of known longitude on Earth, such as the ship's home port. Sailors could then convert the difference in clock time to a distance from that known location in degrees. For example, since Earth takes 24 hours to turn once through all 360° of its longitude, a time aboard ship of one hour earlier than the time at the ship's home port would mean the ship was 15° west of the port.

Sailing techniques were mastered long before sailors knew the earth was round. Chinese sailors probably first developed and used the compass—an instrument that shows north, south, east, and west—in the early 1000s or 1100s to guide their ships. The Arabs then used this technology and passed it on to the Europeans. The Europeans improved the magnetic compass, and during the Age of Exploration, European sailors used it to navigate their way across the unknown seas.

Analyzing the Issue

Imagine standing on board your ship. You are the captain and are in charge of the lives of about 150 crewmembers. Now your ship is in the middle of the ocean, and you have to navigate. All you can see is water—water everywhere. How in the world will you know where to find land? You are facing the same navigation problem that Christopher Columbus, Vasco da Gama, and other explorers faced. What is the solution? One way to navigate would be to use a compass to find direction. Are there other ways?

Believe It or Not!

In the late 1800s, some shipbuilders built ships with iron and steel. However, these metals interfered with the magnetic compasses sailors used. Eventually navigators learned to make the necessary adjustments to the compass so it would work properly.

Compasses

Landing of Columbus

96

EXTENDING THE CONTENT

Global Positioning System The most modern method of finding location on Earth's surface is the use of the Global Positioning System, or GPS. The GPS system consists of a set of 24 satellites arranged in six orbits 12,500 miles (20,200 km) above Earth. Each satellite constantly broadcasts a signal that identifies its location. A GPS receiver on the ground then uses signals from at least four of the 24 satellites to determine the latitude and longitude of the receiver on Earth.

What To Do

After you have organized into groups of six, follow the directions to explore different methods of navigation. You will need one compass per group. Each team will write three methods of getting across the classroom and then challenge classmates to follow and evaluate those methods.

1 Each group of students should pick 3 destinations across the classroom.

2 Within the group, one pair of students will write directions to one of the destinations using *compass* directions. These directions must include direction and distance, such as "go north four steps, then west three steps," and so on until the destination is reached.

3 Another pair of students will write directions to a second destination using *landmarks* for direction. Use large objects in your classroom as landmarks, such as "go to the brown bookshelf and turn left," and so on.

4 Another pair of students will write directions using *direction words* such as "left," "right," and "straight" *and number of steps*. An example might be "go straight for 3 steps and turn left," and so on.

5 Next, exchange directions with another group and navigate the room using them.

Presentation

6 Once all of the teams have finished, each group should discuss the advantages and disadvantages of each navigation method. Then have one person per group give a report to the class of what they decided was the best method and why. Keep track on the board which of the three methods got the best results.

World map, 1507

Go a Step Further

Navigational tools as they developed made sailing a ship easier, but they were not foolproof. Even the explorer Christopher Columbus made some questionable navigational conclusions. His flawed measurements put China roughly where the city of San Diego, California, is now. Research information about different navigational tools that have been used. Create a chart describing the various tools, including the astrolabe, sextant, and gyrocompass. Add illustrations and present your chart to the class.

97

2 TEACH

Interpreting Directions Before students start the activity, make sure they know where north, south, east, and west are in the classroom. Ask students to identify the directions. If necessary, place cards with *north*, *south*, *east*, and *west* on the appropriate classroom walls.

Have students also brainstorm a list of classroom landmarks that could be used to write directions during the activity. List students' responses on the chalkboard, and allow students to refer to the list during the activity. **Ask:** What characteristics does a landmark need in order to be useful for finding directions? *(It must be prominent enough to see. It must be permanent—not like a car outside or a backpack in the classroom that could be moved at any time.)* **L2**

3 ASSESS

Have students complete the **Presentation** activity on page 97.

4 CLOSE

Encourage students to complete the **Go a Step Further** activity. Interested students might also research the navigation methods of other famous explorers and adventurers, such as Lewis and Clark or Charles Lindbergh. Discuss how methods of navigation have changed over time.

Answers

Answers to the **Presentation** activity will vary but may include: Compass directions: advantage—compass directions are exact so navigation is more precise, disadvantage—may not know compass directions, depending on location and tools available; Landmarks: advantage—many landmarks are easy to identify, disadvantage—landmarks are not always available or may change; Left/Right: advantage—no tools or outside landmarks are necessary, disadvantage—the size of a "step" may differ among individuals. Students should explain which method was the best to use and why.

Timesaving Tools

TeacherWorks™ All-In-One Planner and Resource Center

- **Interactive Teacher Edition** Access your Teacher Wraparound Edition and your classroom resources with a few easy clicks.
- **Interactive Lesson Planner** Planning has never been easier! Organize your week, month, semester, or year with all the lesson helps you need to make teaching creative, timely, and relevant.

Use Glencoe's **Presentation Plus!** multimedia teacher tool to easily present dynamic lessons that visually excite your students. Using Microsoft PowerPoint® you can customize the presentations to create your own personalized lessons.

TEACHING TRANSPARENCIES

Graphic Organizer 15 L2

Why It Matters Chapter Transparency 4 L2

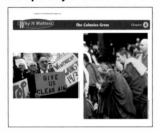

REVIEW AND REINFORCEMENT

Workbook Activity 4 L1

Time Line Activity 4 L2

Vocabulary Activity 4 L1

REVIEW AND REINFORCEMENT

Critical Thinking Skills Activity 4 L2

Take-Home Review Activity 4 L1

ENRICHMENT

Linking Past and Present Activity 4 L2

Primary Source Reading 4 L2

GEOGRAPHY

Geography and History Activity 4 L2

Meeting NCSS Standards

The following standards are highlighted in Chapter 4:

Section 1	VII	Production, Distribution, & Consumption: A, I
Section 2	II	Time, Continuity, & Change: B, C
Section 3	II	Time, Continuity, & Change: A, C
Section 4	IV	Individual Development & Identity: D, E

FOLDABLES™ Study Organizer

Dinah Zike's Foldables are three-dimensional, interactive graphic organizers that help students practice basic writing skills, review key vocabulary terms, and identify main ideas. Additional chapter activities can be found in the **Reading and Study Skills Foldables** booklet.

Chapter 4 Resources

ASSESSMENT AND EVALUATION

Chapter 4 Test Form A L2

Chapter 4 Test Form B L2

Standardized Test Practice Workbook Activity 4 L2

Performance Assessment Activity 4 L1, ELL

ExamView® Pro Testmaker CD-ROM

MULTIMEDIA

- Vocabulary PuzzleMaker CD-ROM
- Interactive Tutor Self-Assessment CD-ROM
- ExamView® Pro Testmaker CD-ROM
- Audio Program
- American History Primary Source Document Library CD-ROM
- MindJogger Videoquiz
- Presentation Plus! CD-ROM
- TeacherWorks CD-ROM
- Interactive Student Edition CD-ROM
- Glencoe Skillbuilder Interactive Workbook CD-ROM, Level 1
- The American Republic to 1877 Video Program
- American Music: Hits Through History

SPANISH RESOURCES

The following Spanish language materials are available in the Spanish Resources Binder:

- Spanish Guided Reading Activities
- Spanish Reteaching Activities
- Spanish Quizzes and Tests
- Spanish Vocabulary Activity
- Spanish Take-Home Review Activity
- Spanish Summaries
- The Declaration of Independence and United States Constitution Spanish Translation

The following videotape programs are available from Glencoe as supplements to Chapter 4:

- **George Washington: Founding Father** (ISBN 1-56501-377-8)*
- **Benjamin Franklin: Citizen of the World** (ISBN 1-56501-426-X)

To order, call Glencoe at 1-800-334-7344. To find classroom resources to accompany many of these videos, check the following home pages:
A&E Television: www.aande.com
The History Channel: www.historychannel.com

*Available individually or in *The American Republic to 1877 Video Library.*

Use our Web site for additional resources. All essential content is covered in the Student Edition.

You and your students can visit tarvol1.glencoe.com, the Web site companion to **The American Republic to 1877.** This innovative integration of electronic and print media offers your students a wealth of opportunities. The student text directs students to the Web site for the following options:

- **Chapter Overviews**
- **Self-Check Quizzes**
- **Student Web Activities**
- **Textbook Updates**

Answers to the student Web activities are provided for you in the **Web Activity Lesson Plans.** Additional Web resources and Interactive Tutor Puzzles are also available.

Chapter 4 Resources

SECTION RESOURCES

Daily Objectives	Reproducible Resources	Multimedia Resources
SECTION 1 **Life in the Colonies** 1. Define the triangular trade and explain how it affected American society. 2. Understand how the regions in the colonies differed from one another. 3. Understand why the use of enslaved workers increased in the colonies.	Reproducible Lesson Plan 4–1 Daily Lecture and Discussion Notes 4–1 Guided Reading Activity 4–1* Section Quiz 4–1* Reteaching Activity 4–1* Reading Essentials and Study Guide 4–1* Enrichment Activity 4–1	Daily Focus Skills Transparency 4–1 Interactive Tutor Self-Assessment CD-ROM ExamView® Pro Testmaker CD-ROM Presentation Plus! CD-ROM
SECTION 2 **Government, Religion, and Culture** 1. Understand why the Navigation Acts angered the colonists. 2. Identify the people who had the right to vote in colonial legislatures.	Reproducible Lesson Plan 4–2 Daily Lecture and Discussion Notes 4–2 Guided Reading Activity 4–2* Section Quiz 4–2* Reteaching Activity 4–2* Reading Essentials and Study Guide 4–2* Enrichment Activity 4–2	Daily Focus Skills Transparency 4–2 American Music: Hits Through History Interactive Tutor Self-Assessment CD-ROM ExamView® Pro Testmaker CD-ROM Presentation Plus! CD-ROM
SECTION 3 **France and Britain Clash** 1. Explain how wars in Europe spread to the American colonies. 2. Understand the purpose of the Albany Plan of Union.	Reproducible Lesson Plan 4–3 Daily Lecture and Discussion Notes 4–3 Guided Reading Activity 4–3* Section Quiz 4–3* Reteaching Activity 4–3* Reading Essentials and Study Guide 4–3* Enrichment Activity 4–3	Daily Focus Skills Transparency 4–3 Interactive Tutor Self-Assessment CD-ROM ExamView® Pro Testmaker CD-ROM Presentation Plus! CD-ROM
SECTION 4 **The French and Indian War** 1. Explain how British fortunes improved after William Pitt took over direction of the war. 2. Describe how Chief Pontiac united his people to fight for their land.	Reproducible Lesson Plan 4–4 Daily Lecture and Discussion Notes 4–4 Guided Reading Activity 4–4* Section Quiz 4–4* Reteaching Activity 4–4* Reading Essentials and Study Guide 4–4* Enrichment Activity 4–4	Daily Focus Skills Transparency 4–4 Vocabulary PuzzleMaker CD-ROM Interactive Tutor Self-Assessment CD-ROM ExamView® Pro Testmaker CD-ROM Presentation Plus! CD-ROM

0:00 OUT OF TIME?
Assign the Chapter 4 **Reading Essentials and Study Guide.**

*Also Available in Spanish

 Blackline Master   Transparency   CD-ROM   DVD

Poster   Music Program   Audio Program   Videocassette

KEY TO ABILITY LEVELS

Teaching strategies have been coded.

L1 BASIC activities for all students
L2 AVERAGE activities for average to above-average students
L3 CHALLENGING activities for above-average students
ELL ENGLISH LANGUAGE LEARNER activities

NATIONAL GEOGRAPHIC Teacher's Corner

INDEX TO NATIONAL GEOGRAPHIC MAGAZINE

The following articles relate to this chapter.

- "Treasure from the Silver Bank," by Tracy Bowden, July 1996.
- "David Thompson," by Priit J. Vesilind, May 1996.
- "The Cruelest Commerce: African Slave Trade," by Colin Palmer, September 1992.

ADDITIONAL NATIONAL GEOGRAPHIC SOCIETY PRODUCTS

To order the following, call National Geographic at 1-800-368-2728:

- *GeoKit: Colonial America* (Kit)
- *Spain in the Americas* (Map)
- *Colonization and Trade in the Americas* (Map)
- *National Geographic Desk Reference* (Book)
- *Indians of North America* (Map)
- *American Indians: A Brief History* (Video)

NGS ONLINE

Access National Geographic's Web site for current events, atlas updates, activities, links, interactive features, and archives.
www.nationalgeographic.com

MEETING SPECIAL NEEDS

In addition to the Differentiated Instruction strategies found in each section, the following resources are also suitable for your special needs students:

- *ExamView® Pro Testmaker CD-ROM* allows teachers to tailor tests by reducing answer choices.
- The *Audio Program* includes the entire narrative of the student edition so that less-proficient readers can listen to the words as they read them.
- The *Reading Essentials and Study Guide* provides the same content as the student edition but is written two grade levels below the textbook.
- *Guided Reading Activities* give less-proficient readers point-by-point instructions to increase comprehension as they read each textbook section.
- *Enrichment Activities* includes a stimulating collection of readings and activities for gifted and talented students.

From the Classroom of . . .

David Mayo
Galvin Middle School
Wakefield, MA

A Cooperative Chapter Review

Student groups will analyze, review, and creatively present their ideas concerning each of four sections of this chapter. First, organize the class into four groups and assign each group one of the chapter's four sections to review. Have groups list the main topics and ideas in their sections. Then divide the list so that each group member is responsible for one part of it. For homework students should write short reports about their items. Have students share their reports. Each group can decide how to present their material to the class: a play, a lecture, or a "chart show," where they share visual charts and pictures explaining the section. Allow students time to rehearse their presentations. For homework, students should begin preparing materials that will be needed, such as props, costumes, speeches, or charts. While groups one and two make presentations, groups three and four should take notes, and vice versa. Once all groups have made their presentations, review the chapter information.

ADDITIONAL RESOURCES FROM GLENCOE

- American Music: Cultural Traditions
- American Art and Architecture
- Outline Map Resource Book
- U.S. Desk Map
- Building Geography Skills for Life
- Inclusion for the Middle School Social Studies Classroom Strategies and Activities
- Teaching Strategies for the American History Classroom (Including Block Scheduling Pacing Guides)
- American Crafts Hands-On Activities
- American Games Hands-On Activities
- American History Flash Cards

Block Schedule

Activities that are suited to use within the block scheduling framework are identified by:

✔ **Performance Assessment**

Refer to Activity 4 in the Performance Assessment Activities and Rubrics booklet.

Why It Matters Activity

Encourage students to think about how the spirit of independence grew in colonial times. How do they think the new nation, government, and culture emerged? How do they think the new American society evolved? As students read the chapter, have them describe and give examples of how the spirit of independence influences American government and culture today.

CHAPTER 4

The Colonies Grow

1607–1770

Why It Matters

Independence was a spirit that became evident early in the history of the American people. The spirit of independence contributed to the birth of a new nation, one with a new government and a culture that was distinct from those of other countries.

The Impact Today

Americans continue to value independence. For example:
- *The right to practice one's own religion freely is safeguarded.*
- *Americans value the right to express themselves freely and to make their own laws.*

The American Republic to 1877 Video The chapter 4 video, "Middle Passage: Voyages of the Slave Trade," examines the beginnings of the slave trade, focusing on the Middle Passage.

The Americas

- **c. 1570** • Iroquois Confederacy formed
- **1651** • First Navigation Act regulates colonial trade
- **1676** • Bacon's Rebellion

1550   1600   1650

World

- **1603** • Tokugawa Shogunate emerges in Japan
- **1610** • Galileo observes planets and stars with telescope
- **1644** • Qing Dynasty established in China

Reading Strategy   **PURPOSE FOR READING**

Graphic organizers, explained previously on page 14, are a way to organize a variety of information. Tell the students a new nation and culture emerged partly because of the diverse peoples and cultural elements that colonization brought together. In the early years, the Middle Colonies were the most diverse of the colonies. Today, diversity is found in regions across the United States. In the left hand column of a two-column organizer, the students will list different regions found in the United States today. In the right hand column, the students are to list examples of diversity in those regions such as place names, words, and customs. **L1**

The South Side of St. John's Street by Joseph B. Smith This painting shows a quiet neighborhood in New York City during the late 1760s.

1700s
• Enslaved Africans brought to America

c. 1740
• Great Awakening peaks

1754
• French and Indian War begins

1763
• Proclamation of 1763

1700   *1750*

1689
• English Bill of Rights signed

1690
• Locke's *Two Treatises of Government*

1702
• England and France at war

1748
• Montesquieu's *The Spirit of Laws*

CHAPTER 4   The Colonies Grow   99

More About the Art

By 1760 New York City had grown to be among the largest colonial cities. Its growth was favored by its sheltered harbor and driven by coastal, river, and ocean trade. This painting shows a different side to bustling New York City, which boasted shipyards, refineries, mills, and a slave market in the 1700s. Have students examine the painting. Ask students to describe how the artist tries to illustrate a prosperous middle-class neighborhood in New York City. *(The homes are large, the people are well dressed, and the buildings and streets are clean.)*

1 FOCUS

Section Overview
This section describes the economic activities of the colonies.

BELLRINGER
Skillbuilder Activity

 Project transparency and have students answer the question.

Daily Focus Skills Transparency 4–1

Reading Preview

Answers to Graphic: New England: small subsistence farms and businesses, fishing, shipbuilding, trade; Middle Colonies: large farms, cash crops, small-scale manufacturing, lumbering, mining, trade; Southern Colonies: large-scale plantations, use of indentured servants and enslaved Africans

Preteaching Vocabulary
Ask students to define the term *triangular trade*. Have them review the map on page 103 to check their definitions.

SECTION 1 Life in the Colonies

Guide to Reading

Main Idea
Each region developed a unique way of life.

Key Terms
subsistence farming, triangular trade, cash crop, diversity, Tidewater, backcountry, overseer

Reading Strategy
Classifying Information As you read Section 1, re-create the diagram below and describe the differences in the economies of the New England, Middle, and Southern Colonies.

Economic Development		
New England	Middle Colonies	Southern Colonies

Read to Learn
- what the triangular trade was and how it affected American society.
- how the regions in the colonies differed from one another.
- why the use of enslaved workers increased in the colonies.

Section Theme
Economic Factors Ways of earning a living varied among the colonies.

Preview of Events

♦1700   ♦1750   ♦1800

1700s
Thousands of enslaved Africans are brought to America

1750
South Carolina and Georgia have the fastest-growing colonial economies

c. 1760
New York City's population reaches 18,000

Colonial spinning wheel

AN American Story

In 1760 Englishman Andrew Burnaby traveled throughout the North American colonies, observing American life. He could not imagine that these colonies would ever join in union for they were as different from one another as "fire and water," and each colony was jealous of the other. "In short, such is the difference of character, of manners, of religion, of interest, of the different colonies, that I think . . . were they left to themselves, there would soon be a civil war, from one end of the continent to the other."

New England Colonies

Although Burnaby believed that the colonies would never unite, the colonies continued to grow. The number of people living in the colonies rose from about 250,000 in 1700 to approximately 2.5 million by the mid-1770s. The population of African Americans increased at an even faster rate—from about 28,000 to more than 500,000.

SECTION RESOURCES

📁 Reproducible Masters
- Reproducible Lesson Plan 4–1
- Daily Lecture and Discussion Notes 4–1
- Guided Reading Activity 4–1
- Section Quiz 4–1
- Reteaching Activity 4–1
- Reading Essentials and Study Guide 4–1
- Enrichment Activity 4-1

📖 Transparencies
- Daily Focus Skills Transparency 4–1

Multimedia
- 🖥 Interactive Tutor Self-Assessment CD-ROM
- 🖥 ExamView® Pro Testmaker CD-ROM
- 🖥 Presentation Plus! CD-ROM

Immigration was important to this growth. Between 1607 and 1775, almost a million people—an estimated 690,000 Europeans and 278,000 Africans—came to live in the colonies. By 1775 about 2,500 Jews lived in the colonies. Most lived in the cities of New York, Philadelphia, Charles Town, Savannah, and Newport, where they were allowed to worship as they pleased.

Another reason for the growing population was that colonial women tended to marry early and have large families. In addition, America, especially New England, turned out to be an unusually healthy place to live.

Most people in New England lived in well-organized towns. In the center of the town stood the meetinghouse, a building used for both church services and town meetings. The meetinghouse faced a piece of land called the green, or common, where cows grazed and the citizen army trained. Farmers lived in the town and worked in fields on its outskirts.

Farming was the main economic activity in all the colonies, but New England farms were smaller than those farther south. Long winters and thin, rocky soil made large-scale farming difficult. Farmers in New England practiced *subsistence farming*, which means that they generally produced just enough to meet the needs of their families, with little left over to sell or exchange. Most Northern farmers relied on their children for labor. Everyone in the family worked—spinning yarn, preserving fruit, milking cows, fencing in fields, and sowing and harvesting grain.

Economics

Commerce in New England

New England also had many small businesses. Some people used the waterpower from the streams on their land to run mills for grinding grain or sawing lumber. Women who made cloth, garments, candles, or soap for their families sometimes made enough of these products to sell or trade. Large towns attracted skilled craftspeople who set themselves up as blacksmiths, shoemakers, furniture makers, gunsmiths, metalsmiths, and printers.

Shipbuilding was an important industry. The lumber for building ships came from the forests of New England and was transported down rivers to the shipyards in coastal towns.

America's *Architecture*

A house design called a "salt box" became popular in many areas. The design featured a square or rectangular house, often with an addition in the back that provided more living space. These houses were called salt boxes because they were similar in shape to the wooden box in which salt was kept in colonial kitchens. **Where was the meetinghouse located in many towns?**

Pineapples symbolized hospitality in colonial America.

Reading Strategy

Outlining the Section Have students outline the section, filling in appropriate material under these four main headings: *New England Colonies, The Middle Colonies, The Southern Colonies,* and *Slavery.* Students may use their outlines for study before doing the section review or taking the section quiz. **L1**

America's *Architecture*

Answer: The meetinghouse was located in the center of town and faced a piece of land called the green, where cows grazed and the citizen army trained.

COOPERATIVE LEARNING ACTIVITY

Making a Display Have students work in groups to create displays or drawings showing a typical New England village with its green, meetinghouse, and farms; a Middle Colony city (New York or Philadelphia) with shops, docks, and ships; and a Southern plantation with a mansion, workshops, slave cabins, dock, and fields. Assign specific tasks (constructing or drawing, researching, writing labels, preparing a "guided tour") to each student within a group. **ELL**

L1, ELL

Guided Reading Activity 4–1

Name _____ Date _____ Class _____

★ **Guided Reading Activity 4-1**

DIRECTIONS: Outlining Locate the heading in your textbook. Then use the information under the heading to help you write each answer. Use another sheet of paper if necessary.

I. New England Colonies
   A. Introduction
      1. What are three reasons the English colonies in America grew at a fast rate?

      2. Why were New England farms fairly small? _____
   B. Commerce in New England—What were two major New England industries?

   C. Colonial Trade—Where did New England ships sail to carry on trade?

   D. Triangular Trade—Why were certain trade routes called the triangular trade routes?
   E. The Middle Passage—What was the Middle Passage? _____
II. The Middle Colonies
   A. Introduction—What two seaports became the largest cities in the colonies?

   B. Industries of the Middle Colonies—What were four industries of the Middle Colonies?
   C. German Immigrants—What did the diversity of the Middle Colonies lead to?

III. The Southern Colonies
   A. Tobacco and Rice
      1. What was the main cash crop of Maryland and Virginia? _____
      2. What was the main cash crop of South Carolina and Georgia? _____
   B. Tidewater and Backcountry—How did the Tidewater and backcountry regions differ? _____
IV. Slavery
   A. Introduction—What were the slave codes? _____
   B. African Traditions—What often happened to families of enslaved Africans?

Picturing History

Between 1761 and 1775, more than 74,000 enslaved people were brought to the colonies. The leading colonies involved in this slave trade were South Carolina, Virginia, and Georgia.
Answer: the leg of the triangular trade in which enslaved Africans were shipped to the West Indies

---

The region also relied on fishing. New Englanders fished for cod, halibut, crabs, oysters, and lobsters. Some ventured far out to sea to hunt whales for oil and whalebone.

Colonial Trade

As the center of the shipping trade in America, northern coastal cities linked the northern colonies with the Southern Colonies, and linked America to other parts of the world. New England ships sailed south along the Atlantic coast, trading with the colonies and with islands in the **West Indies.** They crossed the Atlantic carrying fish, furs, and fruit to trade for manufactured goods in England and Europe.

These colonial merchant ships followed many different trading routes. Some went directly to England and back. Others followed routes that came to be called the triangular trade because the routes formed a triangle. On one leg of such a route, ships brought sugar and molasses from the West Indies to the New England colonies. In New England, the molasses would be made into rum. Next, the rum and other goods were shipped to West Africa and traded for enslaved Africans. Slavery was widely practiced in West Africa.

Many West African kingdoms enslaved those they defeated in war. Some of the enslaved were sold to Arab slave traders. Others were forced to mine gold or work in farm fields. With the arrival of the Europeans, enslaved Africans also began to be shipped to America in exchange for trade goods. On the final leg of the route, the enslaved Africans were taken to the West Indies where they were sold to planters. The profit was used to buy more molasses—and the process started over.

The Middle Passage

The inhumane part of the triangular trade, shipping enslaved Africans to the West Indies, was known as the **Middle Passage.** Olaudah Equiano, a young African forced onto a ship to America, later described the voyage:

❝I was soon put down under the decks, . . . The closeness of the place, and the heat of the climate, added to the number in the ship, which was so crowded that each had scarcely room to turn himself, almost suffocated us. . . . The shrieks of the women, and the groans of the dying, rendered [made] the whole a scene of horror.❞

Slaves packed in a ship

Picturing History

A deck plan (above) reveals tightly packed ranks of slaves on a ship bound from Africa to the Americas. Once docked, the ship's human cargo was replaced with rum or molasses. **What does the term "Middle Passage" refer to?**

DIFFERENTIATED INSTRUCTION

Reading Support Enslaved Africans sang spirituals for comfort and even as a secret means of communicating. Spirituals usually expressed themes of redemption from sin and slavery and hopes of a better life in the future. Check your library for recordings of spirituals that you could play for the class. If possible, have students work with the music teacher to learn some spirituals and perform them for other classes. **L1**

📁 Refer to *Inclusion for the Middle School Social Studies Classroom Strategies and Activities* in the TCR.

Triangular Trade Routes

Trade routes

BRITAIN

BRITISH COLONIES

Rice, tobacco, indigo, furs

Sugar, molasses, fruit

Cloth, manufactured goods

Iron, cloth, weapons

Goods

Molasses

Gulf of Mexico

WEST INDIES

PACIFIC OCEAN

Caribbean Sea

ATLANTIC OCEAN

AFRICA

Enslaved persons, gold, pepper

Enslaved persons

THE MIDDLE PASSAGE

Rum, iron, tools

African Slave Trade 1450–1870

Destination	Total
British America/United States	427,000
Mexico and Central America	224,000
West Indies	4,040,000
Spanish South America	522,000
Guianas	531,000
Brazil	3,647,000
Europe	175,000

Source: *Historical Atlas of the United States;*
Philip D. Curtin, Atlantic Slave Trade.

Geography *Skills*

Triangular trade routes developed among the British colonies, Africa, and the West Indies.
1. **Comparing** What did the colonies export to Africa? What did they import from the West Indies?
2. **Evaluating** Which part of the triangle—import or export—do you think was most important to colonists? Why?

With its trade, shipbuilding, and fishing, New England's economy flourished. Although good farmland was lacking in much of the region, New England's population grew and towns and cities developed.

✓**Reading Check** **Explaining** Where was the shipping hub in America?

The Middle Colonies

The Middle Colonies enjoyed fertile soil and a slightly milder climate than New England's. Farmers in this region cultivated larger areas of

land and produced bigger harvests than did New Englanders. In New York and Pennsylvania, farmers grew large quantities of wheat and other cash crops, crops that could be sold easily in markets in the colonies and overseas.

Farmers sent cargoes of wheat and livestock to New York City and Philadelphia for shipment, and these cities became busy ports. By the 1760s New York, with 18,000 people, and Philadelphia, with 24,000 people, were the largest cities in the American colonies.

Industries of the Middle Colonies

Like the New England Colonies, the Middle Colonies also had industries. Some were home-based crafts such as carpentry and flour

INTERDISCIPLINARY CONNECTIONS ACTIVITY

Science Although the colonists did not have electricity, they did use the power of wind and water in their sawmills and grist mills. Windmills were mostly limited to coastal locations where a good breeze could be counted on much of the time. Using the power of moving water, mills could be located anywhere there was a swift stream. Have students draw diagrams showing how such mills worked. Edwin Tunis's book *Colonial Craftsmen and the Beginning of American Industry* is a good source of information and pictures. **L2,** **ELL**

Reading Check

Answer: crops that could be sold easily for a profit

History *Through Art*

Tapestry weaving was common in many cultures. Specimens have been found dating back to Egypt in 1500 B.C.
Answer: It is a wedding scene.

CURRICULUM CONNECTION

Language Arts Nathaniel Hawthorne (1804–1864) drew on his New England Puritan heritage in writing *The Scarlet Letter* and *The House of Seven Gables*, both of which are set in the colonial period. One ancestor, Major William Hathorne (it was Nathaniel who changed the spelling of the family name), is described in *The Scarlet Letter* as a "grave bearded, sable-cloaked and steeple-crowned progenitor." The major was a magistrate known for his persecution of Quakers. His son John, also a magistrate, presided over the infamous Salem witch trials.

History *Through Art*

Colonists brought traditions from their homelands. One was the display of tapestry, a heavy fabric with a woven pattern or picture. **What is happening in this tapestry?**

making. Others included larger businesses such as lumbering, mining, and small-scale manufacturing.

One iron mill in northern New Jersey employed several hundred workers, many of them from Germany. Other smaller ironworks operated in New Jersey and Pennsylvania.

German Immigrants

Most of the nearly 100,000 German immigrants who came to America in the colonial era settled in Pennsylvania. Using agricultural methods developed in Europe, these immigrants became successful farmers.

The Germans belonged to a number of Protestant groups. Together with the Dutch, Swedish, and other non-English immigrants, they gave the Middle Colonies a cultural diversity, or variety, that was not found in New England. With the diversity came tolerance for religious and cultural differences.

Reading Check **Explaining** What are cash crops?

The Southern Colonies

With their rich soil and warm climate, the Southern Colonies were well suited to certain kinds of farming. Southern farmers could cultivate large areas of land and produce harvests of cash crops. Because most settlers in the Southern Colonies made their living from farming the land, they did not have the need to develop commerce or industry. For the most part, London merchants rather than local merchants managed Southern trade.

Economics
Tobacco and Rice

Tobacco was the principal cash crop of Maryland and Virginia. Most tobacco was sold in Europe, where the demand for it was strong. Growing tobacco and preparing it for sale required a good deal of labor. At first planters used indentured servants to work in the fields. When indentured servants became scarce and expensive, Southern planters used enslaved Africans instead.

Slaveholders with large properties became rich on tobacco. Sometimes, however, a surplus, or extra amounts, of tobacco on the market caused prices to fall and then the growers' profits also fell. In time, some tobacco planters switched to growing other crops such as corn and wheat.

The main cash crop in South Carolina and Georgia was rice. In low-lying areas along the coast, planters built dams to create rice fields, called paddies. These fields were flooded when the rice was young and drained when the rice was ready to harvest. Work in the rice paddies involved standing knee-deep in the mud all day with no protection from the blazing sun or the biting insects.

Reading Strategy   READING THE TEXT

Predicting Predicting allows students to use prior knowledge to make educated guesses. Have students formulate hypotheses on the effect the slave trade had on African societies. Before students begin, point out the following: (1) Europeans provided Africans with guns to use in capturing members of other ethnic groups for the slave trade (*increased violence among African groups*). (2) Most captives were healthy men and women between the ages of 15 and 25 (*robbed African societies of their most economically productive members, as well as those most likely to have children*). (3) African slave traders often received guns, alcohol, and luxury goods in return for captives (*promoted social ills rather than helping develop the economy*). Have students use library resources to check their hypotheses. **L2**

Because rice harvesting required so much strenuous work, rice growers relied on slave labor. Rice proved to be even more profitable than tobacco. As it became popular in southern Europe, the price of rice rose steadily. By the 1750s South Carolina and Georgia had the fastest-growing economies in the colonies.

Tidewater and Backcountry

Most of the large Southern plantations were located in the Tidewater, a region of flat, low-lying plains along the seacoast. Plantations, or large farms, were often located on rivers so crops could be shipped to market by boat.

Each plantation was a self-contained community with fields stretching out around a cluster of buildings. The planter's wife supervised the main house and the household servants. A plantation also included slave cabins, barns and stables, and outbuildings such as carpenter and blacksmith shops and storerooms. Even kitchens were in separate buildings. A large plantation might also have its own chapel and school.

West of the Tidewater lay a region of hills and forests climbing up toward the **Appalachian Mountains.** This region was known as the backcountry and was settled in part by hardy newcomers to the colonies. The backcountry settlers grew corn and tobacco on small farms. They usually worked alone or with their families, although some had one or two enslaved Africans to help.

In the Southern Colonies, the independent small farmers of the backcountry outnumbered the large plantation owners. The plantation owners, however, had greater wealth and more influence. They controlled the economic and political life of the region.

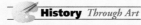 **Reading Check** **Comparing** How were the settlers of the Tidewater different from those of the backcountry?

History *Through Art*

The Old Plantation by an unknown artist
This watercolor from the 1700s shows a traditional African celebration on a Southern plantation. **Where would you be more likely to find enslaved African laborers—in the Tidewater or backcountry? Why?**

Reading Check

Answer: Wealthy and influential tidewater planters had large, self-contained plantations that used slave labor; backcountry farmers had little political and economic influence and worked small, family-run farms.

History *Through Art*

Answer: in the Tidewater because plantations were large and depended on slave labor to handle large quantities of crops

---

3 ASSESS

Assign Section 1 Assessment as homework or as an in-class activity.

Have students use **Interactive Tutor Self-Assessment CD-ROM.**

L2

Section Quiz 4–1

Name _____ Date _____ Class _____

★ **Chapter 4**   Score

Section Quiz 4-1

DIRECTIONS: Matching Match the items in Column A with the items in Column B. Write the correct letters in the blanks. *(10 points each)*

Column A	Column B
_____ 1. important New England industry	A. cash crops
_____ 2. crops that sold easily	B. backcountry
_____ 3. cultural variety	C. slave codes
_____ 4. near Appalachian Mountains	D. shipbuilding
_____ 5. governed slaves	E. diversity

EXTENDING THE CONTENT

Legalizing Slavery The eighteenth century marked a turning point for African Americans. At that time colonial assemblies made slavery in America legal by passing slave codes. Only one factor determined whether a person was subject to slave codes—color. Any African ancestry was enough to classify a person as black.

✓ **Reading Check**

Answer: They governed the behavior and punishment of enslaved people.

L1

Reteaching Activity 4–1

L1, ELL

Reading Essentials and Study Guide 4–1

L3

Enrichment Activity 4–1

4 CLOSE

Have students speculate on how history might have been different if slavery had not been allowed

Slavery

Most enslaved Africans lived on plantations. Some did housework, but most worked in the fields and often suffered great cruelty. The large plantation owners hired overseers, or bosses, to keep the slaves working hard.

By the early 1700s, many of the colonies had issued **slave codes,** strict rules governing the behavior and punishment of enslaved Africans. Some codes did not allow slaves to leave the plantation without written permission from the master. Some made it illegal to teach enslaved people to read or write. They usually allowed slaves to be whipped for minor offenses and hanged or burned to death for serious crimes. Those who ran away were often caught and punished severely.

African Traditions

Although the enslaved Africans had strong family ties, their families were often torn apart. Slaveholders could sell a family member to another slaveholder. Slaves found a source of strength in their African roots. They developed a culture that drew on the languages and customs of their West African homelands.

Some enslaved Africans learned trades such as carpentry, blacksmithing, or weaving. Skilled workers could sometimes set up shops, sharing

their profits with the slaveholders. Those lucky enough to be able to buy their freedom joined the small population of free African Americans.

Criticism of Slavery

Although the majority of white Southerners were not slaveholders, slavery played an important role in the economic success of the Southern Colonies. That success, however, was built on the idea that one human being could own another. Some colonists did not believe in slavery. Many Puritans refused to hold enslaved people. In Pennsylvania, Quakers and Mennonites condemned slavery. Eventually the debate over slavery would erupt in a bloody war, pitting North against South.

✓ **Reading Check** **Describing** What did slave codes do?

Fact • Fiction • Folklore

Banning Slavery

Slavery was first outlawed in the northern colonies. This is not true. Slavery was first outlawed in the colony of Georgia in 1735. Georgia eventually made slavery legal again.

SECTION 1 ASSESSMENT

Checking for Understanding

1. **Key Terms** Use each of these terms in a sentence that will help explain its meaning: subsistence farming, triangular trade, cash crop.
2. **Reviewing Facts** Identify the various economic activities carried on in the Middle Colonies.

Reviewing Themes

3. **Economic Factors** How did New England's natural resources help its commerce?

Critical Thinking

4. **Comparing** How did farming in New England compare with farming in the Southern Colonies? Use a chart like the one below to answer the question.

	Similarities	Differences
New England		
Southern Colonies		

5. **Making Inferences** How do you think plantation owners in the Southern Colonies justified their use of enslaved Africans?

Analyzing Visuals

6. **Geography Skills** Study the map on page 103. What goods were traded from the British Colonies to Great Britain? From the West Indies to the British Colonies?

Interdisciplinary Activity

Informative Writing Imagine you live in New England in the 1750s and are visiting cousins on a farm in the Carolinas. Write a letter to a friend at home describing your visit to the farm.

SECTION 1 ASSESSMENT ANSWERS

1. Student work should reflect correct use of terms.
2. cash crops, small-scale manufacturing, lumbering, mining, trade
3. Streams and rivers powered mills and transported materials; forests provided lumber for shipbuilding; access to the ocean encouraged trading.
4. New England–Similarities: main economic activity; Differences: small subsistence farms worked by family members, long winters; Southern Colonies–Similarities: main economic activity; Differences: large scale plantations, cash crops, slave labor
5. Answers will vary but should indicate that owners felt that it was necessary to keep the economy strong.
6. rice, tobacco, indigo, furs; goods and molasses

Interdisciplinary Activity Letters should describe a plantation.

Olaudah Equiano
(c. 1750–1797)

Olaudah Equiano was 11 years old when he and his sister were kidnapped by slave traders. Olaudah was taken to the West Indies and sold into slavery. His life story includes memories of his childhood in Africa. He wrote his story after receiving the name Gustavus Vassa from one of his masters and buying his freedom. Published during the time of the movement to end slavery, Equiano's work became a best-seller.

READ TO DISCOVER

This selection begins after Olaudah has been kidnapped and forced to endure the terrifying trip across the Atlantic Ocean aboard a slave ship. As you read, think about what life must have been like for Africans who were sold into slavery.

READER'S DICTIONARY

parcel: group
lots: groups
toil: work

The Kidnapped Prince

Right away we were taken to a merchant's yard, where we were all penned up together like so many sheep. When I looked out at the town, everything was new to me. The houses were built with bricks, in stories, and were completely different from any I had seen in Africa. I was still more astonished at seeing people on horseback. . . .

We were not many days in the merchant's custody before we were sold—like this:

Someone beat a drum. Then all the buyers rushed at once into the yard where we were penned to choose the **parcel** of us that they liked best. They rushed from one group of us to another, with tremendous noise and eager faces, terrifying us all.

Three men who were sold were brothers. They were sold in different **lots.** I still remember how they cried when they were parted. Probably they never saw each other again.

I didn't know it, but this happened all the time in slave sales. Parents lost their children; brothers lost their sisters. Husbands lost their wives.

We had already lost our homes, our countries, and almost everyone we loved. The people who did the selling and buying could have done it without separating us from our very last relatives and friends. They already could live in riches from our misery and **toil.** What possible advantage did they gain from this refinement of cruelty?

From *The Kidnapped Prince* by Olaudah Equiano. Adapted by Ann Cameron. Copyright © 1995 by Ann Cameron. Reprinted by permission of Alfred A. Knopf, Inc.

ANALYZING LITERATURE

1. **Recall and Interpret** How did the Africans feel as they were being sold?
2. **Evaluate and Connect** Do you think Olaudah Equiano supports slavery? Explain.

Interdisciplinary Activity

Descriptive Writing Re-read the excerpt and think about what it must have been like to be separated from family members. Write a dialogue you think might occur between two family members as they are about to be separated from each other.

 Block Schedule

Team Teaching This selection from *The Kidnapped Prince* may be implemented in a team-teaching context, in conjunction with English/Language Arts.

Reinforcing Vocabulary

Review the **Reader's Dictionary** terms with students to be sure they understand any unfamiliar terms.

Historical Connection

Olaudah Equiano survived against great odds. Millions of other Africans were killed during capture or perished aboard the vastly overcrowded and unsanitary ships.

Background Information

Setting The excerpt takes place at the end of the voyage from Africa to America.

Characters Equiano is the main character. Other characters include ship captives and various slaveholders.

Plot *The Kidnapped Prince* tells Equiano's story from his life in Africa before his capture through the terrifying voyage and slave auction to his eventual purchase of freedom.

 HISTORY *Online*

Refer to tarvol1.glencoe.com for additional Glencoe Literature titles, lesson plans, and study guides related to this unit.

ANSWERS TO ANALYZING LITERATURE

1. They were penned up together like sheep, then sold with no regard for family groups.
2. Students should recognize that he would not have written about the cruel treatment and separation of family members if he supported slavery. His first-hand experience would teach him its injustice.

Interdisciplinary Activity
Dialogues should reflect an understanding of the family members' fears and sorrow.

1 FOCUS

Section Overview

This section examines colonial government, religion, and culture.

BELLRINGER
Skillbuilder Activity

Project transparency and have students answer the question.

Daily Focus Skills Transparency 4–2

Reading Preview

Answers to Graphic: charter; proprietary; royal

Preteaching Vocabulary
Point out that the term *apprentice* is derived from a Latin word meaning "to grasp." Have students read the definition on page 112, and speculate on the connection between *apprentice* and *grasp*. (*An apprentice tries to grasp the skills of the craft.*)

SECTION 2 Government, Religion, and Culture

Guide to Reading

Main Idea
The ideals of American democracy and freedom of religion took root during the colonial period.

Key Terms
mercantilism, export, import, smuggling, charter colony, proprietary colony, royal colony, apprentice, literacy

Reading Strategy
Organizing Information As you read the section, re-create the diagram below and identify the three types of English colonies.

Types of colonies

Read to Learn
• why the Navigation Acts angered the colonists.
• who had the right to vote in colonial legislatures.

Section Theme
Continuity and Change The roots of American democracy, freedom of religion, and public education are found in the American colonial experience.

Preview of Events

♦1630   ♦1670   ♦1710   ♦1750

1636
Harvard College is established

1693
College of William and Mary is founded

1732
Benjamin Franklin publishes *Poor Richard's Almanack*

c. 1740
Great Awakening sweeps through the colonies

From Poor Richard's Almanack

AN American Story

"Fish and Visitors stink after three days."
"Beware of little Expenses: a small Leak will sink a great Ship."
"No gains without pains."
Benjamin Franklin wrote these and other witty sayings for his annual book, *Poor Richard's Almanack*. The last saying—"No gains without pains"—was particularly true in the American colonies in the late 1600s.

English Colonial Rule

In his writings, Benjamin Franklin celebrated a new American spirit. This spirit signaled that Americans were beginning to view themselves differently from the way Great Britain viewed them.

Trouble was brewing in England—and in the colonies—during the mid-1600s. England's monarchy had been restored with Charles II on the throne, but many people were not satisfied with his rule. James II, Charles's successor,

108   CHAPTER 4   The Colonies Grow

SECTION RESOURCES

📂 Reproducible Masters
• Reproducible Lesson Plan 4–2
• Daily Lecture and Discussion Notes 4–2
• Guided Reading Activity 4–2
• Section Quiz 4–2
• Reteaching Activity 4–2
• Reading Essentials and Study Guide 4–2
• Enrichment Activity 4–2

📄 Transparencies
• Daily Focus Skills Transparency 4–2

Multimedia
🎵 American Music: Hits Through History
💿 Interactive Tutor Self-Assessment CD-ROM
💿 ExamView® Pro Testmaker CD-ROM
💿 Presentation Plus! CD-ROM

attempted to take back the powers Parliament had won during the English Civil War. He also tried to tighten royal control over the colonies.

In 1688 Parliament took action. It forced out James and placed his daughter Mary and her Dutch husband, William of Orange, on the throne. This change, which showed the power of the elected representatives over the monarch, came to be known as the **Glorious Revolution.**

William and Mary signed an **English Bill of Rights** in 1689 guaranteeing certain basic rights to all citizens. This document became part of the heritage of English law that the American colonists shared. It later inspired the people who created the American Bill of Rights.

England viewed its North American colonies as an economic resource. The colonies provided England with raw materials. English manufacturers used these materials to produce finished goods, which they sold to the colonists. This process followed an economic theory called mercantilism. This theory states that as a nation's trade grows, its gold reserves increase, and the nation becomes more powerful. To make money from its trade, England had to export, or sell abroad, more goods than it imported, or bought from foreign markets.

To make certain that only England benefited from trade with the colonies, Parliament passed a series of laws between 1651 and 1673. These laws, called the **Navigation Acts,** directed the flow of goods between England and the colonies. Colonial merchants who had goods to send to England could not use foreign ships—even if those ships offered cheaper rates. The Navigation Acts also prevented the colonists from sending certain products, such as sugar or tobacco, outside England's empire.

Some colonists ignored these laws and began smuggling, or trading illegally with other nations. Controls on trade would later cause even more conflict between the American colonies and England.

✓ **Reading Check** **Examining** Under mercantilism, who controlled trade and who supplied raw materials?

People In History

Benjamin Franklin 1706–1790

Ben Franklin learned the printer's trade as a young man. By the time he was 23, he owned his own newspaper in Philadelphia. Soon afterward he began publishing *Poor Richard's Almanack*, a calendar filled with advice, philosophy, and wise sayings, such as "Early to bed, early to rise, makes a man healthy, wealthy, and wise."

Franklin was deeply interested in science. He invented the lightning rod, bifocal eyeglasses, and the Franklin stove for heating. Energetic and open-minded, Franklin served in the Pennsylvania Assembly for many years. He founded a hospital, a fire department, America's first lending library, and an academy of higher learning that later became the University of Pennsylvania.

Franklin's greatest services to his fellow Americans would come during the 1770s. As a statesman and patriot, Franklin would help guide the colonies toward independence.

CHAPTER 4 The Colonies Grow **109**

2 TEACH

Daily Lecture and Discussion Notes 4–2

Copyright © by The McGraw-Hill Companies, Inc.

Daily Lecture and Discussion Notes

Chapter 4, Section 2

Did You Know? The "Great Awakening" of the 1730s and 1740s called for a greater involvement of faith in God in daily life. On the other side, the "Enlightenment" of the 1770s questioned such involvement of faith and called for a smaller role for God in the daily affairs of people.

I. **English Colonial Rule** *(Pages 108–109)*

A. In the mid-1600s, the English monarchy saw Charles II and then James II rule. James II tried to tighten royal control over the colonies, but in 1688 he was forced out by the English Parliament. Mary, his daughter, and her husband, William, ruled. This power of elected representatives over the monarch was known as the Glorious Revolution.

B. The English Bill of Rights, signed by William and Mary in 1689, guaranteed certain

Reading Strategy

Identifying the Significance of Events After students have read the section, have them explain the importance of each of the following: Glorious Revolution, English Bill of Rights, Navigation Acts, Great Awakening, Enlightenment. Students may work in pairs, with one student giving the explanation and the other identifying the term. **L1**

✓ Reading Check

Answer: Trade was controlled by England, and the colonies served as a source of raw materials.

People In History

At age 13 Benjamin Franklin was apprenticed to his brother James, a printer. Benjamin devoted his spare time to self-education. In 1721 his brother James began the *New England Courant*. At age 15, Benjamin delivered the newspaper by day and wrote anonymous articles at night.

COOPERATIVE LEARNING ACTIVITY

Producing a Play Have students work in groups to produce plays about the lives of colonial children and teens. Possible topics include school, work, games and toys, home chores, and apprenticeships. Divide tasks (writing dialogue, researching, creating props, making costumes, and acting) according to the skills of the group members. As each group presents its play, have classmates write impressions about what was especially effective, as well as suggestions for improvement. **L1,** ELL

Why It Matters

Traveling revivalist ministers toured the colonies, attracting large crowds. They were welcomed for promoting religious zeal, gaining converts, and increasing church membership. This movement provided a sense of connection among the colonists, which proved beneficial during the American Revolution. Some members of the established churches rejected the revival because of its emotionalism. Since other members supported the revival, denominations divided into separate churches.

Ask: How do you think a sense of American nationality affected the colonists? *(Students may note that many colonists began to share the belief that the colonies should be independent from England.)*

History and the Humanities

📁 American Art and Music, Edward Winslow **L2**

🎵 American Music: Hits Through History, "Beausoleil"

Why It Matters

Causes and Effects of the Great Awakening

The Great Awakening

The Great Awakening is the name for the powerful religious revival that swept over the colonies beginning in the 1720s. Christian ministers such as George Whitefield and Jonathan Edwards preached throughout the colonies, drawing huge crowds. The Great Awakening had a lasting effect on the way in which the colonists viewed themselves, their relationships with one another, and their faith.

Jonathan Edwards

Causes

- Jonathan Edwards, George Whitefield, and others preach of the need for a revival of religious belief.
- Awareness of the importance of religion in people's lives grows.
  - A religious revival sweeps through America in the mid-1700s.

🏛 Citizenship

Colonial Government

The English colonists brought with them ideas about government that had been developing in England for centuries. By the 1600s the English people had won political liberties, such as trial by jury, that were largely unknown elsewhere. At the heart of the English system were two principles of government. These principles—limited government and representative government—greatly influenced the development of the United States.

By the time the first colonists reached North America, the idea that government was not all-powerful had become an accepted part of the English system of government. The idea first appeared in the Magna Carta that King John was forced to sign in 1215. The Magna Carta established the principle of limited government, in which the power of the king, or government, was limited. This document provided for protection against unjust punishment and against the loss of life, liberty, and property, except according to law. 📖 *(See page 611 of the Appendix for excerpts from the Magna Carta.)*

As the colonies grew, they relied more and more on their own governments to make local laws. By the 1760s there were three types of colonies in America—charter colonies, proprietary colonies, and royal colonies.

Charter Colonies

Connecticut and Rhode Island, the charter colonies, were established by settlers who had been given a charter, or a grant of rights and privileges. These colonists elected their own governors and the members of the legislature. Great Britain had the right to approve the governor, but the governor could not veto the acts of the legislature.

DIFFERENTIATED INSTRUCTION

Reading Support Each of the thirteen colonies was divided into counties, as are the 50 states today. (In Louisiana they are called parishes.) Have students find out the name of their county, what the county government does, and how it is organized. Have students present their findings in written form and include an organizational chart. **L2**

📁 Refer to *Inclusion for the Middle School Social Studies Classroom Strategies and Activities* in the TCR.

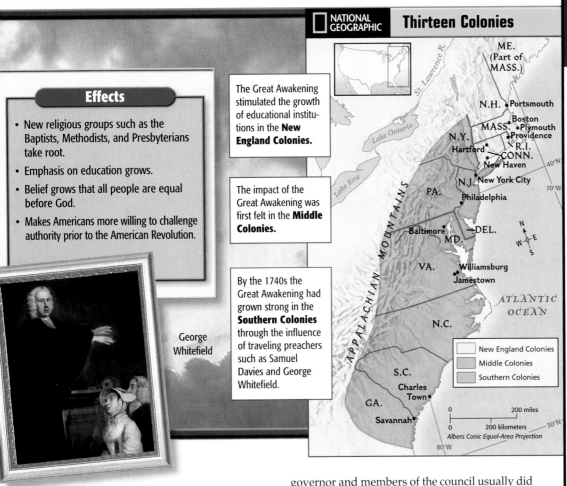

Effects

- New religious groups such as the Baptists, Methodists, and Presbyterians take root.
- Emphasis on education grows.
- Belief grows that all people are equal before God.
- Makes Americans more willing to challenge authority prior to the American Revolution.

George Whitefield

The Great Awakening stimulated the growth of educational institutions in the **New England Colonies.**

The impact of the Great Awakening was first felt in the **Middle Colonies.**

By the 1740s the Great Awakening had grown strong in the **Southern Colonies** through the influence of traveling preachers such as Samuel Davies and George Whitefield.

NATIONAL GEOGRAPHIC — Thirteen Colonies

- New England Colonies
- Middle Colonies
- Southern Colonies

Reading Check

Answer: It established the principle of limited government in which the power of the monarchy or government was limited. As the colonies grew, more of their governments made local laws.

L1, ELL

Guided Reading Activity 4–2

Name _____ Date _____ Class _____

★ **Guided Reading Activity 4-2**

DIRECTIONS: Recalling the Facts Use the information in your textbook to answer the questions. Use another sheet of paper if necessary.

1. What were the major contributions and accomplishments of Benjamin Franklin? _____
2. How did the Navigation Acts ensure that only England could benefit from trade with the American colonies? _____
3. What were the two charter colonies? _____
4. Who established the charter colonies? _____
5. What were the three proprietary colonies? _____
6. Who ruled the proprietary colonies? _____
7. What were the seven royal colonies? _____
8. Who ruled the royal colonies? _____
9. Who had the right to vote in colonial America? _____
10. Why did the Puritans of New England come to America? _____
11. When did the Great Awakening occur? _____
12. What roles did women have in colonial America? _____
13. Where were women allowed to participate in decision making? _____
14. When did the Massachusetts Puritans pass the first public education law? _____
15. What was the main idea of the Enlightenment? _____

Proprietary Colonies

The proprietary colonies—Delaware, Maryland, and Pennsylvania—were ruled by proprietors. These were individuals or groups to whom Britain had granted land. Proprietors were generally free to rule as they wished. They appointed the governor and members of the upper house of the legislature, while the colonists elected the lower house.

Royal Colonies

By the 1760s Georgia, Massachusetts, New Hampshire, New Jersey, New York, North Carolina, South Carolina, and Virginia were royal colonies. Britain directly ruled all royal colonies. In each, the king appointed a governor and council, known as the upper house. The colonists elected an assembly, called the lower house. The governor and members of the council usually did what the British leaders told them to do. However, this often led to conflict with the colonists in the assembly, especially when officials tried to enforce tax laws and trade restrictions.

Voting Rights

Colonial legislatures gave only some people a voice in government. Generally, white men who owned property had the right to vote; however, most women, indentured servants, landless poor, and African Americans could not vote. In spite of these limits, a higher proportion of people was involved in government in the colonies than anywhere in the European world. This strong participation gave Americans training that was valuable when the colonies became independent.

✓ **Reading Check** **Drawing Inferences** How did the Magna Carta affect government in the colonies?

CHAPTER 4   The Colonies Grow   **111**

Cooper, Smith, Wright Many proper names come from occupations. For example, a *cooper* was a person who made wooden tubs or barrels. A *smith* was a metalworker. A *wright* was a person who made something (wheelwright, playwright).

INTERDISCIPLINARY CONNECTIONS ACTIVITY

Daily Life Point out that Benjamin Franklin made a number of contributions to Philadelphia, including building a library, a fire department, and a college. Have students choose a public service that they can perform. Possibilities include cleaning up a stream, a vacant lot, or graffiti; getting a streetlight installed on a dark street or parking lot; setting up a book swap; holding a canned goods drive for the needy. Students should write an article for the local paper to announce the event and to ask for community volunteers if needed. L1, ELL

3 ASSESS

Assign Section 2 Assessment as homework or as an in-class activity.

🌐 Have students use **Interactive Tutor Self-Assessment CD-ROM.**

L2

Section Quiz 4–2

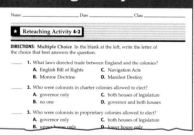

L1

Reteaching Activity 4–2

An Emerging Culture

From the 1720s through the 1740s, a religious revival called the **Great Awakening** swept through the colonies. In New England and the Middle Colonies, ministers called for "a new birth," a return to the strong faith of earlier days. One of the outstanding preachers was **Jonathan Edwards** of Massachusetts. People thought that his sermons were powerful and convincing.

The English preacher **George Whitefield**, who arrived in the colonies in 1739, helped spread the religious revival. Whitefield inspired worshipers in churches and open fields from New England to Georgia. The Great Awakening led to the formation of many new churches.

Family Roles

Throughout the colonies, people adapted their traditions to the new conditions of life in America. Religion, education, and the arts contributed to a new American culture. The family formed the foundation of colonial society.

A colonial farm was both home and workplace. Mothers and fathers cared for their children. Women cooked, made butter and cheese, and preserved food. They spun yarn, made clothes, and tended chickens and cows. Men worked in the fields and built barns, houses, and fences. In many areas, women worked in the fields next to their husbands.

Men were the formal heads of the households. They managed the farms and represented the family in community affairs. In most churches, women could attend church meetings, but could not speak, vote, or serve as clergy. Families often arranged for their sons to work as indentured servants for farmers or to serve as apprentices, or learning assistants, to craft workers who taught them a trade. Married women were considered under their husbands' authority and had few rights.

TECHNOLOGY & History

Colonial Printing Press

Life in the colonies often revolved around local printers who produced pamphlets, small flyers, books, and newspapers. The first printing press in the American colonies was established by Stephen Daye in 1639.

Type is made up of large numbers of single letters that can be moved and reused.

1 A sheet of paper is fitted into the **paper holder**, which is then folded on top of the type form.

2 The **platen** presses the paper onto the inked type.

3 The **horizontal lever** lowered or raised the platen.

4 **Type form** was slid under the raised platen.

5 **Paper** was put in the paper holder. Once the paper was removed, it was hung up to dry on clothes lines. The lines were called flys and the printed papers became known as flyers.

3 horizontal lever

1 paper holder

2 platen

4 type form

5 paper

112

Reading Strategy READING THE TEXT

Comparing and Contrasting Comparing and contrasting helps students see the similarities and differences between people, things, and ideas. Two movements that influenced the belief systems of individuals and groups in the 1700s were the Great Awakening and the Enlightenment. Pair students to research another movement that affected Americans. Then have them create a two-column list for their movement. One column should list the similarities their movement has compared to the Enlightenment or the Great Awakening, and the other column should list the differences. Have students share their lists with the class. **L2**

Women in cities and towns sometimes held jobs outside the home. Young unmarried women might work for wealthy families as maids, cooks, and nurses. Widows might work as teachers, nurses, and seamstresses. They also opened shops and inns. Widows and women who had never married could run businesses and own property, even though they could not vote. 📖 *(See page 594 of the Primary Sources Library for the selection, "What is an American?")*

Education

Most colonists valued education. Children were often taught to read and write at home by their parents. In New England and Pennsylvania, in particular, school systems were set up to make sure that everyone could read and study the Bible. In 1647 the Massachusetts Puritans passed a public education law. Each community with 50 or more households had to have a school supported by taxes.

By 1750, New England had a very high level of literacy, the ability to read and write. Approximately 85 percent of the men and about half of the women could read. Many learned to read from *The New England Primer,* which combined lessons in good conduct with reading and writing.

Many colonial schools were run by widows or unmarried women. In the Middle Colonies, some schools were run by Quakers and other religious groups. In the towns and cities, craftspeople set up night schools for their apprentices.

The colonies' early colleges were founded to train ministers. The first was Harvard College, established in 1636 by the Puritans in Cambridge, Massachusetts. Anglicans founded William and Mary College in Virginia in 1693.

The Enlightenment

By the middle of the 1700s, many educated colonists were influenced by the **Enlightenment.** This movement, which began in Europe, spread the idea that knowledge, reason, and science could improve society. In the colonies, the Enlightenment increased interest in science. People observed nature, staged experiments, and published their findings. The best known American scientist was Benjamin Franklin.

Freedom of the Press

In 1735 John Peter Zenger of the *New York Weekly Journal* faced charges of libel for printing a critical report about the royal governor of New York. Andrew Hamilton argued that free speech was a basic right of English people. He defended Zenger by asking the jury to base its decision on whether Zenger's article was true, not whether it was offensive. The jury found Zenger not guilty. At the time the case attracted little attention, but today it is regarded as an important step in the development of a free press in America.

✓**Reading Check** **Analyzing** What was the impact of the Great Awakening?

SECTION 2 ASSESSMENT

Checking for Understanding

1. **Key Terms** Use each of these terms in a complete sentence that will help explain its meaning: export, charter colony, proprietary colony, apprentice, literacy.
2. **Reviewing the Facts** Identify some contributions of women inside and outside the home.

Reviewing Themes

3. **Continuity and Change** Why did the Navigation Acts anger the colonists?

Critical Thinking

4. **Drawing Conclusions** Why did Andrew Hamilton defend John Peter Zenger and free speech?
5. **Determining Cause and Effect** Re-create the diagram below and describe the effects of the Great Awakening.

Analyzing Visuals

6. **Picturing History** Examine the printing press on page 112. Who established the first printing press in the colonies? How do you think the colonists communicated their ideas before printed material was widely used?

Interdisciplinary Activity

Government Draw a chart that shows the structure of a royal colony, a proprietary colony, and a charter colony.

✓**Reading Check**

Answer: Answers may include that it led to a revival of strong religious beliefs and helped promote a sense of American nationality.

L1, ELL

Reading Essentials and Study Guide 4–2

Study Guide
Chapter 4, Section 2
For use with textbook pages 108–113
GOVERNMENT, RELIGION, AND CULTURE

KEY TERMS	
mercantilism	Theory that states that, when a nation's trade grows, its gold reserves increase, and the nation becomes more powerful *(page 109)*
export	To sell to another country *(page 109)*
import	To buy from a foreign market *(page 109)*
smuggling	To trade illegally *(page 109)*
charter colony	Colonies established by settlers who were given a grant of rights and privileges *(page 110)*
proprietary colony	Colonies governed by individuals or groups to whom the land had been given by England's king *(page 111)*

L3

Enrichment Activity 4–2

Name _____ Date _____ Class _____

★ **Enrichment Activity 4-2** ★ 🔍

Secrets to Business Success
Benjamin Franklin, who was very organized, used the following schedule for the 24 hours of the day.

THE MORNING Question. What good shall I do this day?	5 6	Rise, wash and address *Powerful Goodness!* Contrive day's business, and take the resolution of the day; prosecute the present study, and breakfast.
	7 8 9	Work.
NOON	10 11 12 1	Read, or overlook my accounts, and dine.
	2 3	Work.

4 CLOSE

Developments in England and the colonies gave most colonists more rights and an increasing voice in their own government. Have students list facts from the section about rights and citizen voice in government in England, charter colonies, proprietary colonies, and royal colonies.

SECTION 2 ASSESSMENT ANSWERS

1. Student work should reflect correct use of terms.
2. Answers may include: inside the home: cooking, making clothes, tending livestock, working in the fields; outside the home: working as maids, cooks, nurses, teachers, or shopkeepers
3. The acts restricted trade with all nations except England and limited the ships they could use.
4. Hamilton believed that free speech was a basic right.
5. Answers may include: revival of strong religious belief, religion becoming more important in people's lives, formation of new churches, growing sense of American nationality in colonies.
6. Stephen Daye; Answers may include: writing by hand, posting notices, lectures, and talking in public places.

Interdisciplinary Activity Charts should show differences among the colonies.

TEACH

Analyzing Primary Sources

Have students read Edward Winslow's description of the first Thanksgiving feast. **Ask:** When did the first Thanksgiving feast take place? What were the colonists celebrating? Where did the colonists get the fowl they ate? *(fall of 1621; the harvest; hunters killed them)*

Invite volunteers to compare and contrast their own Thanksgiving celebrations with the first Thanksgiving. *(Student answers will vary, but students should note the differences between the celebrations. For example, most students will celebrate as a family rather than at a community event; guests will be family or close friends rather than a nearby tribe of Native Americans; and most will buy their food. Feasts will last for one afternoon or evening, rather than three days. Thanksgiving today does not specifically celebrate the harvest.)*

Visit the TIME Web site at www.time.com for up-to-date news, weekly magazine articles, editorials, online polls, and an archive of past magazine and Web articles.

TIME NOTEBOOK

What were people's lives like in the past?

What—and who—were people talking about? What did they eat? What did they do for fun? These two pages will give you some clues to everyday life in the U.S. as you step back in time with TIME Notebook.

Profile

EDWARD WINSLOW *was 25 when he sailed on the Mayflower to Massachusetts. Winslow helped found Plymouth Colony, served as the colony's governor three times—and still found time to sit down to the very first Thanksgiving celebrated in the British colonies in the fall of 1621. Here's part of what he wrote about the first big feast:*

"OUR HARVEST BEING GOTTEN IN, OUR GOVERNOR sent four men on the fowling *(hunt for fowl)*, that we might ... rejoice together after we had gathered the fruits of our labors. In one day, they killed as much fowl as ... served the company almost a week. At which time, ... many of the Indians came amongst us ... with some ninety men whom for three days we entertained and feasted...."

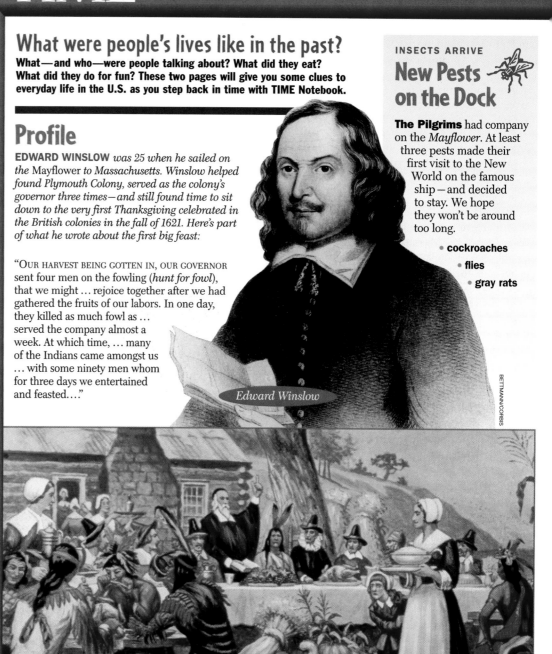

Edward Winslow

INSECTS ARRIVE
New Pests on the Dock

The Pilgrims had company on the *Mayflower*. At least three pests made their first visit to the New World on the famous ship—and decided to stay. We hope they won't be around too long.

- cockroaches
- flies
- gray rats

114

EXTENDING THE CONTENT

Thanksgiving Harvests The Thanksgiving holiday is believed by many scholars to be an extension of the harvest festivals that are traditional in other parts of the world. Governor William Bradford proclaimed a day of thanksgiving and prayer following the first harvest in 1621. Gradually celebrating Thanksgiving after the harvest became an annual custom in New England. The Continental Congress suggested a yearly day of national Thanksgiving during the American Revolution. In 1863 President Abraham Lincoln designated a specific day of Thanksgiving.

COLONIAL EVENTS
Virginia Is Number 1

Here's a list of events that happened first in 1619 in Virginia. One of the facts is wrong. Can you figure out the one that doesn't belong?

1. First boatload of African slaves
2. First labor strike
3. First elected lawmakers
4. First time English settlers can own land
5. First daily newspaper
6. First boatload of women who agreed to marry colonists in exchange for a ticket across the Atlantic

answer: 5

POPULAR FOOD
Have Your Corn Cake – and Eat It Too!

This New World meal is all the rage in the colonies.

Stir one cup of coarse cornmeal grits into three cups of water.

Place on stove. Simmer.

Remove from heat when all the water is absorbed. Let it cool.

Shape the mixture into two round, flat cakes on a floured work surface.

Bake it in a hot oven for 45 minutes.

Serve warm or cold with freshly churned butter.

VERBATIM
WHAT PEOPLE ARE SAYING

❝ ...I found some black people about me, and I believe some were those who had brought me on board and had been receiving their pay.... I asked them if we were not to be eaten by those white men with horrible looks, red faces, and long hair.❞

OLAUDAH EQUIANO,
11-year-old kidnapped from his home in what is now Nigeria and brought to America as an enslaved person, on his first day on the slave ship

❝ For pottage and puddings and custards and pies / Our pumpkins and parsnips are common supplies. We have pumpkins at morning and pumpkins at noon, / If it were not for pumpkin, / We should be undone.❞

AMERICAN FOLK SONG,
a tribute to the pumpkin

NUMBERS
THE COLONIES AT THE TIME

1,500 Number of English children in 1627 who were kidnapped and sent to work as servants in Virginia

80% Percentage of colonists who died in Jamestown, Virginia, during the winter of 1609–10 after getting so hungry they ate rats, snakes, and horsehide

65% Percentage of colonists who could read in 1620

2,500 Number of trees needed to build a ship the size of the *Mayflower*

NORTH WIND PICTURES

0 Number of chairs set at the dinner table for children— only adults sat while eating

50 Number of pounds of tobacco colonists in Virginia were fined if they did not go to church in the early 1600s

Alternative Assessment

Have students read the *Numbers* column. Discuss each fact and what it reflects about life at the time the colonies were being settled, especially the status and lives of children. Tell students to select a fact and write about a related issue today or about how conditions have changed since the early 1600s.

Did you know?

In 1623 a day of fasting and prayer during a period of drought was changed to one of thanksgiving because the rain came during the prayers.

CLOSE

Have students research present-day statistics and one of the facts in the TIME feature. For example, they might find statistics on literacy or deaths from starvation and where they occur. Ask students to share their findings with the class. Discuss whether or not these statistics have relatively improved or worsened since colonial times.

COOPERATIVE LEARNING ACTIVITY

Songwriting and Singing Have students work in groups to write and sing a folk song that would reflect an aspect of present-day life in your community, as the pumpkin song reflects diet in the *Verbatim* section on page 115. Help students divide the work according to abilities, with different students responsible for lyrics and melody. Allow one or more group members to sing the song, unless the entire group chooses to sing it. **L1**

👉 Use the rubric for writing an original song on pages 52–53 in the *Performance Assessment Activities and Rubrics.*

1 FOCUS

Section Overview

This section tells how American colonists and Native Americans became involved in the clash between France and Britain.

BELLRINGER
Skillbuilder Activity

 Project transparency and have students answer the question.

Daily Focus Skills Transparency 4–3

Reading Preview

Answers to Graphic: Answers may include: French and British fur traders clash in French-controlled Ohio; France attacks British-controlled Nova Scotia; Native Americans side with French, but the Iroquois side with British; Washington's militia clashes with French in Ohio.

Preteaching Vocabulary
List *Iroquois Confederacy* and *militia* on the chalkboard. Have students develop questions for which each term is an answer.

France and Britain Clash

Guide to Reading

Main Idea
Rivalry between Great Britain and France led to a long-lasting conflict.

Key Terms
Iroquois Confederacy, militia

Reading Strategy
Organizing Information As you read the section, re-create the diagram below and describe the events that led to conflict in North America.

☐ → ☐ → ☐ → Conflict in North America

Read to Learn
• how wars in Europe spread to the American colonies.
• about the purpose of the Albany Plan of Union.

Section Theme
Continuity and Change American colonists and Native American groups were drawn into the clash between France and Britain.

Preview of Events

◆1740   ◆1750   ◆1760

1745
New England troops seize Fort Louisbourg from France

1753
George Washington sent to Ohio country to protest French actions

1754
Benjamin Franklin proposes Albany Plan of Union

Powderhorn, French and Indian War

★★★★★★★★
AN
American Story
~~~~~~~~~~

In 1689 England and France began competing to be the most powerful nation in Europe. This contest for power went on for generations, with only short intervals of peace. In 1758 writer Nathaniel Ames noted, "The parts of North America which may be claimed by Great Britain or France are of as much worth as either kingdom. That fertile country to the west of the Appalachian Mountains [is the] 'Garden of the World'!"

British-French Rivalry

Britain and France had been competing for wealth for centuries. By 1700 they were two of the strongest powers in Europe. Their long rivalry aroused bitter feelings between British and French colonists in North America.

As the growing population of the American colonies pushed up against French-held territory, hostility between England and France increased. At the same time, some land companies wanted to explore opportunities in the **Ohio River valley.** However, the French, who traded throughout the Ohio country,

---

SECTION RESOURCES

📁 **Reproducible Masters**
• Reproducible Lesson Plan 4–3
• Daily Lecture and Discussion Notes 4–3
• Guided Reading Activity 4–3
• Section Quiz 4–3
• Reteaching Activity 4–3
• Reading Essentials and Study Guide 4–3
• Enrichment Activity 4–3

🖥 **Transparencies**
• Daily Focus Skills Transparency 4–3

Multimedia
🔵 Interactive Tutor Self-Assessment CD-ROM
🔵 ExamView® Pro Testmaker CD-ROM
🔵 Presentation Plus! CD-ROM

regarded this territory as their own. They had no intention of letting British colonists share in their profitable fur trade.

In the 1740s British fur traders went into the Ohio country. They built a fort deep in the territory of the Miami people at a place called Pickawillany. Acting quickly, the French attacked Pickawillany and drove the British traders out of Ohio. The French then built a string of forts along the rivers of the upper Ohio Valley, closer to the British colonies than ever before. Two mighty powers—Great Britain and France— were headed for a showdown in North America.

In the early 1700s, Britain had gained control of Nova Scotia, Newfoundland, and the Hudson Bay region. In the 1740s French troops raided towns in Maine and New York. In response a force of New Englanders went north and captured the important French fortress at **Louisbourg** on Cape Breton Island, north of Nova Scotia. Later Britain returned Louisbourg to France, much to the disgust of the New England colonists.

Native Americans Take Sides

The French traders and the British colonists knew that Native American help would make a difference in their struggle for North America. The side that received the best trade terms from Native Americans and the most help in the war would probably win the contest for control of North America.

The French had many Native American allies. Unlike the British, the French were interested mainly in trading for furs—not in taking over Native American land. The French also had generally better relations with Native Americans. French trappers and fur traders often married Native American women and followed their customs. French missionaries traveled through the area, converting many Native Americans to Catholicism.

During the wars between Great Britain and France, Native Americans often helped the French by raiding British settlements. In 1704, for example, the Abenaki people joined the French in an attack on the British frontier outpost at Deerfield, Massachusetts, in which almost 50 settlers were killed.

North America in 1754

Claimed by Britain
Claimed by Spain
Claimed by France

0   500 miles
0   500 kilometers
Azimuthal Equidistant projection

Geography *Skills*

1. **Analyzing Information** What power claimed the territory of Florida?
2. **Region** What three rivers were located within French territory ?

The Iroquois Confederacy

The most powerful group of Native Americans in the East was the Iroquois Confederacy, based in New York. When the confederacy was first formed in about 1570, it included five nations—the Mohawk, Seneca, Cayuga, Onondaga, and Oneida. Other groups later joined or were conquered by the Iroquois.

The Iroquois managed to remain independent by trading with both the British and the French. By skillfully playing the British and French against each other, the Iroquois dominated the area around the Great Lakes.

By the mid-1700s, however, the Iroquois came under greater pressure as the British moved into the Ohio Valley. Eventually the leaders of the confederacy gave certain trading rights to the

2 TEACH

Daily Lecture and Discussion Notes 4–3

Copyright © by The McGraw-Hill Companies, Inc.

Daily Lecture and Discussion Notes

Chapter 4, Section 3

Did You Know ? George Washington lost most of his teeth over the years by cracking Brazil nuts between his jaws. His first set of dentures was made from cow's teeth and his second set from hippopotamus tusk. Washington's dentures were held in place by being attached to his one remaining natural tooth.

I. **British-French Rivalry** *(Pages 116–118)*

A. The French and British rivalry grew as both countries expanded into each other's territories.

B. In the 1740s, the British fur traders built a fort at Pickawillany in the Ohio River country. In 1752, the French attacked this fort and drove the British out. The French built several more forts along the Ohio River valley to protect what they claimed to be their fur-trading territory.

C. Also in the 1740s, French troops raided towns in Maine and New York. The British captured the French fortress at Louisbourg, north of Nova Scotia, in retaliation. Later they returned Louisbourg to France.

D. Many Native Americans helped France since the French and Native Americans had a better relationship. The Native Americans often raided British settlements.

E. The Iroquois Confederacy was the most powerful Native American group in the East. It consisted of five nations:

1. the Mohawks
2. the Seneca
3. the Cayuga
4. the Onondaga
5. the Oneida

They remained independent until the mid-1700s when the British gained certain trading rights in the Ohio Valley.

Discussion Question

Why did the British and French rivalry grow? *(The rivalry grew as a result of each country wanting to control the territory that they claimed and each country infringing on the other's territory.)*

turn

Summarizing Have students use the following words in a summary of the rivalry between the British and French: *power, profit, fur trade, fishing, land. (Students' summaries should note that these were all sources of conflict.)* **L1**

Geography *Skills*

Answers:
1. Spain
2. Mississippi River, Ohio River, Missouri River (Although the St. Lawrence River is not labeled, it was also controlled by France.)

COOPERATIVE LEARNING ACTIVITY

Researching the Iroquois League Have students work in small groups to prepare reports on the Iroquois League and the legends about its formation. Have students choose their own tasks: researching, writing, drawing illustrations, making a map to show the location of each of the five founding nations, and so on. Give each group a chance to present its report, with visuals, to the class. Select one item from each group to display in the classroom.

✓ **Reading Check**

Answer: The French were traders and did not take Native American lands and were more tolerant of Native American ways.

L1, ELL

Guided Reading Activity 4–3

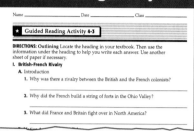

TWO VIEWPOINTS

Answers:

1. Both show allegiance to a monarch, provide a rationale for the explorer's claim, and give a description of the lands.
2. Answers may note that the claim was a formal record.

3 ASSESS

Assign Section 3 Assessment as homework or as an in-class activity.

🌐 Have students use **Interactive Tutor Self-Assessment CD-ROM.**

L2

Section Quiz 4–3

TWO VIEWPOINTS

I Claim This Land!

In the sixteenth century, Europeans became aware of a larger world around them—a world where they could claim new lands and profits. Soon a desire arose in England and France to conquer these lands and the people in them, and a race began to be the first to make those claims.

Drake Claims South and North America for England, June 1579

This country our general named Albion, and that for two causes; the one in respect of the white banks and cliffs, . . . that it might have some affinity [similarity], even in name also, with our own country, which was sometime so called.

Before we went from there, our general caused to be set up, a monument of our being there; as also of her majesties, and successors right and title to that kingdom, namely, a plate of brass, fast nailed to a great and firm post; whereon is [carved] her graces name, and the day and year of our arrival there, and of the free giving up, of the province and kingdom, both by the king and people, into her majesties hands. . . .

Sieur de St. Lusson Claims West and Northwest America for France, 1671

In the name of the Most High, Mighty, and Redoubted Monarch, Louis the Fourteenth of that name, Most Christian King of France and Navarre, I take possession of this place, Ste. Marie of the Sault, as also of Lakes Huron and Superior, the Island of Manitoulin, and all countries, rivers, lakes, and streams . . . both those which have been discovered and those which may be discovered hereafter, in all their length and breadth, bounded on the one side by the seas of the North and of the West, and on the other by the South Sea: Declaring to the nations thereof that from this time forth they are vassals [servants] of his Majesty, bound to obey his laws and follow his customs. . . .

Francis Drake

Learning From History

1. How are the two accounts similar?
2. Why do you think these men held such formal ceremonies when claiming a piece of land?

118

British and reluctantly became their allies. By taking this step, the Iroquois upset the balance of power between the French and British that had been so difficult to establish.

✓ **Reading Check** **Explaining** Why were Native Americans more likely to help the French than help the British?

American Colonists Take Action

A group of Virginians had plans for settling the Ohio Valley. In the fall of 1753 Governor Robert Dinwiddie of Virginia sent a 21-year-old planter and surveyor named **George Washington** into the Ohio country. Washington's mission was to tell the French that they were trespassing on territory claimed by Great Britain and demand that they leave.

Washington delivered the message, but it did no good. "The French told me," Washington said later, "that it was their absolute design to take possession of the Ohio, and by God they would do it."

Washington's First Command

In the spring of 1754, Dinwiddie made Washington a lieutenant colonel and sent him back to the Ohio country with a militia—a group of civilians trained to fight in emergencies—of 150 men. The militia had instructions to build a fort where the Allegheny and Monongahela Rivers meet to form the Ohio River—the site of present-day Pittsburgh. When Washington and his troops arrived, they found the French were already building Fort Duquesne (doo•KAYN) on that spot.

Washington established a small post nearby called **Fort Necessity.** Although greatly outnumbered, the

---

DIFFERENTIATED INSTRUCTION

English Learners Bring to class some books showing frontier forts of the period. Then have students design an ideal fort, including a location near a cliff or other natural barrier. Have them construct the fort using construction paper and other available materials. The project should be placed on a large piece of cardboard on which students can show the important features of the fort's location. **L1, ELL**

📁 Refer to *Inclusion for the Middle School Social Studies Classroom Strategies and Activities* in the TCR.

forces of the inexperienced Washington attacked a French scouting party. The French surrounded Washington's soldiers and forced them to surrender, but the soldiers were later released and they returned to Virginia. Washington's account of his experience in the Ohio country was published, and his fame spread throughout the colonies and Europe. In spite of his defeat, the colonists regarded Washington as a hero who struck the first blow against the French.

The Albany Plan of Union

While Washington struggled with the French, representatives from New England, New York, Pennsylvania, and Maryland met to discuss the threat of war. In June 1754, the representatives gathered in Albany, New York. They wanted to find a way for the colonies to defend themselves against the French. They also hoped to persuade the Iroquois to take their side against the French.

The representatives adopted a plan suggested by Benjamin Franklin. Known as the **Albany Plan of Union,** Franklin's plan called for "one general government" for 11 of the American colonies. An elected legislature would govern these colonies and would have the power to collect taxes, raise troops, and regulate trade. Not a single colonial assembly approved the plan. None of the colonies were willing to give up any

The Albany Plan

The Albany Plan was the first colonial constitution. Actually it was not the first. In 1639, settlers in Connecticut drew up America's first formal constitution, or charter, called the Fundamental Orders of Connecticut. This document laid out a plan for government that gave the people the right to elect the governor, judges, and representatives to make laws.

of their power. The Albany meeting failed to unite the colonists to fight the French. Disappointed, Franklin wrote,

> ❝Everyone cries, a union is necessary, but when they come to the manner and form of the union, their weak noodles [brains] are perfectly distracted.❞

Washington's defeat at Fort Necessity marked the start of a series of clashes and full-scale war. The colonists called it the French and Indian War because they fought two enemies—the French and their Native American allies.

✓ **Reading Check** Analyzing What was the purpose of the Albany Plan of Union?

SECTION 3 ASSESSMENT

Checking for Understanding

1. **Key Terms** Write a short paragraph that uses the terms Iroquois Confederacy and militia.
2. **Reviewing Facts** List two reasons the French felt threatened by British interest in the Ohio River valley.

Reviewing Themes

3. **Continuity and Change** Why did colonists consider George Washington a hero, even after he was defeated by the French?

Critical Thinking

4. **Analyzing Primary Sources** Re-read Benjamin Franklin's quote on this page. What was his reaction to the colonies' refusal to accept the Albany Plan of Union?
5. **Evaluating Information** Re-create the diagram below and explain the powers the legislature would have under the Albany Plan.

Analyzing Visuals

6. **Geography Skills** Study the map on page 117. What countries claimed land in North America? What power controlled most of what is present-day Canada? If you live in North America, what country controlled the region in which you live?

Interdisciplinary Activity

Expository Writing Make a list of five questions that a reporter might have asked Iroquois leaders after they reluctantly sided with the British.

✓ **Reading Check**

Answer: to provide for one general government for the colonies

L1

Reteaching Activity 4–3

L1, ELL

Reading Essentials and Study Guide 4–3

L3

Enrichment Activity 4–3

4 CLOSE

Have students turn the **Read to Learn** phrases (page 116) into questions and write answers to each.

SECTION 3 ASSESSMENT ANSWERS

1. Student work should reflect correct use of terms.
2. Answers may include: tradition of rivalry between the two nations; threat to their profitable fur trade with Native Americans; competition over resources, land, and fishing grounds.
3. His bravery in making the first move against the French made him a hero.
4. Franklin was frustrated that although the colonies expressed their desire for a union, they were unwilling to give up enough power to form one.
5. Answers may include: collect taxes, raise troops, regulate trade.
6. Britain, France, Spain; Britain; Answers will vary depending on one's location in North America.

Interdisciplinary Activity Students' questions should reflect an understanding of the Iroquois position.

TEACH

Understanding Cause and Effect Point out that understanding history involves knowing why events happened. Note that most effects have more than one cause, and that causes can have more than one effect.

After students answer the questions in **Practicing the Skill,** ask them to name another effect. *(Possible responses: Abolitionist movement; Civil War and its destruction; economic and social problems for freed African Americans; economic disaster for former slaveholders after the war)*

Additional Practice
L2

Chapter Skills Activity 4

Name	Date	Class

★ Chapter Skills Activity 4

Understanding Cause and Effect
An event or a condition that makes something happen is a *cause.*
An *effect* is what happens as a result of the cause. For example:

CAUSE		EFFECT
New England lacked good farmland.		Small farms produced few cash crops.

GLENCOE
TECHNOLOGY

CD-ROM
Glencoe Skillbuilder Interactive Workbook CD-ROM, Level 1

This interactive CD-ROM reinforces student mastery of essential social studies skills.

Understanding Cause and Effect

Why Learn This Skill?

You know that if you watch television instead of completing your homework you will receive poor grades. This is an example of a cause-and-effect relationship. The cause—watching television instead of doing homework—leads to an effect—poor grades.

Learning the Skill

A *cause* is any person, event, or condition that makes something happen. What happens as a result is known as an *effect*. These guidelines will help you identify cause and effect.
* Identify two or more events.
* Ask questions about why events occur.
* Look for "clue words" that alert you to cause and effect, such as *because, led to, brought about, produced,* and *therefore.*
* Identify the outcome of events.

Practicing the Skill

Study the cause-and-effect chart about the slave trade on this page. Think about the guidelines listed above. Then answer the questions below.

❶ What were some causes of the development of slavery in the colonies?

❷ What were some of the short-term effects of enslaving Africans?

❸ What was the long-term effect of the development of slavery?

Causes and Effects of the Slave Trade

Causes
* Colonists need to grow cash crops, such as tobacco and rice.
* European demand for tobacco and rice increases.
* Growing tobacco and rice requires large labor force.

Effects
* Africans are robbed of basic human rights.
* Population of enslaved Africans grows.
* Slavery creates feelings of injustice and plants seeds of regional conflict.

Applying the Skill
Understanding Cause and Effect Read an account of a recent event or chain of events in your community newspaper. Determine at least one cause and one effect of that event. Show the cause-and-effect relationship in a chart.

 Glencoe's **Skillbuilder Interactive Workbook CD-ROM, Level 1,** provides instruction and practice in key social studies skills.

ANSWERS TO PRACTICING THE SKILL

❶ colonists' need to grow cash crops, increased demand for tobacco and rice, need for large labor force to grow rice and tobacco

❷ enslaved Africans robbed of basic human rights, African American population grows

❸ created feelings of injustice and sowed seeds of regional conflict

Applying the Skill Charts should show valid cause-and-effect relationships between events or conditions in a news story.

SECTION 4 The French and Indian War

Guide to Reading

Main Idea
England and France fought for control of North America. The French and Indian War resulted from this struggle.

Key Terms
alliance, speculator

Reading Strategy
Organizing Information As you read the section, re-create the diagram below and describe the effects these events had on the conflict between France and Britain.

Turning point	Effect
Pitt takes charge	
Quebec falls	

Read to Learn
• how British fortunes improved after William Pitt took over direction of the war.
• how Chief Pontiac united his people to fight for their land.

Section Theme
Individual Action Victory or loss in war often depended on the actions of a single leader.

Preview of Events

♦1750	♦1755	♦1760	♦1765

1754
French and Indian War begins

1758
French forces driven out of Fort Duquesne

1759
British forces capture Quebec

1763
Proclamation of 1763 established

Native American maize mask

AN American Story

"These lakes, these woods, and mountains were left [to] us by our ancestors. They are our inheritances, and we will part with them to no one. . . . [Y]ou ought to know that He, the Great Spirit and Master of Life, has provided food for us in these spacious lakes and on the woody mountains. . . ."

These words, spoken by Chief Pontiac, served as a warning to the British colonists who wanted to take Native American lands.

The British Take Action

During the French and Indian War, some Native Americans fought on the side of the British. Many others fought against the British. The war that raged in North America through the late 1750s and early 1760s was one part of a larger struggle between England and France for control of world trade and power on the seas.

In 1754 the governor of Massachusetts announced to the colonial assembly that the French were on the way to "making themselves masters of this Continent."

CHAPTER 4   The Colonies Grow   **121**

2 TEACH

Daily Lecture and Discussion Notes 4–4

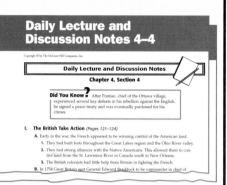

Daily Lecture and Discussion Notes

Chapter 4, Section 4

Did You Know? After Pontiac, chief of the Ottawa village, experienced several key defeats in his rebellion against the English, he signed a peace treaty and was eventually pardoned for his crimes.

I. **The British Take Action** (Pages 121–124)

  A. Early in the war, the French appeared to be winning control of the American land.

   1. They had built forts throughout the Great Lakes region and the Ohio River valley.

   2. They had strong alliances with the Native Americans. This allowed them to control land from the St. Lawrence River in Canada south to New Orleans.

   3. The British colonists had little help from Britain in fighting the French.

  B. In 1754 Great Britain sent General Edward Braddock to be commander in chief of

Prioritizing Important Events

Have students work in pairs or small groups to identify the five most important events in the section and rank their choices in order of importance. Pair English Language Learners with English dominant students. Have the English dominant students select the important events and the English Language Learners rank them. Then compare the results and have each group defend its choices and rankings. **L2, ELL**

Picturing **History**

As the British army tried to retreat during the fighting on July 9, the baggage train came up the narrow road, blocking it and adding to the confusion. During the battle, Braddock had five horses shot from under him.

Answer: A formal style of marching and bright uniforms made the British army an easy target.

The British colonists knew that the French were building well-armed forts throughout the Great Lakes region and the Ohio River valley. Their network of **alliances,** or unions, with Native Americans allowed the French to control large areas of land, stretching from the St. Lawrence River in Canada all the way south to New Orleans. The French and their Native American allies seemed to be winning control of the American frontier. The final showdown was about to begin.

During the early stages of the French and Indian War, the British colonists fought the French and the Native Americans with little help from Britain. In 1754, however, the government in London decided to intervene in the conflict. It was alarmed by the new forts the French were building and by George Washington's defeat at Fort Necessity. In the fall of 1754, Great Britain appointed **General Edward Braddock** commander in chief of the British forces in America and sent him to drive the French out of the Ohio Valley.

Picturing **History**

Native American warriors and French troops, protected by rocks and trees, fire into General Braddock's army, who were crammed together on a forest trail. **What weakness of the British army contributed to Braddock's defeat?**

Braddock Marches to Duquesne

In June 1755, Braddock set out from Virginia with about 1,400 red-coated British soldiers and a smaller number of blue-coated colonial militia. George Washington served as one of his aides. It took Braddock's army several weeks to trek through the dense forest to **Fort Duquesne.** Washington reported that Braddock

> 66halted to level every mole-hill and to erect bridges over every brook, by which means we were four days in getting twelve miles.99

Washington tried to tell Braddock that his army's style of marching was not well suited to fighting in frontier country. Lined up in columns and rows, the troops made easy targets. Braddock ignored the advice.

On July 9 a combined force of Native American warriors and French troops ambushed the British. The French and Native Americans were hidden, firing from behind trees and aiming at the bright uniforms. The British, confused and frightened, could not even see their attackers. One of the survivors of Braddock's army, Captain Orne, later described the "great confusion"

COOPERATIVE LEARNING ACTIVITY

Making a TV News Show Have students prepare a TV news show with "live" coverage of the Battle of Quebec. Roles include roving correspondents to interview the generals and troops during the two-month siege and to cover the brief but bloody battle; news anchors to introduce various parts of the show; reporters covering field hospitals and interviewing civilians within the city walls; and actors for commercials. If possible, videotape the show and play it back on a VCR. Tasks for preparing the show include doing any necessary research, preparing maps and other visuals, writing dialogue, and so on. Tasks should be divided according to the strengths of the students.

The French and Indian War, 1754–1763

Legend:
- British territory
- French territory
- Disputed territory
- ← British troop movements
- ← French troop movements
- ✦ British victory
- ✦ French victory
- • City
- ✶ Fort

Map labels: WOLFE, Gulf of St. Lawrence, Louisbourg, ACADIA, Ft. Beauséjour, Ft. Saint John, Quebec, Halifax, NEW FRANCE, Montreal, AMHERST, Lake Champlain, Crown Point, Ft. Frontenac, Ft. Ticonderoga, Ft. Oswego, Ft. William Henry, ATLANTIC OCEAN, Lake Huron, Lake Ontario, Boston, Ft. Niagara, Lake Erie, Hudson R., New York City, Ft. Duquesne, BRADDOCK, Ft. Necessity, Monongahela R., Alexandria, Allegheny R.

0 — 250 miles
0 — 250 kilometers
Lambert Equal-Area projection

Geography Skills

1. **Movement** After their victory at the French city of Quebec, in what direction did the British troops advance?
2. **Drawing Conclusions** Why would Ft. Duquesne be a valuable fort to control?

---

that overcame Braddock's troops when they were attacked. Braddock called for an orderly retreat, "but the panic was so great he could not succeed." Braddock was killed, and the battle ended in a bitter defeat for the British, who suffered nearly 1,000 casualties. Washington led the survivors back to Virginia.

Britain Declares War on France

The fighting in America helped start a new war in Europe, known as the **Seven Years' War.** After arranging an alliance with Prussia, Britain declared war on France in 1756. Prussia fought France and its allies in Europe while Britain fought France in the Caribbean, India, and North America.

The first years of the war were disastrous for the British and their American colonies. French troops captured several British forts, and their Native American allies began staging raids on frontier farms from New York to Pennsylvania. They killed settlers, burned farmhouses and crops, and drove many families back toward the coast. French forces from Canada captured British forts at Lake Ontario and at Lake George.

Pitt Takes Charge

Great Britain's prospects in America improved after **William Pitt** came to power as secretary of state and then as prime minister. An outstanding military planner, Pitt knew how to pick skilled commanders. He oversaw the war effort from London.

To avoid having to deal with constant arguments from the colonies about the cost of the war, Pitt decided that Great Britain would pay for supplies needed in the war—no matter the cost. In doing so Pitt ran up an enormous debt. After the French and Indian War, the British raised the colonists' taxes to help pay this debt. Pitt had only delayed the moment when the colonists had to pay their share of the bill.

CHAPTER 4   The Colonies Grow   **123**

L1, **ELL**

Guided Reading Activity 4–4

Name _____ Date _____ Class _____

★ **Guided Reading Activity 4-4**

DIRECTIONS: Filling in the Blanks Use your textbook to fill in the blanks using the words in the box. Some words may be used more than once. Use another sheet of paper if necessary.

General Edward Braddock	French Canada	French
Proclamation of 1763	Fort Duquesne	alliance
Ohio River valley	Pontiac's War	Treaty of Paris
Lake Ontario	Pennsylvania	Quebec
roads and bridges	Seven Years' War	secretary of state

The British Take Action

British colonists fought in the French and Indian War. Then (1) _____, commander in chief of the British forces in America, was sent to drive the French from the Ohio Valley. His army was ambushed by the (2) _____.

Geography Skills

Answers:
1. Southwest
2. because of its location on the Allegheny River in the Ohio River valley, as well as its eastern border of mountains

Geography Skills Practice

Ask: Where did Amherst go after he left Halifax? *(to Louisbourg)*

Who?What?Where?When?

James Wolfe James Wolfe's forces at Quebec included many ships and thousands of soldiers. For two months they sailed along the cliffs looking for a way to get at the seemingly impregnable fortress. Then one day Wolfe noticed women washing clothing in the river and later saw the clothes hanging to dry at the top of the cliff. A scout then found the path the women used. It was attention to detail that solved Wolfe's problem.

DIFFERENTIATED INSTRUCTION

Reading Support Have students design a statue, plaque, or monument commemorating a person or an event in the section. Possible topics include British soldiers killed under General Braddock's disastrous leadership, George Washington, the Battle of Quebec, William Pitt, or Chief Pontiac. Students may wish to use library resources to find out more about their chosen topics. **L1**

☞ Refer to *Inclusion for the Middle School Social Studies Classroom Strategies and Activities* in the TCR.

✓ **Reading Check**

Answer: Pitt was an outstanding military planner and knew how to pick good commanders.

✓ **Reading Check**

Answer: the Louisiana Territory and the Port of New Orleans

3 ASSESS

Assign Section 4 Assessment as homework or as an in-class activity.

⊙ Have students use **Interactive Tutor Self-Assessment CD-ROM.**

L2

Section Quiz 4–4

Name _____ Date _____ Class _____

★ Chapter 4   Score ☐

Section Quiz 4-4

DIRECTIONS: Matching Match the items in Column A with the items in Column B. Write the correct letters in the blanks. *(10 points each)*

Column A	Column B
___ 1. one of Edward Braddock's guides	**A.** James Wolfe
___ 2. Britain's prime minister	**B.** George Washington
___ 3. conquered Quebec	**C.** Pontiac
___ 4. conquered Montreal	**D.** William Pitt
___ 5. united Native Americans	**E.** Jeffrey Amherst

L1

Reteaching Activity 4–4

Name _____ Date _____ Class _____

★ **Reteaching Activity 4-4**

DIRECTIONS: Recognizing Causes and Effects After each *Cause,* write the letter of its *Effect* from the Fact Bank.

1. Cause: The French built a number of well-armed forts throughout the Great Lakes region and the Ohio River valley.
Effect: ___

2. Cause: News of Edward Braddock's defeat at Fort Duquesne reached London.
Effect: ___

3. Cause: William Pitt ran up an enor-

5. Cause: Quebec and Montreal were captured by British troops.
Effect: ___

6. Cause: The Treaty of Paris was signed in 1763.
Effect: ___

7. Cause: The British settlers mistreated the Native Americans in the Ohio River valley.
Effect: ___

Pitt wanted more than just a clear path to the Western territories. He also intended to conquer French Canada. He sent British troops to North America under the command of such energetic officers as **Jeffrey Amherst** and **James Wolfe.**

In 1758 Amherst and Wolfe led a British assault that recaptured the fortress at Louisbourg. That same year a group of New Englanders, led by British officers, captured Fort Frontenac at Lake Ontario. Still another British force marched across Pennsylvania and forced the French to abandon Fort Duquesne, which was renamed Fort Pitt.

✓ **Reading Check Describing** What abilities did William Pitt bring to the post of prime minister?

The Fall of New France

The year 1759 brought so many British victories that people said the church bells of London wore thin with joyous ringing. The British captured several French islands in the West Indies and the city of Havana in Cuba. They defeated the French in India, and destroyed a French fleet that had been sent to reinforce Canada. The greatest victory of the year, though, took place in the heart of New France.

The Battle of Quebec

Perched high on a cliff overlooking the St. Lawrence River, **Quebec,** the capital of New France, was thought to be impossible to attack. In September 1759, British general James Wolfe found a way.

One of Wolfe's scouts spotted a poorly guarded path up the back of the cliff. Wolfe's soldiers overwhelmed the guards posted on the path and then scrambled up the path during the night. The British troops assembled outside the fortress of Quebec on a field called the **Plains of Abraham.** There they surprised and defeated the French army. James Wolfe died in the battle. The French commander, the Marquis de Montcalm, was wounded and died the next day.

> *"If you are French . . . join us. If you are English, we declare war against you. Let us have your answer."*
>
> —*Pontiac, 1763*

The Treaty of Paris

The fall of Quebec and General Amherst's capture of Montreal the following year brought the fighting in North America to an end. In the **Treaty of Paris** of 1763, France was permitted to keep some of its sugar-producing islands in the West Indies, but it was forced to give Canada and most of its lands east of the Mississippi River to Great Britain. From Spain, France's ally, Great Britain gained Florida. In return, Spain received French lands west of the Mississippi River—the Louisiana Territory—as well as the port of New Orleans.

The Treaty of Paris marked the end of France as a power in North America. The continent was now divided between Great Britain and Spain, with the Mississippi River marking the boundary. While the Spanish and British were working out a plan for the future of North America, many Native Americans still lived on the lands covered by the European agreement.

✓ **Reading Check Summarizing** What lands did Spain receive under the Treaty of Paris?

INTERDISCIPLINARY CONNECTIONS ACTIVITY

Language Arts In class read aloud all or parts of Henry Wadsworth Longfellow's poem "Evangeline." Allow time for class discussion of the poem. Then have students either write diary entries from the point of view of one of the Acadians or dramatize events in the poem. Included among the many dramatic possibilities are hearing the order for deportation, loading the ships, and Gabriel dying in Evangeline's arms. **L3**

Trouble on the Frontier

The British victory over the French dealt a blow to the Native Americans of the Ohio River valley. They had lost their French allies and trading partners. Although they continued to trade with the British, the Native Americans regarded them as enemies. The British raised the prices of their goods and, unlike the French, refused to pay the Native Americans for the use of their land. Worst of all, British settlers began moving into the valleys of western Pennsylvania.

Pontiac's War

Pontiac, chief of an Ottawa village near Detroit, recognized that the British settlers threatened the Native American way of life. Just as Benjamin Franklin had tried to bring the colonies together with the Albany Plan, Pontiac wanted to join Native American groups to fight the British.

In the spring of 1763, Pontiac put together an alliance. He attacked the British fort at Detroit while other war parties captured most of the other British outposts in the Great Lakes region. That summer Native Americans killed settlers along the Pennsylvania and Virginia frontiers in a series of raids called **Pontiac's War.**

The Native Americans, however, failed to capture the important strongholds of Niagara, Fort Pitt, and Detroit. The war ended in August 1765 after British troops defeated Pontiac's allies, the Shawnee and Delaware people. In July 1766, Pontiac signed a peace treaty and was pardoned by the British.

★ Geography

The Proclamation of 1763

To prevent more fighting, Britain called a halt to the settlers' westward expansion. In the **Proclamation of 1763,** King George III declared that the Appalachian Mountains were the temporary western boundary for the colonies. The proclamation angered many people, especially those who owned shares in land companies. These speculators, or investors, had already bought land west of the mountains. They were furious that Britain ignored their land claims.

Although the end of the French and Indian War brought peace for the first time in many years, the Proclamation of 1763 created friction. More conflicts would soon arise between Britain and the colonists in North America.

✔ **Reading Check** **Examining** Why were many colonists angered by the Proclamation of 1763?

Student Web Activity Visit tarvol1.glencoe.com and click on **Chapter 4— Student Web Activities** for an activity on the French and Indian War.

SECTION 4 ASSESSMENT

Checking for Understanding

1. **Key Terms** Use the terms alliance and speculator in a short paragraph to explain their meaning.
2. **Reviewing the Facts** Name the three nations that were involved in the Seven Years' War.

Reviewing Themes

3. **Individual Action** How did Pontiac plan to defend Native Americans from British settlers? Was his plan successful?

Critical Thinking

4. **Analyzing Information** What did the British hope to gain by issuing the Proclamation of 1763?
5. **Analyzing Information** What actions do you think General Braddock could have taken to increase his army's chances of defeating the French? Re-create the diagram below to organize your answer.

Other strategies and tactics

Analyzing Visuals

6. **Geography Skills** Study the map of the French and Indian War on page 123. What was the result of the battle at Fort Duquesne? What route did British General Wolfe take to reach Quebec?

Interdisciplinary Activity

Geography Sketch a map showing the land claims of Great Britain, France, and Spain in North America after the Treaty of Paris.

CHAPTER 4   The Colonies Grow   **125**

SECTION 4 ASSESSMENT ANSWERS

1. Student work should reflect correct use of terms.
2. Britain, France, and Spain
3. He wanted to join Native American groups together to fight. He put together a successful alliance of Native American peoples.
4. They hoped to stop the fighting between colonists and Native Americans.
5. Answers may include: adapted fighting style to American landscape, not halting the troop movement to clear land and build bridges, supplied troops with appropriate clothing
6. French victory; southwest from the Gulf of St. Lawrence

Interdisciplinary Activity Maps should show approximate territory of each nation as described on page 124.

---

4 CLOSE

Point out that victory or loss in war often hinges on the actions (or inactions) of a single leader. Have students find examples of such leaders and their actions in Section 4.

GLENCOE
TECHNOLOGY

MindJogger Videoquiz
Use **MindJogger Videoquiz** to review the Chapter 4 content.

Available in VHS

Reviewing Key Terms
1.–7. Paragraphs should conform to the directions in the text.

Reviewing Key Facts
8. immigration; colonial women often married early and had large families; more children survived; adults lived longer

9. Tidewater planters had large, self-contained plantations that used slave labor, and they grew large amounts of tobacco and rice; backcountry farmers had less political and economic influence and had small, family-run farms where they grew corn and tobacco.

10. a period of revival of strong religious beliefs

11. Quakers and Mennonites settled in Pennsylvania for religious freedom.

12. New England had thin, rocky soil, so farmers practiced subsistence farming on small farms. The Middle Colonies had more fertile soil, with larger farms and bigger harvests.

13. a group of Native Americans in the East, formed in 1570 with five nations, that grew as other groups joined or were conquered

14. to prevent other countries from profiting from trade with the American colonies

15. European movement based on idea that knowledge, reason, and science could improve society

16. all of Canada and lands east and west of the Mississippi including New Orleans

Chapter Summary
The Colonies Grow

- Between the 1600s and early 1700s, thirteen American colonies are established—some for profit and others by religious groups seeking freedom.

- New England, the Middle Colonies, and the Southern Colonies develop diverse economies.

- Although many different people live in the colonies, their values and beliefs, government, and educational institutions grow out of English traditions.

- Between 1650 and 1750, Parliament passes laws regulating colonial trade.

- In 1754 the French and Indian War begins.

- From 1689 to 1763, France and Britain fight a series of wars.

- Under the terms of the Treaty of Paris, Britain obtains control of much of the continent.

- North America is divided between Great Britain and Spain.

JOIN, or DIE.

126

Reviewing Key Terms
Use all the terms below in one of three paragraphs, each about one of the following: trade, farming, organization of the colonies.

1. subsistence farming
2. cash crop
3. export
4. mercantilism
5. charter colony
6. proprietary colony
7. import

Reviewing Key Facts
8. Why did the colonial population grow rapidly?

9. What differences existed between the Tidewater planters and the backcountry farmers of the South?

10. What was the Great Awakening?

11. What immigrant groups settled in Pennsylvania?

12. How did the soil in the Middle Colonies differ from that in New England? What did that mean for the two regions?

13. What was the Iroquois Confederacy?

14. What was England's reason for the Navigation Acts?

15. What was the Enlightenment?

16. What North American land claims were the French forced to give up in the Treaty of Paris?

17. Why did the Proclamation of 1763 cause friction?

Critical Thinking
18. Comparing How did the economies of the New England and Southern Colonies differ? Re-create the chart below to answer the question.

Northern economy	Southern economy

19. Drawing Conclusions Re-read the People in History feature on page 109. In what ways did Benjamin Franklin represent the Enlightenment way of thinking?

20. Determining Cause and Effect How did the French relationship with Native Americans help them in their conflicts with the British?

21. Analyzing Information Re-read the Two Viewpoints feature on page 118. Why did Drake give the name 'Albion' to the land?

17. It kept colonists from moving west of the Appalachians, and some had already bought land there and were denied access to it.

Critical Thinking
18. Northern economy: more commerce and industry, small family farms; Southern economy: based on agriculture, many large farms dependent on slave labor, little commerce or industry

19. Franklin acquired and spread knowledge and was interested in science.

20. Usually Native Americans sided with the French, who had treated them well and respected their ways.

21. because of the white banks and cliffs and the name of England

Self-Check Quiz
Visit tarvol1.glencoe.com and click on **Chapter 4—
Self-Check Quizzes** to prepare for the chapter test.

 Geography and History Activity

Study the map of North America in 1754 on page 117; then answer these questions.

22. What countries controlled land on the continent?

23. What regions were under Spain's control?

24. Who controlled the land that is now Mexico?

25. What nation controlled the Mississippi River?

Practicing Skills

Determining Cause and Effect *Each of the following three sentences illustrates a cause-and-effect relationship. On a separate sheet of paper, identify the cause(s) and effect(s) in each sentence.*

26. During the 1700s the population of the English colonies grew dramatically as a result of high immigration.

27. To make certain that only England benefited from trade with the colonies, Parliament passed the Navigation Acts.

28. Because worship was so central to the Puritans, they built their towns around the church.

Citizenship Cooperative Activity

29. **Community Volunteers** Work with a partner to make a list of places in your community that need the services of volunteers. These can include libraries, nursing homes, and day care centers. Call each place and ask what the volunteers do, what times of the day and week they are needed, and how a volunteer can get started. Share your findings with the class. Then volunteer some of your time at one of the places you contacted.

Economics Activity

30. Working with a partner, create a map showing a trade route that colonial merchants might use. To get started, examine maps and information from your text and from encyclopedias and historical atlases. Include the physical features that the colonial merchants had to face, including rivers, mountains, lakes, and so on.

 Alternative Assessment

31. **Portfolio Writing Activity** Research and write a report in which you identify racial, ethnic, and religious groups that immigrated to the United States. Choose one group from the 17th century, one group from the 18th century, and one from the 19th century. Identify their reasons for immigrating.

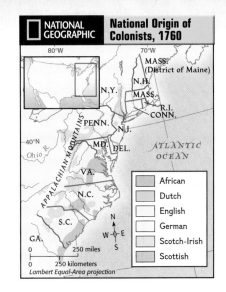

NATIONAL GEOGRAPHIC — **National Origin of Colonists, 1760**

Key:
- African
- Dutch
- English
- German
- Scotch-Irish
- Scottish

0 250 miles
0 250 kilometers
Lambert Equal-Area projection

Standardized Test Practice

Directions: Use the map above to answer the following question.

According to the map, which of the following statements is true?

F The Appalachian Mountains divided North Carolina and South Carolina.

G Virginia had the largest population.

H Most of Delaware's people were English.

J Dutch communities were widespread throughout South Carolina.

Test-Taking Tip:

Make sure that you look at the map's *title* and *key* so that you understand what it represents. Since the map does not show *total population* of the colonies, you can eliminate answer **G**.

CHAPTER 4 The Colonies Grow 127

Citizenship Cooperative Activity

29. Students should provide accurate and useful information about volunteer opportunities.

Economics Activity

30. Each pair of students should create a physical map showing a trade route.

 Alternative Assessment

31. Sample answers: Scotch-Irish came for economic opportunity and African Americans arrived involuntarily as enslaved workers. Reasons for immigrating include political freedom, religious freedom, economic opportunity, and family reunification.

Have students visit the Web site at tarvol1.glencoe.com to review Chapter 4 and take the Self-Check Quiz.

Standardized Test Practice

Answer: H
Question Type: History
Answer Explanation: According to the map, Delaware was comprised of colonists of English descent.

Bonus Question ?

Ask: Suppose the colonies had agreed to the Albany Plan of Union. How might the diverse values and economies have affected the attempts to govern and regulate trade in all the colonies? *(Friction might have developed over such questions as the role of religion in government, slavery, and trade policies.)*

 Geography and History Activity

22. Britain, Spain, and France

23. Mexico, the present-day southwestern states, Florida, Central America, and western coast of South America

24. Spain

25. France

Practicing Skills

26. cause: high immigration; effect: the population of the English colonies grew dramatically

27. cause: to make certain only England benefited from trade with the colonies; effect: Parliament passed the Navigation Acts

28. cause: worship was central to Puritans; effect: built towns around churches

Unit 3 Resources

SUGGESTED PACING CHART

Unit 3 (1 Day)	Chapter 5 (6 Days)	Chapter 6 (6 Days)	Chapter 7 (5 Days)	Unit 3 (2 Days)
Day 1 Introduction	**Day 1** Chapter 5 Intro, Section 1	**Day 1** Chapter 6 Intro, Section 1	**Day 1** Chapter 7 Intro, Section 1	**Day 1** Wrap-Up/Project **Day 2** Unit 3 Assessment
	Day 2 Section 2	**Day 2** Section 2	**Day 2** Section 2	
	Day 3 Section 3	**Day 3** Section 3	**Day 3** Section 3	
	Day 4 Section 4	**Day 4** Section 4	**Day 4** Chapter 7 Review	
	Day 5 Chapter 5 Review	**Day 5** Chapter 6 Review	**Day 5** Chapter 7 Assessment	
	Day 6 Chapter 5 Assessment	**Day 6** Chapter 6 Assessment		

GLENCOE'S ASSESSMENT ADVANTAGE

Use the following tools to easily assess student learning in a variety of ways:

- Performance Assessment Activities and Rubrics
- Chapter and Unit Tests
- Section Quizzes
- Standardized Test Practice Workbook

- www.tarvol1.glencoe.com
- Interactive Tutor Self-Assessment CD-ROM
- MindJogger Videoquiz
- ExamView® Pro Testmaker CD-ROM

TEACHING TRANSPARENCIES

Unit 3 Map Overlay Transparencies
L2

Cause-and-Effect Transparency 3
L2

READING SUPPORT FROM JAMESTOWN EDUCATION

- *Timed Readings Plus in Social Studies* help students increase their reading rate and fluency while maintaining comprehension. The 400-word passages are similar to those found on state and national assessments.

- *Reading in the Content Area: Social Studies* concentrates on six essential reading skills that help students better comprehend what they read. The book includes 75 high-interest nonfiction passages written at increasing levels of difficulty.

- *Reading Fluency* helps students read smoothly, accurately, and expressively.

- *Jamestown's Reading Improvement,* by renowned reading expert Edward Fry, focuses on helping build your students' comprehension, vocabulary, and skimming and scanning skills.

- *Critical Reading Series* provides high-interest books, each written at three reading levels.

For more information about these products, see the Jamestown Education materials in the Classroom Solutions in the front of this Teacher Wraparound Edition. To order these products, call Glencoe at 1-800-334-7344.

Unit 3 Resources

ASSESSMENT

Unit 3 Pretests L2

Unit 3 Posttests L2

INTERDISCIPLINARY ACTIVITIES

American Literature Reading 3 L2

Interdisciplinary Connection 3 L2

Economics and History Activity 3 L2

APPLICATION AND ENRICHMENT

Cooperative Learning Activity 3 L1, ELL

Citizenship Activity 3 L1

HANDS-ON ACTIVITIES

Hands-On History Activity 3 L1

History Simulations and Problem Solving 3 L1

Reading List Generator CD-ROM

GLENCOE BOOKLINK

The Glencoe BookLink CD-ROM is a database that allows you to search more than 15,000 titles to create a customized reading list for your students.

- Reading lists can be organized by students' reading level, author, genre, theme, or area of interest.

- The database provides Degrees of Reading Power™ (DRP) and Lexile™ readability scores for all selections.

- A brief summary of each selection is included.

Leveled reading suggestions for this unit:

For Students at a Grade 6 Reading Level:
- *Why Not, Lafayette?,* by Jean Fritz

For Students at a Grade 7 Reading Level:
- *A Convention of Delegates: The Creation of the Constitution,* by Denis J. Hauptly

For Students at a Grade 8 Reading Level:
- *Come All You Brave Soldiers,* by Clinton Cox

Extending the Content

Readings for the Teacher
- *The American Revolution: Writings from the War of Independence,* by John Rhodehamel, ed. Library of America, 2001.

Multimedia Links
- *American Revolution.* VHS. A&E, 1994.
- *History's Mysteries: Spies of the Revolutionary War.* VHS. The History Channel, 1999.

Unit Overview

Unit 3 describes the American Revolution, its causes, and aftermath. **Chapter 5** focuses on events leading up to the American Revolution. **Chapter 6** describes the battles and strategies of the war. **Chapter 7** examines the steps Americans took after the war to build a new nation.

Unit Objectives

After studying this unit, students will be able to:

1. Explain how changes in British policies in North America caused dissatisfaction among colonists.
2. Describe the outbreak of hostilities between Patriot and British forces.
3. Discuss the preparation of and key points in the Declaration of Independence and the Constitution.

Why It Matters Activity

Have students describe what rights they have as citizens. Ask them to think about how they would feel if these rights were gradually taken away and what they would do to restore them. As students study the unit, have them compare their responses to how the colonists reacted to the British before the American Revolution.

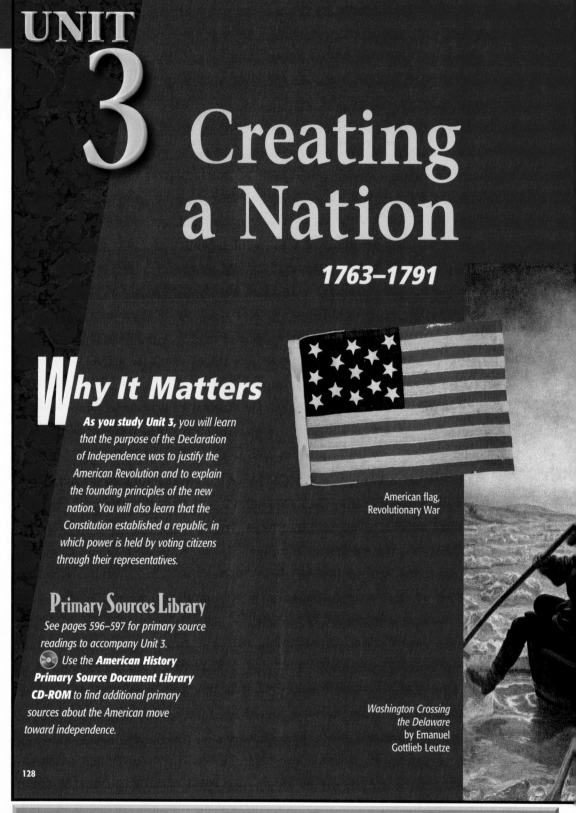

UNIT 3

Creating a Nation

1763–1791

Why It Matters

As you study Unit 3, you will learn that the purpose of the Declaration of Independence was to justify the American Revolution and to explain the founding principles of the new nation. You will also learn that the Constitution established a republic, in which power is held by voting citizens through their representatives.

American flag, Revolutionary War

Primary Sources Library

See pages 596–597 for primary source readings to accompany Unit 3.
Use the **American History Primary Source Document Library CD-ROM** to find additional primary sources about the American move toward independence.

Washington Crossing the Delaware by Emanuel Gottlieb Leutze

128

TEAM TEACHING ACTIVITY

Language Arts Work with a Language Arts teacher to help students research, review, and analyze newspaper articles that were published before and during the American Revolution. Students should look for articles that deal with important events such as the Boston Massacre, the Battle of Lexington, or the meeting of the Second Continental Congress, and report on how a particular newspaper covered the event. Have students also compare the style of eighteenth century reporting with the style that newspapers use today. Have students work in groups and present their findings to the class. **L3**

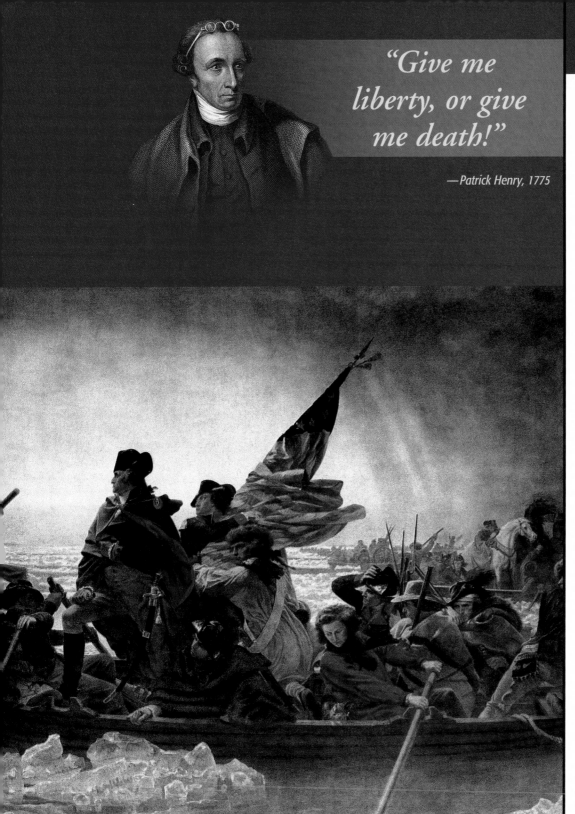

"*Give me liberty, or give me death!*"

—Patrick Henry, 1775

GLENCOE
TECHNOLOGY

CD-ROM
American History
Primary Source
Document Library
CD-ROM
Use the **American History Primary Source Document Library CD-ROM** to access primary source documents related to the independence movement.

More About the Art

Emanuel Leutze's oil painting depicts an important event in the American Revolution—General George Washington leading his troops across the ice-clogged Delaware River on Christmas night in 1776 to surprise a garrison of Hessian troops at Trenton. The American victories at Trenton and Princeton boosted the morale of American forces early in the war. Leutze chose a large canvas to depict this significant event. The original artwork, painted in 1851, was more than 12 feet high and 21 feet wide. Ask students to describe how Leutze draws the viewer's attention to Washington. (*Answers may include that Washington is positioned in the center of the boat and the angle of the American flag draws attention to him.*)

Glencoe Literature Library

As students study the unit, have them read *The Autobiography of Benjamin Franklin* from the **Glencoe Literature Library.** The Glencoe Literature Library consists of novels and other readings for middle school students, along with study guides that offer instructional support and student activities.

SERVICE-LEARNING PROJECT

During the eighteenth century, people in small towns and villages often worked cooperatively at tasks such as growing food, mending fences, and herding animals. Have students work cooperatively to help senior citizens in your community do chores such as yard work, weekly grocery shopping, or small painting or home repair projects. Have students organize themselves into teams of two, three, or four to tackle various jobs. Students should check with the local senior center for the names of people who might need help.

Refer to *Building Bridges: Connecting Classroom and Community through Service-Learning in Social Studies* from the National Council for the Social Studies for information about service-learning.

Timesaving Tools

TeacherWorks™ All-In-One Planner and Resource Center

- **Interactive Teacher Edition** Access your Teacher Wraparound Edition and your classroom resources with a few easy clicks.
- **Interactive Lesson Planner** Planning has never been easier! Organize your week, month, semester, or year with all the lesson helps you need to make teaching creative, timely, and relevant.

Use Glencoe's **Presentation Plus!** multimedia teacher tool to easily present dynamic lessons that visually excite your students. Using Microsoft PowerPoint® you can customize the presentations to create your own personalized lessons.

TEACHING TRANSPARENCIES

Graphic Organizer 9 L2

Why It Matters Chapter Transparency 5 L2

REVIEW AND REINFORCEMENT

Workbook Activity 5 L1

Time Line Activity 5 L2

Vocabulary Activity 5 L1

REVIEW AND REINFORCEMENT

Critical Thinking Skills Activity 5 L2

Take-Home Review Activity 5 L1

ENRICHMENT

Linking Past and Present Activity 5 L2

Primary Source Reading 5 L2

GEOGRAPHY

Geography and History Activity 5 L2

Meeting NCSS Standards

The following standards are highlighted in Chapter 5:

Section 1	X	Civic Ideals & Practices: A, B, C
Section 2	V	Individuals, Groups, & Institutions: B, E
Section 3	V	Individuals, Groups, & Institutions: B, F, G
Section 4	VI	Power, Authority, & Governance: B, C, D, F, I

FOLDABLES™ Study Organizer

Dinah Zike's Foldables are three-dimensional, interactive graphic organizers that help students practice basic writing skills, review key vocabulary terms, and identify main ideas. Additional chapter activities can be found in the **Reading and Study Skills Foldables** booklet.

Chapter 5 Resources

ASSESSMENT AND EVALUATION

**Chapter 5 Test
Form A** L2

**Chapter 5 Test
Form B** L2

**Standardized Test Practice
Workbook Activity 5** L2

**Performance Assessment
Activity 5** L1, ELL

**ExamView® Pro
Testmaker CD-ROM**

MULTIMEDIA

- **Vocabulary PuzzleMaker CD-ROM**
- **Interactive Tutor Self-Assessment CD-ROM**
- **ExamView® Pro Testmaker CD-ROM**
- **Audio Program**
- **American History Primary Source Document Library CD-ROM**
- **MindJogger Videoquiz**
- **Presentation Plus! CD-ROM**
- **TeacherWorks CD-ROM**
- **Interactive Student Edition CD-ROM**
- **Glencoe Skillbuilder Interactive Workbook CD-ROM, Level 1**
- **The American Republic to 1877 Video Program**
- **American Music: Hits Through History**

SPANISH RESOURCES

The following Spanish language materials are available in the Spanish Resources Binder:

- **Spanish Guided Reading Activities**
- **Spanish Reteaching Activities**
- **Spanish Quizzes and Tests**
- **Spanish Vocabulary Activity**
- **Spanish Take-Home Review Activity**
- **Spanish Summaries**
- **The Declaration of Independence and United States Constitution Spanish Translation**

THE HISTORY CHANNEL®

The following videotape programs are available from Glencoe as supplements to Chapter 5:

- **George Washington: Founding Father** (ISBN 1-56501-377-8)*
- **Thomas Jefferson: Philosopher of Freedom** (ISBN 1-56501-502-9)*
- **Benjamin Franklin: Citizen of the World** (ISBN 1-56501-426-X)
- **The American Revolution** (Six Video Set) (ISBN 1-56501-436-7)

To order, call Glencoe at 1-800-334-7344. To find classroom resources to accompany many of these videos, check the following home pages:
A&E Television: www.aande.com
The History Channel: www.historychannel.com

*Available individually or in *The American Republic to 1877 Video Library*.

Use our Web site for additional resources. All essential content is covered in the Student Edition.

You and your students can visit tarvol1.glencoe.com, the Web site companion to **The American Republic to 1877.** This innovative integration of electronic and print media offers your students a wealth of opportunities. The student text directs students to the Web site for the following options:

- **Chapter Overviews**
- **Self-Check Quizzes**
- **Student Web Activities**
- **Textbook Updates**

Answers to the student Web activities are provided for you in the **Web Activity Lesson Plans.** Additional Web resources and Interactive Tutor Puzzles are also available.

Chapter 5 Resources

SECTION RESOURCES

Daily Objectives	Reproducible Resources	Multimedia Resources
SECTION 1 **Taxation Without Representation** 1. Describe why the British had problems in North America after the French and Indian War. 2. Explain how the colonists responded to unpopular British laws.	Reproducible Lesson Plan 5–1 Daily Lecture and Discussion Notes 5–1 Guided Reading Activity 5–1* Section Quiz 5–1* Reteaching Activity 5–1* Reading Essentials and Study Guide 5–1* Enrichment Activity 5–1	Daily Focus Skills Transparency 5–1 Interactive Tutor Self-Assessment CD-ROM ExamView® Pro Testmaker CD-ROM Presentation Plus! CD-ROM
SECTION 2 **Building Colonial Unity** 1. Identify the causes of the Boston Massacre. 2. Explain how Britain tried to maintain its control over the colonies.	Reproducible Lesson Plan 5–2 Daily Lecture and Discussion Notes 5–2 Guided Reading Activity 5–2* Section Quiz 5–2* Reteaching Activity 5–2* Reading Essentials and Study Guide 5–2* Enrichment Activity 5–2	Daily Focus Skills Transparency 5–2 Interactive Tutor Self-Assessment CD-ROM ExamView® Pro Testmaker CD-ROM Presentation Plus! CD-ROM
SECTION 3 **A Call to Arms** 1. Identify the events that took place at the Continental Congress. 2. Describe the early skirmishes of the American Revolution.	Reproducible Lesson Plan 5–3 Daily Lecture and Discussion Notes 5–3 Guided Reading Activity 5–3* Section Quiz 5–3* Reteaching Activity 5–3* Reading Essentials and Study Guide 5–3* Enrichment Activity 5–3	Daily Focus Skills Transparency 5–3 ABC News Interactive™ Historic America Electronic Field Trips Interactive Tutor Self-Assessment CD-ROM ExamView® Pro Testmaker CD-ROM Presentation Plus! CD-ROM
SECTION 4 **Moving Toward Independence** 1. Understand what happened at the Second Continental Congress. 2. Explore why the Declaration of Independence was drafted.	Reproducible Lesson Plan 5–4 Daily Lecture and Discussion Notes 5–4 Guided Reading Activity 5–4* Section Quiz 5–4* Reteaching Activity 5–4* Reading Essentials and Study Guide 5–4* Enrichment Activity 5–4	Daily Focus Skills Transparency 5–4 American Music: Hits Through History Vocabulary PuzzleMaker CD-ROM Interactive Tutor Self-Assessment CD-ROM ExamView® Pro Testmaker CD-ROM Presentation Plus! CD-ROM

0:00 OUT OF TIME?
Assign the Chapter 5 **Reading Essentials and Study Guide.**

*Also Available in Spanish

 Blackline Master   Transparency   CD-ROM   DVD

Poster   Music Program   Audio Program   Videocassette

KEY TO ABILITY LEVELS

Teaching strategies have been coded.

L1 BASIC activities for all students

L2 AVERAGE activities for average to above-average students

L3 CHALLENGING activities for above-average students

ELL ENGLISH LANGUAGE LEARNER activities

NATIONAL GEOGRAPHIC Teacher's Corner

INDEX TO NATIONAL GEOGRAPHIC MAGAZINE

The following articles relate to this chapter.

- "Two Revolutions," by Charles McCarry, July 1989.
- "Yorktown Shipwreck," by John D. Broadwater, June 1988.
- "Thomas Jefferson: Architect of Freedom," by Mike Edwards, February 1976.

ADDITIONAL NATIONAL GEOGRAPHIC SOCIETY PRODUCTS

To order the following, call National Geographic at 1-800-368-2728:

- *GeoKit: Colonial America* (Kit)
- *GeoKit: The American Revolution* (Kit)
- *Colonization and Trade in the Americas* (Map)
- *National Geographic Desk Reference* (Book)
- *Democratic Government Series, "The United States"* (Video)
- *Branches of Government Series* (Video)

NGS ONLINE

Access National Geographic's Web site for current events, atlas updates, activities, links, interactive features, and archives.

www.nationalgeographic.com

MEETING SPECIAL NEEDS

In addition to the Differentiated Instruction strategies found in each section, the following resources are also suitable for your special needs students:

- *ExamView® Pro Testmaker CD-ROM* allows teachers to tailor tests by reducing answer choices.
- The *Audio Program* includes the entire narrative of the student edition so that less-proficient readers can listen to the words as they read them.
- The *Reading Essentials and Study Guide* provides the same content as the student edition but is written two grade levels below the textbook.
- *Guided Reading Activities* give less-proficient readers point-by-point instructions to increase comprehension as they read each textbook section.
- *Enrichment Activities* includes a stimulating collection of readings and activities for gifted and talented students.

From the Classroom of...

Dean Mantz
Lyons Middle School
Sterling, KS

The Stamp Act Revisited

This activity helps students understand how a colonist might have felt during the late 1700s when the Stamp Act was enacted. Students are taxed for their actions (or inactions). Materials needed include play money and a box to serve as a treasury. Evenly distribute the play money among students. Have one student serve as the British tax agent who will collect tax money. Another student can act as an employer who pays students for certain services. (This employer-student will need additional money.) Taxable activities may include turning in an assignment, requesting a hall pass to leave the room, or not being able to answer a question. Students can earn money by correctly answering a question or helping another student who has more money. After about a week of being "taxed," have students discuss their feelings about the tax.

ADDITIONAL RESOURCES FROM GLENCOE

- American Music: Cultural Traditions
- American Art and Architecture
- Outline Map Resource Book
- U.S. Desk Map
- Building Geography Skills for Life
- Inclusion for the Middle School Social Studies Classroom Strategies and Activities
- Teaching Strategies for the American History Classroom (Including Block Scheduling Pacing Guides)
- American Crafts Hands-On Activities
- American Games Hands-On Activities
- American History Flash Cards

Block Schedule

Activities that are suited to use within the block scheduling framework are identified by: ▢

✓ Performance Assessment

Refer to Activity 5 in the Performance Assessment Activities and Rubrics booklet. 📦

Why It Matters Activity

Discuss with students why people in a colony would want to leave or separate from the country of origin. After reading the chapter, have students evaluate whether Britain's actions toward its American colonies justified a war for independence.

GLENCOE
TECHNOLOGY

The American Republic to 1877 Video Program

To learn more about the American Revolution from the perspectives of Loyalists and Tories, have students view the Chapter 5 video "Loyalists and Tories" from **The American Republic to 1877 Video program.**

 Available in DVD and VHS

MindJogger Videoquiz

Use **MindJogger Videoquiz** to preview the Chapter 5 content.

Available in VHS

CHAPTER 5

Road to Independence

1763–1776

Why It Matters

A spirit of independence became evident early in the history of the American people. Far from the established rules and restrictions they had faced in their home countries, the new settlers began to make their own laws and develop their own ways of doing things.

The Impact Today

The ideals of revolutionary America still play a major role in shaping the society we live in. For example:
- *Americans still exercise their right to protest laws they view as unfair.*
- *Citizens have the right to present their views freely.*

 The American Republic to 1877 *Video The chapter 5 video, "Loyalists and Tories," portrays events leading up to the Revolutionary War from a Loyalist's point of view, as well as a Patriot's.*

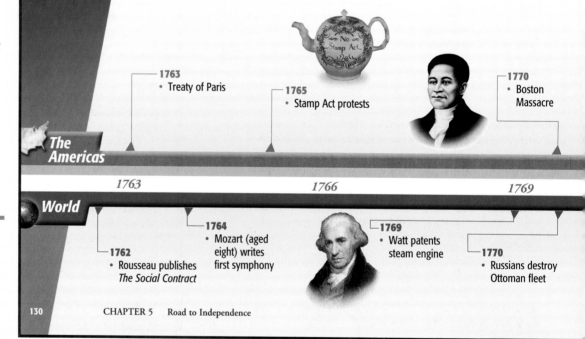

The Americas

1763
- Treaty of Paris

1765
- Stamp Act protests

1770
- Boston Massacre

1763   *1766*   *1769*

World

1762
- Rousseau publishes *The Social Contract*

1764
- Mozart (aged eight) writes first symphony

1769
- Watt patents steam engine

1770
- Russians destroy Ottoman fleet

130   CHAPTER 5   Road to Independence

📖 Reading Strategy   PURPOSE FOR READING

Think/Write–Pair–Share is a stratey to engage students in their subject matter through discussion. During the 1760s and 1770s, British actions, such as the levying of a series of new taxes, angered the American colonists and drove them toward breaking ties with Britain. Give students the topic: "What items would they be willing to give up for the sake of freedom?" Ask them to think silently about this topic, then write down at least three freedoms they would be willing to give up. After writing, each student pairs with a partner to share ideas and thoughts. Conclude this activity with a class "share" discussion. **L1**

Bunker Hill by **Don Troiani** Low on ammunition, Colonel William Prescott gives the order, "Don't fire until you see the whites of their eyes."

FOLDABLES™
Study Organizer

Cause-and-Effect Study Foldable Make this foldable to show the causes and effects of the events that led the Americans to declare independence from Great Britain.

Step 1 Fold one sheet of paper in half from side to side.

> Fold the sheet vertically.

Step 2 Fold again, 1 inch from the top. (**Tip:** The middle knuckle of your index finger is about 1 inch long.)

Step 3 Open and label as shown.

> Draw lines along the fold lines.

Reading and Writing As you read this chapter, fill in the causes (British Actions) and effects (Colonial Reactions) in the correct columns of your foldable.

FOLDABLES™
Study Organizer   Dinah Zike's Foldables

Purpose Students make and use a cause-and-effect foldable to help them organize the events leading to the Declaration of Independence from Great Britain. As students read the chapter and fill in information on their foldable, they analyze the causes and effects of key events.

Have students complete **Reading and Study Skills Foldables** Activity 5. **L1**

HISTORY
Online

Introduce students to chapter content and key terms by having them access **Chapter Overview 5** at tarvol1.glencoe.com

TIME LINE
ACTIVITY

Have students review the time line on pages 130–131 as they read the chapter. Have students identify the events that occurred between 1762 and 1765.

1773
• Boston Tea Party

1774
• First Continental Congress meets

1775
• Battles fought at Lexington and Concord

1776
• Declaration of Independence signed

1772

1775

1772
• Poland partitioned among Russia, Prussia, and Austria

1774
• Louis XVI becomes king of France

HISTORY
Online

Chapter Overview
Visit tarvol1.glencoe.com and click on **Chapter 5— Chapter Overviews** to preview chapter information.

CHAPTER 5   Road to Independence   131

More About the Art

Almost half of the British soldiers who fought in the Battle of Bunker Hill died over the course of three attacks. The battle proved that American militias could hold their own against the British army. Have students read the caption. **Ask: Why do you think Colonel Prescott gave this order to his troops?** *(Because they were low on ammunition, Prescott did not want the troops to fire until the British soldiers got very close. They would then be less likely to shoot and miss.)*

1 FOCUS

Section Overview
This section describes how British laws caused discontent among the colonists.

Reading Preview

Answers to Graphic: Proclamation of 1763: limited freedom by preventing westward movement; Sugar Act: took away right to jury trial in some cases; Stamp Act: taxed without colonists' consent and interfered with affairs of colonial governments

Preteaching Vocabulary
Call on a volunteer to define the term *boycott*. Then have students identify examples of boycotts.

SECTION 1 Taxation Without Representation

Guide to Reading

Main Idea
The British government's actions after winning the French and Indian War angered American colonists.

Key Terms
revenue, writs of assistance, resolution, effigy, boycott, nonimportation, repeal

Reading Strategy
Classifying Information British actions created colonial unrest. As you read Section 1, re-create the diagram below and describe why the colonists disliked these policies.

British action	Colonists' view
Proclamation of 1763	
Sugar Act	
Stamp Act	

Read to Learn
- why the British faced problems in North America after the French and Indian War.
- why the American colonists objected to new British laws.

Section Theme
Civic Rights and Responsibilities The American colonists believed that new British laws denied their civic rights.

Preview of Events

♦1760   ♦1765   ♦1770

1763 Proclamation of 1763

1764 Parliament passes Sugar Act

1765 Parliament enacts Stamp Act

1767 Townshend Acts tax colonial imports

★ AN ★
American Story

St. Edward's crown, worn by George III

Huron and Ottawa warriors silently peered from the woods. They watched about 100 British soldiers camped on Lake Erie's shore. The soldiers—sent by the British Crown—had just stopped to rest on their way to Fort Detroit. They were worried about rumors of Native Americans planning war.

Suddenly the warriors rushed from the forest. The British managed to escape in two boats. War raged on the frontier—and the British were in the thick of it!

Relations with Britain

After winning the French and Indian War, Great Britain controlled a vast territory in North America. To limit settlement of this territory, Britain issued the Proclamation of 1763. Parts of the land acquired through the Treaty of Paris became the provinces of Quebec, East Florida, West Florida, and Grenada (a combination of several Caribbean islands). Most importantly, the Proclamation prohibited colonists from moving west of the Appalachian Mountains.

132   CHAPTER 5   Road to Independence

SECTION RESOURCES

📁 Reproducible Masters
- Reproducible Lesson Plan 5–1
- Daily Lecture and Discussion Notes 5–1
- Guided Reading Activity 5–1
- Section Quiz 5–1
- Reteaching Activity 5–1
- Reading Essentials and Study Guide 5–1
- Enrichment Activity 5–1

📓 Transparencies
- Daily Focus Skills Transparency 5–1

Multimedia
- 💿 Interactive Tutor Self-Assessment CD-ROM
- 💿 ExamView® Pro Testmaker CD-ROM
- 💿 Presentation Plus! CD-ROM

Stopping western settlement provided several advantages for Britain. It allowed the British government, not the colonists, to control westward movement. In this way, westward expansion would go on in an orderly way, and conflict with Native Americans might be avoided. Slower western settlement would also slow colonists moving away from the colonies on the coast—where Britain's important markets and investments were. Finally, closing western settlement protected the interests of British officials who wanted to control the lucrative fur trade. The British planned to keep 10,000 troops in America to protect their interests.

These plans alarmed the colonists. Many feared that the large number of British troops in North America might be used to interfere with their liberties. They saw the Proclamation of 1763 as a limit on their freedom. These two measures contributed to the feeling of distrust that was growing between Great Britain and its colonies.

The financial problems of Great Britain complicated the situation. The French and Indian War left Britain with a huge public debt. Desperate for new revenue, or incoming money, the king and Parliament felt it was only fair that the colonists pay part of the cost. They began plans to tax them. This decision set off a chain of events that enraged the American colonists and surprised British authorities.

Britain's Trade Laws

In 1763 **George Grenville** became prime minister of Britain. He was determined to reduce Britain's debt. He decided to take action against smuggling in the colonies. When the colonists smuggled goods to avoid taxes, Britain lost revenue that could be used to pay debts.

Grenville knew that American juries often found smugglers innocent. In 1763 he convinced Parliament to pass a law allowing smugglers to be sent to vice-admiralty courts. Vice-admiralty courts were run by officers and did not have juries. In 1767 Parliament decided to authorize writs of assistance. These legal documents allowed customs officers to enter any location to search for smuggled goods.

NATIONAL GEOGRAPHIC   **Proclamation of 1763**

HUDSON'S BAY COMPANY

PROVINCE OF QUEBEC

Mississippi R.

Ohio R.

LOUISIANA TERRITORY

APPALACHIAN MOUNTAINS

ATLANTIC OCEAN

FLORIDA

Gulf of Mexico

40°N

70°W

80°W

30°N

90°W

☐ Thirteen Colonies
☐ Other British territory
☐ Spanish territory
— Proclamation Line of 1763

0   300 miles
0   300 kilometers
Lambert Equal-Area projection

Geography *Skills*

1. **Place** What natural feature marked the western boundary of British territory?
2. **Analyzing Information** Who controlled the Louisiana Territory in 1763?

The Sugar Act

With a new law in place to stop smuggling, Grenville tried to increase tax revenue. In 1764 Parliament passed the **Sugar Act**. The act lowered the tax on molasses imported by the colonists. Grenville hoped the lower tax would convince the colonists to pay the tax instead of smuggling. The act also let officers seize goods from smugglers without going to court.

The Sugar Act and the new laws to control smuggling angered the colonists. They believed their rights as Englishmen were being violated. Writs of assistance violated their right to be secure in their home. Vice-admiralty courts violated their right to a jury trial. Furthermore, in trials at vice-admiralty courts, the burden of

2 TEACH

Daily Lecture and Discussion Notes 5–1

Copyright © by The McGraw-Hill Companies, Inc.

Daily Lecture and Discussion Notes

Chapter 5, Section 1

Did You Know? In 1764 Britain issued a complete ban on paper money to all the colonies except for military purposes. Benjamin Franklin tried to convince Parliament that paper money was needed, but he did not succeed. The struggle over the right to issue paper money was a major factor of the American Revolution.

I. **Relations With Britain** *(Pages 132–134)*

A. A feeling of distrust between the colonists and Britain grew due to
1. British soldiers stationed in the colonies and on the frontier
2. the Proclamation of 1763
3. the passing of trade laws and the Sugar Act

Charting Laws Ask small groups of students to make charts of the British colonial laws discussed in this section. Have them create three columns for the charts: one each for the Sugar Act, the Stamp Act, and the Townshend Acts. In each column, they should summarize the law and note its results. **L1**

Geography *Skills*

Answers:
1. the Mississippi River
2. Spain

Geography Skills Practice
Ask: What geographic features bordered the thirteen colonies to the east and west? *(the Atlantic Ocean to the east and the Appalachian Mountains to the west)*

Reading Strategy   READING THE TEXT

Brainstorming Organize the class into groups of five to seven students each. Ask one student in each group to write the following statement on a sheet of paper: We must protest British taxes because . . . Explain that everyone in the group should provide one answer and that students should try not to be influenced by other responses on the page. Then have each group circulate the page with each member completing the statement as quickly as possible. Assign a secretary in each group to present the responses to the class. Afterward, discuss these questions: Which responses were based on fact? Which were more emotional? Which responses might you have heard most often from colonial Americans? **L1**

✓ Reading Check

Answer: to stop the smuggling between the colonies and the French West Indies

L1, ELL

Guided Reading Activity 5–1

Name _____ Date _____ Class _____

★ **Guided Reading Activity 5-1**

DIRECTIONS: Recalling the Facts Use the information in your textbook to answer the questions. Use another sheet of paper if necessary.

1. In 1763 how did Great Britain try to end troubles with the Native Americans?

2. Why did these actions alarm the colonists?
3. Why did George Grenville allow customs officers to obtain general writs of assistance?

4. What was the purpose of the Sugar Act?
5. How did the smuggling courts created by the Sugar Act differ from regular courts?

✓ Reading Check

Answer: He helped start the Sons of Liberty, which protested the Stamp Act.

3 ASSESS

Assign Section 1 Assessment as homework or as an in-class activity.

⊕ Have students use **Interactive Tutor Self-Assessment CD-ROM.**

L2

Section Quiz 5–1

Name _____ Date _____ Class _____

★ **Chapter 5**   Score [ ]

Section Quiz 5-1

DIRECTIONS: Matching Match the items in Column A with the items in Column B. Write the correct letters in the blanks. *(10 points each)*

Column A	Column B
___ 1. revenue	A. Samuel Adams
___ 2. formal expression of opinion	B. effigies
___ 3. organized the Sons of Liberty	C. incoming money
___ 4. rag figures	D. boycott
___ 5. to refuse to buy	E. resolution

DIRECTIONS: Multiple Choice In the blank at the left, write the letter of the

L1

Reteaching Activity 5–1

Name _____ Date _____ Class _____

★ **Reteaching Activity 5-1**

DIRECTIONS: Sequencing Events Number the events in the order in which they occurred. Write the same number for the three events that occurred at the same time.

___ **A.** Parliament passes the Townshend Acts.

___ **B.** Samuel Adams helps start the Sons of Liberty.

___ **C.** Parliament passes the Sugar Act.

___ **D.** Parliament passes the Declaratory Act.

___ **E.** George Grenville takes action against colonial smuggling.

___ **F.** Thousands of merchants, artisans, and farmers sign nonimportation agreements.

---

proof was on defendants to prove their innocence. This contradicted British law, which states that the accused is "innocent until proved guilty."

These measures alarmed the colonists. **James Otis,** a young lawyer in Boston, argued that

> 66no parts of [England's colonies] can be taxed without their consent . . . every part has a right to be represented.99

In his speeches and pamphlets, Otis defined and defended colonial rights.

✓ **Reading Check** **Analyzing** Why did Parliament pass the Sugar Act?

The Stamp Act

In 1765 Parliament passed another law in an effort to raise money. This law, the **Stamp Act,** placed a tax on almost all printed material in the colonies—everything from newspapers and pamphlets to wills and playing cards. All printed material had to have a stamp, which was applied by British officials. Because so many items were taxed, it affected almost everyone in the colonial cities. The Stamp Act convinced many colonists of the need for action.

Opposition to the Stamp Act centered on two points. Parliament had interfered in colonial affairs by taxing the colonies directly. In addition, it taxed the colonists without their consent. In passing the Stamp Act without consulting the colonial legislatures, Parliament ignored the colonial tradition of self-government.

Protesting the Stamp Act

A young member of the Virginia House of Burgesses, **Patrick Henry,** persuaded the burgesses to take action against the Stamp Act. According to tradition, when he was accused of treason, Henry replied,

> 66If this be treason, make the most of it!99

The Virginia assembly passed a resolution—a formal expression of opinion—declaring it had "the only and sole exclusive right and power to lay taxes" on its citizens.

In Boston **Samuel Adams** helped start an organization called the **Sons of Liberty.** Members took to the streets to protest the Stamp Act. People in other cities also organized Sons of Liberty groups.

Throughout the summer of 1765, protesters burned effigies—rag figures—representing unpopular tax collectors. They also raided and destroyed houses belonging to royal officials and marched through the streets shouting that only Americans had the right to tax Americans.

The Stamp Act Congress

In October delegates from nine colonies met in New York at the **Stamp Act Congress.** They drafted a petition to the king and Parliament declaring that the colonies could not be taxed except by their own assemblies.

In the colonial cities, people refused to use the stamps. They urged merchants to boycott—refuse to buy—British and European goods in protest. Thousands of merchants, artisans, and farmers signed nonimportation agreements. In these agreements they pledged not to buy or use goods imported from Great Britain. As the boycott spread, British merchants lost so much business that they begged Parliament to repeal, or cancel, the Stamp Act.

The Act Is Repealed

In March 1766, Parliament gave in to the colonists' demands and repealed the Stamp Act. Yet the colonists' trust in the king and Parliament was never fully restored.

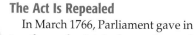
Revenue stamp

While the colonists celebrated their victory over the Stamp Act, Parliament passed another act on the same day it repealed the Stamp Act. The **Declaratory Act** of 1766 stated that Parliament had the right to tax and make decisions for the British colonies "in all cases." The colonists might have won one battle, but the war over making decisions for the colonies had just begun.

✓ **Reading Check** **Evaluating** What role did Samuel Adams play in colonial protests?

DIFFERENTIATED INSTRUCTION

At-Risk Students Ask students to collect and display a variety of everyday items that would have been taxed under British Laws, first under the Stamp Act (for example, newspapers, stationery, and a deck of playing cards) and then under the Townshend Acts (for example, a glass pitcher and a tin of tea). Call on volunteers to pick up an item from the display and explain its importance. Then have the student explain, as a protesting colonist might, why a tax on the item is unfair. **L1**

📁 Refer to *Inclusion for the Middle School Social Studies Classroom Strategies and Activities* in the TCR.

History *Through Art*

Patrick Henry Before the Virginia House of Burgesses by Peter F. Rothermel Patrick Henry gave a fiery speech before the Virginia House of Burgesses in 1765. **Why did Henry deliver the speech?**

New Taxes

Soon after the Stamp Act crisis, Parliament passed a set of laws in 1767 that came to be known as the **Townshend Acts.** In these acts the British leaders tried to avoid some of the problems the Stamp Act caused. They understood that the colonists would not tolerate internal taxes—those levied or paid inside the colonies. As a result the new taxes applied only to imported goods, with the tax being paid at the port of entry. The goods taxed, however, included basic items—such as glass, tea, paper, and lead—that the colonists had to import because they did not produce them.

By this time the colonists were outraged by *any* taxes Parliament passed. They believed that only their own representatives had the right to levy taxes on them. The colonists responded by bringing back the boycott that had worked so well against the Stamp Act. The boycott proved to be even more widespread this time.

Women took an active role in the protest against the Townshend Acts. In towns throughout the colonies, women organized groups to support the boycott of British goods, sometimes calling themselves the **Daughters of Liberty.** They urged Americans to wear homemade fabrics and produce other goods that were available only from Britain before. They believed this would help the American colonies become economically independent.

✓Reading Check **Comparing** How did the Townshend Acts differ from the Stamp Act?

History *Through Art*

Peter Rothermel also created paintings based on religious and literary themes. This work illustrates Rothermel's technique of combining sharp details with shadowy forms in a single painting. **Answer:** Henry wanted the burgesses to formally oppose the Stamp Act.

✓Reading Check

Answer: They taxed imported goods at the point of entry.

L1, ELL

Reading Essentials and Study Guide 5–1

Study Guide
Chapter 5, Section 1
For use with textbook pages 132–135

TAXATION WITHOUT REPRESENTATION

KEY TERMS	
revenue	Incoming money *(page 133)*
writs of assistance	Legal documents that allowed customs officers to search homes and warehouses *(page 133)*
resolution	A formal expression of opinion *(page 134)*
effigy	A life-size rag figure representing a hated person *(page 134)*
boycott	To refuse to buy, use, or have dealings with *(page 134)*
nonimportation	Not to buy or use imported goods *(page 134)*
repeal	To cancel or officially withdraw *(page 134)*

L3

Enrichment Activity 5–1

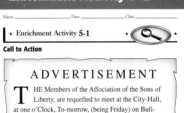

Name _____ Date _____ Class _____

★ **Enrichment Activity 5-1** ★

Call to Action

ADVERTISEMENT

THE Members of the Affociation of the Sons of Liberty, are requefted to meet at the City-Hall, at one o'Clock, To-morrow, (being Friday) on Bufinefs of the utmoft Importance;—And every other Friend to the Liberties and Trade of America, are hereby

4 CLOSE

Ask students which British taxation law they consider the most objectionable and why.

SECTION 1 ASSESSMENT

Checking for Understanding

1. **Key Terms** Write sentences or short paragraphs in which you use the following groups of terms correctly: (1) **revenue** and **writs of assistance;** (2) **resolution, effigy, boycott, nonimportation,** and **repeal.**

2. **Reviewing Facts** State two reasons for the deterioration of relations between the British and the colonists.

Reviewing Themes

3. **Civic Rights and Responsibilities** Why did the colonists think the writs of assistance violated their rights?

Critical Thinking

4. **Identifying Central Issues** Why did British policies following the French and Indian War lead to increased tensions with American colonists?

5. **Determining Cause and Effect** Re-create the diagram below and describe the effects of these British actions.

British Actions		Effects
Sugar Act	⇒	
Stamp Act	⇒	
Townshend Acts	⇒	

Analyzing Visuals

6. **Geography Skills** Review the map on page 133. The Proclamation of 1763 banned colonists from settling west of the Appalachian Mountains. Why did the British government want to halt western movement?

Interdisciplinary Activity

Persuasive Writing Write a letter to the editor of a colonial newspaper in which you attempt to persuade fellow colonists to boycott British goods. Use standard grammar, spelling, sentence structure and punctuation.

SECTION 1 ASSESSMENT ANSWERS

1. Student work should reflect correct use of terms.

2. Colonists felt the Proclamation of 1763 restricted freedom, did not want to pay for the French and Indian War, did not believe in taxation without representation, and were alarmed by British troops stationed in the colonies.

3. Colonists were horrified that government officials could enter their homes without warning.

4. Colonists thought British policies would curtail their freedoms and were angered by Britain's series of taxes.

5. Sugar Act: Colonists alarmed about losing basic rights; Stamp Act:

protests, refusal to use stamps, boycott of British goods; Townshend Acts: boycott of British goods

6. to minimize conflict with Native American groups

Interdisciplinary Activity Letters should be written from a colonist's perspective and include reasons for a boycott.

1 FOCUS

Section Overview

This section describes what happened at the Boston Massacre and the Boston Tea Party.

BELLRINGER
Skillbuilder Activity

Project transparency and have students answer the question.

Daily Focus Skills Transparency 5–2

Reading Preview

Answers to Graphic: prevented the arrival of food and supplies to Boston Harbor; ended town meetings; forced colonists to shelter British soldiers in their homes

Preteaching Vocabulary
Ask a student to read aloud the definition of the term *propaganda* from the textbook glossary. Have another student use the term in a sentence.

SECTION 2 Building Colonial Unity

Guide to Reading

Main Idea
As tensions between colonists and the British government increased, protests grew stronger.

Key Terms
propaganda, committee of correspondence

Reading Strategy
Organizing Information As you read the section, re-create the diagram below and describe how the Intolerable Acts changed life for colonists.

Read to Learn
• why Boston colonists and British soldiers clashed, resulting in the Boston Massacre.
• how the British government tried to maintain its control over the colonies.

Section Theme
Groups and Institutions Colonists banded together to protest British laws.

Preview of Events

♦1770	♦1773	♦1776

1770
Boston Massacre takes place

1772
Samuel Adams sets up a committee of correspondence

1773
Boston Tea Party occurs

1774
Parliament passes the Intolerable Acts

American protest banner

DONT TREAD ON ME

AN American Story

In the spring of 1768, British customs officials in Boston seized the *Liberty,* a ship belonging to John Hancock, a merchant and protest leader. The ship had docked in Boston Harbor to unload a shipment of wine and take on new supplies. The customs officials, however, charged that Hancock was using the ship for smuggling. As news of the ship's seizure spread through Boston, angry townspeople filled the streets. They shouted against Parliament and the taxes it had imposed on them. The *Liberty* affair became one of the events that united the colonists against British policies.

Trouble in Boston

Protests like the *Liberty* affair made British colonial officials nervous. In the summer of 1768, worried customs officers sent word back to Britain that the colonies were on the brink of rebellion. Parliament responded by sending two regiments of troops to Boston. As angry Bostonians jeered, the newly arrived "redcoats" set up camp right in the center of the city.

136   CHAPTER 5   Road to Independence

SECTION RESOURCES

Reproducible Masters
• Reproducible Lesson Plan 5–2
• Daily Lecture and Discussion Notes 5–2
• Guided Reading Activity 5–2
• Section Quiz 5–2
• Reteaching Activity 5–2
• Reading Essentials and Study Guide 5–2
• Enrichment Activity 5–2

Transparencies
• Daily Focus Skills Transparency 5–2

Multimedia
⦿ Interactive Tutor Self-Assessment CD-ROM
⦿ ExamView® Pro Testmaker CD-ROM
⦿ Presentation Plus! CD-ROM

Many colonists, especially those living in Boston, felt that the British had pushed them too far. First the British had passed a series of laws that violated colonial rights. Now they had sent an army to occupy colonial cities.

To make matters worse, the soldiers stationed in Boston acted rudely and sometimes even violently toward the colonists. Mostly poor men, the redcoats earned little pay. Some of them stole goods from local shops or scuffled with boys who taunted them in the streets. The soldiers competed off-hours for jobs that Bostonians wanted. The townspeople's hatred for the soldiers grew stronger every day.

The Boston Massacre

Relations between the redcoats and the Boston colonists grew more tense. Then on March 5, 1770, the tension finally reached a peak. That day a fight broke out between townspeople and soldiers. While some British officers tried to calm the crowd, one man shouted,

> 66 We did not send for you. We will not have you here. We'll get rid of you, we'll drive you away! 99

The angry townspeople moved through the streets, picking up any weapon they could find—sticks, stones, shovels, and clubs. They pushed forward toward the customshouse on King Street.

As the crowd approached, the sentry on duty panicked and called for help. The crowd responded by throwing stones, snowballs, oyster shells, and pieces of wood at the soldiers. "Fire, you bloodybacks, you lobsters," the crowd screamed. "You dare not fire."

After one of the soldiers was knocked down, the nervous and confused redcoats did fire. Several shots rang out, killing five colonists. One Bostonian cried out:

> 66 Are the inhabitants to be knocked down in the streets? Are they to be murdered in this manner? 99

Among the dead was **Crispus Attucks,** a dockworker who was part African, part Native American. The colonists called the tragic encounter the **Boston Massacre.**

The Word Spreads

Colonial leaders used news of the killings as propaganda—information designed to influence opinion—against the British. Samuel Adams put up posters describing the "Boston Massacre" as a slaughter of innocent Americans by bloodthirsty redcoats. An engraving by Paul Revere showed a British officer giving the order to open fire on an orderly crowd. Revere's powerful image strengthened anti-British feeling.

The Boston Massacre led many colonists to call for stronger boycotts on British goods. Aware of the growing opposition to its policies, Parliament repealed all the Townshend Acts taxes except the one on tea. Many colonists believed they had won another victory. They ended their boycotts, except on the taxed tea, and started to trade with British merchants again.

Some colonial leaders, however, continued to call for resistance to British rule. In 1772 Samuel Adams revived the Boston committee of correspondence, an organization used in earlier protests. The committee circulated writings about colonists' grievances against Britain. Soon other committees of correspondence sprang up throughout the colonies, bringing together protesters opposed to British measures. 📖 *(See page 596 of the Primary Sources Library for readings about colonial resistance.)*

✓ **Reading Check** **Explaining** How did the Boston Massacre contribute to the repeal of the Townshend Acts?

Fact · Fiction · Folklore

The Boston Massacre

The British soldiers never stood trial for the massacre. Eight soldiers and the commanding officer at the Boston Massacre *were* jailed and tried for murder. Many Patriots thought it was an act of disloyalty to defend the soldiers. The soldiers' hopes for justice rested in the hands of John Adams, who believed that even the enemy should be given a fair trial. Two of the soldiers were found guilty of manslaughter. The others were found not guilty on grounds of self-defense. Some Patriots questioned Adams's loyalty; others argued that the trial showed even the hated redcoats could receive a fair trial.

CHAPTER 5   Road to Independence   **137**

2 TEACH

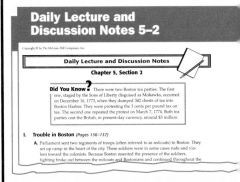

Daily Lecture and Discussion Notes 5–2

Copyright © by The McGraw-Hill Companies, Inc.

Daily Lecture and Discussion Notes

Chapter 5, Section 2

Did You Know There were two Boston tea parties. The first one, staged by the Sons of Liberty disguised as Mohawks, occurred on December 16, 1773, when they dumped 342 chests of tea into Boston Harbor. They were protesting the 3 cents per pound tax on tea. The second one repeated the protest on March 7, 1774. Both tea parties cost the British, in present-day currency, around $3 million.

I. Trouble in Boston *(Pages 136–137)*

A. Parliament sent two regiments of troops (often referred to as redcoats) to Boston. They set up camp in the heart of the city. These soldiers were in some cases rude and violent toward the colonists. Because Boston resented the presence of the soldiers, fighting broke out between the redcoats and Bostonians and continued throughout the

Interpreting Symbols Direct students' attention to the flag on page 136. **Ask:** Why wouldn't you want to step on a snake? *(It could bite you.)* Why might this flag be a warning to Britain? *(It might be telling Britain to leave the colonies alone or risk some sort of violent response.)* **L1**

✓ **Reading Check**

Answer: Britain tried to calm colonial anger and opposition by repealing the Townshend Acts.

L1, ELL

Guided Reading Activity 5–2

Name _____ Date _____ Class _____

★ **Guided Reading Activity 5-2**

DIRECTIONS: Outlining Locate the heading in your textbook. Then use the information under the heading to help you write each answer. Use another sheet of paper if necessary.

I. Trouble in Boston

A. Introduction—Why were Bostonians angry with British troops in their town?

B. The Boston Massacre

1. When did the Boston Massacre take place? _____

2. What did the crowd do as the British soldiers approached them? _____

3. Who was Crispus Attucks? _____

Reading Strategy   **READING THE TEXT**

Rewriting Use the Boston Massacre's events to help students understand that every historical event has two points of view. Have each student write an editorial from the point of view of a person from one side (either a British officer or Samuel Adams). Students should incorporate factual information, as well as opinion, in their editorial. Invite students who represented each side to share their editorials with the class. **L1, ELL** 🎁

British Soldiers *Redcoats* was the name the Patriots used to describe British soldiers. The patriots also called the British *bloodybacks* and *lobsters* to ridicule their bright red uniforms.

The tea the colonists threw into Boston Harbor would be worth more than $700,000 today. **Ask:** Why was East India tea cheaper than colonial tea? *(It was not taxed.)*

3 ASSESS

Assign Section 2 Assessment as homework or as an in-class activity.

🌐 Have students use **Interactive Tutor Self-Assessment CD-ROM.**

L2

Section Quiz 5–2

Name _____ Date _____ Class _____

⭐ Chapter 5   Score ☐

Section Quiz 5-2

DIRECTIONS: Matching Match the items in Column A with the items in Column B. Write the correct letters in the blanks. *(10 points each)*

Column A

_____ 1. participant in Boston Tea Party

_____ 2. Crispus Attucks

_____ 3. ruler of Britain

_____ 4. circulated colonists' grievances

_____ 5. closed Boston Harbor

Column B

A. victim of Boston Massacre
B. committee of correspondence
C. Coercive Acts
D. Samuel Adams
E. George III

DIRECTIONS: Multiple Choice In the blank at the left, write the letter of the

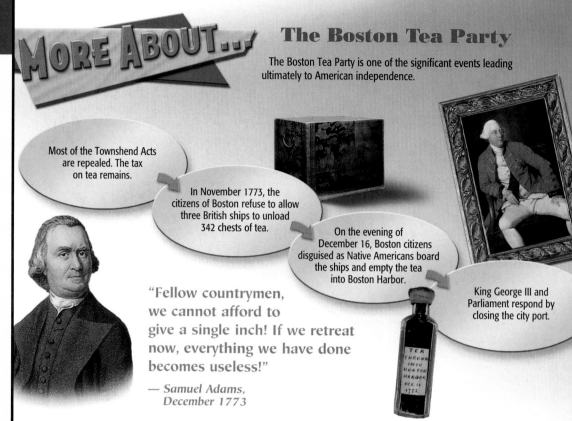

MORE ABOUT... The Boston Tea Party

The Boston Tea Party is one of the significant events leading ultimately to American independence.

Most of the Townshend Acts are repealed. The tax on tea remains.

In November 1773, the citizens of Boston refuse to allow three British ships to unload 342 chests of tea.

On the evening of December 16, Boston citizens disguised as Native Americans board the ships and empty the tea into Boston Harbor.

King George III and Parliament respond by closing the city port.

"Fellow countrymen, we cannot afford to give a single inch! If we retreat now, everything we have done becomes useless!"

— *Samuel Adams,*
December 1773

A Crisis Over Tea

In the early 1770s, some Americans considered British colonial policy a "conspiracy against liberty." The British government's actions in 1773 seemed to confirm that view.

The British East India Company faced ruin. To save the East India Company, Parliament passed the **Tea Act** of 1773. This measure gave the company the right to ship tea to the colonies without paying most of the taxes usually placed on tea. It also allowed the company to bypass colonial merchants and sell its tea directly to shopkeepers at a low price. This meant that East India Company tea was cheaper than any other tea in the colonies. The Tea Act gave the company a very favorable advantage over colonial merchants.

Colonial Demands

Colonial merchants immediately called for a new boycott of British goods. Samuel Adams and others denounced the British monopoly. The Tea Act, they argued, was just another attempt to crush the colonists' liberty.

At large public meetings in Boston and Philadelphia, colonists vowed to stop the East India Company's ships from unloading. The Daughters of Liberty issued a pamphlet declaring that rather than part with freedom, "we'll part with our tea."

Parliament ignored warnings that another crisis was brewing. The East India Company shipped tea to Philadelphia, New York, Boston, and Charles Town. The colonists forced the ships sent to New York and Philadelphia to turn back. The tea sent to Charles Town was seized and stored in a warehouse. In Boston, a showdown began.

The Boston Tea Party

Three tea ships arrived in Boston Harbor in late 1773. The royal governor, whose house had been destroyed by Stamp Act protesters, refused

DIFFERENTIATED INSTRUCTION

Gifted and Talented Colonists persuaded the captains of almost all of the East India Company ships that arrived in American ports loaded with tea to turn back. Ask students with strong interpersonal skills to write or speak what they think a colonist might have said to influence one of these ship's captains. **L3**

📁 Refer to *Inclusion for the Middle School Social Studies Classroom Strategies and Activities* in the TCR.

to let the ships turn back. When he ordered the tea unloaded, Adams and the Boston Sons of Liberty acted swiftly. On December 16, a group of men disguised as Mohawks and armed with hatchets marched to the wharves. At midnight they boarded the ships and threw 342 chests of tea overboard, an event that became known as the **Boston Tea Party.**

Word of this act of defiance spread throughout the colonies. Men and women gathered in the streets to celebrate the bravery of the Boston Sons of Liberty. Yet no one spoke of challenging British rule, and colonial leaders continued to think of themselves as members of the British empire.

The Intolerable Acts

When news of the Boston Tea Party reached London, the reaction was quite different. King **George III** realized that Britain was losing control of the colonies. "We must master them or totally leave them alone." Not prepared to give up, the king and Parliament vowed to punish Boston. In the spring of 1774, Parliament passed the **Coercive Acts,** very harsh laws intended to punish the people of Massachusetts for their resistance.

The Coercive Acts closed Boston Harbor until the Massachusetts colonists paid for the ruined tea. This action prevented the arrival of food and other supplies that normally came by ship. Worse,

the laws took away certain rights of the Massachusetts colonists. For example, the laws banned most town meetings, an important form of self-government in New England. Another provision permitted royal officers to be tried in other colonies or in Britain when accused of crimes.

The Coercive Acts also forced Bostonians to shelter soldiers in their own homes. Parliament planned to isolate Boston with these acts. Instead the other colonies sent food and clothing to demonstrate their support for Boston. The colonists maintained that the Coercive Acts violated their rights as English citizens. These included the rights to no quartering of troops in private homes and no standing army in peacetime without their consent.

The Quebec Act, passed shortly after the Coercive Acts, further angered the colonists. This act set up a permanent government for Quebec and granted religious freedom to French Catholics. Colonists strongly objected to the provision that gave Quebec the area west of the Appalachians and north of the Ohio River. This provision ignored colonial claims to the area. The feelings of the colonists were made clear by *their* name for the new laws—the Intolerable Acts.

✓**Reading Check** **Summarizing** List the effects of the Coercive Acts on the citizens of Boston.

SECTION 2 ASSESSMENT

Checking for Understanding

1. **Key Terms** Use these terms in sentences that relate to the Boston Massacre: propaganda, committee of correspondence.
2. **Reviewing Facts** How did colonial leaders use the Boston Massacre to their advantage?

Reviewing Themes

3. **Groups and Institutions** Why were the committees of correspondence powerful organizations?

Critical Thinking

4. **Drawing Conclusions** Do you think the Boston Tea Party was a turning point in the relationship between the British and the colonists? Explain.
5. **Organizing Information** Re-create the diagram below and describe how colonists showed their opposition to British policies.

Increased colonial opposition

Analyzing Visuals

6. **Picturing History** Examine the material about the Boston Tea Party on page 138. What artifacts are shown? When did the "tea party" take place?

Interdisciplinary Activity

Art Draw a cartoon strip showing the story of the Boston Tea Party. Use at least four cartoon frames to present the sequence of events from your point of view. Compare your cartoon to a classmate's and describe his or her point of view.

SECTION 2 ASSESSMENT ANSWERS

1. Student work should reflect correct use of terms.
2. The event was used as propaganda to drum up support against the British.
3. They spread political ideas and united opposition to British rule.

4. Students should mention that it was the most dramatic act of defiance by the colonists up until that time.
5. use of propaganda, revival of committees of correspondence, calls for new boycotts, and refusal of British shipments of tea

6. a chest and glass container of tea; Dec. 16, 1773

Interdisciplinary Activity Cartoons should show an understanding of the order in which the events took place.

✓**Reading Check**

Answer: Ships carrying food and other goods were prevented from arriving; town meetings were banned; and citizens were forced to house British soldiers.

L1

Reteaching Activity 5–2

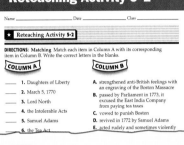

L1, ELL

Reading Essentials and Study Guide 5–2

L3

Enrichment Activity 5–2

4 CLOSE

Discuss the methods Britain used to try to control the colonies.

139

Block Schedule

Team Teaching This selection from *Johnny Tremain* may be implemented in a team-teaching context, in conjunction with English/Language Arts.

Reinforcing Vocabulary

Review the **Reader's Dictionary** terms with students to be sure they understand any unfamiliar terms.

Historical Connection

In Boston, the Sons of Liberty defied the Tea Act of 1773 by dumping the tea cargo of three ships. The Boston Tea Party made a forceful point and inspired other dissatisfied colonists.

Background Information

Setting The excerpt takes place aboard British ships in Boston Harbor on December 16, 1773.

Characters Johnny Tremain, the teenage hero of the novel, is the main character.

Plot The characters assist in confiscating tea from a British ship and dumping it into Boston Harbor.

HISTORY *Online*

Refer to tarvol1.glencoe.com for additional Glencoe Literature titles, lesson plans, and study guides related to this unit.

America's LITERATURE

Esther Forbes (1891–1967)

Esther Forbes wrote a number of books; among them is the prize-winning biography *Paul Revere and the World He Lived In*. As she researched Paul Revere's life, Forbes learned that many young apprentices played a role in the American Revolution. *Johnny Tremain*, a fictional work, tells the story of such an apprentice.

READ TO DISCOVER

In this passage from *Johnny Tremain*, 14-year-old Johnny and his friend Rab have disguised themselves as Mohawks. They join the crowd at Griffin's Wharf in Boston Harbor, where three English ships carrying tea are docked and are unable to leave or unload their cargo.

READER'S DICTIONARY

boatswain: officer on a ship
warped: roped
jargon: strange language
hold: place where cargo is stored on a ship
winch: machine for hauling

Johnny Tremain

There was a **boatswain's** whistle, and in silence one group boarded the *Dartmouth*. The *Eleanor* and the *Beaver* had to be **warped** in to the wharf. Johnny was close to Mr. Revere's heels. He heard him calling for the captain, promising him, in the **jargon** everyone talked that night, that not one thing should be damaged on the ship except only the tea, but the captain and all his crew had best stay in the cabin until the work was over.

Captain Hall shrugged and did as he was told, leaving his cabin boy to hand over the keys to the **hold**. The boy was grinning with pleasure. The "tea party" was not unexpected. . . .

The **winches** rattled and the heavy chests began to appear—one hundred and fifty of them. As some men worked in the hold, others broke open the chests and flung the tea into the harbor. But one thing made them unexpected difficulty. The tea inside the chests was wrapped in heavy canvas. The axes went through the wood easily enough—the canvas made endless trouble. Johnny had never worked so hard in his life.

Then Mr. Revere called the captain to come up and inspect. The tea was utterly gone, but Captain Hall agreed that beyond that there had not been the slightest damage.

It was close upon dawn when the work on all three ships was done. And yet the great, silent audience on the wharf, men, women, and children, had not gone home. As the three groups came off the ships, they formed in fours along the wharf, their axes on their shoulders. Then a hurrah went up and a fife began to play.

Paul Revere

ANALYZING LITERATURE

1. **Recall and Interpret** Why was the "tea party" expected?
2. **Evaluate and Connect** What does the conduct of the "tea party" participants suggest about the protest? Explain your answer.

Interdisciplinary Activity

Expository Writing Write a one-page paper about how you think you would react in Johnny's situation.

ANSWERS TO ANALYZING LITERATURE

1. The ships' captains were aware of the tension between colonists and the British over the Tea Act. This seemed obvious when Captain Hall and other crew members did not resist their visitors.

2. Their conduct suggests that the protest was peaceful since no one was hurt and they only destroyed the tea.

Interdisciplinary Activity
Papers should include a possible reaction, and students should support their choice by explaining their reasoning.

SECTION 3 A Call to Arms

Guide to Reading

Main Idea
Colonial leaders met at Philadelphia in 1774 to discuss a united response to British policies. Seven months later American and British troops met in battle for the first time.

Key Terms
militia, minutemen, Loyalist, Patriot

Reading Strategy
Sequencing Information As you read the section, re-create the diagram below and list six events leading to the Battle of Bunker Hill.

Read to Learn
• what happened at the Continental Congress in Philadelphia.
• how the colonists met British soldiers in the first battle.

Section Theme
Groups and Institutions With the establishment of the Continental Congress, the colonies continued to protest.

Preview of Events

◆1774	◆1775	◆1776

September 1774
First Continental Congress meets

April 19, 1775
Battles of Lexington and Concord are fought

May 10, 1775
Ethan Allen captures Fort Ticonderoga

June 17, 1775
Battle of Bunker Hill is fought

Revolutionary War drum and fife

★ AN
American Story

At first few colonists wanted a complete break with Britain. One of the most popular songs of the time, "The Bold Americans," called for *both* liberty and continued loyalty to the British king:

> We'll honor George, our sovereign, while he sits on the throne.
> If he grants us liberty, no other king we'll own.
> If he will grant us liberty, so plainly shall you see,
> We are the boys that fear no noise! Success to liberty.

As tensions mounted, however, a peaceful compromise was no longer possible.

The Continental Congress

Colonial leaders realized they needed more than boycotts to gain the liberty they sang about in "The Bold Americans." They needed the colonies to act together in their opposition to British policies.

In September 1774, 55 men arrived in the city of Philadelphia. Sent as delegates from all the colonies except Georgia, these men had come to establish a political body to represent American interests and challenge British control. They called the new organization the **Continental Congress.**

CHAPTER 5   Road to Independence   **141**

1 FOCUS

Section Overview
This section examines what happened at the Continental Congress and how the colonies prepared for war.

BELLRINGER
Skillbuilder Activity

 Project transparency and have students answer the question.

Daily Focus Skills Transparency 5–3

Reading Preview

Answers to Graphic: Continental Congress votes for boycott on British goods and called for militias; militias organize, some known as minutemen; King declares colonies were in rebellion; British troops are organized; battles of Lexington and Concord; Patriots capture Fort Ticonderoga

Preteaching Vocabulary
Have students demonstrate their understanding of *Loyalist* and *Patriot* by using each term in a sentence.

SECTION RESOURCES

📁 Reproducible Masters
• Reproducible Lesson Plan 5–3
• Daily Lecture and Discussion Notes 5–3
• Guided Reading Activity 5–3
• Section Quiz 5–3
• Reteaching Activity 5–3
• Reading Essentials and Study Guide 5–3
• Enrichment Activity 5–3

Transparencies
• Daily Focus Skills Transparency 5–3

Multimedia
📼 ABC News Interactive™ Historic America Electronic Field Trips
💿 Interactive Tutor Self-Assessment CD-ROM
💿 ExamView® Pro Testmaker CD-ROM
💿 Presentation Plus! CD-ROM

2 TEACH

Daily Lecture and Discussion Notes 5-3

Copyright © by The McGraw-Hill Companies, Inc.

Daily Lecture and Discussion Notes

Chapter 5, Section 3

Did You Know ? After Paul Revere reached Lexington on his famous April 1775 ride to warn John Hancock and Samuel Adams that the British were coming, he rode to Concord, where he was captured by the British. After being interrogated, they left him horseless and stranded.

I. **The Continental Congress** *(Pages 141–142)*

A. The Continental Congress was a group of prominent colonial leaders who met in September 1774 to establish a political group that would fight for American interests and challenge British rule. Among the delegates who attended were Samuel Adams, John Adams, John Jay, Richard Henry Lee, Patrick Henry, and George Washington.

B. The delegates worked together to draft a statement of grievances. They called for repeal of the 13 acts of Parliament. They voted to boycott all British goods and trade.

Reading Strategy

Responding to a Quote Have a volunteer read aloud the comment from Patrick Henry on page 142. Discuss why it would be important for his opinion to be widely held if the Patriot cause were to succeed. **L2**

Graphic Organizer → Skills

Answer: The Americans had a tradition of self-government and desired their own identity separate from that of Britain. In addition, British policies from 1763 onward angered the colonists, increasing the desire for independence.

Graphic Organizer Skills Practice Ask: What was the most immediate effect after the colonists declared their independence? *(The colonies fought a long war with Great Britain.)*

Reading Check

Answer: to represent the interests of the colonists and challenge British control

---

Causes and Effects of the Revolutionary War

Causes

- Colonists' tradition of self-government
- Americans' desire for a separate identity from Britain
- Proclamation of 1763
- Harsh British policies toward North America after 1763

Effects

- A long war with Great Britain
- Self-government for the United States
- World recognition of United States independence

Graphic Organizer → Skills

Relations between Britain and America worsened during the 1760s and the 1770s.

Analyzing Information Why did the colonists fight for self-government?

Delegates to the Congress

Major political leaders from all the colonies attended the Congress. Massachusetts sent fiery Samuel Adams and his younger cousin **John Adams,** a successful lawyer. New York sent **John Jay,** another lawyer. From Virginia came **Richard Henry Lee** and **Patrick Henry,** two of the most outspoken defenders of colonial rights, as well as **George Washington.**

Patrick Henry summed up the meaning of the gathering:

“The distinctions between Virginians, Pennsylvanians, New Yorkers, and New Englanders are no more. . . . I am not a Virginian, but an American.”

Decisions of the Congress

Although the delegates were hardly united in their views, they realized they needed to work together. First they drafted a statement of

142   CHAPTER 5   Road to Independence

---

grievances calling for the repeal of 13 acts of Parliament passed since 1763. They declared that these laws violated the colonists' rights. Their rights were based on the "laws of nature, the principles of the English constitution, and the several charters" of the colonies. The delegates also voted to boycott all British goods and trade. No British products could be brought into or consumed in the colonies, and no colonial goods could be shipped to Britain.

One of Congress's major decisions was to endorse the Suffolk Resolves. These resolutions had been prepared by Bostonians and others who lived in Suffolk County, Massachusetts. They called on the people of Suffolk County to arm themselves against the British. The people responded by forming militias—groups of citizen soldiers. Many wondered if war was coming. The answer came the following spring.

Reading Check **Explaining** What was the purpose of the Continental Congress?

The First Battles

Colonists expected that if fighting against the British broke out, it would begin in New England. Militia companies in Massachusetts held frequent training sessions, made bullets, and stockpiled rifles and muskets. Some companies, known as minutemen, boasted they would be ready to fight on a minute's notice. In the winter of 1774–1775, a British officer stationed in Boston noted in his diary:

“The people are evidently making every preparation for resistance. They are taking every means to provide themselves with arms.”

Britain Sends Troops

The British also prepared for conflict. King George announced to Parliament that the New England colonies were "in a state of rebellion" and said that "blows must decide" who would control America. By April 1775, British general Sir Thomas Gage had several thousand soldiers under his command in and around Boston, with many more on the way. Gage had instructions to

---

COOPERATIVE LEARNING ACTIVITY

Reviewing the Sides Organize the class into two teams—one to represent the First Continental Congress, the other to represent Parliament. Have students in both groups choose one of the following tasks: summarize the group's feelings about the conflict; identify the basis for those feelings; outline the group's plan of action; or explain how they demonstrated this plan at Lexington, Concord, and Bunker Hill. Students should divide work according to their skills and abilities. Students can research, write, prepare speeches, or illustrate concepts. Have them present their findings as a section review. **L1, ELL**

take away the weapons of the Massachusetts militia and arrest the leaders.

Gage learned that the militia was storing arms and ammunition at **Concord,** a town about 20 miles northwest of Boston. He ordered 700 troops under Lieutenant-Colonel Francis Smith to march

> 66to Concord, where you will seize and destroy all the artillery and ammunition you can find.99

Alerting the Colonists

On the night of April 18, 1775, Dr. Joseph Warren walked the streets of Boston, looking for any unusual activity by the British army. He saw a regiment form ranks in Boston Common and then begin to march out of the city.

Warren rushed to alert **Paul Revere** and **William Dawes,** leading members of the Sons of Liberty. Revere and Dawes rode to Lexington, a town east of Concord, to warn Samuel Adams and John Hancock that the British were coming.

Revere galloped off across the moonlit countryside, shouting, "The regulars are out!" to the people and houses he passed along the way. When he reached Lexington, he raced to tell Adams and Hancock his news. Adams could barely control his excitement. "What a glorious morning this is!" Adams was ready to fight for American independence.

Fighting at Lexington and Concord

At dawn the redcoats approached Lexington. When they reached the center of the town they discovered a group of about 70 minutemen who had been alerted by Revere and Dawes. Led by Captain John Parker, the minutemen had positioned themselves on the town common with muskets in hand. A minuteman reported,

> 66There suddenly appeared a number of the King's troops, about a thousand . . . the foremost of which cried, 'Throw down your arms, ye villains, ye rebels.'99

A shot was fired, and then both sides let loose with an exchange of bullets. When the fighting was over, eight minutemen lay dead.

L1, ELL

Guided Reading Activity 5–3

Name _____ Date _____ Class _____

★ Guided Reading Activity **5-3**

DIRECTIONS: Filling in the Blanks Use your textbook to fill in the blanks using the words in the box. Use another sheet of paper if necessary.

Green Mountain Boys	American	John Hancock	militias
correspondence	April 18, 1775	minutemen	Loyalists
Major John Pitcairn	Boston	70 minutemen	Patriots
Breed's Hill	Concord	gunpowder	Paul Revere
Ethan Allen	Georgia		

The Continental Congress

Delegates from every colony except (1) _____ attended the Continental Congress in September 1774. At the gathering, Patrick Henry stated, "I am not a Virginian, but an (2) _____." The most important decision delegates made concerned armed

Geography *Skills*

Answers:
1. Concord
2. about 6–7 miles

VIDEOCASSETTE
Historic America Electronic Field Trips

View **Chapter 6** to learn more about the battles of Lexington and Concord.

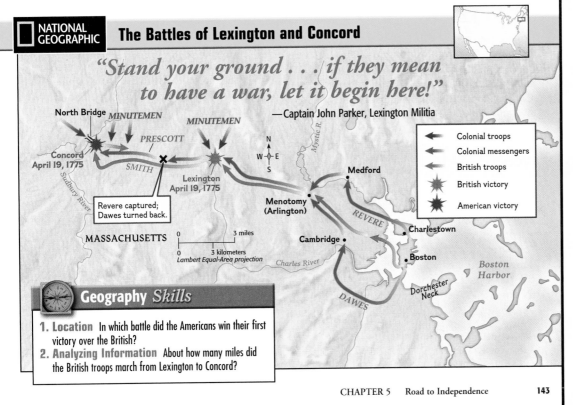

NATIONAL GEOGRAPHIC — The Battles of Lexington and Concord

"Stand your ground . . . if they mean to have a war, let it begin here!"
—Captain John Parker, Lexington Militia

North Bridge MINUTEMEN
MINUTEMEN
PRESCOTT
Concord
April 19, 1775
SMITH
Sudbury River
Revere captured; Dawes turned back.
MASSACHUSETTS
Lexington
April 19, 1775
Mystic R.
Medford
Menotomy (Arlington)
REVERE
Charlestown
Cambridge
Boston
DAWES
Charles River
Dorchester Neck
Boston Harbor

N W E S

0   3 miles
0   3 kilometers
Lambert Equal-Area projection

←	Colonial troops
←	Colonial messengers
←	British troops
✶	British victory
✶	American victory

Geography *Skills*

1. **Location** In which battle did the Americans win their first victory over the British?
2. **Analyzing Information** About how many miles did the British troops march from Lexington to Concord?

Who?What?Where?When?

David Lamson David Lamson, an African American who had fought in the French and Indian War, commanded the forces defending Concord. After the warning at Boston, all the young men of Concord had been pressed into service as minutemen, so the defense of the town fell to older citizens.

DIFFERENTIATED INSTRUCTION

Gifted and Talented Patrick Henry's statement "I am not a Virginian, but an American" reflects a new point of view shared by many delegates to the First Continental Congress. Invite students to picture themselves as delegates from various colonies. Have them, in character, write diary entries kept during the meeting in Philadelphia. The entries should show how their attitudes change—from seeking the best for their own colonies to promoting the good of the colonies as a whole—and why.

L3

📂 Refer to *Inclusion for the Middle School Social Studies Classroom Strategies and Activities* in the TCR.

History *Through Art*

Answer: in order to seize and destroy the weapons of the Massachusetts militia and arrest the leaders

✓ Reading Check

Answer: The colonists hid behind objects and fired at the British as they marched in plain sight along the road.

3 ASSESS

Assign Section 3 Assessment as homework or as an in-class activity.

🔵 Have students use **Interactive Tutor Self-Assessment CD-ROM.**

L2

Section Quiz 5–3

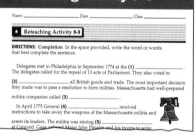

L1

Reteaching Activity 5–3

History *Through Art*

A View of the Town of Concord, 1775 by an unknown artist Two British officers (left) search for fleeing minutemen, while British troops march through Concord. **Why did the British march to Lexington and Concord?**

The British troops continued their march to Concord. When they arrived there, they discovered that most of the militia's gunpowder had already been removed. They destroyed the remaining supplies. At Concord's North Bridge, the minutemen were waiting for them.

Messengers on horseback had spread word of the British movements. All along the road from Concord to Boston, farmers, blacksmiths, saddle makers, and clerks hid behind trees, rocks, and stone fences. As the British marched down the road, the militia fired. A British officer wrote, "These fellows were generally good marksmen, and many of them used long guns made for duck shooting." By the time the redcoats reached Boston, at least 174 were wounded and 73 were dead.

Looking back, the poet Ralph Waldo Emerson wrote in "The Concord Hymn" that the Americans at Lexington and Concord had fired the "shot heard 'round the world." The battle for America's independence from Great Britain had begun.

✓ Reading Check Describing What tactics did the colonists use against the British troops on their march back from Concord to Boston?

144   CHAPTER 5   Road to Independence

More Military Action

Shortly after Lexington and Concord, Benedict Arnold, a captain in the Connecticut militia, was authorized to raise a force of 400 to seize Fort Ticonderoga on Lake Champlain. Ticonderoga was not only strategically located but was rich in military supplies. Arnold learned that Ethan Allen was also mounting an expedition in Vermont to attack the fort. Arnold joined with Allen's force, known as the Green Mountain Boys, and together they caught the British by surprise. The garrison surrendered on May 10, 1775.

Later during the war, Arnold conspired to surrender the key fort of West Point to the British and led British raids against the Americans in Virginia and Connecticut. Arnold became a general in the British army.

Building Forces

After the battles of Lexington and Concord, the committees of correspondence sent out calls for volunteers to join the militias. Soon the colonial militia assembled around Boston was about 20,000 strong. For several weeks, the American and British armies waited nervously to see who would make the next move.

INTERDISCIPLINARY CONNECTIONS ACTIVITY

Daily Life The First Continental Congress drafted a list of grievances toward British policies and actions. As a review, ask students to list anything they have read in the chapter thus far that they think colonists would have considered a "grievance." You might prompt students by giving them the option of thinking of themselves as delegates to the Congress. Conclude by discussing how people express political grievances today. Mention such formats as editorials, demonstrations, and talk radio. **L1**

The Battle of Bunker Hill

On June 16, 1775, about 1,200 militiamen under the command of Colonel William Prescott set up fortifications at Bunker Hill and nearby Breed's Hill, across the harbor from Boston.

The British decided to drive the Americans from their strategic locations overlooking the city. The next day the redcoats crossed the harbor and assembled at the bottom of Breed's Hill. Bayonets drawn, they charged up the hill. With his forces low on ammunition, Colonel Prescott reportedly shouted the order, "Don't fire until you see the whites of their eyes." The Americans opened fire, forcing the British to retreat. The redcoats charged two more times, receiving furious fire. In the end the Americans ran out of gunpowder and had to withdraw.

The British won the **Battle of Bunker Hill** but suffered heavy losses—more than 1,000 dead and wounded. As one British officer wrote in his diary, "A dear bought victory, another such would have ruined us." The British had learned that defeating the Americans on the battlefield would not be quick or easy.

Choosing Sides

As American colonists heard about these battles, they faced a major decision. Should they join the rebels or remain loyal to Britain? Those who

Fact · Fiction · Folklore

The Battle of Bunker Hill

The Battle of Bunker Hill was fought on Breed's Hill. Most of the fighting did actually take place on Breed's Hill. The Patriot soldiers received instructions to set up defensive positions on Bunker Hill. For reasons that are unclear, they set up the positions on nearby Breed's Hill.

chose to stay with Britain, the Loyalists, did not consider unfair taxes and regulations good reasons for rebellion. Some remained loyal to the king because they were officeholders who would lose their positions as a result of the Revolution. Others were people who lived in relative isolation and who had not been part of the wave of discontent that turned so many Americans against Britain. Still others expected Britain to win the war and wanted to gain favor with the British. The Patriots, on the other hand, were determined to fight the British to the end—until American independence was won.

✓**Reading Check** **Describing** What did the British learn from the Battle of Bunker Hill?

SECTION 3 ASSESSMENT

Checking for Understanding

1. **Key Terms** One of the following terms does not belong with the other three. Identify the term that does not belong and explain why. Terms: militia, minutemen, Loyalist, Patriots.

2. **Reviewing Facts** What decisions were made by the First Continental Congress?

Reviewing Themes

3. **Groups and Institutions** Why did the Continental Congress pass a resolution to form militias?

Critical Thinking

4. **Making Inferences** What reasons might Loyalists have had to support Great Britain?

5. **Comparing** Re-create the diagram below and list the differing beliefs of Patriots and Loyalists and those shared by both.

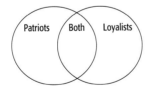

Analyzing Visuals

6. **Chart Skills** Review the cause-and-effect chart on page 142. What event in 1763 was significant to the independence movement?

Interdisciplinary Activity

Expressive Writing Write a one-act play in which a small group of ordinary men, women, and children in a small town react to news of the Battle of Lexington. Remember that reactions varied from colony to colony and that not all colonists wanted independence from Great Britain.

CHAPTER 5   Road to Independence   **145**

L1, ELL

Reading Essentials and Study Guide 5–3

Study Guide

Chapter 5, Section 3

For use with textbook pages 141–145

A CALL TO ARMS

KEY TERMS

militia	Groups of citizen soldiers (page 142)
minutemen	Militia companies, or citizen soldiers, ready to fight on a minute's notice (page 142)
Loyalists	Those colonists who decided to support Britain (page 145)
Patriots	Colonists determined to fight against Britain for American independence (page 145)

DRAWING FROM EXPERIENCE

Have you ever had a disagreement with a friend or family member? What did you do to try

L3

Enrichment Activity 5–3

Name _____ Date _____ Class _____

★ **Enrichment Activity 5-3** ★

Paul Revere, Artisan

Paul Revere (1734–1818), who was famous for warning the minutemen of Lexington that the British troops were coming, was also a businessperson and renowned craft worker who fashioned silver goods. His designs are still popular today.

DIRECTIONS: Analyzing Information Use the table to answer the questions.

Paul Revere's Silver Business

Silver Objects	Period A 1761–1775		Period B 1779–1797	
	Number	Percent	Number	Percent
Flatware	410	35.8	2,069	49.15

Did you know?

The route of the Boston Marathon generally follows the route taken by the British in their retreat from Concord.

4 CLOSE

Review the chart on page 142. Have students choose the action they believe to be the greatest cause for declaring independence.

SECTION 3 ASSESSMENT ANSWERS

1. *Loyalist;* the other groups fought or rebelled against Britain.

2. called for the repeal of several laws; called for a boycott of British goods; voted to form a militia

3. so that the colonies would be ready if fighting broke out

4. Loyalists did not think the colonists could win a struggle with Britain; they thought that a Patriot victory would mean upheaval; they did not see good cause for rebellion.

5. Patriots: determined to fight the British until they gained independence; Loyalists: did not consider

unfair taxes and regulations good enough reasons for rebellion; Both: wanted fair treatment

6. the Proclamation of 1763

Interdisciplinary Activity Plays should focus on the views that colonists held based on what was presented in this section.

TEACH

Distinguishing Fact from Opinion The ability to recognize the difference between verifiable statements (facts) and statements of personal belief (opinion) is important. By evaluating with a checklist, students will be able to classify facts and opinions.

Ask students to rephrase *We have the highest-ranking team in the state* as an opinion. *(Example: We have the best team in the state.)* Call on volunteers to make statements about popular TV shows. Have the class identify each statement as a fact or an opinion.

Additional Practice
L2

Chapter Skills Activity 5

Name _____ Date _____ Class _____

★ Chapter Skills Activity 5

Distinguishing Fact From Opinion

Facts can be verified and checked for accuracy. Opinions express beliefs and cannot be proved or disproved. Expert opinions on a topic, such as a doctor's opinion on health, may be more reliable than other opinions. Words and phrases such as *I believe, I think, probably, might, could, should, best, worst,* and *greatest* help identify opinions.

DIRECTIONS: Read the statements. If the statement is a fact, write **F** and explain how you could check its accuracy. If it is an opinion, write **O** and underline words that suggest it is opinion.

_____ 1. Members of the British Parliament should have considered more carefully the effect of their tax policies on the American colonists. _____

2. The Stamp Act of 1765 required colonists to pay a tax on printed material.

GLENCOE
TECHNOLOGY

CD-ROM
Glencoe Skillbuilder Interactive Workbook CD-ROM, Level 1

This interactive CD-ROM reinforces student mastery of essential social studies skills.

Distinguishing Fact From Opinion

Why Learn This Skill?

Suppose a friend says, "Our school's basketball team is awesome. That's a fact." Actually, it is not a fact; it is an opinion. Knowing how to tell the difference between a fact and an opinion can help you analyze the accuracy of political claims, advertisements, and many other kinds of statements.

Learning the Skill

A **fact** answers a specific question such as: What happened? Who did it? When and where did it happen? Why did it happen? Statements of fact can be checked for accuracy and proven.

An **opinion,** on the other hand, expresses beliefs, feelings, and judgments. Although it may reflect someone's thoughts, we cannot prove or disprove it.

An opinion often begins with phrases such as *I believe, I think, probably, it seems to me,* or *in my opinion.* It often contains words such as *might, could, should,* and *ought* and superlatives such as *best, worst,* and *greatest.* Judgment words that express approval or disapproval—such as *good, bad, poor,* and *satisfactory*—also usually indicate an opinion.

To distinguish between facts and opinions, ask yourself these questions:
* Does this statement give specific information about an event?
* Can I check the accuracy of this statement?
* Does this statement express someone's feelings, beliefs, or judgment?
* Does it include phrases such as *I believe,* superlatives, or judgment words?

Paul Revere's ride

Practicing the Skill

Read each numbered statement below. Tell whether each is a fact or an opinion, and explain how you arrived at your answer.

1. Paul Revere rode to Lexington with the news that the British redcoats were coming.

2. The redcoats were the most feared soldiers in the world at that time.

3. The Daughters of Liberty opposed the Tea Act of 1773.

4. The Boston Tea Party raiders should have sunk the tea ships.

5. George III was a foolish king.

Applying the Skill

Distinguishing Fact from Opinion Analyze 10 advertisements. List at least three facts and three opinions presented in the ads.

 Glencoe's **Skillbuilder Interactive Workbook CD-ROM, Level 1,** provides instruction and practice in key social studies skills.

ANSWERS TO PRACTICING THE SKILL

1. Fact; this is a statement of fact about an event that can be verified.

2. Opinion; this is a belief or judgment that includes superlatives and cannot be verified.

3. Fact: this is a statement of fact about the political position of a group that can be verified.

4. Opinion; the expression *should have* indicates someone's feeling.

5. Opinion; the idea that George III was foolish reflects a personal belief.

Applying the Skill Ask students how easy it would be to check some of the facts for accuracy and why ads seem to be based on opinions.

SECTION 4 Moving Toward Independence

Guide to Reading

Main Idea
The Second Continental Congress voted to approve the Declaration of Independence.

Key Terms
petition, preamble

Reading Strategy
Organizing Information As you read the section, re-create the diagram below and describe the parts of the Declaration of Independence.

Parts of the Declaration of Independence

Read to Learn
• what happened at the Second Continental Congress.
• why the colonists drafted the Declaration of Independence.

Section Theme
Government and Democracy The Declaration of Independence declared the colonies free and independent.

Preview of Events

♦1775   ♦1776   ♦1777

May 10, 1775
Second Continental Congress meets

July 1775
The Congress sends Olive Branch Petition to George III

March 1776
George Washington takes Boston from the British

July 4, 1776
Declaration of Independence is approved

Adams and Jefferson

★ AN ★ American Story

In June 1776, delegates to the Second Continental Congress came to a momentous decision. They agreed to have a committee draw up a document declaring America's independence from Great Britain. Many years later John Adams recalled a conversation with Thomas Jefferson about the writing of the document.

Jefferson: You should do it.
Adams: Oh! no.
Jefferson: Why will you not? You ought to do it. . . .
Adams: You can write ten times better than I can.
Jefferson: Well, if you are decided, I will do as well as I can.

Colonial Leaders Emerge

On May 10, 1775, the **Second Continental Congress** assembled for the first time, declaring independence was a long way off. The conversation between Jefferson and Adams did not occur until more than a year after that first meeting.

CHAPTER 5   Road to Independence   **147**

---

2 TEACH

Supporting Key Ideas Write the following statement on the chalkboard: *By the spring of 1776, the colonies had started to resemble an independent nation.* Have students work together to locate details that support this statement (for example, the Second Continental Congress was meeting; the Continental Army was established). **L2**

you don't say...

Militia From the Latin *miles*, which means "soldier," comes *militia*. During the Revolutionary War, the term referred to all able-bodied men between the ages of 16 and 60 (who were potential soldiers).

The Second Continental Congress acted as a central government for the colonies.

The delegates to the Second Continental Congress included some of the greatest political leaders in America. Among those attending were John and Samuel Adams, Patrick Henry, Richard Henry Lee, and George Washington—all delegates to the First Continental Congress held in 1774. Several distinguished new delegates came as well.

Benjamin Franklin, one of the most accomplished and respected men in the colonies, had been an influential member of the Pennsylvania legislature. In 1765, during the Stamp Act Crisis, he represented the colonies in London and helped secure the repeal of the act.

Fact *Fiction Folklore*

America's Flags

Continental Colors, 1775–1777 The Continental Colors, or Grand Union flag, was the first to represent all the colonies. Its 13 stripes stood for the thirteen colonies. The crosses represented the British flag and symbolized the colonists' loyalty to Great Britain at that time.

John Hancock of Massachusetts, 38 years old, was a wealthy merchant. He funded many Patriot groups, including the Sons of Liberty. The delegates chose Hancock as president of the Second Continental Congress.

Thomas Jefferson, only 32 when the Congress began, had already acquired a reputation as a brilliant thinker and writer. As a member of the Virginia House of Burgesses, Jefferson had become associated with the movement toward independence.

The Second Continental Congress began to govern the colonies. It authorized the printing of money and set up a post office with Franklin in charge. It established committees to communicate with Native Americans and with other countries. Most important, the Congress created the **Continental Army** to fight against Britain in a more organized way than the colonial militias could. On John Adams's recommendation, the Congress unanimously chose George Washington to be the army's commander.

After Washington left to take charge of the colonial forces in Boston, the delegates offered Britain one last chance to avoid all-out war. In July the Congress sent a petition, or formal request, to George III. Called the **Olive Branch Petition,** it assured the king of the colonists' desire for peace. It asked the king to protect the

148 CHAPTER 5 Road to Independence

Reading Strategy **READING THE TEXT**

Visualizing Help students to create pictures in their mind as they read to aid their understanding through visualizing. The Second Continental Congress witnessed several moments of historic impact. Have students visualize any of the following events: the choice of John Hancock as president of the meetings; the choice of George Washington as commander of the new Continental Army; debate over the wisdom of declaring independence; or approval of the draft of Thomas Jefferson's Declaration of Independence. Have each student illustrate or write a paragraph or dialogue describing what they visualize. **L2** 🎒

colonists' rights, which Parliament seemed determined to destroy. George III refused to receive the Olive Branch Petition. Instead he prepared for war, hiring more than 30,000 German troops to send to America and fight beside British troops.

The Colonies Take the Offensive

Meanwhile the Congress learned that British troops stationed in what is now Canada were planning to invade New York. The Americans decided to strike first. Marching north from Fort Ticonderoga, a Patriot force captured Montreal in November. An American attack on Quebec led by Benedict Arnold failed, however. The American forces stayed outside the city of Quebec through the long winter and returned to Fort Ticonderoga in 1776.

Washington reached Boston in July 1775, a few weeks after the Battle of Bunker Hill. He found the members of the militia growing in number every day, but he realized they lacked discipline, organization, and leadership. He began the hard work of shaping these armed civilians into an army.

By March 1776, Washington judged the Continental Army ready to fight. He positioned the army in a semicircle around Boston and gave the order for its cannons to bombard the British forces. The redcoats, under Sir William Howe, hurriedly withdrew from the city and boarded their ships. On March 17 Washington led his jubilant troops into Boston. The British troops sailed to Halifax, Nova Scotia.

Moving Toward Independence

Throughout the colonies in late 1775 and early 1776, some Americans still hoped to avoid a complete break with Britain. Support for the position of absolute independence was growing, however.

In January 1776, **Thomas Paine** published a pamphlet called *Common Sense* that captured the attention of the American colonists. In bold language, Paine called for complete independence from Britain. He argued that it was simply

HISTORY Online

Student Web Activity
Visit tarvol1.glencoe.com and click on **Chapter 5— Student Web Activities** for an activity on the Declaration of Independence.

People In History

Abigail Adams 1744–1818

Born into a comfortable Massachusetts household, Abigail Smith spent her youth reading and studying. At age 19 she married 28-year-old lawyer John Adams, who became a leader in the independence movement. Through her letters to family and friends, Abigail left us a record of her thoughts about the revolution as it developed. She also shared her hopes for the new nation.

As Congress considered a declaration of independence, she teasingly —but seriously—wrote to her husband:

"I long to hear that you have declared an independency . . . I desire you would Remember the Ladies, and be more generous and favorable to them than your ancestors."

Their correspondence during the times they spent apart showed a thoughtful exchange of ideas and a strong respect for one another. Abigail Adams would later become the second of the new nation's first ladies.

CHAPTER 5   Road to Independence   **149**

Guided Reading Activity 5-4

Name _____ Date _____ Class _____

★ Guided Reading Activity 5-4

DIRECTIONS: Recalling the Facts Use the information in your textbook to answer the questions. Use another sheet of paper if necessary.
1. When did the Second Continental Congress assemble? _____
2. Who were four political leaders who attended the Second Continental Congress?
3. What four actions did the Congress take as it began to govern the colonies?
4. Who did the Congress choose to lead the Continental Army? _____
5. What was the Olive Branch Petition? _____
6. Why were George Washington's troops jubilant on March 17, 1776? _____

HISTORY Online

Objectives and answers to the student activity can be found in the **Web Activity Lesson Plan** feature at tarvol1.glencoe.com

People In History

Abigail Adams was a strong supporter of women's rights and was an opponent of slavery. Abigail was the first First Lady to live in the White House. Ask students to describe the causes that recent presidents' wives have supported.

CURRICULUM CONNECTION

Language Arts As Jefferson drafted the Declaration of Independence, he was greatly influenced by other literary works. Six months earlier Thomas Paine, in *Common Sense*, had outlined the steps needed to declare independence. Jefferson also drew many ideas from John Locke's *Two Treatises of Government*.

DIFFERENTIATED INSTRUCTION

English Learners The musical film, *1776*, celebrates the events leading up to the signing of the Declaration of Independence. Invite students to view the video or listen to the soundtrack. Afterward, have students discuss the characters they found most interesting. Ask them to explain how hearing the story of the Declaration of Independence affected their understanding of revolutionary events. **L1,** ELL

📁 Refer to *Inclusion for the Middle School Social Studies Classroom Strategies and Activities* in the TCR.

Picturing History

Answer: Congress voted on Richard Henry Lee's resolution for independence.

✓ Reading Check

Answer: He motivated Americans to fight for their independence from Britain.

History *and the* Humanities

🏳 American Music: Hits Through History, "General Scott's March"

3 ASSESS

Assign Section 4 Assessment as homework or as an in-class activity.

⊕ Have students use **Interactive Tutor Self-Assessment CD-ROM.**

L2

Section Quiz 5–4

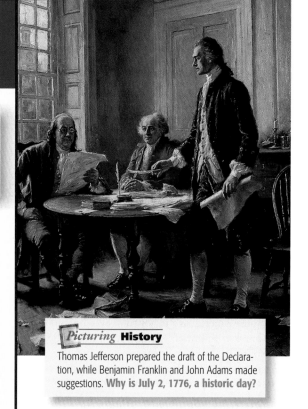

Picturing History

Thomas Jefferson prepared the draft of the Declaration, while Benjamin Franklin and John Adams made suggestions. **Why is July 2, 1776, a historic day?**

❝That these United Colonies are, and of right ought to be, free and independent States . . . and that all political connection between them and the State of Great Britain is, and ought to be, totally dissolved.❞

The Congress debated the resolution. Some delegates still thought the colonies were not ready to form a separate nation. Others argued that war already had begun and a large portion of the American population wanted to separate from Great Britain. Still others feared Great Britain's power to hold down the rebellion.

While the delegates debated the issue, the Congress chose a committee to draft a **Declaration of Independence.** Jefferson was selected to write the document. Jefferson drew on the ideas of thinkers such as English philosopher John Locke to set out the colonies' reasons for proclaiming their freedom. Locke wrote that people were born with certain natural rights to life, liberty, and property; that people formed governments to protect these rights; and that a government interfering with these rights might rightfully be overthrown.

On July 2, 1776, the Congress finally voted on Lee's resolution for independence. Twelve colonies voted for it. New York did not vote but later announced its support. Next the delegates took up Jefferson's draft of the Declaration of Independence. After making some changes, they approved the document on July 4, 1776.

John Hancock, the president of the Congress, was the first to sign the Declaration of Independence. Hancock remarked that he wrote his name large enough for King George to read it without his glasses. Hancock's bold signature stands out on the original document. Eventually 56 delegates signed the paper announcing the birth of the United States.

Copies of the Declaration went out to the newly declared states. Washington had it read to his troops on July 9. In New York American soldiers tore down a statue of George III in celebration. In Worcester, Massachusetts, the reading of the Declaration of Independence was followed by "repeated huzzas [cheers], firing of musketry and cannon, bonfires, and other demonstrations of joy."

"common sense" to stop following the "royal brute," King George III. Paine told the colonists their cause was not just a squabble over taxes but a struggle for freedom—"in a great measure the cause of all mankind." *Common Sense* inspired thousands of Americans. 📖 *(See page 596 of the Primary Sources Library for another excerpt from* Common Sense*.)*

✓ Reading Check **Explaining** Why was Thomas Paine important to the independence movement?

The Colonies Declare Independence

At the Second Continental Congress in Philadelphia, the meeting hall was filled with spirited debate. One central issue occupied the delegates: Should the colonies declare themselves an independent nation, or should they stay under British rule?

In April 1776, North Carolina instructed its delegates to support independence. On June 7 Virginia's Richard Henry Lee proposed a bold resolution:

INTERDISCIPLINARY CONNECTIONS ACTIVITY

Daily Life The Declaration of Independence ends with this promise from those who signed it: ". . . we mutually pledge to each other our lives, our fortunes, and our sacred honor." Have students investigate what happened during the course of the war to the people who made this pledge. Which delegates lost their lives, their fortunes, or their reputations (political or personal) in defense of independence—and how? Encourage students to choose a variety of formats for presenting their information. Follow up with a class discussion of the presentations. **L2**

The Declaration of Independence

The Declaration has four major sections. The preamble, or introduction, states that people who wish to form a new country should explain their reasons for doing so. The next two sections list the rights the colonists believed they should have and their complaints against Britain. The final section proclaims the existence of the new nation.

The Declaration of Independence states what Jefferson and many Americans thought were universal principles. It begins with a description of traditional English political rights.

> ❝We hold these truths to be self-evident, that all men are created equal, that they are endowed by their Creator with certain unalienable Rights, that among these are Life, Liberty, and the pursuit of Happiness.❞

The Declaration states that government exists to protect these rights. If it does not, it goes on to state that "it is the Right of the People to alter or to abolish it and to institute new Government."

The Declaration goes on to list the many grievances Americans held against the king and Parliament. The crimes of George III included "cutting off our trade with all parts of the world" and "imposing taxes on us without our

Independence Day

Congress voted for independence on July 4, 1776. Actually, Congress voted for independence on July 2, 1776. Why, then, is Independence Day celebrated on the fourth? On that day the delegates voted to accept Jefferson's statement, the Declaration of Independence, as the reason why they had voted for independence two days earlier.

consent." Americans, the Declaration says, had "Petitioned for Redress" of these grievances. These petitions, however, were ignored or rejected by Britain.

The Declaration ends by announcing America's new status. Now pledging "to each other our Lives, our Fortunes, and our sacred Honor," the Americans declared themselves a new nation. The struggle for American independence—the American Revolution—had begun. 📖 *(See pages 154–157 for the entire text of the Declaration of Independence.)*

✔**Reading Check** **Summarizing** What grievances against King George III were included in the Declaration of Independence?

SECTION 4 ASSESSMENT

Checking for Understanding

1. **Key Terms** Connect the terms below with the proper document. Then write a sentence in which you use each term. Terms: petition, preamble. Documents: Declaration of Independence, Olive Branch Petition
2. **Reviewing Facts** What was King George III's response to the Olive Branch Petition?

Reviewing Themes

3. **Government and Democracy** Why was the Second Continental Congress more like a government than the First Continental Congress?

Critical Thinking

4. **Analyzing Primary Sources** Based on the quote from the Declaration of Independence on this page, what are the "unalienable Rights" to which Jefferson referred? Give examples.
5. **Organizing Information** Re-create the diagram below and describe each individual's role in the movement toward independence.

	Role
Thomas Jefferson	
Thomas Paine	
Samuel Adams	
Benjamin Franklin	

Analyzing Visuals

6. **Picturing History** Compare the flag on page 148 with the flag on page 128. How are the two flags similar? How are they different? Which of the flags more closely resembles the American flag of today?

Interdisciplinary Activity

Expository Writing Prepare a help-wanted ad to locate a person qualified to write the Declaration of Independence. Describe the responsibilities of the job as well as the experience and character traits that are needed.

✔**Reading Check**

Answer: cutting off trade with other parts of the world and imposing taxes without consent

L1

Reteaching Activity 5–4

★ Reteaching Activity 5-4

DIRECTIONS: Multiple Choice In the blank at the left, write the letter of the choice that best completes the statement or answers the question.

___ 1. Which person was *not* present at the Second Continental Congress?
  A. John Adams   **C.** Benedict Arnold
  B. Patrick Henry   **D.** Richard Henry Lee

___ 2. Who was chosen as commander of the Continental Army?
  A. John Adams   **C.** Benjamin Franklin
  B. George Washington **D.** Thomas Jefferson

___ 3. Which was *not* an action of the Second Continental Congress?
  A. declaring English the official language of America
  B. setting up a post office

L1, ELL

Reading Essentials and Study Guide 5–4

Study Guide

Chapter 5, Section 4
For use with textbook pages 147–151

MOVING TOWARD INDEPENDENCE

KEY TERMS

| petition | Formal request (page 148) |
| preamble | Introduction to the Declaration of Independence (page 151) |

DRAWING FROM EXPERIENCE

Have you ever read the Declaration of Independence? Can you recall any famous quotes from this historic document? What does the Declaration of Independence mean to you?

In the last section, you read about how colonial leaders met in Philadelphia in 1774 and established the First Continental Congress. This section focuses on how the Second Continental Congress declared the colonies free and independent of Britain.

L3

Enrichment Activity 5–4

★ Enrichment Activity 5-4 ★

Common Sense

Thomas Paine supported independence. His pamphlets and news articles made issues sound simple and appealed to the emotions of readers. Thousands of copies of *Common Sense*, his first American pamphlet, were handed from person to person.

4 CLOSE

Call on volunteers to suggest reasons for (pros) and reasons against (cons) a formal declaration of independence.

SECTION 4 ASSESSMENT ANSWERS

1. Preamble/Declaration of Independence; petition/Olive Branch Petition; student work should reflect correct use of terms
2. He prepared for war.
3. It authorized the printing of money; set up a post office; and created the Continental Army.

4. life, liberty, and the pursuit of happiness; accept reasonable examples

5. Thomas Jefferson: wrote Declaration of Independence; Thomas Paine: wrote *Common Sense*; Samuel Adams: delegate to the Second Continental Congress; Benjamin Franklin: representative in London during Stamp Act crisis

6. Students should compare and contrast the flags.

Interdisciplinary Activity Ads might include: ability to express complex ideas, patriotism, belief in the colonists' goal of independence.

1 FOCUS

By the eve of the Revolution, the English colonies were concentrated in a narrow strip of land along the Atlantic coast. **Ask:** *Why do you think colonial settlements were concentrated along or near the coast? (Large numbers of people could not penetrate far inland because the transportation system was not well-developed. Many settlements were also located along coasts and rivers, where they were accessible by water. Students might also note that the royal proclamation in 1763 forbade settlement beyond the Appalachians.)*

2 TEACH

Reading a Map Have students use the map to discuss the geography of settlements and roads in the colonies on the eve of the American Revolution. **Ask:** *Where was most of the road system concentrated at this time? What is the southernmost settlement that could be reached by road? How would the post roads have been useful to both the Continental and the British armies during the Revolution? (in the coastal region; St. Augustine; they would have provided routes along which troops and supplies could move fairly easily)* **L2**

EVE OF REVOLUTION

IN THE EARLY 1770s most colonists thought of themselves as British subjects. However, they also thought of themselves as Virginians or Georgians or New Yorkers. It wasn't until colonists began to unite in opposition to harsh British policies that they began to consider themselves Americans.

STIRRINGS OF REVOLT

In 1772 Samuel Adams convinced a group of Bostonians to join a Committee of Correspondence to communicate with other towns in Massachusetts. Soon, the idea spread. In colony after colony, Americans joined Committees of Correspondence. In this era before radios or telephones, the committees spread opposition to British policies into nearly every county, town, and city.

In 1774 delegates gathered at the Continental Congress in Philadelphia to form an organization to represent their interests as Americans. In addition to stating their grievances and voting to boycott British products, the Patriots decided to organize their own militias.

THE SHOT HEARD 'ROUND THE WORLD

The Revolution's first blow fell early on the morning of April 19, 1775. British redcoats clashed with colonial minutemen at Lexington and Concord. This clash, later called the "shot heard 'round the world," was the first battle of the Revolutionary War. The Battle of Bunker Hill in June showed that the war would be hard, long, and expensive on both sides.

LEARNING *from* GEOGRAPHY

1. **How do you think the geography of the colonies made communication difficult?**
2. **Near what cities did the early battles take place?**

152

The Continental Army was organized in May 1775.

Augusta • Camden
GEORGIA
SOUTH CAROLINA
Wilmington
Savannah • Charles Town • Georgetown
• St. Augustine

American Revolution
——— Proclamation Line of 1763
——— Post road
🇬🇧 British fort or post
✳ Conflict
Scale varies in this perspective

EXTENDING THE CONTENT

The Wilderness Road The Wilderness Road, which followed older buffalo traces and Native American paths, ran west from the Shenandoah Valley, crossing the Appalachian Mountains through the Cumberland Gap into what is now Kentucky. By the time Kentucky became a state in 1792, more than 70,000 settlers had made their way along the Wilderness Road to Kentucky from east coast towns and farms. The Wilderness Road was abandoned in the 1840s when the improved National Road was completed.

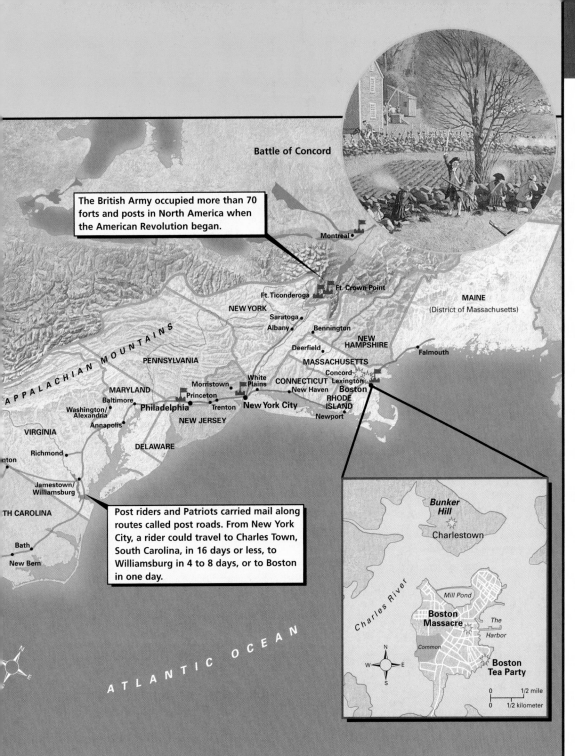

Battle of Concord

The British Army occupied more than 70 forts and posts in North America when the American Revolution began.

Montreal

Ft. Crown Point
Ft. Ticonderoga
NEW YORK
Saratoga
Albany
Bennington
Deerfield
MAINE
(District of Massachusetts)
Falmouth
NEW HAMPSHIRE
PENNSYLVANIA
White Plains
MASSACHUSETTS
Concord
Lexington
CONNECTICUT
New Haven
Boston
A P P A L A C H I A N M O U N T A I N S
Morristown
MARYLAND
Princeton
RHODE ISLAND
Baltimore
Philadelphia
Trenton
New York City
Newport
Washington/
Alexandria
Annapolis
NEW JERSEY
VIRGINIA
DELAWARE
Richmond
Jamestown/
Williamsburg

Post riders and Patriots carried mail along routes called post roads. From New York City, a rider could travel to Charles Town, South Carolina, in 16 days or less, to Williamsburg in 4 to 8 days, or to Boston in one day.

TH CAROLINA
Bath
New Bern

A T L A N T I C O C E A N

Bunker Hill
Charlestown
Charles River
Mill Pond
Boston Massacre
The Harbor
Common
Boston Tea Party

0   1/2 mile
0   1/2 kilometer

153

3 ASSESS

Have students answer the **Learning from Geography** questions.

4 CLOSE

Direct each student to draw an outline map of the American colonies, showing where several of the events in Chapter 5 took place. Students should include the Boston Massacre, the Boston Tea Party, the meetings of the Continental Congress at Philadelphia, and the Battles of Lexington and Concord. Next to each location, have students label what occurred there and when.

NGS ONLINE

Access National Geographic's Web site for current events, atlas updates, activities, links, interactive features, and archives at www.nationalgeographic.com

Did you know?

The English colonies in North America had a population in 1750 of over 1,000,000. As the result of births to settlers and immigration, the population is estimated to have risen to between 2,325,000 and 2,600,000 by 1775.

Answers to Learning from Geography

1. Answers will vary, but should include these two ideas: communication would have been difficult because of the lack of a well-developed system of roads; the most popular forms of transportation at the time—horses, wagons, boats—were slow.

2. Conflict occurred in Lexington and Concord near Boston.

The Declaration of Independence

BELLRINGER
Motivational Activity

Inform students that at the signing of the Declaration of Independence, Benjamin Franklin remarked to John Hancock, "We must indeed all hang together, or, most assuredly, we shall all hang separately." Have students suggest what Franklin meant by this comment. *(If the colonists did not work together for independence, they would all be hanged for treason.)*

What?Who?Where?When?

Earlier Attempt Thomas Jefferson had already addressed most of the issues discussed in the Declaration in *A Summary View of the Rights of British America*, a pamphlet he published in 1774.

ABCNEWS
INTERACTIVE™

VIDEOCASSETTE
Historic America Electronic Field Trips

View **Chapter 7** to learn more about Independence Hall in Philadelphia, Pennsylvania.

In Congress, July 4, 1776. The unanimous Declaration of the thirteen united States of America,

[Preamble]

When in the Course of human events, it becomes necessary for one people to dissolve the political bands which have connected them with another, and to assume among the Powers of the earth, the separate and equal station to which the Laws of Nature and of Nature's God entitle them, a decent respect to the opinions of mankind requires that they should declare the causes which **impel** them to the separation.

[Declaration of Natural Rights]

We hold these truths to be self-evident, that all men are created equal, that they are **endowed** by their Creator with certain unalienable Rights, that among these are Life, Liberty, and the pursuit of Happiness.

That to secure these rights, Governments are instituted among Men, deriving their just powers from the consent of the governed,

That whenever any Form of Government becomes destructive of these ends, it is the Right of the People to alter or to abolish it, and to institute new Government, laying its foundation on such principles and organizing its powers in such form, as to them shall seem most likely to effect their Safety and Happiness. Prudence, indeed, will dictate that Governments long established should not be changed for light and transient causes; and accordingly all experience hath shown, that mankind are more disposed to suffer, while evils are sufferable, than to right themselves by abolishing the forms to which they are accustomed. But when a long train of abuses and usurpations, pursuing invariably the same Object evinces a design to reduce them under absolute **Despotism,** it is their right, it is their duty, to throw off such Government, and to provide new Guards for their future security.

[List of Grievances]

Such has been the patient sufferance of these Colonies; and such is now the necessity which constrains them to alter their former Systems of Government. The history of the present King of Great Britain is a history of repeated injuries and **usurpations,** all having in direct object the establishment of an absolute Tyranny over these States. To prove this, let Facts be submitted to a candid world.

He has refused his Assent to Laws, the most wholesome and necessary for the public good.

What It Means
The Preamble The Declaration of Independence has four parts. The Preamble explains why the Continental Congress drew up the Declaration.

impel *force*

What It Means
Natural Rights The second part, the Declaration of Natural Rights, lists the rights of the citizens. It goes on to explain that, in a republic, people form a government to protect their rights. The Declaration refers to these rights as *unalienable rights*. The word unalienable means nontransferable. An unalienable right is a right that cannot be surrendered.

endowed *provided*

despotism *unlimited power*

What It Means
List of Grievances The third part of the Declaration lists the colonists' complaints against the British government. Notice that King George III is singled out for blame.

usurpations *unjust uses of power*

EXTENDING THE CONTENT

The Declaration of Independence The Continental Congress had copies of the Declaration of Independence made, and messengers rushed them to leaders in each of the thirteen colonies. The leaders then had the Declaration read aloud in public places. The first such reading was given on July 8, 1776, from the steps of the Philadelphia Statehouse—the building where the Continental Congress had debated the document. Philadelphians were summoned to the reading by the ringing of the Liberty Bell.

He has forbidden his Governors to pass Laws of immediate and pressing importance, unless suspended in their operation till his Assent should be obtained; and when so suspended, he has utterly neglected to attend to them.

He has refused to pass other Laws for the accommodation of large districts of people, unless those people would **relinquish** the right of Representation in the Legislature, a right **inestimable** to them and formidable to tyrants only.

relinquish *give up*
inestimable *priceless*

He has called together legislative bodies at places unusual, uncomfortable, and distant from the depository of their Public Records, for the sole purpose of fatiguing them into compliance with his measures.

He has dissolved Representative Houses repeatedly, for opposing with manly firmness his invasions on the rights of the people.

He has refused for a long time, after such dissolutions, to cause others to be elected; whereby the Legislative Powers, incapable of **Annihilation,** have returned to the People at large for their exercise; the State remaining in the mean time exposed to all the dangers of invasion from without, and **convulsions** within.

annihilation *destruction*

convulsions *violent disturbances*

He has endeavoured to prevent the population of these States; for that purpose obstructing the Laws for **Naturalization of Foreigners;** refusing to pass others to encourage their migrations hither, and raising the conditions of new Appropriations of Lands.

Naturalization of Foreigners *process by which foreign-born persons become citizens*

He has obstructed the Administration of Justice, by refusing his Assent to Laws for establishing Judiciary Powers.

He has made Judges dependent on his Will alone, for the **tenure** of their offices, and the amount and payment of their salaries.

tenure *term*

He has erected a multitude of New Offices, and sent hither swarms of Officers to harass our people, and eat out their substance.

The Declaration of Independence **155**

2 TEACH

Analyzing Information Inform students that statements in the Declaration of Natural Rights proclaim some of the most important ideas on which democratic government is based. Then have students identify these statements in the Declaration of Independence. *(Most students will note the following: All people are created equal; all people possess certain basic rights; the purpose of governments is to secure these rights for the people; the power and authority of governments are derived from the people.)* **L1**

What?Where?When?Who?

Serious Editing Congress did not adopt the Declaration of Independence with just a few minor changes in Jefferson's work. Congress cut about a quarter of the document, most notably a scathing attack on slaveholding and the slave trade.

CURRICULUM CONNECTION

World History The Declaration of Independence proved very influential, inspiring the struggle for freedom in other parts of the world. The Marquis de Lafayette, who fought for the colonists in the American Revolution and became a key figure in the French Revolution, hung a copy of the Declaration on his dining room wall. He looked forward to the day when a copy of a French Declaration of Human Rights would hang beside it. The leaders of Latin American independence movements of the early 1800s also were spurred to take action by the democratic sentiments expressed in the Declaration.

The Declaration of Independence

3 ASSESS

Draw a graphic organizer on the chalkboard that shows three large boxes aligned in a horizontal row with arrows connecting the boxes. Title the graphic organizer *The Declaration of Independence.* Tell students that this is the event in a cause-effect-cause chain. Ask students to recreate the graphic organizer and complete it by noting the causes and effects of the Declaration of Independence. Suggest that they add annotations explaining which cause they think made the passage of the Declaration inevitable and which outcome they think was the most important.

Who?What?Where?When?

Only George III Although Parliament was the body that drafted the laws that so upset the colonists, Parliament is not mentioned once in the Declaration of Independence. The List of Grievances singles out George III for blame.

---

quartering *lodging*

render *make*

abdicated *given up*

perfidy *violation of trust*

insurrections *rebellions*

petitioned for redress *asked formally for a correction of wrongs*

unwarrantable jurisdiction *unjustified authority*

consanguinity *originating from the same ancestor*

He has kept among us, in times of peace, Standing Armies without the Consent of our legislature.

He has affected to render the Military independent of and superior to the Civil Power.

He has combined with others to subject us to a jurisdiction foreign to our constitution, and unacknowledged by our laws; giving his Assent to their acts of pretended legislation:

For **quartering** large bodies of troops among us:

For protecting them, by a mock Trial, from Punishment for any Murders which they should commit on the Inhabitants of these States:

For cutting off our Trade with all parts of the world:

For imposing taxes on us without our Consent:

For depriving us in many cases, of the benefits of Trial by Jury:

For transporting us beyond Seas to be tried for pretended offences:

For abolishing the free System of English Laws in a neighbouring Province, establishing therein an Arbitrary government, and enlarging its Boundaries so as to **render** it at once an example and fit instrument for introducing the same absolute rule into these Colonies:

For taking away our Charters, abolishing our most valuable Laws, and altering fundamentally the Forms of our Governments:

For suspending our own Legislature, and declaring themselves invested with Power to legislate for us in all cases whatsoever.

He has **abdicated** Government here, by declaring us out of his Protection and waging War against us.

He has plundered our seas, ravaged our Coasts, burnt our towns, and destroyed the lives of our people.

He is at this time transporting large armies of foreign mercenaries to compleat the works of death, desolation and tyranny, already begun with circumstances of Cruelty & **perfidy** scarcely paralleled in the most barbarous ages, and totally unworthy the Head of a civilized nation.

He has constrained our fellow Citizens taken Captive on the high Seas to bear Arms against their Country, to become the executioners of their friends and Brethren, or to fall themselves by their Hands.

He has excited domestic **insurrections** amongst us, and has endeavoured to bring on the inhabitants of our frontiers, the merciless Indian Savages, whose known rule of warfare, is an undistinguished destruction of all ages, sexes and conditions.

In every stage of these Oppressions We have **Petitioned for Redress** in the most humble terms: Our repeated Petitions have been answered only by repeated injury. A Prince, whose character is thus marked by every act which may define a Tyrant, is unfit to be the ruler of a free People.

Nor have We been wanting in attention to our British brethren. We have warned them from time to time of attempts by their legislature to extend an **unwarrantable jurisdiction** over us. We have reminded them of the circumstances of our emigration and settlement here. We have appealed to their native justice and magnanimity, and we have conjured them by the ties of our common kindred to disavow these usurpations, which, would inevitably interrupt our connections and correspondence. They too have been deaf to the voice of justice and of **consanguinity**. We must, therefore, acquiesce in the necessity, which denounces our Separation, and hold them, as we hold the rest of mankind, Enemies in War, in Peace Friends.

COOPERATIVE LEARNING ACTIVITY

Research Report Inform students that the Declaration of Independence has been a force for change in the United States. Americans have used its ideas to promote measures such as the abolition of slavery and equal rights for women. Then organize students into several small groups. Have groups conduct research to find three examples of individuals or groups using the Declaration of Independence to promote reform. Have groups present their findings in an illustrated report.

[Resolution of Independence by the United States]

We, therefore, the Representatives of the united States of America, in General Congress, Assembled, appealing to the Supreme Judge of the world for the **rectitude** of our intentions, do, in the Name, and by Authority of the good People of these Colonies, solemnly publish and declare, That these United Colonies are, and of Right ought to be Free and Independent States; that they are Absolved from all Allegiance to the British Crown, and that all political connection between them and the State of Great Britain, is and ought to be totally dissolved; and that as Free and Independent States, they have full Power to levy War, conclude Peace, contract Alliances, establish Commerce, and to do all other Acts and Things which Independent States may of right do.

And for the support of this Declaration, with a firm reliance on the Protection of Divine Providence, we mutually pledge to each other our Lives, our Fortunes and our sacred Honor.

John Hancock
President from
Massachusetts

Georgia
Button Gwinnett
Lyman Hall
George Walton

North Carolina
William Hooper
Joseph Hewes
John Penn

South Carolina
Edward Rutledge
Thomas Heyward, Jr.
Thomas Lynch, Jr.
Arthur Middleton

Maryland
Samuel Chase
William Paca
Thomas Stone
Charles Carroll
of Carrollton

Virginia
George Wythe
Richard Henry Lee
Thomas Jefferson
Benjamin Harrison
Thomas Nelson, Jr.
Francis Lightfoot Lee
Carter Braxton

Pennsylvania
Robert Morris
Benjamin Rush
Benjamin Franklin
John Morton
George Clymer
James Smith
George Taylor
James Wilson
George Ross

Delaware
Caesar Rodney
George Read
Thomas McKean

New York
William Floyd
Philip Livingston
Francis Lewis
Lewis Morris

New Jersey
Richard Stockton
John Witherspoon
Francis Hopkinson
John Hart
Abraham Clark

New Hampshire
Josiah Bartlett
William Whipple
Matthew Thornton

Massachusetts
Samuel Adams
John Adams
Robert Treat Paine
Elbridge Gerry

Rhode Island
Stephen Hopkins
William Ellery

Connecticut
Samuel Huntington
William Williams
Oliver Wolcott
Roger Sherman

What It Means
Resolution of Independence The final section declares that the colonies are "Free and Independent States" with the full power to make war, to form alliances, and to trade with other countries.

rectitude *rightness*

What It Means
Signers of the Declaration The signers, as representatives of the American people, declared the colonies independent from Great Britain. Most members signed the document on August 2, 1776.

John Hancock

The Declaration of Independence

Who?What?Where?When?

Two Lees Richard Henry Lee and Francis Lightfoot Lee, two Virginians who signed the Declaration of Independence, were brothers. Their cousin, Henry "Lighthorse Harry" Lee, served with considerable distinction in the Continental Army.

Did you know?

The ideas expressed in the Declaration of Independence reverberated in the twentieth century. When Ho Chi Minh declared Vietnam free of its French colonial rulers in 1945, he quoted freely from the Declaration. And Jawaharlal Nehru, a leader of the struggle for independence in India, considered the Declaration a "landmark in human freedom."

4 CLOSE

Have students explain the purposes of the Declaration of Independence. (*It justified the revolution and put forth the principles on which the new nation was founded.*)

DIFFERENTIATED INSTRUCTION

At-Risk Students Students who have difficulty decoding unfamiliar words sometimes skip over them. The Declaration of Independence is reproduced in its original language and, therefore, contains a number of words that probably are unfamiliar. Point out to students that many of these words are defined in the margin notes. Suggest that students substitute the definitions for the unfamiliar words as they read through the document. Ask volunteers to paraphrase various sections of the document in everyday language. **L1**

☞ Refer to *Inclusion for the Middle School Social Studies Classroom Strategies and Activities* in the TCR.

5 ASSESSMENT and ACTIVITIES

Reviewing Key Terms
Answers may include:

1. The Stamp Act produced **revenue** for Great Britain. *(true)*

2. The colonists never considered a **boycott** of British goods. *(false; some urged merchants to boycott British and European goods to protest the Stamp Act)*

3. The actions of the colonists forced the British Parliament to **repeal** the Stamp Act in 1766. *(true)*

4. The colonists used the killings of the Boston Massacre as **propaganda** against the British. *(true)*

5. The colonial **militias** were made up of professional soldiers. *(false; militias were made up of citizen soldiers)*

6. Some militias were called **minutemen** because all of their battles took five minutes or less. *(false; the minutemen boasted that they could be ready to fight on a minute's notice)*

7. A **Patriot** was a colonist who wanted to remain loyal to Great Britain. *(false; a Patriot was a colonist who wanted to fight for independence from Great Britain)*

8. The introduction to the Declaration of Independence is called the **preamble.** *(true)*

9. An **unalienable right** is a right that cannot be surrendered. *(true)*

Reviewing Key Facts
10. issued the Proclamation of 1763

11. imposed taxes such as the Stamp Act and Townshend Acts; colonists believed that only their own representatives had the right to levy taxes

12. the Boston Tea Party

13. to unite all the American colonies in

Chapter Summary
Road to Independence
Follow the arrows to review the causes and the effects that led to the colonies declaring independence.

Cause: French and Indian War leaves Great Britain in debt

Effect: Britain taxes colonies; Parliament passes Sugar Act and Stamp Act → **Becomes Cause**

Effect: Colonists boycott British goods → **Becomes Cause**

Effect: British send troops to Boston, resulting in the Boston Massacre → **Becomes Cause**

Effect: British repeal import taxes → **Becomes Cause**

Effect: Colonists respond with Boston Tea Party → **Becomes Cause**

Effect: Parliament passes the Coercive Acts → **Becomes Cause**

Effect: First Continental Congress drafts a statement of grievances → **Becomes Cause**

Effect: British troops fight colonists at battles of Lexington and Concord; British defeat colonial forces at Bunker Hill

Congress signs Declaration of Independence

158

protest of British taxes

14. The Declaration of Independence was approved and the struggle for American independence had begun.

15. alter or abolish the government and create a new government

16. the preamble, the list of rights American citizens felt they should have, the list of grievances against the king, the announcement that the United States would be formed as a new and self-governing nation

Critical Thinking
17. British Parliament taxed the colonies directly without their consent.

18. boycotts, the Boston Tea Party, forming the Continental Congresses, raising militias

19. that the colonies had to stop thinking as separate divisions and unite to defeat the British

20. life, liberty, and the pursuit of happiness

Practicing Skills

Distinguishing Fact From Opinion *Read the following statements. Tell whether each is a fact or an opinion.*

21. Great Britain should not have tried to stop the colonists from settling west of the Appalachians.

22. The Stamp Act placed a tax on almost all printed material in the colonies.

23. The Daughters of Liberty urged Americans to wear home-made fabrics.

24. Thomas Jefferson was a better writer than John Adams.

 Geography and History Activity

Study the map on page 133; then answer the following questions.

25. What bodies of water did the Proclamation of 1763 prevent colonists from reaching?

26. What nation claimed the land west of the Mississippi River?

27. The land west of the Appalachian Mountains became part of what province?

28. What natural feature was cited in the Proclamation of 1763 as an approximate boundary?

Citizenship Cooperative Activity

29. Work with a group of classmates to create your own "Declaration of Independence." Use the original Declaration of Independence on pages 154–157 as a guide to create your document. Outline the basic freedoms that you expect to have as a citizen and describe why these freedoms are important to you. Then write at least three responsibilities and/or sacrifices that citizens should be willing to make to enjoy the freedoms you listed. After your group has completed its Declaration of Independence, have the groups come together as a class. Share all the groups' documents and compare the ideas expressed in each.

 Technology Activity

30. **Using the Internet** On the Internet, locate the computer address for the National Archives or the Library of Congress in Washington, D.C. Search each site for documents concerning the drafting of the Declaration of Independence and/or photos of pamphlets produced by the colonies in the 1700s. Print a copy of what you find or sketch a likeness to share with the class.

Online

Self-Check Quiz
Visit **tarvol1.glencoe.com** and click on **Chapter 5— Self-Check Quizzes** to prepare for the chapter test.

Economics Activity

31. How did laws passed by the British after 1763 affect American trade and industry? Write your answer in a one-page paper.

 Alternative Assessment

32. **Persuasive Writing** What do you think a good citizen is? Is it someone who follows the law? Or might it be someone who breaks the law in order to stand up for an ideal? Do you think that people like the Sons of Liberty acted as good citizens? Write a persuasive paper explaining your views.

Standardized Test Practice

Read the following passage and choose the *best* answer to the question that follows.

An English philosopher named John Locke wrote about his belief that people had natural rights. These included the right to life, liberty, and property. In *Two Treatises of Government,* Locke wrote that people created government to protect natural rights. If a government failed in its basic duty of protecting natural rights, people had the right to overthrow the government.

Locke's ideas contributed to the

A Proclamation of 1763.

B Intolerable Acts.

C Declaration of Independence.

D Articles of Confederation.

Test-Taking Tip:
Look for clues in the passage to support your answer. For example, the passage refers to *life, liberty and property.* It also states that *people had the right to overthrow the government.* Which answer does this information best support?

Economics Activity

31. Papers should include the following ideas: the laws restrained American trade and industry so that it would not compete with that of Great Britain and would not cut into revenues collected by the British.

 Alternative Assessment

32. Students should first state what a good citizen is, then use persuasive argument and facts to support their views.

 HISTORY *Online*

Have students visit the Web site at tarvol1.glencoe.com to review Chapter 5 and take the Self-Check Quiz.

Standardized Test Practice

Answer: C
Question Type: Civics
Answer Explanation: As quoted on page 151, the preamble of the Declaration of Independence reflects the ideas of John Locke.

 Bonus Question ?

Ask: Why did Britain fight to keep the American colonies?
(Students may note that Britain had an economic interest in keeping the colonies.)

Practicing Skills

21. opinion   **23.** fact

22. fact   **24.** opinion

 Geography and History Activity

25. the Great Lakes, the Ohio River, and the Mississippi River

26. Spain

27. Province of Quebec

28. the Appalachian Mountains

Citizenship Cooperative Activity

29. Students' declarations should reflect thoughtful insight about the basic freedoms they expect to have and why students should identify responsibilities or sacrifices that are necessary to enjoy their freedoms.

Technology Activity

30. Students should locate at least one photo or document and present what they found to the class.

Chapter 6 Resources

Timesaving Tools

TeacherWorks™ All-In-One Planner and Resource Center

- **Interactive Teacher Edition** Access your Teacher Wraparound Edition and your classroom resources with a few easy clicks.
- **Interactive Lesson Planner** Planning has never been easier! Organize your week, month, semester, or year with all the lesson helps you need to make teaching creative, timely, and relevant.

Use Glencoe's **Presentation Plus!** multimedia teacher tool to easily present dynamic lessons that visually excite your students. Using Microsoft PowerPoint® you can customize the presentations to create your own personalized lessons.

TEACHING TRANSPARENCIES

Graphic Organizer 13 L2

Why It Matters Chapter Transparency 6 L2

REVIEW AND REINFORCEMENT

Workbook Activity 6 L1

Time Line Activity 6 L2

Vocabulary Activity 6 L1

REVIEW AND REINFORCEMENT

Critical Thinking Skills Activity 6 L2

Take-Home Review Activity 6 L1

ENRICHMENT

Linking Past and Present Activity 6 L2

Primary Source Reading 6 L2

GEOGRAPHY

Geography and History Activity 6 L2

Meeting NCSS Standards

The following standards are highlighted in Chapter 6:

Section 1	V	Individuals, Groups, & Institutions: B, E
Section 2	V	Individuals, Groups, & Institutions: B, D
Section 3	III	People, Places, & Environments: A, I
Section 4	V	Individuals, Groups, & Institutions: B, E, F, G

FOLDABLES™ Study Organizer

Dinah Zike's Foldables are three-dimensional, interactive graphic organizers that help students practice basic writing skills, review key vocabulary terms, and identify main ideas. Additional chapter activities can be found in the *Reading and Study Skills Foldables* booklet.

**Chapter 6 Test
Form A** L2

**Chapter 6 Test
Form B** L2

**Standardized Test Practice
Workbook Activity 6** L2

**Performance Assessment
Activity 6** L1, ELL

**ExamView® Pro
Testmaker CD-ROM**

MULTIMEDIA

- Vocabulary PuzzleMaker CD-ROM
- Interactive Tutor Self-Assessment CD-ROM
- ExamView® Pro Testmaker CD-ROM
- Audio Program
- American History Primary Source Document Library CD-ROM
- MindJogger Videoquiz
- Presentation Plus! CD-ROM
- TeacherWorks CD-ROM
- Interactive Student Edition CD-ROM
- Glencoe Skillbuilder Interactive Workbook CD-ROM, Level 1
- The American Republic to 1877 Video Program
- American Music: Hits Through History

SPANISH RESOURCES

The following Spanish language materials are available in the Spanish Resources Binder:

- Spanish Guided Reading Activities
- Spanish Reteaching Activities
- Spanish Quizzes and Tests
- Spanish Vocabulary Activity
- Spanish Take-Home Review Activity
- Spanish Summaries
- The Declaration of Independence and United States Constitution Spanish Translation

---

A&E HOME VIDEO.

Biography®

THE HISTORY CHANNEL®

The following videotape programs are available from Glencoe as supplements to Chapter 6:

- **John Paul Jones: Captain of the High Seas** (ISBN 1-56501-875-3)
- **The American Revolution** (Six Video Set) (ISBN 1-56501-436-7)
- **Benedict Arnold** (ISBN 1-56501-594-0)

To order, call Glencoe at 1-800-334-7344. To find classroom resources to accompany many of these videos, check the following home pages:
A&E Television: www.aande.com
The History Channel: www.historychannel.com

HISTORY Online

Use our Web site for additional resources. All essential content is covered in the Student Edition.

You and your students can visit tarvol1.glencoe.com, the Web site companion to **The American Republic to 1877**. This innovative integration of electronic and print media offers your students a wealth of opportunities. The student text directs students to the Web site for the following options:

- **Chapter Overviews**
- **Self-Check Quizzes**
- **Student Web Activities**
- **Textbook Updates**

Answers to the student Web activities are provided for you in the **Web Activity Lesson Plans.** Additional Web resources and Interactive Tutor Puzzles are also available.

Chapter 6 Resources

SECTION RESOURCES

Daily Objectives	Reproducible Resources	Multimedia Resources
SECTION 1 **The Early Years** 1. Understand why some Americans supported the British. 2. Explain how the Battle of Saratoga marked a turning point in the war.	📁 Reproducible Lesson Plan 6–1 📁 Daily Lecture and Discussion Notes 6–1 📁 Guided Reading Activity 6–1* 📁 Section Quiz 6–1* 📁 Reteaching Activity 6–1* 📁 Reading Essentials and Study Guide 6–1* 📁 Enrichment Activity 6–1	🖼 Daily Focus Skills Transparency 6–1 🖼 American Art and Architecture, Transparency 14 🎵 American Music: Hits Through History 💿 Interactive Tutor Self-Assessment CD-ROM 💿 ExamView® Pro Testmaker CD-ROM 💿 Presentation Plus! CD-ROM
SECTION 2 **The War Continues** 1. Understand why other nations helped the Patriots. 2. Describe how Washington's troops survived the winter at Valley Forge. 3. Recognize the challenges Americans faced at home as a result of the war.	📁 Reproducible Lesson Plan 6–2 📁 Daily Lecture and Discussion Notes 6–2 📁 Guided Reading Activity 6–2* 📁 Section Quiz 6–2* 📁 Reteaching Activity 6–2* 📁 Reading Essentials and Study Guide 6–2* 📁 Enrichment Activity 6–2	🖼 Daily Focus Skills Transparency 6–2 💿 Interactive Tutor Self-Assessment CD-ROM 💿 ExamView® Pro Testmaker CD-ROM 💿 Presentation Plus! CD-ROM
SECTION 3 **The War Moves West and South** 1. Explain how the war involved Native Americans. 2. Describe how a new kind of fighting developed in the South.	📁 Reproducible Lesson Plan 6–3 📁 Daily Lecture and Discussion Notes 6–3 📁 Guided Reading Activity 6–3* 📁 Section Quiz 6–3* 📁 Reteaching Activity 6–3* 📁 Reading Essentials and Study Guide 6–3* 📁 Enrichment Activity 6–3	🖼 Daily Focus Skills Transparency 6–3 💿 Interactive Tutor Self-Assessment CD-ROM 💿 ExamView® Pro Testmaker CD-ROM 💿 Presentation Plus! CD-ROM
SECTION 4 **The War Is Won** 1. Describe how George Washington changed his military strategy. 2. Explain how the Americans won the Revolutionary War despite many disadvantages.	📁 Reproducible Lesson Plan 6–4 📁 Daily Lecture and Discussion Notes 6–4 📁 Guided Reading Activity 6–4* 📁 Section Quiz 6–4* 📁 Reteaching Activity 6–4* 📁 Reading Essentials and Study Guide 6–4* 📁 Enrichment Activity 6–4	🖼 Daily Focus Skills Transparency 6–4 💿 Vocabulary PuzzleMaker CD-ROM 💿 Interactive Tutor Self-Assessment CD-ROM 💿 ExamView® Pro Testmaker CD-ROM 💿 Presentation Plus! CD-ROM

0:00 OUT OF TIME?
Assign the Chapter 6 **Reading Essentials and Study Guide.** 📁

*Also Available in Spanish

📁 Blackline Master	🖼 Transparency	💿 CD-ROM	💿 DVD
📕 Poster	🎵 Music Program	🎧 Audio Program	📼 Videocassette

KEY TO ABILITY LEVELS

Teaching strategies have been coded.

L1 BASIC activities for all students

L2 AVERAGE activities for average to above-average students

L3 CHALLENGING activities for above-average students

ELL ENGLISH LANGUAGE LEARNER activities

NATIONAL GEOGRAPHIC Teacher's Corner

INDEX TO NATIONAL GEOGRAPHIC MAGAZINE

The following articles relate to this chapter.
- "Two Revolutions," by Charles McCarry, July 1989.
- "Yorktown Shipwreck," by John D. Broadwater, June 1988.

ADDITIONAL NATIONAL GEOGRAPHIC SOCIETY PRODUCTS

To order the following, call National Geographic at 1-800-368-2728:
- *GeoKit: American History Series* (Kit)
- *GeoKit: Colonial America* (Kit)
- *GeoKit: The American Revolution* (Kit)
- *Colonization and Trade in the Americas* (Map)
- *National Geographic Desk Reference* (Book)
- *Democratic Government Series, "The United States"* (Video)
- *Branches of Government Series* (Video)

NGS ONLINE

Access National Geographic's Web site for current events, atlas updates, activities, links, interactive features, and archives.
www.nationalgeographic.com

MEETING SPECIAL NEEDS

In addition to the Differentiated Instruction strategies found in each section, the following resources are also suitable for your special needs students:

- *ExamView® Pro Testmaker CD-ROM* allows teachers to tailor tests by reducing answer choices.

- The *Audio Program* includes the entire narrative of the student edition so that less-proficient readers can listen to the words as they read them.

- The *Reading Essentials and Study Guide* provides the same content as the student edition but is written two grade levels below the textbook.

- *Guided Reading Activities* give less-proficient readers point-by-point instructions to increase comprehension as they read each textbook section.

- *Enrichment Activities* includes a stimulating collection of readings and activities for gifted and talented students.

From the Classroom of . . .

Edward McKinney
Hugh Hartman Middle School
Redmond, OR

Covering the Revolution in a Classroom Newspaper

Students will publish a newspaper to further develop the material covered in this chapter. Organize the class into four groups, and have each group be responsible for one of these topics: (1) biographies and fictional interviews of famous people, (2) coverage of specific battles, (3) recipes of the types of food prepared during the Revolutionary era, and (4) articles about weapons used. Each student will research and submit a short story on the group's topic. Stories should be typed using narrow margins so they can be pasted onto 11" × 17" paper. Each group then decides which one of its stories it wants on the front page. The groups' other stories will be placed on the inside pages. Assign one member from each group to work together on designing the newspaper's front page. The rest of the groups should design their own pages. Remind them to include art, illustrations, advertisements, and so on.

ADDITIONAL RESOURCES FROM GLENCOE

- American Music: Cultural Traditions
- American Art and Architecture
- Outline Map Resource Book
- U.S. Desk Map
- Building Geography Skills for Life
- Inclusion for the Middle School Social Studies Classroom Strategies and Activities
- Teaching Strategies for the American History Classroom (Including Block Scheduling Pacing Guides)
- American Crafts Hands-On Activities
- American Games Hands-On Activities
- American History Flash Cards

Block Schedule

Activities that are suited to use within the block scheduling framework are identified by: 🔲

☑ **Performance Assessment**

Refer to Activity 6 in the Performance Assessment Activities and Rubrics booklet.

W*hy It Matters Activity*

Have students brainstorm why winning the war was critical for the colonies. Students should reflect back on their ideas after they have completed the chapter. Then have students think about the challenges a country would face after it won its independence and was no longer a colony.

GLENCOE
TECHNOLOGY

The American Republic to 1877 Video Program
To learn more about the American Revolution and how the colonists won the war, have students view the Chapter 6 video "The American Revolution" from **The American Republic to 1877 Program.**

 Available in DVD and VHS

MindJogger Videoquiz
Use **MindJogger Videoquiz** to preview the Chapter 6 content.

 Available in VHS

CHAPTER
6
The American Revolution
1776–1783

Why It Matters

Although the United States declared its independence in 1776, no country recognized it as an independent nation at that time. It took a war and the efforts of American diplomats to win this recognition.

The Impact Today

In fighting for the principles set forth in the Declaration of Independence, the American Patriots laid the foundation for the United States of America we know today.

The American Republic to 1877 *Video* The chapter 6 video, "The American Revolution," details how the American Patriots were able to defeat a powerful British military.

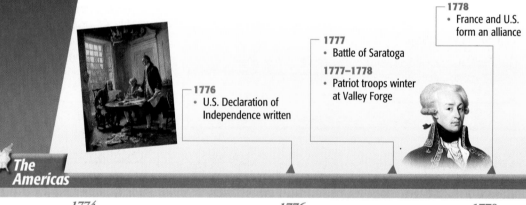

1778
• France and U.S. form an alliance

1777
• Battle of Saratoga

1777–1778
• Patriot troops winter at Valley Forge

1776
• U.S. Declaration of Independence written

The Americas

1774 *1776* *1778*

World

1774
• Joseph Priestley discovers oxygen

1776
• Adam Smith's *Wealth of Nations* published

📖 Reading Strategy **PURPOSE FOR READING**

Carousel brainstorming is a good strategy to help students generate many responses to questions or issues. Organize the class into two groups. One group will support the fight for independence. The other group will oppose it. Divide each of the two groups into smaller groups of 3 or 4. Give two of the small groups a large sheet of paper. Ask one group from the pro-independence side and the other from the anti-independence side to list three reasons supporting its position. Once this is completed, the group passes the sheet to the next small group with the same position. This group adds three additional reasons. Continue this process until each group has added three reasons. Wrap up by displaying the sheets in the classroom and have students identify the strongest arguments. **L1**

FOLDABLES™
Study Organizer

Organizing Information Study Foldable
When you group information into categories on a table, it is easier to compare characteristics of items. Make this foldable to help you compare the attitudes and actions of the Patriots and Loyalists.

Step 1 Fold a sheet of paper into thirds from top to bottom.

> This forms three rows.

Step 2 Open the paper and refold it into fourths from side to side.

> Fold it in half, then in half again.

> This forms four columns.

Step 3 Unfold, turn the paper, and draw lines along the folds.

Step 4 Label your table as shown.

The American Revolution	Patriots	Loyalists
Beginning		
Middle		
End		

Reading and Writing As you read about the American Revolution, write down facts about the attitudes and actions of the Patriots and Loyalists at different times during the war.

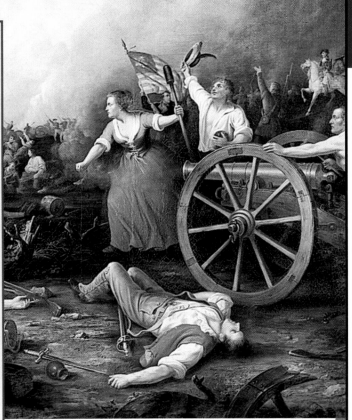

Molly Pitcher at the Battle of Monmouth by Dennis Malone Carter
According to legend, when her husband collapsed, Molly Pitcher immediately took his place in the gun crew and continued firing his cannon.

1780
• Patriots gain victory at Kings Mountain

1781
• British surrender at Yorktown

1783
• Treaty of Paris

1780   *1782*

1779
• Spain declares war on Britain

1780
• Britain declares war on Holland

HISTORY Online

Chapter Overview
Visit tarvol1.glencoe.com and click on Chapter 6—Chapter Overviews to preview chapter information.

FOLDABLES™
Study Organizer — Dinah Zike's Foldables

Purpose This activity requires students to create a table and organize information from the chapter on it. Students group information from the chapter into categories, comparing the attitudes and actions of American Patriots and Loyalists during the Revolutionary War.

 Have students complete **Reading and Study Skills Foldables** Activity 6. **L1**

HISTORY Online

Introduce students to chapter content and key terms by having them access **Chapter Overview 6** at tarvol1.glencoe.com

TIME LINE ACTIVITY

As students read the chapter, have them review the time line on pages 160–161. Have students create a similar time line that identifies the major battles fought during the Revolutionary War.

More About the Art

Dennis Malone Carter (1827–1881) created oil paintings depicting significant moments in American history. The Battle of Monmouth took place on June 28, 1778, as the British attempted to retreat from Philadelphia to New York. It was the last major conflict in the North. Mary had accompanied her husband onto the battlefield. She carried countless pitchers of water to the soldiers fighting in daytime temperatures of close to 100 degrees, earning her the nickname "Molly Pitcher."

1 FOCUS

Section Overview

This section highlights the initial struggles of the Patriots.

BELLRINGER
Skillbuilder Activity

 Project transparency and have students answer the question.

Daily Focus Skills Transparency 6–1

Reading Preview

Answers to Graphic: Advantages: British—strong army, military supplies, wealth; American—fighting on home ground, ideals, Washington as commander; Disadvantages: British—fighting in faraway land, supplies and soldiers need to be transported; American—no regular army or strong navy, few weapons

Preteaching Vocabulary
Ask students the meanings of the **Key Terms.** Assist them in understanding any terms that may be unfamiliar.

SECTION 1 The Early Years

Guide to Reading

Main Idea
The British and the Americans each had advantages and disadvantages as they faced one another in war.

Key Terms
neutral, mercenary, recruit

Reading Strategy
Classifying Information As you read the section, re-create the chart below and describe British and American advantages and disadvantages in the spaces provided.

	Advantages	Disadvantages
British		
American		

Read to Learn
- why some Americans supported the British.
- how the Battle of Saratoga marked a turning point of the war.

Section Theme
Groups and Institutions Although British forces won several battles early in the war, Patriot victories slowed their progress.

Preview of Events

♦1776		♦1777		♦1778
July 1776 American colonies declare independence		December 1776 Patriots capture Hessians at Trenton	October 1777 Burgoyne surrenders at Saratoga	1778 African American regiment forms in Rhode Island

British cannon

★★★★★★
AN
American Story

The mighty British troops sailed to America, confident that they would quickly and easily crush the rebellious colonists. A British officer wrote to his friend, describing a military skirmish:

September 3, 1776

We landed on Long-Island. . . . [I]t was a fine sight to see with what [eagerness] they dispatched the Rebels with their bayonets after we had surrounded them so that they could not resist. . . . The island is all ours, and we shall soon take New-York, for the Rebels dare not look us in the face. I expect the affair will be over [after] this campaign. . . .

The Opposing Sides

Following years of disagreement and negotiation, the tensions between the colonies and England had reached a critical point. After the colonies declared independence from England in July 1776, the war for freedom was unavoidable.

Both the British and the Americans expected the war for independence to be short. The British planned to crush the rebellion by force. Most of the Patriots—Americans who supported independence—believed the British would give up

---

SECTION RESOURCES

🗁 Reproducible Masters
- Reproducible Lesson Plan 6–1
- Daily Lecture and Discussion Notes 6–1
- Guided Reading Activity 6–1
- Section Quiz 6–1
- Reteaching Activity 6–1
- Reading Essentials and Study Guide 6–1
- Enrichment Activity 6-1

🖥 Transparencies
- Daily Focus Skills Transparency 6–1
- American Art and Architecture, Transparency 14

Multimedia
- 🎵 American Music: Hits Through History
- 🎧 Interactive Tutor Self-Assessment CD-ROM
- 🎧 ExamView® Pro Testmaker CD-ROM
- 🎧 Presentation Plus! CD-ROM

after losing one or two major battles. Few Patriots believed John Adams when he predicted in April 1776:

> 66We shall have a long . . . and bloody war to go through.99

At first glance the British had an overwhelming advantage in the war. They had the strongest navy in the world; an experienced, well-trained army; and the wealth of a worldwide empire. Britain also had a much larger population than the United States—over 8 million people in Britain compared to only 2.5 million in the United States.

The colonists suffered serious disadvantages. They lacked a regular army and a strong navy. American soldiers also lacked military experience, and weapons and ammunition were in short supply. Many Patriots belonged to militia groups—local forces—but they were volunteer soldiers who fought for short periods of time before returning home.

The Patriots faced another obstacle. Not all Americans supported the struggle for independence. Some people were neutral, taking neither side in the conflict. The Quakers, for example, would not participate in the war because they opposed all armed conflict. Still other Americans remained loyal to Britain.

The Loyalists

Those who remained loyal to Britain and opposed the war for independence were called Loyalists or Tories. At least one American in five was a Loyalist—perhaps as many as one in three. Some people changed sides during the war, depending on which army was closer. Loyalist strength varied

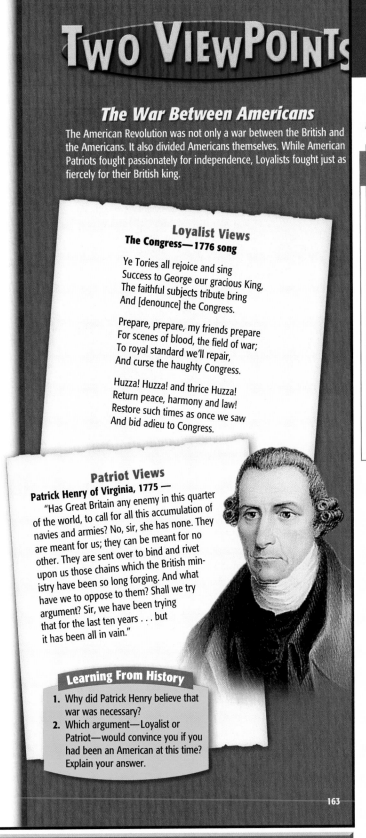

Two ViewPoints

The War Between Americans

The American Revolution was not only a war between the British and the Americans. It also divided Americans themselves. While American Patriots fought passionately for independence, Loyalists fought just as fiercely for their British king.

Loyalist Views
The Congress—1776 song

Ye Tories all rejoice and sing
Success to George our gracious King,
The faithful subjects tribute bring
And [denounce] the Congress.

Prepare, prepare, my friends prepare
For scenes of blood, the field of war;
To royal standard we'll repair,
And curse the haughty Congress.

Huzza! Huzza! and thrice Huzza!
Return peace, harmony and law!
Restore such times as once we saw
And bid adieu to Congress.

Patriot Views
Patrick Henry of Virginia, 1775 —
"Has Great Britain any enemy in this quarter of the world, to call for all this accumulation of navies and armies? No, sir, she has none. They are meant for us; they can be meant for no other. They are sent over to bind and rivet upon us those chains which the British ministry have been so long forging. And what have we to oppose to them? Shall we try argument? Sir, we have been trying that for the last ten years . . . but it has been all in vain."

Learning From History

1. Why did Patrick Henry believe that war was necessary?
2. Which argument—Loyalist or Patriot—would convince you if you had been an American at this time? Explain your answer.

163

2 TEACH

Daily Lecture and Discussion Notes 6–1

Copyright © by The McGraw-Hill Companies, Inc.

Daily Lecture and Discussion Notes

Chapter 6, Section 1

Did You Know Thomas Paine's *Common Sense* was published in 1776 in order to influence Americans to support the Revolution. The pamphlet met this goal. Today, more than 200 years later, *Common Sense* is still in print!

I. **The Opposing Sides** *(Pages 162–166)*

A. In order for the colonies to actually gain their independence from Britain, they had to fight a war. No one expected it to last so long, however.

B. The Patriots, or Americans who supported independence, faced several obstacles:
  1. Britain had a larger population—9 million against 2.5 million.
  2. Britain had the strongest navy in the world and a well-trained army as well.
  3. The Americans did not have a regular army or navy. Many colonists belonged to militias who were basically volunteers and served for short periods of time.
  4. Not all Americans supported the war effort. Some were neutral, some were opposed to fighting, and some were loyal to Britain.

C. The Loyalists, or Tories, supported Britain for several reasons:
  1. Some were members of the Anglican Church and thus loyal to Britain.
  2. Some depended on the British for jobs.
  3. Some feared the changes a new government might bring and feared challenging an existing government.
  4. Some just did not understand the war.
  Loyalist strength varied from region to region but was strongest in the Carolinas and Georgia.

D. Some African Americans were promised their freedom if they fought on the British side, so they became Loyalists.

E. The Patriots had some advantages over the British troops.
  1. They fought on their own ground, not 3,000 miles from home.
  2. They had a personal stake in fighting to protect the freedom of their own land as opposed to the Hessian mercenaries, or hired soldiers, who fought for the British for money.
  3. George Washington was a leader with courage, honesty, and determination.

Discussing Reasons Organize students into pairs. **Ask:** Why might you have wanted to support Britain in the war? Discuss responses that partners present to the class. (*Examples: I work for the British and don't want to lose my job; I don't think the colonies can work together.*) **L1**

Two ViewPoints

Answers:

1. He believed the British troops in America were intended to oppress Americans, and that continuing to argue with the British would have no effect.
2. Student answers will vary but should be supported with examples from one of the viewpoints.

COOPERATIVE LEARNING ACTIVITY

Creating a Board Game Organize the class into groups. Explain that they will create a board game of Revolutionary War battles. Have groups choose a name for the game and discuss how it will be played. Make sure that each group assigns the following tasks to individual group members: drawing a map of the colonies on poster board as a gameboard; illustrating the gameboard; writing the rules of the game; creating playing pieces; and designing playing cards. After groups have completed their games, have them swap games and play another group's game.

L1, ELL

Guided Reading Activity 6–1

Name _____ Date _____ Class _____

★ **Guided Reading Activity 6-1**

DIRECTIONS: Recalling the Facts Use the information in your textbook to answer the questions. Use another sheet of paper if necessary.

1. Who were the Patriots? _____
2. Give two advantages the British had over the Patriots. _____
3. Give two serious disadvantages suffered by the Patriots. _____
4. Who were the Loyalists? _____
5. How did the location of the war help the Americans? _____
6. What was the main difference between Hessian soldiers and Patriots? _____
7. What did Margaret Corbin and Deborah Sampson have in common? _____
8. Who said, "I only regret that I have but one life to lose for my country"? _____
9. Who wrote the inspiring pamphlet *Common Sense*? _____
10. Why did George Washington read words from *The American Crisis* to his troops? _____
11. Why were enslaved African Americans not allowed to enlist in the war? _____
12. When did Washington cross the Delaware to surprise the enemy at Trenton? _____
13. Where did British troops hope to separate New England from the Middle States? _____
14. Who surrendered to the Patriots on October 17, 1777? _____

Linking Past & Present

The Women's Army Corps began in 1942 (as the Women's Auxiliary Army Corps), as did its Navy counterpart, Women Accepted for Voluntary Emergency Service. During World War II, there were also women's corps for the Marines, the Coast Guard, and the Air Force. Approximately 350,000 women served in the United States military during that war.

Did you know?

About 30,000 Hessians fought during the American Revolution. The Hessians were paid about 25 cents a day for their service. The American cause appealed to some Hessians, causing them to desert the British army. Many Hessians stayed in the United States after the war.

Linking Past & Present

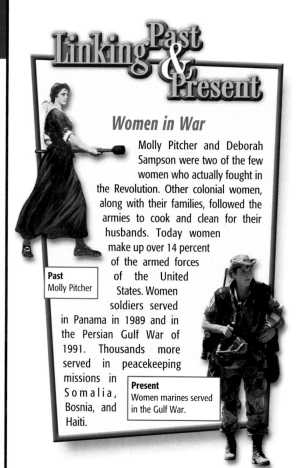

Women in War

Molly Pitcher and Deborah Sampson were two of the few women who actually fought in the Revolution. Other colonial women, along with their families, followed the armies to cook and clean for their husbands. Today women make up over 14 percent of the armed forces of the United States. Women soldiers served in Panama in 1989 and in the Persian Gulf War of 1991. Thousands more served in peacekeeping missions in Somalia, Bosnia, and Haiti.

Past
Molly Pitcher

Present
Women marines served in the Gulf War.

---

from region to region. In general it was strongest in the Carolinas and Georgia and weakest in New England.

Loyalists supported Britain for different reasons. Some remained loyal because they were members of the Anglican Church, headed by the British king. Some depended on the British for their jobs. Many feared the disorder that would come from challenging the established government. Others simply could not understand what all the commotion was about. No other country, one Loyalist complained, "faced a rebellion arising from such trivial causes."

The issue of independence disrupted normal relations. Friends and families were divided over their loyalty to Britain. For example, William Franklin, son of Patriot Benjamin Franklin, was a Loyalist who had served as a royal governor. As one Connecticut Loyalist observed:

"Neighbor was against neighbor, father against son and son against father. He that would not thrust his own blade through his brother's heart was called an infamous villain."

African Americans in the War

Some African Americans also sided with the Loyalists. At the start of the war, the British appealed to enslaved Africans to join them. Lord Dunmore, the royal governor of Virginia, announced that enslaved people who fought on the British side would be freed, and many men answered his call. Eventually some of them ended up free in Canada, and others settled the British colony of Sierra Leone in Africa.

Patriot Advantages

The Americans possessed some advantages. They were fighting on their own ground and fought with great determination to protect it. The British, on the other hand, had to wage war in a faraway land and were forced to ship soldiers and supplies thousands of miles across the Atlantic Ocean.

The makeup of the British army in America also helped the Patriots. The British relied on mercenaries—hired soldiers—to fight. The Americans called the mercenaries **Hessians**, after the region in Germany where most of them lived. To gain support for the war effort, Patriots compared their own troops, who were fighting for the freedom of their own land, to the Hessians, who fought for money. The Patriots had a much greater stake in winning the war than the hired soldiers did. This personal stake gave the Americans an edge over the Hessians in battle.

The Americans' greatest advantage was probably their leader, George Washington. Few could match him for courage, honesty, and determination. The war might have taken a different turn without Washington steering its course.

Raising an Army

The Americans placed great value on liberty and personal freedom for citizens. After throwing off the rule of the British Parliament, they

---

DIFFERENTIATED INSTRUCTION

At-Risk Students Although the Continental forces had some factors in their favor, they also had several needs. Some students may grasp this concept better if they draw representations of what the Continental Army lacked, especially in the early days of the war: a well-trained force, greater numbers of soldiers, blankets and other supplies. Encourage students to consider their drawings as they explain how these needs gave the early advantage to the British. **L1**

📁 Refer to *Inclusion for the Middle School Social Studies Classroom Strategies and Activities* in the TCR.

were unwilling to transfer power to their own Continental Congress. In some ways the American Revolution was really 13 separate wars, with each state pursuing its own interests. As a result Congress experienced difficulty enlisting soldiers and raising money to fight the war.

Although the militia played an essential role in the Patriots' forces, the Americans also needed a regular army—well-trained soldiers who could fight anywhere in the colonies. The Congress established the Continental Army but depended on the states to recruit, or enlist, soldiers.

At first soldiers signed up for one year of army service. General Washington appealed for longer terms. "If we ever hope for success," he said, "we must have men enlisted for the whole term of the war." Eventually the Continental Congress offered enlistments for three years or for the length of the war. Most soldiers, however, still signed up for only a year.

Women also fought with the Patriot forces. **Margaret Corbin** of Pennsylvania accompanied her husband when he joined the Continental Army. After he died in battle, she took his place. Mary Ludwig Hays McCauley also accompanied her husband in battle. The soldiers called her "Moll of the Pitcher," or **Molly Pitcher,** because she carried water pitchers to the soldiers. As a teenager, **Deborah Sampson** of Massachusetts watched her brothers and their friends go off to war. Moved by a sense of adventure, she disguised herself as a boy and enlisted.

✓**Reading Check** **Summarizing** What disadvantages did the Patriots face?

✓**Reading Check**

Answer: They did not have a strong navy or a regular army with experience, were short on weapons and ammunition, and did not have support from all Americans.

Geography *Skills*

Answers:
1. American forces
2. Burgoyne surrendered to the Patriot forces.

Geography Skills Practice
Ask: Who captured Philadelphia in 1777? (*Howe*)

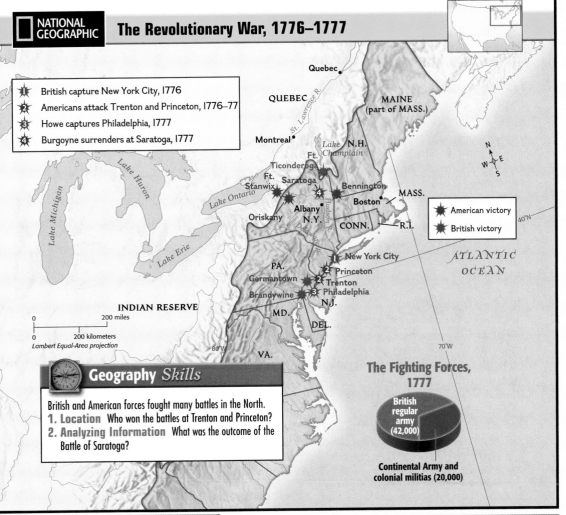

The Revolutionary War, 1776–1777

💥 British capture New York City, 1776
💥 Americans attack Trenton and Princeton, 1776–77
💥 Howe captures Philadelphia, 1777
💥 Burgoyne surrenders at Saratoga, 1777

✦ American victory
✦ British victory

The Fighting Forces, 1777

British regular army (42,000)

Continental Army and colonial militias (20,000)

Geography *Skills*

British and American forces fought many battles in the North.
1. **Location** Who won the battles at Trenton and Princeton?
2. **Analyzing Information** What was the outcome of the Battle of Saratoga?

History *and the* **Humanities**

🎵 American Music: Hits Through History, "The World Turned Upside Down"

🖼 American Art and Architecture, Transparency 14, *Washington Crossing the Delaware* **L3**

Who?What?Where?When?

George Washington George Washington actually lost more battles than he won. However, he met his goal of keeping the army in the field.

Reading Strategy **READING THE TEXT**

Reading Primary and Secondary Sources George Washington found Thomas Paine's *The American Crisis* so empowering that he had it read to his troops. Secure a few copies of *The American Crisis* and have students work in small groups to analyze it. Ask them to find and share 8 to 10 statements by Paine that they think would inspire the Continental soldiers. Encourage them to choose their own format for the presentation but to be prepared to explain why they consider each statement inspirational. **L3, ELL**

People In History

Thomas Paine was born in England in 1737. He met Benjamin Franklin in London, and Franklin encouraged him to go to America. While working for the *Pennsylvania Magazine*, Paine wrote *Common Sense*. After the war Paine left for Europe where he lived in England and France. He wrote *The Rights of Man* in 1791–1792. In this work Paine called for equal political rights for all men and argued for a whole program of social legislation to help the poor. **Ask:** Why do you think Washington read Paine's words to his troops? *(to inspire them to continue the fight for independence)*

you don't say...

Yankee Many scholars believe the word *Yankee* comes from the Dutch Jan Kees, or "John Cheese," a term that other Europeans used to ridicule the Dutch. The Dutch then used the term to ridicule the English settlers of Connecticut, and the English later used it to ridicule the Patriots.

Who?What?Where?When?

The Black Pioneers The British also made an appeal to African Americans, offering freedom and grants of land in Canada for fighting on their side. In response, thousands of African Americans, including a group called the Black Pioneers, took up arms against the Patriots.

People In History

Thomas Paine 1737–1809

In early 1776 Thomas Paine published a pamphlet titled *Common Sense*. The pamphlet moved many American colonists toward independence. After taking part in the retreat across New York and New Jersey, Paine published another pamphlet to help boost Americans' lagging spirits. In *The American Crisis*, written in December 1776, he warned: "These are the times that try men's souls. The summer soldier and the sunshine patriot will in this crisis shrink from the service of their country; but he that stands it now deserves the love and thanks of man and woman."

He reminded Americans that "the harder the conflict, the more glorious the triumph."

Washington had Paine's stirring words read to his troops to inspire them to continue the fight for independence. Throughout the colonies people passed copies of *The American Crisis* from hand to hand and discussed Paine's patriotic ideas.

Fighting in New York

Most of the early battles involved few troops. At Bunker Hill, for example, about 2,200 British soldiers fought 1,200 Americans. The British had not yet won a decisive victory over the Patriots, however, and they realized they would need more troops to end the war quickly.

During the summer of 1776, Britain sent 32,000 troops across the Atlantic to New York. The British commander, **General William Howe,** hoped the sheer size of his army would convince the Patriots to give up. He was soon disappointed.

Defeat on Long Island

Although Washington and the Patriots had fewer than 20,000 troops, they were determined to fight. In late August the two sides clashed in the **Battle of Long Island.** Outnumbered and outmaneuvered, the Continental Army suffered a serious defeat at the hands of the British forces.

One Patriot, **Nathan Hale,** proved himself a hero at Long Island. A teacher from Connecticut, Hale volunteered to spy on British troops and disguised himself as a Dutch schoolteacher. The British discovered his true identity, however, and hanged him. According to tradition, just before his hanging, Hale's last words were,

> **❝**I only regret that I have but one life to lose for my country.**❞**

Although the Americans showed bravery, they ran short of supplies for the army. In the autumn of 1776, a British officer wrote that many of the Patriot soldiers killed on Long Island had not been wearing shoes, socks, or jackets. "They are also in great want of blankets," he said, predicting that the rebels would suffer greatly when "the severe weather sets in."

After the defeat on Long Island, Washington retreated to Manhattan, pursued by the British. By late November, the Continental Army had retreated across New Jersey into Pennsylvania.

A Low Point

In the winter of 1776–1777, the Patriots' cause was near collapse. The size of the Continental Army had dwindled. Some soldiers completed their terms of service and went home. Other soldiers ran away.

166   CHAPTER 6   The American Revolution

CRITICAL THINKING ACTIVITY

Analyzing Information Organize the class into three groups: Patriots, Loyalists, and Neutrals. Have each group discuss its views on the friction between Britain and America and then write three position statements. Have a representative from each group read the group's statements, one at a time. After each statement is read, have the groups discuss the statement. Students may switch groups to support or protest a statement. Continue until all statements have been read. How have the groups changed? How might that change be explained? **L2**

Washington wrote his brother that, if new soldiers were not recruited soon, "I think the game is pretty near up." Still, Washington could not believe that the fight for liberty would truly fail.

✓**Reading Check** Describing Why was the total number of soldiers in the Continental Army decreasing?

Patriot Gains

Washington pleaded with the Continental Congress for more troops. He asked the Congress to enlist free African Americans. Early in the war, the Southern states had persuaded the Congress to not allow African Americans in the Continental Army. Many white people in the South felt uncomfortable about giving guns to African Americans and allowing them to serve as soldiers. In Southern states with large enslaved populations, whites feared revolts.

African Americans Join the Fight

As the need for soldiers grew, some states ignored the ban and enlisted African Americans. Rhode Island raised an all-African American regiment in 1778. By the war's end, every state except South Carolina enlisted African Americans to fight.

Historians estimate that as many as 5,000 African Americans joined the Patriots. Among them were **Lemuel Hayes** and **Peter Salem,** who fought at Concord. African Americans fought for the same reasons as other Americans. They believed in the Patriot cause or they needed the money. Some soldiers were enslaved Africans who had run away from slaveholders. Others fought to earn their freedom.

American Victories in New Jersey

The British army settled in New York for the winter of 1776, leaving some troops in New Jersey at **Trenton** and **Princeton.** Armies usually called a halt to their wars during the winter, and the British did not expect to fight.

Stationed across the Delaware River from the British camp in New Jersey, Washington saw a chance to catch the British off guard. On Christmas night 1776, Washington took 2,400 troops

Fact Fiction Folklore

America's Flags

First Stars and Stripes, 1777–1795 On June 14, 1777, the Continental Congress designed the first Stars and Stripes. The Congress determined that "the Flag of the United States be 13 stripes, alternate red and white; that the Union be 13 stars, white in a blue field representing a new constellation." For Americans past and present, the color red symbolizes courage; white, purity of ideals; and blue, strength and unity of the states.

across the icy river and surprised the enemy at Trenton the next day. The Americans captured more than 900 Hessians. The British sent reinforcements under Lord Charles Cornwallis, but Washington led his troops away from Cornwallis's men. Washington then marched the army to Princeton, where they drove away the British. One discouraged British soldier wrote in his diary,

❝A few days ago [the Americans] had given up the cause for lost. Their late successes have turned the scale and now they are all liberty mad again.❞

✓**Reading Check** Explaining What was the outcome of the battle at Trenton?

A British Plan for Victory

The British worked out a battle plan for 1777. They would take Albany, New York, and gain control of the Hudson River. This would separate New England from the Middle Colonies.

The plan involved a three-pronged attack. General John Burgoyne would lead nearly 8,000 troops south from Canada. A second force, under Lieutenant Colonel Barry St. Leger, would move east from Lake Ontario. A third group, under General Howe, would move north from New York City. The three British forces would meet at Albany and destroy the Patriot troops.

✓**Reading Check**

Answer: Many soldiers were killed; some had completed their terms and went home; others ran away.

✓**Reading Check**

Answer: The Americans captured 900 Hessians.

3 ASSESS

Assign Section 1 Assessment as homework or as an in-class activity.

⊕ Have students use **Interactive Tutor Self-Assessment CD-ROM.**

L2

Section Quiz 6–1

Name _____ Date _____ Class _____

★ Chapter 6   Score ▢

Section Quiz 6-1

DIRECTIONS: Matching Match the items in Column A with the items in Column B. Write the correct letters in the blanks. *(10 points each)*

Column A	Column B
___ 1. American supporters of independence	A. Tories
___ 2. taking neither side	B. Patriots
___ 3. Loyalists	C. enlist
___ 4. mercenaries	D. neutral
___ 5. to recruit	E. hired soldiers

L1

Reteaching Activity 6–1

Name _____ Date _____ Class _____

★ Reteaching Activity 6-1

DIRECTIONS: Completing a Chart Write the number of the names and terms from the Fact Bank in the section of the chart where they belong.

The Early Years of the Revolutionary War		
	Patriots	British
Advantages		
Disadvantages		

EXTENDING THE CONTENT

New York Holding New York City gave Britain an excellent harbor (especially important after the loss of Boston). It also put control of the Hudson River into British hands, allowing much freer shipping to and from Canada and greater possibilities of blocking trade between the Northern and Southern Colonies.

✓ **Reading Check**

Answer: It prevented Britain from putting a wedge between New England and the Middle Colonies.

L1, ELL

Reading Essentials and Study Guide 6–1

L3

Enrichment Activity 6–1

4 CLOSE

Work with students to brainstorm a list of reasons the Patriots might have felt optimistic about the war in the fall of 1777.

The British Capture Philadelphia

Howe planned to take Philadelphia, the American capital, before marching to Albany. After winning battles in September 1777 at Brandywine and Paoli near Philadelphia, Howe's troops captured the city itself, forcing the Continental Congress to flee. In early October Washington attacked the main British camp at nearby Germantown, but he was forced to withdraw. Howe postponed the move north to Albany and decided to spend the winter in Philadelphia.

Patriots Slow the British

Meanwhile problems delayed the British plans to take Albany. In August American soldiers halted St. Leger's advance at Fort Stanwix, New York. Led by **Benedict Arnold,** the Americans forced the British to retreat.

General Burgoyne's army was not making much progress toward Albany either. In July Burgoyne captured Fort Ticonderoga, but trouble followed. Burgoyne, a dashing general who enjoyed good food and fine clothes, traveled with 30 wagons of luxury goods. Loaded down with this heavy baggage, Burgoyne's army moved slowly through the dense forests. To make matters worse, the Americans blocked the British by chopping down trees across their path.

In need of food and supplies, Burgoyne sent 800 troops and Native Americans to capture the American supply base at Bennington, Vermont.

The British troops' brightly colored uniforms made the soldiers easy targets in the woods. A local militia group, the **Green Mountain Boys,** attacked and defeated them. Having lost part of his army and desperately short of supplies, Burgoyne retreated in October to the town of **Saratoga** in New York.

The Battle of Saratoga

At Saratoga Burgoyne faced serious trouble. He expected British forces from the west and south to join him, but they had not arrived. The Americans had stopped St. Leger's army at Fort Stanwix, and Howe's forces were still in Philadelphia. In addition, American troops under the command of **General Horatio Gates** blocked his path to the south. Burgoyne found himself surrounded by an army about three times as large as his own. Burgoyne made a last desperate attack on October 7, but the Americans held firm.

On October 17, 1777, General Burgoyne surrendered. As a Patriot band played "Yankee Doodle," over 5,700 British soldiers handed their weapons to the Americans. The British plan to separate New England from the Middle Colonies had failed. Soon afterward, General Howe resigned as commander of the British troops in America. He was replaced by General Henry Clinton.

✓ **Reading Check** **Analyzing** Why was the Battle of Saratoga an important victory for the Americans?

SECTION 1 ASSESSMENT

Checking for Understanding

1. **Key Terms** Write a short paragraph in which you define the following terms: neutral, mercenary, recruit.
2. **Reviewing Facts** Compare the strengths of the British and American military forces.

Reviewing Themes

3. **Groups and Institutions** What problems did the Continental Congress face in raising an army to fight during the American Revolution?

Critical Thinking

4. **Analyzing Information** Explain why African Americans were willing to enlist in the Continental Army.
5. **Organizing Information** Re-create the chart below and describe each battle, including its outcome, in the space provided.

Battle	Description
Long Island	
Trenton/Princeton	

Analyzing Visuals

6. **Geography Skills** Examine the map on page 165. Which event came first—the British capture of New York or the British capture of Philadelphia?

Interdisciplinary Activity

Descriptive Writing Write a newspaper article that describes the Battle of Saratoga. Include details about British and American strategies and troop movements.

SECTION 1 ASSESSMENT ANSWERS

1. Student work should reflect correct use of terms.
2. British: strong navy, larger population, more experienced; American: fighting on own land for freedom, Washington was a skilled military leader
3. fear that the Continental Congress would control the colonies as the British Parliament had; thus, it had difficulty enlisting soldiers and raising money
4. Some believed in the fight, needed money, or wanted to earn their freedom.
5. Long Island: Continental Army defeated, runs short on supplies, army retreats to Pennsylvania; Trenton/Princeton: Washington takes troops across Delaware River, British army defeated, Patriots evade British, Patriots drive away British at Princeton
6. the British capture of New York

Interdisciplinary Activity Newspaper articles should describe the Battle of Saratoga in detail.

Reading a Military Map

Why Learn This Skill?

In your study of American history, you often have to read maps. A military map shows the areas where battles occurred, routes soldiers took, who won the battles, and who controlled various sites.

Learning the Skill

Military maps use colors, symbols, and arrows to show major battles, troop movements, and defensive positions during a particular battle or over a period of time.

When reading a military map, follow these steps:

• Read the map title. This will indicate the location and time period covered on the map.

• Read the map key. This tells what the symbols on the map represent. For example, battle sites may be symbolized by crossed swords, a burst shell, or a star.
• Study the map itself. This will reveal the actual events or sequence of events that took place. Notice the geography of the area and try to determine how it could affect military strategy.

Practicing the Skill

Analyze the information on the map on this page; then answer the following questions.

1 What troops surrounded Boston Harbor? How do you know this?

2 What action did the American forces take after fighting the Battle of Bunker Hill?

3 Which commander led the British troops to Breed's Hill?

4 In which direction did the British forces move when they left Boston? What parts of the map help you find this information?

Applying the Skill

Reading a Military Map Find a map of a specific battle of the American Revolution in an encyclopedia or other reference book. Create a three-dimensional model of the battle and use moveable pieces to represent troops. Then demonstrate troop movements over the course of the battle.

Glencoe's **Skillbuilder Interactive Workbook CD-ROM, Level 1**, provides instruction and practice in key social studies skills.

TEACH

Reading a Military Map
Students who know how to read details on military maps can gain a clearer understanding of troop movements, battle strategy, and more. Have students apply the directions provided in **Learning the Skill** to the map of Bunker Hill.

Have students suggest symbols for a more recent military map. (*Answers may include: air routes, missile locations, tank movements.*)

Additional Practice

L2

GLENCOE
TECHNOLOGY

CD-ROM
Glencoe Skillbuilder Interactive Workbook CD-ROM, Level 1

This interactive CD-ROM reinforces student mastery of essential social studies skills.

ANSWERS TO PRACTICING THE SKILL

1 American; the symbol that depicts American forces appears around the harbor

2 They retreated.

3 Gage

4 They moved counterclockwise, to the northwest; the compass rose and the arrows

Applying the Skill Students may wish to work in groups, with some students in each group doing the research, others building the model, and the rest using it to demonstrate troop movements.

TEACH

Analyzing Primary Resources

Have students read George Hewes's words describing his participation in the Boston Tea Party. **Ask:** What in Hewes's words shows that the Boston Tea Party was not a riot but an event with order and command? *(Participants were dressed alike. Participants "fell in" and marched in order. Participants were ordered to dispose of the tea in a specific way.)* Discuss with students how reading personal accounts of an event in history helps us to understand what actually happened. **Ask:** Why are personal accounts of an event in history valuable? *(They provide a true account of the events and emotions of the time as seen through the eyes of the writer.)*

Have students keep a diary of the events of a day. Students should chronicle any directions given to them, actions that resulted, and how they felt about the different events of the day. Ask for student volunteers to share their diaries with the class. Have students create a display of submitted sections of student diaries. **L1**

Visit the **TIME** Web site at www.time.com for up-to-date news, weekly magazine articles, editorials, online polls, and an archive of past magazine and Web articles.

TIME NOTEBOOK

What were people's lives like in the past?

What—and who—were people talking about? What did they eat? What did they do for fun? These two pages will give you some clues to everyday life in the U.S. as you step back in time with TIME Notebook.

Eyewitness
The Boston Tea Party

BETTMANN/CORBIS

GEORGE HEWES *is one of hundreds of people roused by Sam Adams on December 16, 1773. Adams whipped the crowd into a rage, resulting in the dumping of 342 cases of untaxed British tea into Boston Harbor. Hewes boarded one of the ships that night and here is what he remembers:*

"IT WAS NOW EVENING, AND I IMMEDIATELY DRESSED MYSELF IN THE costume of an Indian, equipped with a small hatchet . . . and a club, with which, after having painted my face and hands with coal dust in the shop of a blacksmith, I [went] to Griffin's Wharf, where the ships lay that contained the tea. . . . I fell in with many who were dressed, equipped and painted as I was, and who fell in with me and marched in order to the place of our destination. . . . We then were ordered by our commander to open the hatches and take out all the chests of tea and throw them overboard, and we immediately proceeded to execute his orders, first cutting and splitting the chests with our tomahawks, so as to thoroughly expose them to the effects of the water."

1770s WORD PLAY

What's In A Name?

Match the nickname with the person or thing to the right.

1. Sable Genius
2. Molly Pitcher
3. Battalia Pie
4. Brown Bess

a. Mary Hays gave American soldiers water and fired a cannon in the war

b. Benjamin Banneker, African American, built the first American clock

c. Most famous type of gun used in the 1700s

d. Meal made of pigeon, rabbit, sheep tongues, and the red growth on the heads of roosters

answers: 1. b; 2. a; 3. d; 4. c

Benjamin Banneker

NORTH WIND PICTURES

❝I'm obnoxious…and unpopular. You are very much otherwise.❞

JOHN ADAMS,
to Thomas Jefferson in discussing which of them should write the Declaration of Independence in 1776

❝Whilst you are proclaiming peace and goodwill to men… you insist upon retaining [*keeping*] an absolute power over wives.❞

ABIGAIL ADAMS,
in a letter to her husband John around the time of the signing of the Declaration of Independence

❝Yankee Doodle went to town, / A-ridin' on a pony. / Stuck a feather in his cap / And called it Macaroni.❞

YANKEE DOODLE,
opening words from the song written by the British about American soldiers

❝I only regret that I have but one life to lose for my country.❞

NATHAN HALE,
according to tradition, those were the last words of 21-year-old about to be hanged

---

EXTENDING THE CONTENT

The Boston Tea Party The Boston Tea Party was the culmination of colonial protest against what was seen as unfair taxation by England. The resistance to the landing of tea in Boston by Samuel Adams and his followers resulted in similar acts of resistance in other ports. The Coercive Acts, passed by Parliament in 1774, were in response to Boston's refusal to pay for the destroyed tea. The company that shipped the tea thrown overboard in the Boston Tea Party still exists and today markets a tea called "Boston Harbour."

How to Load and Shoot a Cannon

Here are the steps that soldiers follow before firing their cannons at the British:

1 As the officer in charge, you must be loud enough to be heard above the noise of cannon shot.

2 Have six or seven strong people help you as the cannon is difficult to load and shoot. Then you must call out the following commands:

"WORM!" The **wormer**, a soldier with a long piece of iron, must step forward to clean out the barrel of the cannon.

BROWN BROTHERS

"SPONGE!" The **sponger** must stick a wet sheepskin into the cannon barrel to cool it off and put out any sparks from the last use.

"LOAD!" The **loader** then stuffs a bag of powder into the barrel and adds ammunition—a big iron ball or smaller grapeshot.

"RAM!" The **rammer** will push and pack the ammunition down the barrel with a pole.

"PICK AND PRIME!" The **gunner** must now open a bag of gun powder. He puts a little powder in a vent hole.

"GIVE!" The **gunner** must light a fuse.

"FIRE!" The **gunner** lights the powder on top of the barrel with the fuse. The flame jumps through the air vent and ignites the powder inside the cannon.

"STAND BACK!" The **cannon ball** will explode out of the barrel at about 1,000 feet per second.

NUMBERS

THE COLONIES AT THE TIME

60 Seconds it takes a Minuteman soldier to get ready to fight

16 Age of Sibyl Ludington, who in 1777 made a 40-mile midnight ride like Paul Revere's, shouting "The British are coming!"

10,000 The approximate number of enslaved persons who earned their freedom by fighting against the British

200 Number of American doctors with actual medical degrees in 1776

COLONIAL GAMES

Nine Man Morris Scores a Ten!

*What are all the colonial kids playing?
It's that entertaining game* **Nine Man Morris**.

1. Get nine copper coins, nine silver coins, and a friend to play with you.
2. Make a drawing like the one shown on a piece of paper.
3. Give yourself the copper coins and your friend the silver ones.
4. Take turns placing your coins on the dots in the drawing.
5. Be the first to line up three of your coins in a row.
6. Capture one of the other player's coins when you get three in a row.
7. Keep playing until one player is down to two coins. The other player wins!

Alternative Assessment

Have students review the quotations in the *Verbatim* section. Discuss each quotation and how it relates to the people and times. Students should choose a person from the unit to research. Have students search Internet quotation sites or documents in books to develop a list of quotations spoken by the person. The quotations should present a complete representation of the character and beliefs of their chosen individual. Students may want to create a poster with a drawing of the individual surrounded by his or her quotations.

Did you know?

The biggest cannon ever used in combat was the German Dora aimed at Russia during World War II. At least 60 railroad cars were needed to transport the many parts that made up Dora. It took 1,500 men laboring for 20 minutes to load a single 5-ton shell. Dora's gun barrel was 107 feet long. Men could crawl around inside to clean the barrel by hand. It could lob shells 19 miles, and its armor-piercing shells could rip through 90 feet of solid rock.

CLOSE

Have students look in a current almanac to list six facts about an event that occurred within the past year. After each fact students should note why they feel it is an important fact to know.

COOPERATIVE LEARNING ACTIVITY

Creating a News Broadcast Form student groups. Have students choose an event from before or during the American Revolution. Students should research the event and then create an on-the-scene news broadcast. One student should role-play a news anchor and another the on-the-scene reporter. For example, a "live" report of the Boston Tea Party could have the anchor interviewing town officials or citizens asking for their reactions to the rebellion. Have students present their role plays to the class. **L2,** [ELL]

📁 Use the rubric for a role play on pages 58–59 in the *Performance Assessment Activities and Rubrics.*

1 FOCUS

Section Overview

This section describes the Patriots' hardships at war and at home and how Europeans helped the Patriots.

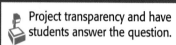

BELLRINGER
Skillbuilder Activity

Project transparency and have students answer the question.

Daily Focus Skills Transparency 6–2

Reading Preview

Answers to Graphic: Lafayette: became an aide to Washington; Pulaski: fought as a calvary officer in the Continental Army; Von Steuben: taught military discipline to Continental Army; De Miralles: lent money to the Patriot cause

Preteaching Vocabulary

Explain that *inflation* is the noun form of *inflate*, which means "to blow into" in Latin. Ask for examples of things that can be inflated.

SECTION 2 The War Continues

Guide to Reading

Main Idea

As the Revolutionary War continued, the Americans received support from European countries.

Key Terms

desert, inflation

Reading Strategy

Classifying Information As you read the section, re-create the chart below and describe how each person helped the Americans fight for independence.

Person	Contribution
Lafayette	
Pulaski	
Von Steuben	
De Miralles	

Read to Learn

- why other nations helped the Patriots.
- how Washington's troops survived the winter at Valley Forge.
- what challenges Americans faced at home as a result of the war.

Section Theme

Groups and Institutions Patriots faced hardships but were encouraged by help from Europeans.

Preview of Events

♦1777   ♦1778   ♦1779

October 1777
Americans win Battle of Saratoga

Winter 1777–1778
Patriot troops suffer at Valley Forge

February 1778
France and U.S. form an alliance

1779
Spain declares war on Britain

★★★★★★★★
AN
American Story

The Continental Congress sent Jonathan Austin of Boston to France to deliver the news of the American victory at Saratoga. Benjamin Franklin was already in France trying to get that country to help the Americans against the British. As soon as Austin arrived, Franklin nervously inquired, "Is Philadelphia taken?" Austin answered, "It is, sir. But, sir, I have greater news than that. General Burgoyne and his whole army are prisoners of war."

French medal showing Benjamin Franklin

Gaining Allies

The victory at Saratoga in October 1777 boosted American spirits. Even more, Saratoga marked a turning point in the war. The European nations, especially France, realized that the United States might actually win its war against Great Britain.

Now was the time for the Americans to seek support from Great Britain's rivals. By late 1777 Benjamin Franklin had been in Paris for a year, trying to get the French to support the Americans' fight for independence. With his skill and

---

SECTION RESOURCES

📁 Reproducible Masters
- Reproducible Lesson Plan 6–2
- Daily Lecture and Discussion Notes 6–2
- Guided Reading Activity 6–2
- Section Quiz 6–2
- Reteaching Activity 6–2
- Reading Essentials and Study Guide 6–2
- Enrichment Activity 6–2

📖 Transparencies
- Daily Focus Skills Transparency 6–2

Multimedia
- 🖥 Interactive Tutor Self-Assessment CD-ROM
- 🖥 ExamView® Pro Testmaker CD-ROM
- 🖥 Presentation Plus! CD-ROM

charm, Franklin gained many friends for the United States. The French gave the Americans money secretly, but they had not committed to an alliance.

France

News of the American victory at Saratoga caused a shift in France's policy. Realizing that the Americans had a chance of defeating Britain, the French announced support for the United States openly. In February 1778, the French and the Americans worked out a trade agreement and an alliance. France declared war on Britain and sent money, equipment, and troops to aid the American Patriots.

Spain

Other European nations also helped the American cause, mostly because they hated the British. Although Spain did not recognize American independence until after the Revolution, Spain declared war on Britain in 1779. The Spanish governor of Louisiana, **Bernardo de Gálvez** (GAHL•vez), raised an army. Gálvez's soldiers forced British troops from Baton Rouge and Natchez. Then the army captured British forts at Mobile in 1780 and Pensacola in 1781. Gálvez's campaign through hundreds of miles of wilderness diverted British troops from other fronts.

Winter at Valley Forge

Word of the French-American alliance did not reach the United States until the spring of 1778. Meanwhile British general Howe and his forces spent the winter in comfort in Philadelphia. Washington set up camp at **Valley Forge,** about 20 miles to the west of the British. Washington and his troops endured a winter of terrible suffering, lacking decent food, clothing, and shelter. Washington's greatest challenge at Valley Forge was keeping the Continental Army together.

Joseph Martin, a young private from Connecticut, spent the winter at Valley Forge. "We had a hard duty to perform," he wrote years later, "and little or no strength to perform it with." Most of the men lacked blankets, shoes, and shirts. Martin made a rough pair of moccasins for himself out of a scrap of cowhide. Although the moccasins hurt his feet, they were better than going barefoot, "as hundreds of my companions had to do, till they might be tracked by their bloods upon the rough, frozen ground."

📖 *(See page 597 for more accounts of the winter at Valley Forge.)*

Not surprisingly, many men deserted, or left without permission, while the Continental Army was camped at Valley Forge. Some officers resigned. The army seemed to be falling apart.

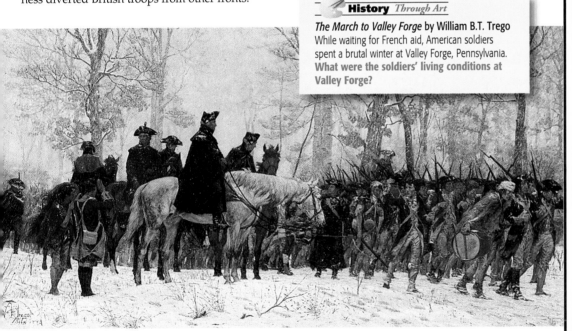

History *Through Art*

The March to Valley Forge by William B.T. Trego
While waiting for French aid, American soldiers spent a brutal winter at Valley Forge, Pennsylvania. **What were the soldiers' living conditions at Valley Forge?**

2 TEACH

Daily Lecture and Discussion Notes 6–2

Copyright © by The McGraw-Hill Companies, Inc.

Daily Lecture and Discussion Notes
Chapter 6, Section 2

Did You Know? The Saratoga battlefield in Stillwater, New York, was established as a New York state park in 1927 on the 150th anniversary of the battles. It was made part of the National Park System in 1938 by Congress.

I. **Gaining Allies** *(Pages 172–175)*

A. European nations helped the American cause. France and Spain were at war with the British in Europe and hated the British. They realized that the Americans had a chance to win their war, so they offered assistance.

B. France at first secretly gave money to help the American war effort and then publicly announced its support. In February 1778, the French and the Americans worked out a trade agreement and an alliance. France declared war on Britain and gave the

Solving Problems Have groups of students create a problem/solution chart. In the left-hand column, they should list problems that the Americans faced (such as the need for allies and financing the war); in the right-hand column, they should note how each problem was handled. Have groups share their charts with the class. **L1**

History *Through Art*

Answer: The soldiers lacked proper clothing, food, and shelter. Supplies, such as shoes, blankets, and shirts were scarce.

What?Who?Where?When?

Illness at Valley Forge Of the approximately 12,000 soldiers at Valley Forge, nearly 2,000 died of various diseases that winter. Dysentery, pneumonia, typhus, and typhoid were the leading killers.

Reading Strategy   READING THE TEXT

Using Graphic Organizers A graphic organizer can be any kind of graphic that is designed to show relationships between words or concepts. This section focuses on the idea of freedom. Organize students into three teams; supply each team with poster board and markers. Within each team have some students specialize in political meanings of freedom, other focus on the status of women, and still others consider the status of African Americans. Then ask each team to create a concept web relating to this section. Have teams begin with the word *freedom* in the center of the poster, then branch out to show the kinds of or lack of freedom discussed, and note a few details about each one. Encourage teams to compare and discuss their webs. **L2**

Guided Reading Activity 6–2

Name _____ Date _____ Class _____

★ **Guided Reading Activity 6-2**

DIRECTIONS: Filling in the Blanks Use your textbook to fill in the blanks using the words in the box. Use another sheet of paper if necessary.

Continental Congress	gold and silver	alliance	France
Casimir Pulaski	Loyalists	Spain	inflation
Bernardo de Gálvez	women	Martha	
Marquis de Lafayette	Valley Forge	slavery	

Gaining Allies

The victory at Saratoga lifted the Patriots' spirits and encouraged **(1)** _____ to form an **(2)** _____ with America in 1778. Then **(3)** _____ declared war on Great Britain in 1779, and **(4)** _____, the Spanish governor of Louisiana, raised an army that forced British soldiers from Baton Rouge and Natchez. While awaiting the arrival of French troops, George Washington and his troops set up camp at **(5)** _____, where they suffered a cold winter with little clothing, shelter, or decent food. Volunteers, including Washington's wife **(6)** _____, helped by making clothes and caring for the sick. Several Europeans, such as French nobleman **(7)** _____ and Polish cavalry officer **(8)** _____, worked for the Patriot cause. The **(9)** _____ had no power to levy taxes. Therefore, Congress printed hundreds of millions of dollars worth of paper money that soon lost its value because there was not enough **(10)** _____ to back it. This caused **(11)** _____.

Life on the Home Front

The war caused many **(12)** _____ to flee their homes in America. The ideals of liberty and freedom caused some **(13)** _____ to question their place in society and some Americans to question **(14)** _____.

Graphic Organizer → Skills

Answer: Students may note that France gained an ally by helping the Americans with their money, reinforcements, and supplies.

3 ASSESS

Assign Section 2 Assessment as homework or as an in-class activity.

🕸 Have students use **Interactive Tutor Self-Assessment CD-ROM.**

L2

Section Quiz 6–2

Name _____ Date _____ Class _____

★ **Chapter 6**   Score ___

Section Quiz 6-2

DIRECTIONS: Matching Match the items in Column A with the items in Column B. Write the correct letters in the blanks. *(10 points each)*

Column A	Column B
___ 1. William Howe's winter camp	A. Valley Forge
___ 2. George Washington's winter camp	B. Judith Sargeant Murray
___ 3. French noble at Valley Forge	C. Loyalists
___ 4. fled the colonies for England	D. Marquis de Lafayette
___ 5. essay writer for women's education	E. Philadelphia

DIRECTIONS: Multiple Choice In the blank at the left, write the letter of the

---

Yet somehow, with strong determination, the Continental Army survived the winter, and conditions gradually improved. The troops built huts and gathered supplies from the countryside. Volunteers—including Washington's wife, Martha—made clothes for the troops and cared for the sick. Washington declared that no army had ever suffered "such uncommon hardships" with such "patience and fortitude." New soldiers joined the ranks in the spring.

❝The army grows stronger every day," one officer wrote. "There is a spirit of discipline among the troops that is better than numbers.❞

In April 1778 Washington told his troops of the Patriots' alliance with France. Everyone's spirits rose at the thought of help from overseas. The Continental Army celebrated with a religious service and a parade.

Help From Overseas

Among the hardy soldiers who spent the winter at Valley Forge was a French nobleman, the **Marquis de Lafayette** (lah•fay•EHT). Filled with enthusiasm for the ideas expressed in the Declaration of Independence, Lafayette had bought a ship and set sail for America. He rushed to join the battle for freedom. Lafayette wrote to his wife and children in France,

❝The future of America is closely bound up with the future of all mankind.❞

Upon his arrival in Philadelphia, Lafayette offered his services and those of his followers to General Washington. Lafayette became a trusted aide to Washington.

Other Europeans also volunteered to work for the Patriot cause. Two Poles—Thaddeus Kosciusko (kawsh•CHUSH•koh), an engineer, and Casimir Pulaski, a cavalry officer—contributed to the American efforts. Pulaski died in 1779, fighting for the Continental Army.

Friedrich von Steuben (STOO•buhn), a former army officer from Germany, also came to help Washington. Von Steuben drilled the Patriot troops at Valley Forge, teaching them military discipline. He turned the ragged Continental Army into a more effective fighting force.

Juan de Miralles (mee•RAH•yays) arrived in Philadelphia in 1778 as a representative of Spain. At his urging, Spain, Cuba, and Mexico sent financial aid to the colonies. Miralles befriended many Patriot leaders and lent money to the cause.

$ Economics

Money Problems

Getting money to finance the war was a major problem. The Continental Congress had no power to raise money through taxes. Although

Causes and Effects of French-American Alliance in 1778

Causes
- Longstanding hostility between Britain and France
- Conflict between Britain and France during French and Indian War
- Victory at Saratoga boosts French confidence in Patriots

Effects
- France lends money to the Continental Congress
- France sends soldiers and ships to help American forces
- Americans win independence

Graphic Organizer → Skills

In 1777 Benjamin Franklin negotiated with French leaders for money and support for the American cause.

Drawing Conclusions Why was it important for France to recognize the independence of the American colonies?

174   CHAPTER 6   The American Revolution

DIFFERENTIATED INSTRUCTION

Reading Support Why would a European nation want to become involved in the Americans' war for independence? Encourage students who enjoy analytical questions to make up a list of pro and con statements that a European leader might consider before committing to the Patriot cause. (You might ask students to do additional research to learn what various nations stood to gain or lose by siding against Britain.) **L2**

📁 Refer to *Inclusion for the Middle School Social Studies Classroom Strategies and Activities* in the TCR.

the Congress received some money from the states and from foreign countries, much more money was needed.

To pay for the war, the Congress and the states printed hundreds of millions of dollars worth of paper money. These bills quickly lost their value, however, because the amount of bills in circulation grew faster than the supply of gold and silver backing them. This led to inflation, which means that it took more and more money to buy the same amount of goods. The Congress stopped issuing the paper money because no one would use it. However, the Americans had no other way to finance the fighting of their war for independence.

✓ **Reading Check** **Describing** How did Lafayette help the Patriot cause?

Life on the Home Front

The war changed the lives of all Americans, even those who stayed at home. With thousands of men away in military service, women took over the duties that had once been the responsibility of their husbands or fathers. Other women ran their husbands' or their own businesses.

Changing Attitudes

The ideals of liberty and freedom that inspired the American Revolution caused some women to question their place in society. In an essay on education, **Judith Sargeant Murray** of Massachusetts argued that women's minds are as good as men's. Girls, therefore, should get as good an education as boys. At a time when most girls received little schooling, this was a radical idea.

Abigail Adams also championed women's interests. She wrote to her husband, John Adams, who was a member of the Second Continental Congress:

❝I cannot say that I think you are very generous to the ladies, for, whilst you are proclaiming peace and good will to men, emancipating all nations, you insist upon retaining an absolute power over wives.❞

Picturing History

Paper notes issued by the Congress and the states rapidly declined in value. By the time these South Carolina bills were printed, their real value was only 10 percent of their face value. **Why did American notes quickly decline in value?**

Treatment of Loyalists

Every state had some Loyalists. Thousands of them fought with the British against the Patriots. To prove their loyalty to Britain, some Loyalists spied and informed on the Patriots.

Many Loyalists, however, fled the American colonies during the Revolutionary War. They packed their belongings and sold whatever they could. Some left hurriedly for England. Others took off for Florida. Still others journeyed to the frontier beyond the Appalachian Mountains and to Canada.

Loyalists who remained in the United States faced difficult times. Their neighbors often shunned them. Some became victims of mob violence. Loyalists who actively helped the British could be arrested and tried as traitors. Patriots executed a few Loyalists, but such extreme measures were unusual.

🏛 Citizenship

Hopes for Equality

The Revolutionary War ideals of freedom and liberty inspired some white Americans to question slavery. As early as the Stamp Act crisis,

✓**Reading Check**

Answer: He came to America with enthusiasm and fellow supporters and became an aide to Washington.

Picturing History

Answer: There were more bills in circulation than the available gold and silver could back.

L3

Enrichment Activity 6–2

Name _____ Date _____ Class _____

★ **Enrichment Activity 6-2** ★ 🔍

The Unusual Battle of the Kegs

During the British occupation of Philadelphia during the Revolutionary War, Americans began experimenting with floating mines. Read the excerpts from a January 1778 satire, which pokes fun at the British. Do you think the writer for the *New Jersey Gazette* really thought the British navy showed "activity, bravery, and military skill" in this action?

Philadelphia has been entertained with the most astonishing instance of the activity, bravery, and military skill of the royal navy of Great Britain. Yesterday . . . several kegs . . . made their appearance [on the Delaware River]. An alarm was immediately spread through the city . . . the Roebuck and other ships of war, whole broadsides were poured into the Delaware. In short, not a wandering ship, stick or drift log but felt the vigor of the British arms. The action began about sunrise, and would have been completed with great success by noon, had not an old market

L1

Reteaching Activity 6–2

Name _____ Date _____ Class _____

★ **Reteaching Activity 6-2**

DIRECTIONS: Completion In the space provided, write the word or words that best complete the sentence.

By late 1777 **(1)** _____ had been in Paris for a year trying unsuccessfully to get France to form an alliance with the United States. After the victory at **(2)** _____, France realized the Patriots might win the war; they declared war on Great Britain and sent money, equipment, and **(3)** _____ to aid the Americans. Soon, **(4)** _____ also declared war on Great Britain.

While British general William Howe and his forces spent the winter in comfort in Philadelphia, George Washington and his troops endured terrible suffering at their camp at **(5)** _____. Because of the lack of decent food, clothing, and shelter,

L1, ELL

Reading Essentials and Study Guide 6–2

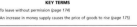

Study Guide

Chapter 6, Section 2

For use with textbook pages 172–176

THE WAR CONTINUES

KEY TERMS	
desert	To leave without permission *(page 174)*
inflation	An increase in money supply causes the price of goods to rise *(page 175)*

DRAWING FROM EXPERIENCE

Have you ever had to ask others for help when you had a problem you could not solve by yourself? How did the people you asked respond? Were they helpful? Did you feel they supported you? How did you feel when you shared your problem with someone who cared and was willing to help?

In the last section, you read about the advantages and disadvantages of the British and the Americans. This section focuses on the hardships the Patriots faced and the help they received.

INTERDISCIPLINARY CONNECTIONS ACTIVITY

Language Arts Have students consider the personality of George Washington. Then have them create quotes that reflect what they think the general might have said about the following topics: the progress of the war thus far; conditions at Valley Forge; alliances with European nations; military experts who have arrived recently from Europe; and the army's financial needs. **L1,** ELL

Analyzing *Political Cartoons*

Answer: The horse represents the Americans, and the rider represents the British. The cartoon presents the spirit felt by Americans as they fought for their independence from Britain.

Models of Civic Virtue To extend the Interdisciplinary Activity on this page, tell students that many Americans look to the Founders as models of civic virtue. Explain that civic virtue involves putting the good of the community ahead of one's personal interests and participating in the democratic process. For example, George Washington wanted to retire after the Revolution but later agreed to serve as president. The signers of the Declaration risked their lives for the benefit of their fellow Americans. Have students research a Founder and create a biographical sketch. The sketches should evaluate the Founder's contributions as models of civic virtue. **L2**

Reading Check

Answer: took over husband's responsibilities, ran family businesses, and worked toward new independence for women

4 CLOSE

Ask students how the Continental Army's experience at Valley Forge reflected problems that many of the Patriots—both military and civilian—faced.

Analyzing *Political Cartoons*

This cartoon, drawn in 1779, shows a rider being thrown by a horse. Cartoonists often use animals as symbols. For example, an eagle is often used to symbolize the United States. The Republican Party is often represented by an elephant, while the Democratic Party symbol is the donkey. **Who do the horse and rider represent? What idea is the cartoon presenting?**

religious groups and other groups had voted to condemn slavery. In 1778 Governor William Livingston of New Jersey asked the legislature to free all enslaved people in the state. Slavery, Livingston said, was "utterly inconsistent with the principles of Christianity and humanity."

African Americans made similar arguments. In New Hampshire enslaved Africans asked the legislature for their freedom

❝so that the name of *slave* may not be heard in a land gloriously contending for the sweets of freedom.❞

From the beginning of the war—at Lexington, Concord, and Bunker Hill—African American soldiers fought for the American cause. To some fighting for freedom, both African American and white, the Revolution seemed to bring nearer the day when slavery would be abolished. Vermont, New Hampshire, Massachusetts, and Pennsylvania attempted to end slavery in their states. The issue of slavery would remain unsettled for many years, however.

Reading Check **Explaining** What contributions did women make during the war?

SECTION 2 ASSESSMENT

Checking for Understanding

1. **Key Terms** Write a short paragraph in which you define the terms desert and inflation correctly. Use standard sentence structure and spelling in your paragraph.
2. **Reviewing Facts** Explain why the French did not publicly support the Americans until after the Battle of Saratoga.

Reviewing Themes

3. **Groups and Institutions** How were the Loyalists treated by the Patriots during the war?

Critical Thinking

4. **Making Inferences** The Americans claimed to fight for liberty and freedom. How did these ideals make women and enslaved Africans question their positions in society?
5. **Determining Cause and Effect** Re-create the diagram below and describe what happened when the Continental Congress tried to finance the war by printing money.

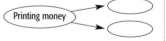

Printing money

Analyzing Visuals

6. **Graphic Organizer Skills** Study the cause-and-effect chart on page 174. In what ways did France help the Americans in their fight for independence? What event led France to aid the Americans in the first place?

Interdisciplinary Activity

Expository Writing Why was Washington such an effective leader? Write a one-page paper describing both his personal and professional characteristics.

SECTION 2 ASSESSMENT ANSWERS

1. Student work should reflect correct use of terms.
2. After the Battle of Saratoga, the French believed the Americans had a chance of defeating Britain.
3. They were shunned by neighbors and were occasionally victims of mob violence; some were arrested and tried as traitors;

a few were executed.
4. These ideals highlighted the fact that they did not have equal rights or the same freedoms and opportunities that white American males had at the time.
5. The bills lost their value due to the lack of gold and silver backing; inflation

6. lent money to the Continental Congress, sent soldiers and ships; the Battle of Saratoga

Interdisciplinary Activity Essays should include ideas about Washington's leadership such as respect, concern for his soldiers, and integrity.

SECTION 3 The War Moves West and South

Guide to Reading

Main Idea
Revolutionary War fighting spreads to the West and South.

Key Terms
blockade, privateer, guerrilla warfare

Reading Strategy
Organizing Information As you read the section, re-create the chart below and describe the significance of key battles in the West and South.

Battle	Significance
Vincennes	
Camden	
Kings Mountain	
Guilford Courthouse	

Read to Learn
• how the war involved Native Americans.
• how a new kind of fighting developed in the South.

Section Theme
Geography and History As the war continued, Patriot victories were won in the West, in the South, and at sea.

Preview of Events

1778	1779	1780	1781

July 1778
George Rogers Clark captures Vincennes

September 1779
The *Serapis* surrenders to John Paul Jones

May 1780
British troops take Charles Town

January 1781
Patriots defeat British at Cowpens

AN American Story

Francis Marion organized a small but expert fighting force in South Carolina. Living off the land, Marion's soldiers harassed British troops by staging daring surprise attacks, sabotaging communication and supply lines, and rescuing American prisoners. After these attacks, Marion withdrew his men to swamps and forests. His habit of disappearing into the swamps to get away from the British earned him his nickname, the Swamp Fox.

The Swamp Fox and his troops

War in the West

At the same time Francis Marion was staging his daring raids in the South, important battles of the Revolutionary War were taking place along the western frontier. Much of this fighting involved Native Americans. Although some helped the Patriots, more sided with the British. For many Native Americans, the British seemed to present less of a threat than the Americans did.

CHAPTER 6   The American Revolution   **177**

SECTION RESOURCES

Reproducible Masters
• Reproducible Lesson Plan 6–3
• Daily Lecture and Discussion Notes 6–3
• Guided Reading Activity 6–3
• Section Quiz 6–3
• Reteaching Activity 6–3
• Reading Essentials and Study Guide 6–3
• Enrichment Activity 6–3

Transparencies
• Daily Focus Skills Transparency 6–3

Multimedia
• Interactive Tutor Self-Assessment CD-ROM
• ExamView® Pro Testmaker CD-ROM
• Presentation Plus! CD-ROM

2 TEACH

Daily Lecture and Discussion Notes 6–3

Copyright © by The McGraw-Hill Companies, Inc.

Daily Lecture and Discussion Notes
Chapter 6, Section 3

Did You Know? Naval hero John Paul Jones is considered to be one of the founders of the United States Navy. He was the first person to hoist the new American flag on a warship. In 1778 Jones sailed into a French bay and exchanged gun salutes with a French ship. This was the first time the United States flag was officially recognized by a foreign government.

I. **War in the West** (Pages 177–178)
   A. The war in the West took place along the frontier, west of the Appalachian Mountains, and involved Native Americans. They often helped the British by raiding American settlements.
   B. George Rogers Clark went to end the attacks. In June 1778, he and 175 soldiers

Reading Strategy

Reviewing Facts Have students turn back to Sections 1 and 2 to review the progress of the American Revolution. Have them list major confrontations. Students should note who won the confrontation, including the significance of the victory. **L2**

✓ Reading Check

Answer: Kaskaskia and Vincennes

What If...

Answers:

1. Answers will vary but should include that many soldiers felt empowered by George Washington and, therefore, might have left the military if he stepped down.

2. Answers may include that many European countries may not have provided support if George Washington stepped down and this would have decreased America's chances of gaining independence.

West of the Appalachian Mountains, the British and their Native American allies were raiding American settlements. Mohawk chief **Joseph Brant** led a number of brutal attacks in southwestern New York and northern Pennsylvania. After the war, Brant served as a representative of the Mohawk people to the Continental Congress and tried to get a fair land settlement for his people. Unable to reach an agreement, Brant and his people moved to Canada.

Henry Hamilton commanded Detroit, the main British base in the West. Some called Hamilton the "hair buyer" because of rumors that he paid Native Americans for the scalps of settlers.

★ Geography
Victory at Vincennes

George Rogers Clark, a lieutenant colonel in the Virginia militia, set out to end the British attacks on western settlers. In June 1778, Clark and 175 soldiers sailed down the Ohio River to the mouth of the Tennessee River. After marching 120 miles, the Patriots seized the British post at Kaskaskia (ka•SKAS•kee•uh) in present-day Illinois. Then, in February 1779, they captured the British town of **Vincennes** (vihn•SEHNZ) in present-day Indiana.

During Clark's absence in December, British troops under Henry Hamilton's command recaptured Vincennes. Clark vowed to get it back. In February, after marching for days through countrysides flooded with icy waters, Clark and his troops surprised the British, forcing Hamilton to surrender. George Rogers Clark's victory at Vincennes strengthened the American position in the West.

✓ **Reading Check** **Explaining** What British outposts did George Rogers Clark's troops capture?

Glory at Sea

As fighting continued on the western frontier, other battles raged at sea. Great Britain used its powerful navy to patrol American waterways,

What If...

Washington Had Stepped Down?

Throughout the Revolutionary War, Washington succeeded in holding his army together, despite many difficulties. He had to deal with low morale among soldiers who lived on poor rations and received low pay. The Continental Congress often interfered with his conduct of military operations. During the gloomy winter at Valley Forge, some congressmen and army officers plotted to replace Washington as commander in chief.

One of his critics was Dr. Benjamin Rush, who served for a time as surgeon general of the Continental Army. In a letter to John Adams, Rush compared Washington unfavorably to the hero of Saratoga, Horatio Gates.

❝I am more convinced than ever of the necessity of discipline and system in the management of our affairs. I have heard several officers who have served under General Gates compare his army to a well-regulated family. The same gentlemen have compared Gen'l Washington's imitation of an army to an unformed mob. Look at the characters of both! The one [Gates] on the pinnacle of military glory—exulting in the success of schemes planned with wisdom, and executed with vigor and bravery. . . . See the other [Washington] outgeneraled and twice beaten. . . .❞

—Dr. Benjamin Rush, October 21, 1777

COOPERATIVE LEARNING ACTIVITY

Organizing a Battle Chart Students may find it hard to distinguish the various battles discussed in this section. To aid their memories, organize the class into groups representing battles along the western frontier and in the South. You also might designate a group to document the naval battle between the *Bonhomme Richard* and the *Serapis*. Have each group complete a column in a classroom battle chart noting dates, giving details of the battles, and relating the battles to the war's progress. Assign students to create a detailed time line of the battle, research important people in the battle, and illustrate the crucial turning point in the battle. **L2**

keeping the ships of the Patriots and the ships of their allies from entering or leaving American harbors. This British blockade prevented supplies and reinforcements from reaching the Continental Army.

Privateers

To break the British naval blockade, the Second Continental Congress ordered the construction of 13 American warships. Only two of these, however, sailed to sea. The Americans destroyed four of their own ships to keep them out of British hands. Others were quickly captured by the British. Several states maintained their own small fleets, but the American navy was too weak to operate effectively.

American privateers captured more British vessels at sea than did the American navy. The privateers were privately owned merchant ships equipped with weapons. The Congress authorized approximately 2,000 ships to sail as privateers and attack enemy shipping. Finding crews for these ships was not difficult. Sailors

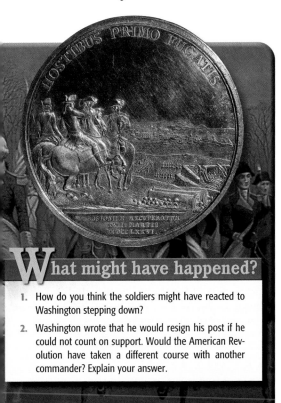

What might have happened?

1. How do you think the soldiers might have reacted to Washington stepping down?

2. Washington wrote that he would resign his post if he could not count on support. Would the American Revolution have taken a different course with another commander? Explain your answer.

from the whaling and fishing ports of New England signed on eagerly for the profitable privateering trade.

John Paul Jones

A daring American naval officer, **John Paul Jones,** began raiding British ports in 1777. He sailed in an old French ship that Benjamin Franklin had obtained for him. Jones gave the ship a French name, *Bonhomme Richard,* in honor of Franklin's *Poor Richard's Almanack.*

Sailing near the coast of Great Britain in September 1779, the *Bonhomme Richard* met a large fleet of British merchant ships escorted by the warship *Serapis.* The *Bonhomme Richard* moved close to the *Serapis* before attacking. The two ships fought for more than three hours. At one point Jones's ship was so badly damaged that the British captain asked whether Jones wished to surrender. Jones is said to have answered, "I have not yet begun to fight."

In the end the *Serapis* surrendered, but the *Bonhomme Richard* sank not long after the battle. Still, his victory made John Paul Jones a naval hero to the American Patriots.

✓ **Reading Check** **Describing** How did John Paul Jones contribute to the war effort?

Struggles in the South

In the early years of the war, the Americans had won some battles in the South. In 1776 they had crushed Loyalists at the Battle of Moore's Creek, near Wilmington, North Carolina, and had saved **Charles Town,** South Carolina, from the British. Although a small battle, its impact was great.

By 1778 the British realized that bringing the American colonies back into the empire would not be easy. As a result they changed their strategy and planned a hard-hitting offensive to finish the war.

The British concentrated their efforts in the South, where there were many Loyalists. They hoped to use British sea power and the support of the Loyalists to win decisive victories in the Southern states. Initially the strategy worked.

CHAPTER 6 The American Revolution 179

CHAPTER 6
Section 3, 177–182

L1, **ELL**

Guided Reading Activity 6–3

Name _____ Date _____ Class _____

★ **Guided Reading Activity 6-3**

DIRECTIONS: Recalling the Facts Use the information in your textbook to answer the questions. Use another sheet of paper if necessary.

1. Explain why more Native Americans sided with the British than with the Patriots.

2. Who set out to end the British attacks on western settlers?

3. Where was the victory that strengthened the American position in the West?

4. What did the British do to prevent supplies and reinforcements from reaching the Continental Army?

5. What were privateers?

6. Describe how privateers helped the American cause.

7. Who was the daring commander of the privateer *Bonhomme Richard*?

8. What response did this commander give to the British captain of the *Serapis* when asked whether he wished to surrender during a long, fierce battle at sea?

9. What strategy did the British use in an attempt to finish the war and bring the colonies back into the empire?

10. Where and when did the worst American defeat of the war take place?

11. Who was in command of the British forces in the South?

12. Why was the hit-and-run technique of guerrilla warfare successful against the British?

13. Who was known as the Swamp Fox?

14. When did Charles Cornwallis retreat north to Virginia?

15. Where did Cornwallis set up camp?

✓ **Reading Check**

Answer: He raided English ports and became a naval hero by causing the surrender of the English vessel *Serapis.*

Did you know?

Many Patriots wore their own clothing, such as breeches, vests, hose, and tricorner hats, rather than uniforms. They carried muskets and knives into battle.

DIFFERENTIATED INSTRUCTION

Reading Support As evidenced by the forces led by Francis Marion, guerrilla warfare was an effective Patriot tactic. Organize the class into groups. Use a wooden surface as a base. Using air-dry clay, have one group make trees found in South Carolina. Have another group make other natural features, such as swamp areas. Have other groups make both Patriot and British soldiers. Have the groups paint their contributions. Create a display of Francis Marion's forces waiting in ambush as the British troops march in file. **L1**

Refer to *Inclusion for the Middle School Social Studies Classroom Strategies and Activities* in the TCR.

Geography Skills

Answers:
1. Vincennes, Cahokia, and Kaskaskia
2. Fort Pitt

Geography Skills Practice
Ask: What waterway did Hamilton's troops follow for part of their trip from Fort Detroit to Vincennes? *(the Wabash River)*

Guerrilla *Guerrilla* is a Spanish word meaning "little war."

What?Who?Where?When?

Medical Practices For every Patriot soldier killed by the British, about nine died from disease or poor medical practices. In some cases, doctors drained about three-fourths of a soldier's blood. Draining "sick" blood to spur the production of "healthy" blood later proved fatal to the Patriots' commander. In 1799 the ailing George Washington gave his permission to be bled three times and died shortly afterward.

NATIONAL GEOGRAPHIC
The Revolutionary War in the West, 1778–1779

- American victory
- British troops
- American troops
- Fort
- Present-day boundaries

Fort Detroit

Lake Erie

Fort Miami

Fort Pitt

Wabash R.

Ohio R.

HAMILTON

CLARK

Cahokia (1778)

Vincennes (Feb. 1779)

Kaskaskia (July 1778)

APPALACHIAN MOUNTAINS

0   200 miles
0   200 kilometers
Lambert Equal-Area projection

"I know the case is desperate, sir . . . no time is to be lost."

—letter to Patrick Henry, February 1779

George Rogers Clark captured the key points of Kaskaskia, Cahokia, and Vincennes, saving the west region for the United States.

Geography Skills

The Revolutionary War spread west of the Appalachian Mountains where American troops won key victories.
1. **Region** What victories did the American forces win in the West?
2. **Analyzing Information** From what fort did Clark's troops set out?

British Victories

In late 1778 General Henry Clinton sent 3,500 British troops from New York to take Savannah, on the coast of Georgia. The British occupied the city and overran most of the state.

Clinton himself headed south with a large army in early 1780 to attack the port of Charles Town, South Carolina. Charles Town surrendered in May, and the British took thousands of prisoners. It marked the worst American defeat of the war. A member of Britain's Parliament gloated, "We look on America as at our feet."

Clinton returned to New York, leaving **General Charles Cornwallis** in command of British forces in the South. The Continental Congress sent forces under General Horatio Gates to face Cornwallis. The two armies met at **Camden,** South Carolina, in August 1780. Although the British won, Cornwallis soon found that he could not control the area he had conquered. He and his troops faced a new kind of warfare.

Guerrilla Warfare

The British received less help than they had expected from Loyalists in Southern states. Instead, as British troops moved through the countryside, small forces of Patriots attacked them. These bands of soldiers appeared suddenly, struck their blows, and then disappeared. This hit-and-run technique of guerrilla warfare caught the British off guard.

One successful guerrilla leader, **Francis Marion,** operated out of the swamps of eastern South Carolina. Known as the Swamp Fox, Marion was quick and smart. One British colonel grumbled that "the devil himself" could not catch Marion.

Help From Spain

When 30-year-old Bernardo de Gálvez became governor of the Spanish territory of Louisiana in January 1777, Spain was neutral. That did not stop Gálvez from helping the colonists. He loaned thousands of dollars to the Americans and opened the port of New Orleans to free trade on the part of the colonists. Gálvez also organized the shipment of tons of supplies

INTERDISCIPLINARY CONNECTIONS ACTIVITY

Civics As the text points out, many Native Americans of this era sided with the British, but some supported the Patriot cause. How political was their reasoning? Students may work independently or in small groups to chart some reasons for supporting either side. Have them discuss questions such as the following: How had each side treated Native Americans before the war? Which side seemed more likely to win? What might Native Americans have to gain from a British victory? From a Patriot victory? **L2,** **ELL**

and ammunition up the Mississippi River to the army of George Rogers Clark in the Northwest Territory. With this help from Gálvez, Clark was able to capture the key points of Kaskaskia, Cahokia, and Vincennes.

In the summer of 1779, Spain declared war on Britain. Gálvez raised an army of Spanish soldiers along with Creoles, Native Americans, and African Americans and marched on British posts along the lower Mississippi. Striking quickly, he captured British forts at Baton Rouge and Natchez. Then, in March 1780, Gálvez forced British Mobile to surrender. In May 1781 he took Pensacola, the British capital of West Florida.

These victories opened supply lines for military goods from Spain, France, Cuba, and Mexico. According to historian Buchanan Parker Thomson, Gálvez had given

66the most vital aid contributed by any one man to the struggling American colonies. In winning this triumphant victory over the last great British outpost, he had not only served his King to the limit of his strength but had made to the United States the most important gift an ally could offer: the security of their southeastern and western frontiers.99

Geography *Skills*

Answers:
1. Cornwallis
2. It kept British fleets from reaching Yorktown and Cornwallis's troops from escaping by sea; it also cut off supplies and reinforcements.

3 ASSESS

Assign Section 3 Assessment as homework or as an in-class activity.

🕙 Have students use **Interactive Tutor Self-Assessment CD-ROM.**

L2

Section Quiz 6–3

L1, ELL

Reteaching Activity 6–3

NATIONAL GEOGRAPHIC

The Revolutionary War in the South, 1778–1781

1️⃣ British capture Savannah, 1778

2️⃣ British capture Charles Town and Camden, but are defeated at Kings Mountain in October 1780 and at Cowpens in January 1781

3️⃣ Washington and Rochambeau rush toward Virginia, August 1781

4️⃣ French Admiral De Grasse keeps British ships away

5️⃣ Cornwallis trapped; the British surrender at Yorktown, 1781

Geography *Skills*

Most of the fighting took place in the South during the latter years of the Revolutionary War.
1. **Location** What British general was trapped at Yorktown, Virginia?
2. **Drawing Conclusions** How did the French navy help the Americans win the war?

⬅ American and allied forces

⬅ British forces

✴ American victory

✴ British victory

★ Fort

Reading Strategy ── READING THE TEXT

Predicting Assign students to groups. Have each group work together to create a wall-length time line. Use wall-length rolls of paper. As a class, discuss important dates from this section to include on each time line. Then discuss events that might occur over the following four years. Encourage students to base their predictions on what they have already learned in this chapter. The predicted events should stand out in design. For example, they could be written in a color different from the rest of the time line. Student groups should add important information about the American Revolution to their time lines. Pictures, illustrations, magazine cuttings, and similar items can be added. Hang the time lines in the class or hallway. L1

✓ **Reading Check**

Answer: The victory brought new support for independence from Southerners because they wanted to see an end to the destruction of their homes brought about by the war.

L1, ELL

Reading Essentials and Study Guide 6–3

Name _____ Date _____ Class _____

Study Guide

Chapter 6, Section 3

For use with textbook pages 177–182

THE WAR MOVES WEST AND SOUTH

KEY TERMS	
blockade	To close off cities and ports with ships (page 179)
privateer	Privately owned merchant ships equipped with weapons (page 179)
guerrilla warfare	A small band of soldiers appears suddenly, attacks, and disappears (page 180)

DRAWING FROM EXPERIENCE

Have you ever wondered what it would be like to have a war fought on American soil or at sea along our coasts? How would your life change? How would you feel if

L3

Enrichment Activity 6–3

Name _____ Date _____ Class _____

★ Enrichment Activity 6-3 ★

Science and Humanity

In 1780 Benjamin Franklin wrote a letter, excerpted below, to Joseph Priestley, a British chemist who supported the American Revolution.

Dear Sir,
... I always rejoice to hear of your being still employed in experimental researches into nature.... The rapid Progress true Science now makes, occasions my regretting sometimes that I was born so soon.... [I]n a thousand years ... [we] may perhaps learn to deprive large masses of their gravity, and give them absolute levity, for the sake of easy transport. Agriculture may diminish its labour and double its produce; all diseases may by sure means be

4 CLOSE

Ask students to speculate about how British military leaders justified their losses to the Patriots at this point in the war.

> *"I shall not spare any effort or trouble . . . for the benefit of the colonies."*
>
> —Bernardo de Gálvez,
> letter May 6, 1778,
> to Patrick Henry

Patriot Victories

After the British victory at Camden, South Carolina, the British moved northward through the Carolinas in September 1780. At **Kings Mountain,** a British officer and more than 1,000 Loyalists defended an outpost against the attack of Patriot sharpshooters. The Patriots forced the British to retreat. The victory brought new support for independence from Southerners. They wanted to see an end to the war that was destroying their homes and farms.

In October 1780, **Nathanael Greene** replaced Gates as commander of the Continental forces in the South. Rather than lead an all-out attack on Cornwallis's forces, Greene split his army in two. In January 1781, one section of the army, led by General Daniel Morgan, defeated the British at **Cowpens,** South Carolina. Another section joined Marion's guerrilla raids. In March Greene reunited his forces to meet Cornwallis's army at **Guilford Courthouse,** in present-day Greensboro, North Carolina. Greene's army was forced to retreat, but the British sustained great losses in the process. General Cornwallis abandoned the Carolina campaign.

British Retreat

Cornwallis decided to march north to Virginia in April 1781. His troops carried out raids throughout the state, nearly capturing Governor Thomas Jefferson and the Virginia legislature in June. Jefferson fled on horseback, just ahead of the advancing British troops.

General Washington sent Lafayette and General Anthony Wayne south to fight Cornwallis. Meanwhile Cornwallis set up camp at Yorktown, which was located on the Virginia coast, and awaited further orders from Clinton in New York. The battle for control of the South was entering its final phase.

✓ **Reading Check** **Evaluating** What effect did the Patriot victory at Kings Mountain produce?

SECTION 3 ASSESSMENT

Checking for Understanding

1. **Key Terms** Write a short paragraph in which you use the following terms: blockade, privateer, guerrilla warfare.
2. **Reviewing Facts** Explain why most Native Americans sided with the British in the conflict.

Reviewing Themes

3. **Geography and History** How did the British navy use the location of the colonies to their advantage?

Critical Thinking

4. **Drawing Conclusions** Why was guerrilla warfare effective against the British?
5. **Analyzing Information** Re-create the diagram below and describe the results of the battle at Guilford Courthouse.

Battle at Guilford Courthouse

Analyzing Visuals

6. **Geography Skills** Study the maps on pages 180 and 181. Who won the battle at Cowpens, South Carolina? At Kings Mountain, South Carolina? Whose forces did George Rogers Clark face at Vincennes?

Interdisciplinary Activity

Art Create a symbol or emblem that captures the spirit of the Patriot soldiers.

SECTION 3 ASSESSMENT ANSWERS

1. Student work should reflect correct use of terms.
2. The British seemed less of a threat than the Americans did. They knew the Americans wanted to expand onto their lands.
3. The colonies bordered the Atlantic, which allowed the British to blockade harbors.
4. Students may suggest that the British, more formal in their fighting style, were not familiar with guerrilla hit-and-run tactics. The British also were unfamiliar with the terrain, giving the guerrillas an added advantage.
5. Greene's troops retreated; Cornwallis abandoned the Carolina campaign due to heavy losses.
6. the Americans; the Americans; Hamilton's forces

Interdisciplinary Activity Symbols and emblems should represent the spirit of the Patriots during the war.

SECTION 4 The War Is Won

Guide to Reading

Main Idea
The American colonies overcame many disadvantages to win independence.

Key Terms
ratify, ambush

Reading Strategy
Organizing Information As you read the section, re-create the diagram below and list the reasons why the Americans were able to defeat the British in the Revolutionary War.

Reasons for the British defeat

Read to Learn
• how George Washington changed his military strategy.
• why the Americans won the Revolutionary War despite many disadvantages.

Section Theme
Groups and Institutions A combined Patriot force secured final victory, ensuring an independent United States.

Preview of Events

| ◆1780 | ◆1781 | ◆1782 | ◆1783 |

┗ **July 1780**
French troops arrive in colonies

┗ **August 1781**
Washington advances toward British at Yorktown

┗ **October 1781**
Cornwallis surrenders at Yorktown

┗ **September 1783**
Treaty of Paris is signed

*General Rochambeau,
French commander*

AN
American Story

A popular children's tune in eighteenth-century Britain went like this:

"If ponies rode men and if grass ate the cows,

And cats should be chased into holes by the mouse . . .

If summer were spring and the other way 'round,

Then all the world would be upside down."

This song would hold special meaning for the British troops in America as the Revolution reached its peak.

Victory at Yorktown

The Revolutionary War was at a critical point. Both armies needed a victory to win the war. While General Washington made plans to attack the British at Yorktown, Virginia, rather than New York City, the Patriots hoped for help from the French.

In July 1780, French warships appeared in the waters off **Newport,** Rhode Island. The ships carried more than 5,000 soldiers under the command of the French general, the **Comte de Rochambeau** (ROH•SHAM•BOH). Cheering crowds greeted the French soldiers, who were well armed and clad in colorful

---

1 FOCUS

Section Overview
This section highlights the events that led to the end of the American Revolution, and identifies the reasons why the Patriots won.

Reading Preview

Answers to Graphic: British were not on home land; American's victory at Yorktown; other nations helped America

Preteaching Vocabulary
⊕ Use the **Vocabulary PuzzleMaker CD-ROM** to create crossword and word search puzzles.

SECTION RESOURCES

📂 **Reproducible Masters**
• Reproducible Lesson Plan 6–4
• Daily Lecture and Discussion Notes 6–4
• Guided Reading Activity 6–4
• Section Quiz 6–4
• Reteaching Activity 6–4
• Reading Essentials and Study Guide 6–4
• Enrichment Activity 6–4

📖 **Transparencies**
• Daily Focus Skills Transparency 6–4

Multimedia
⊕ Vocabulary PuzzleMaker CD-ROM
⊕ Interactive Tutor Self-Assessment CD-ROM
⊕ ExamView® Pro Testmaker CD-ROM
⊕ Presentation Plus! CD-ROM

2 TEACH

Daily Lecture and Discussion Notes 6–4

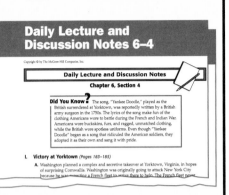

Creating a Story Map Organize students into groups of three or four and have them create a story map of the Revolutionary War. Have students pay attention to the characters' actions and points of view along with the development of the plot. Students should note major turning points as well as the climax of the story. **L2**

Picturing **History**

James Armistead was a courier and spy for the Patriots. He even worked as a servant—gathering military information as he did so—in the headquarters of General Cornwallis.
Answer: They contributed ships, troops, leaders, and money to the Patriot cause.

---

uniforms and plumed caps. The promised French aid had arrived at last. Unfortunately the British fleet arrived soon afterward and trapped the French ships in Newport.

In the autumn of 1780, Washington camped north of New York City waiting for a second fleet of French ships. From this position he could keep a close eye on the British army based in New York that General Clinton commanded. Washington planned to attack Clinton's army as soon as this second French fleet arrived from the West Indies. He had to wait a year to put his plan into action, however, because the fleet did not set sail for America until the summer of 1781.

Change in Plans

Washington had followed reports of the fighting in the South during 1780 and 1781. He knew that the British army commanded by Cornwallis was camped in **Yorktown,** Virginia. Washington also knew that Patriot forces under the Marquis de Lafayette were keeping Cornwallis and his troops bottled up on the Yorktown peninsula.

In August 1781, Washington learned that **Admiral François de Grasse,** the French naval

commander, was heading toward Chesapeake Bay instead of New York. Washington quickly changed his plans. He would advance on the British at Yorktown rather than at New York City.

Washington took steps to keep the new American strategy secret. He wanted Clinton to think the Patriots still planned to attack New York. This, he hoped, would keep Clinton from sending aid to Cornwallis.

General Rochambeau had marched his troops from Newport to join General Washington in July. Washington and Rochambeau then rushed south with their armies. The secrecy was so strict that most of the soldiers did not know where they were going. One soldier wrote,

> ❝We do not know the object of our march, and are in perfect ignorance whether we are going against New York, or . . . Virginia.❞

Washington's troops marched 200 miles in 15 days. General Clinton in New York did not detect the forces heading south toward Virginia. Three groups—Lafayette's troops, Washington's and Rochambeau's main American-French army, and the French fleet under Admiral De Grasse—would meet at Yorktown.

The Siege of Yorktown

Washington wondered whether his complicated plan had fooled Clinton, and whether the French fleet would reach Yorktown in time. On September 5, to his great relief, Washington received news that Admiral De Grasse's ships were nearing Yorktown.

The plan worked perfectly, and the British were thoroughly confused. By the end of September, 14,000 American and French troops had trapped Cornwallis's 7,500 British and Hessian troops at Yorktown. Meanwhile, De Grasse's

Picturing **History**

The Marquis de Lafayette (left) relied on James Armistead (right), an enslaved African American, to gather military information about the British. Armistead was later freed and took the name James Armistead Lafayette.
How did the French help the Patriots win the war?

COOPERATIVE LEARNING ACTIVITY

Discussing the Revolution Use a press-conference format to help students focus on the conclusion of the American Revolution. Call on volunteers to portray Jean Baptiste de Rochambeau, Anthony Wayne, Charles Cornwallis, George Washington, and General Clinton. Have the remainder of the class portray reporters and ask questions about the end of the war. Encourage questions that elicit details about battles. Also encourage discussion of the Treaty of Paris and the significance of a newly independent United States. **L1**

History *Through Art*

Surrender of Lord Cornwallis by **John Trumbull** Trapped by American and French forces, General Charles Cornwallis surrendered at Yorktown. The victory would guarantee America's independence. **What were the two major terms of the Treaty of Paris?**

L1, ELL

Guided Reading Activity 6–4

Name _____ Date _____ Class _____

★ **Guided Reading Activity 6-4**

DIRECTIONS: Outlining Locate the heading in your textbook. Then use the information under the heading to help you write each answer. Use another sheet of paper if necessary.

I. **Victory at Yorktown**
   A. Introduction—In 1780 George Washington camped north of New York City, waiting to attack whose army? _____
   B. Change in Plans
      1. Who commanded the British army at Yorktown, Virginia? _____
      2. Why did Washington decide to attack the British at Yorktown? _____
      3. What three groups would meet for the attack? _____
   C. The Siege of Yorktown—By the end of September, how many American and French troops had trapped how many British and Hessian troops? _____
   D. Cornwallis's Defeat—When did Cornwallis surrender? _____

fleet kept Cornwallis from escaping by sea. General Clinton and the rest of the British army waited in New York, unable to help Cornwallis.

Cornwallis's Defeat

On October 9 the Americans and French began a tremendous bombardment. A Hessian soldier described the dreadful scene in his diary:

> ❝One saw men lying nearly everywhere who were mortally wounded and whose heads, arms, and legs had been shot off. . . . Likewise on watch and on post in the lines, on trench and work details, they were wounded by the fearfully heavy fire.❞

British supplies began running low, and many soldiers were wounded or sick. Cornwallis realized the hopelessness of his situation. On October 19 he surrendered. The Patriots had won the **Battle of Yorktown.**

Handing over their weapons, the British marched between rows of French and American troops—the French in fancy white uniforms on one side and the raggedly clothed Continental Army on the other. A French band played "Yankee Doodle," and a British band responded with a children's tune called "The World Turned Upside Down." Indeed it had.

✓**Reading Check** **Explaining** Why did Washington decide to advance on the British camp at Yorktown?

Independence

The fighting did not really end with Yorktown. The British still held Savannah, Charles Town, and New York, and a few more clashes took place on land and sea. The Patriot victory at Yorktown, however, convinced the British that the war was too costly to pursue.

The two sides sent delegates to Paris to work out a treaty. **Benjamin Franklin, John Adams,** and **John Jay** represented the United States. The American Congress ratified, or approved, the preliminary treaty in April 1783. The final **Treaty of Paris** was signed on September 3, 1783. By that time Britain had also made peace with France and Spain.

The Treaty of Paris was a triumph for the Americans. Great Britain recognized the United States as an independent nation. The territory that the new nation claimed extended from the Atlantic Ocean west to the Mississippi River and from Canada in the north to Spanish Florida in the south. The British promised to withdraw all their troops from American territory. They also agreed to give Americans the right to fish in the waters off the coast of Canada.

The United States, in turn, agreed that British merchants could collect

HISTORY *Online*

Student Web Activity
Visit tarvol1.glencoe.com and click on **Chapter 6— Student Web Activities** for an activity on the Battle of Yorktown.

✓**Reading Check**

Answer: because his original plan had to be changed once he learned that the French fleet was not heading to New York

History *Through Art*

Answer: Britain had to recognize America's independence and withdraw its troops.

HISTORY *Online*

Objectives and answers to the student activity can be found in the **Web Activity Lesson Plan** feature at tarvol1.glencoe.com

Did you know?

For a little more than two years after the Battle of Yorktown, New York remained securely under the control of Sir Guy Carleton and his British forces.

DIFFERENTIATED INSTRUCTION

English Learners Have students research and draw uniforms worn by Continental and British forces. Remind students to color the uniforms correctly. Have them provide labeling as well. Work with students to create a classroom display of the uniforms. Then lead a discussion of why the uniforms were different and in what ways the uniforms might symbolize the two sides of the conflict.
L1, ELL

👉 Refer to *Inclusion for the Middle School Social Studies Classroom Strategies and Activities* in the TCR.

People In History

Peter Francisco was a valiant soldier of the American Revolution. He was wounded five times in battle and he was present at Yorktown for the surrender of General Cornwallis. **Ask:** Where was Peter Francisco from? *(an island in the Portuguese Azores)*

3 ASSESS

Assign Section 4 Assessment as homework or as an in-class activity.

🖥 Have students use **Interactive Tutor Self-Assessment CD-ROM.**

L2

Section Quiz 6–4

L1

Reteaching Activity 6–4

People In History

Peter Francisco 1760–1831

Peter Francisco was found abandoned in Colonial America in 1765 when he was about five years old. It was later learned that he was from an island in the Portuguese Azores. The abandoned boy was adopted by an uncle of Patrick Henry.

When the Revolution began, 16-year-old Fran-cisco joined the Tenth Virginia Regiment and earned a reputation for bravery and dedication to the revolutionary cause. George Washington was reported to have said about Francisco, "Without him we would have lost two crucial battles, perhaps the war, and with it our freedom. He was truly a one-man army."

After the war, Francisco served as sergeant at arms in the Virginia House of Delegates. In 1974 the Portuguese Continental Union of the United States of America began bestowing a "Peter Francisco Award" upon distinguished Americans who have contributed to the Portuguese cause.

---

debts owed by Americans. The treaty also stated that the Congress would advise the states that property taken from Loyalists was to be returned to them.

The Newburgh Conspiracy

After the British surrender, Washington maintained a strong army with headquarters at Newburgh, New York, planning to disband it when the peace treaty was signed. The period following the British surrender at Yorktown was not easy for American soldiers. Anger mounted when Congress refused to fund their pensions and failed to provide other pay. In disgust some officers circulated a letter in March 1783. If their demands were not met, the letter said, the army should refuse to disband.

Shocked and worried, General Washington realized that such an action could lead to a revolt that would threaten to destroy the new nation. He persuaded the angry officers to be patient with Congress. Then he urged Congress to meet the soldiers' just demands: "If, retiring from the field, they [the officers] are to grow old in poverty…then shall I have learned what ingratitude is."

Washington's leadership ended the threat to the new nation, and Congress soon acted on the demands.

Washington's Farewell

British troops left New York City in late November 1783. The war had truly ended, and George Washington could at last give up his command. On December 4 Washington said farewell to his officers at Fraunces' Tavern in Manhattan. "With a heart full of love and gratitude, I now take my leave of you."

Nearly three weeks later Washington formally resigned from the army at a meeting of the Second Continental Congress in Annapolis, Maryland. A witness described the scene: "The spectators all wept, and there was hardly a member of Congress who did not drop tears." Washington said,

> 66 Having now finished the work assigned me I retire . . . and take my leave of all the employments of public life. 99

He returned to his home, Mount Vernon, in time for Christmas. There he planned to live quietly with his family.

📖 Reading Strategy   READING THE TEXT

Brainstorming Have students brainstorm words that describe the ideals of the Declaration of Independence. Make a list of these terms on the chalkboard. Ask how each word applies to today. Students should relate the ideals of liberty and equality to present-day events in their community. Student essays should be well structured and draw a relationship between the ideals of the past and concerns for the common good today. **L2,** ELL

Why the Americans Won

How had the Americans managed to win the Revolutionary War? How had they defeated Britain, the world's strongest power?

The Americans had several advantages in the war. They fought on their own land, while the British had to bring troops and supplies from thousands of miles away. The siege of Yorktown showed how the British depended on support from the sea. When their ships were blocked, the British troops were without support.

The British succeeded in occupying cities but had difficulty controlling the countryside. They had not been successful at Saratoga or in the Carolinas. The Patriots, however, knew the local terrain and where to lay an ambush—a surprise attack.

Help from other nations contributed to the American victory. The success at Yorktown would not have been possible without French soldiers and ships. Loans from France helped the Americans win the war. The Spanish also aided the Patriots by attacking the British in the Mississippi Valley and along the Gulf of Mexico.

Perhaps most important, the American Revolution was a people's movement. Its outcome depended not on any one battle or event but on the determination and spirit of all the Patriots. As the Continental Army marched from New York to Yorktown, crowds came out to watch and wish the troops well. Washington pointed to the crowd and said,

> 66We may be beaten by the English . . . but here is an army they will never conquer.99

The Influence of the American Revolution

In 1776 the American colonists began a revolution, making clear the principles of freedom and rights outlined in the Declaration of Independence. These ideas bounded back across the Atlantic to influence the French Revolution. French rebels in 1789 fought in defense of "Liberty, Equality, and Fraternity." French revolutionaries repeated the principles of the American Declaration of Independence: "Men are born and remain free and equal in rights."

In 1791 the ideals of the American and French Revolutions traveled across the Caribbean and the Atlantic to the French-held island colony of Saint Domingue. Inspired by talk of freedom, enslaved Africans took up arms. Led by Toussaint-Louverture, they shook off French rule. In 1804, Saint Domingue—present-day Haiti—became the second nation in the Americas to achieve independence from colonial rule. "We have asserted our rights," declared the revolutionaries. "We swear never to yield them to any power on earth."

✓**Reading Check** **Summarizing** What were three reasons the Americans were successful in their fight?

SECTION 4 ASSESSMENT

Checking for Understanding

1. **Key Terms** Use each of these terms in a sentence that will help explain its meaning: ratify, ambush.
2. **Reviewing Facts** Describe how the French navy helped George Washington at Yorktown.

Reviewing Themes

3. **Groups and Institutions** What influence did the American Revolution have around the world?

Critical Thinking

4. **Predicting Consequences** What might have happened if the French fleet had not arrived at Yorktown?
5. **Organizing Information** Re-create the diagram below and describe the terms that the Americans agreed to in the Treaty of Paris.

Analyzing Visuals

6. **Picturing History** Look at the painting on page 185. How does the artist focus attention on the figures in the center of the painting?

Interdisciplinary Activity

Geography Create a map of the United States that shows the boundaries of the country at the time of the Treaty of Paris. Use colored pencils to show the lands that the British gave to the Americans.

SECTION 4 ASSESSMENT ANSWERS

1. Student work should reflect correct use of terms.
2. It prevented Cornwallis and his soldiers from escaping by sea.
3. It inspired the ideals of freedom and democracy in France, influencing the French Revolution.
4. Washington's troops may not have been victorious because Cornwallis most likely would have been able to escape by sea.
5. British merchants could collect American debts; Congress would advise the states that property belonging to the Loyalists be returned to them.
6. The troops lined up on the sides focus attention on the center, as does the bright white horse in the center.

Interdisciplinary Activity Student maps should include a key and compass rose. Areas should be well defined.

✓**Reading Check**

Answer: The Americans fought on familiar territory and could control the countryside; they had help from other countries; it was a people's movement built on determination and spirit.

L1, ELL

Reading Essentials and Study Guide 6–4

Study Guide

Chapter 6, Section 4
For use with textbook pages 183–187

THE WAR IS WON

	KEY TERMS
ratify	To approve (page 185)
ambush	A surprise attack (page 186)

DRAWING FROM EXPERIENCE

Have any of your relatives served in a war? In which war did they serve? What role did they play in the war? Were they honored for their service?

In the last section, you read about how Revolutionary War fighting spread to the South and West. This section focuses on how American colonies overcame many disadvantages to win their independence.

L3

Enrichment Activity 6–4

Name _____ Date _____ Class _____

★ Enrichment Activity 6-4

Revolutionary Transportation

While the American Revolution smoldered and raged, inventors developed new ways to travel. Study the two inventions below.

4 CLOSE

Ask students to explain why the end of the Revolutionary War meant a "world turned upside-down" for the British.

Reviewing Key Terms

1. A **mercenary** was a hired soldier, whereas a **recruit** was an enlisted soldier.

2. A **privateer** ship attacked enemy shipping to break the British naval **blockade.**

3. Revolutionary soldiers used the tactics of **guerrilla warfare** to **ambush** English troops.

Reviewing Key Facts

4. Its forces were larger and more experienced; Britain had the most powerful navy in the world.

5. Some were members of the Anglican Church; some depended on England for their jobs; some feared the disorder that was sure to come; others did not understand the issues.

6. Thomas Paine published *The Crisis*, a pamphlet that boosted American spirits and determination for freedom.

7. France and Spain sent money, supplies, and troops to aid the Americans.

8. Problems included a lack of food, clothing, blankets, and shoes; harsh winter conditions; desertion; illness; and a lack of morale.

9. education for girls equal to that for boys

10. They knew that many Americans wanted to take their land.

11. guerrilla warfare

12. the Battle of Yorktown

13. The Americans were familiar with the terrain, allowing them to control the countryside, plan ambushes, and chart routes through the forest.

Chapter Summary
The American Revolution

1776
- Thomas Paine writes the inspiring *Common Sense.*
- The Continental Army is defeated at the Battle of Long Island.
- George Washington leads troops across the Delaware River to surprise the British at Trenton.

1777
- The Patriots defeat the British at Saratoga, New York.
- The British capture Philadelphia.

1778
- France provides money, troops, and equipment to the Patriots.
- The Continental Army suffers from the lack of supplies at Valley Forge.

1779
- John Paul Jones forces the surrender of the British warship *Serapis.*

1780
- The British capture Charles Town and take thousands of prisoners.

1781
- The Americans win the Battle of Yorktown.

1783
- The Treaty of Paris is signed, marking the end of the Revolution.

Reviewing Key Terms

Examine the pairs of words below. Then write a sentence explaining what each of the pairs has in common.

1. mercenary, recruit
2. blockade, privateer
3. guerrilla warfare, ambush

Reviewing Key Facts

4. Why did the British think their military forces were superior to those of the Americans?

5. Why did Loyalists support Britain?

6. How did Thomas Paine help the Patriots during the Revolutionary War?

7. What European nations fought with the Americans against the British?

8. What were some of the problems that troops faced during the winter at Valley Forge?

9. What ideas did Judith Sargeant Murray promote about education?

10. Why did many Native Americans give their support to the British?

11. What fighting method did the Americans use to keep the British from taking the Southern Colonies?

12. Which battle convinced the British that fighting the Americans was too costly?

13. Why was fighting on their own land an advantage for the Patriots?

Critical Thinking

14. **Compare and Contrast** What advantage did the Patriots have over the British mercenaries?

15. **Analyzing Information** How did women help in the war effort?

16. **Drawing Conclusions** Why do you think the British found it easier to capture American cities than to take over the American countryside?

17. **Determining Cause and Effect** Re-create the diagram below and describe two ways America's fight for independence influenced other countries.

Critical Thinking

14. The Patriots had a personal interest in the outcome of the war; the mercenaries were fighting for money.

15. They took over the management of farms and businesses, made clothes for the troops, and cooked and cared for the sick and injured.

16. Patriots had an advantage in rural areas because they were more familiar with the terrain. Guerrilla warfare used this advantage.

17. Ideals of independence helped to fuel the French Revolution and inspired enslaved Africans to fight for freedom on the French-held island of Saint Domingue.

Geography and History Activity

The Treaty of Paris in 1783 established the boundaries of the new United States. The newly independent nation shared land claims on the North American continent with several nations. Study the map below and answer the questions that follow.

18. **Location** What natural landmark formed the new western boundary of the United States?

19. **Region** Which country claimed the most land in North America in 1783? The least land?

NATIONAL GEOGRAPHIC

Land Claims in North America, 1783

Hudson Bay

CANADA

SPANISH LOUISIANA

Mississippi R.

UNITED STATES

NEW SPAIN

Gulf of Mexico

0   500 miles
0   500 kilometers
Azimuthal Equidistant projection

United States	Disputed
British	Spanish
French	Russian

Practicing Skills

Reading a Military Map *Study the military map on page 181. Then answer the questions that follow.*

20. What color symbolizes British troop movement?

21. What symbol represents battles?

22. When did the British capture the city of Savannah?

23. Who was victorious at the Battle of Cowpens?

Self-Check Quiz
Visit tarvol1.glencoe.com and click on **Chapter 6—Self-Check Quizzes** to prepare for the chapter test.

Citizenship Cooperative Activity

24. **Expository Writing** As citizens, we have responsibilities to our communities. For a community to be successful, its citizens must take an active role in it. Write a one-page paper in which you discuss the topic, "My responsibilities to my community."

Economics Activity

25. Look up the word *inflation* in a dictionary or another reference book. Write a definition of the term in your own words. Then write answers to these questions:
   • What happens to the price of goods during periods of inflation?
   • How would inflation affect your standard of living?

Alternative Assessment

26. **Portfolio Writing Activity** Scan the chapter for details about people who came to the United States from other countries to help in the war effort. Record the names in your journal. Then create a chart that shows the people's names, their home countries, and what they did to aid the Americans.

Standardized Test Practice

Directions: Choose the *best* answer to the following question.

What American victory convinced the French to form an alliance with the United States?
A Saratoga   C Bunker Hill
B Ticonderoga   D Trenton

Test-Taking Tip

Remember to eliminate answers that you know are wrong. For example, the Patriots did not win the battle of Bunker Hill; therefore, choice **C** is not correct.

 Alternative Assessment

26. Student charts should include information about people such as Bernardo de Gálvez, Marquis de Lafayette, and Casimir Pulaski.

HISTORY Online

Have students visit the Web site at tarvol1.glencoe.com to review Chapter 6 and take the Self-Check Quiz.

Standardized Test Practice

Answer: A
Question Type: History
Answer Explanation: According to page 173, when the French realized that the Americans had a chance of defeating the British after the Battle of Saratoga, they sent money, equipment, and troops to the Patriots.

Bonus Question ?

Ask: By what nickname was Anthony Wayne known, and why? *(He was called "Mad" Anthony Wayne because of his eagerness for battle.)*

 Geography and History Activity

18. the Mississippi River

19. Spain; Russia

Practicing Skills

20. red   22. 1778
21. a star burst   23. American forces

Citizenship Cooperative Activity

24. Students' papers should include ideas about obeying laws and voting.

Economics Activity

25. Students should research the cost, reliability, and performance of various brands of their chosen product and determine which brand makes the best merchandise.

Timesaving Tools

TeacherWorks™ All-In-One Planner and Resource Center

- **Interactive Teacher Edition** Access your Teacher Wraparound Edition and your classroom resources with a few easy clicks.
- **Interactive Lesson Planner** Planning has never been easier! Organize your week, month, semester, or year with all the lesson helps you need to make teaching creative, timely, and relevant.

Use Glencoe's **Presentation Plus!** multimedia teacher tool to easily present dynamic lessons that visually excite your students. Using Microsoft PowerPoint® you can customize the presentations to create your own personalized lessons.

TEACHING TRANSPARENCIES

Graphic Organizer 15 L2

Why It Matters Chapter Transparency 7 L2

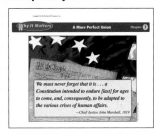

REVIEW AND REINFORCEMENT

Workbook Activity 7 L1

Time Line Activity 7 L2

Vocabulary Activity 7 L1

REVIEW AND REINFORCEMENT

Critical Thinking Skills Activity 7 L2

Take-Home Review Activity 7 L1

ENRICHMENT

Linking Past and Present Activity 7 L2

Primary Source Reading 7 L2

GEOGRAPHY

Geography and History Activity 7 L2

Meeting NCSS Standards

The following standards are highlighted in Chapter 7:

Section 1	VI	Power, Authority, & Governance: A, B, C, D, I
Section 2	V	Individuals, Groups, & Institutions: B, D, E, F, G
Section 3	X	Civic Ideals & Practices: A, F, G

FOLDABLES™ Study Organizer

Dinah Zike's Foldables are three-dimensional, interactive graphic organizers that help students practice basic writing skills, review key vocabulary terms, and identify main ideas. Additional chapter activities can be found in the **Reading and Study Skills Foldables** booklet.

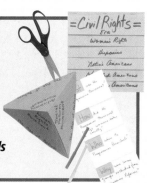

Chapter 7 Resources

ASSESSMENT AND EVALUATION

Chapter 7 Test
Form A L2

Chapter 7 Test
Form B L2

Standardized Test Practice
Workbook Activity 7 L2

Performance Assessment
Activity 7 L1, ELL

ExamView® Pro
Testmaker CD-ROM

MULTIMEDIA

- Vocabulary PuzzleMaker CD-ROM
- Interactive Tutor Self-Assessment CD-ROM
- ExamView® Pro Testmaker CD-ROM
- Audio Program
- American History Primary Source Document Library CD-ROM
- MindJogger Videoquiz
- Presentation Plus! CD-ROM
- TeacherWorks CD-ROM
- Interactive Student Edition CD-ROM
- Glencoe Skillbuilder Interactive Workbook CD-ROM, Level 1
- The American Republic to 1877 Video Program
- American Music: Hits Through History

SPANISH RESOURCES

The following Spanish language materials are available in the Spanish Resources Binder:

- Spanish Guided Reading Activities
- Spanish Reteaching Activities
- Spanish Quizzes and Tests
- Spanish Vocabulary Activity
- Spanish Take-Home Review Activity
- Spanish Summaries
- The Declaration of Independence and United States Constitution Spanish Translation

The following videotape programs are available
from Glencoe as supplements to Chapter 7:
- **George Washington: Founding Father** (ISBN 1-56501-377-8)*
- **Thomas Jefferson: Philosopher of Freedom** (ISBN 1-56501-502-9)*
- **Benjamin Franklin: Citizen of the World** (ISBN 1-56501-426-X)
- **Patrick Henry: Voice of Liberty** (ISBN 1-56501-645-9)

To order, call Glencoe at 1-800-334-7344. To find classroom resources to accompany many of these videos, check the following home pages:
A&E Television: www.aande.com
The History Channel: www.historychannel.com

*Available individually or in The American Republic to 1877 Video Library.

Use our Web site for additional resources. All essential content is covered in the Student Edition.

You and your students can visit tarvol1.glencoe.com, the Web site companion to **The American Republic to 1877**. This innovative integration of electronic and print media offers your students a wealth of opportunities. The student text directs students to the Web site for the following options:

- **Chapter Overviews**
- **Self-Check Quizzes**
- **Student Web Activities**
- **Textbook Updates**

Answers to the student Web activities are provided for you in the **Web Activity Lesson Plans.** Additional Web resources and Interactive Tutor Puzzles are also available.

Chapter 7 Resources

SECTION RESOURCES

Daily Objectives	Reproducible Resources	Multimedia Resources
SECTION 1 **The Articles of Confederation** 1. Examine how the weaknesses of the Articles led to instability. 2. Explain how the Confederation Congress dealt with the western lands.	📁 Reproducible Lesson Plan 7–1 📁 Daily Lecture and Discussion Notes 7–1 📁 Guided Reading Activity 7–1* 📁 Section Quiz 7–1* 📁 Reteaching Activity 7–1* 📁 Reading Essentials and Study Guide 7–1* 📁 Enrichment Activity 7–1	🖼 Daily Focus Skills Transparency 7–1 💿 Interactive Tutor Self-Assessment CD-ROM 💿 ExamView® Pro Testmaker CD-ROM 💿 Presentation Plus! CD-ROM 🎵 American Music: Hits Through History
SECTION 2 **Convention and Compromise** 1. Describe how the Constitutional Convention broke the deadlock over the form the new government would take. 2. Understand how the delegates answered the question of representation.	📁 Reproducible Lesson Plan 7–2 📁 Daily Lecture and Discussion Notes 7–2 📁 Guided Reading Activity 7–2* 📁 Section Quiz 7–2* 📁 Reteaching Activity 7–2* 📁 Reading Essentials and Study Guide 7–2* 📁 Enrichment Activity 7–2	🖼 Daily Focus Skills Transparency 7–2 📼 ABCNews Interactive™ Historic America Electronic Field Trips 💿 Interactive Tutor Self-Assessment CD-ROM 💿 ExamView® Pro Testmaker CD-ROM 💿 Presentation Plus! CD-ROM
SECTION 3 **A New Plan of Government** 1. Understand the roots of the Constitution. 2. Explain how the Constitution limits the power of government.	📁 Reproducible Lesson Plan 7–3 📁 Daily Lecture and Discussion Notes 7–3 📁 Guided Reading Activity 7–3* 📁 Section Quiz 7–3* 📁 Reteaching Activity 7–3* 📁 Reading Essentials and Study Guide 7–3* 📁 Enrichment Activity 7–3	🖼 Daily Focus Skills Transparency 7–3 💿 Vocabulary PuzzleMaker CD-ROM 💿 Interactive Tutor Self-Assessment CD-ROM 💿 ExamView® Pro Testmaker CD-ROM 💿 Presentation Plus! CD-ROM

0:00 OUT OF TIME?
Assign the Chapter 7 **Reading Essentials and Study Guide.** 📁

*Also Available in Spanish

 Blackline Master   Transparency   CD-ROM   DVD

Poster   🎵 Music Program   Audio Program   Videocassette

KEY TO ABILITY LEVELS

Teaching strategies have been coded.

L1 BASIC activities for all students
L2 AVERAGE activities for average to above-average students
L3 CHALLENGING activities for above-average students
ELL ENGLISH LANGUAGE LEARNER activities

NATIONAL GEOGRAPHIC   Teacher's Corner

INDEX TO
NATIONAL GEOGRAPHIC MAGAZINE

The following articles relate to this chapter.

- "L'Enfant's Washington," by Alice J. Hall, August 1991.
- "The Peales: America's First Family of Art," by Otto Friedrich, December 1990.
- "James Madison, Architect of the Constitution," by Alice J. Hall, September 1987.
- "George Washington's Patowmack Canal," by Wilbur E. Garrett, June 1987.

ADDITIONAL NATIONAL GEOGRAPHIC
SOCIETY PRODUCTS

To order the following, call National Geographic at 1-800-368-2728:

- *GeoKit: The American Revolution* (Kit)
- *United States/Territorial Growth* (Map)
- *National Geographic Desk Reference* (Book)
- *Democratic Government Series, "The United States"* (Video)
- *Branches of Government Series* (Video)
- *Washington, D.C.* (Video)

NGS ONLINE

Access National Geographic's Web site for current events, atlas updates, activities, links, interactive features, and archives.
www.nationalgeographic.com

MEETING SPECIAL NEEDS

In addition to the Differentiated Instruction strategies found in each section, the following resources are also suitable for your special needs students:

- *ExamView® Pro Testmaker CD-ROM* allows teachers to tailor tests by reducing answer choices.

- The *Audio Program* includes the entire narrative of the student edition so that less-proficient readers can listen to the words as they read them.

- The *Reading Essentials and Study Guide* provides the same content as the student edition but is written two grade levels below the textbook.

- *Guided Reading Activities* give less-proficient readers point-by-point instructions to increase comprehension as they read each textbook section.

- *Enrichment Activities* includes a stimulating collection of readings and activities for gifted and talented students.

From the Classroom of . . .

Gary Chinn
Rooftop K–8 School
San Francisco, CA

Compromise—My Rights or Yours?

Have students research both sides of the following debate, which formed the basis of the Federalist and Antifederalist standoff: the United States needs a strong central government versus individual states' rights. After researching, students should choose either a "for" or "against" stance toward the statement. Then have them produce posters, advertisements, flyers, or political cartoons to promote either the cause of the Federalists or the cause of the Antifederalists. Each student is responsible for a one-minute presentation, explaining his or her artwork and viewpoint. When presentations are completed, have a group of students collate the artwork into a portfolio that can be used during a class discussion or debate concerning the pros and cons of ratifying the Constitution.

ADDITIONAL RESOURCES FROM GLENCOE

- American Music: Cultural Traditions
- American Art and Architecture
- Outline Map Resource Book
- U.S. Desk Map
- Building Geography Skills for Life
- Inclusion for the Middle School Social Studies Classroom Strategies and Activities
- Teaching Strategies for the American History Classroom (Including Block Scheduling Pacing Guides)
- American Crafts Hands-On Activities
- American Games Hands-On Activities
- American History Flash Cards

Block Schedule

Activities that are suited to use within the block scheduling framework are identified by:

✓ **Performance Assessment**

Refer to Activity 7 in the Performance Assessment Activities and Rubrics booklet. 📦

Why It Matters Activity

Ask students to describe how the Constitution has influenced their lives. Have students think about current controversies about states' rights versus federal power; cases before the Supreme Court involving constitutional issues; or Bill of Rights issues such as free speech and search and seizure. Students may note that even though the Constitution has been interpreted differently to meet the changing needs of the country, it still serves as the framework for government and the justice system.

GLENCOE
TECHNOLOGY

The American Republic to 1877 Video Program

To learn more about the United States Constitution, have students view the Chapter 7 video "Discovering Our Constitution" from **The American Republic to 1877 Video Program.**

 Available in DVD and VHS

MindJogger Videoquiz

Use **MindJogger Videoquiz** to preview the Chapter 7 content.

 Available in VHS

CHAPTER 7
A More Perfect Union
1777–1790

Why It Matters

When the American colonies broke their political ties with Great Britain, they faced the task of forming independent governments at both the state and national levels. In 1788 the Constitution became the official plan of American government.

The Impact Today

Created to meet the needs of a changing nation, the Constitution has been the fundamental law of the United States for more than 200 years. It has served as a model for many constitutions all over the world.

 The American Republic to 1877 *Video* The chapter 7 video, *"Discovering Our Constitution,"* examines how the Constitution has preserved our government and the rights of citizens for over two hundred years.

1777
• Articles of Confederation written

1783
• Treaty of Paris

United States PRESIDENTS

1776   *1779*   *1782*

World

1778
• France goes to war against Britain

1780
• League of Armed Neutrality formed

1784
• Russians found colony on Kodiak Island, Alaska

190   CHAPTER 7   A More Perfect Union

📖 **Reading Strategy** **PURPOSE FOR READING**

Free Writes are an important strategy to explore student background knowledge and engage the student. The Framers of the Constitution created the document that today determines what federal laws can be passed and what individual rights citizens and residents enjoy. Ask students to imagine they are leaders of the new government. Ask: "What 'rights' and 'laws' do you think the citizens of this new government should be governed by?" Emphasize that there are no wrong answers to the questions—it is important that all ideas are accepted. Solicit random student responses and discuss as a class. Wrap up the activity by explaining that in this chapter they will study how the Constitution has influenced their lives. **L1**

FOLDABLES™
Study Organizer

Comparison Study Foldable Make this foldable to help you compare the Articles of Confederation to the U.S. Constitution.

Step 1 Fold a sheet of paper from side to side, leaving a 2-inch tab uncovered along the side.

> Fold it so the left edge lies 2 inches from the right edge.

Step 2 Turn the paper and fold it into thirds.

Step 3 Unfold and cut along the two inside fold lines.

> Cut along the two folds on the front flap to make 3 tabs.

Step 4 Label the foldable as shown.

> A More Perfect Union
> Articles of Confederation | Both | U.S. Constitution

Reading and Writing As you read the chapter, write what you learn about these documents under the appropriate tabs.

George Washington Addressing the Constitutional Convention by J.B. Stearns The Constitution created the basic form of American government.

1787
- Shays's Rebellion
- U.S. Constitution signed
- Northwest Ordinance passed

1788
- U.S. Constitution ratified

Washington 1789–1797

1785
- First hot air balloon crosses English Channel

1788
- British establish penal colony in Australia

1789
- French Revolution begins

1785 — *1788* — *1791*

HISTORY Online

Chapter Overview
Visit tarvol1.glencoe.com and click on **Chapter 7— Chapter Overviews** to preview chapter information.

FOLDABLES™
Study Organizer — Dinah Zike's Foldables

Purpose Students make and use a compare-contrast foldable to collect and organize information about two American plans of government—the Articles of Confederation and the United States Constitution. Students will compare and contrast characteristics of the two documents by using a Venn diagram.

📁 Have students complete **Reading and Study Skills Foldables** Activity 7. **L1**

HISTORY Online

Introduce students to chapter content and key terms by having them access **Chapter Overview 7** at tarvol1.glencoe.com

TIME LINE ACTIVITY

As students read the chapter, have them review the time line on pages 190–191. Ask students whether the Constitution was ratified before or after the beginning of the French Revolution.

More About the Art

The signing of the Constitution was by no means the end of the road to a constitutional government. The states needed to ratify it, and the process took time and debate. After rejecting the Constitution in 1788, North Carolina ratified it on November 21, 1789, after the United States government had already been established. Rhode Island was persuaded to ratify the Constitution on May 29, 1790, by the slimmest margin—34 to 32.

191

1 FOCUS

Section Overview

This section describes how the leaders of the new United States sought to define the power of government.

Reading Preview

Answers to Graphic: Answers will vary but may include: make laws, impose taxes, issue currency, conduct foreign relations, raise troops, and regulate trade.

Preteaching Vocabulary
Call on volunteers to define each of the entries in **Key Terms.** Point out that *bicameral* comes from the Latin prefix *bi-*, meaning "two," and the Latin root, *camera*, meaning "chamber."

The Articles of Confederation

Guide to Reading

Main Idea
The leaders of the new United States worked to define the powers of government.

Key Terms
constitution, bicameral, republic, petition, ordinance, depreciate

Reading Strategy
Organizing Information As you read the section, re-create the diagram below and in the ovals list the powers you think a national government should have.

Powers of government

Read to Learn
- how the weaknesses of the Articles of Confederation led to instability.
- how Congress dealt with the western lands.

Section Theme
Government and Democracy At both state and national levels, the government of the United States tried to define its powers.

Preview of Events

♦1775	♦1780	♦1785	♦1790

1777
Articles of Confederation are written

1781
All states approve Confederation government

1783
Treaty of Paris officially ends American Revolution

1787
Northwest Ordinance is passed

Phillis Wheatley

✭✭✭✭✭✭ AN ✭✭✭
American Story

Many Americans, from colonial times on, spoke out for liberty. One who lent her voice to the pursuit of freedom was poet Phillis Wheatley. Celebrated as the founder of the African American literary tradition, Wheatley wrote many poems supporting the colonists in the Revolutionary War. For many Americans, like Wheatley, the end of the Revolution was a reason for joy. American liberty had survived the challenge of war. But could it meet the demands of peace?

Thirteen Independent States

Although the Americans won their independence, they had trouble winning Britain's respect. Ignoring the terms of the Treaty of Paris, the British kept troops at frontier posts in American territory. The British believed the new American government was weak and ineffective. While Americans were fighting for their independence on the battlefield, they were also creating new governments. After rejecting British rule, they needed to establish their own political institutions.

192   CHAPTER 7   A More Perfect Union

SECTION RESOURCES

📁 Reproducible Masters
- Reproducible Lesson Plan 7–1
- Daily Lecture and Discussion Notes 7–1
- Guided Reading Activity 7–1
- Section Quiz 7–1
- Reteaching Activity 7–1
- Reading Essentials and Study Guide 7–1
- Enrichment Activity 7–1

Transparencies
- Daily Focus Skills Transparency 7–1

Multimedia
- American Music: Hits Through History
- Interactive Tutor Self-Assessment CD-ROM
- ExamView® Pro Testmaker CD-ROM
- Presentation Plus! CD-ROM

State Constitutions

In May 1776 the Continental Congress asked the states to organize their governments, and each moved quickly to adopt a state constitution, or plan of government. By the end of 1776, eight states had drafted constitutions. New York and Georgia followed suit in 1777, and Massachusetts in 1780. Connecticut and Rhode Island retained their colonial charters as state constitutions.

Their experience with British rule made Americans cautious about placing too much power in the hands of a single ruler. For that reason the states adopted constitutions that limited the power of the governor. Pennsylvania even replaced the office of governor with an elected council of 12 members.

Limiting Power

The states took other measures against concentration of power. They divided government functions between the governor (or Pennsylvania's council) and the legislature. Most states established two-house, or bicameral, legislatures to divide the power even further.

The writers of the constitutions not only wanted to prevent abuses of power in the states, but they also wanted to keep power in the hands of the people. State legislators were popularly elected, and elections were frequent. In most states, only white males who were at least 21 years old could vote. These citizens also had to own a certain amount of property or pay a certain amount of taxes. Some states allowed free African American males to vote.

The state constitutions restricted the powers of the governors, which made the legislatures the most powerful branch of government. The state legislatures struggled to make taxes more fair, but there were many disagreements. Going from dependent colonies to self-governing states brought new challenges.

✔ **Reading Check** Explaining Why did some states choose a bicameral legislature?

The Articles of Confederation

Forming a Republic

For Americans, establishing separate state governments was a much easier task than creating a central government. They agreed that their country should be a republic, a government in which citizens rule through elected representatives. They could not agree, however, on the organization and powers of their new republic.

At first most Americans favored a weak central government. They assumed the states would be very much like small, independent countries—similar to the way that the colonies had been set up. The states would act independently on most issues, working together through a central government only to wage war and handle relations with other nations.

Planning a New Government

In 1776 the Second Continental Congress appointed a committee to draw up a plan for a new government. The delegates in the Congress realized they needed a central government to

2 TEACH

Daily Lecture and Discussion Notes 7–1

Copyright © The McGraw-Hill Companies, Inc.

Daily Lecture and Discussion Notes

Chapter 7, Section 1

Did You Know ? The voting age in the United States remained 21 until the passage of the Twenty-Sixth Amendment in 1971, which lowered the age to 18. It was spurred on by Vietnam war protesters in the 1960s who argued that if people were old enough to fight in wars, they were old enough to vote.

I. **Thirteen Independent States** *(Pages 192–193)*

A. Americans needed to establish their own government and gain Britain's respect. This brought new challenges. The British believed the new government was weak and ineffective.

B. States organized their governments and adopted their own state constitutions. The writers wanted to prevent abuses of power and also wanted to keep power in the

Discussing Reasons Organize students into pairs. **Ask: Why is a government important? Should all people just do what they feel is right?** (*Discuss responses that partners present to the class. For example, not everyone agrees about what is right; some people purposely will do wrong.*) **L1, ELL**

✔ **Reading Check**

Answer: They wanted to diffuse rather than concentrate power.

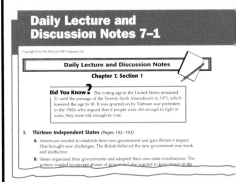

Did you know?

Voting in New Jersey under that state's Constitution, "any person" who met certain property qualifications could vote. Many women used that provision to vote until the state legislature took away that right in 1807.

📖 **Reading Strategy** ▶ **READING THE TEXT**

Questioning Before students begin to take in any new knowledge, prepare them by bringing to mind what they may already know about establishing and defining central government. Organize students into groups and assign each group one of the following questions: How does a new nation . . . plan for a national government, establish new land policies, pay off war debts, and establish relationships with other nations? Encourage students to exchange and answer questions within their group and to create "What if . . ." situations. Then form new groups, making sure that at least one representative from each problem topic is in each new group. Have the experts teach their topic to fellow group members. **L1** 📦

193

Guided Reading Activity 7-1

Name _____ Date _____ Class _____

★ Guided Reading Activity 7-1

DIRECTIONS: Recalling the Facts Use the information in your textbook to answer the questions. Use another sheet of paper if necessary.

1. What were the goals of the writers of the state constitutions?

2. State constitutions made which branch of government the most powerful?

3. What plan for a national government did Congress adopt in November 1777?

4. What could Congress do and not do under this plan?

5. When did the Confederation formally become the government of the United States?

6. Who proposed the 1784 plan to divide the Western territory into 10 self-governing districts?

7. What did the Ordinance of 1785 establish?

8. What area did the Northwest Ordinance create?

9. Why did the value of the money printed during the Revolutionary War plummet?

10. What did Robert Morris propose to help pay the national debt?

11. Why did the British trade policy upset American merchants?

12. What did Spain do to halt American expansion into its territory?

Why It Matters

The Land Ordinance of 1785 reserved one section in each township for use or support of public elementary schools in the future. The administration of public lands later became the responsibility of the United States Department of the Treasury, which was created in 1789. Congress established the General Land Office within the Treasury Department in 1812. In 1849 the General Land Office was transferred to the Department of the Interior. **Ask: What does it mean to survey the land?** *(to take a detailed measurement of an area of land)*

---

coordinate the war effort against Britain. After much debate the Congress adopted the committee's plan, the **Articles of Confederation,** in November 1777.

The Articles, America's first constitution, provided for a new central government under which the states gave up little of their power. For the states, the Articles of Confederation were "a firm league of friendship" in which each state retained "its sovereignty, freedom and independence."

Under the Articles of Confederation, the government—consisting of the Congress—had the authority to conduct foreign affairs, maintain armed forces, borrow money, and issue currency. Yet it could not regulate trade, force citizens to join the army, or impose taxes. If Congress needed to raise money or troops, it had to ask the state legislatures—but the states were not required to contribute. In addition the govern-ment lacked a chief executive. The Confederation government carried on much of its business, such as selling western lands, through congressional committees.

Under the new plan, each state had one vote in Congress, regardless of its population, and all states had to approve the Articles as well as any amendments. Despite this arrangement, the larger states believed that their population warranted having more votes. The states were also divided by whether or not they claimed land in the West. Maryland refused to approve the Articles until New York, Virginia, and other states abandoned claims to lands west of the Appalachian Mountains. Finally the states settled their differences. With Maryland's ratification, all 13 states had approved the Articles. On March 1, 1781, the Confederation formally became the government of the United States.

Why It Matters

Surveying the Land

When the Revolution began, only a few thousand white settlers lived west of the Appalachian Mountains. By the 1790s their numbers had increased to about 120,000. Through the Ordinance of 1785, Congress created a system for surveying—taking a detailed measurement of an area of land—and selling the western lands.

The Ordinance at first applied only to what was then called the Northwest Territory—present-day Ohio, Indiana, Michigan, Illinois, and Wisconsin. It established a system of land survey and settlement that we still use today.

The Land Ordinance led to the sale of large amounts of land and speeded settlement of the Northwest Territory.

DIFFERENTIATED INSTRUCTION

Reading Support Encourage students to consider the new nation's name: United States. Have them work individually or with partners to brainstorm words and images they associate with (1) a union that sought to take its place among the nations of the world *(United)* and (2) the individuality of the former colonies *(States)*. Call on volunteers to share responses as you introduce or review this section. **L2**

📁 Refer to *Inclusion for the Middle School Social Studies Classroom Strategies and Activities* in the TCR.

The Confederation Government

The years between 1781 and 1789 were a critical period for the young American republic. The Articles of Confederation did not provide a government strong enough to handle the problems facing the United States. The Congress had limited authority. It could not pass a law unless nine states voted in favor of it. Any attempt to change the Articles required the consent of all 13 states, making it difficult for the Congress to pass laws when there was any opposition. Despite its weaknesses, the Confederation did accomplish some important things. Under the Confederation government, Americans won their independence and expanded foreign trade. The Confederation also provided for settling and governing the nation's western territories.

Reading Check **Explaining** What powers did the Confederation government have?

New Land Policies

At the beginning of the Revolutionary War, only a few thousand settlers lived west of the Appalachian Mountains. By the 1790s the number was approaching 120,000. These western settlers hoped to organize their lands as states and join the union, but the Articles of Confederation contained no provision for adding new states. Congress realized that it had to extend its national authority over the frontier and bring order to this territory.

During the 1780s all of the states except Georgia gave up their claims to lands west of the Appalachians, and the central government took control of these lands. In 1784 Congress, under

Reading Check

Answer: conduct foreign affairs, maintain armed forces, borrow money, issue currency

What?Where?When?Who?

The Bald Eagle The bald eagle became America's national symbol in 1872. Benjamin Franklin suggested the turkey as the national bird. The American bald eagle, Franklin claimed, was "a bird of bad moral character . . . and often [full of lice]." Franklin stated, "The turkey is . . . a much more respectable bird, withal a true original native of America."

History *and the* Humanities

♪ American Music: Hits Through History, "College Hornpipe/ Belle Catherine"

🗀 American Biographies, *Phillis Wheatley* **L2**

Township: American Building Block

Western lands north of the Ohio River were divided into townships six miles to a side. Each township contained 36 square miles, or "sections."

The Northwest Territory was divided into townships, each with 36 sections.

Northwest Territory
Present-day state boundaries

INTERDISCIPLINARY CONNECTIONS ACTIVITY

Economics At this time many foreign coins were still being used, as well as coins that were struck privately. The only way to determine the value of a coin was to determine the weight of the gold used in making the coin. Have students conduct some research about how the value of paper currency was first determined and how it is determined today. **L2**

Land Speculator The Latin *specula*, which means "watchtower," is part of the etymology of *speculator*. It could be said that a speculator's attempts to second-guess the future are like trying to see far away from the top of a watchtower.

✓ Reading Check

Answer: It created a single Northwest Territory out of the lands north of the Ohio River and east of the Mississippi River.

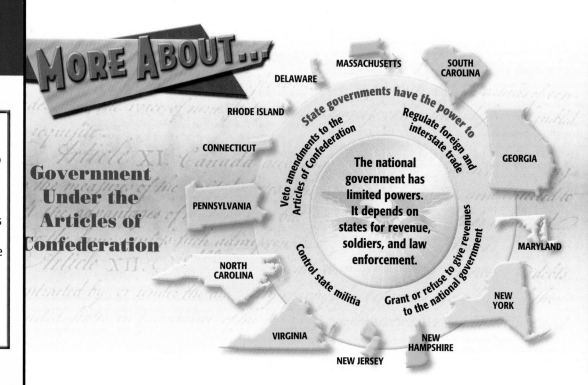

Government Under the Articles of Confederation

a plan proposed by Thomas Jefferson, divided the western territory into self-governing districts. When the number of people in a district reached the population of the smallest existing state, that district could petition, or apply to, Congress for statehood.

The Ordinance of 1785

In 1785 the Confederation Congress passed an ordinance, or law, that established a procedure for surveying and selling the western lands north of the Ohio River. The new law divided this massive territory into townships six miles long and six miles wide. These townships were to be further divided into 36 sections of 640 acres each that would be sold at public auction for at least a dollar an acre.

Land speculators viewed the law as an opportunity to cheaply accumulate large tracts of land. Concerned about lawless people moving into western lands, Richard Henry Lee, the president of Congress, urged that "the rights of property be clearly defined" by the government. Congress drafted another ordinance to protect the interests of hard-working settlers.

The Northwest Ordinance

The Northwest Ordinance, passed in 1787, created a single **Northwest Territory** out of the lands north of the Ohio River and east of the Mississippi River. The lands were to be divided into three to five smaller territories. When the population of a territory reached 60,000, the people could petition for statehood. Each new state would come into the Union with the same rights and privileges as the original 13 states.

The Northwest Ordinance included a bill of rights for the settlers, guaranteeing freedom of religion and trial by jury. It also stated, "There shall be neither slavery nor involuntary servitude in said territory." This clause marked the United States's first attempt to stop the spread of slavery.

The Confederation's western ordinances had an enormous effect on American expansion and development. The Ordinance of 1785 and the Northwest Ordinance opened the way for settlement of the Northwest Territory in a stable and orderly manner.

✓ Reading Check **Explaining** What was the purpose of the Northwest Ordinance?

CRITICAL THINKING ACTIVITY

Identifying Central Issues Have students work in groups of three and list the following, with each member completing one list:
• the reasons a weak national government was created
• the reasons a strong national government was created
• what showed that government under the Articles of Confederation was not working.
Give group members a chance to share their lists, then compare them with those of other groups. **L2**

Trouble on Two Fronts

Despite its accomplishments, the Confederation government had so little power that it could not deal with the country's financial problems. It also failed to resolve problems with Britain and Spain.

📊 Economics

Financial Problems

By 1781 the money printed during the Revolutionary War had depreciated, or fallen in value, so far that it was almost worthless. Unable to collect taxes, both the Continental Congress and the states had printed their own paper money. No gold or silver backed up these bills. The value of the bills plummeted, while the price of food and other goods soared. Between 1779 and 1781, the number of Continental dollars required to buy one Spanish silver dollar rose from 40 to 146. In Boston and some other areas, high prices led to food riots.

Fighting the war left the Continental Congress with a large debt. Congress had borrowed money from American citizens and foreign governments during the war. It still owed the Revolutionary soldiers their pay for military service. Lacking the power to tax, the Confederation could not pay its debts. It requested funds from the states, but the states contributed only a small portion of the money needed.

Robert Morris's Import Tax

In 1781, faced with a total collapse of the country's finances, Congress created a department of finance under Philadelphia merchant **Robert Morris.** While serving in Congress, Morris had proposed a 5 percent tax on imported goods to help pay the national debt.

The plan required that the Articles of Confederation be changed to give Congress the power to levy the tax. Although 12 states approved the plan, Rhode Island's opposition killed the measure. A second effort in 1783 also failed to win unanimous approval. The financial crisis only worsened.

Problems with Britain

The weaknesses of the new American government became more evident as the United States encountered problems with other countries. In the Treaty of Paris of 1783, Britain had promised to withdraw from the lands east of the Mississippi River. Yet British troops continued to occupy several strategic forts in the Great Lakes region.

📷 *Picturing* **History**

Pennsylvania merchant and banker Robert Morris became Superintendent of Finance in May 1781. **What reform did Morris propose to help the nation's finances?**

Continental currency

Robert Morris

📷 *Picturing* **History**

Robert Morris (1734–1806) became politically active before the American Revolution. As a member of the Continental Congress from 1776 to 1778, he signed the Declaration of Independence. He supervised the finances of the Revolutionary War, using his own personal credit. He established the oldest financial institution in the United States, the Bank of North America, in 1781 in Philadelphia. After serving as a delegate to the Constitutional Convention of 1787, he served in the United States Senate. He lost his money in land speculation and spent three years in a prison for debtors.

Answer: a 5 percent tax on imported goods to help pay off the national debt

3 ASSESS

Assign Section 1 Assessment as homework or as an in-class activity.

💿 Have students use **Interactive Tutor Self-Assessment CD-ROM.**

L2

Section Quiz 7–1

Name _____ Date _____ Class _____

★ **Chapter 7**   Score ____

Section Quiz 7-1

DIRECTIONS: Matching Match the items in Column A with the items in Column B. Write the correct letters in the blanks. *(10 points each)*

Column A	Column B
____ **1.** plan of government	**A.** Articles of Confederation
____ **2.** two-house legislatures	**B.** constitution
____ **3.** America's first constitution	**C.** ordinance
____ **4.** law	**D.** depreciated
____ **5.** fallen in value	**E.** bicameral

EXTENDING THE CONTENT

John Dickinson The Articles of Confederation were written by a committee of the Second Continental Congress of the thirteen colonies, headed by John Dickinson. Eight days after Congress voted to accept the Declaration of Independence on July 12, 1776, Dickinson presented a report on the proposed Articles to the Congress. In his initial report, Dickinson proposed a strong central government with equal representation for the states, control over the western lands, and the power to levy taxes. Dickinson's proposed articles were changed substantially before being sent to all the states for ratification in November 1777.

✓ Reading Check

Answer: to halt American expansion into territory it claimed

L1

Reteaching Activity 7–1

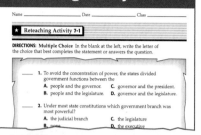

L1, ELL

Reading Essentials and Study Guide 7–1

L3

Enrichment Activity 7–1

4 CLOSE

Have students name strengths and weaknesses of the Articles of Confederation. Ask them to explain why a weak government plan could cause problems for a growing country.

Fact · Fiction · Folklore

John Hanson

The Forgotten President? Who was the first president of the United States? Was it George Washington—or John Hanson? Some historians consider Hanson the first United States president because he was the first to serve in the office in 1781 under the Articles of Confederation. Other historians argue that Hanson was the head of Congress, but not until George Washington began his term in 1789 did the nation have a "true" president.

British trade policy caused other problems. American merchants complained that the British were keeping Americans out of the West Indies and other profitable British markets.

In 1785 Congress sent **John Adams** to London to discuss these difficulties. The British, however, were not willing to talk. They pointed to the failure of the United States to honor *its* promises made in the Treaty of Paris. The British claimed that Americans had agreed to pay Loyalists for the property taken from them during the Revolutionary War. The Congress had, in fact, recommended that the states pay the Loyalists, but the states had refused.

Problems With Spain

If American relations with Great Britain were poor, affairs with Spain were worse. Spain, which held Florida as well as lands west of the Mississippi River, was anxious to halt American expansion into the territory it claimed. As a result, Spain closed the lower Mississippi River to American shipping in 1784. Western settlers depended on the Mississippi River for commerce. As **John Jay,** the American secretary of foreign affairs, had noted a few years earlier:

❝The Americans, almost to a man, believed that God Almighty had made that river a highway for the people of the upper country to go to sea by.❞

In 1786 American diplomats reached an agreement with Spain. Representatives from the Southern states, however, blocked the agreement because it did not include the right to use the Mississippi River.

The weakness of the Confederation and its inability to deal with problems worried many leaders. George Washington described the government as "little more than the shadow without the substance." Many Americans began to agree that the country needed a stronger government.

✓ **Reading Check** **Analyzing** Why did Spain close the lower Mississippi River to American trade?

SECTION 1 ASSESSMENT

Checking for Understanding

1. **Key Terms** Use each of these terms in a complete sentence that will help explain its meaning: constitution, bicameral, republic, petition, ordinance, depreciate.

2. **Reviewing Facts** Describe the country's financial problems after the Revolutionary War.

Reviewing Themes

3. **Government and Democracy** Why did most states limit the power of their governors and divide the legislature into two bodies?

Critical Thinking

4. **Predicting Consequences** What effect do you think the Northwest Ordinance had on Native Americans?

5. **Organizing Information** Re-create the diagram below and summarize the strengths and weaknesses of the Confederation government.

The Articles of Confederation	
Strengths	Weaknesses

Analyzing Visuals

6. **Geography Skills** Study the material on pages 194 and 195 about the Ordinance of 1785. Then answer these questions. What present-day states were created from the Northwest Territory? How many sections are in a township?

Interdisciplinary Activity

Citizenship Imagine you are an American citizen in the 1780s. Create a poster that defends the Articles of Confederation. Be sure to include reasons the Confederation Congress is needed.

198 CHAPTER 7 A More Perfect Union

SECTION 1 ASSESSMENT ANSWERS

1. Student work should reflect correct use of terms.
2. Currency had depreciated; the government could not tax to pay its war debt.
3. British rule made them cautious about giving too much power to single rulers or political bodies.
4. Native Americans were forced to fight or give up their lands and move.
5. Strengths: could conduct foreign affairs, issue currency, borrow money, maintain armed forces; Weaknesses: Congress could not pass a law unless nine states voted in favor of it and the consent of all states was required to change the Articles; it could not regulate trade, force soldiers to join the army, or impose taxes
6. Illinois, Indiana, Michigan, Ohio, and Wisconsin; 36

Interdisciplinary Activity Posters should cite reasons to keep the existing government.

SECTION 2 Convention and Compromise

Guide to Reading

Main Idea
The new Constitution corrected the weaknesses of government under the Articles of Confederation.

Key Terms
depression, manumission, proportional, compromise

Reading Strategy
Organizing Information As you read the section, re-create the diagram below. In the boxes, describe the role each individual played in creating the new plan of government.

	Role
Edmund Randolph	
James Madison	
Roger Sherman	

Read to Learn
• how the Constitutional Convention broke the deadlock over the form the new government would take.
• how the delegates answered the question of representation.

Section Theme
Groups and Institutions National leaders worked to produce a new constitution for the United States.

Preview of Events

◆1783	◆1785	◆1787	◆1789

1784
Rhode Island passes plan to end slavery

September 1786
Daniel Shays leads rebellion

May 1787
Delegates meet to revise Articles of Confederation

September 1787
Delegates sign draft of Constitution

George Washington

★★★★★★★★★★
AN American Story

By 1786 many Americans observed that the Confederation was not working. George Washington himself agreed that the United States was really "thirteen Sovereignties pulling against each other."

In the spring of 1787, Washington joined delegates from Virginia and 11 other states who gathered in Philadelphia to address this problem. Rhode Island decided not to participate. The delegates came "for the sole and express purpose of revising the Articles of Confederation."

Economic Depression

The call to revise the Articles of Confederation came while the young nation faced difficult problems. Many Americans believed that the Confederation government was too weak to deal with these challenges.

After the Revolutionary War ended, the United States went through a depression, a period when economic activity slowed and unemployment

CHAPTER 7   A More Perfect Union   **199**

---

1 FOCUS

Section Overview
This section explains how weaknesses in the Articles of Confederation prompted national leaders to create a new Constitution.

BELLRINGER
Skillbuilder Activity

 Project transparency and have students answer the question.

Daily Focus Skills Transparency 7–2

Reading Preview

Answers to Graphic: Randolph: introduced the Virginia Plan; Madison: put forth the basic ideas of the Virginia Plan; Sherman: proposed the Great Compromise

Preteaching Vocabulary
Point out that the term *compromise* can be used as a noun or a verb. Have students write two sentences, one using *compromise* as a noun, the other as a verb.

SECTION RESOURCES

📁 **Reproducible Masters**
• Reproducible Lesson Plan 7–2
• Daily Lecture and Discussion Notes 7–2
• Guided Reading Activity 7–2
• Section Quiz 7–2
• Reteaching Activity 7–2
• Reading Essentials and Study Guide 7–2
• Enrichment Activity 7–2

📄 **Transparencies**
• Daily Focus Skills Transparency 7–2

Multimedia
▣ ABCNews Interactive™ Historic America Electronic Field Trips
◉ Interactive Tutor Self-Assessment CD-ROM
◉ ExamView® Pro Testmaker CD-ROM
◉ Presentation Plus! CD-ROM

2 TEACH

Identifying Relationships Have students discuss how a government might find out that some of its decisions are not working. Invite students to speculate about the relationship between Shays's Rebellion and the move a few months later to revise the Articles of Confederation and then replace them with the Constitution. *(Students may suggest that the rebellion made it clear that the Articles of Confederation were not working and made citizens fearful enough to give up some freedoms for safety.)* **L1**

Picturing **History**

Donations for the militia did not come from average citizens because many of them sympathized with the farmers. Instead, Boston merchants paid for the force that put down Shays's Rebellion. **Answer:** People were worried that the government could not control unrest and prevent violence.

Picturing **History**

Only through donations was Massachusetts able to raise a militia to defeat Shays. **Why did Shays's Rebellion frighten many Americans?**

increased. Southern plantations had been damaged during the war, and rice exports dropped sharply. Trade also fell off when the British closed the profitable West Indies (Caribbean) market to American merchants. What little money there was went to pay foreign debts, and a serious currency shortage resulted.

Difficult Times for Farmers

American farmers suffered because they could not sell their goods. They had problems paying the requests for money that the states levied to meet Revolutionary War debts. As a result state officials seized farmers' lands to pay their debts and threw many farmers into jail. Grumblings of protest soon grew into revolt.

Shays's Rebellion

Resentment grew especially strong in Massachusetts. Farmers viewed the new government as just another form of tyranny. They wanted the government to issue paper money and make new policies to relieve debtors. In a letter to state officials, some farmers proclaimed:

> **❝**Surely your honours are not strangers to the distresses [problems] of the people but . . . know that many of our good inhabitants are now confined in [jail] for debt and taxes.**❞**

In 1786 angry farmers lashed out. Led by **Daniel Shays,** a former Continental Army captain, they forced courts in western Massachusetts to close so judges could not confiscate farmers' lands.

In January 1787 Shays led more than 1,000 farmers toward the federal arsenal in **Springfield,** Massachusetts, for arms and ammunition. The state militia ordered the advancing farmers to halt, then fired over their heads. The farmers did not stop, and the militia fired again, killing four rebels. Shays and his followers scattered, and the uprising was over.

Shays's Rebellion frightened many Americans. They worried that the government could not control unrest and prevent violence. On hearing of the rebellion, George Washington wondered whether "mankind, when left to themselves, are unfit for their own government." Thomas Jefferson, minister to France at the time, had a different view. "A little rebellion, now and then," he wrote, "is a good thing."

The Issue of Slavery

The Revolutionary War brought attention to the contradiction between the American battle for liberty and the practice of slavery. Between 1776 and 1786, 11 states—all except South Carolina and Georgia—outlawed or heavily taxed the importation of enslaved people.

Although slavery was not a major source of labor in the North, it existed and was legal in all the Northern states. Many individuals and groups began to work to end the institution of slavery. In 1774 Quakers in Pennsylvania organized the first American antislavery society. Six

---

COOPERATIVE LEARNING ACTIVITY

Writing Editorials Direct students' attention to the statements made by George Washington and Thomas Jefferson in response to Shays's Rebellion. Invite two groups of students to create editorials that expand upon those statements. Have an editorial director lead the writing and a representative from each group present it to the class for discussion. **L1**

years later Pennsylvania passed a law that provided for the gradual freeing of enslaved people.

Between 1783 and 1804, Connecticut, Rhode Island, New York, and New Jersey passed laws that gradually ended slavery. Still, free African Americans faced discrimination. They were barred from many public places. Few states gave free African Americans the right to vote. The children of most free blacks had to attend separate schools. Free African Americans established their own institutions—churches, schools, and mutual-aid societies—to seek opportunity.

The states south of Pennsylvania clung to the institution of slavery. The plantation system of the South had been built on slavery, and many Southerners feared that their economy could not survive without it. Nonetheless, an increasing number of slaveholders began freeing the enslaved people that they held after the war. Virginia passed a law that encouraged manumission, the freeing of individual enslaved persons, and the state's population of free African Americans grew.

The abolition of slavery in the North divided the new country on the critical issue of whether people should be allowed to hold other human beings in bondage. This division came at the time when many American leaders had decided that the Articles of Confederation needed strengthening. In the summer of 1787, when state representatives assembled to plan a new government, they compromised on this issue. It would take years of debate, bloodshed, and ultimately a war to settle the slavery question.

✔**Reading Check** **Explaining** Why did Southern states support slavery?

A Call for Change

The American Revolution had led to a union of 13 states, but it had not yet created a nation. Some leaders were satisfied with a system of independent state governments that resembled the old colonial governments. Others saw a strong national government as the solution to America's problems. They demanded a reform of the Articles of Confederation.

Two Americans active in the movement for change were **James Madison,** a Virginia planter, and **Alexander Hamilton,** a New York lawyer. In September 1786, Hamilton proposed calling a convention in Philadelphia to discuss trade issues. He also suggested that this convention consider what possible changes were needed to make

❝the Constitution of the Federal Government adequate to the exigencies [needs] of the Union.❞

At first George Washington was not enthusiastic about the movement to revise the Articles of Confederation. When he heard the news of Shays's Rebellion, Washington changed his mind. After Washington agreed to attend the Philadelphia convention, the meeting took on greater significance.

✔**Reading Check** **Evaluating** Why did Madison and Hamilton call for a convention in 1787?

Picturing **History**

Philadelphia preachers Richard Allen (left) and Absalom Jones (right) founded the Free African Society and later set up the first African American churches. **What challenges did free African Americans face?**

201

✔**Reading Check**

Answer: Southerners feared that their economy would not survive without it.

✔**Reading Check**

Answer: to discuss trade issues and address changes to the Articles of Confederation to meet the needs of the Union

Picturing **History**

Born in slavery, Richard Allen was freed after his master became a Methodist. In 1784 Allen was ordained a Methodist minister and became an itinerant preacher. After he and Absalom Jones founded an independent Methodist church for black members, Allen was appointed its first bishop. In the early 1800s, some African American movements encouraged immigration to Africa. Allen and Jones opposed this idea, stating that since "our ancestors (not of choice) were the first successful cultivators of the wilds of America, we their descendants feel ourselves entitled to participate in the blessings of her soil. . . ." **Answer:** Answers may include: they were barred from public places; few had the right to vote; and children had to attend separate schools.

L1, ELL

Guided Reading Activity 7–2

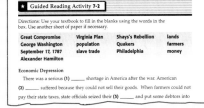

Name _____ Date _____ Class _____

★ **Guided Reading Activity 7-2**

Directions: Use your textbook to fill in the blanks using the words in the box. Use another sheet of paper if necessary.

Great Compromise	Virginia Plan	Shays's Rebellion	lands
George Washington	population	Quakers	farmers
September 17, 1787	slave trade	Philadelphia	money
Alexander Hamilton			

Economic Depression

There was a serious **(1)** _____ shortage in America after the war. American **(2)** _____ suffered because they could not sell their goods. When farmers could not pay their state taxes, state officials seized their **(3)** _____ and put some debtors into

**ABCNEWS
INTERACTIVE™**

**VIDEOCASSETTE
Historic America Electronic Field Trips**

View **Chapter 7** to learn more about Philadelphia's Independence Hall.

Did you know?

The oldest person to sign the Constitution was Benjamin Franklin (81). The youngest person was Jonathan Dayton (26).

The Constitutional Convention

The Philadelphia meeting began in May 1787 and continued through one of the hottest summers on record. The 55 delegates included planters, merchants, lawyers, physicians, generals, governors, and a college president. Three of the delegates were under 30 years of age, and one, Benjamin Franklin, was over 80. Many were well educated. At a time when only one white man in 1,000 went to college, 26 of the delegates had college degrees. Native Americans, African Americans, and women were not considered part of the political process, so none attended.

Several men stood out as leaders. The presence of George Washington and Benjamin Franklin ensured that many people would trust the Convention's work. Two Philadelphians also played key roles. James Wilson often read Franklin's speeches and did important work on the details of the Constitution. Gouverneur Morris, a powerful speaker and writer, wrote the final draft of the Constitution.

From Virginia came Edmund Randolph and James Madison. Both were keen supporters of a strong national government. Madison's careful notes are the major source of information about the Convention's work. Madison is often called the **Father of the Constitution** because he was the author of the basic plan of government that the Convention adopted.

Organization

The Convention began by unanimously choosing George Washington to preside over the meetings. It also decided that each state would have one vote on all questions. A simple majority vote of those states present would make decisions. No meetings could be held unless delegates from at least seven of the 13 states were present. The delegates decided to close their doors to the public and keep the sessions secret. This was a key decision because it made it possible for the delegates to talk freely.

The Virginia Plan

After the rules were adopted, the Convention opened with a surprise. It came from the Virginia delegation. Edmund Randolph proposed

America's *Architecture*

Independence Hall The Pennsylvania State House, later known as Independence Hall, was the site of the signing of the Declaration of Independence and of the Constitutional Convention. Independence Hall was restored in 1950 and is now maintained as a museum. **Why do you think this site was used for many important events?**

INTERDISCIPLINARY CONNECTIONS ACTIVITY

Language Arts *The Prince of Parthia* by Thomas Godfrey was presented in Philadelphia in 1767. This historical drama, the first written by an American and performed by professional actors, is set in the ancient Middle East. Mercy Otis Warren's 1775 play *The Group* is a satire written to ridicule British sympathizers and corrupt officials. Like Warren, many playwrights of the era chose contemporary subjects. Have students research various playwrights and dramas in the library and determine how drama changed during early American history. Students should present their findings to the class. **L2**

People In History

James Madison 1751–1836

James Madison, only 36 at the time of the Constitutional Convention, was the best prepared of the delegates. In the months before the convention, he had made a detailed study of government. He read hundreds of books on history, politics, and economics. He also corresponded with Thomas Jefferson.

Madison looked for ways to build a strong but fair system of government. He knew that republics were considered weaker than monarchies because kings or queens could use their authority to act quickly and decisively. Who would provide the same leadership in a republic? At the same time, Madison was concerned about protecting the people from misuse of power. As he searched for solutions, Madison worked out a new plan that included a system of balances among different functions of government. The delegates adopted many of Madison's ideas in what would become the United States Constitution.

that the delegates create a strong national government instead of revising the Articles of Confederation. He introduced the **Virginia Plan,** which was largely the work of James Madison. The plan called for a two-house legislature, a chief executive chosen by the legislature, and a court system. The members of the lower house of the legislature would be elected by the people. The members of the upper house would be chosen by the lower house. In both houses the number of representatives would be proportional, or corresponding in size, to the population of each state. This would give Virginia many more delegates than Delaware, the state with the smallest population.

Delegates from Delaware, New Jersey, and other small states immediately objected to the plan. They preferred the Confederation system in which all states were represented equally.

Delegates unhappy with the Virginia Plan rallied around **William Paterson** of New Jersey. On June 15 he presented an alternative plan that revised the Articles of Confederation, which was all the convention was empowered to do.

The New Jersey Plan

The **New Jersey Plan** kept the Confederation's one-house legislature, with one vote for each state. Congress, however, could set taxes and regulate trade—powers it did not have under the Articles. Congress would elect a weak executive branch consisting of more than one person.

Paterson argued that the Convention should not deprive the smaller states of the equality they had under the Articles. Thus, his plan was designed simply to amend the Articles.

✓**Reading Check** **Explaining** Why did some delegates criticize the Virginia Plan?

Compromise Wins Out

The convention delegates had to decide whether they were simply revising the Articles of Confederation or writing a constitution for a new national government. On June 19 the states voted to work toward a national government based on the Virginia Plan, but they still had to resolve the thorny issue of representation that divided the large and small states.

CHAPTER 7   A More Perfect Union   **203**

✓**Reading Check**

Answer: Representation was proportional, and critics wanted all states represented equally.

People In History

James Madison (1751–1836) argued passionately for ideas contained in the Constitution. Despite his zealous support for the Constitution, later in his life he felt awkward about being called the "Father of the Constitution." After one especially fiery speech, Madison complained to a friend, "Why didn't you pull me when you heard me going like that?" His friend replied, "I would rather have laid a finger on the lightning."

Did you know

Philadelphia took great efforts to give the delegates a quiet atmosphere during the convention. The city went so far as to cover the paved road around the hall with dirt to reduce noise.

CURRICULUM CONNECTION

Science As the Constitutional Convention drew to a close, delegates saw the demonstration of a possible new form of transportation. Meeting at the Delaware River on August 22, they boarded a steam-powered boat built by John Fitch and rode along at 3 mph (4.8 kph).

Reading Strategy   READING THE TEXT

Reading and Saying Something Write the following generalization on the chalkboard: The Constitution shows more of what the delegates did not want than what they did want. Have students skim the section to locate facts and details that either support or challenge this generalization. Have each student write a paragraph supporting their conclusions. **L2**

Picturing History

Independence Hall is also known as the Old State House. It stands only a block from the site of Carpenters' Hall, where the First Continental Congress met in 1774.
Answer: nine

3 ASSESS

Assign Section 2 Assessment as homework or as an in-class activity.

🕐 Have students use **Interactive Tutor Self-Assessment CD-ROM.**

L2

Section Quiz 7–2

Name	Date	Class

⭐ Chapter 7 ___ Score

Section Quiz 7-2

DIRECTIONS: Matching Match the items in Column A with the items in Column B. Write the correct letters in the blanks. *(10 points each)*

Column A	Column B
___ 1. led a rebellion	A. manumission
___ 2. antislavery society	B. Roger Sherman
___ 3. freeing of individual enslaved persons	C. James Madison
___ 4. author of Virginia Plan	D. Daniel Shays
___ 5. proposed Great Compromise	E. Quakers

DIRECTIONS: Multi...

L1

Reteaching Activity 7–2

Name	Date	Class

⭐ **Reteaching Activity 7-2**

DIRECTIONS: Determining Cause and Effect After each *Cause*, write the letter of its *Effect* from the Fact Bank.

1. Cause: Rice exports dropped sharply; trade fell off when Great Britain closed the West Indian market to Americans; the little bit of money available went to pay foreign debt.
Effect: ___

2. Cause: American farmers could not pay the taxes levied by the states.
Effect: ___

3. Cause: Daniel Shays led Shays's Rebellion, during which four rebels

6. Cause: The proceedings of the convention were kept secret.
Effect: ___

7. Cause: In the Virginia Plan, the number of representatives in the legislature would correspond to a state's population.
Effect: ___

8. Cause: Southern states refused to abolish slavery.

Picturing History

Delegates to the Constitutional Convention met in this room at Independence Hall. **How many states had to ratify the Constitution before it went into effect?**

Discussion and Disagreement

As the convention delegates struggled to deal with difficult questions, tempers and temperatures grew hotter. How were the members of Congress to be elected? How would state representation be determined in the upper and lower houses? Were enslaved people to be counted as part of the population on which representation was based?

🏛 Citizenship
The Great Compromise

Under Franklin's leadership, the convention appointed a "grand committee" to try to resolve their disagreements. **Roger Sherman** of Connecticut suggested what came to be known as the **Great Compromise.** A compromise is an agreement between two or more sides in which each side gives up some of what it wants.

Sherman proposed a two-house legislature. In the lower house—the House of Representatives—the number of seats for each state would vary according to the state's population. In the upper house—the Senate—each state would have two members.

The Three-Fifths Compromise

Another major compromise by the delegates dealt with counting enslaved people. Southern states wanted to include the enslaved in their population counts to gain delegates in the House of Representatives. Northern states objected to this idea because enslaved people were legally considered property. Some delegates from Northern states argued that the enslaved, as property, should be counted for the purpose of taxation but not representation. However, neither side considered giving enslaved people the right to vote.

The committee's solution, known as the **Three-Fifths Compromise,** was to count each enslaved person as three-fifths of a free person for both taxation and representation. In other words, every five enslaved persons would equal three free persons. On July 12 the convention delegates voted to approve the Three-Fifths Compromise. Four days later, they agreed that each state should elect two senators.

EXTENDING THE CONTENT

Public Scrutiny of Political Figures Today many political commentators and reporters comment on the personal lives and personalities of government officials. During the Constitutional Convention, William Pierce, a delegate from Georgia, recorded vivid impressions of his colleagues. Pierce described Roger Sherman as "the oddest-shaped character I ever remember to have met with. He is awkward, un-meaning and unaccountably strange in his manner . . . and yet he deserves infinite praise—no Man has a better heart or a clearer Head." Pierce characterized Robert Morris as a man "who never once spoke on any point" and who later wound up in debtors' prison. Pierce praised Benjamin Franklin as "the greatest philosopher of the present age."

Slave Trade

The convention needed to resolve another difficult issue that divided the Northern and Southern states. Having banned the slave trade within their borders, Northern states wanted to prohibit it throughout the nation. Southern states considered slavery and the slave trade essential to their economies. To keep the Southern states in the nation, Northerners agreed that the Congress could not interfere with the slave trade until 1808. Beginning that year Congress could limit the slave trade if it chose to.

Bill of Rights

George Mason of Virginia proposed a bill of rights to be included in the Constitution. Some delegates worried that without the protection of a bill of rights the new national government might abuse its power. However, most of the delegates believed that the Constitution, with its carefully defined listing of government powers, provided adequate protection of individual rights. Mason's proposal was defeated.

Approving the Constitution

The committees finished their work on the Constitution in late summer. On September 17, 1787, the delegates assembled in the Philadelphia State House to sign the document. Franklin made a final plea for approval:

> ❝I consent to this Constitution because I expect no better, and because I am not sure, that it is not the best.❞

Three delegates refused to sign—Elbridge Gerry of Massachusetts, and Edmund Randolph and George Mason of Virginia. Gerry and Mason would not sign without a bill of rights.

The Confederation Congress then sent the approved draft of the Constitution to the states for consideration. To amend the Articles of Confederation had required unanimous approval of the states. Getting a unanimous vote had proved slow and frustrating. Therefore, the delegates agreed to change the approval process for the Constitution. When 9 of the 13 states had approved, the new government of the United States would come into existence. 📖 *(See pages 232–253 for the entire text of the Constitution.)*

✓**Reading Check** **Analyzing** Who refused to sign the Constitution? Explain why.

Student Web Activity
Visit tarvol1.glencoe.com and click on **Chapter 7—Student Web Activities** for an activity on the Constitutional Convention.

SECTION 2 ASSESSMENT

Checking for Understanding

1. **Key Terms** Use the terms that follow to write a newspaper article about the main events of the Constitutional Convention: depression, manumission, proportional, compromise.

2. **Reviewing Facts** Explain what caused Shays's Rebellion. What was one effect?

Reviewing Themes

3. **Groups and Institutions** How did the Great Compromise satisfy both the small and the large states on the question of representation?

Critical Thinking

4. **Summarizing Information** You are asked to write a 30-second news broadcast to announce the agreement made in the Great Compromise. What would you include in the broadcast?

5. **Analyzing Information** Re-create the diagram below and identify arguments for and against ratifying the Constitution.

Ratification	
Arguments for	Arguments against

Analyzing Visuals

6. **Picturing History** Examine the images that appear on pages 202 and 204. What do they show? Where are they located? Why are these places important in the nation's history?

Interdisciplinary Activity

Government Create a political cartoon that illustrates the view of either the Northern states or the Southern states on how enslaved people should be counted for representation.

✓**Reading Check**

Answer: Elbridge Gerry, Edmund Randolph, and George Mason; Gerry and Mason would not sign the Constitution without a bill of rights.

Objectives and answers to the student activity can be found in the **Web Activity Lesson Plan** feature at tarvol1.glencoe.com

L1, ELL

Reading Essentials and Study Guide 7-2

Study Guide

Chapter 7, Section 2
For use with textbook pages 199–205

CONVENTION AND COMPROMISE

KEY TERMS

Depression	A period of slow economic activity and increased unemployment (page 199)
manumission	The freeing of individual enslaved persons (page 201)
proportional	To match up in size (page 203)
compromise	An agreement between two or more sides in which each side gives up some of what it wants (page 204)

DRAWING FROM EXPERIENCE

Have you ever had a disagreement with someone? Did you and the other person agree to compromise, that is give up something to gain something more important? What did you give up? What did...

L3

Enrichment Activity 7-2

Name _____ Date _____ Class _____

⭐ **Enrichment Activity 7-2** ⭐ 🔍 ⭐

The Founders

When the Constitutional Convention met, a young delegate from Georgia, William Pierce, wrote brief character sketches of his fellow delegates. Below are selections from these sketches.

Alexander Hamilton "Colo. [Colonel] Hamilton is deservedly celebrated for his talents... [He] requires time to think...

James Madison "Mr. Madison is a character who has long been in public life, and what is very remarkable every Person seems to acknowledge his greatness...

Benjamin Franklin "Dr. Franklin is well-known to be the greatest philosopher of the present age.... He is ... a most extraordinary Man and tells a story in a style...

4 CLOSE

Call on volunteers to name as many ways as they can in which the Constitution reflects compromise.

SECTION 2 ASSESSMENT ANSWERS

1. Student work should reflect correct use of terms.

2. Farmers wanted the government to help them. Possible effects: some farmers were killed; support grew for government; increased support for revision of Articles

3. In the House of Representatives, seats are based on a state's population; in the Senate, each state has two seats.

4. information about the role of Roger Sherman and the two-house legislature

5. For: a strong national government, proportional representation, an end to the slave trade; Against: independent state governments, equal representation, a continuation of the slave trade

6. Independence Hall in Philadelphia, Pennsylvania; the Declaration of Independence and the Constitution were signed here.

Interdisciplinary Activity Cartoons should present valid views.

205

Critical Thinking
SKILLBUILDER

TEACH

Making Comparisons Making comparisons is a life skill that people utilize in everyday transactions. In this chapter students compare the powers of the federal government under the Articles of Confederation and under the Constitution. As students examine the chart, call on volunteers to explain the importance of each power being compared.

In this lesson students should see that charting is a valuable way to record details for easy comparison.

Additional Practice

L2

Chapter Skills Activity 7

Name _____ Date _____ Class _____

★ Chapter Skills Activity 7

Making Comparisons

Making a comparison involves looking at similarities and differences.

DIRECTIONS: While James Madison attended the Constitutional Convention, he corresponded with Thomas Jefferson, in France, about the importance of including a bill of rights to the Constitution. Compare the similarities and differences in their points of view. Then answer the questions on a separate sheet of paper.

> My own opinion has always been in favor of a bill of rights ... At the same time ... I have not viewed it in an important light ... Wherever the real power lies in

> .... Let me add that a bill of rights is what the people are entitled to against every government on earth ... I think our governments will remain

GLENCOE
TECHNOLOGY

CD-ROM

Glencoe Skillbuilder Interactive Workbook CD-ROM, Level 1

This interactive CD-ROM reinforces student mastery of essential social studies skills.

Critical Thinking
SKILLBUILDER

Making Comparisons

Why Learn This Skill?

Suppose you want to buy a portable compact disc (CD) player, and you must choose among three models. You would probably compare characteristics of the three models, such as price, sound quality, and size, to figure out which model is best for you. When you study American history, you often compare people or events from one time period with those from a different time period.

Learning the Skill

When making comparisons, you examine two or more groups, situations, events, or documents. Then you identify similarities and differences. For example, the chart on this page compares two documents, specifically the powers each gave the federal government. The Articles of Confederation were implemented before the United States Constitution, which replaced the Articles.

When making comparisons, you first decide what items will be compared and determine which characteristics you will use to compare them. Then you identify similarities and differences in these characteristics.

Practicing the Skill

Analyze the information on the chart on this page. Then answer the following questions.

1. What items are being compared?

2. Which document allowed the government to organize state militias?

3. Which document allowed the government to coin money? Regulate trade?

4. In what ways are the two documents different?

5. In what ways are the two documents similar?

Powers of the Federal Government	Articles of Confederation	United States Constitution
Declare war; make peace	✔	✔
Coin money	✔	✔
Manage foreign affairs	✔	✔
Establish a postal system	✔	✔
Impose taxes		✔
Regulate trade		✔
Organize a court system		✔
Call state militias for service		✔
Protect copyrights		✔
Take other necessary actions to run the federal government		✔

Applying the Skill

Making Comparisons On the editorial page of your local newspaper, find two letters to the editor that express different viewpoints on the same issue. Read the letters and identify the similarities and differences between the two points of view.

 Glencoe's **Skillbuilder Interactive Workbook CD-ROM, Level 1,** provides instruction and practice in key social studies skills.

ANSWERS TO PRACTICING THE SKILL

1. the powers of the federal government as identified in the Articles of Confederation and the United States Constitution

2. the United States Constitution

3. both documents; the United States Constitution

4. The Constitution specifies powers that are not named in the Articles.

5. Both documents give the federal government the power to declare war and make peace, coin money, manage foreign affairs, and establish a postal system.

Applying the Skill Students' comparisons should correctly identify the similarities and differences in the writers' points of view.

SECTION 3 A New Plan of Government

Guide to Reading

Main Idea
The United States system of government rests on the Constitution.

Key Terms
Enlightenment, federalism, article, legislative branch, executive branch, Electoral College, judicial branch, checks and balances, ratify, Federalist, Antifederalist, amendment

Reading Strategy
Organizing Information Re-create the diagram below. In the boxes explain how the system of checks and balances works.

	Has check or balance over:	Example
President		
Congress		
Supreme Court		

Read to Learn
• about the roots of the Constitution.
• how the Constitution limits the power of government.

Section Theme
Civic Rights and Responsibilities The Constitution outlines the responsibilities and the limits of the three branches of the national government.

Preview of Events

♦1680   ♦1720   ♦1760   ♦1800

1689 English Bill of Rights established

1690 Locke publishes *Two Treatises of Civil Government*

1748 Montesquieu writes *The Spirit of Laws*

1787 Constitutional Convention meets in Philadelphia

Washington's chair, Constitutional Convention

AN American Story

As Benjamin Franklin was leaving the last session of the Constitutional Convention, a woman asked, "What kind of government have you given us, Dr. Franklin? A republic or a monarchy?" Franklin answered, "A republic, Madam, if you can keep it." Franklin's response indicated that a republic—a system of government in which the people elect representatives to exercise power for them—requires citizens to take an active role.

Roots of the Constitution

After four long and difficult months, Franklin and the other delegates had produced a new constitution. The document provided the framework for a strong central government for the United States.

Although a uniquely American document, the Constitution has roots in many other civilizations. The delegates had studied and discussed the history of political development at length—starting with ancient Greece—so that their new government could avoid the mistakes of the past.

CHAPTER 7   A More Perfect Union   **207**

1 FOCUS

Section Overview
This section outlines the responsibilities and limits of the national government.

BELLRINGER
Skillbuilder Activity

Project transparency and have students answer the question.

Daily Focus Skills Transparency 7–3

Reading Preview

Answers to Graphic: President: Congress and Supreme Court; can veto laws and appoint justices; Congress: President, Supreme Court; can override the president's veto and Senate approves Supreme Court appointments; Supreme Court: Congress, President; can rule on congressional law and presidential acts

Preteaching Vocabulary
⊙ Use the **Vocabulary PuzzleMaker CD-ROM** to create crossword and word search puzzles.

SECTION RESOURCES

📂 **Reproducible Masters**
• Reproducible Lesson Plan 7–3
• Daily Lecture and Discussion Notes 7–3
• Guided Reading Activity 7–3
• Section Quiz 7–3
• Reteaching Activity 7–3
• Reading Essentials and Study Guide 7–3
• Enrichment Activity 7–3

🖨 **Transparencies**
• Daily Focus Skills Transparency 7–3

Multimedia
⊙ Vocabulary PuzzleMaker CD-ROM
⊙ Interactive Tutor Self-Assessment CD-ROM
⊙ ExamView® Pro Testmaker CD-ROM
⊙ Presentation Plus! CD-ROM

2 TEACH

Identifying Branches Brainstorm with students a list of current topics in the national news. Have partners or small groups of students choose various topics and decide which branch of government is most directly involved in each topic. **L2**

✓ Reading Check

Answer: The English Bill of Rights provided an important model for Americans, many of whom felt that the United States Constitution also needed a bill of rights.

What?Who?Where?When?

Senatorial Terms The people now elect senators, but unlike the president, senators have no limit on the number of terms they can serve. In recent years citizens have debated setting term limits for senators. Some people feel that having a limited term of activity would encourage senators to work harder for the people they represent.

Many ideas embedded in the Constitution came from the study of European political institutions and political writers. British ideas and institutions particularly influenced the delegates.

The Framers who shaped the document were familiar with the parliamentary system of Britain, and many had participated in the colonial assemblies or their state assemblies. They valued the individual rights guaranteed by the British judicial system. Although the Americans had broken away from Britain, they respected many British traditions.

British System of Government

The **Magna Carta** (1215) had placed limits on the power of the monarch. England's lawmaking body, Parliament, emerged as a force that the king had to depend on to pay for wars and to finance the royal government. Like Parliament, the colonial assemblies controlled their colony's funds. For that reason the assemblies had some control over colonial governors.

The English Bill of Rights of 1689 provided another important model for Americans. Many Americans felt that the Constitution also needed a bill of rights.

Framers of the Constitution got many ideas on the nature of people and government from European writers of the Enlightenment. The Enlightenment was a movement of the 1700s that promoted knowledge, reason, and science as the means to improve society. James Madison and other architects of the Constitution were familiar with the work of **John Locke** and **Baron de Montesquieu** (MAHN•tuhs•KYOO), two important philosophers.

Locke, an English philosopher, believed that all people have **natural rights.** These natural rights include the rights to life, liberty, and property. In his *Two Treatises of Civil Government* (1690), he wrote that government is based on an agreement, or contract, between the people and the ruler. Many Americans interpreted natural rights to mean the rights of Englishmen defined in the Magna Carta and the English Bill of Rights. The Framers viewed the Constitution as a contract between the American people and their government. The contract protected the people's natural rights by limiting the government's power.

> *"[E]very man has a property in his own person. This nobody has any right to but himself."*
>
> —*John Locke*, The Second Treatise of Government *(1690)*

In *The Spirit of Laws* (1748), the French writer Montesquieu declared that the powers of government should be separated and balanced against each other. This separation would keep any one person or group from gaining too much power. The powers of government should also be clearly defined and limited to prevent abuse. Following the ideas of Montesquieu, the Framers of the Constitution carefully specified and divided the powers of government.

✓ Reading Check **Describing** How did the English Bill of Rights influence Americans?

The Federal System

The Constitution created a federal system of government that divided powers between the national, or federal, government and the states. Under the Articles of Confederation the states retained their sovereignty. Under the Constitution the states gave up some of their powers to the federal government while keeping others.

Shared Powers

Federalism, or sharing power between the federal and state governments, is one of the distinctive features of the United States government.

COOPERATIVE LEARNING ACTIVITY

Painting the Past Organize the class into groups of four or five students. Ask each group to create a mural that illustrates the sources from which the Framers of the Constitution drew their ideas. Allow students to decide how to distribute work in each group. Students can illustrate part of the mural, provide additional research, gather supplies, sketch scene outlines, color sketches, and so on. Prepare a "gallery walk" in which the artists explain the completed mural to onlookers. **L1,** **ELL**

Under the Constitution, the federal government gained broad powers to tax, regulate trade, control the currency, raise an army, and declare war. It could also pass laws that were "necessary and proper" for carrying out its responsibilities.

However, the Constitution left important powers in the hands of the states. The states had the power to pass and enforce laws and regulate trade within their borders. They could also establish local governments, schools, and other institutions affecting the welfare of their citizens. Both federal and state governments also had the power to tax and to build roads.

The Constitution Becomes Supreme Law of the Land

The Constitution and the laws that Congress passed were to be "the supreme law of the land." No state could make laws or take actions that went against the Constitution. Any dispute between the federal government and the states was to be settled by the federal courts on the basis of the Constitution. Under the new federal system, the Constitution became the final and supreme authority.

✓ **Reading Check** **Describing** What is the principle of federalism?

The Organization of Government

Influenced by Montesquieu's idea of a division of powers, the Framers divided the federal government into three branches—legislative, executive, and judicial. The first three articles, or parts, of the Constitution describe the powers and responsibilities of each branch.

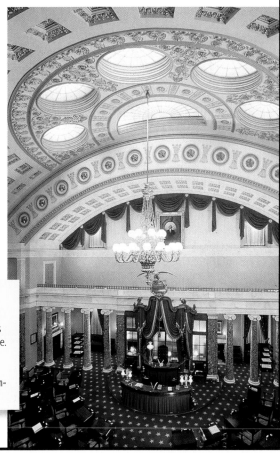

America's *Architecture*

The Old Senate Chamber The U.S. Senate met in the Old Senate Chamber from 1810 until 1859. The two-story chamber is semicircular in shape and measures 75 feet long and 50 feet wide. Two visitors galleries overlook the chamber. After the Senate moved to its present location, the room was occupied by the Supreme Court, from 1860 to 1935. **What branches of government conducted business in the chamber?**

The Legislative Branch

Article I of the Constitution establishes Congress, the legislative branch, or lawmaking branch, of the government. Congress is composed of the House of Representatives and the Senate. As a result of the Great Compromise between large and small states, each state's representation in the House is proportional to its population. Representation in the Senate is equal—two senators for each state.

The powers of Congress include collecting taxes, coining money, and regulating trade. Congress can also declare war and "raise and support armies." Finally it makes all laws needed to fulfill the functions given to it as stated in the Constitution.

The Executive Branch

Memories of King George III's rule made some delegates reluctant to establish a powerful executive, or ruler. Others believed that the

✓**Reading Check**

Answer: Powers are divided and shared between the states and the national government.

L1, ELL

Guided Reading Activity 7-3

Name _____ Date _____ Class _____

★ Guided Reading Activity 7-3

DIRECTIONS: Outlining Locate the heading in your textbook. Then use the information under the heading to help you write each answer. Use another sheet of paper if necessary.

I. Roots of the Constitution
   A. British System of Government
      1. What British document provided an important model for the Americans? _____
      2. What idea did the Enlightenment promote? _____
II. The Federal System
   A. Shared Powers—What is federalism? _____
   B. The Constitution Becomes Supreme Law of the Land—Under the new system, what became the final and supreme authority in disputes between the federal government and state governments? _____
III. The Organization of Government
   A. The Legislative Branch—What are the powers of Congress? _____
   B. The Executive Branch—Who or what indirectly elects the president and vice president? _____
   C. The Judicial Branch—Which courts are included in the judicial branch? _____
   D. System of Checks and Balances—What does the separation of powers prevent? _____
   E. National Citizens—What did the new government pledge? _____
IV. The Constitutional Debate
   A. Federalists—What are the names of two highly respected men who were Federalists? _____
   B. Antifederalists—Why did the Antifederalists fear an energetic central government? _____
   C. Protecting Rights—What was the strongest criticism against the new Constitution? _____
V. Adopting the Constitution
   1. What two states were important to the future of the new government? _____
   2. When would a bill of rights be added? _____

America's *Architecture*

The Old Senate Chamber was located in the original north wing of the Capitol. William Thornton, a physician, designed the Capitol in 1792. The cornerstone was laid by George Washington on September 18, 1793. **Answer:** the legislative and judicial branches

DIFFERENTIATED INSTRUCTION

Gifted and Talented Have students use computers and their textbooks, along with other secondary sources, to create physical/cultural geography databases that provide information about the delegates to the Constitutional Convention. Database fields might include the region and city where delegates lived, their age, their wealth, and their education. Then have students create quizzes for their classmates. Questions should address geographic issues and patterns such as whether the majority of delegates were urban or rural, whether they came from particular regions, and the distribution of such characteristics as age or income. Students should print their quizzes and exchange them with their classmates to complete. **L3**

📁 Refer to ***Inclusion for the Middle School Social Studies Classroom Strategies and Activities*** in the TCR.

CURRICULUM CONNECTION

Science Modern technology has helped preserve the Constitution document. It is scanned by electronic scanners frequently to detect any minor changes in the ink or parchment. These periodic measurements enable curators to detect if any deterioration has taken place that is invisible to the human eye.

Did you know?

One of the delegates at the Constitutional Convention suggested that a presidential term last 15 years. In 1945 President Franklin D. Roosevelt came the closest to fulfilling this idea. Roosevelt took office in 1933 and died in office 12 years later.

Picturing **History**

The Supreme Court has the final say in deciding what the Constitution means. **What types of cases does the Supreme Court hear?**

Confederation had failed, in part, because it lacked an executive branch or president. They argued that a strong executive would serve as a check, or limit, on Congress.

Article II of the Constitution established the executive branch, headed by the president, to carry out the nation's laws and policies. The president serves as commander in chief of the armed forces and conducts relations with foreign countries.

The president and a vice president are elected by a special group called the Electoral College, made up of presidential electors. Each state's voters select electors to cast their votes for the president and vice president. Each state has as many electors as it has senators and representatives in Congress. The president and vice president chosen by the electors serve a four-year term.

The Judicial Branch

Article III of the Constitution deals with the judicial branch, or court system, of the United States. The nation's judicial power resides in "one supreme Court" and any other lower federal courts that Congress might establish. The Supreme Court and the federal courts hear cases involving the Constitution, laws passed by Congress, and disputes between states.

System of Checks and Balances

The most distinctive feature of the United States government is the separation of powers. The Constitution divides government power among the legislative, executive, and judicial branches. To keep any one branch from gaining too much power, the Framers built in a system of checks and balances. The three branches of government have roles that check, or limit, the others so that no single branch can dominate the government.

Both the House and the Senate must pass a bill for it to become law. The president can check Congress by vetoing, or rejecting, the bill. However, Congress can then check the president by overriding, or voting down, the veto. To override a veto, two-thirds of the members of both houses of Congress must vote for the bill.

The system of checks and balances also applies to the Supreme Court. The president appoints Supreme Court justices, and the Senate must approve the appointments.

INTERDISCIPLINARY CONNECTIONS ACTIVITY

Civics Irish playwright George Bernard Shaw described the Constitution as "one of the few modern political documents drawn up by men who were forced by the sternest circumstances to think about what they really had to face, instead of chopping logic in a university classroom." In a class brainstorming session, ask students to recall the history of the American Revolution and of the early nation. Have them suggest some of the practical issues reflected in the Constitution. Ask students if they agree with Shaw. **L2**

Over time, the Court became a check on Congress and the president by ruling on the constitutionality of laws and presidential acts. The system has been successful in maintaining a balance of power among the branches of the federal government and limiting abuses of power.

National Citizens

The Constitution created citizens of the United States. It set up a government in which the people choose their officials—directly or indirectly. Officials answer to the people rather than to the states. The new government pledged to protect the personal freedoms of its citizens.

With these revolutionary changes, Americans showed the world that it was possible for a people to change its form of government through discussion and choice—rather than through chaos, force, or war. The rest of the world watched the new nation with interest to see whether its experiment in self-government would really work.

☑ **Reading Check** **Explaining** Why does the Constitution divide government power among the legislative, executive, and judicial branches?

🗣 Citizenship

The Constitutional Debate

The delegates at Philadelphia had produced the Constitution, but its acceptance depended upon the will of the people. Gaining approval of the Constitution, with its radical new plan of government, was not going to be easy. Supporters and opponents prepared to defend their positions.

Before the Constitution could go into effect, nine states needed to ratify, or approve, it. State legislatures set up special ratifying conventions to consider the document. By late 1787 these conventions started to meet. Rhode Island stood apart. Its leaders opposed the Constitution from the beginning and therefore did not call a convention to approve it.

A great debate now took place throughout the country. In newspapers, at public meetings, and in ordinary conversations, Americans discussed the arguments for and against the new Constitution.

Great Seal of the United States

The Great Seal of the United States is the official seal of the United States government. The seal appears on important government documents. First adopted in 1782, it remains in use today. The face of the seal shows an American eagle with its wings spread. The seal also includes the motto *E pluribus unum* ("From many, one"). Most Americans don't know it, but they often carry around the seal. The one-dollar bill has both sides of the Great Seal on its back.

The United States has had several versions of the Great Seal.

The Great Seal and the number thirteen

On the Great Seal are
13 stars in the crest above the eagle
13 stripes on the eagle's shield
13 arrows in the eagle's left claw
13 olives and leaves in the eagle's right claw
13 letters in *E Pluribus Unum*
13 letters in the motto above the eye, *Annuit Coeptis*

Federalists

Supporters of the new Constitution were called Federalists. Better organized than their opponents, Federalists enjoyed the support of two of the most respected men in America—George Washington and Benjamin Franklin.

CHAPTER 7 A More Perfect Union **211**

☑ **Reading Check**
Answer: to keep any one branch from gaining too much power

Linking Past & Present

Ask students where they might have seen the seal of the United States. *(Answers will vary depending on government documents students have seen. Many may have seen it on a one dollar bill.)* Ask why the number 13 is so prominently featured on the seal. *(The new nation began as 13 colonies.)* Ask how these numbers might differ if they were adopted today for the first time. *(It might have 50 of all of these items or a smaller number symbolizing something other than number of states.)*

Did you know?

The Constitution is stored at the National Archives Building in Washington, D.C. During the daytime, pages one and four of the document are displayed in a bullet-proof case. At night the pages are lowered into a vault behind five-ton doors that can withstand a nuclear explosion. The entire Constitution is displayed for only one day a year, September 17, which is the anniversary of its signing.

CRITICAL THINKING ACTIVITY

Predicting Have students work in groups to predict what might have happened to the United States without the new Constitution. Would it have survived as a nation? Would it have been able to defend itself and win wars? If it survived, what would it be like? Would it be a world leader today? Encourage groups to share their predictions with the class. **L2**

Picturing History

Mercy Otis Warren was not afraid to criticize the government. Before the American Revolution, she wrote plays that ridiculed Tories and their policies. Several of her satirical dramas were published in Massachusetts.
Answer: The strongest criticism was that it lacked a bill of rights to protect individual freedoms.

3 ASSESS

Assign Section 3 Assessment as homework or as an in-class activity.

🖱 Have students use **Interactive Tutor Self-Assessment CD-ROM.**
L2

Section Quiz 7–3

Reteaching Activity 7–3

Three of the nation's most gifted political thinkers—James Madison, Alexander Hamilton, and **John Jay**—also backed the Constitution.

Madison, Hamilton, and Jay teamed up to write a series of essays explaining and defending the Constitution. These essays appeared in newspapers around the country and were widely read by Americans of every persuasion. Called *The Federalist Papers,* they were later published as a book and sent to delegates at the remaining ratifying conventions. 📖 *(See pages 614–615 of the Appendix for excerpts from* The Federalist Papers.*)* Jefferson described the series of essays as

66the best commentary on the principles of government which was ever written.99

Antifederalists

The Federalists called those who opposed ratification Antifederalists. Although not as well organized as the Federalists, the Antifederalists

Picturing History

Antifederalist Mercy Otis Warren feared that the Constitution would make the central government too powerful. **What was the biggest criticism of the Constitution by Antifederalists?**

had some dedicated supporters. They responded to the Federalists with a series of their own essays, now known as the *Antifederalist Papers.* Their main argument was that the new Constitution would take away the liberties Americans had fought to win from Great Britain. The Constitution would create a strong central government, ignore the will of the states and the people, and favor the wealthy few over the common people. Antifederalists preferred local government close to the people. An energetic central government, they feared, would be government by a small, educated group of individuals. They agreed with Patrick Henry, who warned that the Constitution was "incompatible with the genius of republicanism."

Protecting Rights

Perhaps the strongest criticism of the Constitution was that it lacked a bill of rights to protect individual freedoms. Antifederalists believed that no government could be trusted to protect the freedom of its citizens. Several state conventions took a stand and announced that they would not ratify the Constitution without the addition of a bill of rights.

Mercy Otis Warren, a Massachusetts opponent of the Constitution, expressed the problem faced by many Antifederalists. She admitted the need for a strong government but feared it.

66We have struggled for liberty and made costly sacrifices . . . and there are still many among us who [value liberty] too much to relinquish . . . the rights of man for the dignity of government.99

In many ways the debate between Federalists and Antifederalists came down to their different fears. Federalists feared disorder without a strong central government. They believed that more uprisings like Shays's Rebellion would occur. They looked to the Constitution to create a national government capable of maintaining order. The Antifederalists feared oppression more than disorder. They worried about the concentration of power that would result from a strong national government.

✓ **Reading Check** **Explaining** According to the Antifederalists, why was a bill of rights important?

EXTENDING THE CONTENT

Scared Silent An incident related by William Pierce of Georgia illustrates the Constitutional Convention's obsession with secrecy. A delegate apparently dropped his copy of a paper containing one of the major proposals, the Virginia Plan of Union. Another delegate found it and turned it over to the presiding officer, George Washington. Just before adjourning for the day, Washington admonished the delegates about carelessness and tossed the paper on the table saying, "Let him who owns it take it." Washington then left the room "with a dignity so severe that every person seemed alarmed," Pierce wrote. But no one owned up to losing the paper.

Analyzing *Political Cartoons*

A cartoon published in 1788 celebrates New Hampshire becoming the ninth state to ratify the Constitution. **From the cartoon, which was the first state to ratify?**

The Ninth *PILLAR* erected !
"The Ratification of the Conventions of nine States, shall be sufficient for the establishment of this Constitution, between the States so ratifying the same." *Art.* vii.

INCIPIENT MAGNI PROCEDERE MENSES.

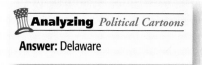

Adopting the Constitution

On December 7, 1787, Delaware became the first state to approve the Constitution. On June 21, 1788, the ninth state—New Hampshire—ratified it. In theory that meant that the new government could go into effect. However, without the support of the two largest states—New York and Virginia—the future of the new government was not promising. Neither state had ratified yet, and both had strong Antifederalist groups.

In Virginia, **Patrick Henry** gave fiery speeches against the proposed Constitution. It did not, he charged, sufficiently limit the power of the federal government. Still, Virginia ratified the Constitution at the end of June 1788, after being assured that the Constitution would include a bill of rights amendment. An amendment is something added to a document.

That left three states—New York, North Carolina, and Rhode Island—to ratify. In July 1788, New York finally ratified it by a narrow margin. North Carolina ratified in November 1789, and Rhode Island ratified in May 1790.

After ratification came the celebrations. Boston, New York, and Philadelphia held big parades accompanied by cannon salutes and ringing church bells. Smaller celebrations took place in hundreds of American towns.

The task of creating the Constitution had ended. The Bill of Rights would be added in 1791, after the new government took office. Now it was time for the nation to elect leaders and begin the work of government.

✓ **Reading Check** **Explaining** Why was the support of New York and Virginia vital to ratifying the Constitution?

Analyzing *Political Cartoons*

Answer: Delaware

✓ **Reading Check**

Answer: They were the two largest states.

L1, ELL

Reading Essentials and Study Guide 7–3

Study Guide

Chapter 7, Section 3
For use with textbook pages 207–213

A NEW PLAN OF GOVERNMENT

KEY TERMS	
Enlightenment	Movement of the 1700s that promoted knowledge, reason, and science as means to improve society *(page 208)*
federalism	Sharing power between federal and state governments *(page 208)*
article	Part of the Constitution *(page 209)*
legislative branch	Lawmaking branch of the government *(page 209)*
executive branch	Branch of government headed by the president that carries out laws and policies *(page 210)*
Electoral College	Special group of presidential electors *(page 210)*
judicial branch	Court system that enforces the laws *(page 210)*

L3

Enrichment Activity 7–3

Name _____ Date _____ Class _____

★ **Enrichment Activity 7-3** ★

Checks and Balances

Major Features of the American System of Checks and Balances

SECTION 3 ASSESSMENT

Checking for Understanding

1. **Key Terms** Define the following terms: Enlightenment, federalism, article, Electoral College, checks and balances, ratify, Federalist, Antifederalist, amendment.

2. **Reviewing Facts** What influence did John Locke have on American government?

Reviewing Themes

3. **Civic Rights and Responsibilities** Why did the Framers of the Constitution believe that a division of powers and a system of checks and balances were necessary in a government?

Critical Thinking

4. **Finding the Main Idea** What do you think was the most important reason for establishing a strong central government under the Constitution?

5. **Comparing** Re-create the diagram below. Describe the differences between Hamilton's and Henry's views on the Constitution.

Views on the Constitution	
Hamilton	Henry

Analyzing Visuals

6. **Political Cartoons** Study the political cartoon on this page. Then answer the questions that follow. What do the pillars represent? How do the last two pillars appear?

Interdisciplinary Activity

Citizenship Refer to the Bill of Rights on pages 244–245. Collect photographs from newspapers or magazines that illustrate the freedoms guaranteed in the Bill of Rights. Put your photos on a poster entitled "Pictures of Liberty."

4 CLOSE

Have students work in pairs and prepare one-sentence summaries of the Federalist and Antifederalist viewpoints.

SECTION 3 ASSESSMENT ANSWERS

1. Student work should reflect correct use of terms.

2. Locke wrote that government is based on a contract between the people and the ruler. The Framers viewed the Constitution as a contract protecting the people's natural rights by limiting the government's power.

3. to keep any one branch from gaining too much power

4. Answers should mention that it could address issues that affected the nation as a whole.

5. Hamilton: supported the Constitution and worked to build support with the Federalist Papers; Henry: opposed the Constitution, saying it did not sufficiently limit the power of the federal government

6. the states that ratified the Constitution; they are rising to join the other states.

Interdisciplinary Activity Pictures should clearly demonstrate the freedoms guaranteed in the Bill of Rights.

CHAPTER
7 ASSESSMENT and ACTIVITIES

Reviewing Key Terms

1. The states needed to **ratify** the **Constitution.**

2. The **legislative branch** consists of a **bicameral** legislature.

3. The **executive branch** is headed by the president, who today is elected by the **Electoral College.**

Reviewing Key Facts

4. strengths: it could conduct foreign affairs, issue currency, borrow money, maintain armed forces; weaknesses: it couldn't regulate trade, make soldiers join the army, impose taxes

5. Damage to plantations cut rice exports; trade slowed; foreign debts had to be paid; there was a currency shortage; higher taxes forced farmers out of business.

6. It created a single territory for lands north of the Ohio River and east of Mississippi River. When population of an area reached 60,000, the area could apply for statehood.

7. two houses with proportional representation; members of lower house elected by people; members of upper house chosen by lower house

8. Paterson

9. A slave counted as three-fifths of a person for purposes of taxation and representation.

10. all powers not specifically granted to the Federal government

11. They did not think that the Constitution, as written, protected individual rights.

12. In the *Federalist Papers*, Federalists defended the Constitution, saying the United States needed a strong central government. In the

Chapter Summary

A More Perfect Union

1777
- Congress adopts the Articles of Confederation to coordinate the war effort against Britain.

1781
- The Articles of Confederation formally become the government of the United States.

1784
- Spain closes the lower Mississippi River to American shipping.

1785
- The Land Ordinance provides a method for settlement of public lands north of the Ohio River.

1787
- Congress provides for the organization of the Northwest Territory and outlines the steps that a territory must take in order to become a state.

- Delegates meet in Philadelphia and draft the Constitution.

- Delaware becomes the first state to ratify the Constitution.

1788
- New Hampshire becomes the ninth state to vote for ratification.

1790
- The last of the 13 states—Rhode Island—votes for ratification.

1791
- Bill of Rights is added to the Constitution.

214

Reviewing Key Terms

For each of the pairs of terms below, write a sentence or short paragraph showing how the two are related.

1. constitution, ratify
2. bicameral, legislative branch
3. executive branch, Electoral College

Reviewing Key Facts

4. Summarize the strengths and weaknesses of the Articles of Confederation.

5. What caused the depression after the Revolution?

6. How did the Northwest Ordinance provide for the country's expansion?

7. According to the Virginia Plan, how was the legislature to be set up?

8. Who supported the New Jersey Plan?

9. What was the Three-Fifths Compromise?

10. What powers did the Constitution leave in the hands of the state governments?

11. Why did some states want a bill of rights added to the Constitution?

12. How did the *Federalist Papers* and the *Antifederalist Papers* influence ideas on systems of U.S. government?

13. How does the system of checks and balances work?

Critical Thinking

14. **Comparing** Who had the most power under the Articles of Confederation? Re-create the diagram below. In the boxes, describe the powers given to the state and national governments.

State Governments	National Government

15. **Analyzing Themes: Groups and Institutions** Were the people who attended the Constitutional Convention representative of the American public? Explain.

16. **Drawing Conclusions** Why did Madison want checks and balances built into the Constitution?

17. **Analyzing Information** Refer to the grievances listed in the Declaration of Independence on pages 154–157. How were these grievances addressed in the Constitution?

Antifederalist Papers, Antifederalists built resistance to a strong central government, fearing that a strong central government would take away liberties that Americans had won from Britain.

13. Each branch has a role that limits other branches.

Critical Thinking

14. State Governments: regulate trade, force soldiers to join the army, impose taxes; National Government: conduct foreign affairs, issue currency, borrow money,

maintain armed forces

15. No; women, African Americans, and Native Americans were not included.

16. to keep any one branch from dominating the government

17. Leaders were elected and made subject to law; powers were divided and a system of checks and balances set up; some powers were reserved for states; and a bill of individual rights was written.

Geography and History Activity

Examine the map of the Northwest Territory on page 195. Then answer the questions that follow.

18. How many miles long and wide was a township?
19. How many miles long and wide was a section?
20. How many acres were in a section?

Practicing Skills

Making Comparisons *The two statements that follow reflect the opinions of an Antifederalist and a Federalist toward the ratification of the Constitution. Read the opinions; then answer the questions.*

"These lawyers and men of learning, and moneyed men . . . make us poor illiterate people swallow down the pill, expect to get into Congress themselves; they expect to be the managers of this Constitution, and get all the power and all the money into their own hands, and then they will swallow up all of us little folks. . . . This is what I am afraid of."

— Amos Singletary, farmer

"I am a plain man, and get my living by the plough. . . . I did not go to any lawyer, to ask his opinion; I formed my own opinion, and was pleased with this Constitu-tion. . . . I don't think the worse of the Constitution because lawyers, and men of learning, and moneyed men, are fond of it."

— Jonathan Smith, farmer

21. Who is the Antifederalist? How do you know?
22. How are the two opinions similar? How are they different?
23. In your opinion, does the Antifederalist or the Federalist make the stronger argument? Explain.

Citizenship Cooperative Activity

24. **Interviewing** In groups of three, interview students from your school and adults from your community to find out what they know about the powers of government speci-fied in the Constitution. Prepare a list of questions to use in your interviews. To keep the interviews brief, you might use yes/no questions, such as "Does the Constitu-tion give the government the power to regulate high-ways?" Compile the answers and present a report to your class.

Self-Check Quiz
Visit <u>tarvol1.glencoe.com</u> and click on **Chapter 7—Self-Check Quizzes** to prepare for the chapter test.

Economics Activity

25. For a week, keep track of the number of times that you read about or hear about the topics of unemployment and inflation. Write down the source from which you heard or read this information. After each entry, indicate whether the economic news was good.

Alternative Assessment

26. **Portfolio Writing Activity** Review the Bill of Rights to the Constitution (first 10 amendments) on pages 244–245. Summarize each in your journal. Next, choose the amendment from the Bill of Rights that you think is the most important. Write a paragraph in which you explain your choice. Finally, knowing what you know about today's society, write a short description of a right you think the Framers of the Constitution should have included.

Standardized Test Practice

Directions: Choose the *best* answer to the following multiple choice question.

Each of the states enacted state constitutions in the late 1700s. All state constitutions

A established equal rights for all persons living in the state.

B set up legislative and executive branches of state government.

C granted women the right to vote.

D agreed that states would be supervised by the federal government.

Test-Taking Tip:

Eliminate answers that do not make sense. For example, *equal rights for all* (choice A) is a fairly new concept. During the 1700s, women and enslaved people had few rights.

Economics Activity

25. Entries should describe real events that involve unemployment and inflation.

Alternative Assessment

26. Students should summarize each amendment and choose one that they think is the most important and explain why. Rights suggested should not already be included in the Bill of Rights.

HISTORY
Online

Have students visit the Web site at <u>tarvol1.glencoe.com</u> to review Chapter 7 and take the Self-Check Quiz.

Standardized Test Practice

Answer: B
Question Type: Civics
Answer Explanation: According to page 193, states took several meas-ures against concentration of power by dividing government functions.

Bonus Question ?

Ask: How many total essays were included in *The Federalist Papers*? *(85)*

Geography and History Activity

18. 6   **19.** 1   **20.** 640

Practicing Skills

21. Amos Singletary; he opposed the Constitution, fearing that it would give the government too much power.
22. Both express distrust of lawyers, the highly educated, and the wealthy. The opinions differ in that Smith has confidence in the Constitution, whereas Singletary

fears that it would be used to increase the wealth and power of the country's leaders.

23. Opinions will vary, but should be supported with arguments.

Citizenship Cooperative Activity

24. Have students discuss what their interviews revealed about how informed people are about the Constitution.

215

Beginning the Handbook

Inform students that when members of the first Congress gathered in New York in 1789, a bill of rights had not been added to the Constitution. These amendments were important because a number of states made their ratification conditional on such an addition. Other states had threatened to revoke their ratification if the bill of rights proved too radical. Have students speculate why Congress moved so quickly to inaugurate the new government. *(The country was eager for a new government. Congress perhaps felt that if the process of government had begun, it would be harder for wavering states to leave the Union.)*

Did you know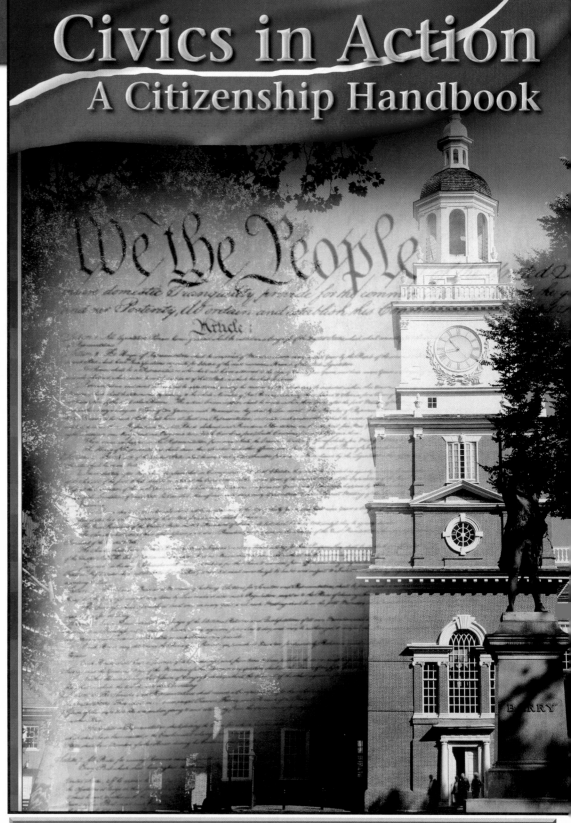

Constitutions vary from country to country. For example, Article XXIII of Japan's constitution guarantees academic freedom. During the era of communism, the constitution of communist countries emphasized economic and social rights such as the right to work, the right to choose an occupation, and the right to leisure.

Civics in Action
A Citizenship Handbook

EXTENDING THE CONTENT

Constitutions The United States has the oldest written national constitution still in effect. Compared to other written constitutions, it might be characterized as succinct. The average federal constitution contains about 26,500 words, whereas the United States Constitution with its 27 amendments has fewer than 7,500 words.

SECTION 1 The Constitution

Guide to Reading

Main Idea
For more than 200 years, the Constitution has provided the framework for the United States government and has helped preserve the basic rights of American citizens.

Key Terms
preamble, domestic tranquility, popular sovereignty, republicanism, federalism, enumerated powers, reserved powers, concurrent powers, amendment, implied powers, judicial review

Read to Learn
• why the Constitution is the nation's most important document.
• the goals of the Constitution.
• the principles that form the basis of the Constitution.

Goals of the Constitution

The Preamble, or introduction, to the Constitution reflects the basic principle of American government—the right of the people to govern themselves. It also lists six goals for the United States government:

66. . .to form a more perfect Union, establish Justice, insure domestic Tranquility, provide for the common defence [defense], promote the general Welfare, and secure the Blessings of Liberty to ourselves and our Posterity.99

These goals guided the Constitution's Framers as they created the new government. They remain as important today as they were when the Constitution was written.

To Form a More Perfect Union Under the Articles of Confederation, the states functioned almost like independent nations. For the most part, they did not work together on important matters such as defense and finances. This lack of unity could have been dangerous for the nation during times of crisis. To form "a more perfect Union" the Framers believed the states needed to agree to operate as a single country and cooperate on major issues.

To Establish Justice For the Framers, treating each citizen equally was one of the fundamental principles on which to build the new nation.

The Constitution provides a national system of courts to protect the people's rights, and to hear cases involving violations of federal law and disputes between the states.

To Insure Domestic Tranquility Shays's Rebellion began in 1786 and shocked Americans. The United States had become a self-governing nation, yet a group of people had resorted to violence to express their anger over government policies. The Constitution provides a strong central government to "insure domestic Tranquility"—that is, to keep peace among the people.

To Provide for the Common Defense The Articles of Confederation required nine states to approve any decision by the Confederation Congress to build an army or navy. The Constitution gives the federal government the power to maintain armed forces to protect the country and its citizens from attack.

To Promote the General Welfare The Declaration of Independence states that the purpose of government is to promote "Life, Liberty, and the pursuit of Happiness" for the people of the nation. The Constitution includes ways to "promote the general Welfare"—or well-being—of the people by maintaining order, protecting individual liberties, regulating commerce and bankruptcies, and promoting science and technology by granting patents.

1 FOCUS

BELLRINGER
Motivational Activity

Provide pairs of students with board games, such as chess or checkers. Have pairs play the game, but tell them there are no rules. They are to make up their own rules as they go along. After a few minutes, initiate a discussion about the needs for rules and organization. Conclude by asking students to consider why the Constitution might be regarded as a rule book for government.

Reading Preview

Preteaching Vocabulary
Ask students to write definitions of each of the entries listed in the **Key Terms.** Have them check their definitions as they read the section. When they have finished, have them discuss similarities and differences among *enumerated powers*, *reserved powers*, *concurrent powers*, and *implied powers*.

Did you know?

Not many governments have had the stability that the United States Constitution has provided. France, for example, has had more than a dozen constitutions. Peru, independent since 1821, has had 12.

SECTION RESOURCES

Reproducible Masters
• *Civics in Action: Activities, Quizzes, and Tests,* Constitution Pretest
• *Civics in Action: Activities, Quizzes, and Tests,* Guided Reading Activity 1
• *Civics in Action: Activities, Quizzes, and Tests,* Section 1 Quiz

• *Civics in Action: Activities, Quizzes, and Tests,* Enrichment Activity 1
• *Supreme Court Cases Studies, Marbury* v. *Madison*

Transparencies
• *Civics in Action: Activities, Quizzes, and Tests,* Transparency 1

2 TEACH

Discussing Precedents Have groups of students recall aspects of self-government with which American colonists had experimented. (*Answers include the Mayflower Compact, the Articles of Confederation, and organizations such as the Virginia House of Burgesses.*) Explain that this handbook will help them see how those experiments helped shape the American system of government. **L1,** ELL

✓ Reading Check

Answer: to introduce the Constitution and identify its goals

Chart *Skills*

Answer: Although each government branch has its own responsibilities, a system of checks and balances keeps the legislative, executive, and judicial branches from becoming too powerful.

Chart Skills Practice
Ask: How is republicanism reflected in popular sovereignty? (*People are the source of power and elect their political representatives.*)

To Secure the Blessings of Liberty The American colonists fought the Revolutionary War to gain their liberty. The Framers believed that preserving liberty should also be a major goal of the Constitution. The Constitution guarantees that no American's basic rights will be taken away now or for posterity (generations not yet born).

✓ Reading Check **Analyzing** What is the purpose of the Preamble?

Major Principles

The principles outlined in the Constitution were the Framers' solution to the problems of a representative government. The Constitution rests on seven major principles: (1) popular sovereignty, (2) republicanism, (3) limited govern-

Major Principles of the Constitution

Popular Sovereignty	People are the source of the government's power.
Republicanism	People elect their political representatives.
Limited Government	The Constitution limits the actions of government by specifically listing powers it does and does not have.
Federalism	In this government system, power is divided between national and state governments.
Separation of Powers	Each of the three branches of government has its own responsibilities.
Checks and Balances	Each branch of government holds some control over the other two branches.
Individual Rights	Basic liberties and rights of all citizens are guaranteed in the Bill of Rights.

Chart *Skills*

The Principles outlined in the Constitution were the Framers' solution to the complex problems presented by a representative government.

Analyzing Information What is the relationship between checks and balances and separation of powers?

218

---

ment, (4) federalism, (5) separation of powers, (6) checks and balances, and (7) individual rights.

Popular Sovereignty The Declaration of Independence states that governments derive their powers from "the consent of the governed." The opening words of the Constitution, "We the people," reinforce this idea of popular sovereignty—or "authority of the people."

Republicanism Under republicanism, voters hold sovereign power. The people elect representatives and give them the responsibility to make laws and conduct government. For most Americans today, the terms *republic* and *representative democracy* mean the same thing: a system of limited government where the people are the ultimate source of governmental power.

Limited Government The Framers saw both benefits and risks in creating a powerful national government. They agreed that the nation needed strong central authority but feared misuse of power. They wanted to prevent the government from using its power to give one

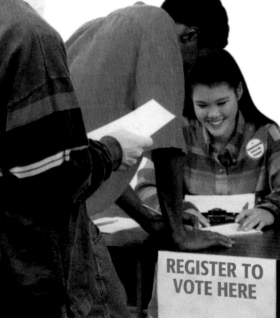

Voting is a basic political right of all citizens.

REGISTER TO VOTE HERE

COOPERATIVE LEARNING ACTIVITY

Exploring Key Concepts Organize the class into groups of four students, one group for each of the Constitution's underlying principles: popular sovereignty, limited government, federalism, and separation of powers. Have each group define the principle and locate at least one part of the Constitution that addresses that principle. Students should create a role play showing that principle in the lives of Americans today. Allow time for presentations of each group's work. Follow up with a class vote about which principle they think affects their lives the most right now.

The Federal System

National Government	National & State Governments	State Governments
Enumerated Powers	**Concurrent Powers**	**Reserved Powers**
• Regulate trade	• Enforce the laws	• Regulate trade within the state
• Coin Money	• Establish courts	• Establish local government systems
• Provide an army and navy	• Collect taxes	• Conduct elections
• Conduct Foreign affairs	• Borrow money	• Establish public school systems
• Set up federal courts	• Provide for the general welfare	

What?Where?When?Who?

Nobility The power to award titles of nobility is denied to Congress. This clause was written into the Constitution to prevent the development of a noble class in the United States.

Popular Students may hear much grumbling about governmental issues today that they may wonder why we say that the government is empowered by popular sovereignty. Point out that *popular* comes from the Latin word *populus*, meaning "the people." The same Latin word also gives us *population* and *populate*.

The Living Constitution

Refer to *The Living Constitution* for student activities and information related to the Constitution.

---

group special advantages or to deprive another group of its rights. By creating a limited government, they made certain the government would have only those powers granted by the people.

Article I of the Constitution states the powers that the government has and the powers that it does not have. Other limits on government appear in the Bill of Rights, which guarantees certain rights and liberties to the people.

Limited government can be described as the "rule of law." No people or groups are above the law. Government officials must obey the law.

Federalism When the states banded together under the Constitution, they gave up some independence. States could no longer print their own money or tax items imported from other states. Nevertheless, each state governed itself much as it had in the past.

This system, in which the power to govern is shared between the national government and the states, is called the federal system, or federalism. Our federal system allows the people of each state to deal with their needs in their own way. At the same time, it lets the states act together to deal with matters that affect all Americans.

The Constitution defines three types of government powers. Enumerated powers belong only to the federal government. These include the power to coin money, regulate interstate and foreign trade, maintain the armed forces, and create federal courts (Article I, Section 8).

The second kind of powers are those retained by the states, known as reserved powers. They include such rights as the power to establish

schools, pass marriage and divorce laws, and regulate trade within a state. Although reserved powers are not listed specifically in the Constitution, the Tenth Amendment says that all powers not specifically granted to the federal government "are reserved to the States."

The third set of powers defined by the Constitution are concurrent powers—powers shared by the state and federal governments. Among these powers are the right to raise taxes, borrow money, provide for public welfare, and administer criminal justice.

When conflicts arise between state law and federal law, the Constitution declares that the Constitution is "the supreme Law of the Land." Conflicts between state law and federal law must be settled in a federal court.

Separation of Powers To prevent any single group or institution in government from gaining too much authority, the Framers divided the federal government into three branches: **legislative, executive,** and **judicial.** Each branch has its own functions and powers. The legislative branch, Congress, makes the laws. The executive branch, headed by the president, carries out the laws. The judicial branch, consisting of the Supreme Court and other federal courts, interprets and applies the laws.

Checks and Balances As an additional safeguard, the Framers established a system of **checks and balances** in which each branch of government can check, or limit, the power of the other branches. This system helps maintain a

Citizenship Handbook   **219**

DIFFERENTIATED INSTRUCTION

English Learners Committing the Preamble of the Constitution to memory provides a useful language model for students' spoken language development. To aid in this memory task, structure the activity by asking students to write the words *who*, *why*, and *what* in their notebooks. Have students write the various phrases of the Preamble under the words to which they are most closely related. **L1,** ELL

☞ Refer to *Inclusion for the Middle School Social Studies Classroom Strategies and Activities* in the TCR.

CURRICULUM CONNECTION

Civics Administering criminal justice is a controversial shared power. The Framers regarded execution by beheading and drawing and quartering as "cruel and unusual punishments." More recently, opponents have argued that any form of capital punishment is "cruel and unusual." The Supreme Court has not upheld that view. As a result, some states impose a death penalty; others do not.

✓ Reading Check

Answer: the authority of the people

How the Constitution is Amended

STEP 1: Amendment Proposed by:

A two-thirds vote of both houses of Congress

OR

A constitutional convention called by Congress on petition of two-thirds of the 50 states

STEP 2: Amendment Ratified by:

Three-fourths of the 50 state legislatures

OR

Three-fourths of special constitutional conventions called by the 50 states

New amendment to the Constitution

Graphic Organizer → Skills

Amending the Constitution allows it to be able to adapt to changing times.

Analyzing Information What role do the states play in the amendment process?

balance in the power of the three branches. For example, Congress can pass a law. Then the president can reject the law by vetoing it. However, Congress can override, or reverse, the president's veto if two-thirds of the members of both houses vote again to approve the law.

Over the years, the Supreme Court has acquired the power to determine the meaning of the Constitution and to declare that a law or a government policy goes against the Constitution. In doing so, the Court provides a check on the powers of Congress and the president. Judicial decisions—those made by the courts—can be overruled by amending the Constitution. The president and the Senate provide a check on the judicial branch through their power to appoint and approve federal judges. Congress can also change a law so that it no longer conflicts with the Constitution, or it can amend the Constitution. The Fourteenth Amendment, passed by Congress in 1866, overturned the Supreme Court's ruling in the *Dred Scott* decision, which had ruled that enslaved African Americans were not citizens.

Individual Rights The Bill of Rights became part of the Constitution in 1791. These first 10 amendments protect basic liberties and rights that you may take for granted—including freedom of speech, freedom of the press, freedom of assembly, freedom of religion, and the right to a trial by jury.

The 17 amendments that follow the Bill of Rights expand the rights of Americans and adjust certain provisions of the Constitution. Included among them are amendments that abolish slavery, define citizenship, guarantee the right to vote to all citizens, authorize an income tax, and set a two-term limit on the presidency.

✓ Reading Check
Explaining What is popular sovereignty?

A Living Constitution

Two years after the Constitutional Convention, Benjamin Franklin wrote, "Our Constitution is in actual operation; everything appears to promise that it will last; but in this world nothing is certain but death and taxes."

Reading Strategy — READING THE TEXT

Using Graphic Organizers Federalism can be graphically illustrated in many ways. After reading the section on federalism, ask students to graphically represent federalism. Encourage them to reflect shared powers as well as independent powers in their graphics. **L1**

Civics in Action
A Citizenship Handbook
Section 1, 217–222

Despite Franklin's uncertainty about the Constitution's future, it is still very much alive today. The Constitution has survived because the Framers wrote a document that the nation could alter and adapt to meet changing needs. The result is a flexible document that can be interpreted in different ways in keeping with the conditions of a particular time. The Constitution's flexibility allows the government to deal with matters the Framers never anticipated—such as regulating nuclear power plants or developing a space program. In addition the Constitution contains a provision for amending—changing or adding to—the document.

Amending the Constitution The Framers intentionally made the amendment process difficult to discourage minor or frequent changes being made. Although thousands of amendments—changes to the Constitution—have been proposed since 1788, only 27 of them have actually become part of the Constitution.

An amendment may be proposed in two ways: by the vote of two-thirds of both houses of Congress or by two-thirds of the state legislatures asking for a special convention on the amendment. The second method has never been used. Ratification of an amendment requires approval by three-fourths of the states. The Constitution can be ratified by the approval of state legislatures or by special state conventions.

Only the Twenty-first Amendment—which repealed the Eighteenth Amendment, banning the sale of alcoholic beverages—was ratified by state conventions. Voters in each state chose the delegates to the special conventions.

Interpreting the Constitution The Constitution includes two provisions that give Congress the power to act as needed to meet changing conditions. The first of these provisions is what is known as the "elastic clause" (Article I, Section 8). It directs Congress to "make all Laws which shall be necessary and proper" for executing all the powers of government. Congress has interpreted this clause to mean that it has certain implied powers, powers not specifically defined in the Constitution. Over the years,

Congress has drawn on its implied powers to pass laws to deal with the needs of society.

The second provision used to expand congressional authority, the "commerce clause" (Article I, Section 8), gives Congress the power to "regulate Commerce with foreign Nations, and among the several States." Congress has used this clause to expand its powers into a number of areas, such as regulation of the airline industry, radio and television, and nuclear energy.

Powers of the Presidency The Constitution describes the role and the powers of the president in general terms. This has allowed the executive branch to extend its powers. In 1803, for example, President Thomas Jefferson approved a treaty with France that enabled the United States to buy an enormous tract of land.

The Bill of Rights

1	Guarantees freedom of religion, speech, assembly, and press, and the right of people to petition the government
2	Protects the rights of states to maintain a militia and of citizens to bear arms
3	Restricts quartering of troops in private homes
4	Protects against "unreasonable searches and seizures"
5	Assures the right not to be deprived of "life, liberty, or property, without due process of law"
6	Guarantees the right to a speedy and public trial by an impartial jury
7	Assures the right to a jury trial in cases involving the common law (the law established by previous court decisions)
8	Protects against excessive bail, or cruel and unusual punishment
9	Provides that people's rights are not restricted to those specified in the first eight Amendments
10	Restates the Constitution's principle of federalism by providing that powers not granted to the national government nor prohibited to the states are reserved to the states and to the people

Citizenship Handbook **221**

Check The verb *check* comes from Persian and is related to the royal title *shah*. It is also a sports term, relating to a blocking action in hockey.

Who?What?Where?When?

James Madison Known as "the Father of the Constitution," Madison believed that the Constitution would have to be altered as new situations arose but that this had to depend on the majority. He wrote: "If the will of the majority cannot be trusted where there are diversified and conflicting interests, it can be trusted nowhere."

Did you know?

Although the required 11 states ratified the Bill of Rights by 1791, Connecticut, Georgia, and Massachusetts waited until 1939 to grant their approval.

CRITICAL THINKING ACTIVITY

Analyzing Information The First Amendment guarantees freedom of religion. Have students research this freedom. Ask students to analyze how the freedom of religion impacts Americans in a one-page report. Students may cite examples of how the freedom of religion affects their own lives at school and home. **L2**

Who?What?Where?When?

William Marbury President John Adams, on the night before Thomas Jefferson became president, appointed William Marbury as a judge. When Secretary of State James Madison denied Marbury's commission, Marbury asked the Supreme Court to intervene, but the Supreme Court refused. The Court ruled that the law allowing Marbury to apply directly to the Supreme Court was unconstitutional.

3 ASSESS

Assign Section 1 Assessment as homework or as an in-class activity.

4 CLOSE

Have students offer one-sentence definitions of the terms *legislative, executive, judicial, checks and balances,* and *amendment.*

"I have finally been included in 'We the people.'"

—Barbara Jordan, U.S. representative from Texas, 1972–1978

The Courts The role of the judicial branch has also grown as powers implied in the Constitution have been put into practice. In 1803 Chief Justice John Marshall expanded the powers of the Supreme Court by striking down an act of Congress in the case of *Marbury* v. *Madison.* In that decision the Court defined its right to determine whether a law violates the Constitution. Although not mentioned in the Constitution, judicial review has become a major power of the judicial branch.

The process of amending the Constitution and applying its principles in new areas helps keep our government functioning well. In 1974 Barbara Jordan, an African American member of Congress and a constitutional scholar, spoke in ringing tones of her faith in the Constitution:

❝I felt somehow for many years that George Washington and Alexander Hamilton just left me out by mistake. But through the process of amendment, interpretation, and court decision I have finally been included in 'We the people.'❞

✔ **Reading Check** **Explaining** What are implied powers?

SECTION 1 ASSESSMENT

Checking for Understanding

1. **Key Terms** Write complete sentences using each group of terms below. Group 1: **republicanism, federalism.** Group 2: **enumerated powers, concurrent powers.** Group 3: **preamble, amendment.**
2. **Reviewing Facts** Explain the origin of judicial review.

Reviewing Themes

3. **Government and Democracy** What is the importance of federalism in the Constitution?

Critical Thinking

4. **Analyzing Information** Why was it so important for basic freedoms to be guaranteed in the Constitution?
5. **Comparing** Re-create the diagram below and describe how each branch of government has power over another branch.

Branch	Power
Legislative	
Executive	
Judicial	

Analyzing Visuals

6. **Reading a Table** Refer to the table on page 218. How are popular sovereignty and republicanism related?

Interdisciplinary Activity

Civics The Bill of Rights guarantees certain basic rights to all Americans. Select one of the 10 amendments that make up the Bill of Rights (see page 221) and research its history. Present your findings in a one-page essay.

SECTION 1 ASSESSMENT ANSWERS

1. Student work should reflect correct use of terms.
2. In *Marbury* v. *Madison* the Supreme Court defined its right to determine whether a law violates the Constitution.
3. Power is shared between the national and state governments.
4. to prevent the government from becoming too powerful and freedoms are part of the national identity
5. Legislative: can override a president's veto; Executive: can veto an act of Congress and control who is appointed to courts; Judicial: the Court can declare a law unconstitutional
6. Both are defined by the power of the people.

Interdisciplinary Activity Essays may focus on how the amendment has been interpreted and how it affects Americans today.

SECTION 2
The Federal Government

Guide to Reading

Main Idea

The government of the United States has three branches: the legislative branch, the executive branch, and the judicial branch.

Key Terms

appropriate, impeach, constituents

Read to Learn

• the goals of the three branches of the government.
• the powers of the three branches of the government.

1 FOCUS

BELLRINGER
Motivational Activity

Ask students to consider how our government would be different if we did not have a division of responsibility among the three branches. How would the government function if one group conducted all legislative, executive, and judicial functions?

Reading Preview

Preteaching Vocabulary
Ask students to use each **Key Term** in a sentence that demonstrates its meaning as defined in the Glossary.

Did you know?

Since January 1789, Americans have voted every other year on persons to represent them in their national government. This has not stopped despite a civil war, two world wars, and an economic depression. The American people reaffirm in every election James Madison's belief in the people's right to choose the government they would live by.

The Legislative Branch

Congress, the legislative branch of the government, makes the nation's laws. It also has the power to "lay and collect taxes" and to declare war. Congress has two houses, the House of Representatives and the Senate.

The House and Senate Today the House of Representatives has 435 voting members and five nonvoting delegates from the District of Columbia, Puerto Rico, Guam, American Samoa, and the Virgin Islands. The number of representatives from each state is determined by the state's population. Representatives, who must be at least 25 years old, serve two-year terms.

The Senate consists of 100 senators, two from each state. Senators, who must be at least 30 years old, serve six-year terms. The senators' terms are staggered, which means that one-third of the Senate seats come up for election every two years.

Seal of the U.S. Congress

The Role of Congress Congress has two primary functions: to make the nation's laws and to control government spending. The government cannot spend any money unless Congress *appropriates*, or sets aside, funds. All tax and spending bills must originate in the House of Representatives and gain approval in both the House and the Senate before moving on to the president for signature.

Congress also serves as a watchdog over the executive branch, monitoring its actions and investigating possible abuses of power. The House of Representatives can *impeach*, or bring formal charges against, any federal official it suspects of wrongdoing or misconduct. If an official is impeached, the Senate acts as a court and tries the accused official. Officials who are found guilty may be removed from office.

The Senate also holds certain special powers. Only the Senate can ratify treaties made by the president and confirm presidential appointments of federal officials, such as department heads, ambassadors, and federal judges.

All members of Congress have the responsibility of representing their *constituents*, the people of their home states and districts. As a constituent you can expect your senators and representatives to promote and protect your state's interests as well as those of the nation.

Congress at Work Thousands of **bills**, or proposed laws, are introduced in Congress every year. Because individual members of Congress

SECTION RESOURCES

📖 Reproducible Masters

• *Civics in Action: Activities, Quizzes, and Tests,* Guided Reading Activity 2
• *Civics in Action: Activities, Quizzes, and Tests,* Section 2 Quiz
• *Civics in Action: Activities, Quizzes, and Tests,* Enrichment Activity 2

📄 Transparencies

• *Civics in Action: Activities, Quizzes, and Tests,* Transparencies 1, 2, and 3

2 TEACH

Charting Powers Have partners or small groups make charts of the federal government's powers. Ask them to create three columns for the charts—one each for the legislative, the executive, and the judicial branches of government—noting the powers of each in the appropriate column. Students can share their charts during class discussion and use them for review. **L1, ELL**

The Living Constitution

Refer to **The Living Constitution** for student activities and information related to the Constitution.

you don't say...

Veto *Veto* is a Latin word meaning "I forbid." It originated in the Senate of ancient Rome to protect the rights of commoners.

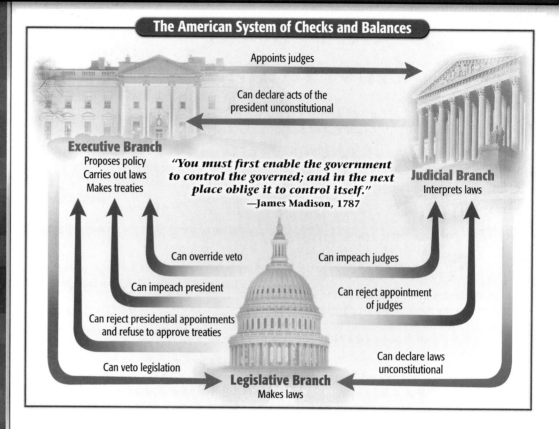

The American System of Checks and Balances

Appoints judges

Can declare acts of the president unconstitutional

Executive Branch
Proposes policy
Carries out laws
Makes treaties

"You must first enable the government to control the governed; and in the next place oblige it to control itself."
—James Madison, 1787

Judicial Branch
Interprets laws

Can override veto

Can impeach judges

Can impeach president

Can reject appointment of judges

Can reject presidential appointments and refuse to approve treaties

Can veto legislation

Can declare laws unconstitutional

Legislative Branch
Makes laws

---

cannot possibly study all these bills carefully, both houses use committees of selected members to evaluate proposed legislation.

Standing committees are permanent committees in both the House and the Senate that specialize in a particular topic, such as agriculture, commerce, or veterans' affairs. These committees usually are broken down into **subcommittees** that focus on a particular aspect of a problem or issue.

The House and the Senate sometimes form temporary **select committees** to deal with issues requiring special attention. These committees meet only until they complete their task.

Occasionally the House and the Senate form **joint committees** with members from both houses. These committees meet to consider specific issues, such as the system of federal taxation. One type of joint committee, a **conference committee,** has a special function. If the House

and the Senate pass different versions of the same bill, a conference committee tries to work out a compromise bill acceptable to both houses.

When it receives a bill, a committee can kill it by rejecting it outright, "pigeonhole" it by setting it aside without reviewing it, or prepare it for consideration by the full House or Senate. While preparing bills, committees hold public hearings at which citizens can present arguments and documents supporting or opposing the bills.

Once a bill is approved by a committee in either house of Congress, it is sent to the full Senate or House for debate. After debate the bill may be passed, rejected, or returned to committee for further changes.

When both houses pass a bill, the bill goes to the president. If the president approves the bill and signs it, it becomes law. If the president vetoes the bill, it does not become law,

224 Citizenship Handbook

Reading Strategy ⟩ READING THE TEXT

Synthesizing Have students work together to develop a set of 5 to 10 rules to use in the classroom. Offer the following as an example of such rules: During class discussion, students should not talk unless they raise their hands and the teacher recognizes them. Point out that rules should be acceptable to a two-thirds majority of the class. After students have completed the task, ask them to discuss the most difficult problems they faced in developing the rules. **L1**

unless Congress **overrides** (cancels) the presidential veto by a vote of two-thirds of the members in each house.

✓**Reading Check** **Sequencing** List the basic steps of how a bill becomes a law.

The Executive Branch

The executive branch of government includes the president, the vice president, and various executive offices, departments, and agencies. The executive branch carries out the laws that Congress passes.

Chief Executive The president plays a number of different roles in government, each of which has specific powers and responsibilities. These roles include the nation's chief executive, chief diplomat, commander in chief, chief of state, and legislative leader.

As chief executive, the president is responsible for carrying out the nation's laws. Many executive departments and agencies assist the president in this job.

Chief Diplomat As chief diplomat, the president directs foreign policy, appoints ambassadors, and negotiates treaties with other nations. Treaties must be approved by a two-thirds vote of the Senate before they go into effect.

Commander in Chief As commander in chief of the armed forces, the president can use the military to intervene or offer assistance in crises at home and around the world. The president cannot declare war; only Congress holds this power. The president can send troops to other parts of the world for up to 60 days but must notify Congress when doing so. The troops may remain longer only if Congress gives approval or declares war.

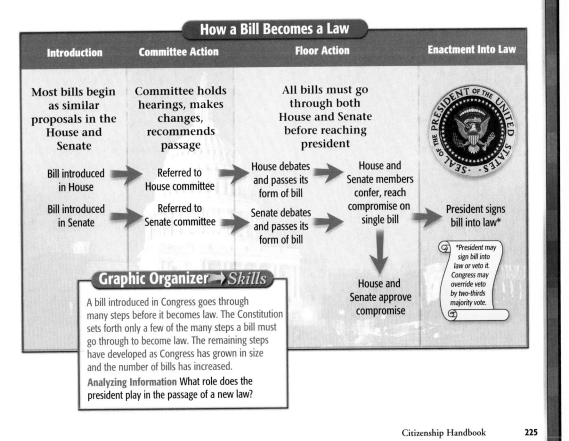

How a Bill Becomes a Law

Introduction	Committee Action	Floor Action	Enactment Into Law
Most bills begin as similar proposals in the House and Senate	Committee holds hearings, makes changes, recommends passage	All bills must go through both House and Senate before reaching president	

Bill introduced in House → Referred to House committee → House debates and passes its form of bill → House and Senate members confer, reach compromise on single bill → President signs bill into law*

Bill introduced in Senate → Referred to Senate committee → Senate debates and passes its form of bill →

House and Senate approve compromise

*President may sign bill into law or veto it. Congress may override veto by two-thirds majority vote.

Graphic Organizer → Skills

A bill introduced in Congress goes through many steps before it becomes law. The Constitution sets forth only a few of the many steps a bill must go through to become law. The remaining steps have developed as Congress has grown in size and the number of bills has increased.

Analyzing Information What role does the president play in the passage of a new law?

✓**Reading Check**

Answer: A bill is introduced in both houses; referred to committee in both houses; debated, marked up, and passed; compromise version worked out; compromise approved; president signs into law.

Graphic Organizer → Skills

Answer: The president may sign a passed bill into law or may try to keep it from becoming law by vetoing it.

**Graphic Organizer Skills Practice
Ask:** How many votes are necessary to override a presidential veto?
(a vote of two-thirds of the members in each house)

CURRICULUM CONNECTION

Civics Some presidents have used the veto sparingly; others have used it often. Franklin D. Roosevelt, for example, vetoed 635 pieces of legislation (only 9 of which were overridden). On the other hand, Richard M. Nixon vetoed 43 bills (with 7 overrides), and John F. Kennedy vetoed 21 (with no overrides).

DIFFERENTIATED INSTRUCTION

Reading Support Certain words from Section 2—*committee, office, department, agency, cabinet*—suggest the need for effective interaction among group members. Brainstorm with students for a list of characteristics of effective group work. The following ideas can prompt their thinking: chances for everyone to participate, a respect for one another's ideas, and working for the benefit of all. Discuss how each characteristic can benefit the work of a committee, an agency, and so on.
L2

📁 Refer to ***Inclusion for the Middle School Social Studies Classroom Strategies and Activities*** in the TCR.

✓ Reading Check

Answer: a group consisting of the heads of executive departments that helps the president make decisions and set policy

Cabinet *Cabinet* is French in origin; it refers to a small room for private meetings. Today the media covers cabinet meetings, but the term retains the idea of a close, private talk with trusted advisers.

Chief of State As chief of state, the president serves a symbolic role as the representative of all Americans. The president fulfills this role when receiving foreign ambassadors or heads of state, visiting foreign nations, or bestowing honors on Americans.

Legislative Leader The president serves as a legislative leader by proposing laws to Congress and working to see that they are passed. In the annual State of the Union address, the president presents goals for legislation.

The Executive Branch at Work Many executive offices, departments, and independent agencies help the president carry out and enforce the nation's laws. The Executive Office of the President (EOP) is made up of individuals and agencies that directly assist the president. Presidents rely heavily on the EOP for advice and for gathering information.

The executive branch also includes 14 executive departments, each responsible for a different area of government. For example, the

Picturing **History**

President George W. Bush describes a legislative program in the annual State of the Union message to Congress. **What powers does the president hold in his role as commander in chief?**

Department of State plans and carries out foreign policy, and the Department of the Interior manages and protects the nation's public lands and natural resources. The heads, or secretaries, of these departments are members of the president's **cabinet,** a group that helps the president make decisions and set government policy.

The independent agencies manage federal programs in many fields. These include aeronautics and space, banking, communications, farm credit, and trade. Government corporations are government agencies that are run like privately owned businesses. One government corporation whose services you may often use is the United States Postal Service.

✓ Reading Check **Describing** What is the president's cabinet?

The Judicial Branch

Article III of the Constitution called for the creation of a Supreme Court and "such inferior [lower] courts as Congress may from time to time ordain and establish." In 1789 Congress passed a **Judiciary Act,** which added a series of district courts to the federal court system. Congress added appeals courts, sometimes called circuit courts, in 1891 to ease the workload of the Supreme Court.

Lower Federal Courts At the lowest level of the federal court system are the United States **district courts.** These courts consider criminal and civil cases that come under federal, rather than state, authority. The criminal cases include such offenses as kidnapping and federal tax evasion. Civil cases cover claims against the federal government and cases involving constitutional rights, such as free speech. There are 91 district courts in the nation, with at least one in every state.

The next level of federal courts, the **appeals courts,** reviews district court decisions in which the losing side has asked for a review of the verdict. If an appeals court disagrees with the lower court's decision, it can either overturn the verdict or order a retrial. There are 14 appeals courts in the United States.

INTERDISCIPLINARY CONNECTIONS ACTIVITY

Politics Ask students to list 10 states of their choice and rank their choices in order of geographic size. Students may use almanacs, encyclopedias, and other reference books. Then have them find out how many members of the House of Representatives each state sends to Washington, D.C. Ask students to reorder their lists accordingly. Then discuss the differences between the lists, emphasizing the value of two kinds of representation: one based on population (for the House of Representatives), the other on a set number (for the Senate). **L2**

The Supreme Court The **Supreme Court** stands at the top of the American legal system. Article III of the Constitution created the Supreme Court as one of three coequal branches of the national government, along with Congress and the president.

The Supreme Court is composed of nine justices: the chief justice of the United States and eight associate justices. Congress sets this number and has the power to change it. Over the years it has varied from 5 to 10, but it has been 9 since 1869.

The Constitution does not describe the duties of the justices. Instead, the duties have developed from laws, through tradition, and as the needs and circumstances of the nation have developed. The main duty of the justices is to hear and rule on cases. This duty involves them in three decision-making tasks: deciding which cases to hear from among the thousands appealed to the Court each year; deciding the case itself; and determining an explanation for the decision, called the Court's **opinion.**

Shaping Public Policy The Supreme Court is both a political and a legal institution. It is a legal institution because it is responsible for settling disputes and interpreting the meaning of laws. The Court is a political institution because when it applies the law to specific disputes, it often determines what national policy will be. For example, when the Court rules that certain parts of the Social Security Act must apply to men and women equally, it is determining government policy.

Judicial Review As you have read, the Supreme Court's power to examine the laws and actions of local, state, and national governments and to cancel them if they violate the Constitution is called judicial review. The Supreme Court first assumed the power of judicial review in the case of *Marbury* v. *Madison* (1803). Since then, the Court has invalidated, or canceled, nearly 200 provisions of federal law.

The Supreme Court may also review presidential policies. In the case of *Ex parte Milligan* (1866), the Court ruled President Lincoln's suspension of certain civil rights during the Civil War was unconstitutional.

Judicial review of state laws and actions may have as much significance as the Court's activities at the federal level. In *Brown* v. *Board of Education of Topeka* (1954), the Court held that laws requiring or permitting racially segregated schools in four states were unconstitutional. The *Brown* decision cleared the way for the end of segregated schools throughout the nation.

✓ **Reading Check** **Describing** How was the court system set up?

✓ **Reading Check**

Answer: At the lowest level of the federal court system are the district courts which handle federal criminal and civil cases. Appeals courts review district court decisions and can either overturn the verdict or order a retrial. The Supreme Court examines the laws and actions of local, state, and national governments and reviews presidential policies.

Who?What?Where?When?

Sandra Day O'Connor In 1981 Sandra Day O'Connor became the first female Supreme Court justice. President Ronald Reagan appointed her, saying, "She is truly a person for all seasons, possessing those unique qualities of temperament, fairness, intellectual capacity, and devotion to the public good, which had characterized the 101 brethren who had preceded her." Ruth Bader Ginsburg, appointed by President Bill Clinton, joined O'Connor on the Court in 1993.

SECTION 2 ASSESSMENT

Checking for Understanding

1. **Key Terms** Use each of these terms in a complete sentence that helps explain its meaning: appropriate, impeach, constituents.
2. **Reviewing Facts** List three responsibilities of the president.

Reviewing Themes

3. **Government and Democracy** Why is Congress's power to appropriate money important?

Critical Thinking

4. **Analyzing Information** Which branch of government do you think is most powerful? Explain why you think so.
5. **Analyzing Information** Re-create the diagram below and provide five different kinds of Congressional committees.

Analyzing Visuals

6. **Reading a Flowchart** Refer to the flowchart on page 225. What do committees do to a bill?

Interdisciplinary Activity

Current Events Research in newspapers and news magazines about bills that are being debated in Congress. Find out what the bill will do if it is passed. Write a one-page paper about the bill and what has happened to it as it has gone through Congress.

Citizenship Handbook **227**

SECTION 2 ASSESSMENT ANSWERS

1. Student work should reflect correct use of terms.
2. Answers may include: the president is responsible for carrying out the nation's laws; the president directs foreign policy; and the president serves as a representative for all Americans.
3. All tax and spending bills must start in the House of Representatives. Without funds, the government has no power.
4. Answers should describe one branch of government and give reasons why students think it is the most powerful.
5. standing, subcommittee, select, joint, conference

6. Committees hold hearings, make changes, and recommend passage.

Interdisciplinary Activity Papers should reflect students' research about a current bill being debated in Congress. Students should note how the bill has changed from its original version.

3 ASSESS

Assign Section 2 Assessment as homework or as an in-class activity.

4 CLOSE

Ask students to suggest a scenario in which all three branches of government would become involved in making and administering a law.

1 FOCUS

BELLRINGER
Motivational Activity

Ask students to list the rights they possess as American citizens. *(Most students will mention the right to speak freely, right to worship, right to vote, right to a fair trial, and right to be treated equally regardless of race or religion.)* Point out that we "pay" for American citizenship by performing certain duties and responsibilities.

Reading Preview

Preteaching Vocabulary
Have students use the Glossary to look up definitions of each of the **Key Terms.** Then ask them to explain how *citizen* and *naturalization* are related.

✓ Reading Check

Answer: The government must follow procedures established by law and guaranteed by the Constitution, treating all people according to these principles.

SECTION 3 — Citizens' Rights and Responsibilities

Guide to Reading

Main Idea
Citizens of the United States have both rights and responsibilities.

Key Terms
due process of law, citizen, naturalization

Read to Learn
- where the rights of citizens come from.
- the rights and responsibilities of United States citizens.

The Rights of American Citizens

❝We hold these truths to be self-evident, that all men are created equal, that they are endowed by their Creator with certain unalienable Rights, that among these are Life, Liberty, and the pursuit of Happiness.❞

These words from the Declaration of Independence continue to inspire Americans. They have encouraged Americans to pursue the ideals expressed in the Declaration and to create a Constitution and a Bill of Rights that protect these rights. The rights of Americans fall into three broad categories: the right to be protected from unfair actions of the government, to have equal treatment under the law, and to have basic freedoms.

Due Process The Fifth Amendment states that no person shall "be deprived of life, liberty, or property, without due process of law." Due process of law means that the government must follow procedures established by law and guaranteed by the Constitution, treating all people according to these principles.

Equal Protection All Americans, regardless of race, religion, or political beliefs, have the right to be treated the same under the law. The Fourteenth Amendment requires every state to grant its citizens "equal protection of the laws."

Basic Freedoms The basic freedoms involve the liberties outlined in the First Amendment—freedom of speech, freedom of religion, freedom of the press, freedom of assembly, and the right to petition. In a democratic society, power exists in the hands of the people. Therefore, its citizens must be free to exchange ideas freely.

The First Amendment allows citizens to criticize the government, in speech or in the press, without fear of punishment. It also states that the government cannot endorse a religion, nor can it prohibit citizens from practicing a religion if they choose to do so. In addition, the Ninth Amendment states that the rights of Americans are not limited to those mentioned in the Constitution. This has allowed basic freedoms to expand over the years through the passage of other amendments and laws. The Twenty-sixth Amendment, for example, extends the right to vote to American citizens 18 years of age.

Limits on Rights Our rights are not unlimited. The government can establish laws or rules to restrict certain standards to protect the health, safety, security, and moral standards of a community. Moreover, rights may be limited to prevent one person's rights from interfering with the rights of others. The restrictions of rights, however, must be reasonable and must apply to everyone equally.

✓ **Reading Check** Summarizing What is due process of law?

SECTION RESOURCES

📁 **Reproducible Masters**
- *Civics in Action: Activities, Quizzes, and Tests,* Constitution Posttest
- *Civics in Action: Activities, Quizzes, and Tests,* Guided Reading Activity 3
- *Civics in Action: Activities, Quizzes, and Tests,* Section 3 Quiz

- *Civics in Action: Activities, Quizzes, and Tests,* Enrichment Activity 3

📖 **Transparencies**
- *Civics in Action: Activities, Quizzes, and Tests,* Transparency 4

Citizen Participation

A citizen is a person who owes loyalty to and is entitled to the protection of a state or nation. How do you become an American citizen? Generally, citizenship is granted to anyone born within the borders of the United States. Citizenship is also granted to anyone born outside the United States if one parent is a United States citizen. A person of foreign birth can also become a citizen through the process of naturalization.

To qualify, applicants must be at least 18 years old. They must have been lawfully admitted for permanent residence and have lived in the United States for at least five years. They must possess good moral character and accept the principles of the Constitution. Applicants must also understand English and demonstrate an understanding of the history and principles of the government of the United States. Before being admitted to citizenship, applicants must be willing to give up any foreign allegiance and must promise to obey the Constitution and the laws of the United States.

As citizens of the United States, we are expected to carry out certain duties and responsibilities. **Duties** are things we are required to do by law. **Responsibilities** are things we should do. Fulfilling both our duties and our responsibilities helps ensure that we have a good government and that we continue to enjoy our rights.

Duties One of the duties of all Americans is to obey the law. Laws serve three important functions. They help maintain order; they protect the health, safety, and property of all citizens; and they make it possible for people to live together peacefully. If you disobey laws, for example, you endanger others and interfere with the smooth functioning of society. If you believe a law needs to be changed, you can work through your elected representatives to improve it.

Americans also have a duty to pay taxes. The government uses tax money to defend the nation, provide health insurance for people over 65, and build roads and bridges. Americans benefit from services provided by the government.

Flag Etiquette

★ The flag should be raised and lowered by hand and displayed only from sunrise to sunset. On special occasions, it may be displayed at night.

★ The flag may be displayed on all days, weather permitting, particularly on national and state holidays and on historic and special occasions.

★ No flag should be flown above the American flag or to the right of it at the same height.

★ The flag may be flown at half-mast to mourn the death of public officials.

★ The flag should never touch the ground or floor beneath it.

★ The flag may be flown upside down only to signal distress.

★ When the flag becomes old and tattered, it should be destroyed by burning. According to an approved custom, the Union (the white stars on the blue field) is first cut from the flag; then the two pieces, which no longer form a flag, are burned.

Another duty of citizens is to defend the nation. All males aged 18 and older must register with the government in case they are needed for military service. The nation no longer has a **draft,** or required military service, but a war could make the draft necessary again.

The Constitution guarantees all Americans the right to a trial by a jury of their peers (equals). For this reason you should be prepared to serve on a jury when you become eligible at the age of 18. Having a large group of jurors on hand is necessary to guarantee the right to a fair and speedy trial. You also have a duty to serve as a witness at a trial if called to do so.

Responsibilities The responsibilities of citizens are not as clear-cut as their duties. Because responsibilities are voluntary, people are not arrested or punished if they do not fulfill these obligations. The quality of our government and of our lives will diminish, however, if our responsibilities are not carried out.

Citizenship Handbook   **229**

2 TEACH

Reading Strategy

Comparing and Contrasting Concepts Ask students to speculate about the differences among a freedom, a right, and a responsibility. Call on volunteers to give examples to support their ideas. As students read and discuss this section, encourage them to modify their ideas. **L1**

The Living Constitution

Refer to *The Living Constitution* for student activities and information related to the Constitution.

CURRICULUM CONNECTION

Economics Income taxes account for nearly half the money collected by the federal government, whereas sales taxes are the source of about half of the revenue of state governments.

Draft This use of the noun *draft* comes from Old English and refers to a drawing or pulling, for example, as draftees' names or numbers might be drawn from a container.

COOPERATIVE LEARNING ACTIVITY

Depicting Citizenship Ask groups of students to create collages that depict Americans exercising the rights, duties, and/or responsibilities of their citizenship. Each group should choose a slogan as a basis for selecting that group's illustrations. Tasks could include gathering used magazines and newspapers to clip pictures; working on layout; providing necessary lettering; and selecting and gluing pictures. Have group representatives explain their finished collages. **L1**

Answer: the process by which a person of foreign birth can become a citizen

CURRICULUM CONNECTION

Civics Today we recognize the secret ballot as a protection of our right to make our electoral choices unhindered and without fear. When it was first introduced, however, some Southern states used it to deny voting rights to African Americans. Illiteracy rates were high among African Americans at the time, and to cast a secret ballot a voter had to be able to read.

3 ASSESS

Assign Section 3 Assessment as homework or as an in-class activity.

4 CLOSE

Have students brainstorm a list of rights they believe people throughout the world should have.

Keep in mind that government exists to serve you. Therefore, one of your responsibilities as a citizen is to know what the government is doing and to voice your opinion when you feel strongly about something the government has done or has failed to do. When the government learns that most people favor or oppose an action, it usually follows their wishes.

You also need to be informed about your rights and to exercise them when necessary. Knowing your rights helps preserve them. Other responsibilities include respecting diversity, accepting responsibility for your actions, and supporting your family.

Vote, Vote, Vote! Perhaps your most important responsibility as an American citizen will be to vote when you reach the age of 18. Voting allows you to participate in government and guide its direction. When you vote for people to represent you in government, you will be exercising your right of self-government. If you disapprove of the job your representatives are doing, it will be your responsibility to help elect other people in the next election. You can also let your representatives know how you feel about issues through letters, telephone calls, and petitions.

While not everyone holds public office, everyone can participate in government in other ways. Working on a political campaign, volunteering

Citizens taking part in a town meeting

to help in a hospital or a library, and participating in a local park cleanup are all ways to take responsibility and to make a contribution to good government and a well-run community.

Respecting Others' Rights To enjoy your rights to the fullest, you must be prepared to respect the rights of others. Respecting the rights of others also means respecting the rights of people with whom you disagree. Respecting and accepting others regardless of race, religion, beliefs, or other differences is essential in a democracy. All Americans are entitled to the same respect and good treatment.

✓ **Reading Check** **Identifying** What is naturalization?

SECTION 3 ASSESSMENT

Checking for Understanding

1. **Key Terms** Use each of these terms in a complete sentence that helps explain its meaning: **due process of law, citizen, naturalization.**
2. **Reviewing Facts** Why are personal responsibilities important?

Reviewing Themes

3. **Government and Democracy** Summarize three of the freedoms granted in the First Amendment.

Critical Thinking

4. **Analyzing Information** The Fifth Amendment states that people have the right of "due process of law." Why is this phrase important?
5. **Analyzing Information** Re-create the diagram below and provide the three categories of American rights.

Analyzing Visuals

6. **Analyzing a Chart** Refer to the chart on page 229. For what reason may the flag be flown at half-mast?

Interdisciplinary Activity

Civics One responsibility of being an American citizen is to become involved in the democratic system. Make a poster showing how students can get involved in their community's democracy. Display your poster in a prominent place in school.

SECTION 3 ASSESSMENT ANSWERS

1. Student work should reflect correct use of terms.
2. Fulfilling responsibilities helps to improve the quality of government and society.
3. Students should summarize three of the following: freedom of speech, freedom of religion, freedom of the press, freedom

of assembly, and the right to petition.
4. People are guaranteed the protections written in the Constitution.
5. the right to be protected from unfair actions of the government, the right to have equal treatment under the law, and the right to have basic freedoms

6. to mourn the death of public officials

Interdisciplinary Activity Posters should demonstrate ways to become involved in a democracy. Work with students to plan the display for the finished posters.

Handbook Assessment

✓ Reviewing Key Terms

Write the key term that completes each sentence. Then write a sentence for each term not chosen.

a. popular sovereignty   **d.** amendment
b. enumerated powers   **e.** implied powers
c. reserved powers   **f.** judicial review

1. A(n)_____ is a change to the Constitution.
2. Those powers that are suggested but not directly stated in the Constitution are called _____.
3. _____ is the Supreme Court's power to review all congressional acts and executive actions.
4. Those powers mentioned specifically in the Constitution are called _____.

✓ Reviewing Key Facts

5. List the six goals of government stated in the Preamble.
6. How does one become a naturalized citizen?
7. Explain why the amendment process is so difficult.
8. Explain why responsible citizenship is important. Provide examples of responsible citizenship.
9. How does the Constitution protect individual rights?
10. Summarize the basic freedoms outlined in the First Amendment.

✓ Critical Thinking

11. **Analyzing Information** Analyze how limited government, republicanism, and popular sovereignty are important parts of the Constitution.
12. **Identifying Options** Describe five possible ways a person can fulfill his or her responsibilities in society and at home.
13. **Comparing** Some people argue that there should be a limit on the number of terms a senator or representative can serve. What are some of the advantages of the present system, which does not limit these terms? What are some of the disadvantages?
14. **Predicting Consequences** Re-create the diagram below and predict what might have happened to the U.S. if the Framers had not provided for a system of checks and balances.

✓ Citizenship Cooperative Activity

15. **Examining Citizens' Rights** Working with a partner, choose one of the following rights and trace its historical development in the United States from the time the Constitution was ratified to the present:

    suffrage   freedom of speech
    freedom of religion   equal protection of law

16. **Civic Planning** Constitutions provide a plan for organizing and operating governments. What plan provides the rules for your local government? Contact a local government official to find out about the basic plan of your city or town. Share your findings with the class.

✓ Alternative Assessment

17. **Portfolio Writing Activity** Part of your responsibility as an American citizen is to be informed about what the government is doing and to voice your opinion about its actions. Compose a letter to the editor of your local newspaper. In your letter, express your opinion about an issue in your community.

Standardized Test Practice

Directions: Choose the *best* answer to the following question.

Under the Constitution, the president chooses judges to serve on the Supreme Court, but each choice must be approved by the Senate. This is an example of what principle of government?

A Checks and balances
B Federalism
C Separation of powers
D Judicial Review

Test-Taking Tip:

What do you think would happen if the president could choose all judges without anyone else's approval? The writers of the Constitution wanted to make sure that none of the three branches of government became too powerful. Which answer shows this idea?

---

9. It protects the people from unfair actions of the government and allows for basic freedoms and equal treatment under the law.
10. freedom of speech, religion, the press, assembly, and the right to petition

✓ Critical Thinking

11. The Framers feared misuse of government power and restricted it (limited government); governments receive their power by the will of the people (popular sovereignty) and the voters hold sovereign power (republicanism).
12. Answers may include: become informed about issues, vote, work on a campaign, volunteer, and respect differences of others.
13. advantages: legislators may demonstrate more experience and consistency in policy; disadvantages: legislators may become unwilling to consider new ideas and be less responsive to the needs of constituents
14. Students may note that the president could prevent a bill from becoming law or Congress could create laws that were unconstitutional.

✓ Citizenship Cooperative Activity

15. Students should identify the key historical developments for the specific right they choose.
16. Students should research the basic government plan of their city or town.

✓ Alternative Assessment

17. Letters should demonstrate awareness of a community issue.

Standardized Test Practice

Answer: A
Question Type: Civics
Answer Explanation: According to page 220, this is a check on the judicial branch.

✓ Reviewing Key Terms

1. d   **2.** e   **3.** f   **4.** b

Students should write sentences for *popular sovereignty* and *reserved powers*.

✓ Reviewing Key Facts

5. to form a more perfect union, establish justice, insure domestic tranquility, provide for the common defense, promote the general welfare, and secure the blessings of liberty

6. Applicants must be at least 18 years old; be lawfully admitted for permanent residence and have lived in the U.S. for at least five years; accept the Constitution's principles; understand English and principles of government; give up foreign allegiance and promise to obey the laws of the U.S.

7. The Framers wanted to discourage frequent or trivial changes to the Constitution.

8. Students may note how obeying laws and voting helps maintain the quality of government and society.

The Constitution of the United States

The Constitution of the United States is truly a remarkable document. It was one of the first written constitutions in modern history. The Framers wanted to devise a plan for a strong central government that would unify the country, as well as preserve the ideals of the Declaration of Independence. The document they wrote created a representative legislature, the office of president, a system of courts, and a process for adding amendments. For over 200 years, the flexibility and strength of the Constitution has guided the nation's political leaders. The document has become a symbol of pride and a force for national unity.

The entire text of the Constitution and its amendments follows. Those passages that have been set aside, outdated by the passage of time, or changed by the adoption of amendments are printed in blue. Also included are explanatory notes that will help clarify the meaning of each article and section.

James Madison, author of the Constitution

Preamble

We the People of the United States, in Order to form a more perfect Union, establish Justice, insure domestic Tranquility, provide for the common defence, promote the general Welfare, and secure the Blessings of Liberty to ourselves and our Posterity, do ordain and establish this Constitution for the United States of America.

Article I

Section 1

All legislative Powers herein granted shall be vested in a Congress of the United States, which shall consist of a Senate and House of Representatives.

Section 2

[1.] The House of Representatives shall be composed of Members chosen every second Year by the People of the several States, and the Electors in each State shall have the Qualifications requisite for Electors of the most numerous Branch of the State Legislature.

[2.] No person shall be a Representative who shall not have attained to the Age of twenty five Years, and been seven Years a Citizen of the United States, and who shall not, when elected, be an Inhabitant of that State in which he shall be chosen.

[3.] Representatives and direct Taxes shall be apportioned among the several States which may be included within this Union, according to their respective Numbers, which shall be determined by adding to the whole Number of free Persons, including those bound to Service for a Term of Years, and excluding Indians not taxed, three fifths of all other Persons. The actual Enumeration shall be made within three Years after the first Meeting of the Congress of the United States, and within every subsequent Term of ten Years, in such Manner as they shall by Law direct. The Number of Representatives shall not exceed one for every thirty Thousand, but each State shall have at Least one Representative; and until such enumeration shall be made, the State of New Hampshire shall be entitled to chuse three; Massachusetts eight, Rhode-Island and Providence Plantations one, Connecticut five, New-York six, New Jersey four, Pennsylvania eight, Delaware one, Maryland six, Virginia ten, North Carolina five, South Carolina five, and Georgia three.

[4.] When vacancies happen in the Representation from any State, the Executive Authority thereof shall issue Writs of Election to fill such Vacancies.

[5.] The House of Representatives shall chuse their Speaker and other Officers; and shall have the sole Power of Impeachment.

The Preamble introduces the Constitution and sets forth the general purposes for which the government was established. The Preamble also declares that the power of the government comes from the people.

The printed text of the document shows the spelling and punctuation of the parchment original.

Article I. The Legislative Branch

The Constitution contains seven divisions called articles. Each article covers a general topic. For example, Articles I, II, and III create the three branches of the national government—the legislative, executive, and judicial branches. Most of the articles are divided into sections.

> **Section 2. House of Representatives**
> **Division of Representatives Among the States** The number of representatives from each state is based on the size of the state's population. Each state is entitled to at least one representative. *What are the qualifications for members of the House of Representatives?*

Vocabulary

preamble: *introduction*
constitution: *principles and laws of a nation*
enumeration: *census or population count*
impeachment: *bringing charges against an official*

The Constitution of the United States **233**

TEACH

Analyzing Information Have students research data from the 1990 and 2000 censuses. Students should create a chart that identifies the populations of each state and the number of representatives each state had in 1990. Then students should list the populations each state had in 2000 and whether or not that state lost or gained representation in the House of Representatives. Have students identify which states gained the most seats and speculate as to why those states are gaining populations. **L2**

> **Answer:** A member of the House of Representatives must be at least 25 years old, be a United States citizen for at least seven years, and be an inhabitant of the state from which he or she was elected.

 VIDEOCASSETTE
Historic America Electronic Field Trips

View **Chapter 7** to learn more about Independence Hall.

EXTENDING THE CONTENT

Sergeants-at-Arms House and Senate sergeants-at-arms are the police officers of Congress. They enforce the rules and maintain order. When they walk down the aisle of the legislature, carrying a ceremonial staff called a mace, Congress must be orderly. Any member of Congress who persists in disorderly conduct is guilty of contempt. The sergeants-at-arms also maintain security within the Capitol and associated buildings and supervise the Capitol police force. Sometimes the sergeants-at-arms round up members for floor votes, personally escorting to the floor any member who refuses to attend.

United States Constitution

Analyzing Information Write on the chalkboard the following, which George Washington supposedly said to Thomas Jefferson in defense of the Senate: "We pour legislation into the senatorial saucer to cool it." Have students speculate on what Washington meant by this. *(The Senate was seen as the more deliberative of the two houses of Congress.)* **L1**

Answer: the Senate

Who?What?Where?When?

Senior Senator The oldest senator from each state is not known as the senior senator. It is the senator who has served the longest time in the upper house who is known as the senior senator.

Section 3. The Senate
Number of Members, Terms of Office, and Voting Procedure Originally, senators were chosen by the state legislators of their own states. The Seventeenth Amendment changed this, so that senators are now elected by the people. There are 100 senators, 2 from each state. The vice president serves as president of the Senate.

John Adams, the first vice president

Section 3. The Senate
Trial of Impeachment One of Congress's powers is the power to impeach—to accuse government officials of wrongdoing, put them on trial, and if necessary remove them from office. *Which body has the power to decide the official's guilt or innocence?*

Vocabulary

president pro tempore: *presiding officer of Senate who serves when the vice president is absent*
indictment: *charging a person with an offense*
quorum: *minimum number of members that must be present to conduct sessions*
adjourn: *to suspend a session*
immunity privilege: *members cannot be sued or prosecuted for anything they say in Congress*
emoluments: *salaries*
bill: *draft of a proposed law*
revenue: *income raised by government*

234   The Constitution of the United States

Section 3
[1.] The Senate of the United States shall be composed of two Senators from each State, chosen by the Legislature thereof, for six Years; and each Senator shall have one Vote.
[2.] Immediately after they shall be assembled in Consequence of the first Election, they shall be divided as equally as may be into three Classes. The Seats of the Senators of the first Class shall be vacated at the Expiration of the second Year, of the second Class at the Expiration of the fourth Year, and of the third Class at the Expiration of the sixth Year, so that one third may be chosen every second Year; and if Vacancies happen by Resignation, or otherwise, during the Recess of the Legislature of any State, the Executive thereof may make temporary Appointments until the next Meeting of the Legislature, which shall then fill such Vacancies.
[3.] No Person shall be a Senator who shall not have attained to the Age of thirty Years, and been nine Years a Citizen of the United States, and who shall not, when elected, be an Inhabitant of that State for which he shall be chosen.
[4.] The Vice President of the United States shall be President of the Senate, but shall have no Vote, unless they be equally divided.
[5.] The Senate shall chuse their other Officers, and also a President pro tempore, in the Absence of the Vice President, or when he shall exercise the Office of the President of the United States.
[6.] The Senate shall have the sole Power to try all Impeachments. When sitting for that Purpose, they shall be on Oath or Affirmation. When the President of the United States is tried, the Chief Justice shall preside: And no Person shall be convicted without the Concurrence of two thirds of the Members present.
[7.] Judgment in Cases of Impeachment shall not extend further than to removal from Office, and disqualification to hold and enjoy any Office of honor, Trust or Profit under the United States: but the Party convicted shall nevertheless be liable and subject to Indictment, Trial, Judgment and Punishment, according to Law.

Section 4
[1.] The Times, Places and Manner of holding Elections for Senators and Representatives, shall be prescribed in each State by the Legislature thereof; but the Congress may at any time by Law make or alter such Regulations, except as to the Places of chusing Senators.
[2.] The Congress shall assemble at least once in every Year, and such Meeting shall be on the first Monday in December, unless they shall by Law appoint a different Day.

CRITICAL THINKING ACTIVITY

Analyzing Information Remind students that representation in the House of Representatives is based on each state's population. Then have students ascertain the number of members in the House currently representing their state, and also the numbers in 1990 and 1985. This information is readily available in many almanacs. Ask students to discuss how a change in the number of House seats might affect a state. **L2**

234

Section 5

[1.] Each House shall be the Judge of the Elections, Returns and Qualifications of its own Members, and a Majority of each shall constitute a Quorum to do Business; but a smaller Number may adjourn from day to day, and may be authorized to compel the Attendance of absent Members, in such Manner, and under such Penalties as each House may provide.

[2.] Each House may determine the Rules of its Proceedings, punish its Members for disorderly Behaviour, and, with the Concurrence of two thirds, expel a Member.

[3.] Each House shall keep a Journal of its Proceedings, and from time to time publish the same, excepting such Parts as may in their Judgment require Secrecy; and the Yeas and Nays of the Members of either House on any question shall, at the Desire of one fifth of those Present, be entered on the Journal.

[4.] Neither House, during the Session of Congress, shall, without the Consent of the other, adjourn for more than three days, nor to any other Place than that in which the two Houses shall be sitting.

Section 6

[1.] The Senators and Representatives shall receive a Compensation for their Services, to be ascertained by Law, and paid out of the Treasury of the United States. They shall in all Cases, except Treason, Felony and Breach of the Peace, be privileged from Arrest during their Attendance at the Session of their respective Houses, and in going to and returning from the same; and for any Speech or Debate in either House, they shall not be questioned in any other Place.

[2.] No Senator or Representative shall, during the Time for which he was elected, be appointed to any civil Office under the Authority of the United States, which shall have been created, or the Emoluments whereof shall have been encreased during such time; and no Person holding any Office under the United States, shall be a Member of either House during his Continuance in Office.

Section 7

[1.] All Bills for raising Revenue shall originate in the House of Representatives; but the Senate may propose or concur with Amendments as on other Bills.

[2.] Every Bill which shall have passed the House of Representatives and the Senate, shall, before it become a Law, be presented to the President of the United States; If he approve he shall sign it, but if not he shall return it, with his Objections to that House in which it shall have originated, who shall enter the Objections at large on their Journal, and proceed to reconsider it. If after such Reconsideration two thirds of that House shall agree to pass the Bill, it shall be sent, together with the Objections, to the other House, by which it shall likewise be reconsidered, and if approved by two thirds

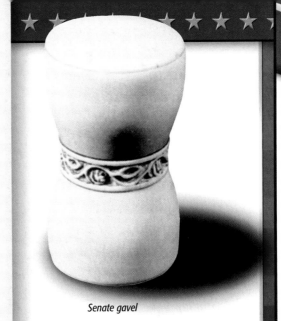

Senate gavel

Section 6. Privileges and Restrictions

Pay and Privileges To strengthen the federal government, the Founders set congressional salaries to be paid by the United States Treasury rather than by members' respective states. Originally, members were paid $6 per day. In 2002, all members of Congress received a base salary of $150,000.

Section 7. Passing Laws

Revenue Bills All tax laws must originate in the House of Representatives. This ensures that the branch of Congress that is elected by the people every two years has the major role in determining taxes.

Section 7. Passing Laws

How Bills Become Laws A bill may become a law only by passing both houses of Congress and by being signed by the president. The president can check Congress by rejecting—vetoing—its legislation. *How can Congress override the president's veto?*

The Constitution of the United States **235**

Constructing a Chart Have students construct a chart categorizing the legislative powers of Congress. Suggest that they list powers under the following categories: *Monetary, Commerce, Regulatory, Judicial, War, Implied.* **L1**

Answer: A bill can become law, despite not being signed by the president, if two-thirds of the House of Representatives and two-thirds of the Senate approve the bill.

Who?What?Where?When?

Jeannette Rankin Republican and pacifist Jeannette Rankin of Montana was the first woman elected to the House of Representatives in 1916. In 1917, along with 49 House colleagues, Rankin voted against the United States entering World War I. On December 8, 1941, the day after the bombing of Pearl Harbor, she was the only member of Congress to vote against declaring war on Japan.

COOPERATIVE LEARNING ACTIVITY

Understanding Ideas Organize students into groups of five to consider one of the expressed powers of Congress: taxing and spending; regulating commerce, foreign policy and national defense; providing for the nation's growth, and so on. Have each group discuss why the power it selected was delegated to Congress rather than to the executive branch. **L2**

Writing Letters Point out that because of the heavy volume of legislation, both houses of Congress have committees that do much of the work in preparing bills. Each committee deals with a particular issue, such as banking, foreign affairs, or natural resources. Encourage students to write letters asking representatives and senators from your state about the committees on which they serve. Invite volunteers to share the replies they receive. **L2**

Answer: Article 1, Section 8, Clause 11

Did you know?

When the first Congress was called to assemble in New York City in 1789, it took nearly a month for enough members to arrive to make a quorum.

Section 8. Powers Granted to Congress

Expressed Powers Expressed powers are those powers directly stated in the Constitution. Most of the expressed powers of Congress are listed in Article I, Section 8. These powers are also called enumerated powers because they are numbered 1–18. *Which clause gives Congress the power to declare war?*

Civil War money

Vocabulary

resolution: *legislature's formal expression of opinion*
naturalization: *procedure by which a citizen of a foreign nation becomes a citizen of the United States*
tribunal: *a court*
letter of marque: *authority given to a citizen to outfit an armed ship and use it to attack enemy ships in time of war*
reprisal: *taking by force property or territory belonging to another country or to its citizens*
insurrection: *rebellion*

236   The Constitution of the United States

of that House, it shall become a Law. But in all such Cases the Votes of both Houses shall be determined by yeas and Nays, and the Names of the Persons voting for and against the Bill shall be entered on the Journal of each House respectively. If any Bill shall not be returned by the President within ten Days (Sundays excepted) after it shall have been presented to him, the Same shall be a Law, in like Manner as if he had signed it, unless the Congress by their Adjournment prevent its Return, in which Case it shall not be a Law.

[3.] Every Order, Resolution, or Vote to which the Concurrence of the Senate and House of Representatives may be necessary (except on a question of Adjournment) shall be presented to the President of the United States; and before the Same shall take Effect, shall be approved by him, or being disapproved by him, shall be repassed by two thirds of the Senate and House of Representatives, according to the Rules and Limitations prescribed in the Case of a Bill.

Section 8

[1.] The Congress shall have the Power To lay and collect Taxes, Duties, Imposts and Excises, to pay the Debts and provide for the common Defence and general Welfare of the United States; but all Duties, Imposts and Excises shall be uniform throughout the United States;

[2.] To borrow Money on the credit of the United States;

[3.] To regulate Commerce with foreign Nations, and among the several States, and with the Indian Tribes;

[4.] To establish an uniform Rule of Naturalization, and uniform Laws on the subject of Bankruptcies throughout the United States;

[5.] To coin Money, regulate the Value thereof, and of foreign Coin, and fix the Standard of Weights and Measures;

[6.] To provide for the Punishment of counterfeiting the Securities and current Coin of the United States;

[7.] To establish Post Offices and post Roads;

[8.] To promote the Progress of Science and useful Arts, by securing for limited Times to Authors and Inventors the exclusive Right to their respective Writings and Discoveries;

[9.] To constitute Tribunals inferior to the supreme Court;

[10.] To define and punish Piracies and Felonies committed on the high Seas, and Offences against the Law of Nations;

[11.] To declare War, grant Letters of Marque and Reprisal, and make Rules concerning Captures on Land and Water;

CRITICAL THINKING ACTIVITY

Synthesizing Information Call on students to list the qualifications for serving in Congress as set forth in the Constitution. Then ask students what other qualifications, if any, they think should be applied to members of Congress. Discuss with students whether they would like to serve in Congress. **L1**

[12.] To raise and support Armies, but no Appropriation of Money to that Use shall be for a longer Term than two Years;

[13.] To provide and maintain a Navy;

[14.] To make Rules for the Government and Regulation of the land and naval Forces;

[15.] To provide for calling forth the Militia to execute the Laws of the Union, suppress Insurrections and repel Invasions;

[16.] To provide for organizing, arming, and disciplining, the Militia, and for governing such Part of them as may be employed in the Service of the United States, reserving to the States respectively, the Appointment of the Officers, and the Authority of training the Militia according to the discipline prescribed by Congress;

[17.] To exercise exclusive Legislation in all Cases whatsoever, over such District (not exceeding ten Miles square) as may, by Cession of particular States, and the Acceptance of Congress, become the Seat of Government of the United States, and to exercise like Authority over all Places purchased by the Consent of the Legislature of the State in which the Same shall be, for the Erection of Forts, Magazines, Arsenals, dock-Yards, and other needful Buildings;—And

[18.] To make all Laws which shall be necessary and proper for carrying into Execution the foregoing Powers, and all other Powers vested by this Constitution in the Government of the United States, or in any Department or Officer thereof.

Section 9

[1.] The Migration or Importation of such Persons as any of the States now existing shall think proper to admit, shall not be prohibited by the Congress prior to the Year one thousand eight hundred and eight, but a Tax or duty may be imposed on such Importation, not exceeding ten dollars for each Person.

[2.] The Privilege of the Writ of Habeas Corpus shall not be suspended, unless when in Cases of Rebellion or Invasion the public Safety may require it.

[3.] No Bill of Attainder or ex post facto Law shall be passed.

[4.] No Capitation, or other direct, Tax shall be laid, unless in Proportion to the Census or Enumeration herein before directed to be taken.

[5.] No Tax or Duty shall be laid on Articles exported from any State.

[6.] No Preference shall be given by any Regulation of Commerce or Revenue to the Ports of one State over those of another: nor shall Vessels bound to, or from, one State, be obliged to enter, clear, or pay Duties in another.

Seal of the U.S. Navy

Section 8. Powers Granted to Congress

Elastic Clause The final enumerated power is often called the "elastic clause." This clause gives Congress the right to make all laws "necessary and proper" to carry out the powers expressed in the other clauses of Article I. It is called the elastic clause because it lets Congress "stretch" its powers to meet situations the Founders could never have anticipated.

What does the phrase "necessary and proper" in the elastic clause mean? Almost from the beginning, this phrase was a subject of dispute. The issue was whether a strict or a broad interpretation of the Constitution should be applied. The dispute was first addressed in 1819, in the case of *McCulloch* v. *Maryland*, when the Supreme Court ruled in favor of a broad interpretation.

Section 9. Powers Denied to the Federal Government

Habeas Corpus A writ of habeas corpus issued by a judge requires a law official to bring a prisoner to court and show cause for holding the prisoner. A bill of attainder is a bill that punished a person without a jury trial. An "ex post facto" law is one that makes an act a crime after the act has been committed. *What does the Constitution say about bills of attainder?*

Evaluating Issues Article I, Section 9, prohibits the suspension of the writ of habeas corpus. Discuss with students the protection this offers. Ask students if they think this is an outdated principle today or still necessary to the Constitution. *(Most students will see this is a major principle of our legal system.)* **L2**

Answer: No bills of attainder shall be passed.

CURRICULUM CONNECTION

Civics On many occasions when the United States has intervened militarily, Congress has not issued a declaration of war. These "undeclared wars" of the twentieth century include the conflicts in Korea and Vietnam. Both wars were fought on the president's authority to support governments against external aggression.

EXTENDING THE CONTENT

The Capitol The interior of the Capitol is a combination of new and old. Many of the furnishings and works of art date from the mid-1800s. However, signs of modern technology are everywhere. Roll-call votes are counted electronically. In addition, members of both houses have access to computers and other electronic information services. There are even electric subways connecting many of the office buildings on Capitol Hill.

United States Constitution

FOCUS

BELLRINGER
Motivational Activity

Point out that one of the difficult questions for the Framers of the Constitution concerned the Chief Executive—exactly how much power should the president have? Have students discuss why the Framers set up an office of president with limited powers. *(Discussion should focus on the Framers' fear of a single leader with uncontrolled powers.)*

Did you know?

One of the most important traditional measures of the president's standing with the public is the Gallup presidential approval survey, or poll. Since 1945 the Gallup Organization has polled members of the public monthly—and sometimes more often—about whether they approve or disapprove of the president's handling of the job.

> ### Section 10. Powers Denied to the States
> **Limitations on Power** Section 10 lists limits on the states. These restrictions were designed, in part, to prevent an overlapping in functions and authority with the federal government.

United States coins

Article II. The Executive Branch

Article II creates an executive branch to carry out laws passed by Congress. Article II lists the powers and duties of the presidency, describes qualifications for office and procedures for electing the president, and provides for a vice president.

Vocabulary

appropriations: *funds set aside for a specific use*
emolument: *payment*
impost: *tax*
duty: *tax*

238   The Constitution of the United States

[7.] No Money shall be drawn from the Treasury, but in Consequence of Appropriations made by Law; and a regular Statement and Account of the Receipts and Expenditures of all public Money shall be published from time to time.

[8.] No Title of Nobility shall be granted by the United States: And no Person holding any Office of Profit or Trust under them, shall, without the Consent of the Congress, accept of any present, Emolument, Office, or Title, of any kind whatever, from any King, Prince, or foreign State.

Section 10

[1.] No State shall enter into any Treaty, Alliance, or Confederation; grant Letters of Marque and Reprisal; coin Money; emit Bills of Credit; make any Thing but gold and silver Coin a Tender in Payment of Debts; pass any Bill of Attainder, ex post facto Law, or Law impairing the Obligation of Contracts, or grant any Title of Nobility.

[2.] No State shall, without the Consent of the Congress, lay any Imposts or Duties on Imports or Exports, except what may be absolutely necessary for executing it's inspection Laws: and the net Produce of all Duties and Imposts, laid by any State on Imports and Exports, shall be for the Use of the Treasury of the United States; and all such Laws shall be subject to the Revision and Controul of the Congress.

[3.] No State shall, without the Consent of Congress, lay any Duty of Tonnage, keep Troops, or Ships of War in time of Peace, enter into any Agreement or Compact with another State, or with a foreign Power, or engage in War, unless actually invaded, or in such imminent Danger as will not admit of delay.

Article II

Section 1

[1.] The executive Power shall be vested in a President of the United States of America. He shall hold his Office during the Term of four Years, and, together with the Vice President, chosen for the same Term, be elected, as follows

[2.] Each State shall appoint, in such Manner as the Legislature thereof may direct, a Number of Electors, equal to the whole Number of Senators and Representatives to which the State may be entitled in the Congress: but no Senator or Representative, or Person holding an Office of Trust or Profit under the United States, shall be appointed an Elector.

[3.] The Electors shall meet in their respective States, and vote by Ballot for two Persons, of whom one at least shall not be an Inhabitant of the same State with

---

EXTENDING THE CONTENT

Two-Term Limits The Constitution originally did not limit the number of terms the Chief Executive could serve. George Washington served two terms, as did all presidents until Franklin D. Roosevelt. Many people opposed Roosevelt's four terms in office. This opposition eventually led to the ratification of the Twenty-second Amendment in 1951, which limited presidents to two terms.

themselves. And they shall make a List of all the Persons voted for, and of the Number of Votes for each; which List they shall sign and certify, and transmit sealed to the Seat of the Government of the United States, directed to the President of the Senate. The President of the Senate shall, in the Presence of the Senate and House of Representatives, open all the Certificates, and the Votes shall then be counted. The Person having the greatest Number of Votes shall be the President, if such Number be a Majority of the whole Number of Electors appointed; and if there be more than one who have such Majority, and have an equal Number of Votes, then the House of Representatives shall immediately chuse by Ballot one of them for President; and if no person have a Majority, then from the five highest on the List the said House shall in like Manner chuse the President. But in chusing the President, the Votes shall be taken by States, the Representation from each State having one Vote; A quorum for this Purpose shall consist of a Member or Members from two thirds of the States, and a Majority of all the States shall be necessary to a Choice. In every Case, after the Choice of the President, the Person having the greatest Number of Votes of the Electors shall be the Vice President. But if there should remain two or more who have equal Votes, the Senate shall chuse from them by Ballot the Vice President.

[4.] The Congress may determine the Time of chusing the Electors, and the Day on which they shall give their Votes; which Day shall be the same throughout the United States.

[5.] No Person except a natural born Citizen, or a Citizen of the United States, at the time of the Adoption of this Constitution, shall be eligible to the Office of President; neither shall any Person be eligible to that Office who shall not have attained to the Age of thirty five Years, and been fourteen Years a Resident within the United States.

[6.] In Case of the Removal of the President from Office, or of his Death, Resignation, or Inability to discharge the Powers and Duties of the said Office, the Same shall devolve on the Vice President, and the Congress may by Law provide for the Case of Removal, Death, Resignation or Inability, both of the President and Vice President, declaring what Officer shall then act as President, and such Officer shall act accordingly, until the Disability be removed, or a President shall be elected.

[7.] The President shall, at stated Times, receive for his Services, a Compensation, which shall neither be encreased nor diminished during the Period for which he shall have been elected, and he shall not receive within that Period any other Emolument from the United States, or any of them.

[8.] Before he enter on the Execution of his Office, he shall take the following Oath or Affirmation:—"I do solemnly swear (or affirm) that I will faithfully execute the Office of President of the United States, and will to the best of my Ability, preserve, protect and defend the Constitution of the United States."

Section 1. President and Vice President

Former Method of Election The Twelfth Amendment, added in 1804, changed the method of electing the president stated in Article II, Section 1, paragraph 3. The Twelfth Amendment requires that the electors cast separate ballots for president and vice president.

George Washington, the first president

Section 1. President and Vice President

Qualifications The president must be a citizen of the United States by birth, at least 35 years of age, and a resident of the United States for 14 years.

Section 1. President and Vice President

Vacancies If the president dies, resigns, is removed from office by impeachment, or is unable to carry out the duties of the office, the vice president assumes the duties of the president. The Twenty-Fifth Amendment sets procedures for presidential succession.

Section 1. President and Vice President

Salary Originally, the president's salary was $25,000 per year. The president's current salary is $400,000 plus a $50,000 nontaxable expense account per year. The president also receives living accommodations in two residences—the White House and Camp David.

The Constitution of the United States **239**

TEACH

Reading Strategy

Classifying Information Have students read Article II to find the powers of the president. Suggest that they classify these powers under the headings *Executive, Legislative, Diplomatic, Military,* and *Judicial.* **L1**

Making Judgments Ask students to discuss why the Framers of the Constitution made the president commander in chief of the armed forces and any state militias called to serve the United States. (*The Framers wanted to ensure civilian control of the military.*) **L2**

Did you know?

The electors in the Electoral College almost always vote as expected. Exceptions are rare: there have only been nine "faithless electors" among the more than 17,000 electors chosen since 1789. Most recently, in 1988 Democratic nominee Michael Dukakis was denied one of his 112 electoral votes when a West Virginia elector cast her ballot for Dukakis's running mate, Lloyd Bentsen. She gave her vice presidential vote to Dukakis.

CRITICAL THINKING ACTIVITY

Determining Cause and Effect Discuss examples showing the increase in presidential power during this century. For example, increasing globalization has expanded the President's foreign relations responsibilities, such as negotiating international treaties, military policing interventions, and waging "undeclared wars" (without the authorization of Congress). Write the following statement on the chalkboard: "The increase in presidential power during the twentieth century has been largely related to crises, whether domestic or foreign." **Ask:** Do you think this is the true cause of the increase in presidential power? Why or why not? If not, what do you think caused the increase? **L3**

United States Constitution

FOCUS

Did you know?

In the first election, the American people had no problem selecting a president. George Washington was the unanimous choice, winning 69 electoral votes—the maximum possible in 1789. No other president has matched that feat, although Franklin D. Roosevelt came close in 1936 with 98.5 percent of the electoral vote. Most other presidential elections have been more competitive, sometimes creating issues the Founders did not foresee.

Section 2. Powers of the President

Military, Cabinet, Pardons Mention of "the principal officer in each of the executive departments" is the only suggestion of the president's cabinet to be found in the Constitution. The cabinet is an advisory body, and its power depends on the president. Section 2, Clause 1 also makes the president—a civilian—the head of the armed services. This established the principle of civilian control of the military.

Section 2. Powers of the President

Treaties and Appointments An executive order is a command issued by a president to exercise a power which he has been given by the U.S. Constitution or by a federal statute. In times of emergency, presidents sometimes have used the executive order to override the Constitution of the United States and the Congress. During the Civil War, President Lincoln suspended many fundamental rights guaranteed in the Constitution and the Bill of Rights. He closed down newspapers that opposed his policies and imprisoned some who disagreed with him. Lincoln said that these actions were justified to preserve the Union.

Impeachment ticket

Article III. The Judicial Branch

The term *judicial* refers to courts. The Constitution set up only the Supreme Court but provided for the establishment of other federal courts. The judiciary of the United States has two different systems of courts. One system consists of the federal courts, whose powers derive from the Constitution and federal laws. The other includes the courts of each of the 50 states, whose powers derive from state constitutions and laws.

240   The Constitution of the United States

Section 2

[1.] The President shall be Commander in Chief of the Army and Navy of the United States, and of the Militia of the several States, when called into the actual Service of the United States; he may require the Opinion, in writing, of the principal Officer in each of the executive Departments, upon any Subject relating to the Duties of their respective Offices, and he shall have Power to grant Reprieves and Pardons for Offences against the United States, except in Cases of Impeachment.

[2.] He shall have Power, by and with the Advice and Consent of the Senate, to make Treaties, provided two thirds of the Senators present concur; and he shall nominate, and by and with the Advice and Consent of the Senate, shall appoint Ambassadors, other public Ministers and Consuls, Judges of the supreme Court, and all other Officers of the United States, whose Appointments are not herein otherwise provided for, and which shall be established by Law: but the Congress may by Law vest the Appointment of such inferior Officers, as they think proper, in the President alone, in the Courts of Law, or in the Heads of Departments.

[3.] The President shall have Power to fill up all Vacancies that may happen during the Recess of the Senate, by granting Commissions which shall expire at the End of their next Session.

Section 3

He shall from time to time give to the Congress Information of the State of the Union, and recommend to their Consideration such Measures as he shall judge necessary and expedient; he may, on extraordinary Occasions, convene both Houses, or either of them, and in Case of Disagreement between them, with Respect to the Time of Adjournment, he may adjourn them to such Time as he shall think proper; he shall receive Ambassadors and other public Ministers; he shall take Care that the Laws be faithfully executed, and shall Commission all the Officers of the United States.

Section 4

The President, Vice President and all civil Officers of the United States, shall be removed from Office on Impeachment for, and Conviction of, Treason, Bribery, or other high Crimes and Misdemeanors.

Article III

Section 1

The judicial Power of the United States, shall be vested in one supreme Court, and in such inferior Courts as the Congress may from time to time ordain and establish. The Judges, both of the supreme and inferior Courts, shall hold their Offices during good Behaviour, and shall, at stated Times, receive for their Services, a Compensation, which shall not be diminished during their Continuance in Office.

EXTENDING THE CONTENT

Minorities and the Supreme Court Until the late 1900s, all Supreme Court justices were white males. The first African American justice, Thurgood Marshall, was named to the Court by President Lyndon Johnson in 1967. President Ronald Reagan nominated the first woman justice, Sandra Day O'Connor, in 1981.

Section 2

[1.] The judicial Power shall extend to all Cases, in Law and Equity, arising under this Constitution, the Laws of the United States, and Treaties made, or which shall be made, under their Authority;—to all Cases affecting Ambassadors, other public Ministers and Consuls;—to all Cases of admiralty and maritime Jurisdiction;—to Controversies to which the United States shall be a Party;—to Controversies between two or more States;—between a State and Citizens of another State;—between Citizens of different States,—between Citizens of the same State claiming Lands under Grants of different States, and between a State, or the Citizens thereof, and foreign States, Citizens or Subjects.

[2.] In all Cases affecting Ambassadors, other public Ministers and Consuls, and those in which a State shall be Party, the supreme Court shall have original Jurisdiction. In all the other Cases before mentioned, the supreme Court shall have appellate Jurisdiction, both as to Law and Fact, with such Exceptions, and under such Regulations as the Congress shall make.

[3.] The Trial of all Crimes, except in Cases of Impeachment, shall be by Jury; and such Trial shall be held in the State where the said Crimes shall have been committed; but when not committed within any State, the Trial shall be at such Place or Places as the Congress may by Law have directed.

Section 3

[1.] Treason against the United States, shall consist only in levying War against them, or in adhering to their Enemies, giving them Aid and Comfort. No Person shall be convicted of Treason unless on the Testimony of two Witnesses to the same overt Act, or on Confession in open Court.

[2.] The Congress shall have Power to declare the Punishment of Treason, but no Attainder of Treason shall work Corruption of Blood, or Forfeiture except during the Life of the Person attainted.

Article IV

Section 1

Full Faith and Credit shall be given in each State to the public Acts, Records, and judicial Proceedings of every other State. And the Congress may by general Laws prescribe the Manner in which such Acts, Records and Proceedings shall be proved, and the Effect thereof.

Section 2. Jurisdiction

Statute Law Federal courts deal mostly with "statute law," or laws passed by Congress, treaties, and cases involving the Constitution itself.

Section 2. Jurisdiction

The Supreme Court A Court with "original jurisdiction" has the authority to be the first court to hear a case. The Supreme Court primarily has "appellate jurisdiction" and mostly hears cases appealed from lower courts.

Article IV. Relations Among the States

Article IV explains the relationship of the states to one another and to the national government. This article requires each state to give citizens of other states the same rights as its own citizens, addresses admitting new states, and guarantees that the national government will protect the states.

Vocabulary

original jurisdiction: *authority to be the first court to hear a case*

appellate jurisdiction: *authority to hear cases that have been appealed from lower courts*

treason: *violation of the allegiance owed by a person to his or her own country, for example, by aiding an enemy*

The Constitution of the United States **241**

TEACH

Analyzing Ideas Point out that federal judges are appointed for life and can be removed only by their death, resignation, or impeachment. Ask students why they think the Framers of the Constitution made judgeships lifetime appointments. *(The Framers believed that judges who felt secure in their positions would be more likely to make unpopular, but correct, decisions.)* **L2**

Writing Reports Encourage students to listen to excerpts from "May It Please the Court," recordings of the Supreme Court in session. Have them write a brief report on the case or cases they listened to. **L2**

CURRICULUM CONNECTION

Civics The judiciary is only briefly described in the Constitution. The federal court system was established by the Judiciary Act of 1789.

CRITICAL THINKING ACTIVITY

Predicting Outcomes Have students discuss the pros and cons of federal judges being elected rather than appointed. Direct them to list the possible outcomes they foresee if the federal judiciary was subject to the electoral process. Encourage students to share and compare their lists. **L3**

FOCUS

Inform students that one political scientist has called the supremacy clause (Article VI, Section 2) "the most important single provision of the Constitution." Ask students to think about why this might be so. *(This clause made it clear that the national Constitution and laws are supreme over state constitutions.)*

TEACH

Expressing Viewpoints Have students speculate about why the Framers of the Constitution established the amendment process as they did. *(The Framers wanted to make the Constitution flexible, but not so easy to amend that it would not be respected.)* Ask students to discuss the following questions: Should the amendment process be made easier? Why or why not? **L2**

Answer: a change to the Constitution

Section 3. New States and Territories

New States Congress has the power to admit new states. It also determines the basic guidelines for applying for statehood. Two states, Maine and West Virginia, were created within the boundaries of another state. In the case of West Virginia, President Lincoln recognized the West Virginia government as the legal government of Virginia during the Civil War. This allowed West Virginia to secede from Virginia without obtaining approval from the Virginia legislature.

Section 4. Federal Protection for States

Republic Government can be classified in many different ways. The ancient Greek philosopher Aristotle classified government based on the question: Who governs? According to Aristotle, all governments belong to one of three major groups: (1) autocracy—rule by one person; (2) oligarchy—rule by a few persons; or (3) democracy—rule by many persons. A republic is a form of democracy in which the people elect representatives to make laws and conduct government.

Article V. The Amendment Process

Article V spells out the ways that the Constitution can be amended, or changed. All of the 27 amendments were proposed by a two-thirds vote of both houses of Congress. Only the Twenty-first Amendment was ratified by constitutional conventions of the states. All other amendments have been ratified by state legislatures. *What is an amendment?*

Vocabulary

extradition: *surrender of a criminal to another authority*
amendment: *a change to the Constitution*
ratification: *process by which an amendment is approved*

Section 2

[1.] The Citizens of each State shall be entitled to all Privileges and Immunities of Citizens in the several States.

[2.] A Person charged in any State with Treason, Felony, or other Crime, who shall flee from Justice, and be found in another State, shall on Demand of the executive Authority of the State from which he fled, be delivered up, to be removed to the State having Jurisdiction of the Crime.

[3.] No Person held to Service or Labour in one State, under the Laws thereof, escaping into another, shall, in Consequence of any Law or Regulation therein, be discharged from such Service or Labour, but shall be delivered up on Claim of the Party to whom such Service or Labour may be due.

Section 3

[1.] New States may be admitted by the Congress into this Union; but no new State shall be formed or erected within the Jurisdiction of any other State; nor any State be formed by the Junction of two or more States, or Parts of States, without the Consent of the Legislatures of the States concerned as well as of the Congress.

[2.] The Congress shall have Power to dispose of and make all needful Rules and Regulations respecting the Territory or other Property belonging to the United States; and nothing in this Constitution shall be so construed as to Prejudice any Claims of the United States, or of any particular State.

Section 4

The United States shall guarantee to every State in this Union a Republican Form of Government, and shall protect each of them against Invasion; and on Application of the Legislature, or of the Executive (when the Legislature cannot be convened) against domestic Violence.

Article V

The Congress, whenever two thirds of both Houses shall deem it necessary, shall propose Amendments to this Constitution, or, on the Application of the Legislatures of two thirds of the several States, shall call a Convention for proposing Amendments, which, in either Case, shall be valid to all Intents and Purposes, as Part of this Constitution, when ratified by the Legislatures of three fourths of the several States, or by Conventions in three fourths thereof, as the one or the other Mode of Ratification may be proposed by the Congress; Provided that no Amendment which may be made prior to the Year One thousand eight hundred and eight shall in any Manner affect the first and fourth Clauses in the Ninth Section of the first Article; and that no State, without its Consent, shall be deprived of its equal Suffrage in the Senate.

Article VI

[1.] All Debts contracted and Engagements entered into, before the Adoption of this Constitution, shall be as valid against the United States under this Constitution, as under the Confederation.

[2.] This Constitution, and the Laws of the United States which shall be made in Pursuance thereof; and all Treaties made, or which shall be made, under the Authority of the United States, shall be the supreme Law of the Land; and the Judges in every State shall be bound thereby, any Thing in the Constitution or Laws of any State to the Contrary notwithstanding.

[3.] The Senators and Representatives before mentioned, and the Members of the several State Legislatures, and all executive and judicial Officers, both of the United States and of the several States, shall be bound by Oath or Affirmation, to support this Constitution; but no religious Test shall ever be required as a Qualification to any Office or public Trust under the United States.

Article VII

The Ratification of the Conventions of nine States, shall be sufficient for the Establishment of this Constitution between the States so ratifying the Same.

Done in Convention by the Unanimous Consent of the States present the Seventeenth Day of September in the Year of our Lord one thousand seven hundred and Eighty seven and of the Independence of the United States of America the Twelfth. In witness whereof We have hereunto subscribed our Names,

Article VI. National Supremacy

Article VI contains the "supremacy clause." This clause establishes that the Constitution, laws passed by Congress, and treaties of the United States "shall be the supreme Law of the Land." The "supremacy clause" recognized the Constitution and federal laws as supreme when in conflict with those of the states.

Article VII. Ratification

Article VII addresses ratification and declares that the Constitution would take effect after it was ratified by nine states.

Biographical Sketches Ask students to research and write a brief biographical sketch of one of the signers of the Constitution. Suggest that students focus on such factors as background, education, family life, and so on, that might reveal the person's motivation in taking part in the Constitutional Convention. **L2**

Researching the Constitution Encourage volunteers to research the number of amendments to the California state constitution, a relatively easy constitution to amend. Have them report to the class, using California as an example of what happens when a constitution is easily amended. Encourage students to discuss which system is better. In particular, have them discuss the type of issues that should be addressed in the constitution and which should be left to the legislative process. **L3**

Did you know?

The first five states to ratify the Constitution—Delaware, Pennsylvania, New Jersey, Georgia, and Connecticut—did so quickly and by large majorities.

Signers
George Washington, *President and Deputy from Virginia*

New Hampshire
John Langdon
Nicholas Gilman

Massachusetts
Nathaniel Gorham
Rufus King

Connecticut
William Samuel Johnson
Roger Sherman

New York
Alexander Hamilton

New Jersey
William Livingston
David Brearley
William Paterson
Jonathan Dayton

Pennsylvania
Benjamin Franklin
Thomas Mifflin
Robert Morris
George Clymer
Thomas FitzSimons
Jared Ingersoll
James Wilson
Gouverneur Morris

Delaware
George Read
Gunning Bedford, Jr.
John Dickinson
Richard Bassett
Jacob Broom

Maryland
James McHenry
Daniel of St. Thomas Jenifer
Daniel Carroll

Virginia
John Blair
James Madison, Jr.

North Carolina
William Blount
Richard Dobbs Spaight
Hugh Williamson

South Carolina
John Rutledge
Charles Cotesworth Pinckney
Charles Pinckney
Pierce Butler

Georgia
William Few
Abraham Baldwin

Attest: William Jackson, **Secretary**

EXTENDING THE CONTENT

Signers of the Constitution Of the 55 delegates who attended the Constitutional Convention, only 38 signed the document. A thirty-ninth signature—that of John Dickinson—was written by George Read at Dickinson's request. Elbridge Gerry of Massachusetts and Edmund Randolph and George Mason of Virginia refused to sign, while 13 other delegates left the Convention early.

United States Constitution

FOCUS

BELLRINGER
Motivational Activity

Write the word *change* on the chalkboard. Have students discuss why the Framers included a process for changing the Constitution. *(They realized that the needs of the people would eventually change.)*

Answer: freedom of religion, freedom of speech, freedom of the press, freedom to peaceably assemble, and freedom to petition the government for a redress of grievances.

Answer: The debate centers on whether Americans have a right to bear arms, whether they're serving in an official state militia or not.

Answer: "Presentment" or "indictment" means to formally charge a person with committing a crime. The grand jury evaluates whether there is enough evidence to bring the accused person to trial.

Bill of Rights

The first 10 amendments are known as the Bill of Rights (1791). These amendments limit the powers of government. The First Amendment protects the civil liberties of individuals in the United States. The amendment freedoms are not absolute, however. They are limited by the rights of other individuals. *What freedoms does the First Amendment protect?*

Amendment 2
Right to Bear Arms This amendment is often debated. Originally, it was intended to prevent the national government from repeating the actions of the British, who tried to take weapons away from the colonial militia, or armed forces of citizens. This amendment seems to support the right of citizens to own firearms, but the Supreme Court has ruled that it does not prevent Congress from regulating the interstate sale of weapons. *Why is the Second Amendment's meaning debated?*

Amendment 5
Rights of Accused Persons This amendment contains important protections for people accused of crimes. One of the protections is that government may not deprive any person of life, liberty, or property without due process of law. This means that the government must follow proper constitutional procedures in trials and in other actions it takes against individuals. *According to Amendment V, what is the function of a grand jury?*

Vocabulary

quarter: *to provide living accommodations*
probable cause: *police must have a reasonable basis to believe a person is linked to a crime*
warrant: *document that gives police particular rights or powers*
common law: *law established by previous court decisions*
bail: *money that an accused person provides to the court as a guarantee that he or she will be present for a trial*

Amendment I
Congress shall make no law respecting an establishment of religion, or prohibiting the free exercise thereof; or abridging the freedom of speech, or of the press; or the right of the people peaceably to assemble, and to petition the Government for a redress of grievances.

Amendment II
A well regulated Militia, being necessary to the security of a free State, the right of the people to keep and bear Arms, shall not be infringed.

Amendment III
No Soldier shall, in time of peace be quartered in any house, without the consent of the Owner, nor in time of war, but in a manner to be prescribed by law.

Amendment IV
The right of the people to be secure in their persons, houses, papers, and effects, against unreasonable searches and seizures, shall not be violated, and no Warrants shall issue, but upon probable cause, supported by Oath or affirmation, and particularly describing the place to be searched, and the persons or things to be seized.

Amendment V
No person shall be held to answer for a capital, or otherwise infamous crime, unless on a presentment or indictment of a Grand Jury, except in cases arising in the land or naval forces, or in the Militia, when in actual service in time of War or public danger; nor shall any person be subject for the same offence to be twice put in jeopardy of life or limb; nor shall be compelled in any criminal case to be a witness against himself, nor be deprived of life, liberty, or property, without due process of law; nor shall private property be taken for public use without just compensation.

EXTENDING THE CONTENT

The Bill of Rights Critics of the Constitution felt that it did not go far enough in protecting individual rights and liberties. To answer these objections, supporters of the Constitution promised to introduce a series of amendments listing the rights of individuals. On June 8, 1789, James Madison kept this promise by proposing 12 amendments to the Constitution, 10 of which were adopted and are now known as the Bill of Rights. One amendment not adopted concerned pay raises for members of Congress. It eventually became part of the Constitution as the Twenty-seventh Amendment.

Amendment VI

In all criminal prosecutions, the accused shall enjoy the right to a speedy and public trial, by an impartial jury of the State and district wherein the crime shall have been committed, which district shall have been previously ascertained by law, and to be informed of the nature and cause of the accusation; to be confronted with the witnesses against him; to have compulsory process for obtaining Witnesses in his favor, and to have the assistance of counsel for his defence.

Amendment VII

In Suits at common law, where the value in controversy shall exceed twenty dollars, the right of trial by jury shall be preserved, and no fact tried by a jury, shall be otherwise reexamined in any Court of the United States, than according to the rules of common law.

Amendment VIII

Excessive bail shall not be required, nor excessive fines imposed, nor cruel and unusual punishments inflicted.

Amendment IX

The enumeration in the Constitution, of certain rights, shall not be construed to deny or disparage others retained by the people.

Amendment X

The powers not delegated to the United States by the Constitution, nor prohibited by it to the States, are reserved to the States respectively, or to the people.

Amendment XI

The Judicial power of the United States shall not be construed to extend to any suit in law or equity, commenced or prosecuted against one of the United States by Citizens of another State, or by Citizens or Subjects of any Foreign State.

Amendment 6

Right to a Speedy, Fair Trial A basic protection is the right to a speedy, public trial. The jury must hear witnesses and evidence on both sides before deciding the guilt or innocence of a person charged with a crime. This amendment also provides that legal counsel must be provided to a defendant. In 1963, the Supreme Court ruled, in *Gideon* v. *Wainwright*, that if a defendant cannot afford a lawyer, the government must provide one to defend him or her. *Why is the right to a "speedy" trial important?*

Amendment 9

Powers Reserved to the People This amendment prevents government from claiming that the only rights people have are those listed in the Bill of Rights.

Amendment 10

Powers Reserved to the States The final amendment of the Bill of Rights protects the states and the people from an all-powerful federal government. It establishes that powers not given to the national government—or denied to the states—by the Constitution belong to the states or to the people.

Amendment 11

Suits Against States The Eleventh Amendment (1795) limits the jurisdiction of the federal courts. The Supreme Court had ruled that a federal court could try a lawsuit brought by citizens of South Carolina against the state of Georgia. This case, *Chisholm* v. *Georgia*, decided in 1793, raised a storm of protest, leading to passage of the Eleventh Amendment.

TEACH

Analyzing Ideas Ask students to identify areas of concern that they would like to see addressed by a constitutional amendment. Write suggestions on the chalkboard and have students discuss each in terms of the following questions: Why is an amendment needed? Would it be better for Congress to pass laws or the courts to establish precedents on this issue? **L2**

Answer: The requirement of a "speedy" trial ensures that an accused person will not be held in jail for a lengthy period as a means of punishing the accused without a trial.

CURRICULUM CONNECTION

Civics Some lawyers maintain that the mass media threaten a defendant's Sixth Amendment rights. Extensive coverage of a crime on television and in the newspapers, these lawyers argue, makes it difficult to find jurors who are truly impartial.

CRITICAL THINKING ACTIVITY

Expressing Problems Clearly Point out that the Fifth Amendment protects the right of people charged with crimes to remain silent. In some countries, however, silence is equated with an admittance of guilt. Ask students to write a paragraph that supports or challenges the following statement: The Fifth Amendment is little more than a shield for the guilty. **L3**

United States Constitution

Identifying Alternatives Point out that the Electoral College has been criticized as being obsolete, and various reforms have been suggested for changing it or abolishing it altogether. Lead a discussion about the 2000 presidential election that continued the debate over the role of the Electoral College. Ask students to research, discuss, and assess alternatives to the Electoral College. **L3**

Answer: the House of Representatives

What?Where?When?Who?

The Republican Party The nickname of the Republican Party is the GOP, which stands for the Grand Old Party. The term began to be used around the time of the 1880 Republican convention. Prime Minister William Gladstone of Great Britain was fondly referred to as the Grand Old Man, and some Republican admirers of the prime minister applied the same term of affection to their political party.

Amendment 12
Election of President and Vice President The Twelfth Amendment (1804) corrects a problem that had arisen in the method of electing the president and vice president. This amendment provides for the Electoral College to use separate ballots in voting for president and vice president. *If no candidate receives a majority of the electoral votes, who elects the president?*

Ballot and ballot marker

Amendment 13
Abolition of Slavery Amendments Thirteen (1865), Fourteen (1868), and Fifteen (1870) often are called the Civil War amendments because they grew out of that great conflict. The Thirteenth Amendment outlaws slavery.

Vocabulary

majority: *more than half*
devolve: *to pass on*
abridge: *to reduce*
insurrection: *rebellion against the government*
emancipation: *freedom from slavery*

Amendment XII

The electors shall meet in their respective states and vote by ballot for President and Vice-President, one of whom, at least, shall not be an inhabitant of the same state with themselves; they shall name in their ballots the person voted for as President, and in distinct ballots the person voted for as Vice-President, and they shall make distinct lists of all persons voted for as President, and of all persons voted for as Vice-President, and of the number of votes for each, which lists they shall sign and certify, and transmit sealed to the seat of the government of the United States, directed to the President of the Senate;—The President of the Senate shall, in the presence of the Senate and House of Representatives, open all the certificates and the votes shall then be counted;—The person having the greatest number of votes for President, shall be the President, if such number be a majority of the whole number of Electors appointed; and if no person have such majority, then from the persons having the highest numbers not exceeding three on the list of those voted for as President, the House of Representatives shall choose immediately, by ballot, the President. But in choosing the President, the votes shall be taken by states, the representation from each state having one vote; a quorum for this purpose shall consist of a member or members from two-thirds of the states, and a majority of all the states shall be necessary to a choice. And if the House of Representatives shall not choose a President whenever the right of choice shall devolve upon them, before the fourth day of March next following, then the Vice-President shall act as President, as in the case of the death or other constitutional disability of the President. The person having the greatest number of votes as Vice-President, shall be the Vice-President, if such number be a majority of the whole number of Electors appointed, and if no person have a majority, then from the two highest numbers on the list, the Senate shall choose the Vice-President; a quorum for the purpose shall consist of two-thirds of the whole number of Senators, and a majority of the whole number shall be necessary to a choice. But no person constitutionally ineligible to the office of President shall be eligible to that of Vice-President of the United States.

Amendment XIII

Section 1
Neither slavery nor involuntary servitude, except as a punishment for crime whereof the party shall have been duly convicted, shall exist within the United States, or any place subject to their jurisdiction.

Section 2
Congress shall have power to enforce this article by appropriate legislation.

EXTENDING THE CONTENT

Racial Discrimination and the Constitution The Thirteenth, Fourteenth, and Fifteenth Amendments represent attempts to use the Constitution to end slavery, to extend citizenship to former enslaved persons, and to guarantee African Americans the right to vote. Literacy tests, poll taxes, and grandfather clauses, however, continued to keep large numbers of African Americans from voting in many Southern states even after Reconstruction.

Amendment XIV

Section 1

All persons born or naturalized in the United States, and subject to the jurisdiction thereof, are citizens of the United States and of the State wherein they reside. No State shall make or enforce any law which shall abridge the privileges or immunities of citizens of the United States; nor shall any State deprive any person of life, liberty, or property, without due process of law; nor deny to any person within its jurisdiction the equal protection of the laws.

Section 2

Representatives shall be apportioned among the several States according to their respective numbers, counting the whole number of persons in each State, excluding Indians not taxed. But when the right to vote at any election for the choice of electors for President and Vice President of the United States, Representatives in Congress, the Executive and Judicial officers of a State, or the members of the Legislature thereof, is denied to any of the male inhabitants of such State, being twenty-one years of age, and citizens of the United States, or in any way abridged, except for participation in rebellion, or other crime, the basis of representation therein shall be reduced in the proportion which the number of such male citizens shall bear to the whole number of male citizens twenty-one years of age in such State.

Section 3

No person shall be a Senator or Representative in Congress, or elector of President and Vice President, or hold any office, civil or military, under the United States, or under any State, who, having previously taken an oath, as a member of Congress, or as an officer of the United States, or as a member of any State legislature, or as an executive or judicial officer of any State, to support the Constitution of the United States, shall have engaged in insurrection or rebellion against the same, or given aid or comfort to the enemies thereof. But Congress may by a vote of two-thirds of each House, remove such disability.

Section 4

The validity of the public debt of the United States, authorized by law, including debts incurred for payment of pensions and bounties for service in suppressing insurrection or rebellion, shall not be questioned. But neither the United States nor any State shall assume or pay any debt or obligation incurred in aid of insurrection or rebellion against the United States, or any claim for the loss or emancipation of any slave; but all such debts, obligations and claims shall be held illegal and void.

Amendment 14

Rights of Citizens The Fourteenth Amendment (1868) originally was intended to protect the legal rights of the freed slaves. Today it protects the rights of citizenship in general by prohibiting a state from depriving any person of life, liberty, or property without "due process of law." In addition, it states that all citizens have the right to equal protection of the law in all states.

Amendment 14. Section 2

Representation in Congress This section reduced the number of members a state had in the House of Representatives if it denied its citizens the right to vote. Later civil rights laws and the Twenty-Fourth Amendment guaranteed the vote to African Americans.

Amendment 14. Section 3

Penalty for Engaging in Insurrection The leaders of the Confederacy were barred from state or federal offices unless Congress agreed to remove this ban. By the end of Reconstruction all but a few Confederate leaders were allowed to return to public life.

Amendment 14. Section 4

Public Debt The public debt acquired by the federal government during the Civil War was valid and could not be questioned by the South. However, the debts of the Confederacy were declared to be illegal. *Could former slaveholders collect payment for the loss of their slaves?*

The Constitution of the United States **247**

United States Constitution

Time Lines Have students make a time line that includes each of the amendments, the year of ratification, and significant concurrent political, economic, and social events. Encourage students to display and compare their time lines. **L2**

Answer: Former slaveholders could not collect compensation for the loss of their slaves.

CURRICULUM CONNECTION

Civics Section 1 of the Fourteenth Amendment sets out two of the three alternative requirements of American citizenship: birth on American soil and naturalization. The third possible requirement is birth to a parent who is an American citizen.

EXTENDING THE CONTENT

Due Process of Law References to due process of law are made in the Fifth and Fourteenth Amendments. As a result of Supreme Court rulings, two types of due process have developed. Procedural due process requires that government use fair procedures in enforcing the law. Substantive due process requires that the laws under which the government acts be fair.

United States Constitution

Amendment 15
Right to Vote The Fifteenth Amendment (1870) prohibits the government from denying a person's right to vote on the basis of race. Despite the law, many states denied African Americans the right to vote by such means as poll taxes, literacy tests, and white primaries. During the 1950s and 1960s, Congress passed successively stronger laws to end racial discrimination in voting rights.

Internal Revenue Service

Amendment 17
Direct Election of Senators The Seventeenth Amendment (1913) states that the people, instead of state legislatures, elect United States senators. *How many years are in a Senate term?*

Vocabulary

apportionment: *distribution of seats in House based on population*
vacancy: *an office or position that is unfilled or unoccupied*

248   The Constitution of the United States

Section 5
The Congress shall have power to enforce, by appropriate legislation, the provisions of this article.

Amendment XV

Section 1
The right of citizens of the United States to vote shall not be denied or abridged by the United States or by any State on account of race, color, or previous condition of servitude.

Section 2
The Congress shall have power to enforce this article by appropriate legislation.

Amendment XVI
The Congress shall have power to lay and collect taxes on incomes, from whatever source derived, without apportionment among the several States and without regard to any census or enumeration.

Amendment XVII

Section 1
The Senate of the United States shall be composed of two Senators from each State, elected by the people thereof, for six years; and each Senator shall have one vote. The electors in each State shall have the qualifications requisite for electors of the most numerous branch of the State legislatures.

Section 2
When vacancies happen in the representation of any State in the Senate, the executive authority of such State shall issue writs of election to fill such vacancies: *Provided,* That the legislature of any State may empower the executive thereof to make temporary appointments until the people fill the vacancies by election as the legislature may direct.

Section 3
This amendment shall not be so construed as to affect the election or term of any Senator chosen before it becomes valid as part of the Constitution.

EXTENDING THE CONTENT

The Poll Tax After the Civil War, poll taxes were levied in many Southern states. Although the poll tax kept many low-income white males from voting, its major purpose was to keep African Americans away from the polls. Not until the 1960s did Congress take firm action to enforce the guarantee of the Fifteenth Amendment and end this kind of racial discrimination.

Amendment XVIII

Section 1

After one year from ratification of this article, the manufacture, sale, or transportation of intoxicating liquors within, the importation thereof into, or the exportation thereof from the United States and all territory subject to the jurisdiction thereof for beverage purposes is hereby prohibited.

Section 2

The Congress and the several States shall have concurrent power to enforce this article by appropriate legislation.

Section 3

This article shall be inoperative unless it shall have been ratified as an amendment to the Constitution by the legislatures of the several States, as provided in the Constitution, within seven years from the date of the submission hereof to the States by the Congress.

Amendment XIX

Section 1

The right of citizens of the United States to vote shall not be denied or abridged by the United States or by any State on account of sex.

Section 2

Congress shall have power by appropriate legislation to enforce the provisions of this article.

Amendment XX

Section 1

The terms of the President and Vice President shall end at noon on the 20th day of January, and the terms of the Senators and Representatives at noon on the 3d day of January, of the years in which such terms would have ended if this article had not been ratified; and the terms of their successors shall then begin.

Section 2

The Congress shall assemble at least once in every year, and such meeting shall begin at noon on the 3d day of January, unless they shall by law appoint a different day.

Amendment 18
Prohibition of Alcoholic Beverages The Eighteenth Amendment (1919) prohibited the production, sale, or transportation of alcoholic beverages in the United States. Prohibition proved to be difficult to enforce. This amendment was later repealed by the Twenty-first Amendment.

Amendment 19
Woman Suffrage The Nineteenth Amendment (1920) guaranteed women the right to vote. By then women had already won the right to vote in many state elections, but the amendment put their right to vote in all state and national elections on a constitutional basis.

Amendment 20
"Lame-Duck" Amendment The Twentieth Amendment (1933) sets new dates for Congress to begin its term and for the inauguration of the president and vice president. Under the original Constitution, elected officials who retired or who had been defeated remained in office for several months. For the outgoing president, this period ran from November until March. Such outgoing officials had little influence and accomplished little, and they were called lame ducks because they were so inactive. *What date was fixed as Inauguration Day?*

Writing Reports Point out that a number of states preceded the national government in giving women the vote. Encourage students to research the fight for woman suffrage in these states. Ask them to present their findings in written reports. **L2**

Answer: January 20

Did you know?

Not all U.S. citizens over the age of 18 are eligible to vote. Forty-six states and the District of Columbia prohibit prison inmates from voting while serving a felony sentence. Ten states prohibit all ex-offenders from voting for the rest of their lives, while five other states prohibit only some ex-offenders from voting. An estimated 3.9 million Americans have currently or permanently lost their right to vote.

The Constitution of the United States   **249**

CRITICAL THINKING ACTIVITY

Analyzing Information Make sure that students understand the "lame-duck" issue by reminding them that lame ducks are presidents and members of Congress waiting to leave office after retiring or failing to gain reelection. Since lame ducks often were members of the defeated party, they were in a position to affect legislation even though they no longer spoke for the majority of voters. Then ask students to note how the Twentieth Amendment addressed this problem. *(It shortened the waiting period between Election Day and the beginning of a new term.)* **L1**

Categorizing Information Have students categorize on a chart the amendments according to the following headings: *Personal Freedoms, Relations Among States, Process of Government,* and *Citizenship.* They should keep in mind the substance of the amendment and its effect on American life. Remind students that some amendments might fit in more than one category. **L1**

CURRICULUM CONNECTION

Health Although Prohibition caused many problems, it did succeed in reducing the consumption of alcohol in the United States, thus decreasing the number of alcohol-related deaths and accidents.

Amendment 20. Section 3
Succession of President and Vice President This section provides that if the president-elect dies before taking office, the vice president-elect becomes president.

John Tyler was the first vice president to become president when a chief executive died.

Amendment 21
Repeal of Prohibition Amendment The Twenty-first Amendment (1933) repeals the Eighteenth Amendment. It is the only amendment ever passed to overturn an earlier amendment. It is also the only amendment ratified by special state conventions instead of state legislatures.

Vocabulary

president-elect: *individual who is elected president but has not yet begun serving his or her term*
District of Columbia: *site of nation's capital, occupying an area between Maryland and Virginia*

Section 3

If, at the time fixed for the beginning of the term of the President, the President elect shall have died, the Vice President elect shall become President. If a President shall not have been chosen before the time fixed for the beginning of his term, or if the President elect shall have failed to qualify, then the Vice President elect shall act as President until a President shall have qualified; and the Congress may by law provide for the case wherein neither a President elect nor a Vice President elect shall have qualified, declaring who shall then act as President, or the manner in which one who is to act shall be selected, and such person shall act accordingly until a President or Vice President shall have qualified.

Section 4

The Congress may by law provide for the case of the death of any of the persons from whom the House of Representatives may choose a President whenever the right of choice shall have devolved upon them, and for the case of the death of any of the persons from whom the Senate may choose a Vice President whenever the right of choice shall have devolved upon them.

Section 5

Sections 1 and 2 shall take effect on the 15th day of October following the ratification of this article.

Section 6

This article shall be inoperative unless it shall have been ratified as an amendment to the Constitution by the legislatures of three-fourths of the several States within seven years from the date of its submission.

Amendment XXI

Section 1

The eighteenth article of amendment to the Constitution of the United States is hereby repealed.

Section 2

The transportation or importation into any State, Territory, or possession of the United States for delivery or use therein of intoxicating liquors, in violation of the laws thereof, is hereby prohibited.

Section 3

This article shall be inoperative unless it shall have been ratified as an amendment to the Constitution by conventions in the several States, as provided in the Constitution, within seven years from the date of the submission hereof to the States by the Congress.

COOPERATIVE LEARNING ACTIVITY

Debate Organize students into groups to debate the pros and cons of Prohibition. Give groups time to prepare their arguments and encourage group members to be responsible for a different part of the research. As each group presents its argument, note major points on the chalkboard. When groups have completed the debate, lead the class in a discussion of the following question: Is Prohibition an issue that should have been addressed in a constitutional amendment? Why or why not? **L1**

Amendment XXII

Section 1
No person shall be elected to the office of the President more than twice, and no person who had held the office of President, or acted as President, for more than two years of a term to which some other person was elected President shall be elected to the office of the President more than once. But this Article shall not apply to any person holding the office of President when this Article was proposed by the Congress, and shall not prevent any person who may be holding the office of President, or acting as President, during the term within which this Article becomes operative from holding the office of President or acting as President during the remainder of such term.

Section 2
This article shall be inoperative unless it shall have been ratified as an amendment to the Constitution by the legislatures of three-fourths of the several States within seven years from the date of its submission to the States by the Congress.

Amendment XXIII

Section 1
The District constituting the seat of Government of the United States shall appoint in such manner as the Congress may direct:

A number of electors of President and Vice President equal to the whole number of Senators and Representatives in Congress to which the District would be entitled if it were a State, but in no event more than the least populous State; they shall be in addition to those appointed by the States, but they shall be considered, for the purposes of the election of President and Vice President, to be electors appointed by a State; and they shall meet in the District and perform such duties as provided by the twelfth article of amendment.

Section 2
The Congress shall have power to enforce this article by appropriate legislation.

Amendment 22

Limit on Presidential Terms The Twenty-second Amendment (1951) limits presidents to a maximum of two elected terms. It was passed largely as a reaction to Franklin D. Roosevelt's election to four terms between 1933 and 1945.

Presidential campaign buttons

Amendment 23

Presidential Electors for the District of Columbia The Twenty-third Amendment (1961) allows citizens living in Washington, D.C., to vote for president and vice president, a right previously denied residents of the nation's capital. The District of Columbia now has three presidential electors, the number to which it would be entitled if it were a state.

Expressing Viewpoints Write the following statement on the chalkboard: *That the people of Washington, D.C., have no representation in Congress is a violation of their democratic rights.* Call on volunteers to express their views on this statement. **L2**

Did you know?

The United States has had a disabled president several times in its history. In the 1880s James Garfield remained bedridden for 79 days before dying from injuries sustained by an assassin's bullet. In the twentieth century Woodrow Wilson had a stroke and was incapacitated for the last several months of his presidency.

The Constitution of the United States **251**

CRITICAL THINKING ACTIVITY

Evaluating Information Have students list the advantages and disadvantages of the two-term limit for presidents. Ask volunteers to present and defend their lists. Then have students discuss the following: Should there be presidential term limits? If so, how many terms should the president be limited to? Should members of Congress have term limits? Why or why not? **L2**

United States Constitution

Answer: the president pro tempore of the Senate (the vice president) and the Speaker of the House of Representatives

Who?What?Where?When?

Gerald R. Ford Gerald R. Ford became the thirty-eighth president of the United States in 1974. He was the only president who was not elected either president or vice president. He replaced Spiro T. Agnew when Agnew resigned as vice president, then replaced President Richard Nixon, who resigned on August 9, 1974.

Amendment 24

Abolition of Poll Tax The Twenty-fourth Amendment (1964) prohibits poll taxes in federal elections. Prior to the passage of this amendment, some states had used such taxes to keep low-income African Americans from voting. In 1966 the Supreme Court banned poll taxes in state elections as well.

Amendment 25

Presidential Disability and Succession The Twenty-fifth Amendment (1967) established a process for the vice president to take over leadership of the nation when a president is disabled. It also set procedures for filling a vacancy in the office of vice president.

This amendment was used in 1973, when Vice President Spiro Agnew resigned from office after being charged with accepting bribes. President Richard Nixon then appointed Gerald R. Ford as vice president in accordance with the provisions of the 25th Amendment. A year later, President Nixon resigned during the Watergate scandal and Ford became president. President Ford then had to fill the vice presidency, which he had left vacant upon assuming the presidency. He named Nelson A. Rockefeller as vice president. Thus individuals who had not been elected held both the presidency and the vice presidency. *Whom does the president inform if he or she cannot carry out the duties of the office?*

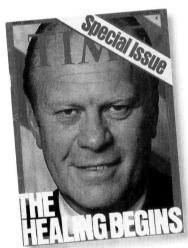

President Gerald Ford

Amendment XXIV

Section 1

The right of citizens of the United States to vote in any primary or other election for President or Vice President, for electors for President or Vice President, or for Senator or Representative in Congress, shall not be denied or abridged by the United States or any State by reason of failure to pay any poll tax or other tax.

Section 2

The Congress shall have power to enforce this article by appropriate legislation.

Amendment XXV

Section 1

In case of the removal of the President from office or his death or resignation, the Vice President shall become President.

Section 2

Whenever there is a vacancy in the office of the Vice President, the President shall nominate a Vice President who shall take the office upon confirmation by a majority vote of both Houses of Congress.

Section 3

Whenever the President transmits to the President pro tempore of the Senate and the Speaker of the House of Representatives his written declaration that he is unable to discharge the powers and duties of his office, and until he transmits to them a written declaration to the contrary, such powers and duties shall be discharged by the Vice President as Acting President.

Section 4

Whenever the Vice President and a majority of either the principal officers of the executive departments or of such other body as Congress may by law provide, transmit to the President pro tempore of the Senate and the Speaker of the House of Representatives their written declaration that the President is unable to discharge the powers and duties of his office, the Vice President shall immediately assume the power and duties of the office of Acting President.

Thereafter, when the President transmits to the President pro tempore of the Senate and the Speaker of the House of Representatives his written declaration that no inability exists, he shall resume the powers and duties of his office unless the Vice President and a majority of either the principal officers of the executive department or of such other body as Congress may by law provide, transmit within four days to the President pro tempore of the Senate and the Speaker of the House of Represen-

EXTENDING THE CONTENT

The Twenty-fifth Amendment The assassination of President John F. Kennedy made the need for a constitutional amendment on presidential disability apparent. Kennedy's successor, Lyndon Johnson, had once had a heart attack, and the two men in line of succession after Johnson were both over 70 years old. Congress quickly passed the Twenty-fifth Amendment, which was submitted to the states in mid-1965 and was ratified early in 1967.

tatives their written declaration that the President is unable to discharge the powers and duties of his office. Thereupon Congress shall decide the issue, assembling within forty-eight hours for that purpose if not in session. If the Congress, within twenty-one days after receipt of the latter written declaration, or, if Congress is not in session, within twenty-one days after Congress is required to assemble, determines by two-thirds vote of both Houses that the President is unable to discharge the powers and duties of his office, the Vice President shall continue to discharge the same as Acting President; otherwise, the President shall resume the power and duties of his office.

Amendment XXVI

Section 1
The right of citizens of the United States, who are eighteen years of age or older, to vote shall not be denied or abridged by the United States or by any State on account of age.

Section 2
The Congress shall have power to enforce this article by appropriate legislation.

Amendment XXVII
No law, varying the compensation for the services of Senators and Representatives, shall take effect, until an election of representatives shall have intervened.

Amendment 26
Eighteen-Year-Old Vote The Twenty-sixth Amendment (1971) guarantees the right to vote to all citizens 18 years of age and older.

Amendment 27
Restraint on Congressional Salaries The Twenty-seventh Amendment (1992) makes congressional pay raises effective during the term following their passage. James Madison offered the amendment in 1789, but it was never adopted. In 1982 Gregory Watson, then a student at the University of Texas, discovered the forgotten amendment while doing research for a school paper. Watson made the amendment's passage his crusade.

What?Where?When?Who?
The Twenty-sixth Amendment
Many people used the Vietnam War to justify the adoption of the Twenty-sixth Amendment. These people argued that those old enough to fight and die for their country were also old enough to vote.

CURRICULUM CONNECTION

Geography Why do states such as Maine and Minnesota consistently turn out 60 percent of their voters in presidential elections when the national average is about 50 percent? Some states make it easy for voters to get on the election rolls. Maine, Minnesota, and Wisconsin permit registration at the voting place on Election Day. North Dakota permits citizens to vote without registering.

Joint meeting of Congress

COOPERATIVE LEARNING ACTIVITY

Writing a School Constitution Have students form a group to write a constitution for your school. Students should begin the document with a preamble that lists goals for school government. Each group member should write an article describing one branch of the school government. Be certain that groups list the functions of each branch. Then, as a group, have students decide if they think some powers should be denied to the school government and list these in another article. Finally, have students decide if a bill of rights is necessary. If so, have students list the rights they think should be added. **L1**

Unit 4 Resources

SUGGESTED PACING CHART

Unit 4 (1 Day)	Chapter 8 (5 Days)	Chapter 9 (6 Days)	Chapter 10 (5 Days)	Unit 4 (2 Days)
Day 1 Introduction	**Day 1** Chapter 8 Intro, Section 1 **Day 2** Section 2 **Day 3** Section 3 **Day 4** Chapter 8 Review **Day 5** Chapter 8 Assessment	**Day 1** Chapter 9 Intro, Section 1 **Day 2** Section 2 **Day 3** Section 3 **Day 4** Section 4 **Day 5** Chapter 9 Review **Day 6** Chapter 9 Assessment	**Day 1** Chapter 10 Intro, Section 1 **Day 2** Section 2 **Day 3** Section 3 **Day 4** Chapter 10 Review **Day 5** Chapter 10 Assessment	**Day 1** Wrap-Up/Project **Day 2** Unit 4 Assessment

Use the following tools to easily assess student learning in a variety of ways:

- Performance Assessment Activities and Rubrics
- Chapter and Unit Tests
- Section Quizzes
- Standardized Test Practice Workbook

- www.tarvol1.glencoe.com
- Interactive Tutor Self-Assessment CD-ROM
- MindJogger Videoquiz
- ExamView® Pro Testmaker CD-ROM

TEACHING TRANSPARENCIES

READING SUPPORT FROM
JAMESTOWN EDUCATION

Unit 4 Map Overlay Transparencies
L2

Cause-and-Effect Transparency 4
L2

- *Timed Readings Plus in Social Studies* help students increase their reading rate and fluency while maintaining comprehension. The 400-word passages are similar to those found on state and national assessments.

- *Reading in the Content Area: Social Studies* concentrates on six essential reading skills that help students better comprehend what they read. The book includes 75 high-interest nonfiction passages written at increasing levels of difficulty.

- *Reading Fluency* helps students read smoothly, accurately, and expressively.

- *Jamestown's Reading Improvement,* by renowned reading expert Edward Fry, focuses on helping build your students' comprehension, vocabulary, and skimming and scanning skills.

- *Critical Reading Series* provides high-interest books, each written at three reading levels.

For more information about these products, see the Jamestown Education materials in the Classroom Solutions in the front of this Teacher Wraparound Edition. To order these products, call Glencoe at 1-800-334-7344.

Unit 4 Resources

Unit 4 Pretests L2

Unit 4 Posttests L2

INTERDISCIPLINARY ACTIVITIES

American Literature Reading 4 L2

Interdisciplinary Connection 4 L2

Economics and History Activity 4 L2

APPLICATION AND ENRICHMENT

Cooperative Learning Activity 4 L1, ELL

Citizenship Activity 4 L2

HANDS-ON ACTIVITIES

Hands-On History Activity 4 L1

History Simulations and Problem Solving 4 L1

Reading List Generator CD-ROM

GLENCOE BOOKLINK

The Glencoe BookLink CD-ROM is a database that allows you to search more than 15,000 titles to create a customized reading list for your students.

- Reading lists can be organized by students' reading level, author, genre, theme, or area of interest.

- The database provides Degrees of Reading Power™ (DRP) and Lexile™ readability scores for all selections.

- A brief summary of each selection is included.

Leveled reading suggestions for this unit:

For Students at a Grade 6 Reading Level:
- **The Lewis and Clark Expedition,** by Patrick McGrath

For Students at a Grade 7 Reading Level:
- **1812: The War Nobody Won,** by Albert Marrin

For Students at a Grade 8 Reading Level:
- **Erie Canal,** by Ralph K. Andrist

Extending the Content

Readings for the Teacher
- **Lewis and Clark: Voyage of a Discovery,** by Stephen E. Ambrose. National Geographic Society, 1998.
- **From Africa to America: African American History from the Colonial Era to the Early Republic 1526–1790,** by William Dillon Pierson. Prentice Hall International, 1996.

Multimedia Links
- **Thomas Jefferson.** VHS. PBS Home Video: Turner Home Entertainment.

Unit Overview

Unit 4 describes the challenges faced by the new American government. **Chapter 8** explores the organization and policies of Washington's administration. **Chapter 9** describes the War of 1812. **Chapter 10** describes the industrial and westward growth of the nation.

Unit Objectives

After studying this unit, students will be able to:
1. List highlights of the new government.
2. Identify and discuss the importance of various aspects of the Jefferson era.
3. Discuss the Industrial Revolution and its effects; explain how sectionalism developed and summarize the Monroe Doctrine.

Why It Matters Activity

Ask students to think about how the affairs of foreign countries impact the policies of the United States government. Discuss how foreign policy issues affect the lives of Americans.

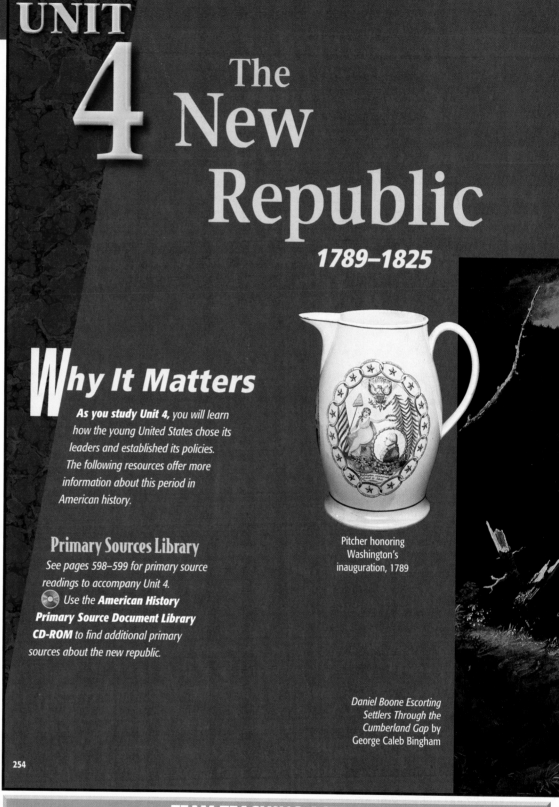

UNIT 4
The New Republic

1789–1825

Why It Matters

As you study Unit 4, you will learn how the young United States chose its leaders and established its policies. The following resources offer more information about this period in American history.

Primary Sources Library

See pages 598–599 for primary source readings to accompany Unit 4.

Use the **American History Primary Source Document Library CD-ROM** to find additional primary sources about the new republic.

Pitcher honoring Washington's inauguration, 1789

Daniel Boone Escorting Settlers Through the Cumberland Gap by George Caleb Bingham

254

TEAM TEACHING ACTIVITY

Science Have the class work with the Science or Health teacher (or the school nurse) to investigate how diseases such as cholera and yellow fever—a deadly threat in early cities—have been brought under control in the developing world. Cholera—which is spread by fecal-contaminated food and water—is still prevalent in parts of Asia, Africa, and South America where public sanitation is poor. Yellow fever, caused by a virus carried by mosquitoes, has been largely eliminated. Discuss how modern transportation methods provide a means for quicker transfer of dangerous diseases from continent to continent. **L2**

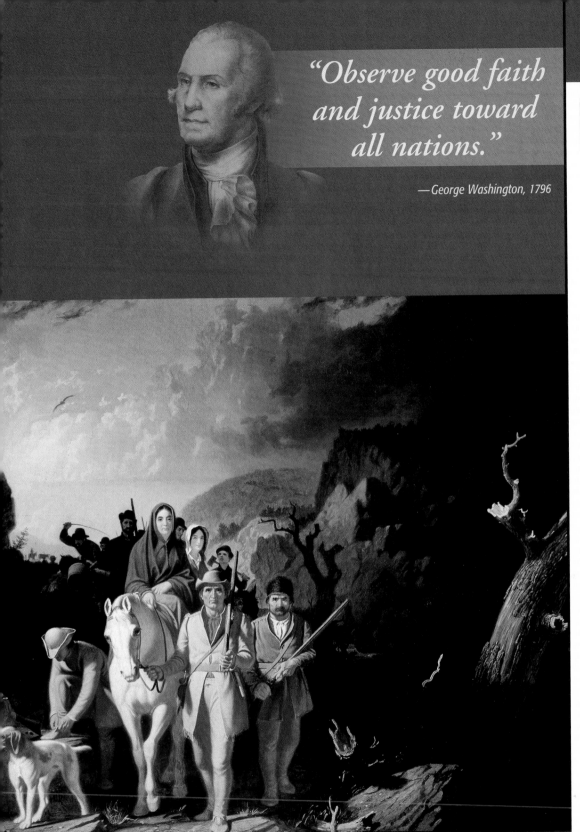

> *"Observe good faith and justice toward all nations."*
>
> —George Washington, 1796

GLENCOE TECHNOLOGY

CD-ROM
**American History
Primary Source
Document Library
CD-ROM**

Use the **American History Primary Source Document Library CD-ROM** to access primary source documents related to issues facing the new American government and westward expansion.

More About the Art

George Caleb Bingham painted this oil on canvas work in 1851 and 1852. The painting shows Daniel Boone hero-ically leading his people through hos-tile terrain to a promised land in the West. The woman on the horse sym-bolizes the civilizing influence that will develop the culture of the frontier. Bingham shows the rocks and trees parting and a heavenly light shining down on the settlers, symbolizing the support of Providence for American settlement of the frontier. **Ask: What might the surrounding darkness symbolize?** *(Accept reasonable suggestions. Answers may include: danger, uncertainty, or unfavorable circumstances—fatigue, hunger, illness—preceding arrival in Kentucky.)*

Glencoe Literature Library

As students study the unit, have them read *Little Women* by Louisa May Alcott from the **Glencoe Literature Library.** The Glencoe Literature Library consists of novels and other readings for middle school students, along with study guides that offer instructional support and student activities.

SERVICE-LEARNING PROJECT

Help students understand the importance of becoming an actively involved citizen. Have students visit a city council or county board meeting. As a class, discuss the importance to residents of the decisions made at the council or county meeting. Discuss a community issue important to your class. Have students write letters to the local paper expressing their views on the issue. Plan a way to make the issue and its possible solution known to local government. **L2**

Refer to **Building Bridges: Connecting Classroom and Community through Service-Learning in Social Studies** from the National Council for the Social Studies for information about service-learning.

Timesaving Tools

TeacherWorks™ All-In-One Planner and Resource Center

- **Interactive Teacher Edition** Access your Teacher Wraparound Edition and your classroom resources with a few easy clicks.
- **Interactive Lesson Planner** Planning has never been easier! Organize your week, month, semester, or year with all the lesson helps you need to make teaching creative, timely, and relevant.

Use Glencoe's **Presentation Plus!** multimedia teacher tool to easily present dynamic lessons that visually excite your students. Using Microsoft PowerPoint® you can customize the presentations to create your own personalized lessons.

TEACHING TRANSPARENCIES

Graphic Organizer 3 L2

Why It Matters Chapter Transparency 8 L2

REVIEW AND REINFORCEMENT

Workbook Activity 8 L1

Time Line Activity 8 L2

Vocabulary Activity 8 L1

REVIEW AND REINFORCEMENT

Critical Thinking Skills Activity 8 L2

Take-Home Review Activity 8 L1

ENRICHMENT

Linking Past and Present Activity 8 L2

Primary Source Reading 8 L2

GEOGRAPHY

Geography and History Activity 8 L2

Meeting NCSS Standards

The following standards are highlighted in Chapter 8:

Section 1	VI	Power, Authority, & Governance: A, B, E, F, H, I
Section 2	III	People, Places, & Environments: B, H, I
Section 3	VI	Power, Authority, & Governance: A, B, C, D, F, H

FOLDABLES™ Study Organizer

Dinah Zike's Foldables are three-dimensional, interactive graphic organizers that help students practice basic writing skills, review key vocabulary terms, and identify main ideas. Additional chapter activities can be found in the ***Reading and Study Skills Foldables*** booklet.

Chapter 8 Resources

ASSESSMENT AND EVALUATION

**Chapter 8 Test
Form A** L2

**Chapter 8 Test
Form B** L2

**Standardized Test Practice
Workbook Activity 8** L2

**Performance Assessment
Activity 8** L1, ELL

**ExamView® Pro
Testmaker CD-ROM**

MULTIMEDIA

- Vocabulary PuzzleMaker CD-ROM
- Interactive Tutor Self-Assessment CD-ROM
- ExamView® Pro Testmaker CD-ROM
- Audio Program
- American History Primary Source Document
  Library CD-ROM
- MindJogger Videoquiz
- Presentation Plus! CD-ROM
- TeacherWorks CD-ROM
- Interactive Student Edition CD-ROM
- Glencoe Skillbuilder Interactive Workbook
  CD-ROM, Level 1
- The American Republic to 1877 Video Program
- American Music: Hits Through History

SPANISH RESOURCES

**The following Spanish language materials are
available in the Spanish Resources Binder:**

- Spanish Guided Reading Activities
- Spanish Reteaching Activities
- Spanish Quizzes and Tests
- Spanish Vocabulary Activity
- Spanish Take-Home Review Activity
- Spanish Summaries
- The Declaration of Independence and United States Constitution
  Spanish Translation

The following videotape programs are available
from Glencoe as supplements to Chapter 8:

- **George Washington: Founding Father** (ISBN 1-56501-377-8)*
- **Thomas Jefferson: Philosopher of Freedom** (ISBN 1-56501-502-9)*

To order, call Glencoe at 1-800-334-7344. To find classroom resources to
accompany many of these videos, check the following home pages:
A&E Television: www.aande.com
The History Channel: www.historychannel.com

*Available individually or in *The American Republic to 1877 Video Library.*

Use our Web site for additional resources. All essential content is
covered in the Student Edition.

You and your students can visit tarvol1.glencoe.com, the Web site
companion to **The American Republic to 1877.** This innovative integration of electronic and print media offers your students a wealth of
opportunities. The student text directs students to the Web site for the
following options:

- **Chapter Overviews**   • **Student Web Activities**
- **Self-Check Quizzes**   • **Textbook Updates**

Answers to the student Web activities are provided for you in the **Web
Activity Lesson Plans.** Additional Web resources and Interactive Tutor
Puzzles are also available.

Chapter 8 Resources

SECTION RESOURCES

Daily Objectives	Reproducible Resources	Multimedia Resources
SECTION 1 **The First President** 1. Describe what actions were taken to launch the new government. 2. Explain how Hamilton proposed to strengthen the economy.	Reproducible Lesson Plan 8–1 Daily Lecture and Discussion Notes 8–1 Guided Reading Activity 8–1* Section Quiz 8–1* Reteaching Activity 8–1* Reading Essentials and Study Guide 8–1* Enrichment Activity 8–1	Daily Focus Skills Transparency 8–1 Interactive Tutor Self-Assessment CD-ROM ExamView® Pro Testmaker CD-ROM Presentation Plus! CD-ROM
SECTION 2 **Early Challenges** 1. Understand how the federal government asserted its power in the West. 2. Examine how the United States tried to stay out of European conflicts.	Reproducible Lesson Plan 8–2 Daily Lecture and Discussion Notes 8–2 Guided Reading Activity 8–2* Section Quiz 8–2* Reteaching Activity 8–2* Reading Essentials and Study Guide 8–2* Enrichment Activity 8–2	Daily Focus Skills Transparency 8–2 Interactive Tutor Self-Assessment CD-ROM ExamView® Pro Testmaker CD-ROM Presentation Plus! CD-ROM
SECTION 3 **The First Political Parties** 1. Describe how political parties got started and what positions they supported. 2. Explain how John Adams and Thomas Jefferson became candidates of opposing parties in the election of 1796.	Reproducible Lesson Plan 8–3 Daily Lecture and Discussion Notes 8–3 Guided Reading Activity 8–3* Section Quiz 8–3* Reteaching Activity 8–3* Reading Essentials and Study Guide 8–3* Enrichment Activity 8–3	Daily Focus Skills Transparency 8–3 American Music: Hits Through History Vocabulary PuzzleMaker CD-ROM Interactive Tutor Self-Assessment CD-ROM ExamView® Pro Testmaker CD-ROM Presentation Plus! CD-ROM

0:00 OUT OF TIME?
Assign the Chapter 8 **Reading Essentials and Study Guide.**

*Also Available in Spanish

 Blackline Master   Transparency   ⊙ CD-ROM   ⊙ DVD

🔲 Poster   🎵 Music Program   ⊙ Audio Program   ▭ Videocassette

KEY TO ABILITY LEVELS

Teaching strategies have been coded.

L1 BASIC activities for all students
L2 AVERAGE activities for average to above-average students
L3 CHALLENGING activities for above-average students
ELL ENGLISH LANGUAGE LEARNER activities

NATIONAL GEOGRAPHIC Teacher's Corner

INDEX TO NATIONAL GEOGRAPHIC MAGAZINE

The following articles relate to this chapter.

- "L'Enfant's Washington," by Alice J. Hall, August 1991.
- "The Peales: America's First Family of Art," by Otto Friedrich, December 1990.

ADDITIONAL NATIONAL GEOGRAPHIC SOCIETY PRODUCTS

To order the following, call National Geographic at 1-800-368-2728:

- *National Geographic Desk Reference* (Book)
- *Washington, D.C.* (Video)

NGS ONLINE

Access National Geographic's Web site for current events, atlas updates, activities, links, interactive features, and archives.
www.nationalgeographic.com

MEETING SPECIAL NEEDS

In addition to the Differentiated Instruction strategies found in each section, the following resources are also suitable for your special needs students:

- *ExamView® Pro Testmaker CD-ROM* allows teachers to tailor tests by reducing answer choices.
- The *Audio Program* includes the entire narrative of the student edition so that less-proficient readers can listen to the words as they read them.
- The *Reading Essentials and Study Guide* provides the same content as the student edition but is written two grade levels below the textbook.
- *Guided Reading Activities* give less-proficient readers point-by-point instructions to increase comprehension as they read each textbook section.
- *Enrichment Activities* includes a stimulating collection of readings and activities for gifted and talented students.

From the Classroom of...

Carolyn Steinbrink
Shenandoah Middle School
Shenandoah, IA

Illustrating Reading Assignments

Students will illustrate the main ideas of the chapter. They will need several sheets of plain paper and colored pens and pencils for this activity. First, have students write a list of the main ideas and topics they encountered in their reading assignment, such as Washington's actions as president, the Whiskey Rebellion, the rise of political parties, and so on. As students read, have them create a design incorporating these topics. The design itself should relate to the main ideas of the reading. For example, Washington's accomplishments as president could be listed on branches of a cherry tree or within the pillars of the White House. The finished product could be as simple as a sketch of a road with the topics arranged on highway signs in chronological order. As you discuss the chapter in class, have students share their artwork and explain their topics.

ADDITIONAL RESOURCES FROM GLENCOE

- American Music: Cultural Traditions
- American Art and Architecture
- Outline Map Resource Book
- U.S. Desk Map
- Building Geography Skills for Life
- Inclusion for the Middle School Social Studies Classroom Strategies and Activities
- Teaching Strategies for the American History Classroom (Including Block Scheduling Pacing Guides)
- American Crafts Hands-On Activities
- American Games Hands-On Activities
- American History Flash Cards

Block Schedule

Activities that are suited to use within the block scheduling framework are identified by:

✓ **Performance Assessment**

Refer to Activity 8 in the Performance Assessment Activities and Rubrics booklet.

Why It Matters Activity

Ask students to speculate on the possible problems the new government might encounter. Have each student state one problem they think Washington faced that a president today may also encounter.

GLENCOE
TECHNOLOGY

The American Republic to 1877 Video Program
To learn more about George Washington and the first presidency, have students view the Chapter 8 video "George Washington" from **The American Republic to 1877 Video Program.**

Available in DVD and VHS

MindJogger Videoquiz
Use **MindJogger Videoquiz** to preview the Chapter 8 content.

Available in VHS

CHAPTER 8

A New Nation
1789–1800

Why It Matters

George Washington's administration faced the huge task of making the new government work. The Constitution had created the office of the presidency, but Washington established many procedures and customs.

The Impact Today

President Washington set many examples that presidents still follow. These include creating a cabinet, directing foreign affairs, and serving as chief legislator.

The American Republic to 1877 Video *The chapter 8 video, "George Washington," examines the issues that arose upon the establishment of the office of president.*

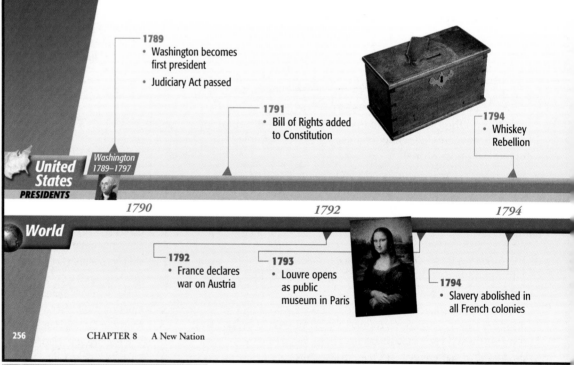

United States PRESIDENTS

Washington 1789–1797

1789
• Washington becomes first president
• Judiciary Act passed

1791
• Bill of Rights added to Constitution

1794
• Whiskey Rebellion

1790　　　*1792*　　　*1794*

World

1792
• France declares war on Austria

1793
• Louvre opens as public museum in Paris

1794
• Slavery abolished in all French colonies

Reading Strategy 〉 PURPOSE FOR READING

Mindstreaming is a useful strategy to bring out students' background knowledge or review prior material before starting a new unit. State that the Constitution set the framework for the new government. Critically missing from the Constitution was a set of laws identifying the rights of the people. Organize the students into pairs: Student A and Student B. Have Student A talk for one minute, telling everything he or she remembers about causes of the American Revolution. Student B listens and encourages but says nothing. Reverse the roles and Student B adds new information and repeats what Student A has said. Finally, ask volunteers to present their information to the class. **L1**

Boston Harbor as Seen From Constitution Wharf by Robert Salmon
Salmon recorded the emerging cities and scenic harbors of the young nation.

FOLDABLES™
Study Organizer

Summarizing Study Foldable Make this foldable and use it as a journal to help you record the major events that occurred as the new nation of the United States formed.

Step 1 Fold a sheet of paper from top to bottom.

Step 2 Then fold it in half from side to side.

Step 3 Label the foldable as shown.

Journal of American Firsts

Reading and Writing As you read the chapter, find the "firsts" experienced by the new nation, and record them in your foldable journal. For example, list the precedents set by President Washington and identify the first political parties.

FOLDABLES™
Study Organizer — Dinah Zike's Foldables

Purpose Students will make and use a foldable to summarize key concepts after reading the chapter. This reading strategy requires students to read with the purpose of identifying and recording important "firsts" that occurred as the new nation of the United States was launched.

Have students complete **Reading and Study Skills Foldables** Activity 8. **L1**

HISTORY
Online

Introduce students to chapter content and key terms by having them access **Chapter Overview 8** at tarvol1.glencoe.com

TIME LINE
ACTIVITY

As students read the chapter, have them review the time line on pages 256–257. Have students identify how many years had passed from the time that the Bill of Rights was added to the Constitution to other world and United States events.

1795
• Nation's first chief justice, John Jay, retires from court

1800
• Convention of 1800 resolves U.S./French conflicts

1798
• Alien and Sedition Acts passed
• XYZ affair

Adams 1797–1801

1796

1798

1796
• Jenner develops smallpox vaccine

1799
• Rosetta stone discovered

HISTORY
Online

Chapter Overview
Visit tarvol1.glencoe.com and click on **Chapter 8— Chapter Overviews** to preview chapter information.

More About the Art

Artist Robert Salmon specialized in maritime scenes, often showing detailed depictions of clipper ships. Salmon was born in Whitehaven, England. He began his artistic career painting scenes from Liverpool and Greenock, England. He sailed to the United States in 1828 and soon began painting scenes from Boston Harbor. It is estimated that he completed about 1,000 paintings in his lifetime. *Boston Harbor* is an example of Salmon's polished and carefully detailed painting style.

257

1 FOCUS

Section Overview

This section explains the task faced by the Washington administration of establishing a new government.

Reading Preview

Answers to Graphic: Washington: nominated first chief justice of the Supreme Court, appointed cabinet heads; Congress: created the executive departments, established a federal court system, approved Bill of Rights, created a national bank

Preteaching Vocabulary
Have students look in a dictionary for the word *cabinet*. Ask them to choose the meaning they think will apply to this section.

Guide to Reading

Main Idea
President Washington and the first Congress tackled the work of establishing a new government.

Key Terms
precedent, cabinet, national debt, bond, speculator, unconstitutional, tariff

Reading Strategy
Classifying Information As you read the section, re-create the diagram below and list the actions taken by Congress and Washington's first administration.

Actions	
Washington	Congress

Read to Learn
• what actions were taken to launch the new government.
• how Hamilton proposed to strengthen the economy.

Section Theme
Government and Democracy President Washington and Congress took actions that shaped the future of government in our nation.

Preview of Events

♦1789   ♦1790   ♦1791   ♦1792

April 6, 1789
George Washington is elected president

April 30, 1789
Washington takes the oath of office

September 1789
Judiciary Act sets up federal court system

December 1791
Bill of Rights added to the Constitution

Washington banner

February 22nd 1732
December 14th 1799

AN American Story

Celebrations erupted in the streets of Philadelphia, New York, Boston, and Charleston in 1789. News of the Constitution's ratification was greeted with relief and enthusiasm. All that was needed now was a leader to guide the new nation.

On April 6 the new Senate counted the presidential ballots. To no one's surprise, the votes were unanimous. Senator John Langdon wrote to General George Washington: "Sir, I have the honor to transmit to Your Excellency the information of your unanimous election to the office of President of the United States of America." Washington was ready to begin the difficult task of leading the country.

President Washington

The 57-year-old president-elect made his way slowly toward New York City, then the nation's capital. After the Constitutional Convention, George Washington had looked forward to a quiet retirement. Instead his fellow citizens elected him to the highest office in the land. On April 30, 1789, Washington took the oath of office as the first president of the United States under the federal Constitution (there had been several presidents under the Articles of Confederation). John Adams became vice president. 📖 *(See page 598 of the Primary Sources Library for an excerpt of an account of Washington's First Inaugural.)*

Perhaps no office in the new government created more suspicion among the people than the office of president. Many Americans feared that a president would try to become king, but they trusted Washington. They believed that his leadership had brought them victory in the Revolutionary War.

Washington was aware of the difficulties he faced. He knew that the precedents, or traditions, he established as the nation's first president would shape the future of the United States. "No slip will pass unnoticed," he remarked. One precedent he established concerned the way people should address him. Vice President Adams supported "His Highness the President of the United States," but ultimately it was decided that "Mr. President" would be more appropriate.

Washington and the new Congress also had many decisions to make about the structure of government. For example, the Constitution gave Congress the power to establish executive departments, but it did not state whether the department heads would report to the president or to Congress.

The First Congress

During the summer of 1789, Congress set up three departments in the executive branch of government. The State Department would handle relations with other nations, the Treasury Department would deal with financial matters, and the War Department would provide for the nation's defense. Congress also created the office of attorney general to handle the government's legal affairs and the office of postmaster general to direct the postal service.

To head the departments, Washington chose prominent political figures of the day—**Thomas Jefferson** as secretary of state, **Alexander Hamilton** as secretary of the treasury, and **Henry Knox** as secretary of war. He appointed **Edmund Randolph** as attorney general. Washington met regularly with the three department heads and the attorney general, who together became known as the cabinet.

Congress created the executive departments; opinion was divided, however, on how much power the president should have over them. For example, should the president be able to replace an official that he had appointed and the Senate had confirmed? Senators were evenly divided in voting on the issue.

Vice President Adams broke the tie by voting to allow the president the authority to dismiss cabinet officers without the Senate's approval. This decision strengthened the president's position. It also helped create a greater separation between the legislative and executive branches of government by establishing the president's authority over the executive branch.

Judiciary Act

The first Congress also had to decide how to set up the nation's court system. The Constitution briefly mentioned a supreme court but had left further details about the courts to Congress.

Disagreements arose between those favoring a uniform, national legal system and those favoring state courts. The two groups reached a compromise in the **Judiciary Act of 1789.** With this act, Congress established a federal court system with 13 district courts and three circuit courts to serve the nation. State laws would remain, but the federal courts would have the power to reverse state decisions.

The Supreme Court would be the final authority on many issues. Washington nominated **John Jay** to lead the Supreme Court as chief justice, and the Senate approved Jay's nomination. With the Judiciary Act, Congress had taken the first steps toward creating a strong and independent national judiciary.

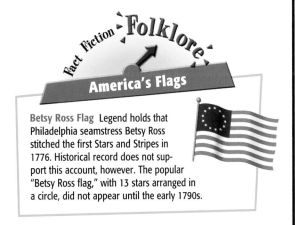

Fact Fiction Folklore

America's Flags

Betsy Ross Flag Legend holds that Philadelphia seamstress Betsy Ross stitched the first Stars and Stripes in 1776. Historical record does not support this account, however. The popular "Betsy Ross flag," with 13 stars arranged in a circle, did not appear until the early 1790s.

CHAPTER 8   A New Nation   **259**

Reading Strategy

Finding Main Points Have students turn each subheading into a question. For example, "Judiciary Act" would become "What was the Judiciary Act?" Have students read the section and write one sentence summarizing the answer to each question. **L1**

When?Who?What?Where?

The Election of 1789 George Washington was chosen by the electors from just 10 states. Election problems prevented New York from casting its ballot, and Rhode Island and North Carolina had not yet ratified the Constitution.

COOPERATIVE LEARNING ACTIVITY

Presenting the National Capital Organize the class into small groups. Each group should choose an important building or monument in Washington, D.C. Have each group find or draw a picture of its building or make a model of it. Each group should also write a paragraph about it. Some groups may choose to draw a diagram of the interior of the building. One group might choose to draw a map of the capital marking the location of various points of interest. Tasks within groups should be divided according to the skills of the members. **L1, ELL**

Guided Reading Activity 8–1

Name _____ Date _____ Class _____

★ **Guided Reading Activity 8-1**

DIRECTIONS: Recalling the Facts Use the information in your textbook to answer the questions. Use another sheet of paper if necessary.

1. When and where was George Washington inaugurated as president?

2. Who was the first vice president?
3. Why were people willing to trust Washington as president?

4. What executive departments were set up by Congress in 1789?

5. Who was the first head of the department described below?
   a) handled relations with other nations
   b) dealt with financial matters
   c) provided for the nation's defense
6. How was the president's authority over the executive branch established?

7. What did Congress establish with the Judiciary Act of 1789?
8. Who was the first chief justice of the United States?
9. What was the Bill of Rights?
10. When was the Bill of Rights added to the Constitution?
11. What are bonds?
12. Why did the South object to Alexander Hamilton's plan to repay the bonds?
13. How did Hamilton win the support of the South?
14. Between which two states was the new capital district located?
15. What were three other proposals Hamilton made to build a strong economy?

16. Why did Thomas Jefferson and James Madison oppose Hamilton's economic program?

People In History

In 1753 Benjamin Banneker built a clock entirely of wood, including hand-carved gears. The clock is reported to have kept near-perfect time for decades. Between 1792 and 1802, Banneker wrote a yearly almanac that included weather and tide predictions. Banneker sent Thomas Jefferson a copy of his first almanac, along with a letter requesting the abolition of slavery.

People In History

Benjamin Banneker 1731–1806

Black Heritage USA 15c

Benjamin Banneker was born into a free African American family in Maryland. He attended a private Quaker school, but was largely self-educated. When his father died, Banneker sold the family farm and devoted the rest of his life to mathematics and natural sciences.

Banneker's skill in mathematics prompted Thomas Jefferson to give him a job surveying the land for the new national capital at Washington, D.C. When French architect Pierre L'Enfant was removed from the project, he took his detailed maps with him. Banneker amazed everyone by redrawing the missing maps from memory! From 1792 to 1802 he made astronomical and tide calculations for a yearly almanac. Banneker became a symbol for racial justice in a land not yet ready to grant him the rights of citizenship, granted to others in the Bill of Rights.

The Bill of Rights

Americans had long feared strong central governments. They had fought a revolution to throw off one and did not want to replace it with another. Many people insisted the Constitution needed to include guarantees of personal liberties. Some states had supported the Constitution on the condition that a bill of rights be added.

To fulfill the promises made during the fight for ratification of the Constitution, James Madison introduced a set of amendments during the first session of Congress. Congress passed 12 amendments, and the states ratified 10 of them. In December 1791, these 10 amendments were added to the Constitution and became known as the **Bill of Rights.**

The Bill of Rights limits the powers of government. Its purpose is to protect the rights of individual liberty, such as freedom of speech, and rights of persons accused of crimes, including trial by jury. The Tenth Amendment protects the rights of states and individuals by saying that powers not specifically given to the federal government "are reserved to the States respectively, or to the people." With the Tenth Amendment, Madison hoped to use the states as an important line of defense against a too-powerful national government. 📖 *(See pages 244–245 for the entire text of the Bill of Rights.)*

✓ **Reading Check** **Describing** Why was the Bill of Rights created?

Ⓢ Economics

Financial Problems

Washington himself rarely proposed laws, and he almost always approved the bills that were passed by Congress. The first president concentrated on foreign affairs and military matters and left the government's economic policies to his dynamic secretary of the treasury, Alexander Hamilton.

The new nation faced serious financial problems. The national debt—the amount the nation's government owed—was growing. Hamilton tried to find a way to improve the government's financial reputation and to strengthen the nation at the same time.

DIFFERENTIATED INSTRUCTION

Reading Support Speculators bought the old state war bonds at 10 to 20 cents on the dollar and later sold them at full value, making huge profits. Have students solve word problems to calculate possible profits. Example: A man buys a bond worth $50. At 10 cents per dollar, how much did he pay for the bond? *($5.00)* Ignoring interest, what was the profit? *($45.00)* If he bought 100 bonds, what was the profit? *($4,500.00)* **L2**

📁 Refer to *Inclusion for the Middle School Social Studies Classroom Strategies and Activities* in the TCR.

Hamilton's Plan

In 1790 Hamilton proposed that the new government pay off the millions of dollars in debts owed by the Confederation government to other countries and to individual American citizens. The states had fought for the nation's independence, Hamilton argued, so the national government should pay for the cost of their help. Hamilton also believed that federal payment of state debts would give the states a strong interest in the success of the national government.

Opposition to the Plan

Congress agreed to pay money owed to other nations, but Hamilton's plan to pay off the debt to American citizens unleashed a storm of protest. When the government had borrowed money during the American Revolution, it had issued bonds—paper notes promising to repay the money in a certain length of time. While waiting for the payment, many of the original bond owners—shopkeepers, farmers, and soldiers—had sold the bonds for less than their value. They were purchased by speculators, people who risk money in order to make a larger profit. Hamilton proposed that these bonds be paid off at their original value. Opponents believed that Hamilton's plan would make speculators rich, and

66established at the expense of national justice, gratitude, and humanity.**99**

The original bond owners felt betrayed by the government because they had lost money on their bonds while new bond owners profited.

Even stronger opposition came from the Southern states, which had accumulated much less debt than the Northern states. Southern states complained that they would have to pay more than their share under Hamilton's plan.

Compromise Results in a Capital

To win support for his plan, Hamilton compromised. He agreed to a proposal from Southern leaders to locate the new nation's capital in the South after moving to Philadelphia while workmen prepared the new city for the federal government. A special district would be laid out between Virginia and Maryland along the banks of the Potomac River. This district became **Washington, D.C.** In return, Southerners supported his plan to pay off the state debts.

✓**Reading Check** Explaining Why did Hamilton's plan to pay off the debt to American citizens cause such a storm of protest?

America's *Architecture*

The Capitol is the seat of the United States Congress in Washington, D.C. Built on a hill popularly called Capitol Hill, the Capitol contains floor space equivalent to over 16 acres. The dome of the United States Capitol, finished in 1863, is one of the most famous landmarks in the United States. Other important parts of the Capitol include the Rotunda directly under the dome, the Senate Chamber in the north wing, the House Chamber in the south wing, and the National Statuary Hall.

✓**Reading Check**

Answer: Hamilton proposed repayment of war bonds at their original level. Because average citizens had sold the bonds far under their original value to speculators, it was believed that Hamilton's plan would make speculators unfairly rich.

America's *Architecture*

During the War of 1812, British troops captured and set fire to the Capitol. The building's restoration was completed in 1826.

3 ASSESS

Assign Section 1 Assessment as homework or as an in-class activity.

⊙ Have students use **Interactive Tutor Self-Assessment CD-ROM.**

L2

Section Quiz 8–1

Name _____ Date _____ Class _____

★ Chapter 8   Score

Section Quiz 8-1

DIRECTIONS: Matching Match the items in Column A with the items in Column B. Write the correct letters in the blanks. *(10 points each)*

Column A	Column B
___ 1. precedents	A. national debt
___ 2. first attorney general	B. tariff
___ 3. amount the government owes	C. traditions
___ 4. tax on imports	D. Henry Knox
___ 5. first secretary of war	E. Edmund Randolph

L1

Reteaching Activity 8–1

Name _____ Date _____ Class _____

★ Reteaching Activity 8-1

DIRECTIONS: Matching Match each item in Column A with its corresponding item in Column B. Write the correct letters in the blanks.

COLUMN A	COLUMN B
___ 1. New York City	A. first secretary of war
___ 2. John Adams	B. executive branch department heads and the attorney general
___ 3. Thomas Jefferson	C. first 10 amendments to the Constitution guaranteeing personal liberties
___ 4. Alexander Hamilton	D. people who risk money to make a larger profit
___ 5. Henry Knox	E. the temporary capital of the United
___ 6. Edmund Randolph	

INTERDISCIPLINARY CONNECTIONS ACTIVITY

Civics Have students find out about the 14 departments that are now part of the cabinet (State, Treasury, Defense, Justice, Interior, Agriculture, Commerce, Labor, Housing and Urban Development, Transportation, Energy, Education, Health and Human Services, Veterans Affairs). Ask students to write a paragraph describing the duties of each department and to use an almanac or the Internet to find the names of the current secretaries. (The head of the Department of Justice is called the attorney general, not secretary.) **L2**

4 CLOSE

A member of the House of Representatives reacted to the job ahead—launching the new government—by exclaiming, "We are in a wilderness!" Have students explain the statement, giving specific examples from the section.

Building the Economy

Hamilton made other proposals for building a strong national economy. He asked Congress to create a national bank, the Bank of the United States. Both private investors and the national government would own the Bank's stock.

The Fight Over the Bank

In 1792 there were only eight other banks in the nation. All eight had been established by state governments. Madison and Jefferson opposed the idea of a national bank. They believed it would benefit the wealthy. They also charged that the Bank was unconstitutional— that it was inconsistent with the Constitution. Hamilton argued that although the Constitution did not specifically say that Congress could create a bank, Congress still had the power to do so. In the end the president agreed with Hamilton and signed the bill creating the national bank.

Tariffs and Taxes

At the time, most Americans earned their living by farming. Hamilton thought the development of manufacturing would make America's economy stronger. He proposed a tariff—a tax on imports—to encourage people to buy American products. This protective tariff would protect American industry from foreign competition.

The South, having little industry to protect, opposed protective tariffs. Hamilton did win support in Congress for some low tariffs to raise money rather than to protect industries. By the 1790s the revenue from tariffs provided 90 percent of the national government's income.

The final portion of Hamilton's economic program concerned the creation of national taxes. The government needed additional funds to operate and to make interest payments on the national debt. At Hamilton's request Congress approved a variety of taxes, including one on whiskey distilled in the United States.

Hamilton's economic program gave the national government new financial powers. However, his proposals split Congress and the nation. The opponents—including Jefferson and Madison—feared a national government with strong economic powers dominated by the wealthy class. They had a very different vision of what America should become.

✓ **Reading Check** **Comparing** Summarize the arguments for and against protective tariffs.

SECTION 1 ASSESSMENT

Checking for Understanding

1. **Key Terms** Write a paragraph for each group of terms below. Group 1: precedent, cabinet. Group 2: national debt, bond, speculator. Group 3: unconstitutional, tariff.
2. **Reviewing Facts** Name three things that Hamilton wanted to do to create a stable economic system and strengthen the economy.

Reviewing Themes

3. **Government and Democracy** What compromise did Congress reach in establishing a court system?

Critical Thinking

4. **Analyzing Primary Sources** Hamilton said about Washington, "He consulted much, pondered much, resolved slowly, resolved surely." Did this make Washington a good first president? Explain.
5. **Comparing** Re-create the diagram below. Compare the views of Hamilton and Jefferson. In the boxes, write "for" or "against" for each issue.

Issue	Hamilton	Jefferson
National bank		
Protective tariff		
National taxes		

Analyzing Visuals

6. **Picturing History** Examine the picture of the U.S. Capitol on page 261. The Capitol is one of the most widely recognized buildings in the world. What members of the government serve in the Capitol? What does the U.S. Capitol symbolize to you?

Interdisciplinary Activity

Expository Writing You have been given the task of choosing the first cabinet members. Write a job description for the secretaries of state, treasury, and war. Then interview classmates to see who would be best suited for each position.

SECTION 1 ASSESSMENT ANSWERS

1. Student work should reflect correct use of terms.
2. Answers may include: pay off debts, form a national bank, enact tariffs, and create national taxes.
3. The Judiciary Act of 1789 kept state laws in place, but gave federal courts power to reverse state decisions.
4. Answers should show that it is important to consult others, think carefully about actions, and take action with confidence.
5. National Bank: Hamilton–for, Jefferson–against; Protective tariff: Hamilton–for, Jefferson–against; National taxes: Hamilton–for, Jefferson–against
6. members of the Senate and the House of Representatives; answers may include an idea of national unity, democracy, and American pride

Interdisciplinary Activity Job descriptions should list characteristics and experience suitable for these positions.

SECTION 2 Early Challenges

Guide to Reading

Main Idea
In the 1790s, the new government struggled to keep peace at home and avoid war abroad.

Key Terms
neutrality, impressment

Reading Strategy
Classifying Information As you read the section, re-create the diagram below and list results of government actions during the early Republic.

Government action	Results
Treaty of Greenville	
Proclamation of Neutrality	
Jay's Treaty	
Pinckney's Treaty	

Read to Learn
• how the federal government asserted its power in the West.
• how the United States tried to stay out of European conflicts.

Section Theme
Geography and History The new government clashed over control of the Northwest Territory.

Preview of Events

◆1790   ◆1792   ◆1794   ◆1796

November 1791
Little Turtle defeats St. Clair's forces

March 1793
Washington begins second term

July 1794
Western farmers revolt in Whiskey Rebellion

August 1794
Battle of Fallen Timbers occurs

October 1795
Spain opens Mississippi River to American shipping

AN American Story

Far removed from the bustle of trade and shipping along the Atlantic coast, farmers on the western frontier lived quite differently. In fact, western ways seemed almost primitive to travelers from the East. They seemed to notice only the poor roads and the boring diet of corn and salted pork. Living in scattered, isolated homesteads, frontier farmers were proud of their self-reliance. They wanted no "eastern" tax collectors heading their way.

Drawing of tax collector

The Whiskey Rebellion

Hamilton's taxes led to rebellion in western Pennsylvania. The farmers were in an uproar over having to pay a special tax on the whiskey they made from surplus corn. In the backcountry most farmers lived by bartering—exchanging whiskey and other items they produced for goods they needed. They rarely had cash. How could they pay a tax on whiskey?

The farmers' resistance was mostly peaceful—until July 1794, when federal officers stepped up efforts to collect the tax. Then a large mob of people armed with swords, guns, and pitchforks attacked tax collectors and burned down buildings.

CHAPTER 8   A New Nation   **263**

1 FOCUS

Section Overview
This section examines problems encountered by the new United States government.

BELLRINGER
Skillbuilder Activity

Project transparency and have students answer the question.

Daily Focus Skills Transparency 8–2

Reading Preview

Answers to Graphic: Treaty of Greenville: Native Americans gave up most of their lands in present-day Ohio for white settlement; Proclamation of Neutrality: prohibited American citizens from fighting in the war between France and England; Jay's Treaty: British agreed to withdraw from American soil; Pinckney's Treaty: gave Americans free navigation of the Mississippi River

Preteaching Vocabulary
Explain that the term *neutrality* comes from a Latin word meaning "neither." Have students explain the relationship between the two terms.

SECTION RESOURCES

📁 **Reproducible Masters**
• Reproducible Lesson Plan 8–2
• Daily Lecture and Discussion Notes 8–2
• Guided Reading Activity 8–2
• Section Quiz 8–2
• Reteaching Activity 8–2
• Reading Essentials and Study Guide 8–2
• Enrichment Activity 8–2

🖨 **Transparencies**
• Daily Focus Skills Transparency 8–2

Multimedia
🔘 Interactive Tutor Self-Assessment CD-ROM
🔘 ExamView® Pro Testmaker CD-ROM
🔘 Presentation Plus! CD-ROM

2 TEACH

Reading Strategy

Taking Notes Have students write a one-paragraph summary of each of the four main parts of the section and answer the review questions by referring only to their paragraphs. **L1**

✓ Reading Check

Answer: It set a precedent for government to use force when necessary in order to maintain social order.

L1, ELL

✓ Reading Check

Answer: Native Americans turned to Britain and Spain to help them in their cause.

The armed protest, called the **Whiskey Rebellion,** alarmed government leaders. President Washington and his advisers decided to crush the challenge. The rebellion collapsed as soon as the army crossed the Appalachian Mountains.

By his action, Washington served notice to those who opposed government actions. If citizens wished to change the law, they had to do so peacefully, through constitutional means. Government would use force when necessary to maintain the social order.

✓ Reading Check **Explaining** How did the Whiskey Rebellion affect the way government handled protesters?

★ Geography

Struggle Over the West

The new government faced difficult problems in the West. The Native Americans who lived between the Appalachian Mountains and the Mississippi River denied that the United States had any authority over them. On many occasions Native Americans turned to Britain and Spain to help them in their cause. Both countries welcomed the opportunity to prevent American settlement of the region.

Washington worried about European ambitions in the Northwest Territory. He hoped that signing treaties with the Native American tribes in the area would lessen the influence of the British and Spanish. American settlers ignored the treaties and continued to move onto lands promised to the Native Americans. Fighting broke out between the two groups.

Washington sent an army under General Arthur St. Clair to restore order in the Northwest Territory. In November 1791, St. Clair's forces were badly beaten by Little Turtle, chief of the Miami people. More than 600 American soldiers died in a battle by the Wabash River.

Many Americans believed that an alliance with France would enable them to defeat the combined forces of the British, Spanish, and Native Americans in the West. The British, who still had forts in the region, wanted to hold on to the profitable fur trade. The possibility of French

involvement in the region pushed the British to make a bold bid for control of the West. In 1794 the British government urged Native Americans to destroy American settlements west of the Appalachians. The British also began building a new fort in Ohio.

Battle of Fallen Timbers

The Native Americans demanded that all settlers north of the Ohio River leave the territory. Washington sent another army headed by Anthony Wayne, a former Revolutionary War general, to challenge their demands. In August 1794 his army defeated over 1,000 Native Americans under Shawnee chief Blue Jacket at the **Battle of Fallen Timbers** (near present-day Toledo, Ohio). The Battle of Fallen Timbers crushed the Native Americans' hopes of keeping their land. In the **Treaty of Greenville** (1795), the Native Americans agreed to surrender most of the land in present-day Ohio.

✓ Reading Check **Describing** What did Native American groups do to fight more effectively in the Northwest?

Problems With Europe

Shortly after Washington was inaugurated in 1789, the French Revolution began. At first most Americans cheered upon hearing the news. The French had helped the Americans in their struggle for independence, and their revolution seemed to embody many of the ideals of the American Revolution.

By 1793 the French Revolution had turned bloody. The leaders had executed the king and queen of France and thousands of French citizens. Public opinion in the United States started to divide. The violence of the French Revolution, as well as its attack on religion and disregard of individual liberties, offended many Americans. Others hailed the new republic as a copy of the United States.

When Britain and France went to war in 1793, some Americans, particularly in the South, sympathized with France. Others, especially manufacturers and merchants who traded with the British, favored Britain. Hamilton, Adams, and their supporters generally sided with the

---

Reading Strategy   READING THE TEXT

Understanding Vocabulary Students should be familiar with different types of words. Homophones are words that sound the same but have different meanings and different spellings. For example, *base* is a foundation whereas *bass* is a deep tone. Homographs are words that have different meanings and origins but are spelled the same. For example, a fan may be an admirer, but it also may be a cooling device. As students read the section, have them list any homophones and homographs they can find. With partners, have them create an illustrated booklet of three homophones and three homographs, using captions and pictures to describe the differences between the words. **L1, ELL**

British. Jefferson was pro-French. A French victory, Jefferson reasoned, would help drive the British out of North America.

Washington hoped that the nation could maintain its neutrality—that is, that it would not take sides in the conflict between France and Britain. As time went on, however, neutrality became increasingly difficult.

Washington Proclaims Neutrality

The French tried to involve the United States in their conflict with Britain. In April 1793, they sent diplomat **Edmond Genêt** (zhuh•NAY) to the United States. His mission was to recruit American volunteers to attack British ships.

NATIONAL GEOGRAPHIC
Native American Campaigns

Battle of Fallen Timbers, 1794
Ft. Miami
St. Clair's defeat, 1791
Ft. Defiance
Greenville Treaty Line, 1795
Wabash R.
Ft. Recovery
Land ceded by Native Americans
NORTHWEST TERRITORY
Ft. Washington (Cincinnati)
Ohio R.
Lake Erie
N.Y.
PA.
VA.
KY.

0   50 miles
0   50 kilometers
Lambert Equal-Area projection

← Route of General Arthur St. Clair
← Route of General Anthony Wayne
✷ Battle
■ Fort

Geography *Skills*

General Anthony Wayne's forces marched north from Fort Washington to fight the Shawnee chief Blue Jacket.
1. Location When and where was St. Clair defeated?
2. Location On what lake was Fort Miami located?

President Washington took action to discourage American involvement. On April 22 he issued a **Proclamation of Neutrality.** It prohibited American citizens from fighting in the war and barred French and British warships from American ports. Genêt's plans eventually failed, but he did manage to sign up a few hundred Americans to serve on French ships. These ships seized British vessels and stole their cargoes before Washington ended their adventures by closing American ports.

Outraged by the French attacks at sea, the British began capturing American ships that traded with the French. The British also stopped American merchant ships and forced their crews into the British navy. This practice, known as impressment, infuriated the Americans. British attacks on American ships and sailors, along with the challenge in the West, pushed the nation closer to war with Great Britain.

A Controversial Treaty

President Washington decided to make one last effort to come to a peaceful solution with Britain. He sent John Jay, chief justice of the Supreme Court, to negotiate.

The British were willing to listen to Jay's proposals. War with the United States would only make it harder to carry on the war with France, and the United States was Britain's best market.

Picturing **History**

Upon signing the Treaty of Greenville, 12 Native American nations received $20,000 worth of goods to share. **How did the treaty affect white settlement?**

Geography *Skills*

Answers:
1. by the Wabash River near Fort Recovery in 1791
2. Lake Erie

Picturing **History**

Answer: It provided the opportunity to settle in most of present-day Ohio.

3 ASSESS

Assign Section 2 Assessment as homework or as an in-class activity.

🅰 Have students use **Interactive Tutor Self-Assessment CD-ROM.**

L2

Section Quiz 8–2

Name _____ Date _____ Class _____

★ Chapter 8   Score

Section Quiz 8-2

DIRECTIONS: Matching Match the items in Column A with the items in Column B. Write the correct letters in the blanks. *(10 points each)*

Column A
_____ **1.** tax protest
_____ **2.** pro-French
_____ **3.** to not take sides
_____ **4.** forced into British navy
_____ **5.** agreement with Spain

Column B
A. neutrality
B. the Whiskey Rebellion
C. Pinckney's Treaty
D. Thomas Jefferson
E. impressment

L1

Reteaching Activity 8–2

Name _____ Date _____ Class _____

★ Reteaching Activity 8-2

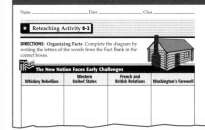

DIRECTIONS: Organizing Facts Complete the diagram by writing the letters of the words from the Fact Bank in the correct boxes.

The New Nation Faces Early Challenges			
Whiskey Rebellion	Western United States	French and British Relations	Washington's Farewell

---

DIFFERENTIATED INSTRUCTION

At-Risk Students Have students draw a political cartoon dealing with some aspect of the section. Possibilities include the Whiskey Rebellion from the point of view of farmers in western Pennsylvania, treaties with Native Americans from the point of view of the Native Americans, and Jay's Treaty from the point of view of those who opposed it. **L1**

📂 Refer to *Inclusion for the Middle School Social Studies Classroom Strategies and Activities* in the TCR.

✓ **Reading Check**

Answer: It did not deal with impressment or the British interference with trade.

✓ **Reading Check**

Answer: The Address influenced American leaders to avoid foreign alliances for more than 100 years.

L1, ELL

Reading Essentials and Study Guide 8-2

Study Guide
Chapter 8, Section 2
For use with textbook pages 263–266
EARLY CHALLENGES

KEY TERMS
neutrality   Not taking sides in a conflict (page 265)
impressment   The act of forcing men into military service (page 265)

DRAWING FROM EXPERIENCE
Have you ever been in a situation where two of your friends were arguing and you did not want to take a side? Why did you want to stay neutral, or stay out of the argument?
In the last section, you read about how Washington and Congress established a cabinet of advisers and an economic plan for the new government. This section focuses on how the new government asserted its power in the West and tried to stay out of European conflicts.

L3

Enrichment Activity 8-2

★ Enrichment Activity 8-2 ★

Name _____ Date _____ Class _____

Give Me Liberty!

4 CLOSE

Lt. Colonel Henry Lee spoke this tribute upon Washington's death: "First in war, first in peace, first in the hearts of his countrymen." Have students cite examples supporting the statement.

Chief Justice John Jay

In **Jay's Treaty** the British agreed to withdraw from American soil, to pay damages for ships they had seized, and to allow some American ships to trade with British colonies in the Caribbean. The treaty also provided for settlement of debts from before 1776.

Despite these gains few Americans approved of Jay's Treaty. They protested that the treaty did not deal with the issue of impressment and did not mention British interference with American trade. Although Washington found fault with the treaty, he realized it would end an explosive crisis with Great Britain. He sent the treaty to the Senate, which narrowly approved it after a fierce debate.

Treaty With Spain

When Jay's Treaty was made, Spanish leaders realized that the United States and Great Britain could work together against the Spanish Empire in North America. Thomas Pinckney was sent to Spain to try to settle the differences between the two nations. In 1795 **Pinckney's Treaty** gave the Americans free navigation of the Mississippi River and the right to trade at New Orleans.

✓ **Reading Check** Describing Why did many Americans protest Jay's Treaty?

Washington's Farewell

In September 1796, Washington announced he would not seek a third term. By choosing to serve only two terms, Washington set a precedent that later presidents would follow.

Plagued with a variety of ailments, the 64-year-old president looked forward to retirement at Mount Vernon. He also felt troubled over the divisions that had developed in American politics and with what he considered a grave danger to the new nation—the growth of political parties.

Washington's "Farewell Address" was published in a Philadelphia newspaper. In it he attacked the evils of political parties and entanglement in foreign affairs. He also urged his fellow citizens to

❝observe good faith and justice toward all nations . . . Tis our policy to steer clear of permanent alliances.❞

Washington's parting words influenced the nation's foreign policy for more than 100 years. The text is still read aloud in the United States Senate each year on Washington's birthday. 📖
(See page 615 of the Appendix for an excerpt from Washington's Farewell Address.)

✓ **Reading Check** Explaining What was the impact of Washington's Farewell Address?

SECTION 2 ASSESSMENT

Checking for Understanding

1. **Key Terms** Use the terms neutrality and impressment in a sentence about Washington's administration.
2. **Reviewing Facts** What message was Washington sending to the American people when he used force to stop the Whiskey Rebellion?

Reviewing Themes

3. **Geography and History** How did the Treaty of Greenville affect the land claims of Native Americans in the Northwest Territory?

Critical Thinking

4. **Predicting Consequences** What did the United States have to gain by remaining neutral in foreign affairs?
5. **Determining Cause and Effect** Re-create the diagram below. In the boxes, list the cause and effects of the Whiskey Rebellion.

Cause → Cause/Effect **Whiskey Rebellion** → Effects

Analyzing Visuals

6. **Geography and History** Review the map on page 265. The Native American nations surrendered land that makes up a large part of what present-day state?

Interdisciplinary Activity

Descriptive Writing A tribute is a speech showing respect and gratitude. Write a one-paragraph tribute that you might have delivered if you had been asked to speak at George Washington's funeral.

SECTION 2 ASSESSMENT ANSWERS

1. Student work should reflect correct use of terms.
2. The government would not tolerate violent protests. Laws had to be changed peacefully, through constitutional means.
3. It allowed settlers to take Native Americans' land.
4. Americans would not be killed in battle; less money and property loss; better relations with other nations
5. Cause: farmers resistance to a tax imposed on whiskey; Effects: 500 people riot; armed troops sent to crush the rebellion; citizens aware that federal force used to maintain peace; citizens made aware that changes in laws need to occur through peaceful and constitutional means
6. Ohio

Interdisciplinary Activity Tributes should cite some of Washington's achievements and his strengths as a leader.

SECTION 3 The First Political Parties

Guide to Reading

Main Idea
By the election of 1796, two distinct political parties with different views about the role of the national government had formed.

Key Terms
partisan, implied powers, caucus, alien, sedition, nullify, states' rights

Reading Strategy
Classifying Information As you read Section 3, create a diagram like the one below and list the differences between the Federalists and the Democratic-Republicans.

Issue	Federalists	Democratic-Republicans
Role of federal government		

Read to Learn
• how political parties got started and what positions they supported.
• how John Adams and Thomas Jefferson became candidates of opposing parties in the election of 1796.

Section Theme
Government and Democracy Different values fueled the rise of the nation's first political parties.

Preview of Events

♦1796　　　　　　　♦1798　　　　　　　♦1800

1796
Federalists nominate Adams for president; Democratic-Republicans nominate Jefferson

1797
John Adams becomes president

1798
Congress passes Alien and Sedition Acts

1800
Convention of 1800

George Washington

AN American Story

The Washington presidency was known for its dignity and elegance. The president rode in a coach drawn by horses and accompanied by mounted attendants. He and his wife, Martha, lived in the finest house in Philadelphia, the new nation's capital. They entertained a great deal, holding weekly receptions. Each year a ball was held on Washington's birthday. The president wore a black velvet suit with gold buckles, yellow gloves, powdered hair, an ostrich plume in his hat, and a sword in a white leather sheath. Despite these extravagances, Washington's character and military record were admired by most Americans.

Opposing Views

Although hailed by Americans as the nation's greatest leader, George Washington did not escape criticism during his two terms as president. From time to time, harsh attacks on his policies and on his personality appeared in newspapers. One paper even called Washington "the scourge and the misfortune of his country."

CHAPTER 8　A New Nation　**267**

1 FOCUS

Section Overview
This section examines disagreements between the Federalists and Democratic-Republicans.

BELLRINGER
Skillbuilder Activity

Project transparency and have students answer the question.

Daily Focus Skills Transparency 8–3

Reading Preview

Answers to Graphic: Federalists: strong role of federal government, loose interpretation of the Constitution, Democratic-Republicans: weak role of federal government with strong state governments, strict interpretation of the Constitution

Preteaching Vocabulary
Use the **Vocabulary PuzzleMaker CD-ROM** to create crossword and word search puzzles.

SECTION RESOURCES

📂 Reproducible Masters
• Reproducible Lesson Plan 8–3
• Daily Lecture and Discussion Notes 8–3
• Guided Reading Activity 8–3
• Section Quiz 8–3
• Reteaching Activity 8–3
• Reading Essentials and Study Guide 8–3
• Enrichment Activity 8–3

📊 Transparencies
• Daily Focus Skills Transparency 8–3

Multimedia
🎵 American Music: Hits Through History
💿 Vocabulary PuzzleMaker CD-ROM
💿 Interactive Tutor Self-Assessment CD-ROM
💿 ExamView® Pro Testmaker CD-ROM
💿 Presentation Plus! CD-ROM

2 TEACH

Daily Lecture and Discussion Notes 8–3

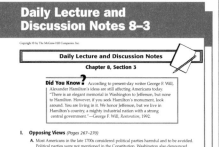

Copyright © The McGraw-Hill Companies, Inc.

Daily Lecture and Discussion Notes

Chapter 8, Section 3

Did You Know? According to present-day writer George F. Will, Alexander Hamilton's ideas are still affecting Americans today: "There is an elegant memorial in Washington to Jefferson, but none to Hamilton. However, if you seek Hamilton's monument, look around. You are living in it. We honor Jefferson, but we live in Hamilton's country, a mighty industrial nation with a strong central government."—George F. Will, *Restoration*, 1992

I. **Opposing Views** *(Pages 267–270)*

　A. Most Americans in the late 1700s considered political parties harmful and to be avoided. Political parties were not mentioned in the Constitution. Washington also denounced them.

　B. By 1796, Americans were beginning to divide into opposing groups and form political

Choosing a Party Have students select the political party they would have joined and defend their choice orally or in writing. **L1**

📁 Use the rubric for giving an oral presentation on pages 37–38 in the *Performance Assessment Activities and Rubrics.*

Graphic Organizer ➔ Skills

Answer: The two parties emerged based on different philosophies of government, conflicting interpretations of the Constitution, different economic and regional interests, and disagreement over foreign affairs.

Graphic Organizer Skills Practice Ask: Why do you think Hamilton and Jefferson were not able to work together in the Washington administration? *(Their views were too different on critical issues.)*

Causes and Effects of Political Parties

Causes

- Different philosophies of government
- Conflicting interpretations of the Constitution
- Different economic and regional interests
- Disagreement over foreign affairs

Effects

- Federalists and Democratic-Republicans propose different solutions
- The two parties nominate candidates
- Political parties become a way of American life

Graphic Organizer ➔ Skills

Thomas Jefferson and Alexander Hamilton emerged as the leaders of the two opposing parties.

Analyzing Information How did the first two political parties emerge?

Most attacks on Washington had come from supporters of Thomas Jefferson. They were trying to discredit the policies of Washington and Hamilton by attacking the president. By 1796 Americans were beginning to divide into opposing groups and to form political parties.

At that time, many Americans considered political parties harmful. Parties—or "factions" as they were called—were to be avoided as much as strong central government. The nation's founders did not even mention political parties in the Constitution.

Washington had denounced political parties and warned that they would divide the nation. To others it seemed natural that people would disagree about issues and that those who held similar views would band together.

In Washington's cabinet Hamilton and Jefferson often took opposing sides on issues. They disagreed on economic policy and foreign relations, on the power of the federal government, and on interpretations of the Constitution. Even

Washington had been **partisan**—favoring one side of an issue. Although he believed he stood above politics, Washington usually supported Hamilton's positions.

Political Parties Emerge

In Congress and the nation at large, similar differences existed. By the mid-1790s, two distinct political parties had taken shape.

The name **Federalist** had first described someone who supported ratification of the Constitution. By the 1790s the word was applied to the group of people who supported the policies of the Washington administration.

Generally Federalists stood for a strong federal government. They admired Britain because of its stability and distrusted France because of the violent changes following the French Revolution. Federalist policies tended to favor banking and shipping interests. Federalists received the strongest support in the Northeast, especially in New England, and from wealthy plantation owners in the South.

Efforts to turn public opinion against Federalist policies began seriously in late 1791 when Philip Freneau (Freh•NOH) began publishing the *National Gazette.* Jefferson, then secretary of state, helped the newspaper get started. Later he and Madison organized people who disagreed with Hamilton. They called their party the **Republicans,** or the **Democratic-Republicans.**

The Republicans wanted to limit government's power. They feared that a strong federal government would endanger people's liberties. They supported the French and condemned what they regarded as the Washington administration's pro-British policies. Republican policies appealed to small farmers and urban workers, especially in the Middle Atlantic states and the South.

▮Citizenship
Views of the Constitution

One difference between Federalists and Republicans concerned the basis of government power. In Hamilton's view the federal government had **implied powers,** powers that were not expressly forbidden in the Constitution.

COOPERATIVE LEARNING ACTIVITY

Holding a Panel Discussion Organize the class into small groups with half of each group representing the Federalists and the other half the Democratic-Republicans. Have each group present a panel discussion in which students try to recruit people to their own party. Remind students that to be effective recruiters, they cannot just disparage the beliefs of the other party; they must offer some attractive arguments for people to join their party. Students should prepare their arguments together before presenting the discussion. **L2** 📦

Hamilton used the idea of implied powers to justify a national bank. He argued that the Constitution gave Congress the power to issue money and regulate trade, and a national bank would clearly help the government carry out these responsibilities. Therefore, creating a bank was within the constitutional power of Congress.

Jefferson and Madison disagreed with Hamilton. They believed in a strict interpretation of the Constitution. They accepted the idea of implied powers, but in a much more limited sense than Hamilton did: Implied powers are those powers that are "absolutely necessary" to carry out the expressed powers.

The People's Role

The differences between the parties, however, went even deeper. Federalists and Republicans had sharply opposing views on the role ordinary people should play in government.

Federalists supported representative government, in which elected officials ruled in the people's name. They did not believe that it was wise to let the public become too involved in politics. Hamilton said:

> **❝**The people are turbulent and changing. . . . They seldom judge or determine right.**❞**

Public office, Federalists thought, should be held by honest and educated men of property who would protect everyone's rights. Ordinary people were too likely to be swayed by agitators.

In contrast, the Republicans feared a strong central government controlled by a few people. They believed that liberty would be safe only if ordinary people participated in government. As Jefferson explained:

> **❝**I am not among those who fear the people; they, and not the rich, are our dependence [what we depend on] for continued freedom.**❞**

Washington's Dilemma

Washington tried to get his two advisers to work out their differences. Knowing Jefferson was discontented, Washington wrote:

> **❝**I have a great sincere esteem and regard for you both, and ardently wish that some line could be marked out by which both [of] you could walk.**❞**

Nevertheless, by 1793 Jefferson was so unhappy that he resigned as secretary of state. In 1795, Alexander Hamilton resigned, too, as secretary of the treasury. The rival groups and their points of view moved further apart.

The Election of 1796

In the presidential election of 1796, candidates sought office for the first time as members of a party. To prepare for the election, the Federalists and the Republicans held meetings called caucuses. At the caucuses members of

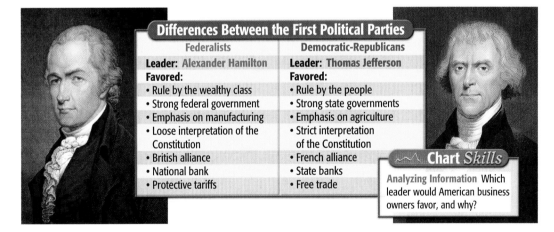

Differences Between the First Political Parties

Federalists	Democratic-Republicans
Leader: Alexander Hamilton	**Leader:** Thomas Jefferson
Favored:	**Favored:**
• Rule by the wealthy class	• Rule by the people
• Strong federal government	• Strong state governments
• Emphasis on manufacturing	• Emphasis on agriculture
• Loose interpretation of the Constitution	• Strict interpretation of the Constitution
• British alliance	• French alliance
• National bank	• State banks
• Protective tariffs	• Free trade

 Chart *Skills*

Analyzing Information Which leader would American business owners favor, and why?

L1, ELL

Guided Reading Activity 8–3

Name _____ Date _____ Class _____

★ **Guided Reading Activity 8-3**

DIRECTIONS: Outlining Locate the heading in your textbook. Then use the information under the heading to help you write each answer. Use another sheet of paper if necessary.

I. Opposing Views

  A. Introduction—Which two cabinet members often took opposing sides of issues?

  B. Political Parties Emerge

    1. By the 1790s to whom was the word *Federalist* applied?_____

    2. Which two leaders organized people into the Republican Party?_____

  C. Views of the Constitution—Which party believed in a strict interpretation of the Constitution?

  D. The People's Role—Who did the Federalists think should hold public office?

  E. Washington's Dilemma—What did Washington hope would happen between Jefferson and Hamilton?

  F. The Election of 1796—What were the results of the presidential election of 1796?

II. President John Adams

  A. The XYZ Affair

    1. How did France punish the United States for signing Jay's Treaty with Great Britain?

    2. How did John Adams respond to the story about three French agents who demanded a bribe and a loan for France?

    3. How did Congress prepare for war with France?

  B. Alien and Sedition Acts—In what year were the Alien and Sedition Acts passed?

  C. Domestic and Foreign Affairs

    1. According to the Kentucky and Virginia Resolutions, what rights did the states have?

    2. What were the political results of Adams's decision to seek peace with France?

Chart *Skills*

Answer: Hamilton; He favored rule by the wealthy, emphasized manufacturing, believed in strong tariffs to encourage the sale of manufactured products in the states, and favored a national bank.

Chart Skills Practice
Ask: Which party would appeal to someone who favored states' rights? *(the Democratic-Republican Party)*

History *and the* Humanities

American Music: Hits Through History, "College Hornpipe/Belle Catherine"

DIFFERENTIATED INSTRUCTION

Reading Support Write this saying on the chalkboard: "Liberty for the whale means death for the minnow." Have students explain its meaning. Then have them relate the statement to each political party, and discuss which party would support or refute it. **L2**

👉 Refer to *Inclusion for the Middle School Social Studies Classroom Strategies and Activities* in the TCR.

✓ Reading Check

Answer: the Federalist Party

Objectives and answers to the student activity can be found in the **Web Activity Lesson Plan** feature at tarvol1.glencoe.com

What?Who?Where?When?

Modern Political Parties Today's Democratic Party traces its roots to Jefferson's Democratic-Republicans. The modern Republican Party, however, was not founded until 1854.

Did you know?

The Internet was first used for voting during the 2000 Arizona Democratic Primary. Voters who voted via the Internet received a confidential personal identification number by mail prior to the election. Voters could log on to the voting Web site four days prior to Election Day and vote. As a result of Internet voting, voter turnout increased by 600 percent.

Student Web Activity
Visit tarvol1.glencoe.com and click on **Chapter 8— Student Web Activities** for an activity on the first political parties.

Congress and other leaders chose their party's candidates for office.

The Federalists nominated Vice President John Adams as their candidate for president and Charles Pinckney for vice president. The Republicans put forth former secretary of state Jefferson for president and Aaron Burr for vice president. Adams and Jefferson, who had been good friends, became rivals. The Federalists expected to carry New England. The Republicans' strength lay in the South, which would give most of its votes to Jefferson.

In the end Adams received 71 electoral votes, winning the election. Jefferson finished second with 68 votes. Under the provisions of the Constitution at that time, the person with the second-highest number of electoral votes became vice president. Jefferson therefore became the new vice president. The administration that took office on March 4, 1797, had a Federalist president and a Republican vice president.

✓ Reading Check **Explaining** Which political party would a Boston factory owner most likely support?

Fact Fiction Folklore

American Heroes

Did Johnny Appleseed scatter apple seeds in the wilderness? There was a real Johnny Appleseed. Johnny, whose real name was John Chapman, was born in Massachusetts in 1774. When the rich lands west of the Ohio River were opened for settlement in the early 1800s, he was the among the first to explore the new territory. Johnny Appleseed did not scatter seeds as he wandered, as many people believe. As he traveled, he would spot good sites for planting. There he would clear the land and plant the seeds. His orchards varied in size. Some covered about an acre. Others covered many acres. When settlers arrived, they found Johnny Appleseed's young apple trees ready for sale.

President John Adams

John Adams had spent most of his life in public service. One of Massachusetts's most active patriots, he later became ambassador to France and to Great Britain. He helped to negotiate the Treaty of Paris that ended the Revolution. Under Washington, he served two terms as vice president.

The XYZ Affair

When Adams took office, he inherited the dispute with France. The French regarded Jay's Treaty, signed in 1794, as an American attempt to help the British in their war with France. To punish the United States, the French seized American ships that carried cargo to Britain.

Adams wanted to avoid war with France. In the fall of 1797, he sent a delegation to Paris to try to resolve the dispute. French foreign minister **Charles de Talleyrand,** however, refused to meet with the Americans. Instead, Talleyrand sent three agents who demanded a bribe and a loan for France from the Americans. "Not a sixpence," the Americans replied and sent a report of the incident to the United States. Adams was furious. Referring to the three French agents as X, Y, and Z, the president urged Congress to prepare for war. The incident became known as the **XYZ affair.**

Undeclared War With France

Congress responded with a program to strengthen the armed forces. It established the Navy Department in April 1798 and set aside money for building warships. Congress also increased the size of the army. George Washington was appointed commanding general.

Between 1798 and 1800, United States and French naval vessels clashed on a number of occasions, although war was not formally declared. Adams's representatives negotiated an agreement with France in September 1800 that ensured peace.

In the view of most Americans, France had become an enemy. The Republican Party, friendly toward France in the past, hesitated to turn around and condemn France. As a result, in the 1798 elections, Americans voted some Republicans out of office.

INTERDISCIPLINARY CONNECTIONS ACTIVITY

Art Ask each student to draw a Federalist and a Democratic-Republican. Then have them write a short statement for each of their characters that expresses the views of each group. Create a bulletin board display with the cutout characters and their statements. **L2**

📁 Use the rubric for creating a bulletin board display on pages 40–41 in the *Performance Assessment Activities and Rubrics.*

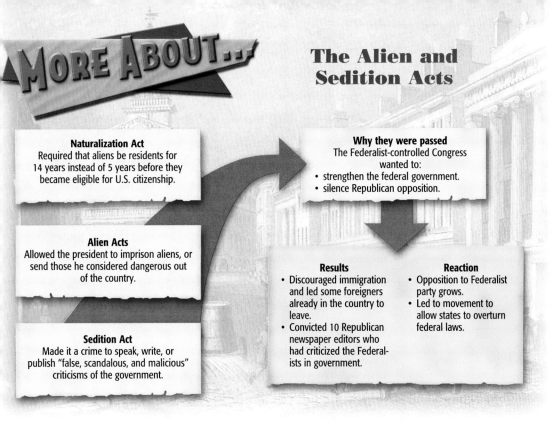

MORE ABOUT... The Alien and Sedition Acts

Naturalization Act
Required that aliens be residents for 14 years instead of 5 years before they became eligible for U.S. citizenship.

Alien Acts
Allowed the president to imprison aliens, or send those he considered dangerous out of the country.

Sedition Act
Made it a crime to speak, write, or publish "false, scandalous, and malicious" criticisms of the government.

Why they were passed
The Federalist-controlled Congress wanted to:
• strengthen the federal government.
• silence Republican opposition.

Results
• Discouraged immigration and led some foreigners already in the country to leave.
• Convicted 10 Republican newspaper editors who had criticized the Federalists in government.

Reaction
• Opposition to Federalist party grows.
• Led to movement to allow states to overturn federal laws.

The Alien and Sedition Acts, passed by Congress in 1798, were supported by the Federalists and intended to silence opposition to an expected war with France. The Federalists backed the English government in most international affairs. **Ask:** Do you think acts restricting free speech would be tolerated today? *(Students may note how the influence of the Internet has affected people's views about free speech restrictions.)*

3 ASSESS

Assign Section 3 Assessment as homework or as an in-class activity.

🌐 Have students use **Interactive Tutor Self-Assessment CD-ROM.**

L2

Section Quiz 8–3

Name _____ Date _____ Class _____

★ Chapter 8   Score ⬜

Section Quiz 8-3

DIRECTIONS: Matching Match the items in Column A with the items in Column B. Write the correct letters in the blanks. *(10 points each)*

Column A
_____ 1. political parties
_____ 2. to legally overturn
_____ 3. French foreign minister
_____ 4. Federalist
_____ 5. Democratic-Republican

Column B
A. Alexander Hamilton
B. Charles de Talleyrand
C. nullify
D. Thomas Jefferson
E. factions

L1

Reteaching Activity 8–3

Name _____ Date _____ Class _____

★ **Reteaching Activity 8-3**

DIRECTIONS: Organizing Facts The numbered items are characteristics of the first political parties. Write the number of each item in the appropriate section of the chart.

The First Political Parties

	Federalist	Republican
Political Leaders		

Alien and Sedition Acts

The threat of war with France made Americans more suspicious of aliens, immigrants living in the country who were not citizens. Many Europeans who came to the United States in the 1790s supported the ideals of the French Revolution. Some Americans questioned whether these aliens would remain loyal if the United States went to war with France.

Federalists in Congress responded with strict laws to protect the nation's security. In 1798 they passed a group of measures known as the **Alien and Sedition Acts.** Sedition refers to activities aimed at weakening established government.

📖 Citizenship
Domestic and Foreign Affairs

For some Americans, fears of a strong central government abusing its power seemed to be coming true. The Republicans looked to the states to preserve the people's liberties and stand up to what they regarded as Federalist tyranny. Madison and Jefferson drafted documents of protest that were passed by the Virginia and Kentucky legislatures.

The Virginia and Kentucky Resolutions of 1798 and 1799 claimed that the Alien and Sedition Acts could not be put into action because they violated the Constitution. The Kentucky Resolutions further suggested that states might nullify—legally overturn—federal laws considered unconstitutional.

The resolutions affirmed the principle of states' rights—limiting the federal government to those powers clearly assigned to it by the Constitution and reserving to the states all other powers not expressly forbidden to them. The issue of states' rights would arise again and again in the nation's early history.

As the election of 1800 approached, the Federalists found themselves under attack. They urged Adams to step up the war with France. They hoped to benefit politically from the

CHAPTER 8   A New Nation   **271**

📖 Reading Strategy ▶ READING THE TEXT

Rewriting Thomas Jefferson was a firm believer in states' rights. He once said, "I believe the States can best govern our home concerns, and the General Government our foreign ones." Ask students to restate Jefferson's quote and explain how Jefferson's words apply to the issues of the time, in particular to the establishment of a national bank. Ask students to write a one-page essay responding to Jefferson's statement. Student essays should express a position for or against states' rights and include supportive examples. **L3**

Analyzing *Political Cartoons*

Answer: They are amused by the fight.

✓ **Reading Check**

Answer: It split the party, allowing Jefferson the opportunity to win the 1800 presidential election.

L1, ELL

Reading Essentials and Study Guide 8–3

Study Guide
Chapter 8, Section 3
For use with textbook pages 267–272

THE FIRST POLITICAL PARTIES

KEY TERMS	
partisan	Favoring one side of an issue (*page 268*)
implied powers	Powers that were not specifically mentioned in the Constitution (*page 268*)
caucus	Meetings held by political parties to choose the party's candidates for office (*page 269*)
alien	Immigrants living in a country who are not citizens (*page 271*)
sedition	Activities aimed at weakening established government (*page 271*)
nullify	To cancel (*page 271*)
states' rights	A theory in the Kentucky and Virginia Resolutions of 1798 and

L2

Enrichment Activity 8–3

★ Enrichment Activity 8-3 ★

Monticello
Thomas Jefferson spent more than 50 years designing and re-designing Monticello, which had three stories, Greek columns and the first dome in an American home. The drawing to the right shows Jefferson's original first-floor plan and the additions to the first floor made over the years.

4 CLOSE

Ask: Why did Federalists want to step up the war with France? (*to stir up patriotic fervor in their favor*)

① Matthew Lyon ② Roger Griswold ③ painting

Analyzing *Political Cartoons*

Fighting in Congress *The Sedition Act led to hard feelings, even violence. This cartoon provides a humorous look at a fight in Congress. Federalist Roger Griswold attacks Republican Matthew Lyon with a cane. Lyon seizes a pair of fire tongs and fights back. On the wall is a painting named "Royal Sport" showing animals fighting.* **How are the other members of Congress reacting to the fight?**

patriotic feelings that war would unleash. Adams refused to rush to war, especially for his own political gain. Instead he appointed a new commission to seek peace with France.

In 1800 the French agreed to a treaty and stopped attacks on American ships. Although the agreement with France was in the best interest of the United States, it hurt Adams's chance for re-election. Rather than applauding the agreement, Hamilton and his supporters now opposed their own president. With the Federalists split, the Republican prospects for capturing the presidency improved. The way was prepared for Thomas Jefferson in the election of 1800.

✓ **Reading Check** **Summarizing** *How did the peace agreement with France affect the Federalists?*

SECTION 3 ASSESSMENT

Checking for Understanding

1. **Key Terms** Write a short newspaper article about the election of 1796 in which you use the following terms: *partisan, implied powers, caucus.*
2. **Reviewing Facts** Who was elected president in 1796, and who became vice president?

Reviewing Themes

3. **Government and Democracy** How were the Federalists different from the Republicans in how they felt about a powerful central government?

Critical Thinking

4. **Drawing Conclusions** Do you think the development of political parties was necessary? Why or why not?
5. **Classifying Information** Re-create the diagram below. Provide information about the election of 1796 in the spaces provided.

Presidential Election of 1796	
Candidate	
Party	
Electoral votes	
Winner (check column)	
Vice President (check column)	

Analyzing Visuals

6. **Graphic Organizer Skills** Study the diagram on page 271. Who are aliens? Why were the Alien and Sedition Acts passed? How did their passage affect the Federalist Party?

Interdisciplinary Activity

Art Choose the presidential candidate for whom you would have voted in 1796. Design a campaign poster or button using words and illustrations to help promote your candidate.

272 CHAPTER 8 A New Nation

SECTION 3 ASSESSMENT ANSWERS

1. Student work should reflect correct use of terms.
2. John Adams; Thomas Jefferson
3. Federalists supported a strong federal government; Republicans supported strong state governments.
4. Some students may answer yes because people will always dis- agree on some issues. Some students may answer no because parties divide the nation.
5. John Adams, Federalists, 71 electoral votes, winner; Thomas Jefferson, Democratic-Republicans, 68 electoral votes, vice president
6. people from other countries who are not United States citizens; to strengthen the federal government and silence Republican opposition; opposition to the Federalist Party increased

Interdisciplinary Activity Posters and buttons should accurately represent the beliefs of each party and candidate.

Social Studies SKILLBUILDER

Reading a Flowchart

Why Learn This Skill?

Sometimes determining a sequence of events can be confusing, particularly when many events occur at the same time. A flowchart can help you understand what is going on in a series of events.

Learning the Skill

Flowcharts show the steps in a process or a sequence of events. For example, a flowchart could be used to show the movement of goods through a factory, of people through a training program, or of a bill through Congress. The following steps explain how to read a flowchart:

- Read the title or caption of the flowchart to find out what you are studying.
- Read all of the labels or sentences on the flowchart.
- Look for numbers indicating a sequence, or arrows showing the direction of movement.

Practicing the Skill

Read the flowchart on this page. It shows a sequence of events that took place in the Northwest Territory. Analyze the information in the flowchart; then answer the following questions.

❶ What symbol is used to show the sequence of the events?

❷ What actions taken by the British set off the sequence of events that are reflected in the title of the chart?

❸ What action did Washington take in response to trouble in the Ohio Valley?

❹ What information from the chapter could you add to the flowchart to continue the sequence of events?

Conflicts in the Northwest Territory

1790s
Great Britain holds forts in the Ohio Valley.

British stir up trouble between Native Americans and American settlers in the Ohio Valley.

President Washington sends troops into the Northwest Territory.

Federal troops are defeated by Miami chief Little Turtle.

Applying the Skill

Making a Flowchart Imagine that a student who is new to your school asks you how to sign up for a sport or social club. Draw a flowchart outlining the steps the student should follow.

 Glencoe's **Skillbuilder Interactive Workbook CD-ROM, Level 1,** provides instruction and practice in key social studies skills.

Social Studies SKILLBUILDER

TEACH

Reading a Flowchart This skill teaches students how to read a flowchart. Point out that this flowchart reads from top to bottom, but that others may go from left to right. A more complicated one might go in more than one direction.

Have students think of everyday things they do that might be explained in a flowchart (*anything having a process or sequence of events*).

Additional Practice
L2

Chapter Skills Activity 8

Name _____ Date _____ Class _____

★ Chapter Skills Activity 8

Reading a Flowchart
A flowchart can make a sequence of events or the steps in a process easy to follow. To read a flowchart, look for numbers or arrows that indicate sequence.

DIRECTIONS: This flowchart shows the sequence of events in the conflict between the United States and France that led to undeclared war between the two nations. Analyze the information in the chart. Then answer the questions below.

Conflict Between the United States and France

GLENCOE TECHNOLOGY

 CD-ROM
Glencoe Skillbuilder Interactive Workbook CD-ROM, Level 1

This interactive CD-ROM reinforces student mastery of essential social studies skills.

ANSWERS TO PRACTICING THE SKILL

❶ arrow

❷ The British took control of forts and stirred up trouble between Native Americans and American settlers in the Ohio Valley.

❸ He sent troops into the Northwest Territory.

❹ General Anthony Wayne is sent to gain control of the Ohio River valley; Shawnee are defeated at Battle of Fallen Timbers; Native Americans are forced to sign treaty opening Ohio to white settlement.

Applying the Skill Students' flowcharts should outline a logical sequence of events associated with joining a school club.

GLENCOE TECHNOLOGY

MindJogger Videoquiz
Use **MindJogger Videoquiz** to review the Chapter 8 content.

Available in VHS

Reviewing Key Terms

Students' puzzles will vary but should reflect the instructions.

1. tradition
2. group consisting of the secretary of state, the secretary of the treasury, the secretary of war, and the attorney general
3. a tax on imports
4. the condition of not taking sides in a conflict
5. the British practice of stopping American merchant ships and forcing their crews into the British navy
6. a meeting at which members of Congress and other leaders choose their party's candidates for office
7. term referring to activities aimed at weakening established government
8. theory stating that the people of each state have the right to nullify a federal law within that state

Reviewing Key Facts

9. to supply the government with additional funds to operate and to make interest payments on the national debt; some feared a national government with strong economic powers dominated by the wealthy class

10. It established a strong federal judiciary by establishing the federal court system with 13 district courts and 3 circuit courts.

11. They protested the whiskey tax.

12. powers that were not expressly forbidden in the Constitution

---

Chapter Summary
A New Nation

Federal Government
- First Congress establishes three executive departments
- Judiciary Act of 1789 passes
- Bill of Rights added to the Constitution
- Nation's capital moves to Washington, D.C.
- National bank created
- Congress approves tariffs

Early Challenges
- Whiskey Rebellion put down
- Force and treaties slow Native American resistance to settlement
- Washington maintains American neutrality
- Treaty with Spain allows access to the Mississippi River

The New Nation

First Political Parties
- Federalists emerge, promoting a strong central government
- Republicans want to leave more power in the hands of the states.

President John Adams
- Federalist John Adams becomes second president
- American and French naval forces fight an undeclared war
- Federalists in Congress pass the Alien and Sedition Acts
- Virginia and Kentucky Resolutions advocate states' rights

274

---

13. The French began seizing American ships that carried cargo to British ports; the XYZ affair

14. John Adams; Thomas Jefferson

Critical Thinking

15. In addition to guaranteeing the freedoms of speech, press, and religion, the Bill of Rights protects the rights of states and individuals by saying that powers not specifically given to the federal government "are reserved to the States respectively, or to the people."

Reviewing Key Terms

On graph paper, create a word search puzzle using the following terms. Crisscross the terms vertically and horizontally, then fill in the remaining squares with extra letters. List the definition of each term below the puzzle as clues. Share your puzzle with a classmate.

1. precedent
2. cabinet
3. tariff
4. neutrality
5. impressment
6. caucus
7. sedition
8. states' rights

Reviewing Key Facts

9. Why did Hamilton want national taxes? Why did some oppose the taxes?

10. What was the importance of the Judiciary Act of 1789?

11. What caused farmers in western Pennsylvania to revolt during the Whiskey Rebellion?

12. According to Hamilton, what are implied powers?

13. What actions by France led to an undeclared war with the United States?

14. Who was elected president in 1796? Who was elected vice president?

Critical Thinking

15. **Analyzing Themes: Government and Democracy** Refer to the grievances listed in the Declaration of Independence. How were these grievances addressed in the Bill of Rights?

16. **Analyzing Information** What did President Washington say in his Farewell Address about political parties and foreign policy?

17. **Comparing** Re-create the diagram below. Compare the positions of the Federalists and Democratic-Republicans on the national bank. In the boxes list the leaders and their positions.

National Bank	
Federalists	Democratic-Republicans
Leader:	Leader:
Position:	Position:

---

16. He said that political parties were evil and warned against entanglements in foreign affairs.

17. Federalists: Hamilton—believed in the constitutionality of a national bank even though the power was not specified in the Constitution; Democratic-Republicans: Jefferson/Madison—believed a national bank to be unconstitutional

Practicing Skills

18. arrows

Practicing Skills

Reading a Flowchart *Alexander Hamilton promoted the creation of a national bank. Study the flowchart below. Then answer the questions that follow.*

How Banks Work Today

People deposit savings in banks and receive interest.

Workers receive payment for work.

Banks loan money to businesses and receive interest.

Businesses use loan money to make products and pay workers.

18. What is used to show the sequence of events?
19. What happens after workers receive payment for work?
20. What two parts on this flowchart show who receives interest on their money?

 Geography and History Activity

Study the map on page 265. Then answer the questions that follow.

21. **Movement** In which direction did St. Clair's troops move?
22. **Location** Along what river was Ft. Washington located?

Citizenship Cooperative Activity

23. **Researching** Work in groups of four to discuss and develop answers to these questions:
    • How does the Bill of Rights reflect the principle of limited government?
    • What are two individual rights protected in the Bill of Rights?
    • Why would it be necessary to change the Constitution?

Self-Check Quiz
Visit tarvol1.glencoe.com and click on **Chapter 8— Self-Check Quizzes** to prepare for the chapter test.

Economics Activity

24. **Math Practice** When you deposit money in a bank, you receive interest—a payment for lending money to the bank. To figure simple interest, you need to know what the interest rate is. Say, for example, a local bank is offering simple interest on savings accounts at 6 percent per year. If you deposit $100, how much will you have in the account at the end of one year? At the end of four years?

 Technology Activity

25. **Using a Computerized Card Catalog** Search your local library's computerized card catalog for sources on Mount Vernon, George Washington's home. Find the sources on the library shelves, then use the information you found to write a two-paragraph description that Washington might have written if he had ever wanted to sell his home.

 Alternative Assessment

26. Review the chapter and make a list of the differences between the Federalist and Republican parties. Based on your list, create a symbol to represent each of the parties.

Standardized Test Practice

Directions: Choose the *best* answer to the following question.

Certain grievances listed in the Declaration of Independence were addressed in the Bill of Rights. Which amendment addressed the quartering of troops?

A   1st Amendment
B   3rd Amendment
C   8th Amendment
D   12th Amendment

Test-Taking Tip

Read the question carefully. The 12th Amendment was not part of the Bill of Rights, so it can be eliminated as a possibility.

 Technology Activity

25. Students' paragraphs should reflect knowledge about Mount Vernon.

 Alternative Assessment

26. Students should sketch symbols that represent the positions and views of the Federalist and Republican Parties.

HISTORY Online

Have students visit the Web site at tarvol1.glencoe.com to review Chapter 8 and take the Self-Check Quiz.

Standardized Test Practice

Answer: B
Question Type: Civics
Answer Explanation: The Third Amendment to the United States Constitution is based on the principle that people have a right to privacy in their own homes.

Bonus Question ?

Ask: What salary did George Washington receive as president? What does the president receive today? *($25,000; $400,000 plus a $50,000 nontaxable expense account per year)*

---

19. People deposit savings in banks and receive interest.

20. Banks receive interest on loans, and people receive interest on savings.

 Geography and History Activity

21. northwest
22. the Ohio River

Citizenship Cooperative Activity

23. Answers will vary but may include: the Bill of Rights protects individual liberties and limits the role of government in the lives of citizens; freedom of speech and the right to a speedy and fair trial; to meet the changing needs of the country.

Economics Activity

24. $106; $124

Chapter 9 Resources

Timesaving Tools

TeacherWorks™ All-In-One Planner and Resource Center

- **Interactive Teacher Edition** Access your Teacher Wraparound Edition and your classroom resources with a few easy clicks.
- **Interactive Lesson Planner** Planning has never been easier! Organize your week, month, semester, or year with all the lesson helps you need to make teaching creative, timely, and relevant.

Use Glencoe's **Presentation Plus!** multimedia teacher tool to easily present dynamic lessons that visually excite your students. Using Microsoft PowerPoint® you can customize the presentations to create your own personalized lessons.

TEACHING TRANSPARENCIES

Graphic Organizer 1 L2

Why It Matters Chapter Transparency 9 L2

REVIEW AND REINFORCEMENT

Workbook Activity 9 L1

Time Line Activity 9 L2

Vocabulary Activity 9 L1

REVIEW AND REINFORCEMENT

Critical Thinking Skills Activity 9 L2

Take-Home Review Activity 9 L1

ENRICHMENT

Linking Past and Present Activity 9 L2

Primary Source Reading 9 L2

GEOGRAPHY

Geography and History Activity 9 L2

Meeting NCSS Standards

The following standards are highlighted in Chapter 9:

Section 1	VI	Power, Authority, & Governance: B, C, I
Section 2	III	People, Places, and Environments: A, B, H, I
Section 3	IX	Global Connections: B, E
Section 4	VI	Power, Authority, & Governance: B, C, D, F

FOLDABLES™ Study Organizer

Dinah Zike's Foldables are three-dimensional, interactive graphic organizers that help students practice basic writing skills, review key vocabulary terms, and identify main ideas. Additional chapter activities can be found in the **Reading and Study Skills Foldables** booklet.

Chapter 9 Resources

ASSESSMENT AND EVALUATION

Chapter 9 Test Form A L2

Chapter 9 Test Form B L2

Standardized Test Practice Workbook Activity 9 L2

Performance Assessment Activity 9 L1, ELL

ExamView® Pro Testmaker CD-ROM

MULTIMEDIA

- Vocabulary PuzzleMaker CD-ROM
- Interactive Tutor Self-Assessment CD-ROM
- ExamView® Pro Testmaker CD-ROM
- Audio Program
- American History Primary Source Document Library CD-ROM
- MindJogger Videoquiz
- Presentation Plus! CD-ROM
- TeacherWorks CD-ROM
- Interactive Student Edition CD-ROM
- Glencoe Skillbuilder Interactive Workbook CD-ROM, Level 1
- The American Republic to 1877 Video Program
- American Music: Hits Through History

SPANISH RESOURCES

The following Spanish language materials are available in the Spanish Resources Binder:

- Spanish Guided Reading Activities
- Spanish Reteaching Activities
- Spanish Quizzes and Tests
- Spanish Vocabulary Activity
- Spanish Take-Home Review Activity
- Spanish Summaries
- The Declaration of Independence and United States Constitution Spanish Translation

The following videotape programs are available from Glencoe as supplements to Chapter 9:

- **Lewis and Clark** (ISBN 1-56501-592-4)*
- **Tecumseh: The Dream of Confederacy** (ISBN 0-7670-1247-X)

To order, call Glencoe at 1-800-334-7344. To find classroom resources to accompany many of these videos, check the following home pages:
A&E Television: www.aande.com
The History Channel: www.historychannel.com

*Available individually or in *The American Republic to 1877 Video Library.*

Use our Web site for additional resources. All essential content is covered in the Student Edition.

You and your students can visit tarvol1.glencoe.com, the Web site companion to **The American Republic to 1877.** This innovative integration of electronic and print media offers your students a wealth of opportunities. The student text directs students to the Web site for the following options:

- **Chapter Overviews**
- **Student Web Activities**
- **Self-Check Quizzes**
- **Textbook Updates**

Answers to the student Web activities are provided for you in the **Web Activity Lesson Plans.** Additional Web resources and Interactive Tutor Puzzles are also available.

Chapter 9 Resources

SECTION RESOURCES

Daily Objectives	Reproducible Resources	Multimedia Resources
SECTION 1 **The Republicans Take Power** 1. Discuss how the election of 1800 was resolved. 2. Explain how the Supreme Court was strengthened.	Reproducible Lesson Plan 9–1 Daily Lecture and Discussion Notes 9–1 Guided Reading Activity 9–1* Section Quiz 9–1* Reteaching Activity 9–1* Reading Essentials and Study Guide 9–1* Enrichment Activity 9–1	Daily Focus Skills Transparency 9–1 Interactive Tutor Self-Assessment CD-ROM ExamView® Pro Testmaker CD-ROM Presentation Plus! CD-ROM
SECTION 2 **The Louisiana Purchase** 1. Discuss how the United States expanded in the early 1800s. 2. Review the expeditions of explorers such as Lewis and Clark.	Reproducible Lesson Plan 9–2 Daily Lecture and Discussion Notes 9–2 Guided Reading Activity 9–2* Section Quiz 9–2* Reteaching Activity 9–2* Reading Essentials and Study Guide 9–2* Enrichment Activity 9–2	Daily Focus Skills Transparency 9–2 ABCNews Interactive™ Historic America Electronic Field Trips Interactive Tutor Self-Assessment CD-ROM ExamView® Pro Testmaker CD-ROM Presentation Plus! CD-ROM
SECTION 3 **A Time of Conflict** 1. Explain why Tecumseh built a Native American confederacy. 2. Discuss why the War Hawks wanted to go to war.	Reproducible Lesson Plan 9–3 Daily Lecture and Discussion Notes 9–3 Guided Reading Activity 9–3* Section Quiz 9–3* Reteaching Activity 9–3* Reading Essentials and Study Guide 9–3* Enrichment Activity 9–3	Daily Focus Skills Transparency 9–3 Interactive Tutor Self-Assessment CD-ROM ExamView® Pro Testmaker CD-ROM Presentation Plus! CD-ROM
SECTION 4 **The War of 1812** 1. Describe how the British seized and set fire to Washington, D.C. 2. Explain why Andrew Jackson fought a battle after the war was over.	Reproducible Lesson Plan 9–4 Daily Lecture and Discussion Notes 9–4 Guided Reading Activity 9–4* Section Quiz 9–4* Reteaching Activity 9–4* Reading Essentials and Study Guide 9–4* Enrichment Activity 9–4	Daily Focus Skills Transparency 9–4 Vocabulary PuzzleMaker CD-ROM Interactive Tutor Self-Assessment CD-ROM ExamView® Pro Testmaker CD-ROM Presentation Plus! CD-ROM

0:00 OUT OF TIME?
Assign the Chapter 9 **Reading Essentials and Study Guide.**

*Also Available in Spanish

 Blackline Master   Transparency   ⊙ CD-ROM   ⊙ DVD

� Poster   Music Program   ⊛ Audio Program   ▭ Videocassette

KEY TO ABILITY LEVELS

Teaching strategies have been coded.

L1 BASIC activities for all students

L2 AVERAGE activities for average to above-average students

L3 CHALLENGING activities for above-average students

ELL ENGLISH LANGUAGE LEARNER activities

NATIONAL GEOGRAPHIC Teacher's Corner

INDEX TO NATIONAL GEOGRAPHIC MAGAZINE

The following articles relate to this chapter.

- "The Way West," by John G. Mitchell, September 2000.
- "L'Enfant's Washington," by Alice J. Hall, August 1991.
- "The Peales: America's First Family of Art," by Otto Friedrich, December 1990.
- "Thomas Jefferson: Architect of Freedom," by Mike Edwards, February 1976.

NATIONAL GEOGRAPHIC SOCIETY PRODUCTS

To order the following, call National Geographic at 1-800-368-2728:

- *GeoKit: Lewis and Clark* (Kit)
- *GeoKit: Westward Movement* (Kit)
- *The West That Was* (Video)
- *Exploration* (Map)
- *United States/ Territorial Growth* (Map)
- *National Geographic Desk Reference* (Book)
- *Washington, D.C.* (Video)

NGS ONLINE

Access National Geographic's Web site for current events, atlas updates, activities, links, interactive features, and archives.

www.nationalgeographic.com

MEETING SPECIAL NEEDS

In addition to the Differentiated Instruction strategies found in each section, the following resources are also suitable for your special needs students:

- *ExamView® Pro Testmaker CD-ROM* allows teachers to tailor tests by reducing answer choices.

- The *Audio Program* includes the entire narrative of the student edition so that less-proficient readers can listen to the words as they read them.

- The *Reading Essentials and Study Guide* provides the same content as the student edition but is written two grade levels below the textbook.

- *Guided Reading Activities* give less-proficient readers point-by-point instructions to increase comprehension as they read each textbook section.

- *Enrichment Activities* includes a stimulating collection of readings and activities for gifted and talented students.

From the Classroom of...

Rick Wilson
Brunswick Jr. High School
Brunswick, ME

"Who Has?" "I Have." (Around-the-World Chapter Review)

Students will identify the major people and events in Chapter 9 by playing a game using index cards. First, write a "Who has . . .?" question—such as, "Who has the name of the man inaugurated as president on March 4, 1801?"—on the front of an index card. Then write the answer to that question on the back of a different card: "I have Thomas Jefferson." Continue this process of writing a "Who has . . . ?" question on the front of one card and the "I have . . . " answer on the back of a different card—one card for every student. The last step involves writing your last "I have . . . " answer on the back of the first card, completing the circle "around the world." You may want to play the game several times, redistributing the cards and seeing how much faster the class can complete it a second or third time.

ADDITIONAL RESOURCES FROM GLENCOE

- American Music: Cultural Traditions
- American Art and Architecture
- Outline Map Resource Book
- U.S. Desk Map
- Building Geography Skills for Life
- Inclusion for the Middle School Social Studies Classroom Strategies and Activities
- Teaching Strategies for the American History Classroom (Including Block Scheduling Pacing Guides)
- American Crafts Hands-On Activities
- American Games Hands-On Activities
- American History Flash Cards

Block Schedule

Activities that are suited to use within the block scheduling framework are identified by:

Performance Assessment

Refer to Activity 9 in the Performance Assessment Activities and Rubrics booklet.

Why It Matters Activity

The two main political parties in the Jefferson era were the Federalists and the Democratic-Republicans (often referred to in the text as "Republicans"). Have students research present-day political parties. Ask them to identify each party's position on the role of government in the economy and foreign affairs.

GLENCOE TECHNOLOGY

The American Republic to 1877 Video Program

To learn more about Sacagawea and her role in the Lewis and Clark expedition, have students view the Chapter 9 video "The True Story of Sacagawea" from **The American Republic to 1877 Video Program.**

 Available in DVD and VHS

MindJogger Videoquiz

Use **MindJogger Videoquiz** to preview the Chapter 9 content.

Available in VHS

276

CHAPTER 9

The Jefferson Era

1800–1816

Why It Matters

In 1801 the Democratic-Republican Party took control of the nation's government. The Federalists—the party of Alexander Hamilton and John Adams—were now on the sidelines and played the role of critics to the Republican administration.

The Impact Today

Politicians today operate within the party system that took shape at that time.
• While the two main parties have changed, each still works to win votes and gain power.
• If the people vote to change the party in power, the newly elected representatives take office peacefully and the government continues.

The American Republic to 1877 *Video* The chapter 9 video, "The True Story of Sacagawea," tells the story of the Shoshone woman who helped guide the Lewis and Clark expedition.

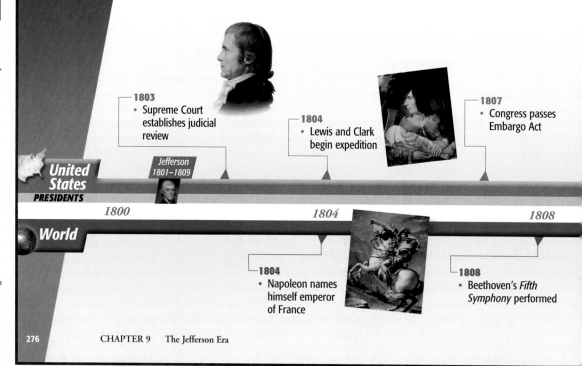

1803
• Supreme Court establishes judicial review

1804
• Lewis and Clark begin expedition

1807
• Congress passes Embargo Act

Jefferson 1801–1809

United States PRESIDENTS

1800   *1804*   *1808*

World

1804
• Napoleon names himself emperor of France

1808
• Beethoven's *Fifth Symphony* performed

276   CHAPTER 9   The Jefferson Era

Reading Strategy   PURPOSE FOR READING

Think/Write–Pair–Share is a simple strategy that engages students through writing and discussion. Begin by pointing out that Thomas Jefferson was an accomplished scholar, writer, political leader, architect, and inventor, but many people know of him only as the third president of the United States. Ask students to think about what they know about Jefferson and write this down. After writing, pair students with a partner and have them share ideas and thoughts. Conclude this activity with a class-wide "share" discussion. **L1**

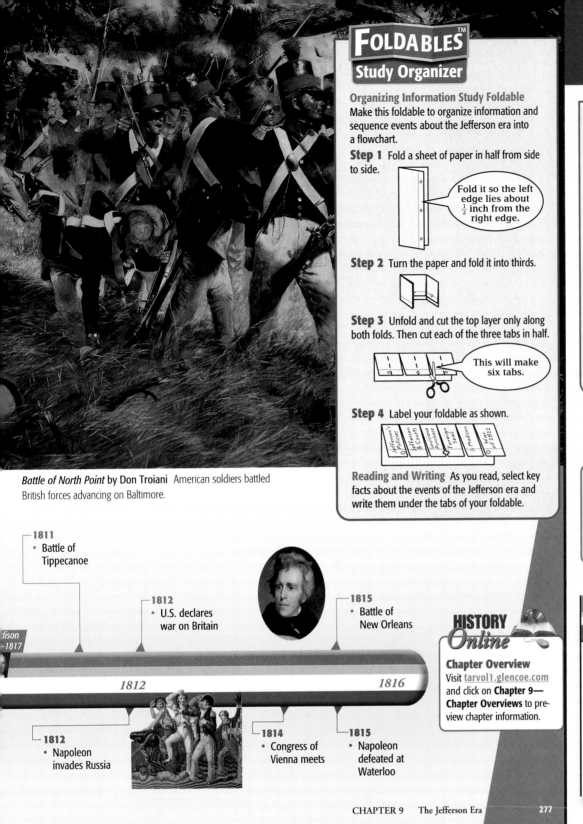

Battle of North Point by Don Troiani American soldiers battled British forces advancing on Baltimore.

FOLDABLES™
Study Organizer

Organizing Information Study Foldable
Make this foldable to organize information and sequence events about the Jefferson era into a flowchart.

Step 1 Fold a sheet of paper in half from side to side.

> Fold it so the left edge lies about ½ inch from the right edge.

Step 2 Turn the paper and fold it into thirds.

Step 3 Unfold and cut the top layer only along both folds. Then cut each of the three tabs in half.

> This will make six tabs.

Step 4 Label your foldable as shown.

Jefferson's Policies | Jefferson & Courts | Louisiana Purchase | Foreign Seas | J. Madison | War of 1812

Reading and Writing As you read, select key facts about the events of the Jefferson era and write them under the tabs of your foldable.

FOLDABLES™
Study Organizer **Dinah Zike's Foldables**

Purpose Students make and use a foldable to organize events during the administration of President Thomas Jefferson. As students read the chapter, they are required to interpret information by describing important events. When students have completed the activity, they should have a flowchart that outlines the history of the country during the Jefferson era.

Have students complete *Reading and Study Skills Foldables* Activity 9. **L1**

HISTORY
Online

Introduce students to chapter content and key terms by having them access **Chapter Overview 9** at tarvol1.glencoe.com

TIME LINE
ACTIVITY

Have students review the time line on pages 276–277 as they read the chapter. Ask students to determine the number of years between Thomas Jefferson taking office and sending Lewis and Clark on their famous expedition. *(roughly three years; Jefferson took office in 1801 and sent Lewis and Clark on their expedition in 1804.)*

1811
• Battle of Tippecanoe

1812
• U.S. declares war on Britain

1815
• Battle of New Orleans

1812

1816

...dison
...–1817

1812
• Napoleon invades Russia

1814
• Congress of Vienna meets

1815
• Napoleon defeated at Waterloo

HISTORY
Online

Chapter Overview
Visit tarvol1.glencoe.com and click on **Chapter 9— Chapter Overviews** to preview chapter information.

More About the Art

Battle of North Point depicts a little-known but important battle between American militia and British troops during the War of 1812. Fresh from torching Washington, D.C., nearly three weeks before, British troops advanced on Baltimore in early September of 1814. The clash of American and British troops at North Point, east of the city, slowed the British advance, giving the Americans time to reinforce their defenses around the city. Partly as the result of the American success at North Point, the British did not capture Baltimore.

1 FOCUS

Section Overview
This section describes the election of 1800 and the policies of President Thomas Jefferson.

BELLRINGER
Skillbuilder Activity

Project transparency and have students answer the question.

Daily Focus Skills Transparency 9–1

Reading Preview

Answers to Graphic: allowed Alien and Sedition Acts to expire, repealed Naturalization Act, reduced the size of the army and navy, cut federal spending, repealed federal internal taxes

Preteaching Vocabulary
Refer students to **Key Terms.** Have students write questions for which each term is an answer.

SECTION 1 The Republicans Take Power

Guide to Reading

Main Idea
The election of 1800 marked the transfer of power from one political party to another through a democratic election.

Key Terms
laissez-faire, customs duties, judicial review

Reading Strategy
Organizing Information As you read the section, use a diagram like the one shown here to identify ways Republicans tried to reduce the role of government.

Ways the Republicans reduced government

Read to Learn
• how the election deadlock of 1800 was resolved.
• how John Marshall strengthened the Supreme Court.

Section Theme
Government and Democracy Jefferson believed that a large federal government threatened liberty.

Preview of Events

♦1800	♦1801	♦1802	♦1803
1800 Thomas Jefferson and John Adams contend for presidency	1801 Judiciary Act expands court system	March 1801 Jefferson is inaugurated	1803 *Marbury* v. *Madison* sets precedent for judicial review

AN American Story

Abigail Adams in the unfinished White House

In 1801 Washington, D.C., was slowly rising from a swampy site on the Potomac River. The nation's new capital had only two noteworthy buildings—the president's mansion (later called the White House) and the still-unfinished Capitol. Between them stretched about two miles of muddy streets on which pigs and chickens roamed freely.

Very few people liked being in Washington. It was hot and steamy in the summer, and the river and swamps were a breeding ground for mosquitoes. Abigail Adams called the new capital "the very dirtiest Hole."

The Election of 1800

The Federalist and Republican parties fought a bitter election campaign in 1800. Federalists supported President Adams for a second term and Charles Pinckney of South Carolina for vice president. Republicans nominated **Thomas Jefferson** for president and **Aaron Burr** of New York as his running mate.

The election campaign of 1800 differed greatly from campaigns of today. Neither Adams nor Jefferson traveled around the country making speeches about

SECTION RESOURCES

📁 **Reproducible Masters**
• Reproducible Lesson Plan 9–1
• Daily Lecture and Discussion Notes 9–1
• Guided Reading Activity 9–1
• Section Quiz 9–1
• Reteaching Activity 9–1
• Reading Essentials and Study Guide 9–1
• Enrichment Activity 9–1

📄 **Transparencies**
• Daily Focus Skills Transparency 9–1

Multimedia
🔘 Interactive Tutor Self-Assessment CD-ROM
🔘 ExamView® Pro Testmaker CD-ROM
🔘 Presentation Plus! CD-ROM

why he should be elected. That would have been considered in bad taste. Instead the candidates and their allies wrote hundreds of letters to leading citizens and friendly newspapers to publicize their views. The letter-writing campaign, however, was not polite.

Federalists charged the Republican Jefferson, who believed in freedom of religion, as being "godless." Republicans warned that the Federalists would bring back monarchy. Federalists, they claimed, represented the interests of wealthy people with property.

Election Deadlock

When members of the Electoral College voted, Jefferson and Burr each received 73 votes. Because of this tie, the House of Representatives had to decide the election. At the time the electors voted for each presidential and vice-presidential candidate individually rather than voting for a party's candidates as a team.

In the House, Federalists saw a chance to prevent the election of Jefferson by supporting Burr. For 35 ballots, the election remained tied. Finally, at Alexander Hamilton's urging, one Federalist decided not to vote for Burr. Jefferson became president, and Burr became vice president.

To prevent another showdown between a presidential and a vice-presidential candidate, Congress passed the Twelfth Amendment to the Constitution in 1803. This amendment, ratified in 1804, requires electors to vote for the president and vice president on separate ballots. 📖

(See page 246 for the entire text of the Twelfth Amendment.)

Jefferson's Inauguration

On March 4, 1801, the day of the inauguration, Jefferson dressed in everyday clothes. He left his boardinghouse and walked to the Senate to be sworn in as president. President Adams did not attend the ceremony. He had slipped out of the presidential mansion and left the city so he would not have to watch Thomas Jefferson become president.

In his Inaugural Address, Jefferson tried to bridge the gap between the developing political parties and reach out to Federalists with healing words. "We are all Republicans, we are all Federalists," he said. Then he outlined some of his goals, which included "a wise and frugal government" and "the support of state governments in all their rights." Jefferson had long been a supporter of states' rights. He believed that a large federal government threatened liberty and that vigilant states could best protect freedom.

Jefferson believed in reducing the power and size of the federal government. These ideas were similar to the French philosophy of laissez-faire (leh•say FEHR), which means "let (people) do (as they choose)."

✓**Reading Check** **Describing** What does the Twelfth Amendment to the Constitution require?

America's *Architecture*

Monticello Thomas Jefferson had many talents, including being a skilled architect. He designed buildings at the University of Virginia and his home at Monticello. Construction on Monticello began in 1769, following Jefferson's first design. Remodeling and enlarging the house began in 1796 and was completed by 1809.

"*All my wishes end, where I hope my days will end, at Monticello.*"
—*Thomas Jefferson*

COOPERATIVE LEARNING ACTIVITY

Presenting Jefferson: Inventor/Architect Organize the class into small groups and have each group use library resources to find examples of some of Jefferson's inventions and of buildings he designed. Have each group prepare an illustrated booklet containing drawings and descriptive captions of inventions and buildings. Tasks such as drawing, writing, and finding resources should be assigned according to the skills of group members. **L1,** ELL 🎲

2 TEACH

Daily Lecture and Discussion Notes 9–1

Copyright © by The McGraw-Hill Companies, Inc.

Daily Lecture and Discussion Notes

Chapter 9, Section 1

Did You Know ❓ Chief Justice John Marshall's home, which he built in Richmond, Virginia, still stands. Many of his personal belongings are there, including his black robe, which he wore on the bench for 34 years.

I. **The Election of 1800** (Pages 278–279)

  A. The election campaign of 1800 between Adams/Pinckney and Jefferson/Burr was very different from those of today. Candidates and their friends wrote letters to leading citizens and newspapers to spread their views. The Federalists and Republicans fought a bitter letter-writing campaign.

  B. The election was deadlocked. Both Jefferson and Burr received 73 electoral votes, so the House of Representatives had to decide the election.

Ranking Events Have each student choose three events from the section and rank them in order of importance. Call on volunteers to read their lists. Then have a class discussion in which students decide whether they agree or disagree with the volunteers' rankings. **L1**

✓**Reading Check**

Answer: It requires electors to vote for president and vice president on separate ballots.

America's *Architecture*

Monticello has a total of 43 rooms.

L1, ELL

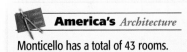

Guided Reading Activity 9–1

Name _____ Date _____ Class _____

★ **Guided Reading Activity 9-1**

DIRECTIONS: Outlining Locate the heading in your textbook. Then use the information under the heading to help you write each answer. Use another sheet of paper if necessary.

  I. The Election of 1800

  A. Election Deadlock

  1. Why did the House of Representatives decide the election of 1800?

  2. What does the Twelfth Amendment require?

  B. Jefferson's Inauguration—What is laissez-faire?

✓ **Reading Check**

Answer: He reduced the size of the army and navy and eliminated certain taxes to decrease the power of the federal government.

3 ASSESS

Assign Section 1 Assessment as homework or as an in-class activity.

⊙ Have students use **Interactive Tutor Self-Assessment CD-ROM.**

L2

Section Quiz 9–1

L1

Reteaching Activity 9–1

Linking Past & Present

The Nation's Capital, Washington, D.C.

The United States government moved to the new capital city of Washington, D.C., in 1800. Being located along the Potomac River, Washington was expected to emerge as a great trading city. However, growth was so slow that many thought the government should move to a larger city.

Washington, D.C., in 1803

Washington, D.C., today

Instead of trade, the driving force of the city's economy has become the federal government.

Jefferson's Policies

Thomas Jefferson had strong ideas about how to make the United States a success. He believed that the strength of the United States was its independent farmers. As long as most people owned their own property, they would fight to protect their rights and to preserve the republic. For this reason, Jefferson favored expanding the nation westward to acquire more land. He also believed the federal government should be kept small. He distrusted standing armies and wanted to reduce the size of the military.

Jefferson's Cabinet

When Jefferson entered office, he surrounded himself with men who shared his Republican principles. His secretary of state was his friend and fellow Virginian, James Madison. For secretary of the treasury, he chose **Albert Gallatin.** This Pennsylvanian had a grasp of financial matters that equaled Alexander Hamilton's.

The new government soon ended two unpopular Federalist measures. It allowed the Alien and Sedition acts to expire and repealed the Naturalization Act. For Republicans both acts were symbols of a federal government that threatened individual liberties.

Cutting Costs

Jefferson and Gallatin aimed to reduce the national debt that the Federalists had left. They scaled down military expenses. They cut the army by one-third and reduced the navy from 25 to 7 ships. By slashing spending Jefferson and Gallatin significantly lowered the national debt within a few years.

Jefferson and Gallatin also persuaded Congress to repeal all federal internal taxes, including the hated whiskey tax. At that point government funds would come only from customs duties—taxes on foreign imported goods—and from the sale of western lands.

The entire federal government in 1801 consisted of only a few hundred people. This was exactly how Jefferson thought it should be. In his view the responsibilities of the national government should be limited to delivering the mail, collecting customs duties, and conducting a census every 10 years.

✓ **Reading Check** **Explaining** How did the changes that Jefferson made when he became president reflect his views about government?

Jefferson and the Courts

Jefferson hoped that some Federalists would support his policies. However, bitter feelings between the parties continued during his administration. Much of the ill will resulted from a fight over control of the federal courts.

280 CHAPTER 9 The Jefferson Era

DIFFERENTIATED INSTRUCTION

Reading Support Have students use library references to find the value of United States imports and exports from 1800 to 1820. Have them make a line graph showing this information, using different colors for the two lines and providing a key. **L2**

▭ Refer to *Inclusion for the Middle School Social Studies Classroom Strategies and Activities* in the TCR.

HISTORY Online

Student Web Activity
Visit tarvol1.glencoe.com and click on **Chapter 9— Student Web Activities** for an activity on the history of the Supreme Court.

Judiciary Act of 1801

Before Jefferson took office, the Federalists passed the Judiciary Act of 1801. The act set up regional courts for the United States with 16 judges and many other judicial officials. In his last days as president, John Adams made hundreds of appointments to these positions, and the Federalist-controlled Congress approved them. Adams also asked **John Marshall,** his secretary of state, to serve as chief justice of the United States. By these actions Adams shut President-elect Jefferson out of the appointment process and ensured that Federalists would control the courts.

Adams and Marshall worked around the clock in the final hours of the Federalist government, processing the papers for these judicial appointments. The appointments could not take effect, however, until the papers (commissions) for these last-minute "midnight judges" were delivered. When Jefferson became president on March 4, a few of the commissions had not yet been delivered. He told Secretary of State Madison not to deliver them. One commission was addressed to William Marbury.

Marbury v. *Madison*

To force the delivery of his commission, Marbury took his case directly to the Supreme Court, which he claimed had jurisdiction as a result of the Judiciary Act of 1789. John Marshall wrote an opinion turning down Marbury's claim. He noted that the Constitution did not give the Court jurisdiction to decide Marbury's case.

In his opinion, Marshall set out three principles of judicial review: (a) The Constitution is the supreme law of the land. (b) When there is a conflict between the Constitution and any other law, the Constitution must be followed. (c) The judicial branch has a duty to uphold the Constitution. It must be able to determine when a federal law conflicts with the Constitution and to nullify, or cancel, unconstitutional laws.

Marshall not only extended the power of the Court, he also broadened federal power at the expense of the states. In *McCulloch* v. *Maryland* (1819), the Court held that the elastic clause allows Congress to do more than the Constitution expressly authorizes it to do. In *Gibbons* v. *Ogden* (1824) the Court held that federal law takes precedence over state law in interstate transportation. 📖 *(See the Supreme Court Case Summaries beginning on page 624 for more on these cases.)*

✓**Reading Check** **Summarizing** Summarize the court case that established judicial review.

Objectives and answers to the student activity can be found in the **Web Activity Lesson Plan** feature at tarvol1.glencoe.com

✓**Reading Check**

Answer: *Marbury* v. *Madison* established the Supreme Court's right to review and rule on acts of the other branches of government.

L1

Reading Essentials and Study Guide 9–1

L3

Enrichment Activity 9–1

SECTION 1 ASSESSMENT

Checking for Understanding

1. **Key Terms** Write a short paragraph in which you explain the terms laissez-faire, customs duties, and judicial review.

2. **Reviewing Facts** Explain how Jefferson cut government spending.

Reviewing Themes

3. **Government and Democracy** How did the judicial branch under Jefferson serve as a check on the executive and legislative branches?

Critical Thinking

4. **Identifying Central Issues** How was the deadlock in the presidential election of 1800 finally resolved?

5. **Determining Cause and Effect** Re-create the diagram below. In the boxes list the effects that came from the appointment of the "midnight judges."

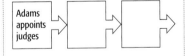

Analyzing Visuals

6. **Analyzing Architecture** Examine the photograph of Monticello on page 279. Who lived there? What do you think gives Monticello its unique look? Explain.

Interdisciplinary Activity

Expository Writing A letter of recommendation is written to discuss the positive qualities of a person. Write a letter from John Adams to Thomas Jefferson about John Marshall. Address Marshall's skills and leadership qualities.

4 CLOSE

Ask students to describe Jefferson's probable reaction to today's federal government.

SECTION 1 ASSESSMENT ANSWERS

1. Student work should reflect correct use of terms.

2. He cut the size of the army and navy, reduced the national debt, and kept the number of government workers low.

3. With the establishment of judicial review, the Supreme Court could review and rule on acts of the other branches of government.

4. The House of Representatives decided the election. Hamilton swayed the vote in Jefferson's favor.

5. Jefferson tells Madison not to send out commissions appointing judges; Marbury takes his case to the Supreme Court to force delivery of his commission, resulting in *Marbury* v. *Madison*.

6. Thomas Jefferson; Answers should describe some aspect of Monticello.

Interdisciplinary Activity Letters should discuss the positive qualities of John Marshall.

1 FOCUS

Section Overview
This section examines why the United States purchased the Louisiana Territory from France.

BELLRINGER
Skillbuilder Activity

Project transparency and have students answer the question.

Daily Focus Skills Transparency 9–2

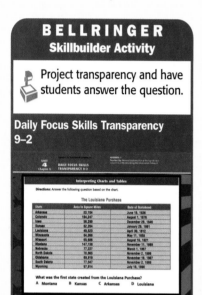

Reading Preview

Answers to Graphic: Louisiana Territory; upper Mississippi Valley and present-day Colorado

Preteaching Vocabulary
Inform students that the word *secede* comes from a Latin word meaning "to go away." Encourage volunteers to use *secede* correctly in a sentence.

SECTION 2 The Louisiana Purchase

Guide to Reading

Main Idea
The Louisiana Purchase opened a vast area to exploration and settlement.

Key Terms
Conestoga wagon, secede

Reading Strategy
Classifying Information As you read, re-create the diagram below and describe the areas that Lewis and Clark, and Zebulon Pike explored.

Explorer	Region explored
Meriwether Lewis and William Clark	
Zebulon Pike	

Read to Learn
- how the United States expanded in the early 1800s.
- how Lewis and Clark led an expedition to explore the Louisiana Territory.

Section Theme
Geography and History The purchase of the Louisiana Territory doubled the nation's size.

Preview of Events

1804	1805	1806	1807
October 1803 Senate ratifies Louisiana Purchase treaty	**May 1804** Lewis and Clark begin expedition	**September 1806** Lewis and Clark return to St. Louis	**November 1806** Zebulon Pike sights Pikes Peak

---

✦ AN American Story

Conestoga wagon

Why did Americans risk everything they had to travel west? An English visitor, Harriet Martineau, observed: "The pride and delight of Americans is in their quantity of land. . . . The possession of land is the aim of all action . . . and the cure for all social evils. . . . If a man is disappointed in politics or love, he goes and buys land. If he disgraces himself, he betakes himself to a lot in the West. . . ."

Western Territory

During the early 1800s, more and more Americans moved west in search of land and adventure. These pioneers headed over the mountains into Kentucky and Tennessee and the less settled areas of the Northwest Territory. Most of these pioneers were farmers. They made a long and exhausting journey over the Appalachian Mountains. Pioneers had to trudge along crude, muddy roads or cut their way through dense forests.

282   CHAPTER 9   The Jefferson Era

SECTION RESOURCES

📂 Reproducible Masters
- Reproducible Lesson Plan 9–2
- Daily Lecture and Discussion Notes 9–2
- Guided Reading Activity 9–2
- Section Quiz 9–2
- Reteaching Activity 9–2
- Reading Essentials and Study Guide 9–2
- Enrichment Activity 9–2

🕯 Transparencies
- Daily Focus Skills Transparency 9–2

Multimedia
- ABCNews Interactive™ Historic America Electronic Field Trips
- Interactive Tutor Self-Assessment CD-ROM
- ExamView® Pro Testmaker CD-ROM
- Presentation Plus! CD-ROM

Settlers loaded their household goods into Conestoga wagons, sturdy vehicles topped with white canvas. For these westward-bound pioneers, their two most valued possessions were a rifle for protection and hunting and an ax to hack their way through the dense forests.

In 1800 the territory of the United States extended only as far west as the Mississippi River. The area to the west of the river—known as the **Louisiana Territory**—belonged to Spain. It was an enormous area of land, anchored to the south by the city of New Orleans and extending west to the Rocky Mountains. Its northern boundaries remained undefined.

Many of the pioneers settled down and established farms along rivers that fed into the upper Mississippi River. They needed the river to ship their crops to markets. The Spanish allowed the Americans to sail on the lower Mississippi and trade in **New Orleans.** For the western farmers, this right was vital. The goods they sent downriver were unloaded in New Orleans and sent by ship to markets on the East Coast.

The French Threat

In 1802 the Spanish suddenly changed their policy. They refused to allow American goods to move into or past New Orleans. That same year, President Jefferson confirmed that Spain and France had made a secret agreement that transferred the Louisiana Territory to France.

This agreement posed a serious threat for the United States. France's leader, **Napoleon Bonaparte,** had plans for empires in Europe and the Americas. Jefferson was alarmed. He believed French control would jeopardize American trade on the Mississippi River. Jefferson authorized Robert Livingston, the new minister to France, to offer as much as $10 million for New Orleans and West Florida in order to gain control of the territory. Jefferson believed that France had gained Florida as well as Louisiana in its secret agreement with Spain.

Revolt in Santo Domingo

Napoleon had recognized the importance of Santo Domingo as a Caribbean naval base from which he could control an American empire. Events in Santo Domingo ended Napoleon's dream of a Western empire. Inspired by the ideas of the French Revolution, enslaved Africans and other laborers in Santo Domingo had revolted against the island's plantation owners. After fierce and bitter fighting, the rebels, led by **Toussaint-Louverture** (TOO•SA LOO•vuhr•TYUR), declared the colony an independent republic. Toussaint set up a new government.

In 1802 Napoleon sent troops to regain control. The French captured Toussaint but could not regain control of the island. By 1804, the French were driven out of Santo Domingo and the country regained its original name of Haiti.

✔ **Reading Check** **Explaining** Why was the Mississippi River important to western farmers?

The Nation Expands

Without Santo Domingo, Napoleon had little use for Louisiana. The French also needed money to finance Napoleon's plans for war against Britain. The French believed they had something to sell that the United States might want to buy.

French foreign minister Charles de Talleyrand informed the American diplomats that the entire Louisiana Territory was for sale. Livingston and James Monroe, Jefferson's new special representative, were taken completely by surprise. Accepting the offer went far beyond what they were authorized to do, but the deal was too good to pass up. After a few days of negotiation, the parties agreed on a price of $15 million.

The Louisiana Purchase pleased Jefferson. The new territory would provide cheap and abundant land for farmers for generations to come. He worried, however, whether the purchase was legal. The Constitution said nothing about acquiring new territory. By what authority could he justify the purchase? Livingston wrote from Paris, urging Jefferson to accept the deal before Napoleon changed his mind. Jefferson decided the government's treaty-making powers allowed the purchase of the new territory. The Senate gave its approval in October 1803. With the ratification of the treaty, the size of the United States doubled.

CHAPTER 9 The Jefferson Era 283

2 *TEACH*

Daily Lecture and Discussion Notes 9–2

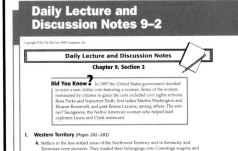

Copyright © by The McGraw-Hill Companies, Inc.

Daily Lecture and Discussion Notes

Chapter 9, Section 2

Did You Know? In 1997 the United States government decided to mint a new dollar coin featuring a woman. Some of the women nominated by citizens to grace the coin included civil rights activists Rosa Parks and Sojourner Truth, first ladies Martha Washington and Eleanor Roosevelt, and poet Emma Lazarus, among others. The winner? Sacagawea, the Native American woman who helped lead explorers Lewis and Clark westward.

I.   Western Territory *(Pages 282–283)*

A. Settlers in the less settled areas of the Northwest Territory and in Kentucky and Tennessee were pioneers. They loaded their belongings onto Conestoga wagons and made the long, tiring journey over the Appalachian Mountains to the area west of the

◀ Reading Strategy ▶

Finding Answers As students read the section, have them find answers to the following questions: Why did Jefferson want to buy New Orleans? Why did the French want to sell the Louisiana Territory? What did the Lewis and Clark expedition achieve? **L1**

✔**Reading Check**

Answer: They needed the river to ship their crops to market.

 VIDEOCASSETTE
Historic America Electronic Field Trips

View **Chapter 5** to learn more about the historic city of New Orleans.

◀ Reading Strategy ▶ READING THE TEXT

Summarizing Information Summarizing information teaches students to reduce information and to rethink what they have read. Have students read the paragraphs under "The Nation Expands" and then summarize what they have just read. Remind them that only the main ideas should be included in a summary. Tell students that to determine whether they have accurately summarized the paragraphs, they should ask themselves: Can my summary be easily understood by someone who has not read the selection? **L1, ELL**

Guided Reading Activity 9–2

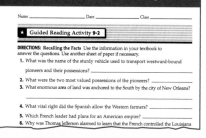

Name _____ Date _____ Class _____

★ **Guided Reading Activity 9-2**

DIRECTIONS: Recalling the Facts Use the information in your textbook to answer the questions. Use another sheet of paper if necessary.

1. What was the name of the sturdy vehicle used to transport westward-bound pioneers and their possessions?

2. What were the two most valued possessions of the pioneers?

3. What enormous area of land was anchored to the South by the city of New Orleans?

4. What vital right did the Spanish allow the Western farmers?

5. Which French leader had plans for an American empire?

6. Why was Thomas Jefferson alarmed to learn that the French controlled the Louisiana

Geography Skills

Answers:
1. the Rocky Mountains
2. the Missouri River, the Platte River, the Arkansas River, the Red River (with the Mississippi River and the Rio Grande serving as borders)

3 ASSESS

Assign Section 2 Assessment as homework or as an in-class activity.

◉ Have students use **Interactive Tutor Self-Assessment CD-ROM.**

L2

Section Quiz 9–2

Name _____ Date _____ Class _____

★ **Chapter 9**   Score ___

Section Quiz 9-2

DIRECTIONS: Matching Match the items in Column A with the items in Column B. Write the correct letters in the blanks. *(10 points each)*

Column A	Column B
___ 1. area west of the Mississippi River	**A.** Toussaint-Louverture
___ 2. trade center	**B.** Napoleon Bonaparte
___ 3. France's leader	**C.** Louisiana Territory
___ 4. revolt leader	**D.** New Orleans
___ 5. Lewis and Clark's guide	**E.** Sacagawea

DIRECTIONS: Multiple Choice In the blank at the left, write the letter of the

The Louisiana Purchase and Western Exploration

★Geography

Lewis and Clark

Jefferson wanted to know more about the mysterious lands west of the Mississippi. Even before the Louisiana Purchase was complete, he persuaded Congress to sponsor an expedition to explore the new territory. Jefferson was particularly interested in the expedition as a scientific venture. Congress was interested in commercial possibilities and in sites for future forts.

To head the expedition, Jefferson chose his private secretary, 28-year-old **Meriwether Lewis.** Lewis was well qualified to lead this journey of exploration. He had joined the militia during the Whiskey Rebellion and had been in the army since that time. The expedition's co-leader was **William Clark,** 32, a friend of Lewis's from military service. Both Lewis and Clark were knowledgeable amateur scientists and had conducted business with Native Americans. Together they assembled a crew that included expert river men, gunsmiths, carpenters, scouts, and a cook. Two

men of mixed Native American and French heritage served as interpreters. An African American named York rounded out the group.

The expedition left **St. Louis** in the spring of 1804 and slowly worked its way up the **Missouri River.** Lewis and Clark kept a journal of their voyage and made notes on what they saw and did.

Along their journey they encountered Native American groups. One young Shoshone woman named **Sacagawea** (SA•kuh•juh•WEE•uh) joined their group as a guide. After 18 months and nearly 4,000 miles, Lewis and Clark reached the Pacific Ocean. After spending the winter there, both explorers headed back east along separate routes.

Geography Skills

The purchase of the Louisiana Territory doubled the size of the United States. Americans quickly set out to explore the region and lands farther west.
1. **Place** What geographical barrier did Lewis and Clark have to cross in order to reach the Pacific Ocean?
2. **Region** What rivers flowed through the Louisiana Territory?

DIFFERENTIATED INSTRUCTION

Reading Support Have students use library sources to learn more about Fort Clatsop and the Pacific Northwest where Lewis and Clark spent the winter. Have students build a model of the fort and the surrounding area using cardboard, construction paper, and other materials. Students should label different features on the model. Then have students create quizzes based on their models. Quiz questions should address geographic issues and patterns, such as how the expedition obtained food and resources, what Native American groups lived in the region, and how geography determined where they lived. Have students exchange their quizzes with other students. **L2**

When the expedition returned in September 1806, it had collected valuable information on people, plants, animals, and the geography of the West. Perhaps most important, the journey provided inspiration to a nation of people eager to move westward.

Pike's Expedition

Even before Lewis and Clark returned, Jefferson sent others to explore the wilderness. Lieutenant **Zebulon Pike** led two expeditions between 1805 and 1807, traveling through the upper Mississippi River valley and into the region that is now the state of Colorado. In Colorado he found a snow-capped mountain he called Grand Peak. Today this mountain is known as Pikes Peak. During his expedition Pike was captured by the Spanish but was eventually released.

Federalists Plan to Secede

Many Federalists opposed the Louisiana Purchase. They feared that the states carved out of the new territory would become Republican, reducing the Federalists' power. A group of Federalists in Massachusetts plotted to secede—withdraw—from the Union. They wanted New England to form a separate "Northern Confederacy."

The plotters realized that to have any chance of success, the Northern Confederacy would have to include New York as well as New England. The Massachusetts Federalists needed a powerful friend in that state who would back their plan. They turned to Aaron Burr, who had been cast aside by the Republicans for his refusal to withdraw from the 1800 election. The Federalists gave Burr their support in 1804, when he ran for governor of New York.

Burr and Hamilton

Alexander Hamilton had never trusted Aaron Burr. Now Hamilton was concerned about rumors that Burr had secretly agreed to lead New York out of the Union. Hamilton accused Burr of plotting treason. When Burr lost the election for governor, he blamed Hamilton and challenged him to a duel. In July 1804, the two men—armed with pistols—met in Weehawken, New Jersey. Hamilton hated dueling and pledged not to shoot at his rival. Burr, however, did fire and aimed to hit Hamilton. Seriously wounded, Hamilton died the next day. Burr fled to avoid arrest.

✓Reading Check **Summarizing** Why did France sell the Louisiana Territory to the United States?

SECTION 2 ASSESSMENT

Checking for Understanding

1. **Key Terms** Write a short paragraph in which you describe the terms Conestoga wagon and secede.

2. **Reviewing Facts** What European countries controlled the Louisiana Territory up until 1800?

Reviewing Themes

3. **Geography and History** Why were the Mississippi River and New Orleans important to the United States?

Critical Thinking

4. **Determining Cause and Effect** How do you think the Lewis and Clark expedition helped to prepare people who wanted to move west?

5. **Organizing Information** Create a diagram like the one below that lists the benefits of acquiring the Louisiana Territory in 1803.

Analyzing Visuals

6. **Geography Skills** Review the map on page 284. What was the farthest western point that the Lewis and Clark expedition reached? What is the straight-line distance between St. Louis and Pikes Peak?

Interdisciplinary Activity

Descriptive Writing Accurate descriptions and drawings in their journals made Lewis and Clark's observations valuable. Find an example of plants or animals nearby. Carefully draw and describe what you see.

CHAPTER 9 The Jefferson Era **285**

SECTION 2 ASSESSMENT ANSWERS

1. Student work should reflect correct use of terms.
2. Spain
3. Farmers needed to ship their goods down the Mississippi River to New Orleans to get them to markets.
4. Answers will vary but may include the following: provided maps,

descriptions and locations of landforms, locations and information about Native American groups, distribution of animals and plants.

5. The territory provided cheap and abundant land for farmers; the United States would control the entire Mississippi River, which was

important for western farmers; the United States acquired the port of New Orleans.

6. Pacific Ocean; about 775 miles (1,250 km)

Interdisciplinary Activity Students' drawings and descriptions of animals or plants should be detailed.

✓Reading Check

Answer: The French needed money to finance Napoleon's plans for war against Britain.

L1

Reteaching Activity 9–2

Name _____ Date _____ Class _____

★ Reteaching Activity 9-2

DIRECTIONS: Sequencing Events Number the events in the order in which they occurred.

____ A. The Lewis and Clark expedition leaves St. Louis.

____ B. Thomas Jefferson authorizes American diplomats to offer $10 million for New Orleans and West Florida.

____ C. Meriwether Lewis and William Clark return from their expedition.

____ D. Jefferson persuades Congress to sponsor an expedition into the Louisiana Territory.

____ E. The Federalists support Aaron Burr in his bid to become governor of New York.

____ F. The Spanish refuse to allow Americans to move into

L1, ELL

Reading Essentials and Study Guide 9–2

Study Guide

Chapter 9, Section 2

For use with textbook pages 282–285

THE LOUISIANA PURCHASE

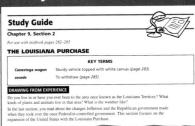

KEY TERMS	
Conestoga wagon	Sturdy vehicle topped with white canvas (*page 283*)
secede	To withdraw (*page 285*)

DRAWING FROM EXPERIENCE

Do you live in or have you ever been to the area once known as the Louisiana Territory? What kinds of plants and animals live in that area? What is the weather like?

In the last section, you read about the changes Jefferson and the Republican government made when they took over the once Federalist-controlled government. This section focuses on the expansion of the United States with the Louisiana Purchase.

L3

Enrichment Activity 9–2

Name _____ Date _____ Class _____

★ Enrichment Activity 9-2

Packing for a New Life

When settlers loaded up their goods to travel westward in Conestoga wagons, they could not bring all of their possessions. Study the diagram that shows the goods carried in a Conestoga wagon.

1. Rope
2. Pickax
3. Ax
4. Rifle
5. Lantern
6. Knife
7. Hatchet
8. Shovel
9. Pitchfork
10. Crosscut saw
11. Hammer

4 CLOSE

Ask students whether they consider Jefferson's purchase of the Louisiana Territory his greatest accomplishment.

1 FOCUS

Have students brainstorm a list of reasons why the Louisiana Territory would have been important to Americans during Jefferson's time. **Ask: What information were Lewis and Clark collecting for Jefferson?** *(Answers may include information about Native American groups, possible locations of fort sites, animals and plants, and commercial possibilities in the territory.)*

2 TEACH

Reading a Map Have students describe, in their own words, the routes that Lewis and Clark traveled. Students should use the map numbers to identify what happened at different locations along the journey. Then have students identify what geographic features would have helped or hindered Lewis and Clark as they traveled through the Louisiana Territory. *(The Missouri, Yellowstone, and Columbia Rivers would have made traveling easier but crossing through the Rocky Mountains could have been difficult.)* **L2**

GEOGRAPHY & HISTORY

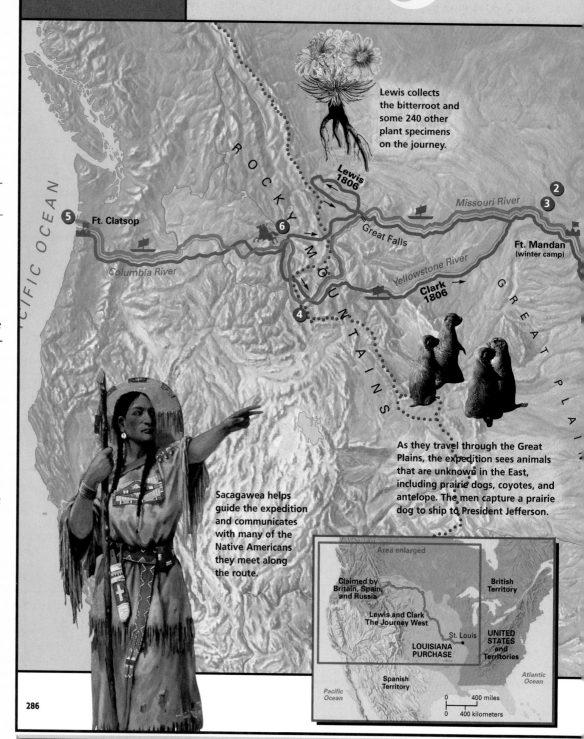

Lewis collects the bitterroot and some 240 other plant specimens on the journey.

Lewis 1806

Missouri River

Great Falls

Yellowstone River

Clark 1806

Ft. Mandan (winter camp)

ROCKY MOUNTAINS

GREAT PLAINS

5 Ft. Clatsop

6

Columbia River

PACIFIC OCEAN

2
3

4

As they travel through the Great Plains, the expedition sees animals that are unknown in the East, including prairie dogs, coyotes, and antelope. The men capture a prairie dog to ship to President Jefferson.

Sacagawea helps guide the expedition and communicates with many of the Native Americans they meet along the route.

Area enlarged

Claimed by Britain, Spain, and Russia

British Territory

Lewis and Clark The Journey West

St. Louis

UNITED STATES and Territories

LOUISIANA PURCHASE

Spanish Territory

Pacific Ocean

Atlantic Ocean

0   400 miles
0   400 kilometers

286

EXTENDING THE CONTENT

The Cajuns Among those living in the Louisiana Territory was a group of French-speaking people from Acadia, an area of eastern Canada. Called Acadians, they had been driven from their Canadian homes in the 1750s after they refused to swear loyalty to Britain. They eventually settled along the bayous in the southern area of the Louisiana Territory, making a living from fishing and trapping. In time, they became known as Cajuns, a slurred version of the word *Acadians*.

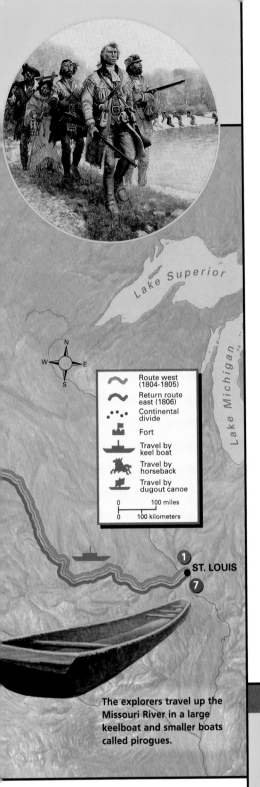

The explorers travel up the Missouri River in a large keelboat and smaller boats called pirogues.

INTO THE UNKNOWN

LEWIS AND CLARK In 1803 President Jefferson set up the Corps of Discovery to find a water route to the Pacific and explore the recently acquired Louisiana Purchase. In the spring of 1804, William Clark and Meriwether Lewis, with a company of recruits, set off from St. Louis.

1804 THE JOURNEY WEST

1 **MAY 14** The members of the Corps of Discovery, which number over 45, embark on the expedition, which would eventually cover nearly 7,700 miles.

2 **NOVEMBER** The explorers set up a winter camp near the villages of the Mandans and Hidatsas. Sacagawea, a Shoshone woman who had been kidnapped by the Hidatsa, joins the expedition.

1805

3 **APRIL 7** Lewis and Clark send a group back on the keelboat with reports and specimens of some of the plants and animals that were unknown in the East. The expedition continues in smaller boats.

4 **AUGUST 12** Lewis realizes that there is no Northwest Passage—or river route—to the Pacific. The Corps continues on horseback.

5 **DECEMBER 25** The expedition celebrates Christmas in its new winter quarters, Fort Clatsop.

1806 THE RETURN TRIP

6 **JULY 3** The expedition splits into smaller units to explore more of the Louisiana Territory. They reunite on August 12.

7 **SEPTEMBER 23** The Corps of Discovery finally arrives back in St. Louis. The explorers had established peaceful contact with many Native Americans and accumulated a wealth of geographic information. Fur traders and others, armed with the new knowledge, soon start heading west.

Route west (1804-1805)
Return route east (1806)
Continental divide
Fort
Travel by keel boat
Travel by horseback
Travel by dugout canoe
0   100 miles
0   100 kilometers

Lake Superior

Lake Michigan

ST. LOUIS

LEARNING from GEOGRAPHY

1. **What obstacles do you think would have been the most difficult for the expedition?**

2. **Write a paragraph that describes the importance of teamwork in helping the Corps of Discovery reach its goals.**

287

NATIONAL GEOGRAPHIC
GEOGRAPHY & HISTORY

3 ASSESS

Have students answer the **Learning from Geography** questions.

4 CLOSE

Have students create a graphic organizer that shows the causes and effects of the Lewis and Clark expedition.

NGS ONLINE

Access National Geographic's Web site for current events, atlas updates, activities, links, interactive features, and archives at www.nationalgeographic.com

Did you know?

Presiding at his last official ceremony in the White House, President Bill Clinton awarded a posthumous promotion to William Clark to the rank of Army Captain and gave the title of honorary Army Sergeant to Sacagawea and to Clark's enslaved African, York.

Answers to Learning from Geography

1. Answers will vary but may include navigating the terrain, maintaining a food supply, and communicating with different Native American groups.

2. Students' paragraphs should describe how teamwork helped the Corps of Discovery achieve its goals.

1 FOCUS

Section Overview

This section examines the foreign and domestic conflicts that arose during the early 1800s.

BELLRINGER
Skillbuilder Activity

 Project transparency and have students answer the question.

Daily Focus Skills Transparency 9–3

Reading Preview

Answers to Graphic: war with Tripoli; Embargo Act; conflict with Native Americans

Preteaching Vocabulary
Point out that a hawk is a bird of prey. Then have students suggest why supporters of war are called *hawks*.

SECTION 3 · A Time of Conflict

Guide to Reading

Main Idea
Between 1800 and 1815 the United States experienced rapid expansion as well as the challenge of war.

Key Terms
tribute, neutral rights, impressment, embargo, War Hawks, nationalism

Reading Strategy
Organizing Information As you read the section, re-create the diagram below and describe in the box the actions the United States took in each of these situations.

U.S. actions →
- Demand for tribute
- Attack on *Chesapeake*
- Tecumseh's confederation

Read to Learn
- why Tecumseh built a confederacy among Native American nations.
- why the War Hawks wanted to go to war.

Section Theme
Global Connections The nation's neutrality was challenged.

Preview of Events

♦1804   ♦1808   ♦1812

1804 Barbary pirates seize the U.S. warship *Philadelphia*

1807 The British navy attacks the American vessel *Chesapeake*; Congress passes the Embargo Act

1811 Harrison defeats the Prophet at Tippecanoe

1812 Madison asks Congress to declare war on Britain

American sailors

★ AN ★ American Story

The floors of the oceans are littered with the remains of once-mighty ships and the unmarked graves of unlucky sailors who sank with them in the 1700s. Seafarer Francis Rogers described the terror of a storm in this journal entry: "The sky seemed all on fire and [all around] were such swift darting rays of lightning, flying in long bright veins, with inexpressible fury as was very frightful."

Americans in Foreign Seas

Despite the dangers of sea travel in the early 1800s, the livelihoods of many Americans depended on trade with foreign nations. In 1785 the American ship *Empress of China* returned to New York from China with a highly prized cargo of tea and silk. The goods sold for a fabulous profit. Soon ships from New York, Philadelphia, and especially New England were sailing regularly to China and India carrying furs and other goods. In the following years, American merchant ships sailed far and wide, making calls in South America, Africa, and lands along the Mediterranean Sea.

288   CHAPTER 9   The Jefferson Era

SECTION RESOURCES

📁 Reproducible Masters
- Reproducible Lesson Plan 9–3
- Daily Lecture and Discussion Notes 9–3
- Guided Reading Activity 9–3
- Section Quiz 9–3
- Reteaching Activity 9–3
- Reading Essentials and Study Guide 9–3
- Enrichment Activity 9–3

🖼 Transparencies
- Daily Focus Skills Transparency 9–3

Multimedia
- 🅢 Interactive Tutor Self-Assessment CD-ROM
- 🅢 ExamView® Pro Testmaker CD-ROM
- 🅢 Presentation Plus! CD-ROM

War between the French and British in the mid-1790s gave an additional boost to American shipping. Rather than risk capture or destruction by the enemy, many French and British merchant ships remained at home. American shippers profited from the situation and increased their trade. By 1800 the United States had almost 1,000 merchant ships trading around the world.

Barbary Pirates

Sailing in foreign seas was not without danger. In the Mediterranean, for example, ships had to be on guard for pirates from Tripoli and the other **Barbary Coast states** of North Africa. For years these Barbary pirates had been terrorizing the Mediterranean. They demanded tribute, or protection money, from European governments to let their ships pass safely.

War With Tripoli

The United States, too, had paid tribute for safe passage—but not enough. In 1801 the ruler of Tripoli asked for more money from the United States. When President Jefferson refused, the ruler chopped down the flagpole of the American consulate—a declaration of war. Jefferson sent ships to the Mediterranean and blockaded, or closed off, Tripoli. The American fleet, however, was not powerful enough to defeat the Barbary pirates, and the conflict continued.

In 1804 the pirates seized the U.S. warship *Philadelphia* and towed it into Tripoli Harbor. They threw the captain and crew into jail. **Stephen Decatur,** a 25-year-old United States Navy captain, took action. Slipping into the heavily guarded harbor with a small raiding party, Decatur burned the captured ship to prevent the pirates from using it. A British admiral praised the deed as the "most bold and daring act of the age."

Negotiations finally ended the conflict with Tripoli in June 1805. Tripoli agreed to stop demanding tribute, but the United States had to pay a ransom of $60,000 for the release of the American prisoners.

✓**Reading Check** **Explaining** Why did Tripoli declare war on the United States?

Writing Headlines Have students compose a newspaper headline for each major part of the section. Remind them that dramatic events, such as Decatur's burning of the *Philadelphia*, sell newspapers. **L1**

✓**Reading Check**

Answer: because the United States would not agree to increase the amount of tribute paid to Tripoli

Imports and Exports, 1800–1820

- Nonintercourse Act
- Embargo Act
- War of 1812
- Panic of 1819

1 Exports: goods sold
2 Imports: goods purchased
3 Balance of trade: difference between the value of a nation's exports and its imports

Millions of Dollars (y-axis: 20, 40, 60, 80, 100, 120, 140, 160, 180)
Year (x-axis: 1800, 1805, 1810, 1815, 1820)

Chart *Skills*

1. **Analyzing Information** When did U.S. exports reach their lowest level?
2. **Determining Cause and Effect** How did the Embargo Act affect imports and exports?

Chart *Skills*

Answers:
1. 1814
2. Both imports and exports significantly decreased.

COOPERATIVE LEARNING ACTIVITY

Protesting the Action of the Barbary Pirates Have students work in small groups to organize a campaign to convince President Jefferson that paying tribute to the Barbary pirates is a bad idea. Have each student choose a specific role in the project: writing letters, preparing and designing posters, preparing a brief argument to get people to sign a petition, and writing and delivering speeches. **L2**

Guided Reading Activity 9–3

Name _____ Date _____ Class _____

★ **Guided Reading Activity 9-3**

DIRECTIONS: Filling in the Blanks Use your textbook to fill in the blanks using the words in the box. Use another sheet of paper if necessary.

General William Henry Harrison	Philadelphia	Tecumseh
Napoleon Bonaparte	impressed	United States
declaration of war	Embargo Act	Chesapeake
Nonintercourse Act	James Madison	neutral rights
Stephen Decatur	Tripoli	

Americans in Foreign Seas

By 1800 the **(1)** _____ was second only to Great Britain in the number of merchant ships trading around the world. When Thomas Jefferson refused to pay more money for protection of American ships in the Mediterranean, the ruler of **(2)** _____ chopped down the flagpole of the American consulate. In 1804 **(3)** _____ slipped into Tripoli Harbor and burned the **(4)** _____ to prevent Barbary pirates from using it.

Freedom of the Seas

In the war between Great Britain and France, the United States had **(5)** _____, the right to sail the seas and not take sides. In need of sailors, British naval patrols stopped American ships and **(6)** _____ thousands of American citizens into service. When the British attacked the **(7)** _____ in June 1807, many Americans called for war against Great Britain. Instead Congress passed the **(8)** _____, which banned imports from and exports to *all* foreign countries. The **(9)** _____, passed on March 1, 1809, prohibited trade only with Great Britain and France.

War Fever

When **(10)** _____ took office as president in 1809, the cries for war with Great Britain were growing louder. **(11)** _____ tricked the United States when he promised to end France's trade restrictions. Aware of the growing power of the Shawnee brothers **(12)** _____ and the Prophet, the American governor of the Indiana Territory, **(13)** _____, feared a Native American alliance with the British. On June 1, 1812, Madison asked Congress for a **(14)** _____.

Embargo Americans enraged by the embargo made anagrams of the word *embargo* that reflected their anger: "O Grab Me," "Go Bar 'Em," and "Mobrage." One cartoon of the time shows a snapping turtle (the embargo) clenching a merchant's trousers in its jaws, preventing the man from loading his cargo. The merchant's speech balloon reads, "Oh! this cursed Ograbme."

Freedom of the Seas

Riding the wave of four successful years as president, Jefferson won reelection easily in 1804. Jefferson received 162 electoral votes to only 14 for his Federalist opponent, Charles Pinckney. His second term began with the nation at peace. Across the sea, however, Great Britain and France were already involved in a war that threatened to interfere with American trade.

The thriving foreign trade of the United States depended on being able to sail the seas freely. The nation had resolved the threat from the Barbary pirates. Now it was challenged at sea by the two most powerful nations in Europe.

Neutral Rights Violated

When Britain and France went to war in 1803, America enjoyed a prosperous commerce with both countries. As long as the United States remained neutral, shippers could continue doing business. A nation not involved in a conflict had neutral rights—the right to sail the seas and not take sides.

For two years American shipping continued to prosper. By 1805, however, the warring nations had lost patience with American "neutrality." Britain blockaded the French coast and threatened to search all ships trading with France. France later announced that it would search and seize ships caught trading with Britain.

American Sailors Kidnapped

The British needed sailors for their naval war. Conditions in the British Royal Navy were terrible. British sailors were poorly paid, poorly fed, and badly treated. Many of them deserted. Desperately in need of sailors, the British often used force to get them. British naval patrols claimed the right to stop American ships at sea and search for any sailors on board suspected of being deserters from the British navy.

This practice of forcing people to serve in the navy was called impressment. While some of those taken were deserters from the British navy, the British also impressed thousands of native-born and naturalized American citizens.

Attack on the *Chesapeake*

Quite often the British would lie in wait for American ships outside an American harbor. This happened in June 1807 off the coast of **Virginia.** A British warship, the *Leopard,* intercepted the American vessel *Chesapeake* and demanded to search the ship for British deserters. When the *Chesapeake*'s captain refused, the British opened fire, killing 3, wounding 18, and crippling the American ship.

As news of the attack spread, Americans reacted with an anti-British fury not seen since the Revolutionary War. Secretary of State **James Madison** called the attack an outrage. Many demanded war against Britain. Although President Jefferson did not intend to let Great Britain's actions go unanswered, he sought a course of action other than war.

A Disastrous Trade Ban

Britain's practice of impressment and its violation of America's neutral rights had led Jefferson to ban some trade with Britain. The attack on the *Chesapeake* triggered even stronger measures. In December 1807, the Republican Congress passed the **Embargo Act.** An embargo prohibits trade with another country. Although Great Britain was the target of this act, the embargo banned imports from and exports to *all* foreign countries. Jefferson wanted to prevent Americans from using other countries as go-betweens in the forbidden trade.

With the embargo, Jefferson and Madison hoped to hurt Britain but avoid war. They believed the British depended on American agricultural products. As it turned out, the embargo of 1807 was a disaster. The measure wiped out all American commerce with other nations. Worse, it proved ineffective against Britain. The British simply traded with Latin America for its agricultural goods.

The embargo clearly had not worked. On March 1, 1809, Congress repealed it. In its place Congress enacted the much weaker **Nonintercourse Act.** The new act prohibited trade only with Britain and France and their colonial possessions. It was no more popular or successful than the Embargo Act.

DIFFERENTIATED INSTRUCTION

Gifted and Talented Have each student choose a person from the section and write several diary entries that the person might have made. Encourage students to think about how their chosen character might have felt and how they themselves would have felt in the same situation. Remind students to use correct grammar, spelling, sentence structure, and punctuation. **L3**

📁 Refer to ***Inclusion for the Middle School Social Studies Classroom Strategies and Activities*** in the TCR.

Jefferson Leaves Office

Following Washington's precedent, Jefferson made it clear in mid-1808 that he would not be a candidate for a third term. With Jefferson's approval the Republicans chose James Madison as their candidate for president. The Federalists nominated Charles Pinckney and hoped that anger over the embargo would help their party. Pinckney carried most of New England, but the Federalist ticket collected little support from the other regions. Madison won with 122 electoral votes to Pinckney's 47 votes.

✓**Reading Check** **Evaluating** How effective was the Embargo Act?

War Fever

James Madison did not take office as president under the most favorable conditions. At home and abroad, the nation was mired in the embargo crisis. Meanwhile Britain continued to claim the right to halt American ships, and cries for war with Britain grew louder.

Closer to War

In 1810 Congress passed a law permitting direct trade with either France or Britain, depending on which country first lifted its trade restrictions against America. Napoleon seized the opportunity and promised to end France's trade restrictions.

Unfortunately for Madison, Napoleon had tricked the American administration. The French continued to seize American ships, selling them and pocketing the proceeds. Americans were deeply divided. To some it seemed as if the nation was on the verge of war—but it was hard to decide if the enemy should be Britain or France. Madison knew that France had tricked him, but he continued to see Britain as the bigger threat to the United States.

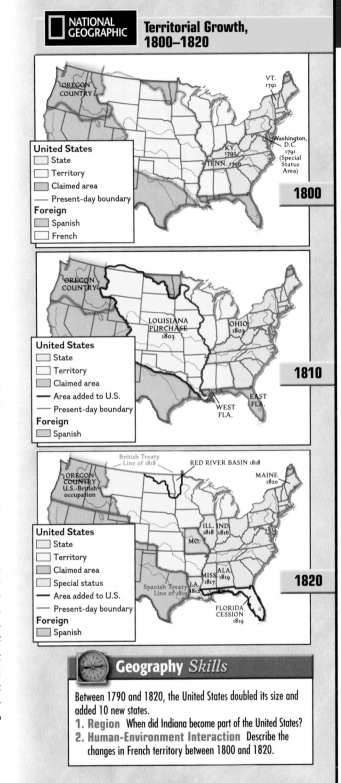

NATIONAL GEOGRAPHIC **Territorial Growth, 1800–1820**

1800

United States
- State
- Territory
- Claimed area
- Present-day boundary

Foreign
- Spanish
- French

1810

United States
- State
- Territory
- Claimed area
- Area added to U.S.
- Present-day boundary

Foreign
- Spanish

1820

United States
- State
- Territory
- Claimed area
- Special status
- Area added to U.S.
- Present-day boundary

Foreign
- Spanish

Geography *Skills*

Between 1790 and 1820, the United States doubled its size and added 10 new states.

1. **Region** When did Indiana become part of the United States?
2. **Human-Environment Interaction** Describe the changes in French territory between 1800 and 1820.

✓**Reading Check**

Answer: It was ineffective because American trade with other countries was wiped out and Britain traded with South America for its agricultural products.

 Geography *Skills*

Answers:
1. 1816
2. France owned the vast Louisiana Territory in 1800. With its sale to the United States in 1803, France no longer held any territory in the present-day United States.

Geography Skills Practice
Ask: Who occupied the Oregon Country in 1820? *(both Britain and the United States)*

What?Where?When?Who?

Embargoes Throughout its history, the United States has used the embargo as a political weapon. In 1980 President Jimmy Carter placed an embargo on the sale of American grain to the Soviet Union because the country's troops had invaded Afghanistan. The embargo was meant to put pressure on the Soviet Union to withdraw its troops.

INTERDISCIPLINARY CONNECTIONS ACTIVITY

Geography Have students interpret information from physical maps of the United States to find the expanse of terrain that a wagon would have to cross to go from the eastern states to the Far West. Then ask students to write a list of the obstacles that various features of the terrain would present for settlers. *(Answers may include: mountains such as the Appalachians and Rockies and large rivers such as the Mississippi would be hard to cross. It would be difficult to find water in desert areas.)* **L2**

Conestoga Conestoga is the name of a Native American group whose population was reduced by epidemics from about 5,000 in 1600 to 20 people in 1763. White settlers massacred these last few.

Did you know?

Wagons with wooden wheels gave passengers a bumpy ride over rough terrain. When the wagons came to especially rocky stretches, people often had to get out and walk.

Tecumseh Tecumseh is the anglicized version of *Tek-am-thi*, which is Shawnee for "Panther Passing Across." His father chose that name because Tecumseh was born just as a shooting star of great brilliance passed overhead. According to Shawnee legend, shooting stars were panthers looking for a deep hole or cave in which to sleep.

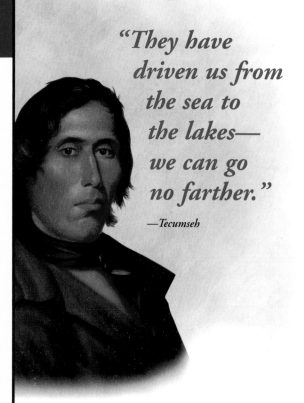

"They have driven us from the sea to the lakes— we can go no farther."

—*Tecumseh*

Frontier Conflicts

While Madison was trying to decide how to resolve the difficulties with European powers, news arrived about problems in the West. **Ohio** had become a state in 1803. Between 1801 and 1810, white settlers continued to press for more land in the Ohio Valley. Native Americans had given up many millions of acres. Now the settlers were moving onto lands that had been guaranteed to Native Americans by treaty.

As tensions increased, some Native Americans began renewing their contacts with British agents and fur traders in Canada. Others pursued a new strategy. A powerful Shawnee chief named **Tecumseh** (tuh•KUHM•suh) built a confederacy among Native American nations in the Northwest. Tecumseh believed that a strong alliance—with the backing of the British in Canada—could put a halt to white movement onto Native American lands.

A commanding speaker, Tecumseh possessed great political skills. In his view, the United States

government's treaties with separate Native American nations were worthless. "The Great Spirit gave this great island to his red children," he said. No one nation had the right to give it away.

Tecumseh had a powerful ally—his brother, known as **the Prophet.** The Prophet urged Native Americans everywhere to return to the customs of their ancestors. They should, he said, give up practices learned from the white invaders—wearing western dress, using plows and firearms, and especially drinking alcohol. The Prophet attracted a huge following among Native Americans. He founded a village at a site in northern Indiana, near present-day Lafayette, where the Tippecanoe and Wabash Rivers meet. It was called Prophetstown.

A Meeting With Harrison

The American governor of the Indiana Territory, **General William Henry Harrison,** became alarmed by the growing power of the two Shawnee brothers. He feared they would form an alliance with the British.

In a letter to Tecumseh, Harrison warned that the United States had many more warriors than all the Indian nations could put together. "Do not think that the redcoats can protect you; they are not able to protect themselves." Tecumseh sent word that he would reply in person.

A few weeks later, Tecumseh came to Harrison and spoke to the white people assembled there:

❝Brothers: Since the peace was made, you have killed some of the Shawnees, Winnebagoes, Delawares, and Miamis, and you have taken our land from us; and I do not see how we can remain at peace if you continue to do so. You try to force the red people to do some injury; it is you who are pushing them on to do mischief. You try to keep the tribes apart, and make distinctions among them. You wish to prevent the Indians from uniting.❞

The Battle of Tippecanoe

In 1811 while Tecumseh was in the South trying to expand his confederacy, Harrison decided to attack Prophetstown on the

Reading Strategy   READING THE TEXT

Predicting Have students brainstorm how history might have unfolded if the United States had declared war on Britain in the early 1800s because of impressment. Ask them to consider issues such as whether the United States would have been strong enough to defeat Britain at that time or whether the Louisiana Purchase would have happened if the United States had been involved in a long war. Have students present their ideas in an oral presentation. **L3**

📂 Use the rubric for giving an oral presentation on pages 50–51 in the **Performance Assessment Activities and Rubrics.**

Tippecanoe River. After more than two hours of battle, the Prophet's forces fled the area in defeat. The **Battle of Tippecanoe** was proclaimed a glorious victory for the Americans. Harrison acquired the nickname "Tippecanoe" and used it as a patriotic rallying cry when he ran for president in 1840.

Harrison's victory at the Battle of Tippecanoe, however, resulted in something the American people had hoped to prevent. Tecumseh now joined forces with the British troops. White settlers in the region claimed that the British had supplied Tecumseh's confederacy with guns. As a result, the rallying cry of the settlers became "On to Canada!"

War Hawks

Back in the nation's capital, President Madison faced demands for a more aggressive policy toward the British. The most insistent voices came from a group of young Republicans elected to Congress in 1810. Known as the War Hawks, they came from the South and the West. The War Hawks pressured the president to declare war against Britain.

While the War Hawks wanted to avenge British actions against Americans, they were also eager to expand the nation's power. Their nationalism—or loyalty to their country— appealed to a renewed sense of American patriotism. The leading War Hawks were **Henry**

3 ASSESS

Assign Section 3 Assessment as homework or as an in-class activity.

Have students use **Interactive Tutor Self-Assessment CD-ROM.**

L2

Section Quiz 9–3

Name _____ Date _____ Class _____

★ Chapter 9   Score

Section Quiz 9-3

DIRECTIONS: Matching Match the items in Column A with the items in Column B. Write the correct letters in the blanks. *(10 points each)*

Column A	Column B
____ 1. tribute	**A.** the Prophet
____ 2. United States Navy captain	**B.** protection money
____ 3. powerful Shawnee leader	**C.** William Henry Harrison
____ 4. Tecumseh's brother and ally	**D.** Stephen Decatur
____ 5. attacked Prophetstown	**E.** Tecumseh

L1

Reteaching Activity 9–3

Name _____ Date _____ Class _____

★ Reteaching Activity 9-3

DIRECTIONS: Organizing Facts Complete the diagram by writing the numbers of the words from the Fact Bank in the correct boxes.

A Time of Conflicts

The Barbary Coast	Acts Against the United States by Great Britain

The Trade Ban	The American Frontier

TECHNOLOGY & History

The Conestoga Wagon

By the mid-1700s, sturdy Conestoga wagons transported settlers and their freight over the Appalachian Mountains. These wagons were first built in the Conestoga Creek region of Lancaster, Pennsylvania. As people pushed even farther westward, the Conestoga was seen rolling across the plains toward Oregon and California. *Why did Conestoga wagons have a high front and back?*

1 Six to eight draft horses or a dozen oxen pull the wagon. The driver rides or walks beside the animals.

2 The boat-shaped wagon's high front and back keep goods from falling out on steep mountain trails.

3 A **toolbox** attached to the side of the wagon holds spare parts for needed repairs.

4 A white canvas cloth stretches over the hoops, or **wagon bows**. This cover protects passengers and cargo from heat, rain, and snow.

5 Broad **wheels** help keep the heavy wagon from being mired in the mud.

The average Conestoga wagon was 21 feet long, 11 feet high, and 4 feet in width and depth. It could carry up to 12,000 pounds of cargo.

3 toolbox   4 wagon bows

2

5 wheels

1

EXTENDING THE CONTENT

Tecumseh is believed to have been born at Old Piqua, a Shawnee village on the Mad River, northeast of present-day Dayton. Besides forging a Native American confederacy in Ohio, Indiana, and Michigan, Tecumseh also inspired the Creek Nation, who rose up against colonists throughout Alabama, Georgia, and Mississippi. Many colonists, including William Henry Harrison, held Tecumseh in high regard. In a private report to the War Department, Harrison described Tecumseh as "one of those uncommon geniuses which spring up occasionally to produce revolutions and overturn the established order of things."

✓Reading Check

Answer: They wanted to expand the nation's power while avenging British actions against Americans.

Geography *Skills*

Answers:
1. before 1750
2. Natchez

L1, ELL

Reading Essentials and Study Guide 9–3

L3

Enrichment Activity 9–3

4 CLOSE

President Jefferson wrote, "Never did a prisoner, released from his chains, feel such relief as I shall on shaking off the shackles of power." Have students explain Jefferson's relief at leaving the presidency.

294

Clay from Kentucky and **John Calhoun** from South Carolina, both in their 30s. Hunger for land heightened war fever. Westerners wanted to move north into the fertile forests of southern Canada. A war with Britain might make Canadian land available. Southerners wanted Spanish Florida.

The War Hawks urged major military spending. Through their efforts Congress quadrupled the army's size. The Federalists in the Northeast, however, remained strongly opposed to the war.

Declaring War

By the spring of 1812, Madison concluded that war with Britain was inevitable. In a message to Congress on June 1, he cited "the spectacle of injuries and indignities which have been heaped on our country" and asked for a declaration of war.

In the meantime the British had decided to end their policy of search and seizure of American ships. Unfortunately, because of the amount of time it took for news to travel across the Atlantic, this change in policy was not known in Washington. Word of the breakthrough arrived too late. Once set in motion, the war machine could not be stopped.

✓Reading Check **Explaining** Why did the War Hawks call for war with Britain?

NATIONAL GEOGRAPHIC

Land Taken from Native Americans

Geography *Skills*

1. **Region** During which of the three time periods was the largest amount of land taken along the Atlantic coast?
2. **Location** Which people lived nearest to the Red River?

SECTION 3 ASSESSMENT

Checking for Understanding

1. **Key Terms** Write two paragraphs in which you use all of the following terms: **tribute, neutral rights, impressment, embargo, War Hawks, nationalism.**
2. **Reviewing Facts** Describe the negotiations that ended the war between the United States and Tripoli.

Reviewing Themes

3. **Global Connections** How did the conflict in Europe help the American shipping industry prosper?

Critical Thinking

4. **Determining Cause and Effect** How did frontier battles with Native Americans intensify Americans' anti-British feelings?
5. **Sequencing Information** Re-create the diagram below and list key events in the nation's effort to remain neutral in the war between France and Britain.

Analyzing Visuals

6. **Geography Skills** Examine the maps that appear on page 291. When did Tennessee gain statehood? Which of the maps shows the territory gained from the Louisiana Purchase? In what year was Florida ceded to the United States?

Interdisciplinary Activity

Art Choose a side in the argument about war with Great Britain. Draw a political cartoon supporting your point of view.

294 CHAPTER 9 The Jefferson Era

SECTION 3 ASSESSMENT ANSWERS

1. Student work should reflect correct use of terms.
2. Tripoli agreed to stop demanding tribute, but the U.S. had to pay a ransom for the release of American prisoners.
3. By remaining neutral, the U.S. could trade with both France and Britain. Both countries kept most of their trading ships in port to avoid capture, so Americans increased their trade.
4. The British sided with Native Americans; this interference angered many Americans.
5. 1805: the U.S. remained neutral in the war between Britain and France; June 1807: Britain's attack on the Chesapeake does not result in war.; Dec. 1807: Embargo Act passed; 1809: Nonintercourse Act passed
6. 1796; 1810 map; 1819

Interdisciplinary Activity Political cartoons should encourage support for or opposition to war.

America's LITERATURE

Block Schedule

Team Teaching This selection from *Night Flying Woman* may be implemented in a team-teaching context, in conjunction with English/Language Arts.

Ignatia Broker (1919–1987)

Ignatia Broker was born on the White Earth Ojibway Reservation in Minnesota. She grew up hearing the stories of her people. She decided that one day she would tell others about Ojibway traditions. Through her writing, Broker passed on many Ojibway tales about "the purity of man and nature and keeping them in balance."

READ TO DISCOVER

Night Flying Woman tells the story of Oona, Ignatia Broker's great-great-grandmother. Oona was still a child when the Ojibway were forced to leave their land and find a new home. As you read, look for the ways in which Oona overcomes her fear of her latest home. What gives the Ojibway people faith that they will continue as a people?

READER'S DICTIONARY

fretful: worrisome, anxious, uneasy

A-wa-sa-si: a storyteller traveling with Oona's people

Ojibway: a Native American nation

Night Flying Woman

The next morning, very early, Grandfather, Oldest Uncle, and Father walked into the thick forest. Oona did not see them leave, for she was sleeping soundly. When Mother told her that they were gone, Oona looked at the forest fearfully. It seemed very unfriendly. She thought, "It has swallowed up my grandfather and father." She became **fretful.**

Mother said, "Daughter, look at the forest again but do not look and see only the dark and shadows. Instead, look at the trees, each one, as many as you can. Then tell me what you think.". . .

As Oona looked at the trees, she heard the si-si-gwa-d—the murmuring that the trees do when they brush their branches together. It was a friendly sound, and the sun sent sparkles through the si-si-gwa-d that chased the shadows. Suddenly the forest seemed different to Oona, and she knew that Grandfather, Oldest Uncle, and Father had gone into a friendly place. . . .

A-wa-sa-si said, "The forests have never failed the **Ojibway.** . . . As long as the Ojibway are beneath, the trees will murmur with contentment. When the Ojibway and the Animal Brothers are gone, the forest will weep and this will be reflected in the sound of the si-si-gwa-d. . . . In each generation of

Ojibway there will be a person who will hear the si-si-gwa-d, who will listen and remember and pass it on to the children. Remembering our past and acting accordingly will ensure that we, the Ojibway, will always people the earth. The trees have patience and so they have stood and have seen many generations of Ojibway. Yet will there be more, and yet will they see more."

From Night Flying Woman: An Ojibway Narrative *by Ignatia Broker. Copyright © 1983 by the Minnesota Historical Society. Reprinted by permission.*

ANALYZING LITERATURE

1. **Recall and Interpret** What sound did Oona hear in the forest? How did the sound affect Oona's feelings about the forest?
2. **Evaluate and Connect** What does Ignatia Broker in *Night Flying Woman* say about the importance of the past? Explain your answer.

Interdisciplinary Activity

Art Create a painting or drawing that shows the forest as Oona saw it. Use symbols to hint at the coming of the Europeans.

Reinforcing Vocabulary

Review the **Reader's Dictionary** terms with students to be sure they understand any unfamiliar terms.

Historical Connection

The Ojibway occupied areas around the Great Lakes. By the 1830s the westward movement of the United States' frontier had encroached on Ojibway lands.

Background Information

Setting This excerpt describes Ojibway families as they leave for a new home where they will not be in conflict with white people.

Characters The major character is Ni-bo-wi-se-gwe; Oona is her nickname.

Plot This book is about the traditions of the Ojibway people.

Refer to tarvol1.glencoe.com for additional Glencoe Literature titles, lesson plans, and study guides related to this unit.

ANSWERS TO ANALYZING LITERATURE

1. Si-si-gwa-d, the sound of the branches brushing together; it made her feel that the forest was friendly, not threatening.
2. The past is something people can remember and pass on to their children, thus ensuring the continuation and preservation of certain stories and memories.

Interdisciplinary Activity
Drawings should reflect Oona's feeling that the forest was a friendly place. Drawings should also depict the coming of the Europeans in some way.

SECTION 4 The War of 1812

Section Overview

This section describes the War of 1812 and its impact on the United States.

BELLRINGER
Skillbuilder Activity

Project transparency and have students answer the question.

Daily Focus Skills Transparency 9–4

Reading Preview

Answers to Graphic: Lake Erie: American naval forces destroy British naval forces; Washington, D.C.: the British burned government buildings; New Orleans: British were defeated.

Preteaching Vocabulary
Use the **Vocabulary PuzzleMaker CD-ROM** to create crossword and word search puzzles.

Guide to Reading

Main Idea
Beginning in 1812 the United States was at war with Britain. Fighting took place in the United States, in Canada, and at sea.

Key Terms
frigate, privateer

Reading Strategy
Taking Notes As you read the section, re-create the diagram below and in the boxes describe each battle's outcome.

Battle	Outcome
Lake Erie	
Washington, D.C.	
New Orleans	

Read to Learn
• how the British seized and set fire to Washington, D.C.
• why Andrew Jackson fought a battle after the war was over.

Section Theme
Government and Democracy The end of the War of 1812 produced a new spirit of nationalism.

Preview of Events

◆1812	◆1813	◆1814	◆1815

June 1812
United States declares war on Britain

September 1813
Perry defeats the British navy on Lake Erie

August 1814
The British burn Washington, D.C.

January 1815
American forces win the Battle of New Orleans

Madison peace medal

AN American Story

While President Madison awarded peace medals to Native Americans who supported the United States against the British, Congressional War Hawks could be heard singing:

Ye Parliaments of England,
Ye lords and commons, too,
Consider well what you're about,
And what you're goin' to do;

You're now at war with Yankees,
And I'm sure you'll rue the day
Ye roused the sons of liberty,
In North Americay.

War Begins

Despite their swaggering songs, the War Hawks did not achieve the quick victory they boldly predicted. The Americans committed a series of blunders that showed how unprepared they were for war. The regular army now consisted of fewer than 7,000 troops. The states had between 50,000 and 100,000 militia, but the units were poorly trained, and many states opposed "Mr. Madison's war." The military commanders, veterans of the American Revolution, were too old for warfare, and the government in Washington provided no leadership. The Americans also underestimated the strength of the British and their Native American allies.

SECTION RESOURCES

📁 Reproducible Masters
• Reproducible Lesson Plan 9–4
• Daily Lecture and Discussion Notes 9–4
• Guided Reading Activity 9–4
• Section Quiz 9–4
• Reteaching Activity 9–4
• Reading Essentials and Study Guide 9–4
• Enrichment Activity 9–4

📖 Transparencies
• Daily Focus Skills Transparency 9–4

Multimedia
⊕ Vocabulary PuzzleMaker CD-ROM
⊕ Interactive Tutor Self-Assessment CD-ROM
⊕ ExamView® Pro Testmaker CD-ROM
⊕ Presentation Plus! CD-ROM

The war started in July 1812, when **General William Hull** led the American army from **Detroit** into Canada. Hull was met by Tecumseh and his warriors. Fearing a massacre by the Native Americans, Hull surrendered Detroit to a small British force in August. Another attempt by General William Henry Harrison was unsuccessful as well. Harrison decided that the Americans could make no headway in Canada as long as the British controlled Lake Erie.

Naval Battles

Oliver Hazard Perry, commander of the **Lake Erie** naval forces, had his orders. He was to assemble a fleet and seize the lake from the British. From his headquarters in Put-in-Bay, Ohio, Perry could watch the movements of the enemy ships. The showdown came on September 10, 1813, when the British ships sailed out to face the Americans. In the bloody battle that followed, Perry and his ships defeated the British naval force. After the battle, Perry sent General William Henry Harrison the message, "We have met the enemy and they are ours."

With Lake Erie in American hands, the British and their Native American allies tried to pull back from the Detroit area. Harrison and his troops cut them off. In the fierce **Battle of the Thames** on October 5, the great leader Tecumseh was killed.

The Americans also attacked the town of York (present-day Toronto, Canada), burning the parliament buildings. Canada remained unconquered, but by the end of 1813 the Americans had won some victories on land and at sea.

To lower the national debt, the Republicans had reduced the size of the navy. However, the navy still boasted three of the fastest frigates, or warships, afloat. Americans exulted when the *Constitution*, one of these frigates, destroyed two British vessels—the *Guerrière* in August 1812 and the *Java* four months later. After seeing a shot bounce off the *Constitution*'s hull during battle, a sailor nicknamed the ship "Old Ironsides."

American privateers, armed private ships, also staged spectacular attacks on British ships and captured numerous vessels. These victories were more important for morale than for their strategic value.

BROTHER JONATHAN *Administering a Salutary Cordial to JOH*

Ⓐ John Bull represents Britain Ⓑ Brother Jonathan represents the United States

Analyzing *Political Cartoons*

The cartoon shows Brother Jonathan forcing John Bull to drink a tankard of American medicine. Brother Jonathan was used to represent Americans in many cartoons, beginning with the American Revolution.
Why is the name "Perry" on the tankard?

CHAPTER 9   The Jefferson Era   **297**

2 TEACH

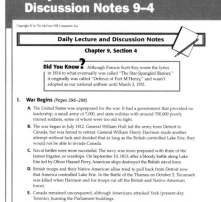

Daily Lecture and Discussion Notes 9–4

Copyright © by The McGraw-Hill Companies, Inc.

Daily Lecture and Discussion Notes

Chapter 9, Section 4

Did You Know? Although Francis Scott Key wrote the lyrics in 1814 to what eventually was called "The Star-Spangled Banner," it originally was called "Defence of Fort M'Henry," and wasn't adopted as our national anthem until March 3, 1931.

I. War Begins (Pages 296–298)

  A. The United States was unprepared for the war. It had a government that provided no leadership, a small army of 7,000, and state militias with around 700,000 poorly trained soldiers, some of whom were too old to fight.

  B. The war began in July 1812. General William Hull led the army from Detroit to Canada, but was forced to retreat. General William Henry Harrison made another attempt without luck and decided that as long as the British controlled Lake Erie, they would not be able to invade Canada.

  C. Naval battles were more successful. The navy was more prepared with three of the fastest frigates, or warships. On September 10, 1813, after a bloody battle along Lake Erie led by Oliver Hazard Perry, American ships destroyed the British naval force.

  D. British troops and their Native American allies tried to pull back from Detroit now that America controlled Lake Erie. In the Battle of the Thames on October 5, Tecumseh was killed when Harrison and his troops cut off the British and Native American forces.

  E. Canada remained unconquered, although Americans attacked York (present-day Toronto), burning the Parliament buildings.

  F. The war at sea saw more victories. In August 1812, the American warship *Constitution* destroyed a British vessel and four months later destroyed another British ship. American privateers attacked and captured numerous vessels.

  G. The Native Americans had some setbacks. When Tecumseh died, hopes of a Native American confederation also died. In March 1814, at the Battle of Horseshoe Bend, Indiana, Jackson attacked and defeated the Creeks. They were forced to give up most of their lands in the United States.

Discussion Question
Why do you think America wanted to seize Canada from the British? *(Answers will vary, but should include the idea that Canada was a vast land. If America could conquer the region, the United States would grow in size and in resources.)*

turn

Making a Chart Have students work in pairs to make a chart showing the major events and people in the War of 1812 and the issues surrounding these events. Events should be arranged in chronological order. **L3**

Analyzing *Political Cartoons*

Answer: because the Americans defeated the British naval forces at the Battle of Lake Erie under the command of Perry

COOPERATIVE LEARNING ACTIVITY

Making a Mural Have students work together in small groups to create a mural showing various dramatic events from the War of 1812. Each group should be responsible for a different section of the mural. Students may use events from the text or do further research on other events of the period. Among the many possibilities are the Battle of Lake Erie, the shelling of the *Guerrière* and the *Java*, and the defeat of the Creek at the Battle of Horseshoe Bend. **L1**

✓ Reading Check

Answer: Answers may vary, but students may note that the United States was unprepared because its forces were small and many Americans opposed the war.

L1, ELL

Guided Reading Activity 9–4

Name _____ Date _____ Class _____

★ **Guided Reading Activity 9-4**

DIRECTIONS: Recalling the Facts Use the information in your textbook to answer the questions. Use another sheet of paper if necessary.

1. How many troops were in the regular army at the start of the War of 1812?

2. What did Americans underestimate in their eagerness for war?

3. When did the war start? _____

4. Who led American naval forces to victory in the battle for Lake Erie?

5. Where was Tecumseh killed?

Geography *Skills*

Answers:
1. by blockading the coast
2. the Americans under Jackson

you don't say...

Uncle Sam During the War of 1812, Samuel Wilson, an army meat inspector from Troy, New York, stamped "U.S." for United States on the barrels of salted meat he approved. One day government inspectors asked a meat packer what the initials stood for. The worker did not know, so he said that the initials represented his boss, "Uncle Sam." "Uncle" Samuel Wilson soon became a symbol of the federal government.

Setbacks for Native Americans

With the death of Tecumseh in 1813, hopes for a Native American confederation died. In his travels two years before his death, Tecumseh had discussed plans for a confederation with the Creeks in the Mississippi Territory.

In March 1814, a lanky Tennessee planter named **Andrew Jackson** attacked the Creeks. Jackson's forces slaughtered more than 550 of the Creek people. Known as the **Battle of Horseshoe Bend,** the defeat broke the Creeks' resistance and forced them to give up most of their lands to the United States.

✓ **Reading Check** **Evaluating** Do you think the United States was prepared to wage war? Explain.

The British Offensive

British fortunes improved in the spring of 1814. They had been fighting a war with Napoleon and had won. Now they could send more forces to America.

Attack on Washington, D.C.

In August 1814, the British sailed into Chesapeake Bay. Their destination was Washington, D.C. On the outskirts of Washington, D.C., the British troops quickly overpowered the American militia and then marched into the city. "They proceeded, without a moment's delay, to burn and destroy everything in the most distant degree connected with government," reported a British officer.

NATIONAL GEOGRAPHIC — **The War of 1812**

Fort
American forces
British forces
American victory
British victory
British naval blockade

1 The British navy blockades the coast, 1812
2 Perry defeats the British on Lake Erie, 1813
3 Harrison defeats British and Native American forces at the Battle of Thames, 1813
4 The British burn Washington, D.C. Americans recapture the city and defeat the British at Ft. McHenry, 1814
5 Americans win the Battle of Lake Champlain, 1814
6 Jackson defeats the British at New Orleans, 1815

Geography *Skills*

1. **Movement** How did the British navy strengthen the British land troops?
2. **Analyzing Information** Who won the Battle of New Orleans?

DIFFERENTIATED INSTRUCTION

English Learners A number of patriotic songs came out during the War of 1812. Have volunteers read some of the titles from Chapter 6 of *Music for Patriots, Politicians, and Presidents* by Vera Brodsky Lawrence (New York: Macmillan, 1975). You might ask the music teacher to teach one or more songs to the class. **L1, ELL**

📁 Refer to ***Inclusion for the Middle School Social Studies Classroom Strategies and Activities*** in the TCR.

People In History

Dolley Madison 1768-1849

Born in North Carolina, Dolley Payne grew up in Virginia until, at age 15, her family moved to Philadelphia. There she married John Todd, Jr. As Dolley Todd, she gave birth to two children, but lost her husband and one child in 1793 during a yellow fever epidemic.

The following year she married James Madison. While her husband was secretary of state, Dolley Madison served as unofficial first lady for the widower president, Thomas Jefferson. She became the nation's official first lady when James Madison was elected president in 1808. During the War of 1812

she showed remarkable bravery. In 1814, as the British approached the capital, she refused to leave the executive mansion until she had packed up many valuable government documents, a painting of George Washington, and other priceless valuables.

The Capitol and the president's mansion were among the buildings burned. Watching from outside the city, President Madison and his cabinet saw the night sky turn orange. Fortunately a violent thunderstorm put out the fires before they could do more damage. August 24, 1814, was a low point for the Americans.

Baltimore Holds Firm

Much to everyone's surprise, the British did not try to hold Washington. They left the city and sailed north to Baltimore. Baltimore, however, was ready and waiting—with barricaded roads, a blocked harbor, and some 13,000 militiamen. The British attacked in mid-September. They were kept from entering the town by a determined defense and ferocious bombardment from Fort McHenry in the harbor.

During the night of September 13–14, a young attorney named **Francis Scott Key** watched as the bombs burst over Fort McHenry. Finally "by the dawn's early light," Key was able to see that the American flag still flew over the fort. Deeply moved by patriotic feeling, Key wrote a poem called "The Star-Spangled Banner." In 1931, Congress designated "The Star-Spangled Banner" as the National Anthem. 📖 *(See page 616 of the Appendix for an excerpt from "The Star-Spangled Banner.")*

Defeat at Plattsburgh

Meanwhile, in the north, General Sir George Prevost led more than 10,000 British troops into New York State from Canada. The first British goal was to capture Plattsburgh, a key city on the shore of Lake Champlain. The invasion was stopped when an American naval force on Lake Champlain defeated the British fleet on the lake in September 1814. Knowing the American ships could use their control of the lake to bombard them and land troops behind them, the British retreated to Canada.

After the Battle of Lake Champlain, the British decided the war in North America was too costly and unnecessary. Napoleon had been defeated in Europe. To keep fighting the United States would gain little and was not worth the effort.

The War Ends

American and British representatives signed a peace agreement in December 1814 in Ghent, Belgium. The **Treaty of Ghent** did not change any existing borders. Nothing was mentioned about the impressment of sailors, but, with Napoleon's defeat, neutral rights had become a dead issue.

Before word of the treaty had reached the United States, one final—and ferocious—battle

CHAPTER 9   The Jefferson Era   **299**

People In History

Dolley Payne Todd married James Madison in 1794, while he was a member of Congress. Dolley was well-known as a Washington social leader. While her husband was in office, she often hosted gatherings where people of different points of view could discuss politics. **Ask: What happened to the Capitol and the president's mansion during the War of 1812?** *(They were burned.)*

3 ASSESS

Assign Section 4 Assessment as homework or as an in-class activity.

🖳 Have students use **Interactive Tutor Self-Assessment CD-ROM.**

L2

Section Quiz 9–4

L1

Reteaching Activity 9–4

Reading Strategy   READING THE TEXT

Identifying the Main Idea Provide students with the words to the "Star Spangled Banner." Then lead a class discussion in which students analyze the lyrics, line by line, to determine how the words relate to the nighttime bombardment of Fort McHenry by British ships. Ask students to determine the main idea of the song. *(The fort had not been captured that night, and the American flag still flew over it at sunrise.)* Then ask students to give their opinions on whether this is a good song to represent the United States as its national anthem. **L2**

✓ Reading Check

Answer: No, it did not change existing borders, nor did it address the impressment of sailors.

L1, ELL

Reading Essentials and Study Guide 9–4

Study Guide
Chapter 9, Section 4
For use with textbook pages 296–300

THE WAR OF 1812

KEY TERMS

frigate Warship (page 297)

privateer Armed private ship (page 297)

DRAWING FROM EXPERIENCE

Do you know the words to our country's national anthem? Who wrote the words? Why were the words written?

In the last section, you read about the events that led to the War of 1812. This section focuses on the events of the War of 1812 and how the war affected the United States.

ORGANIZING YOUR THOUGHTS

Use the chart below to help you take notes as you read the summaries that follow. Think about which country was better prepared militarily during the War of 1812.

L3

Enrichment Activity 9–4

★ Enrichment Activity **9-4** ★

Tecumseh

By the time he was 37 years old, Tecumseh, a Shawnee, supported complete resistance to all white people.

DIRECTIONS: Understanding and Synthesizing Ideas Read each Tecumseh quotation. On a separate sheet of paper, define or explain any proper nouns in the quotation. Then paraphrase the main message of the quotation.

Tecumseh's Ideas

1. Where today are the Pequots? Where the Narragansetts, the Mohawks, the Pocanets and many other once powerful tribes of our people? They have vanished before the avarice [greed] and oppression of the white man, as snow before a summer sun.

4 CLOSE

When the Madisons returned to the capital, Dolley said, "We shall rebuild Washington. The enemy cannot frighten a free people." Have students explain her statement.

---

occurred at New Orleans. In December 1814, British army troops moved toward New Orleans. Awaiting them behind earthen fortifications was an American army led by Andrew Jackson.

On January 8, 1815, the British troops advanced. The redcoats were no match for Jackson's soldiers, who shot from behind bales of cotton. In a short but gruesome battle, hundreds of British soldiers were killed. At the **Battle of New Orleans,** Americans achieved a decisive victory. Andrew Jackson became a hero, and his fame helped him win the presidency in 1828.

American Nationalism

New England Federalists had opposed "Mr. Madison's war" from the start. In December 1814, unhappy New England Federalists gathered in Connecticut at the **Hartford Convention.** A few favored secession. Most wanted to remain within the Union, however. To protect their interests, they drew up a list of proposed amendments to the Constitution.

After the convention broke up, word came of Jackson's spectacular victory at New Orleans, followed by news of the peace treaty. In this moment of triumph, the Federalist grievances seemed unpatriotic. The party lost respect in the eyes of the public. Most Americans felt proud and self-confident at the end of the War of 1812.

Fact ▸ Fiction Folklore

America's Flags

The First Star-Spangled Banner, 1779–1818 The Stars and Stripes flag gained two more stars and two more stripes in 1795, after Kentucky and Vermont joined the Union.

Congress realized that the flag would become too large if a stripe were added for every new state. It decided in 1818 to keep the stripes at 13—for the thirteen original colonies—and to add a star for each new state.

The young nation had gained new respect from other nations in the world. Americans felt a new sense of patriotism and a strong national identity.

Although the Federalist Party weakened, its philosophy of strong national government was carried on by the War Hawks who were part of the Republican Party. They favored trade, western expansion, the energetic development of the economy, and a strong army and navy.

✓ **Reading Check** **Analyzing** Did the Treaty of Ghent resolve any major issues? Explain.

SECTION 4 ASSESSMENT

Checking for Understanding

1. **Key Terms** Write a short paragraph in which you use the terms **frigate** and **privateer.**
2. **Reviewing Facts** Who won the Battle of Lake Champlain? Why was it an important victory?

Reviewing Themes

3. **Government and Democracy** Why did the Federalist Party lose support after the War of 1812?

Critical Thinking

4. **Drawing Conclusions** Why did people from the North, South, and the West feel differently about going to war with Britain?
5. **Determining Cause and Effect** Recreate the diagram below. In the ovals, list four effects that the War of 1812 had on the United States.

Effects of the War of 1812

Analyzing Visuals

6. **Geography Skills** Study the map on page 298. On what lake did Perry defeat the British? Which battle—Lake Champlain or Thames—took place later in time?

Interdisciplinary Activity

Music Imagine if Francis Scott Key had been at the Battle of New Orleans instead of in Baltimore. Rewrite the first verse of "The Star-Spangled Banner" based on what occurred in that battle.

SECTION 4 ASSESSMENT ANSWERS

1. Student work should reflect correct use of terms.
2. the Americans; it secured the northern border of the United States and persuaded Britain to end the War of 1812
3. It looked unpatriotic because it had opposed the war and wanted to amend the Constitution.

4. Answers will vary. Westerners and Southerners thought war might make more land available and wanted to avenge British actions against Americans. Northerners saw little benefit in war.
5. The Federalist Party lost power; there was a new spirit of nationalism; Americans felt themselves as

equals with other countries; philosophy of strong government carried on by War Hawks
6. Battle of Lake Erie; Lake Champlain

Interdisciplinary Activity Words to songs should reflect what occurred at the Battle of New Orleans.

Writing a Journal

Why Learn This Skill?

Journal writing is personal writing with a casual style. What you write *on* is not as important as what you write *about*—your experiences, interests, and even your feelings.

Learning the Skill

A journal is a written account that records what you have learned or experienced. In the journal you can express your feelings about a subject, summarize key topics, describe difficulties or successes in solving particular problems, and draw maps or other visuals. To help you get started writing in your journal, follow these steps:

- As you read your textbook, jot down notes or questions about a specific topic or event. Then look for details and answers about it as you continue reading.
- Describe your feelings as you read a selection or look at a photograph. Are you angry, happy, frustrated, sad? Explain why.
- Ask yourself if drawing a map or flowchart would help you understand an event better. If so, draw in your journal.

William Clark's journal

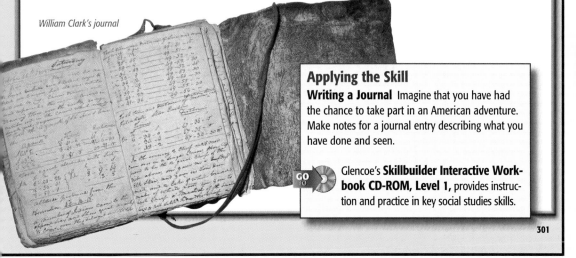

Practicing the Skill

The following excerpt describes the burning of Washington, D.C., during the War of 1812. Read the excerpt, then use the following questions to help you write entries in your own journal.

f [T]his was a night of dismay to the inhabitants of Washington. They were taken completely by surprise.... The first impulse of course tempted them to fly.... [T]he streets were ... crowded with soldiers and senators, men, women, and children, horses, carriages, and carts loaded with household furniture, all hastening towards a wooden bridge which crosses the Potomac. The confusion ... was terrible, and the crowd upon the bridge was such to endanger its giving way. ™

① What is particularly interesting about this description?

② What are your feelings as you read the excerpt?

③ Draw a map or other visual to help you understand the situation described here.

Applying the Skill

Writing a Journal Imagine that you have had the chance to take part in an American adventure. Make notes for a journal entry describing what you have done and seen.

 Glencoe's **Skillbuilder Interactive Workbook CD-ROM, Level 1,** provides instruction and practice in key social studies skills.

301

TEACH

Writing a Journal Point out that much of what we know about history, especially social history, comes from journals of the men, women, and children of the past discussing topics such as work, school, home life, religion, and community events.

Call on volunteers to share the notes they wrote for **Applying the Skill.** Discuss whether the notes are more appropriate for journal writing or narratives and why.

Additional Practice

L2

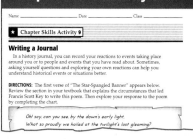

Chapter Skills Activity 9

Name _____ Date _____ Class _____

★ Chapter Skills Activity **9**

Writing a Journal

In a history journal, you can record your reactions to events taking place around you or to people and events that you have read about. Sometimes, asking yourself questions and exploring your own reactions can help you understand historical events or situations better.

DIRECTIONS: The first verse of "The Star-Spangled Banner" appears below. Review the section in your textbook that explains the circumstances that led Francis Scott Key to write this poem. Then explore your response to the poem by completing the chart.

Oh! say, can you see, by the dawn's early light,
What so proudly we hailed at the twilight's last gleaming?

GLENCOE
TECHNOLOGY

CD-ROM
Glencoe Skillbuilder Interactive Workbook CD-ROM, Level 1

This interactive CD-ROM reinforces student mastery of essential social studies skills.

ANSWERS TO PRACTICING THE SKILL

① Accept any reasonable answer.

② Accept any reasonable answer.

③ Drawings should show that students understand the excerpt.

Applying the Skill Students' notes should be based on information from the chapter regarding a specific American adventure. Although the notes should be based on factual information, students' notes may be creative and imaginative.

CHAPTER 9 ASSESSMENT and ACTIVITIES

Reviewing Key Terms

1.–6. Paragraphs should conform to directions in the text. Accept all paragraphs using the meaning of the terms correctly.

Reviewing Key Facts

7. passed the Twelfth Amendment that requires electors to vote for the president and vice president on separate ballots

8. The revolt in Santo Domingo was costly in terms of lives and money. The revolt was a major factor in the sale of the Louisiana Territory to the United States.

9. It stopped American commerce with other nations.

10. a group of Republicans in Congress from the South and West who urged war with Britain

11. It had a negative effect. With the death of Tecumseh, hopes for a Native American confederation died.

Critical Thinking

12. It established the Supreme Court's right of judicial review, in which the judiciary branch could review the acts of other branches of government.

13. Mississippi River on the east, British Canada on the north, the Oregon Country on the northwest, Spanish territory from the southern boundary of the Oregon Country to the Gulf of Mexico west of New Orleans

14. View of War Hawks: wanted to avenge British acts against Americans and expand American power; View of Federalists: strong opposition to the war

Chapter Summary
The Jefferson Era

1801
- Thomas Jefferson inaugurated as third president

1803
- *Marbury* v. *Madison* sets precedent for judicial review
- Louisiana Territory purchased from France
- Ohio becomes a state

1804
- Twelfth Amendment ratified
- Lewis and Clark expedition sets off from St. Louis
- Thomas Jefferson wins reelection

1807
- American ship *Chesapeake* attacked by British navy
- Congress passes the Embargo Act

1809
- James Madison becomes president

1811
- Harrison defeats the Prophet at Tippecanoe

1812
- U.S. declares war on Britain
- British navy blockades coast

1813
- Perry defeats British navy on Lake Erie
- Tecumseh killed at the Battle of the Thames

1814
- British burn Washington, D.C.
- Treaty of Ghent ends war with Britain

302

Reviewing Key Terms

On a sheet of paper, use all of the following terms to write several short, historically accurate paragraphs related to the information in the chapter. Use standard grammar and punctuation.

1. laissez-faire
2. impressment
3. embargo
4. nationalism
5. judicial review
6. secede

Reviewing Key Facts

7. What did Congress do to prevent a deadlock in presidential elections?

8. How did events in Santo Domingo (Haiti) influence American expansion?

9. How did the Embargo Act of 1807 hurt the United States?

10. Who were the War Hawks?

11. What effect did Tecumseh's death have on Native Americans?

Critical Thinking

12. Analyzing Themes: Government and Democracy Summarize the importance of the *Marbury* v. *Madison* decision.

13. Analyzing Information What were the boundaries of the Louisiana Territory?

14. Comparing Re-create the diagram below. In the boxes, describe the differences between the War Hawks and Federalists in their views of the War of 1812.

War of 1812	
View of War Hawks	View of Federalists

Geography and History Activity

Study the maps of territorial growth on page 291 and answer the following questions.

15. Location In what year did Mississippi become a state?

16. Region What three Southern states were admitted to the nation between 1810 and 1820?

Geography and History Activity

15. 1817

16. Louisiana, Mississippi, and Alabama

Practicing Skills

17. Writing a Journal By the late 1700s, more than 55,000 Americans had crossed the mountains into Kentucky and Tennessee. Write entries for a journal for such a trip. Explain why you are enduring such hardships to move to new land.

Citizenship Cooperative Activity

18. Analyzing Current Events With a partner, choose a recent event for which you will be able to locate primary and secondary sources of information. Compare the primary source with one secondary source. Prepare a report for the class in which you describe the event and compare the information in the primary and secondary sources.

Economics Activity

19. Work in small groups to prepare an international trade map. Your map should show United States imports during the early 1800s from each of the major continents. What major ports were merchants sailing to during this time? What products were they bringing back to the United States? Your map should include the names of important ports, the countries where they were located, symbols to represent the different products, a map key to explain the symbols, and other information such as distances or major shipping routes.

Technology Activity

20. Using a Spreadsheet Search the library for information about the modern city of New Orleans. Make a database using the spreadsheet. Beginning in column B, label four columns as follows: 1) Street names; 2) Buildings; 3) Foods; 4) Sites. Beginning in row two, label rows as follows: 1) Spanish; 2) French. Fill in the spreadsheet with the information you find.

Alternative Assessment

21. Portfolio Writing Activity Review the chapter for information about the expedition of Lewis and Clark. Imagine that you had the chance to accompany them on their adventure. Write a letter home describing what you have done and seen. Be sure to include how you were affected by the land and the people you encountered.

Self-Check Quiz
Visit **tarvol1.glencoe.com** and click on **Chapter 9—Self-Check Quizzes** to prepare for the chapter test.

Standardized Test Practice

Use the map below to choose the *best* answer to the question.

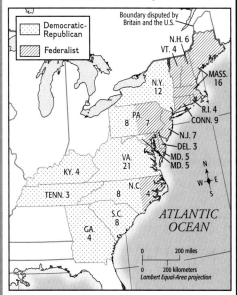

Which of the following statements about the election of 1800 is true?

F Federalists won Georgia's electoral votes.

G New Hampshire supported the Democratic-Republican ticket.

H Connecticut had seven electoral votes.

J Pennsylvania was one of the states that split its votes.

Test-Taking Tip:

Double-check all answer choices to make sure that you have chosen the best answer. Make sure that your answer choice is supported by information on the map. Check each choice against the map. Only one is correct.

Alternative Assessment

21. Students' letters should include accurate information about the Lewis and Clark expedition as presented in the chapter.

HISTORY Online

Have students visit the Web site at **tarvol1.glencoe.com** to review Chapter 9 and take the Self-Check Quiz.

Standardized Test Practice

Answer: J
Question Type: History
Answer Explanation: According to the map, eight of Pennsylvania's electoral votes were allotted to the Democratic-Republicans and seven votes went to the Federalists.

Bonus Question ?

Ask: As Lewis and Clark traveled down the Columbia River, they knew they were getting close to the ocean when they saw salmon in the river. Why? *(Salmon are an ocean-dwelling fish and travel only in freshwater to lay their eggs.)*

Practicing Skills

17. Accept answers that reflect moving to improve their lives, getting a better job, excitement of a new life, and so on.

Citizenship Cooperative Activity

18. Reports should show information about the event and compare the primary and secondary sources.

Economics Activity

19. Maps should include all the major continents, important ports and the countries where they were located, symbols for products, and any other pertinent information.

Technology Activity

20. Students should locate information about New Orleans that reflects Spanish and French influence and present it in spreadsheet form.

Chapter 10 Resources

TeacherWorks™ All-In-One Planner and Resource Center

- **Interactive Teacher Edition** Access your Teacher Wraparound Edition and your classroom resources with a few easy clicks.
- **Interactive Lesson Planner** Planning has never been easier! Organize your week, month, semester, or year with all the lesson helps you need to make teaching creative, timely, and relevant.

Use Glencoe's **Presentation Plus!** multimedia teacher tool to easily present dynamic lessons that visually excite your students. Using Microsoft PowerPoint® you can customize the presentations to create your own personalized lessons.

TEACHING TRANSPARENCIES

Graphic Organizer 5 L2

Why It Matters Chapter Transparency 10 L2

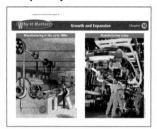

REVIEW AND REINFORCEMENT

Workbook Activity 10 L1

Time Line Activity 10 L2

Vocabulary Activity 10 L1

REVIEW AND REINFORCEMENT

Critical Thinking Skills Activity 10 L2

Take-Home Review Activity 10 L1

ENRICHMENT

Linking Past and Present Activity 10 L2

Primary Source Reading 10 L2

GEOGRAPHY

Geography and History Activity 10 L2

Meeting NCSS Standards

The following standards are highlighted in Chapter 10:

Section 1 VII Production, Distribution, & Consumption: A, B, I

Section 2 VIII Science, Technology, & Society: A

Section 3 IV Individual Development & Identity: B, F

FOLDABLES™

Study Organizer

Dinah Zike's Foldables are three-dimensional, interactive graphic organizers that help students practice basic writing skills, review key vocabulary terms, and identify main ideas. Additional chapter activities can be found in the **Reading and Study Skills Foldables** booklet.

Chapter 10 Resources

ASSESSMENT AND EVALUATION

Chapter 10 Test Form A L2

Chapter 10 Test Form B L2

Standardized Test Practice Workbook Activity 10 L2

Performance Assessment Activity 10 L1, ELL

ExamView® Pro Testmaker CD-ROM

MULTIMEDIA

- Vocabulary PuzzleMaker CD-ROM
- Interactive Tutor Self-Assessment CD-ROM
- ExamView® Pro Testmaker CD-ROM
- Audio Program
- American History Primary Source Document Library CD-ROM
- MindJogger Videoquiz
- Presentation Plus! CD-ROM
- TeacherWorks CD-ROM
- Interactive Student Edition CD-ROM
- Glencoe Skillbuilder Interactive Workbook CD-ROM, Level 1
- The American Republic to 1877 Video Program
- American Music: Hits Through History

SPANISH RESOURCES

The following Spanish language materials are available in the Spanish Resources Binder:

- Spanish Guided Reading Activities
- Spanish Reteaching Activities
- Spanish Quizzes and Tests
- Spanish Vocabulary Activity
- Spanish Take-Home Review Activity
- Spanish Summaries
- The Declaration of Independence and United States Constitution Spanish Translation

---

The following videotape programs are available from Glencoe as supplements to Chapter 10:

- **The Best of the Real West** (five video set) (ISBN 1-56501-352-2)
- **The Mighty Mississippi** (ISBN 0-7670-1090-6)
- **Textiles: Birth of an American Industry** (ISBN 0-7670-0624-0)

To order, call Glencoe at 1-800-334-7344. To find classroom resources to accompany many of these videos, check the following home pages:
A&E Television: www.aande.com
The History Channel: www.historychannel.com

Use our Web site for additional resources. All essential content is covered in the Student Edition.

You and your students can visit tarvol1.glencoe.com, the Web site companion to **The American Republic to 1877**. This innovative integration of electronic and print media offers your students a wealth of opportunities. The student text directs students to the Web site for the following options:

- **Chapter Overviews**
- **Student Web Activities**
- **Self-Check Quizzes**
- **Textbook Updates**

Answers to the student Web activities are provided for you in the **Web Activity Lesson Plans.** Additional Web resources and Interactive Tutor Puzzles are also available.

Chapter 10 Resources

SECTION RESOURCES

Daily Objectives	Reproducible Resources	Multimedia Resources
SECTION 1 **Economic Growth** 1. Describe how the Industrial Revolution began in the United States. 2. Describe how the United States changed as it became more economically independent.	Reproducible Lesson Plan 10–1 Daily Lecture and Discussion Notes 10–1 Guided Reading Activity 10–1* Section Quiz 10–1* Reteaching Activity 10–1* Reading Essentials and Study Guide 10–1* Enrichment Activity 10–1	Daily Focus Skills Transparency 10–1 American Music: Hits Through History ABCNews Interactive™ Historic America Electronic Field Trips Interactive Tutor Self-Assessment CD-ROM ExamView® Pro Testmaker CD-ROM Presentation Plus! CD-ROM
SECTION 2 **Westward Bound** 1. Explain how transportation improved in the early 1800s. 2. Understand how Western settlements affected the nation's economy and politics.	Reproducible Lesson Plan 10–2 Daily Lecture and Discussion Notes 10–2 Guided Reading Activity 10–2* Section Quiz 10–2* Reteaching Activity 10–2* Reading Essentials and Study Guide 10–2* Enrichment Activity 10–2	Daily Focus Skills Transparency 10–2 Interactive Tutor Self-Assessment CD-ROM ExamView® Pro Testmaker CD-ROM Presentation Plus! CD-ROM
SECTION 3 **Unity and Sectionalism** 1. Describe why sectional differences grew in the 1820s. 2. Identify the effect the Monroe Doctrine had on foreign policy.	Reproducible Lesson Plan 10–3 Daily Lecture and Discussion Notes 10–3 Guided Reading Activity 10–3* Section Quiz 10–3* Reteaching Activity 10–3* Reading Essentials and Study Guide 10–3* Enrichment Activity 10–3	Daily Focus Skills Transparency 10–3 Vocabulary PuzzleMaker CD-ROM Interactive Tutor Self-Assessment CD-ROM ExamView® Pro Testmaker CD-ROM Presentation Plus! CD-ROM

0:00 OUT OF TIME?
Assign the Chapter 10 **Reading Essentials and Study Guide.**

*Also Available in Spanish

 Blackline Master   Transparency   CD-ROM   DVD

Poster   Music Program   Audio Program   Videocassette

KEY TO ABILITY LEVELS

Teaching strategies have been coded.

L1 BASIC activities for all students

L2 AVERAGE activities for average to above-average students

L3 CHALLENGING activities for above-average students

ELL ENGLISH LANGUAGE LEARNER activities

NATIONAL GEOGRAPHIC Teacher's Corner

INDEX TO NATIONAL GEOGRAPHIC MAGAZINE

The following articles relate to this chapter.

- "The Way West," by John G. Mitchell, September 2000.
- "The Cherokee," by Geoffrey Norman, May 1995.
- "Powwow," by Michael Parfit, June 1994.
- "The Cruelest Commerce: African Slave Trade," by Colin Palmer, September 1992.
- "Philadelphia's African Americans," by Roland L. Freeman, August 1990.

ADDITIONAL NATIONAL GEOGRAPHIC SOCIETY PRODUCTS

To order the following, call National Geographic at 1-800-368-2728:

- *GeoKit: Lewis and Clark* (Kit)
- *GeoKit: Westward Movement* (Kit)
- *The West That Was* (Video)
- *Exploration* (Map)
- *United States/Territorial Growth* (Map)
- *National Geographic Desk Reference* (Book)
- *Washington, D.C.* (Video)

NGS ONLINE

Access National Geographic's Web site for current events, atlas updates, activities, links, interactive features, and archives.

www.nationalgeographic.com

MEETING SPECIAL NEEDS

In addition to the Differentiated Instruction strategies found in each section, the following resources are also suitable for your special needs students:

- *ExamView® Pro Testmaker CD-ROM* allows teachers to tailor tests by reducing answer choices.
- The *Audio Program* includes the entire narrative of the student edition so that less-proficient readers can listen to the words as they read them.
- The *Reading Essentials and Study Guide* provides the same content as the student edition but is written two grade levels below the textbook.
- *Guided Reading Activities* give less-proficient readers point-by-point instructions to increase comprehension as they read each textbook section.
- *Enrichment Activities* includes a stimulating collection of readings and activities for gifted and talented students.

From the Classroom of...

Michael Branch
Van Devender Junior High
Parkersburg, WV

Westward Journey

Give students the following scenario: You and your spouse are part of a small caravan of wagons traveling west. Because your wagon is falling behind, you must eliminate eight of the items listed on the chalkboard to reduce your load. Remind students to keep what is important. Write the following list: 1. two barrels of bacon; 2. pans you received as a wedding present; 3. four bolts of cloth; 4. small Franklin metal stove; 5. crate of lead and gunpowder; 6. 100 feet of heavy rope; 7. barrel of flour; 8. spare tools; 9. case of salted dried beef; 10. trunk of winter clothing; 11. small anvil and hammer; 12. spare wheel rim; 13. plow; 14. heirloom table and chairs; 15. set of axes; 16. set of books; 17. spinning wheel; 18. barrel of molasses. Ask: What were the reasons you discarded these items? What were the two most important items you kept?

ADDITIONAL RESOURCES FROM GLENCOE

- American Music: Cultural Traditions
- American Art and Architecture
- Outline Map Resource Book
- U.S. Desk Map
- Building Geography Skills for Life
- Inclusion for the Middle School Social Studies Classroom Strategies and Activities
- Teaching Strategies for the American History Classroom (Including Block Scheduling Pacing Guides)
- American Crafts Hands-On Activities
- American Games Hands-On Activities
- American History Flash Cards

Block Schedule

Activities that are suited to use within the block scheduling framework are identified by:

✓ **Performance Assessment**

Refer to Activity 10 in the Performance Assessment Activities and Rubrics booklet. 📀

Why It Matters Activity

Westward expansion was a major factor in the growth of American economic and military power. Discuss with students how westward expansion affected the area in which they live. Did people from their area primarily become settlers who moved west, or was their region a part of the frontier that was settled during the nineteenth century?

GLENCOE
TECHNOLOGY

The American Republic to 1877 Video Program

To learn more about what it was like to attend school during the nineteenth century, have students view the Chapter 10 video "The One-Room Schoolhouse" from **The American Republic to 1877 Video program.**

 Available in DVD and VHS

MindJogger Videoquiz

Use **MindJogger Videoquiz** to preview the Chapter 10 content.

 Available in VHS

CHAPTER 10 Growth and Expansion

1790–1825

Why It Matters

During the early 1800s, manufacturing took on a stronger role in the American economy. During the same period, people moved westward across the continent in larger and larger numbers. In 1823 the United States proclaimed its dominant role in the Americas with the Monroe Doctrine.

The Impact Today

These developments were important factors in shaping the nation. Today the United States is one of the leading economic and military powers in the world.

The American Republic to 1877 Video The chapter 10 video, "The One-Room Schoolhouse," depicts a typical school day in the nineteenth century.

1790
• First U.S. Census

1793
• Eli Whitney invents cotton gin

1807
• Robert Fulton designs first practical steamboat

United States PRESIDENTS

Washington 1789–1797

Adams 1797–1801

Jefferson 1801–1809

Madison 1809–1817

1790   *1800*   *1810*

World

1792
• Russia invades Poland

1804
• Haiti claims independence from France

📖 Reading Strategy ⟩ PURPOSE FOR READING

Quick free write is a pre-reading activity for an upcoming topic or lesson. Begin by pointing out that the westward expansion of the United States involved individuals and families who were willing to leave their friends and homes for a chance to make a new life on the frontier. Ask: What five things would you need to consider before deciding to move to the frontier? Have students respond in a quick free write. Encourage students to include drawings if they wish. Conclude by having students do another free write after completing the chapter. **L1**

Valley of the Yosemite by Albert Bierstadt Bierstadt's panoramic scenes of the American West capture the vastness of the landscape.

FOLDABLES™
Study Organizer

Cause-and-Effect Study Foldable Make this foldable to help you analyze the causes and effects of growth in the East and expansion into the West of the United States.

Step 1 Fold one sheet of paper in half from top to bottom.

Step 2 Fold it in half again, from side to side.

Step 3 Unfold the paper once. Sketch an outline of the United States across both tabs and label them as shown.

Expansion | Growth

West | East

Step 4 Cut up the fold of the top flap only.

Expansion | Growth

West | East

This cut will make two tabs.

Reading and Writing As you read the chapter, list causes and effects of eastern growth and western expansion under the appropriate tabs of your foldable.

FOLDABLES™
Study Organizer
Dinah Zike's Foldables

Purpose This foldable helps students analyze information by identifying cause-and-effect relationships in the chapter material. Direct students to identify the causes and effects of two separate events occurring in the United States between 1790 and 1825. These two separate events were economic growth in the East and expansion in the West.

📁 Have students complete **Reading and Study Skills Foldables** Activity 10. **L1**

HISTORY Online

Introduce students to chapter content and key terms by having them access **Chapter 10 Overview** at tarvol1.glencoe.com

TIME LINE ACTIVITY

Have students review the time line on pages 304–305 as they read the chapter. Ask students to list advances in technology or transportation that occurred between 1790 and 1830 that aided Western expansion. *(1793: invention of cotton gin made it possible to cultivate more land in the South and West; 1807: Robert Fulton invents the first practical steamboat, which spurs the growth of river transportation; 1825: completion of the Erie Canal, linking the Great Lakes region with the East Coast)*

1825
• Erie Canal completed

1819
• Florida ceded to U.S.

1820
• Missouri Compromise passed

1823
• Monroe Doctrine issued

Monroe 1817–1825

J.Q. Adams 1825–1829

1820   *1830*

1815
• Battle of Waterloo crushes Napoleon

1819
• Bolívar defeats Spanish forces at Boyacá

1821
• Peru claims independence from Spain

HISTORY Online

Chapter Overview
Visit tarvol1.glencoe.com and click on **Chapter 10— Chapter Overviews** to preview chapter information.

More About the Art

Albert Bierstadt (1830–1902) was born in Germany and moved to Massachusetts with his family when he was a young boy. He returned to Germany to study painting, but kept a studio in New York City from 1861 to 1879. Bierstadt was always attracted to mountains as a subject for his paintings. He became best known for depicting American western landscapes in his work. Throughout his life, Bierstadt made many trips to the West. Paintings such as *Valley of the Yosemite* feature highly detailed landscapes and emphasize the unspoiled natural splendors of the West.

1 FOCUS

Section Overview
This section describes how industry changed cities and the American economy.

Reading Preview

Answers to Graphic: Cities grew as people moved to work in factories and mills; changes in the factory system allowed products to be produced faster and cheaper; inventions allowed agriculture to expand; the United States gained wealth, power, and independence.

Preteaching Vocabulary
Have students look up *revolution* in a dictionary and choose the meaning they think will fit best in the term *Industrial Revolution*.

SECTION 1 Economic Growth

Guide to Reading

Main Idea
The rise of industry and trade led to the growth of cities.

Key Terms
Industrial Revolution, capitalism, capital, free enterprise, technology, cotton gin, patent, factory system, interchangeable parts

Reading Strategy
Organizing Information As you read the section, re-create the diagram below and describe in the ovals changes brought about by the Industrial Revolution.

Industrial Revolution

Read to Learn
• how the Industrial Revolution began in the United States.
• how the United States changed as it became more economically independent.

Section Theme
Economic Factors The Industrial Revolution changed the way goods were made.

Preview of Events

♦1790	♦1800	♦1810	♦1820
1793 Eli Whitney invents the cotton gin	**1807** Congress passes Embargo Act	**1814** Francis Lowell opens textile plant in Massachusetts	**1816** Second National Bank is chartered

★ AN American Story

Both men and women in the early 1800s valued hard work. An English journalist described the farmers of Long Island in 1818: "Every man can use an axe, a saw, and a hammer. Scarcely one who cannot do any job at rough carpentering, and mend a plough and wagon. . . . " Another European noted the daily activities of American women in 1823: "They take care of everything pertaining to the domestic economy, for example, making candles, boiling soap, preparing starch, canning berries, fruit and cucumbers, baking, and spinning, sewing, and milking the cows."

American blacksmith, early 1800s woodcut

The Growth of Industry

During the colonial era, workers were in short supply. Americans learned to develop tools that made work easier and more efficient. American methods and inventions won the admiration of Europeans. One observer exclaimed:

❝The axe here [in America] . . . is a combination axe, wedge, and sledgehammer; what an accomplished woodchopper can do with this instrument! There are some among them who can chop and split five and one-half loads of wood a day, including stacking them.❞

SECTION RESOURCES

📂 Reproducible Masters
• Reproducible Lesson Plan 10–1
• Daily Lecture and Discussion Notes 10–1
• Guided Reading Activity 10–1
• Section Quiz 10–1
• Reteaching Activity 10–1
• Reading Essentials and Study Guide 10–1
• Enrichment Activity 10–1

📖 Transparencies
• Daily Focus Skills Transparency 10–1

Multimedia
📺 ABC News Interactive™ Historic America Electronic Field Trips
🎵 American Music: Hits Through History
💿 Interactive Tutor Self-Assessment CD-ROM
💿 ExamView® Pro Testmaker CD-ROM
💿 Presentation Plus! CD-ROM

People working in their homes or in workshops made cloth and most other goods. Using hand tools, they produced furniture, farm equipment, household items, and clothing.

In the mid-1700s, however, the way goods were made began to change. These changes appeared first in Great Britain. British inventors created machinery to perform some of the work involved in cloth making, such as spinning. The machines ran on waterpower, so British cloth makers built mills along rivers and installed the machines in these mills. People left their homes and farms to work in the mills and earn wages. The changes this system brought about were so great that this historic development is known as the Industrial Revolution.

The Industrial Revolution in New England

The Industrial Revolution began to take root in the United States around 1800, appearing first in New England—Massachusetts, Rhode Island, Connecticut, Vermont, and New Hampshire. New England's soil was poor, and farming was difficult. As a result, people were willing to leave their farms to find work elsewhere. Also, New England had many rushing rivers and streams. These provided the waterpower necessary to run the machinery in the new factories.

New England's geographic location also proved to be an advantage. It was close to other resources, including coal and iron from nearby Pennsylvania. New England also had many ports. Through these ports passed the cotton

2 TEACH

Daily Lecture and Discussion Notes 10–1

Copyright © by The McGraw-Hill Companies, Inc.

Daily Lecture and Discussion Notes

Chapter 10, Section 1

Did You Know? Eli Whitney, who invented the cotton gin, was not only an inventor. At different times in his life, he was a blacksmith, a nail maker, and the country's only maker of ladies' hatpins.

I.   The Growth of Industry (Pages 306–308)

　A. The Industrial Revolution began in the mid-1700s in Britain. It was a period during which machinery and technology changed how people worked and produced goods.

　B. The Industrial Revolution took hold in the United States in New England around 1800.

　　1. Rivers and streams provided waterpower to run machinery in factories.

　　2. New England was near needed resources, such as coal and iron from Pennsylvania.

Finding Changes Among the several umbrella terms that could characterize this section is the term *change*. Write the term on the chalkboard and have students brainstorm the changes discussed in the section. **L1,** ELL

TECHNOLOGY & History

Textile Mill Factory jobs were hazardous to people's health and safety. Some workers lost their hearing from the din of the machinery. Tiny particles of fiber filled the air people breathed, causing lung cancer and other respiratory diseases. The huge and powerful machines had no safety devices, so the workers had to be careful. If a worker made a mistake, he or she could have lost a hand or an arm.
Answer: waterpower

TECHNOLOGY & History

Textile Mill

The Lowell factory system was designed to bring work and workers together. A typical Lowell textile mill in 1830 housed 4,500 spindles, 120 power looms, and more than 200 employees under one roof. *What type of energy powered the mills?*

Gears

1 The first steps in textile production **clean** the raw cotton and turn loose cotton into crude yarn.

2 The **spinning** process transforms the yarn into thread.

3 At the **weaving** stage, power **looms** interlace the threads into coarse cloth or fabric.

4 Fabric is measured and batched for **dyeing**. Vegetable dyes were the earliest known dyes.

3 weaving looms

4 dyeing

2 spinning

1 clean

307

COOPERATIVE LEARNING ACTIVITY

Making a Flowchart Note that one innovation often creates a need for another. Have students do research as needed on the following six innovations and then create an illustrated flowchart explaining the relationships among them: flying shuttle, spinning jenny, water frame, spinning mule, power loom, cotton gin. Have students choose their own role in the project: researching, making the chart, drawing the illustrations, writing descriptive paragraphs. **L2,** ELL

The Lowell Girls The women who worked in the Lowell mills stayed in well-kept, supervised company boardinghouses. Women living in these company houses were not allowed to drink or play cards. They were required to be in bed by ten o'clock and to attend church on Sunday. The women were encouraged to read books, write letters, and listen to lectures. The Lowell girls received weekly wages of about $3.00, about half of which went for room and board. **Ask:** Why do you think there were rules at the boardinghouses? *(Answers may include that the women were young and away from their parents' guidance.)*

✓ Reading Check

Answer: because the machines used waterpower

History *and the* Humanities

🎵 American Music: Hits Through History, "Welcome Gospel Kindred"

---

shipped from Southern states to New England factories, as well as the finished cloth bound for markets throughout the nation.

Also necessary to strong industrial growth is an economic system that allows competition to flourish with a minimum of government interference. The economic system of the United States is called capitalism. Under capitalism, individuals put their capital, or money, into a business in hopes of making a profit.

Free enterprise is another term used to describe the American economy. In a system of free enterprise, people are free to buy, sell, and produce whatever they want. They can also work wherever they wish. The major elements of free enterprise are competition, profit, private property and economic freedom. Business owners have the freedom to produce the products that they think will be the most profitable. Buyers also compete to find the best products at the lowest prices.

New Technology

Workers, waterpower, location, and capital all played roles in New England's Industrial Revolution. Yet without the invention of new machines and technology—scientific discoveries that simplify work—the Industrial Revolution could not have taken place.

Inventions such as the spinning jenny and the water frame, which spun thread, and the power loom, which wove the thread into cloth, made it possible to perform many steps in making cloth by machine, saving time and money. Because these new machines ran on waterpower, most mills were built near rivers. In 1785, for the first time, a steam engine provided power for a cotton mill.

In 1793 **Eli Whitney** of Massachusetts invented the cotton gin, a simple machine that quickly and efficiently removed the seeds from the cotton fiber. The cotton gin enabled one worker to clean cotton as fast as 50 people working by hand.

In 1790 Congress passed a patent law to protect the rights of those who developed "useful and important inventions." A patent gives an inventor the sole legal right to the invention and

308   CHAPTER 10   Growth and Expansion

What Life Was Like...

The Lowell Girls

Cloth for manufactured goods such as shirts and sheets is produced at textile mills (cloth factories). The mills in Lowell, Massachusetts, drew about 80 percent of their workers from young women, many in their teens, known as the "Lowell girls."

its profits for a certain period of time. One of the first patents went to Jacob Perkins for a machine to make nails.

✓ **Reading Check** **Analyzing** Why were the first mills in Great Britain built near rivers?

New England Factories

The British tried to keep their new industrial technology a secret. They even passed laws prohibiting their machinery as well as their skilled mechanics from leaving the country. However, a few enterprising workers managed to slip away to the United States.

In Britain **Samuel Slater** had worked in a factory that used machines invented by Richard Arkwright for spinning cotton threads. Slater

---

DIFFERENTIATED INSTRUCTION

Gifted and Talented As American cities grew, thousands of people lived in close proximity to one another. Conflicts often arose between different groups. The causes of these problems were often differences in religion, social class, and political beliefs. Organize students into nine groups and have each group conduct research on one of these three causes of urban problems in the 1600s, 1700s, or 1800s. Have the groups stand together according to conflict and then according to time period. Each time they should discuss what their topics have in common. **L3**

Working Conditions

The young women who worked in Lowell's mills endured difficult working conditions. They put in long hours—from sunrise to sunset—for low wages. The volume of the factory machinery was earsplitting and the work was monotonous. The women usually performed one task over and over again.

Magazine

The Lowell Offering was a magazine written for and about the mill girls.

On the Job

Lucy Larcom started working in the mills when she was 11 years old. She later recalled her life at Waltham:

❝We did not call ourselves ladies. We did not forget that we were working girls, wearing aprons suitable to our work, and that there was some danger of our becoming drudges.❞

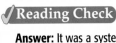

VIDEOCASSETTE
Historic America Electronic Field Trips

View **Chapter 4** to learn more about Lowell's mills.

✓ **Reading Check**

Answer: It was a system of bringing all of the steps in making a product together in one place to increase efficiency.

The War of 1812 and the Industrial Revolution Point out to students that the War of 1812 played an important role in the coming of the Industrial Revolution in the United States. Explain that the war kept Americans from buying British goods and that American industries had to increase their output to meet demand. After the war, British goods flowed into the United States at low prices, hurting the American companies. Congress responded with the Tariff of 1816, which protected American industries and allowed them to grow. Ask students to analyze the war's impact on economic change in relation to the other causes of the Industrial Revolution in the United States. Ask them which factors they think were most important in bringing about the Industrial Revolution. **L2**

---

memorized the design of Arkwright's machines and slipped out of Britain in 1789. Once in the United States, Slater took over the management of a cotton mill in Pawtucket, Rhode Island. There he duplicated Arkwright's machines. Using these machines the mill made cotton thread. Women working in their homes wove the thread into cloth. Slater's mill marked an important step in the Industrial Revolution in America.

In 1814 **Francis Cabot Lowell** opened a textile plant in Waltham, Massachusetts. The plan he implemented went several steps beyond Slater's mill. For the first time, all the stages of cloth making were performed under one roof. Lowell's mill launched the factory system, a system bringing manufacturing steps together in one place to increase efficiency. The factory system was a significant development in the way goods were made—and another important part of the Industrial Revolution.

Interchangeable Parts

The inventor Eli Whitney started the use of interchangeable parts. These were identical machine parts that could be quickly put together to make a complete product. Because all the parts were alike, they could be manufactured with less-skilled labor, and they made machine repair easier. Interchangeable parts opened the way for producing many different kinds of goods on a mass scale and for reducing the price of the goods.

✓ **Reading Check** **Describing** How did the factory system work?

CHAPTER 10   Growth and Expansion   **309**

INTERDISCIPLINARY CONNECTIONS ACTIVITY

Economics Pay for factory workers depended not on the job, but on the worker's age and gender. Lowell girls (among the best-paid women) made from $2.50 to $3.00 per week; men earned $4.00 for the same job. Note that despite modern legislation, women still struggle for equal pay. Have students research the current gender gap in earnings by locating and using primary and secondary sources. **L3**

Geography *Skills*

Answers:
1. New York, Pennsylvania, Virginia
2. Alabama

✓ Reading Check

Answer: In the Northeast produce was usually marketed locally on small farms. In the South cotton production took place on larger plantations.

3 ASSESS

Assign Section 1 Assessment as homework or as an in-class activity.

⊕ Have students use **Interactive Tutor Self-Assessment CD-ROM.**

L2

Section Quiz 10–1

L1

Reteaching Activity 10–1

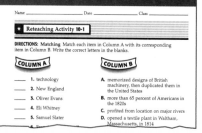

NATIONAL GEOGRAPHIC **Population of the United States, 1820**

Population by State in 1820
- ☐ Less than 100,000
- ☐ 100,000 – 500,000
- ☐ 500,000 – 1 million
- ☐ More than 1 million
- • Cities with 25,000 or more
- ☐ Territories with unknown population

0 400 miles
0 400 kilometers
Albers Conic Equal-Area projection

Population Growth, 1800–1840

Year	Population (in millions)
1800	5.3
1810	7.2
1820	9.6
1830	12.9
1840	17.1

Source: *Historical Statistics of the United States.*

Urban and Rural Population, 1820

Rural 92.8 %
Urban 7.2 %

Geography *Skills*

The tremendous growth in population helped to spur the growth of industry.
1. **Analyzing Information** What states had passed one million in population by 1820?
2. **Comparing** Which state had the larger population—Missouri or Alabama?

Agriculture Expands

Although many New Englanders went to work in factories, most Americans still lived and worked on farms. In the 1820s more than 65 percent of Americans were farmers.

In the Northeast, farms tended to be small, and the produce was usually marketed locally. In the South, cotton production increased dramatically. The demand for cotton had grown steadily with the development of the textile industries of New England and Europe. Southern plantation owners used enslaved workers to plant, tend, and pick the cotton. The cotton gin—which made it possible to clean the cotton faster and less expensively than by hand—encouraged the planters to raise larger crops. Between 1790 and 1820, cotton production soared from 3,000 to more than 300,000 bales a year.

In the West, agriculture also expanded. Southern farmers seeking new land moved west to plant cotton. Western farmers north of the Ohio River concentrated on raising pork and cash crops such as corn and wheat.

✓ Reading Check **Describing** How was the Northeast different from the South in what it produced?

Economic Independence

Most new industries were financed by small investors—merchants, shopkeepers, and farmers. These people invested some of their

310   CHAPTER 10   Growth and Expansion

Reading Strategy   READING THE TEXT

Identifying Cause and Effect The cause-and-effect structure is used to explore the reasons for something happening and to examine the results of previous events. Whitney's cotton gin (and others like it) made it profitable to grow more cotton, and production increased dramatically. While some planters did grow rich, social and economic problems resulted from the cotton boom. First, slavery, which had been declining because of economic problems in the South, rebounded. Second, reliance on cotton meant a lack of economic diversity for the region. Have students think about the cause-and-effect relationships surrounding the cotton boom. Then ask students to identify at least one possible effect that resulted from each problem. **L2**

money in the hope of earning profits if the new businesses succeeded. Low taxes, few government regulations, and competition encouraged people to invest in new industries.

Large businesses called **corporations** began to develop rapidly in the 1830s, when some legal obstacles to their formation were removed. The rise of these new corporations made it easier to sell **stock**—shares of ownership in a company—to finance improvement and development.

The charter of the First Bank of the United States had expired in 1811. In 1816 Congress chartered the **Second Bank of the United States,** also chartered for 20 years. The Bank had the power to make large loans to businesses. State banks and frontier people criticized the Bank on the grounds that it was a monopoly used by the rich and powerful for their own gain. Those who believed in strict interpretation of the Constitution also criticized it because they believed Congress did not have the power to charter such a bank.

Cities Come of Age

The growth of factories and trade spurred the growth of towns and cities. The new industrial towns grew quickest. Many developed along rivers and streams to take advantage of the waterpower. Older cities like New York, Boston, and Baltimore also grew as centers of commerce and trade. In the West, towns like Pittsburgh, Cincinnati, and Louisville profited from their locations on major rivers. As farmers in the West shipped more and more of their products by water, these towns grew rapidly.

Cities and towns looked quite different from modern urban areas. Buildings were made of wood or brick. Streets and sidewalks were unpaved, and barnyard animals often roamed freely. There were no sewers to carry waste and dirty water away, so the danger of diseases such as cholera and yellow fever was very real. In 1793, for example, a yellow fever epidemic in Philadelphia killed thousands of people.

Fire posed another threat to cities. Sparks from a fireplace or chimney could easily ignite a wooden building and spread to others. Few towns or cities had organized fire companies, and fires could be disastrous.

Cities and towns of the period also had advantages, however. Some people left farming because cities and towns offered a variety of jobs and steady wages. As cities grew they added libraries, museums, and shops that were unavailable in the countryside. For many, the jobs and attractions of city life outweighed any of the dangers.

✓ **Reading Check** **Analyzing** Why did cities such as Pittsburgh and Louisville grow?

✓**Reading Check**

Answer: They grew because farmers in the West increased the amount of product they shipped by water.

L1, ELL

Reading Essentials and Study Guide 10–1

L3

Enrichment Activity 10–1

4 CLOSE

Ask students if they would have chosen to stay on the family farm or move to a city if they had lived in the early 1800s. Ask them to explain why or why not.

SECTION 1 ASSESSMENT

Checking for Understanding

1. **Key Terms** Use each of these terms in a sentence that will help explain its meaning: Industrial Revolution, capital, technology, cotton gin, patent, factory system, interchangeable parts.

2. **Reviewing Facts** Describe the reasons New England was ideal for the development of factories.

Reviewing Themes

3. **Economic Factors** How did the cotton gin affect cotton production?

Critical Thinking

4. **Categorizing Information** Re-create the diagram below and describe the characteristics and benefits of the free enterprise system.

Free enterprise system

5. **Determining Cause and Effect** Was new technology necessary for the Industrial Revolution? Explain.

Analyzing Visuals

6. **Geography Skills** Study the map and the graphs on page 310. What do the cities shown on the map have in common? Which state had the larger population in 1820—Georgia or Ohio?

Interdisciplinary Activity

Expository Writing Study the map and graphs on page 310. Create a quiz for your classmates based on the information presented. Trade quizzes with a classmate and answer those questions.

SECTION 1 ASSESSMENT ANSWERS

1. Student work should reflect correct use of terms.

2. Poor soil caused people to leave their farms to find work; rivers provided waterpower to run machinery; ports for passage; proximity to resources

3. It made cleaning quicker and more efficient.

4. Students may note the benefits of competition: buyers compete to find products at the lowest prices; profit: owners produce profitable products; private property: people can work wherever they want; economic freedom: people can buy, sell, and produce whatever they want.

5. Yes; without technology, production might have continued, on a small scale.

6. They are all coastal cities; Ohio

Interdisciplinary Activity Quizzes should reflect information about canals or states.

TEACH

Analyzing Primary Sources

Have students read Sagoyewatha's speech on page 312. **Ask:** What two things does Sagoyewatha say the whites have done to his people? *(He says whites took their land and are now trying to force them to accept white religion.)* **Ask:** Why does Sagoyewatha think the whites are hypocritical about religion? *(He says the whites tell Native Americans there is just one way to worship God, but the whites have many different religions.)* **Ask:** What is Sagoyewatha's tone in his speech? *(Students should conclude that Sagoyewatha is angry and critical of the actions of whites, but his tone is respectful and controlled. He does not show open hostility, even calling the whites, "Brothers.")*

Have students write a short essay in which they discuss something they perceive to be an injustice, explaining why they think as they do. The subject can be something personal, or a local or national issue. Encourage students to share and discuss in class what they have written. **L1**

Visit the **TIME** Web site at www.time.com for up-to-date news, weekly magazine articles, editorials, online polls, and an archive of past magazine and Web articles.

312

What were people's lives like in the past?

What—and who—were people talking about? What did they eat? What did they do for fun? These two pages will give you some clues to everyday life in the U.S. as you step back in time with TIME Notebook.

Profile

SAGOYEWATHA *is the great Iroquois leader some call Red Jacket. Why? Because he fought with the British in the Revolutionary War. Sagoyewatha means "He Causes Them to Be Awake." Below is part of a speech Sagoyewatha delivered in 1805 to a group of religious leaders from Boston:*

"BROTHERS, OUR (NATIVE AMERICAN) SEATS were once large and yours (colonists) were small. You have now become a great people, and we have scarcely a place left to spread our blankets. You have got our country but are not satisfied; you want to force your religion upon us....

Brothers, continue to listen. You say there is but one way to worship and serve the Great Spirit. If there is but one religion, why do you white people differ so much about it?...

Brothers, we...also have a religion which was given to our forefathers and has been handed down to us, their children...."

Sagoyewatha

VERBATIM

WHAT PEOPLE ARE SAYING

❝We are one.❞
❝Mind your business.❞
FIRST OFFICIAL U.S. COIN,
sayings are on the front and back of the coin minted in 1787

❝I die hard, but I am not afraid to go.❞
GEORGE WASHINGTON,
on his deathbed in 1799

❝My mother and myself begged Mr. Carter not to sell this child out of Fredg [*plantation*], he gave us his word and honor that he would not, but as soon as we left him, he sold the child.❞
JAMES CARTER,
African American slave of Landon Carter, writing around 1790 about his sister, whom he never saw again

❝May the Lord bless King George, convert him, and take him to heaven, as we want no more of him.❞
REVEREND JOHN GRUBER,
to his Baltimore congregation during the War of 1812

HULTON GETTY

TIME INC. PICTURE COLLECTION

1790s WORD PLAY

Ahoy There!

BETTMANN/CORBIS

The U.S.S. Constitution, the world's largest frigate, or warship, was launched in 1797 with a crew of 450 and 54 cannons. Want to join the crew? First, you must prove you can understand a sailor's vocabulary. Match each word or phrase in the first column with its original meaning.

1. Keel over
2. Try a new tack
3. Let the cat out of the bag
4. Mind your p's and q's
5. Shipshape

a. Sailors who do wrong are disciplined with a cat-o'-nine-tails whip that's kept in a red sack

b. Putting a ship in for repair

c. Bartenders keep track of what sailors drink and owe by marking numbers under "pints" and "quarts"

d. The course or direction boats take into the wind

e. Good condition

answers: 1. b; 2. d; 3. a; 4. c; 5. e

312

EXTENDING THE CONTENT

The Iroquois Sagoyewatha was a chief of the Seneca, one of the five Native American nations that formed the Iroquois Confederacy, or Iroquois League. By the early 1600s, five once-warring nations in what is now northern New York State had formed a union that offered mutual support, but allowed each group to claim a certain portion of their vast territory. The Mohawk were in the east, overlooking the present Mohawk River Valley. The Seneca were in the west, on lands that reached beyond the Genesee River. The Oneida, Onondaga, and Cayuga occupied lands in between. In about 1722 the Tuscorora joined the confederation, which then became known as the Six Nations.

NATIVE AMERICAN LIFE

Sports Story

GEORGE CATLIN *is a white man with a strong interest in Native American life. This lawyer has made a name for himself as an artist, painting portraits of Native American leaders, families, and everyday Western life. Here he paints with words, telling us about a game (one the French call lacrosse) played by Choctaw men:*

"EACH PARTY (TEAM) HAD THEIR GOAL MADE WITH TWO UPRIGHT POSTS, about 25 feet high and six feet apart, set firm in the ground, with a pole across at the top. These goals were about 40 to 50 rods (660–825 feet) apart. At a point just halfway between was another small stake, driven down, where the ball was to be thrown up at the firing of a gun, to be struggled for by the players … who were some 600 or 700 in numbers, and were (trying) to catch the ball in their sticks, and throw it home and between their respective stakes. …For each time that the ball was passed between the stakes of either party, one was counted for their game…until the successful party arrived to 100, which was the limit of the game, and accomplished at an hour's sun."

NATIONAL GALLERY OF ART

RIGHT: George Catlin *painted this picture of a 15-year-old Native American girl. Her name, Ka-te-qua, means "female eagle."*

BELOW: *Painting by* **George Catlin** *of* **Choctaw athletes** *playing their version of lacrosse.*

NUMBERS

U.S. AT THE TIME

30 **Number of treaties that took away Native American land or moved their borders. The treaties were between the U.S. and the Creeks, Choctaws, and Chickasaws between 1789 and 1825**

$158 million
The price the U.S. spent to fight the War of 1812

First Elizabeth Seton founds the Sisters of Charity, a Roman Catholic order, in 1809

First Mary Kies becomes the first woman to receive a U.S. patent in 1809 for a method of weaving straw with silk

---

$3,820.33 Amount paid to Paul Revere for providing the U.S.S. *Constitution* with copper parts and a ship's bell in 1797

---

45 feet Length of the dinosaur dug up by Lewis and Clark on their 1804 expedition

---

NY PUBLIC LIBRARY/TIME INC. PICTURE COLLECTION

313

Have students read the description of lacrosse written by George Catlin. Then challenge students to write a similar short description of the rules of any game or sport, as if explaining it to someone who had never seen it played before. Have students who write about the same game or sport compare and contrast their descriptions.

Did you know?

The 200-year old U.S.S. *Constitution*–the oldest commissioned warship in existence today–is often called "Old Ironsides." The name stuck after a sea battle with a British ship, *Guerrière,* during the War of 1812. When cannonballs fired at the *Constitution* seemed to just bounce off its sides (its tough hull was 63 cm [25 inches] thick at the waterline), a British sailor was supposed to have said in astonishment, "Her sides are made of iron!"

CLOSE

Ask students to brainstorm the names of famous Native American leaders other than Sagoyewatha (such as Geronimo, Seattle, Pontiac, and Crazy Horse). As students call out the names, have the class give one reason for that leader's fame.

COOPERATIVE LEARNING ACTIVITY

Examining Coins The first official United States coin had "We are one," on one side, and "Mind your business," on the other. What messages do American coins carry today? Have students look at pennies, nickels, dimes, quarters, and coin dollars and list the mottos or slogans on each. Lead a discussion of the meaning of the words and mottos. *(Front of all coins: "Liberty," which refers to a belief in freedom, and "In God We Trust," the national motto that affirms a belief in divine guidance. Back of all coins: "e pluribus unum," a Latin phrase meaning "out of many, one" which refers to the creation of the United States from the original thirteen colonies.)* 📖 **L2**

1 FOCUS

Section Overview

This section describes advances in transportation in the first part of the nineteenth century and how they aided westward expansion.

BELLRINGER
Skillbuilder Activity

Project transparency and have students answer the question.

Daily Focus Skills Transparency 10–2

Reading Preview

Answers to Graphic: National Road: connected areas of the Midwest to the East; John Fitch: helped develop the steamboat; Erie Canal: linked New York City with the Great Lakes region and inspired the building of other canals; Students should note that each led to improved transportation and increased settlement.

Preteaching Vocabulary

Ask students which three of the **Key Terms** have to do with transportation. *(turnpike, canal, lock)*

SECTION 2 Westward Bound

Guide to Reading

Main Idea

The huge amount of territory added to the United States during the early 1800s gave the country a large store of natural resources and provided land for more settlers.

Key Terms

census, turnpike, canal, lock

Reading Strategy

Taking Notes As you read the section, re-create the diagram below and describe why each was important to the nation's growth and development.

	Significance
National Road	
John Fitch	
Erie Canal	

Read to Learn

- how land and water transportation improved in the early 1800s.
- how settlements in the West affected the nation's economy and politics.

Section Theme

Science and Technology Expansion of transportation systems helped settlement spread westward.

Preview of Events

♦1800	♦1810	♦1820	♦1830

1806
Congress approves funds for national road

1807
Fulton's *Clermont* steams to Albany

1820
U.S. population stands at 9.6 million

1825
Erie Canal is completed

Pioneer homestead, Smoky Mountains

★★★★★★★★★★★
AN
American Story

During the 1800s, settlers poured into the frontier west of the Appalachians. The typical frontier family moved from place to place as the line of settlement pushed ever westward. Their home often consisted of a three-sided shack or a log cabin with a dirt floor and no windows or door. A pile of leaves in the loft of the cabin often served as a bed. Loneliness, poverty, and an almost primitive lifestyle were daily companions to many frontier people.

Moving West

The first census—the official count of a population—of the United States in 1790 revealed a population of nearly four million. Most of the Americans counted lived east of the Appalachian Mountains and within a few hundred miles of the Atlantic coast.

Within a few decades this changed. The number of settlers heading west increased by leaps and bounds. In 1811 a Pennsylvania resident reported seeing 236 wagons filled with people and their possessions on the road to Pittsburgh. A man in Newburgh, New York, counted 60 wagons rolling by in a single day. In 1820, just 30 years after the first census, the population of the

---

SECTION RESOURCES

📁 **Reproducible Masters**
- Reproducible Lesson Plan 10–2
- Daily Lecture and Discussion Notes 10–2
- Guided Reading Activity 10–2
- Section Quiz 10–2
- Reteaching Activity 10–2
- Reading Essentials and Study Guide 10–2
- Enrichment Activity 10–2

📑 **Transparencies**
- Daily Focus Skills Transparency 10–2

Multimedia
- ⓘ Interactive Tutor Self-Assessment CD-ROM
- ⓘ ExamView® Pro Testmaker CD-ROM
- ⓘ Presentation Plus! CD-ROM

United States had more than doubled, to about 10 million people, with nearly 2 million living west of the Appalachians.

Traveling west was not easy in the late 1790s and early 1800s. The 363-mile trip from **New York City** to **Buffalo** could take as long as three weeks. A pioneer family heading west with a wagonload of household goods faced hardship and danger along the way.

Roads and Turnpikes

The nation needed good inland roads for travel and for the shipment of goods. Private companies built many turnpikes, or toll roads. The fees travelers paid to use those roads helped to pay for construction. Many of the roads had a base of crushed stone. In areas where the land was often muddy, companies built "corduroy roads," consisting of logs laid side by side, like the ridges of corduroy cloth. 📖 *(See page 599 of the Primary Sources Library for an account of a typical stagecoach journey.)*

When Ohio joined the Union in 1803, the new state asked the federal government to build a road to connect it with the East. In 1806 Congress approved funds for a **National Road** to the West

and five years later agreed on the route. Because work on the road stopped during the War of 1812, the first section, from Maryland to western Virginia, did not open until 1818. In later years the National Road reached Ohio and continued on to Vandalia, Illinois. Congress viewed the National Road as a military necessity, but it did not undertake other road-building projects.

★ Geography

River Travel

River travel had definite advantages over wagon and horse travel. It was far more comfortable than travel over the bumpy roads, and pioneers could load all their goods on river barges—if they were heading downstream in the direction of the current.

River travel had two problems, however. The first related to the geography of the eastern United States. Most major rivers in the region flowed in a north-south direction, not east to west, where most people and goods were headed. Second, traveling upstream by barge against the current was extremely difficult and slow.

People In History

Robert Fulton 1765–1815

Robert Fulton grew up in Lancaster, Pennsylvania. At an early age he created his own lead pencils and rockets. While living in Europe in the late 1790s, Fulton designed and built a submarine called the *Nautilus* to be used in France's war against Britain. Submarine warfare became common later.

Fulton returned to the United States and developed a steamboat engine that was more powerful and provided a smoother ride than previous engines. On August 17, 1807, Fulton's *Clermont* made its first successful run. By demonstrating the usefulness of two-way river travel, Fulton launched the steamboat

era. Although his engine was considered a great success, trouble followed after Fulton received a monopoly and government money. Eventually, the collapse of the monopoly led to lower prices, growth of competition, and introduction of new technology to improve the steamboat.

CHAPTER 10   Growth and Expansion   **315**

Daily Lecture and Discussion Notes 10–2

Copyright © by The McGraw-Hill Companies, Inc.

Daily Lecture and Discussion Notes
Chapter 10, Section 2

Did You Know ? The first turnpike, the Lancaster Turnpike, was built in 1793. The word *turnpike* comes from the Middle English of the 1500s. A turnpike was a revolving frame bearing spikes and serving as a barrier. Turnpikes today use toll booths as barriers.

I.   Moving West *(Pages 314–317)*

   A. In 1790 most of the nearly 4 million people of the United States lived east of the Appalachian Mountains and near the Atlantic coast. In 1820 the population had more than doubled to about 10 million with almost 2 million living west of the Appalachian Mountains.

   B. Travel west was difficult. A pioneer family faced many hardships along the way.

   C. Good inland roads were needed. Private companies built turnpikes, or toll roads. In

Making Graphic Organizers

After students have read the section, work with them to make a graphic organizer for each major part. The first graphic organizer, for example, might consist of a central oval called "land travel." Surrounding ovals might consist of "turnpikes," "crushed stone," and so on. **L1, ELL**

People In History

Designing steamboats was Robert Fulton's second career. He began as an artist who painted miniature portraits of people such as Benjamin Franklin. After several years Fulton abandoned the fine arts to work in what he called the "useful arts." Fulton worked on canals, then on designing experimental submarines, called "plunging boats." Have students discuss how the steamboat aided river travel.

COOPERATIVE LEARNING ACTIVITY

Impact on the Environment Have students work together in small groups to learn about the environmental impact of westward settlement. Have them use library sources to discover what different immigrant groups did as they moved west during the nineteenth century. How did they grow food? How did they use the land to their advantage? In what kind of houses did they live? Allow each member of the group to research their favorite aspect of the subject. Have each group give a presentation on one particular immigrant group and how it interacted with the environment in the nineteenth century. **L2**

L1, ELL

Guided Reading Activity 10–2

★ Guided Reading Activity 10-2

DIRECTIONS: Filling in the Blanks Use your textbook to fill in the blanks using the words in the box. Use another sheet of paper if necessary.

Clermont	New York City	north-south	Robert Fulton
mules or horses	Erie Canal	4 million	five
the Atlantic coast	National Road	10 million	four
De Witt Clinton	the great rivers	steamboats	turnpikes

Moving West

The 1790 census of the United States showed a population of nearly (1) _____. Most Americans lived within a few hundred miles of (2) _____. By 1820 the population of the United States had increased to about (3) _____ people. The 363-mile trip from (4) _____ to Buffalo took a pioneer family about three weeks by wagon. Private companies built (5) _____, which charged fees to offset their costs. In 1806 Congress approved funds for a (6) _____ to the West. Although river travel was more comfortable, rivers allowed travel in only a (7) _____ direction. In 1802 Robert Livingston hired (8) _____ to develop a more powerful steamboat. In 1807 the (9) _____ made the 150-mile trip from New York City to Albany in only 32 hours.

Canals

Led by (10) _____, New York officials planned to link New York City with the Great Lakes region. Thousands of laborers worked on the construction of the 363-mile (11) _____. At first this waterway did not allow the passage of (12) _____. Instead, teams of (13) _____ hauled the boats and barges.

Western Settlement

Between 1791 and 1803, (14) _____ new states were admitted to the Union. Between 1816 and 1821, (15) _____ new states were created. Pioneers tended to settle in communities along (16) _____ with others from their home communities.

Why It Matters

Nearly $7 million in federal funds was spent on the National Road, which was also called the Cumberland Road. It was eventually replaced in the nineteenth century by railroad lines. In the twentieth century, U.S. Highway 40 was built, largely following the path of the National Road. There are now plans to restore a part of the National Road to its early nineteenth-century condition, as a historical landmark. **Ask: How did the National Road help with westward expansion?** *(It provided a more convenient route for goods and people to move west.)*

Steam engines were already being used in the 1780s and 1790s to power boats in quiet waters. Inventor James Rumsey equipped a small boat on the Potomac River with a steam engine. John Fitch, another inventor, built a steamboat that navigated the Delaware River. Neither boat, however, had enough power to withstand the strong currents and winds found in large rivers or open bodies of water.

In 1802 Robert Livingston, a political and business leader, hired **Robert Fulton** to develop a steamboat with a powerful engine. Livingston wanted the steamboat to carry cargo and passengers up the **Hudson River** from New York City to **Albany.**

In 1807 Fulton had his steamboat, the *Clermont,* ready for a trial. Powered by a newly designed engine, the *Clermont* made the 150-mile trip from New York to Albany in the unheard-of time of 32 hours. Using only sails, the trip would have taken four days.

About 140-feet long and 14-feet wide, the *Clermont* offered great comforts to its passengers. They could sit or stroll about on deck, and at

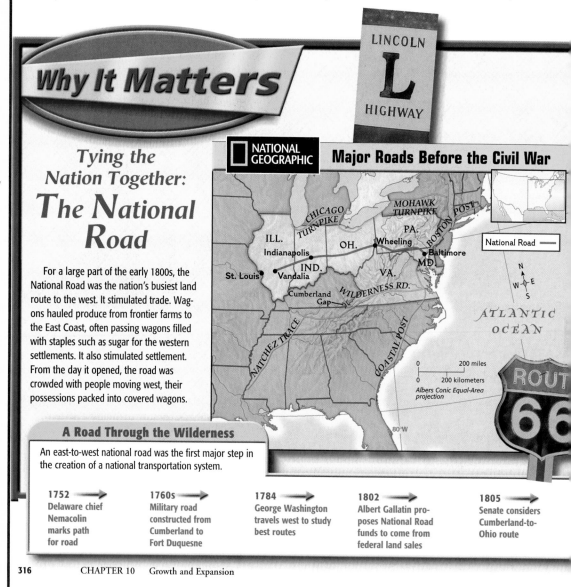

Why It Matters

Tying the Nation Together: The National Road

For a large part of the early 1800s, the National Road was the nation's busiest land route to the west. It stimulated trade. Wagons hauled produce from frontier farms to the East Coast, often passing wagons filled with staples such as sugar for the western settlements. It also stimulated settlement. From the day it opened, the road was crowded with people moving west, their possessions packed into covered wagons.

NATIONAL GEOGRAPHIC — **Major Roads Before the Civil War**

National Road ———

200 miles
200 kilometers
Albers Conic Equal-Area projection

A Road Through the Wilderness

An east-to-west national road was the first major step in the creation of a national transportation system.

1752 →	1760s →	1784 →	1802 →	1805 →
Delaware chief Nemacolin marks path for road	Military road constructed from Cumberland to Fort Duquesne	George Washington travels west to study best routes	Albert Gallatin proposes National Road funds to come from federal land sales	Senate considers Cumberland-to-Ohio route

---

DIFFERENTIATED INSTRUCTION

Reading Support Have students make labeled diagrams showing how canal locks work. Students should be able to explain their diagrams orally or in writing. Explanations should include the reason that locks are necessary. Students should not have trouble finding diagrams to use for reference; the subject is covered in encyclopedias. Challenge students to find the name of a canal built between 1859 and 1869 that has no locks. *(the Suez Canal)* **L2**

📁 Refer to *Inclusion for the Middle School Social Studies Classroom Strategies and Activities* in the TCR.

night they could relax in the sleeping compartments below deck. The engine was noisy, but its power provided a fairly smooth ride.

Steamboats ushered in a new age in river travel. They greatly improved the transport of goods and passengers along major inland rivers. Shipping goods became cheaper and faster. Steamboats also contributed to the growth of river cities like Cincinnati and St. Louis.

✓ **Reading Check** **Comparing** What advantages did steamboat travel have over wagon and horse travel?

Canals

Although steamboats represented a great improvement in transportation, their routes depended on the existing river system. Steamboats could not effectively tie the eastern and western parts of the country together.

In New York, business and government officials led by De Witt Clinton came up with a plan to link New York City with the Great Lakes

✓ **Reading Check**

Answer: It was more comfortable than traveling on bumpy roads, and pioneers could load all their belongings onto steamboats.

What?Who?Where?When?

Federal Road Building Another federal road project was completed much later than the National Road. In the 1950s truckers asked Congress for modern high-speed highways. Increased car and truck use on such highways would benefit the construction, oil, and auto industries. To justify financing the interstate highway system with federal funds, Congress decided that interstates were necessary for defense.

Did you know?

In 1815, goods could be sent by land route from Cincinnati to New York City in 52 days. By the 1840s, after the canal-building boom, goods could be sent from Cincinnati to New York City, using an all-water route that included the Erie Canal, in just 18–20 days.

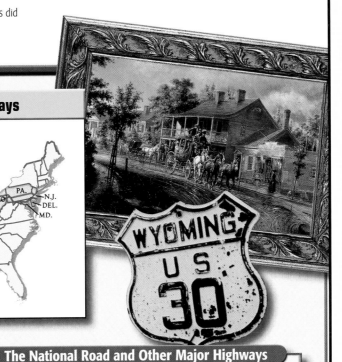

NATIONAL GEOGRAPHIC
American Highways

- Route 40
- Lincoln Highway
- Route 66

By 1926, the long-distance motorist could use transcontinental highways for car travel.

The National Road and Other Major Highways

	Official Status	From/To	Length in miles/km
National Road	1806	Cumberland, Md./Vandalia, Ill.	780/1,255
Lincoln Highway*	1913	New York City/San Francisco	3,390/5,456
Route 40	1926	Atlantic City, N.J./San Francisco	3,020/4,860
Route 66	1926	Chicago/Santa Monica, Calif.	2,450/3,943

*first transcontinental road for automobiles

1811 → Construction begins at Cumberland	1818 → Cumberland-to-Wheeling section completed	1825 → Construction in Ohio begins	1833 → Route to Columbus, Ohio, completed	1850 → National Road stops at Vandalia

CHAPTER 10   Growth and Expansion   **317**

INTERDISCIPLINARY CONNECTIONS ACTIVITY

Geography Have students break into groups of three to report on the Erie Canal. Have each group create a map of New York State that shows the Hudson River and the route of the Erie Canal between Albany and Buffalo. Maps should include major towns and cities along the canal. Have students choose one city along the route and research the way the canal affected the economy and development of that city. Students in each group can divide the project tasks (research, map drawing, and writing a report) according to their skills. **L2, ELL**

Geography *Skills*

Answers:
1. Lake Erie and the Hudson River
2. 360

✓ Reading Check

Answer: Albany and Buffalo

3 ASSESS

Assign Section 2 Assessment as homework or as an in-class activity.

🔘 Have students use **Interactive Tutor Self-Assessment CD-ROM.**

L2

Section Quiz 10–2

NATIONAL GEOGRAPHIC   Canals, 1820–1860

Canal Mileage, 1850

NY and PA, 1,757 miles

OH, 792 miles
IN, 214 miles
IL, 100 miles
Other states, 800 miles

Geography *Skills*

In the early 1800s, Americans shipped many goods along canals, which helped to unite the country.
1. **Location** What two bodies of water did the Erie Canal connect?
2. **Analyzing Information** About how many miles long was the Erie Canal?

---

region. They would build a canal—an artificial waterway—across New York State, connecting Albany on the Hudson River with Buffalo on **Lake Erie.**

Building the Erie Canal

Thousands of laborers, many of them Irish immigrants, worked on the construction of the 363-mile **Erie Canal.** Along the canal they built a series of locks—separate compartments where water levels were raised or lowered. Locks provided a way to raise and lower boats at places where canal levels changed.

After more than two years of digging, the Erie Canal opened on October 26, 1825. Clinton boarded a barge in Buffalo and journeyed on the canal to Albany. From there, he headed down the Hudson River to New York City. As crowds cheered, the officials poured water from Lake Erie into the Atlantic. The East and Midwest were joined.

In its early years, the canal did not allow steamboats because their powerful engines could

damage the earthen embankments along the canal. Instead, teams of mules or horses hauled the boats and barges. A two-horse team pulled a 100-ton barge about 24 miles in one day—astonishingly fast compared to travel by wagon. In the 1840s the canal banks were reinforced to accommodate steam tugboats pulling barges.

The success of the Erie Canal led to an explosion in canal building. By 1850 the United States had more than 3,600 miles of canals. Canals lowered the cost of shipping goods. They brought prosperity to the towns along their routes. Perhaps most important, they helped unite the growing country.

✓ Reading Check   **Identifying** What two cities did the Erie Canal connect?

318   CHAPTER 10   Growth and Expansion

Reading Strategy   READING THE TEXT

Making Inferences When students make inferences, they use their reason and their experience to take educated guesses. Review the fact that people from the same community or region tended to settle in certain areas. For example, mainly New Englanders settled western New York State, and primarily people from Kentucky and Tennessee moved into frontier Indiana. Ask students to infer why settlers from certain regions clustered together in the same area. (*Possible answers: they traveled to areas that were fairly nearby; they chose land and soil that was similar to what they were used to; after some settlers had become established, later groups were attracted to areas with large numbers of people from back home.*) **L2**

Western Settlement

Americans moved westward in waves. The first wave began before the 1790s and led to the admission of four new states between 1791 and 1803—Vermont, Kentucky, Tennessee, and Ohio. A second wave of westward growth began between 1816 and 1821. Five new western states were created—Indiana, Illinois, Mississippi, Alabama, and Missouri.

The new states reflected the dramatic growth of the region west of the Appalachians. Ohio, for example, had only 45,000 settlers in 1800. By 1820 it had 581,000.

Pioneer families tended to settle in communities along the great rivers, such as the Ohio and the Mississippi, so that they could ship their crops to market. The expansion of canals, which criss-crossed the land in the 1820s and 1830s, allowed people to live farther away from the rivers.

People also tended to settle with others from their home communities. Indiana, for example, was settled mainly by people from Kentucky and Tennessee, while Michigan's pioneers came mostly from New England.

Western families often gathered together for social events. Men took part in sports such as wrestling. Women met for quilting and sewing parties. Both men and women participated in cornhuskings—gatherings where farm families shared the work of stripping the husks from ears of corn.

Life in the West did not include the conveniences of Eastern town life, but the pioneers had not come west to be pampered. They wanted to make a new life for themselves and their families. America's population continued to spread westward in the years ahead.

Legendary Heroes

Paul Bunyan and John Henry Legends have grown around mythical figures like Paul Bunyan. Imaginary stories were passed along about how this giant lumberjack dug the Mississippi River and performed other incredible feats. Yet some of the famous characters in American folklore were real people. There was a John Henry who worked on the railroads. He was an African American renowned for his strength and skill in driving the steel drills into solid rock. He is best remembered for something that probably never happened. According to legend, John Henry defeated a steel-driving machine, but the effort killed him.

✓ **Reading Check** **Identifying** What states were formed between 1791 and 1803?

SECTION 2 ASSESSMENT

Checking for Understanding

1. **Key Terms** Use the following terms to write a short newspaper article about the opening of the Erie Canal: turnpike, canal, lock.

2. **Reviewing Facts** Describe the improvements for transportation in the westward expansion during the early 1800s.

Reviewing Themes

3. **Science and Technology** How did steam-powered boats improve river travel?

Critical Thinking

4. **Drawing Conclusions** How did better transportation affect westward expansion?

5. **Comparing** What forms of communication and transportation linked East to West in the early 1800s? What links exist today? Re-create the diagram below and compare the links.

Links	
Early 1800s	Today

Analyzing Visuals

6. **Geography Skills** Study the information on the National Road on pages 316 and 317. When did construction of the National Road begin? To what city did it extend? How long was the National Road?

Interdisciplinary Activity

Geography Create a chart that lists the major means of transportation that helped the United States grow. Include the advantages and disadvantages of each type of transportation.

✓ **Reading Check**

Answer: Vermont, Kentucky, Tennessee, and Ohio

L1

Reteaching Activity 10–2

★ Reteaching Activity **10-2**

DIRECTIONS: Sequencing Events For each section below, number the events in the order in which they occurred.

SECTION I

___ **A.** The *Clermont* makes the trip up the Hudson River from New York City to Albany in only 32 hours.

___ **B.** Congress approves funds for a National Road.

___ **C.** Wagon travel from New York City to Buffalo takes as long as three weeks.

___ **D.** Thousands of laborers work on the construction of the Erie Canal.

___ **E.** Private companies build...

L1, ELL

Reading Essentials and Study Guide 10–2

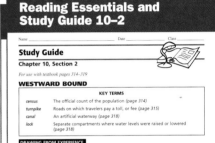

Study Guide
Chapter 10, Section 2
For use with textbook pages 314–319

WESTWARD BOUND

KEY TERMS	
census	The official count of the population *(page 314)*
turnpike	Roads on which travelers pay a toll, or fee *(page 315)*
canal	An artificial waterway *(page 318)*
lock	Separate compartments where water levels were raised or lowered *(page 318)*

DRAWING FROM EXPERIENCE

What is the farthest you have ever traveled? What kind of transportation did you use

L3

Enrichment Activity 10–2

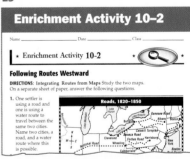

★ Enrichment Activity 10-2

Following Routes Westward

DIRECTIONS: Integrating Routes from Maps Study the two maps. On a separate sheet of paper, answer the following questions.

1. One settler is using a road and one is using a water route to travel between the same two cities. Name two cities, a road, and a water route where this is possible.

Roads, 1820–1850

4 CLOSE

Ask students to explain why it could be said that Fulton "reversed the rivers."

SECTION 2 ASSESSMENT ANSWERS

1. Student work should reflect correct use of terms.

2. Steamboats and canals made transportation on inland waterways easier; the Erie Canal shipped goods between the East Coast and the Great Lakes region; the National Road became a new land route between the East and the Midwest.

3. Steamboats could withstand currents and winds to travel more quickly on rivers.

4. It shortened the travel time and made travel more comfortable, which made western travel more attractive.

5. Early 1800s: roads, canals, steamboats and barges, wagons, horseback; Today: roads, motor vehicles, trains, canals, boats, airplanes

6. 1811; Vandalia, Illinois; 780 miles

Interdisciplinary Activity Charts should include different means of transportation and advantages and disadvantages.

319

TEACH

Reading a Diagram This skill teaches students what to look for when interpreting a diagram. After they have answered the questions in **Practicing the Skill,** challenge students to think of another question that could be asked about the diagram. *(Possible responses: What was the Clermont's width and length? Who made the Clermont's boiler? What was the function of the boiler?)*

Additional Practice
L2

Chapter Skills Activity 10

GLENCOE
TECHNOLOGY

 CD-ROM
Glencoe Skillbuilder Interactive Workbook CD-ROM, Level 1

This interactive CD-ROM reinforces student mastery of essential social studies skills.

Social Studies
SKILLBUILDER

Reading a Diagram

Why Learn This Skill?

Suppose you buy a new bicycle and discover that you must assemble the parts before you can ride it. A *diagram,* or a drawing that shows how the parts fit together, would make this job much easier.

Learning the Skill

To read a diagram, follow these steps:
- Read the title to find out what the diagram shows.
- Read all labels carefully to clearly determine their meanings.
- Read the legend and identify symbols and colors used in the diagram.
- Look for numbers indicating a sequence of steps, or arrows showing movement.

Practicing the Skill

Analyze the diagram of the Clermont, *then answer the following questions.*

❶ What type of energy was used to power this ship?

❷ What was the purpose of the paddle wheels?

Applying the Skill
Making a Diagram Draw a diagram showing either how to make macaroni and cheese or how to tie a pair of shoes. Label your diagram.

 Glencoe's **Skillbuilder Interactive Workbook CD-ROM, Level 1,** provides instruction and practice in key social studies skills.

The *Clermont* Steamboat

On August 17, 1807, the *Clermont* steamed up the Hudson River from New York City on its way to Albany, New York. The trip took only 32 hours—a commercial success!

The *Clermont* was about 140 feet (43 m) long and 14 feet (4.3 m) wide.

The steam is released from the boiler as pressurized energy, which powered the **pistons** that moved the paddle wheels.

Water is heated into steam inside the **boiler.**

Two side **paddle wheels** pushed the steamboat upriver.

ANSWERS TO PRACTICING THE SKILL

❶ steam (pressurized energy)

❷ They pushed the steamboat upriver.

Applying the Skill Students will draw and label a diagram of either how to make macaroni and cheese or how to tie a pair of shoes.

SECTION 3 Unity and Sectionalism

Guide to Reading

Main Idea
As the nation grew, differences in economic activities and needs increased sectionalism.

Key Terms
sectionalism, internal improvements, American System, disarmament, demilitarize, court-martial

Reading Strategy
Organizing Information As you read the section, re-create the diagram below and list four issues that created sectional conflict.

Read To Learn
• why sectional differences grew in the 1820s.
• what effect the Monroe Doctrine had on foreign policy.

Section Theme
Individual Action Senators Calhoun, Webster, and Clay represented different regions and different interests.

Preview of Events

◆1815	◆1820	◆1825

1816 James Monroe elected president

1820 Missouri Compromise passed

1823 Monroe Doctrine issued

James Monroe pocket watch

AN American Story

Following the War of 1812, Americans felt buoyed by a new sense of pride and faith in the United States. In his Inaugural Address on March 4, 1817, President James Monroe expressed this feeling of proud nationalism: "If we look to the history of other nations, ancient or modern, we find no example of a growth so rapid, so gigantic, of a people so prosperous and happy."

The Era of Good Feelings

The absence of major political divisions after the War of 1812 helped forge a sense of national unity. In the 1816 presidential election, James Monroe, the Republican candidate, faced almost no opposition. The Federalists, weakened by doubts of their loyalty during the War of 1812, barely existed as a national party. Monroe won the election by an overwhelming margin.

Although the Federalist Party had almost disappeared, many of its programs gained support. Republican president James Madison, Monroe's predecessor, had called for tariffs to protect industries, for a national bank, and for other programs.

CHAPTER 10   Growth and Expansion   **321**

1 FOCUS

Section Overview
This section discusses the differences in the economic and political interests of different sections of the country.

BELLRINGER
Skillbuilder Activity

Project transparency and have students answer the question.

Daily Focus Skills Transparency 10–3

Reading Preview

Answers to Graphic: Mesoamerica: *Olmec, Mayan, Toltec, Aztec cultures;* North American Southwest: *Hohokam and Anasazi cultures;* North American Midwest: *Adena, Hopewell, and Mississippian cultures*

Preteaching Vocabulary
Have students write a paragraph using at least three of the Key Terms and Names.

SECTION RESOURCES

📁 Reproducible Masters
• Reproducible Lesson Plan 10–3
• Daily Lecture and Discussion Notes 10–3
• Guided Reading Activity 10–3
• Section Quiz 10–3
• Reteaching Activity 10–3
• Reading Essentials and Study Guide 10–3
• Enrichment Activity 10–3

📄 Transparencies
• Daily Focus Skills Transparency 10–3

Multimedia
🔘 Vocabulary PuzzleMaker CD-ROM
🔘 Interactive Tutor Self-Assessment CD-ROM
🔘 ExamView® Pro Testmaker CD-ROM
🔘 Presentation Plus! CD-ROM

2 TEACH

Daily Lecture and Discussion Notes 10–3

Daily Lecture and Discussion Notes
Chapter 10, Section 3

Did You Know? Aaron Burr and Alexander Hamilton were not the only leaders in early America to fight a duel. In 1809 Kentucky state legislator and Republican Henry Clay and his Federalist party colleague, Humphrey Marshall, disagreed over an embargo of British-made goods. Clay challenged Marshall to a duel. The two men fired three rounds at each other, and both suffered minor wounds. Neither man changed his mind about the embargo.

I. **The Era of Good Feelings** (Pages 321–322)
   A. James Monroe won the 1816 presidential election easily. He had been involved in national politics since the American Revolution.
   B. The Federalist Party was almost nonexistent, but its programs gained support. Political differences seemed to disappear during this Era of Good Feelings, and Monroe's presidency also symbolized the era. He traveled around the nation as far south as Savannah and as far west as Detroit. In 1820 Monroe was reelected, receiving all but one electoral vote.

Discussion Question
Why did Monroe so easily win the elections of 1816 and 1820? (He hardly had opposition from the Federalist Party. Also, because of the Era of Good Feelings, people were satisfied with Monroe, so they elected him to a second term.)

II. **Sectionalism Grows** (Pages 322–324)
   A. Regional differences soon arose, and the Era of Good Feelings disappeared. People felt a strong tie to the region in which they lived. This promoted sectionalism, or loyalty to a region.
   B. Differences arose over slavery and national policies. Slavery was opposed in the North and protected in the South. National policies—such as tariffs, a national bank, and internal improvements, or federal, state, and privately funded projects to develop the nation's transportation system—were not accepted in all regions of the Union.
   C. John Calhoun, a planter from South Carolina, was the spokesperson from the South. Early on he favored support for internal improvements, developing industries, and a national bank. In the 1820s, he backed state sovereignty, or the belief that states should have power over the federal government, and was against high tariffs. Calhoun said high tariffs raised the prices of manufactured goods planters could not produce themselves and tariffs protected unproductive corporations.

Writing Questions Have students write five questions that can be answered with information in the section. Then have students work in pairs and use their questions to quiz each other on knowledge of section content. Remind students to use correct grammar, spelling, sentence structure, and punctuation. **L1**

✓ Reading Check

Answer: It was a time of strong nationalism and an absence of sectional conflict.

Political differences seemed to fade away, causing a Boston newspaper to call these years the **Era of Good Feelings.** The president himself symbolized these good feelings.

Monroe had been involved in national politics since the American Revolution. He wore breeches and powdered wigs—a style no longer in fashion. With his sense of dignity, Monroe represented a united America, free of political strife.

Early in his presidency, Monroe toured the nation. No president since George Washington had done this. He paid his own expenses and tried to travel without an official escort. Everywhere Monroe went, local officials greeted him and celebrated his visit.

Monroe arrived in Boston, the former Federalist stronghold, in the summer of 1817. About 40,000 well-wishers cheered him, and John Adams, the second president, invited Monroe to his home. Abigail Adams commended the new president's "unassuming manner."

Monroe did not think the demonstrations were meant for him personally. He wrote Madison that they revealed a "desire in the body of the people to show their attachment to the union."

Two years later Monroe continued his tour, traveling as far south as Savannah and as far west as Detroit. In 1820 President Monroe won reelection, winning all but one electoral vote.

✓ **Reading Check** **Describing** Why was this period called the Era of Good Feelings?

Sectionalism Grows

The Era of Good Feelings did not last long. Regional differences soon came to the surface, ending the period of national harmony.

Most Americans felt a strong allegiance to the region where they lived. They thought of themselves as Westerners or Southerners or Northerners. This sectionalism, or loyalty to their region, became more intense as differences arose over national policies.

The conflict over slavery, for example, had always simmered beneath the surface. Most white Southerners believed in the necessity and value of slavery. Northerners increasingly opposed it. To protect slavery, Southerners stressed the importance of states' rights. States' rights are provided in the Constitution. Southerners believed they had to defend these rights against the federal government infringing on them.

The different regions also disagreed on the need for tariffs, a national bank, and internal improvements. Internal improvements were federal, state, and privately funded projects, such as canals and roads, to develop the nation's transportation system. Three powerful voices emerged in Congress in the early 1800s as spokespersons for their regions: John C. Calhoun, Daniel Webster, and Henry Clay.

John C. Calhoun

John C. Calhoun, a planter from South Carolina, was one of the War Hawks who had called for war with Great Britain in 1812. Calhoun remained a nationalist for some time after the war. He favored support for internal improvements and developing industries, and he backed a national bank. At the time, he believed these programs would benefit the South.

In the 1820s, however, Calhoun's views started to change, and he emerged as one of the chief supporters of **state sovereignty**, the idea that states have autonomous power. Calhoun

Fact · Fiction · Folklore

America's Flags

Flag of 1818 By 1818 the number of states had reached 20. In April President Monroe signed a bill that set the basic design of the flag. Each newly admitted state added a star to the field of blue. The addition of a new star took place on the Fourth of July following the state's year of entry.

The Great Star Flag Congress did not state how the stars should be arranged, so flagmakers used various designs. The Great Star Flag placed the stars in the form of a five-pointed star.

COOPERATIVE LEARNING ACTIVITY

Writing a Biography Have students work in small groups to study Calhoun, Webster, or Clay. Each group should write a short biography of the person, write a description of an important event in his life or make a drawing of it, and recite aloud a portion of one of his speeches. Assign the various tasks according to the skills of group members. **L1, ELL**

The Missouri Compromise, 1820

State
- Free
- Slave

Territory
- Free
- Slave

Oregon Country

Maine, 1820

Missouri, 1821

Missouri Compromise Line (36°30' N)

36°30'N

MEXICO

0   500 miles
0   500 kilometers
Azimuthal Equidistant projection

Geography *Skills*

After 1820 all new states north of 36°30'N were to be admitted as free states.

1. Region Did Missouri enter the Union as a free state or a slave state?

2. Analyzing Information Was Maine a slave state or a free state in 1820?

Guided Reading Activity 10–3

Name _____ Date _____ Class _____

★ **Guided Reading Activity 10-3** _____

DIRECTIONS: Outlining Locate the heading in your textbook. Then use the information under the heading to help you write each answer. Use another sheet of paper if necessary.

I. The Era of Good Feelings Why did a Boston newspaper call the years of James Monroe's presidency the "Era of Good Feelings"? _____

II. Sectionalism Grows
  A. Introduction—On what points did the different regions disagree? _____
  B. John C. Calhoun—What did Calhoun believe about high tariffs? _____
  C. Daniel Webster—What region did the great orator Daniel Webster represent? _____
  D. Henry Clay—How did Clay try to bring conflicting interests together? _____
  E. The Missouri Compromise—What were the terms of the Missouri Compromise? _____

III. The American System
  A. Introduction—What did Clay's American System include? _____
  B. McCulloch v. Maryland—How did the Supreme Court rule in *McCulloch v. Maryland*? _____

IV. Foreign Affairs
  A. Relations With Britain—Through Adams's efforts, where did Americans gain the right to settle? _____
  B. Relations With Spain—What did General Jackson do in April 1818? _____
  C. Adams-Onis Treaty—What did Jackson's raid demonstrate to the Spanish? _____

V. Latin American Republics
  A. Bolívar and San Martín—What are the achievements of José de San Martín? _____
  B. The Monroe Doctrine—What did the president state in the Monroe Doctrine? _____

became a strong opponent of nationalist programs such as high tariffs. Calhoun and other Southerners argued that tariffs raised the prices that they had to pay for the manufactured goods they could not produce for themselves. They also argued that high tariffs protected inefficient manufacturers.

Daniel Webster

First elected to Congress in 1812 to represent his native New Hampshire, **Daniel Webster** later represented Massachusetts in both the House and the Senate. Webster began his political career as a supporter of free trade and the shipping interests of New England. In time, Webster came to favor the Tariff of 1816—which protected American industries from foreign competition—and other policies that he thought would strengthen the nation and help the North.

Webster gained fame as one of the greatest orators of his day. As a United States senator, he spoke eloquently in defense of the nation as a whole against sectional interests. In one memorable speech Webster declared, "Liberty and Union, now and forever, one and inseparable!"

Henry Clay

Another leading War Hawk, **Henry Clay** of Kentucky, became Speaker of the House of Representatives in 1811 and a leader who represented the interests of the Western states. He also served as a member of the delegation that negotiated the Treaty of Ghent, ending the War of 1812. Above all, Henry Clay became known as the national leader who tried to resolve sectional disputes through compromise.

The Missouri Compromise

Sectional tension reached new heights in 1820 over the issue of admitting new states to the Union. The problem revolved around slavery. The South wanted Missouri, part of the Louisiana Purchase, admitted as a slave state. Northerners wanted Missouri to be free of

Geography *Skills*

Answers:
1. slave state
2. free state

Geography Skills Practice
Ask: Which parallel separated the North and South in the Missouri Compromise? *(36°30'N)*

Who?What?Where?When?

Henry Clay Henry Clay first won election to the House of Representatives in 1811. When the session began, the other representatives disregarded his lack of experience and elected him Speaker of the House.

DIFFERENTIATED INSTRUCTION

English Learners The standardization of currency included many of the coins provided for in the Mint Act of 1792. Those were coins valued at $10.00, $5.00, $2.50, $1.00, 50¢, 25¢, 10¢, 5¢, 1¢, and 1/2¢. Our currency system is a decimal system, based on the dollar. Present the list of coins, expressed in words, and have students express each as a decimal. **L1, ELL**

📁 Refer to *Inclusion for the Middle School Social Studies Classroom Strategies and Activities* in the TCR.

Linking Past & Present

Many people today believe in alternative remedies. These remedies include acupuncture, herbalism, and chiropractic healing.

✔ Reading Check

Answer: the issue of whether new states would be admitted to the Union as slave states or free states; most white Southerners believed in the necessity and value of slavery, whereas Northerners increasingly opposed slavery

Did you know?

The acceptance of Missouri as a new slave state required the votes of northern members of Congress who were willing to compromise. Fourteen northern members of Congress joined southern members in a vote to admit Missouri as a slave state. But these votes were costly. Almost all of the Northerners who voted to admit the slave state were voted out of office by angry constituents in the next election.

slavery. The issue became the subject of debate throughout the country, exposing bitter regional divisions that would plague national politics for decades.

While Congress considered the Missouri question, Maine—still part of Massachusetts—also applied for statehood. The discussions about Missouri now broadened to include Maine.

Some observers feared for the future of the Union. Eventually Henry Clay helped work out a compromise that preserved the balance between North and South. The **Missouri Compromise,** reached in March 1820, provided for the admission of Missouri as a slave state and Maine as a

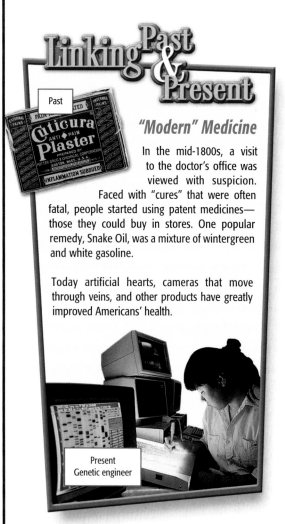

Linking Past & Present

Past

"Modern" Medicine

In the mid-1800s, a visit to the doctor's office was viewed with suspicion. Faced with "cures" that were often fatal, people started using patent medicines—those they could buy in stores. One popular remedy, Snake Oil, was a mixture of wintergreen and white gasoline.

Today artificial hearts, cameras that move through veins, and other products have greatly improved Americans' health.

Present
Genetic engineer

324 CHAPTER 10 Growth and Expansion

free state. The agreement banned slavery in the remainder of the Louisiana Territory north of the 36°30'N parallel.

✔ Reading Check **Identifying** What issue did the Missouri Compromise address? How did the Northern and Southern attitudes towards slavery differ?

The American System

Though he was a spokesperson for the West, Henry Clay believed his policies would benefit *all* sections of the nation. In an 1824 speech, he called his program the "American System." The American System included a protective tariff; a program of internal improvements, especially the building of roads and canals, to stimulate trade; and a national bank to control inflation and to lend money to build developing industries.

Clay believed that the three parts of his plan would work together. The tariff would provide the government with money to build roads and canals. Healthy businesses could use their profits to buy more agricultural goods from the South, then ship these goods northward along the nation's efficient new transportation system.

Not everyone saw Clay's program in such positive terms. Former president Jefferson believed the American System favored the wealthy manufacturing classes in New England. Many people in the South agreed with Jefferson. They saw no benefits to the South from the tariff or internal improvements.

In the end, little of Clay's American System went into effect. Congress eventually adopted some internal improvements, though not on the scale Clay had hoped for. Congress had created the Second National Bank in 1816, but it remained an object of controversy.

McCulloch v. *Maryland*

The Supreme Court also became involved in sectional and states' rights issues at this time. The state of Maryland imposed a tax on the Baltimore branch of the Second Bank of the United States—a federal institution. The Bank refused to pay the state tax, and the case, *McCulloch* v. *Maryland,* reached the Court in 1819.

INTERDISCIPLINARY CONNECTIONS ACTIVITY

Daily Life Several colorful characters lived in the late 1700s and early 1800s. Among them were John Chapman (Johnny Appleseed), Davy Crockett, Mike Fink, and Jean Lafitte. Have students, working in small groups, choose and read about a character, and decide on a way to present their findings to the class, such as role-playing, drawings, written reports, or a combination of forms. Groups should include factual information and tall tales in their presentations. Tasks should be divided according to the skills of group members. **L1,** ELL

Analyzing *Political Cartoons*

English cartoonist James Gillray shows European leaders carving up the world (above). American cartoonist David Claypoole Johnston portrays Andrew Jackson as a ruthless general (right). **What opinions are the cartoonists expressing?**

Speaking for the Court, Chief Justice **John Marshall** ruled that Maryland had no right to tax the Bank because it was a federal institution. He argued that the Constitution and the federal government received their authority directly from the people, not by way of the state governments. Those who opposed the *McCulloch* decision argued that it was a "loose construction" of the Constitution, which says that the federal government can "coin" money—gold, silver, and other coins—but the Constitution does not mention paper money. In addition, the Constitutional Convention had voted *not* to give the federal government the authority to charter corporations, including banks. 📖 *(See page 625 of the Appendix for a summary of McCulloch v. Maryland.)*

Gibbons v. *Ogden*

Another Supreme Court case, ***Gibbons* v. *Ogden,*** established that states could not enact legislation that would interfere with Congressional power over interstate commerce. The Supreme Court's rulings strengthened the national government. They also contributed to the debate over sectional issues. People who supported states' rights believed that the decisions increased federal power at the expense of state power. Strong nationalists welcomed the rulings' support for national power. 📖 *(See page 624 of the Appendix for a summary of Gibbons v. Ogden.)*

✓**Reading Check** **Examining** Why was the Court's decision in *Gibbons* v. *Ogden* significant?

Foreign Affairs

The War of 1812 heightened Americans' pride in their country. Abigail Adams, wife of John Adams, wrote from England to her sister back in Massachusetts:

❝Do you know that European birds have not half the melody of ours? Nor is their fruit half so sweet, nor their flowers half so fragrant, nor their manners half so pure, nor their people half so virtuous.❞

At the same time, many Americans realized that the United States needed peace with Britain to grow and develop. It had to put differences aside and establish a new relationship with the "Old World."

Analyzing *Political Cartoons*

Answer: the opinion that the major European powers, such as Britain, France, and Spain, were dividing up control of the world in pursuit of empires; the opinion that Jackson was a harsh and difficult man

✓**Reading Check**

Answer: The ruling strengthened the national government and contributed to the debate over sectional issues.

Where?Who?What?When?

Canadian-American Border Canada and the United States share more than 6,400 kilometers (3,977 miles) of common border. Relations between the two countries have generally been good since the Rush-Bagot Treaty of 1817 and the Convention of 1818. The border is demilitarized today, with millions of Canadians and Americans crossing regularly to work, shop, and vacation.

Reading Strategy   READING THE TEXT

Comparing and Contrasting Have students compare and contrast the needs of the North, South, and West as they review the material in "The American System." Then organize students into three groups, with one group representing the interests of the North, one the interests of the South, and the last the interests of the West. Have students participate in a panel debate in which they try to come to a compromise on the components of the American system, while representing the interests of their section. **L2**

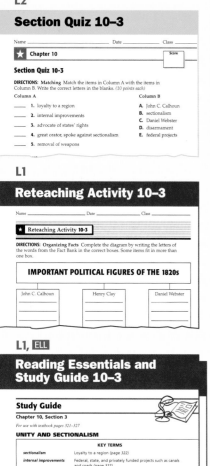

3 ASSESS

Assign Section 3 Assessment as homework or as an in-class activity.

🌐 Have students use **Interactive Tutor Self-Assessment CD-ROM.**

L2

Section Quiz 10–3

L1

Reteaching Activity 10–3

L1, ELL

Reading Essentials and Study Guide 10–3

Relations With Britain

In the years following the War of 1812, President Monroe and his secretary of state, John Quincy Adams, moved to resolve long-standing disputes with Great Britain and Spain.

In 1817, in the **Rush-Bagot Treaty,** the United States and Britain agreed to set limits on the number of naval vessels each could have on the Great Lakes. The treaty provided for the disarmament—the removal of weapons—along an important part of the border between the United States and British **Canada.**

The second agreement with Britain, the **Convention of 1818,** set the boundary of the Louisiana Territory between the United States and Canada at the 49th parallel. The convention created a secure and demilitarized border—a border without armed forces. Through Adams's efforts, Americans also gained the right to settle in the **Oregon Country.**

Relations With Spain

Spain owned East Florida and also claimed West Florida. The United States contended that West Florida was part of the Louisiana Purchase. In 1810 and 1812, Americans simply added parts of West Florida to Louisiana and Mississippi. Spain objected but took no action.

In April 1818, General **Andrew Jackson** invaded Spanish East Florida, seizing control of two Spanish forts. Jackson had been ordered to stop Seminole raids on American territory from Florida. In capturing the Spanish forts, however, Jackson went beyond his instructions.

Luis de Onís, the Spanish minister to the United States, protested forcefully and demanded the punishment of Jackson and his officers. Secretary of War Calhoun said that Jackson should be court-martialed—tried by a military court—for overstepping instructions. Secretary of State John Quincy Adams disagreed.

✚Geography
Adams-Onís Treaty

Although Secretary of State Adams had not authorized Jackson's raid, he did nothing to stop it. Adams guessed that the Spanish did not want war and that they might be ready to settle the

Florida dispute. He was right. For the Spanish the raid had demonstrated the military strength of the United States.

Already troubled by rebellions in **Mexico** and South America, Spain signed the **Adams-Onís Treaty** in 1819. Spain gave East Florida to the United States and abandoned all claims to West Florida. In return the United States gave up its claims to Spanish Texas and took over responsibility for paying the $5 million that American citizens claimed Spain owed them for damages.

The two countries also agreed on a border between the United States and Spanish possessions in the West. The border extended northwest from the Gulf of Mexico to the 42nd parallel and then west to the Pacific, giving the United States a large piece of territory in the Pacific Northwest. America had become a transcontinental power.

✓**Reading Check** **Identifying** What areas did the United States obtain from Spain?

Latin American Republics

While the Spanish were settling territorial disputes with the United States, they faced a series of challenges within their empire. In the early

Miguel Hidalgo

Americans and Mexico At first the new independent government of Mexico welcomed American settlers into its northern frontier areas, such as Texas. But the number of American settlers became so great that Mexico decided to cut off all migration from the United States into the area of Texas in 1830. Americans still continued to arrive. These defiant American settlers became a driving force in splitting Texas from the rest of Mexico during the 1830s.

1800s, Spain controlled a vast colonial empire that included what is now the southwestern United States, Mexico and Central America, and all of South America except Brazil.

In the fall of 1810 a priest, **Miguel Hidalgo** (ee• DAHL• goh), led a rebellion against the Spanish government of Mexico. Hidalgo called for racial equality and the redistribution of land. The Spanish defeated the revolutionary forces and executed Hidalgo. In 1821 Mexico gained its independence, but independence did not bring social and economic change.

Bolívar and San Martín

Independence in South America came largely as a result of the efforts of two men. **Simón Bolívar,** also known as "the Liberator," led the movement that won freedom for the present-day countries of Venezuela, Colombia, Panama, Bolivia, and Ecuador. **José de San Martín** successfully achieved independence for Chile and Peru. By 1824 the revolutionaries' military victory was complete, and most of South America had liberated itself from Spain. Portugal's large colony of Brazil gained its independence peacefully in 1822. Spain's empire in the Americas had shrunk to Cuba, Puerto Rico, and a few other islands in the Caribbean.

The Monroe Doctrine

In 1822 Spain had asked France, Austria, Russia, and Prussia— the Quadruple Alliance —for help in its fight against revolutionary forces in South America. The possibility of increased European involvement in North America led President Monroe to take action.

Student Web Activity
Visit tarvol1.glencoe.com and click on **Chapter 10— Student Web Activities** for an activity on the democratic movements in the Americas.

The president issued a statement, later known as the **Monroe Doctrine,** on December 2, 1823. While the United States would not interfere with any existing European colonies in the Americas, Monroe declared, it would oppose any new ones. North and South America "are henceforth not to be considered as subjects for future colonization by any European powers."

In 1823 the United States did not have the military power to enforce the Monroe Doctrine. The Monroe Doctrine nevertheless became an important element in American foreign policy and has remained so for more than 170 years. (*See page 616 of the Appendix for an excerpt from the Monroe Doctrine.*)

✓**Reading Check** **Evaluating** How did the Monroe Doctrine affect foreign policy?

SECTION 3 ASSESSMENT

Checking for Understanding

1. **Key Terms** Write a short paragraph in which you use the following key terms: sectionalism, internal improvements, American System, disarmament, demilitarize.

2. **Reviewing Facts** Describe the disagreement between the North and South that resulted in the Missouri Compromise.

Reviewing Themes

3. **Individual Action** What action did Daniel Webster take that shows he placed his concerns for the nation above his sectional interests?

Critical Thinking

4. **Identifying Central Issues** Explain the debate involved in *Gibbons* v. *Ogden* and the final decision.

5. **Determining Cause and Effect** Describe the chain of events in Latin America and Europe that led to the adoption of the Monroe Doctrine. Show your answers in a diagram like the one below.

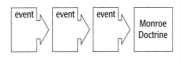

Analyzing Visuals

6. **Geography Skills** Use the map on page 323 to answer these questions. Which parallel did the Missouri Compromise line follow? How many slave states were there in 1820? How many free states?

Interdisciplinary Activity

Art Design a flag to represent either the North, South, or West during the early 1800s. Use photos, symbols, or mottoes that might have been popular with the people who lived in these regions.

L3

Enrichment Activity 10–3

DIRECTIONS: Integrating Information Follow the directions below.

1. Color the countries in blue that made up the colony known as Rio de la Plata.
2. Color in red the South American countries that were never under Spanish rule.
3. Circle the name of the country that is still held by France.
4. What countries made up New Granada? _____
5. What colony eventually became Chile and Peru? _____
6. On a separate sheet of paper, describe one or more shared features of location for each colony.

Activity **DIRECTIONS: Creating a Multimedia Presentation** Explore the cultures of the countries in South America. With your teacher, form groups of three or four students. Select a South American country and do research to find out what kinds of homes people live in, what foods they eat, what kind of art and music they enjoy, and what kinds of clothes they wear. Present what your group discovers to the class in a creative way, using photographs, drawings, and cassettes or videos.

Objectives and answers to the student activity can be found in the **Web Activity Lesson Plan** feature at tarvol1.glencoe.com

✓**Reading Check**

Answer: It changed foreign policy by stating that the United States would take action against European nations that tried to build new colonies in the Americas.

4 CLOSE

Have students explain why it was in the nation's best interest to make peace with European powers.

SECTION 3 ASSESSMENT ANSWERS

1. Student work should reflect correct use of terms.

2. The South wanted Missouri to be admitted as a slave state, while the North wanted it admitted as a free state.

3. He supported policies, such as the Tariff of 1816, that he thought would strengthen the United States, not just the North.

4. The case involved a debate over sectional issues between nationalists and those supporting states' rights. States could not enact legislation interfering with congressional power over interstate commerce.

5. increased nationalism and self-confidence on the part of the United States; many rebellions against the rule of Spain occurred in Spanish colonies; Spain asked for help in its fight against revolutionaries

6. 36°30′N; 12; 12

Interdisciplinary Activity Flags should have elements that make them unique to one of the regions.

GLENCOE TECHNOLOGY

MindJogger Videoquiz

Use **MindJogger Videoquiz** to review the Chapter 10 content.

Available in VHS

Reviewing Key Terms

Students' puzzles will vary. Definitions should include:

1. the time in history when goods were produced in mills with the help of machines

2. a system bringing manufacturing steps together in one place to increase efficiency

3. loyalty to one's region

4. the removal of weapons

5. no armed forces

6. to try by a military court

Reviewing Key Facts

7. overcrowding, unsanitary conditions, disease, threat of fire

8. New England's poor soil, rushing rivers and streams, abundant ports, and proximity to resources such as coal and iron made it a suitable landscape for the Industrial Revolution, during which many people left farming for factory work.

9. They linked the Great Lakes to the Atlantic Coast and allowed people to ship their goods at a lower cost.

10. Business interests in the North favored them; agricultural and slavery interests in the South did not.

11. Answers include supply of workers, capital, inventions, and technology.

12. a set of policies proposed by Henry Clay that were supposed to benefit all sections of the United States: protective tariffs, the building of canals and roads, and a national bank

Chapter Summary
Growth and Expansion

1790
- Samuel Slater builds first cotton mill in America

1793
- Eli Whitney invents the cotton gin

1801
- John Marshall is appointed chief justice of the Supreme Court

1807
- Robert Fulton builds the *Clermont*

1811
- National Road is begun

1816
- James Monroe elected president
- Second National Bank is chartered

1817
- Rush-Bagot Treaty is signed

1818
- Convention of 1818 agreement is signed

1819
- Adams-Onís Treaty is signed
- Supreme Court rules on *McCulloch* v. *Maryland*

1820
- Missouri Compromise is adopted

1823
- Monroe Doctrine is announced

1825
- Erie Canal is opened

Reviewing Key Terms

On a sheet of paper, create a crossword puzzle using the following terms. Use the terms' definitions as your crossword clues.

1. Industrial Revolution
2. factory system
3. sectionalism
4. disarmament
5. demilitarize
6. court-martial

Reviewing Key Facts

7. What problems did cities face as a result of rapid growth during the Industrial Revolution?

8. How did the landscape of New England affect how and where people lived in the late 1700s and early 1800s?

9. How did canals boost the economy of the Great Lakes region?

10. How did North and South differ on the issue of tariffs?

11. Identify factors in the United States that made it ideal for the free enterprise system.

12. What was the American System?

13. Explain the debate involved in *McCulloch* v. *Maryland* and the final decision in the case. Why was the decision significant?

14. How did James Monroe change the nation's foreign policy?

Critical Thinking

15. **Analyzing Themes: Economic Factors** How did the Industrial Revolution help to make the United States more economically independent in the early 1800s?

16. **Analyzing Themes: Global Connections** Why did Secretary of State John Quincy Adams allow General Jackson's invasion into Spanish East Florida in 1818?

17. **Determining Cause and Effect** How did the development of roads boost the growth of the United States? Use a diagram like the one shown to organize your answer.

```
        Roads
       /     \
   (    )   (    )
```

---

13. The debate involved the Second Bank of the United States, a federal institution, refusing to pay a state tax. In ruling that a state could not tax the Bank, the Court put forth a decision that helped strengthen the national government.

14. Monroe announced the Monroe Doctrine, which became one of the foundations of U.S. policy in Latin America. It was a statement of policy on the activities and rights of European powers in the Western Hemisphere.

Critical Thinking

15. The United States was able to produce more goods for use domestically and for trade with other nations. As a result the United States became less dependent economically on other nations.

16. He figured that Spain would not want to go to war and would peacefully settle the Florida dispute.

17. stimulated settlements farther west; increased trade between different regions

Geography and History Activity

In 1819 Spain ceded Florida to the United States in the Adams-Onís Treaty. The Spanish had established colonies in Florida beginning in the 1500s. Study the map and answer the questions that follow.

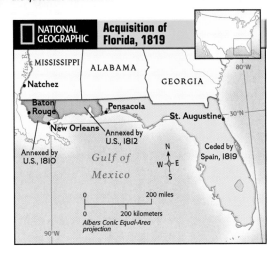

NATIONAL GEOGRAPHIC
Acquisition of Florida, 1819

MISSISSIPPI
ALABAMA
GEORGIA
Natchez
Baton Rouge
Pensacola
New Orleans
St. Augustine
Annexed by U.S., 1812
Annexed by U.S., 1810
Gulf of Mexico
Ceded by Spain, 1819
N W E S
0 200 miles
0 200 kilometers
Albers Conic Equal-Area projection
80°W · 30°N · 90°W

18. **Region** When was the largest portion of Florida acquired from Spain?
19. **Location** What body of water blocked further expansion of Florida to the west?
20. **Movement** In what direction did the United States acquire the various parts of Florida?

Practicing Skills

Reading a Diagram *Study the diagram of the textile mill on page 307. Use the diagram to answer these questions.*

21. What is the first step in the production of textiles?
22. At what stage does the thread become cloth?
23. What process turns the yarn into thread?
24. When would a cotton gin be necessary in this process?
25. Now choose one of the inventions mentioned in the chapter. Prepare a diagram that traces the development of that invention to a similar device in use today. For example, you might diagram the development of a modern cruise ship, showing all the improvements made from start to finish.

Citizenship Cooperative Activity

26. **Exploring Your Community's Past** Working with two other students, contact a local historical society to learn about your community's history. Then interview people in your neighborhood to learn about their roots in the community. Find out when their families first settled there. Write a history of the community and give a copy of it to the historical society.

Economics Activity

27. **Using the Internet** Search the Internet for information about how to apply for a patent for an invention. Create a step-by-step list of directions describing the process.

Alternative Assessment

28. **Portfolio Writing Activity** Review Section 2 of the chapter for information about what it was like to live in the West in the early 1800s. Record your notes in your journal. Use your notes to write a postcard to a friend describing your social life.

Standardized Test Practice

Directions: Choose the *best* answer to the following question.

The South opposed protective tariffs for which reason?

A They thought tariffs would not work.
B They had very little industry to protect.
C They thought foreign goods were better.
D Their main business was smuggling.

Test-Taking Tip:

Eliminate answers that do not make sense. For example, it is not realistic that the main business for the entire South was smuggling. Therefore, answer **D** cannot be correct.

Economics Activity

27. Students should use the Internet to find information about products made during the Industrial Revolution.

Alternative Assessment

28. Students' postcards should include information presented in Section 2 of Chapter 10.

HISTORY Online

Have students visit the Web site at tarvol1.glencoe.com to review Chapter 10 and take the Self-Check Quiz.

Standardized Test Practice

Answer: B
Question Type: Economics
Answer Explanation: According to pages 322-323, some Southerners argued that tariffs raised prices they had to pay for the manufactured goods they could not produce for themselves.

Bonus Question ?

Ask: Which American inventor of the early 1800s invented a torpedo-firing submarine? *(Robert Fulton)*

Geography and History Activity

18. 1819
19. Mississippi River
20. west to east

Practicing Skills

21. clean cotton, turn loose cotton into yarn
22. weaving
23. spinning
24. cleaning stage
25. Students' diagrams should reflect their research.

Citizenship Cooperative Activity

26. Students' reports should show evidence of research and an interview.

Unit 5 Resources

SUGGESTED PACING CHART

Unit 5 (1 Day)	Chapter 11 (5 Days)	Chapter 12 (6 Days)	Chapter 13 (6 Days)	Chapter 14 (5 Days)	Unit 5 (2 Days)
Day 1 Introduction	**Day 1** Chapter 11 Intro, Section 1 **Day 2** Section 2 **Day 3** Section 3 **Day 4** Chapter 11 Review **Day 5** Chapter 11 Assessment	**Day 1** Chapter 12 Intro, Section 1 **Day 2** Section 2 **Day 3** Section 3 **Day 4** Section 4 **Day 5** Chapter 12 Review **Day 6** Chapter 12 Assessment	**Day 1** Chapter 13 Intro, Section 1 **Day 2** Section 2 **Day 3** Section 3 **Day 4** Section 4 **Day 5** Chapter 13 Review **Day 6** Chapter 13 Assessment	**Day 1** Chapter 14 Intro, Section 1 **Day 2** Section 2 **Day 3** Section 3 **Day 4** Chapter 14 Review **Day 5** Chapter 14 Assessment	**Day 1** Wrap-Up/Project **Day 2** Unit 5 Assessment

GLENCOE'S ASSESSMENT ADVANTAGE

Use the following tools to easily assess student learning in a variety of ways:

- Performance Assessment Activities and Rubrics
- Chapter and Unit Tests
- Section Quizzes
- Standardized Test Practice Workbook

- www.tarvol1.glencoe.com
- Interactive Tutor Self-Assessment CD-ROM
- MindJogger Videoquiz
- ExamView® Pro Testmaker CD-ROM

TEACHING TRANSPARENCIES

Unit 5 Map Overlay Transparencies L2

Cause-and-Effect Transparency 5 L2

READING SUPPORT FROM JAMESTOWN EDUCATION

- *Timed Readings Plus in Social Studies* help students increase their reading rate and fluency while maintaining comprehension. The 400-word passages are similar to those found on state and national assessments.

- *Reading in the Content Area: Social Studies* concentrates on six essential reading skills that help students better comprehend what they read. The book includes 75 high-interest nonfiction passages written at increasing levels of difficulty.

- *Reading Fluency* helps students read smoothly, accurately, and expressively.

- *Jamestown's Reading Improvement,* by renowned reading expert Edward Fry, focuses on helping build your students' comprehension, vocabulary, and skimming and scanning skills.

- *Critical Reading Series* provides high-interest books, each written at three reading levels.

For more information about these products, see the Jamestown Education materials in the Classroom Solutions in the front of this Teacher Wraparound Edition. To order these products, call Glencoe at 1-800-334-7344.

Unit 5 Resources

ASSESSMENT

Unit 5 Pretests L2

Unit 5 Posttests L2

INTERDISCIPLINARY ACTIVITIES

American Literature Reading 5 L2

Interdisciplinary Connection 5 L2

Economics and History Activity 5 L2

APPLICATION AND ENRICHMENT

Cooperative Learning Activity 5 L1, ELL

Citizenship Activity 5 L1

HANDS-ON ACTIVITIES

Hands-On History Activity 5 L1

History Simulations and Problem Solving 5 L1

Reading List Generator CD-ROM

GLENCOE BOOKLINK

The Glencoe BookLink CD-ROM is a database that allows you to search more than 15,000 titles to create a customized reading list for your students.

- Reading lists can be organized by students' reading level, author, genre, theme, or area of interest.

- The database provides Degrees of Reading Power™ (DRP) and Lexile™ readability scores for all selections.

- A brief summary of each selection is included.

Leveled reading suggestions for this unit:

For Students at a Grade 6 Reading Level:
- ***The Underground Railroad: Life on the Road to Freedom,*** by Ellen Hansen

For Students at a Grade 7 Reading Level:
- ***The Great American Gold Rush,*** by Rhoda Blumberg

For Students at a Grade 8 Reading Level:
- ***Beyond the Mississippi: Early Westward Expansion of the United States,*** by Angela M. Herb

Extending the Content

Readings for the Teacher
- ***The Cherokee Removal: A Brief History With Documents,*** by Theda Perdue. Bedford/St. Martin's, 1995.
- ***Hidden in Plain View: A Secret Story of Quilts and the Underground Railroad,*** by Jacqueline L. Tobin and Raymond G. Dobard. Doubleday, 1999.

Multimedia Links
- ***Harriet Tubman: Conductor on the Underground Railway.*** Audiocassette. Recorded Book, 1999.

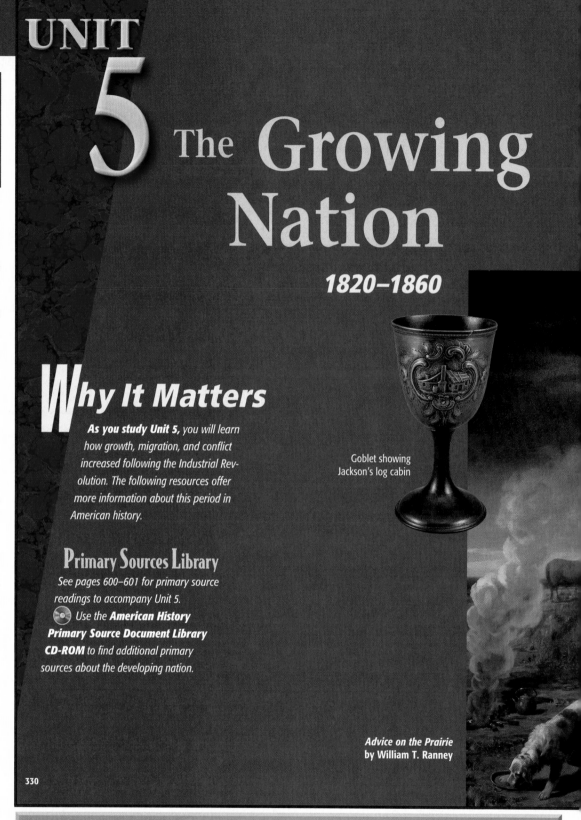

UNIT

5 The Growing Nation

1820–1860

Goblet showing Jackson's log cabin

Advice on the Prairie by William T. Ranney

Unit Overview

Unit 5 surveys the growth and change of the United States from 1820 to 1860. **Chapter 11** describes Andrew Jackson's impact on the country. **Chapter 12** focuses on westward expansion. **Chapter 13** traces the sectional differences between the Northern and Southern states. **Chapter 14** examines religious, educational, and cultural reform movements.

Unit Objectives

After studying this unit, students will be able to:
1. Describe key political and social events of the Jackson era.
2. Explain the concept of Manifest Destiny.
3. Compare and contrast the economy and people of the North with those of the South.
4. Discuss the social history of the early and mid-1800s.

Why It Matters Activity

Have students discuss the impact that technology, such as the Internet, has had on the growth of the United States. Ask students to compare and contrast the similarities and differences between the Industrial Revolution and the changes brought about by technology.

Why It Matters

As you study Unit 5, you will learn how growth, migration, and conflict increased following the Industrial Revolution. The following resources offer more information about this period in American history.

Primary Sources Library

See pages 600–601 for primary source readings to accompany Unit 5.

Use the **American History Primary Source Document Library CD-ROM** to find additional primary sources about the developing nation.

330

TEAM TEACHING ACTIVITY

Science Have students work with the Science teacher to make a simple device that can be used to send "telegraph" messages using Morse code. Materials needed include wire, nails, screws, one or two dry-cell batteries, a block of wood, and small pieces of flexible metal. Two books that have copies of the code and directions for building a transmitter are *Table Top Science*, by S.H. Fisher (Garden City, N.Y.: The Natural History Press, 1972) and *Science in Action: The World of Numbers*, edited by Sue Lyon (New York: Marshall Cavendish Corporation, 1988).

"Liberty and Union, now and forever. . . ."

—*Daniel Webster, 1830*

GLENCOE TECHNOLOGY

CD-ROM
American History Primary Source Document Library CD-ROM

Use the **American History Primary Source Document Library CD-ROM** to access primary source documents related to westward expansion.

More About the Art

Although William T. Ranney devoted his career to depicting the West, he spent very little time on the frontier. He studied art in New York City and served as an apprentice to a tinsmith in Fayetteville, North Carolina. His only experience on the frontier was in 1836, when he joined the Texas army in its fight for independence against Mexico. He then returned to his home in Brooklyn until 1853, when he moved his family to West Hoboken, New Jersey. He maintained an interest in frontier life. *Advice on the Prairie* shows a family traveling West on the Oregon Trail. Draw students' attention to the baby at the center of the painting, representing a new generation to be raised in the West.

Glencoe Literature Library

As students study the unit, have them read *The True Confessions of Charlotte Doyle* by Avi from the **Glencoe Literature Library.** The Glencoe Literature Library consists of novels and other readings for middle school students, along with study guides that offer instructional support and student activities.

SERVICE-LEARNING PROJECT

Organizations still work for reform or to correct remaining injustices in the United States today. Encourage students to conduct research on reform or watchdog organizations that seek democracy, fairness, and justice for people. Then have students choose one organization and perform services for it such as volunteering at its main office, distributing literature, participating in a campaign, or some other service that helps the organization work toward its objectives. Have students write a one-page report telling how the activities of the group are effective in the community. **L1**

Refer to ***Building Bridges: Connecting Classroom and Community through Service-Learning in Social Studies*** from the National Council for the Social Studies for information about service-learning.

Chapter 11 Resources

Timesaving Tools

TeacherWorks™ All-In-One Planner and Resource Center

- **Interactive Teacher Edition** Access your Teacher Wraparound Edition and your classroom resources with a few easy clicks.
- **Interactive Lesson Planner** Planning has never been easier! Organize your week, month, semester, or year with all the lesson helps you need to make teaching creative, timely, and relevant.

Use Glencoe's **Presentation Plus!** multimedia teacher tool to easily present dynamic lessons that visually excite your students. Using Microsoft PowerPoint® you can customize the presentations to create your own personalized lessons.

TEACHING TRANSPARENCIES

Graphic Organizer 14 L2

Why It Matters Chapter Transparency 11 L2

REVIEW AND REINFORCEMENT

Workbook Activity 11 L1

Time Line Activity 11 L2

Vocabulary Activity 11 L1

REVIEW AND REINFORCEMENT

Critical Thinking Skills Activity 11 L2

Take-Home Review Activity 11 L1

ENRICHMENT

Linking Past and Present Activity 11 L2

Primary Source Reading 11 L2

GEOGRAPHY

Geography and History Activity 11 L2

Meeting NCSS Standards

The following standards are highlighted in Chapter 11:

Section 1	II	Time, Continuity, & Change: B, C, D, E
Section 2	V	Individuals, Groups, & Institutions: A, B, D, E, F
Section 3	VII	Production, Distribution, & Consumption: A, B, C, D, F

FOLDABLES™ Study Organizer

Dinah Zike's Foldables are three-dimensional, interactive graphic organizers that help students practice basic writing skills, review key vocabulary terms, and identify main ideas. Additional chapter activities can be found in the **Reading and Study Skills Foldables** booklet.

Chapter 11 Resources

ASSESSMENT AND EVALUATION

Chapter 11 Test Form A L2

Chapter 11 Test Form B L2

Standardized Test Practice Workbook Activity 11 L2

Performance Assessment Activity 11 L1, ELL

ExamView® Pro Testmaker CD-ROM

MULTIMEDIA

- Vocabulary PuzzleMaker CD-ROM
- Interactive Tutor Self-Assessment CD-ROM
- ExamView® Pro Testmaker CD-ROM
- Audio Program
- American History Primary Source Document Library CD-ROM
- MindJogger Videoquiz
- Presentation Plus! CD-ROM
- TeacherWorks CD-ROM
- Interactive Student Edition CD-ROM
- Glencoe Skillbuilder Interactive Workbook CD-ROM, Level 1
- The American Republic to 1877 Video Program
- American Music: Hits Through History

SPANISH RESOURCES

The following Spanish language materials are available in the Spanish Resources Binder:

- Spanish Guided Reading Activities
- Spanish Reteaching Activities
- Spanish Quizzes and Tests
- Spanish Vocabulary Activity
- Spanish Take-Home Review Activity
- Spanish Summaries
- The Declaration of Independence and United States Constitution Spanish Translation

The following videotape program is available from Glencoe as a supplement to Chapter 11:
- **Andrew Jackson: A Man for the People** (ISBN 1-56501-647-5)*

To order, call Glencoe at 1-800-334-7344. To find classroom resources to accompany many of these videos, check the following home pages:
A&E Television: www.aande.com
The History Channel: www.historychannel.com

*Available individually or in *The American Republic to 1877 Video Library.*

Use our Web site for additional resources. All essential content is covered in the Student Edition.

You and your students can visit tarvol1.glencoe.com, the Web site companion to **The American Republic to 1877.** This innovative integration of electronic and print media offers your students a wealth of opportunities. The student text directs students to the Web site for the following options:

- **Chapter Overviews**   • **Student Web Activities**
- **Self-Check Quizzes**   • **Textbook Updates**

Answers to the student Web activities are provided for you in the **Web Activity Lesson Plans.** Additional Web resources and Interactive Tutor Puzzles are also available.

Chapter 11 Resources

SECTION RESOURCES

Daily Objectives	Reproducible Resources	Multimedia Resources
SECTION 1 **Jacksonian Democracy** 1. Explain why the nation's sixth president was chosen by the House of Representatives. 2. Identify the changes President Jackson brought to the American political system.	Reproducible Lesson Plan 11–1 Daily Lecture and Discussion Notes 11–1 Guided Reading Activity 11–1* Section Quiz 11–1* Reteaching Activity 11–1* Reading Essentials and Study Guide 11–1* Enrichment Activity 11–1	Daily Focus Skills Transparency 11–1 Interactive Tutor Self-Assessment CD-ROM ExamView® Pro Testmaker CD-ROM Presentation Plus! CD-ROM
SECTION 2 **Conflicts Over Land** 1. Understand how Native Americans were forced off their lands in the Southeast. 2. Explain how President Jackson defied the Supreme Court.	Reproducible Lesson Plan 11–2 Daily Lecture and Discussion Notes 11–2 Guided Reading Activity 11–2* Section Quiz 11–2* Reteaching Activity 11–2* Reading Essentials and Study Guide 11–2* Enrichment Activity 11–2	Daily Focus Skills Transparency 11–2 Interactive Tutor Self-Assessment CD-ROM ExamView® Pro Testmaker CD-ROM Presentation Plus! CD-ROM
SECTION 3 **Jackson and the Bank** 1. Examine the reasons why Jackson wanted to destroy the Bank of the United States. 2. Understand why the Whigs came to power in 1840.	Reproducible Lesson Plan 11–3 Daily Lecture and Discussion Notes 11–3 Guided Reading Activity 11–3* Section Quiz 11–3* Reteaching Activity 11–3* Reading Essentials and Study Guide 11–3* Enrichment Activity 11–3	Daily Focus Skills Transparency 11–3 Vocabulary PuzzleMaker CD-ROM Interactive Tutor Self-Assessment CD-ROM ExamView® Pro Testmaker CD-ROM Presentation Plus! CD-ROM

`0:00` OUT OF TIME?
Assign the Chapter 11 **Reading Essentials and Study Guide.**

*Also Available in Spanish

Blackline Master	Transparency	CD-ROM	DVD
Poster	Music Program	Audio Program	Videocassette

KEY TO ABILITY LEVELS

Teaching strategies have been coded.

L1 BASIC activities for all students
L2 AVERAGE activities for average to above-average students
L3 CHALLENGING activities for above-average students
ELL ENGLISH LANGUAGE LEARNER activities

NATIONAL GEOGRAPHIC
Teacher's Corner

INDEX TO NATIONAL GEOGRAPHIC MAGAZINE

The following articles relate to this chapter.

- "The Way West," by John G. Mitchell, September 2000.
- "The Cherokee," by Geoffrey Norman, May 1995.
- "Powwow," by Michael Parfit, June 1994.
- "The Cruelest Commerce: African Slave Trade," by Colin Palmer, September 1992.
- "Philadelphia's African Americans," by Roland L. Freeman, August 1990.

ADDITIONAL NATIONAL GEOGRAPHIC SOCIETY PRODUCTS

To order the following, call National Geographic at 1-800-368-2728:

- *GeoKit: Lewis and Clark* (Kit)
- *GeoKit: Westward Movement* (Kit)
- *The West That Was* (Video)
- *Exploration* (Map)
- *United States/Territorial Growth* (Map)
- *National Geographic Desk Reference* (Book)

NGS ONLINE

Access National Geographic's Web site for current events, atlas updates, activities, links, interactive features, and archives.
www.nationalgeographic.com

MEETING SPECIAL NEEDS

In addition to the Differentiated Instruction strategies found in each section, the following resources are also suitable for your special needs students:

- *ExamView® Pro Testmaker CD-ROM* allows teachers to tailor tests by reducing answer choices.

- The *Audio Program* includes the entire narrative of the student edition so that less-proficient readers can listen to the words as they read them.

- The *Reading Essentials and Study Guide* provides the same content as the student edition but is written two grade levels below the textbook.

- *Guided Reading Activities* give less-proficient readers point-by-point instructions to increase comprehension as they read each textbook section.

- *Enrichment Activities* includes a stimulating collection of readings and activities for gifted and talented students.

From the Classroom of . . .

Winnie Cohran
Drakes Creek Middle School
Bowling Green, KY

Create an Andrew Jackson Mural

To help students review the main issues and events of the chapter, have them make a mural using a large sheet of paper and colored pencils or pens. Students can work individually or in pairs. First, have students cut the paper into five irregularly shaped pieces (similar to puzzle pieces). On each piece of paper, have students label an issue or event and then illustrate it. For example, a student might write "Indian Removal Act" and then draw pictures of footsteps, or "Jackson Attacks Bank of United States" illustrated with dollar bill signs. Have students use different colors for each piece. Each student or group should present the mural to the class and explain it. Murals can be taped together and displayed in class.

ADDITIONAL RESOURCES FROM GLENCOE

- American Music: Cultural Traditions
- American Art and Architecture
- Outline Map Resource Book
- U.S. Desk Map
- Building Geography Skills for Life
- Inclusion for the Middle School Social Studies Classroom Strategies and Activities
- Teaching Strategies for the American History Classroom (Including Block Scheduling Pacing Guides)
- American Crafts Hands-On Activities
- American Games Hands-On Activities
- American History Flash Cards

Block Schedule

Activities that are suited to use within the block scheduling framework are identified by:

✓ **Performance Assessment**

Refer to Activity 11 in the Performance Assessment Activities and Rubrics booklet.

Why It Matters Activity

Tell students that many states dropped the property requirements for voting before and during Jackson's term. Encourage students to discuss people they know who are eligible to vote. Remind them, if necessary, that all citizens 18 or older are eligible to vote. Ask them which adults they know would not be able to vote if changes had not occurred during and after the Jackson era. They may name famous people as well as those they know personally.

GLENCOE
TECHNOLOGY

The American Republic to 1877 Video Program

To learn more about the Jackson era, have students view the Chapter 11 Video, "Old Hickory" from **The American Republic to 1877 Video Program.**

 Available in DVD and VHS

MindJogger Videoquiz

Use **MindJogger Videoquiz** to preview the Chapter 11 content.

Available in VHS

CHAPTER 11 The Jackson Era

1824–1845

Why It Matters

The struggle for political rights took shape in the 1820s and 1830s, when many people questioned the limits of American democracy.

The Impact Today

In the years since the Jackson era:
• Women, African Americans, and other minorities have won the right to vote and to participate in the political process.
• Today every United States citizen aged 18 or older, regardless of gender, race, or wealth, has the right to vote.

 The American Republic to 1877 Video The chapter 11 video, "Old Hickory," chronicles events in Andrew Jackson's military and political careers.

1823
• President Monroe outlines Monroe Doctrine

1830
• Indian Removal Act passed
• Webster-Hayne debate

1833
• Force Bill passed

United States PRESIDENTS

Monroe 1817–1825

J. Q. Adams 1825–1829

Jackson 1829–1837

1820   *1825*   *1830*

World

1822
• Brazil gains independence from Portugal

1826
• French scientist Niépce produces first photograph

1829
• Louis Braille publishes reading system for the blind

1833
• Slavery abolished in British colonies

332   CHAPTER 11   The Jackson Era

📖 **Reading Strategy** ❭ **PURPOSE FOR READING**

Brainstorming and **one-sentence summaries** are useful for students to represent many ideas concisely. Begin by asking: "Why do you think the right to vote is important in a democracy?" As students brainstorm, write their responses on the chalkboard. After 2 or 3 minutes, ask the students to pick one of the brainstormed items and in a one-sentence summary explain their choice. Use the sentence frame: I think _____ is important because _____. **L1**

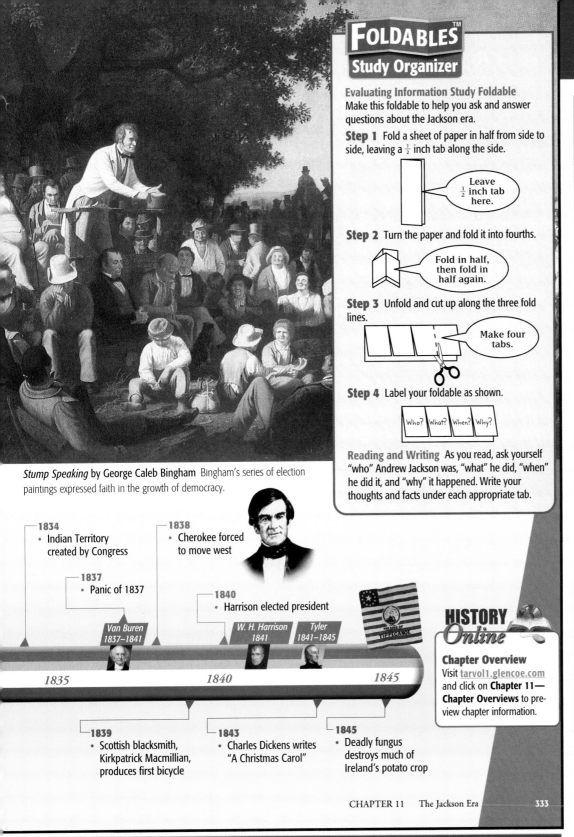

Stump Speaking by George Caleb Bingham Bingham's series of election paintings expressed faith in the growth of democracy.

FOLDABLES™ Study Organizer

Evaluating Information Study Foldable
Make this foldable to help you ask and answer questions about the Jackson era.

Step 1 Fold a sheet of paper in half from side to side, leaving a ½ inch tab along the side.

Leave ½ inch tab here.

Step 2 Turn the paper and fold it into fourths.

Fold in half, then fold in half again.

Step 3 Unfold and cut up along the three fold lines.

Make four tabs.

Step 4 Label your foldable as shown.

Who? What? When? Why?

Reading and Writing As you read, ask yourself "who" Andrew Jackson was, "what" he did, "when" he did it, and "why" it happened. Write your thoughts and facts under each appropriate tab.

FOLDABLES™ Study Organizer — Dinah Zike's Foldables

Purpose When making this foldable, students are required to ask themselves questions about the Jackson era. This reading strategy requires students to ask questions of the chapter material as they read it, helping them focus on the main ideas and better understand the material.

Have students complete **Reading and Study Skills Foldables** Activity 11. **L1**

HISTORY Online

Introduce students to chapter content and key terms by having them access **Chapter Overview 11** at tarvol1.glencoe.com

TIME LINE ACTIVITY

As students read the chapter, have them review the time line on pages 332–333. Ask students whether the Indian Territory was created before or after the passage of the Indian Removal Act. Have them discuss how these events might be related.

1834
• Indian Territory created by Congress

1837
• Panic of 1837

1838
• Cherokee forced to move west

1840
• Harrison elected president

Van Buren 1837–1841

W. H. Harrison 1841

Tyler 1841–1845

1835   *1840*   *1845*

1839
• Scottish blacksmith, Kirkpatrick Macmillian, produces first bicycle

1843
• Charles Dickens writes "A Christmas Carol"

1845
• Deadly fungus destroys much of Ireland's potato crop

HISTORY Online

Chapter Overview
Visit tarvol1.glencoe.com and click on **Chapter 11— Chapter Overviews** to preview chapter information.

More About the Art

George Caleb Bingham (1811–1879), a chronicler of the frontier, received his best inspiration from the spirited life along the Missouri and Mississippi Rivers. His best known paintings fall into two categories: activity on the river and frontier politics. Examples of the latter include *County Election* (1852) and *Verdict of the People* (1855) as well as *Stump Speaking*.

1 FOCUS

Section Overview

This section discusses the changes that occurred to the political system during the Jackson presidency.

BELLRINGER
Skillbuilder Activity

Project transparency and have students answer the question.

Daily Focus Skills Transparency 11–1

Reading Preview

Answers to Graphic: Democratic Republicans: Jackson—favored states' rights; National Republicans: Adams—favored strong federal government

Preteaching Vocabulary
Call on volunteers to define each of the **Key Terms,** and then use the textbook glossary to check the accuracy of the definitions. Then have students discuss the difference between *majority* and *plurality*.

SECTION 1 Jacksonian Democracy

Guide to Reading

Main Idea
The United States's political system changed under Andrew Jackson.

Key Terms
favorite son, majority, plurality, mudslinging, landslide, suffrage, bureaucracy, spoils system, caucus, nominating convention, tariff, nullify, secede

Reading Strategy
As you read Section 1, create a chart like the one below and in the boxes describe the political parties in 1828.

	Candidate	Views
Democratic Republicans		
National Republicans		

Read to Learn
• why the nation's sixth president was chosen by the House.
• what political changes came under President Jackson.

Section Theme
Continuity and Change James Monroe's decision not to seek a third term was followed by two hotly contested presidential elections.

Preview of Events

1825	1830	1835

1825
John Quincy Adams wins presidency in House election

1828
Andrew Jackson elected president

1830
Webster and Hayne debate

1832
South Carolina threatens to secede

Jackson sewing box

AN
American Story

The presidential campaign of 1828 was one of the most vicious in American history. Supporters of John Quincy Adams in Philadelphia distributed a pamphlet titled "Some Account of Some of the Bloody Deeds of General Jackson." One illustration in the pamphlet showed a ferocious-looking Andrew Jackson plunging his sword through the body of a helpless civilian. Meanwhile Jackson's supporters falsely accused John Quincy Adams of kidnapping a young American girl and selling her to the ruler of Russia.

The Election of 1824

From 1816 to 1824, the United States had only one political party, the Jeffersonian Republicans. Within the party, however, differences arose among various groups that had their own views and interests. In 1824 James Monroe was finishing his second term as president but declined to run for a third term. Four candidates from the Republican Party competed for the presidency.

334 CHAPTER 11 The Jackson Era

SECTION RESOURCES

Reproducible Masters
• Reproducible Lesson Plan 11–1
• Daily Lecture and Discussion Notes 11–1
• Guided Reading Activity 11–1
• Section Quiz 11–1
• Reteaching Activity 11–1
• Reading Essentials and Study Guide 11–1
• Enrichment Activity 11–1

Transparencies
• Daily Focus Skills Transparency 11–1

Multimedia
🖲 Interactive Tutor Self-Assessment CD-ROM
🖲 ExamView® Pro Testmaker CD-ROM
🖲 Presentation Plus! CD-ROM

The four candidates' opinions differed on the role of the federal government. They also spoke for different parts of the country. The Republican Party nominated **William H. Crawford,** a former congressman from Georgia. However, Crawford's poor health weakened him as a candidate.

The other three Republicans in the presidential race were favorite son candidates, meaning they received the backing of their home states rather than that of the national party. Two of these candidates—**Andrew Jackson** and **Henry Clay**—came from the West. Clay, of Kentucky, was Speaker of the House of Representatives. He fought for his program of internal improvements, high tariffs, and a stronger national bank.

General Andrew Jackson of Tennessee was not a Washington politician, but he was a hero of the War of 1812. Raised in poverty, he claimed to speak for the Americans who had been left out of politics.

John Quincy Adams of Massachusetts, son of former president John Adams, received support from merchants of the Northeast.

Striking a Bargain

In the election Jackson received the largest number of popular votes. However, no candidate received a majority, or more than half, of the electoral votes. Jackson won 99 electoral votes, which gave him a plurality, or largest single share. Under the terms of the Twelfth Amendment to the Constitution, when no candidate receives a majority of electoral votes, the House of Representatives selects the president.

While the House was preparing to vote on the next president, Henry Clay met with Adams. Clay agreed to use his influence as Speaker of the House to defeat Jackson. In return Clay may have hoped to gain the position of secretary of state.

With Clay's help Adams was elected president in the House. Adams quickly named Clay as secretary of state, traditionally the stepping-stone to the presidency. Jackson's followers accused the two men of making a **"corrupt bargain"** and stealing the election.

The Adams Presidency

In **Washington, D.C.,** the "corrupt bargain" had cast a shadow over Adams's presidency. Outside the capital Adams's policies ran against popular opinion. Adams wanted a stronger navy and government funds for scientific expeditions. Adams also wanted the federal government to direct economic growth.

Such ideas horrified those who desired a more limited role for the federal government, and Congress turned down many of Adams's proposals. This was especially true after the congressional elections of 1826, when enemies of Adams controlled both the House and Senate.

✓ Reading Check **Describing** Why were Adams and Clay accused of making a "corrupt bargain"?

The Election of 1828

By the election of 1828, the party had divided into two separate parties: the **Democratic-Republicans,** who supported Jackson, and the **National Republicans,** who supported Adams. Jackson's Democratic-Republicans, or Democrats, favored states' rights and mistrusted

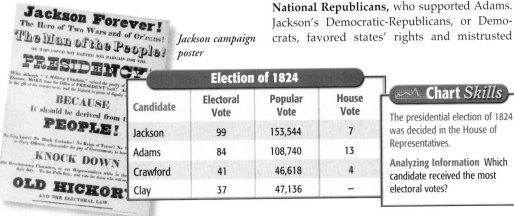

Jackson campaign poster

Election of 1824

Candidate	Electoral Vote	Popular Vote	House Vote
Jackson	99	153,544	7
Adams	84	108,740	13
Crawford	41	46,618	4
Clay	37	47,136	—

Chart *Skills*

The presidential election of 1824 was decided in the House of Representatives.

Analyzing Information Which candidate received the most electoral votes?

2 TEACH

Daily Lecture and Discussion Notes 11–1

Copyright © by The McGraw-Hill Companies, Inc.

Daily Lecture and Discussion Notes

Chapter 11, Section 1

Did You Know ? In United States history, there have been two instances in which both a father and son became presidents: John Adams and John Quincy Adams, and George H. Bush and George W. Bush. So there have been two women who have been both the wife of a president as well as the mother of one: Abigail Adams and Barbara Bush.

I. The Election of 1824 *(Pages 334–335)*

A. John Quincy Adams was elected president in 1824. William Crawford, Andrew Jackson, and Henry Clay were the other Republican Party candidates. No candidate received a majority of the electoral votes, so the House of Representatives selected the president.

 1. Clay and Adams struck a deal. Clay agreed to use his influence as speaker of the house to defeat Jackson, hoping to gain the secretary of state post in return. Adams did name Clay as secretary of state.

 2. Andrew Jackson's followers accused the two men of making a corrupt bargain and stealing the election.

B. During the Adams presidency, his policies ran against popular opinion. He wanted a stronger navy, scientific expeditions supported by government funds, and direct federal involvement in economic growth.

C. Congress turned down many of his proposals. Some members of Congress wanted a more limited role for the federal government.

Discussion Question

Why do you think Clay and Adams got together to defeat Jackson in the election of 1824? *(Answers will vary, but should include the idea that both were politicians, while Jackson was a war hero. Clay also had ulterior motives to improve his political status. If Adams won the presidency, then he would make Clay the secretary of state. Adams won, and Clay became secretary of state.)*

II. The Election of 1828 *(Pages 335–336)*

A. The election was a vicious campaign between Jackson and Adams. The party divided into two: the Democratic-Republicans nominated Jackson, and the National Republicans nominated Adams. Democratic-Republicans favored states' rights.

turn

Using Vocabulary Have students use each of the words in Key Terms plus *Democratic-Republicans* and *National Republicans* in writing a summary of the section. **L1**

✓ Reading Check

Answer: Critics charged that Clay helped Adams get elected president in exchange for becoming Adams's secretary of state.

Chart *Skills*

Answer: Jackson

Chart Skills Practice
Ask: How many House votes did Adams receive? *(13)*

✓ Reading Check

Answer: He accused Adams of betraying the people. Like Adams, Jackson also used slogans, buttons, rallies, and events such as barbecues to build enthusiasm during the campaign.

Did you know?

During his presidency Andrew Jackson surrounded himself with a group of trusted advisers. Because they met in the White House kitchen, Jackson's critics referred to the group as the "kitchen cabinet." Martin Van Buren was the only member of this influential group who also belonged to the president's official cabinet. Like Jackson, many later presidents—often mistakenly—put their trust in their kitchen cabinet of friends rather than in officially appointed cabinet members.

you don't say...

Political Terms *Caucus* probably is derived from the Algonquin word *cau-cauasu*, which means "counselor" or "adviser." The first recorded use of the word to mean a meeting of political leaders came in the 1770s.

---

strong central government. Many Democrats were individualists from the frontier, immigrants, or laborers in the big cities.

The National Republicans wanted a strong central government. They supported federal measures, such as road building and the Bank of the United States, that would shape the nation's economy. Many were merchants or farmers.

During the campaign both parties resorted to mudslinging, attempts to ruin their opponent's reputation with insults. The Democratic-Republicans accused Adams of betraying the people. They put out a handbill calling the election a contest "between an honest patriotism, on the one side, and an unholy, selfish ambition, on the other."

The National Republicans fought back. They created a vicious campaign song to play up embarrassing incidents in Jackson's life. One involved Jackson's order in the War of 1812 to execute several soldiers who had deserted.

Mudslinging was not the only new element introduced in the 1828 campaign. Election slogans, rallies, buttons, and events such as barbecues were also used to arouse enthusiasm. All of these new features became a permanent part of American political life.

Jackson Triumphs

In the election of 1828, Jackson received most of the votes cast by voters of the new frontier states. He also received many votes in the South, where his support for states' rights was popular. John C. Calhoun of South Carolina, who had served as Adams's vice president, switched parties to run with Jackson. Calhoun also championed states' rights. Jackson won the election in a landslide, an overwhelming victory, with 56 percent of the popular vote and 178 electoral votes.

✓ Reading Check **Summarizing** How did Jackson try to get the support of people in the election of 1828?

Jackson as President

Andrew Jackson was everything most Americans admired—a patriot, a self-made man, and a war hero. On March 4, 1829, thousands of farmers, laborers, and other ordinary Americans crowded into the nation's capital to hear Jack-

son's Inaugural Address. After Jackson's speech a crowd joined him at a White House reception. They filled the elegant rooms of the mansion, trampling on the carpets with muddy shoes, spilling food on sofas and chairs. They were there to shake the hand of the general who seemed just like them.

"Old Hickory"

Like many of his supporters, Andrew Jackson had been born in a log cabin. His parents, poor farmers, died before he was 15. As a teenager Jackson fought with the Patriots in the American Revolution. Before he was 30, he was elected to Congress from Tennessee.

Jackson gained fame during the War of 1812. He defeated the Creek Nation in the Battle of Horseshoe Bend and defeated the British at the Battle of New Orleans. His troops called him "Old Hickory" because he was as tough as a hickory stick.

Small farmers, craft workers, and others who felt left out of the expanding American economy loved Jackson. They felt that his rise from a log cabin to the White House demonstrated the American success story. His popularity with the common man changed politics in Washington, D.C.

🔲 Citizenship
New Voters

President Andrew Jackson promised "equal protection and equal benefits" for all Americans—at least for all white American men. During his first term, a spirit of equality spread through American politics.

In the nation's early years, most states had limited suffrage, or the right to vote, for men who owned property or paid taxes. By 1815 many states had loosened or soon would loosen the property requirements for voting. In the 1820s democracy expanded as people who had not been allowed to vote voted for the first time. Between 1824 and 1828, the percentage of white males voting in presidential elections increased from 26.9 to 57.6 percent. For the first time, white male sharecroppers, factory workers, and many others were brought into the political process.

DIFFERENTIATED INSTRUCTION

At-Risk Students Challenge students to compose a song that Jackson supporters could have sung at rallies during his campaign. The song could focus on his own qualifications and achievements or on the shortcomings of his opponent. Allow time for students to sing the song for the class. **L1**

📁 Refer to **Inclusion for the Middle School Social Studies Classroom Strategies and Activities** in the TCR.

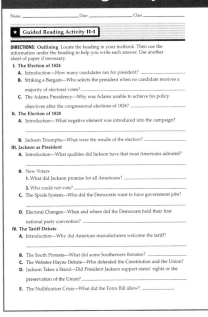

Ⓐ Andrew Jackson Ⓑ Nicholas Biddle Ⓒ Henry Clay Ⓓ John C. Calhoun

The expansion of suffrage continued, and in 1840 more than 80 percent of white males voted in the presidential election. However, women still could not vote, and African Americans and Native Americans had few rights of any kind.

Another development in the broadening of democracy involved presidential electors. By 1828, 22 of the 24 states changed their constitutions to allow the people, rather than the state legislatures, to choose presidential electors.

The Spoils System

Democrats carried the spirit of democracy into government. They wanted to open up government jobs to people from all walks of life. They were disturbed that the federal government had become a bureaucracy, a system in which nonelected officials carry out laws. Democrats argued that ordinary citizens could handle any government job.

President Jackson fired many federal workers and replaced them with his supporters. The discharged employees protested vehemently. They charged that Jackson was acting like a tyrant, hiring and firing people at will. Jackson responded that a new set of federal employees would be good for democracy.

One Jackson supporter explained it another way: "To the victors belong the spoils." In other words, because the Jacksonians had won the election, they had the right to the spoils—benefits of victory—such as handing out government jobs to supporters. The practice of replacing government employees with the winning candidate's supporters became known as the spoils system.

Electoral Changes

Jackson's supporters worked to make the political system more democratic as well. They abandoned the unpopular caucus system. In this system major political candidates were chosen by committees made up of members of Congress. The caucuses were replaced by nominating conventions in which delegates from the states selected the party's presidential candidate.

The Democrats held their first national party convention in 1832 in **Baltimore, Maryland.** The convention drew delegates from each state in the Union. The delegates decided to nominate the candidate who could gather two-thirds of the vote, and Jackson won the nomination. This system allowed many people to participate in the selection of political candidates.

✓ **Reading Check** **Describing** What is a caucus system?

INTERDISCIPLINARY CONNECTIONS ACTIVITY

Language Arts The election of Andrew Jackson marked a turning point in American politics. Have students use library sources to research and write a well-structured essay addressing how government and people's relationship to government changed, along with describing the emergence of the modern Democratic Party. Remind students to use standard grammar, spelling, and punctuation.

3 ASSESS

Assign Section 1 Assessment as homework or as an in-class activity.

🌐 Have students use **Interactive Tutor Self-Assessment CD-ROM.**

L2

Section Quiz 11–1

L1

Reteaching Activity 11–1

Analyzing *Political Cartoons*

King Andrew Some people called Andrew Jackson "a man of the people." Others called him a power-hungry ruler. **What symbols does the cartoonist use to suggest items of royalty?**

to nullify, or cancel, a federal law it considered against state interests. Some Southerners called for the Southern states to secede, or break away, from the United States and form their own government. When Calhoun explored this idea, troubling questions arose. The United States had been a nation for nearly 50 years. What if a state disagreed with the federal government? Did a state have the right to go its own way?

Calhoun drew from the ideas that Madison and Jefferson wrote in the Virginia and Kentucky Resolutions of 1798–1799. Calhoun argued that since the federal government was a creation of the states, the states themselves are the final authority of the constitutionality of federal laws. The alternative to state sovereignty, Calhoun pointed out, is to allow the Supreme Court or Congress to tell the people what our Constitution means and what orders we must obey.

💲Economics

The Tariff Debate

Americans from different parts of the country disagreed strongly on some issues. One such issue was the tariff, a fee paid by merchants who imported goods. While president, Jackson faced a tariff crisis that tested the national government's powers.

In 1828 Congress passed a very high tariff on manufactured goods from Europe. Manufacturers in the United States—mostly in the Northeast—welcomed the tariff. Because tariffs made European goods more expensive, American consumers were more likely to buy American-made goods.

Southerners, however, hated the new tariff. They called it the Tariff of Abominations—something hateful. These critics argued that, while tariffs forced consumers to buy American goods, tariffs also meant higher prices.

The South Protests

Southern politicians and plantation owners were ready to act. Vice President John C. Calhoun argued that a state or group of states had the right

The Webster–Hayne Debate

In January 1830, Senator Daniel Webster delivered a stinging attack on nullification. Webster stood on the floor of the Senate to challenge a speech given by Robert Hayne, a young senator from South Carolina. Hayne had defended the idea that the states had a right to nullify acts of the federal government, and even to secede.

In his response, Webster defended the Constitution and the Union. He argued that nullification could only mean the end of the Union. Webster closed with the ringing statement, "Liberty and Union, now and forever, one and inseparable!"

Jackson Takes a Stand

Nobody knew exactly where President Jackson stood on the issue of nullification. Many Southerners hoped that Jackson might side with them. In April 1830 supporters of states' rights invited the president to speak at a dinner. The

Reading Strategy   READING THE TEXT

Predicting Discuss the spoils system with students. Have them speculate on the possible negative and positive aspects of the system. Ask students to write a list of positives and a list of negatives. *(Positive: helps job of president to have loyal workers, cooperation makes it easier to get work done; Negative: people could be given jobs on the basis of their support rather than on their qualifications, experienced people would be replaced with workers new to the job)* **L3**

guests, including Calhoun, waited anxiously for Jackson to speak. Finally, the president rose to his feet and spoke directly to Calhoun.

❝Our federal union . . . must be preserved!❞

The states' rights supporters were shocked and disappointed, but Calhoun answered the president's challenge. He raised his glass and said,

❝The Union—next to our liberty, most dear.❞

He meant that the fate of the Union must take second place to a state's liberty to overrule the Constitution if its interests were threatened.

Calhoun realized that Jackson would not change his views. Wishing to return to Congress to speak for Southern interests, Calhoun won election to the Senate in December 1832. Not long after, he resigned the vice presidency.

The Nullification Crisis

Southern anger over the tariff continued to build. The Union seemed on the verge of splitting apart. In 1832 Congress passed a new, lower tariff, hoping that the protest in the South would die down. It did not.

South Carolina, Calhoun's home state, had led the fight against the so-called Tariff of Abominations. Now South Carolina took the battle one step further. The state legislature passed the **Nullification Act,** declaring that it would not pay the "illegal" tariffs of 1828 and 1832. The South Carolina legislators threatened to secede from the Union if the federal government tried to interfere with their actions.

To ease the crisis, Jackson supported a compromise bill proposed by Henry Clay that would gradually lower the tariff over several years. At the same time, Jackson made sure that the South would accept Clay's compromise. Early in 1833 he persuaded Congress to pass the **Force Bill,** which allowed the president to use the United States military to enforce acts of Congress.

In response, South Carolina accepted the new tariff. However, to show that they had not been defeated, state leaders voted to nullify the Force Act. Calhoun and his followers claimed a victory for nullification, which had, they insisted, forced the revision of the tariff. For the time being, the crisis between a state and the federal government was over. Yet South Carolina and the rest of the South would remember the lesson of the nullification crisis—that the federal government would not allow a state to go its own way without a fight.

✓**Reading Check** **Summarizing** Why did South Carolina pass the Nullification Act?

SECTION 1 ASSESSMENT

Check for Understanding

1. **Key Terms** Use each of these terms in a complete sentence that will help explain its meaning: favorite son, majority, plurality, mudslinging, landslide, suffrage, spoils system, secede.

2. **Reviewing Facts** Why did the House of Representatives select the president in the 1824 presidential election?

Reviewing Themes

3. **Continuity and Change** What election practices used in the 1828 presidential campaign are still used today?

Critical Thinking

4. **Drawing Conclusions** What was the main reason President Adams was not popular with the Democratic-Republicans?

5. **Organizing Information** Re-create the diagram below and describe the changes that took place in the political system under Andrew Jackson.

Changes

Analyzing Visuals

6. **Analyzing Political Cartoons** Look at the cartoon on page 338. What symbols are used to represent the United States? How does the cartoonist use labels? What does the cartoonist want readers to think of President Jackson?

Interdisciplinary Activity

Interviewing Prepare a list of five questions that you might have asked President Jackson if you had interviewed him.

✓**Reading Check**

Answer: to protest the tariffs of 1828 and 1832

L1, ELL

Reading Essentials and Study Guide 11–1

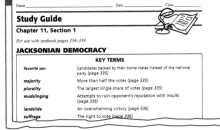

L3

Enrichment Activity 11–1

4 CLOSE

Have students choose the candidate they would have selected in the elections of 1824 and 1828 and defend their choice.

SECTION 1 ASSESSMENT ANSWERS

1. Student work should reflect correct use of terms.

2. No candidate received a majority of electoral votes.

3. mudslinging, election slogans, rallies, buttons, staged events to arouse voter enthusiasm

4. He tried to make the federal government too powerful.

5. Answers may include: a more democratic process for nominating political candidates, expansion of suffrage, and the spoils system.

6. The eagle and the Constitution; the cartoonist uses labels to stand for an item, institution, or concept. The cartoonist wants readers to think Jackson is assuming the powers of a king.

Interdisciplinary Activity Questions should take into account Jackson's personality and activities as described in the section.

339

TEACH

Analyzing Primary Sources
Point out that primary sources include not only written materials but also paintings, photographs, and artifacts.

Ask students whether their textbook is a primary source. *(No, but it contains many primary sources.)* Ask students why two eyewitness accounts of the same event might be very different. *(Answers may include: people have different biases; one person might be intentionally trying to deceive; one person might be better at remembering details.)*

Additional Practice

L2

Chapter Skills Activity 11

Name _____ Date _____ Class _____

★ **Chapter Skills Activity 11**

Analyzing Primary Sources

DIRECTIONS: The following excerpt is from an eyewitness account of the inauguration of Andrew Jackson in 1829. Read the excerpt and answer the questions below.

> . . . Some one came and informed us the crowd before the President's house was so far lessened that they thought we might enter. This time we effected our purpose. But what a scene did we witness! . . .
> . . . Ladies and gentlemen only had been expected at this levee, not the people en masse. But it was the people's day, and the people's President, and the people would rule. . . . I fear, enlightened freemen as they are, they will be found, as they have been found in all ages and countries where they get the power in their hands, that of all tyrants, they are the most ferocious,

GLENCOE
TECHNOLOGY

CD-ROM
Glencoe Skillbuilder Interactive Workbook CD-ROM, Level 1

This interactive CD-ROM reinforces student mastery of essential social studies skills.

Analyzing Primary Sources

Why Learn This Skill?

Historians determine what happened in the past by combing through bits of evidence to reconstruct events. This evidence—both written and illustrated—is called *primary sources.* Examining primary sources can help you understand history.

Choctaw forced from their land

Learning the Skill

Primary sources are records of events made by the people who witnessed them. They include letters, diaries, photographs and pictures, news articles, and legal documents. To analyze primary sources, follow these steps:

- Identify when and where the document was written.
- Read the document for its content and try to answer the five "W" questions: Who is it about? What is it about? When did it happen? Where did it happen? Why did it happen?
- Identify the author's opinions.

Practicing the Skill

The primary source that follows comes from Speckled Snake, an elder of the Creek Nation, in 1829. He was more than 100 years old at the time

he said these words. Read the quote, then answer the questions that follow.

> 66Brothers! I have listened to many talks from our Great Father. When he first came over the wide waters, he was but a little man. . . . But when the white man had warmed himself before the Indians' fire and filled himself with their hominy, he became very large. With a step he bestrode the mountains and his feet covered the plains and the valleys. His hand grasped the eastern and the western sea, and his head rested on the moon. Then he became our Great Father. Brothers, I have listened to a great many talks from our Great Father. But they always began and ended in this—'Get a little further; you are too near me.'99

❶ What events are described?

❷ Who was affected by these events?

❸ What is the general feeling of the person who stated this opinion?

Applying the Skill
Analyzing Primary Sources Find a primary source from your past—a photograph, a report card, an old newspaper clipping, or your first baseball card. Bring this source to class and explain what it shows about that time in your life.

 Glencoe's **Skillbuilder Interactive Workbook CD-ROM, Level 1,** provides instruction and practice in key social studies skills.

ANSWERS TO PRACTICING THE SKILL

❶ the coming of white people and the forcing of Native Americans from their land

❷ Native Americans

❸ The writer feels disgust, anger, distrust, and resentment because the white settlers have overpowered

the Native Americans and taken their lands, pushing them farther and farther west.

Applying the Skill Students should use a primary source from their past and explain what it shows about that time in their lives.

SECTION 2 Conflicts Over Land

Guide to Reading

Main Idea

As more white settlers moved into the Southeast, conflict arose between the Native Americans who lived there and the United States government.

Key Terms

relocate, guerrilla tactics

Reading Strategy

As you read Section 2, create a chart like the one below that describes what happened to each group of Native Americans as the United States expanded.

	Description
Cherokee	
Sauk/Fox	
Seminole	

Read to Learn

• how Native American peoples were forced off their lands in the Southeast.
• how President Jackson defied the Supreme Court.

Section Theme

Groups and Institutions In the 1830s many Native American peoples were forced to relocate.

Preview of Events

♦1830	♦1833	♦1836	♦1839
1830 Congress passes the Indian Removal Act	**1832** Black Hawk leads Sauk and Fox people to Illinois	**1835** Seminole refuse to leave Florida	**1838** Cherokee driven from their homelands on the Trail of Tears

Sequoya

AN American Story

The Cherokee held their land long before European settlers arrived. Through treaties with the United States government, the Cherokee became a sovereign nation within Georgia. By the early 1800s the Cherokee had their own schools, their own newspaper, and their own written constitution. Sequoya's invention of a Cherokee alphabet enabled many of the Cherokee to read and write in their own language. The Cherokee farmed some of Georgia's richest land, and in 1829 gold was discovered there. Settlers, miners, and land speculators began trespassing on Cherokee territory in pursuit of riches.

Moving Native Americans

While the United States had expanded westward by the 1830s, large numbers of Native Americans still lived in the eastern part of the country. In Georgia, Alabama, Mississippi, and Florida lived the "Five Civilized Tribes"—the Cherokee, Creek, Seminole, Chickasaw, and Choctaw. The tribes had established farming societies with successful economies.

CHAPTER 11   The Jackson Era   **341**

---

1 FOCUS

Section Overview

This section describes the relocation of Native Americans during the 1830s.

BELLRINGER
Skillbuilder Activity

 Project transparency and have students answer the question.

Daily Focus Skills Transparency 11-2

Reading Preview

Answers to Graphic: Cherokee: legally challenged removal and won, were forced to move anyway; Sauk/Fox: tried to reclaim land, were driven off; Seminole: waged guerrilla war until the United States allowed the Seminole to stay in Florida

Preteaching Vocabulary
Explain the meaning of the term *relocate*. Have students predict what or whom will relocate in Chapter 11.

SECTION RESOURCES

📂 Reproducible Masters

• Reproducible Lesson Plan 11–2
• Daily Lecture and Discussion Notes 11–2
• Guided Reading Activity 11–2
• Section Quiz 11–2
• Reteaching Activity 11–2
• Reading Essentials and Study Guide 11–2
• Enrichment Activity 11–2

🖐 Transparencies

• Daily Focus Skills Transparency 11–2

Multimedia

🔘 Interactive Tutor Self-Assessment CD-ROM
🔘 ExamView® Pro Testmaker CD-ROM
🔘 Presentation Plus! CD-ROM

2 TEACH

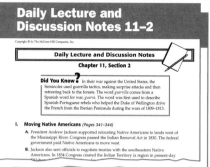
Reading Strategy

Classifying Responses Have
students review the section and
list the three main ways Native
Americans responded to the
Indian Removal Act. *(accepted
payment and agreed to move; sued
the government; resisted forcefully)*
Ask: How were the outcomes of
each response alike? *(Most ended
with relocation of the Native
Americans.)* **L1**

Geography *Skills*

Answers:
1. Seminole
2. Choctaw, Chickasaw

Geography Skills Practice
Ask: Where were Native Americans
sent? *(to reservations or to Indian
Territory)*

Because the area west of the Mississippi was
dry and seemed unsuitable for farming, few
white Americans lived there. Many settlers
wanted the federal government to relocate
Native Americans living in the Southeast. They
proposed to force the Native Americans to
leave their land and move west of the Mississippi River. President Andrew Jackson, a man
of the frontier himself, supported the settlers'
demand for Native American land.

Indian Removal Act

Congress responded by passing the **Indian
Removal Act** in 1830. The act allowed the federal government to pay Native Americans to
move west. Jackson then sent officials to negotiate treaties with Native Americans of the Southeast. Most felt compelled to accept payment for
their lands. In 1834 Congress created the **Indian
Territory,** an area in present-day Oklahoma, for
Native Americans from the Southeast.

NATIONAL GEOGRAPHIC — **Removal of Native Americans, 1820–1840**

1. Chief Black Hawk led Native Americans back to Illinois in 1832, but they were driven away.
2. The Cherokee took their refusal to move to the Supreme Court – and won. Federal troops forced them to leave anyway.
3. Chief Osceola led the Seminole in rebellion.

Ceded by Native Americans
Ceded to Native Americans
Common Removal Route
Cherokee Removal Route
Chickasaw Removal Route
Choctaw Removal Route
Creek Removal Route
Seminole Removal Route
Fort
Borders as of 1840

Dade Massacre 1835

Seminole area, 1740–1822
Seminole area, 1822–1842
Seminole Reservation, 1823–1832
Fort
Battle

Geography *Skills*

Between 1830 and 1840, the U.S. government moved about
60,000 Native Americans to reservations.
1. Movement What group was forced to move farthest
from its homeland?
2. Analyzing Information Which groups were forced to
move from Mississippi?

Reading Strategy — READING THE TEXT

Summarizing Information Summarizing information teaches students to reduce information and
to rethink what they have read. As students read this section, have them summarize what they
learn about Osceola and Seminole wars. When they finish, have students work in small groups to
compare what they have written.

Name _____ Date _____ Class _____

⭐ **Guided Reading Activity 11-2**

DIRECTIONS: Filling in the Blanks Use your textbook to fill in the blanks using the words in the box. Use another sheet of paper if necessary.

General Winfield Scott	Trail of Tears	Illinois
Indian Removal Act	1,500	Chief Justice John Marshall
100 million	Indian Territory	Black Hawk
Osceola	Cherokee	17,000
Seminole		

Moving Native Americans

After Congress passed the **(1)** _____ in 1830, Jackson sent federal officials to negotiate treaties with Native Americans in the Southeast. In 1834 Congress created the **(2)** _____, an area in present-day Oklahoma. President Jackson supported Georgia's efforts to remove the **(3)** _____ even after **(4)** _____ ruled against Georgia. Most of the **(5)** _____ Cherokee refused to give up their land. In 1838 **(6)** _____ and an army of 7,000 federal troops went to Georgia to remove the Cherokee from their homes and lead them west. Thousands of Cherokee died on the forced journey west, which became known as the **(7)** _____ .

Native American Resistance

In 1832 the Sauk chieftain **(8)** _____ led a force of Sauk and Fox people back to **(9)** _____, their homeland. Most of the Sauk and Fox were killed by the state militia. The **(10)** _____ of Florida were the only Native Americans who successfully resisted their removal. Chief **(11)** _____ and his people went to war against the United States rather than leave Florida. By 1842 more than **(12)** _____ American soldiers had died, and the government gave up. Native Americans gave up more than **(13)** _____ acres in exchange for $68 million and 32 million acres.

The Cherokee Nation

The Cherokee Nation, however, refused to give up its land. In treaties of the 1790s, the federal government had recognized the Cherokee people in the state of Georgia as a separate nation with their own laws. Georgia, however, refused to recognize Cherokee laws.

The Cherokee sued the state government and eventually took their case to the Supreme Court. In *Worcester* v. *Georgia* (1832), Chief Justice John Marshall ruled that Georgia had no right to interfere with the Cherokee. Only the federal government had authority over matters involving the Cherokee. 📖 *(See page 627 of the Appendix for a summary of* Worcester v. Georgia.*)*

President Jackson had supported Georgia's efforts to remove the Cherokee. He vowed to ignore the Supreme Court's ruling. "John Marshall has made his decision," Jackson reportedly said. "Now let him enforce it."

The Trail of Tears

In 1835 the federal government persuaded a few Cherokee to sign a treaty giving up their people's land. Yet most of the 17,000 Cherokee refused to honor the treaty. They wrote a protest letter to the government and people of the United States.

History *Through Art*

Trail of Tears by Robert Lindneux Native Americans who were forced from their land traveled west in the 1830s. **Why was the forced march called the "Trail of Tears"?**

❝We are aware that some persons suppose it will be for our advantage to [re]move beyond the Mississippi. . . . Our people universally think otherwise. . . . We wish to remain on the land of our fathers.❞

The Cherokee plea for understanding did not soften the resolve of President Jackson or the white settlers of the area. In 1838 **General Winfield Scott** and an army of 7,000 federal troops came to remove the Cherokee from their homes and lead them west.

Scott threatened to use force if the Cherokee did not leave. He told them he had positioned troops all around the country so that resistance and escape were both hopeless. "Chiefs, head men, and warriors—Will you then, by resistance, compel us to resort to arms?" The Cherokee knew that fighting would only lead to their destruction. Filled with sadness and anger, their leaders gave in, and the long march to the West began. One man in Kentucky wrote of seeing hundreds of Cherokee marching by:

CHAPTER 11   The Jackson Era   **343**

History *Through Art*

Although created a century after the event, Robert Lindneux's painting captures the defeat and sadness of the Cherokee people.
Answer: because the Cherokee were forced to leave their homes, and thousands died on the march

CURRICULUM CONNECTION

Economics The Cherokee Nation in Georgia enjoyed economic success. The nation owned 22,000 head of cattle, 2,000 spinning wheels, 700 looms, 10 sawmills, and 1,300 enslaved persons.

DIFFERENTIATED INSTRUCTION

Gifted and Talented Have each student choose an event discussed in the section (such as the Trail of Tears). Ask them what it would have been like to live through the event. Then have students write a first-person narrative describing their experiences. Encourage them to share their narratives with the rest of the class. **L3**

📂 Refer to *Inclusion for the Middle School Social Studies Classroom Strategies and Activities* in the TCR.

People In History

In 1837, under a flag of truce, Osceola went with several chiefs to attend a meeting with General T.S. Jesup. Osceola and the Seminoles were seized and imprisoned. **Ask: In which present-day state did the Seminole live?** *(Florida)*

✓ **Reading Check**

Answer: to resettle Native Americans west of the Mississippi River

Objectives and answers to the student activity can be found in the **Web Activity Lesson Plan** feature at tarvol1.glencoe.com

3 ASSESS

Assign Section 2 Assessment as homework or as an in-class activity.

⊙ Have students use **Interactive Tutor Self-Assessment CD-ROM.**

L2

Section Quiz 11–2

Name	Date	Class
★ Chapter 11		Score

Section Quiz 11-2

DIRECTIONS: Matching Match the items in Column A with the items in Column B. Write the correct letters in the blanks. *(10 points each)*

Column A	Column B
____ 1. Indian Territory	A. led Sauk and Fox warriors
____ 2. Osceola	B. marched the Trail of Tears
____ 3. Black Hawk	C. sent to remove Cherokee
____ 4. Winfield Scott	D. present-day Oklahoma
____ 5. Cherokee	E. led Seminole rebellion

DIRECTIONS: Multiple Choice In the blank at the left, write the letter of the

People In History

Osceola 1804–1838

Osceola was born in 1804. His ancestors were Creek, African American, British, Irish, and Scottish. After President Jackson signed the Indian Removal Act in 1830, Osceola became the leader of the Seminoles and led successful attacks on United States forts. Hiding in the swampy lands of the Everglades, the Seminoles grew tired, sick, and hungry. Osceola attempted to surrender but was captured. He and his family were imprisoned at Fort Moultrie, South Carolina, where he died of a throat infection in 1838. Although he had waged a war against the United States, the public considered Osceola an honorable hero and a victim of trickery, and he was given a funeral with full military honors.

❝Even [the] aged . . . nearly ready to drop in the grave, were traveling with heavy burdens attached to their backs, sometimes on frozen ground and sometimes on muddy streets, with no covering for their feet.❞

Brutal weather along the way claimed thousands of Cherokee lives. Their forced journey west became known to the Cherokee people as the Trail Where They Cried. Historians call it the **Trail of Tears.**

✓ **Reading Check** **Explaining** What was the purpose of the Indian Removal Act?

Native American Resistance

In 1832 the Sauk chieftain, **Black Hawk,** led a force of Sauk and Fox people back to Illinois, their homeland. They wanted to recapture this area, which had been given up in a treaty. The Illinois state militia and federal troops responded with force, gathering nearly 4,500 soldiers. They chased the Fox and Sauk to the Mississippi River and slaughtered most of the Native Americans as they tried to flee westward into present-day Iowa.

The Seminole people of Florida were the only Native Americans who successfully resisted their removal. Although they were pressured in the early 1830s to sign treaties giving up their land, the Seminole chief, **Osceola,** and some of his people refused to leave Florida. The Seminole decided to go to war against the United States instead.

In 1835 the Seminole joined forces with a group of African Americans who had run away to escape slavery. Together they attacked white settlements along the Florida coast. They used guerrilla tactics, making surprise attacks and then retreating back into the forests and swamps. In December 1835, Seminole ambushed soldiers under the command of Major Francis Dade. Only a few of the 110 soldiers survived the attack. The Dade Massacre pressured the call for more troops and equipment to fight the Seminole.

By 1842 more than 1,500 American soldiers had died in the Seminole wars. The government gave up and allowed some of the Seminole to remain in Florida. Many Seminole, however,

Student Web Activity Visit tarvol1.glencoe.com and click on **Chapter 11— Student Web Activities** for an activity on the Trail of Tears.

INTERDISCIPLINARY CONNECTIONS ACTIVITY

Daily Life The Cherokee and Seminole were not the only Southern Native Americans to be removed from lands east of the Mississippi River during the 1830s. The Choctaw, Chickasaw, and Creek peoples were also driven from their lands. Have students do research for a report on one of these groups. Students may describe the culture as a whole or the circumstances of the group's removal, or they may choose to do a biographical sketch of one of the leaders. **L2**

📁 Use the rubric for doing a research report on pages 56–57 in the *Performance Assessment Activities and Rubrics.*

"We told them to let us alone and keep away from us; but they followed on."

—Black Hawk, Sauk leader (far right), pictured here with his son, Whirling Thunder

had died in the long war, and many more were captured and forced to move westward. After 1842 only a few scattered groups of Native Americans lived east of the Mississippi. Most had been removed to the West. Native Americans had given up more than 100 million acres of eastern land to the federal government. They had received in return about $68 million and 32 million acres in lands west of the Mississippi River. There they lived, divided by tribes, in reservations. Eventually, these reservations, too, would face intrusion from white civilization.

The area of present-day Oklahoma became part of the United States in 1803 with the Louisiana Purchase. The United States set aside this area as the home for various Native American groups.

The Five Civilized Tribes were relocated in the eastern half of present-day Oklahoma on lands claimed by several Plains groups, including the Osage, Comanche, and Kiowa. United States Army leaders got agreements from the Plains groups to let the Five Civilized Tribes live in peace. Settled in their new homes, the Five Tribes developed their governments, improved their farms, and built schools. The Five Tribes also developed a police force called the Lighthorsemen. This law enforcement unit maintained safety for the region.

✓ **Reading Check** **Comparing** How was the response of the Seminoles different from that of the Cherokee when they were removed from their lands?

✓ Reading Check

Answer: The Seminoles responded by attacking the white settlements on their land, and the Cherokee took action in the United States court system.

L1

Reteaching Activity 11–2

L1, ELL

Reading Essentials and Study Guide 11–2

L3

Enrichment Activity 11–2

SECTION 2 ASSESSMENT

Checking for Understanding

1. **Key Terms** Use the terms **relocate** and **guerrilla tactics** in complete sentences that will explain their meanings.

2. **Analyzing** Analyze how President Jackson reacted to the Supreme Court decision supporting the Cherokees' rights.

Reviewing Themes

3. **Groups and Institutions** How were the Seminole able to resist relocation?

Critical Thinking

4. **Drawing Conclusions** How was Georgia's policy toward the Cherokee different from the previous federal policy?

5. **Organizing Information** Re-create the diagram below to show how the Cherokee were eventually removed from their land.

Analyzing Visuals

6. **Geography Skills** Study the maps on page 342. Which groups of Native Americans were located in Alabama? What does the inset map show? In what area of Florida was the Seminole reservation?

Interdisciplinary Activity

Persuasive Writing Write a letter to Andrew Jackson telling him why the Native Americans should or should not be allowed to stay in their homelands.

CHAPTER 11   The Jackson Era   **345**

4 CLOSE

Have students make questions out of the **Read to Learn** items, and then answer the questions.

SECTION 2 ASSESSMENT ANSWERS

1. Student work should reflect correct use of terms.

2. He ignored the ruling because he believed the Native Americans should be moved west of the Mississippi.

3. They waged a guerrilla war until the United States allowed the Seminole survivors to stay in Florida.

4. The previous federal policy had recognized the Cherokee people in the state of Georgia as a separate nation with their own laws.

5. Most Cherokee refused to sign; Cherokee protested to federal government; Federal troops removed the Cherokee.

6. Cherokee and Creek; Seminole areas in Florida; central

Interdisciplinary Activity Letters will vary, but should present convincing reasons for the position taken.

1 FOCUS

Have students brainstorm a list of reasons the United States government might order soldiers to move Cherokee families from their homes and relocate them from their homeland in Georgia to a territory 800 miles away. **Ask:** Who might benefit from the removal of Native Americans? *(Students may answer settlers who wanted the land or who had experienced conflict with the Cherokee.)*

2 TEACH

Analyzing a Graphic Have students refer to the graph, Forced Migration, and the information in Trail of Tears. **Ask:** The majority of relocated Native Americans belonged to what tribe? *(Cherokee)* Which tribe had the least number of its members relocated? Why? *(Seminole; they fought removal until the government allowed them to remain on their lands.)* **L1**

Did you know?

The state of Oklahoma entered the Union in 1907. It was created from the Indian and Oklahoma territories. The state seal displays a large circle with a five-pointed star in its center. Within the points of the star are five symbols representing the Cherokee, Seminole, Choctaw, Chickasaw, and Creek peoples.

NATIONAL GEOGRAPHIC **GEOGRAPHY & HISTORY**

Cherokee Trail of Tears
(East to West)

• • • • June 6–19, 1838

– – – September 28, 1838– January 17, 1839

——— October 11, 1838– January 7, 1839

– – – October 23, 1838– March 24, 1839

□ Historic site

0   50 miles
0   50 kilometers

The Cherokee supplemented their meager diet with ground acorns and other foods they found along the route.

ILLINOIS
Ohio River

MISSOURI

Cherokee Nation Territory prior to Oklahoma statehood

Springfield

Hopkinsv

Cherokee Outlet

Ozark Plateau

Nashville

Tulsa
Tahlequah • Stilwell
Fort Gibson • Fayetteville

Mississippi River

TENNESSEE

Fort Coffee   Fort Smith

Lewisburg

Memphis

OKLAHOMA

Little Rock ⊛

Decatur

Arkansas River

MISSISSIPPI

ARKANSAS

ALABAM

Removal and Relocation

Indian Territory

Cherokee
Chickasaw

Choctaw   Creek

ATLANTIC OCEAN

John Ross (left), the principal chief of the Cherokee, opposed the removal of his people. Rebecca Neugin (right) was one of the Cherokee forced to march west to Oklahoma. In this 1931 photograph, Neugin is 96 years old.

Gulf of Mexico

Seminole

0   300 miles
0   300 kilometers

346

EXTENDING THE CONTENT

Displacement Removal actually began on a smaller scale in the early 1800s, before the Indian Removal Act of 1830 legitimized and accelerated it. Removal was just the beginning of Native American hardships. Native peoples displaced from the east had great difficulty in adapting their ways of life to a very different environment on the Great Plains, and the Plains Native Americans resented the influx of new tribes into their territories. White settlers eventually moved into the Plains territory, causing further hostilities.

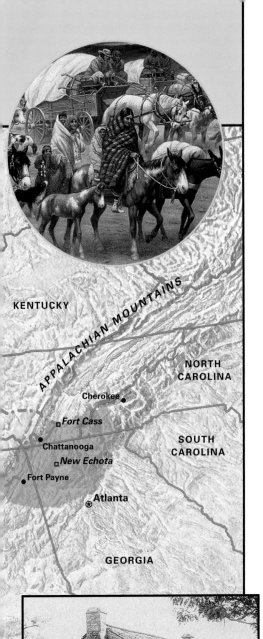

TRAIL OF TEARS

LONG BEFORE EUROPEAN EXPLORERS ARRIVED, the Cherokee, Chickasaw, Choctaw, Creek, and Seminole were living in eastern North America. The Native Americans built permanent communities, practiced agriculture, and developed complex tribal governments—thereby earning the name of Five Civilized Tribes.

REMOVAL

As white settlers moved into the southeastern states, they began demanding the land held by Native Americans. In 1830, Congress passed the Indian Removal Act to move the Five Civilized Tribes west of the Mississippi. Under pressure, the Choctaw, Chickasaw, and Creek moved west while the Cherokee and the Seminole resisted.

RESISTANCE

Despite protests from the Cherokee people, they were forced to march west. In 1838, 13 ragged groups trekked to Fort Gibson in the newly created Indian Territory (see maps). Along the journey, which became known as the "Trail of Tears," 4,000 Cherokee died of cold, hunger, or disease.

Some of the Seminole refused to abandon their homeland and waged a guerrilla war in the Florida Everglades until the government gave up its efforts to resettle them in 1842.

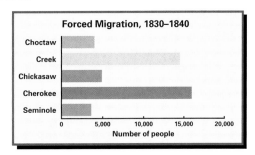

Forced Migration, 1830–1840

Number of people

Most Cherokee farmers lived in log cabins.

LEARNING *from* GEOGRAPHY

1. **To what present-day state were the Five Civilized Tribes forced to move?**

2. **Through what cities did the Cherokee travel during the removal that began on June 6, 1838?**

347

3 ASSESS

Have students answer the **Learning from Geography** questions.

4 CLOSE

Have groups of students research the ways in which the Five Civilized Tribes met their survival needs in their original homelands. Tell students to learn about the geography, wildlife, and climate of the southeastern states and of Oklahoma. Then, have them hold a panel discussion about why the relocated tribes might have difficulty surviving by their traditional means.

NGS ONLINE

Access National Geographic's Web site for current events, atlas updates, activities, links, interactive features, and archives at www.nationalgeographic.com

Answers to Learning *from* Geography

1. Oklahoma

2. Decatur, Memphis, Little Rock

1 FOCUS

Section Overview

This section examines how economic issues affected politics in the mid 1800s.

BELLRINGER
Skillbuilder Activity

 Project transparency and have students answer the question.

Daily Focus Skills Transparency 11–3

Reading Preview

Answers to Graphic: Jackson vetoes the bill to renew the Bank's charter; Jackson orders the withdrawal of all government deposits from the Bank.

Preteaching Vocabulary
Use the **Vocabulary PuzzleMaker CD-ROM** to create crossword and word search puzzles.

Guide to Reading

Main Idea
Economic issues affected the presidencies of Andrew Jackson and Martin Van Buren.

Key Terms
veto, depression, laissez-faire, log cabin campaign

Reading Strategy
Sequencing Information As you read the section, re-create the diagram below. In the spaces provided, describe the steps Andrew Jackson took that put the Bank of the United States out of business.

☐ → ☐ → Jackson stops Bank

Read to Learn
- why Jackson wanted to destroy the Bank of the United States.
- how the Whigs came to power in 1840.

Section Theme
Economic Factors Economic issues influenced politics in the mid-1800s.

Preview of Events

♦1830 — ♦1835 — ♦1840 — ♦1845

1832
Andrew Jackson challenges the Bank of the United States

1836
Martin Van Buren is elected president

1837
Panic of 1837 strikes the nation

1841
Vice President John Tyler becomes president

Bank note issued in the mid-1800s

AN American Story

President Andrew Jackson made many enemies. His most outspoken rivals, the Whigs, were strong in Congress. They accused "King Andrew" of increasing his power and spreading corruption with the spoils system. In response, Jackson declared that the president was responsible for the protection of "the liberties and rights of the people and the integrity of the Constitution against the Senate, or the House of Representatives, or both together."

War Against the Bank

Jackson had another great battle during his presidency. For years, he had attacked the Bank of the United States as being an organization of wealthy Easterners over which ordinary citizens had no control. The Bank of the United States was a powerful institution. It held the federal government's money and controlled much of the country's money supply. Although the Bank had been chartered by Congress, it was run by private bankers rather than elected officials.

SECTION RESOURCES

📁 Reproducible Masters
- Reproducible Lesson Plan 11-3
- Daily Lecture and Discussion Notes 11-3
- Guided Reading Activity 11-3
- Section Quiz 11-3
- Reteaching Activity 11-3
- Reading Essentials and Study Guide 11-3
- Enrichment Activity 11-3

📊 Transparencies
- Daily Focus Skills Transparency 11-3

Multimedia
- Vocabulary PuzzleMaker CD-ROM
- Interactive Tutor Self-Assessment CD-ROM
- ExamView® Pro Testmaker CD-ROM
- Presentation Plus! CD-ROM

The Bank's president, **Nicholas Biddle,** represented everything Jackson disliked. Jackson prided himself on being a self-made man who started with nothing. Biddle, on the other hand, came from a wealthy family and had a good education and social standing.

In 1832 Jackson's opponents gave him the chance to take action against the Bank. Senators **Henry Clay** and **Daniel Webster,** friends of Biddle, planned to use the Bank to defeat Jackson in the 1832 presidential election. They persuaded Biddle to apply early for a new charter—a government permit to operate the Bank—even though the Bank's current charter did not expire until 1836.

Clay and Webster believed the Bank had popular support. They thought that an attempt by Jackson to veto its charter would lead to his defeat and allow Henry Clay to be elected president.

When the bill to renew the Bank's charter came to Jackson for signature, he was sick in bed. Jackson told his friend **Martin Van Buren,** "The bank, Mr. Van Buren, is trying to kill me. But I will kill it!" Jackson vetoed, or rejected, the bill.

Jackson, like many others, still felt the Bank was unconstitutional despite the Supreme Court's decision to the contrary in *McCulloch* v. *Maryland* (1819). In a message to Congress, Jackson angrily denounced the Bank, arguing that

66. . . when laws . . . make the rich richer and the potent more powerful, the humble members of society—the farmers, mechanics, and laborers—who have neither the time nor the means of securing like favors to themselves, have a right to complain of the injustice of their Government.99

The Election of 1832

Webster and Clay were right about one thing. The Bank of the United States did play a large part in the campaign of 1832. Their strategy for

Analyzing *Political Cartoons*

Many cartoons from the period depicted Jackson's battle against the Second Bank of the United States. **Does this cartoon support the president or the Bank? Explain.**

Ⓐ The Bank   Ⓑ President Jackson   Ⓒ American people

Matching Have students create matching quizzes using the people and terms in the section and a brief definition or identification of each. Then have pairs of students exchange quizzes and try to complete each other's quiz. **L1,** ELL

Analyzing *Political Cartoons*

Answer: It supports the president because the Bank is depicted negatively as a monster.

Reading Strategy   READING THE TEXT

Rewriting When students rewrite information, it helps them internalize it. Have students read the quote on p. 349. Ask students to rewrite the quote in their own words.

Guided Reading Activity 11–3

★ **Guided Reading Activity 11-3**

DIRECTIONS: Recalling the Facts Use the information in your textbook to answer the questions. Use another sheet of paper if necessary.

1. Why did President Andrew Jackson attack the Bank of the United States?

2. Who was president of the Bank?

3. What did Jackson do when the bill to renew the Bank's charter came to him for his signature?

4. How did Jackson "kill" the Bank once he was reelected?

5. Whom did the Democrats select to succeed Jackson as president in 1836?

William Henry Harrison

Miniature log cabin

Picturing **History**

Answer: to show Harrison was a man of the people

---

3 ASSESS

Assign Section 3 Assessment as homework or as an in-class activity.

🔊 Have students use **Interactive Tutor Self-Assessment CD-ROM.**

L2

Section Quiz 11–3

★ **Chapter 11**   Score

Section Quiz 11-3

DIRECTIONS: Matching Match the items in Column A with the items in Column B. Write the correct letters in the blanks. *(10 points each)*

Column A	Column B
____ 1. Andrew Jackson's rivals	**A.** Martin Van Buren's home state
____ 2. Bank president	**B.** Whigs
____ 3. veto	**C.** William Henry Harrison
____ 4. New York	**D.** reject
____ 5. 1840 Whig candidate	**E.** Nicholas Biddle

DIRECTIONS: Multiple Choice In the blank at the left, write the letter of the

L1

Reteaching Activity 11–3

★ **Reteaching Activity 11-3**

DIRECTIONS: Organizing Facts The numbered items in the Fact Bank are characteristics of United States presidents in the mid-1800s. Write the number of each item in the appropriate section of the chart.

Presidents in the Mid-1800s

Andrew Jackson	Martin Van Buren	William Henry Harrison	John Tyler	James Polk

---

Picturing **History**

In the 1840 election campaign, the Whigs marched in street parades, often carrying miniature log cabins on poles. **Why did Harrison's supporters make the log cabin their symbol?**

---

gaining support for Clay as president, however, backfired. Most people supported Jackson's veto of the bank charter bill. Jackson was re-elected, receiving 55 percent of the popular vote and collecting 219 electoral votes to Clay's 49. Martin Van Buren was elected vice president.

Once re-elected, Jackson decided on a plan to "kill" the Bank ahead of the 1836 schedule. He ordered the withdrawal of all government deposits from the Bank and placed the funds in smaller state banks. In 1836 he refused to sign a new charter for the Bank, and it closed.

💲 Economics

The Panic of 1837

When Jackson decided not to run for a third term in 1836, the Democrats selected Martin Van Buren of New York, Jackson's friend and vice president, as their candidate. Van Buren faced bitter opposition from the Whigs, a new political party that included former National Republicans and other anti-Jackson forces. Jackson's great popularity and his personal support helped Van Buren easily defeat several Whig opponents. Van Buren was inaugurated in 1837.

Shortly after Van Buren's election, the country entered a severe economic depression, a period in which business and employment fall to a very low level. The depression began with the **Panic of 1837,** a time when land values dropped sharply, investments declined suddenly, and banks failed. Thousands of businesses closed and hundreds of thousands of people lost their jobs. In the South, cotton prices fell to record lows. Farmers plunged into debt and lost their land. In the cities, many people could not afford food or rent. In February 1837, people in New York put up signs voicing their anger:

> 66 Bread, Meat, Rent, and Fuel!
> Their prices must come down!
> The Voice of the People shall be heard
> and will prevail! 99

President Van Buren believed in the principle of laissez-faire—that government should interfere as little as possible in the nation's economy. Van Buren did persuade Congress to establish an independent federal treasury in 1840. The government would no longer deposit its money with private individual banks as it had started to do during President Jackson's war with the Bank of the United States. Instead the government would store its money in the federal treasury. The private banks had used government funds to back their banknotes. The new treasury system would prevent banks from using government funds in this way and so help guard against further bank crises.

Van Buren and his supporters hailed the new law as a "second declaration of independence." However, criticism of the act came from members

350   CHAPTER 11   The Jackson Era

DIFFERENTIATED INSTRUCTION

Reading Support Today's national debt is over $5 trillion ($5,700,000,000,000), and our population is about 281 million (281,000,000). Have students express both figures in numerals. Then have them figure out how much every man, woman, and child in the United States would have to contribute to pay off the debt if it were distributed equally *(about $21,000).* Ask students to calculate how much their own family would have to contribute *($21,000 times the number of family members).* **L2**

of Van Buren's own Democratic Party as well as from Whigs. The split in the Democratic Party meant the Whigs had a chance to win the presidency in 1840.

✓**Reading Check** **Explaining** What was the new treasury system supposed to prevent?

The Whigs Come to Power

The Democrats had controlled the presidency for 12 years. However, with the country still in the depths of depression, the Whigs thought they had a chance to win the election in 1840. They nominated **William Henry Harrison,** a hero of the War of 1812, to run against President Van Buren. **John Tyler**, a planter from Virginia, was Harrison's running mate. Because Harrison had gained national fame defeating Tecumseh's followers in the Battle of Tippecanoe, the Whigs' campaign slogan was "Tippecanoe and Tyler Too."

To win the election, Harrison had to gain the support of the laborers and farmers who had voted for Jackson. The Whigs adopted a log cabin as their symbol. Political cartoons in newspapers showed Harrison, a wealthy man from Virginia, in front of a log cabin. The Whigs wanted to show that their candidate was a "man of the people."

The Whigs also ridiculed Van Buren as "King Martin," a wealthy snob who had spent the people's money on fancy furniture for the White House. The log cabin campaign seemed to work, and Harrison went on to defeat Van Buren by a wide margin.

William Henry Harrison was inaugurated in 1841 as the first Whig president. The Whigs were still celebrating their victory when Harrison died of pneumonia on April 4, 1841. John Tyler of Virginia became the first vice president to gain the presidency because the elected president died in office.

Although Tyler had been elected vice president as a Whig, he had once been a Democrat. As president, Tyler, a strong supporter of states' rights, vetoed several bills sponsored by Whigs in Congress, including a bill to recharter the Bank of the United States. His lack of party loyalty outraged Whigs. Most of Tyler's cabinet resigned, and Whig leaders in Congress expelled Tyler from the party.

It seemed that the Whigs could not agree on their party's goals. Increasingly, Whigs voted according to sectional ties—North, South, and West—not party ties. This division may explain why the Whig candidate, Henry Clay, lost the election of 1844 to Democratic candidate **James Polk.** After only four years, the Whigs were out of power again.

✓**Reading Check** **Describing** How did John Tyler become president?

SECTION 3 ASSESSMENT

Checking for Understanding

1. **Key Terms** Use each of these terms in a complete sentence that will help explain its meaning: veto, depression, laissez-faire, log cabin campaign.

2. **Reviewing Facts** List Jackson's reasons for wanting to "kill" the Bank of the United States.

Reviewing Themes

3. **Economic Factors** Why did President Van Buren do little to solve the nation's economic problems during the depression?

Critical Thinking

4. **Analyzing Information** What tactics did the Whigs borrow from Jackson's campaign to win the election of 1840?

5. **Organizing Information** Re-create the diagram below to show how the Panic of 1837 affected the presidency of Martin Van Buren.

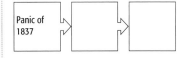

Analyzing Visuals

6. **Analyzing Political Cartoons** Study the cartoon on page 349. Do you think the Bank of the United States is portrayed positively or negatively? Explain your answer.

Interdisciplinary Activity

Art Write a campaign slogan for Van Buren or Harrison in the election of 1840. Then design a campaign button that incorporates your slogan.

✓**Reading Check**

Answer: It was supposed to prevent banks from using government funds to back their banknotes.

✓**Reading Check**

Answer: He was vice president when President Harrison died in office.

L1, ELL

Reading Essentials and Study Guide 11–3

L3

Enrichment Activity 11–3

4 CLOSE

Ask students which of Jackson's nicknames they think is more fitting: King Andrew or Old Hickory. Explain.

SECTION 3 ASSESSMENT ANSWERS

1. Student work should reflect correct use of terms.

2. He believed it favored the rich and hurt the poor and that it had too much power.

3. He believed in the principle of laissez-faire, that government should not interfere in the nation's economy.

4. They tried to appeal to the "common man" by portraying Harrison as a man of the people. They ridiculed Van Buren, calling him King Martin to suggest that he was interested only in the welfare of the rich.

5. Supporters turn against him; he loses 1840 election, ending his presidency.

6. Answers may include that it is negative because it is portrayed as an ugly, green monster.

Interdisciplinary Activity

Students' slogans and buttons should show an understanding of each candidate's platform.

CHAPTER 11 ASSESSMENT and ACTIVITIES

Reviewing Key Terms

Students' puzzles will vary but should conform to the written instructions.

1. largest single share
2. an overwhelming victory
3. the right to vote
4. more than half
5. cancel
6. break away
7. a period in which business and employment fall to a very low level

Reviewing Key Facts

8. Jackson's supporters: favored states' rights, suspicious of a strong central government; Adams's supporters: supported a strong central government, supported measures such as road building and a national bank

9. mudslinging, election slogans, rallies, buttons, staged events to arouse enthusiasm

10. Women, African Americans, and Native Americans were still excluded from voting. Only white male property owners could vote before the 1800s.

11. Nominating conventions replaced caucuses, which were made up of members of Congress. Delegates from the states selected the party's presidential candidate at nominating conventions, allowing more people to participate.

12. The South, with little manufacturing, bought its manufactured goods from abroad. The tariffs made them expensive.

13. escaped slaves

14. Businesses closed. Many people lost their jobs. Southern cotton prices fell.

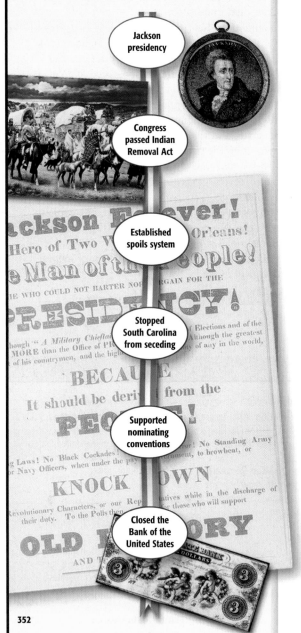

Chapter Summary
The Jackson Era

- Jackson presidency
- Congress passed Indian Removal Act
- Established spoils system
- Stopped South Carolina from seceding
- Supported nominating conventions
- Closed the Bank of the United States

352

Reviewing Key Terms

On graph paper, create a word search puzzle using the following terms. Crisscross the terms vertically and horizontally. Then fill in the remaining squares with extra letters. List the definitions below the puzzle as clues. Share your puzzle with a classmate.

1. plurality
2. landslide
3. suffrage
4. majority
5. nullify
6. secede
7. depression

Reviewing Key Facts

8. How did the supporters of Jackson and Adams differ in their beliefs?

9. What were some of the political tactics used by Democratic-Republicans and the National Republicans in the election of 1828?

10. Which Americans were prohibited from voting in most states before the 1800s?

11. How did nominating conventions make the selection of political candidates more democratic?

12. Why was the South against high tariffs?

13. Who did the Seminoles join forces with as they fought against forced removal from their land?

14. How did the Panic of 1837 affect the nation's economy?

15. Why was Harrison's log cabin campaign successful?

Critical Thinking

16. **Drawing Conclusions** President Andrew Jackson promised "equal protection and equal benefits" for all Americans. Do you think he included Native Americans in his promise? Why or why not?

17. **Analyzing Themes: Groups and Institutions** What agreement did the Cherokee Nation make with the federal government that Georgia refused to recognize?

18. **Organizing Information** Re-create the chart below. List the issues that Jackson dealt with during his presidency. Then describe how he responded to each issue.

Issues	Jackson's response

15. By focusing on the "common man," it appealed to the same voters that were attracted to Jackson.

Critical Thinking

16. No; he supported their relocation, showing that he did not consider them to have the same rights as other Americans.

17. In treaties of the 1790s, the federal government acknowledged the Cherokee in Georgia as a separate nation with its own laws.

18. Federal employees: fired many and replaced with supporters; Electoral change: replaced caucuses with nominating conventions; Nullification: opposed nullification and supported preservation of the Union; Indian Removal: ordered forcible removal when tribes did not leave voluntarily; National Bank: He ordered all government deposits to be withdrawn and placed the money in state banks; by 1836 the Bank was forced to close

Geography and History Activity

The issue of states' rights was debated in the election of 1828. Study the map below and answer the questions that follow.

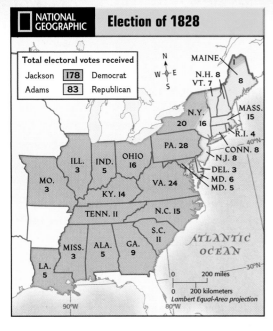

Election of 1828

NATIONAL GEOGRAPHIC

Total electoral votes received

Jackson **178** Democrat
Adams **83** Republican

19. Region Which general areas of the United States voted for Andrew Jackson in the election of 1828?

20. Location Which candidate won more votes in Adams's home state of Massachusetts?

21. Place Which three states divided their total electoral count between the two candidates?

Practicing Skills

Analyzing Primary Sources In an annual message to Congress in 1835, President Andrew Jackson spoke the words below. Read the excerpt and answer the questions that follow.

❝All preceding experiments for the improvement of the Indians have failed. It seems now to be an established fact that they cannot live in contact with a civilized community and prosper. . . . A country west of Missouri and Arkansas has been assigned to them, into which the white settlements are not to be pushed.❞

Self-Check Quiz
Visit tarvol1.glencoe.com and click on **Chapter 11— Self-Check Quizzes** to prepare for the chapter test.

22. Whose opinion is stated in the excerpt?

23. What is the speaker's attitude toward Native Americans?

24. According to the speaker, why should Native Americans be assigned to a country west of Missouri and Arkansas?

Citizenship Cooperative Activity

25. Becoming an Informed Voter With a partner, choose an election in your community. Outline how you would become informed on the candidates and/or the issues. Then follow your outline and become an informed voter. Share your outline and your findings with the class.

Economics Activity

26. Look in a dictionary to find definitions of "recession" and "depression." Write a paragraph to explain the difference between the two.

Standardized Test Practice

Directions: Choose the *best* answer to the following question.

Which of the following statements expresses an opinion about Andrew Jackson?

A Jackson served two terms as president.

B He spoke out against South Carolina's Nullification Act.

C Because of Jackson, the United States has the best system of filling government positions.

D Jackson supported the Indian Removal Act.

Test-Taking Tip

An opinion is a person's belief. It is not a proven fact (such as answer A). Opinions often contain subjective words, like *easier* or *best*.

Citizenship Cooperative Activity

25. Students' outlines should show organized planning and evidence of research.

Economics Activity

26. Students' paragraphs should show knowledge of the terms.

 HISTORY *Online*

Have students visit the Web site at tarvol1.glencoe.com to review Chapter 11 and take the Self-Check Quiz.

Standardized Test Practice

Answer: C
Question Type: History
Answer Explanation: Only C states an opinion. The other statements are facts.

Bonus Question ?

Ask: Who was the first president to be born a United States citizen? *(Martin Van Buren)*

 Geography and History Activity
19. the West and the South
20. Adams
21. Maine, New York, Maryland

Practicing Skills

22. Andrew Jackson's

23. The speaker's attitude is negative. He considers them uncivilized and less important than the whites.

24. White settlers would not move to that country, and Native Americans could not prosper if they lived among whites.

Timesaving Tools

TeacherWorks™ All-In-One Planner and Resource Center

- **Interactive Teacher Edition** Access your Teacher Wraparound Edition and your classroom resources with a few easy clicks.
- **Interactive Lesson Planner** Planning has never been easier! Organize your week, month, semester, or year with all the lesson helps you need to make teaching creative, timely, and relevant.

Use Glencoe's **Presentation Plus!** multimedia teacher tool to easily present dynamic lessons that visually excite your students. Using Microsoft PowerPoint® you can customize the presentations to create your own personalized lessons.

TEACHING TRANSPARENCIES

Graphic Organizer 10 L2

Why It Matters Chapter Transparency 12 L2

REVIEW AND REINFORCEMENT

Workbook Activity 12 L1

Time Line Activity 12 L2

Vocabulary Activity 12 L1

REVIEW AND REINFORCEMENT

Critical Thinking Skills Activity 12 L2

Take-Home Review Activity 12 L1

ENRICHMENT

Linking Past and Present Activity 12 L2

Primary Source Reading 12 L2

GEOGRAPHY

Geography and History Activity 12 L2

Meeting NCSS Standards

The following standards are highlighted in Chapter 12:

Section 1 VII Production, Distribution, & Consumption: B, E, G, H, I

Section 2 III People, Places, & Environments: A, H, I

Section 3 I Culture: A, B, C, E

Section 4 V Individuals, Groups, & Institutions: B, C, D, F, G

FOLDABLES™ Study Organizer

Dinah Zike's Foldables are three-dimensional, interactive graphic organizers that help students practice basic writing skills, review key vocabulary terms, and identify main ideas. Additional chapter activities can be found in the **Reading and Study Skills Foldables** booklet.

Chapter 12 Resources

ASSESSMENT AND EVALUATION

Chapter 12 Test Form A L2

Chapter 12 Test Form B L2

Standardized Test Practice Workbook Activity 12 L2

Performance Assessment Activity 12 L1, ELL

ExamView® Pro Testmaker CD-ROM

MULTIMEDIA

- Vocabulary PuzzleMaker CD-ROM
- Interactive Tutor Self-Assessment CD-ROM
- ExamView® Pro Testmaker CD-ROM
- Audio Program
- American History Primary Source Document Library CD-ROM
- MindJogger Videoquiz
- Presentation Plus! CD-ROM
- TeacherWorks CD-ROM
- Interactive Student Edition CD-ROM
- Glencoe Skillbuilder Interactive Workbook CD-ROM, Level 1
- The American Republic to 1877 Video Program
- American Music: Hits Through History

SPANISH RESOURCES

The following Spanish language materials are available in the Spanish Resources Binder:

- Spanish Guided Reading Activities
- Spanish Reteaching Activities
- Spanish Quizzes and Tests
- Spanish Vocabulary Activity
- Spanish Take-Home Review Activity
- Spanish Summaries
- The Declaration of Independence and United States Constitution Spanish Translation

---

The following videotape programs are available from Glencoe as supplements to Chapter 12:

- **The Alamo** (ISBN 1-56501-784-6)
- **The Best of the Real West** (ISBN 1-56501-352-2)
- **The Battle of the Alamo** (ISBN 1-56501-357-3)
- **California and the Dream Seekers** (2 Pack) (ISBN 0-7670-0555-4)

To order, call Glencoe at 1-800-334-7344. To find classroom resources to accompany many of these videos, check the following home pages:
A&E Television: www.aande.com
The History Channel: www.historychannel.com

Use our Web site for additional resources. All essential content is covered in the Student Edition.

You and your students can visit tarvol1.glencoe.com, the Web site companion to **The American Republic to 1877.** This innovative integration of electronic and print media offers your students a wealth of opportunities. The student text directs students to the Web site for the following options:

- **Chapter Overviews**
- **Self-Check Quizzes**
- **Student Web Activities**
- **Textbook Updates**

Answers to the student Web activities are provided for you in the **Web Activity Lesson Plans.** Additional Web resources and Interactive Tutor Puzzles are also available.

Chapter 12 Resources

SECTION RESOURCES

Daily Objectives	Reproducible Resources	Multimedia Resources
SECTION 1 **The Oregon Country** 1. Explain why large numbers of settlers headed for the Oregon country. 2. Understand how the idea of Manifest Destiny contributed to the nation's growth.	Reproducible Lesson Plan 12–1 Daily Lecture and Discussion Notes 12–1 Guided Reading Activity 12–1* Section Quiz 12–1* Reteaching Activity 12–1* Reading Essentials and Study Guide 12–1* Enrichment Activity 12–1	Daily Focus Skills Transparency 12–1 American Music: Hits Through History Interactive Tutor Self-Assessment CD-ROM ExamView® Pro Testmaker CD-ROM Presentation Plus! CD-ROM
SECTION 2 **Independence for Texas** 1. Understand why problems arose between the Mexican government and the American settlers in Texas. 2. Describe how Texas achieved independence from Mexico and later became a state.	Reproducible Lesson Plan 12–2 Daily Lecture and Discussion Notes 12–2 Guided Reading Activity 12–2* Section Quiz 12–2* Reteaching Activity 12–2* Reading Essentials and Study Guide 12–2* Enrichment Activity 12–2	Daily Focus Skills Transparency 12–2 ABCNews InterActive™ Historic America Electronic Field Trips Interactive Tutor Self-Assessment CD-ROM ExamView® Pro Testmaker CD-ROM Presentation Plus! CD-ROM
SECTION 3 **War With Mexico** 1. Explain why Americans began to settle in the Southwest. 2. Describe how the United States acquired New Mexico and California.	Reproducible Lesson Plan 12–3 Daily Lecture and Discussion Notes 12–3 Guided Reading Activity 12–3* Section Quiz 12–3* Reteaching Activity 12–3* Reading Essentials and Study Guide 12–3* Enrichment Activity 12–3	Daily Focus Skills Transparency 12–3 Interactive Tutor Self-Assessment CD-ROM ExamView® Pro Testmaker CD-ROM Presentation Plus! CD-ROM
SECTION 4 **New Settlers in California and Utah** 1. Understand how the hopes of getting rich quick drew thousands of people to California. 2. Describe how the search for religious freedom led to the settlement of Utah.	Reproducible Lesson Plan 12–4 Daily Lecture and Discussion Notes 12–4 Guided Reading Activity 12–4* Section Quiz 12–4* Reteaching Activity 12–4* Reading Essentials and Study Guide 12–4* Enrichment Activity 12–4	Daily Focus Skills Transparency 12–4 Vocabulary PuzzleMaker CD-ROM Interactive Tutor Self-Assessment CD-ROM ExamView® Pro Testmaker CD-ROM Presentation Plus! CD-ROM

0:00 OUT OF TIME?
Assign the Chapter 12 **Reading Essentials and Study Guide.**

*Also Available in Spanish

 Blackline Master   Transparency   CD-ROM   DVD

 Poster   Music Program   Audio Program   Videocassette

KEY TO ABILITY LEVELS

Teaching strategies have been coded.

L1   BASIC activities for all students
L2   AVERAGE activities for average to above-average students
L3   CHALLENGING activities for above-average students
ELL   ENGLISH LANGUAGE LEARNER activities

Block Schedule

Activities that are suited to use within the block scheduling framework are identified by:

Chapter 12 Resources

NATIONAL GEOGRAPHIC Teacher's Corner

INDEX TO NATIONAL GEOGRAPHIC MAGAZINE

The following articles relate to this chapter.

- "The Way West," by John G. Mitchell, September 2000.
- "Tex-Mex Border," by Richard Conniff, February 1996.
- "The Cherokee," by Geoffrey Norman, May 1995.
- "Powwow," by Michael Parfit, June 1994.
- "The American Prairie: Roots of the Sky," by Douglas H. Chadwick, October 1993.
- "Along the Santa Fe Trail," by Rowe Findley, February 1989.
- "Life and Death on the Oregon Trail: The Itch to Move West," by Boyd Gibbons, August 1986.

ADDITIONAL NATIONAL GEOGRAPHIC SOCIETY PRODUCTS

To order the following, call National Geographic at 1-800-368-2728:

- *GeoKit: Lewis and Clark* (Kit)
- *GeoKit: Westward Movement* (Kit)
- *The West That Was* (Video)
- *Exploration* (Map)
- *United States Territorial Growth* (Map)
- *National Geographic Desk Reference* (Book)
- *American Indians: A Brief History* (Video)

NGS ONLINE

Access National Geographic's Web site for current events, atlas updates, activities, links, interactive features, and archives.

www.nationalgeographic.com

MEETING SPECIAL NEEDS

In addition to the Differentiated Instruction strategies found in each section, the following resources are also suitable for your special needs students:

- *ExamView® Pro Testmaker CD-ROM* allows teachers to tailor tests by reducing answer choices.
- The *Audio Program* includes the entire narrative of the student edition so that less-proficient readers can listen to the words as they read them.
- The *Reading Essentials and Study Guide* provides the same content as the student edition but is written two grade levels below the textbook.
- *Guided Reading Activities* give less-proficient readers point-by-point instructions to increase comprehension as they read each textbook section.

From the Classroom of...

Sharon Owens
Westerville School District
Westerville, OH

Manifest Destiny Road Trip

Organize students into groups of four or five. Have them consult modern road maps and plan a trip out West that duplicates, as closely as possible, one of the trails presented on maps in this chapter, such as the Oregon or California Trails. Each student is responsible for researching at least one location along the route and making a short report on how the pioneers might have seen it versus how it appears today. For example, one student might research Fort Boise and compare it to present-day Boise, Idaho. Another student might research the Columbia River, examining how much more developed it is today than it was in the 1840s. Groups can present their trips to the class. Have them use visual aids, such as a drawing of their trail that includes those points of interest they have researched.

ADDITIONAL RESOURCES FROM GLENCOE

- American Music: Cultural Traditions
- American Art and Architecture
- Outline Map Resource Book
- U.S. Desk Map
- Building Geography Skills for Life
- Inclusion for the Middle School Social Studies Classroom Strategies and Activities
- Teaching Strategies for the American History Classroom (Including Block Scheduling Pacing Guides)
- American Crafts Hands-On Activities
- American Games Hands-On Activities
- American History Flash Cards

✓ **Performance Assessment**

Refer to Activity 12 in the Performance Assessment Activities and Rubrics booklet.

Why It Matters Activity

Tell students that Manifest Destiny refers to the mid-1800s idea that the purpose of the United States was to extend its borders to the Pacific. On a map, show students the states of Oregon, Texas, New Mexico, and California. Encourage students to discuss how it would affect the United States' position in the world if these states belonged to other countries. Ask students to discuss how these states affect the political and economic power of the United States.

GLENCOE TECHNOLOGY

The American Republic to 1877 Video Program

To learn more about Manifest Destiny and the history of Texas, have students view the Chapter 12 video, "Whose Destiny?" from **The American Republic to 1877 Video Program.**

 Available in DVD and VHS

MindJogger Videoquiz

Use **MindJogger Videoquiz** to preview the Chapter 12 content.

 Available in VHS

CHAPTER 12
Manifest Destiny

1818–1853

Why It Matters

The United States was made up of people who had emigrated from many places in the world. Many Americans remained on the move as the United States extended its political borders and grew economically.

The Impact Today

The United States grew in size and wealth, setting the stage for the nation's rise to great economic and political power.

The American Republic to 1877 *Video* *The chapter 12 video, "Whose Destiny?," chronicles the influence of Manifest Destiny on the history of Texas.*

1809
• Elizabeth Ann Seton founds Sisters of Charity

1820
• Missouri Compromise

1824
• Russia surrenders land south of Alaska

United States PRESIDENTS

Madison 1809–1817
Monroe 1817–1825
J.Q. Adams 1825–1829
Jackson 1829–1837

1810   *1820*   *1830*

World

1821
• Mexico declares independence from Spain

1828
• Russia declares war on Ottoman Empire

1830
• France occupies Algeria

Reading Strategy   PURPOSE FOR READING

In **pre- and post response activities,** students identify what they know before the activity and then identify what they learned from the activity. Begin by saying: "The fertile land, resources, and economic opportunities in western lands attracted settlers from the United States. Eventually, these lands were taken from Native Americans and countries that had settled and claimed them." Ask students to generate a list detailing how westward expansion affected Native Americans. Have them share their list with a partner. As a class, discuss the ideas generated in the pre-reading discussions. After reading, students write again verifying their lists and adding new information. **L1**

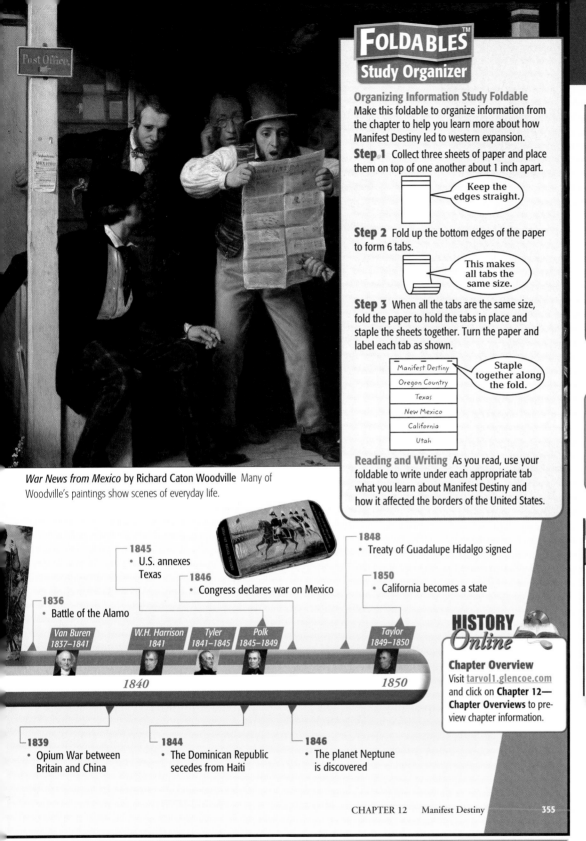

War News from Mexico by Richard Caton Woodville Many of Woodville's paintings show scenes of everyday life.

FOLDABLES™ Study Organizer

Organizing Information Study Foldable
Make this foldable to organize information from the chapter to help you learn more about how Manifest Destiny led to western expansion.

Step 1 Collect three sheets of paper and place them on top of one another about 1 inch apart.

> Keep the edges straight.

Step 2 Fold up the bottom edges of the paper to form 6 tabs.

> This makes all tabs the same size.

Step 3 When all the tabs are the same size, fold the paper to hold the tabs in place and staple the sheets together. Turn the paper and label each tab as shown.

| Manifest Destiny |
| Oregon Country |
| Texas |
| New Mexico |
| California |
| Utah |

> Staple together along the fold.

Reading and Writing As you read, use your foldable to write under each appropriate tab what you learn about Manifest Destiny and how it affected the borders of the United States.

FOLDABLES™ Study Organizer — Dinah Zike's Foldables

Purpose This activity requires students to create a table and organize information from the chapter in it. Students group information from the chapter into categories comparing the effects of Manifest Destiny on the borders of the United States.

📁 Have students complete *Reading and Study Skills Foldables* Activity 12. **L1**

HISTORY Online

Introduce students to chapter content and key terms by having them access **Chapter Overview 12** at tarvol1.glencoe.com

TIME LINE ACTIVITY

As students read the chapter, have them review the time line on pages 354–355. Ask students whether Texas was a colony of Spain, a part of Mexico, or an independent nation when the Battle of the Alamo was fought. Have them use the time line to explain their answers.

1845
• U.S. annexes Texas

1848
• Treaty of Guadalupe Hidalgo signed

1846
• Congress declares war on Mexico

1850
• California becomes a state

1836
• Battle of the Alamo

| Van Buren 1837–1841 | W.H. Harrison 1841 | Tyler 1841–1845 | Polk 1845–1849 | Taylor 1849–1850 |

1840   *1850*

HISTORY Online

Chapter Overview
Visit tarvol1.glencoe.com and click on **Chapter 12—Chapter Overviews** to preview chapter information.

1839
• Opium War between Britain and China

1844
• The Dominican Republic secedes from Haiti

1846
• The planet Neptune is discovered

CHAPTER 12 Manifest Destiny 355

More About the Art

Although Richard Caton Woodville (1825–1855) began his career training to be a doctor, he always had a passion for drawing and painting. In 1845 he went to Germany to study art at the Dusseldorf Academy. Much of his work portrays scenes from Baltimore, his hometown. Some of his more important works include *The Sailor's Wedding, Politics in an Oyster House,* and *War News from Mexico.*

1 FOCUS

Section Overview

This section explains how economics played a part in the settlement of the Oregon country.

BELLRINGER
Skillbuilder Activity

 Project transparency and have students answer the question.

Daily Focus Skills Transparency 12–1

Reading Preview

Answers to Graphic: 1819: Adams-Onís Treaty; 1825: Adams becomes President; 1836: Whitman builds mission in Oregon; 1846: United States and Britain set Oregon boundary

Preteaching Vocabulary
Call on volunteers to define each of the entries in **Key Terms**. Ask students to use the textbook glossary to check the accuracy of the definitions.

356

SECTION 1 The Oregon Country

Guide to Reading

Main Idea
Manifest Destiny is the idea that the United States was meant to extend its borders from the Atlantic Ocean to the Pacific Ocean.

Key Terms
joint occupation, mountain man, rendezvous, emigrant, Manifest Destiny

Reading Strategy
Sequencing Information As you read Section 1, re-create the diagram below and in the boxes list key events that occurred.

1819	1825	1836	1846

Read to Learn
• why large numbers of settlers headed for the Oregon Country.
• how the idea of Manifest Destiny contributed to the nation's growth.

Section Theme
Economic Factors Many fur traders and pioneers moved to Oregon for economic opportunities.

Preview of Events

♦1820   ♦1830   ♦1840   ♦1850

1819
Adams-Onís Treaty is signed

1836
Marcus Whitman builds mission in Oregon

1840s
"Oregon fever" sweeps through Mississippi Valley

1846
U.S. and Britain set the Oregon Boundary at 49°N

Doll owned by a young pioneer

AN American Story

On an April morning in 1851, 13-year-old Martha Gay said good-bye to her friends, her home, and the familiar world of Springfield, Missouri. She and her family were beginning a long, hazardous journey. The townsfolk watched as the Gays left in four big wagons pulled by teams of oxen. "Farewell sermons were preached and prayers offered for our safety," Martha wrote years later. "All places of business and the school were closed . . . and everybody came to say good-bye to us." This same scene occurred many times in the 1840s and 1850s as thousands of families set out for the Oregon Country.

Rivalry in the Northwest

The **Oregon Country** was the huge area that lay between the Pacific Ocean and the Rocky Mountains north of **California.** It included all of what is now Oregon, Washington, and Idaho plus parts of Montana and Wyoming. The region also contained about half of what is now the Canadian province of British Columbia.

356   CHAPTER 12   Manifest Destiny

SECTION RESOURCES

📁 Reproducible Masters
• Reproducible Lesson Plan 12–1
• Daily Lecture and Discussion Notes 12–1
• Guided Reading Activity 12–1
• Section Quiz 12–1
• Reteaching Activity 12–1
• Reading Essentials and Study Guide 12–1
• Enrichment Activity 12–1

Transparencies
• Daily Focus Skills Transparency 12–1

Multimedia
📺 American Music: Hits Through History
💿 Interactive Tutor Self-Assessment CD-ROM
💿 ExamView® Pro Testmaker CD-ROM
💿 Presentation Plus! CD-ROM

In the early 1800s, four nations laid claim to the vast, rugged land known as the Oregon Country. The United States based its claim on Robert Gray's discovery of the **Columbia River** in 1792 and on the Lewis and Clark expedition. Great Britain based its claim on British explorations of the Columbia River. Spain, which had also explored the Pacific coast in the late 1700s, controlled California to the south. Russia had settlements that stretched south from **Alaska** into Oregon.

Adams-Onís Treaty

Many Americans wanted control of the Oregon Country to gain access to the Pacific Ocean. Secretary of State **John Quincy Adams** played a key role in promoting this goal. In 1819 he negotiated the **Adams-Onís Treaty** with Spain. In the treaty the Spanish agreed to set the limits of their territory at what is now California's northern border and gave up any claim to Oregon. In 1824 Russia also surrendered its claim to the land south of Alaska. Only Britain remained to challenge American control of Oregon.

In 1818 Adams had worked out an agreement with Britain for joint occupation of the area. This meant that people from both the United States and Great Britain could settle there. When Adams became president in 1825, he proposed that the two nations divide Oregon along the 49°N line of latitude. Britain refused, insisting on a larger share of the territory. Unable to resolve their dispute, the two countries agreed to extend the joint occupation. In the following years, thousands of Americans streamed into Oregon, and they pushed the issue toward resolution.

Mountain Men

The first Americans to reach the Oregon Country were not farmers but fur traders. They had come to trap beaver, whose skins were in great demand in the eastern United States and in Europe. The British established several trading posts in the region, as did merchant **John Jacob Astor** of New York. In 1808 Astor organized the American Fur Company. The American Fur Company soon became the most powerful of the fur companies in America. It allowed him to build up trade with the East Coast, the Pacific Northwest, and China.

At first the merchants traded for furs that the Native Americans supplied. Gradually American adventurers joined the trade. These people, who spent most of their time in the Rocky Mountains, came to be known as mountain men.

The tough, independent mountain men made their living by trapping beaver. Many had Native American wives and adopted Native American ways. They lived in buffalo-skin lodges and dressed in fringed buckskin pants, moccasins, and beads.

Some mountain men worked for fur-trading companies; others sold their furs to the highest bidder. Throughout the spring and early summer they ranged across the mountains, setting traps and then collecting the beaver pelts. In late summer they gathered for a rendezvous (RAHN•dih•voo), or meeting.

For the mountain men, the annual rendezvous was the high point of the year. They met with the trading companies to exchange their "hairy

"To explore unknown regions . . . was [the mountain men's] chief delight."

—Clerk in a fur trade company

2 TEACH

Reading Strategy

Describing Characteristics
Mountain men and pioneers alike were independent, resourceful, hardworking, and determined—characteristics that people often attribute to Americans in general. Write those traits on the chalkboard and ask students to find examples of each in the section. **L1**

Who?What?Where?When?

Mountain Men Fur traders placed ads in newspapers to recruit men for trapping. One ad called for a hundred men to work for one, two, or three years under the leadership of an army major.

Reading Strategy   READING THE TEXT

Writing Free Writes Ask students to imagine what would have enticed them to move to the Oregon country. Students should find many of Oregon's attractions in the section. Ask students to write which attributes would have encouraged them to move and why.

L1, ELL

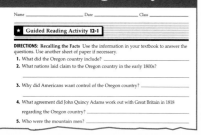

Guided Reading Activity 12-1

Name _____ Date _____ Class _____

★ **Guided Reading Activity 12-1**

DIRECTIONS: Recalling the Facts Use the information in your textbook to answer the questions. Use another sheet of paper if necessary.
1. What did the Oregon country include? _____
2. What nations laid claim to the Oregon country in the early 1800s? _____
3. Why did Americans want control of the Oregon country? _____
4. What agreement did John Quincy Adams work out with Great Britain in 1818 regarding the Oregon country? _____
5. Who were the mountain men? _____

✓ **Reading Check**

Answer: the territories from Alaska into Oregon

History *and the* Humanities

♪ American Music: Hits Through History, "Nabucca's Quick Step"

✓ **Reading Check**

Answer: They traveled along the Oregon Trail in prairie schooners.

Where?When?Who?What?

Oregon The following quote from a Missouri farmer gives one man's reasons to pack up and head to Oregon: "Out in Oregon I can get me a square mile of land. And a quarter section for each of you all. Dad burn me, I am done with this country. Winters it's frost and snow to freeze a body; summers the overflow from Old Muddy drowns half my acres; taxes take the yield of them that are left. What say, Maw, it's God's country."

banknotes"—beaver skins—for traps, guns, coffee, and other goods. They met old friends and exchanged news. They relaxed by competing in races and various other contests—including swapping stories about who had been on the most exciting adventures.

As they roamed searching for beaver, the mountain men explored the mountains, valleys, and trails of the West. Jim Beckwourth, an African American from Virginia, explored Wyoming's Green River. Robert Stuart and Jedediah Smith both found the **South Pass,** a broad break through the Rockies. South Pass later became the main route that settlers took to Oregon.

To survive in the wilderness, a mountain man had to be skillful and resourceful. Trapper Joe Meek told how, when faced with starvation, he once held his hands "in an anthill until they were covered with ants, then greedily licked them off." The mountain men took pride in joking about the dangers they faced.

In time the mountain men killed off most of the beaver and could no longer trap. Some went to settle on farms in Oregon. With their knowledge of the western lands, though, some mountain men found new work. Jim Bridger, Kit Carson, and others acted as guides to lead the parties of settlers now streaming west.

✓ **Reading Check** **Identifying** What North American territories did Russia control in the early 1800s?

Fact • Fiction • Folklore

Alaska

Is Alaska the largest state? If you calculate by area, Alaska is far and away the largest state, with more than 570,000 square miles. It is approximately 2,000 miles from east to west. If placed on top of the mainland area of the United States, it would stretch from Atlanta to Los Angeles. Population is another matter. Alaska's population of 626,932 makes it the third least populous state. There is about 1.0 person per square mile in Alaska, compared to more than 79 people per square mile for the rest of the United States.

358   CHAPTER 12   Manifest Destiny

Settling Oregon

Americans began traveling to the Oregon Country to settle in the 1830s. Reports of the fertile land persuaded many to make the journey. Economic troubles at home made new opportunities in the West look attractive.

The Whitman Mission

Among the first settlers of the Oregon Country were missionaries who wanted to bring Christianity to the Native Americans. Dr. Marcus Whitman and his wife, Narcissa, went to Oregon in 1836 and built a mission among the Cayuse people near the present site of Walla Walla, Washington.

New settlers unknowingly brought measles to the mission. An epidemic killed many of the Native American children. Blaming the Whitmans for the sickness, the Cayuse attacked the mission in November 1847 and killed them and 11 others. Despite this, the flood of settlers continued into Oregon.

The Oregon Trail

In the early 1840s, "Oregon fever" swept through the Mississippi Valley. The depression caused by the Panic of 1837 had hit the region hard. People formed societies to gather information about Oregon and to plan to make the long trip. The "great migration" had begun. Tens of thousands of people made the trip. These pioneers were called emigrants because they left the United States to go to Oregon.

Before the difficult 2,000-mile journey, these pioneers stuffed their canvas-covered wagons, called **prairie schooners,** with supplies. From a distance these wagons looked like schooners (ships) at sea. Gathering in Independence or other towns in Missouri, they followed the **Oregon Trail** across the Great Plains, along the Platte River, and through the South Pass of the Rocky Mountains. On the other side, they took the trail north and west along the Snake and Columbia Rivers into the Oregon Country.

✓ **Reading Check** **Explaining** How did most pioneers get to Oregon?

DIFFERENTIATED INSTRUCTION

Reading Support Travel on the 2,000-mile (3,200-km) Oregon Trail was slow. Wagons went from 1 to 2 miles an hour (1.6 to 3.2 kph). Today the same trip could be completed traveling by car and averaging 60 miles per hour (97 kph). Have students create a pictograph comparing the pioneers' trip with a modern trip by car. **L1**

📁 Refer to *Inclusion for the Middle School Social Studies Classroom Strategies and Activities* in the TCR.

MORE ABOUT...

The Oregon Trail

The Importance of the Trail The Oregon Trail was much more than just a trail to Oregon. It served as the most practical route to the western United States. The pioneers traveled in large groups, often of related families. Some went all the way to Oregon in search of farmland. Many others split off for California in search of gold.

The Journey The trip west lasted five or six months. The pioneers had to start in the spring and complete the trip before winter snows blocked the mountain passes. The trail crossed difficult terrain. The pioneers walked across seemingly endless plains, forded swift rivers, and labored up high mountains.

Problems Along the Way Although the pioneers feared attacks by Native Americans, such attacks did not often occur. More often Native Americans assisted the pioneers, serving as guides and trading necessary food and supplies. About 1 in 10 of the pioneers died on the trail, perishing from disease, overwork, hunger, or accidents.

When did use of the trail stop? With the building of a transcontinental railroad in 1869, the days of using the Oregon Trail as a corridor to the West were over.

"We are creeping along slowly, one wagon after another, the same old gait, the same thing over, out of one mud hole into another all day."
—*Amelia Stewart Knight, 1853*

"After Laramie we entered the great American desert, which was hard on the teams. Sickness became common. . . ."
—*Catherine Sager Pringle, 1844*

One of the many stories of endurance on the way west to Oregon is that of Janette Riker. In Montana in September 1849, her father and two brothers went hunting and never came back. She was left alone. To survive the coming winter, Janette built a hut, which she heated with the family stove and firewood that she chopped. To add to the provisions from the wagon, she butchered an ox and salted the meat. Finally Native Americans discovered her. They were so impressed that she had made it through the winter alone that they agreed to take her where she wanted to go. **Ask:** What are five possible hardships that pioneers faced during their journey west? (*Answers may include difficult terrain, disease, hunger, attacks from animals, and cold weather.*)

3 ASSESS

Assign Section 1 Assessment as homework or as an in-class activity.

🖝 Have students use **Interactive Tutor Self-Assessment CD-ROM.**

L2

Section Quiz 12-1

Name	Date	Class
⭐ Chapter 12		Score

Section Quiz 12-1

DIRECTIONS: Matching Match the items in Column A with the items in Column B. Write the correct letters in the blanks. *(10 points each)*

Column A	Column B
_____ 1. American merchant	A. mountain men
_____ 2. fur trappers	B. meeting
_____ 3. rendezvous	C. Dr. Marcus Whitman
_____ 4. missionary	D. Manifest Destiny
_____ 5. national mission	E. John Jacob Astor

The Division of Oregon

Most American pioneers headed for the fertile **Willamette Valley** south of the Columbia River. Between 1840 and 1845, the number of American settlers in the area increased from 500 to 5,000, while the British population remained at about 700. The question of ownership of Oregon arose again.

Expansion of Freedom

Since colonial times many Americans had believed their nation had a special role to fulfill. For years people thought the nation's mission should be to serve as a model of freedom and democracy. In the 1800s that vision changed. Many believed that the United States's mission was to spread freedom by occupying the entire continent. In 1819 John Quincy Adams expressed what many Americans were thinking when he said expansion to the Pacific was as inevitable "as that the Mississippi should flow to the sea."

Manifest Destiny

In the 1840s New York newspaper editor John O'Sullivan put the idea of a national mission in more specific words. O'Sullivan declared it was

CHAPTER 12   Manifest Destiny   **359**

INTERDISCIPLINARY CONNECTIONS ACTIVITY

Language Arts Have each student find a biography of someone from the period, read it, and write a book report. Subjects may include the following people: Jim Beckwourth, Jim Bridger, Kit Carson, John J. Astor, Jedediah Smith, Marcus and Narcissa Whitman, John Sager and his family. John and his brothers and sisters were orphaned on the Oregon Trail and were taken to the Whitman mission by members of their wagon train. (At least one book has 13-year-old John and his younger siblings—one a baby and one with a broken leg—proceeding alone to the mission, which makes a dramatic story but is not true.) **L2**

✔ Reading Check

Answer: Some people thought the United States had a special purpose to spread freedom by extending its boundaries to the Pacific Ocean.

L1

Reteaching Activity 12–1

Name _____ Date _____ Class _____

★ Reteaching Activity 12-1

DIRECTIONS: Organizing Facts The items in the Fact Bank describe or name mountain men or pioneers of the Oregon country. Complete the web diagram by writing the letter of each item in the correct circle.

Mountain Men · Oregon Country · Pioneers

L1, ELL

Reading Essentials and Study Guide 12–1

Study Guide

Chapter 12, Section 1
For use with textbook pages 356–360

THE OREGON COUNTRY

KEY TERMS	
joint occupation	The agreement allowing both the United States and Britain to settle in the Oregon territory (page 357)
mountain man	A person who spends most of his time in the mountains (page 357)
rendezvous	A meeting (page 357)
emigrant	People who leave the United States to live in another country (page 358)
Manifest Destiny	The idea that the United States had a special purpose to extend its boundaries from the Atlantic Ocean to the Pacific Ocean (page 360)

DRAWING FROM EXPERIENCE

L3

Enrichment Activity 12–1

Name _____ Date _____ Class _____

★ Enrichment Activity 12-1

Rendezvous

The mountain men's rendezvous, where they traded furs for other goods, was often the highlight of the year for these early explorers of the Oregon country. Alfred Jacob Miller, an American painter, painted scenes of the rendezvous and described it in notes. Below are excerpts from his notes on a painting of an 1837 rendezvous, near Green River, Oregon.

This was . . . our final destination. Here we rested for a month under the shadows of the great spurs of Wind River Mountains, encamping among 3000 Snake and other Indians who had all assembled at this place . . . [to] trade buffalo robes and peltries for dry goods, ammunition, tobacco, etc. It had . . .

directions, some of them dressed in barbaric magnificence.
. . . The American Fur company's great tent is elevated and trading goes briskly forward. Here the trapper gets his outfit and gangs of them depart under a "bourgeois" for the beaver streams to trap the valuable animal. Here we saw all the . . .

4 CLOSE

Have students evaluate John Quincy Adams's statement that American expansion to the Pacific was a "law of nature."

Fact → Fiction Folklore

The Presidency

Who was the first "dark horse" president? A dark horse is a little-known contender who unexpectedly wins. In 1844 the Democrats passed over Martin Van Buren, John C. Calhoun, and other party leaders. Instead, they nominated James K. Polk, the governor of Tennessee. The Whigs were confident that their candidate, the celebrated Henry Clay, would win the election easily. Contrary to all expectations, Polk won the election, becoming at age 49 the youngest president in American history up to that time.

America's "Manifest Destiny to overspread and to possess the whole of the continent which Providence has given us." O'Sullivan meant that the United States was clearly destined—set apart for a special purpose—to extend its boundaries all the way to the Pacific.

"Fifty-four Forty or Fight"

The settlers in Oregon insisted that the United States should have sole ownership of the area. More and more Americans agreed. As a result Oregon became a significant issue in the 1844 presidential election.

James K. Polk received the Democratic Party's nomination for president, partly because he supported American claims for sole ownership of Oregon. Democrats campaigned using the slogan "Fifty-four Forty or Fight." The slogan referred to the line of latitude that Democrats believed should be the nation's northern border in Oregon.

Henry Clay of the Whig Party, Polk's principal opponent, did not take a strong position on the Oregon issue. Polk won the election because the antislavery Liberty Party took so many votes from Clay in New York that Polk won the state. Polk won 170 electoral votes to 105 for Clay.

Reaching a Settlement

Filled with the spirit of Manifest Destiny, President Polk was determined to make Oregon part of the United States. Britain would not accept a border at "Fifty-four Forty," however. To do so would have meant giving up its claim entirely. Instead, in June 1846, the two countries compromised, setting the boundary between the American and British portions of Oregon at latitude 49°N.

During the 1830s Americans sought to fulfill their Manifest Destiny by looking much closer to home than Oregon. At that time much attention was also focused on Texas.

✔ **Reading Check** **Explaining** In what way did some people think of Manifest Destiny as a purpose?

SECTION 1 ASSESSMENT

Checking for Understanding

1. **Key Terms** Use each of these terms in a complete sentence that will help explain its meaning: joint occupation, mountain man, rendezvous, emigrant, Manifest Destiny.

2. **Reviewing Facts** Name the four countries that claimed parts of the Oregon Country.

Reviewing Themes

3. **Economic Factors** How did the fur trade in Oregon aid Americans who began settling there?

Critical Thinking

4. **Making Generalizations** How did the idea of Manifest Destiny help Americans justify their desire to extend the United States to the Pacific Ocean?

5. **Determining Cause and Effect** Re-create the diagram below. In the box, describe how the fur trade led to interest in Oregon.

Cause	→	
The fur trade develops		

Analyzing Visuals

6. **Picturing History** Study the painting on page 359. Do you think it provides a realistic portrayal of the journey west?

Interdisciplinary Activity

Informative Writing Imagine you and your family are traveling to the Oregon Country in the 1840s. A friend will be making the same trip soon. Write a letter telling your friend what to expect on the journey.

SECTION 1 ASSESSMENT ANSWERS

1. Student work should reflect correct use of terms.
2. United States, Great Britain, Spain, Russia
3. Fur trappers and traders served as guides to lead parties of settlers west.

4. Many Americans believed that it was the destiny or mission of the United States to spread freedom by occupying the North American continent.
5. Reports of fertile land encouraged many to move there.

6. Student opinions will vary.

Interdisciplinary Activity Students' letters should refer to some of the hardships of travel over the Oregon Trail.

Understanding Latitude and Longitude

Why Learn This Skill?

Your new friend invites you to her house. In giving directions, she says, "I live on Summit Street at the southwest corner of Indiana Avenue." She has pinpointed her exact location. We use a similar system of lines of latitude and longitude to pinpoint locations on maps and globes.

Learning the Skill

The imaginary horizontal lines that circle the globe from east to west are called lines of **latitude.** Because the distance between the lines of latitude is always the same, they are also called *parallels.* The imaginary vertical lines that intersect the parallels are lines of **longitude,** also called *meridians.*

Lines of longitude run from the North Pole to the South Pole. They are numbered in degrees east or west of a starting line called the Prime Meridian, which is at 0° longitude. On the opposite side of the earth from the Prime Meridian is the International Date Line, or 180° longitude.

The point at which parallels and meridians intersect is the grid address, or coordinates, of an exact location. The coordinates for Salt Lake City, for example, are 41°N and 112°W.

NATIONAL GEOGRAPHIC — Oregon Country

Practicing the Skill

Analyze the information on the map on this page, then answer the following questions.

1. What are the approximate coordinates of Fort Victoria?

2. At what line of latitude was the Oregon Country divided between the United States and Britain?

3. What geographic feature lies at about 42°N and 115°W?

Applying the Skill

Understanding Latitude and Longitude Turn to the atlas map of the United States on pages RA2 and RA3. Find your city or the city closest to it. Identify the coordinates as closely as possible. Now list the coordinates of five other cities and ask a classmate to find the cities based on your coordinates.

Glencoe's **Skillbuilder Interactive Workbook CD-ROM, Level 1,** provides instruction and practice in key social studies skills.

TEACH

Understanding Latitude and Longitude This skill teaches students how to use latitude and longitude to locate places. Point out that on maps 0° latitude (Equator), 0° longitude (Prime Meridian), and 180° are not labeled north, south, east, or west because they are lines of reference. Note also that not all the lines of latitude or longitude are labeled. To find coordinates, students will have to estimate distance between lines. Astoria, for example, is a little less than halfway between 120°W and 130°W, so it is a little less than 125°W, or about 124°W. **Ask: Is the boundary of 1846 a parallel or a meridian?** *(parallel)*

Additional Practice
L2

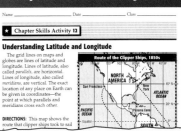

Chapter Skills Activity 12

GLENCOE
TECHNOLOGY

CD-ROM
Glencoe Skillbuilder Interactive Workbook CD-ROM, Level 1

This interactive CD-ROM reinforces student mastery of essential social studies skills.

ANSWERS TO PRACTICING THE SKILL

1. 48°N, 125°W

2. 49°N

3. the Great Salt Lake

Applying the Skill Students should find the coordinates of their city or the city closest to it and have a partner find other cities based on their coordinates.

1 FOCUS

Section Overview

This section describes how Mexico's offer of huge tracts of fertile land brought American settlers to Texas.

Reading Preview

Answers to Graphic: Oct. 1835: Battle at Gonzales; Dec. 1835: Texans liberate San Antonio; Feb. 1836: Siege of Alamo begins; Mar. 1836: declaration of independence of the Republic of Texas; Apr. 1836: Battle at San Jacinto; May 1836: Santa Anna signs treaty; Sept. 1836: Sam Houston elected president of independent Texas

Preteaching Vocabulary
Write *empresario* on the chalkboard. Then have a volunteer skim the section to find the term and read it in context.

Guide to Reading

Main Idea
Texans won their independence from Mexico and asked to be admitted to the United States.

Key Terms
Tejano, empresario, decree, annex

Reading Strategy
Sequencing Information As you read Section 2, re-create the diagram below and, in the boxes, list key events that occurred in Texas.

1835   1836
Oct. | Dec. | Mar. | May
Feb. | Apr. | Sept.

Read to Learn
• why problems arose between the Mexican government and the American settlers in Texas.
• how Texas achieved independence and later became a state.

Section Theme
Geography and History Mexico's offers of huge tracts of fertile land brought American settlers to Texas.

Preview of Events

♦1820   ♦1830   ♦1840

1821
Moses Austin receives land grant in Texas

1833
Santa Anna becomes president of Mexico

March 1836
The Alamo falls to Mexican troops

September 1836
Sam Houston is elected president of Texas

Davy Crockett

AN
American Story

Davy Crockett was a backwoodsman from Tennessee. His skill as a hunter and story-teller helped get him elected to three terms in Congress. But when he started his first political campaign, Crockett was doubtful about his chances of winning. "The thought of having to make a speech made my knees feel mighty weak and set my heart to flut-tering." Fortunately for Crockett, the other candidates spoke all day and tired out the audience. "When they were all done," Crockett boasted, "I got up and told some laugh-able story, and quit. . . . I went home, and didn't go back again till after the election was over." In the end, Crockett won the election by a wide margin.

A Clash of Cultures

Davy Crockett of Tennessee won notice for his frontier skills, his sense of humor, and the shrewd common sense he often displayed in politics. When he lost his seat in Congress in 1835, he did not return to Tennessee. Instead he went southwest to Texas.

SECTION RESOURCES

📁 **Reproducible Masters**
• Reproducible Lesson Plan 12–2
• Daily Lecture and Discussion Notes 12–2
• Guided Reading Activity 12–2
• Section Quiz 12–2
• Reteaching Activity 12–2
• Reading Essentials and Study Guide 12–2
• Enrichment Activity 12–2

✎ **Transparencies**
• Daily Focus Skills Transparency 12–2

Multimedia
📼 ABC News Interactive™ Historic America Electronic Field Trips
💿 Interactive Tutor Self-Assessment CD-ROM
💿 ExamView® Pro Testmaker CD-ROM
💿 Presentation Plus! CD-ROM

Crockett thought he could make a new start there. He also wanted to help the Texans win their independence from Mexico. Little did he know his deeds in Texas would bring him greater fame than his adventures on the frontier or his years in Congress.

Conflict over Texas began in 1803, when the United States bought the Louisiana Territory from France. Americans claimed that the land in present-day Texas was part of the purchase. Spain protested. In 1819, in the **Adams-Onís Treaty**, the United States agreed to drop any further claim to the region.

Land Grants

At the time, few people lived in Texas. Most residents—about 3,000—were Tejanos (teh•HAH•nohs), or Mexicans who claimed Texas as their home. Native Americans, including Comanches, Apaches, and Kiowas, also lived in the area.

Because the Spanish wanted to promote the growth of Texas, they offered vast tracts of land to people who agreed to bring families to settle

on the land. The people who obtained these grants from the government and recruited the settlers were called empresarios.

Moses Austin, a businessman who had developed a mining operation in Missouri, applied for and received the first land grant in 1821. Before he could establish his colony, however, Moses contracted pneumonia and died. After Mexico declared independence from Spain, Austin's son, **Stephen F. Austin,** asked the Mexican government to confirm his father's land grant. Once he received confirmation, he began to organize the colony.

Stephen F. Austin recruited 300 American families to settle the fertile land along the Brazos River and the Colorado River of Texas. The first settlers came to be called the **Old Three Hundred.** Many received 960 acres, with additional acres for each child. Others received larger ranches. Austin's success made him a leader among the American settlers in Texas.

From 1823 to 1825, Mexico passed three colonization laws. All these laws offered new settlers large tracts of land at extremely low prices and

People In History

Stephen F. Austin 1793–1836

Stephen F. Austin earned the name "Father of Texas" because of his leadership in populating the Mexican territory of Texas. After attending college he worked as a businessperson. Austin organized the first land grant colony in Texas in 1821. Austin offered large tracts of land to settlers, and his colony grew quickly.

Austin often played the role of spokesperson with the Mexican government, sometimes on behalf of colonists who were not part of his settlement. He served as their advocate, even when he disagreed with their opinions. For example, he negotiated for permission to continue slavery in the province of Texas after it was banned by Mexican law. He also served

nearly a year in prison for promoting independence for the Texans.

After Texas won its war for independence, Austin ran for the office of president. He was defeated but was appointed secretary of state. He died just a few months later. The state of Texas honored Stephen F. Austin by naming its capital city—Austin—after its founding father.

CHAPTER 12   Manifest Destiny   **363**

COOPERATIVE LEARNING ACTIVITY

Making an Illustrated Time Line Have students work together to make a large, illustrated time line of this section for the bulletin board. As a class, students should decide which events to include. Assign some students to make the actual time line. Then organize the remainder of the class into small groups, each working on one event. In each group some students may do any necessary research; others should make the illustrations; others should write brief captions describing the event. **L1, ELL** 📓

What If...

Answers:

1. Answers will vary, but students should note that the stand at the Alamo encouraged Texans to continue to fight for their independence.
2. If the defenders of the Alamo had surrendered, then the battle might not have provided Texan leaders time to meet and declare the independence of the Republic of Texas.

ABCNEWS INTERACTIVE™

 VIDEOCASSETTE
Historic America Electronic Field Trips

View **Chapter 10** to learn more about the Alamo.

you don't say...

Texas The name *Texas* comes from a Native American word meaning "friend" or "ally." Spanish speakers changed it to *tejas* and English speakers to *Texas*.

What If...

The Defenders Had Not Stayed at the Alamo?

William Travis and almost 200 other defenders were determined to hold the Alamo. Travis wrote several messages to the people of Texas and the United States asking them for assistance. Travis's appeal was unsuccessful. Texas military forces were not yet well organized and were badly scattered. Travis's letter of February 24, 1836, is one of the finest statements of courage in American history.

The defenders—mostly volunteers—were free to leave whenever they chose. But they decided to defend the Alamo for a cause in which they believed.

Santa Anna hoped the fall of the Alamo would convince other Texans that it was useless to resist his armies. Instead, the heroism of those in the Alamo inspired other Texans to carry on the struggle. "Remember the Alamo!" became the battle cry of Houston's army.

Travis's Appeal for Aid at the Alamo,
February 24, 1836

> To the People of Texas and All Americans in the World—
>
> Fellow Citizens and Compatriots:
>
> I am besieged by a thousand or more of the Mexicans under Santa Anna. I have sustained a continual Bombardment & cannonade for 24 hours & have not lost a man. The enemy has demanded a surrender at discretion, otherwise the garrison are to be put to the sword if the fort is taken. I have answered the demand with a cannon shot, and our flag still waves proudly from the walls. I shall never surrender or retreat.
>
> Then, I call on you in the name of Liberty, of patriotism, & of everything dear to the American character, to come to our aid with all dispatch. The enemy is receiving reinforcements daily & will no doubt increase to three or four thousand in four or five days. If this call is neglected I am determined to sustain myself as long as possible & die like a soldier who never forgets what is due to his honor & that of his country.
>
> Victory or Death
> William Barret Travis
> Lt. Col. Comdt.

reduced or no taxes for several years. In return the colonists agreed to learn Spanish, become Mexican citizens, convert to Catholicism—the religion of Mexico—and obey Mexican law.

Mexican leaders hoped to attract settlers from all over, including other parts of Mexico. Most Texas settlers, however, came from the United States.

Growing Tension

By 1830 Americans in Texas far outnumbered Mexicans. Further, these American colonists had not adopted Mexican ways. In the meantime the United States had twice offered to buy Texas from Mexico.

The Mexican government viewed the growing American influence in Texas with alarm. In 1830 the Mexican government issued a decree, or official order, that stopped all immigration from the United States. At the same time, the decree encouraged the immigration of Mexican and European families with generous land grants. Trade between Texas and the United States was discouraged by placing a tax on goods imported from the United States.

These new policies angered the Texans. The prosperity of many citizens depended on trade with the United States. Many had friends and relatives who wanted to come to Texas. In addition, those colonists who held slaves were uneasy about the Mexican government's plans to end slavery.

Attempt at Reconciliation

Some of the American settlers called for independence. Others hoped to stay within Mexico but on better terms. In 1833 **General Antonio López de Santa Anna** became president of

364 CHAPTER 12 Manifest Destiny

DIFFERENTIATED INSTRUCTION

Gifted and Talented Have students list the quarrels between the two sides: Americans' failure to learn Spanish, convert to Catholicism, and obey Mexican law; Mexico's forbidding further American settlement and taxing of goods imported from the United States; and Mexico's plan to end slavery. Then have students write a letter to a newspaper editor describing the quarrels from the Mexican point of view. Remind students to use standard grammar, spelling, sentence structure, and punctuation. **L3**

☞ Refer to ***Inclusion for the Middle School Social Studies Classroom Strategies and Activities*** in the TCR.

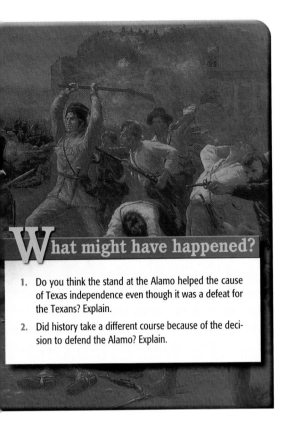

What might have happened?

1. Do you think the stand at the Alamo helped the cause of Texas independence even though it was a defeat for the Texans? Explain.

2. Did history take a different course because of the decision to defend the Alamo? Explain.

The Struggle for Independence

During 1835 unrest grew among Texans and occasionally resulted in open conflict. Santa Anna sent an army into Texas to punish the Texans for criticizing him. In October some Mexican troops tried to seize a cannon held by Texans at the town of **Gonzales.** During the battle the Texans decorated the front of the cannon with a white flag that bore the words "Come and Take It." After a brief struggle, Texans drove back the Mexican troops. Texans consider this to be the first fight of the Texan Revolution.

The Texans called on volunteers to join their fight. They offered free land to anyone who would help. Davy Crockett and many others—including a number of African Americans and Tejanos—answered that call.

In December 1835, the Texans scored an important victory. They liberated **San Antonio** from the control of a larger Mexican force. The Texas army at San Antonio included more than 100 Tejanos. Many of them served in a scouting company commanded by Captain Juan Seguín. Born in San Antonio, Seguín was an outspoken champion of the Texans' demand for independence.

Despite these victories, the Texans encountered problems. With the Mexican withdrawal, some Texans left San Antonio, thinking the war was won. Various groups argued over who was in charge and what course of action to follow. In early 1836, when Texas should have been making preparations to face Santa Anna, nothing was being done.

The Battle of the Alamo

Santa Anna marched north, furious at the loss of San Antonio. When his army reached San Antonio in late February 1836, it found a small Texan force barricaded inside a nearby mission called the **Alamo.**

Although the Texans had cannons, they lacked gunpowder. Worse, they had only about 180 soldiers to face Santa Anna's army of several thousand. The Texans did have brave leaders, though, including Davy Crockett, who had arrived with a band of sharpshooters from Tennessee, and a tough Texan named Jim Bowie. The commander, William B. Travis, was only 26

Mexico. Stephen F. Austin traveled to Mexico City with the Texans' demands, which were to remove the ban on American settlers and to make Texas a separate state.

Santa Anna agreed to the first request but refused the second. Austin sent a letter back to Texas, suggesting that plans for independence get underway. The Mexican government intercepted the letter and arrested Austin. While Austin was in jail, Santa Anna named himself dictator and overthrew Mexico's constitution of 1824. Without a constitution to protect their rights, Texans felt betrayed. Santa Anna reorganized the government, placing greater central control over Texas. This loss of local power dismayed many people.

✓**Reading Check** **Explaining** What role did empresarios play in colonization?

✓**Reading Check**

Answer: They arranged for settlers to settle on tracts of land granted by the Mexican government.

L1, ELL

Guided Reading Activity 12–2

Name _____ Date _____ Class _____

★ Guided Reading Activity 12-2

DIRECTIONS: Outlining Locate the heading in your textbook. Then use the information under the heading to help you write each answer. Use another sheet of paper if necessary.

I. A Clash of Cultures
  A. Introduction—Why did Americans believe that they had the right to claim Texas?
  B. Land Grants—What name was given to the first American families, carefully recruited by Stephen F. Austin, to settle in Texas?
  C. Growing Tension—What was the purpose of the 1830 decree issued by Mexico?
  D. Attempt at Reconciliation—What demands did Austin present to the Mexican president Antonio López de Santa Anna in their 1833 meeting?

II. The Struggle for Independence
  A. Introduction
    1. What do Texans consider the first fight of the Texan Revolution?
    2. Where did Texans score an important victory in 1835?
  B. The Battle of the Alamo
    1. When was the Battle of the Alamo?
    2. Who led the Mexican forces and who led the Texans at the Alamo?
    3. Although they lost the battle and their lives, what had the defenders of the Alamo done for Texas?
  C. Texas Declares Its Independence
    1. What happened on March 2, 1836?
    2. What was the Goliad Massacre?
  D. The Battle of San Jacinto—What was the battle cry of Texans at the battle of San Jacinto?

III. The Lone Star Republic
  A. Introduction—Who was elected president of Texas in 1836?
  B. Texas Becomes a State—When did Texas officially become a state?

CURRICULUM CONNECTION

Economics As an additional incentive for American settlers in Texas, the Mexican government promised protection from lawsuits filed in the United States for failure to pay debts. Such a large number of bankrupt families decided to take the opportunity to start over that vacated homes with signs reading "Gone to Texas" became a familiar sight throughout the South.

INTERDISCIPLINARY CONNECTIONS ACTIVITY

Geography The landscape of the Oregon Trail and the climate of Texas influenced how and where pioneers settled. Geography still has an effect on national and world events. Have students think about a major world event that occurred during the last five years and discuss how geography influenced it. **L2**

HISTORY Online

Objectives and answers to the student activity can be found in the **Web Activity Lesson Plan** feature at tarvol1.glencoe.com

Who?What?Where?When?

Sam Houston Sam Houston aided his country well. He was elected governor of Tennessee and was a United States senator from Texas for over 13 years. Serving later as governor of Texas, he is the only man ever elected governor of two different states of the Union.

you don't say...

Words from Mexico *Bronco, corral,* and *rodeo* all came from Mexican vaqueros, or cowhands. The source of the Alamo's name is disputed. Some historians think it was named after a group of Spanish soldiers who were based there and who came originally from Alamo de Parras in Mexico. Other historians note that *álamo* is the Spanish word for "cottonwood" and think the mission was named after the cottonwood trees that grew nearby.

"We must now act or abandon all hope!"

—Sam Houston, before the Battle of San Jacinto

years old, but he was determined to hold his position. Travis managed to send messages out through Mexican lines. He wrote several messages to the people of Texas and the United States, asking them for assistance. In his last message, Travis described the fighting that had already taken place and repeated his request for assistance. He warned that

❝the power of Santa Anna is to be met here, or in the colonies; we had better meet them here than to suffer a war of devastation to rage in our settlements.❞

Travis concluded with the statement that he and his troops were determined to hold the Alamo.

For 12 long days, the defenders of the Alamo kept Santa Anna's army at bay with rifle fire. The Mexicans launched two assaults but had to break them off. During the siege, 32 volunteers from Gonzales slipped through the Mexican lines to join the Alamo's defenders.

On March 6, 1836, Mexican cannon fire smashed the Alamo's walls, and the Mexicans launched an all-out attack. The Alamo defenders killed many Mexican soldiers as they crossed

open land and tried to mount the Alamo's walls. The Mexicans were too numerous to hold back, however, and they finally entered the fortress, killing William Travis, Davy Crockett, Jim Bowie, and all the other defenders. Only a few women and children and some servants survived to tell of the battle.

In the words of Santa Anna's aide, "The Texans fought more like devils than like men." The defenders of the Alamo had killed hundreds of Mexican soldiers. But more important, they had bought Texans some much needed time.

Texas Declares Its Independence

During the siege of the Alamo, Texan leaders were meeting at Washington-on-the-Brazos, where they were drawing up a new constitution. There, on March 2, 1836—four days before the fall of the Alamo—American settlers and Tejanos firmly declared independence from Mexico and established the Republic of Texas.

The Texas Declaration of Independence was similar to the Declaration of the United States, which had been written 60 years earlier. The Texas Declaration stated that the government of Santa Anna had violated the liberties guaranteed under the Mexican Constitution. The declaration charged that Texans had been deprived of freedom of religion, the right to trial by jury, the right to bear arms, and the right to petition. It noted that the Texans' protests against these policies were met with force. The Mexican government had sent a large army to drive Texans from their homes. Because of these grievances, the declaration proclaimed the following:

❝The people of Texas, in solemn convention assembled, appealing to a candid world for the necessities of our condition, do hereby resolve and declare that our political connection with the Mexican nation has forever ended; and that the people of Texas do now constitute a free, sovereign, and independent republic....❞

Student Web Activity
Visit tarvol1.glencoe.com and click on **Chapter 12—Student Web Activities** for an activity on the fight for Texas independence.

Reading Strategy   READING THE TEXT

Evaluating Information During the controversy over the admission of Texas as a state, some Northerners claimed that the move to bring Texas into the Union was a conspiracy by the Southern "slavocracy" to expand slavery. Have students consider that theory in light of Texas's geographic location. *(Students should note that Texas is near the Southern states and that it is more probable that a majority of the American settlers in Texas were from states in which slavery was widespread and merely continued the practice in their new homes.)* **L2**

With Mexican troops in Texas, it was not possible to hold a general election to ratify the constitution and vote for leaders of the new republic. Texas leaders set up a temporary government. They selected officers to serve until regular elections could be held.

David G. Burnet, an early pioneer in Texas, was chosen president and Lorenzo de Zavala, vice president. De Zavala had worked to establish a democratic government in Mexico. He moved to Texas when it became clear that Santa Anna would not make reforms.

The government of the new republic named **Sam Houston** as commander in chief of the Texas forces. Houston had come to Texas in 1832. Raised among the Cherokee people, he became a soldier, fighting with Andrew Jackson against the Creek people. A politician as well, Houston had served in Congress and as governor of Tennessee.

Houston wanted to prevent other forts from being overrun by the Mexicans. He ordered the troops at **Goliad** to abandon their position. As they retreated, however, they came face to face with Mexican troops led by General Urrea. After a fierce fight, several hundred Texans surrendered. On Santa Anna's orders, the Texans were executed a few days later. This action outraged Texans, who called it the "Goliad Massacre."

The Battle of San Jacinto

Houston moved his small army eastward about 100 miles, watching the movements of Santa Anna and waiting for a chance to strike. Six weeks after the Alamo, he found the opportunity.

After adding some new troops, Houston gathered an army of about 900 at **San Jacinto** (SAN juh•SIHN•toh), near the site of present-day Houston. Santa Anna was camped nearby with an army of more than 1,300. On April 21 the Texans launched a surprise attack on the Mexican camp, shouting, "Remember the Alamo! Remember Goliad!" They killed more than 600 soldiers and captured about 700 more—including Santa Anna. On May 14, 1836, Santa Anna signed a treaty that recognized the independence of Texas.

Reading Check **Identifying** Who was commander in chief of the Texas forces?

The Lone Star Republic

Texans elected Sam Houston as their president in September 1836. Mirabeau Lamar, who had built a fort at Velasco and had fought bravely at the Battle of San Jacinto, served as vice president. Houston sent a delegation to Washington, D.C., asking the United States to annex—take control of—Texas. The nation's president Andrew Jackson refused, however, because the addition of another slave state would upset the balance of slave and free states in Congress. For the moment Texas would remain an independent country.

Texas War for Independence, 1835–1836

Geography *Skills*

In 1836 General Santa Anna led Mexico's main forces across the Rio Grande into Texas.
1. **Location** At which battles did Texans win victories?
2. **Analyzing Information** What battle immediately followed the Alamo?

CHAPTER 12 Manifest Destiny **367**

✔ **Reading Check**

Answer: Sam Houston

Geography *Skills*

Answers:
1. San Antonio, Gonzales, and San Jacinto
2. Refugio

Geography Skills Practice
Ask: What was the date of the last battle shown on the map? *(April 21, 1836)*

3 ASSESS

Assign Section 2 Assessment as homework or as an in-class activity.

⊕ Have students use **Interactive Tutor Self-Assessment CD-ROM.**

L2

Section Quiz 12–2

L1

Reteaching Activity 12–2

Santa Anna Santa Anna tried to escape after his defeat at San Jacinto by dressing in an ordinary soldier's uniform and hiding in a marsh. He was captured the day after the battle by Texan soldiers who did not recognize him. When they brought Santa Anna back to camp, his identity was revealed by Mexican prisoners who saluted "El Presidente."

Reading Check

Answer: Sam Houston

L1, ELL

Reading Essentials and Study Guide 12–2

L3

Enrichment Activity 12–2

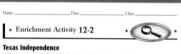

4 CLOSE

Ask students why Houston's troops shouted "Remember the Alamo" and "Remember Goliad." *(Texans who died at those places were considered martyrs and heroes; troops were inspired to avenge their deaths.)*

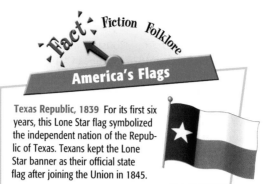

Fact — Fiction — Folklore

America's Flags

Texas Republic, 1839 For its first six years, this Lone Star flag symbolized the independent nation of the Republic of Texas. Texans kept the Lone Star banner as their official state flag after joining the Union in 1845.

The Question of Annexation

Despite rapid population growth, the new republic faced political and financial difficulties. The Mexican government refused to honor Santa Anna's recognition of independence, and fighting continued between Texas and Mexico. In addition Texas had an enormous debt and no money to repay it.

Many Texans still hoped to join the United States. Southerners favored the annexation of Texas, but Northerners objected that Texas would add another slave state to the Union. President Martin Van Buren, like Jackson, did not want to inflame the slavery issue or risk war with Mexico. He put off the question of annexing Texas.

John Tyler, who became the nation's president in 1841, was the first vice president to become president upon the death of a chief executive. He succeeded William Henry Harrison, who died in April, just one month after taking office. Tyler supported adding Texas to the Union and persuaded Texas to reapply for annexation. However, the Senate was divided over slavery and failed to ratify the annexation treaty.

Texas Becomes a State

The situation changed with the 1844 presidential campaign. The feeling of Manifest Destiny was growing throughout the country. The South favored annexation of Texas. The North demanded that the United States gain control of the Oregon country from Britain. The Democratic candidate, James K. Polk, supported both actions. The Whig candidate, Henry Clay, initially opposed adding Texas to the Union. When he finally came out for annexation, it lost him votes in the North—and the election.

After Polk's victory, supporters of annexation pressed the issue in Congress. They proposed and passed a resolution to annex Texas. On December 29, 1845, Texas officially became a state of the United States.

Reading Check **Identifying** Who was president of the Texas Republic?

SECTION 2 ASSESSMENT

Checking for Understanding

1. **Key Terms** Write a short history about events in Texas using the following terms: Tejano, empresario, decree, annex.

2. **Reviewing Facts** Name the four things that American settlers agreed to do in exchange for receiving land in Texas.

Reviewing Themes

3. **Geography and History** Why did Northerners and Southerners disagree on the annexation of Texas?

Critical Thinking

4. **Analyzing Information** How did the fall of the Alamo help the cause of Texas independence, even though it was a defeat for the Texans?

5. **Categorizing Information** Re-create the diagram below. In the boxes, describe two causes of the war between Mexico and Americans in Texas.

Causes

```
[   ]
        → War
[   ]
```

Analyzing Visuals

6. **Sequencing** Study the map on page 367. Place these battles in order, starting with the earliest: Gonzales, San Jacinto, the Alamo, Goliad.

Interdisciplinary Activity

Descriptive Writing Look at the painting of the Battle of the Alamo on page 365. Write one paragraph that describes what is happening in the picture.

368 CHAPTER 12 Manifest Destiny

SECTION 2 ASSESSMENT ANSWERS

1. Student work should reflect correct use of terms.
2. learn Spanish, become Mexican citizens, convert to Catholicism, obey Mexican law
3. Northerners objected because it would add another slave state to the Union; Southerners favored it for the same reason.

4. Answers may include: gained time to organize; motivated Texas rebels
5. Answers may include: Colonists disobeyed colonization laws, Mexico halted U.S. immigration, Santa Anna threw out Mexico's constitution and centralized control, Texans

moved for independence.

6. Gonzales, Alamo, Goliad, San Jacinto

Interdisciplinary Activity Descriptions should contain details about the painting.

SECTION 3 War with Mexico

Guide to Reading

Main Idea
American settlement in the Southwest led to conflict with Mexico.

Key Terms
rancho, ranchero, Californios, cede

Reading Strategy
Taking Notes As you read the section, describe the actions and achievements of each of the individuals in the table.

	Actions taken
William Becknell	
Jedediah Smith	
John C. Frémont	

Read to Learn
• why Americans began to settle in the Southwest.
• how the United States acquired New Mexico and California.

Section Theme
Culture and Traditions New Mexico, California, and Texas were Spanish lands with Spanish cultures and traditions.

Preview of Events

♦1820	♦1830	♦1840	♦1850
1821 Mexico gains independence	**1833** Mexico abolishes missions	**1845** The United States annexes Texas	**1846** Congress declares war on Mexico

Wagon wheel

★★★★★★★★★
AN
American Story

Long lines of covered wagons stretched as far as the eye could see. "All's set!" a driver called out. "All's set!" everyone shouted in reply.

"Then the 'Heps!' of drivers—the cracking of whips—the trampling of feet—the occasional creak of wheels—the rumbling of wagons—form a new scene of [intense] confusion," reported Josiah Gregg. Gregg was one of the traders who traveled west on the Santa Fe Trail in the 1830s to sell cloth, knives, and other goods in New Mexico.

The New Mexico Territory

In the early 1800s, **New Mexico** was the name of a vast region sandwiched between the Texas and California territories. It included all of present-day New Mexico, Arizona, Nevada, and Utah and parts of Colorado and Wyoming.

Native American peoples had lived in the area for thousands of years. Spanish conquistadors began exploring there in the late 1500s and made it part of Spain's colony of Mexico. In 1610 the Spanish founded the settlement of **Santa Fe.** Missionaries followed soon after.

When Mexico won its independence in 1821, it inherited the New Mexico province from Spain. The Mexicans, however, had little control over the distant province. The inhabitants of New Mexico mostly governed themselves.

CHAPTER 12   Manifest Destiny   **369**

---

1 FOCUS

Section Overview
This section examines how the United States obtained New Mexico and California.

Reading Preview

Answers to Graphic: William Becknell: first American trader in Santa Fe, blazed Santa Fe trail; Jedediah Smith: visited and wrote about San Gabriel Mission; John C. Frémont: visited and wrote about California

Preteaching Vocabulary
Point out that the word *rancho* means not only "ranch" but "a hut or group of huts for ranch workers." Have students look up the etymology of the word and speculate on the links between the various roots.

SECTION RESOURCES

📂 Reproducible Masters
• Reproducible Lesson Plan 12–3
• Daily Lecture and Discussion Notes 12–3
• Guided Reading Activity 12–3
• Section Quiz 12–3
• Reteaching Activity 12–3
• Reading Essentials and Study Guide 12–3
• Enrichment Activity 12–3

📑 Transparencies
• Daily Focus Skills Transparency 12–3

Multimedia
• Interactive Tutor Self-Assessment CD-ROM
• ExamView® Pro Testmaker CD-ROM
• Presentation Plus! CD-ROM

2 TEACH

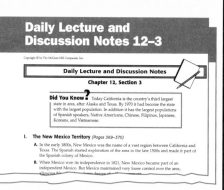
Finding Similarities Have students list similarities between New Mexico and California and in the way Americans settled in the two places. **L1**

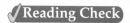

Reading Check

Answer: the New Mexico Territory

History *Through Art*

Skilled at handling cattle, vaqueros were indispensable laborers in the cattle industry of the Southwest, and a romantic figure in American folklore. Settlers from the United States first met vaqueros on Texas ranches about 1820. Some United States cowboys mastered vaquero skills, learning to use lariats, saddles, spurs, and branding irons.

Answer: After Mexico gained its independence from Spain, more settlers arrived in California, which was a state in the Mexican nation. In 1833 Mexico abolished missions and sold land to ranchers.

The Spanish had tried to keep Americans away from Santa Fe, fearing that Americans would want to take over the area. The Mexican government changed this policy, welcoming American traders into New Mexico. It hoped that the trade would boost the economy of the province.

The Santa Fe Trail

William Becknell, the first American trader to reach Santa Fe, arrived in 1821 with a pack of mules loaded with goods. Becknell sold the merchandise he brought for many times what he would have received for it in St. Louis.

Becknell's route came to be known as the **Santa Fe Trail.** The trail left the Missouri River near Independence, Missouri, and crossed the prairies to the Arkansas River. It followed the river west toward the Rocky Mountains before turning south into New Mexico Territory. Because the trail was mostly flat, on later trips Becknell used wagons to carry his merchandise.

Other traders followed Becknell, and the Santa Fe Trail became a busy trade route for hundreds of wagons. Americans brought cloth and firearms, which they exchanged in Santa Fe for silver, furs, and mules. The trail remained in use until the arrival of the railroad in 1880.

As trade with New Mexico increased, Americans began settling in the region. In the United States, the idea of Manifest Destiny captured the popular imagination, and many people saw New Mexico as territory worth acquiring. At the same time, they eyed another prize—the Mexican territory of California, which would provide access to the Pacific.

✓**Reading Check** **Describing** Where did the Santa Fe Trail end?

California's Spanish Culture

Spanish explorers and missionaries from Mexico had been the first Europeans to settle in California. In the 1760s Captain Gaspar de Portolá and Father Junípero Serra began building a string of missions that eventually extended from San Diego to Sonoma.

The mission system was a key part of Spain's plan to colonize California. The Spanish used the missions to convert Native Americans to Christianity. By 1820, California had 21 missions, with about 20,000 Native Americans living in them.

In 1820 American mountain man Jedediah Smith visited the San Gabriel Mission east of present-day Los Angeles. Smith reported that the Native Americans farmed thousands of acres and worked at weaving and other crafts. He described the missions as "large farming and grazing establishments." Another American in Smith's party called the Native Americans "slaves in every sense of the word."

History *Through Art*

Vaqueros in a Horse Corral by James Walker Mexican American cowhands, or vaqueros, work on a ranch in the Southwest. **Why did the number of ranchos grow in the 1820s and 1830s?**

Reading Strategy | READING THE TEXT

Reading Maps, Graphs and Charts Have students use library resources to find the information they need to prepare a map showing the missions established by Father Junípero Serra. (During Serra's lifetime, nine missions were built; eventually there were 21.)

California After 1821

After Mexico gained its independence from Spain in 1821, **California** became a state in the new Mexican nation. At the time only a few hundred Spanish settlers lived in California, but emigrants began arriving from Mexico. The wealthier settlers lived on ranches devoted to raising cattle and horses.

In 1833 the Mexican government passed a law abolishing the missions. The government gave some of the lands to Native Americans and sold the remainder. Mexican settlers bought these lands and built huge properties called ranchos.

The Mexican settlers persuaded Native Americans to work their lands and tend their cattle in return for food and shelter. The California ranchos were similar to the plantations of the South, and the rancheros—ranch owners—treated Native American workers almost like slaves.

Manifest Destiny and California

Americans had been visiting California for years. Most arrived on trading or whaling ships, although a few hardy travelers like Jedediah Smith came overland from the East. Soon more began to arrive.

At first the Mexican authorities welcomed Americans in California. The newcomers included agents for American shipping companies, fur traders from Oregon, and merchants from New Mexico. In the 1840s families began to arrive in California to settle. They made the long journey from Missouri on the Oregon Trail and then turned south after crossing the Rocky Mountains. Still, by 1845 the American population of California numbered only about 700. Most Americans lived in the Sacramento River valley.

Some American travelers wrote glowing reports of California. **John C. Frémont,** an army officer who made several trips through California in the 1840s, wrote of the region's mild climate, scenic beauty, and abundance of natural resources.

Americans began to talk about adding California to the nation. Shippers and manufacturers hoped to build ports on the Pacific coast for trade with China and Japan. Many Americans

John C. Frémont's strong belief in westward expansion advanced the cause of Manifest Destiny.

saw the advantage of extending United States territory to the Pacific. That way the nation would be safely bordered by the sea instead of by a foreign power. In 1845 Secretary of War William Marcy wrote that

> **❝**if the people [of California] should desire to unite their destiny with ours, they would be received as brethren [brothers].**❞**

President James Polk twice offered to buy California and New Mexico from Mexico, but Mexico refused. Soon, the United States would take over both regions by force.

✓ Reading Check Examining What was the purpose of the California missions?

War With Mexico

President James K. Polk was determined to get the California and New Mexico territories from Mexico. Their possession would guarantee that the United States had clear passage to the Pacific Ocean—an important consideration because the British still occupied part of Oregon. Polk's main reason, though, involved fulfilling the nation's Manifest Destiny. Like many Americans, Polk saw California and New Mexico as rightfully belonging to the United States.

CHAPTER 12 Manifest Destiny **371**

L1, ELL

Guided Reading Activity 12–3

Name _____ Date _____ Class _____

★ **Guided Reading Activity 12-3**

DIRECTIONS: Filling in the Blanks Use your textbook to fill in the blanks using the words in the box. Use another sheet of paper if necessary.

Guadalupe Hidalgo	Santa Fe Trail	capital	John Slidell
William Becknell	war with Mexico	1833	Santa Fe
mission system	Spanish explorers	1840s	declared war
Republic of California	New Mexico	half	Pacific
Zachary Taylor			

The New Mexico Territory

In the early 1800s, the area of (1) _____ included all of present-day New Mexico, Arizona, Nevada, and Utah and parts of Colorado and Wyoming. The Spanish tried to keep Americans away from (2) _____, fearing that Americans would want to take over the area. (3) _____, the first American trader to reach Santa Fe, arrived in 1821. The route he took became known as the (4) _____.

California's Spanish Culture

Missionaries and (5) _____ were the first Europeans to settle in California. A key part of Spain's plan to colonize California was the (6) _____. In (7) _____ the Mexican government passed a law abolishing the missions and sold some of the land to Mexican settlers. American families began arriving in the (8) _____. Many Americans saw the benefits of extending the United States territory to the (9) _____.

War With Mexico

President Polk sent an agent, (10) _____, to Mexico to settle several disputes. When the Mexican government refused to negotiate, Polk ordered General (11) _____ to march soldiers to the disputed borderland. Mexican soldiers attacked the American soldiers in 1846, and Congress (12) _____. The American people were divided over the (13) _____.

In the summer of 1846, General Stephen Watts Kearny captured the (14) _____ of New Mexico without firing a shot. A small group of Americans in Sonoma proclaimed the independent (15) _____. The Treaty of (16) _____ was signed in February 1848, ending the war with Mexico. The war cost Mexico (17) _____ of its territory.

SECTION 12-3

✓ Reading Check

Answer: to colonize California and convert Native Americans to Christianity

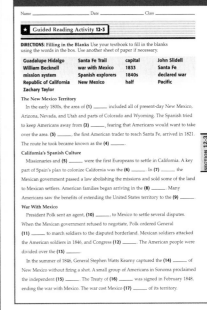

Did you know?

Cattle on Mexican ranches were raised mainly for their hides and fat, which was used in candle making.

DIFFERENTIATED INSTRUCTION

English Learners Encourage students to research, collect, and bring to school recordings or sheet music of Western songs or music from the mid-1800s, both those of United States settlers and of Mexican residents. Encourage students to perform or listen to the music, comparing and contrasting pieces from the two cultures. **L1,** ELL

📂 Refer to *Inclusion for the Middle School Social Studies Classroom Strategies and Activities* in the TCR.

Geography *Skills*

Answers:
1. Bear Flag Revolt
2. There are more blue symbols that represent American victories than there are green symbols that signify Mexican victories.

CURRICULUM CONNECTION

Civics In 1846 American forces may have provoked Mexico into an attack, which allowed President Polk to demand and obtain from Congress a declaration of war. A similar event occurred in 1964 when United States ships may have provoked a North Vietnamese attack. This event led President Lyndon Johnson to demand and obtain quickly from Congress a resolution permitting the United States to fight without the constitutionally required declaration of war. To prevent this from ever happening again, Congress passed the War Powers Act in 1973.

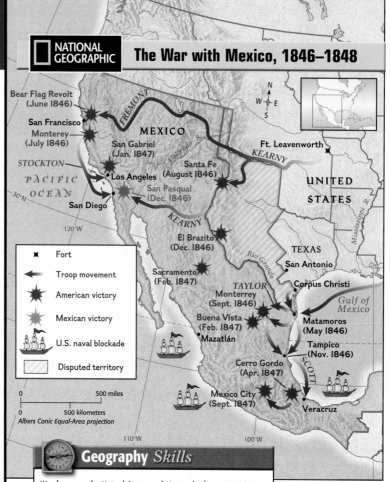

NATIONAL GEOGRAPHIC
The War with Mexico, 1846–1848

Legend:
- Fort
- Troop movement
- American victory
- Mexican victory
- U.S. naval blockade
- Disputed territory

0   500 miles
0   500 kilometers
Albers Conic Equal-Area projection

Geography *Skills*

War between the United States and Mexico broke out in 1846 near the Rio Grande.
1. **Location** Which battle occurred farthest north?
2. **Making Inferences** What information on the map can you use to infer which side won the war?

After Mexico refused to sell California and New Mexico, President Polk plotted to pull the Mexican provinces into the Union through war. He wanted, however, to provoke Mexico into taking military action first. This way Polk could justify the war to Congress and the American people.

Relations between Mexico and the United States had been strained for some years. When the United States annexed Texas in 1845, the situation worsened. Mexico, which had never recognized the independence of Texas, charged that the annexation was illegal.

Another dispute concerned the Texas-Mexico border. The United States insisted that the **Rio Grande** formed the border. Mexico claimed that the border lay along the **Nueces** (nu•AY•suhs) **River,** 150 miles farther north. Because of this dispute, Mexico had stopped payments to American citizens for losses suffered during Mexico's war for independence.

Polk sent an agent, John Slidell, to Mexico to propose a deal. Slidell was authorized to offer $30 million for California and New Mexico in return for Mexico's acceptance of the Rio Grande as the Texas boundary. In addition, the United States would take over payment of Mexico's debts to American citizens.

Conflict Begins

The Mexican government refused to discuss the offer and announced its intention to reclaim Texas for Mexico. In response Polk ordered **General Zachary Taylor** to march his soldiers across the disputed borderland between the Nueces River and the Rio Grande. Taylor followed the order and built a fort there on his arrival. On April 24, Mexican soldiers attacked a small force of Taylor's soldiers. Taylor sent the report the president wanted to hear: "Hostilities may now be considered as commenced."

Polk called an emergency meeting of his cabinet, and the cabinet agreed that the attack was grounds for war with Mexico. On May 11, 1846, the president told Congress that Mexico had "invaded our territory and shed American blood upon the American soil." Congress passed a declaration of war against Mexico.

372   CHAPTER 12   Manifest Destiny

INTERDISCIPLINARY CONNECTIONS ACTIVITY

Language Arts Have students use primary and secondary sources to research and write biographies of Father Serra, the leader of five missionaries on Portolá's expedition, who began exploring California in the 1760s. Tell students to include anecdotes about his travels. Encourage them to illustrate the biographies with drawings of an incident in his life. **L2**

American Attitudes Toward the War

The American people were divided over the war with Mexico. Polk's party, the Democrats, generally supported the war. Many Whigs opposed it, calling Polk's actions aggressive and unjust. Northerners accused Democrats of waging the war to spread slavery.

Illinois congressman Abraham Lincoln demanded to know the exact spot where the first attack against American troops had occurred. Lincoln, like many who opposed the war, claimed that the spot was clearly in Mexico and that Polk therefore had no grounds for blaming the war on Mexico.

Frederick Douglass, an African American leader in the antislavery movement, called the war "disgraceful" and "cruel." Douglass shared the belief that if the United States expanded into the West, the Southern states would carry slavery into the new territories.

Newspapers generally supported the war, and volunteers quickly signed up for military service. As time went on, however, antiwar feeling grew, particularly in the North.

Polk's War Plan

President Polk had a three-part plan for the war with Mexico. First, American troops would drive Mexican forces out of the disputed border region in Texas and make the border secure. Second, the United States would seize New Mexico and California. Finally, American forces would take **Mexico City,** the capital of Mexico.

Zachary Taylor accomplished the first goal. His army captured the town of Matamoros in May 1846 and **Monterrey** in September 1846. The Americans pushed forward and entered the bishop's palace. The Mexican flag was lowered, and a mighty cheer erupted from American forces remaining on the plain below. In February 1847, Taylor defeated the Mexicans again at Buena Vista. The Texas border was secure.

While Taylor made progress in northern Mexico, American forces also advanced farther west. General **Stephen Watts Kearny** led his troops to New Mexico and California. In the summer of 1846, Kearny led about 1,500 cavalry soldiers along the Santa Fe Trail from Fort Leavenworth to New Mexico. The Mexican governor fled, allowing the Americans to capture New Mexico's capital, Santa Fe, on August 18, 1846, without firing a shot. Kearny and his army then headed across the deserts of New Mexico and Arizona to California.

California and the Bear Flag Republic

In June 1846, a small group of Americans had seized the town of Sonoma north of San Francisco and proclaimed the independent Republic of California. They called the new country the **Bear Flag Republic** because their flag showed a bear and a star on a white background. John C. Frémont and mountain man **Kit Carson,** who were already out West on a military expedition in California, joined the Americans in Sonoma.

Though unaware of the outbreak of war with Mexico, Frémont declared that he would conquer California. Frémont's actions outraged many Californios, the Mexicans who lived in California. They might have supported a revolt for local control of government, but they opposed what looked like an attempt by a band of Americans to seize land.

Naval Intervention

In July 1846, a United States Navy squadron under Commodore John Sloat captured the ports of Monterey and San Francisco. Sloat declared California annexed to the United States, and the American flag replaced the Bear Flag in California.

Sloat's fleet sailed for San Diego, carrying Frémont and Carson. The Americans captured San Diego and moved north to Los Angeles. Carson

California Bear Flag

373

3 ASSESS

Assign Section 3 Assessment as homework or as an in-class activity.

🖲 Have students use **Interactive Tutor Self-Assessment CD-ROM.**

L2

Section Quiz 12–3

Name _____ Date _____ Class _____

⭐ Chapter 12 — Score ☐

Section Quiz 12-3

DIRECTIONS: Matching Match the items in Column A with the items in Column B. Write the correct letters in the blanks. *(10 points each)*

Column A	Column B
_____ **1.** opposed war with Mexico	**A.** Native Americans
_____ **2.** mission slaves	**B.** Bear Flag Republic
_____ **3.** ranch owners	**C.** Whigs
_____ **4.** Republic of California	**D.** Winfield Scott
_____ **5.** captured Mexico City	**E.** rancheros

DIRECTIONS: Multiple Choice In the blank at the left, write the letter of the choice that best completes the statement or answers the question. *(10 points each)*

_____ **6.** Which trail left the Missouri River near Independence, Missouri, and crossed the prairies to the Arkansas River?
  A. Independence Trail   **C.** Missouri Trail
  B. Arkansas River Trail   **D.** Santa Fe Trail

_____ **7.** Who was an army officer that wrote of California's mild climate, scenic beauty, and abundance of resources?
  A. William Becknell   **C.** Josiah Gregg
  B. John C. Frémont   **D.** Jedediah Smith

_____ **8.** What did President James K. Polk use as grounds for declaring war against Mexico?
  A. annexation of Texas   **C.** attack of Zachary Taylor's forces
  B. declaration of the border   **D.** nonpayment of debts

_____ **9.** What city did Americans capture without firing a shot?
  A. Santa Fe   **C.** Sonoma
  B. Monterrey   **D.** San Francisco

_____ **10.** The United States mainland reached its present size with the
  A. Mexican Cession.   **C.** Gadsden Purchase.
  B. capture of Veracruz.   **D.** Treaty of Guadalupe Hidalgo.

CRITICAL THINKING ACTIVITY

Identifying Central Issues Have students offer support for the position of the Mexican government, shared by many Americans, that the war was the result of deliberate provocation and that it was wrong to take land by force. Then ask them to support President Polk's view. Following the class discussion, organize students into groups to discuss and decide which position has more merit. Have a member of each group report the conclusion and the rationale of the group. **L2**

✓ **Reading Check**

Answer: California and New Mexico

L1

Reteaching Activity 12–3

Name _____ Date _____ Class _____

★ Reteaching Activity **12-3**

DIRECTIONS: Sequencing Events Number the events in the order in which they occurred.

___ **A.** William Becknell reaches Santa Fe.

___ **B.** Mexico stops payments on its debt to the United States because of the dispute over the Texas-Mexico border.

___ **C.** A small group of Americans seize the California town of Sonoma and proclaim the independent Republic of California.

___ **D.** The United States controls all of California.

___ **E.** In an attempt to provoke Mexico, James K. Polk orders General Zachary Taylor to lead a small army of soldiers across the disputed border.

___ **F.** Zachary Taylor secures the Texas border with a victory at Buena Vista.

L1, ELL

Reading Essentials and Study Guide 12–3

Study Guide

Chapter 12, Section 3

For use with textbook pages 369–374

WAR WITH MEXICO

KEY TERMS	
rancho	An expansive section of land that includes large properties (page 371)
ranchero	A person who owns a rancho (page 371)
Californios	Mexican people who lived in California (page 373)
cede	To give up or relinquish (page 374)

DRAWING FROM EXPERIENCE

Have you ever tried to learn another language or about a culture different from your own? What might be some difficulties in understanding that group of people? Could some aspects of the culture conflict with your own background? How could the conflict be resolved? What impact could other cultures make on your own culture?

L3

Enrichment Activity 12–3

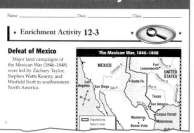

Name _____ Date _____ Class _____

★ Enrichment Activity **12-3**

Defeat of Mexico

Major land campaigns of the Mexican War (1846–1848) were led by Zachary Taylor, Stephen Watts Kearny, and Winfield Scott in southwestern North America.

4 CLOSE

After the war Frederick Douglass wrote, ". . . we are not the people to rejoice; we ought rather to blush and hang our heads for shame." Have students explain what he meant.

---

headed east with the news of California's annexation. On his way he met and joined Kearny's force, marching west from Santa Fe.

After Sloat's ships left, many Californios in San Diego rose up in arms against the Americans who had taken over the city. General Kearny and his troops arrived in the midst of the rebellion. They faced a stiff fight but eventually won. By January 1847, California was fully controlled by the United States.

The Capture of Mexico City

With their victories in New Mexico and California, the Americans met their first two goals in the war. President Polk then launched the third part of his war plan—an attack on Mexico City.

Polk gave the task of capturing Mexico City to General **Winfield Scott.** In March 1847, Scott's army landed on the coast of the Gulf of Mexico, near the Mexican port of **Veracruz.** Scott captured Veracruz after a three-week siege and then set out to march the 300 miles to Mexico City.

The Americans had to fight their way toward Mexico City, battling not only the Mexican army but also bands of armed citizens. Scott reached the outskirts of Mexico City with his troops towards the end of August 1847. By mid-September the Americans had taken Mexico City. The Mexican government surrendered.

The United States lost 1,721 men to battle and more than 11,000 to disease in the war with Mexico. Mexico's losses were far greater. The war cost the United States nearly $100 million, but here, too, Mexico paid a higher price. The war would cost Mexico half its territory.

The Peace Treaty

Peace talks between the United States and Mexico began in January 1848. The **Treaty of Guadalupe Hidalgo** (GWAH•duhl•OOP hih•DAL•goh) was signed in February 1848.

In the treaty Mexico gave up all claims to Texas and agreed to the Rio Grande as the border between Texas and Mexico. Furthermore, in what was called the **Mexican Cession,** Mexico ceded—gave—its provinces of California and New Mexico to the United States. In return the United States gave Mexico $15 million.

In 1853 the United States paid Mexico an additional $10 million for the **Gadsden Purchase,** a strip of land along the southern edge of the present-day states of Arizona and New Mexico. With the Gadsden Purchase, the United States mainland reached its present size. All that remained was to settle the newly acquired territories.

✓ **Reading Check** **Describing** What lands did Mexico cede to the United States?

SECTION 3 ASSESSMENT

Checking for Understanding

1. **Key Terms** Write a short paragraph in which you use the following terms: rancho, ranchero, Californios, cede.

2. **Reviewing Facts** According to the Mexican government, where did the border between Texas and Mexico lie?

Reviewing Themes

3. **Culture and Traditions** Why did the Spanish establish missions in the Southwest? What happened to the mission land after Mexico gained its independence?

Critical Thinking

4. **Analyzing Primary Sources** Explain the meaning of this sentence in your own words: "If the people [of California] should desire to unite their destiny with ours, they would be received as brethren [brothers]."

5. **Categorizing Information** Re-create the diagram below and describe the three parts of Polk's strategy and how they were accomplished.

Analyzing Visuals

6. **Geography Skills** List the battles that appear on the map on page 372 in order from first to last. Identify whether each was a Mexican victory or a U.S. victory.

Interdisciplinary Activity

Science Settlers traveling west encountered new wildlife, vegetation, and landforms. Choose one region of the west and investigate as a traveling scientist would. List plants and animals you would see there. Write a report summarizing what you have observed.

374 CHAPTER 12 Manifest Destiny

SECTION 3 ASSESSMENT ANSWERS

1. Student work should reflect correct use of terms.

2. along the Nueces

3. to colonize and convert Native Americans to Christianity; some was given to Native Americans and the rest was sold

4. The U.S. would welcome California into the Union.

5. Drive Mexican forces out of disputed area in Texas—Taylor captures Monterrey and Buena Vista securing Texas border; Seize New Mexico and California—Kearny captures New Mexico's capital, and Sloat declares California annexed to the U.S.; Take capital of Mexico—Scott's army takes the capital.

6. Students should list each battle in order and identify it as a Mexican or U.S. victory.

Interdisciplinary Activity Reports should list several plant and animal species native to the West.

SECTION 4 New Settlers in California and Utah

Guide to Reading

Main Idea
The lure of gold and the promise of religious freedom drew many settlers westward.

Key Terms
forty-niners, boomtown, vigilante

Reading Strategy
Organizing Information As you read Section 4, re-create the diagram below. In the boxes, describe who these groups and individuals were and what their role was in the settlement of California and Utah.

	What was their role?
Forty-niners	
Mormons	
Brigham Young	

Read to Learn
• how the hopes of getting rich drew thousands of people to California.
• how the search for religious freedom led to the settlement of Utah.

Section Theme
Groups and Institutions In the mid-1800s, people went to California in search of gold, and Mormons settled in Utah in search of religious freedom.

Preview of Events

♦1846	♦1848	♦1850

1846
Mormons migrate to the Great Salt Lake area

1848
Gold is discovered at Sutter's Mill

1850
California applies for statehood

1 FOCUS

Section Overview
This section describes how the search for gold and religious freedom led to settlements in California and Utah.

BELLRINGER
Skillbuilder Activity

Project transparency and have students answer the question.

Daily Focus Skills Transparency 12–4

Reading Preview

Answers to Graphic: Forty-niners: people who came to California after gold was discovered; Mormons: religious group whose migration to present-day Utah was the largest single migration in American history; Brigham Young: Mormon leader and governor of Utah Territory

Preteaching Vocabulary
Use the **Vocabulary PuzzleMaker CD-ROM** to create crossword and word search puzzles.

AN
American Story

Gold miner's cradle

James Marshall was building a sawmill on the South Fork of the American River in California. He worked for John Sutter, who owned a vast tract of land about 35 miles from present-day Sacramento. On January 24, 1848, Marshall saw something shining in a ditch. "I reached my hand down and picked it up," he wrote later. "It made my heart thump, for I was certain it was gold." Looking around, he found other shiny pieces. Marshall rushed to show the glittering pieces to Sutter, who determined that they were gold. Sutter tried to keep the discovery a secret, but word soon leaked out. The great California Gold Rush was underway!

California Gold Rush

People from all over the world flocked to California in search of quick riches. More than 80,000 people came to California looking for gold in 1849 alone. Those who arrived in 1849 were called forty-niners. An official in Monterey reported that "the farmers have thrown aside their plows, the lawyers their

CHAPTER 12 Manifest Destiny **375**

SECTION RESOURCES

📂 Reproducible Masters
• Reproducible Lesson Plan 12–4
• Daily Lecture and Discussion Notes 12–4
• Guided Reading Activity 12–4
• Section Quiz 12–4
• Reteaching Activity 12–4
• Reading Essentials and Study Guide 12–4
• Enrichment Activity 12–4

⚡ Transparencies
• Daily Focus Skills Transparency 12–4

Multimedia
⊕ Vocabulary PuzzleMaker CD-ROM
⊕ Interactive Tutor Self-Assessment CD-ROM
⊕ ExamView® Pro Testmaker CD-ROM
⊕ Presentation Plus! CD-ROM

2 TEACH

Daily Lecture and Discussion Notes 12–4

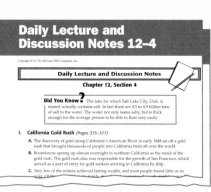

Copyright © by The McGraw-Hill Companies, Inc.

Daily Lecture and Discussion Notes

Chapter 12, Section 4

Did You Know? The lake for which Salt Lake City, Utah, is named actually contains salt. In fact there are 4.5 to 4.9 billion tons of salt in the water. The water not only tastes salty, but is thick enough for the average person to be able to float very easily.

I. California Gold Rush *(Pages 375–377)*

   A. The discovery of gold along California's American River in early 1848 set off a gold rush that brought thousands of people into California from all over the world.

   B. Boomtowns sprang up almost overnight in northern California as the result of the gold rush. The gold rush also was responsible for the growth of San Francisco, which served as a port of entry for gold-seekers arriving in California by ship.

   C. Very few of the miners achieved lasting wealth, and most people found little or no gold. Of the

Making a Graph Have students make a bar graph showing California's population in 1848 (20,000) and in 1852 (220,000).

📁 Use the rubric for making a graph on pages 42–43 in the *Performance Assessment Activities and Rubrics.*

Linking Past & Present

In May 2001 the oldest known pair of Levi's jeans, dating back to the 1800s, was sold to Levi Strauss & Co. for $46,532, the highest price ever paid for a pair of denim jeans.

L1, ELL

Guided Reading Activity 12–4

Name _____ Date _____ Class _____

★ **Guided Reading Activity 12-4**

DIRECTIONS: Recalling The Facts Use the information in your textbook to answer the questions. Use another sheet of paper if necessary.

1. How many people came to California in search of gold in 1848 and 1849?

2. Who were the forty-niners? _____

3. Where did the forty-niners come from? _____

4. What was the name given to the communities that seemed to spring up overnight? _____

5. What city grew from a tiny village to a city of about 20,000 people during

---

Linking Past & Present

Jeans

In 1873 Levi Strauss, a dry goods merchant living in San Francisco, and Jacob Davis, a Nevada tailor, developed and began to market denim pants reinforced with small copper tacks called rivets. Levi's popular denims—called blue jeans today—are known for their durability and quality.

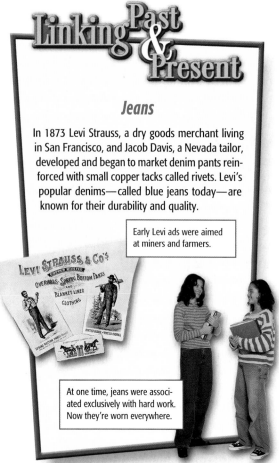

Early Levi ads were aimed at miners and farmers.

At one time, jeans were associated exclusively with hard work. Now they're worn everywhere.

briefs, the doctors their pills, the priests their prayer books, and all are now digging gold." By the end of 1848, they had taken $6 million in gold from the American River.

Many of the gold seekers came to California by sea. Others came overland, traveling on the Oregon Trail or the Santa Fe Trail and then pushing westward through California's **Sierra Nevada** mountain range.

Americans made up about 80 percent of the forty-niners. Others came from Mexico, South America, Europe, and Australia. About 300 men arrived from China, the first large group of Asian immigrants to come to America. Although some eventually returned to China, others remained, establishing California's Chinese American community.

The Californios

The Treaty of Guadalupe Hidalgo ending the war with Mexico made **Californios** (Mexican Californians) citizens of the United States. The treaty also guaranteed them the rights to their lands. But these rights would soon be weakened.

The Land Law of 1851 set up a group of people to review the Californios' land rights. The Californios had to prove what land they owned. When a new settler claimed the rights to a Californio's land, the two parties would go to court. Some Californios were able to prove their claims. Many, however, lost their land.

Life in California

As people rushed to a new area to look for gold, they built new communities, called boomtowns, almost overnight. At one site on the Yuba River where only two houses stood in September 1849, a miner arrived the next year to find a town of 1,000 people "with a large number of hotels, stores, groceries, bakeries, and . . . gambling houses." The miners gave some of the boomtowns colorful names such as Shinbone Peak and You Bet.

Cities also flourished during the Gold Rush. As ships arrived daily with gold seekers and adventurers, San Francisco grew from a tiny village to a city of about 20,000 people.

Most of the hopeful forty-niners had no experience in mining. Rushing furiously from place to place, they attacked hillsides with pickaxes and shovels and spent hours bent over streambeds, "washing" or "panning" the water to seek gold dust and nuggets.

The California Gold Rush more than doubled the world's supply of gold. For all their effort, however, very few of the forty-niners achieved lasting wealth. Most of the miners found little or no gold. Many of those who did lost their riches through gambling or wild spending.

Merchants, however, made huge profits. They could charge whatever they liked because the miners had no place else to go to buy food and other essential items. Eggs sold for $10 a dozen. A Jewish immigrant named **Levi Strauss** sold the miners sturdy pants made of denim. His "Levi's" made him rich.

Reading Strategy | READING THE TEXT

Reading Maps, Graphs, and Charts American culture has diverse roots. Different groups of people have made various contributions to the national identity. Organize students into small groups. Have students use their textbooks and other library sources to study the contributions of different ethnic, racial, and religious groups during the 1600s, 1700s, and 1800s. Have students come together to create a chart identifying the groups, their contributions, and the century in which the contributions were made. **L3**

Gold Rush Society

Very few women lived in the mining camps, which were populated by men of all races and walks of life. Lonely and suffering from the hardships of mining, many men spent their free hours drinking, gambling, and fighting.

Mining towns had no police or prisons, so lawbreakers posed a real threat to business owners and miners. One miner wrote,

❝Robberies and murders were of daily occurrence. Organized bands of thieves existed in the towns and in the mountains.❞

Concerned citizens formed vigilance committees to protect themselves. The vigilantes (VIH•juh•LAN•tees) took the law into their own hands, acting as police, judge, jury, and sometimes executioner.

Economic and Political Progress

The Gold Rush ended within a few years but had lasting effects on California's economy. Agriculture, shipping, and trade expanded to meet the miners' needs for food and other goods. Many people who had come looking for gold stayed to farm or run a business. California's population soared, increasing from about 20,000 in 1848 to more than 220,000 only four years later.

Such rapid growth brought the need for more effective government. Zachary Taylor, the Mexican War hero and now president, urged the people of California to apply for statehood. They did so, choosing representatives in September 1849 to write a constitution. Once their constitution was approved, Californians elected a governor and state legislators.

California applied to Congress for statehood in March 1850. Because California's constitution banned slavery, however, the request caused a crisis in Congress. The Southern states objected to making California a state because it would upset the balance of free and slave states. California did not become a state until Congress worked out a compromise six months later.

✓ Reading Check **Explaining** Why did the forty-niners come to California?

A Religious Refuge in Utah

A visitor to the Utah Territory in the 1850s wrote admiringly: "The whole of this small nation occupy themselves as usefully as the working bees of a hive." This account described the **Mormons,** or members of the Church of Jesus Christ of Latter-day Saints. Mormons had come to Utah to fulfill their vision of the godly life.

The First Mormons

Joseph Smith founded the church in 1830 in New York State. He had visions that led him to launch a new Christian church. He hoped to use these visions to build an ideal society.

Smith believed that property should be held in common. He also supported polygamy, the idea that a man could have more than one wife. This angered a large number of people. Mormons eventually gave up this practice.

Smith formed a community in New York, but unsympathetic neighbors disapproved of the

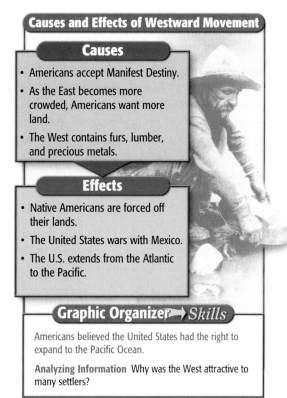

Causes and Effects of Westward Movement

Causes
- Americans accept Manifest Destiny.
- As the East becomes more crowded, Americans want more land.
- The West contains furs, lumber, and precious metals.

Effects
- Native Americans are forced off their lands.
- The United States wars with Mexico.
- The U.S. extends from the Atlantic to the Pacific.

Graphic Organizer → Skills

Americans believed the United States had the right to expand to the Pacific Ocean.

Analyzing Information Why was the West attractive to many settlers?

CHAPTER 12   Manifest Destiny   **377**

✓ Reading Check

Answer: to find gold

Graphic Organizer → Skills

Answer: It contained land, furs, lumber, and precious metals.

3 ASSESS

Assign Section 4 Assessment as homework or as an in-class activity.

🔵 Have students use **Interactive Tutor Self-Assessment CD-ROM.**

L2

Section Quiz 12–4

Name _____ Date _____ Class _____

★ Chapter 12   Score

Section Quiz 12-4

DIRECTIONS: Matching Match the items in Column A with the items in Column B. Write the correct letters in the blanks. *(10 points each)*

Column A	Column B
_____ 1. gold seekers	A. boomtowns
_____ 2. Gold Rush communities	B. Levi Strauss
_____ 3. pants maker	C. Mormons
_____ 4. vigilance committees for security	D. forty-niners
_____ 5. settled near the Great Salt Lake, Utah	E. vigilante

L1

Reteaching Activity 12–4

Name _____ Date _____ Class _____

★ Reteaching Activity 12-4

DIRECTIONS: Organizing Facts The numbered items in the Fact Bank describe settlers to the Western territories of California and Utah. Write the number of each item in the appropriate section of the chart.

California and Utah Settlers	
Forty-Niners	**Mormons**

DIFFERENTIATED INSTRUCTION

Reading Support The Mormons did a great deal of advance planning before leaving Illinois for Utah. Have students brainstorm the preparations needed to get thousands of people across the Mississippi River, through the plains, and over the Rocky Mountains to their new homes. Then have students check their ideas in library resources. **L2**

📁 Refer to *Inclusion for the Middle School Social Studies Classroom Strategies and Activities* in the TCR.

Analyzing *Political Cartoons*

Answer: Students may note that the cartoon shows how people quickly hurried west.

✓**Reading Check**

Answer: because the Mormons established farms and industries and sold supplies to forty-niners

L1, ELL

Reading Essentials and Study Guide 12–4

L3

Enrichment Activity 12–4

4 CLOSE

Have students find out why there is a monument to seagulls in Salt Lake City. *(In 1848 the Mormons' crops were attacked by crickets. Seagulls arrived and ate the insects, and the crops were saved.)*

Analyzing *Political Cartoons*

Cartoons of the period often showed Americans rushing to California in hopes of striking it rich. **What idea do you think the cartoonist is presenting?**

Mormons' religion. They forced the Mormons to move on. From New York the Mormons went to Ohio, then to Missouri, and then Illinois.

In 1844 a mob in Illinois killed Smith, and **Brigham Young** took over as head of the Mormons. Young decided the Mormons should move again, this time near the **Great Salt Lake** in present-day Utah. Although part of Mexico at that time, no Mexicans had settled in the region because of its harsh terrain.

A Haven in the Desert

The Mormon migration to the Great Salt Lake area began in 1846. About 12,000 Mormons made the trek—the largest single migration in American history. In the midst of the desert they set up communities in an area they called **Deseret.**

With hard work and determination, the Mormons made Deseret flourish. They planned their towns carefully and built irrigation canals to water their farms. They also founded industries so they could be self-sufficient. Mormon merchants sold supplies to the forty-niners who passed through Utah on their way to California.

In 1848 the United States acquired the Salt Lake area as part of the settlement of the war with Mexico. In 1850 Congress established the Utah Territory, and President Millard Fillmore made Brigham Young its governor.

Utah was not easily incorporated into the United States. The Mormons often had conflicts with federal officials. In 1857 and 1858, war almost broke out between the Mormons and the United States Army. Utah did not become a state until 1896.

✓**Reading Check** **Explaining** Why was Deseret able to grow economically?

SECTION 4 ASSESSMENT

Checking for Understanding

1. **Key Terms** Use each of these terms in a complete sentence that will help explain its meaning: **forty-niners, boomtown, vigilante.**

2. **Reviewing Facts** Why was California's entry into the Union delayed?

Reviewing Themes

3. **Groups and Institutions** What steps did Californians take to apply for statehood? When was California admitted?

Critical Thinking

4. **Predicting Consequences** How might the history of California have been different if the Gold Rush had not happened?

5. **Organizing Information** Re-create the diagram below. In the boxes, describe how the Gold Rush helped California's economy grow.

Growth of California

Analyzing Visuals

6. **Graphic Organizer Skills** Study the cause-and-effect chart on page 377. Are each of the effects of the westward movement positive? Explain.

Interdisciplinary Activity

Art Boomtowns sprang up almost overnight as gold seekers flocked to the West. Draw a scene of a boomtown. Include a written description of the activities that took place in the town.

378 CHAPTER 12 Manifest Destiny

SECTION 4 ASSESSMENT ANSWERS

1. Student work should reflect correct use of terms.
2. It was a free state, so the Southern states objected to it entering the Union.
3. wrote and approved a constitution, elected a governor and legislators, applied for statehood; September 1850

4. Answers will vary but students may speculate that without the surge in population, California probably would not have become a state as early as it did. Fewer people would have settled there, so the economy might not have developed as rapidly.

5. increased population, agriculture, and trade
6. Student opinions will vary, but may indicate that westward movement was not good for Mexico or the Native Americans.

Interdisciplinary Activity Illustrations should incorporate descriptions of boomtowns presented in the section.

America's LITERATURE

Hamlin Garland (1860–1940)

Hamlin Garland was born in rural Wisconsin and grew up on farms in Iowa and South Dakota. At the age of 24, he moved to Boston to begin his writing career. Although he gave up the life of a prairie farmer, Garland's work—fiction and nonfiction—reflects his background and his concern for the hard, lonely lives of pioneer men and women.

READ TO DISCOVER

A Son of the Middle Border is Garland's autobiography. The following excerpt describes one of the many westward moves that the Garland family made. As you read, pay attention to the emotions that the author expresses when he sees the plains for the first time.

READER'S DICTIONARY

middle border: the advancing frontier across the Mississippi River

habitation: residence

blue-joint: type of prairie grass

A Son of the Middle Border

Late in August my father again loaded our household goods into wagons, and with our small herd of cattle following, set out toward the west, bound once again to overtake the actual line of the **middle border.**

This journey has an unforgettable epic charm as I look back upon it. Each mile took us farther and farther into the unsettled prairie, until in the afternoon of the second day, we came to a meadow so wide that its western rim touched the sky without revealing a sign of man's **habitation** other than the road in which we travelled.

The plain was covered with grass tall as ripe wheat and when my father stopped his team and came back to us and said, "Well, children, here we are on The Big Prairie," we looked about us with awe, so endless seemed this spread of wild oats and waving **blue-joint.**

Far away dim clumps of trees showed, but no chimney was in sight, and no living thing moved save our own cattle and the hawks lazily wheeling in the air. My heart filled with awe as well as wonder. . . .

Sunset came at last, but still he drove steadily on through the sparse settlements. Just at nightfall we came to a beautiful little stream and stopped to let the horses drink.

I heard its rippling, reassuring song on the pebbles. Thereafter all is dim and vague to me until my mother called out sharply, "Wake up, children! Here we are!"

Struggling to my feet I looked about me. Nothing could be seen but the dim form of a small house. On every side the land melted into blackness, silent and without boundary.

Child's doll made of cornhusks

ANALYZING LITERATURE

1. **Recall and Interpret** Give two details that Garland uses to describe "The Big Prairie."
2. **Evaluate and Connect** How does Garland feel about the prairie and the move west? Explain.

Interdisciplinary Activity

Descriptive Writing Write a poem about a vast empty place that you know, or base your poem on a place you have read about.

America's LITERATURE

Block Schedule

Team Teaching This selection from *A Son of the Middle Border* may be implemented in a team-teaching context, in conjunction with English/Language Arts.

Reinforcing Vocabulary

Review the **Reader's Dictionary** terms with students to be sure they understand any unfamiliar terms.

Historical Connection

At first considered uninhabitable, the Great Plains was the last section of the nation to be settled. Farming on the plains presented special challenges, including the unpredictability of rain.

Background Information

Setting This excerpt takes place on the vast and magnificent plains of South Dakota.

Characters The main characters are Garland and his father, mother, brother, and sisters.

Plot Garland remembers his family's move westward to the plains in the late 1800s.

HISTORY Online

Refer to tarvol1.glencoe.com for additional Glencoe Literature titles, lesson plans, and study guides related to this unit.

379

ANSWERS TO ANALYZING LITERATURE

1. Answers may include any two of the following: "so wide that its western rim touched the sky," no sign of habitation, "covered with grass tall as ripe wheat," "wild oats and waving blue-joint," "dim clumps of trees, . . . but no chimney," "hawks lazily wheeling."

2. He felt exalted and full of awe, and thought the move was exciting and unforgettable.

Interdisciplinary Activity
Students' poems should use expressive language.

GLENCOE TECHNOLOGY

MindJogger Videoquiz
Use **MindJogger Videoquiz** to review the Chapter 12 content.

Available in VHS

Reviewing Key Terms

1.–5. Articles should use all words and accurately describe events.

Reviewing Key Facts

6. Both agreed to set the boundary at the 49th parallel.

7. He did not want to upset the balance of slave and free states.

8. If the United States was bordered by the Pacific Ocean rather than by a foreign power, the threat to security would be lessened.

9. The United States and Mexico disagreed over the location of each country's borders, and many Americans felt that it was the United States's destiny to expand throughout the North American continent.

10. Miners coming to California needed food and supplies. Merchants could sell these goods for high prices because the miners had nowhere else to buy them.

11. He spoke on behalf of colonists even when he disagreed with their opinions.

Critical Thinking

12. The economic opportunities offered by fertile and valuable natural resources near Oregon encouraged many people in the East to leave their economic troubles and move west.

13. In the peace talks after the war, the United States gained California and New Mexico, and the Rio Grande was recognized as the border between Texas and Mexico.

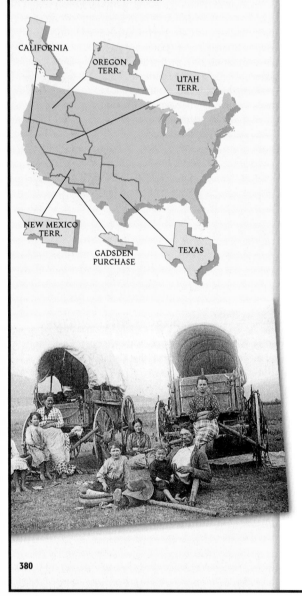

Chapter Summary
Manifest Destiny

Through war and negotiations, the United States acquires Texas, Oregon, California, Utah, and the remainder of the Southwest. By 1850 thousands and thousands of settlers cross the Great Plains for new homes.

380

Reviewing Key Terms

Use the vocabulary terms to create a newspaper article in which you describe events in the Southwest during this era.

1. emigrant
2. Tejano
3. empresario
4. ranchero
5. forty-niner

Reviewing Key Facts

6. What agreement did the United States and Great Britain reach about the Oregon Territory?

7. Why did President Jackson refuse to annex Texas?

8. Why did some Americans think that making California part of the United States would strengthen the security of the nation?

9. Explain the two main causes of the United States's war with Mexico.

10. Why did merchants earn such large profits during the Gold Rush?

11. Analyzing Information Reread the feature on page 363 about Stephen F. Austin. Why was Austin a good spokesperson for American settlers in Texas?

Critical Thinking

12. Determining Cause and Effect How did economic troubles in the East affect settlement in the Oregon area?

13. Analyzing Themes: Geography and History How did the war with Mexico change the U.S. border and its land holdings?

14. Drawing Conclusions What reactions do you think the governments of Great Britain and Mexico had to the American idea of Manifest Destiny?

15. Comparing How did the negotiations between the United States and Britain over the Oregon Territory differ from those between the United States and Mexico over the Southwest?

16. Determining Cause and Effect Re-create the diagram below. In the box, explain what led to the need for a more effective government in California.

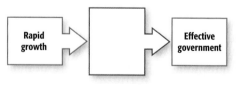

Rapid growth → → Effective government

14. Students may say that these two countries had probably used the same justification at some time in history to gain land; these countries might have thought that this notion was a potential threat to them; or they might have seen it as an excuse to justify expansion at any cost—even war.

15. The United States compromised with Britain. They went to war with Mexico and negotiated terms after defeating them.

16. desire to apply for statehood

The Oregon and California Trails

NATIONAL GEOGRAPHIC

Self-Check Quiz
Visit **tarvol1.glencoe.com** and click on **Chapter 12—Self-Check Quizzes** to prepare for the chapter test.

 Technology Activity

21. **Using a Database** Search your library's card catalog for books and reports containing information about Salt Lake City and the state of Utah. Use this information to make an alphabetical directory of historic sites to visit. Your list might include museums, sites of businesses, or other places of interest.

 Alternative Assessment

22. **Portfolio Writing Activity** If you were asked to make a film about one event described in this chapter, what would it be? In your journal describe the event and make a list of at least three people from history who would be in your movie. Then suggest the names of modern movie or TV stars you think would be suitable for these roles.

 Alternative Assessment

22. Movie ideas should be based on events discussed in this chapter. Students should list at least three characters and cast modern movie or television actors to play their roles.

HISTORY *Online*

Have students visit the Web site at tarvol1.glencoe.com to review Chapter 12 and take the Self-Check Quiz.

Geography and History Activity

Study the routes of the western trails shown on the map above. Then answer the questions that follow.

17. **Region** Which mountains did settlers have to cross to reach Oregon's Pacific coast? California's Pacific coast?

18. **Location** In what city did the Oregon Trail begin? In what city did it end?

Citizenship Cooperative Activity

19. **Analyzing Issues** With a partner, read the newspaper to find out what problems your state faces. Perhaps your state has a large budget deficit, or the crime rate has increased sharply. List the problems and describe what you would do if you were governor. List your options and the advantages and disadvantages of each one. Choose a solution and explain why it is the best option.

Practicing Skills

20. **Understanding Latitude and Longitude** Turn to the map of the world on pages RA14–RA15 of the Reference Atlas. What is the largest land area both west of the Prime Meridian and entirely north of the Equator?

Standardized Test Practice

Directions: Choose the *best* answer to the following question.

The discovery of gold in California led to which of the following?

A   Discovery of gold in the Black Hills of the Dakotas

B   Increased western expansion and foreign immigration

C   Annexation of California as a slave state

D   War with Mexico over the independence of California

Test-Taking Tip:

This question is a good example of *cause and effect.* Think about other times in history when people have discovered something of value in an area. What effect did this discovery have on people's behavior?

Standardized Test Practice

Answer: B
Question Type: History
Answer Explanation: Expansion and immigration are discussed on pages 375–376.

Bonus Question ?

Ask: Which defender of the Alamo designed a knife that still carries his name? *(Jim Bowie, bowie knife)*

 Geography and History Activity

17. Rockies, Cascades; Rockies, Sierra Nevada

18. Independence; Portland

Citizenship Cooperative Activity

19. Answers should show evidence of research concerning local issues and how problems would be solved.

Practicing Skills

20. North America

 Technology Activity

21. Students should locate information about Salt Lake City and Utah and compile a directory of points of interest.

Block Schedule

This activity may be implemented within either a traditional class period or a block scheduling framework.

1 FOCUS

Have students discuss how settlers might have felt leaving their homes and people they knew in search of a better life. **Ask:** Would you have made the decision to go to Oregon or California, like the family described on this page? Explain why. *(Answers will vary. Accept any answer and the reasons that support it as the basis for class discussion.)*

Did you know?

Successful emigrant groups who traveled together in wagon trains had written constitutions and laws that they could refer to when emigrants disagreed over issues. Almost all wagon trains had regulations, including rules for camping and restrictions on gambling.

THINKING CRITICALLY
You Decide

Let's Go West

Put yourself on a farm in Missouri in the 1840s. You work hard, but this year has been the most difficult. The crops have failed, and surviving winter will be a challenge. You meet other farmers traveling past your home on their way to the Oregon country or California. They speak of free, fertile land and new opportunities. Married settlers can claim a square mile, 640 acres, of the Oregon country at no cost. After much thought, you too decide to move your family west.

Analyzing the Issue

You, together with your spouse and two children, have decided to join a wagon train—a group of other families moving west. You will be traveling about 2,000 miles over rough country, finding your way with only the aid of natural landmarks. You will travel to either the Oregon country or to California. The trip will take about five months and must be completed before winter. Your goal is to survive and to make sure your family survives. Not knowing exactly what to expect, you have some research to do and decisions to make.

Believe It or Not!

Along the Oregon Trail, travelers lacked firewood for fuel over long parts of the trail. Looking for an alternative, they discovered dried buffalo dung burned well and was plentiful. The buffalo droppings—called chips—served another purpose too. Children would throw the chips back and forth for fun—the first, pioneer-type Frisbees?

Advice on the Prairie by William T. Ranney, 1853

Inside of Conestoga Wagon

382

EXTENDING THE CONTENT

The Oregon Trail Many emigrants were forced to leave keepsakes, heirlooms, or wedding gifts along the Oregon Trail to help the weary oxen. Parts of the Oregon Trail were littered with piles of "leeverites"— items that people were forced to "leave `er right here" to lighten the wagons.

What To Do

After you have organized into groups of four to six, follow the directions to make decisions about your trip. Decide upon specific tasks for each member of your group and who will research the following items.

Research the following:

1 Your destination and departure date

2 What route you should follow (A map will need to be drawn.)

3 A set of "rules for the road" (For example, up at dawn, on the road by seven, careful use of water, drive at least 15 miles per day, walk nearly all the way, etc.)

4 What supplies you will carry with you (You will need to research and estimate the weights of supplies because you may only take with you what you can carry in your wagon. The wagon dimensions are 4 feet by 10 feet, and at least 1,000 pounds of food is needed for a four-person family. Be careful not to overload your wagon—you do not want the wagon to break down or your animals to become exhausted.)

5 What mode of power will your wagon use?
- mules (most sure-footed, but expensive and hard to control)
- horses (can pull wagons faster, but can easily become ill)
- oxen (slowest, strongest, and have most endurance)

Presentation

6 Once you have collected your data, make your decisions and prepare your presentation. The format of the presentation is up to the group.

Go a Step Further

The Oregon Trail is the nation's longest graveyard. In 25 years, thousands died from illness, accidents, and drownings. Using your experience with this activity, answer this question: What do you think was the major cause for failure for wagon trains traveling west? Answer the question by writing the story of one such possible failure.

383

2 TEACH

Creating a Map Before beginning the activity, have members of each group research the routes to California and the Oregon Country. Have students choose a route and draw maps showing their routes. Maps should include major rivers, mountain ranges, and deserts, as well as forts or settlements along the way (if any) where additional provisions might be available. Tell students to take into account the type of terrain they will cross and the climate in the areas they will travel through when making decisions. **L1**

3 ASSESS

Have students answer the **Go a Step Further** question on page 383.

4 CLOSE

Invite students to write a short diary entry detailing one day along the trail west. Have students share their diary entries in short oral readings.

Answers

Students should explain their decisions once they have collected the data. Students should describe how their decisions would help them survive their trips to California or the Oregon Country. Information about their decisions may be presented in a graph or a poster.

Chapter 13 Resources

Timesaving Tools

TeacherWorks™ All-In-One Planner and Resource Center

- **Interactive Teacher Edition** Access your Teacher Wraparound Edition and your classroom resources with a few easy clicks.
- **Interactive Lesson Planner** Planning has never been easier! Organize your week, month, semester, or year with all the lesson helps you need to make teaching creative, timely, and relevant.

Use Glencoe's **Presentation Plus!** multimedia teacher tool to easily present dynamic lessons that visually excite your students. Using Microsoft PowerPoint® you can customize the presentations to create your own personalized lessons.

TEACHING TRANSPARENCIES

Graphic Organizer 13 L2

Why It Matters Chapter Transparency 13 L2

REVIEW AND REINFORCEMENT

Workbook Activity 13 L1

Time Line Activity 13 L2

Vocabulary Activity 13 L1

REVIEW AND REINFORCEMENT

Critical Thinking Skills Activity 13 L2

Take-Home Review Activity 13 L1

ENRICHMENT

Linking Past and Present Activity 13 L2

Primary Source Reading 13 L2

GEOGRAPHY

Geography and History Activity 13 L2

Meeting NCSS Standards

The following standards are highlighted in Chapter 13:

Section 1 VII Production, Distribution, & Consumption: A, B, E, H, I

Section 2 III People, Places, & Environments: D, G, H, I, J, K

Section 3 VIII Science, Technology, & Society: A, B, C

Section 4 I Culture: A, B, C, D, E

FOLDABLES™ Study Organizer

Dinah Zike's **Foldables** are three-dimensional, interactive graphic organizers that help students practice basic writing skills, review key vocabulary terms, and identify main ideas. Additional chapter activities can be found in the **Reading and Study Skills Foldables** booklet.

Chapter 13 Resources

ASSESSMENT AND EVALUATION

Chapter 13 Test Form A L2

Chapter 13 Test Form B L2

Standardized Test Practice Workbook Activity 13 L2

Performance Assessment Activity 13 L1, ELL

ExamView® Pro Testmaker CD-ROM

MULTIMEDIA

- Vocabulary PuzzleMaker CD-ROM
- Interactive Tutor Self-Assessment CD-ROM
- ExamView® Pro Testmaker CD-ROM
- Audio Program
- American History Primary Source Document Library CD-ROM
- MindJogger Videoquiz
- Presentation Plus! CD-ROM
- TeacherWorks CD-ROM
- Interactive Student Edition CD-ROM
- Glencoe Skillbuilder Interactive Workbook CD-ROM, Level 1
- The American Republic to 1877 Video Program
- American Music: Hits Through History

SPANISH RESOURCES

The following Spanish language materials are available in the Spanish Resources Binder:

- Spanish Guided Reading Activities
- Spanish Reteaching Activities
- Spanish Quizzes and Tests
- Spanish Vocabulary Activity
- Spanish Take-Home Review Activity
- Spanish Summaries
- The Declaration of Independence and United States Constitution Spanish Translation

---

THE HISTORY CHANNEL®

The following videotape program is available from Glencoe as a supplement to Chapter 13:

- **Civil War Journal** (Set 1) (ISBN 1-56501-200-3)

To order, call Glencoe at 1-800-334-7344. To find classroom resources to accompany many of these videos, check the following home pages:
A&E Television: www.aande.com
The History Channel: www.historychannel.com

HISTORY Online

Use our Web site for additional resources. All essential content is covered in the Student Edition.

You and your students can visit tarvol1.glencoe.com , the Web site companion to **The American Republic to 1877.** This innovative integration of electronic and print media offers your students a wealth of opportunities. The student text directs students to the Web site for the following options:

- **Chapter Overviews**
- **Self-Check Quizzes**
- **Student Web Activities**
- **Textbook Updates**

Answers to the student Web activities are provided for you in the **Web Activity Lesson Plans.** Additional Web resources and Interactive Tutor Puzzles are also available.

Chapter 13 Resources

SECTION RESOURCES

Daily Objectives	Reproducible Resources	Multimedia Resources
SECTION 1 **The North's Economy** 1. Understand how advances in technology shaped the economy of the North. 2. Explain how new kinds of transportation and communication spurred economic growth.	▭ Reproducible Lesson Plan 13–1 ▭ Daily Lecture and Discussion Notes 13–1 ▭ Guided Reading Activity 13–1* ▭ Section Quiz 13–1* ▭ Reteaching Activity 13–1* ▭ Reading Essentials and Study Guide 13–1* ▭ Enrichment Activity 13–1	🖎 Daily Focus Skills Transparency 13–1 💿 Interactive Tutor Self-Assessment CD-ROM 💿 ExamView® Pro Testmaker CD-ROM 💿 Presentation Plus! CD-ROM
SECTION 2 **The North's People** 1. Summarize how working conditions in industries changed. 2. Compare and contrast how immigration affected American economic, political, and cultural life.	▭ Reproducible Lesson Plan 13–2 ▭ Daily Lecture and Discussion Notes 13–2 ▭ Guided Reading Activity 13–2* ▭ Section Quiz 13–2* ▭ Reteaching Activity 13–2* ▭ Reading Essentials and Study Guide 13–2* ▭ Enrichment Activity 13–2	🖎 Daily Focus Skills Transparency 13–2 💿 Interactive Tutor Self-Assessment CD-ROM 💿 ExamView® Pro Testmaker CD-ROM 💿 Presentation Plus! CD-ROM
SECTION 3 **Southern Cotton Kingdom** 1. Explore how settlement expanded in the South. 2. Determine why the economy of the South relied on agriculture.	▭ Reproducible Lesson Plan 13–3 ▭ Daily Lecture and Discussion Notes 13–3 ▭ Guided Reading Activity 13–3* ▭ Section Quiz 13–3* ▭ Reteaching Activity 13–3* ▭ Reading Essentials and Study Guide 13–3* ▭ Enrichment Activity 13–3	🖎 Daily Focus Skills Transparency 13–3 💿 Interactive Tutor Self-Assessment CD-ROM 💿 ExamView® Pro Testmaker CD-ROM 💿 Presentation Plus! CD-ROM
SECTION 4 **The South's People** 1. Describe what life was like on Southern plantations. 2. Understand how enslaved workers maintained strong family and cultural ties.	▭ Reproducible Lesson Plan 13–4 ▭ Daily Lecture and Discussion Notes 13–4 ▭ Guided Reading Activity 13–4* ▭ Section Quiz 13–4* ▭ Reteaching Activity 13–4* ▭ Reading Essentials and Study Guide 13–4* ▭ Enrichment Activity 13–4	🖎 Daily Focus Skills Transparency 13–4 🎵 American Music: Hits Through History 💿 Vocabulary PuzzleMaker CD-ROM 💿 Interactive Tutor Self-Assessment CD-ROM 💿 ExamView® Pro Testmaker CD-ROM 💿 Presentation Plus! CD-ROM

0:00 OUT OF TIME?
Assign the Chapter 13 **Reading Essentials and Study Guide.** ▭

*Also Available in Spanish

 Blackline Master   Transparency   💿 CD-ROM   ⦿ DVD

 Poster   Music Program   Audio Program   ▣ Videocassette

KEY TO ABILITY LEVELS

Teaching strategies have been coded.

L1 BASIC activities for all students
L2 AVERAGE activities for average to above-average students
L3 CHALLENGING activities for above-average students
ELL ENGLISH LANGUAGE LEARNER activities

NATIONAL GEOGRAPHIC — Teacher's Corner

INDEX TO NATIONAL GEOGRAPHIC MAGAZINE

The following articles relate to this chapter.

- "The Way West," by John G. Mitchell, September 2000.
- "America's Poet: Walt Whitman," by Joel L. Swerdlow, December 1994.
- "C.S.S. *Alabama*," by Max Guerout, December 1994.
- "The Cruelest Commerce: African Slave Trade," by Colin Palmer, September 1992.
- "Philadelphia's African Americans," by Roland L. Freeman, August 1990.

ADDITIONAL NATIONAL GEOGRAPHIC SOCIETY PRODUCTS

To order the following, call National Geographic at 1-800-368-2728:

- *GeoKit: The Civil War* (Kit)
- *GeoKit: Westward Movement* (Kit)
- *GeoKit: Immigration* (Kit)
- *The West That Was* (Video)
- *United States/Territorial Growth* (Map)
- *National Geographic Desk Reference* (Book)
- *Immigration: The Triumph of Hope* (Video)
- *Steal Away: The Harriet Tubman Story* (Video)

NGS ONLINE

Access National Geographic's Web site for current events, atlas updates, activities, links, interactive features, and archives.

www.nationalgeographic.com

MEETING SPECIAL NEEDS

In addition to the Differentiated Instruction strategies found in each section, the following resources are also suitable for your special needs students:

- *ExamView® Pro Testmaker CD-ROM* allows teachers to tailor tests by reducing answer choices.

- The *Audio Program* includes the entire narrative of the student edition so that less-proficient readers can listen to the words as they read them.

- The *Reading Essentials and Study Guide* provides the same content as the student edition but is written two grade levels below the textbook.

- *Guided Reading Activities* give less-proficient readers point-by-point instructions to increase comprehension as they read each textbook section.

From the Classroom of...

Gerald Schuchard
Flandreau Indian School
Flandreau, SD

Immigration and Geography—Regional Comparisons

Remind students that one of the major themes of geography is regional comparison, and that we can learn a great deal about how geography affects people by comparing regions of the world. Review the chapter's content regarding immigration to the United States between 1840 and 1860. Explain that many immigrants—at least those who had the money to choose where they lived—selected certain regions of the country to live in partly because of the similarities of those regions to regions in their home countries. To illustrate this concept, have students consult encyclopedias or weather-related Internet sites, or use other resource materials to collect information on climatic conditions in Germany. Then have them compare this data to information they find on climatic regions in the United States. Many German immigrants settled in New York and Pennsylvania. Ask students to compare the climatic data of these two states to the climate found in Germany. Ask students, "If you were moving to another land, how important would climate be to you?"

ADDITIONAL RESOURCES FROM GLENCOE

- American Music: Cultural Traditions
- American Art and Architecture
- Outline Map Resource Book
- U.S. Desk Map
- Building Geography Skills for Life
- Inclusion for the Middle School Social Studies Classroom Strategies and Activities
- Teaching Strategies for the American History Classroom (Including Block Scheduling Pacing Guides)
- American Crafts Hands-On Activities
- American Games Hands-On Activities
- American History Flash Cards

Block Schedule

Activities that are suited to use within the block scheduling framework are identified by:

☑ **Performance Assessment**

Refer to Activity 13 in the Performance Assessment Activities and Rubrics booklet.

Why It Matters Activity

Preview the economic and cultural differences that occurred in the United States in the 1800s. Discuss how those regional differences helped to polarize the nation. Ask students if they believe regional differences still impact the nation today. Students should evaluate their ideas as they work through the chapter.

GLENCOE
TECHNOLOGY

The American Republic to 1877 Video Program
To learn more about children working on farms in the pre-Civil War South, have students view the Chapter 13 video "Young People of the South" from **The American Republic to 1877 Video Program.**

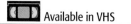 Available in DVD and VHS

MindJogger Videoquiz
Use **MindJogger Videoquiz** to preview the Chapter 13 content.

Available in VHS

CHAPTER 13 North **North** and **and South** South

1820–1860

Why It Matters

At the same time that national spirit and pride were growing throughout the country, a strong sectional rivalry was also developing. Both North and South wanted to further their own economic and political interests.

The Impact Today

Differences still exist between the regions of the nation but are no longer as sharp. Mass communication and the migration of people from one region to another have lessened the differences.

The American Republic to 1877 Video The chapter 13 video, "Young People of the South," describes what life was like for children in the South.

1820
• U.S. population reaches 10 million

1826
• *The Last of the Mohicans* published

1834
• McCormick reaper patented

1837
• Steel-tipped plow invented

United States
PRESIDENTS

Monroe 1817–1825

J.Q. Adams 1825–1829

Jackson 1829–1837

Van Buren 1837–1841

W.H. Harrison 1841

1820　　*1830*　　*1840*

World

1820
• Antarctica discovered

1825
• World's first public railroad opens in England

📖 Reading Strategy　**PURPOSE FOR READING**

Venn diagrams are a way for students to compare and/or contrast two or more items. Review with students that the overlapping circles in a Venn diagram are for recording similarities; information about differences belongs in the rest of the diagram. Point out to students that the differences in lifestyle between the North and the South set the stage for the American Civil War. Have the students use a Venn diagram to list the similarities and differences between the North and the South. **L1**

The Oliver Plantation by unknown artist During the mid-1800s, plantations in southern Louisiana were entire communities in themselves.

FOLDABLES™
Study Organizer

Compare-and-Contrast Study Foldable
Make this foldable to help you analyze the similarities and differences between the development of the North and the South.

Step 1 Mark the midpoint of the side edge of a sheet of paper.

Draw a mark at the midpoint.

Step 2 Turn the paper and fold the outside edges in to touch at the midpoint.

Step 3 Turn and label your foldable as shown.

Northern
Economy & People
Economy & People
Southern

Reading and Writing As you read the chapter, collect and write information under the appropriate tab that will help you compare and contrast the people and economics of the Northern and Southern states.

FOLDABLES™
Study Organizer **Dinah Zike's Foldables**

Purpose Students make and use a compare-contrast foldable to help them organize the similarities and differences between the development of the North and the South. As students read the chapter and fill in information on their foldable, they analyze the similarities and the differences of the people and economies of the Northern and Southern states.

◤ Have students complete *Reading and Study Skills Foldables* Activity 13. **L1**

HISTORY
Online

Introduce students to chapter content and key terms by having them access **Chapter Overview 13** at tarvol1.glencoe.com

1845
• Alexander Cartwright sets rules for baseball

1849
• Thoreau writes "Civil Disobedience"

1860
• U.S. population climbs to over 30 million

| Tyler 1841–1845 | Polk 1845–1849 | Taylor 1849–1850 | Fillmore 1850–1853 | Pierce 1853–1857 | Buchanan 1857–1861 |

1850   *1860*

HISTORY
Online

Chapter Overview
Visit tarvol1.glencoe.com and click on **Chapter 13— Chapter Overviews** to preview chapter information.

1845
• Beginning of Irish potato famine

1848
• Revolution in Austrian Empire

1857
• Sepoy Rebellion begins in India

1859
• Darwin's *On the Origin of Species* published

TIME LINE
ACTIVITY

As students read the chapter, have them review the time line on pages 384–385. **Ask: How much did the population increase from 1820 to 1860?** *(by more than 20 million people)*

More About the Art

Self-sufficient plantations, like the Oliver Plantation, were found throughout Louisiana and other Southern states. Covering several hundred acres, these large plantation complexes included a grand mansion surrounded by gardens, outbuildings, sugar mills, slave cabins, and fields of sugar, tobacco, or cotton. Many plantation mansions were built using a "raised cottage" design. While the ground floor was used primarily for storage, the main living space was on the second floor where available breezes offered relief from the heat of the day.

1 FOCUS

Section Overview

This section examines the advances in technology, transportation, and communication that shaped the North's economy in the 1800s.

Reading Preview

Answers to Graphic: Any five: power-driven loom; sewing machine; clipper ship; steamboat; wider, deeper canals; more roads; steam-powered locomotive; network of railroad tracks; telegraph; steel-tipped plow; mechanical reaper

Preteaching Vocabulary
Point out that the word *telegraph* comes from the Greek words *tele* (at a distance, far off) and *graphein* (to write). Encourage students to define *telegraph* based on this information.

The North's Economy

Guide to Reading

Main Idea
During the 1800s, advances in technology and transportation shaped the North's economy.

Key Terms
clipper ship, telegraph, Morse code

Reading Strategy
Organizing Information As you read the section, re-create the diagram below and list examples of advances in transportation and technology.

Read to Learn
- how advances in technology shaped the economy of the North.
- how new kinds of transportation and communication spurred economic growth.

Section Theme
Economic Factors Advances in technology and transportation shaped the North's economy.

Preview of Events

♦1830	♦1840	♦1850	♦1860
1834 Cyrus McCormick patents reaper	**1844** Samuel Morse sends first telegraph message	**1846** Elias Howe patents a sewing machine	**1860** About 3,000 steamboats are operating

Samuel Morse's telegraph key

AN American Story

In the 1840s, telegraph wires and railroads began to cross the nation. But traveling by rail had its discomforts, as writer Charles Dickens describes: "[T]here is a great deal of jolting, a great deal of noise, a great deal of wall, not much window, a locomotive engine, a shriek, and a bell. . . . In the center of the carriage there is usually a stove . . . which is for the most part red-hot. It is insufferably close; and you see the hot air fluttering between yourself and any other object you may happen to look at, like the ghost of smoke. . . ."

Technology and Industry

In 1800 most Americans worked on farms. Items that could not be made at home were manufactured—by hand, one at a time—by local blacksmiths, shoemakers, and tailors. By the early 1800s, changes took place in the Northern states. Power-driven machinery performed many tasks that were once done by hand. Industrialization and technology were changing the way Americans worked, traveled, and communicated.

Industrialization

The industrialization of the North developed in three phases. In the first, manufacturers made products by dividing the tasks involved among the workers. One worker would spin thread all day and another would weave cloth—instead of having one person spin and then weave. During the second phase, manufacturers built factories to bring specialized workers together. This allowed products to be made more quickly than before.

In the third phase, factory workers used machinery to perform some of their work. Many of the new machines ran on waterpower or steam power. For example, power-driven looms took over the task of weaving. The worker's job changed from weaving to tending the machine, which produced more fabric in less time.

Mass production of cotton textiles began in New England in the early 1800s. After **Elias Howe** invented the sewing machine in 1846, machine operators could produce clothing on a large scale from fabrics made by machine. Other types of industries developed during the same period. By 1860 the Northeast's factories produced at least two-thirds of the country's manufactured goods.

Improved Transportation

Improvements in transportation contributed to the success of many of America's new industries. Between 1800 and 1850, construction crews built thousands of miles of roads and canals. The canals opened new shipping routes by connecting many lakes and rivers. The growth of the railroads in the 1840s and 1850s also helped to speed the flow of goods. Inventor **Robert Fulton** demonstrated a reliable steamboat in 1807. Steamboats carried goods and passengers more cheaply and quickly along inland waterways than could flatboats or sail-powered vessels.

In the 1840s canal builders began to widen and deepen canals to accommodate steamboats. By 1860 about 3,000 steamboats traveled the major rivers and canals of the country as well as the Great Lakes. Steamboats spurred the growth of cities such as Cincinnati, Buffalo, and Chicago.

In the 1840s sailing ships were improved. The clipper ships—with sleek hulls and tall sails—were the pride of the open seas. They could sail 300 miles per day, as fast as most steamships of the day. The ships got their name because they "clipped" time from long journeys. Before the clippers, the voyage from New York to Great Britain took about 21 to 28 days. A clipper ship could usually make that trip in half the time.

Picturing History

A clipper ship, the *Flying Cloud,* set a new record by sailing from New York to California in less than 90 days. **How did clipper ships get their name?**

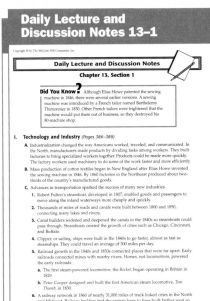

Daily Lecture and Discussion Notes 13–1

Copyright © by The McGraw-Hill Companies, Inc.

Daily Lecture and Discussion Notes

Chapter 13, Section 1

Did You Know? Although Elias Howe patented the sewing machine in 1846, there were several earlier versions. A sewing machine was introduced by a French tailor named Barthelemy Thimonnier in 1830. Other French tailors were frightened that the machine would put them out of business, so they destroyed his 80-machine shop.

I. Technology and Industry *(Pages 386–389)*

  A. Industrialization changed the way Americans worked, traveled, and communicated. In the North, manufacturers made products by dividing tasks among workers. They built factories to bring specialized workers together. Products could be made more quickly. The factory workers used machinery to do some of the work faster and more efficiently.

  B. Mass production of cotton textiles began in New England after Elias Howe invented the sewing machine in 1846. By 1860 factories in the Northeast produced about two-thirds of the country's manufactured goods.

  C. Advances in transportation spurred the success of many new industries.

    1. Robert Fulton's steamboat, developed in 1807, enabled goods and passengers to move along the inland waterways more cheaply and quickly.

    2. Thousands of miles of roads and canals were built between 1800 and 1850, connecting many lakes and rivers.

    3. Canal builders widened and deepened the canals in the 1840s so steamboats could pass through. Steamboats created the growth of cities such as Chicago, Cincinnati, and Buffalo.

    4. Clipper, or sailing, ships were built in the 1840s to go faster, almost as fast as steamships. They could travel an average of 300 miles per day.

    5. Railroad growth in the 1840s and 1850s connected places that were far apart. Early railroads connected mines with nearby rivers. Horses, not locomotives, powered the early railroads.

      a. The first steam-powered locomotive, the *Rocket,* began operating in Britain in 1829.

      b. Peter Cooper designed and built the first American steam locomotive, *Tom Thumb,* in 1830.

    6. A railway network in 1860 of nearly 31,000 miles of track linked cities in the North and Midwest. Railway builders tied the eastern lines to lines built farther west so that by 1860, a network united the East and the Midwest.

turn

Creating a Concept Web Work with students to create a concept web showing the interrelationships between technology, transportation, and advances in agriculture. The central oval should be labeled *Industrialized Economy of the North.* **L1**

Picturing History

Merchants used clipper ships in the tea trade between the United States and China.
Answer: They clipped time from the length of voyages.

Reading Strategy | READING THE TEXT

Using Graphic Organizers Have students work together in small groups to create a mural illustrating the concept web they created. (See Creating a Concept Web, above right.) Each group should choose a different aspect to illustrate—steamboats, clipper ships, trains, telegraph and printing press, agricultural technology, and so on. If necessary, have some students do research. Others can be responsible for making drawings, while still others can write captions and labels. **L1, ELL**

L1 ELL

Guided Reading Activity 13–1

Name _____ Date _____ Class _____

★ **Guided Reading Activity 13-1**

DIRECTIONS: Filling in the Blank Use your textbook to fill in the blanks using the words in the box. Use another sheet of paper if necessary.

Robert Fulton	machinery	canals	31,000 miles
telegraph	thresher	factories	Samuel Morse
steel-tipped plow	Peter Cooper	dividing	sewing machine
mechanical reaper			

Technology and Industry

First, manufacturers made products by **(1)** _____. Then manufacturers built **(2)** _____ to bring specialized workers together. Finally, factory workers used **(3)** _____ to perform some of their work. After Elias Howe invented the **(4)** _____ in 1846, operators could produce clothing on a large scale from fabrics made by machine. The invention of the steamboat by **(5)** _____ in 1807 meant that goods and passengers could be transported more quickly. In the 1840s **(6)** _____ were widened and deepened to accommodate steamboats. In 1830 **(7)** _____ built the first American steam locomotive. By 1860 the United States had almost **(8)** _____ of railway tracks that helped speed the flow of goods from the East to the Midwest. On May 24, 1844, **(9)** _____ successfully demonstrated the use of his **(10)** _____ system.

Agriculture

The **(11)** _____ easily cut through the hard-packed sod of the prairies; the **(12)** _____ sped up the harvesting of wheat; and the **(13)** _____ quickly separated the grain from the stalk.

Geography *Skills*

Answers:
1. St. Joseph
2. Answers may include Indianapolis, Louisville, Cairo, and Jackson (Tennessee and Mississippi).

What?Where?When?Who?

Air Brakes Air brakes to stop locomotives were not invented until the 1860s. Before George Westinghouse invented them, brakemen had to stop railcars by hand. Standing on the roof of a car, the brakeman slowed or stopped the train by turning a cast-iron wheel connected to a shaft that ran down to the brakes. Many brakemen lost their lives falling from the top of railcars as they wrestled with the wheel while the train sped around dangerous curves.

NATIONAL GEOGRAPHIC **Major Railroads, 1860**

Americans loved their railroads in spite of irregular schedules, frequent breakdowns, and being showered with sparks from the locomotives.

Trains clipped along at 20 to 30 miles per hour by 1860.

In 1833 the 136-mile Charleston and Hamburg line was the longest railroad in the world.

Gulf of Mexico

ATLANTIC OCEAN

300 miles
300 kilometers
Albers Conic Equal-Area projection

Geography *Skills*

Shippers could send large quantities of goods faster over railroads than they could over earlier canal, river, and wagon routes.
1. **Location** To what westernmost city did the railroads extend by 1860?
2. **Location** What cities might a train traveler pass through on a trip from Chicago to New Orleans?

Locomotives

The development of railroads in the United States began with short stretches of tracks that connected mines with nearby rivers. Early trains were pulled by horses rather than by locomotives. The first steam-powered passenger locomotive, the *Rocket*, began operating in Britain in 1829.

Peter Cooper designed and built the first American steam locomotive in 1830. Called the *Tom Thumb*, it got off to a bad start. In a race against a horse-drawn train in **Baltimore**, the *Tom Thumb's* engine failed. Engineers soon improved the engine, and within 10 years steam locomotives were pulling trains in the United States.

A Railway Network

In 1840 the United States had almost 3,000 miles of railroad track. By 1860 it had almost 31,000 miles, mostly in the North and the **Midwest.** One railway linked New York City and Buffalo. Another connected Philadelphia and Pittsburgh. Yet another linked Baltimore with Wheeling, Virginia (now West Virginia).

DIFFERENTIATED INSTRUCTION

At-Risk Students In 1860, using 1,600 workers, the last 38 miles of track were laid between New York City and Jamestown, New York. A great celebration was held in Jamestown when the last rail had been laid. Have students design posters announcing the coming of the steam locomotive to Jamestown. The posters should be very visual and highlight the advantages of the railroad to this western New York town. **L1**

☞ Refer to *Inclusion for the Middle School Social Studies Classroom Strategies and Activities* in the TCR.

Railway builders connected these eastern lines to lines being built farther west in Ohio, Indiana, and Illinois. By 1860 a network of railroad track united the Midwest and the East.

Moving Goods and People

Along with canals, the railways transformed trade in the nation's interior. The changes began with the opening of the Erie Canal in 1825 and the first railroads of the 1830s. Before this time agricultural goods were carried down the Mississippi River to New Orleans and then shipped to other countries or to the East Coast of the United States.

The development of the east-west canal and the rail network allowed grain, livestock, and dairy products to move directly from the Midwest to the East. Because goods now traveled faster and more cheaply, manufacturers in the East could offer them at lower prices.

The railroads also played an important role in the settlement and industrialization of the Midwest. Fast, affordable train travel brought people into Ohio, Indiana, and Illinois. As the populations of these states grew, new towns and industries developed.

Picturing **History**

The defeat of the train *Tom Thumb* in 1830 did not mean the end of the steam engine. The first successful use of a steam locomotive in the United States took place in South Carolina in 1831. **In 1860 which regions of the United States had the most miles of railroad track?**

Faster Communication

The growth of industry and the new pace of travel created a need for faster methods of communication. The telegraph—an apparatus that used electric signals to transmit messages—filled that need.

Samuel Morse, an American inventor, had been seeking support for a system of telegraph lines. On May 24, 1844, Morse got the chance to demonstrate that he could send messages instantly along wires. As a crowd in the U.S. capital watched, Morse tapped in the words, "What hath God wrought!" A few moments later, the telegraph operator in Baltimore sent the same message back in reply. The telegraph worked! Soon telegraph messages were flashing back and forth between Washington and Baltimore.

Morse transmitted his message in Morse code, a series of dots and dashes representing the letters of the alphabet. A skilled Morse code operator could rapidly tap out words in the dot-and-dash alphabet. Americans adopted the telegraph eagerly. A British visitor marveled at the speed with which Americans formed telegraph companies and erected telegraph lines. Americans, he wrote, were driven to "annihilate [wipe out] distance" in their vast country. By 1852 the United States was operating about 23,000 miles of telegraph lines.

✓ **Reading Check** **Explaining** How did canals and railways change transportation?

Samuel Morse

Picturing **History**

Early railroads were expensive to build and maintain. Although state governments funded canal building, private enterprise provided the money for early railroads.
Answer: East and Midwest

✓ **Reading Check**

Answer: They allowed more direct ways to get from the East Coast to the Midwest.

3 ASSESS

Assign Section 1 Assessment as homework or as an in-class activity.

🔵 Have students use **Interactive Tutor Self-Assessment CD-ROM.**

L2

Section Quiz 13–1

Name	Date	Class
★ Chapter 13		Score

Section Quiz 13-1

DIRECTIONS: Matching Match the items in Column A with the items in Column B. Write the correct letters in the blanks. *(10 points each)*

Column A	Column B
_____ **1.** invented the sewing machine	**A.** Robert Fulton
_____ **2.** clipper ship	**B.** the *Rocket*
_____ **3.** changed river travel	**C.** Elias Howe
_____ **4.** steam-powered locomotive	**D.** Samuel Morse
_____ **5.** sent the first telegraph message	**E.** the *Flying Cloud*

L1

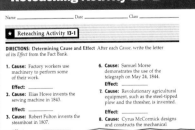

Reteaching Activity 13–1

Name	Date	Class
★ **Reteaching Activity 13-1**		

DIRECTIONS: Determining Cause and Effect After each *Cause*, write the letter of its *Effect* from the Fact Bank.

1. Cause: Factory workers use machinery to perform some of their work.
Effect: _____

2. Cause: Elias Howe invents the sewing machine in 1843.
Effect: _____

3. Cause: Robert Fulton invents the steamboat in 1807.
Effect: _____

6. Cause: Samuel Morse demonstrates the use of the telegraph on May 24, 1844.
Effect: _____

7. Cause: Revolutionary agricultural equipment, such as the steel-tipped plow and the thresher, is invented.
Effect: _____

8. Cause: Cyrus McCormick designs and constructs the mechanical

INTERDISCIPLINARY CONNECTIONS ACTIVITY

Science The first successful transatlantic telegraph cable was laid in 1858. Financed by Cyrus Field, a wealthy New York paper manufacturer, it stretched from Newfoundland to Ireland. The telegraph, however, would not have been possible without the discovery of electricity. Have students research early experiments with electricity and how it helped with the development of the telegraph. Students should report their findings in well-structured essays.

389

✓ **Reading Check**

Answer: McCormick's mechanical reaper

L1, ELL

Reading Essentials and Study Guide 13–1

Study Guide

Chapter 13, Section 1
For use with textbook pages 386–390
THE NORTH'S ECONOMY

KEY TERMS	
clipper ship	Fast sailing ships with tall sails and sleek hulls (page 387)
telegraph	An apparatus that used electric signals to transmit messages (page 389)
Morse code	A series of dots and dashes representing the alphabet developed by Samuel Morse (page 389)

DRAWING FROM EXPERIENCE

When you need food or clothes, how do you get them? Do you grow your own food or sew your clothes? What inventions changed the way people produced food and clothing in the 1800s? This section focuses on how advances in technology and transportation shaped the economy of the North.

ORGANIZING YOUR THOUGHTS

Use the chart below to help you take notes as you read the summaries that follow. Think about how the economy of the North was affected by advances in technology and transportation.

Segment of Economy	Inventions/Developments
Transportation	
Communication	
Farming	
Manufacturing	

L3

Enrichment Activity 13–1

Name _____ Date _____ Class _____

★ Enrichment Activity 13–1 ★

Communicating in Code

AMERICAN MORSE

Samuel F.B. Morse and Alfred Vail developed a code to make it easy to communicate on the telegraph. Morse code uses a combination of dots and dashes to represent letters, numbers, and punctuation.

The message STAND BY looks like this in American Morse code:

S T A N D B Y

The first message, WHAT HATH GOD WROUGHT looks like this in American Morse code:

W H A T H A T H

4 CLOSE

Railroads were viewed as a threat to business by turnpike investors and canal backers. **Ask:** Who else might have lost income because of the railroads? *(innkeepers along roads; farmers who raised horses; wagon makers, saddle makers, wheelwrights, and so on)*

Agriculture

The railroads gave farmers access to new markets to sell their products. Advances in technology allowed farmers to greatly increase the size of the harvest they produced.

In the early 1800s, few farmers had ventured into the treeless **Great Plains** west of Missouri, Iowa, and Minnesota. Even areas of mixed forest and prairie west of Ohio and Kentucky seemed too difficult for farming. Settlers worried that their wooden plows could not break the prairie's matted sod and that the soil was not fertile.

Revolution in Agriculture

Three revolutionary inventions of the 1830s changed farming methods and encouraged settlers to cultivate larger areas of the West. One was the steel-tipped plow that **John Deere** invented in 1837. Far sturdier than the wooden plow, Deere's plow easily cut through the hard-packed sod of the prairies. Equally important was the mechanical reaper, which sped up the harvesting of wheat, and the thresher, which quickly separated the grain from the stalk.

McCormick's Reaper

Born on a Virginia farm, **Cyrus McCormick** became interested in machines that would ease the burden of farmwork. After years of tinkering, McCormick designed and constructed the mechanical reaper and made a fortune manufacturing and selling it.

For hundreds of years, farmers had harvested grain with handheld sickles. McCormick's reaper could harvest grain much faster than a hand-operated sickle. Because farmers could harvest wheat so quickly, they began planting more of it. Growing wheat became profitable.

McCormick's reaper ensured that raising wheat would remain the main economic activity in the Midwestern prairies. New machines and railroads helped farmers plant more acres in "cash" crops—crops planted strictly for sale. Midwestern farmers began growing more wheat and shipping it east by train and canal barge. Farmers in the Northeast and Middle Atlantic states increased their production of fruits and vegetables that grew well in Eastern soils.

Despite improvements in agriculture, however, the North turned away from farming and increasingly toward industry. It was difficult making a living farming the rocky soil of New England, but industry flourished in the area. The number of people who worked in factories continued to rise—and so did problems connected with factory labor.

✓ **Reading Check** **Identifying** What innovation sped the harvesting of wheat?

SECTION 1 ASSESSMENT

Checking for Understanding

1. **Key Terms** Use each of these terms in a sentence that will help explain its meaning: clipper ship, telegraph, Morse code.

2. **Reviewing Facts** Identify and describe the three phases of industrialization in the North.

Reviewing Themes

3. **Economic Factors** How did improvements in transportation affect the price of goods?

Critical Thinking

4. **Determining Cause and Effect** How did the steel-tipped plow aid settlers on the Great Plains?

5. **Analyzing Consequences** How might failure to improve transportation have affected the economic and social development of the nation? Re-create the diagram below and list the possible effects.

Effects	
Social	Economic

Analyzing Visuals

6. **Geography Skills** Study the map on page 388, then answer this question: Through what two cities in Mississippi did major rail lines pass?

Interdisciplinary Activity

Math Research the number of acres of wheat harvested in the United States before and after McCormick introduced his reaper. Then create a chart or graph to illustrate your findings.

390 CHAPTER 13 North and South

SECTION 1 ASSESSMENT ANSWERS

1. Student work should reflect correct use of terms.

2. (a) division of tasks among workers, (b) building factories to bring specialized workers together, (c) use of machinery

3. They reduced prices because goods traveled faster and more cheaply.

4. Wooden plows could not break through the tough sod. When the steel plow was invented, it solved this problem. The sturdy plow easily cut through hard-packed sod.

5. Social: less interaction of people from different backgrounds and areas of the country; Economic: less industry, employment, transport of goods, and slower growth of cities

6. Jackson; Vicksburg

Interdisciplinary Activity Graphs and charts should compare wheat production before and after the invention of the McCormick reaper.

SECTION 2 The North's People

Guide to Reading

Main Idea
Many cities grew tremendously during this period.

Key Terms
trade union, strike, prejudice, discrimination, famine, nativist

Reading Strategy
Determining Cause and Effect As you read the section, re-create the diagram below and list two reasons for the growth of cities.

Growth of cities

Read to Learn
• how working conditions in industries changed.
• how immigration affected American economic, political, and cultural life.

Section Theme
Geography and History Growth of industry and an increase in immigration changed the North.

Preview of Events

♦1820	♦1830	♦1840	♦1850	♦1860

1827
Freedom's Journal, first African American newspaper, is published

1833
The General Trades Union of New York is formed

1854
American Party (Know-Nothings) forms

1860
Population of New York City passes 800,000

12-year-old factory worker

★★★★★★★
AN
American Story

"At first the hours seemed very long, but I was so interested in learning that I endured it very well; when I went out at night the sound of the mill was in my ears," a Northern mill worker wrote in 1844. The worker compared the noise of the cotton mill to the ceaseless, deafening roar of Niagara Falls. The roar of machinery was only one feature of factory life workers had to adjust to. Industrialization created new challenges for the men, women, and children who worked in the nation's factories.

Northern Factories

Between 1820 and 1860, more and more of America's manufacturing shifted to mills and factories. Machines took over many of the production tasks.

In the early 1800s, in the mills established in **Lowell, Massachusetts,** the entire production process was brought together under one roof—setting up the factory system. In addition to textiles and clothing, factories now produced such items as shoes, watches, guns, sewing machines, and agricultural machinery.

CHAPTER 13   North and South   **391**

---

1 FOCUS

Section Overview
This section explains how the growth of industry along with an increase in immigration changed Northern cities.

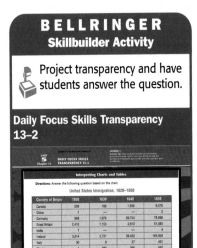
Reading Preview

Answers to Graphic: Any two: growth of factories; growth of trade and shipping; increased immigration

Preteaching Vocabulary
Point out that the term *strike* was first used in a labor context in 1768 when British sailors protested by striking, or taking down, the sails. Encourage students to describe what happens when a strike occurs.

---

2 TEACH

Reading Strategy

Synthesizing Information As students read the section, have them answer the following questions. **Ask:** Why could workers of the mid-1800s be called wage slaves? What similar experiences did women, African Americans, and immigrants face? What was the agenda of the Know-Nothing Party? *(poor conditions in factories, no laws protecting safety or limiting hours, little or no choice but to accept their lot; discrimination and prejudice; called for stricter citizenship laws and wanted to ban foreign-born citizens from holding public office)*
L2

History *Through Art*

Answer: Most African Americans could not vote or attend public schools. They were barred from other public facilities, forced to use segregated schools and hospitals, and could get only low-paying jobs.

Working Conditions

As the factory system developed, working conditions worsened. Factory owners wanted their employees to work longer hours in order to produce more goods. By 1840 factory workers averaged 11.4 hours a day. As the workday grew longer, on-the-job accidents became more and more common.

Factory work involved many dangerous conditions. For example, the long leather belts that connected the machines to the factory's water-powered driveshaft had no protective shields. Workers often suffered injuries such as lost fingers and broken bones from the rapidly spinning belts. Young children working on machines with powerful moving parts were especially at risk.

Workers often labored under unpleasant conditions. In the summer, factories were miserably hot and stifling. The machines gave off heat, and

History *Through Art*

Young Man in White Apron by John Mackie Falconer The artist of this painting was known for his watercolors depicting New York City workers such as this African American clerk. **How did prejudice affect the lives of African Americans in the North?**

392

air-conditioning had not yet been invented. In the winter, workers suffered because most factories had no heating.

Factory owners often showed more concern for profits than for the comfort and safety of their employees. Employers knew they could easily replace an unhappy worker with someone else eager for a job. No laws existed to regulate working conditions or to protect workers.

Attempts to Organize

By the 1830s workers began organizing to improve working conditions. Fearing the growth of the factory system, skilled workers had formed trade unions—organizations of workers with the same trade, or skill. Steadily deteriorating working conditions led unskilled workers to organize as well.

In the mid-1830s skilled workers in New York City staged a series of strikes, refusing to work in order to put pressure on employers. Workers wanted higher wages and to limit their workday to 10 hours. Groups of skilled workers formed the General Trades Union of New York.

In the early 1800s going on strike was illegal. Striking workers could be punished by the law, or they could be fired from their jobs. In 1842 a Massachusetts court ruled that workers did have the right to strike. It would be many years, however, before workers received other legal rights.

African American Workers

Slavery had largely disappeared from the North by the 1830s. However, racial prejudice—an unfair opinion not based on facts—and discrimination—unfair treatment of a group—remained in Northern states. For example, in 1821 New York eliminated the requirement that white men had to own property in order to vote—yet few African Americans were allowed to vote. Both Rhode Island and Pennsylvania passed laws prohibiting free African Americans from voting.

Most communities would not allow free African Americans to attend public schools and barred them from public facilities as well. Often African Americans were forced into segregated, or separate, schools and hospitals.

Reading Strategy — READING THE TEXT

Writing Free Writes Ask each student to write a letter to the editor describing the problems facing one of the groups discussed in this section. The letters should be written from the point of view of a family or an individual, and should make suggestions for ways to improve conditions. Remind students to use standard grammar, spelling, sentence structure, and punctuation. Before presenting the letter to the class, the group should critique it and revise it as necessary.

A few African Americans rose in the business world. Henry Boyd owned a furniture manufacturing company in Cincinnati, Ohio. In 1827 Samuel Cornish and John B. Russwurm founded *Freedom's Journal,* the first African American newspaper, in New York City. In 1845 Macon B. Allen became the first African American licensed to practice law in the United States. The overwhelming majority of African Americans, however, were extremely poor.

Women Workers

Women had played a major role in the developing mill and factory systems. However, employers discriminated against women, paying them less than male workers. When men began to form unions, they excluded women. Male workers wanted women kept out of the workplace so that more jobs would be available for men.

Some female workers attempted to organize in the 1830s and 1840s. In Massachusetts the Lowell Female Labor Reform Organization, founded by a weaver named **Sarah G. Bagley,** petitioned the state legislature for a 10-hour workday in 1845. Because most of the petition's signers were women, the legislature did not consider the petition.

Most of the early efforts by women to achieve equality and justice in the workplace failed. They paved the way, however, for later movements to correct the injustices against female workers.

✔**Reading Check** **Describing** How did conditions for workers change as the factory system developed?

The Rise of Cities

The growth of factories went hand in hand with the growth of Northern cities. People looking for work flocked to the cities, where most of the factories were located. The population of New York City, the nation's largest city, passed 800,000, and Philadelphia, more than 500,000 in 1860.

Between 1820 and 1840, communities that had been small villages became major cities, including St. Louis, Pittsburgh, Cincinnati, and Louisville. All of them profited from their location on the

Growth of Cities

Cities grow along fall lines A "fall line" is the boundary between an upland region and a lower region where rivers and streams move down over rapids or waterfalls to the lower region. Cities sprang up along fall lines for a number of reasons. Boats could not travel beyond the fall line, so travelers and merchants had to transfer their goods to other forms of transportation there. Early manufacturers also took advantage of the falls to power their mills. Fall-line cities include Richmond, Virginia; Trenton, New Jersey; and Augusta, Georgia.

Mississippi River or one of the river's branches. These cities became centers of the growing trade that connected the farmers of the Midwest with the cities of the Northeast. After 1830 the Great Lakes became a center for shipping, creating major new urban centers. These centers included Buffalo, Detroit, Milwaukee, and Chicago.

Immigration

Immigration—the movement of people into a country—to the United States increased dramatically between 1840 and 1860. American manufacturers welcomed the tide of immigrants, many of whom were willing to work for long hours and for low pay.

The largest group of immigrants to the United States at this time traveled across the Atlantic from Ireland. Between 1846 and 1860 more than 1.5 million Irish immigrants arrived in the country, settling mostly in the Northeast.

The Irish migration to the United States was brought on by a terrible potato famine. A **famine** is an extreme shortage of food. Potatoes were the main part of the Irish diet. When a devastating blight, or disease, destroyed Irish potato crops in the 1840s, starvation struck the country. More than one million people died.

Although most of the immigrants had been farmers in Ireland, they were too poor to buy land in the United States. For this reason many Irish immigrants took low-paying factory jobs in

L1, ELL

Guided Reading Activity 13–2

Name _____ Date _____ Class _____

★ **Guided Reading Activity 13-2**

DIRECTIONS: Outlining Locate the heading in your textbook. Then use the information under the heading to help you write each answer. Use another sheet of paper if necessary.

I. Northern Factories
  A. Working Conditions—What kind of unpleasant conditions did factory workers labor under?
  B. Attempts to Organize
    1. What kinds of organizations did skilled factory workers form to improve working conditions?
    2. What did some New York City workers do in the 1830s to get higher wages?
  C. African American Workers
    1. What two attitudes toward free African Americans remained in the North

✔**Reading Check**

Answer: Factory employees worked longer hours under worsening conditions.

Did you know?

The women who worked in New England's textile mills were the first American women to work in factories. Today women make up 56 percent of the total civilian labor force. Inequality still exists, however. On average, women earn approximately 76 cents for every dollar men earn.

What?Where?When?Who?

City Life Despite the problems, urban life had much to offer. Perhaps the biggest attraction was the prospect of finding work. To many people from rural America and Europe, even a low-paying factory job seemed like an opportunity to move ahead. Cities were also exciting places where a newcomer could meet different kinds of people and be part of the urban hustle and bustle.

DIFFERENTIATED INSTRUCTION

Reading Support Make library resources available to students to use for reference in creating collages showing living and working conditions discussed in the section. Materials needed are a 9" × 12" piece of cardboard, newspapers, magazines, tissue paper, foil, gift wrap, glue, paintbrush, waxed paper, and scissors. Have students experiment with cutting and tearing shapes out of the various materials (for example, tear a shape of a factory from the newspaper). **L1**

📁 Refer to *Inclusion for the Middle School Social Studies Classroom Strategies and Activities* in the TCR.

So many Irish people immigrated to New York City that it soon became the city with the largest Irish population in the world. In just a few decades, more Irish people lived in America than lived in Ireland. **Ask: Why did most Irish immigrants work in cities?** *(They were too poor to buy land for farming.)*

Answer:
1. Ireland
2. 1850 and 1860

3 ASSESS

Assign Section 2 Assessment as homework or as an in-class activity.

● Have students use **Interactive Tutor Self-Assessment CD-ROM.**

L2

Section Quiz 13–2

MORE ABOUT... Immigration

Newcomers came to America from many different countries in the mid-1800s, but the overwhelming majority came from Ireland and Germany.

Annual Immigration, 1820–1860

Sources of U.S. Immigration

1820–1840
- Great Britain 14%
- Germany 22%
- Ireland 35%
- All other nations 29%

1841–1860
- Great Britain 16%
- Germany 32%
- Ireland 39%
- All other nations 13%

Graph Skills

Immigration to the United States increased dramatically between 1820 and 1860.

1. **Identifying** Which country provided the most immigrants between 1840 and 1860?
2. **Analyzing information** From the graph, in which years did immigration surpass 100,000?

Northern cities. The men who came from Ireland worked in factories or performed manual labor, such as working on the railroads. The women, who accounted for almost half of the immigrants, became servants and factory workers.

The second-largest group of immigrants in the United States between 1820 and 1860 came from Germany. Some sought work and opportunity. Others had left their homes because of the failure of a democratic revolution in Germany in 1848.

Between 1848 and 1860 more than one million German immigrants—many in family groups—settled in the United States. Many arrived with enough money to buy farms or open their own businesses. They prospered in

many parts of the country, founding their own communities and self-help organizations. Some German immigrants settled in New York and Pennsylvania, but many moved to the Midwest and the western territories.

The Impact of Immigration

The immigrants who came to the United States between 1820 and 1860 changed the character of the country. These people brought their languages, customs, religions, and ways of

394   CHAPTER 13   North and South

INTERDISCIPLINARY CONNECTIONS ACTIVITY

Daily Life When the first census was taken in 1790, about 95 percent of Americans lived on farms. By 1850 the population was 85 percent rural. Today our population is largely urban and suburban. Have students find the information they need to create a graph showing the changing nature of the United States population from 1790 to the present. Students may work in small groups, each taking a different block of time to show on a graph. Have each group use the same scale so that changes are apparent when the graphs are placed side by side. **L2**

life with them, some of which filtered into American culture.

Before the early 1800s, the majority of immigrants to America had been either Protestants from Great Britain or Africans brought forcibly to America as slaves. At the time, the country had relatively few Catholics, and most of these lived around Baltimore, New Orleans, and St. Augustine. Most of the Irish immigrants and about one-half of the German immigrants were Roman Catholics.

Many Catholic immigrants settled in cities of the Northeast. The Church gave the newcomers more than a source of spiritual guidance. It also provided a center for the community life of the immigrants.

The German immigrants brought their language as well as their religion. When they settled, they lived in their own communities, founded German-language publications, and established musical societies.

Immigrants Face Prejudice

In the 1830s and 1840s, anti-immigrant feelings rose. Some Americans feared that immigrants were changing the character of the United States too much.

People opposed to immigration were known as nativists because they felt that immigration threatened the future of "native"—American-born—citizens. Some nativists accused immigrants of taking jobs from "real" Americans and were angry that immigrants would work for lower wages. Others accused the newcomers of bringing crime and disease to American cities. Immigrants who lived in crowded slums served as likely targets of this kind of prejudice.

The Know-Nothing Party

The nativists formed secret anti-Catholic societies, and in the 1850s they joined to form a new political party: the American Party. Because members of nativist groups often answered questions about their organization with the statement "I know nothing," their party came to be known as the **Know-Nothing Party.**

The Know-Nothings called for stricter citizenship laws—extending the immigrants' waiting period for citizenship from 5 to 21 years—and wanted to ban foreign-born citizens from holding office.

In the mid-1850s the Know-Nothing movement split into a Northern branch and a Southern branch over the question of slavery. At this time the slavery issue was also dividing the Northern and Southern states of the nation.

✓ **Reading Check** **Identifying** What two nations provided the largest number of immigrants to the United States during this era?

SECTION 2 ASSESSMENT

Checking for Understanding

1. **Key Terms** Use each of these terms in a complete sentence that will help explain its meaning: trade union, strike, prejudice, discrimination, famine, nativist.

2. **Reviewing Facts** What was the nation's largest city in 1860?

Reviewing Themes

3. **Geography and History** How did German and Irish immigrants differ in where they settled?

Critical Thinking

4. **Making Inferences** How do you think nativists would have defined a "real" American?

5. **Determining Cause and Effect** Re-create the diagram below and list reasons workers formed labor unions.

Analyzing Visuals

6. **Graph Skills** Study the graphs on page 394. What country provided about 1 of 4 immigrants to the U.S. between 1820 and 1840?

Interdisciplinary Activity

Geographic Patterns Study the graphs on page 394. Create a quiz for your classmates based on the geographic patterns of immigration to the U.S. as shown on the graphs. Trade quizzes with a classmate and answer those questions.

CHAPTER 13 North and South **395**

✓ **Reading Check**

Answer: Germany and Ireland

L1

Reteaching Activity 13–2

L1, ELL

Reading Essentials and Study Guide 13–2

L3

Enrichment Activity 13–2

4 CLOSE

Ask students to explain why nativists could be said to have forgotten their own origins.

SECTION 2 ASSESSMENT ANSWERS

1. Student work should reflect correct use of terms.
2. New York City
3. Irish settled mostly in cities in the Northeast. They were too poor to buy land, so they took factory jobs. Germans settled in New York, Pennsylvania, the Midwest, and the western territories. Many arrived with money to buy farms and open businesses.
4. Answers will vary but may include that a "real" American was a Protestant born in the United States.
5. poor conditions; long hours; unfair wages; fear of factory system
6. Germany

Interdisciplinary Activity Questions and answers should show accurate analysis of information.

TEACH

Reading a Circle Graph This skill teaches students how to read a circle graph. A circle graph is most useful for showing parts of a whole, rather than a progression or changes over time. When you have several graphs together, as on this page, you can do both.

If you have students make their own circle graphs, review the use of a protractor. To find the size of the angle of a wedge, students must multiply the part number by 360 and divide that figure by the total.

Additional Practice

L2

Chapter Skills Activity 13

GLENCOE
TECHNOLOGY

CD-ROM
Glencoe Skillbuilder Interactive Workbook CD-ROM, Level 1

This interactive CD-ROM reinforces student mastery of essential social studies skills.

Social Studies
SKILLBUILDER

Reading a Circle Graph

Why Learn This Skill?

Have you ever watched someone dish out pieces of pie? When the pie is cut evenly, everybody gets the same size slice. If one slice is cut a little larger, however, someone else gets a smaller piece. A **circle graph** is like a pie cut in slices. Often, a circle graph is called a *pie chart.*

Learning the Skill

In a circle graph, the complete circle represents a whole group—or 100 percent. The circle is divided into "slices," or wedge-shaped sections representing parts of the whole.

The size of each slice is determined by the percentage it represents.

To read a circle graph, follow these steps:
- Study the labels or key to determine what the parts or "slices" represent.
- Compare the parts of the graph to draw conclusions about the subject.
- When two or more circle graphs appear together, read their titles and labels. Then compare the graphs for similarities and differences.

Practicing the Skill

Read the graphs on this page. Then answer the following questions.

❶ What do the four graphs represent?

❷ What percentage of workers were in agriculture in 1840? In 1870?

Agricultural and Nonagricultural Workers, 1840–1870

1840: 69%, 16%, 15%
1850: 64%, 20%, 16%
1860: 59%, 23%, 18%
1870: 53%, 26%, 21%

Agricultural | Manufacturing | Other

Source: Historical Statistics of the United States.

❸ During what decade did the percentage of workers in manufacturing increase the most?

❹ What can you conclude from the graphs about the relationship between manufacturing and agricultural workers from 1840 to 1870?

Applying the Skill

Reading a Circle Graph Find a circle graph related to the economy in a newspaper or magazine. Compare its sections. Then draw a conclusion about the economy.

Glencoe's **Skillbuilder Interactive Workbook CD-ROM, Level 1,** provides instruction and practice in key social studies skills.

396

ANSWERS TO PRACTICING THE SKILL

❶ agricultural and nonagricultural workers in 1840, 1850, 1860, and 1870

❷ 69 percent, 53 percent

❸ between 1860 and 1870

❹ number of manufacturing workers increased, number of agricultural workers decreased (or agricultural workers made up a larger, though decreasing, percentage of workers than nonagricultural workers)

Applying the Skill Students should correctly analyze an economic circle graph using the steps outlined in **Learning the Skill.**

SECTION 3 Southern Cotton Kingdom

Guide to Reading

Main Idea
Cotton was vital to the economy of the South.

Key Terms
cotton gin, capital

Reading Strategy
Comparing As you read the section, re-create the diagram. In the ovals, give reasons why cotton production grew while industrial growth was slower.

Cotton production   Industry

Read to Learn
• how settlement expanded in the South.
• why the economy of the South relied on agriculture.

Section Theme
Science and Technology Technology, a favorable climate, and rising demand led to the cotton boom in the Deep South.

Preview of Events

| ♦1780 | ♦1800 | ♦1820 | ♦1840 | ♦1860 |

1793
Eli Whitney invents cotton gin

1800s
Removal of Native Americans spurs expansion of cotton production

1860
The South remains largely rural and dependent on cotton

Stem of cotton

AN American Story

Cotton was "king" in the South before 1860. "Look which way you will, you see it; and see it moving," wrote a visitor to Mobile, Alabama. "Keel boats, ships, brigs, schooners, wharves, stores, and press-houses, all appeared to be full." Cotton was also the main topic of conversation: "I believe that in the three days that I was there . . . I must have heard the word *cotton* pronounced more than 3,000 times."

Rise of the Cotton Kingdom

In 1790 the South seemed to be an underdeveloped agricultural region with little prospect for future growth. Most Southerners lived along the Atlantic coast in Maryland, Virginia, and North Carolina in what came to be known as the **Upper South.**

By 1850 the South had changed. Its population had spread inland to the states of the **Deep South**—Georgia, South Carolina, Alabama, Mississippi, Louisiana, and Texas. The economy of the South was thriving. Slavery, which had disappeared from the North, grew stronger than ever in the South.

CHAPTER 13   North and South   **397**

1 FOCUS

Section Overview
This section describes how new technology, favorable climate, and high demand led to the cotton boom in the Deep South.

Reading Preview

Answers to Graphic: Cotton production: cotton gin decreased processing time, farmers grew more cotton; Industry: farming was more profitable so no new businesses started, lack of capital

Preteaching Vocabulary
Have students define *capital* in their own words.

SECTION RESOURCES

Reproducible Masters
• Reproducible Lesson Plan 13–3
• Daily Lecture and Discussion Notes 13–3
• Guided Reading Activity 13–3
• Section Quiz 13–3
• Reteaching Activity 13–3
• Reading Essentials and Study Guide 13–3
• Enrichment Activity 13–3

Transparencies
• Daily Focus Skills Transparency 13–3

Multimedia
• Interactive Tutor Self-Assessment CD-ROM
• ExamView® Pro Testmaker CD-ROM
• Presentation Plus! CD-ROM

2 TEACH

Daily Lecture and Discussion Notes 13–3

Copyright © by The McGraw-Hill Companies, Inc.

Daily Lecture and Discussion Notes
Chapter 13, Section 3

Did You Know? Cotton is still an important industry in the United States. Today 98 percent of cotton is grown in 14 states, with Texas producing the largest share. Each year, over 14.5 million acres of cotton are harvested on 35,000 family farms, producing 16.9 million bales. Each bale weighs about 500 pounds.

I. **Rise of the Cotton Kingdom** (Pages 397–399)

A. The economy of the South thrived by 1850 because of cotton. It became the leading cash crop. Tobacco and rice had been profitable in colonial times, but tobacco depended on foreign markets and the price fluctuated. Rice could not be grown in the dry inland areas. In the Deep South—Georgia, South Carolina, Alabama, Louisiana, Mississippi, and Texas—cotton helped the economy prosper, and slavery grew stronger.

B. Eli Whitney revolutionized ...

Reading Strategy

Finding Main Points Have students turn the **Read to Learn** items into questions and find the main points that answer those questions. **L1**

Geography *Skills*

Answers:
1. Arkansas, Louisiana, Mississippi, Alabama, Tennessee, and Georgia
2. Cotton production increased. By 1860 most of the state produced up to 45 bales of cotton per square mile.

L1, ELL

Guided Reading Activity 13–3

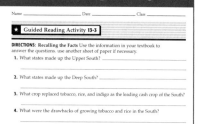

Name _____ Date _____ Class _____

★ **Guided Reading Activity 13-3**

DIRECTIONS: Recalling the Facts Use the information in your textbook to answer the questions. use another sheet of paper if necessary.

1. What states made up the Upper South? _____

2. What states made up the Deep South? _____

3. What crop replaced tobacco, rice, and indigo as the leading cash crop of the South?

4. What were the drawbacks of growing tobacco and rice in the South?

NATIONAL GEOGRAPHIC **Cotton Production, 1820–1860**

1820
Area produces up to 45 bales per square mile

1860
Area produces up to 45 bales per square mile
Area produces more than 45 bales per square mile

Cotton production as a percentage of U.S. exports

7.1% **1800**
32% **1820**
51.6% **1840**
57.5% **1860**

Source: *Historical Statistics of the United States.*

Geography *Skills*

1. **Human-Environment Interaction** What states included areas that produced more than 45 bales of cotton per square mile?
2. **Human-Environment Interaction** Describe the changes in South Carolina's areas of cotton production from 1820 to 1860.

Cotton Rules the Deep South

In colonial times, rice, indigo, and tobacco made up the South's main crops. After the American Revolution, demand for these crops decreased. European mills, however, wanted Southern cotton. But cotton took time and labor to produce. After harvest, workers had to painstakingly separate the plant's sticky seeds from the cotton fibers.

Cotton production was revolutionized when **Eli Whitney** invented the cotton gin in 1793. The cotton gin was a machine that removed seeds from cotton fibers, dramatically increasing the amount of cotton that could be processed. A worker could clean 50 pounds of cotton a day with the machine—instead of 1 pound by hand. Furthermore the gin was small enough for one person to carry from place to place.

Whitney's invention had important consequences. The cotton gin led to the demand for more workers. Because the cotton gin processed cotton fibers so quickly, farmers wanted to grow more cotton. Many Southern planters relied on slave labor to plant and pick the cotton.

398   CHAPTER 13   North and South

COOPERATIVE LEARNING ACTIVITY

Researching Developments Form four or five classroom groups with the goal of having each group research and provide written and oral reports on subjects such as the development of the cotton gin, Eli Whitney, cotton farming today, products made from cotton, and so on. Students should divide tasks, such as organizing, researching, illustrating, and presenting, according to the skills of group members. **L2, ELL**

By 1860 the economies of the Deep South and the Upper South had developed in different ways. Both parts of the South were agricultural, but the Upper South still produced tobacco, hemp, wheat, and vegetables. The Deep South was committed to cotton and, in some areas, to rice and sugarcane.

The value of enslaved people increased because of their key role in producing cotton and sugar. The Upper South became a center for the sale and transport of enslaved people throughout the region.

✓**Reading Check** **Describing** What effect did the cotton gin have on the South's economy?

Industry in the South

The economy of the South prospered between 1820 and 1860. Unlike the industrial North, however, the South remained overwhelmingly rural, and its economy became increasingly different from the Northern economy. The South accounted for a small percentage of the nation's manufacturing value by 1860. In fact, the entire South had a lower value of manufactured goods than the state of Pennsylvania.

Barriers to Industry

Why was there little industry in the South? One reason was the boom in cotton sales. Because agriculture was so profitable, Southerners remained committed to farming rather than starting new businesses.

Another stumbling block was the lack of capital—money to invest in businesses—in the South. To develop industries required money, but many Southerners had their wealth invested in land and slaves. Planters would have had to sell slaves to raise the money to build factories. Most wealthy Southerners were unwilling to do this. They believed that an economy based on cotton and slavery would continue to prosper.

In addition the market for manufactured goods in the South was smaller than it was in the North. A large portion of the Southern

TECHNOLOGY & History

Answer: It increased the amount of cotton that could be processed, so more cotton could be grown, thereby increasing the need for enslaved persons to plant and harvest it.

✓**Reading Check**

Answer: It increased the demand for enslaved African Americans and kept the South committed to cotton production.

3 ASSESS

Assign Section 3 Assessment as homework or as an in-class activity.

⊕ Have students use **Interactive Tutor Self-Assessment CD-ROM.**

L2

Section Quiz 13–3

Name _____ Date _____ Class _____

⭐ **Chapter 13**   Score ▢

Section Quiz 13-3

DIRECTIONS: Matching Match the items in Column A with the items in Column B. Write the correct letters in the blanks. *(10 points each)*

Column A	Column B
___ 1. Southern "king"	A. sugarcane
___ 2. rich man's crop	B. tobacco
___ 3. led to need for more enslaved labor	C. capital
___ 4. profitable colonial crop	D. cotton gin
___ 5. money to invest	E. cotton

L1

Reteaching Activity 13–3

Name _____ Date _____ Class _____

⭐ **Reteaching Activity 13-3**

DIRECTIONS: Comparing and Contrasting After each statement of fact, write the letter of a fact from the Fact Bank that makes a comparison or contrast.

1. **Fact:** In 1790 the South seemed to be an underdeveloped agricultural region with little prospect for future growth.

Comparison or Contrast: ___

2. **Fact:** In the colonial period, tobacco was the most profitable crop in Virginia; Georgia and South Carolina produced rice and indigo.

Comparison or Contrast: ___

3. **Fact:** In the late 1700s, a worker

4. **Fact:** By 1860 the Upper South still produced tobacco, hemp, wheat, and vegetables.

Comparison or Contrast: ___

5. **Fact:** In the industrial North, large numbers of people moved to the cities to be near factories and work.

Comparison or Contrast: ___

6. **Fact:** In the 1840s and 1850s, the North experienced a railroad boom

TECHNOLOGY & History

The Cotton Gin

In 1793 Eli Whitney visited Catherine Greene, a Georgia plantation owner. She asked him to build a device that removed the seeds from cotton pods. Whitney called the machine the cotton gin—"gin" being short for engine. *How did the invention of the cotton gin affect slavery?*

Eli Whitney

① Cotton bolls are dumped into the **hopper.**

② A hand **crank** turns a **cylinder** with wire teeth. The teeth pull the cotton past a grate.

① hopper

③ grate

② cylinder

② crank

④ brushes

③ Slots in the **grate** allow the cotton but not its seeds to pass through.

④ A second cylinder with **brushes** pulls the cotton off the toothed cylinder and sends it out of the gin.

DIFFERENTIATED INSTRUCTION

Reading Support Between 1820 and 1860, it is estimated that 50 percent of the African Americans living in the Upper South were taken by slaveholders to new cotton fields in the new slave states along the Gulf of Mexico and the Mississippi River. Have students put themselves in the position of an African American of the time and write a poem or diary entry expressing their pain at being separated from family and friends. **L2**

☞ Refer to *Inclusion for the Middle School Social Studies Classroom Strategies and Activities* in the TCR.

✓ Reading Check

Answer: money to invest in business; more available capital allows for more investment in businesses, which results in economic growth

L1, ELL

Reading Essentials and Study Guide 13–3

Study Guide

Chapter 13, Section 3
For use with textbook pages 397–400

SOUTHERN COTTON KINGDOM

KEY TERMS	
cotton gin	A machine that removed seeds from cotton fibers (page 398)
capital	Money to invest in businesses (page 399)

DRAWING FROM EXPERIENCE

What is the economy based on where you live? Is it mostly agricultural, fishing, mining, manufacturing, or something else? How does the economy in your area affect the way you live? In the last section, you read about how the growth of industry and increased immigration changed the North. This section focuses on the factors that led to the cotton boom in the South.

ORGANIZING YOUR THOUGHTS

L3

Enrichment Activity 13–3

Name _____ Date _____ Class _____

★ **Enrichment Activity 13–3** ★

The Decade That Cotton Became King

The graph below shows cotton production for 1850 in states of the cotton belt.

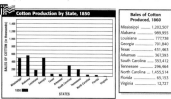

Cotton Production by State, 1850	Bales of Cotton Produced, 1860
	Mississippi 1,202,507
	Alabama 989,955
	Louisiana 777,738
	Georgia 701,840
	Texas 431,463
	Arkansas 367,393
	South Carolina 353,412
	Tennessee 296,464
	North Carolina 1,455,514
	Florida 65,153
	Virginia 12,727

DIRECTIONS: Comparing Data The chart on the right shows cotton production for states in 1860. Add the bars for 1860 to the graph above for each state. Be sure to add the new data to the map key. Compare the 1850 and 1860 data. Then answer the questions on a separate sheet of paper.

1. About how many times more cotton was produced in Virginia in 1860 than in 1850?
2. By about how much did cotton production in Mississippi increase between 1850 and 1860?
3. Did North Carolina or South Carolina show the smaller increase in production between 1850 and 1860?
4. Which states produced the most cotton in 1850 and in 1860?
5. How did cotton production in South Carolina in 1860 compare with cotton production in Georgia that year?

Activity DIRECTIONS: Writing a Report Study each state's pattern of growth in cotton production from 1850 to 1860. Then make a prediction on the basis of what you see. Explain your reasoning in a report that recommends either investing or not investing in cotton. If possible include a graph to explain your predictions. What historic event will affect your report?

4 CLOSE

How do you think the growth and production of cotton, along with Southern resistance to industrial growth, became critical issues in the debate about slavery?

400

---

population consisted of enslaved people with no money to buy merchandise. So the limited local market discouraged industries from developing.

Yet another reason for the lack of industry is that some Southerners did not want industry to flourish there. One Texas politician summed up the Southerners' point of view this way:

> ❝We want no manufactures; we desire no trading, no mechanical or manufacturing classes. As long as we have our rice, our sugar, our tobacco and our cotton, we can command wealth to purchase all we want.❞

Southern Factories

While most Southerners felt confident about the future of the cotton economy, some leaders wanted to develop industry in the region. They argued that, by remaining committed to cotton production, the South was becoming dependent on the North for manufactured goods. These Southerners also argued that factories would revive the economy of the Upper South, which was less prosperous than the cotton states.

One Southerner who shared this view was **William Gregg,** a merchant from Charleston, South Carolina. After touring New England's textile mills in 1844, Gregg opened his own textile factory in South Carolina.

In Richmond, Virginia, **Joseph Reid Anderson** took over the Tredegar Iron Works in the 1840s and made it one of the nation's leading producers of iron. Years later during the Civil War, Tredegar provided artillery and other iron products for the Southern forces.

The industries that Gregg and Anderson built stood as the exception rather than the rule in the South. In 1860 the region remained largely rural and dependent on cotton.

Southern Transportation

Natural waterways provided the chief means for transporting goods in the South. Most towns were located on the seacoast or along rivers. There were few canals, and roads were poor.

Like the North, the South also built railroads, but to a lesser extent. Southern rail lines were short, local, and did not connect all parts of the region in a network. As a result Southern cities grew more slowly than cities in the North and Midwest, where railways provided the major routes of commerce and settlement. By 1860 only about one-third of the nation's rail lines lay within the South. The railway shortage would have devastating consequences for the South during the Civil War.

✓ Reading Check **Explaining** What is capital? Why is it important for economic growth?

SECTION 3 ASSESSMENT

Checking for Understanding

1. **Key Terms** Use each of these terms in a sentence that will help explain its meaning: cotton gin, capital.
2. **Reviewing Facts** How did the lack of capital affect industrial growth?

Reviewing Themes

3. **Science and Technology** Why did the invention of the cotton gin increase the demand for enslaved Africans?

Critical Thinking

4. **Predicting Consequences** If slavery had been outlawed, how do you think it would have affected the South's economy?
5. **Comparing** How did agriculture in the Upper South differ from agriculture in the Deep South? Re-create the diagram below and describe the differences.

Agriculture	
Upper South	Deep South

Analyzing Visuals

6. **Geography Skills** Look at the maps and the graphs on page 398. What area of Florida specialized in cotton? Did cotton make up more than 50 percent of U.S. exports in 1820?

Interdisciplinary Activity

Informative Writing Research and write a report on a machine mentioned in the chapter—perhaps the steam locomotive, steamboat, or another steam-driven machine. Illustrate your report if you wish. Keep the report in your portfolio.

SECTION 3 ASSESSMENT ANSWERS

1. Student work should reflect correct use of terms.
2. Lack of capital limited growth. Southern farmers had their capital invested in land and enslaved workers, leaving little for industrial investment.
3. Because farmers could process their cotton more quickly, they wanted to grow more. As a result, they needed more enslaved Africans to plant and harvest the crop.
4. Paid workers would increase the price of cotton, or lower profits. More Southerners might have turned to developing industry.
5. Upper South: tobacco, hemp, wheat, vegetables; Deep South: mostly cotton, some rice and sugarcane
6. the northern central area; no

Interdisciplinary Activity Reports should show evidence of research performed.

SECTION 4 The South's People

Guide to Reading

Main Idea
The South's population consisted of wealthy slaveholding planters, small farmers, poor whites, and enslaved African Americans.

Key Terms
yeoman, tenant farmer, fixed cost, credit, overseer, spiritual, slave code

Reading Strategy
Organizing Information As you read the section, re-create the diagram below and describe the work that was done on Southern plantations.

Working on a plantation

Read to Learn
• about the way of life on Southern plantations.
• how enslaved workers maintained strong family and cultural ties.

Section Theme
Culture and Traditions Most of the people in the South worked in agriculture in the first half of the 1800s.

Preview of Events

♦1800	♦1820	♦1840	♦1860

1808
Congress outlaws the slave trade

1831
Nat Turner leads rebellion in Virginia

1859
Arkansas orders free blacks to leave

1860
Population of Baltimore reaches 212,000

1 FOCUS

Section Overview
This section examines the different groups of people who lived in the South.

BELLRINGER
Skillbuilder Activity

Project transparency and have students answer the question.

Daily Focus Skills Transparency 13–4

Reading Preview

Answers to Graphic: domestic work; skilled labor; care of farm animals; fieldwork

Preteaching Vocabulary
Use the **Vocabulary PuzzleMaker CD-ROM** to create crossword and word search puzzles.

AN
American Story

Planters gathered in the bright Savannah sunshine. They were asked to bid on a strong slave who could plow their fields. Fear and grief clouded the enslaved man's face because he had been forced to leave his wife and children. Later, he wrote this letter: "My Dear wife I [write] . . . with much regret to inform you that I am Sold to a man by the name of Peterson. . . . Give my love to my father and mother and tell them good Bye for me. And if we Shall not meet in this world, I hope to meet in heaven. My Dear wife for you and my Children my pen cannot express the [grief] I feel to be parted from you all."

Plow

Small Farms

Popular novels and films often portray the South before 1860 as a land of stately plantations owned by rich white slaveholders. In reality most white Southerners were either small farmers without slaves or planters with a handful of slaves. Only a few planters could afford the many enslaved Africans and

CHAPTER 13   North and South   **401**

SECTION RESOURCES

📁 Reproducible Masters
• Reproducible Lesson Plan 13–4
• Daily Lecture and Discussion Notes 13–4
• Guided Reading Activity 13–4
• Section Quiz 13–4
• Reteaching Activity 13–4
• Reading Essentials and Study Guide 13–4
• Enrichment Activity 13–4

Transparencies
• Daily Focus Skills Transparency 13–4

Multimedia
📣 American Music: Hits Through History
🖥 Vocabulary PuzzleMaker CD-ROM
🖥 Interactive Tutor Self-Assessment CD-ROM
🖥 ExamView® Pro Testmaker CD-ROM
🖥 Presentation Plus! CD-ROM

2 TEACH

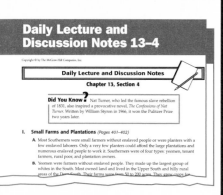
Comparing Lifestyles Have students compare and contrast the lifestyles of the various types of Southerners: plantation owners, yeomen, tenant farmers, rural poor, enslaved African Americans, free African Americans. Students may wish to present this information in chart form. **L2**

Picturing **History**

Plantations were far apart and travel was slow; so when a planter held a party, most of the guests would stay at the host's manor house for several days or even weeks, enjoying the various entertainment provided.
Answer: oversaw enslaved domestic workers; supervised buildings and gardens; some served as plantation's accountant

✓ Reading Check

Answer: yeomen

---

the lavish mansions shown in fictional accounts of the Old South. Most white Southerners fit into one of four categories: yeomen, tenant farmers, the rural poor, or plantation owners.

Small Farmers and the Rural Poor

The farmers who did not have slaves—yeomen—made up the largest group of whites in the South. Most yeomen owned land. Although they lived throughout the region, they were most numerous in the Upper South and in the hilly rural areas of the Deep South, where the land was unsuited to large plantations.

A yeoman's farm usually ranged from 50 to 200 acres. Yeomen grew crops both for their own use and to sell, and they often traded their produce to local merchants and workers for goods and services.

Most Southern whites did not live in elegant mansions or on large plantations. They lived in far simpler homes, though the structure of their homes changed over time. In the early 1800s many lived in cottages built of wood and plaster with thatched roofs. Later many lived in one-story frame houses or log cabins.

Not all Southern whites owned land. Some rented land, or worked as tenant farmers, on landlords' estates. Others—the rural poor—lived in crude cabins in wooded areas where they could clear a few trees, plant some corn, and keep a hog or a cow. They also fished and hunted for food.

The poor people of the rural South were stubbornly independent. They refused to take any job that resembled the work of enslaved people. Although looked down on by other whites, the rural poor were proud of being self-sufficient.

✓ Reading Check **Identifying** What group made up the largest number of whites in the South?

Plantations

A large plantation might cover several thousand acres. Well-to-do plantation owners usually lived in comfortable but not luxurious farmhouses. They measured their wealth partly by the number of enslaved people they controlled and partly by such possessions as homes, furnishings, and clothing. A small group of plantation owners—about 4 percent—held 20 or more slaves in 1860. The large majority of slaveholders held fewer than 10 enslaved workers.

A few free African Americans possessed slaves. The Metoyer family of Louisiana owned thousands of acres of land and more than 400 slaves. Most often, these slaveholders were free African Americans who purchased their own family members in order to free them.

Picturing **History**
Wealthy Southerners pose for the camera in front of an elegant plantation home. **What were the duties of the wife of a plantation owner?**

Atlanta, Georgia, business street, c. 1860

COOPERATIVE LEARNING ACTIVITY

Creating a Documentary Organize the class into small groups, each of which is to plan a segment for a documentary on Southern life. If making an actual film would be impractical, groups may present their ideas in the form of storyboards, which are a series of sketches representing the scenes intended to be shown in the final product. Students may use library resources as well as the information presented in the text. 📦 **L2**

Economics
Plantation Owners

The main economic goal for large plantation owners was to earn profits. Such plantations had fixed costs—regular expenses such as housing and feeding workers and maintaining cotton gins and other equipment. Fixed costs remained about the same year after year.

Cotton prices, however, varied from season to season, depending on the market. To receive the best prices, planters sold their cotton to agents in cities such as **New Orleans, Charleston, Mobile,** and **Savannah.** The cotton exchanges, or trade centers, in Southern cities were of vital importance to those involved in the cotton economy. The agents of the exchanges extended credit—a form of loan—to the planters and held the cotton for several months until the price rose. Then the agents sold the cotton. This system kept the planters always in debt because they did not receive payment for their cotton until the agents sold it.

Plantation Wives

The wife of a plantation owner generally was in charge of watching over the enslaved workers who toiled in her home and tending to them when they became ill. Her responsibilities also included supervising the plantation's buildings and the fruit and vegetable gardens. Some wives served as accountants, keeping the plantation's financial records.

Women often led a difficult and lonely life on the plantation. When plantation agriculture spread westward into Alabama and Mississippi, many planters' wives felt they were moving into a hostile, uncivilized region. Planters traveled frequently to look at new land or to deal with agents in New Orleans or **Memphis.** Their wives spent long periods alone at the plantation.

Work on the Plantation

Large plantations needed many different kinds of workers. Some enslaved people worked in the house, cleaning, cooking, doing laundry, sewing, and serving meals. They were called domestic slaves. Other African Americans were trained as blacksmiths, carpenters, shoemakers,

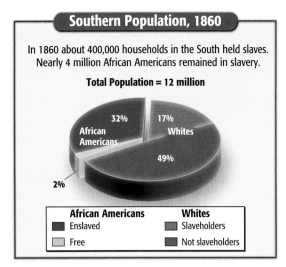

Southern Population, 1860

In 1860 about 400,000 households in the South held slaves. Nearly 4 million African Americans remained in slavery.

Total Population = 12 million

African Americans 32%
Whites 17%
49%
2%

African Americans	Whites
Enslaved	Slaveholders
Free	Not slaveholders

or weavers. Still others worked in the pastures, tending the horses, cows, sheep, and pigs. Most of the enslaved African Americans, however, were field hands. They worked from sunrise to sunset planting, cultivating, and picking cotton and other crops. They were supervised by an overseer—a plantation manager.

Reading Check **Explaining** Why were many slaves needed on a plantation?

Life Under Slavery

Enslaved African Americans endured hardship and misery. They worked hard, earned no money, and had little hope of freedom. One of their worst fears was being sold to another planter and separated from their loved ones. In the face of these brutal conditions, enslaved African Americans maintained their family life as best they could and developed a culture all their own. They resisted slavery through a variety of ingenious methods, and they looked to the day when they would be liberated.

Life in the Slave Cabins

Enslaved people had few comforts beyond the bare necessities. Josiah Henson, an African American who escaped from slavery, described the quarters where he had lived.

Guided Reading Activity 13–4

Name _____ Date _____ Class _____

★ **Guided Reading Activity 13-4**

DIRECTIONS: Filling in the Blanks Use your textbook to fill in the blanks using the words in the box. Use another sheet of paper if necessary.

Underground Railroad	yeoman	tenant farmers	charity
Harriet Tubman	overseer	opportunities	network
profits	slave codes	family life	accountants
domestic slaves	field hands	read or write	

Small Farms and Plantations

Farmers who did not have enslaved labor, (1) _____ made up the largest group of whites in the South. Some Southern whites rented or worked as (2) _____ on landlords' estates.

Plantations

The main economic goal for large plantations was to earn (3) _____. Some wives of plantation owners served as (4) _____, keeping the plantation's financial records. Enslaved people who worked in the house, cleaning, cooking, and doing laundry were called (5) _____. Most enslaved people, however, were (6) _____, supervised by an (7) _____.

Life Under Slavery

Enslaved African Americans maintained their (8) _____ as best they could. To ensure stability, enslaved African Americans created a (9) _____ of relatives and friends, who made up their extended family. The (10) _____ aimed to prevent the dreaded slave rebellion. These laws made it a crime to teach enslaved people to (11) _____. (12) _____ and Frederick Douglass were two African American leaders who escaped enslavement. The (13) _____, a network of "safe houses," offered assistance to runaway slaves.

Life in the Cities

Several large cities in the South provided free African Americans new (14) _____, though they did not have the same rights as other citizens. Many southern states had (15) _____ schools for those who could not afford to pay for education.

Reading Check

Answer: There were many jobs to keep the plantation running such as tending to animals, planting, cultivating, and doing housework.

When?Who?What?Where?

Nineteenth Century In the early 1850s, Indiana, Iowa, and Illinois bordered slave states. All three had laws that banned African Americans, whether free or enslaved, from entering their states.

DIFFERENTIATED INSTRUCTION

English Learners Students may enjoy reading aloud some African or African American folktales. There are many versions of the Brer Rabbit stories available. (Brer Rabbit's roots come from the East African stories of Kalulu the Rabbit, whose wit alternately gets him into trouble and rescues him.)
L1, ELL

📁 Refer to *Inclusion for the Middle School Social Studies Classroom Strategies and Activities* in the TCR.

MORE ABOUT...

In *Twelve Years a Slave*, Solomon Northup described the life of a field hand on a Southern plantation: "The hands are required to be in the cotton fields as soon as it is light in the morning, and, with the exception of ten or fifteen minutes, which is given them at noon to swallow their allowance of cold bacon, they are not permitted to be a moment idle until it is too dark to see, and when the moon is full, they often times labor till the middle of night." **Ask: How did enslaved people cope with the injustices in their lives?** *(They maintained family and culture as well as finding comfort and hope of freedom in their religious beliefs.)*

Did you know?

In North America whites attempted to wipe out African culture. Slaveholders deliberately mixed Africans of different ethnic groups. By mixing Africans who had different languages and customs, the slaveholders hoped to prevent a sense of ethnic identity from fostering a unified rebellion.

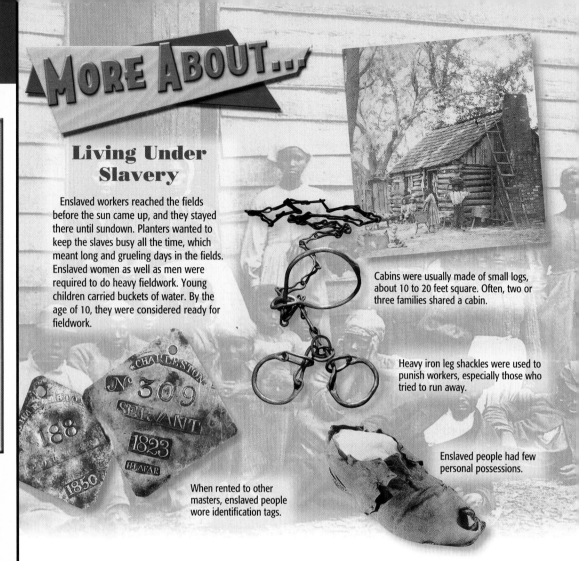

MORE ABOUT...

Living Under Slavery

Enslaved workers reached the fields before the sun came up, and they stayed there until sundown. Planters wanted to keep the slaves busy all the time, which meant long and grueling days in the fields. Enslaved women as well as men were required to do heavy fieldwork. Young children carried buckets of water. By the age of 10, they were considered ready for fieldwork.

Cabins were usually made of small logs, about 10 to 20 feet square. Often, two or three families shared a cabin.

Heavy iron leg shackles were used to punish workers, especially those who tried to run away.

Enslaved people had few personal possessions.

When rented to other masters, enslaved people wore identification tags.

66We lodged in log huts and on the bare ground. Wooden floors were an unknown luxury. In a single room were huddled, like cattle, ten or a dozen persons, men, women and children. . . .

Our beds were collections of straw and old rags, thrown down in the corners and boxed in with boards, a single blanket the only covering. . . . The wind whistled and the rain and snow blew in through the cracks, and the damp earth soaked in the moisture till the floor was miry [muddy] as a pigsty.99

Family Life

Enslaved people faced constant uncertainty and danger. American law in the early 1800s did not protect enslaved families. At any given time a husband or wife could be sold away, or a slaveholder's death could lead to the breakup of an enslaved family. Although marriage between enslaved people was not recognized by law, many couples did marry. Their marriage ceremonies included the phrase "until death or separation do us part"—recognizing the possibility that a marriage might end with the sale of one spouse.

INTERDISCIPLINARY CONNECTIONS ACTIVITY

Music One of the most popular composers of the times was Stephen Foster, who became famous for his songs idealizing the South. Foster used African American melodies to create lively songs. He wrote mostly for the popular minstrel shows, which incorporated the songs, dances, and instruments of African Americans (although the shows used white actors in blackface and depicted African Americans in a demeaning way). Ask a music teacher to present some of Foster's songs to the class. Then discuss how the songs paint a rosy picture of the South that was in stark contrast with the actual conditions. **L1**

To provide some measure of stability in their lives, enslaved African Americans established a network of relatives and friends, who made up their extended family. If a father or mother were sold away, an aunt, uncle, or close friend could raise the children left behind. Large, close-knit extended families became a vital feature of African American culture.

African American Culture

Enslaved African Americans endured their hardships by extending their own culture, fellowship, and community. They fused African and American elements into a new culture.

The growth of the African American population came mainly from children born in the United States. In 1808 Congress had outlawed the slave trade. Although slavery remained legal in the South, no new slaves could enter the United States. By 1860 almost all the enslaved people in the South had been born there.

These native-born African Americans held on to their African customs. They continued to practice African music and dance. They passed traditional African folk stories to their children. Some wrapped colored cloths around their heads in the African style. Although a large number of enslaved African Americans accepted Christianity, they often followed the religious beliefs and practices of their African ancestors as well.

African American Christianity

For many enslaved African Americans, Christianity became a religion of hope and resistance. They prayed fervently for the day when they would be free from bondage.

The passionate beliefs of the Southern slaves found expression in the spiritual, an African American religious folk song. The song "Didn't My Lord Deliver Daniel," for example, refers to the biblical story of Daniel who was saved from the lions' den.

> 66Didn't my Lord deliver Daniel,
> deliver Daniel, deliver Daniel,
> Didn't my Lord deliver Daniel,
> An' why not every man?99

Spirituals provided a way for the enslaved African Americans to communicate secretly among themselves. Many spirituals combined Christian faith with laments about earthly suffering.

Slave Codes

Between 1830 and 1860 life under slavery became even more difficult because the slave codes—the laws in the Southern states that controlled enslaved people—became more severe. In existence since the 1700s, slave codes aimed to prevent the event white Southerners dreaded most—the slave rebellion. For this reason slave codes prohibited slaves from assembling in large groups and from leaving their master's property without a written pass.

Slave codes also made it a crime to teach enslaved people to read or write. White Southerners feared that a literate slave might lead other African Americans in rebellion. A slave who did not know how to read and write, whites believed, was less likely to rebel.

Resistance to Slavery

Some enslaved African Americans did rebel openly against their masters. One was **Nat Turner,** a popular religious leader among his fellow slaves. Turner had taught himself to read and write. In 1831 Turner led a group of followers on a brief, violent rampage in Southhampton County, Virginia. Before being captured Turner and his followers killed at least 55 whites. Nat Turner was hanged, but his rebellion frightened white Southerners and led them to pass more severe slave codes.

Armed rebellions were rare, however. African Americans in the South knew that they would only lose in an armed uprising. For the most part enslaved people resisted slavery by working slowly or by pretending to be ill. Occasionally resistance took more active forms, such as setting fire to a plantation building or breaking tools. Resistance helped enslaved African Americans endure their lives by striking back at white masters—and perhaps establishing boundaries that white people would respect.

CHAPTER 13   North and South   **405**

CURRICULUM CONNECTION

Music African music with its liveliness and inventiveness, influenced many new musical forms that developed outside of Africa. Among these are jazz, blues, bebop, soul, mambo, and reggae. Jazz drumming in particular is based on the drumming style typical of the southern Guineas on the coast of Africa.

Did you know?

African American spirituals, still popular today, influenced other forms of music. For example, the sorrowful songs that were related to spirituals, such as "Nobody Knows the Trouble I've Seen," developed into blues music. The more joyous spirituals, such as "Roll, Jordan, Roll," influenced gospel music.

History and the Humanities

American Music: Hits Through History, "Joshua Fit the Battle of Jericho"

Reading Strategy   READING THE TEXT

Responding and Reflecting Another side of slavery is revealed in the following quote from historian Thomas A. Bailey: "The dark taint of slavery also left its mark on whites. . . . White Southerners increasingly lived in a state of imagined siege, surrounded by potentially rebellious blacks inflamed by abolitionist propaganda. . . . Their fears bolstered an intoxicating theory of biological superiority and turned the South into a reactionary backwater in an era of progress . . . The defenders of slavery were forced to degrade themselves along with their victims." Discuss this quote with students and ask them to explain it in their own words. **L2**

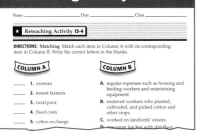
People In History

Harriet Tubman 1820–1913

Born as a slave in Maryland, Harriet Tubman worked in plantation fields until she was nearly 30 years old. Then she made her break for freedom, escaping to the North with the help of the Underground Railroad.

Realizing the risks of being captured, Tubman courageously made 19 trips back into the South during the 1850s to help other enslaved people escape. Altogether she assisted more than 300 individuals—including her parents—to escape from slavery.

While she did not establish the Underground Railroad, she certainly became its most famous and successful conductor. Tubman was known as the "Moses of her people." Despite huge rewards offered in the South for her capture and arrest, Tubman always managed to elude her enemies.

Escaping Slavery

Some enslaved African Americans tried to run away to the North. A few succeeded. **Harriet Tubman** and **Frederick Douglass,** two African American leaders who were born into slavery, gained their freedom when they fled to the North.

Yet for most enslaved people, getting to the North was almost impossible, especially from the Deep South. Most slaves who succeeded in running away escaped from the Upper South. **The Underground Railroad**—a network of "safe houses" owned by free blacks and whites who opposed slavery—offered assistance to runaway slaves.

Some slaves ran away to find relatives on nearby plantations or to escape punishment. Rarely did they plan to make a run for the North. Moses Grandy, who did escape, spoke about the problems runaways faced:

❝They hide themselves during the day in the woods and swamps; at night they travel. . . . [I]n these dangerous journeys they are guided by the north-star, for they only know that the land of freedom is in the north.❞

Most runaways were captured and returned to their owners. Discipline was severe; the most common punishment was whipping.

✔ Reading Check
Explaining How did the African American spiritual develop?

City Life and Education

Although the South was primarily agricultural, it was the site of several large cities by the mid-1800s. By 1860 the population of **Baltimore** had reached 212,000 and the population of New Orleans had reached 168,000. The ten largest cities in the South were either seaports or river ports.

With the coming of the railroad, many other cities began to grow as centers of trade. Among the cities located at the crossroads of the railways were Columbia, South Carolina; Chattanooga, Tennessee; Montgomery, Alabama; Jackson, Mississippi; and Atlanta, Georgia. The population of Southern cities included white city dwellers, some enslaved workers, and many of the South's free African Americans.

EXTENDING THE CONTENT

The North and South Economies The economies of the North and the South were interconnected. The South depended on the North for most manufactured goods. The North relied on the South for raw materials. For example, the Northern textile industry could not operate without Southern cotton. Further, Southern cotton, indigo, and rice accounted for about 60 percent of all American exports. Most of these exports were carried overseas by Northern merchant ships.

The cities provided free African Americans with opportunities to form their own communities. African American barbers, carpenters, and small traders offered their services throughout their communities. Free African Americans founded their own churches and institutions. In New Orleans they formed an opera company.

Although some free African Americans prospered in the cities, their lives were far from secure. Between 1830 and 1860 Southern states passed laws that limited the rights of free African Americans. Most states would not allow them to migrate from other states. Although spared the horrors of slavery, free African Americans were denied an equal share in economic and political life.

Education

Plantation owners and those who could afford to do so often sent their children to private schools. One of the best known was the academy operated by Moses Waddel in Willington, South Carolina. Students attended six days a week. The Bible and classical literature were stressed, but the courses also included mathematics, religion, Greek, Latin, and public speaking.

During this era, no statewide public school systems existed. However, cities such as Charleston, Louisville, and Mobile did establish excellent public schools.

By the mid-1800s, education was growing. Hundreds of public schools were operating in North Carolina by 1860. Even before that, the Kentucky legislature set up a funding system for public schools. Many states also had charity schools for students whose parents could not afford to pay.

Although the number of schools and teachers in the South grew, the South lagged behind other sections of the country in **literacy,** the number of people who can read and write. One reason for this was the geography of the South. Even in the more heavily populated Southern states there were few people per square mile. Virginia and North Carolina had fewer than 15 white inhabitants per square mile. In contrast, Massachusetts had 124 inhabitants per square mile.

It was too great a hardship for many Southern families to send their children great distances to attend school. In addition, many Southerners believed education was a private matter, not a state function; therefore, the state should not spend money on education.

✓ **Reading Check** **Describing** What Southern city had surpassed 200,000 in population by the year 1860?

HISTORY Online

Student Web Activity
Visit tarvol1.glencoe.com and click on **Chapter 13— Student Web Activities** for an activity on family life in the South.

HISTORY Online

Objectives and answers to the student activity can be found in the **Web Activity Lesson Plan** feature at tarvol1.glencoe.com

✓**Reading Check**

Answer: Baltimore

L1, ELL

Reading Essentials and Study Guide 13–4

Study Guide
Chapter 13, Section 4
For use with textbook pages 401–407
THE SOUTH'S PEOPLE

KEY TERMS	
yeomen	Farmers who did not have slaves (page 402)
tenant farmers	Farmers who rented land and worked on a landlord's estate (page 402)
fixed cost	Regular expenses that remain about the same each year (page 403)
credit	A form of loan (page 403)
overseer	A plantation manager (page 403)
spiritual	An African American religious folk song (page 405)
slave code	Law in the Southern states that controlled enslaved people (page 405)

L3

Enrichment Activity 13–4

Name _____ Date _____ Class _____

★ **Enrichment Activity 13-4** ★

New Orleans, City of Music
In New Orleans African Americans have a long history of contributions to American music. Free African Americans established an opera company in New Orleans before the Emancipation Proclamation. They created moving spirituals in their churches and later developed jazz, a musical form that is often called the only truly original American music.
DIRECTIONS: Use the words in the Word Bank to complete the musical crossword puzzle. You may use your dictionary if you wish.

spiritual	aria	libretto	score	improvisation
syncopation	New Orleans	ragtime	Dixieland	swing

Across:
1. jazz term describing

4 CLOSE

Have students summarize the economic differences among plantation owners, yeomen, and enslaved workers.

SECTION 4 ASSESSMENT

Checking for Understanding

1. **Key Terms** Use the following terms to create a newspaper article about life in the South during this period of time: **yeoman, tenant farmer, overseer, spiritual, slave code.**

2. **Reviewing Facts** List two differences between yeomen and plantation owners.

Reviewing Themes

3. **Culture and Traditions** Why were extended families vital to African American culture?

Critical Thinking

4. **Making Generalizations** If you were a plantation owner, what would you tell your son or daughter if he or she asked why you held slaves?

5. **Classifying Information** Re-create the diagram below and in the boxes briefly explain how the slave codes operated.

Slave codes	
Control education	Control assembly

Analyzing Visuals

6. Look at the pictures on pages 402 and 404. Write a paragraph explaining what you think the pictures portray about life in the South.

Interdisciplinary Activity

Geography Research the economic activity of one of the Southern states. Draw a map of the state, and use symbols to represent each resource and show its location in the state.

CHAPTER 13   North and South   **407**

SECTION 4 ASSESSMENT ANSWERS

1. Student work should reflect correct use of terms.
2. Yeomen: did not have enslaved labor, had small farms; Plantation owners: held enslaved workers, larger farms, wealthier
3. They provided stability. If a parent was sold, the extended family raised the children.

4. Answers will vary but might include to support the family; because it was acceptable in the South.
5. Control education: made it a crime to teach enslaved people to read or write; Control assembly: prohibited enslaved people from assembling

or leaving their owner's property.

6. Students may note differences in lifestyles.

Interdisciplinary Activity Student maps should be correct and include a key of any symbols used.

CHAPTER 13
ASSESSMENT and ACTIVITIES

ASSESSMENT and ACTIVITIES

GLENCOE TECHNOLOGY

MindJogger Videoquiz
Use **MindJogger Videoquiz** to review the Chapter 13 content.

 Available in VHS

Reviewing Key Terms
Students' puzzles will vary but should conform to the written instructions. Students may use the following definitions as clues:

1. an apparatus that uses electric signals to transmit messages

2. a person opposed to immigration

3. a plantation manager

4. farmers who did not have enslaved workers

5. a form of loan

Reviewing Key Facts

6. Before canals and railroads were in use, agricultural goods were transported down the Mississippi to New Orleans and then shipped to other countries or to the East Coast. After canals and railroads, products were transported directly from the Midwest to the East.

7. Communication was made faster.

8. Factories grew, and there was an increase in immigration and trade.

9. to get higher wages and to limit the number of hours worked

10. They were paid less than male workers, and unions excluded them.

11. Many men left Germany after the failure of a democratic revolution.

12. It increased production.

13. agriculture was very profitable, lack of capital to invest in businesses, market for manufactured goods was small

Chapter Summary
North and South

North	South

Economy

North:
- Growth of industrialization.
- Specialization and machinery allow for mass production.

South:
- Cotton is leading cash crop.
- Industry limited due to lack of capital and market demand.

Transportation

North:
- Roads, canals, and railroads being built.
- Locomotives improve during this era.

South:
- Natural waterways chief means of transportation.
- Canals and roads are poor.
- Railroads are limited.

Way of Life

North:
- Many people move to cities to find work.
- Cities grow crowded and many live in unhealthy and unsafe conditions.
- African Americans suffer discrimination and have few rights.

South:
- Plantation owners farm large tracts of land; plantations are generally self-sufficient.
- Yeomen make up the largest group of whites.
- Tenant farmers farm small tracts of land.
- Enslaved African Americans do most of the work on plantations.

14. a network of forested routes and safe homes along a northern route leading to freedom for enslaved African Americans

15. to prevent slave rebellions and to control slaves

Critical Thinking

16. Goods could be transported more quickly and cheaply, which meant higher profits.

17. advantages: availability of jobs and social activities; dis-

Reviewing Key Terms
On graph paper, create a word search puzzle using the following terms. Crisscross the terms vertically and horizontally, then fill in the remaining squares with extra letters. Use the terms' definitions as clues to find the words in the puzzle.

1. telegraph
2. nativist
3. overseer
4. yeoman
5. credit

Reviewing Key Facts

6. How did the development of the canal and rail network alter the trade route between the Midwest and the East Coast?

7. How did the the telegraph influence long-distance communication?

8. Provide three reasons why cities grew in the early 1800s.

9. What was the goal of workers going on strike?

10. In what ways were women in the workforce discriminated against?

11. Why did immigration from Germany increase after 1848?

12. How did the cotton gin affect cotton production?

13. Why was there little industry in the South?

14. What was the Underground Railroad?

15. What was the purpose of the slave codes?

Critical Thinking

16. **Analyzing Themes: Economic Factors** How did improvements in transportation affect the economy of the North?

17. **Comparing** Discuss one advantage and one disadvantage of city life in the North.

18. **Comparing** Re-create the diagram below and compare the use of railroads in the North and South before 1860.

	North	South
Use of railroads		

19. **Analyzing Information** Describe ways in which enslaved African Americans held on to their African customs.

advantages: overcrowded, expensive, run-down housing, threat of disease and fire

18. The North relied heavily on railroads for commerce and settlement. The South mainly used natural waterways to transport goods.

19. They merged African and American elements into a new culture, practiced African music and dance, passed African folk stories and proverbs on to their children, and followed ancestral religious beliefs.

Practicing Skills

Reading a Circle Graph *Study the circle graphs below; then answer these questions.*

Populations of the North and South in 1860

North
- 98% white
- 2% African American

South
- 66% white
- 34% African American

Source: *Historical Statistics of the United States.*

20. What does the information in the two graphs represent?

21. In what part of the country did African Americans make up more than one-third of the population?

22. Can you use the graphs to draw a conclusion about the total population of each region? Why or why not?

Geography and History Activity

Study the map on page 388 and answer the questions that follow.

23. **Movement** In which direction would a train travel from Chattanooga, Tennessee, to Lynchburg, Virginia?

24. **Location** What was the easternmost city on the New York Central line?

25. **Movement** What cities would a train passenger pass through taking the most direct Memphis-to-Baltimore route?

Citizenship Cooperative Activity

26. **Community Issues** Working with two other students, contact the office of your local government to find out what is being done to solve local problems and how volunteers can help. Find out when the town board or city council meets. After you obtain the information, interview people in the neighborhood to find out what they think about various problems the community faces. Tell them about the town board or city council meetings, and encourage them to attend or to become involved in community activities. Compare your findings about community issues with the other groups.

Self-Check Quiz
Visit tarvol1.glencoe.com and click on **Chapter 13— Self-Check Quizzes** to prepare for the chapter test.

Economics Activity

27. Although railroads helped the economy, why might investors in turnpikes and canals view them as a threat?

Technology Activity

28. **Research and Writing** Use your text, encyclopedias, and other library resources for information about the lives of enslaved and free African Americans during this era. Write a report at least two pages in length in which you identify various political, economic, and social factors that affected their lives. Compare the effects these factors had on their lives.

Alternative Assessment

29. **Portfolio Writing Activity** Write a conversation between a Southerner and Northerner who meet on a train in the mid-1800s. Have them talk about the differences between their lives. Use the notes from your journal in the script.

Standardized Test Practice

Directions: Choose the *best* answer to the following question.

Organizations of workers having the same skills or working within the same trade are called

A   nativists.

B   trade unions.

C   yeomen.

D   congressional committees.

Test-Taking Tip

Use the process of elimination to answer this question: Which answers can you rule out as definitely wrong?

Economics Activity

27. Railway travel would take away from road and canal travel. Investors in these other two industries would be afraid of losing money.

Technology Activity

28. Students may note that political factors include prohibited from voting; social factors include segregation; economic factors include lacking the freedom to choose where they worked. Students should note that free African Americans had more economic opportunities than enslaved people, but they too were limited.

Alternative Assessment

29. Scripts should reflect students' understanding of the differences between the lives of Northerners and Southerners.

HISTORY Online

Have students visit the Web site at tarvol1.glencoe.com to review Chapter 13 and take the Self-Check Quiz.

Standardized Test Practice

Answer: B
Question Type: Economics
Answer Explanation: On page 392 attempts to organize unions are described.

Bonus Question ?

Ask: Who wrote *The New American Practical Navigator*, a book that revolutionized ship navigation in the 1800s? *(Nathaniel Bowditch)*

Practicing Skills

20. the populations of the North and South in 1860

21. the South

22. No, because specific numbers of people in each region are not given. Only percentages of the total population are given. Also, the graphs do not account for other groups living in the North and South. The graphs only account for whites and African Americans.

Geography and History Activity

23. northeast

24. Boston

25. Chattanooga, Lynchburg, and Washington, D.C.

Citizenship Cooperative Activity

26. Students should attend local meetings and encourage community members to get involved.

Chapter 14 Resources

Timesaving Tools

TeacherWorks™ All-In-One Planner and Resource Center

- **Interactive Teacher Edition** Access your Teacher Wraparound Edition and your classroom resources with a few easy clicks.
- **Interactive Lesson Planner** Planning has never been easier! Organize your week, month, semester, or year with all the lesson helps you need to make teaching creative, timely, and relevant.

Use Glencoe's **Presentation Plus!** multimedia teacher tool to easily present dynamic lessons that visually excite your students. Using Microsoft PowerPoint® you can customize the presentations to create your own personalized lessons.

TEACHING TRANSPARENCIES

Graphic Organizer 6 L2

Why It Matters Chapter Transparency 16 L2

REVIEW AND REINFORCEMENT

Workbook Activity 14 L1

Time Line Activity 14 L2

Vocabulary Activity 14 L1

REVIEW AND REINFORCEMENT

Critical Thinking Skills Activity 14 L2

Take-Home Review Activity 14 L1

ENRICHMENT

Linking Past and Present Activity 14 L2

Primary Source Reading 14 L2

GEOGRAPHY

Geography and History Activity 14 L2

Meeting NCSS Standards

The following standards are highlighted in Chapter 14:

Section 1   X   Civic Ideals & Practices: A, B, C, E, F, G, I, J

Section 2   IV   Individual Development & Identity: A, B, C, D, E, F, G

Section 3   V   Individuals, Groups, & Institutions: A, B, C, D, E, F, G

FOLDABLES™

Study Organizer

Dinah Zike's Foldables are three-dimensional, interactive graphic organizers that help students practice basic writing skills, review key vocabulary terms, and identify main ideas. Additional chapter activities can be found in the *Reading and Study Skills Foldables* booklet.

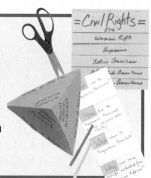

Chapter 14 Resources

ASSESSMENT AND EVALUATION

Chapter 14 Test Form A L2

Chapter 14 Test Form B L2

Standardized Test Practice Workbook Activity 14 L2

Performance Assessment Activity 14 L1, ELL

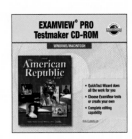

EXAMVIEW® PRO Testmaker CD-ROM
WINDOWS/MACINTOSH

American Republic

- QuickTest Wizard does all the work for you
- Choose ExamView tests or create your own
- Complete editing capability

MULTIMEDIA

- Vocabulary PuzzleMaker CD-ROM
- Interactive Tutor Self-Assessment CD-ROM
- ExamView® Pro Testmaker CD-ROM
- Audio Program
- American History Primary Source Document Library CD-ROM
- MindJogger Videoquiz
- Presentation Plus! CD-ROM
- TeacherWorks CD-ROM
- Interactive Student Edition CD-ROM
- Glencoe Skillbuilder Interactive Workbook CD-ROM, Level 1
- The American Republic to 1877 Video Program
- American Music: Hits Through History

SPANISH RESOURCES

The following Spanish language materials are available in the Spanish Resources Binder:

- Spanish Guided Reading Activities
- Spanish Reteaching Activities
- Spanish Quizzes and Tests
- Spanish Vocabulary Activity
- Spanish Take-Home Review Activity
- Spanish Summaries
- The Declaration of Independence and United States Constitution Spanish Translation

---

THE HISTORY CHANNEL®

The following videotape programs are available from Glencoe as supplements to Chapter 14:

- **Susan B. Anthony: Rebel for the Cause** (ISBN 1-56501-646-7)
- **Underground Railroad** (ISBN 0-7670-1679-3)

To order, call Glencoe at 1-800-334-7344. To find classroom resources to accompany many of these videos, check the following home pages:
A&E Television: www.aande.com
The History Channel: www.historychannel.com

HISTORY Online

Use our Web site for additional resources. All essential content is covered in the Student Edition.

You and your students can visit tarvol1.glencoe.com, the Web site companion to **The American Republic to 1877.** This innovative integration of electronic and print media offers your students a wealth of opportunities. The student text directs students to the Web site for the following options:

- **Chapter Overviews**
- **Self-Check Quizzes**
- **Student Web Activities**
- **Textbook Updates**

Answers to the student Web activities are provided for you in the **Web Activity Lesson Plans.** Additional Web resources and Interactive Tutor Puzzles are also available.

Chapter 14 Resources

SECTION RESOURCES

Daily Objectives	Reproducible Resources	Multimedia Resources
SECTION 1 **Social Reform** 1. Understand how religious and philosophical ideas inspired various reform movements. 2. Explain why educational reformers thought all citizens should attend school.	Reproducible Lesson Plan 14–1 Daily Lecture and Discussion Notes 14–1 Guided Reading Activity 14–1* Section Quiz 14–1* Reteaching Activity 14–1* Reading Essentials and Study Guide 14–1* Enrichment Activity 14–1	Daily Focus Skills Transparency 14–1 American Art and Architecture, Transparencies 10 and 11 Interactive Tutor Self-Assessment CD-ROM ExamView® Pro Testmaker CD-ROM Presentation Plus! CD-ROM
SECTION 2 **The Abolitionists** 1. Describe the ways some Americans worked to eliminate slavery. 2. Explore the reasons why many Americans feared the end of slavery.	Reproducible Lesson Plan 14–2 Daily Lecture and Discussion Notes 14–2 Guided Reading Activity 14–2* Section Quiz 14–2* Reteaching Activity 14–2* Reading Essentials and Study Guide 14–2* Enrichment Activity 14–2	Daily Focus Skills Transparency 14–2 American Music: Hits Through History ABC News Interactive™ Historic America Electronic Field Trips Interactive Tutor Self-Assessment CD-ROM ExamView® Pro Testmaker CD-ROM Presentation Plus! CD-ROM
SECTION 3 **The Women's Movement** 1. Examine how the antislavery and the women's rights movements were related. 2. Evaluate what progress women made toward equality during the 1800s.	Reproducible Lesson Plan 14–3 Daily Lecture and Discussion Notes 14–3 Guided Reading Activity 14–3* Section Quiz 14–3* Reteaching Activity 14–3* Reading Essentials and Study Guide 14–3* Enrichment Activity 14–3	Daily Focus Skills Transparency 14–3 Vocabulary PuzzleMaker CD-ROM Interactive Tutor Self-Assessment CD-ROM ExamView® Pro Testmaker CD-ROM Presentation Plus! CD-ROM

0:00 OUT OF TIME?
Assign the Chapter 14 **Reading Essentials and Study Guide.**

*Also Available in Spanish

 Blackline Master   Transparency   CD-ROM   DVD

Poster   Music Program   Audio Program   Videocassette

KEY TO ABILITY LEVELS

Teaching strategies have been coded.

L1   BASIC activities for all students

L2   AVERAGE activities for average to above-average students

L3   CHALLENGING activities for above-average students

ELL   ENGLISH LANGUAGE LEARNER activities

NATIONAL GEOGRAPHIC Teacher's Corner

INDEX TO NATIONAL GEOGRAPHIC MAGAZINE

The following articles relate to this chapter.

- "The Cherokee," by Geoffrey Norman, May 1995.
- "Powwow," by Michael Parfit, June 1994.
- "The Cruelest Commerce: African Slave Trade, " by Colin Palmer, September 1992.

ADDITIONAL NATIONAL GEOGRAPHIC SOCIETY PRODUCTS

To order the following, call National Geographic at 1-800-368-2728:

- *GeoKit: The Civil War* (Kit)
- *GeoKit: Immigration* (Kit)
- *United States/Territorial Growth* (Map)
- *National Geographic Desk Reference* (Book)
- *Steal Away: The Harriet Tubman Story* (Video)
- *Immigration: The Triumph of Hope* (Video)

NGS ONLINE

Access National Geographic's Web site for current events, atlas updates, activities, links, interactive features, and archives.
www.nationalgeographic.com

MEETING SPECIAL NEEDS

In addition to the Differentiated Instruction strategies found in each section, the following resources are also suitable for your special needs students:

- *ExamView® Pro Testmaker CD-ROM* allows teachers to tailor tests by reducing answer choices.
- The *Audio Program* includes the entire narrative of the student edition so that less-proficient readers can listen to the words as they read them.
- The *Reading Essentials and Study Guide* provides the same content as the student edition but is written two grade levels below the textbook.
- *Guided Reading Activities* give less-proficient readers point-by-point instructions to increase comprehension as they read each textbook section.
- *Enrichment Activities* includes a stimulating collection of readings and activities for gifted and talented students.

From the Classroom of...

Debbie Behling
Angleton Middle School East
Angleton, TX

Who Am I?

Introduce this chapter by going around the room and asking students these questions: "If you could change anything in the world today, what would you change? Why?" Give students some time to think of several answers to avoid duplicate responses. Then assign each student an individual reformer from this chapter. After students have read the chapter, have them write on an index card a "Who Am I?" question about their reformer. Remind students of the types of things that they and their classmates said needed reform today and include those issues in their questions when possible. Collect the cards and save them. As a review at the end of the chapter, organize the class into teams and have a quiz show. Use the cards to see which teams can answer the "Who Am I?" questions correctly, and award points based on the responses.

ADDITIONAL RESOURCES FROM GLENCOE

- American Music: Cultural Traditions
- American Art and Architecture
- Outline Map Resource Book
- U.S. Desk Map
- Building Geography Skills for Life
- Inclusion for the Middle School Social Studies Classroom Strategies and Activities
- Teaching Strategies for the American History Classroom (Including Block Scheduling Pacing Guides)
- American Crafts Hands-On Activities
- American Games Hands-On Activities
- American History Flash Cards

Block Schedule

Activities that are suited to use within the block scheduling framework are identified by:

Performance Assessment

Refer to Activity 14 in the Performance Assessment Activities and Rubrics booklet.

Why It Matters Activity

Explain that reform occurs when there is a collective agreement among a group of people to address a social issue. As students read the chapter, have them consider how each reform movement still impacts them today.

GLENCOE
TECHNOLOGY

The American Republic to 1877 Video Program

To learn more about the women in reform movements, have students view the Chapter 14 video "Women and Reform" from **The American Republic to 1877 Video Program.**

 Available in DVD and VHS

MindJogger Videoquiz

Use **MindJogger Videoquiz** to preview the Chapter 14 content.

 Available in VHS

CHAPTER 14

The Age of Reform
1820–1860

Why It Matters

The idea of reform—the drive to improve society and the lives of Americans—grew during the mid-1800s. Reformers set out to improve the lives of the disadvantaged, especially enslaved people and the urban poor.

The Impact Today

The spirit of reform is alive and well in the modern world. Individual freedom became a key goal during the last half of the twentieth century. Civil rights movements have advanced racial equality. In many countries the women's movement has altered traditional female roles and opportunities.

 The American Republic to 1877 Video The chapter 14 video, "Women and Reform," chronicles the role of women in the reform movements of the 1800s.

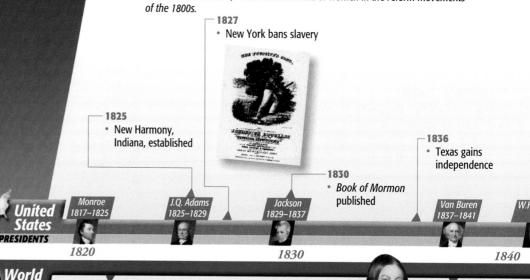

1827
• New York bans slavery

1825
• New Harmony, Indiana, established

1830
• Book of Mormon published

1836
• Texas gains independence

United States PRESIDENTS

Monroe 1817–1825 · J.Q. Adams 1825–1829 · Jackson 1829–1837 · Van Buren 1837–1841 · W.H. H. 184

1820 · *1830* · *1840*

World

1821
• Mexico becomes independent nation

1837
• Victoria becomes queen of England

410   CHAPTER 14   The Age of Reform

Reading Strategy   PURPOSE FOR READING

Concept maps are a special kind of web diagram. To do a concept map, write the main idea in the center of the page. It may be a word or a phrase. Then write related ideas on branches that radiate from this central idea. Tell students to write the word "Reform" on their concept maps. As a group activity, have the students complete the concept map. *(Possible answers include: dedicated people; fighting injustice; changing the government; changing society.)* **L1**

410

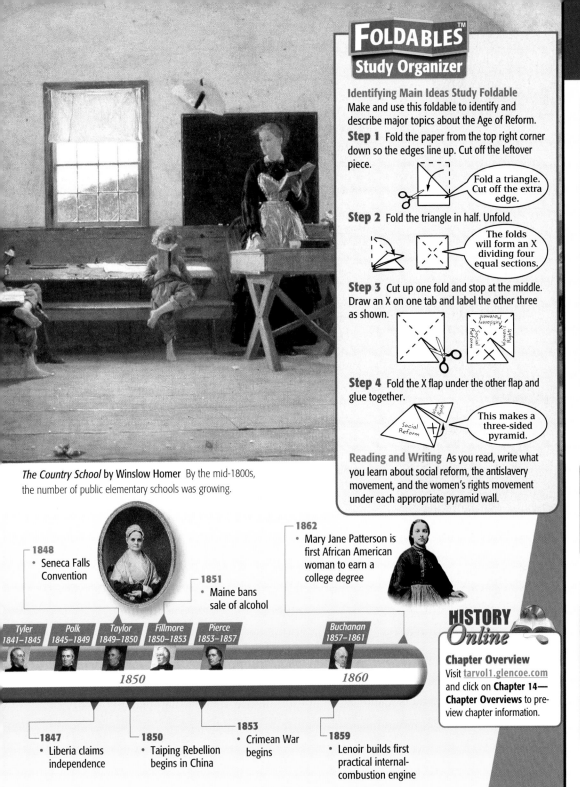

The Country School by Winslow Homer By the mid-1800s, the number of public elementary schools was growing.

FOLDABLES™
Study Organizer

Identifying Main Ideas Study Foldable
Make and use this foldable to identify and describe major topics about the Age of Reform.

Step 1 Fold the paper from the top right corner down so the edges line up. Cut off the leftover piece.

> Fold a triangle. Cut off the extra edge.

Step 2 Fold the triangle in half. Unfold.

> The folds will form an X dividing four equal sections.

Step 3 Cut up one fold and stop at the middle. Draw an X on one tab and label the other three as shown.

Antislavery Movement
Social Reform
Women's Rights

Step 4 Fold the X flap under the other flap and glue together.

Social Reform
Women's Rights

> This makes a three-sided pyramid.

Reading and Writing As you read, write what you learn about social reform, the antislavery movement, and the women's rights movement under each appropriate pyramid wall.

FOLDABLES™
Study Organizer
Dinah Zike's Foldables

Purpose Students will make and use a foldable to summarize the main ideas after reading the chapter. This reading strategy requires students to read with the purpose of discovering and recording major topics about the Age of Reform. As students read, they record what they learned about social reform, the antislavery movement, and the women's rights movement.

📁 Have students complete **Reading and Study Skills Foldables** Activity 14. **L1**

HISTORY Online

Introduce students to chapter content and key terms by having them access **Chapter Overview 14** at tarvol1.glencoe.com

TIME LINE ACTIVITY

As students read the chapter, have them review the time line on pages 410–411. Have students create a chart that lists the presidents and their terms served in chronological order.

1848
• Seneca Falls Convention

1851
• Maine bans sale of alcohol

1862
• Mary Jane Patterson is first African American woman to earn a college degree

| Tyler 1841–1845 | Polk 1845–1849 | Taylor 1849–1850 | Fillmore 1850–1853 | Pierce 1853–1857 | Buchanan 1857–1861 |

1850   *1860*

HISTORY Online

Chapter Overview
Visit tarvol1.glencoe.com and click on **Chapter 14— Chapter Overviews** to preview chapter information.

1847
• Liberia claims independence

1850
• Taiping Rebellion begins in China

1853
• Crimean War begins

1859
• Lenoir builds first practical internal-combustion engine

CHAPTER 14   The Age of Reform   411

More About the Art

Early in his career, Winslow Homer (1836–1910) focused on everyday life in his paintings, such as the schoolroom scene on page 411, rather than the high drama of his marine paintings, most of which were created after 1880. The country school was a unique environment where children of all ages were placed in the same classroom and taught by the same teacher. Often boys sat on one side of the room and girls on the other. **Ask: How does this classroom compare to your classroom?** *(Students should describe how their classroom is arranged.)*

1 FOCUS

Section Overview

This section examines the religious and moral basis for the reform movements of the 1800s.

Reading Preview

Answers to Graphic: Lyman Beecher: led the temperance movement; Horace Mann: promoted longer school terms, better trained teachers, and improved curriculum; Thomas Gallaudet: developed a method for educating hearing-impaired individuals; Dorothea Dix: led a reform movement to improve the care of prisoners and people with mental illness

Preteaching Vocabulary
Revival comes from the Latin *re* meaning "again" and *vivere*, meaning "to live." Have students research the meaning of other **Key Terms.**

SECTION 1 Social Reform

Guide to Reading

Main Idea
During the early 1800s, many religious and social reformers attempted to improve American life and education and help people with disabilities.

Key Terms
utopia, revival, temperance, normal school, transcendentalist

Reading Strategy
Taking Notes As you read section 1, re-create the diagram below and identify these reformers' contributions.

	Contributions
Lyman Beecher	
Horace Mann	
Thomas Gallaudet	
Dorothea Dix	

Read to Learn
- how religious and philosophical ideas inspired various reform movements.
- why educational reformers thought all citizens should go to school.

Section Theme
Civic Rights and Responsibilities Many reformers worked for change during this era.

Preview of Events

◆1820	◆1830	◆1840	◆1850

1825
Robert Owen establishes New Harmony, Indiana

1835
Oberlin College admits African Americans

1837
Horace Mann initiates education reform

1843
Dorothea Dix reveals abuses of mentally ill

Henry David Thoreau

AN American Story

According to folklore, Henry David Thoreau sat on the hard, wooden bench in the jail cell, but he did not complain about its stiffness. He felt proud that he had stood up for his beliefs. Thoreau had refused to pay a one-dollar tax to vote, not wanting his money to support the Mexican War. As he looked through the cell bars, he heard a voice. "Why are you here?" asked his friend Ralph Waldo Emerson. Thoreau replied, "Why are you *not* here?" He would later write, "Under a government which imprisons any unjustly, the true place for a just man is also a prison."

The Reforming Spirit

Thoreau represented a new spirit of reform in America. The men and women who led the reform movement wanted to extend the nation's ideals of liberty and equality to all Americans. They believed the nation should live up to the noble goals stated in the Declaration of Independence and the Constitution.

The spirit of reform brought changes to American religion, politics, education, art, and literature. Some reformers sought to improve society by forming utopias, communities based on a vision of a perfect society. In 1825 Robert Owen established New Harmony, Indiana, a village dedicated to cooperation rather than competition among its members.

SECTION RESOURCES

📂 Reproducible Masters
- Reproducible Lesson Plan 14–1
- Daily Lecture and Discussion Notes 14–1
- Guided Reading Activity 14–1
- Section Quiz 14–1
- Reteaching Activity 14–1
- Reading Essentials and Study Guide 14–1
- Enrichment Activity 14–1

📖 Transparencies
- Daily Focus Skills Transparency 14–1
- American Art and Architecture, Transparencies 10 and 11

Multimedia
- ① Interactive Tutor Self-Assessment CD-ROM
- ② ExamView® Pro Testmaker CD-ROM
- ③ Presentation Plus! CD-ROM

Founded on high hopes and sometimes impractical ideas, few of the utopian communities lasted more than a few years. The Shakers, the Mormons, and other religious groups also built their own communities. Only the Mormons established a stable, enduring community.

The Religious Influence

In the early 1800s, a wave of religious fervor—known as the **Second Great Awakening**—stirred the nation. The first Great Awakening had spread through the colonies in the mid-1700s.

The new religious movement began with frontier camp meetings called revivals. People came from miles around to hear eloquent preachers, such as Charles Finney, and to pray, sing, weep, and shout. The experience often made men and women eager to reform both their own lives and the world. The Second Great Awakening increased church membership. It also inspired people to become involved in missionary work and social reform movements.

📖 *(See page 601 of the Appendix for a primary source account of a revival meeting.)*

War Against Alcohol

Religious leaders stood at the forefront of the war against alcohol. Public drunkenness was common in the early 1800s. Alcohol abuse was widespread, especially in the West and among urban workers. **Lyman Beecher,** a Connecticut minister and crusader against the use of alcohol, wanted to protect society against "rum-selling, tippling folk, infidels, and ruff-scruff."

Reformers blamed alcohol for poverty, the breakup of families, crime, and even insanity. They called for temperance, drinking little or no alcohol. The movement gathered momentum in 1826 when the American Society for the Promotion of Temperance was formed.

Beecher and other temperance crusaders used lectures, pamphlets, and revival-style rallies to warn people of the dangers of liquor. The **temperance movement** gained a major victory in 1851, when Maine passed a law banning the manufacture and sale of alcoholic beverages. Other states passed similar laws. Many Americans resented these laws, however, and most were repealed, or canceled, within several years.

The temperance movement would reemerge in the early 1900s and lead to a constitutional amendment banning alcohol.

✔ **Reading Check** **Analyzing** What were the effects of the Second Great Awakening?

Reforming Education

In the early 1800s, only New England provided free elementary education. In other areas parents had to pay fees or send their children to schools for the poor—a choice some parents refused out of pride. Some communities had no schools at all.

The leader of educational reform was **Horace Mann,** a lawyer who became the head of the Massachusetts Board of Education in 1837. During his term Mann lengthened the school year to six months, made improvements in the school curriculum, doubled teachers' salaries, and developed better ways of training teachers.

Partly due to Mann's efforts, Massachusetts in 1839 founded the nation's first state-supported normal school, a school for training high-school graduates as teachers. Other states soon adopted the reforms that Mann had pioneered.

Education for Some

By the 1850s most states had accepted three basic principles of public education: that schools should be free and supported by taxes, that teachers should be trained, and that children should be required to attend school.

These principles did not immediately go into effect. Schools were poorly funded, and many teachers lacked training. In addition, some people opposed compulsory, or required, education.

Most females received a limited education. Parents often kept their daughters from school because of the belief that a woman's role was to become a wife and mother and that this role did not require an education. When girls did go to school, they often studied music or needlework rather than science, mathematics, and history, which were considered "men's" subjects.

In the West, where settlers lived far apart, many children had no school to attend. African Americans in all parts of the country had few opportunities to go to school.

2 TEACH

Daily Lecture and Discussion Notes 14–1

Copyright © by The McGraw-Hill Companies, Inc.

Daily Lecture and Discussion Notes

Chapter 14, Section 1

Did You Know? The Perkins Institute taught several people who became famous, including Helen Keller, who was blind and deaf. Inventor Alexander Graham Bell referred her to the school. The director of Perkins sent Anne Sullivan, a recent Perkins graduate, to become Keller's resident tutor, and together they became a famous teacher/student pairing because of Keller's great achievements in learning.

I. The Reforming Spirit *(Pages 412–413)*

A. Religious and social reform brought change to the American way of life. Some Americans looked to improve society by forming utopias, or communities based on a vision of a perfect society.

Matching Have students write matching-style quizzes using the vocabulary words and people, places, and movements discussed in the section. Students may then exchange quizzes and try to answer each other's quizzes. **L1**

✔ **Reading Check**

Answer: increased church membership; inspired people to become involved in the social reforms and missionary work

 History *and the* **Humanities**

 American Art and Architecture, Transparency 10, *The Great Blue Heron;* Transparency 11, *The Buffalo Chase, Mouth of the Yellowstone* **L3**

Reading Strategy READING THE TEXT

Visualizing Artists often use their work to comment on society or politics. Have students research artistic works from the first half of the nineteenth century. Have them analyze examples of how art has influenced society or has been a force for change. Have them also identify examples of art that apply to specific American issues and examples that communicate universal themes. **L2**

What *Life* Was Like...

One-Room Schoolhouse School attendance often depended on the needs of the farm. Have students explain why they think school attendance would be affected by planting seasons and harvesting seasons.

3 ASSESS

Assign Section 1 Assessment as homework or as an in-class activity.

⊕ Have students use **Interactive Tutor Self-Assessment CD-ROM.**

L2

Section Quiz 14–1

What *Life* Was Like...

One-Room Schoolhouse

Until education became widespread, many children learned to read and write in one-room schoolhouses. Students of all ages learned mostly by rote—one group recited while the rest studied their lessons. The popular McGuffey *Readers* provided moral lessons as well as lessons in reading and grammar.

Lunch pail, left
Hornbook, center
Page from McGuffey's, right

Higher Education

Dozens of new colleges and universities were created during the age of reform. Most admitted only men. Religious groups founded many colleges between 1820 and 1850, including Amherst and Holy Cross in Massachusetts and Trinity and Wesleyan in Connecticut.

Slowly, higher education became available to groups who were previously denied the opportunity. Oberlin College of Ohio, founded in 1833, admitted both women and African Americans to the student body. In 1837 a teacher named Mary Lyon in Massachusetts opened Mount Holyoke, the first permanent women's college in America. The first college for African Americans—Ashmun Institute, which later became Lincoln University—opened in Pennsylvania in 1854.

People With Special Needs

Some reformers focused on the problem of teaching people with disabilities. **Thomas Gallaudet** (ga•luh•DEHT), who developed a method to educate people who were hearing impaired, opened the Hartford School for the Deaf in Connecticut in 1817.

At about the same time, **Dr. Samuel Gridley Howe** advanced the cause of those who were visually impaired. He developed books with large raised letters that people with sight impairments could "read" with their fingers. Howe headed the Perkins Institute, a school for the blind, in Boston.

When schoolteacher **Dorothea Dix** began visiting prisons in 1841, she found the prisoners were often living in inhumane conditions—

414 CHAPTER 14 The Age of Reform

DIFFERENTIATED INSTRUCTION

Reading Support The early 1800s saw many new social and cultural movements emerge. One of these was the Second Great Awakening. Organize the class into small groups. Have each group discuss and speculate how the Second Great Awakening might have affected different social groups in different parts of the United States. Each member of the group should contribute to the discussion. As a class, have students discuss their group's ideas and speculations. **L2**

📁 Refer to *Inclusion for the Middle School Social Studies Classroom Strategies and Activities* in the TCR.

chained to the walls with little or no clothing, often in unheated cells. To her further horror, she learned that some of the inmates were guilty of no crime—they were mentally ill persons. Dix made it her life's work to educate the public as to the poor conditions for both the mentally ill and for prisoners.

✔ **Reading Check** **Identifying** How did Dr. Samuel Howe help the visually impaired?

Cultural Trends

The changes in American society influenced art and literature. Earlier generations of American painters and writers looked to Europe for their inspiration and models. Beginning in the 1820s American artists developed their own style and explored American themes.

The American spirit of reform influenced transcendentalists. Transcendentalists stressed the relationship between humans and nature as well as the importance of the individual conscience. Writers such as Margaret Fuller, Ralph Waldo Emerson, and Henry David Thoreau were leading transcendentalists. Through her writings, Fuller supported rights for women. In his poems and essays, Emerson urged people to listen to the inner voice of conscience and to break the bonds of prejudice. Thoreau put his beliefs into practice through **civil disobedience** —refusing to obey laws he thought were unjust. In 1846 Thoreau went to jail rather than pay a tax to support the Mexican War.

The transcendentalists were not the only important writers of the period. Many poets created impresive works during this period. Henry Wadsworth Longfellow wrote narrative, or story, poems, such as the *Song of Hiawatha*. Poet Walt Whitman captured the new American spirit and confidence in his *Leaves of Grass*. Emily Dickinson wrote simple, deeply personal poems. In a poem called "Hope," written in 1861, she compares hope with a bird:

> 66 'Hope' is the thing with feathers—
> That perches in the soul—
> And sings the tune without the words—
> And never stops—at all— 99

Women writers of the period were generally not taken seriously, yet they were the authors of the most popular fiction. Harriet Beecher Stowe wrote the most successful best-seller of the mid-1800s, *Uncle Tom's Cabin*. Stowe's novel explores the injustice of slavery—an issue that took on new urgency during the age of reform.

✔ **Reading Check** **Describing** What was one of the subjects that Margaret Fuller wrote about?

SECTION 1 ASSESSMENT

Checking for Understanding

1. **Key Terms** Use each of these terms in a sentence that helps explain its meaning: utopia, revival, temperance, normal school, transcendentalist.

2. **Reviewing Facts** What were the three accepted principles of public education in the 1850s?

Reviewing Themes

3. **Civic Rights and Responsibilities** How did Thoreau act on his beliefs? What impact might such acts have had on the government?

Critical Thinking

4. **Drawing Conclusions** What did Thomas Jefferson mean when he said that the United States could not survive as a democracy without educated and well-informed citizens?

5. **Determining Cause and Effect** Re-create the diagram below and describe two ways the religious movement influenced reform.

```
┌──────────┐      ┌──────┐
│ Religious │─────┤      │
│ movement  │      └──────┘
└──────────┘      ┌──────┐
                  │      │
                  └──────┘
```

Analyzing Visuals

6. **Picturing History** Study the painting of the school room on page 414. What is pictured that you still use in school today?

Interdisciplinary Activity

Research Interview your grandparents or other adults who are over 50 years old to find out what they remember about their public school days. Before you do the interview, write six questions about the information that interests you.

SECTION 1 ASSESSMENT ANSWERS

1. Student work should reflect correct use of terms.

2. Schools should be free and supported by taxes, teachers should be trained, and school attendance should be mandatory.

3. He went to jail rather than pay a tax to support the Mexican War. If people refused to obey laws they thought were unjust, then the laws would have to be changed.

4. Uneducated people cannot effectively and intelligently make decisions about governing themselves.

5. People wanted to reform their own lives; the reform spirit motivated people to become involved in social reform and missionary work.

6. Student answers may include the following: books, tables, and writing instruments.

Interdisciplinary Activity Encourage students to share the results of their interviews with the class.

✔ **Reading Check**

Answer: He developed books with raised letters so that they could "read" with their fingers.

✔ **Reading Check**

Answer: rights for women

L1

Reteaching Activity 14–1

L1, ELL

Reading Essentials and Study Guide 14–1

L3

Enrichment Activity 14–1

4 CLOSE

Have students summarize the goals of the major reform movements discussed in the section.

415

TEACH

Analyzing Primary Sources

Have students read the words of John James Audubon. **Ask: How does Audubon view the hunters?** *(They are quite expert in hunting. However, Audubon uses the term "destruction," which gives the idea that far more birds than necessary were killed.)* Discuss with students how reading Audubon's personal writings adds interest and meaning. **Ask: How does reading Audubon's observations make his descriptions more personal to you?** *(Answers should reflect the idea that Audubon's writings include emotions felt at the time of his observations.)*

Take students out to the school yard. Tell them to listen and observe carefully. Students should make a list of everything they see and hear. Then have them write an account of their time spent outside. Suggest that they add drawings of what they saw. Have students share their observations with the class. **L1**

Visit the **TIME** Web site at www.time.com for up-to-date news, weekly magazine articles, editorials, online polls, and an archive of past magazine and Web articles.

TIME NOTEBOOK

What were people's lives like in the past?

What—and who—were people talking about? What did they eat? What did they do for fun? These two pages will give you some clues to everyday life in the U.S. as you step back in time with TIME Notebook.

PHOTO RESEARCHERS INC., NEW YORK

Profile

"*My best friends solemnly regard me as a madman.*" That's what the artist **JOHN JAMES AUDUBON** *(left) writes about himself in his journal. And he does seem to be a bit peculiar. After all, he put a band around a bird's foot so he could tell if it returned from the South in the spring. No one's ever done that before. Audubon is growing more famous thanks to his drawings. His love of the wild and his skill as an artist have awakened a new sense of appreciation for American animal life both here and in Europe. Here is what he wrote recently while on a trip to New Orleans:*

ACADEMY OF NATURAL SCIENCES OF PHILADELPHIA/CORBIS

"I TOOK A WALK WITH MY GUN THIS afternoon to see… millions of Golden Plovers [medium-sized shorebirds] coming from the northeast and going nearly south— the destruction… was really astonishing—the Sportsmen here are more numerous and at the same time more expert at shooting on the wing than anywhere in the United States."

Personalities Meet Some Concord Residents

YEARS AGO, ONE OF THE FIRST BATTLES OF THE REVOLUTIONARY WAR was fought at Concord, Massachusetts. But now the sparks that fly are of a more intellectual variety. If you want to visit Concord, you should read some of the works of its residents.

Nathaniel Hawthorne
This writer's novel *The Scarlet Letter* moved some readers, and outraged others.

Henry Wadsworth Longfellow
Writes poems about Paul Revere, Hiawatha, and a village blacksmith.

Louisa May Alcott
Author of *Little Women* who published her first book at age 16.

Louisa May Alcott

THE SCHLESINGER LIBRARY, RADCLIFFE COLLEGE

416

SPORTS
Baseball for Beginners

Want to take up the new game of baseball? Keep your eye on the ball—because the rules keep changing!

1845
- canvas bases are set 90 feet apart in a diamond shape
- only nine men play on each side
- pitches are thrown underhanded
- a ball caught on the first bounce is an "out"

1846
- at first base, a fielder can tag the bag before the runner reaches it and so make an out

1847
- players may no longer throw the ball at a runner to put him out

AMERICAN SCENE
Americans Living on Farms

1790: 95% of Americans live on farms

1820: 93% live on farms

1850: 85% live on farms

EXTENDING THE CONTENT

The Audubon Society John James Audubon (1785–1851) was born in Santo Domingo (now Haiti), but grew up in France. He came to America in 1803 to avoid fighting for Napoleon. Eventually he decided to put his childhood pastime—drawing wildlife, especially birds—to work. He spent hours outdoors watching and sketching birds engaged in their daily activities. Unable to find an American publisher that met his standards, he went to London where he found a brilliant craftsperson to do the engravings for *Birds of America*, a classic reference work. The Audubon Society, a national conservation organization, is named in his honor.

TIME
NOTEBOOK

MILESTONES

PEOPLE AND EVENTS OF THE TIME

Frederick Douglass

BROWN BROTHERS

EMIGRATED. In 1845, to England, **FREDERICK DOUGLASS**, former slave, author, and abolitionist leader, to escape danger in reaction to his autobiography, *Narrative of the Life of Frederick Douglass.*

MOVED. HENRY DAVID THOREAU, writer, to Walden Pond, Concord, Massachusetts, in 1845. Thoreau intends to build his own house on the shore of the pond and earn his living by the labor of his hands only. "Many of the so-called comforts of life," writes Thoreau, "are not only not indispensable, but positive hindrances to the elevation of mankind."

AILING. EDGAR ALLAN POE, in Baltimore, 1847, following the death of his wife, Virginia. Other than a poem on death, Poe has written little this year, devoting his dwindling energies to lawsuits against other authors he claims copied his work.

INVENTED. Samuel F.B. Morse has revolutionized communications with a series of dots and dashes in 1844.

Edgar Allan Poe

BETTMANN/CORBIS

CHILD LABOR

Letter From a Mill Worker

Mary Paul is a worker in her teens at a textile mill in Lowell, Massachusetts. Mary works 12 hours a day, 6 days a week. She sent this letter to her father:

Dear Father,

I am well which is one comfort. My life and health are spared while others are cut off. Last Thursday one girl fell down and broke her neck which caused instant death. Last Tuesday we were paid. In all I had six dollars and sixty cents, paid $4.68 for board [rent and food]....At 5 o'clock in the morning the bell rings for the folks to get up and get breakfast. At half past six it rings for the girls to get up and at seven they are called into the mill. At half past 12 we have dinner, are called back again at one and stay till half past seven.... If any girl wants employment, I advise them to come to Lowell.

BETTMANN/CORBIS

417

NUMBERS

U.S. AT THE TIME

9,022 **Miles of railways operating in 1850**

3 **Number of U.S. Presidents in 1841—Van Buren's term ended, Harrison died, and Tyler took his place**

29 **Number of medical schools Elizabeth Blackwell, a woman, applied to before being accepted at one in 1847**

700 **Number of New England whaling ships at sea in 1846**

$8 **Approximate yearly cost for a newspaper subscription in 1830**

50% **Approximate percentage of the American workforce in 1820 under the age of 10**

COOPERATIVE LEARNING ACTIVITY

Creating a Game Show Have students prepare a game similar to the 1950s game show "What's My Line?" Students should create a list of questions to identify the individuals studied in this unit. Have one student play the famous guest from the past and another act as game show moderator. Three students should act as contestants. Questions are asked of the guest until the name of the guest is correctly identified. Determine the number of questions allowed. Time limits for identification can also be established. **L2**

SECTION 2 The Abolitionists

Section Overview

This section examines the abolitionist movement during the early and mid-1800s.

BELLRINGER
Skillbuilder Activity

Project transparency and have students answer the question.

Daily Focus Skills Transparency 14–2

Reading Preview

Answers to Graphic: William Lloyd Garrison: founded *The Liberator*, the New England Antislavery Society, and the American Antislavery Society; Samuel Cornish and John Russwurm: started *Freedom's Journal;* Sarah and Angelina Grimké: bought freedom for family's slaves; Frederick Douglass: spoke and wrote against slavery; Sojourner Truth: involved in the abolitionist and women's rights movements

Preteaching Vocabulary
List this section's **Key Terms** on the chalkboard. Have students develop questions for which each term is an answer.

Guide to Reading

Main Idea
Many reformers turned their attention to eliminating slavery.

Key Terms
abolitionist, Underground Railroad

Reading Strategy
Organizing Information As you read Section 2, identify five abolitionists. Below each name, write a sentence describing his or her role in the movement.

Abolitionists

Read to Learn
• how some Americans worked to eliminate slavery.
• why many Americans feared the end of slavery.

Section Theme
Individual Action Leaders such as Harriet Tubman and William Lloyd Garrison strengthened the abolitionist movement.

Preview of Events

♦1815	♦1830	♦1845	♦1860
1816 American Colonization Society is formed	1822 First African Americans settle in Liberia	1831 William Lloyd Garrison founds *The Liberator*	1847 Liberia becomes an independent country

AN American Story

William Lloyd Garrison, a dramatic and spirited man, fought strongly for the right of African Americans to be free. On one occasion Garrison was present when Frederick Douglass, an African American who had escaped from slavery, spoke to a white audience about life as a slave. Douglass electrified his listeners with a powerful speech. Suddenly Garrison leaped to his feet. "Is this a man," he demanded of the audience, "or a thing?" Garrison shared Douglass's outrage at the notion that people could be bought and sold like objects.

William Lloyd Garrison

Early Efforts to End Slavery

The spirit of reform that swept the United States in the early 1800s was not limited to improving education and expanding the arts. It also included the efforts of abolitionists like Garrison and Douglass—members of the growing band of reformers who worked to abolish, or end, slavery.

Even before the American Revolution, some Americans had tried to limit or end slavery. At the Constitutional Convention in 1787, the delegates had reached a compromise on the difficult issue, agreeing to let each state decide whether to allow slavery. By the early 1800s, Northern states had ended slavery, but it continued in the South.

SECTION RESOURCES

📂 **Reproducible Masters**
• Reproducible Lesson Plan 14–2
• Daily Lecture and Discussion Notes 14–2
• Guided Reading Activity 14–2
• Section Quiz 14–2
• Reteaching Activity 14–2
• Reading Essentials and Study Guide 14–2
• Enrichment Activity 14–2

📖 **Transparencies**
• Daily Focus Skills Transparency 14–2

Multimedia
🎵 American Music: Hits Through History
💿 Interactive Tutor Self-Assessment CD-ROM
💿 ExamView® Pro Testmaker CD-ROM
💿 Presentation Plus! CD-ROM

The religious revival and the reform movement of the early and mid-1800s gave new life to the antislavery movement. Many Americans came to believe that slavery was wrong. Yet not all Northerners shared this view. The conflict over slavery continued to build.

Many of the men and women who led the antislavery movement came from the Quaker faith. One Quaker, Benjamin Lundy, wrote:

❝ I heard the wail of the captive. I felt his pang of distress, and the iron entered my soul. ❞

Lundy founded a newspaper in 1821 to spread the abolitionist message.

American Colonization Society

The first large-scale antislavery effort was not aimed at abolishing slavery but at resettling African Americans in Africa or the Caribbean. The **American Colonization Society,** formed in 1816 by a group of white Virginians, worked to free enslaved workers gradually by buying them from slaveholders and sending them abroad to start new lives.

The society raised enough money from private donors, Congress, and a few state legislatures to send several groups of African Americans out of the country. Some went to the west coast of Africa, where the society had acquired land for a colony. In 1822 the first African American settlers arrived in this colony, called **Liberia,** Latin for "place of freedom."

In 1847 Liberia became an independent country. American emigration to Liberia continued until the Civil War. Some 12,000 to 20,000 African Americans settled in the new country between 1822 and 1865.

The American Colonization Society did not halt the growth of slavery. The number of enslaved people continued to increase at a steady pace, and the society could only resettle a small number of African Americans. Furthermore, most African Americans did not want to go to Africa. Many were from families that had lived in America for several generations. They simply wanted to be free in American society. African Americans feared that the society aimed to strengthen slavery.

✓ **Reading Check** **Explaining** How did the American Colonization Society fight slavery?

The Movement Changes

Reformers realized that the gradual approach to ending slavery had failed. Moreover, the numbers of enslaved persons had sharply increased because the cotton boom in the Deep South made planters increasingly dependent on slave labor. Beginning in about 1830, the American antislavery movement took on new life. Soon it became the most pressing social issue for reformers.

William Lloyd Garrison

Abolitionist **William Lloyd Garrison** stimulated the growth of the antislavery movement. In 1829 Garrison left Massachusetts to work for the country's leading antislavery newspaper in Baltimore. Impatient with the paper's moderate position, Garrison returned to Boston in 1831 to found his own newspaper, *The Liberator.*

" *I looked at my hands to see if I was the same person now that I was free . . . I felt like I was in heaven.*"

—*Harriet Tubman, on her escape from slavery, 1849*

419

2 TEACH

Daily Lecture and Discussion Notes 14–2

Identifying People and Movements Write the following on the chalkboard: American Colonization Society, William Lloyd Garrison, Sarah and Angelina Grimké, David Walker, Frederick Douglass, Sojourner Truth, Underground Railroad, Harriet Tubman, Elijah Lovejoy. Have students write a sentence or two identifying each person or movement. **L1**

✓ **Reading Check**

Answer: by buying enslaved workers from slaveholders and then sending them abroad to live in freedom

---

COOPERATIVE LEARNING ACTIVITY

Dramatizing Escape Organize the class into small groups for this activity. Have each group first research to find out more about what it was like to be an enslaved African American on the run, and then choose an escape episode to dramatize. Stories can be those of people using the Underground Railroad or of those attempting escape on their own. Some students should do the research, while others write dialogue, make props and costumes, or play roles in the dramatization. **L2, ELL**

L1, ELL

Guided Reading Activity 14–2

Name _____ Date _____ Class _____

★ **Guided Reading Activity 14-2**

DIRECTIONS: Recalling the Facts Use the information in your textbook to answer the questions. Use another sheet of paper if necessary.

1. What compromise regarding slavery was reached by the delegates at the 1787 Constitutional Convention? _____
2. Who founded a newspaper in 1815 to spread the abolitionist message? _____
3. What was the aim of the American Colonization Society? _____
4. Where did many African Americans settle between 1822 and 1865? _____
5. Why did William Lloyd Garrison leave Massachusetts in 1829? _____
6. When did Garrison found his own newspaper? _____
7. What was the name of Garrison's newspaper? _____
8. What reform did Garrison call for? _____
9. Who were Sarah and Angelina Grimké? _____
10. How did the Grimké sisters receive their family inheritance and what did they do with it? _____
11. When did free African Americans hold their first convention? _____
12. What African American abolitionist edited an antislavery newspaper called the *North Star*? _____
13. What escaped enslaved African American worked for abolition and women's rights after changing her name from Isabella Baumfree? _____
14. What was the Underground Railroad? _____
15. Who was the most famous conductor of the Underground Railroad? _____
16. Why did Southerners believe abolition threatened their way of life? _____
17. What economic concerns fed the fear of abolition in the North? _____
18. How did Southerners fight abolition? _____

TWO VIEWPOINTS

Answers:

1. Answers may include that she shared personal experiences that were painful.
2. the laws of the state forbade it; he felt a moral obligation not to because he felt they had no ability to support themselves
3. Truth's excerpt describes the painful memories of being enslaved, and Jeter's excerpt mentions possible benefits to being enslaved.

History *and the* Humanities

♪ American Music: Hits Through History, "Joshua Fit the Battle of Jericho"

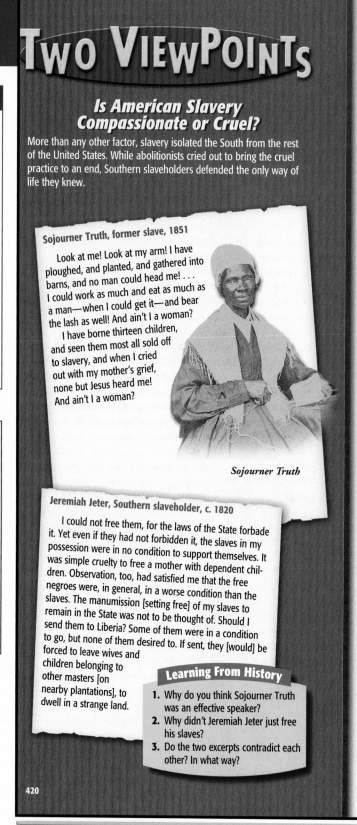

TWO VIEWPOINTS

Is American Slavery Compassionate or Cruel?

More than any other factor, slavery isolated the South from the rest of the United States. While abolitionists cried out to bring the cruel practice to an end, Southern slaveholders defended the only way of life they knew.

Sojourner Truth, former slave, 1851

Look at me! Look at my arm! I have ploughed, and planted, and gathered into barns, and no man could head me! . . . I could work as much and eat as much as a man—when I could get it—and bear the lash as well! And ain't I a woman?

I have borne thirteen children, and seen them most all sold off to slavery, and when I cried out with my mother's grief, none but Jesus heard me! And ain't I a woman?

Sojourner Truth

Jeremiah Jeter, Southern slaveholder, c. 1820

I could not free them, for the laws of the State forbade it. Yet even if they had not forbidden it, the slaves in my possession were in no condition to support themselves. It was simple cruelty to free a mother with dependent children. Observation, too, had satisfied me that the free negroes were, in general, in a worse condition than the slaves. The manumission [setting free] of my slaves to remain in the State was not to be thought of. Should I send them to Liberia? Some of them were in a condition to go, but none of them desired to. If sent, they [would] be forced to leave wives and children belonging to other masters [on nearby plantations], to dwell in a strange land.

Learning From History

1. Why do you think Sojourner Truth was an effective speaker?
2. Why didn't Jeremiah Jeter just free his slaves?
3. Do the two excerpts contradict each other? In what way?

420

Garrison was one of the first white abolitionists to call for the "immediate and complete emancipation [freeing]" of enslaved people. Promising to be "as harsh as truth, and as uncompromising as justice," he denounced the slow, gradual approach of other reformers. In the first issue of his paper he wrote: "I will not retreat a single inch—AND I WILL BE HEARD."

Garrison *was* heard. He attracted enough followers to start the New England Antislavery Society in 1832 and the American Antislavery Society the next year. The **abolitionist movement** grew rapidly. By 1838 the antislavery societies Garrison started had more than 1,000 chapters, or local branches.

The Grimké Sisters

Among the first women who spoke out publicly against slavery were **Sarah** and **Angelina Grimké.** Born in South Carolina to a wealthy slaveholding family, the sisters moved to Philadelphia in 1832.

In the North the Grimké sisters lectured and wrote against slavery. At one antislavery meeting, Angelina Grimké exclaimed,

❝As a Southerner, I feel that it is my duty to stand up . . . against slavery. I have seen it! I have seen it!❞

The Grimkés persuaded their mother to give them their share of the family inheritance. Instead of money or land, the sisters asked for several of the enslaved workers, whom they immediately freed.

Angelina Grimké and her husband, abolitionist Theodore Weld, wrote *American Slavery As It Is* in 1839. This collection of firsthand accounts of life under slavery was one of the most influential abolitionist publications of its time.

DIFFERENTIATED INSTRUCTION

At-Risk Students Have students choose an event or a person discussed in the section and create a monument honoring that person or event. Students may execute their work in clay, papier-mâché, soap, or whatever medium they prefer. Students should give brief oral presentations of their monument. **L1**

📁 Refer to *Inclusion for the Middle School Social Studies Classroom Strategies and Activities* in the TCR.

African American Abolitionists

Although white abolitionists drew public attention to the cause, African Americans themselves played a major role in the abolitionist movement from the start. The abolition of slavery was an especially important goal to the free African Americans of the North.

Most African Americans in the North lived in poverty in cities. Although they were excluded from most jobs and were often attacked by white mobs, a great many of these African Americans were intensely proud of their freedom and wanted to help those who were still enslaved.

African Americans took an active part in organizing and directing the American Antislavery Society, and they subscribed in large numbers to William Lloyd Garrison's *The Liberator.* In 1827 Samuel Cornish and John Russwurm started the country's first African American newspaper, *Freedom's Journal.* Most of the other newspapers that African Americans founded before the Civil War also promoted abolition.

Born a free man in North Carolina, writer **David Walker** of Boston published an impassioned argument against slavery, challenging African Americans to rebel and overthrow slavery by force. "America is more our country than it is the whites'—we have enriched it with our blood and tears," he wrote.

In 1830 free African American leaders held their first convention in Philadelphia. Delegates met "to devise ways and means for the bettering of our condition." They discussed starting an African American college and encouraging free African Americans to emigrate to Canada.

Frederick Douglass

Frederick Douglass, the most widely known African American abolitionist, was born enslaved in Maryland. After teaching himself to read and write, he escaped from slavery in Maryland in 1838 and settled first in Massachusetts and then in New York.

As a runaway, Douglass could have been captured and returned to slavery. Still, he joined the Massachusetts Antislavery Society and traveled widely to address abolitionist meetings. A powerful speaker, Douglass often moved listeners to tears with his message. At an Independence Day gathering he told the audience:

> 66What, to the American slave, is your Fourth of July? I answer: a day that reveals to him, more than all other days in the year, the gross injustice and cruelty to which he is the constant victim. To him, your celebration is a sham . . . your national greatness, swelling vanity; your sounds of rejoicing are empty and heartless . . . your shouts of liberty and equality, hollow mockery.99

For 16 years, Douglass edited an antislavery newspaper called the *North Star.* Douglass won admiration as a powerful and influential speaker and writer. He traveled abroad, speaking to huge antislavery audiences in London and the West Indies.

Douglass returned to the United States because he believed abolitionists must fight slavery at its source. He insisted that African Americans receive not just their freedom but full equality with whites as well. In 1847 friends helped Douglass purchase his freedom from the slaveholder from whom he had fled in Maryland.

Sojourner Truth

"I was born a slave in Ulster County, New York," Isabella Baumfree began when she told her story to audiences. Called "Belle," she lived in the cellar of a slaveholder's house. She escaped in 1826 and gained official freedom in 1827 when New York banned slavery. She eventually settled in New York City.

In 1843 Belle chose a new name. "**Sojourner Truth** is my name," she said, "because from this day I will walk in the light of [God's] truth." She began to work in the movements for abolitionism and for women's rights.

✓**Reading Check** **Explaining** Why did Frederick Douglass return to the United States?

HISTORY Online

Objectives and answers to the student activity can be found in the **Web Activity Lesson Plan** feature at tarvol1.glencoe.com

✓**Reading Check**

Answer: He believed that he needed to fight slavery at its source.

ABCNEWS INTERACTIVE

 VIDEOCASSETTE
Historic America Electronic Field Trips

View **Chapter 9** to learn more about the home of Frederick Douglass.

Who?What?Where?When?

Frederick Douglass After the Civil War, Douglass was a leading supporter of the women's rights movement, fought against racial segregation laws and practices, and held important government posts such as United States minister and consul general to Haiti. *My Bondage and My Freedom*, published in 1855, was the second volume of Frederick Douglass's autobiography. Douglass felt the need to tell his life story because, although white abolitionists could detail slavery's history and depict its horrors, Douglass noted, "they cannot speak from experience as I can."

HISTORY Online Student Web Activity Visit tarvol1.glencoe.com and click on **Chapter 14—Student Web Activities** for an activity on the abolitionist movement.

INTERDISCIPLINARY CONNECTIONS ACTIVITY

Literature Have each student choose a book and read it for a book report. Subjects may include groups and people discussed in the section, historical fiction about the period, or accounts of other people and events of the time. Some students might like to read *Uncle Tom's Cabin.* Caution anyone who does decide to read it that, although it was considered radical in its time, by today's standards the book is guilty of racism and stereotyping. **L2**

MORE ABOUT...

Henry Brown's box measured 2 feet 6 inches deep, 2 feet wide, and 3 feet long. It was lined with a feltlike material, nailed, and bound with five hickory hoops. Brown used a small tool to drill holes in the box for air and packed a day's worth of water and biscuits for the journey. Have students explain why Southern slaveholders saw the Underground Railroad as organized theft. *(Slaveholders considered their slaves property. Therefore, slaveholders thought that they were being stolen from by those who worked on the Underground Railroad.)*

What?Where?When?Who?

Desegregation During the Civil War, Sojourner Truth tried to desegregate public transportation. Desegregated public transportation would not exist until almost 100 years later. Bus desegregation came about in Montgomery, Alabama, because of the efforts of another African American woman, Rosa Parks. Her refusal to sit at the back of a bus led to her arrest and a subsequent successful boycott of the city's buses by African Americans, who constituted the majority of the city's bus riders.

MORE ABOUT...

The Underground Railroad

The Underground Railroad was neither "underground" nor a "railroad." It was a secret organization to help African Americans escape from slavery. The escape of Henry Brown is one of the most remarkable stories in the history of the Underground Railroad.

Henry Brown Henry "Box" Brown escaped slavery by having himself sealed into a small box and shipped from Richmond to Philadelphia. Although "this side up" was marked on the crate, he spent a good part of the trip upside down. When news of his escape spread, he wrote an autobiography and spoke to many anti-slavery groups.

RESURRECTION OF HENRY BOX BROWN, AT PHILADELPHIA.

"It all seemed a comparatively light price to pay for liberty."
—Henry "Box" Brown

After his wife and children were sold to a slaveholder in another state, Brown was determined to escape.

Another man transported the crate, with Brown in it, to a shipping company in Richmond, Virginia.

From there, the crate was sent to the Philadelphia Anti-Slavery Office.

Twenty-six hours later, the top of the crate was pried off and Brown emerged, a free man.

Philadelphia, PA

Richmond, VA

The Underground Railroad

Some abolitionists risked prison—even death—by secretly helping African Americans escape from slavery. The network of escape routes from the South to the North came to be called the Underground Railroad.

The Underground Railroad had no trains or tracks. Instead, passengers on this "railroad" traveled through the night, often on foot, and went north—guided by the North Star. The runaway slaves followed rivers and mountain chains, or felt for moss growing on the north side of trees.

Songs such as "Follow the Drinkin' Gourd" encouraged runaways on their way to freedom. A hollowed-out gourd was used to dip water for drinking. Its shape resembled the Big Dipper, which pointed to the North Star.

❝When the river ends in between two hills,
Follow the drinkin' gourd,
For the Ole Man's waitin' for to carry you
to freedom.
Follow the drinkin' gourd.❞

During the day passengers rested at "stations"—barns, attics, church basements, or other places where fugitives could rest, eat, and hide until the next night's journey. The railroad's "conductors" were whites and African Americans who helped guide the escaping slaves to freedom in the North.

In the early days, many people made the journey north on foot. Later they traveled in wagons, sometimes equipped with secret compartments. African Americans on the Underground Railroad hoped to settle in a free state in the North

Reading Strategy | READING THE TEXT

Comparing and Contrasting Abolitionists such as William Lloyd Garrison, Frederick Douglass, and others did not agree on how to end slavery. Most rejected the American Colonization Society's answer of shipping African Americans to Liberia. Some abolitionists called for an immediate end to slavery. Others hoped for a more gradual approach to eliminate what they considered the scourge of American society. Have students make a list that compares and contrasts the different ideas for ending slavery. **L2**

or to move on to Canada. Once in the North, however, fugitives still feared capture. Henry Bibb, a runaway who reached Ohio, arrived at "the place where I was directed to call on an Abolitionist, but I made no stop: so great were my fears of being pursued."

After her escape from slavery, Harriet Tubman became the most famous conductor on the Underground Railroad. Slaveholders offered a large reward for Tubman's capture or death.

The Underground Railroad helped only a tiny fraction of the enslaved population. Most who used it as a route to freedom came from the states located between the northern states and the Deep South. Still, the Underground Railroad gave hope to those who suffered in slavery. It also provided abolitionists with a way to help some enslaved people to freedom.

Clashes Over Abolitionism

The antislavery movement led to an intense reaction against abolitionism. Southern slaveholders—and many Southerners who did not have slaves—opposed abolitionism because they believed it threatened the South's way of life, which depended on enslaved labor. Many people in the North also opposed the abolitionist movement.

Geography *Skills*

Answers:
1. Ohio River
2. about 790 miles (1,260 km)

Geography Skills Practice
Ask: Through what city did the Underground Railroad route from Marietta to Windsor pass?
(Cleveland)

3 ASSESS

Assign Section 2 Assessment as homework or as an in-class activity.

⏺ Have students use **Interactive Tutor Self-Assessment CD-ROM.**

L2

Section Quiz 14–2

Name _____ Date _____ Class _____

⭐ Chapter 14 — Score

Section Quiz 14-2

DIRECTIONS: Matching Match the items in Column A with the items in Column B. Write the correct letters in the blanks. *(10 points each)*

Column A	Column B
___ 1. worked to end slavery	A. William Lloyd Garrison
___ 2. American Colonization Society colony	B. Sojourner Truth
___ 3. founded *The Liberator*	C. Angelina Grimké
___ 4. a Southerner against slavery	D. abolitionists
___ 5. "Belle"	E. Liberia

L1

Reteaching Activity 14–2

Name _____ Date _____ Class _____

⭐ Reteaching Activity 14-2

DIRECTIONS: Matching Match each item in Column A with its corresponding item in Column B. Write the correct letters in the blanks.

COLUMN A	COLUMN B
___ 1. Benjamin Lundy	A. the United States's first African American newspaper
___ 2. William Lloyd Garrison	B. abolitionist newspaper editor who was killed by angry proslavery whites
___ 3. David Walker	C. bought enslaved people then sent them abroad to start new lives
___ 4. Frederick Douglass	D. guided hundreds of enslaved African Americans to freedom
___ 5. Sojourner Truth	

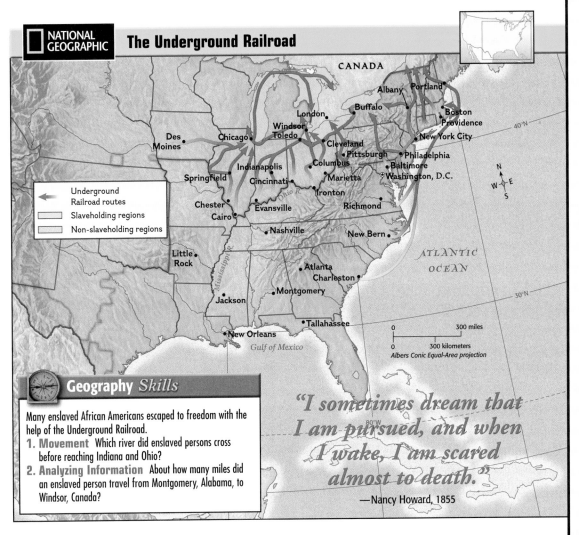

NATIONAL GEOGRAPHIC — **The Underground Railroad**

Geography *Skills*

Many enslaved African Americans escaped to freedom with the help of the Underground Railroad.
1. **Movement** Which river did enslaved persons cross before reaching Indiana and Ohio?
2. **Analyzing Information** About how many miles did an enslaved person travel from Montgomery, Alabama, to Windsor, Canada?

"I sometimes dream that I am pursued, and when I wake, I am scared almost to death."
—Nancy Howard, 1855

Underground Railroad routes
Slaveholding regions
Non-slaveholding regions

EXTENDING THE CONTENT

Harriet Tubman Harriet Tubman had to be quick-witted to avoid capture. Once, she noticed slave catchers approaching as she and her group were about to get on a northbound train. Quickly she herded everyone onto a southbound train, knowing that no one would expect to find runaways heading south. Using her experiences as a conductor on the Underground Railroad, Tubman became a valuable scout and spy for the Union Army during the Civil War. After the war she lived in Auburn, New York, where she established a home for elderly African Americans.

4 CLOSE

It was against the law to help a runaway slave. In fact the law said that those who did not return slaves to their owners could be arrested, fined, and jailed as criminals. Ask students what they would do if they had to decide whether to help a runaway slave.

Opposition in the North

Even in the North, abolitionists never numbered more than a small fraction of the population. Many Northerners saw the antislavery movement as a threat to the nation's social order. They feared the abolitionists could bring on a destructive war between the North and the South. They also claimed that, if the enslaved African Americans were freed, they could never blend into American society.

Economic fears further fed the backlash against abolitionism. Northern workers worried that freed slaves would flood the North and take jobs away from whites by agreeing to work for lower pay.

Opposition to abolitionism sometimes erupted into violence against the abolitionists themselves. In the 1830s a Philadelphia mob burned the city's antislavery headquarters to the ground and set off a bloody race riot. In Boston a mob attacked abolitionist William Lloyd Garrison and threatened to hang him. Authorities saved his life by locking him in jail.

Elijah Lovejoy was not so lucky. Lovejoy edited an abolitionist newspaper in Illinois. Three times angry whites invaded his offices and wrecked his presses. Each time Lovejoy installed new presses and resumed publication. The fourth time the mob set fire to the building. When Lovejoy came out of the blazing building, he was shot and killed.

The South Reacts

Southerners fought abolitionism by mounting arguments in defense of slavery. They claimed that slavery was essential to the South. Slave labor, they said, had allowed Southern whites to reach a high level of culture.

Southerners also argued that they treated enslaved people well. Some Southerners argued that Northern workers were worse off than slaves. The industrial economy of the North employed factory workers for long hours at low wages. These jobs were repetitive and often dangerous, and Northern workers had to pay for their goods from their small earnings. Unlike the "wage slavery" of the North, Southerners said that the system of slavery provided food, clothing, and medical care to the workers.

Other defenses of slavery were based on racism. Many whites believed that African Americans were better off under white care than on their own. "Providence has placed [the slave] in our hands for his own good," declared one Southern governor.

The conflict between proslavery and antislavery groups continued to mount. At the same time, a new women's rights movement was growing, and many leading abolitionists were involved in that movement as well.

✓ Reading Check
Explaining Why did many Northerners oppose the abolition of slavery?

SECTION 2 ASSESSMENT

Checking for Understanding

1. **Key Terms** Write a short paragraph in which you use these key terms: abolitionist, Underground Railroad.
2. **Reviewing Facts** Describe the American Colonization Society's solution to slavery.

Reviewing Themes

3. **Individual Action** What role did Harriet Tubman play in the antislavery movement?

Critical Thinking

4. **Comparing** Compare the arguments of Northerners with Southerners who opposed abolitionism.
5. **Organizing Information** Use a diagram like the one below to identify actions that abolitionists took to free enslaved people.

Freeing of enslaved people

Analyzing Visuals

6. **Geography Skills** Study the map of the Underground Railroad on page 423. Why do you think more enslaved people escaped from the border states than from the Deep South?

Interdisciplinary Activity

Informative Writing Research the life of an abolitionist. Write a one-page biography that describes important events in his or her life.

SECTION 2 ASSESSMENT ANSWERS

1. Student work should reflect correct use of terms.
2. purchase enslaved workers and resettle them in Africa or the Caribbean
3. She led slaves to freedom on the Underground Railroad.
4. Northerners: African Americans could not blend into society and they would take jobs from whites; Southerners: slavery was essential to economy, African Americans were better off under white care.
5. Answers may include: founding of abolitionist newspapers and societies; buying enslaved workers and relocating them; providing safe houses along the Underground Railroad; speaking out against slavery
6. It was less distance to travel to safety.

Interdisciplinary Activity Reports should include details about events in the person's life.

SECTION 3 The Women's Movement

Guide to Reading

Main Idea
Women reformers campaigned for their own rights.

Key Terms
suffrage, coeducation

Reading Strategy
Taking Notes As you read the section, use a chart like the one below to identify the contributions these individuals made to women's rights.

	Contributions
Lucretia Mott	
Elizabeth Cady Stanton	
Susan B. Anthony	
Elizabeth Blackwell	

Read to Learn
• how the antislavery and the women's rights movements were related.
• what progress women made toward equality during the 1800s.

Section Theme
Groups and Institutions Women in the 1800s made some progress toward equality.

Preview of Events

◆1830	◆1860	◆1890

1837
Mary Lyon establishes Mount Holyoke Female Seminary

1848
First women's rights convention held in Seneca Falls, New York

1857
Elizabeth Blackwell founds the New York Infirmary for Women and Children

1869
Wyoming Territory grants women the right to vote

Mary Lyon, pioneer in higher education for women

AN
American Story

Women who fought to end slavery began to recognize their own bondage. On April 19, 1850, about 400 women met at a Quaker meetinghouse in the small town of Salem, Ohio. They came together "to assert their rights as independent human beings." One speaker stated: "I use the term *Woman's Rights,* because it is a technical phrase. I like not the expression. It is not Woman's *Rights* of which I design to speak, but of Woman's *Wrongs.* I shall claim nothing for ourselves because of our sex. . . . [W]e should demand *our* recognition as equal members of the human family. . . ."

Women and Reform

Many women abolitionists also worked for women's rights. They launched a struggle to improve women's lives and win equal rights. Like many of the women reformers, **Lucretia Mott** was a Quaker. Quaker women enjoyed a certain amount of equality in their own communities. Mott gave lectures in Philadelphia calling for temperance, peace, workers' rights, and abolition. Mott

CHAPTER 14   The Age of Reform   **425**

1 FOCUS

Section Overview
This section describes the efforts of women to gain social, economic, and political rights.

BELLRINGER
Skillbuilder Activity

Project transparency and have students answer the question.

Daily Focus Skills Transparency 14–3

Reading Preview

Answers to Graphic: Lucretia Mott: gave speeches and helped organize the first women's rights convention; Elizabeth Cady Stanton: encouraged and won a demand for woman suffrage at the Seneca Falls Convention; Susan B. Anthony: worked for women's rights and temperance; Elizabeth Blackwell: first woman to receive a medical degree in the United States

Preteaching Vocabulary
⊙ Use the **Vocabulary PuzzleMaker CD-ROM** to create crossword and word search puzzles.

SECTION RESOURCES

📂 **Reproducible Masters**
• Reproducible Lesson Plan 14–3
• Daily Lecture and Discussion Notes 14–3
• Guided Reading Activity 14–3
• Section Quiz 14–3
• Reteaching Activity 14–3
• Reading Essentials and Study Guide 14–3
• Enrichment Activity 14–3

📖 **Transparencies**
• Daily Focus Skills Transparency 14–3

Multimedia
⊙ Vocabulary PuzzleMaker CD-ROM
⊙ Interactive Tutor Self-Assessment CD-ROM
⊙ ExamView® Pro Testmaker CD-ROM
⊙ Presentation Plus! CD-ROM

Daily Lecture and Discussion Notes 14–3

Copyright © by The McGraw-Hill Companies, Inc.

Daily Lecture and Discussion Notes

Chapter 14, Section 3

Did You Know? With the issue of a new dollar coin in 1979, Susan B. Anthony became the first woman to be depicted on United States currency. Unfortunately, the coin was not very popular due to its size, which was too similar to that of a quarter.

I. Women and Reform (Pages 425–427)

A. Women abolitionists were the first to also campaign for women's rights, to improve women's lives, and win equal rights.

1. Lucretia Mott, a Quaker, gave lectures in Philadelphia, helped fugitive slaves, and organized the Philadelphia Female Anti-Slavery Society.

2. Elizabeth Cady Stanton met Mott at a world antislavery convention and along with a few other women worked for women's rights.

Reading Strategy

Finding Inequalities As students read the section, have them list (a) the inequalities or problems women faced, (b) the names of the women reformers discussed, and (c) the "firsts" mentioned in the section. **L1**

Why It Matters

The Seneca Falls Convention was held at the Wesleyan Methodist Church on July 19 and 20, 1848. All of the resolutions in the Declaration of the Seneca Falls Convention were passed unanimously except for woman suffrage. The declaration was signed by 100 people–68 women and 32 men. The convention helped establish the cause of women's rights as an organized movement. **Ask: What changes did the Seneca Falls Declaration demand?** *(an end to laws that discriminated against women, the freedom for women to enter all-male professions, and woman suffrage)*

Why It Matters

The Seneca Falls Convention

Throughout the nation's history, women had fought side by side with the men to build a new nation and to ensure freedom. Even though the Declaration of Independence promised equality for all, the promise rang hollow for women.

Female reformers began a campaign for their own rights. In 1848 Lucretia Mott and Elizabeth Cady Stanton organized the Seneca Falls Convention. One of the resolutions demanded suffrage, or the right to vote, for women. This marked the beginning of a long, hard road to gain equal rights.

Photo Gallery

Raising the Status of Women

Lucretia Mott (below) and Susan B. Anthony were leaders in the effort to allow women a greater role in American society.

"We hold these truths to be self-evident: that all men and women are created equal."
— *Declaration of the Seneca Falls Convention, 1848*

Gaining the Right to Vote, 1848–1920

The Seneca Falls Convention led to the growth of the woman suffrage movement.

1848 → Seneca Falls Convention

1850 → First national women's rights convention held in Worcester, Massachusetts

1866 → Susan B. Anthony forms Equal Rights Association

1869 → Women granted voting rights in Wyoming Territory

1878 → Woman suffrage amendment first introduced in U.S. Congress

1884 → Belva Lockwood runs for president

also helped fugitive slaves and organized the Philadelphia Female Anti-Slavery Society. At the world antislavery convention in London, Mott met **Elizabeth Cady Stanton.** There the two female abolitionists joined forces to work for women's rights.

The Seneca Falls Convention

In July 1848, Elizabeth Cady Stanton, Lucretia Mott, and a few other women organized the first women's rights convention in **Seneca Falls, New York.** About 200 women and 40 men attended.

The convention issued a Declaration of Sentiments and Resolutions modeled on the Declaration of Independence. The women's document declared: "We hold these truths to be self-evident: that all men and women are created equal."

The women's declaration called for an end to all laws that discriminated against women. It demanded that women be allowed to enter the all-male world of trades, professions, and businesses. The most controversial issue at the Seneca Falls Convention concerned suffrage, or the right to vote.

Elizabeth Stanton insisted that the declaration include a demand for woman suffrage, but delegates thought the idea of women voting was too radical. Lucretia Mott told her friend, "Lizzie, thee will make us ridiculous." Frederick Douglass stood with Stanton and argued powerfully for women's right to vote. After a heated debate the convention voted to include the demand for woman suffrage in the United States. *(See page 617 of the Appendix for excerpts of the Seneca Falls Declaration.)*

Reading Strategy   READING THE TEXT

Brainstorming Organize the class into small groups. Have each group write on a sheet of paper the question, "Why should women and men be treated equally?" Ask each group to circulate the paper among members with each member writing a response to the question. Continue circulating the paper until each member has written at least two responses. Then have each group select a writer/editor to summarize and compile the group's arguments into a position statement to be read aloud to the class. **L2**

Maria Mitchell gained world renown when she discovered a comet in 1847. She became a professor of astronomy and the first woman elected to the American Academy of Arts and Sciences.

Mary Ann Shadd Cary was the first African American woman in the nation to earn a law degree.

Helen Keller overcame the challenges of an illness that left her deaf, blind, and mute to help others with similar disabilities.

Elizabeth Blackwell was the first woman to receive a medical degree in the United States.

Susette La Flesche was a member of the Omaha tribe and campaigned for Native American rights.

1893 →	1896 →	1910–1918 →	1919 →	1920 →
Colorado adopts woman suffrage	Utah joins the Union, granting women full suffrage	States including Washington, Kansas, and Michigan adopt woman suffrage	House and Senate pass the federal woman suffrage amendment	Tennessee ratifies the Nineteenth Amendment, called the Susan B. Anthony Amendment. It becomes law on August 26, 1920.

The Movement Grows

The Seneca Falls Convention paved the way for the growth of the **women's rights movement.** During the 1800s women held several national conventions. Many reformers—male and female—joined the movement.

Susan B. Anthony, the daughter of a Quaker abolitionist in rural New York, worked for women's rights and temperance. She called for equal pay for women, college training for girls, and coeducation—the teaching of boys and girls together. Anthony organized the country's first women's temperance association, the Daughters of Temperance.

Susan B. Anthony met Elizabeth Cady Stanton at a temperance meeting in 1851. They became lifelong friends and partners in the struggle for women's rights. For the rest of the century, Anthony and Stanton led the women's movement. They worked with other women to win the right to vote. Beginning with Wyoming in 1890, several states granted women the right to vote. It was not until 1920, however, that woman suffrage became a reality everywhere in the United States.

✓**Reading Check** **Explaining** What is suffrage?

Progress by American Women

Pioneers in women's education began to call for more opportunity. Early pioneers such as Catherine Beecher and Emma Hart Willard believed that women should be educated for

CHAPTER 14   The Age of Reform   **427**

DIFFERENTIATED INSTRUCTION

Reading Support Point out that the women who worked for women's rights were shouted at, ridiculed, and taunted. Ask students to think about problems or injustices in today's world. Is there a cause with which students are deeply concerned? After discussing the question, ask them to write a description of the cause and the actions they would take to promote the cause. **L1**

Refer to *Inclusion for the Middle School Social Studies Classroom Strategies and Activities* in the TCR.

427

✓ **Reading Check**

Answer: Emma Willard

L1 [ELL]

Reading Essentials and Study Guide 14–3

Study Guide

Chapter 14, Section 3
For use with textbook pages 425–428
THE WOMEN'S MOVEMENT

KEY TERMS	
suffrage	The right to vote (page 426)
coeducation	The teaching of boys and girls together (page 427)

DRAWING FROM EXPERIENCE

Do girls and boys in your family follow the same rules? Do girls and boys in your family have similar educational opportunities? Are the opinions of girls and boys in your family encouraged? Do girls and boys share equally in the chores and decision making?

In the last section, you read about the movement by abolitionists to end slavery in the United States. This section focuses on the progress toward equality made by the women's rights movement in the 1800s.

L3

Enrichment Activity 14–3

Name _____ Date _____ Class _____

★ **Enrichment Activity 14-3** ★

Women's Right to Vote

The *Declaration of Sentiments and Resolutions* was approved by the Seneca Falls Convention in 1848. Read the excerpts below.

> 1. The history of mankind is a history of repeated injuries and usurpations [unlawful seizing] on the part of man toward woman. . . . To prove this, let facts be submitted to a candid world.
> 2. He has never permitted her to exercise her inalienable right to the elective franchise.
> 3. He has compelled her to submit to laws in the formation of which she has no voice. . . .
> 4. He has made her, if married, in the eye of the law, civilly dead.
> 5. He has taken from her all right of property, even to the wages she earns. . . .
> 6. He has denied her the facilities for obtaining a thorough education. . . .
> 7. Now in view of this denial of the rights of one half the people of this country . . . we insist that they have immediate admission to all the rights and privileges which belong to them as citizens of the United States.

DIRECTIONS: Analyzing and Paraphrasing Information For each of the underlined passages in the *Declaration of Sentiments and Resolutions*, rewrite the sentence in your own words.

1. _____
2. _____
3. _____
4. _____
5. _____
6. _____
7. _____

8. Place the number of each statement in the appropriate box.

Definition of Problem	Examples of Problem	Solution to Problem

Activity **DIRECTIONS: Creating a Presentation** The women's movement has had a number of prominent spokespersons over the years. Use the media center to find important people in the women's movement. Pick one and prepare a creative presentation to tell your class more about your choice. You might present a dramatic reading, prepare a portrait and a picture history of the person, write a song or poem, or create a short skit with a partner.

4 CLOSE

Have students write essays responding to the following: In what ways were women like enslaved people? How was their condition different? Remind students to use standard grammar, spelling, sentence structure, and punctuation.

---

their traditional roles in life. They also thought that women could be capable teachers. The Milwaukee College for Women set up courses based on Beecher's ideas "to train women to be healthful, intelligent, and successful wives, mothers, and housekeepers."

Education

After her marriage Emma Willard educated herself in subjects considered suitable only for boys, such as science and mathematics. In 1821 Willard established the Troy Female Seminary in upstate New York. Willard's Troy Female Seminary taught mathematics, history, geography, and physics, as well as the usual homemaking subjects.

Mary Lyon established Mount Holyoke Female Seminary in Massachusetts in 1837. She modeled its curriculum on that of nearby Amherst College. Some young women began to make their own opportunities. They broke the barriers to female education and helped other women do the same.

Marriage and Family Laws

During the 1800s women made some gains in the area of marriage and property laws. New York, Pennsylvania, Indiana, Wisconsin, Mississippi, and the new state of California recognized the right of women to own property after their marriage.

Some states passed laws permitting women to share the guardianship of their children jointly with their husbands. Indiana was the first of several states that allowed women to seek divorce if their husbands were chronic abusers of alcohol.

Breaking Barriers

In the 1800s women had few career choices. They could become elementary teachers—although school boards often paid lower salaries to women than to men. Breaking into fields such as medicine and the ministry was more difficult. Some strong-minded women, however, succeeded in entering these all-male professions.

Hoping to study medicine, **Elizabeth Blackwell** was turned down by more than 20 schools. Finally accepted by Geneva College in New York, Blackwell graduated at the head of her class. She went on to win acceptance and fame as a doctor.

Despite the accomplishments of notable women, gains in education, and changes in state laws, women in the 1800s remained limited by social customs and expectations. The early feminists—like the abolitionists, temperance workers, and other activists of the age of reform—had just begun the long struggle to achieve their goals.

✓ **Reading Check** **Identifying** Who established the Troy Female Seminary?

SECTION 3 ASSESSMENT

Checking for Understanding

1. **Key Terms** Define the following terms: suffrage, coeducation.
2. **Reviewing Facts** How did the fight to end slavery help spark the women's movement?

Reviewing Themes

3. **Groups and Institutions** Discuss three specific goals of the women's rights movement.

Critical Thinking

4. **Making Generalizations** What qualities do you think women such as Sojourner Truth, Susan B. Anthony, Elizabeth Cady Stanton, and Elizabeth Blackwell shared?
5. **Organizing Information** Re-create the diagram below and list the areas where women gained rights.

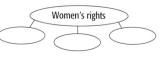

Analyzing Visuals

6. **Sequencing Information** Study the information on the feature on the Seneca Falls Convention on pages 426–427. When did Wyoming women gain the right to vote? What "first" did Elizabeth Blackwell accomplish?

Interdisciplinary Activity

Music Write and record a song designed to win supporters for the women's rights movement. Include lyrics that will draw both men and women supporters.

428   CHAPTER 14   The Age of Reform

SECTION 3 ASSESSMENT ANSWERS

1. Student work should reflect correct use of terms.
2. Many women working for the abolitionist cause became aware of the inequality and discrimination in their own lives.
3. Answers may include any three of the following: freedom to enter all-male professions; suffrage; improved property rights; marriage and divorce laws; equal pay; college training; coeducation.
4. Answers may include self-confidence, intelligence, perseverance, patience, and commitment.
5. Answers may include: the opening of women's colleges; recognition of the right to own property after marriage; and laws allowing shared guardianship of children.
6. 1869; first woman to receive a medical degree in the United States

Interdisciplinary Activity Songs should express some of the goals of the women's movement.

Technology SKILLBUILDER

Evaluating a Web Site

Why Learn This Skill?

The Internet has become a valuable research tool. It is convenient to use, and the information contained on the Internet is plentiful. However, some Web site information is not necessarily accurate or reliable. When using the Internet as a research tool, the user must distinguish between quality information and inaccurate or incomplete information.

Learning the Skill

There are a number of things to consider when evaluating a Web site. Most important is to check the accuracy of the source and content. The author and publisher or sponsor of the site should be clearly indicated. The user must also determine the usefulness of the site. The information on the site should be current, and the design and organization of the site should be appealing and easy to navigate.

To evaluate a Web site, ask yourself the following questions:

- Are the facts on the site documented?
- Is more than one source used for background information within the site?
- Does the site contain a bibliography?
- Are the links within the site appropriate and up-to-date?
- Is the author clearly identified?
- Does the site explore the topic in-depth?
- Does the site contain links to other useful resources?
- Is the information easy to access? Is it properly labeled?
- Is the design appealing?

Practicing the Skill

Visit the Web site featured on this page at <u>www.nationalgeographic.com/features/99/railroad/</u> and answer the following questions.

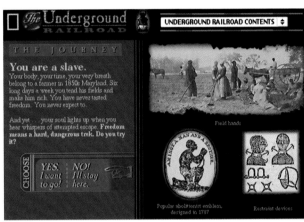

❶ Who is the author or sponsor of the Web site?

❷ What links does the site contain? Are they appropriate to the topic?

❸ Does the site explore the topic in-depth? Why or why not?

❹ Is the design of the site appealing? Why or why not?

❺ What role did William Still play on the Underground Railroad? How easy or difficult was it to locate this information?

Applying the Skill

Comparing Web Sites Locate two other Web sites about the Underground Railroad. Evaluate them for accuracy and usefulness. Then compare them to the site featured above.

Technology SKILLBUILDER

Technology SKILLBUILDER

TEACH

Evaluating a Web Site This skill helps students evaluate whether information found on a Web site is accurate or reliable. After students have read **Learning the Skill,** have them access the Web site noted in **Practicing the Skill.** Ask students to preview the Web site by viewing its pages and answering the questions listed in **Learning the Skill.** Finally, have students answer the **Practicing the Skill** questions.

Point out to students the advantages of researching on the Internet—the wide variety of sites available, visuals, ability to download information, links to other sites, and how search engines can find information from a variety of sources. Discuss the potential for sites to be slanted by personal and political views and the need to carefully evaluate Web sites for their accuracy and objectivity. Also, discuss copyright laws with students and how they apply to information obtained over the Internet.

Additional Practice
L2

ANSWERS TO PRACTICING THE SKILL

❶ the National Geographic Society

❷ links to information about Africans in America throughout history and the Underground Railroad; yes, they are appropriate for learning more about the Underground Railroad

❸ There is a list of sources that include books, other publications, and other Web sites.

❹ Students should explain how they feel about the site's design.

❺ Still campaigned for the freedom of enslaved people; it was easy to locate by clicking on *Faces of Freedom* and *William Still.*

Applying the Skill Students' evaluations should follow the criteria listed in **Learning the Skill.**

GLENCOE TECHNOLOGY

MindJogger Videoquiz
Use **MindJogger Videoquiz** to review the Chapter 14 content.

 Available in VHS

Reviewing Key Terms

Students' puzzles will vary but should conform to the written instructions. Students may use the following definitions as clues:

1. a community based on a vision of a perfect society

2. religious frontier camp meetings

3. drinking little or no alcohol

4. a school for training high-school graduates as teachers

5. one who stresses the relationship between humans and nature as well as the importance of the individual conscience

6. the refusal to obey laws that one thinks to be unjust

7. a reformer who worked to abolish, or end, slavery

8. the network of slavery escape routes out of the South

9. the right to vote

10. movement during the 1800s consisting of reformers working for women's rights

11. the teaching of boys and girls together

Reviewing Key Facts

12. a perfect society

13. poverty, breakup of families, crime, insanity

14. Schools should be free and supported by taxes; teachers should be trained; children should be required to attend school.

15. They no longer looked to Europe for inspiration. They began exploring American themes.

Chapter Summary
The Age of Reform

Utopian communities
- Groups start small voluntary communities to put their idealistic ideas into practice.

Religion
- Great revival meetings, the building of new churches, and the founding of scores of colleges and universities mark the Second Great Awakening.

Temperance
- Reformers work to control consumption of alcohol.

Education
- A movement grows to improve education, make school attendance compulsory, and help students with special needs.

Abolition
- Reformers work to help enslaved people escape to freedom and to ban slavery.

Women's rights
- Reformers call for equal rights, including the right to vote.

The Arts
- Writers and painters turn their attention to the American scene.

430

16. He called for "immediate and complete emancipation" of enslaved people and denounced the gradual approach of other reformers.

17. to help enslaved people escape to freedom

18. Beecher called for more educational opportunities for women and supported the idea that women would make good teachers.

Reviewing Key Terms

On graph paper, create a word search puzzle using the following terms. Crisscross the terms vertically and horizontally, then fill in the remaining squares with extra letters. Use the terms' definitions as clues to find the words in the puzzle. Share your puzzle with a classmate.

1. utopia
2. revival
3. temperance
4. normal school
5. transcendentalist
6. civil disobedience
7. abolitionist
8. Underground Railroad
9. suffrage
10. women's rights movement
11. coeducation

Reviewing Key Facts

12. What were the founders of utopias hoping to achieve?

13. What problems in society did reformers in the temperance movement blame on the manufacture and sale of alcoholic beverages?

14. What were the basic principles of public education?

15. What was unique about the subject matter that American artists and writers of the mid-1800s used?

16. How did William Lloyd Garrison's demands make him effective in the anti-slavery movement?

17. What was the purpose of the Underground Railroad?

18. What role did Catherine Beecher play in education for women?

Critical Thinking

19. **Analyzing Information** What role did Dorothea Dix play regarding prison inmates and people with mental illness?

20. **Making Generalizations** What was the significance of the Seneca Falls Convention?

21. **Organizing Information** Re-create the diagram below and describe the contributions Frederick Douglass made to the abolitionist movement.

Critical Thinking

19. She educated the public about the poor conditions for prisoners and the mentally ill.

20. It was the first women's rights convention in the United States and called for an end to laws that discriminated against women, the freedom for women to enter all-male professions, and woman suffrage.

21. a powerful abolitionist speaker; founded an antislavery newspaper; said that African Americans should not only have freedom but also full equality

Practicing Skills

Evaluating a Web Site *Review the information about evaluating a Web site on page 429. Visit the Web site* www.greatwomen.org/index.php *and answer the following questions.*

22. What information is presented on this Web site?

23. What categories are used to organize the information?

24. What links does the site contain? Are they appropriate to the topic?

25. Do you think the site explores the topic in depth? Explain.

 Geography and History Activity

Use the map on page 423 to answer the following questions.

26. **Region** What other country did passengers on the Underground Railroad travel to?

27. **Location** From what Southern ports did African Americans flee by ship?

28. **Location** What kinds of places were used as "stations" of the Underground Railroad?

29. **Human-Environment Interaction** Why do you think the routes of the Underground Railroad included many coastal cities?

 Technology Activity

30. **Using the Internet** Search the Internet for a modern organization founded to support women's rights. Write a brief description of the organization, including its name, location, and a description of its purpose or activities.

Citizenship Cooperative Activity

31. **The Importance of Voting** Work with a partner to complete this activity. You know that the right to vote belongs to every United States citizen. In your opinion, what do citizens forfeit if they do not exercise their right to vote? Write a one-page paper that answers this question and share your paper with the other students.

Economics Activity

32. Goods are the items people buy. Services are activities done for others for a fee. List five goods you have purchased in the past month. List five services you purchased.

Self-Check Quiz

Visit **tarvol1.glencoe.com** and click on **Chapter 14— Self-Check Quizzes** to prepare for the chapter test.

 Alternative Assessment

33. **Portfolio Writing Activity** Write a poem designed to win supporters for one of the reform movements discussed in Chapter 14.

Standardized Test Practice

Directions: Choose the *best* answer to the following question.

School Enrollment, 1850–2000

In percent of persons of elementary and high school age

Source: *Historical Statistics of the United States; Statistical Abstract.*

According to the graph above, the greatest increase in the percentage of school enrollment occurred between

F 1850 and 1880.   **H** 1900 and 1950.

G 1850 and 1900.   **J** 1950 and 2000.

Test-Taking Tip

Use the information on the *graph* to help you answer this question. Look carefully at the information on the bottom and the side of a bar graph to understand what the bars represent. Process of elimination is helpful here. For example, answer F cannot be correct because this time period is not shown on the graph.

 Technology Activity

30. Students should write a brief description of a modern organization that supports women's rights.

Citizenship Cooperative Activity

31. Students' papers should show support for their opinions.

Economics Activity

32. Lists will vary, but should show an understanding of the difference between goods and services.

 Alternative Assessment

33. Poems should show support for a reform movement discussed in the chapter.

HISTORY Online

Have students visit the Web site at tarvol1.glencoe.com to review Chapter 14 and take the Self-Check Quiz.

Standardized Test Practice

Answer: H
Question Type: Culture/Environment
Answer Explanation: According to the graph, from 1900 to 1950 enrollment increased by more than 25 percent.

Bonus Question ?

Ask: Who said, "A foolish consistency is the hobgoblin of little minds"? *(Ralph Waldo Emerson)*

Practicing Skills

22. information about the National Women's Hall of Fame

23. women of the hall; nominate; support; shop; visit; our history; our mission; news & events; contact us; book of lives and legacies

24. There are links to Choice One and Buck & Pulleyn. These are appropriate because they are links to the company that made this site possible and the company that designed it.

25. Answers may include that it contains historical background, current events, and numerous biographic entries.

 Geography and History Activity

26. Canada

27. Charleston and New Bern

28. Many "stations" were located in northern coastal cities.

29. There was less of a risk of being captured due to the large populations.

431

Unit 6 Resources

Unit 6 (1 Day)	Chapter 15 (6 Days)	Chapter 16 (7 Days)	Chapter 17 (6 Days)	Unit 6 (2 Days)
Day 1 Introduction	**Day 1** Chapter 15 Intro, Section 1	**Day 1** Chapter 16 Intro, Section 1	**Day 1** Chapter 17 Intro, Section 1	**Day 1** Wrap-Up/Project **Day 2** Unit 6 Assessment
	Day 2 Section 2	**Day 2** Section 2	**Day 2** Section 2	
	Day 3 Section 3	**Day 3** Section 3	**Day 3** Section 3	
	Day 4 Section 4	**Day 4** Section 4	**Day 4** Section 4	
	Day 5 Chapter 15 Review	**Day 5** Section 5	**Day 5** Chapter 17 Review	
	Day 6 Chapter 15 Assessment	**Day 6** Chapter 16 Review	**Day 6** Chapter 17 Assessment	
		Day 7 Chapter 16 Assessment		

GLENCOE'S ASSESSMENT ADVANTAGE

Use the following tools to easily assess student learning in a variety of ways:

- Performance Assessment Activities and Rubrics
- Chapter and Unit Tests
- Section Quizzes
- Standardized Test Practice Workbook

- www.tarvol1.glencoe.com
- Interactive Tutor Self-Assessment CD-ROM
- MindJogger Videoquiz
- ExamView® Pro Testmaker CD-ROM

TEACHING TRANSPARENCIES

Unit 6 Map Overlay Transparencies
L2

Cause-and-Effect Transparency 6
L2

READING SUPPORT FROM JAMESTOWN EDUCATION

- *Timed Readings Plus in Social Studies* help students increase their reading rate and fluency while maintaining comprehension. The 400-word passages are similar to those found on state and national assessments.

- *Reading in the Content Area: Social Studies* concentrates on six essential reading skills that help students better comprehend what they read. The book includes 75 high-interest nonfiction passages written at increasing levels of difficulty.

- *Reading Fluency* helps students read smoothly, accurately, and expressively.

- *Jamestown's Reading Improvement,* by renowned reading expert Edward Fry, focuses on helping build your students' comprehension, vocabulary, and skimming and scanning skills.

- *Critical Reading Series* provides high-interest books, each written at three reading levels.

For more information about these products, see the Jamestown Education materials in the Classroom Solutions in the front of this Teacher Wraparound Edition. To order these products, call Glencoe at 1-800-334-7344.

Unit 6 Resources

ASSESSMENT

Unit 6 Pretests L2

Unit 6 Posttests L2

INTERDISCIPLINARY ACTIVITIES

American Literature Reading 6 L2

Interdisciplinary Connection 6 L2

Economics and History Activity 6 L2

APPLICATION AND ENRICHMENT

Cooperative Learning Activity 6 L1, **ELL**

Citizenship Activity 6 L1

HANDS-ON ACTIVITIES

Hands-On History Activity 6 L1

History Simulations and Problem Solving 6 L1

Reading List Generator CD-ROM

GLENCOE BOOKLINK

The Glencoe BookLink CD-ROM is a database that allows you to search more than 15,000 titles to create a customized reading list for your students.

- Reading lists can be organized by students' reading level, author, genre, theme, or area of interest.

- The database provides Degrees of Reading Power™ (DRP) and Lexile™ readability scores for all selections.

- A brief summary of each selection is included.

Leveled reading suggestions for this unit:

For Students at a Grade 6 Reading Level:
- *The Slopes of War,* by N.A. Perez

For Students at a Grade 7 Reading Level:
- *Undying Glory: The Story of the Massachusetts 54th Regiment,* by Clinton Cox

For Students at a Grade 8 Reading Level:
- *The Day Fort Sumter Was Fired On,* by Jim Haskins

Extending the Content

Readings for the Teacher
- ***Black Voices from Reconstruction 1865–1877,*** by John David Smith. Millbrook Press, 1996.
- ***An Illustrated History of the Civil War,*** by William C. Davis. Courage Books, 1997.

Multimedia Links
- ***Civil War Combat.*** VHS. Graystone Communications, Inc. A & E Television Networks.
- ***The History Makers: Abraham Lincoln.*** VHS. Cromwell Productions.

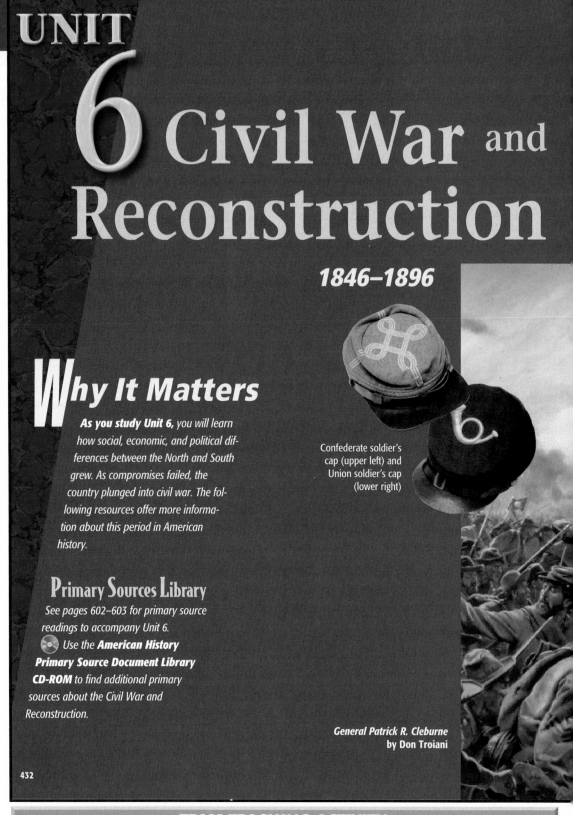

Unit Overview

Unit 6 examines the causes and effects of the Civil War. **Chapter 15** focuses on the issue of slavery in the West. **Chapter 16** discusses the strategies and battles of the Civil War. **Chapter 17** examines Reconstruction.

Unit Objectives

After studying this unit, students will be able to:

1. Explain how differences between the North and the South led to the Civil War.

2. Detail the major campaigns and strategies of the war.

3. Describe the Reconstruction policies and their effects on the former Confederacy.

Why It Matters Activity

Discuss the definition of civil war as an armed conflict between geographical regions or political groups of the same nation. Ask students to identify places where civil wars are currently taking place. Evaluate whether a civil war could occur today in the United States.

UNIT
6 Civil War and Reconstruction

1846–1896

Why It Matters

As you study Unit 6, you will learn how social, economic, and political differences between the North and South grew. As compromises failed, the country plunged into civil war. The following resources offer more information about this period in American history.

Confederate soldier's cap (upper left) and Union soldier's cap (lower right)

Primary Sources Library

See pages 602–603 for primary source readings to accompany Unit 6.

Use the **American History Primary Source Document Library CD-ROM** to find additional primary sources about the Civil War and Reconstruction.

General Patrick R. Cleburne by Don Troiani

432

TEAM TEACHING ACTIVITY

Science The importance of sanitary procedures in medicine, particularly surgery, was just beginning to be developed during the Civil War era. As a result, many soldiers died from infections caused by unsanitary procedures. Work with the Science teacher to coordinate the study of medical discoveries during this era. For example, Louis Pasteur's work with bacteria led to more sanitary operating room procedures and to the first use of antiseptics in surgical procedures. Students may also document the unsanitary conditions of field hospitals during the Civil War. **L2**

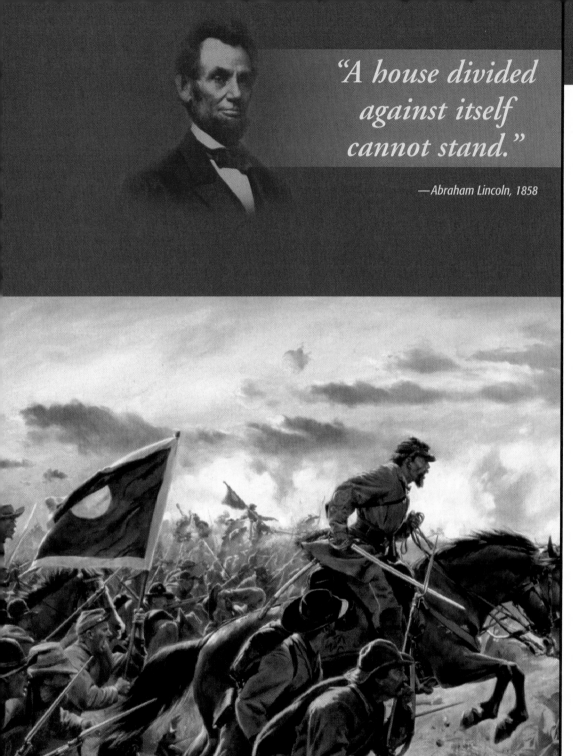

"A house divided against itself cannot stand."

—Abraham Lincoln, 1858

GLENCOE
TECHNOLOGY

CD-ROM
American History Primary Source Document Library CD-ROM

Use the **American History Primary Source Document Library CD-ROM** to access primary source documents related to the Civil War and Reconstruction.

More About the Art

Hoping to strike at Sherman's supply lines and improve the Confederate army's morale, General John Bell Hood ordered a frontal assault against the Armies of the Ohio and Cumberland outside of Franklin, Tennessee. The assault was disastrous, resulting in a Confederate defeat with a loss of more than 6,000 men, including General Patrick Cleburne. Have students describe how the cutting off of supply lines can affect a battle's outcome. *(It would prevent the army from receiving food, weapons, and additional troops.)*

Glencoe Literature Library

As students study the unit, have them read *Cezanne Pinto* by Mary Stolz from the **Glencoe Literature Library.** The Glencoe Literature Library consists of novels and other readings for middle school students, along with study guides that offer instructional support and student activities.

SERVICE-LEARNING PROJECT

Have students read about the daily life of a soldier from any period in American history. Have students contact their local Veteran's Administration hospital and ask about visiting several patients. Students can visit with patients and listen to stories about their experiences. Have students write about the similarities and differences of the soldier they visit with those of the soldier whom they read about. Students may want to consider serving as a volunteer for the hospital after the project is completed. **L2**

Refer to **Building Bridges: Connecting Classroom and Community through Service-Learning in Social Studies** from the National Council for the Social Studies for information about service-learning.

Chapter 15 Resources

TeacherWorks™ All-In-One Planner and Resource Center

- **Interactive Teacher Edition** Access your Teacher Wraparound Edition and your classroom resources with a few easy clicks.
- **Interactive Lesson Planner** Planning has never been easier! Organize your week, month, semester, or year with all the lesson helps you need to make teaching creative, timely, and relevant.

Use Glencoe's **Presentation Plus!** multimedia teacher tool to easily present dynamic lessons that visually excite your students. Using Microsoft PowerPoint® you can customize the presentations to create your own personalized lessons.

TEACHING TRANSPARENCIES

Graphic Organizer 14 L2

Why It Matters Chapter Transparency 15 L2

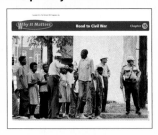

REVIEW AND REINFORCEMENT

Workbook Activity 15 L1

Time Line Activity 15 L2

Vocabulary Activity 15 L1

REVIEW AND REINFORCEMENT

Critical Thinking Skills Activity 15 L2

Take-Home Review Activity 15 L1

ENRICHMENT

Linking Past and Present Activity 15 L2

Primary Source Reading 15 L2

GEOGRAPHY

Geography and History Activity 15 L2

🌐 Meeting NCSS Standards

The following standards are highlighted in Chapter 15:

Section 1	VI	Power, Authority, & Governance: A, B, C, D, F, I
Section 2	II	Time, Continuity, & Change: A, B, C, E
Section 3	II	Time, Continuity, & Change: A, B, C, E
Section 4	III	People, Places, & Environments: A, B, D, H, I

FOLDABLES™ Study Organizer

Dinah Zike's **Foldables** are three-dimensional, interactive graphic organizers that help students practice basic writing skills, review key vocabulary terms, and identify main ideas. Additional chapter activities can be found in the **Reading and Study Skills Foldables** booklet.

Chapter 15 Resources

ASSESSMENT AND EVALUATION

Chapter 15 Test Form A L2

Chapter 15 Test Form B L2

Standardized Test Practice Workbook Activity 15 L2

Performance Assessment Activity 15 L1, ELL

ExamView® Pro Testmaker CD-ROM

MULTIMEDIA

- Vocabulary PuzzleMaker CD-ROM
- Interactive Tutor Self-Assessment CD-ROM
- ExamView® Pro Testmaker CD-ROM
- Audio Program
- American History Primary Source Document Library CD-ROM
- MindJogger Videoquiz
- Presentation Plus! CD-ROM
- TeacherWorks CD-ROM
- Interactive Student Edition CD-ROM
- Glencoe Skillbuilder Interactive Workbook CD-ROM, Level 1
- The American Republic to 1877 Video Program
- American Music: Hits Through History

SPANISH RESOURCES

The following Spanish language materials are available in the Spanish Resources Binder:

- Spanish Guided Reading Activities
- Spanish Reteaching Activities
- Spanish Quizzes and Tests
- Spanish Vocabulary Activity
- Spanish Take-Home Review Activity
- Spanish Summaries
- The Declaration of Independence and United States Constitution Spanish Translation

The following videotape programs are available from Glencoe as supplements to Chapter 15:

- **American Civil War** (ISBN 0-7670-0102-8)
- **Images Of The Civil War** (ISBN 1-56501-171-6)

To order, call Glencoe at 1-800-334-7344. To find classroom resources to accompany many of these videos, check the following home pages:
A&E Television: www.aande.com
The History Channel: www.historychannel.com

HISTORY Online

Use our Web site for additional resources. All essential content is covered in the Student Edition.

You and your students can visit tarvol1.glencoe.com, the Web site companion to **The American Republic to 1877.** This innovative integration of electronic and print media offers your students a wealth of opportunities. The student text directs students to the Web site for the following options:

- **Chapter Overviews**
- **Student Web Activities**
- **Self-Check Quizzes**
- **Textbook Updates**

Answers to the student Web activities are provided for you in the **Web Activity Lesson Plans.** Additional Web resources and Interactive Tutor Puzzles are also available.

Chapter 15 Resources

SECTION RESOURCES

Daily Objectives	Reproducible Resources	Multimedia Resources
SECTION 1 **Slavery and the West** 1. Describe how the debate over slavery was related to the admission of new states. 2. Understand what the Compromise of 1850 accomplished.	Reproducible Lesson Plan 15–1 Daily Lecture and Discussion Notes 15–1 Guided Reading Activity 15–1* Section Quiz 15–1* Reteaching Activity 15–1* Reading Essentials and Study Guide 15–1* Enrichment Activity 15–1	Daily Focus Skills Transparency 15–1 Interactive Tutor Self-Assessment CD-ROM ExamView® Pro Testmaker CD-ROM Presentation Plus! CD-ROM
SECTION 2 **A Nation Dividing** 1. Explain how the Fugitive Slave Act and the Kansas-Nebraska Act further divided the North and South. 2. Describe how popular sovereignty led to violence.	Reproducible Lesson Plan 15–2 Daily Lecture and Discussion Notes 15–2 Guided Reading Activity 15–2* Section Quiz 15–2* Reteaching Activity 15–2* Reading Essentials and Study Guide 15–2* Enrichment Activity 15–2	Daily Focus Skills Transparency 15–2 Interactive Tutor Self-Assessment CD-ROM ExamView® Pro Testmaker CD-ROM Presentation Plus! CD-ROM
SECTION 3 **Challenges to Slavery** 1. Understand why the Republican Party was formed. 2. Describe how the *Dred Scott* decision, the Lincoln-Douglas debates, and John Brown's raid affected Americans.	Reproducible Lesson Plan 15–3 Daily Lecture and Discussion Notes 15–3 Guided Reading Activity 15–3* Section Quiz 15–3* Reteaching Activity 15–3* Reading Essentials and Study Guide 15–3* Enrichment Activity 15–3	Daily Focus Skills Transparency 15–3 Interactive Tutor Self-Assessment CD-ROM ExamView® Pro Testmaker CD-ROM Presentation Plus! CD-ROM
SECTION 4 **Secession and War** 1. Explain how the 1860 election led to the breakup of the Union. 2. Understand why secession led to the Civil War.	Reproducible Lesson Plan 15–4 Daily Lecture and Discussion Notes 15–4 Guided Reading Activity 15–4* Section Quiz 15–4* Reteaching Activity 15–4* Reading Essentials and Study Guide 15–4* Enrichment Activity 15–4	Daily Focus Skills Transparency 15–4 American Music: Hits Through History Vocabulary PuzzleMaker CD-ROM Interactive Tutor Self-Assessment CD-ROM ExamView® Pro Testmaker CD-ROM Presentation Plus! CD-ROM

0:00 OUT OF TIME?
Assign the Chapter 15 **Reading Essentials and Study Guide.**

*Also Available in Spanish

 Blackline Master   Transparency   CD-ROM   DVD

 Poster   Music Program   Audio Program   Videocassette

KEY TO ABILITY LEVELS

Teaching strategies have been coded.

L1 BASIC activities for all students
L2 AVERAGE activities for average to above-average students
L3 CHALLENGING activities for above-average students
ELL ENGLISH LANGUAGE LEARNER activities

NATIONAL GEOGRAPHIC Teacher's Corner

INDEX TO NATIONAL GEOGRAPHIC MAGAZINE

The following articles relate to this chapter.

- "African Rituals in Colonial America," Geographica, February 1997.
- "C.S.S. *Alabama*," by Max Guerout, December 1994.
- "The Cruelest Commerce: African Slave Trade," by Colin Palmer, September 1992.

ADDITIONAL NATIONAL GEOGRAPHIC SOCIETY PRODUCTS

To order the following, call National Geographic at 1-800-368-2728:

- *GeoKit: The Civil War* (Kit)
- *GeoKit: Immigration* (Kit)
- *United States/Territorial Growth* (Map)
- *National Geographic Desk Reference* (Book)
- *Steal Away: The Harriet Tubman Story* (Video)
- *Immigration: The Triumph of Hope* (Video)

NGS ONLINE

Access National Geographic's Web site for current events, atlas updates, activities, links, interactive features, and archives.
www.nationalgeographic.com

MEETING SPECIAL NEEDS

In addition to the Differentiated Instruction strategies found in each section, the following resources are also suitable for your special needs students:

- **ExamView® Pro Testmaker CD-ROM** allows teachers to tailor tests by reducing answer choices.

- The **Audio Program** includes the entire narrative of the student edition so that less-proficient readers can listen to the words as they read them.

- The **Reading Essentials and Study Guide** provides the same content as the student edition but is written two grade levels below the textbook.

- **Guided Reading Activities** give less-proficient readers point-by-point instructions to increase comprehension as they read each textbook section.

- **Enrichment Activities** includes a stimulating collection of readings and activities for gifted and talented students.

From the Classroom of...

John Deluca
Drexel Hill Middle School
Drexel Hill, Pennsylvania

A Mock Trial of John Brown—
American Martyr or Radical?

A mock trial of John Brown will enable students to scrutinize the events that led to the Civil War. Students can examine the viewpoints of both the North and South concerning issues that divided the nation. First, organize the class into four groups. Assign each group a topic to research, such as the Compromise of 1850, the *Dred Scott* decision, the Kansas-Nebraska Act, or the Fugitive Slave Act of 1850. Have students role-play real people they find in their research. For example, a student could play the role of Stephen Douglas explaining the Kansas-Nebraska Act or Robert E. Lee discussing the capture of Brown. Some fictional characters could also be developed for the trial scene. Have characters take the stand one-by-one and let the rest of the class question them on activities that led to Brown's raid and eventually to the outbreak of the Civil War. Encourage students to examine different sides to all the issues discussed.

ADDITIONAL RESOURCES FROM GLENCOE

- American Music: Cultural Traditions
- American Art and Architecture
- Outline Map Resource Book
- U.S. Desk Map
- Building Geography Skills for Life
- Inclusion for the Middle School Social Studies Classroom Strategies and Activities
- Teaching Strategies for the American History Classroom (Including Block Scheduling Pacing Guides)
- American Crafts Hands-On Activities
- American Games Hands-On Activities
- American History Flash Cards

Block Schedule

Activities that are suited to use within the block scheduling framework are identified by:

☑ **Performance Assessment**

Refer to Activity 15 in the Performance Assessment Activities and Rubrics booklet.

Why It Matters Activity

Civil rights issues were paramount during the years surrounding the Civil War. Discuss the issues leading to the Civil War. Have students name current civil rights issues. Then help them to draw parallels between the issues impacting the nation then and now.

GLENCOE TECHNOLOGY

The American Republic to 1877 Video Program

To learn more about how enslaved African Americans escaped to freedom, have students view the Chapter 15 video "Secrets of the Underground Railroad" from **The American Republic to 1877 Video program.**

 Available in DVD and VHS

MindJogger Videoquiz

Use **MindJogger Videoquiz** to preview the Chapter 15 content.

 Available in VHS

CHAPTER 15

Road to Civil War

1820–1861

Why It Matters

Slavery was a major cause of the worsening division between the North and South in the period before the Civil War. The struggle between the North and South turned more hostile, and talk grew of separation and civil war.

The Impact Today

"If slavery is not wrong, nothing is wrong," Abraham Lincoln wrote in a letter to A.G. Hodges in 1864. By studying this era of our history, we can better understand the state of racial relations today and develop ways for improving them.

 The American Republic to 1877 *Video* The chapter 15 video, "Secrets of the Underground Railroad," tells how enslaved African Americans escaped to freedom.

1850
• Compromise of 1850 passed

1845
• Texas becomes a state

1852
• *Uncle Tom's Cabin* published

United States PRESIDENTS

| W.H. Harrison 1841 | Tyler 1841–1845 | Polk 1845–1849 | Taylor 1849–1850 | Fillmore 1850–1853 |

1840   *1845*   *1850*

World

1845
• Many people begin emigrating to escape potato famine in Ireland

1848
• Marx publishes *The Communist Manifesto*

Reading Strategy   **PURPOSE FOR READING**

Quick free write is a pre-reading activity for an upcoming topic or lesson. Ask students: Do you understand the meanings of the words *conflict* and *resolution*. Lead a short class discussion to ensure their understanding. Assign students to write a paragraph explaining the resolution to a personal conflict they have recently experienced. **L1**

African Americans in 1850 About 425,000 African Americans in the United States were free while 3.2 million lived in slavery.

FOLDABLES™
Study Organizer

Sequencing Events Study Foldable Make and use this foldable to sequence some of the key events that led to the Civil War.

Step 1 Fold a sheet of paper in half from side to side, leaving a ½ inch tab along the side.

> Leave ½ inch tab here.

Step 2 Turn the paper and fold it into fourths.

> Fold in half, then fold in half again.

Step 3 Unfold and cut up along the three fold lines.

> Make four tabs.

Step 4 Label your foldable as shown.

Slavery & the West	Acts of 1850 & 1854	Dred Scott & Lincoln/ Douglas Debates	1860 Election

The Road to Civil War

Reading and Writing As you read, write facts about the events under each appropriate tab of your foldable. How did these events lead to the Civil War?

FOLDABLES™
Study Organizer — Dinah Zike's Foldables

Purpose Students make and use a foldable to organize events leading up to the Civil War. As students read the chapter, they are required to sequence and describe important events. When students have completed the activity, they should have a flow-chart that outlines the events leading up to the Civil War.

📁 Have students complete **Reading and Study Skills Foldables** Activity 11. **L1**

HISTORY Online

Introduce students to chapter content and key terms by having them access **Chapter Overview 15** at tarvol1.glencoe.com

TIME LINE ACTIVITY

As students read the chapter, have them review the time line on pages 434–435. Have students identify how each of the events on the time line of the United States created conflict between the North and South.

1854
• Kansas-Nebraska Act passed

1857
• *Dred Scott* decision

1860
• Lincoln elected president

1861
• Civil War begins

1859
• Raid on Harpers Ferry

Pierce 1853–1857

Buchanan 1857–1861

1855

1860

HISTORY Online

Chapter Overview
Visit tarvol1.glencoe.com and click on **Chapter 15— Chapter Overviews** to preview chapter information.

1856
• Bessemer patents steel process

1861
• Alexander II frees serfs in Russia

1863
• French troops occupy Mexico City

CHAPTER 15   Road to Civil War   **435**

More About the Photo

By the early 1850s, the technology of photography made it possible to combine sharp photographic details with the ability to produce multiple copies of photographs from a single negative. The tintype proved to be a durable and relatively inexpensive means by which to produce pictures. For the first time, photographs were available to people who did not necessarily have wealth. More photographers began to pursue photography as a hobby or career, recording various aspects and conditions of everyday life. Discuss with students what information or details they see in this picture that reflect the conditions of African American life in the 1850s.

1 FOCUS

Section Overview

This section describes the growing division in the country over the issue of slavery.

Reading Preview

Answers to Graphic: The Missouri Compromise: Missouri, a slave state, and Maine, a free state; slavery prohibited from any territory acquired in the Louisiana Purchase north of 36°30'N latitude, except Missouri; The Compromise of 1850: California a free state; no restrictions on slavery in New Mexico Territory, and slave trade abolished in District of Columbia

Preteaching Vocabulary
Ask students to read the definition of *sectionalism* on page 437. Have them compare this to the definition of *nationalism*.

SECTION 1 Slavery and the West

Guide to Reading

Main Idea
As new states entered the Union, the question of whether to admit them as free states or slave states arose.

Key Terms
sectionalism, fugitive, secede, abstain

Reading Strategy
Organizing Information As you read the section, re-create the table below and describe how these compromises answered the question of admitting new states.

Admission of new states	
The Missouri Compromise	The Compromise of 1850

Read to Learn
• how the debate over slavery was related to the admission of new states.
• what the Compromise of 1850 accomplished.

Section Theme
Government and Democracy Controversy over slavery grew during the early and mid-1800s.

Preview of Events

◆1820	◆1830	◆1840	◆1850

1820
Missouri Compromise is passed

1845
Texas becomes a state

1848
Free-Soil Party nominates Martin Van Buren

1850
Compromise of 1850 diverts war

CAUTION!!
COLORED PEOPLE
OF BOSTON, ONE & ALL,
You are hereby respectfully CAUTIONED and advised, to avoid conversing with the
Watchmen and Police Officers of Boston,
For since the recent ORDER OF THE MAYOR & ALDERMEN, they are empowered to act as
KIDNAPPERS AND
Slave Catchers,
And they have already been actually employed in KIDNAPPING, CATCHING, AND KEEPING SLAVES. Therefore, if you value your LIBERTY, and the Welfare of the Fugitives among you, Shun them in every possible manner, as so many HOUNDS on the track of the most unfortunate of your race.
Keep a Sharp Look Out for KIDNAPPERS, and have TOP EYE open.
APRIL 24, 1851.

Poster warning African Americans

★★★★★★★★★
AN
American Story

"The deed is done. The . . . chains of slavery are forged for [many] yet unborn. Humble yourselves in the dust, ye high-minded citizens of Connecticut. Let your cheeks be red as crimson. On *your* representatives rests the stigma of this foul disgrace." These biting, fiery words were published in a Connecticut newspaper in 1820. They were in response to members of Congress who had helped pave the way for the admission of Missouri as a slaveholding state.

The Missouri Compromise

The request by slaveholding **Missouri** to join the Union in 1819 caused an angry debate that worried former president Thomas Jefferson and Secretary of State John Quincy Adams. Jefferson called the dispute "a fire-bell in the night" that "awakened and filled me with terror." Adams accurately predicted that the bitter debate was "a mere preamble—a title-page to a great tragic volume."

Many Missouri settlers had brought enslaved African Americans into the territory with them. By 1819 the Missouri Territory included about 50,000 whites

436 CHAPTER 15 Road to Civil War

---

and 10,000 slaves. When Missouri applied to Congress for admission as a state, its constitution allowed slavery.

In 1819, 11 states permitted slavery and 11 did not. The Senate—with two members from each state—was therefore evenly balanced between slave and free states. The admission of a new state would upset that balance.

In addition, the North and the South, with their different economic systems, were competing for new lands in the western territories. At the same time, a growing number of Northerners wanted to restrict or ban slavery. Southerners, even those who disliked slavery, opposed these antislavery efforts. They resented the interference by outsiders in Southerners' affairs. These differences between the North and the South grew into sectionalism—an exaggerated loyalty to a particular region of the country.

Clay's Proposal

The Senate suggested a way to resolve the crisis by allowing Missouri's admittance as a slave state while simultaneously admitting Maine as a free state. Maine, formerly part of Massachusetts, had also applied for admission to the Union. The Senate also sought to settle the issue of slavery in the territories for good. It proposed prohibiting slavery in the remainder of the Louisiana Purchase north of 36°30'N latitude.

Speaker of the House **Henry Clay** of Kentucky skillfully maneuvered the Senate bill to passage in 1820 by dividing it into three proposals. The **Missouri Compromise** preserved the balance between slave and free states in the Senate and brought about a lull in the bitter debate in Congress over slavery.

✓Reading Check **Explaining** What is sectionalism?

New Western Lands

For the next 25 years, Congress managed to keep the slavery issue in the background. In the 1840s, however, this heated debate moved back into Congress. Once again the cause of the dispute was the issue of slavery in new territories. The territories involved were **Texas,** which had won its independence from Mexico in 1836, and **New Mexico** and **California,** which were still part of Mexico.

Many Southerners hoped to see Texas, where slavery already existed, join the Union. As a result, the annexation of Texas became the main issue in the presidential election of 1844. Democrat **James Polk** of Tennessee won the election and pressed forward on acquiring Texas, and Texas became a state in 1845. At the same time, support for taking over New Mexico and California also grew in the South. The federal government's actions on these lands led to war with Mexico.

Conflicting Views

Just months after the Mexican War began, Representative David Wilmot of Pennsylvania introduced a proposal in Congress. Called the **Wilmot Proviso,** it specified that slavery should be prohibited in any lands that might be acquired from Mexico. Southerners protested furiously. They wanted to keep open the possibility of introducing slavery to California and New Mexico.

Senator **John C. Calhoun** of South Carolina countered with another proposal. It stated that neither Congress nor any territorial government had the authority to ban slavery from a territory or regulate it in any way.

Polk campaign banner

2 TEACH

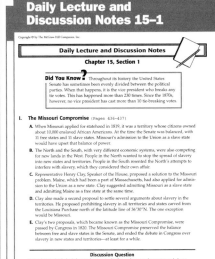

Daily Lecture and Discussion Notes 15–1

Copyright © by The McGraw-Hill Companies, Inc.

Daily Lecture and Discussion Notes

Chapter 15, Section 1

Did You Know? Throughout its history the United States Senate has sometimes been evenly divided between the political parties. When that happens, it is the vice president who breaks any tie votes. This has happened more than 230 times. Since the 1870s, however, no vice president has cast more than 10 tie-breaking votes.

I. The Missouri Compromise (Pages 436–437)

A. When Missouri applied for statehood in 1819, it was a territory whose citizens owned about 10,000 enslaved African Americans. At the time the Senate was balanced, with 11 free states and 11 slave states. Missouri's admission to the Union as a slave state would have upset that balance of power.

B. The North and the South, with very different economic systems, were also competing for new lands in the West. People in the North wanted to stop the spread of slavery into new states and territories. People in the South resented the North's attempts to interfere with slavery, which they considered their own affair.

C. Representative Henry Clay, Speaker of the House, proposed a solution to the Missouri problem. Maine, which had been a part of Massachusetts, had also applied for admission to the Union as a new state. Clay suggested admitting Missouri as a slave state and admitting Maine as a free state at the same time.

D. Clay also made a second proposal to settle several arguments about slavery in the territories. He proposed prohibiting slavery in all territories and states carved from the Louisiana Purchase north of the latitude line of 36°30'N. The one exception would be Missouri.

E. Clay's two proposals, which became known as the Missouri Compromise, were passed by Congress in 1820. The Missouri Compromise preserved the balance between free and slave states in the Senate, and ended the debate in Congress over slavery in new states and territories—at least for a while.

Discussion Question

Why do you think the balance of power in the Senate between free states and slave states was so important? (Answers will vary, but should include the idea that the North and South had different political and economic interests. Each section felt that its interests would be ignored if senators from the other section were in control of the Senate.)

turn

Compromising Discuss the definition of compromise, pointing out that an effective compromise satisfies all parties involved. Pair students to make a graphic organizer for each compromise mentioned in this section. Have pairs show the following on the graphic organizer: name of the compromise, parties involved, what each party gave up, what each party received, the features of the final compromise. **L2**

✓Reading Check

Answer: a strong loyalty to a particular region of the country

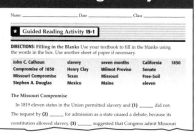

✓ **Reading Check**

Answer: The Wilmot Proviso specified that slavery would be prohibited in any lands acquired from Mexico. Calhoun's proposal, however, stated that government did not have the authority to ban or regulate slavery anywhere.

3 ASSESS

Assign Section 1 Assessment as homework or as an in-class activity.

◉ Have students use **Interactive Tutor Self-Assessment CD-ROM.**

L2

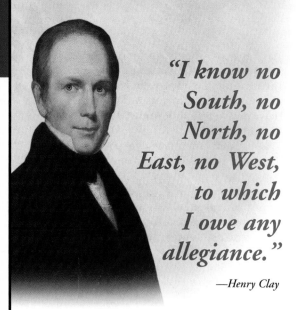

"I know no South, no North, no East, no West, to which I owe any allegiance."

—*Henry Clay*

Neither Wilmot's nor Calhoun's proposal passed, but both caused bitter debate. By the time of the 1848 presidential election, the United States had gained the territories of California and New Mexico from Mexico but had taken no action on the issue of slavery in those areas.

The Free-Soil Party

The debate over slavery led to the formation of a new political party. In 1848 the Whigs chose **Zachary Taylor,** a Southerner and a hero of the Mexican War, as their presidential candidate. The Democrats selected Senator Lewis Cass of Michigan. Neither candidate took a stand on slavery in the territories.

This failure to take a position angered voters. Many antislavery Democrats and Whigs left their parties and joined with members of the old Liberty Party to form the **Free-Soil Party.** The new party proclaimed "Free Soil, Free Speech, Free Labor, and Free Men," and endorsed the Wilmot Proviso. The party nominated former president **Martin Van Buren** as its presidential candidate.

Whig candidate Zachary Taylor won the election by successfully appealing to both slave and free states. Taylor defeated Cass 163 to 127 in electoral votes. Van Buren captured only 14 percent of the popular vote in the North, but several candidates of the Free-Soil Party won seats in Congress.

California

Once in office President Taylor urged leaders in the two territories of California and New Mexico to apply for statehood immediately. Once these lands had become states, he reasoned, their citizens could decide whether to allow slavery. New Mexico did not apply for statehood, but California did in 1850.

Taylor's plan ran into trouble when California's statehood became tangled up with other issues before Congress. Antislavery forces wanted to abolish slavery in the District of Columbia, the nation's capital. Southerners wanted a strong national law requiring states to return fugitive, or runaway, slaves to their masters. Another dispute involved the New Mexico–Texas border.

The greatest obstacle to Taylor's plan was concern over the balance of power in the Senate. In 1849 the nation included 15 slave states and 15 free states. If California entered as a free state—and New Mexico, Oregon, and Utah followed as free states, which seemed likely—the South would be hopelessly outvoted in the Senate. As tension grew, some Southerners began talking about having their states secede from, or leave, the United States.

✓ **Reading Check** **Explaining** How was John C. Calhoun's proposal different from the Wilmot Proviso?

A New Compromise

In January 1850, Henry Clay, now a senator, presented a multi-part plan to settle all the issues dividing Congress. First, California would be admitted as a free state. Second, the New Mexico Territory would have no restrictions on slavery. Third, the New Mexico–Texas border dispute would be settled in favor of New Mexico. Fourth, the slave trade, but not slavery itself, would be abolished in the District of Columbia. Finally, Clay pushed for a stronger fugitive slave law.

Clay's proposal launched an emotional debate in Congress that raged for seven months. Opening that debate were Clay and two other distinguished senators—John C. Calhoun of South Carolina and **Daniel Webster** of Massachusetts.

DIFFERENTIATED INSTRUCTION

Reading Support The West was the final destination of many immigrant groups. Have students create maps showing were immigrants settled around the country. Students should use library resources to determine what religious, racial, and ethnic groups settled in the United States and why they settled in specific areas. Have students complete this activity for the eighteenth and nineteenth centuries. The information about the identity of the group, the reasons for settling, and the years the group settled in the areas should be written on the maps. **L2**

Calhoun opposed Clay's plan. He believed that the only way to save the Union was to protect slavery. If Congress admitted California as a free state, Calhoun warned, the Southern states had to leave the Union.

Three days later Webster gave an eloquent speech in support of Clay's plan. He argued that antislavery forces lost little in agreeing to the compromise:

❝I would rather hear of natural blasts and mildews, war, pestilence, and famine, than to hear gentlemen talk of secession.❞

Webster reasoned that geography would prevent slavery from taking root in the new territories, since most of the land was not suited for plantations. What was most important was to preserve the Union.

The Compromise of 1850

Clay's plan could not pass as a complete package. Too many members of Congress objected to one part of it or another. President Taylor also opposed the plan and threatened to use force against the South if states tried to secede.

Then in July President Taylor suddenly died. The new president, **Millard Fillmore,** supported some form of compromise. At the same time, **Stephen A. Douglas,** a young senator from Illinois, took charge of efforts to resolve the crisis. Douglas divided Clay's plan into a series of

Fiction
Fact · Folklore

Before They Were Presidents

Like Zachary Taylor, did most presidents make the military their profession? Some presidents *did* make the military their principal profession. Washington, William Henry Harrison, Grant, and Eisenhower, as well as Taylor, all made a career in the military. However, more presidents came from the ranks of attorneys than from any other profession. More than half of all presidents, including Jefferson and Lincoln, made their living in the practice of law.

measures that Congress could vote on separately. In this way members of Congress would not have to support proposals they opposed.

President Fillmore persuaded several Whig representatives to abstain—not to cast votes—on measures they opposed. Congress finally passed a series of five separate bills in August and September of 1850. Taken together these laws, known as the **Compromise of 1850,** contained the five main points of Clay's original plan. Fillmore called the compromise a "final settlement" of the conflict between North and South. The president would soon be proved wrong.

✓**Reading Check** **Explaining** How did the Compromise of 1850 affect the New Mexico Territory?

SECTION 1 ASSESSMENT

Checking for Understanding

1. **Key Terms** Use each of these social studies terms in a sentence that will help explain its meaning: sectionalism, fugitive, secede, abstain.

2. **Reviewing Facts** List the provisions of the Missouri Compromise.

Reviewing Themes

3. **Government and Democracy** Why was the Free-Soil Party created?

Critical Thinking

4. **Analyzing Information** What was the Wilmot Proviso? Why was it controversial?

5. **Comparing** Re-create the table below and describe what the North and South each gained from the Compromise of 1850.

Compromise of 1850	
Northern gains	Southern gains

Analyzing Visuals

6. **Examining Artifacts** Look at the campaign banner on page 437. Compare it to a modern political button or advertisement you have seen. In what ways are they similar? In what ways are they different?

Interdisciplinary Activity

Government Create a poster for the Free-Soil Party presidential candidate. Include slogans or symbols to gain popular support.

SECTION 1 ASSESSMENT ANSWERS

1. Student work should reflect correct use of terms.

2. Missouri admitted as slave state and Maine as free state; prohibited slavery in Louisiana Purchase territory in areas north of 36°30' N latitude, except Missouri

3. to take a stand opposing the extension of slavery

4. a proposal to prohibit slavery in any lands acquired from Mexico; some wanted to introduce slavery in those lands

5. North: California admitted as a free state, slave trade abolished in District of Columbia; South: no restrictions on slavery in New Mexico, slavery not abolished

in District of Columbia, stronger fugitive slave law

6. Similarities: use of candidates' names or photos; Differences: use of logos or advertising techniques

Interdisciplinary Activity Posters should address the slavery issue.

✓**Reading Check**

Answer: There were no restrictions on slavery, and the New Mexico–Texas border dispute favored New Mexico.

L1

Reteaching Activity 15–1

★ Reteaching Activity **15-1**

DIRECTIONS: Organizing Facts The items in the Fact Bank list the characteristics of plans made in Congress during the first part of the 1800s to settle issues over slavery. In the blanks on the chart, write the letter of each item in the correct category.

Plans to Avoid Conflict Over Slavery		
Missouri Compromise	Wilmot Proviso/Calhoun's Proposal	Compromise of 1850 (Clay's Five-Part Plan)

L1, ELL

Reading Essentials and Study Guide 15–1

Study Guide

Chapter 15, Section 1

For use with textbook pages 436–439

SLAVERY AND THE WEST

KEY TERMS	
sectionalism	Exaggerated loyalty to a particular region of the country (page 437)
fugitive	Someone who runs away from the law (page 438)
secede	To separate or leave the Union (page 438)
abstain	To not cast a vote (page 439)

DRAWING FROM EXPERIENCE

Have you ever had to give up something to get something you wanted more? How did you decide which item was more important? What were some times when you would not compromise? This section focuses on how the Northern states and the Southern states debated and compromised over the issue of slavery in new states.

L3

Enrichment Activity 15–1

★ Enrichment Activity **15-1**

Representation in the House

As new lands were added to the United States, the issue of equal voting power in the Senate for the free states and slave states became very important. Yet the voting power of states in the House of Representatives, whose membership was based on population, could not be controlled by compromises. The table below shows membership in the House of Representatives.

DIRECTIONS: Analyzing a Table Use the information in the table to fill in the following information.

1. Free states had _____ representatives in the House in 1800, but slave states had only _____

Representation in the House of Representatives, 1800–1850		
Year	Number of Members from Free States	Number of Members from Slave States
1800	76	65

4 CLOSE

Ask students to reexamine the graphic organizers they created at the beginning of this section. Have them point out parts of each compromise that had the potential to lead to civil war.

439

TEACH

Recognizing Bias This skill illustrates how bias prevents someone from looking at a situation in a reasonable and truthful way. By analyzing two excerpts, students apply the steps to recognizing bias.

Have students work in pairs to apply these steps to the quotations in Section 1 to determine each speaker's bias. Discuss the quotations and the biases. Point out to students how their own biases can influence their interpretation of bias.

Additional Practice
L2

Chapter Skills Activity 15

Name _____ Date _____ Class _____

★ Chapter Skills Activity 15

Recognizing Bias

To recognize bias, ask yourself questions such as: Does the author consider more than one point of view? Why did the author write the piece? How might the author's background influence his or her viewpoint?

DIRECTIONS: In the passage below, Nellie Thomas describes the lives of enslaved African Americans on her grandfather's plantation in South Carolina. Read the passage and answer the questions that follow on a separate sheet of paper.

. . . Grandfather held his slaves as part of his official family. He owned them in families and encouraged the making of family ties among them. By these natural methods of economic conservation there were before very long many Negroes in the "quarters." As Grandfather was his own overseer, he gave his personal

GLENCOE
TECHNOLOGY

CD-ROM
Glencoe Skillbuilder Interactive Workbook CD-ROM, Level 1

This interactive CD-ROM reinforces student mastery of essential social studies skills.

Critical Thinking
SKILLBUILDER

Recognizing Bias

Why Learn This Skill?

Cats make better pets than dogs. If you say this, then you are stating a bias. A bias is a prejudice. It can prevent you from looking at a situation in a reasonable or truthful way.

Learning the Skill

Most people have feelings and ideas that affect their point of view. This viewpoint, or *bias,* influences the way they interpret events. For this reason, an idea that is stated as a fact may really be only an opinion. Recognizing bias will help you judge the accuracy of what you read. There are several things you should look for that will help you recognize bias. Identify the author of the statement and examine his or her views and possible reasons for writing the material. Look for language that reflects an emotion or opinion—words such as *all, never, best, worst, might,* or *should.* Examine the writing for imbalances—leaning only to one viewpoint and failing to provide equal coverage of other possible viewpoints.

Practicing the Skill

Read the excerpts on this page. The first excerpt is from an 1858 newspaper editorial. The second is from a speech by Senator John C. Calhoun of South Carolina. Then answer the four questions that follow.

66 Popular sovereignty for the territories will never work. Under this system, each territory would decide whether or not to legalize slavery. This method was tried in the territory of Kansas and all it produced was bloodshed and violence. 99

— *The Republican Leader,* 1858

66 . . . [T]he two great divisions of society are not rich and poor, but white and black; and all the former, the poor as well as the rich, belong to the upper classes, and are respected and treated as such. 99

— Senator Calhoun

❶ Is Senator Calhoun expressing a proslavery or antislavery bias?

❷ What statements indicate the racism in Calhoun's bias?

❸ What political party's view does the editorial represent?

❹ What biases or beliefs are expressed in the editorial?

Applying the Skill

Recognizing Bias Look through the letters to the editor in your local newspaper. Write a short report analyzing one of the letters for evidence of bias.

 Glencoe's **Skillbuilder Interactive Workbook CD-ROM, Level 1,** provides instruction and practice in key social studies skills.

ANSWERS TO PRACTICING THE SKILL

❶ proslavery

❷ by saying that rich and poor whites are of the upper classes and that the divisions of society are black and white

❸ Republican

❹ Popular sovereignty does not work.

Applying the Skill Have students work through the steps to identify bias before they write their reports.

SECTION 2 A Nation Dividing

Guide to Reading

Main Idea
Growing tensions led to differences that could not be solved by compromise.

Key Terms
popular sovereignty, border ruffians, civil war

Reading Strategy
As you read the section, re-create the table below and describe how Southerners and Northerners reacted to the Kansas-Nebraska Act.

Kansas-Nebraska Act	
Southern reaction	Northern reaction

Read to Learn
• how the Fugitive Slave Act and the Kansas-Nebraska Act further divided the North and South.
• how popular sovereignty led to violence.

Section Theme
Continuity and Change As they grew farther apart, Northerners and Southerners sought compromise.

Preview of Events

◆1850   ◆1853   ◆1856

1850
Fugitive Slave Act is passed

1852
Uncle Tom's Cabin is published

1854
Kansas-Nebraska Act is passed

1856
Charles Sumner attacked in Senate

Anthony Burns

AN American Story

On May 24, 1854, the people of Boston erupted in outrage. Federal officers had seized Anthony Burns, a runaway slave who lived in Boston, to send him back to slavery. Abolitionists tried to rescue Burns from the federal courthouse, and city leaders attempted to buy his freedom. All efforts failed. Local militia units joined the marines and cavalry in Boston to keep order. Federal troops escorted Burns to a ship that would carry him back to Virginia and slavery. In a gesture of bitter protest, Bostonians draped buildings in black and hung the American flag upside down.

The Fugitive Slave Act

The **Fugitive Slave Act** of 1850 required all citizens to help catch runaways. Anyone who aided a fugitive could be fined or imprisoned. People in the South believed the law would force Northerners to recognize the rights of Southerners. Instead, enforcement of the law led to mounting anger in the North, convincing more people of the evils of slavery.

After passage of the Fugitive Slave Act, slaveholders stepped up their efforts to catch runaway slaves. They even tried to capture runaways who had lived in freedom in the North for years. Sometimes they seized African Americans who were not escaped slaves and forced them into slavery.

CHAPTER 15   Road to Civil War   **441**

1 FOCUS

Section Overview
This section describes how compromises continued to fail, leading to increased tensions between the North and South.

Reading Preview

Answers to Graphic: Southern reaction: supported bill; Northern reaction: protested passage of act, demanded Congress vote down the bill

Preteaching Vocabulary
Lead students to understand that *popular* means "of or carried on by the common people" and *sovereignty* means "supreme, independent political authority." Combining the two meanings, *popular sovereignty*, means "let the people decide."

SECTION RESOURCES

📂 **Reproducible Masters**
• Reproducible Lesson Plan 15–2
• Daily Lecture and Discussion Notes 15–2
• Guided Reading Activity 15–2
• Section Quiz 15–2
• Reteaching Activity 15–2
• Reading Essentials and Study Guide 15–2
• Enrichment Activity 15–2

🖥 **Transparencies**
• Daily Focus Skills Transparency 15–2

Multimedia
🅢 Interactive Tutor Self-Assessment CD-ROM
🅢 ExamView® Pro Testmaker CD-ROM
🅢 Presentation Plus! CD-ROM

2 TEACH

Creating a Graphic Organizer

Ask students to create a cause-and-effect graphic organizer showing the effects of the Fugitive Slave Act and the Kansas-Nebraska Act. Use the organizers as the basis for discussing why the nation was dividing. **L1**

People In History

As the popularity of *Uncle Tom's Cabin* grew, Southern critics unsuccessfully began to denounce Harriet Beecher Stowe's work. Stowe, however, stood steadfast in the wave of criticism and continued to write, producing about a book each year from 1862 to 1884. **Ask: Why were Southerners more critical of Stowe's work than Northerners were?** *(Stowe encouraged people to turn against slavery, an institution largely supported by Southerners.)*

✓ Reading Check

Answer: to help runaway enslaved African Americans make their way to freedom

People In History

Harriet Beecher Stowe 1811–1896

Writer Harriet Beecher Stowe called the Fugitive Slave Act a "nightmare abomination." Stowe, the daughter of a New England minister, spent part of her childhood in Cincinnati. There, on the banks of the Ohio River, she saw enslaved people being loaded onto ships to be taken to slave markets. As an adult and the wife of a religion professor, she wrote many books and stories about social reform. Her most famous work was a novel about the evils of slavery. *Uncle Tom's Cabin* was published in 1852. Packed with dramatic incidents and vivid characters, the novel shows slavery as a cruel and brutal system.

Uncle Tom's Cabin quickly became a sensation, selling over 300,000 copies in the first year of publication. The book had such an impact on public feelings about slavery that when Abraham Lincoln was introduced to Stowe during the Civil War, he said, so, you "wrote the book that started this great war."

Resistance to the Law

In spite of the penalties, many Northerners refused to cooperate with the law's enforcement. The Underground Railroad, a network of free African Americans and whites, helped runaways make their way to freedom. Antislavery groups tried to rescue African Americans who were being pursued or to free those who were captured. In Boston, members of one such group followed federal agents shouting, "Slave hunters—there go the slave hunters." People contributed funds to buy the freedom of African Americans. Northern juries refused to convict those accused of breaking the Fugitive Slave Law.

✓ **Reading Check** **Explaining** What was the purpose of the Underground Railroad?

The Kansas–Nebraska Act

Franklin Pierce, a New Hampshire Democrat who supported the Fugitive Slave Act, became president in 1853. Pierce intended to enforce the Fugitive Slave Act, and his actions hardened the opposition.

In 1854 the dispute over slavery erupted in Congress again. The cause was a bill introduced by Stephen A. Douglas, the Illinois senator who had forged the Compromise of 1850.

Hoping to encourage settlement of the West and open the way for a transcontinental railroad, Douglas proposed organizing the region west of Missouri and Iowa as the territories of **Kansas** and **Nebraska.** Douglas was trying to work out a plan for the nation to expand that both the North and the South would accept. Instead his bill reopened the conflict about slavery in the territories.

Because of their location, Kansas and Nebraska seemed likely to become free states. Both lay north of 36°30'N latitude, the line established in the Missouri Compromise as the boundary of slavery. Douglas knew that Southerners would object to having Kansas and Nebraska become free states because it would give the North an advantage in the Senate. As a result Douglas proposed abandoning the Missouri Compromise and letting the settlers in each territory vote on whether to allow slavery. He called this popular sovereignty—allowing the people to decide.

COOPERATIVE LEARNING ACTIVITY

Mediating Conflict Organize the class into groups of four to devise alternative compromises that might have avoided the bloodshed following the Kansas-Nebraska Act. Ask each group to role-play a debate over an alternative compromise. Make sure students accurately represent the point of view of the person whose role they are playing. If the sides cannot agree on an alternative plan with the help of the mediator, then the mediator should assume the role of binding arbitrator, who evaluates the different positions and imposes a decision. Have each group analyze the process of compromise and binding arbitration. **L3**

Passage of the Act

Many Northerners protested strongly. Douglas's plan to repeal the Missouri Compromise would allow slavery into areas that had been free for more than 30 years. Opponents of the bill demanded that Congress vote down the bill.

Southerners in Congress, however, provided solid support for the bill. They expected that Kansas would be settled in large part by slaveholders from Missouri who would vote to keep slavery legal. With some support from Northern Democrats and the backing of President Pierce, Congress passed the **Kansas–Nebraska Act** in May 1854.

Division Grows

Northern Democrats in the House split almost evenly on the vote, revealing deep divisions in the party. Many Northerners became convinced that compromise with the South was no longer possible. Sam Houston, senator from Texas, predicted that the bill "will convulse [upset] the country from Maine to the Rio Grande."

✓**Reading Check** **Describing** Write a definition of "popular sovereignty" in your own words.

Conflict in Kansas

Right after passage of the Kansas–Nebraska Act, proslavery and antislavery groups rushed supporters into Kansas. In the spring of 1855, when elections took place in Kansas, a proslavery legislature was elected.

Although only about 1,500 voters lived in Kansas at the time, more than 6,000 people cast ballots in the elections. Thousands of proslavery supporters from Missouri had crossed the border just to vote in the election. These Missourians traveled in armed groups and became known as border ruffians. Soon after the election, the new Kansas legislature passed laws supporting slavery. One law even restricted political office to proslavery candidates.

The antislavery people refused to accept these laws. Instead they armed themselves, held their own elections, and adopted a constitution that banned slavery. By January 1856, rival governments existed in Kansas, one for and one against slavery. Each asked Congress for recognition. To confuse matters further, President Pierce and the Senate favored the proslavery government, while the House backed the forces opposed to slavery.

L1, ELL

Guided Reading Activity 15–2

Name _____ Date _____ Class _____

★ **Guided Reading Activity 15-2**

DIRECTIONS: Outlining Locate heading in your textbook. Then use the information under the heading to help you write each answer. Use another sheet of paper if necessary.

I. The Fugitive Slave Act
  A. Introduction
    1. What did the Fugitive Slave Act of 1850 require?
    2. What did free African Americans and whites who opposed slavery set up to help runaways escape?
    3. Who wrote *Uncle Tom's Cabin*?
    4. What did *Uncle Tom's Cabin* show about slavery?

Geography *Skills*

Answers:
1. It more than doubled the territories open to slavery.
2. Washington, Oregon, and Minnesota

✓**Reading Check**

Answer: Answers will vary, but should show evidence of understanding *popular sovereignty*.

3 ASSESS

Assign Section 2 Assessment as homework or as an in-class activity.

💿 Have students use **Interactive Tutor Self-Assessment CD-ROM.**

L2

Section Quiz 15–2

Name _____ Date _____ Class _____

★ **Chapter 15** Score ☐

Section Quiz 15-2

DIRECTIONS: Matching Match the items in Column A with the items in Column B. Write the correct letters in the blanks. *(10 points each)*

Column A	Column B
___ **1.** bought freedom of enslaved people	**A.** 36°30′N latitude
___ **2.** boundary of slavery	**B.** "Bleeding Kansas"
___ **3.** allowing the people to decide	**C.** John Brown
___ **4.** caused over 200 deaths	**D.** popular sovereignty
___ **5.** violent abolitionist	**E.** antislavery groups

DIRECTIONS: Multiple Choice In the blank at the [...] write the letter of th[...]

NATIONAL GEOGRAPHIC **Slavery and Sectionalism**

The Compromise of 1850

OREGON TERR.
MINNESOTA TERR.
UNORGANIZED TERR.
CALIF. (1850)
UTAH TERR.
NEW MEXICO TERR.

☐ Free states
☐ Slave states
☐ Territory closed to slaveholding
☐ Territory open to slaveholding
☐ Indian Territory

Kansas–Nebraska Act, 1854

WASHINGTON TERR.
OREGON TERR.
NEBRASKA TERR.
KANSAS TERR.

Geography *Skills*

1. **Region** How did the Kansas–Nebraska Act change the amount of territory open to slaveholding?
2. **Analyzing Information** What territories were non-slaveholding in 1854?

DIFFERENTIATED INSTRUCTION

At-Risk Students When *Uncle Tom's Cabin* was published as a novel in 1852, George Aiken dramatized the story into a play. Countless stage versions of this story were enacted before the Civil War. Have students find a copy of the play *Uncle Tom's Cabin* at the library. Choose different students to read parts aloud in class. **L1**

📂 Refer to **Inclusion for the Middle School Social Studies Classroom Strategies and Activities** in the TCR.

✓ **Reading Check**

Answer: a conflict between citizens of the same country

L1

Reteaching Activity 15–2

Name _____ Date _____ Class _____

★ Reteaching Activity 15-2

DIRECTIONS: Recognizing Causes and Effects After each *Cause*, write the letter of its *Effect* from the Fact Bank.

1. Cause: The Fugitive Slave Act is strictly enforced.
Effect: _____

2. Cause: Harriet Beecher Stowe writes *Uncle Tom's Cabin*, a novel that illustrates the brutality of slavery.
Effect: _____

3. Cause: In 1854 Senator Stephen A. Douglas proposes a bill to organize the territories of Kansas and Nebraska.

5. Cause: Southerners, some Northern Democrats, and President Franklin Pierce support the repeal of the Missouri Compromise.
Effect: _____

6. Cause: A proslavery legislature in Kansas passes laws supporting slavery.
Effect: _____

7. Cause: Violence erupts first in Lawrence, Kansas, and then in Pottawatomie Creek.

L1, **ELL**

Reading Essentials and Study Guide 15–2

Study Guide

Chapter 15, Section 2
For use with textbook pages 441–444

A NATION DIVIDING

KEY TERMS	
popular sovereignty	The idea that allows the people to make their own decisions about the area in which they live (page 442)
border ruffians	Armed groups from another state that cross a border solely to vote (page 443)
civil war	A conflict between citizens of the same country (page 444)

DRAWING FROM EXPERIENCE

Have you ever been part of one group that split into two smaller groups because of a disagreement? Did you or anyone try to bring the group back together? Could the disagreement be resolved?
In the last section, you read how Western states were added to the Union with compromises from...

L3

Enrichment Activity 15–2

Name _____ Date _____ Class _____

★ Enrichment Activity 15-2 ★

Runaway!

The Fugitive Slave Act of 1850 was supported by many Southerners but hated, attacked, and ignored by many Northerners. The poster, or placard, shown to the right was posted in 1851.

DIRECTIONS: Interpreting Information
Posters were a little like newspaper articles in the 1800s. They often provided information to answer the questions *Who?*, *What?*, *When?*, *Where?*, and *Why?* Study the poster and then fill in the information below with as much detail as you can.

CAUTION!!
COLORED PEOPLE
OF BOSTON, ONE & ALL,
You are hereby respectfully CAUTIONED and advised, to avoid conversing with the
Watchmen and Police Officers of Boston,
For since the recent ORDER OF THE MAYOR & ALDERMEN, they are empowered to act as
KIDNAPPERS

4 CLOSE

Ask students to speculate about what the federal government could have done, if anything, to prevent the violence that erupted over the Kansas-Nebraska Act.

444

John Brown

"Bleeding Kansas"

With proslavery and antislavery forces in Kansas arming themselves, the outbreak of violence became inevitable. In May 1856, 800 slavery supporters attacked the town of Lawrence, the antislavery capital. They sacked the town, burned the hotel and the home of the governor, and destroyed two newspaper offices. Soon after, forces opposed to slavery retaliated.

John Brown, a fervent abolitionist, believed God had chosen him to end slavery. When he heard of the attack on Lawrence, Brown went into a rage. He vowed to "strike terror in the hearts of the proslavery people." One night Brown led four of his sons and two other men along Pottawatomie Creek, where they seized and killed five supporters of slavery.

More violence followed as armed bands roamed the territory. Newspapers began referring to "Bleeding Kansas" and "the Civil War in Kansas." A **civil war** is a conflict between citizens of the same country. Not until October of 1856 did John Geary, the newly appointed territorial governor, stop the bloodshed in Kansas. He suppressed guerrilla forces and used 1,300 federal troops.

Violence in Congress

The violence that erupted in Kansas spilled over to the halls of Congress as well. Abolitionist senator **Charles Sumner** of Massachusetts delivered a speech entitled "The Crime Against Kansas." Sumner lashed out against proslavery forces in Kansas. He also criticized proslavery senators, repeatedly attacking Andrew P. Butler of South Carolina.

Two days after the speech, Butler's distant cousin, Representative **Preston Brooks,** walked into the Senate chamber. He hit Sumner again and again over the head and shoulders with a cane. Sumner fell to the floor, unconscious and bleeding. He suffered injuries so severe that he did not return to the Senate for several years. The Brooks-Sumner incident and the fighting in "Bleeding Kansas" revealed the rising level of hostility between North and South.

✓ **Reading Check** **Explaining** What is a civil war?

SECTION 2 ASSESSMENT

Checking for Understanding

1. **Key Terms** Use each of these terms in a sentence that will help explain its meaning: popular sovereignty, border ruffians, civil war.
2. **Reviewing Facts** Describe how Northern abolitionists reacted to the Fugitive Slave Act.

Reviewing Themes

3. **Continuity and Change** How did popular sovereignty lead to violence in Kansas?

Critical Thinking

4. **Predicting Consequences** Could the violence in Kansas have been prevented if Congress had not abandoned the Missouri Compromise? Explain.
5. **Organizing Information** Re-create the diagram below and list the steps that led to bloodshed in Kansas.

Step → Step → Bloodshed in Kansas
Step →
Step

Analyzing Visuals

6. **Geography Skills** Study the maps on page 443. From which territory or territories were the Nebraska and Kansas Territories formed? Was the Utah territory closed to slaveholding?

Interdisciplinary Activity

Descriptive Writing With members of your class, choose a scene from *Uncle Tom's Cabin* to portray in a one-act play. Write a short script, assign roles, and present it to the class.

SECTION 2 ASSESSMENT ANSWERS

1. Student work should reflect correct use of terms.
2. refused to accept the terms, aided runaways, refused to convict those accused of breaking the law
3. Outsiders corrupted the election, and fighting broke out over the results.
4. Students should state yes or no and use evidence to support their answers.
5. Answers may include: passage of Kansas-Nebraska Act; supporters and antislavery groups rush to Kansas; Missouri proslavery residents vote in Kansas; proslavery legislature elected; laws supporting slavery passed in Kansas; antislavery groups hold elections and adopt constitution; and two rival state governments exist.
6. Unorganized Territory; no

Interdisciplinary Activity
Scripts should include convincing dialogue.

SECTION 3 Challenges to Slavery

Guide to Reading

Main Idea
Social, economic, and political differences divided the North and South.

Key Terms
arsenal, martyr

Reading Strategy
Sequencing Information As you read the section, re-create the diagram below and list major events for each year.

1846	1854	1856	1858
□	□	□	□

Read to Learn
• why the Republican Party was formed.
• how the *Dred Scott* decision, the Lincoln-Douglas debates, and John Brown's raid affected Americans.

Section Theme
Continuity and Change The slavery issues continued to drive the North and South further apart.

Preview of Events

♦1854   ♦1856   ♦1858   ♦1860

1854
Republican Party is formed

1856
James Buchanan is elected president

1857
Dred Scott decision states that all slaves are property

1859
John Brown raids Harpers Ferry, Virginia

Kansas Free-Soil poster

***
★★★★★★★
AN
American Story
***

Many people considered John Brown to be a radical murderer, while others viewed him as a fighter for the cause of freedom. When he was executed in 1859, the *Anglo-African Magazine* wrote that, as John Brown left the jail, "a black woman, with a little child in her arms, stood near his way. . . . He stopped for a moment in his course, stooped over, and with the tenderness of one whose love is as broad as the brotherhood of man, kissed the child affectionately."

A New Political Party

Even before Brown's raid, other events had driven the North and South further apart. After the Kansas–Nebraska Act, the Democratic Party began to divide along sectional lines, with Northern Democrats leaving the party. Differing views over the slavery issue destroyed the Whig Party.

In 1854 antislavery Whigs and Democrats joined forces with Free-Soilers to form the **Republican Party.** The new party was determined to rally "for the establishment of liberty and the overthrow of the Slave Power."

CHAPTER 15   Road to Civil War   **445**

2 TEACH

Creating a Diagram Discuss the reasons why a third party could develop in a two-party political system, such as the United States. Explain that the Kansas-Nebraska Act changed the political parties in the United States. Ask students to work in small groups to create a poster-size diagram of the changes in the political parties outlined in this section. Post the diagrams on the bulletin board to be used in the "CLOSE" activity. **L1, ELL**

✓ Reading Check

Answer: It wanted to ban slavery from expanding into the new territories.

Picturing **History**

Answer: The Court ruled that Scott was an enslaved person who had no right to bring a lawsuit; an enslaved person was property and Congress could not take the property away without "due process of law"; and Congress had no power to prohibit slavery in any territory.

The Republicans challenged the proslavery Whigs and Democrats, choosing candidates to run in the state and congressional elections of 1854. Their main message was that the government should ban slavery from new territories.

The Republican Party quickly showed its strength in the North. In the election, the Republicans won control of the House of Representatives and of several state governments. In the South the Republicans had almost no support.

Northern Democrats suffered a beating. Almost three-fourths of the Democratic candidates from free states lost in 1854. The party was increasingly becoming a Southern party.

The Election of 1856

Democrats and Republicans met again in the presidential election of 1856. The Whig Party, disintegrating over the slavery issue, did not offer a candidate of its own.

The Republicans chose **John C. Frémont** of California as their candidate for president. Frémont had gained fame as an explorer in the West. The party platform called for free territories and its campaign slogan became "Free soil, free speech, and Frémont."

The Democratic Party nominated **James Buchanan** of Pennsylvania, an experienced diplomat and former member of Congress. The party endorsed the idea of popular sovereignty.

DRED SCOTT
SUBJECT OF THE DECISION OF
THE SUPREME COURT OF THE
UNITED STATES IN 1857 WHICH
DENIED CITIZENSHIP TO THE
NEGRO, VOIDED THE MISSOURI
COMPROMISE ACT, BECAME
ONE OF THE EVENTS THAT
RESULTED IN THE CIVIL WAR.

Picturing **History**

Family members (left) honor the memory of Dred Scott. Scott (above), who lived in slavery, had appealed to the Supreme Court in hopes of being granted his freedom. **How did the Court rule?**

The American Party, or Know Nothings, had grown quickly between 1853 and 1856 by attacking immigrants. The Know Nothings nominated former president Millard Fillmore.

The presidential vote divided along rigid sectional lines. Buchanan won the election, winning all of the Southern states except Maryland and received 174 electoral votes compared to 114 for Frémont and 8 for Fillmore. Frémont did not receive a single electoral vote south of the Mason-Dixon line, but he carried 11 of the 16 free states.

✓ Reading Check **Explaining** What stand did the new Republican party take on the issue of slavery?

The *Dred Scott* Decision

President Buchanan took office on March 4, 1857. Two days later the Supreme Court announced a decision about slavery and the territories that shook the nation.

Dred Scott was an enslaved African American bought by an army doctor in Missouri, a slave state. In the 1830s the doctor moved his household to Illinois, a free state, and then to the Wisconsin Territory, where slavery was banned by the Northwest Ordinance of 1787. Later the family returned to Missouri, where the doctor died. In 1846, with the help of antislavery lawyers, Scott sued for his freedom. He claimed he should be free because he had once lived on free soil. Eleven years later, in the midst of growing anger over the slavery issue, the case reached the Supreme Court.

The case attracted enormous attention. While the immediate issue was Dred Scott's status, the

---

Reading Strategy ▶ READING THE TEXT

Reading Maps, Graphs, and Charts Conflicts can be resolved in many different ways. Organize students into three groups. Have the groups research how conflicts were resolved between racial, ethnic, and religious groups. Within each group, students should research how conflicts were resolved in the 1600s, 1700s, and 1800s. As a class, create a chart that identifies the different racial, ethnic, and religious groups, the resolutions, and the centuries in which the resolutions occurred. **L3**

"This Union can exist forever divided into free and slave states, as our fathers made it."
—Stephen Douglas

"I believe that this government cannot endure permanently half slave and half free."
—Abraham Lincoln

L1, ELL

Guided Reading Activity 15–3

Name _____ Date _____ Class _____

★ Guided Reading Activity **15-3**

DIRECTIONS: **Recalling the Facts** Use the information in your textbook to answer the questions. Use another sheet of paper if necessary.
1. Who joined forces to form the Republican Party in 1854? _____
2. What was the main message of Republican candidates in the elections of 1854? _____
3. What did the results of the elections reveal about the Democratic Party? _____
4. Whom did each party nominate in the presidential election of 1856?
  a) Republican: _____
  b) Democratic: _____
  c) American: _____

Court also had the opportunity to rule on the question of slavery in territories. Many Americans hoped that the Court would resolve the issue for good.

The Court's Decision

The Court's decision electrified the nation. Chief Justice **Roger B. Taney** (TAW•nee) said that Dred Scott was still a slave. As a slave, Scott was not a citizen and had no right to bring a lawsuit. Taney could have stopped there, but he decided to address the broader issues.

Taney wrote that Scott's residence on free soil did not make him free. An enslaved person was property, and the Fifth Amendment prohibits Congress from taking away property without "due process of law."

Finally, Taney wrote that Congress had no power to prohibit slavery in any territory. The Missouri Compromise—which had banned slavery north of 36°30'N latitude—was unconstitutional. For that matter, so was popular sovereignty. Not even the voters in a territory could prohibit slavery because that would amount to taking away a person's property. In effect, the decision meant that the Constitution protected slavery. 📖 *(See page 624 of the Appendix for a summary of the* Dred Scott *decision.)*

Reaction to the Decision

Rather than settling the issue, the Supreme Court's decision divided the country even more. Many Southerners were elated. The Court had reaffirmed what many in the South had always maintained: Nothing could legally prevent the

spread of slavery. Northern Democrats were pleased that the Republicans' main issue—restricting the spread of slavery—had been ruled unconstitutional.

Republicans and other antislavery groups were outraged, calling the *Dred Scott* decision "a wicked and false judgment" and "the greatest crime" ever committed in the nation's courts.

Lincoln and Douglas

In the congressional election of 1858, the Senate race in Illinois was the center of national attention. The contest pitted the current senator, Democrat Stephen A. Douglas, against Republican challenger **Abraham Lincoln.** People considered Douglas a likely candidate for president in 1860. Lincoln was nearly an unknown.

Douglas, a successful lawyer, had joined the Democratic Party and won election to the House in 1842 and to the Senate in 1846. Short, stocky, and powerful, Douglas was called "the Little Giant." He disliked slavery but thought that the controversy over it would interfere with the nation's growth. He believed the issue could be resolved through popular sovereignty.

Born in the poor backcountry of Kentucky, Abraham Lincoln moved to Indiana as a child, and later to Illinois. Like Douglas, Lincoln was intelligent, ambitious, and a successful lawyer. He had little formal education—but excellent political instincts. Although Lincoln saw slavery as morally wrong, he admitted there was no easy way to eliminate slavery where it already existed. He was certain, though, that slavery should not be allowed to spread.

3 ASSESS

Assign Section 3 Assessment as homework or as an in-class activity.

🔘 Have students use **Interactive Tutor Self-Assessment CD-ROM.**

L2

Section Quiz 15–3

Name _____ Date _____ Class _____

★ Chapter 15   Score ☐

Section Quiz 15-3

DIRECTIONS: **Matching** Match the items in Column A with the items in Column B. Write the correct letters in the blanks. *(10 points each)*

Column A	Column B
___ 1. sued for freedom	A. John C. Frémont
___ 2. 1856 Republican candidate	B. Millard Fillmore
___ 3. 1856 Democratic candidate	C. Stephen A. Douglas
___ 4. 1856 Know-Nothing candidate	D. Dred Scott
___ 5. "the Little Giant"	E. James Buchanan

DIRECTIONS: **Multiple Choice** In the blank at the left, write the letter of the

L1

Reteaching Activity 15–3

Name _____ Date _____ Class _____

★ Reteaching Activity **15-3**

DIRECTIONS: **Organizing Facts** The items in the Fact Bank describe Stephen Douglas and Abraham Lincoln before the 1858 congressional election. Complete the chart by writing the letter of each item in the correct place on the chart.

Lincoln-Douglas Debates	
Abraham Lincoln	**Stephen Douglas**

DIFFERENTIATED INSTRUCTION

Gifted and Talented Discuss the effects of the *Dred Scott* decision, the Lincoln-Douglas debates, and John Brown's raid. Have students imagine living in the North or the South during the time period covered in this section and think about what it would have been like. Have students decide which event would have had the most impact on their lives. Then have students write a poem or short story describing the event and its personal impact. **L3**

👉 Refer to *Inclusion for the Middle School Social Studies Classroom Strategies and Activities* in the TCR.

✓ **Reading Check**

Answer: It stated that neither Congress nor voters had any power to prohibit slavery in any territory.

L1, ELL

Reading Essentials and Study Guide 15–3

Study Guide

Chapter 15, Section 3
For use with textbook pages 445–448

CHALLENGES TO SLAVERY

KEY TERMS	
arsenal	A storage place for weapons and ammunition (page 448)
martyr	A person who dies for a great cause (page 448)

DRAWING FROM EXPERIENCE

Have you ever taken an argument to someone else to settle? Were you pleased or disappointed with the result? Did you think the decision was fair?

In the last section, you read about the growing division of the country over slavery. This section focuses on decisions and beliefs about slavery that drive the North and South even further apart.

ORGANIZING YOUR THOUGHTS

Use the chart below to ...

L3

Enrichment Activity 15–3

Name _____ Date _____ Class _____

★ Enrichment Activity 15-3 ★

Dred Scott

The Supreme Court decision on the case of *Dred Scott v. Sanford* caused an uproar. Eventually, it became one of only four Supreme Court decisions that were overturned by a constitutional amendment. Study the poster below that appeared in 1857.

DIRECTIONS:
Understanding Information
Answer the following questions.

1. What is the poster announcing?

2. At what point in the case was this announcement made?

3. Exactly when and where is the meeting to be held?

4. Who will speak at the meeting? Who else of note will attend?

5. Who is invited?

6. What is the cost?

A PUBLIC MEETING
WILL BE HELD ON
THURSDAY EVENING, 2D INSTANT.

7 o'clock in **ISRAEL CHURCH**, to consider atrocious decision of the Supreme Court in the

DRED SCOTT CASE

and other outrages to which the colored people are subject under the Justices of the United States.

C.L. REMOND,
ROBERT PURVIS,

and others will be speakers on the occasion. Mrs. MOTT, Mr. M'KIM and B.S. JONES of Ohio, have also accepted invitations to be present.

All persons are invited to attend.
Admittance is free.

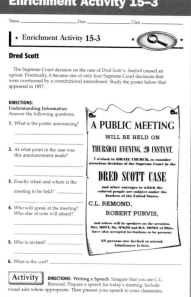

Activity | **DIRECTIONS: Writing a Speech** Imagine that you are C.L. Remond. Prepare a speech for today's meeting. Include visual aids where appropriate. Then present your speech to your classmates.

4 CLOSE

Ask students to form the same groups as in the "TEACH" activity on page 446 to complete their diagrams of the political parties. Tell students to add the following to their diagrams for each political party: party platform, major party leaders, party supporters.

448

The Lincoln–Douglas Debates

Not as well known as Douglas, Lincoln challenged the senator to a series of debates. Douglas reluctantly agreed. The two met seven times in August, September, and October of 1858 in cities and villages throughout Illinois. Thousands came to these debates. The main topic, of course, was slavery.

During the debate at Freeport, Lincoln pressed Douglas about his views on popular sovereignty. Could the people of a territory legally exclude slavery before achieving statehood? Douglas replied that the people could exclude slavery by refusing to pass laws protecting slaveholders' rights. Douglas's response, which satisfied antislavery followers but lost him support in the South, became known as the **Freeport Doctrine.**

Douglas claimed that Lincoln wanted African Americans to be fully equal to whites. Lincoln denied this. Still, Lincoln said, "in the right to eat the bread . . . which his own hand earns, [an African American] is my equal and the equal of [Senator] Douglas, and the equal of every living man." The real issue, Lincoln said, is "between the men who think slavery a wrong and those who do not think it wrong. The Republican Party thinks it wrong."

Following the debates, Douglas won a narrow victory in the election. Lincoln lost the election but gained a national reputation.

The Raid on Harpers Ferry

After the 1858 elections, Southerners began to feel threatened by growing Republican power. In late 1859, an act of violence greatly increased their fears. On October 16 the abolitionist John Brown led 18 men, both whites and African Americans, on a raid on Harpers Ferry, Virginia. His target was an arsenal, a storage place for weapons and ammunition. Brown—who had killed five proslavery Kansans in 1856—hoped to start a rebellion against slaveholders by arming enslaved African Americans. His raid had been financed by a group of abolitionists.

Brown and his men were quickly defeated by local citizens and federal troops. Brown was convicted of treason and murder and was sentenced to hang. His execution caused an uproar in the North. Some antislavery Northerners, including Republican leaders, denounced Brown's use of violence. Others viewed Brown as a hero. Writer Ralph Waldo Emerson called Brown a martyr—a person who dies for a great cause.

John Brown's death became a rallying point for abolitionists. When Southerners learned of Brown's connection to abolitionists, their fears of a great Northern conspiracy against them seemed to be confirmed. The nation was on the brink of disaster.

✓ **Reading Check** **Explaining** How did the *Dred Scott* decision regulate the spread of slavery?

SECTION 3 ASSESSMENT

Checking for Understanding

1. **Key Terms** Use the terms arsenal and martyr in a paragraph about John Brown's raid on Harpers Ferry.
2. **Reviewing Facts** Discuss stages in the development of the Republican Party.

Reviewing Themes

3. **Continuity and Change** How did the *Dred Scott* decision reverse a previous decision made by Congress? What was the reaction of Republicans?

Critical Thinking

4. **Making Inferences** Why did Lincoln emerge as a leader after the Lincoln-Douglas debates?
5. **Organizing Information** Re-create the table shown here, and describe the positions taken by Lincoln and Douglas in their debates.

Lincoln–Douglas Debates	
Lincoln's position	Douglas's position

Analyzing Visuals

6. **Examining Artifacts** Examine the poster on page 445. What is the poster advertising? Explain why some of the phrases are in larger type.

Interdisciplinary Activity

Government Draw a political cartoon that illustrates Lincoln's statement "A house divided against itself cannot stand."

SECTION 3 ASSESSMENT ANSWERS

1. Student work should reflect correct use of terms.
2. Northern Democrats left the party; the Whig Party dissolved; antislavery Whigs and Democrats joined Free-Soilers to form the Republican Party.
3. It ruled the Missouri Compromise unconstitutional by stating that Congress could not prohibit slavery in any territory; they were outraged.
4. He gained a national reputation.
5. Lincoln: government could not endure half slave and half free, all people have the right to enjoy the benefits of their work; Douglas: could exclude slavery by refusing to pass laws protecting slaveholders' rights
6. the free state of Kansas; *slavery* is in larger print because it was an important issue and *mass meeting* is enlarged because it emphasizes group support

Interdisciplinary Activity Cartoons should illustrate the idea.

SECTION **4** Secession and War

Guide to Reading

Main Idea
In 1860 Abraham Lincoln's election as president of the United States was followed by Southern states leaving the Union.

Key Terms
secession, states' rights

Reading Strategy
Sequencing Information As you read the section, re-create the time line below and list the major events at each time.

Nov. 1860		Feb. 1861		April 1861
	Dec. 1860		March 1861	

Read to Learn
• how the 1860 election led to the breakup of the Union.
• why secession led to the Civil War.

Section Theme
Geography and History The election of 1860 clearly divided the nation along sectional lines.

Preview of Events

♦1860   ♦1861   ♦1862

Nov. 1860
Abraham Lincoln is elected president

Dec. 1860
South Carolina secedes

February 1861
Southern states form the Confederate States of America

April 1861
Confederate forces attack Fort Sumter; the Civil War begins

Secessionist ribbon

AN *American Story*

After John Brown's raid on Harpers Ferry, calls for secession grew. South Carolina's *Charleston Mercury* declared "The day of compromise is passed . . . [T]here is no peace for the South in the Union." The *Nashville Union and American* said, "The South will hold the whole party of Republicans responsible for the bloodshed at Harpers Ferry." Republicans refused to take the threat of secession seriously. Secession is only a scare tactic, they argued, aimed at frightening voters from casting their ballot for Abraham Lincoln. To many Southerners, however, the election of Lincoln would be a final signal that their position in the Union was hopeless.

The Election of 1860

Would the Union break up? That was the burning question in the months before the presidential election of 1860. The issue of slavery was seriously discussed and eventually caused a break in the Democratic Party. As the election approached, a northern wing of the Democratic Party nominated Stephen

CHAPTER 15   Road to Civil War   **449**

1 FOCUS

Section Overview
This section details the final events that culminated in the secession of the Southern states from the Union.

BELLRINGER
Skillbuilder Activity

 Project transparency and have students answer the question.

Daily Focus Skills Transparency 15–4

Reading Preview

Answers to Graphic: November 1860: Abraham Lincoln is elected president; December 1860: South Carolina secedes; February 1861: Southern states form the Confederate States of America; March 1861: Lincoln gives Inaugural Address; April 1861: Confederate forces attack Fort Sumter; the Civil War begins

Preteaching Vocabulary
🕮 Use the **Vocabulary PuzzleMaker CD-ROM** to create crossword and word search puzzles.

SECTION RESOURCES

📖 Reproducible Masters
• Reproducible Lesson Plan 15–4
• Daily Lecture and Discussion Notes 15–4
• Guided Reading Activity 15–4
• Section Quiz 15–4
• Reteaching Activity 15–4
• Reading Essentials and Study Guide 15–4
• Enrichment Activity 15–4

🖥 Transparencies
• Daily Focus Skills Transparency 15–4

Multimedia
📻 American Music: Hits Through History
🕮 Vocabulary PuzzleMaker CD-ROM
🕮 Interactive Tutor Self-Assessment CD-ROM
🕮 ExamView® Pro Testmaker CD-ROM
🕮 Presentation Plus! CD-ROM

CHAPTER 15
Section 4, 449–453

2 TEACH

Daily Lecture and Discussion Notes 15-4

Copyright © by The McGraw-Hill Companies, Inc.

Daily Lecture and Discussion Notes

Chapter 15, Section 4

Did You Know? Although Mary Todd Lincoln was the First Lady of the United States during the Civil War, the South considered Varina Howell Davis, Jefferson Davis's wife, First Lady of the Confederate States during the same time. After her husband's death in 1889, she wrote her memoirs and moved to New York City to support herself by writing magazine articles. She died in 1905.

I. The Election of 1860 (Pages 449–450)

    A. In the months leading up to the election of 1860, the issue of slavery split the Democratic Party along sectional lines. A Northern wing of the Democratic Party nominated Stephen Douglas, supporter of popular sovereignty. Southern Democrats nominated John C. Breckinridge of Kentucky, who supported the *Dred Scott* decision. Moderates from the North and South formed the Union Party and nominated John...

Predicting Outcomes Ask students to create a chart of the election of 1860, listing the candidates and how the states voted. Have students use the map in the Chapter Assessment and Activities to find this information. Then have them add a column to their charts to predict which states will secede from the Union. Tell students to keep these charts to use for the "CLOSE" activity. **L1**

TWO VIEWPOINTS

Answers:

1. the issue of whether slavery was right and should have been extended or whether it was wrong and should not have been extended
2. a divorced husband and wife
3. Both hinted that war may be necessary to resolve the issue.

✓ Reading Check

Answer: the issue of slavery

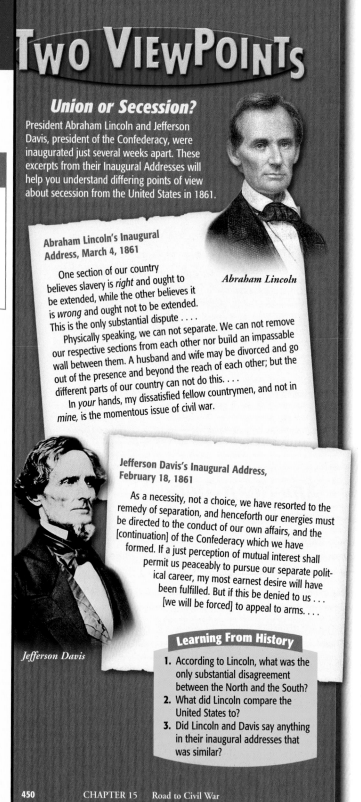

TWO VIEWPOINTS

Union or Secession?

President Abraham Lincoln and Jefferson Davis, president of the Confederacy, were inaugurated just several weeks apart. These excerpts from their Inaugural Addresses will help you understand differing points of view about secession from the United States in 1861.

Abraham Lincoln's Inaugural Address, March 4, 1861

One section of our country believes slavery is *right* and ought to be extended, while the other believes it is *wrong* and ought not to be extended. This is the only substantial dispute . . . .

Physically speaking, we can not separate. We can not remove our respective sections from each other nor build an impassable wall between them. A husband and wife may be divorced and go out of the presence and beyond the reach of each other; but the different parts of our country can not do this. . . .

In *your* hands, my dissatisfied fellow countrymen, and not in *mine*, is the momentous issue of civil war.

Abraham Lincoln

Jefferson Davis's Inaugural Address, February 18, 1861

As a necessity, not a choice, we have resorted to the remedy of separation, and henceforth our energies must be directed to the conduct of our own affairs, and the [continuation] of the Confederacy which we have formed. If a just perception of mutual interest shall permit us peaceably to pursue our separate political career, my most earnest desire will have been fulfilled. But if this be denied to us . . . [we will be forced] to appeal to arms. . . .

Jefferson Davis

Learning From History

1. According to Lincoln, what was the only substantial disagreement between the North and the South?
2. What did Lincoln compare the United States to?
3. Did Lincoln and Davis say anything in their inaugural addresses that was similar?

450   CHAPTER 15   Road to Civil War

Douglas for the presidency and supported popular sovereignty. Southern Democrats—vowing to uphold slavery—nominated John C. Breckinridge of Kentucky and supported the *Dred Scott* decision. Moderates from both the North and South who had formed the Constitutional Union Party nominated John Bell of Tennessee. This party took no position on slavery.

Lincoln Nominated

The Republicans nominated Abraham Lincoln. Their platform, designed to attract voters from many quarters, was that slavery should be left undisturbed where it existed, but that it should be excluded from the territories. Many Southerners feared, however, that a Republican victory would encourage slave revolts.

Lincoln Elected

With the Democrats divided, Lincoln won a clear majority of the electoral votes—180 out of 303. He received only 40 percent of the popular vote, but this was more than any other candidate. Douglas was second with 30 percent of the vote.

The vote was along purely sectional lines. Lincoln's name did not even appear on the ballot in most Southern states, but he won every Northern state. Breckinridge swept the South, and Bell took most border states. Douglas won only the state of Missouri and three of New Jersey's seven electoral votes.

In effect, the more populous North had outvoted the South. The victory for Lincoln was a short-lived one, however, for the nation Lincoln was to lead would soon disintegrate.

✓ **Reading Check Examining** What caused the split in the Democratic Party in 1860?

Reading Strategy | READING THE TEXT

Sequencing Information Organize the class into groups of six to create a bulletin board time line illustrating factors leading to the Civil War. Have groups skim the chapter to determine what factors to include on the time line. Have students choose the following roles: identify dates; draw the time line listing dates, people, and events; illustrate the people; illustrate the events; write short descriptions of people; write short descriptions of events. Have groups construct the time line on the bulletin board. **L1, ELL**

450

The South Secedes

Lincoln and the Republicans had promised not to disturb slavery where it already existed. Many people in the South, however, did not trust the party, fearing that the Republican administration would not protect Southern rights. On December 20, 1860, the South's long-standing threat to leave the Union became a reality when South Carolina held a special convention and voted to secede.

Attempt at Compromise

Even after South Carolina's action, many people still wished to preserve the Union. The question was *how*. As other Southern states debated secession—withdrawal from the Union—leaders in Washington, D.C., worked frantically to fashion a last-minute compromise. On December 18, 1860, Senator **John Crittenden** of Kentucky proposed a series of amendments to the Constitution. Central to Crittenden's plan was a provision to protect slavery south of 36°30'N latitude—the line set by the Missouri Compromise—in all territories "now held or hereafter acquired."

Republicans considered this unacceptable. They had just won an election on the principle that slavery would not be extended in any territories. "Now we are told," Lincoln said,

❝the government shall be broken up, unless we surrender to those we have beaten.❞

Leaders in the South also rejected the plan. "We spit upon every plan to compromise," exclaimed one Southern leader. "No human power can save the Union," wrote another.

The Confederacy

By February 1861, Texas, Louisiana, Mississippi, Alabama, Florida, and Georgia had joined South Carolina and also seceded. Delegates from these states and South Carolina met in Montgomery, Alabama, on February 4 to form a new nation and government. Calling themselves the **Confederate States of America,** they chose **Jefferson Davis,** a senator from Mississippi, as their president.

Southerners justified secession with the theory of states' rights. The states, they argued, had voluntarily chosen to enter the Union. They defined the Constitution as a contract among the independent states. Now because the national government had violated that contract—by refusing to enforce the Fugitive Slave Act and by denying the Southern states equal rights in the territories—the states were justified in leaving the Union.

Reactions to Secession

Many Southerners welcomed secession. In Charleston, South Carolina, people rang church bells, fired cannons, and celebrated in the streets. A newspaper in Atlanta, Georgia, said the South "will never submit" and would defend its liberties no matter what the cost.

Other Southerners, however, were alarmed. A South Carolinian wrote,

❝My heart has been rent [torn] by . . . the destruction of my country—the dismemberment of that great and glorious Union.❞

Virginian Robert E. Lee expressed concern about the future. "I see only that a fearful calamity is upon us," he wrote.

In the North some abolitionists preferred to allow the Southern states to leave. If the Union could be kept together only by compromising on slavery, they declared, then let the Union be destroyed. Most Northerners, however, believed that the Union must be preserved. For Lincoln the issue was "whether in a free government the minority have the right to break up the government whenever they choose."

Presidential Responses

Lincoln had won the election, but he was not yet president. James Buchanan's term ran until March 4, 1861. In December 1860, Buchanan sent a message to Congress saying that the Southern states had no right to secede. Then he added that he had no power to stop them from doing so.

As Lincoln prepared for his inauguration on March 4, 1861, people in both the North and the South wondered what he would say and do. They wondered, too, what would happen in Vir-

L1, ELL

Guided Reading Activity 15–4

Name _____ Date _____ Class _____

★ **Guided Reading Activity 15-4**

DIRECTIONS: Filling in the Blanks Use your textbook to fill in the blanks using the words in the box. Some words may be used more than once. Use another sheet of paper if necessary.

John Breckinridge	Charleston Harbor	Texas	Confederate States of America
Abraham Lincoln	federal property	Georgia	popular sovereignty
Jefferson Davis	Civil War	slavery	December 20, 1860
John Crittenden	states' rights	shooting	unarmed expedition
75,000 troops	April 12, 1861	36°30′N	33 hours

The Election of 1860

The issue of **(1)** _____ caused the Democrats to split. Before the election of 1860, a northern wing of the Democratic Party chose Stephen A. Douglas as their candidate and endorsed **(2)** _____. Southern Democrats chose **(3)** _____ as their candidate, while the Republicans chose **(4)** _____.

The South Secedes

On **(5)** _____, South Carolina voted to secede. As other Southern states debated secession, Senator **(6)** _____ of Kentucky proposed a plan to protect slavery in territories south of **(7)** _____ latitude. By February 1, 1861, **(8)** _____, Louisiana, Mississippi, Alabama, Florida, and **(9)** _____ had also seceded. The seceded states called themselves the **(10)** _____ and elected **(11)** _____ as their president. Southerners justified secession with the theory of **(12)** _____. In his Inaugural Address, Abraham Lincoln said that secession would not be permitted, vowing to hold **(13)** _____ in the South and to enforce the nation's laws.

Fort Sumter

Confederate troops demanded the surrender of Fort Sumter, a United States fort on an island guarding the **(14)** _____. In response, Lincoln sent an **(15)** _____ with much-needed supplies to the fort. Lincoln left the decision to start **(16)** _____ up to the Confederacy. On **(17)** _____, Confederate guns opened fire on the fort. The Union garrison held out for **(18)** _____ before surrendering. Following the attack, President Lincoln issued a call for **(19)** _____ to fight to save the Union. The **(20)** _____ had begun.

History *and the* Humanities

🏳 American Music: Hits Through History: "John Brown's Dream"

Who?What?Where?When?

Jefferson Davis Jefferson Davis was a leading spokesperson for states' rights. While in the Senate, he defended slavery, including its constitutional protection in the territories. He also advocated reinstituting the slave trade. Though he favored secession, he did not immediately welcome being chosen as president of the Confederacy.

DIFFERENTIATED INSTRUCTION

Reading Support Many songs were used as rallying cries at the beginning of the Civil War. Have students decide whether each song rallied the North or the South. Assign individual students to write the lyrics of a patriotic song favoring either the North or the South. Ask volunteers to read aloud their lyrics to the class and allow the class to decide whether the song best represents the North or the South. **L2**

👉 Refer to *Inclusion for the Middle School Social Studies Classroom Strategies and Activities* in the TCR.

Geography Skills

Answers:
1. Missouri, Kentucky, Maryland, Delaware
2. Virginia, North Carolina, Tennessee, Arkansas

✓ Reading Check

Answer: They believed their states' rights had been violated by the federal government, nullifying the contract between the states and the Union.

3 ASSESS

Assign Section 4 Assessment as homework or as an in-class activity.

🌐 Have students use **Interactive Tutor Self-Assessment CD-ROM.**

L2

Section Quiz 15–4

L1

Reteaching Activity 15–4

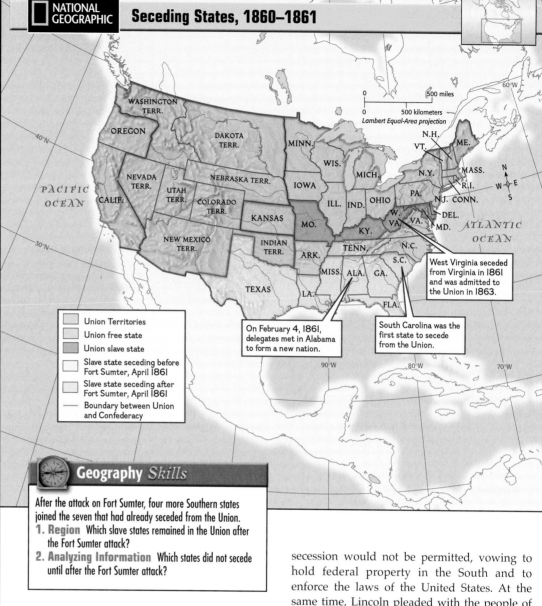

NATIONAL GEOGRAPHIC   Seceding States, 1860–1861

West Virginia seceded from Virginia in 1861 and was admitted to the Union in 1863.

On February 4, 1861, delegates met in Alabama to form a new nation.

South Carolina was the first state to secede from the Union.

- ☐ Union Territories
- ☐ Union free state
- ☐ Union slave state
- ☐ Slave state seceding before Fort Sumter, April 1861
- ☐ Slave state seceding after Fort Sumter, April 1861
- — Boundary between Union and Confederacy

Geography Skills

After the attack on Fort Sumter, four more Southern states joined the seven that had already seceded from the Union.
1. **Region** Which slave states remained in the Union after the Fort Sumter attack?
2. **Analyzing Information** Which states did not secede until after the Fort Sumter attack?

ginia, North Carolina, Kentucky, Tennessee, Missouri, and Arkansas. These slave states had chosen to remain in the Union, but the decision was not final. If the United States used force against the Confederate States of America, the remaining slave states also might secede. In his Inaugural Address, the new president mixed toughness and words of peace. He said that

secession would not be permitted, vowing to hold federal property in the South and to enforce the laws of the United States. At the same time, Lincoln pleaded with the people of the South for reconciliation:

❝We are not enemies, but friends. We must not be enemies. Though passion may have strained, it must not break our bonds of affection.❞

✓ Reading Check **Explaining** How did the seceding states justify their right to leave the Union?

452   CHAPTER 15   Road to Civil War

INTERDISCIPLINARY CONNECTIONS ACTIVITY

Health More soldiers died from sickness during the Civil War than from bullets. Improper food and sanitation caused diarrhea, dysentery, measles, smallpox, typhoid, gangrene, and chicken pox, killing more than 400,000 soldiers. Have students investigate the causes, symptoms, and cures for the sicknesses noted above. **L2**

Fort Sumter

The South soon tested President Lincoln's vow to hold federal property. Confederate forces had already seized some United States forts within their states. Although Lincoln did not want to start a war by trying to take the forts back, allowing the Confederates to keep them would amount to admitting their right to secede.

On the day after his inauguration, Lincoln received a dispatch from the commander of **Fort Sumter,** a United States fort on an island guarding Charleston Harbor. The message warned that the fort was low on supplies and that the Confederates demanded its surrender.

The War Begins

Lincoln responded by sending a message to Governor Francis Pickens of South Carolina. He informed Pickens that he was sending an unarmed expedition with supplies to Fort Sumter. Lincoln promised that Union forces would not "throw in men, arms, or ammunition" unless they were fired upon. The president thus left the decision to start shooting up to the Confederates.

Confederate president Jefferson Davis and his advisers made a fateful choice. They ordered their forces to attack Fort Sumter before the Union supplies could arrive. Confederate guns opened fire on the fort early on April 12, 1861. Union captain Abner Doubleday witnessed the attack from inside the fort:

66 Showers of balls . . . and shells . . . poured into the fort in one incessant stream, causing great flakes of masonry to fall in all directions. 99

High seas had prevented Union relief ships from reaching the besieged fort. The Union garrison held out for 33 hours before surrendering on April 14. Thousands of shots were exchanged during the siege, but there was no loss of life on either side. The Confederates hoisted their flag over the fort, and all the guns in the harbor sounded a triumphant salute.

News of the attack galvanized the North. President Lincoln issued a call for 75,000 troops to fight to save the Union, and volunteers quickly signed up. Meanwhile, Virginia, North Carolina, Tennessee, and Arkansas voted to join the Confederacy. The Civil War had begun.

✓**Reading Check** **Explaining** What action did Lincoln take after the attack on Fort Sumter?

HISTORY Online
Student Web Activity
Visit tarvol1.glencoe.com and click on **Chapter 15— Student Web Activities** for an activity on the period leading up to the Civil War.

SECTION 4 ASSESSMENT

Checking for Understanding

1. **Key Terms** Write a newspaper article about the election of 1860, using the terms states' rights and secession.

2. **Reviewing Facts** Who served as the president of the Confederate States of America?

Reviewing Themes

3. **Geography and History** What role did sectionalism play in Lincoln's winning the 1860 election?

Critical Thinking

4. **Drawing Conclusions** Do you think either Northerners or Southerners believed that secession would *not* lead to war? Explain.

5. **Organizing Information** Re-create the diagram below. In the ovals, describe the events leading to the firing on Fort Sumter.

Analyzing Visuals

6. **Geography Skills** Examine the map on page 452. How many states made up the Confederacy? Which state seceded earlier—Mississippi or Arkansas?

Interdisciplinary Activity

Expository Writing Reread the excerpts on pages 450 and 452 from Lincoln's first inaugural address. Write a paragraph expressing in your own words what Lincoln said about government, union, liberty, and equality.

SECTION 4 ASSESSMENT ANSWERS

1. Student work should reflect correct use of terms.
2. Jefferson Davis
3. He won in every Northern state; votes in the South were divided among three other candidates.

4. Students should support their answers with valid reasoning.
5. Dispatch received warning that fort is low on supplies and Confederates demand its surrender; Lincoln sends expedition with supplies; Davis decides to attack Fort Sumter; Civil War begins.
6. 11 states; Mississippi

Interdisciplinary Activity Students should offer valid paraphrases.

Objectives and answers to the student activity can be found in the **Web Activity Lesson Plan** feature at tarvol1.glencoe.com

✓**Reading Check**

Answer: He issued a call for 75,000 troops to fight to save the Union.

L1, ELL

Reading Essentials and Study Guide 15–4

Study Guide
Chapter 15, Section 4
For use with textbook pages 449–453
SECESSION AND WAR

KEY TERMS

secession	Withdrawal from the Union (page 451)
states' rights	The rights of the state overrule the rights of the federal government (page 451)

DRAWING FROM EXPERIENCE

Have you ever had to make a difficult decision? Did it affect other people? What kind of difficult decisions do you think your parents have to make? What difficult decisions do your teachers, police, or the president of the United States have to make?

In the last section, you read about the decisions on slavery that caused growing division in the United States. This section focuses on how the Southern states separated from the Union.

L3

Enrichment Activity 15–4

Name _____ Date _____ Class _____

★ Enrichment Activity 15-4 ★

A Battle of Songs

A popular Confederate song at the start of the Civil War was "The Bonny Blue Flag." Soon, Northerners wrote "The Northern Bonny Blue Flag" for the same melody. Read the following stanzas.

Northern	Southern
We're fighting for our Union,	We are a band of brothers,
We're fighting for our trust,	And native to the soil,
We're fighting for that happy land,	Fighting for the property
Where sleeps our fathers' dust.	We gained by honest toil;
It cannot be dissevered,	And when our rights were threatened,
Though it cost us bloody wars,	The cry rose near and far:
We never can give up the land	"Hurrah for the Bonny Blue Flag
Where floats the Stripes and Stars.	That bears a single star!"
Hurrah! hurrah! For equal rights, hurrah!	Hurrah! hurrah! For Southern rights, hurrah!

4 CLOSE

Have students correct the charts they created in the "TEACH" activity to accurately show which states seceded from the Union. Ask volunteers to discuss the accuracy of their predictions.

TEACH

Analyzing Primary Sources

Have students read Amelia Stewart's diary entry of her family's difficult trip to Oregon. **Ask:** What happened to Lucy? *(She was accidentally left behind and rescued by another wagon train family.)* Discuss the details in the excerpt that show how difficult travel along the Oregon Trail was. **Ask:** What other problems do you think the travelers faced in their long journey to Oregon? *(Possible answers may include: disease, conflict with Native Americans, death of a family member, traveling in the mountains, bad weather, lack of food, and so on.)* Have students look at a relief map. Note the geography along the Oregon Trail.

Have students select a section of the Oregon Trail. Students should then create a diary entry based on the area they are crossing. Weather and geography should be elements included in their diary entry. Compile the diary entries creating a journal log about crossing the Oregon Trail. **L1**

Visit the **TIME** Web site at www.time.com for up-to-date news, weekly magazine articles, editorials, online polls, and an archive of past magazine and Web articles.

TIME NOTEBOOK

What were people's lives like in the past?

What—and who—were people talking about? What did they eat? What did they do for fun? These two pages will give you some clues to everyday life in the U.S. as you step back in time with TIME Notebook.

Profile

It's 1853, and **AMELIA STEWART** *is heading west to Oregon with her husband and seven children in a covered wagon. How hard can the five-month trip be? Here are two entries from her diary:*

MONDAY, AUGUST 8 We have to make a drive of 22 miles without water today. Have our cans filled to drink. Here we left, unknowingly, our [daughter] Lucy behind, not a soul had missed her until we had gone some miles, when we stopped a while to rest the cattle; just then another train drove up behind us, with Lucy. She was terribly frightened and said she was sitting under the bank of the river when we started, busy watching some wagons cross, and did not know that we were ready....It was a lesson for all of us.

FRIDAY, AUGUST 12 Lost one of our oxen. We were traveling slowly along, when he dropped dead in the yoke....I could hardly help shedding tears, when we drove round this poor ox who had helped us along thus far, and had given us his very last step.

FRONTIER FOOD
Trail Mix
Hard Tack for a Hard Trip

INGREDIENTS: 3 cups flour • 3 tsp. salt • 1 cup water

Mix all ingredients and stir until it becomes too difficult. Knead the dough; add more flour until mixture is very dry. Roll to 1/2-inch thickness and cut into 3" squares, poke with a skewer [pin] to make several holes in each piece (for easy breaking). Bake 30 minutes in a hot oven until hard. Store for up to 10 years.

454

CLOTHED. Hundreds of miners in 1850 by **LEVI STRAUSS**. Using canvas he originally intended to make into tents, Levi made sturdy, tough pants with lots of pockets—perfect clothing for the rough work of mining. Can you imagine anyone in the city ever wearing them?

MARCHED. Just under 100 camels in 1857, from San Antonio to Los Angeles, led by hired Turkish, Greek, and Armenian camel drivers. It is hoped the desert beasts will help the U.S. Army open the West.

MAILED. Thousands of letters carried by **PONY EXPRESS** in 1860 from Missouri to California in an extremely short time—only 10 days! Riders switch to fresh horses every 10 or 15 miles and continue through the night, blizzards, and attacks by outlaws.

EXTENDING THE CONTENT

Life on the Trail Life along the Oregon Trail was long, extremely difficult, and often tragic. Though often starting as part of a wagon train, individual families would be left behind to care for a sick family member or repair a wagon. Children were born along the trail, and family members died. Tolls were charged to ferry wagons across rivers or to travel along sections of the trail. Treasured family items and furniture were left behind as oxen labored to pull heavy wagons up steep embankments and mountains.

Word Watch

Can you talk "Western"? Match the words below to their meaning.

1. maverick
2. Hangtown fry
3. grubstake
4. bonanza
5. palo alto
6. pard or rawwheel

a. gold rush favorite, made of eggs, bacon, and oysters

b. inexperienced '49er; eastern type not used to wearing boots

c. a lucky discovery of gold; a source of sudden wealth

d. a style of hat worn by gold rush miners

e. an individual who takes an independent stand, from the name of a Texas cattleman who left his herd unbranded

f. food provided by an investor to a gold prospector in exchange for a share of whatever gold the prospector finds

answers: 1. e; 2. a; 3. f; 4. c; 5. d; 6. b

The Price of a Life

This notice appeared in 1852.

CREDIT SALE OF A CHOICE GANG OF 41
SLAVES!
COMPRISING MECHANICS, LABORERS, ETC.,

FOR THE SETTLEMENT OF A CO-PARTNERSHIP OF RAILROAD CONTRACTORS.

BY J. A. BEARD & MAY, J. A. BEARD, AUCT'R.

WILL BE SOLD AT AUCTION, AT BANKS' ARCADE, MAGAZINE STREET.

SALE OF SLAVES AND STOCK

The Negroes and Stock listed below are a Prime Lot, and belong to the ESTATE OF THE LATE LUTHER McGOWAN, and will be sold on Monday, Sept. 22nd, 1852, at the Fair Grounds, in Savannah, Georgia, at 1:00 P.M. The Negroes will be taken to the grounds two days previous to the Sale, so that they may be inspected by prospective buyers.

On account of the low prices listed below, they will be sold for cash only, and must be taken into custody within two hours after sale.

No.	Name	Age	Remarks	Price
1	Lunesta	27	Prime Rice Planter	
2	Violet	16	Housework and Nursemaid	$1,275.00
3	Lizzie	30	Rice, Unsound	900.00
4	Minda	27	Cotton, Prime Woman	300.00
5	Adam	28	Cotton, Prime Young Man	1,200.00
6	Abel	41	Rice Hand, Eyesight Poor	1,100.00
7	Tanney	22	Prime Cotton Hand	675.00
8	Flementina	39	Good Cook	950.00

CHICAGO HISTORICAL SOCIETY/PHOTO RESEARCHERS INC.

NUMBERS

U.S. AT THE TIME

$81,249,700
Estimated value of gold mined in 1852

BROWN BROTHERS

89 Days
it takes the American clipper ship, the *Flying Cloud*, to go from Boston around Cape Horn to San Francisco in 1851—a trip that normally takes eight or nine months

12 Poems
included in Walt Whitman's new collection, called *Leaves of Grass* (1855)

33 Number of states
in 1859 after Oregon enters the union

100 Seats in Congress
won by the Republicans in 1854, the year the party was created

300,000
Copies of Harriet Beecher Stowe's novel, *Uncle Tom's Cabin*, sold in 1852

UNCLE TOM'S CABIN;
OR,
LIFE AMONG THE LOWLY.
BY
HARRIET BEECHER STOWE.

VOL. I.
FIFTIETH THOUSAND.

BOSTON:
JOHN P. JEWETT & COMPANY.
CLEVELAND, OHIO:
JEWETT, PROCTOR & WORTHINGTON.
1852.

NORTH WIND PICTURE ARCHIVES

455

GLENCOE TECHNOLOGY

MindJogger Videoquiz
Use **MindJogger Videoquiz** to review the Chapter 15 content.

Available in VHS

Reviewing Key Terms

1.–10. Students should write five true statements and five false statements, each of which should include one of the ten terms. Students should provide a written explanation for each false statement.

Reviewing Key Facts

11. to ease tension between the North and South by preserving the balance between slave and free states in Congress

12. California: admitted as free state; no restrictions on slavery in New Mexico Territory; New Mexico–Texas border dispute resolved in favor of New Mexico; slave trade abolished in District of Columbia; fugitive slave law was strengthened

13. to abandon the Missouri Compromise and let settlers in each territory decide by popular sovereignty

14. Lincoln became a national figure following a series of debates with Stephen Douglas.

15. a Supreme Court decision that considered enslaved African Americans not to be free just because they lived on free soil, declared enslaved African Americans were property, and stated that neither Congress nor voters could prohibit slavery in any territory; that the Constitution now protected slavery

16. The issue of slavery divided the Democratic Party into three factions: Northern Democrats nominated Stephen Douglas, Southern Democrats nominated John C. Breckinridge, moderate Democrats formed the Constitutional Union

456

Chapter Summary
Road to Civil War

1820
- Missouri Compromise passed

1844
- Polk elected president

1845
- Texas becomes a state

1848
- Free-Soil Party nominates Van Buren

1850
- Compromise of 1850 passed

1852
- *Uncle Tom's Cabin* published

1854
- Kansas-Nebraska Act passed
- Republican Party formed

1856
- Violence erupts in Kansas
- Buchanan elected president

1857
- *Dred Scott* decision handed down

1858
- Lincoln-Douglas debates held

1859
- John Brown attacks Harpers Ferry

1860
- Lincoln is elected president
- South Carolina becomes first state to secede

1861
- Confederate States of America formed
- Fort Sumter attacked

Reviewing Key Terms

Write five true and five false statements using the terms below. Use only one term in each statement. Indicate which statements are true and which are false. Below each false statement explain why it is false.

1. sectionalism
2. secede
3. border ruffians
4. arsenal
5. secession
6. fugitive
7. popular sovereignty
8. civil war
9. martyr
10. states' rights

Reviewing Key Facts

11. What was the purpose of the Missouri Compromise?

12. List the five parts of the Compromise of 1850.

13. What was Stephen Douglas's solution to the slavery issue in the Kansas and Nebraska territories?

14. How did Abraham Lincoln become a national figure in politics?

15. What was the *Dred Scott* decision? What did it mean for those opposed to slavery?

16. Why were there four parties and candidates in the presidential election of 1860?

17. How did Lincoln plan to prevent secession?

Critical Thinking

18. **Finding the Main Idea** Why was the balance of free and slave states in the Senate such an important issue?

19. **Drawing Conclusions** Why did Northerners protest Douglas's plan to repeal the Missouri Compromise?

20. **Determining Cause and Effect** Re-create the diagram below. List three ways pro- or antislavery groups changed the structure of political parties in the 1850s.

```
(    )   (    )   (    )
        ↓    ↓    ↓
      Political parties change
```

21. **Analyzing Themes: Geography and History** How did the North's larger population give it an edge over the South in the 1860 election?

Party and nominated John Bell, Republicans nominated Abraham Lincoln.

17. He vowed to hold federal property in the South and enforce the laws of the United States.

Critical Thinking

18. If the balance was upset, one section of the country would have more decision-making power than the other.

19. because it would allow slavery into areas that had been free for more than 30 years

20. The Democratic Party divided along sectional lines; the Whig Party dissolved; the antislavery Whigs and Democrats joined the Free-Soil Party to form the Republican Party.

21. The North had more electoral votes even if the South had not been divided among three candidates.

Geography and History Activity

The election of 1860 divided the nation along sectional lines. Study the map below; then answer the questions that follow.

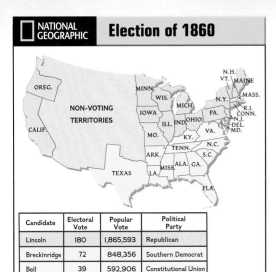

NATIONAL GEOGRAPHIC **Election of 1860**

Candidate	Electoral Vote	Popular Vote	Political Party
Lincoln	180	1,865,593	Republican
Breckinridge	72	848,356	Southern Democrat
Bell	39	592,906	Constitutional Union
Douglas	12	1,382,713	Northern Democrat

22. Location Which states supported Douglas?

23. Region In what region(s) was the Republican Party strongest?

24. Region In what region did Breckinridge find support?

Practicing Skills

25. Recognizing Bias Find written material about a topic of interest in your community. Possible sources include editorials, letters to the editor, and pamphlets from political candidates and interest groups. Write a short report analyzing the material for evidence of bias.

Technology Activity

26. Using the Internet Search the Internet for a list of political parties in existence today. Make a table that briefly summarizes each party's current goals. Then research to find the date that the party was founded. Include this information on your table, too. Then compare your table to the political parties discussed in Chapter 15.

Self-Check Quiz
Visit **tarvol1.glencoe.com** and click on **Chapter 15— Self-Check Quizzes** to prepare for the chapter test.

Citizenship Cooperative Activity

27. Making Compromises With a partner, think of a controversial issue that is a source of disagreement today. Take opposite sides on the issue; then work together to come up with a list of three compromises that would make the solution to this problem acceptable to both sides. Share the issue and your compromises with the class.

Alternative Assessment

28. Portfolio Writing Activity Write a report that answers these questions: Why was Congress in conflict over the question of statehood for California? How did the Compromise of 1850 address this question? What role did Clay, Calhoun, and Webster play in the Compromise?

Standardized Test Practice

Directions: Use the map of the Compromise of 1850 on page 443 to choose the *best* answer to the following question.

Which of the following statements is true?

A The Compromise of 1850 allowed the Oregon Territory to be open to slaveholding.

B The Compromise of 1850 did not make any land on the Pacific Ocean open to slaveholding.

C The Compromise of 1850 made every state touching the southern border of the United States open to slaveholding.

D The Compromise of 1850 gave the Minnesota Territory the authority to choose whether it would allow slaveholding.

Test-Taking Tip

Remember to use the information on the map to support your answer. Don't rely only on your memory. Check each answer choice against the map. Only one choice is correct.

Alternative Assessment

28. Admission of California as a free state would tip the balance of power in the Senate in favor of the free states. The Compromise made concessions to Southern states and California was admitted as a free state. Clay outlined the Compromise, Webster supported Clay, and Calhoun rejected the Compromise as unfair to the South.

HISTORY Online

Have students visit the Web site at tarvol1.glencoe.com to review Chapter 15 and take the Self-Check Quiz.

Standardized Test Practice

Answer: B
Question Type: Geography
Answer Explanation: The map on page 443 shows the states and territories that were impacted by the Compromise of 1850. The Oregon Territory is shown closed to slaveholding. California, which became a state in 1850, is a free state. No other territories or states are found along the coast of the Pacific Ocean.

Bonus Question ?

Ask: What was Frederick Douglass's last name before he changed it to Douglass when he escaped to the North? *(Bailey)*

Geography and History Activity

22. Missouri (He also received three of New Jersey's seven electoral votes.)

23. Northeast, upper Midwest, and West Coast

24. South

Practicing Skills

25. Reports should show an understanding of how to recognize bias.

Technology Activity

26. Students' tables should contain a list of the major political parties and some of the lesser-known parties, a brief description of their goals, and each party's founding date.

Citizenship Cooperative Activity

27. Students should choose a controversial issue and identify three compromises that would be acceptable to both sides.

Chapter 16 Resources

Timesaving Tools

TeacherWorks™ All-In-One Planner and Resource Center

- **Interactive Teacher Edition** Access your Teacher Wraparound Edition and your classroom resources with a few easy clicks.
- **Interactive Lesson Planner** Planning has never been easier! Organize your week, month, semester, or year with all the lesson helps you need to make teaching creative, timely, and relevant.

Use Glencoe's **Presentation Plus!** multimedia teacher tool to easily present dynamic lessons that visually excite your students. Using Microsoft PowerPoint® you can customize the presentations to create your own personalized lessons.

TEACHING TRANSPARENCIES

Graphic Organizer 15 L2

Why It Matters Chapter Transparency 16 L2

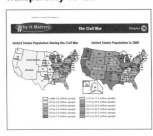

REVIEW AND REINFORCEMENT

Workbook Activity 16 L1

Time Line Activity 16 L2

Vocabulary Activity 16 L1

REVIEW AND REINFORCEMENT

Critical Thinking Skills Activity 16 L2

Take-Home Review Activity 16 L1

ENRICHMENT

Linking Past and Present Activity 16 L2

Primary Source Reading 16 L2

GEOGRAPHY

Geography and History Activity 16 L2

Meeting NCSS Standards

The following standards are highlighted in Chapter 16:

Section 1 VI Power, Authority, & Governance: A, B, C, D, F, H, I
Section 2 III People, Places, & Environments: A, B, H, I, K
Section 3 V Individuals, Groups, & Institutions: A, E, F, G
Section 4 VII Production, Distribution, & Consumption: D, F, G, I, J
Section 5 IV Individual Development & Identity: A, B, C, D, E, F, G

FOLDABLES™ Study Organizer

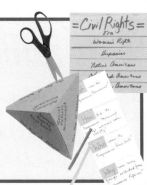

Dinah Zike's Foldables are three-dimensional, interactive graphic organizers that help students practice basic writing skills, review key vocabulary terms, and identify main ideas. Additional chapter activities can be found in the **Reading and Study Skills Foldables** booklet.

Chapter 16 Resources

ASSESSMENT AND EVALUATION

Chapter 16 Test
Form A L2

Chapter 16 Test
Form B L2

Standardized Test Practice
Workbook Activity 16 L2

Performance Assessment
Activity 16 L1, ELL

ExamView® Pro
Testmaker CD-ROM

MULTIMEDIA

- Vocabulary PuzzleMaker CD-ROM
- Interactive Tutor Self-Assessment CD-ROM
- ExamView® Pro Testmaker CD-ROM
- Audio Program
- American History Primary Source Document Library CD-ROM
- MindJogger Videoquiz
- Presentation Plus! CD-ROM
- TeacherWorks CD-ROM
- Interactive Student Edition CD-ROM
- Glencoe Skillbuilder Interactive Workbook CD-ROM, Level 1
- The American Republic to 1877 Video Program
- American Music: Hits Through History

SPANISH RESOURCES

The following Spanish language materials are available in the Spanish Resources Binder:

- Spanish Guided Reading Activities
- Spanish Reteaching Activities
- Spanish Quizzes and Tests
- Spanish Vocabulary Activity
- Spanish Take-Home Review Activity
- Spanish Summaries
- The Declaration of Independence and United States Constitution Spanish Translation

---

The following videotape programs are available from Glencoe as supplements to Chapter 16:

- **Abraham Lincoln: Preserving the Union** (ISBN 0-7670-0034-X)
- **American Civil War** (ISBN 0-7670-0102-8)
- **Images of the Civil War** (ISBN 1-56501-171-6)

To order, call Glencoe at 1-800-334-7344. To find classroom resources to accompany many of these videos, check the following home pages:
A&E Television: www.aande.com
The History Channel: www.historychannel.com

Use our Web site for additional resources. All essential content is covered in the Student Edition.

You and your students can visit tarvol1.glencoe.com, the Web site companion to **The American Republic to 1877.** This innovative integration of electronic and print media offers your students a wealth of opportunities. The student text directs students to the Web site for the following options:

- **Chapter Overviews**
- **Student Web Activities**
- **Self-Check Quizzes**
- **Textbook Updates**

Answers to the student Web activities are provided for you in the **Web Activity Lesson Plans.** Additional Web resources and Interactive Tutor Puzzles are also available.

Chapter 16 Resources

SECTION RESOURCES

Daily Objectives	Reproducible Resources	Multimedia Resources
SECTION 1 **The Two Sides** 1. Explain why the border states played an important part in the war. 2. Compare Northern and Southern populations, industries, resources, and war aims.	Reproducible Lesson Plan 16–1 Daily Lecture and Discussion Notes 16–1 Guided Reading Activity 16–1* Section Quiz 16–1* Reteaching Activity 16–1* Reading Essentials and Study Guide 16–1* Enrichment Activity 16–1	Daily Focus Skills Transparency 16–1 Interactive Tutor Self-Assessment CD-ROM ExamView® Pro Testmaker CD-ROM Presentation Plus! CD-ROM
SECTION 2 **Early Years of the War** 1. Identify Northern and Southern successes and failures in the early years of the war. 2. Explain how the North's naval blockade hurt the South.	Reproducible Lesson Plan 16–2 Daily Lecture and Discussion Notes 16–2 Guided Reading Activity 16–2* Section Quiz 16–2* Reteaching Activity 16–2* Reading Essentials and Study Guide 16–2* Enrichment Activity 16–2	Daily Focus Skills Transparency 16–2 American Music: Hits Through History Interactive Tutor Self-Assessment CD-ROM ExamView® Pro Testmaker CD-ROM Presentation Plus! CD-ROM
SECTION 3 **A Call for Freedom** 1. Describe why Lincoln issued the Emancipation Proclamation. 2. Understand the role that African Americans played in the Civil War.	Reproducible Lesson Plan 16–3 Daily Lecture and Discussion Notes 16–3 Guided Reading Activity 16–3* Section Quiz 16–3* Reteaching Activity 16–3* Reading Essentials and Study Guide 16–3* Enrichment Activity 16–3	Daily Focus Skills Transparency 16–3 Interactive Tutor Self-Assessment CD-ROM ExamView® Pro Testmaker CD-ROM Presentation Plus! CD-ROM
SECTION 4 **Life During the Civil War** 1. Describe what life was like for soldiers during the Civil War. 2. Identify the role that women played in the war. 3. Compare how the war affected the economies of the North and the South.	Reproducible Lesson Plan 16–4 Daily Lecture and Discussion Notes 16–4 Guided Reading Activity 16–4* Section Quiz 16–4* Reteaching Activity 16–4* Reading Essentials and Study Guide 16–4* Enrichment Activity 16–4	Daily Focus Skills Transparency 16–4 American Art and Architecture, Transparency 15 Interactive Tutor Self-Assessment CD-ROM ExamView® Pro Testmaker CD-ROM Presentation Plus! CD-ROM
SECTION 5 **The Way to Victory** 1. Identify the battles that turned the tide of the war in 1863. 2. Cite the events that led to the South's surrender in 1865.	Reproducible Lesson Plan 16–5 Daily Lecture and Discussion Notes 16–5 Guided Reading Activity 16–5* Section Quiz 16–5* Reteaching Activity 16–5* Reading Essentials and Study Guide 16–5* Enrichment Activity 16–5	Daily Focus Skills Transparency 16–5 ABC News Interactive™ Historic America Electronic Field Trips Vocabulary PuzzleMaker CD-ROM Interactive Tutor Self-Assessment CD-ROM ExamView® Pro Testmaker CD-ROM Presentation Plus! CD-ROM

`0:00` OUT OF TIME?
Assign the Chapter 16 **Reading Essentials and Study Guide.**

*Also Available in Spanish

  Blackline Master   Transparency   CD-ROM   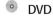 DVD

Poster   Music Program   Audio Program   Videocassette

NATIONAL GEOGRAPHIC Teacher's Corner

INDEX TO NATIONAL GEOGRAPHIC MAGAZINE

The following articles relate to this chapter.

- "Colonial Florida Fort Recalls a Shining Moment in Black History," Geographica, February 1997.
- "C.S.S. *Alabama*," by Max Guerout, December 1994.
- "The Cruelest Commerce: African Slave Trade," by Colin Palmer, September 1992.

ADDITIONAL NATIONAL GEOGRAPHIC SOCIETY PRODUCTS

To order the following, call National Geographic at 1-800-368-2728:

- *GeoKit: The Civil War* (Kit)
- *GeoKit: Immigration* (Kit)
- *United States/Territorial Growth* (Map)
- *National Geographic Desk Reference* (Book)
- *Battlefields of the Civil War* (Map)

NGS ONLINE

Access National Geographic's Web site for current events, atlas updates, activities, links, interactive features, and archives.

www.nationalgeographic.com

KEY TO ABILITY LEVELS

Teaching strategies have been coded.

L1 BASIC activities for all students
L2 AVERAGE activities for average to above-average students
L3 CHALLENGING activities for above-average students
ELL ENGLISH LANGUAGE LEARNER activities

MEETING SPECIAL NEEDS

In addition to the Differentiated Instruction strategies found in each section, the following resources are also suitable for your special needs students:

- *ExamView® Pro Testmaker CD-ROM* allows teachers to tailor tests by reducing answer choices.
- The *Audio Program* includes the entire narrative of the student edition so that less-proficient readers can listen to the words as they read them.

From the Classroom of...

Terri Cook
Carthage Junior High School
Carthage, MO

Write a Wartime Letter

Explain to students that a majority of Civil War soldiers were very literate. Letters between soldiers on the battlefields and their friends back home were widespread. If possible, find Civil War resources showing several letters and share them with the class. Then have students choose a character, such as a soldier, doctor, nurse, spy, soldier's mother, soldier's father, or friend back home. Have students, in character, write a letter to the fictional person. They may research a particular battle or life in the mid-1860s to add more details to their letters. Have them use pencils and unlined paper, explaining that ballpoint pens were not yet invented and that ink was hard to transport. By showing students facsimiles of envelopes, stamps, and stationery from the period, you can also ask them to imitate the designs and styles of these in their own correspondence. Have students share their letters with the rest of the class.

ADDITIONAL RESOURCES FROM GLENCOE

- American Music: Cultural Traditions
- American Art and Architecture
- Outline Map Resource Book
- U.S. Desk Map
- Building Geography Skills for Life
- Inclusion for the Middle School Social Studies Classroom Strategies and Activities
- Teaching Strategies for the American History Classroom (Including Block Scheduling Pacing Guides)
- American Crafts Hands-On Activities
- American Games Hands-On Activities
- American History Flash Cards

Block Schedule

Activities that are suited to use within the block scheduling framework are identified by:

Performance Assessment

Refer to Activity 16 in the Performance Assessment Activities and Rubrics booklet.

Why It Matters Activity

Have students explain how they think the Civil War changed what freedom meant for Americans. Challenge students to reevaluate their answers after they have completed the chapter.

GLENCOE
TECHNOLOGY

The American Republic to 1877 Video Program

To learn more about the Civil War, have students view the Chapter 16 video "The Face of War" from **The American Republic to 1877 Video Program.**

 Available in DVD and VHS

MindJogger Videoquiz

Use **MindJogger Videoquiz** to preview the Chapter 16 content.

Available in VHS

CHAPTER
16 The Civil War
1861–1865

Why It Matters

The Civil War—a war in which Americans fought other Americans—transformed the United States. It shattered the economy of the South while contributing to the rapid economic growth of the North and the West. African Americans gained freedom when slavery was abolished, but the war left a legacy of bitterness between North and South that lasted for generations.

The Impact Today

Key events during this era still shape our lives today. For example:
- *The institution of slavery was abolished.*
- *The war established the power of the federal government over the states.*

 The American Republic to 1877 *Video* The chapter 16 video, "The Face of War," gives insight into the realities of the Civil War.

1861
- Confederate States of America formed
- Conflict at Fort Sumter, South Carolina, begins Civil War

1862
- Robert E. Lee named commander of Confederate armies

1863
- Emancipation Proclamation issued
- Battle of Gettysburg

United States PRESIDENTS

Lincoln 1861–1865

1861   *1862*   *1863*

World

1861
- Charles Dickens's *Great Expectations* published
- Victor Emmanuel II recognized as king of unified Italy

1862
- Otto von Bismarck named premier of Prussia

1863
- Discovery of Lake Victoria as source of Nile River
- International Red Cross established

458   CHAPTER 16   The Civil War

📖 Reading Strategy / PURPOSE FOR READING

Carousel brainstorming is a strategy to help students generate background knowledge on a topic. Begin by saying: "The Civil War ended slavery in the United States and strengthened the power of the federal government over individual states. The war had an impact on most Americans." Divide the students into groups of 5 or 6. Give each group a large piece of chart paper and have each group generate a list on *How war affects the lives of people*. Each group member must write at least one item on the paper. Wrap up by displaying the sheets in the classroom and having students do a "gallery walk" reading everyone's ideas. You may also follow up with a class discussion. **L1**

Fight for the Colors by Don Troiani Troiani has painted many dramatic war scenes, such as this one of the Battle of Gettysburg.

Organizing Information Study Foldable
Make this foldable to help you organize what you learn about the Civil War.

Step 1 Fold a sheet of paper in half from side to side.

Fold it so the left edge lies about ½ inch from the right edge.

Step 2 Turn the paper and fold it into thirds.

Step 3 Unfold and cut the top layer only along both folds.

This will make three tabs.

Step 4 Label your foldable as shown.

Before the War | During the War | After the War
The Civil War

Reading and Writing As you read the chapter, list events that occurred before, during, and after the Civil War under the appropriate tabs of your foldable.

1864
• Sherman's "march to the sea" begins
• Lincoln reelected president

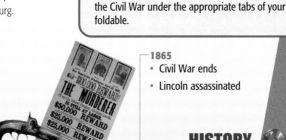

1865
• Civil War ends
• Lincoln assassinated

1864   *1865*

1864
• Maximilian installed as emperor of Mexico

1865
• Lewis Carroll publishes *Alice's Adventures in Wonderland*

HISTORY Online

Chapter Overview
Visit tarvol1.glencoe.com and click on **Chapter 16—Chapter Overviews** to preview chapter information.

CHAPTER 16   The Civil War   459

FOLDABLES™
Study Organizer **Dinah Zike's Foldables**

Purpose This activity requires students to create a foldable and organize information from the chapter on it. Students are required to record events that occurred before, during, and after the Civil War on the appropriate tabs of the foldable.

Have students complete *Reading and Study Skills Foldables* Activity 11. **L1**

HISTORY Online

Introduce students to chapter content and key terms by having them access **Chapter Overview 16** at tarvol1.glencoe.com

TIME LINE ACTIVITY

Have students review the time line on pages 458–459 before they read the chapter. **Ask:** Abraham Lincoln issued the Emancipation Proclamation how many years after the Civil War started? *(two years)*

More About the Art

Born in 1949, Don Troiani developed a passion for both art and history at a young age. Troiani's interest in military heritage lends credibility and authenticity to his paintings. *Fight for the Colors* depicts a scene from the Battle of Gettysburg, a battle that marked the turning point of the Civil War. Have students describe what the fighting was like at Gettysburg based upon the painting. *(Students should note that soldiers used guns and bayonets, and fought in hand-to-hand combat.)*

1 FOCUS

Section Overview

This section describes the North and the South at the start of the Civil War.

Reading Preview

Answers to Graphic: Union strengths: larger population, better banking system and railroad network, leadership of Lincoln, more industry, resources, and ships; Union weaknesses: North would have to invade, support for secession in South; Confederacy strengths: support of white population, knowledge of terrain, military leadership; Confederacy weaknesses: smaller population, few factories and trains, belief in states' rights weakened central government

Preteaching Vocabulary
Have students identify the *border states* and explain why they were important to the North.

SECTION 1 The Two Sides

Guide to Reading

Main Idea
Both the North and the South had strengths and weaknesses that helped determine their military strategies.

Key Terms
border state, blockade, offensive, Rebel, Yankee

Reading Strategy
Classifying Information As you read the section, complete a chart like the one shown here by listing the strengths and weaknesses of the Union and the Confederacy.

	Union	Confederacy
Strengths		
Weaknesses		

Read to Learn
• why the border states played an important part in the war.
• how the North and South compared in terms of population, industry, resources, and war aims.

Section Theme
Government and Democracy The Southern states seceded from the Union to protect states' rights.

Preview of Events

♦1861	♦1862	♦1863

February 1861
The Confederacy forms

April 1861
Four more states join the Confederacy

Summer 1861
Confederate forces total 112,000; Union 187,000

June 1863
West Virginia joins Union

Confederate soldier, 1861

★ AN American Story ★

Union sergeant Driscoll directed his troops at Malvern Hill on July 1, 1862. The enemy fought fiercely, especially one young Confederate soldier. Driscoll raised his rifle, took aim, and shot the boy. As he passed the spot where the boy had fallen, Driscoll turned the daring soldier over to see what he looked like. The boy opened his eyes and faintly murmured, "Father," then his eyes fluttered shut, never to open again. A Union captain later wrote, "I will forever recollect the frantic grief of Driscoll; it was harrowing to witness. He [had killed] his son, who had gone South before the war."

Like the Driscolls, many families were divided by the war. Neither side imagined, however, that the war would cost such a terrible price in human life. During the four years of fighting, hundreds of thousands of Americans were killed in battle.

Choosing Sides

By February 1861, seven states had left the Union and formed the Confederacy. After the Confederate bombardment of Fort Sumter, President Abraham Lincoln issued a call for troops to save the Union. His action caused Virginia, North Carolina, Tennessee, and Arkansas to join the Confederacy. These four states brought needed soldiers and supplies to the Confederacy. For its capital,

---

SECTION RESOURCES

📁 Reproducible Masters
• Reproducible Lesson Plan 16–1
• Daily Lecture and Discussion Notes 16–1
• Guided Reading Activity 16–1
• Section Quiz 16–1
• Reteaching Activity 16–1
• Reading Essentials and Study Guide 16–1
• Enrichment Activity 16–1

📑 Transparencies
• Daily Focus Skills Transparency 16–1

Multimedia
🔘 Interactive Tutor Self-Assessment CD-ROM
🔘 ExamView® Pro Testmaker CD-ROM
🔘 Presentation Plus! CD-ROM

the Confederacy chose **Richmond,** Virginia, a city only about 100 miles from the Union capital of Washington, D.C.

Four states that allowed slavery—Missouri, Kentucky, Maryland, and Delaware—remained in the Union. The people of these border states were divided over which side to support. Missouri, Kentucky, and Maryland had such strong support for the South that the three states teetered on the brink of secession.

Losing the border states would seriously damage the North. All had strategic locations. Missouri could control parts of the Mississippi River and major routes to the West. Kentucky controlled the Ohio River. Delaware was close to the important Northern city of Philadelphia.

Maryland, perhaps the most important of the border states, was close to Richmond. Vital railroad lines passed through Maryland. Most significantly, Washington, D.C., lay within the state. If Maryland seceded, the North's government would be surrounded.

Maryland's key role became clear in April 1861. A mob in Baltimore attacked Northern troops; Confederate sympathizers burned railroad bridges and cut the telegraph line to Washington, isolating the capital from the rest of the North. Northern troops soon arrived, but the nation's capital had suffered some anxious days.

Remaining With the Union

Lincoln had to move cautiously to avoid upsetting people in the border states. If he announced that he aimed to end slavery, for instance, groups supporting the Confederacy might take their states out of the Union. If he ordered Northern troops into Kentucky, Confederate sympathizers there would claim the state had been invaded and swing it to the South.

In some ways Lincoln acted boldly. He suspended some constitutional rights and used his power to arrest people who supported secession. In the end Lincoln's approach worked. The border states stayed in the Union, but many of their citizens joined armies of the South.

A Secession From the South

Most white Southerners favored secession. Still, pockets of Union support existed in parts of Tennessee and Virginia. People in the

History *Through Art*

7th New York Militia at Jersey City on April 19, 1861 by E.L. Henry The 7th New York Militia was one of the first fully equipped and trained units at the outbreak of the war. **Why were troops ordered to the nation's capital in early 1861?**

CHAPTER 16
Section 1, 460–464

2 TEACH

Daily Lecture and Discussion Notes 16–1

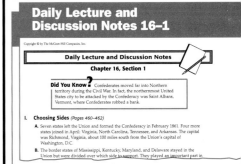

Copyright © by The McGraw-Hill Companies, Inc.

Daily Lecture and Discussion Notes

Chapter 16, Section 1

Did You Know? Confederates moved far into Northern territory during the Civil War. In fact, the northernmost United States city to be attacked by the Confederacy was Saint Albans, Vermont, where Confederates robbed a bank.

I. **Choosing Sides** *(Pages 460–462)*

A. Seven states left the Union and formed the Confederacy in February 1861. Four more states joined in April: Virginia, North Carolina, Tennessee, and Arkansas. The capital was Richmond, Virginia, about 100 miles south from the Union's capital of Washington, D.C.

B. The border states of Mississippi, Kentucky, Maryland, and Delaware stayed in the Union but were divided over which side to support. They played an important part in

Writing a Newspaper Article
Ask groups of students to design and create the front page of a newspaper announcing the beginning of the Civil War. Recommend that each group include on their front pages a banner headline, some form of illustration, a story that includes eyewitness accounts, and announcements from the Union and Confederate governments about the outbreak of war. **L1**

Use the rubric for writing a newspaper article on pages 35–36 in the *Performance Assessment Activities and Rubrics.*

History *Through Art*

Answer: to protect Washington, D.C., and vital railroad lines passing through Maryland, and to prevent Maryland from leaving the Union

---

Reading Strategy   READING THE TEXT

Using Graphic Organizers Have students create a graphic organizer about the strengths and weaknesses of the North and South. They should scan the section for information on strengths and weaknesses and cooperatively categorize each strength and weakness into the following categories: cultural, social, economic, and political factors. Students should decide which type of graphic organizer they want to use. **L2**

Guided Reading Activity 16–1

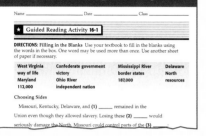

Name _____ Date _____ Class _____

★ **Guided Reading Activity 16-1**

DIRECTIONS: Filling in the Blanks Use your textbook to fill in the blanks using the words in the box. One word may be used more than once. Use another sheet of paper if necessary.

West Virginia way of life	Confederate government victory	Mississippi River border states	Delaware North
Maryland 112,000	Ohio River independent nation	187,000	resources

Choosing Sides

Missouri, Kentucky, Delaware, and **(1)** _____ remained in the Union even though they allowed slavery. Losing these **(2)** _____ would seriously damage the North. Missouri could control parts of the **(3)** _____ .

✓ Reading Check

Answer: It was near important railroad lines, it was close to Richmond, the Confederacy's capital, and Washington, D.C., lay within the state.

〰 Graph *Skills*

Answer: railroad mileage and manufactured goods

Graph Skills Practice
Ask: About how many more farms did the North have compared to the South? *(The North had about twice the amount of farms.)*

you don't say...

Johnny Reb and Billy Yank
Northern troops called the Southern soldier *Johnny Reb* or *Reb*, after the term *rebel*. Southerners called the Northerners *Billy Yank* or *Yankees*.

Appalachian region generally opposed secession. In western Virginia a movement to secede from the state and rejoin the Union grew. In 1861, 48 Virginia counties organized themselves as a separate state called **West Virginia.** Congress admitted this state to the Union in 1863.

✓ Reading Check **Explaining** Why was Maryland strategically important?

Comparing North and South

When the war began, both sides had advantages and disadvantages. How they would use those strengths and weaknesses would determine the war's outcome.

The North enjoyed the advantages of a larger population, more industry, and more abundant resources than the South. It had a better banking system, which helped to raise money for the war. The North also possessed more ships, and almost all the members of the regular navy remained loyal to the Union. Finally, the North had a larger and more efficient railway network.

The North also faced disadvantages. Bringing the Southern states back into the Union would be difficult. The North would have to invade and hold the South—a large area filled with a hostile population. Furthermore, the Southern people's support for the war remained strong. Recalling the example of the American Revolution, when the smaller, weaker colonies had won independence from wealthy Great Britain, many believed the South had a good chance of winning.

One Northern advantage was not obvious until later. Both sides greatly underestimated Abraham Lincoln. His dedication, intelligence, and humanity would lead the North to victory.

One of the main advantages of the South was the strong support its white population gave the war. Southerners also had the advantage of fighting in familiar territory—defending their land, their homes, and their way of life.

The military leadership of the South, at least at first, was superior to the North's. Southern families had a strong tradition of military training and service, and military college graduates provided the South with a large pool of officers. Overseeing the Southern effort was Confederate president **Jefferson Davis,** a West Point graduate and an experienced soldier.

The South faced material disadvantages. It had a smaller population of free men to draw upon in building an army. It also possessed very few factories to manufacture weapons and other supplies, and it produced less than half as much food as the North. With less than half the miles of railroad tracks and vastly fewer trains than the North, the Confederate government had difficulty delivering food, weapons, and other supplies to its troops.

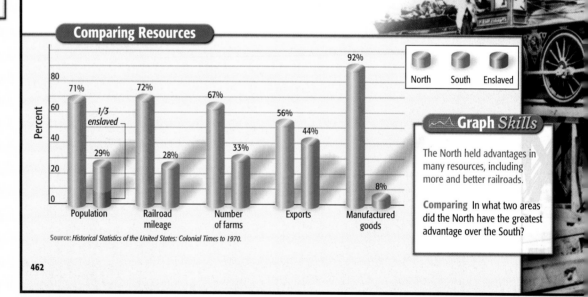

Comparing Resources

Percent

71% 29% *1/3 enslaved* — 72% 28% 67% 33% 56% 44% 92% 8%

Population | Railroad mileage | Number of farms | Exports | Manufactured goods

North · South · Enslaved

Source: *Historical Statistics of the United States: Colonial Times to 1970.*

〰 Graph *Skills*

The North held advantages in many resources, including more and better railroads.

Comparing In what two areas did the North have the greatest advantage over the South?

462

DIFFERENTIATED INSTRUCTION

Gifted and Talented Review the definition of personification with students. Have students choose a border state to personify. Then ask students to write a short paragraph describing how the state feels about being a border state. Encourage students to describe their feelings geographically, emotionally, historically, socially, and politically. Allow students to read their paragraphs aloud to the class and have the rest of the students guess which border state is being described. **L3**

📂 Refer to *Inclusion for the Middle School Social Studies Classroom Strategies and Activities* in the TCR.

The belief in **states' rights**—a founding principle of the Confederacy—also hampered the South's efforts. The individual states refused to give the Confederate government sufficient power. As a result, the government found it difficult to fight the war effectively.

War Aims and Strategy

The North and the South entered the Civil War with different aims. The main goal of the North at the outset was to bring the Southern states back into the Union. Ending slavery was not a major Northern goal at first, but this changed as the war continued.

The Union's plan for winning the war included three main strategies. First the North would blockade, or close, Southern ports to prevent supplies from reaching the South—and to prevent the South from earning money by exporting cotton. Second, the Union intended to gain control of the Mississippi River to cut Southern supply lines and to split the Confederacy. Third, the North planned to capture Richmond, Virginia, the Confederate capital.

For the South, the primary aim of the war was to win recognition as an independent nation. Independence would allow Southerners to preserve their traditional way of life—a way of life that included slavery.

To achieve this goal, the South worked out a defensive strategy. It planned to defend its homeland, holding on to as much territory as possible until the North tired of fighting. The South expected that Britain and France, which imported large quantities of Southern cotton, would pressure the North to end the war to restore their cotton supply.

During the war Southern leaders sometimes changed strategy and took the offensive—went on the attack. They moved their armies northward to threaten Washington, D.C., and other Northern cities, hoping to persuade the North it could not win the war.

☑ **Reading Check** **Explaining** What role did Jefferson Davis play in the war?

American People at War

The Civil War was more than a war between the states. It often pitted brother against brother, parents against their children, and neighbor against neighbor.

American Against American

The leaders from both North and South—and their families—felt these divisions. President Lincoln's wife, Mary Todd Lincoln, had several relatives who fought in the Confederate army. John Crittenden, a senator from Kentucky, had two sons who became generals in the war—one for the Confederacy and one for the Union. Officers on both sides—including Confederate general Robert E. Lee, and Union generals George McClellan and William Tecumseh Sherman—had attended the United States Military Academy at West Point, never dreaming that they would one day command forces against each other.

Who Were the Soldiers?

Most of the soldiers were young. The average age of a recruit was 25 years old, but about 40 percent were 21 or younger. Ted Upson of Indiana was only 16 when he begged his father to let him join the Union army. His father replied, "This Union your ancestors and mine helped to make must be saved from destruction." 📖 *(See page 603 for an additional primary source reading about Civil War soldiers.)*

CHAPTER 16   The Civil War   **463**

☑ **Reading Check**

Answer: He was the Confederate president.

Did you know?

The railroad was an integral part of the movement and preservation of field armies during the Civil War. A railcar mounted with a heavy cannon for bombardment of forts was first used during the Civil War.

3 ASSESS

Assign Section 1 Assessment as homework or as an in-class activity.

🖱 Have students use **Interactive Tutor Self-Assessment CD-ROM.**

L2

Section Quiz 16–1

Name _____ Date _____ Class _____

⭐ Chapter 16   Score [ ]

Section Quiz 16-1

DIRECTIONS: Matching Match the items in Column A with the items in Column B. Write the correct letters in the blanks. *(10 points each)*

Column A

_____ 1. Confederate capital

_____ 2. Union's first strategy

_____ 3. to go on the attack

_____ 4. Confederate soldiers

_____ 5. Union soldiers

Column B

A. offensive
B. Yankees
C. Rebels
D. Richmond, Virginia
E. blockade Southern ports

DIRECTIONS: Multiple Choice In the blank at the left, write the letter of the choice that best completes the statement or answers the question. *(10 points each)*

_____ 6. Perhaps the most important border state was
    A. Kentucky.   C. Missouri.
    B. Delaware.   D. Maryland.

_____ 7. In order to rejoin the Union in 1861, 48 counties organized themselves as a separate state called
    A. Washington, D.C.   C. Virginia.
    B. West Virginia.   D. North Carolina.

_____ 8. For the South the primary aim of the war was to win recognition
    A. for having good soldiers.   C. as an independent nation.
    B. as slaveholders.   D. as a wealthy area.

_____ 9. What was one of the main advantages of the South?
    A. a small population of free men   C. its belief in states' rights
    B. the strong support of its white population   D. its industrial base

_____ 10. Most soldiers, both Confederate and Union, came from
    A. farms.   C. slums.
    B. the East Coast.   D. cities.

INTERDISCIPLINARY CONNECTIONS ACTIVITY

Economics Pair students to research and create a series of graphs showing the differences between the North and the South in 1861. Have them use the graph on page 462 as an example. Encourage students to compare as many categories as possible, such as number of enslaved persons, number of factories, and types of exports and imports. Display completed graphs on a bulletin board titled *Sectionalism in 1861*. **L2**

🗁 Use the rubric for creating a graph on pages 42–43 in the ***Performance Assessment Activities and Rubrics.***

L1

Reteaching Activity 16–1

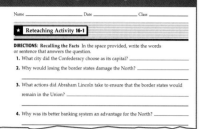

Name _____ Date _____ Class _____

★ Reteaching Activity 16-1

DIRECTIONS: **Recalling the Facts** In the space provided, write the words or sentence that answers the question.
1. What city did the Confederacy choose as its capital? _____
2. Why would losing the border states damage the North? _____
3. What actions did Abraham Lincoln take to ensure that the border states would remain in the Union? _____
4. Why was its better banking system an advantage for the North? _____

L1, ELL

Reading Essentials and Study Guide 16–1

Study Guide

Chapter 16, Section 1
For use with textbook pages 460–464
THE TWO SIDES

KEY TERMS	
border state	A slave state that remained in the Union *(page 461)*
blockade	To close *(page 463)*
offensive	On the attack *(page 463)*
Rebel	Confederate soldier *(page 464)*
Yankee	Union soldier *(page 464)*

DRAWING FROM EXPERIENCE

Have you ever played chess or checkers? What kind of strategy, or plan, did you use to play the game?

L3

Enrichment Activity 16–1

Name _____ Date _____ Class _____

★ Enrichment Activity 16-1 ★ 🔍 ★

Civil War Resources
The North and the South did not have equal resources to fight a war. Study the graphs below.

Resources of the North and the South, 1860s

Number of States Total: 34	Population Total: 31.5 million	Railroad Mileage Total: 31,000 miles	Value of Manufactured Goods Total: $1.9 billion	Value of Exports Total: $316 million
South 32% North 68%	South 29% North 71%	South 29% North 71%	South 8% North 92%	North 34% South 66%

4 CLOSE

Comparing Ask students to review the newspaper articles they created in the "TEACH" activity. Have them compare their articles with information learned from the section.

"I think it is to be a long war...."

—*General William Tecumseh Sherman*

William Stone from Louisiana rushed to join the Confederate army after the attack on Fort Sumter. His sister Kate wrote that he was

❝ . . . wild to be off to Virginia. He so fears that the fighting will be over before he can get there. ❞

Soldiers came from every region and all walks of life. Most, though, came from farms. Almost half of the North's troops and more than 60 percent of the South's had owned or worked on farms. The Union army did not permit African

Americans to join at first, but they did serve later. Lincoln's early terms of enlistment asked governors to supply soldiers for 90 days. When the conflict did not end quickly, soldiers' terms became longer.

By the summer of 1861 the Confederate army had about 112,000 soldiers, who were sometimes called **Rebels.** The Union had about 187,000 soldiers, or **Yankees,** as they were also known. By the end of the war, about 850,000 men fought for the Confederacy and about 2.1 million men fought for the Union. The Union number included just under 200,000 African Americans. About 10,000 Hispanic soldiers fought in the conflict.

False Hopes

When the war began, each side expected an early victory. A Confederate soldier from a town in Alabama expected the war to be over well within a year because "we are going to kill the last Yankee before that time if there is any fight in them still." Northerners were just as confident that they would beat the South quickly.

Some leaders saw the situation more clearly. Northern general William Tecumseh Sherman wrote, "I think it is to be a long war—very long—much longer than any politician thinks." The first spring of the war proved that Sherman's prediction was accurate.

✔Reading Check **Comparing** Which side had the larger fighting force?

SECTION 1 ASSESSMENT

Checking for Understanding

1. **Key Terms** Write a short paragraph in which you use all of the following key terms: border state, blockade, offensive, Rebel, Yankee.
2. **Reviewing Facts** Why were the border states important to the North?

Reviewing Themes

3. **Government and Democracy** How did a strong belief in states' rights affect the South during the war?

Critical Thinking

4. **Predict** What do you think would be the South's greatest advantage in the war?
5. **Comparing** Create a diagram like the one shown here. Then compare Northern and Southern aims and strategies.

	North	South
Aims		
Strategies		

Analyzing Visuals

6. **Making Generalizations** Review the graph on page 462 and write a general conclusion based on the data presented in the graph.

Interdisciplinary Activity

Expository Writing You are a Southerner (or a Northerner) in 1861. Write a journal entry that explains your reasons for joining the Confederate (or Union) army.

SECTION 1 ASSESSMENT ANSWERS

1. Student work should reflect correct use of terms.
2. They controlled crucial land and water routes and were near Washington, D.C.
3. States refused to give the Confederate government needed power.
4. Answers will vary but may include knowledge of the land and fighting for a cause.
5. Northern aims: bring South back into the Union; Northern strategies: blockade ports, control Mississippi River, capture Richmond; Southern aims: gain independence, preserve slavery; Southern strategies: outlast North, gain support from Britain and France, move armies north
6. Answers may include that the North had more resources.

Interdisciplinary Activity Accept valid reasons.

America's LITERATURE

Block Schedule

Team Teaching This selection from *The Red Badge of Courage* may be implemented in a team-teaching context, in conjunction with English/Language Arts.

Stephen Crane (1871–1900)

Stephen Crane began his career in journalism while still in his teens. Later, as a reporter, Crane covered several wars in the late 1890s. He had not yet seen a battlefield, however, when he wrote *The Red Badge of Courage.* Even so, he described the experience of war so realistically that even combat veterans admired his work.

READ TO DISCOVER

What is it like to be a soldier facing battle for the first time? Henry Fleming, the young recruit in *The Red Badge of Courage,* offers some answers as he thinks about his role in the war. What battle does Henry fight with himself before he fights in an actual Civil War battle?

READER'S DICTIONARY

Huns: soldiers known for their fierce fighting

haversack: bag soldiers used to carry personal items

obliged: felt it necessary to do something

confronted: faced

lurking: lying in wait

tumult: uproar

The Red Badge of Courage

Various veterans had told him tales. Some talked of . . . tremendous bodies of fierce soldiery who were sweeping along like the **Huns.** Others spoke of tattered and eternally hungry men. . . . "They'll charge through hell's fire an' brimstone t' git a holt on a **haversack . . .**" he was told. From the stories, the youth imagined the red, live bones sticking out through slits in the faded uniforms.

Still, he could not put a whole faith in veterans' tales, for recruits were their prey. They talked much of smoke, fire, and blood, but he could not tell how much might be lies. They persistently yelled "Fresh fish!" at him, and were in no wise to be trusted.

However, he perceived now that it did not greatly matter what kind of soldiers he was going to fight. . . . There was a more serious problem. He lay in his bunk pondering upon it. He tried to mathematically prove to himself that he would not run from a battle.

Previously he had never felt **obliged** to wrestle too seriously with this question. In his life he had taken certain things for granted, never challenging his belief in ultimate success. . . . But here he was **confronted** with a thing of moment. It had suddenly appeared to him that perhaps in a battle he might run.

He was forced to admit that as far as war was concerned he knew nothing of himself. . . .

A little panic-fear grew in his mind. As his imagination went forward to a fight, he saw hideous possibilities. He contemplated the **lurking** menaces of the future, and failed in an effort to see himself standing stoutly in the midst of them. He recalled his visions of broken-bladed glory, but in the shadow of the impending **tumult** he suspected them to be impossible pictures.

Medal of Honor

ANALYZING LITERATURE

1. **Recall and Interpret** How did Henry view the veterans and their war tales?
2. **Evaluate and Connect** What feelings do you think you might have just before going into battle?

Interdisciplinary Activity

Descriptive Writing Write a conversation between two young soldiers before their first battle. Save your work for your portfolio.

465

Reinforcing Vocabulary

Review the **Reader's Dictionary** terms with students to be sure they understand any unfamiliar terms.

Historical Connection

The bloodiest conflict in the nation's history, the Civil War, lasted 4 years and claimed the lives of more than 600,000 soldiers—equal to 2 percent of the population.

Background Information

Setting The excerpt takes place before a Civil War battle.

Characters The major character in the excerpt is Henry Fleming, the young recruit who is the hero of the book.

Plot As young Fleming faces the rigors of combat for the first time, he learns the meaning of heroism.

HISTORY *Online*

Refer to tarvol1.glencoe.com for additional Glencoe Literature titles, lesson plans, and study guides related to this unit.

ANSWERS TO ANALYZING LITERATURE

1. He knew veterans told tales that could be lies to young recruits. He thought veterans were not to be trusted.

2. Students should describe their feelings about going into battle.

Interdisciplinary Activity

Call on pairs of volunteers to read the conversations aloud.

SECTION 2 Early Years of the War

1 FOCUS

Section Overview

This section describes how geography affected Northern and Southern war strategies.

BELLRINGER
Skillbuilder Activity

Project transparency and have students answer the question.

Daily Focus Skills Transparency 16–2

Reading Preview

Answers to Graphic: First Battle of Bull Run (Manassas): Confederate victory; *Monitor* v. *Merrimack:* neither ship sank, but the Union kept the *Merrimack* in its harbor so it never again threatened Union ships; Antietam: Union victory

Preteaching Vocabulary
Ask students to identify each of the **Key Terms** as a liability or an asset in fighting a war.

Guide to Reading

Main Idea
Neither the Union nor the Confederate forces gained a strong advantage during the early years of the war.

Key Terms
blockade runner, ironclad, casualty

Reading Strategy
Classifying Information As you read, describe the outcome of each of these battles on a chart like the one shown.

Battle	Outcome
First Battle of Bull Run (Manassas)	
Monitor v. *Merrimack*	
Antietam	

Read to Learn
• what successes and failures the North and the South had in the early years of the war.
• how the North's naval blockade hurt the South.

Section Theme
Geography and History The North and the South fought the war differently in different geographic regions.

Preview of Events

♦1861	♦1862	♦1863

July 1861
First Battle of Bull Run (Manassas)

February 1862
Grant captures Fort Henry and Fort Donelson

April 1862
Battle of Shiloh

September 1862
Battle of Antietam

★★★★★★★★
AN
American Story

Civil War cannon

Sunday, July 21, 1861, was a pleasant, sunny day in Washington, D.C. Hundreds of cheerful residents, food baskets in hand, left the city and crossed the Potomac River to spend the day in Virginia. They planned to picnic while watching the first battle between the Union and the Confederate armies. Expecting to see Union troops crush the Rebels, they looked forward to a quick victory. The Confederate soldiers also expected a quick victory. They "carried dress suits with them, and any quantity of fine linen. Every soldier, nearly, had a servant with him, and a whole lot of spoons and forks, so as to live comfortably and elegantly in camp...."

First Battle of Bull Run

This first major battle of the Civil War was fought in northern Virginia, about five miles from a town called Manassas Junction near Bull Run—a small river in the area. Usually called the **First Battle of Bull Run**, it began when about 30,000 inexperienced Union troops commanded by General Irvin McDowell attacked a smaller, equally inexperienced Confederate force led by General P.G.T. Beauregard.

466 CHAPTER 16 The Civil War

SECTION RESOURCES

📁 **Reproducible Masters**
• Reproducible Lesson Plan 16–2
• Daily Lecture and Discussion Notes 16–2
• Guided Reading Activity 16–2
• Section Quiz 16–2
• Reteaching Activity 16–2
• Reading Essentials and Study Guide 16–2
• Enrichment Activity 16–2

📖 **Transparencies**
• Daily Focus Skills Transparency 16–2

Multimedia
🎵 American Music: Hits Through History
💿 Interactive Tutor Self-Assessment CD-ROM
💿 ExamView® Pro Testmaker CD-ROM
💿 Presentation Plus! CD-ROM

President Lincoln meets General McClellan and other Union officers.

The Yankees drove the Confederates back at first. Then the Rebels rallied, inspired by reinforcements under General Thomas Jackson. Jackson, who was seen holding out heroically "like a stone wall," became known thereafter as **"Stonewall" Jackson.** The Confederates unleashed a savage counterattack that forced the Union lines to break.

The Confederates surged forward with a strange, unearthly scream that came to be known as the Rebel yell. Terrified, the Northern soldiers began to drop their guns and packs and run. One observer, Representative Albert Riddle, reported:

> 66 A cruel, crazy, mad, hopeless panic possessed them. . . . The heat was awful . . . the men were exhausted—their mouths gaped, their lips cracked and blackened with the powder of the cartridges they had bitten off in the battle, their eyes staring in frenzy. 99

The Union army began an orderly retreat that quickly became a mad stampede when the retreating Union troops collided with the civilians, fleeing in panic back to Washington, D.C. The Confederates, though victorious, were too disorganized and weakened to pursue the retreating Yankees. Regardless, the South rejoiced. Edmund Ruffin of Virginia thought it meant "the close of the war."

A Shock for the North

The outcome of the battle shocked the North. Northerners began to understand that the war could be a long, difficult, and costly struggle. Although discouraged by the results, President Abraham Lincoln was also determined. Within days he issued a call for more volunteers for the army. He signed two bills requesting a total of one million soldiers, who would serve for three years. Volunteers soon crowded into recruiting offices. Lincoln also appointed a new general, **George B. McClellan,** to head the Union army of the East—called the **Army of the Potomac**—and to organize the troops.

✓**Reading Check** Explaining How did the First Battle of Bull Run change people's views about the war?

War at Sea

Even before Bull Run, Lincoln had ordered a naval blockade of Southern ports. An effective blockade would prevent the South from exporting its cotton and from importing the supplies necessary to continue the war.

CHAPTER 16   The Civil War   **467**

COOPERATIVE LEARNING ACTIVITY

Creating a Civil War Trivia Game Organize the class into groups of three. As a group have students create and write the rules of a Civil War trivia game using information in this section. Have students choose from the following roles: design question cards, design playing pieces and any other game pieces described in the rules, and design game boards. Students should determine the trivia questions and answers to be used in the game and write them on the question cards. Have groups trade and play the completed games. **L2**

---

2 TEACH

Daily Lecture and Discussion Notes 16–2

Copyright © by The McGraw-Hill Companies, Inc.

Daily Lecture and Discussion Notes

Chapter 16, Section 2

Did You Know? General William Tecumseh Sherman was once asked which was his worst experience in battle during the Civil War. Without hesitation, he replied "Shiloh!"

I. **First Battle of Bull Run** *(Pages 466–467)*

 A. The first major battle of the Civil War was called the First Battle of Bull Run. It was fought in northern Virginia near a river called Bull Run.

 B. The Confederates were victorious. Union troops attacked Confederate forces led by General P.G.T. Beauregard. Next, the Rebels rallied under General Thomas "Stonewall" Jackson's reinforcement troops and counterattacked the Yankees. Then, the Union army retreated back to Washington, D.C., first in an orderly fashion and then in a panic.

 C. The Confederate victory shocked the North. Northerners realized that the war could be a long, hard, and costly one. Abraham Lincoln called for one million army volunteers to serve for three years. He also appointed General B. McClellan to head the Union army of the East called the Army of the Potomac.

Discussion Question
Why did Lincoln call for one million volunteers to serve for three years and appoint a new general for the Union troops? *(After the defeat at the First Battle of Bull Run, he knew he had to be better prepared. He was determined to have a strong army of well-trained men committed for a longer length of service. He also wanted good leadership so that the North would be ready for the fighting that now appeared would be longer than people first expected it would.)*

II. **War at Sea** *(Pages 467–468)*

 A. Lincoln ordered a blockade of Southern ports to prevent the South from exporting its cotton and importing necessary supplies such as guns, ammunition, and food. It did not close off all Southern ports, but it did reduce trade by two-thirds. Over time the North also built more ships to better enforce the blockade.

 B. A new era in naval warfare began when the North's *Monitor* and the South's *Merrimack,* renamed *Virginia,* exchanged fire in March 1862. Both ships were wooden ships covered with thick iron plates, making them sturdy and hard to sink. The Union was the victor because the *Merrimack* never again threatened Northern ships.

turn

◀ **Reading Strategy** ▶

Outlining Ask students to make an outline of this section using the subheads. Then have them complete the outlines by listing the strategies used by the North and the South. **L1**

✓**Reading Check**

Answer: Because of the Southern victory, Northerners began to realize that the war could be long, difficult, and costly.

Did you know

Before the war General Thomas "Stonewall" Jackson was an instructor at the Virginia Military Institute. In 1859 he commanded a contingent of V.M.I. cadets serving as guards at John Brown's execution.

Guided Reading Activity 16–2

Name _____ Date _____ Class _____

★ **Guided Reading Activity 16-2**

DIRECTIONS: Recalling the Facts Use the information in your textbook to answer the questions. Use another sheet of paper if necessary.
1. Where was the first major battle of the Civil War? _____
2. Who were the two generals who led the South in this battle? _____

3. Who won this battle? _____
4. What was the Union army of the East called? _____
5. Who headed the Union army of the East? _____
6. Why did Abraham Lincoln order a blockade of Southern ports? _____
7. How did the South challenge the blockade? _____
8. What was the North's first strategic goal in the West? _____
9. How long did the Battle of Shiloh last? _____
10. Who was victorious in the Battle of Shiloh? _____
11. Why was David Farragut's capture of New Orleans significant? _____
12. What was George McClellan's goal in March 1862? _____
13. What was McClellan's operation known as? _____
14. How did McClellan's delays benefit the Confederates? _____
15. Who commanded the South's army for the Seven Days battles? _____
16. What was the outcome of McClellan's offensive? _____
17. What took place on August 29, 1862? _____
18. Who was victorious? _____
19. What advantage over the South did the North have when it launched an offensive into Maryland in September 1862? _____
20. When was the single bloodiest day of the war? _____
21. How did Lincoln react to McClellan's repeated hesitance? _____

✓ Reading Check

Answer: It was the first battle between metal-covered ships.

What?Where?When?Who?

The Monitor The Swedish-born inventor John Ericsson invented the *Monitor*. The original *Monitor* served as the inspiration for 60 more *Monitor*-type ironclads built during the war. It housed 2 guns to the *Merrimack*'s 10, but they were mounted on a revolving turret.

Enforcing the Blockade

When the war began, the North did not have enough ships to blockade the South's entire 3,500-mile coastline. Many Confederate ships, called blockade runners, could sail in and out of Southern ports. In time, the North built more ships and became better able to enforce the blockade.

The blockade caused serious problems for the South. Although the blockade could never close off all Southern trade, it did reduce the trade by more than two-thirds. Goods such as coffee, shoes, nails, and salt—as well as guns and ammunition—were in short supply throughout the war.

The *Monitor* Versus the *Merrimack*

The South did not intend to let the blockade go unchallenged. Southerners salvaged the *Merrimack*, a Union warship that Northern forces had abandoned when Confederate forces seized the naval shipyard in **Norfolk, Virginia.** The Confederates rebuilt the wooden ship, covered it with thick iron plates, and renamed it the *Virginia*.

On March 8, 1862, this ironclad warship attacked a group of Union ships off the coast of Virginia. The North's wooden warships could not damage the Confederate ship—shells simply bounced off its sides.

Some Northern leaders feared the South would use the ironclad warship to destroy much of the Union navy, steam up the Potomac River, and bombard Washington, D.C. However, the North had already built an ironclad ship of its own, the *Monitor*. Described as looking like a "tin can on a shingle," the *Monitor* rushed south to engage the Confederate ship in battle.

On March 9, the two ironclads exchanged fire, but neither ship could sink the other. The Union succeeded in keeping the *Merrimack* in the harbor, so it never again threatened Northern ships. The battle marked a new age in naval warfare—the first battle between two metal-covered ships.

✓ Reading Check **Explaining** What was significant about the battle between the *Merrimack* and the *Monitor*?

War in the West

After the First Battle of Bull Run in July 1861, the war in the East settled into a stalemate as each side built its strength. Generals focused on training raw recruits, turning civilians into soldiers. For a while the action shifted to the West.

Early Victories for the North

One of the North's primary goals in the West was to gain control of the Mississippi and Tennessee Rivers. This would split the Confederacy and hinder Southern efforts to transport goods.

The Union launched its operations in the West from Cairo, Illinois. The city was strategically located where the Ohio and Mississippi Rivers meet. In addition, Cairo was only a short distance from the Cumberland and Tennessee Rivers. The Union commander at Cairo was **Ulysses S. Grant.**

Ironclads marked the beginning of the modern, armored, self-propelled warship.

DIFFERENTIATED INSTRUCTION

English Learners Have students skim this section to find the successes and failures of the North and the South in the early years of the Civil War. Ask them to illustrate this information as a poster-size graphic organizer. Encourage students to use both type and graphics as they create their organizers.
L1, ELL

☞ Refer to *Inclusion for the Middle School Social Studies Classroom Strategies and Activities* in the TCR.

Early in 1862, Grant was ordered to move against Confederate forces under General Albert Sidney Johnson in Kentucky and Tennessee. On February 6, with the aid of a fleet of newly made ironclads under Andrew Foote, Grant captured Fort Henry on the Tennessee River. Ten days later Grant captured Fort Donelson on the Cumberland. When the Confederate commander at Fort Donelson realized he was trapped, he asked Grant for his terms. Grant's reply was,

❝No terms except unconditional and immediate surrender can be accepted.❞

"Unconditional Surrender" Grant became the North's new hero.

Grant's victories helped secure the lower Tennessee River. They also opened a path for Union troops to march into Tennessee, Mississippi, and Alabama. The victories drove the Confederates out of Kentucky, where the South had been attempting to persuade Kentuckians to secede from the Union.

✦ Geography
The Battle of Shiloh

General Grant and about 40,000 troops then headed south along the Tennessee River toward Corinth, Mississippi, an important railroad junction. In early April 1862, the Union army camped at Pittsburg Landing, 20 miles from Corinth. Nearby was a church named Shiloh. Additional Union forces came from Nashville to join Grant.

Confederate leaders decided to strike first, before the reinforcements arrived. Early in the morning of April 6, Confederate forces led by Albert Sidney Johnston and P.G.T. Beauregard launched a surprise attack on the Union troops. The **Battle of Shiloh** lasted two days, with some of the most bitter, bloody fighting of the war. The first day, the Confederates drove Grant and his troops back to the Tennessee River. The second day, the Union forces recovered. Aided by the 25,000 troops from Nashville and shelling by gunboats on the river, they defeated the Confederates, who withdrew to Corinth.

Names of Battles

Many Civil War battles have two names. The Union named battles after the nearest body of water. The Confederacy named them after the nearest settlement. Therefore, the battle called the Battle of Bull Run (a river) in the North was known as the Battle of Manassas (a settlement) in the South.

The losses in the Battle of Shiloh were enormous. Together the two armies suffered more than 20,000 casualties—people killed or wounded. Confederate general Johnston also died in the bloodbath. One Confederate soldier lamented that the battle "was too shocking [and] too horrible."

After their narrow victory at Shiloh, Union forces gained control of Corinth on May 30. Memphis, Tennessee, fell to Union armies on June 6. The North seemed well on its way to controlling the Mississippi River.

New Orleans Falls

A few weeks after Shiloh, the North won another important victory. On April 25, 1862, Union naval forces under **David Farragut** captured New Orleans, Louisiana, the largest city in the South. Farragut, who was of Spanish descent, had grown up in the South but remained loyal to the Union. His capture of New Orleans, near the mouth of the Mississippi River, meant that the Confederacy could no longer use the river to carry its goods to sea. Together with Grant's victories to the north, Farragut's capture of New Orleans gave Union forces control of almost all the Mississippi River.

✓ **Reading Check** Analyzing Why was control of the Mississippi River important to the Union?

War in the East

In the East, General McClellan was training the Army of the Potomac to be an effective fighting force. An expert at training soldiers,

CHAPTER 16   The Civil War   **469**

CHAPTER 16
Section 2, 466–472

✓ **Reading Check**

Answer: Control of the Mississippi River would split the Confederacy and hinder Southern efforts to transport goods.

As the Union troops were driven back at the Battle of Shiloh, they established a line along an area known as the Sunken Road. The Union forces withstood 12 attacks against this position. The area became known as the Hornets' Nest because of the intensity of the gunfire and the grazing of bullets. Southern troops organized 62 artillery pieces to fire on the Hornets' Nest, the largest concentration of artillery yet assembled in the war. The shells splintered trees and boulders. An Iowa lieutenant said that it was "a mighty hurricane sweeping everything before it." After six hours, 2,200 Union soldiers surrendered.

📖 History and the Humanities

🎵 American Music: Hits Through History; "Johnny Comes Marching Home" and "Battle Hymn of the Republic" medley

INTERDISCIPLINARY CONNECTIONS ACTIVITY

Daily Life Ask students to create a time line from the following information on a day in the life of a Civil War soldier (who was not engaged in battle): 5:00 A.M.—Reveille played; 5:15 A.M.—Roll call and special orders; 5:30 A.M.–8:00 A.M.—Breakfast, tend horses, infirmary calls, cleanup duty, and necessary chores; 8:00 A.M.–2:00 P.M.—Two hours of sentry-duty out of six hours; 8:00 A.M.–12:00 P.M.—Drill if not on sentry duty; 12:00 P.M.—Dinner followed by more drill; 4:30 P.M.—Polish weapons and care for uniforms; 5:45 P.M.—Retreat ceremony with roll call, inspection, and dress parade; 7:30 P.M.—Supper; 8:30 P.M.—Assembly and last roll call; 9:00 P.M.—Taps sounded and lights out. **L2,** ELL

469

Geography *Skills*

Answers:
1. Tennessee
2. Fort Sumter, First Bull Run, and Second Bull Run

Geography Skills Practice
Ask: On what date was the battle between the *Monitor* and the *Merrimack* fought? *(March 9, 1862)*

CURRICULUM CONNECTION

Science The single most-important invention used by McClellan's army was an inch-long slug that expanded into the barrel's rifled grooves and spun at great speed from the muzzle. The spin allowed the ball to travel farther and more accurately than musket balls fired from smooth-barreled weapons. The ball was accurate at 250 yards (229 m), five times as far as any other one-person weapon.

NATIONAL GEOGRAPHIC

The Early Battles, 1861–1862

1. Ft. Sumter falls to Confederate troops.
2. Union blockade cuts Confederate flow of trade and supplies.
3. With about 23,000 casualties, Shiloh is the bloodiest battle fought thus far.
4. Antietam costs more casualties than any other single day of the war — over 23,000 killed or wounded.

- Union troops
- Confederate troops
- Union victory
- Confederate victory
- Indecisive battle
- Union naval blockade
- Boundary between Union and Confederacy

Geography *Skills*

1. **Analyzing Information** In what state was the Battle of Shiloh fought?
2. **Summarizing** In what battles were Confederate forces victorious?

McClellan thoroughly reorganized and drilled the Army of the Potomac. However, when faced with the prospect of battle, McClellan was cautious and worried that his troops were not ready. He hesitated to fight because of reports that overestimated the size of the Rebel forces. Finally, in March 1862, the Army of the Potomac was ready for action. Its goal was to capture Richmond, the Confederate capital.

Union Defeat at Richmond

Instead of advancing directly overland to Richmond as Lincoln wished, McClellan moved his huge army by ship to a peninsula between the York and the James Rivers southeast of the city. From there he began a major offensive known as the **Peninsular Campaign.** The operation took many weeks. Time passed and opportunities to attack slipped away as General McClellan readied his troops and tried to evaluate the enemy's strength. Lincoln, constantly prodding McClellan to fight, ended one message with an urgent plea: "You must act." Complaining of his difficult situation, McClellan did

Reading Strategy — READING THE TEXT

Reading Primary and Secondary Sources Have students use library resources to find writings by Northerners and Southerners during the Civil War. In a class discussion, evaluate the validity of the authors' points of view based on their language and logic. Compare this information to that found in their textbooks and other writings. Have students explain whether or not the authors provide valid and reliable sources of information about the Civil War. **L2**

not act. His delays allowed the Confederates to prepare their defense of Richmond.

McClellan and his army inched slowly toward Richmond, getting so close that the troops could hear the city's church bells. At the end of June, the Union forces finally met the Confederates in a series of encounters known as the Seven Days' Battles. In these battles Confederate general **Robert E. Lee** took command of the army opposing McClellan. Before the battles began, Lee's cavalry leader, **James E.B. (J.E.B.) Stuart,** performed a daring tactic. He led his 1,200 troops in a circle around the Union army, gathering vital information about Union positions and boosting Southern morale. Stuart lost only one man in the action. General Lee then boldly countered Union advances and eventually drove the Yankees back to the James River. The Union troops had failed to capture Richmond.

Gloom in the North

Reports from Richmond disheartened the North. Despite the good news of Union victories in the West, failure to take the Confederate capital left Northerners with little hope. There was another call for volunteers—300,000 this time—

but the response was slow. The Southern strategy of making the North weary of war seemed to be working.

The defeat had not been complete, however. McClellan's army had been pushed back, but it was larger than Lee's and still only 25 miles from Richmond. When McClellan failed to renew the attack, President Lincoln ordered him to move his army back to northern Virginia and join the troops led by Major General John Pope.

Stonewall Jackson's forces moved north to attack Pope's supply base at Manassas. Jackson's troops marched 50 miles in two days and were then joined by the rest of Lee's army. On August 29, 1862, Pope attacked the approaching Confederates and started the Second Battle of Bull Run. The battle ended in a Confederate victory. Richmond was no longer threatened. Indeed, the situation of the two sides was completely reversed. Lee and the Confederates now stood only 20 miles from Washington, D.C.

The Battle of Antietam

Following these Southern victories, Confederate president **Jefferson Davis** ordered Lee to launch an offensive into Maryland, northwest of

Wounded soldiers at a military hospital at Alexandria, Virginia.

CHAPTER 16   The Civil War   **471**

EXTENDING THE CONTENT

Boys on the Battlefield Boys under the age of 16 served in both the Union and Confederate armies. Most entered the army as musicians, where they played drums and bugles. Their music woke soldiers in the morning and called them to breakfast. It signaled order and told troops how and when to maneuver in battle. Because of this, the young boys were often the target of enemy fire. The boys also helped soldiers by performing such chores as cutting hair, carrying water, and helping the wounded. One of the most famous boys was John Lincoln Clem. At age 10, Clem joined the 22nd Michigan Infantry. His drum was destroyed by a shell at Shiloh, and he avoided capture at the Battle of Chickamauga by killing a Confederate colonel. After a military career, he was buried at Arlington National Cemetery, remembered as "The Drummer Boy of Chickamauga."

Objectives and answers to the student activity can be found in the **Web Activity Lesson Plan** feature at tarvol1.glencoe.com

✓ **Reading Check**

Answer: Northern forces were driven back to the James River, failing to capture Richmond.

L3

Enrichment Activity 16–2

HISTORY Online
Student Web Activity
Visit tarvol1.glencoe.com and click on **Chapter 16— Student Web Activities** for an activity on the Second Battle of Bull Run.

Washington. He hoped another victory would win aid from Great Britain and France. Lee also issued a proclamation urging the people of Maryland to join the Confederacy, but he received no response.

As Lee's army marched into Maryland in September 1862, McClellan and 80,000 Union troops moved slowly after them. On September 13 the North had an extraordinary piece of good luck. In a field near Frederick, Maryland, two Union soldiers found a copy of Lee's orders for his army wrapped around three cigars. The bundle had probably been dropped by a Southern officer.

Now McClellan knew exactly what Lee planned to do. He also learned that Lee's army was divided into four parts. This provided McClellan with an opportunity to overwhelm Lee's army one piece at a time.

Once again, McClellan was overly cautious. He waited four days before he decided to attack the Confederates. This enabled Lee to gather most of his forces together near Sharpsburg, Maryland, along the Antietam Creek.

The Union and the Confederate armies clashed on September 17 in the **Battle of Antietam.** It was the single bloodiest day of the entire war. A Union officer wrote that

❝In the time that I am writing, every stalk of corn in [cornfields to the north] was cut as closely as could have been with a knife, and the slain lay in rows precisely as they had stood in their ranks a few minutes before.❞

By the time the fighting ended, close to 6,000 Union and Confederate soldiers lay dead or dying, and another 17,000 were seriously wounded. Although both armies suffered heavy losses, neither was destroyed.

The day after the battle, Lee withdrew to Virginia. The Confederate retreat allowed the Union troops to claim victory. However, McClellan, who had been ordered by President Lincoln to "destroy the rebel army," did not pursue the Confederate troops. The president, disgusted with McClellan's failure to follow up his victory, removed McClellan from his command in November. Lincoln placed General **Ambrose Burnside** in command.

Antietam had a profound impact on the war. The Army of the Potomac finally gained some confidence, having forced Lee and his soldiers back south. More important, the battle marked a major change in Northern war aims. President Lincoln used the battle to take action against slavery.

✓ **Reading Check** **Summarizing** What was the outcome of the Seven Days' Battles?

★ Enrichment Activity 16-2

A Clash of Iron
In March 1862, the first battle between ironclad ships took place off the Virginia coast. The Union sent its newly-built USS *Monitor* to attack the Confederate ship CSS *Virginia*, a ship that had been captured from the Union, fortified with iron, and renamed. The *Virginia* was the Confederate name for the *Merrimack*. The picture below shows the ships at war.

Ironclad Ships		
	Monitor	**Merrimack/Virginia**
Approximate relative size	small	large
Source of power	steam	steam
General design	flat; sat low in water; round turret	flat base with slanted sides; triangular peak; high smokestack
Offensive weapons	cannons; main gun in turret	cannons; guns forward and to side of peaked area
Defenses	iron-covered deck; cannonballs roll off flat deck	iron-covered deck; slanted sides of turret deflect cannonballs

DIRECTIONS: Drawing Conclusions Based on the designs, which ship do you think was better prepared for attack? Which was better prepared for defense? Give reasons for your answers.

Activity **DIRECTIONS: Writing a Letter** What do you think it would have been like inside one of these ships? You are assigned to the *Monitor* or the *Merrimack*. Write a letter to your family at home telling about your experiences. Include specific details to give a feeling of being there.

4 CLOSE

Ask students to refer to the outlines they created in the "TEACH" activity to determine which side, the North or the South, had the greatest geographic advantage.

SECTION 2 ASSESSMENT

Checking for Understanding

1. **Key Terms** Use each of these terms in a sentence that will help explain its meaning: **blockade runner, ironclad, casualty.**

2. **Reviewing Facts** Explain why the North wanted to blockade the South.

Reviewing Themes

3. **Geography and History** What was the North's main goal in the western campaign?

Critical Thinking

4. **Analyzing Information** Why was Union general McClellan not effective as a military commander?

5. **Drawing Conclusions** Why was control of the Mississippi River important? Use a web like the one shown here.

Control of the Mississippi River

Analyzing Visuals

6. **Geography Skills** Study the map on page 470. Who claimed victory at the First Battle of Bull Run? When was the Battle of Shiloh fought?

Interdisciplinary Activity

Art Draw a cartoon that would accompany a front-page newspaper story describing the battle between the *Merrimack* and the *Monitor*.

SECTION 2 ASSESSMENT ANSWERS

1. Student work should reflect correct use of terms.
2. to prevent exports of cotton and imports of supplies needed to fight the war
3. to gain control of the Mississippi and Tennessee Rivers
4. McClellan did not act fast enough, and this gave the Confederates time to prepare for attacks.
5. It bound the Confederacy geographically and served as a transportation route for goods and troops.
6. the Confederacy; April 6–7, 1862

Interdisciplinary Activity Cartoons should illustrate the battle between the *Merrimack* and the *Monitor*.

SECTION 3 A Call for Freedom

Guide to Reading

Main Idea
The Civil War provided opportunities for African Americans to contribute to the war effort.

Key Terms
emancipate, ratify

Reading Strategy
Classifying Information As you read the section, complete a table like the one shown describing what the Emancipation Proclamation and the Thirteenth Amendment to the Constitution were meant to accomplish.

	Goal
Emancipation Proclamation	
Thirteenth Amendment	

Read to Learn
• why Lincoln issued the Emancipation Proclamation.
• what role African Americans played in the Civil War.

Section Theme
Groups and Institutions The North's main goal from the start of the war was to preserve the Union, not to abolish slavery.

Preview of Events

◆1862   ◆1863   ◆1864   ◆1865

1862
African Americans allowed to serve in the Union army

January 1863
Lincoln signs the Emancipation Proclamation

July 1863
Nearly half of the 54th Massachusetts Regiment is wiped out

1865
Thirteenth Amendment is ratified

Lincoln portrait, by artist Peter Baumgras

AN American Story

President Lincoln shook many hands on New Year's Day of 1863, as a reception was held to commemorate the official signing of the Emancipation Proclamation. Diplomats, cabinet members, and army officers filed past the president, and when he finally left the reception he noted that his arm was very stiff. As the document was presented, Lincoln remarked, "Now, this signature is one that will be closely examined and if they find my hand trembled, they will say 'he had some compunctions [second thoughts].' But, any way, it is going to be done!"

Emancipation

From the start of the war through the brutal Battle of Antietam, the Northerners' main goal was to preserve the Union rather than to destroy slavery. Abolitionists did not control the North, or even the Republican Party. Abraham Lincoln and other Republican leaders insisted on many occasions that they would act only to prevent the expansion of slavery.

CHAPTER 16   The Civil War   **473**

2 TEACH

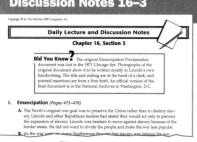
Developing a Story Map Have students work in small groups to create a story map detailing the story leading up to the Emancipation Proclamation. Review with students the four steps of plot development in story maps: 1) introduction of the problem, 2) roadblocks, 3) climax or high point, and 4) solution. Ask groups to present their completed story maps to the class. Discuss how the "plot thickened" to enable President Lincoln to issue the Emancipation Proclamation. **L1**

Did you know?

Heavy death tolls in battle led Civil War soldiers to devise the first dog tags for identification. Soldiers printed their names and addresses on handkerchiefs or paper, which they pinned to their clothing before going into battle.

Why It Matters

The Emancipation Proclamation

On January 1, 1863, President Lincoln issued the Emancipation Proclamation to a nation divided by war. The proclamation stated that all enslaved people in the states controlled by the Confederacy were free.

"If my name ever goes into history, it will be for this act."
— *Abraham Lincoln, 1863*

"The Emancipation Proclamation is the greatest event of our nation's history."
— *Frederick Douglass, 1864*

The Legacy of Freedom

Where America stands today on the issues of human freedom was fueled by the Emancipation Proclamation.

1863	1865	1868	1870	1954
Emancipation Proclamation issued	Thirteenth Amendment abolishes slavery	Fourteenth Amendment guarantees citizens equal protection	Fifteenth Amendment strengthens voting rights	*Brown* v. *Board of Education of Topeka, Kansas* ruling outlaws school segregation

Although Lincoln considered slavery immoral, he hesitated to move against slavery because of the border states. Lincoln knew that making an issue of slavery would divide the people and make the war less popular. In August 1862, Abraham Lincoln responded to pressure to declare an end to slavery.

66 If I could save the Union without freeing *any* slave, I would do it; and if I could save it by freeing *all* the slaves, I would do it; and if I could save it by freeing some and leaving others alone, I would also do that. 99

That was his official position. His personal wish was "that all men everywhere could be free."

As the war went on, attitudes toward slavery began to change. More Northerners believed that slavery was helping the war effort in the South. Enslaved people in the Confederacy raised crops used to feed the armies and did the heavy work in the trenches at the army camps. In the North's view, anything that weakened slavery struck a blow against the Confederacy.

As early as May 1861, some African Americans in the South escaped slavery by going into territory held by the Union army. In 1861 and 1862, Congress passed laws that freed enslaved people who were held by those active in the rebellion against the Union.

Citizenship

The Emancipation Proclamation

Lincoln was keenly aware of the shift in public opinion. He also knew that striking a blow against slavery would make Britain and France

474   CHAPTER 16   The Civil War

COOPERATIVE LEARNING ACTIVITY

Creating a Battle Diorama Organize the class into groups of four to create a diorama of the attack on Fort Wagner by the all-African American 54th Massachusetts. Describe this fort to students as a Confederate fort made of piled-up sand with timber and sandbags that sat at the entrance to Charleston Harbor. The fort mounted 11 heavy guns and numerous mobile field pieces that could be run into position when needed. The only possible approach was up the beach from the south. Allow students to choose from the following roles: create three-dimensional battlefield with fort, create the battle figures, create the artillery and weapons, and create labels for all items displayed. Have groups assemble their dioramas. 📦 **L1, ELL**

As news of the proclamation spread throughout the Confederacy, thousands of enslaved people fled to freedom. About 200,000 freed African Americans served as soldiers, sailors, and laborers for the Union forces.

Union Forces

More than 2 million soldiers served in the Union army, and more than 100,000 sailors served in the Union navy. About 200,000 African Americans served with the Union.

Union Soldiers

Union Sailors

African Americans made up nearly 10% of Union soldiers

African Americans made up about 18% of Union sailors

The proclamation established that the war was being fought not only to preserve the Union, but to end slavery. Few enslaved people were freed by the action, however.

Name _____ Date _____ Class _____

★ Guided Reading Activity 16-3

DIRECTIONS: Using Outlining Locate the heading in your textbook. Then use the information under the heading to help you write each answer. Use another sheet of paper if necessary.

I. Emancipation

A. Introduction

1. Why did Abraham Lincoln hesitate to move against slavery? _____

2. How did Northerners' attitudes toward slavery change as the war went on? _____

B. The Emancipation Proclamation—Why did Lincoln wait to issue the Emancipation Proclamation? _____

C. Effects of the Proclamation

1. Why did the proclamation not actually free any enslaved people? _____

2. What effect did Lincoln hope the proclamation would have on the enslaved? _____

3. What effect did the proclamation have in Europe? _____

4. Which amendment, ratified in 1865, truly freed enslaved African Americans?

II. African Americans in the War

A. In the South

1. By the end of the war, what portion of the Confederacy's enslaved population had fled to Union areas? _____

2. What was the main reason Southerners did not want to use African Americans as soldiers? _____

B. Helping the North—Before they were allowed to serve as soldiers in the Union army, how did African Americans aid the Union war effort? _____

C. African American Soldiers

1. What was the 54th Massachusetts? _____

2. How did the events of July 18, 1863, win respect for African American troops?

1955 →	1963 →	1964 →	2001 →	2003 →
Rosa Parks refuses to give up her bus seat; Montgomery, Alabama	March on Washington	Twenty-fourth Amendment ends use of poll tax; Civil Rights Act passed	Colin Powell named secretary of state	Scheduled work on national monument to Martin Luther King, Jr., begins

---

less likely to aid the South. Moreover, Lincoln became convinced that slavery helped the South continue fighting. Every enslaved person who worked enabled a white Southerner to fight in the Confederate army.

Lincoln also had political reasons for taking action on slavery. He believed it was important that the president rather than the antislavery Republicans in Congress make the decision on ending slavery. Lincoln told the members of his cabinet, "I must do the best I can, and bear the responsibility."

By the summer of 1862, Lincoln had decided to emancipate—or free—all enslaved African Americans in the South. He waited for the right moment so that he would not appear to be acting in desperation when the North seemed to be losing the war. On September 22, 1862, five days

after the Union forces turned back the Confederate troops at the Battle of Antietam, Lincoln announced his plan to issue an order freeing all enslaved people in the Confederacy. On January 1, 1863, Lincoln signed the **Emancipation Proclamation,** which said that

66 …all persons held as slaves within any state…in rebellion against the United States, shall be then, thenceforward, and forever free. 99

Effects of the Proclamation

Because the Emancipation Proclamation applied only to areas that the Confederacy controlled, it did not actually free anyone. Lincoln knew, however, that many enslaved people would hear about the proclamation. He hoped

Why It Matters

Lincoln's preliminary Emancipation Proclamation gave the Confederate states 3 months to end the war without losing their enslaved workers. Lincoln offered this as a means of providing a more peaceful and conservative way of ending slavery. In December 1862 Lincoln proposed to Congress that it should approve a series of constitutional amendments providing for gradual, compensated emancipation and colonization of freed enslaved people. **Ask: How do you think history might have been altered if the Confederacy had accepted Lincoln's initial proposal?** *(Slavery might have continued and the sectional problems of the United States might not have been solved.)*

DIFFERENTIATED INSTRUCTION

Reading Support Make available to students a copy of the Emancipation Proclamation. Working in pairs, students should choose a part of the proclamation they think is the most important and rewrite it in their own words. Then have pairs write a song using these words to sing to the class. **L2**

☞ Refer to *Inclusion for the Middle School Social Studies Classroom Strategies and Activities* in the TCR.

Nearly 200,000 African Americans joined Union forces.

✓ **Reading Check**

Answer: It abolished slavery in the United States.

Who?What?Where?When?

African Americans Even when African Americans were finally allowed to become Union soldiers, they were not immediately allowed into combat. At first, African American units were used as labor battalions and supply troops.

3 ASSESS

Assign Section 3 Assessment as homework or as an in-class activity.

💿 Have students use **Interactive Tutor Self-Assessment CD-ROM.**

L2

Section Quiz 16–3

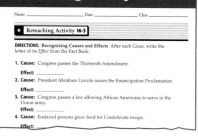

L1

Reteaching Activity 16–3

---

that knowledge of it would encourage them to run away from their slaveholders. Even before the Emancipation Proclamation, some 100,000 African Americans had left slavery for the safety of Union lines. 📖 *(See page 617 of the Appendix for the text of the Emancipation Proclamation.)*

Despite the limitations of the Emancipation Proclamation, African Americans in the North greeted it joyfully. On the day it was signed, a crowd of African Americans gathered at the White House to cheer the president. Frederick Douglass wrote, "We shout for joy that we live to record this righteous decree."

The proclamation had the desired effect in Europe as well. The Confederacy had been seeking support from its trading partners, Britain and France. However, the British took a strong position against slavery. Once Lincoln proclaimed emancipation, Britain and France decided to withhold recognition of the Confederacy.

In 1864 Republican leaders in Congress prepared a constitutional amendment to abolish slavery in the United States. In 1865 Congress passed the **Thirteenth Amendment,** which was **ratified,** or approved, the same year by states loyal to the Union. It was this amendment that truly freed enslaved Americans. 📖 *(See page 246 for the complete text of the Thirteenth Amendment.)*

✓ **Reading Check** **Explaining** What did the Thirteenth Amendment do?

African Americans in the War

Early in the war, Lincoln opposed enlisting African Americans as soldiers. The Emancipation Proclamation announced Lincoln's decision to permit African Americans to join the Union army. In the South, as well as in the North, the Civil War was changing the lives of all African Americans.

In the South

When the war began, over 3.5 million enslaved people lived in the Confederacy. Making up more than 30 percent of the region's population and the bulk of its workforce, enslaved workers labored on plantations and in vital iron, salt, and lead mines. Some worked as nurses in military hospitals and cooks in the army. By the end of the war, about one-sixth of the enslaved population had fled to areas controlled by Union armies.

The possibility of a slave rebellion terrified white Southerners. For this reason most Southerners refused to use African Americans as soldiers—for then they would be given weapons.

Near the end of the war, however, the Confederate military became desperate. Robert E. Lee and some others supported using African Americans as soldiers and believed that those who fought should be freed. The Confederate Congress passed a law in 1865 to enlist enslaved people, although the law did not include automatic freedom. The war ended before any regiments could be organized.

Helping the North

The story was different in the North. At the start of the war, African Americans were not permitted to serve as soldiers in the Union army. This disappointed many free African Americans who had volunteered to fight for the Union.

Yet African Americans who wished to help the war effort found ways to do so. Although the army would not accept them, the Union navy

476 CHAPTER 16 The Civil War

📖 **Reading Strategy** | **READING THE TEXT**

Reading Primary and Secondary Sources Have students research to find primary sources such as letters, diary entries, or contemporary newspaper and magazine articles that shed light on what life was like in the army and navy for African Americans during the Civil War. Direct students to share what they find in class in short oral summaries. Use the information as a springboard for a class discussion about the pros and cons of serving under such circumstances. **L2**

did. African Americans who had escaped slavery often proved to be especially useful as guides and spies because of their knowledge of the South. Some women, such as **Harriet Tubman,** who had helped hundreds escape slavery by way of the Underground Railroad, repeatedly spied behind Confederate lines.

In 1862 Congress passed a law allowing African Americans to serve in the Union army. As a result both free African Americans and those who had escaped slavery began enlisting. In the Emancipation Proclamation, Lincoln supported the use of African American soldiers, and more African Americans began enlisting.

By the end of the war, African American volunteers made up nearly 10 percent of the Union army and about 18 percent of the navy. In all, nearly 200,000 African Americans served. About 37,000 lost their lives defending the Union. By becoming soldiers, African Americans were taking an important step toward securing civil rights.

African American Soldiers

African American soldiers were organized into regiments separate from the rest of the Union army. Most commanding officers of these regiments were white. African Americans received lower pay than white soldiers at first, but protests led to equal pay in 1864.

One of the most famous African American regiments was the **54th Massachusetts,** led by white abolitionists. On July 18, 1863, the 54th spearheaded an attack on a Confederate fortification near Charleston, South Carolina. Under heavy fire, the troops battled their way to the top of the fort. The Confederates drove them back with heavy fire. Nearly half of the 54th were wounded, captured, or killed. Their bravery won respect for African American troops.

Lincoln's political opponents criticized the use of African American soldiers. Lincoln replied by quoting General Grant, who had written to Lincoln that "[they] will make good soldiers and taking them from the enemy weakens him in the same proportion they strengthen us."

Many white Southerners, outraged by African American soldiers, threatened to execute any they captured. In a few instances, this threat was carried out. However, enslaved workers were overjoyed when they saw that the Union army included African American soldiers. As one African American regiment entered Wilmington, North Carolina, a soldier wrote, "Men and women, old and young, were running throughout the streets, shouting and praising God. We could then truly see what we have been fighting for."

✓ **Reading Check** Comparing How were African American soldiers treated differently than white soldiers?

SECTION 3 ASSESSMENT

Checking for Understanding

1. **Key Terms** Use the vocabulary terms that follow to write a paragraph about the Thirteenth Amendment: emancipate, ratify.
2. **Reviewing Facts** Summarize President Lincoln's reasons for issuing the Emancipation Proclamation.

Reviewing Themes

3. **Groups and Institutions** How did African Americans help the war effort in the North? What roles did they play in the South?

Critical Thinking

4. **Comparing** How did President Lincoln's political stand on slavery differ from his personal stand during the war?
5. **Determining Cause and Effect** Re-create the diagram below and list the factors that caused Lincoln to change his war goals to include freeing enslaved persons.

The Emancipation Proclamation

Analyzing Visuals

6. **Picturing History** Study the pictures of the African American soldiers on pages 475 and 476. Do you think that these soldiers have fought in battle? Explain your reasoning.

Interdisciplinary Activity

Citizenship It is 1865 and you have heard about the passage of the Thirteenth Amendment. Using material, thread, beads, and/or felt letters, create a banner that you anticipate carrying in a parade after the Civil War is over.

CHAPTER 16   The Civil War   **477**

✓**Reading Check**

Answer: They were organized into separate units commanded by white officers, and they received lower pay.

L1, ELL

Reading Essentials and Study Guide 16–3

Study Guide

Chapter 16, Section 3
For use with textbook pages 473–477
A CALL FOR FREEDOM

KEY TERMS	
emancipate	To free (page 475)
ratify	To approve (page 476)

DRAWING FROM EXPERIENCE

Have you ever been treated unfairly? Has someone you know been allowed to do something that you were not allowed to do? How did you feel?

In the last section, you read about the battles fought between the North and South in different geographic regions. This section focuses on the contributions of African Americans to the war effort.

L3

Enrichment Activity 16–3

Name _____ Date _____ Class _____

★ **Enrichment Activity 16-3** ★

Charleston

Henry Timrod, who has sometimes been called the "Poet Laureate of the Confederacy," was born in Charleston, South Carolina, in 1828. The poem excerpted below was published by Timrod in 1862.

Charleston

In the broad sunlight of heroic deeds
The City bides [awaits] the foe. . . .
And down the dunes a thousand guns lie couched [resting]
Unseen beside the flood [along the shore],
Like tigers in some Orient jungle crouched,
That wait and watch for blood.
Meanwhile, through streets still echoing with trade,

Whose hands may one day wield the patriot's blade
As lightly as the pen.
And maidens with such eyes as would grow dim
Over a bleeding hound
Seem each one to have caught the strength of him

4 CLOSE

Discuss the following quotation made by American historian Henry Adams while he was in London: "The Emancipation Proclamation has done more for us here than all our former victories and all our diplomacy. It is creating an almost convulsive reaction in our favor."

SECTION 3 ASSESSMENT ANSWERS

1. Student work should reflect correct use of terms.
2. to weaken the South by encouraging enslaved people to run away, to encourage Britain and France to not support the South, to earn public support
3. North: served in military, acted as guides and spies; South: raised crops, labored in mines, worked as nurses and as cooks in the army
4. political: first priority to restore Union; personal: opposed slavery
5. public opinion changed; ending slavery would make Britain and France less likely to aid the South; slavery helped the South
6. Students should support their answers using the pictures.

Interdisciplinary Activity Banners should reflect students' views.

1 FOCUS

Section Overview
This section describes how the war affected civilians and soldiers.

Reading Preview

Answers to Graphic: Velázquez: Confederate soldier and spy; Dix: organized Northern women to serve as military nurses; Barton: treated wounded Union soldiers

Preteaching Vocabulary
Write the entries listed under **Key Terms** on the chalkboard. Have volunteers skim the section to find each term and paraphrase its meaning for the class.

SECTION 4 Life During the Civil War

Guide to Reading

Main Idea
Civilians as well as soldiers had an impact on the war effort.

Key Terms
habeas corpus, draft, bounty, greenback, inflation

Reading Strategy
Classifying Information As you read the section, complete a table like the one shown by describing the roles of these individuals during the war.

	Role
Loretta Janeta Velázquez	
Dorothea Dix	
Clara Barton	

Read to Learn
- what life was like for the soldiers.
- what role women played in the war.
- how the war affected the economies of the North and the South.

Section Themes
Economic Factors The Civil War strained the Northern and Southern economies.

Preview of Events

♦1861	♦1862	♦1863	♦1864
1861 Union Congress passes income tax	**April 1862** Confederate Congress passes draft law	**March 1863** The Union passes draft law	**July 1863** Angry mobs oppose the draft in New York City

---

Union soldier and family, 1861

AN American Story

A soldier's life was not easy—whether in battle or in the mess tent! A Louisiana soldier wrote, "No soldier will forget his first horse-meat breakfast. It was comical to see the facial expression as they viewed the platters of hot steak fried in its own grease or the "chunk" of boiled mule as it floated in a bucket of "stew." However, there seemed to be perfect good humor as they one after the other 'tackled the job.'. . .Occasionally would some stalwart fellow throw back his head and utter a long and loud 'Ye-ha, ye-ha, yehaw!' in imitation of a . . . mule."

The Lives of Soldiers

In both the North and the South, civilians and soldiers suffered terrible hardships and faced new challenges. In touching letters to their families and friends at home, soldiers described what they saw and how they felt—their boredom, discomfort, sickness, fear, and horror.

At the start of the war, men in both the North and the South rushed to volunteer for the armies. Their enthusiasm did not last.

478 CHAPTER 16   The Civil War

478

Most of the time the soldiers lived in camps. Camp life had its pleasant moments of songs, stories, letters from home, and baseball games. Often, however, a soldier's life was dull, a routine of drills, bad food, marches, and rain.

During lulls between battles, Confederate and Union soldiers sometimes forgot that they were enemies. A Southern private described a Fourth of July on the front lines in 1862:

> 66 Our boys and Yanks made a bargain not to fire at each other . . . and talked over the fight, and traded tobacco and coffee and newspaper as peacefully and kindly as if they had not been engaged . . . in butchering one another. 99

The Reality of War

In spite of fleeting moments of calm, the reality of war was never far away. Both sides suffered terrible losses. The new rifles used during the Civil War fired with greater accuracy than the muskets of earlier wars.

Medical facilities were overwhelmed by the thousands of casualties in each battle. After the Battle of Shiloh, many wounded soldiers lay in the rain for more than 24 hours waiting for medical treatment. A Union soldier recalled, "Many had died there, and others were in the last agonies as we passed. Their groans and cries were heart-rending."

Faced with such horrors, many men deserted. About one of every 11 Union soldiers and one of every 8 Confederates ran away because of fear, hunger, or sickness.

Rebel soldiers suffered from a lack of food and supplies. One reason for Lee's invasion of Maryland in 1862 was to allow his army to feed off Maryland crops. A woman who saw the Confederates march to Antietam recalled the "gaunt starvation that looked from their cavernous eyes."

Reading Check **Explaining** Why did many soldiers desert from the armies?

Women and the War

Many Northern and Southern women took on new responsibilities during the war. They became teachers, office workers, salesclerks, and government workers. They worked in factories

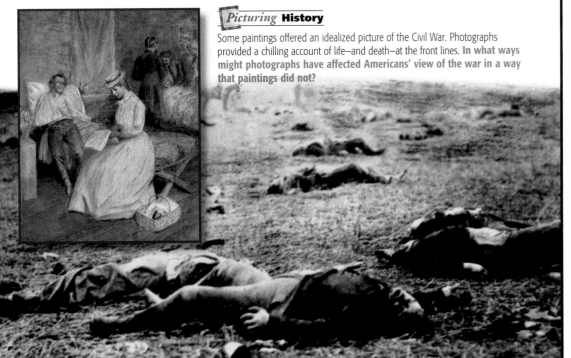

Picturing **History**

Some paintings offered an idealized picture of the Civil War. Photographs provided a chilling account of life—and death—at the front lines. **In what ways might photographs have affected Americans' view of the war in a way that paintings did not?**

COOPERATIVE LEARNING ACTIVITY

Designing a Newspaper Page Organize the class into groups of four to create a newspaper page highlighting selected topics about the Civil War. Have each group choose whether to describe a Northern or Southern newspaper and decide on a name for the newspaper. Then allow group members to choose from the following roles: draw a political cartoon, design an advertisement to raise money for the war effort, write an article on women's roles in the war, and write an interview with a person living at that time. Have each group either paste up the completed pieces of the newspaper page onto newsprint or compose the page on a computer using desktop publishing software. **L1, ELL**

L1, ELL

Guided Reading Activity 16–4

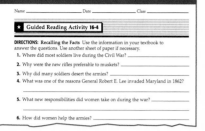

Name _____ Date _____ Class _____

★ **Guided Reading Activity 16-4**

DIRECTIONS: Recalling the Facts Use the information in your textbook to answer the questions. Use another sheet of paper if necessary.

1. Where did most soldiers live during the Civil War? _____
2. Why were the new rifles preferable to muskets? _____
3. Why did many soldiers desert the armies? _____
4. What was one of the reasons General Robert E. Lee invaded Maryland in 1862?
5. What new responsibilities did women take on during the war? _____
6. How did women help the armies? _____

Clara Barton's life of helping others began at the age of 11, when she began two years of nursing a brother who had been badly injured in an accident. After the Civil War, she supervised a four-year search for missing soldiers. Barton also became involved with social issues of her day, supporting the woman suffrage movement and becoming an activist in the movement to gain rights for African Americans. **Ask: In what ways does the Red Cross help people today?** (Answers may include provide food, water, and shelter for disaster victims and maintain a blood supply.)

History *and the* Humanities

American Art and Architecture, Transparency 15, *A Rainy Day in Camp* **L3**

American Art and Music, Mathew Brady **L2**

People In History

Clara Barton 1821–1921

When the Civil War began, Clara Barton, a U.S. Patent Office clerk, began collecting provisions for the Union army. In 1862 she began to deliver supplies directly to the front and to tend to the wounded and dying during battle.

Arriving at Antietam, Barton watched as surgeons dressed the soldiers' wounds with cornhusks because they did not have bandages. Barton was able to give the doctors a wagonload of bandages and other medical supplies. As the battle raged around her, Barton comforted the wounded and helped the doctors with their work.

As night neared, the medical staff had trouble working. From her supply wagon, Barton fetched lanterns and the doctors went back to work.

At Antietam and many other battles, Barton showed courage on the battlefield and gave aid to many. In 1881 Barton organized the American Red Cross and served as its first president for more than 20 years.

and managed farms. They also suffered the loss of husbands, fathers, sons, and brothers. As **Mary Chesnut** of South Carolina wrote:

> ❝ Does anyone wonder [why] so many women die? Grief and constant anxiety kill nearly as many women at home as men are killed on the battle-field. ❞

Women performed many jobs that helped the soldiers and the armies. They rolled bandages, wove blankets, and made ammunition. Many women collected food, clothing, and medicine to distribute to the troops. They also raised money for supplies.

Life at Home

For the most part, Northerners saw the war from a distance, since most of the battles took place in the South. News from the battlefront and letters home from the soldiers kept the war in people's minds.

Almost every woman who stayed at home was touched in some way by the war. But while everyday life in the North suffered little disruption, life in the South was dramatically changed. The fighting and the ever-tightening blockade

disrupted everyday life. Those who lived in the paths of marching armies lost crops and homes. As one Southerner noted: the South had depended upon the outside world "for everything from a hairpin to a toothpick, and from a cradle to a coffin." As the war dragged on, shortages became more commonplace.

The South ran out of almost everything. Shortages in feed for animals and salt for curing meant that little meat was available. Shortages in meat were matched by shortages in clothing, medicine, and even shelter.

Spies

Some women were spies. While Harriet Tubman spied for the North, **Rose O'Neal Greenhow** entertained Union leaders in Washington, D.C., picking up information about Union plans that she passed to the South. Greenhow was caught, convicted of treason, and exiled.

Belle Boyd, of Front Royal, Virginia, informed Confederate generals of Union army movements in the Shenandoah Valley. Some women disguised themselves as men and became soldiers. **Loretta Janeta Velázquez** fought for the South at the First Battle of Bull Run and at Shiloh. Later she became a Confederate spy.

DIFFERENTIATED INSTRUCTION

Reading Support Write the following organizational structure of Civil War armies on the chalkboard: Company = 100 soldiers; Regiment = 10 companies; Brigade = 5 regiments; Division = 3 brigades; Corps = 3 divisions

Ask students to calculate and record how many soldiers made up each unit (regiment, brigade, division, corps), using company as a base. **Ask: How many companies are in a brigade?** *(50)* **How many regiments are in a division?** *(15)* **How many companies are in a corps?** *(450)* **L2**

Treating the Sick and Wounded

In the Civil War, for the first time, thousands of women served as nurses. At first many doctors did not want women nurses on the grounds that women were too delicate for such work. Men also disapproved of women doing what was considered male work, and felt it was improper for women to tend the bodies of unknown men.

Strong-minded women disregarded these objections. In the North **Dorothea Dix** organized large numbers of women to serve as military nurses. Another Northerner, **Clara Barton**, became famous for her work with wounded soldiers. In the South **Sally Tompkins** established a hospital for soldiers in Richmond, Virginia.

Nursing was hard work. Kate Cummings of Alabama, who nursed the wounded in Corinth after the Battle of Shiloh, wrote, "Nothing that I had ever heard or read had given me the faintest idea of the horrors witnessed here." Yet women did a remarkable job in the war.

✓ **Reading Check** **Describing** What role did Sally Tompkins play in the war effort?

Opposition to the War

The war efforts of the Union and the Confederate governments faced opposition. Politicians objected to wartime policies, and ordinary citizens protested the way the war affected their lives.

When the war began, Northern Democrats split into two groups. One group supported most of Lincoln's wartime policies. The other, the "Peace Democrats," favored negotiating with the Confederacy. The Peace Democrats warned that continuing the war would lead to "terrible social change and revolution." They also appealed to racist feelings among Northern whites. Republican newspapers called the Peace Democrats "Copperheads." When Union armies fared poorly, support for the Copperheads rose.

Some Republicans suspected Copperheads of aiding the Confederates. The president ordered the arrest of anyone interfering with the war effort, such as discouraging men from enlisting in the army. Several times Lincoln suspended the right of habeas corpus, which guarantees accused individuals the right to a hearing before being jailed. Lincoln defended his actions, asking "Must I shoot a simple-minded soldier boy who deserts while I must not touch a hair of a wily agitator who induces him to desert?"

Enlistments Decline

As the war dragged on, the number of volunteers declined. Enlisting enough soldiers became a problem, and both the Confederacy and the Union tried new measures.

In April 1862, the Confederate Congress passed a draft law that required men between ages 18 and 35 to serve in the army for three years. A person could avoid the draft by hiring a

Picturing **History**

This 1862 photo shows a Union soldier with his family at the front near Washington, D.C. Most soldiers on both sides, however, faced long separations from their families. **What other hardships did Civil War soldiers face?**

✓**Reading Check**

Answer: She established a hospital for soldiers in Richmond, Virginia.

Picturing **History**

The army hired its own photographers to produce pictures of things such as field fortifications, bridges, and major buildings. Civilian photographers also photographed the war.
Answer: lack of food and supplies, boredom, sickness, discomfort, fear, horror, bad weather

Did you know?

Some women disguised themselves as men and enlisted in the Confederate and Union armies. Jennie Hodgers, for example, signed on with an Illinois regiment as "Albert Cashier."

INTERDISCIPLINARY CONNECTIONS ACTIVITY

Art Ask students to select a family, school, or community event and illustrate that event with a series of photographs. Students who do not have cameras can be paired with students who have. Another alternative is to give students the choice of illustrating an event with photographs or by making a series of drawings. Ask students to present their photographic essays with and without captions. **L1,** ELL

✓ **Reading Check**

Answer: The number of volunteers declined as the war continued.

TECHNOLOGY & History

Civil War Camera Photographic methods were first invented in 1839 in England and France. Americans produced some of the first war photographs during the Mexican War. By 1861 the camera was common throughout the United States.

Answer: Answers will vary, but students should note the changes in technology such as size, automation, film processing, and so on.

3 ASSESS

Assign Section 4 Assessment as homework or as an in-class activity.

🕮 Have students use **Interactive Tutor Self-Assessment CD-ROM.**

L2

Section Quiz 16–4

substitute. Later, Congress exempted one white man on every plantation with 20 or more enslaved people. This led ordinary people to complain of "a rich man's war but a poor man's fight." In reality people from all levels of society served in both armies.

Union states encouraged enlistment by offering *bounties*—payments to encourage volunteers. In March 1863, when this system failed, the North turned to a draft. All men from age 20 to 45 had to register, and the army drew the soldiers it needed from this pool of names. A person could avoid the draft by hiring a substitute or by paying the government $300.

Draft laws aroused opposition, with protests erupting into riots in several Northern cities. The worst disturbance took place in New York City in July 1863. Angry mobs, opposed to the draft and to fighting to free African Americans, went on a rampage of burning, looting, and killing. After four days of terror, more than 100 people were dead. Troops from the Army of the Potomac had to be rushed in to end the rioting.

No disturbance as severe took place in the South, but many opposed the draft. The strong opposition led Jefferson Davis, the president of the Confederacy, to proclaim military law and suspend habeas corpus as Lincoln had done early in the war. Davis's action outraged Southerners who feared that they would lose the liberties for which they had gone to war.

✓ **Reading Check** **Examining** Why did the governments institute a draft?

💲**Economics**

War and the Economy

The Civil War strained the Northern and the Southern economies. The North, with its greater resources, was better able to cope with wartime demands than the South was.

TECHNOLOGY & History

Civil War Camera

Photographer Mathew Brady and his many assistants recorded the camps, lives, and deaths of soldiers in more than 10,000 photos. *What is the biggest difference between this camera and a more modern one?*

Photographer Mathew Brady

1 The photographer looks at the subject through a **glass plate.**

2 A **plate holder** is inserted into the back panel.

3 The photographer opens the **lens**. The lens creates a reversed, upside-down image on the "wet" plate.

4 The **body** of the camera protects the wet plate.

The plate holder and the exposed wet plate are removed from the back panel, then developed into a negative in the photographer's "traveling" **darkroom.**

3 lens
1 glass plate
2 plate holder
4 body

Reading Strategy | READING THE TEXT

Writing Free Writes Have students research the point of view that someone in one of the following groups might have had about the war: Southern farmers, Southern shopkeepers, Southern merchant ship owners, Northern farmers, free Northern African American laborers, Northern textile plant owners. Tell students to then write an essay explaining how such a person feels about the war and why. **L3**

Both the Union and the Confederacy financed the war by borrowing money, increasing taxes, and printing paper money. The North borrowed more than $2 billion, mainly by selling war bonds that promised high interest. The South borrowed more than $700 million. It issued so many bonds that people stopped buying them.

Both sides imposed new taxes as well. The Union passed an income tax in 1861. When Southern states did not provide sufficient funds, the Confederacy also imposed an income tax.

Because neither borrowing nor taxes raised enough money, both sides began printing paper money. Northern money was called greenbacks because of its color. The Confederacy also issued paper money—several times the amount printed in the North.

The North Prospers

During the war prices rose faster than wages in the North. This inflation—a general increase in prices—caused great hardship for working people. Overall, however, the Northern economy boomed. The need for a steady supply of food for Union troops helped farmers prosper.

Factory production grew as manufacturers responded to the demands of war. The army needed many items, from guns and ammunition to shoes and uniforms. Greater use of machinery and the standardization of parts made it possible for the North to produce what it needed.

Economic Troubles in the South

The Civil War is often called the first "modern" war because it required the total commitment of resources. Such a war has an impact on every part of life. However, the impact was more devastating on the South than on the North.

The South struggled to carry out its war effort. Its government encouraged factories to supply arms and ammunition, but the South lacked the industry to provide other necessities.

The economy of the South suffered far more than that of the North. Because most fighting occurred in the South, Southern farmland was overrun and rail lines were torn up. By the end of the war, large portions of the South lay in ruins and thousands of people were homeless.

The North's blockade of Southern ports caused severe shortages of essential goods. A scarcity of food led to riots in Atlanta, Richmond, and other cities. Inflation, too, was much worse in the South. During the course of the war, prices rose 9,000 percent—compared to a rise of 80 percent in the North.

These conditions affected soldiers. Worries about their families caused many men to desert. A Mississippi soldier who overstayed his leave to help his family wrote the governor: "We are poor men and are willing to defend our country but our families [come] first."

✓ **Reading Check** **Explaining** What is inflation?

✓ **Reading Check**

Answer: a general increase in prices

L1

Reteaching Activity 16–4

Name _____ Date _____ Class _____

★ Reteaching Activity 16-4

DIRECTIONS: Completing a Chart Write the number of the names and terms from the Fact Bank in the section of the chart where they belong. Some numbers will be used twice.

The Civil War		
	Union	Confederacy
Soldiers		
Spies		
Nurses		
Economics		

L1, ELL

Reading Essentials and Study Guide 16–4

Study Guide

Chapter 16, Section 4

For use with textbook pages 478–483

LIFE DURING THE CIVIL WAR

KEY TERMS	
habeas corpus	The right to a hearing before being jailed *(page 481)*
draft	A law that required men to serve in the army *(page 481)*
bounty	Payments to volunteers who enlist in the army *(page 482)*
greenback	Northern paper money *(page 483)*
inflation	General increase in prices *(page 483)*

DRAWING FROM EXPERIENCE

Did you know that there has never been a war of ground troops on American soil since the Civil War? All other wars have been fought in foreign countries. How might your life change if you

L3

Enrichment Activity 16–4

Name _____ Date _____ Class _____

★ Enrichment Activity 16-4 ★

Arriving in America

Even as the Civil War raged and news of fighting spread throughout the world, immigrants, hoping for better, more peaceful lives, continued to arrive in the United States. Study the table of immigration during the war years.

Immigration to the United States, 1860–1866				
Year	Great Britain	Ireland	Germany	All Other Countries
1860	29,737	48,637	54,491	20,775
1861	19,675	23,797	31,661	16,785
1862	24,639	23,351	27,529	16,466
1863	66,882	55,916	33,162	20,322
1864	53,428	63,523	57,276	19,191

4 CLOSE

Ask students to explain the following quote made by a colonel of a New York regiment: "We started out in the spring . . . smart, well provided with everything. . . . And we were returning before the autumn, sad, weary, covered with mud, with uniforms in rags."

SECTION 4 ASSESSMENT

Checking for Understanding

1. **Key Terms** Use each of these terms in a complete sentence that will help explain its meaning: habeas corpus, draft, bounty, greenback, inflation.

2. **Reviewing Facts** Why was life on the home front more difficult for Southerners?

Reviewing Themes

3. **Economic Factors** How did the war affect the economy of the South?

Critical Thinking

4. **Making Inferences** Why do you think President Lincoln believed the Copperheads were a threat to the Union war effort?

5. **Analyzing Information** Describe three ways that both the North and South raised money for the war. Use a chart like the one shown below.

Money raised for the war

Analyzing Visuals

6. **Picturing History** Study the photograph of the family on page 481. Why do you think some families accompanied the armies in the field?

Interdisciplinary Activity

Economics List three sectors of the economy that welcomed women during the Civil War. Describe the jobs women held and the contributions they made.

SECTION 4 ASSESSMENT ANSWERS

1. Students work should reflect correct use of terms.

2. Because most of the fighting took place in the South, much of the land lay in ruins, farmland was destroyed, cities were burned, and thousands of people were made homeless.

3. inflation; infrastructure and land destroyed; shortage of essential goods

4. By splitting Union loyalties, Copperheads could give the Confederacy an edge. The Copperheads also appealed to racist feelings and discouraged men from enlisting.

5. borrowed money, increased taxes, printed money

6. Accept all reasonable answers, such as to decrease the time they were apart, or to provide food and other supplies for their loved ones.

Interdisciplinary Activity Answers will vary, but may include education, government, industry, and agriculture.

TEACH

Taking Notes This skill demonstrates how to take notes. As students read Section 5, have them take notes using the main heads found in the text. Students may want to use an outline to help them organize the information. Remind students that although they do not have to write complete sentences, they should be able to understand what they have written. After students read the section, ask questions about what they have read. Students should use their notes to help answer the questions.

Additional Practice

L2

Chapter Skills Activity 16

Name _____ Date _____ Class _____

★ **Chapter Skills Activity 16**

Taking Notes
Notes contain the key points of something that you want to remember. You can take notes while listening to your teacher or reading a book. Notes are especially helpful when you write them in an order and language that you will understand.

DIRECTIONS: Read the excerpt below that is taken from the Emancipation Proclamation signed by Abraham Lincoln during the Civil War. Then fill in the blanks as if you were taking notes on this text.

... That on the 1st day of January, in the year of our Lord 1863, all persons held as slaves within any state or designated part of a state ... in rebellion against the United States, shall be then, thenceforward, and forever free; and the executive government of the United States, including the military and ...

GLENCOE
TECHNOLOGY

CD-ROM
Glencoe Skillbuilder Interactive Workbook CD-ROM, Level 1

This interactive CD-ROM reinforces student mastery of essential social studies skills.

Taking Notes

Why Learn This Skill?

One of the best ways to remember something is to write it down. Taking notes—writing down information in a brief and orderly form—not only helps you remember, but it also makes your studying easier.

Learning the Skill

There are several styles of note taking, but all explain and put information in a logical order. When you are taking notes, it will help to keep in mind these guidelines:

Identify the subject and write it at the top of the page. In your text, for example, look at the chapter title, section title, and other headings.

Select specific information for your notes. For example, anything your teacher writes on the chalkboard or shows you from a transparency should be included. If your teacher emphasizes a point or spends a large amount of time on a topic, this is also a clue to its importance.

Paraphrase the information. That means putting the information in your own words rather than trying to take it down word for word. Doing so helps you think about what the speaker or writer means.

To save time, you might want to develop different strategies. One way is to create a personal "shorthand." For example, use symbols, arrows, or rough drawings: "+" for "and." Practice your shorthand in all of your classes.

Write legible and neat notes so that you will be able to understand them when you read them again.

Practicing the Skill

Review the guidelines for taking notes. Then read Section 5, entitled "The Way to Victory." After you have carefully read the section, follow the guidelines and create shorthand notes for the subsection entitled "The Tide of War Turns," which begins on page 486.

Applying the Skill
Taking Notes Scan a local newspaper for a short editorial or article about your local government. Take notes by using shorthand or by creating an outline. Summarize the article, using only your notes.

 Glencoe's **Skillbuilder Interactive Workbook CD-ROM, Level 1,** provides instruction and practice in key social studies skills.

ANSWERS TO PRACTICING THE SKILL

Students' notes should reflect the information presented in "The Tide of War Turns."

Applying the Skill Notes should include a brief statement that summarizes the main issues in the editorial or article; the names of any local officials, business leaders, or citizens' groups involved; a sentence regarding the pros and cons of any issues.

SECTION 5 The Way to Victory

Guide to Reading

Main Idea
After four years of war that claimed the lives of more than 600,000 Americans, the Northern forces defeated the Southern forces.

Key Terms
entrenched, total war

Reading Strategy
Organizing Information Use a web like the one shown to describe the strategy Grant adopted to defeat the Confederacy.

Grant's strategy

Read to Learn
• what battles turned the tide of the war in 1863.
• what events led the South to surrender in 1865.

Section Theme
Individual Action Brave soldiers from both the North and the South fought gallantly during the Civil War.

Preview of Events

♦1862	♦1863	♦1864	♦1865
December 1862 Lee wins the Battle of Fredericksburg	**July 1863** Battle of Gettysburg	**March 1864** Grant takes over Union command	**April 1865** Lee surrenders to Grant

Confederate soldier

AN American Story

"My shoes are gone; my clothes are almost gone. I'm weary, I'm sick, I'm hungry. My family have been killed or scattered, and may be now wandering helpless and unprotected in a strange country. And I have suffered all this for my country. I love my country. I would die—yes, I would die willingly because I love my country. But if this war is ever over, I'll…[n]ever love another country!" A Confederate soldier expressed these thoughts during difficult times in 1863.

Southern Victories

Gone were the parades and masses of volunteers, the fancy uniforms and optimism of the first years of the war. From 1862 until 1865, the soldiers and civilians faced a grim conflict marked by death, destruction, and wrenching change. What endured on each side was a fierce dedication to its own cause.

The winter of 1862–1863 saw gloom in the North and hope in the South. Robert E. Lee's **Army of Northern Virginia** seemed unbeatable. Lee's grasp of strategy made him more than a match for weak Union generals.

CHAPTER 16   The Civil War   **485**

1 FOCUS

Section Overview
This section describes how Northern forces defeated Southern forces.

BELLRINGER
Skillbuilder Activity

Project transparency and have students answer the question.

Daily Focus Skills Transparency 16–5

Reading Preview

Answers to Graphic: seize Vicksburg to control the Mississippi River; crush Lee's army in Virginia; advance to Atlanta, Georgia, and crush Confederate forces in the Deep South

Preteaching Vocabulary
Use the **Vocabulary PuzzleMaker CD-ROM** to create crossword and word search puzzles.

SECTION RESOURCES

Reproducible Masters
• Reproducible Lesson Plan 16–5
• Daily Lecture and Discussion Notes 16–5
• Guided Reading Activity 16–5
• Section Quiz 16–5
• Reteaching Activity 16–5
• Reading Essentials and Study Guide 16–5
• Enrichment Activity 16–5

Transparencies
• Daily Focus Skills Transparency 16–5

Multimedia
⊙ Vocabulary PuzzleMaker CD-ROM
⊙ Interactive Tutor Self-Assessment CD-ROM
⊙ ExamView® Pro Testmaker CD-ROM
⊙ Presentation Plus! CD-ROM

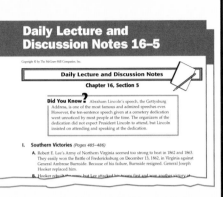
Reading Strategy

Describing Leaders Ask students to skim the section to choose one Union leader and one Confederate leader they believe had the most significant effect on the outcome of the Civil War. Then have them write a paragraph on each one, describing the outstanding leadership characteristics and the specific role each leader played during the Civil War. Ask volunteers to share their paragraphs with the class. **L1**

Reading Check

Answer: Fredericksburg

you don't say...

Burnsides Sideburns are named for the Union commander Ambrose E. Burnside. His distinctive muttonchop whiskers inspired a fashion, which became known as burnsides. Before long the 2 syllables had been transposed.

Fredericksburg and Chancellorsville

Lee needed little skill to win the **Battle of Fredericksburg.** On December 13, 1862, Union general **Ambrose Burnside** clashed with Lee near the Virginia town. Burnside had the larger army, but the Confederates were entrenched, or set up in a strong position, on a number of hills south of the town. Repeated attacks failed to overcome Lee's troops as thousands of Union soldiers fell on the hillside. Devastated by his failure, Burnside resigned his command and was replaced by General **Joseph Hooker.**

Hooker rebuilt the army and in early May 1863, launched a campaign against Lee. Before Hooker could mount a major attack, Lee struck at **Chancellorsville,** Virginia, a few miles west of Fredericksburg. Boldly dividing his troops for an assault on the Union forces, Lee won another victory—but it proved costly. The battle's heavy casualties included General Stonewall Jackson.

On May 2, Jackson and his troops attacked Union troops at dusk. One of the Confederate companies fired on Jackson's party by mistake, wounding the general in the left arm. Jackson's arm had to be amputated and he died a week later.

✓ Reading Check Describing At what Virginia town did Lee defeat Burnside's forces?

Fact • Fiction • Folklore

America's Flags

Confederate Battle Flag, 1861 During the early Civil War battles, soldiers had difficulty distinguishing between the Confederate and Union flags. As a result, Southern soldiers began to carry this battle flag. It had 13 stars, although there were only 11 states in the Confederacy. The other two stars represented the border states of Kentucky and Missouri.

Seventeenth Flag of the Union, 1863 The Union flag of 1863 held 35 stars. Like all the Union flags of the Civil War, it retained stars for the seceded Southern states.

486 CHAPTER 16 The Civil War

The Tide of War Turns

Despite his own heavy losses, Lee decided to invade the North. Another victory—one on Northern soil—might persuade Britain and France to aid the Confederacy.

The Battle of Gettysburg

In June, Lee began moving north with an army of 75,000. Union general Hooker wanted to advance against Richmond, but Lincoln told him to attack Lee's army. When Hooker failed to do this, Lincoln replaced him with General **George Meade.** Meade's mission was to find and fight Lee's forces and to protect Washington and Baltimore from Confederate attack.

The two armies met by accident on July 1, 1863, near the small town of Gettysburg, Pennsylvania. The three-day **Battle of Gettysburg** began when Union cavalry surprised Rebel infantry raiding the town for shoes. Outnumbered, the Northerners fought desperately to hold the town before retreating to Cemetery Ridge, a line of hills south of Gettysburg. The next day the Rebels launched another assault, but a counterattack saved the Union position.

On the third and final day of battle, Lee decided to launch an attack, determined to "create a panic and virtually destroy the [Union] army."

This last attack, led by General George Pickett, is remembered as **Pickett's Charge.** About 14,000 Confederate soldiers advanced across about one-half mile of open ground toward the Union lines. They made easy targets for Union fire as they marched. Barely half of the Rebels returned from the charge. Lee knew the battle was lost. "It's all my fault," he told his troops as they retreated to Virginia.

Victory at Vicksburg

Meanwhile, a great battle was taking place at **Vicksburg, Mississippi.** Vicksburg stood on a high bluff above the Mississippi River. To gain control of the river, one of the North's major war goals, the Union needed to seize Vicksburg. For several months, Union forces under **Ulysses S. Grant** had laid siege to the town. Finally, on July 4, 1863, Vicksburg surrendered.

COOPERATIVE LEARNING ACTIVITY

Illustrating a Time Line Assign each group of four students a time period of American history to illustrate. Time periods should include the Age of Exploration, colonization, the American Revolution, the early Republic, Westward expansion, and the Civil War. Have students in each group choose one of the following activities: draw famous scenes; write a description of daily life; and draw a map of North America. Have each group post the completed information on the appropriate place on the time line with approximate dates for each time period. **L1, ELL**

NATIONAL GEOGRAPHIC
Turning Points, 1862–1863

Union victories at Vicksburg and Gettysburg marked the turning points of the Civil War.

1 Siege of Vicksburg ends with a Confederate surrender. Union isolates western Confederacy.

2 After Gettysburg, Southern troops never again penetrated so deeply into Union territory.

Union troops ⟵
Confederate troops ⟵
Union naval blockade
Union victory ✷
Confederate victory ✷
Indecisive battle ✷
Boundary between Union and Confederacy

Geography *Skills*

1. Location What was the only major battle fought on Union soil?

2. Analyzing Information Why was success at Vicksburg so important to the Union?

With the surrender of Vicksburg and then Port Hudson—a Confederate fort in Louisiana—the Union now held the entire Mississippi River. Texas, Louisiana, and Arkansas were sealed off from the Confederacy.

The Union victories at Gettysburg and Vicksburg marked a turning point in the war. They drove Lee's army out of Pennsylvania, secured the Mississippi as a Union highway, and cut the South in two. Nevertheless, the South still had troops and a will to fight. The war would continue for two more terrible years.

Lincoln at Gettysburg

On November 19, 1863, at a ceremony dedicating a cemetery at Gettysburg, scholar Edward Everett spoke for two hours. Then in a two-minute speech, called the **Gettysburg Address,** President Lincoln beautifully expressed what the war had come to mean:

> 66 It is for us the living . . . to be here dedicated to the great task remaining before us . . . that these dead shall not have died in vain— that this nation, under God, shall have a new birth of freedom—and that government of the people, by the people, for the people shall not perish from the earth. 99

CHAPTER 16   The Civil War   **487**

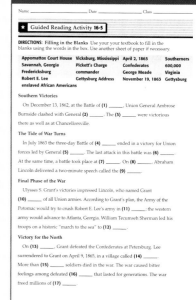

Guided Reading Activity 16–5

Name _____ Date _____ Class _____

★ Guided Reading Activity **16-5**

DIRECTIONS: Filling in the Blanks Use your your textbook to fill in the blanks using the words in the box. Use another sheet of paper if necessary.

Appomattox Court House	Vicksburg, Mississippi	April 2, 1865	Southerners
Savannah, Georgia	Pickett's Charge	Confederates	600,000
Fredericksburg	commander	George Meade	Virginia
Robert E. Lee	Gettysburg Address	November 19, 1863	Gettysburg
enslaved African Americans			

Southern Victories

On December 13, 1862, at the Battle of **(1)** _____, Union General Ambrose Burnside clashed with General **(2)** _____. The **(3)** _____ were victorious there as well as at Chancellorsville.

The Tide of War Turns

In July 1863 the three-day Battle of **(4)** _____ ended in a victory for Union forces led by General **(5)** _____. The last attack in this battle was **(6)** _____. At the same time, a battle took place in **(7)** _____. On **(8)** _____, Abraham Lincoln delivered a two-minute speech called the **(9)** _____.

Final Phase of the War

Ulysses S. Grant's victories impressed Lincoln, who named Grant **(10)** _____ of all Union armies. According to Grant's plan, the Army of the Potomac would try to crush Robert E. Lee's army in **(11)** _____; the western army would advance to Atlanta, Georgia. William Tecumseh Sherman led his troops on a historic "march to the sea" to **(12)** _____.

Victory for the North

On **(13)** _____, Grant defeated the Confederates at Petersburg. Lee surrendered to Grant on April 9, 1865, in a village called **(14)** _____. More than **(15)** _____ soldiers died in the war. The war caused bitter feelings among defeated **(16)** _____ that lasted for generations. The war freed millions of **(17)** _____.

Geography *Skills*

Answers:
1. Gettysburg
2. It gave the Union control of the Mississippi River.

Geography Skills Practice
Ask: Which battle took place in northern Georgia? *(Chickamauga)*

ABCNEWS INTERACTIVE™

VIDEOCASSETTE
Historic America Electronic Field Trips

View **Chapter 8** to learn more about the Battle of Gettysburg.

DIFFERENTIATED INSTRUCTION

Gifted and Talented Ask students to think about what it might have been like to hear the news about Lincoln's assassination. Then have students write a first-person account from the perspective of a Northerner or a Southerner. Students should describe how the event would impact them personally and emotionally. Have them include thoughts about what they think the event would mean for their region of the country. **L3**

📁 Refer to ***Inclusion for the Middle School Social Studies Classroom Strategies and Activities*** in the TCR.

NATIONAL GEOGRAPHIC **The Civil War: Battles and Strategies**

✓ Reading Check

Answer: Vicksburg and Port Hudson

Where? When? Who? What?

Chattanooga Taking Chattanooga was important to the Union. Chattanooga guarded the gateway to the eastern Confederacy and the Southern war industries in Georgia. From this city the Confederate army could mount expeditions into Tennessee and Kentucky. The Union could use the city to mount raids into Georgia and further divide the South.

Did you know?

The extreme left flank of the Union lines at Gettysburg—a hill called Little Round Top—was commanded by Colonel Joshua Lawrence Chamberlain, a college professor who had taken a leave from teaching to fight in the war. Chamberlain knew that if the Confederates took Little Round Top, they would have a view of the whole Union line. Although greatly outnumbered, Chamberlain's forces withstood numerous attacks. Finally, Chamberlain led his troops in a bayonet charge that drove the Confederates from the hill. Chamberlain received the Medal of Honor for his bravery at Gettysburg.

☐ Union Control
☐ Confederate Control
⚓ Union naval blockade

The Anaconda Plan From the beginning the Northern war strategy was to invade the South and divide it. As the plan—called the Anaconda Plan—progressed, the North blocked Southern supply lines and isolated Confederate troops.

1861

Early Stages Confederate troops won most of the battles in the first year of the Civil War.

1863

Union Gains Union control of the Mississippi River cut off Texas and Arkansas, the South's leading food producers, from the Confederacy.

1865

Final Stages By 1865 the Union controlled large parts of the Confederacy.

Lives Lost More lives were lost in the Civil War than in any other major American conflict. Deadly weapons, poor medical practices, infection and disease all contributed to this.

World War II 407,000

Civil War 620,000

World War I 107,000

Vietnam War 58,000

Korean War 54,000

Revolutionary War 25,000

Mexican War 13,000

Other major wars 5,000

The speech helped war-weary Americans look beyond the images of the battlefield and focus on their shared ideals. 📖 *(See page 618 of the Appendix for the entire text of the Gettysburg Address.)*

✓ **Reading Check Identifying** What battle victories gave the Union control of the Mississippi River?

Final Phases of the War

In November 1863, Grant and General **William Tecumseh Sherman** won an important victory at Chattanooga, Tennessee. Following the Northern triumphs at Vicksburg and Gettysburg, Chattanooga further weakened the Confederates. The following March, President Lincoln turned to Grant for help.

Ulysses S. Grant was small and unimpressive in appearance. His early army career was not impressive either, and in 1854 he had been forced to resign because of a drinking problem. When the war began, he rejoined the army. His victories in the West and his willingness to attack hard impressed President Lincoln. "I can't spare this man," the president said. "He fights." After the victory at Chattanooga, Lincoln named Grant commander of all the Union armies.

Grant devised a plan to attack the Confederacy on all fronts. The Army of the Potomac would try to crush Lee's army in Virginia. The western army, under Sherman, would advance to Atlanta, Georgia, and crush the Confederate forces in the Deep South. If the plan succeeded, they would destroy the Confederacy.

INTERDISCIPLINARY CONNECTIONS ACTIVITY

Art Although Mathew Brady revolutionized the artistic documentation of the Civil War through his photography, many artists of the time captured this historic event through fine art. For example, Winslow Homer's paintings *Veteran in a New Field* and *Prisoners from the Front* were completed from sketches he drew from the field. Using either the Student Edition or the media center, have students research a fine art piece that stirs personal feelings about the Civil War. Then have students present the fine art piece to the class. **L2,** ELL

The Final Battles, 1864–1865

Map showing the eastern United States with battle sites:
The Wilderness May 5–6, 1864; Cold Harbor June 3, 1864; Petersburg siege June 5, 1864–April 3, 1865; Appomattox Court House April 9, 1865; Nashville Dec. 15–16, 1864; Franklin Nov. 30, 1864; Bentonville March 19–21, 1865; Wilmington February 12–22, 1865; Kennesaw Mountain June 27, 1864; Atlanta July 20–Sept. 2, 1864; Sherman's March to the Sea 1864; Mobile Bay August 2–23, 1864

Legend:
- Union troops
- Confederate troops
- Boundary between Union and Confederacy
- Union victory
- Confederate victory
- Indecisive battle

0 300 miles
0 300 kilometers
Azimuthal Equal-Area projection

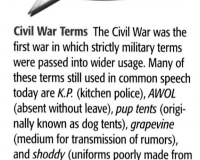

you don't say...

Civil War Terms The Civil War was the first war in which strictly military terms were passed into wider usage. Many of these terms still used in common speech today are *K.P.* (kitchen police), *AWOL* (absent without leave), *pup tents* (originally known as dog tents), *grapevine* (medium for transmission of rumors), and *shoddy* (uniforms poorly made from recycled woolen fibers known as shoddy, which came to denote any article of inferior quality).

Who?What?Where?When?

General Sherman Civil War historian Shelby Foote said of Sherman: "[He] was maybe the first truly modern general. He was the first one to understand that civilians were the backers-up of things and that if you went against civilians, you'd deprive the army of what kept it going."

Grant soon put his strategy into effect. In May and June of 1864, Grant's army of 115,000 men smashed into Lee's 64,000 troops in a series of three battles near Richmond, Virginia—the Battles of the Wilderness, Spotsylvania Courthouse, and Cold Harbor. Each time, Confederate lines held, but each time Grant quickly resumed the attack.

The battles cost the North thousands of men. Critics called Grant a butcher, but he said, "I propose to fight it out on this line if it takes all summer." Lincoln supported Grant.

After Cold Harbor, Grant swung south of Richmond to attack **Petersburg,** an important railroad center. If it fell, Richmond would be cut off from the rest of the Confederacy. Grant's assault turned into a nine-month siege.

The Election of 1864

To the war-weary North, the events of the first half of 1864 were discouraging. Grant was stuck outside Richmond and Petersburg, and Sherman was stuck outside Atlanta. Sentiment for a negotiated peace grew. The Democrats wanted to make peace with the South, even though that might result in Confederate independence. Lincoln was determined to push for restoring the Union.

In the summer of 1864, Lincoln's chances for reelection did not look good. "I am going to be beaten and unless some great change takes place, badly beaten," he said.

Great changes did take place. In August, David Farragut led a Union fleet into **Mobile Bay**. The Union now controlled the Gulf of Mexico. In September, news arrived that Sherman

CHAPTER 16   The Civil War   **489**

Reading Strategy   READING THE TEXT

Reading Primary and Secondary Sources Have students use library resources to find and analyze Lincoln's second Inaugural Address. Students should write a one-page essay that explains Lincoln's ideas about the Union, liberty, equality, and the responsibility of government. **L2**

Linking Past & Present

The G.H. Bent Company made hardtack for Union troops but reduced the production of it after the war. In 1999 the cracker company established an Internet site. Soon thousands of Civil War reenactors posted links to it on their Web sites. Within a year, sales skyrocketed from 120 boxes to over 4,000 boxes sold.

✓ Reading Check

Answer: Sherman and his troops marched from Atlanta to Savannah, destroying anything that could be of use to the Confederacy.

3 ASSESS

Assign Section 5 Assessment as homework or as an in-class activity.

🖲 Have students use **Interactive Tutor Self-Assessment CD-ROM.**

L2

Section Quiz 16–5

L1

Reteaching Activity 16–5

Linking Past & Present

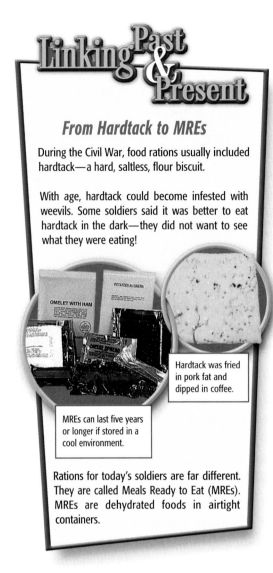

From Hardtack to MREs

During the Civil War, food rations usually included hardtack—a hard, saltless, flour biscuit.

With age, hardtack could become infested with weevils. Some soldiers said it was better to eat hardtack in the dark—they did not want to see what they were eating!

Hardtack was fried in pork fat and dipped in coffee.

MREs can last five years or longer if stored in a cool environment.

Rations for today's soldiers are far different. They are called Meals Ready to Eat (MREs). MREs are dehydrated foods in airtight containers.

had captured Atlanta. Then in October, General Sheridan's Union forces completed a campaign that drove the Rebels out of the Shenandoah Valley in Virginia. With these victories the end of the war was in sight. Lincoln easily won reelection, taking 55 percent of the popular vote.

Total War

Leaving Atlanta in ruins, Sherman convinced Grant to let him try a bold plan. Sherman's army began the historic "march to the sea" to **Savannah, Georgia.** As the army

advanced, it abandoned its supply lines and lived off the land it passed through. Union troops took what food they needed, tore up railroad lines and fields, and killed animals in an effort to destroy anything useful to the South. They cut a path of destruction sometimes 50 miles wide. This method of waging war was known as **total war.** Sherman said:

> 66 We are not only fighting hostile armies, but a hostile people, and must make old and young, rich and poor, feel the hard hand of war. 99

After capturing Savannah in December, Sherman turned north. The army marched through South Carolina, devastating the state. Sherman planned to join Grant's forces in Virginia.

✓ Reading Check Describing What was the "march to the sea"?

Victory for the North

In his second Inaugural Address on March 4, 1865, Lincoln spoke of the coming peace:

> 66 With malice toward none, with charity for all . . . let us strive on to finish the work we are in, to bind up the nation's wounds . . . to do all which may achieve and cherish a just and lasting peace among ourselves and with all nations. 99

Throughout the fall and winter of 1864, Grant continued the siege of Petersburg. Lee and his troops defended the town, but sickness, hunger, casualties, and desertion weakened them. Finally, on April 2, 1865, the Confederate lines broke and Lee withdrew his troops.

Richmond fell the same day. Rebel troops, government officials, and many residents fled the Confederate capital. As they left, they set fire to much of the city to keep it from falling into Union hands.

On April 4 Lincoln visited Richmond and walked its streets. One elderly African American man approached the president, took off his hat, and bowed. Tearfully, he said, "May God bless you." Lincoln removed his own hat and bowed in return.

EXTENDING THE CONTENT

Sherman's March In December 1864 Sherman's troops left Savannah and headed for South Carolina. One phase of Sherman's plan of total war called for a demoralization of Confederate soldiers in the field by attacks on the home front. Sherman wrote, "The simple fact that a man's home has been visited by the enemy makes a soldier in Lee's or Johnson's army very, very anxious to get home." South Carolina Governor Zebulon Vance received letters from soldiers stating their concern for their home and families. They asked him to do something to prevent the desertion of those who felt the need to leave the army to protect their families. Governor Vance, however, could do little to stop the Union troops.

Surrender at Appomattox

Lee moved his army west of Richmond, hoping to link up with the small Confederate force that was trying to stop Sherman's advance. But the Union army blocked his escape route. Realizing the situation was hopeless, Lee said:

❝ There is nothing left for me to do but go and see General Grant, and I would rather die a thousand deaths. ❞

On April 9, 1865, Lee and his troops surrendered to Grant in a small Virginia village called **Appomattox Court House.** Grant's terms were generous. The Confederate soldiers had to lay down their arms, but then were free to go home. Grant allowed them to keep their horses so that they could, as he said, "put in a crop to carry themselves and their families through the next winter." Grant also ordered three days' worth of food sent to Lee's hungry troops.

Several days after Lee's surrender, the Confederate forces in North Carolina surrendered to General Sherman. Jefferson Davis, the president of the Confederacy, was captured in Georgia on May 10. The Civil War was over at last.

Results of the War

The Civil War was the most devastating conflict in American history. More than 600,000 soldiers died, and the war caused billions of dollars of damage, most of it in the South. The war also created bitter feelings among defeated Southerners that lasted for generations.

The war had other consequences as well. The North's victory saved the Union. The federal government was strengthened and was now clearly more powerful than the states. Finally, the war freed millions of African Americans. How the nation would treat these new citizens remained to be seen.

✓**Reading Check** **Identifying** Where did General Lee surrender?

Picturing **History**

The Commanders Ulysses S. Grant (below) and Robert E. Lee (right), had the greatest respect for one another. Lee answered critics of Grant's military ability by saying, "I doubt his superior can be found in all history." **What forced Lee to surrender to Grant?**

SECTION 5 ASSESSMENT

Checking for Understanding

1. **Key Terms** Use the following terms in complete sentences that will help explain their meaning: entrenched, total war.
2. **Reviewing Facts** Identify the reasons that Gettysburg and Vicksburg were important battles.

Reviewing Themes

3. **Individual Action** What thoughts about peace did Lincoln express in his second Inaugural Address?

Critical Thinking

4. **Drawing Conclusions** How did the Union's victory strengthen the federal government?
5. **Analyzing Information** Use a chart like the one shown to explain the significance of each battle listed.

Battle	Importance
Gettysburg	
Vicksburg	
Mobile Bay	
Richmond	

Analyzing Visuals

6. **Geography Skills** Study the map of the final battles on page 489. In which directions did Sherman's army travel from Atlanta to Savannah and then to Bentonville?

Interdisciplinary Activity

Expository Writing Refer to Lincoln's Gettysburg Address on page 618. Write three paragraphs discussing Lincoln's ideas on liberty, equality, union, and government.

CHAPTER 16   The Civil War   **491**

✓**Reading Check**

Answer: Appomattox Court House, Virginia

Picturing **History**

Answer: He was confronted by the Union army and could not escape.

L1, ELL

Reading Essentials and Study Guide 16–5

Study Guide

Chapter 16, Section 5
For use with textbook pages 485–491

THE WAY TO VICTORY

KEY TERMS	
entrenched	Set up in a strong position *(page 486)*
total war	Destroying anything useful to the opposition *(page 490)*

DRAWING FROM EXPERIENCE

What have you learned about President Abraham Lincoln? What were some of the qualities that made him a good president? Do you know how he died?

In the last section, you read about the effects of the Civil War on the economies of the North and South. This section focuses on the brave soldiers who fought during the Civil War.

ORGANIZING YOUR THOUGHTS

L3

Enrichment Activity 16–5

Name _____ Date _____ Class _____

★ **Enrichment Activity 16-5** ★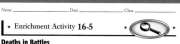

Deaths in Battles

Hundreds of thousands of people died as a result of the Civil War. Deaths from diseases greatly exceeded combat deaths. The table below shows financial costs and battle deaths of major United States wars.

Battle Deaths and Costs of Major Wars Fought by the United States (estimated)			
	Number of Battle Deaths	Total Costs (Millions of Dollars)	Original Costs (Millions of Dollars)
Vietnam War (1959–1983)	47,318	352,000	140,600
Korean War	33,629	164,000	54,000
World War II	291,557	664,000	288,000
World War I	53,402	112,000	26,000

4 CLOSE

Ask students to speculate about how the outcome of the war would have been different if the two leaders they chose in the "TEACH" activity had not been involved in the war.

SECTION 5 ASSESSMENT ANSWERS

1. Student work should reflect correct use of terms.
2. At Gettysburg Lee's army was driven from Pennsylvania; at Vicksburg the Mississippi River was secured, and the South was cut in two.
3. that people should work together to build a lasting peace

4. The war demonstrated that the federal government would not tolerate states acting on their own.
5. Gettysburg: Lee failed to beat the Union army on Northern soil, which he hoped would help the South get foreign support; Vicksburg: the Union gained control of the Mississippi River;

Mobile Bay: the Union gained control of the Gulf of Mexico; Richmond: Union capture of the Confederate capital
6. southeast and northeast

Interdisciplinary Activity Paragraphs should address ideas about liberty, equality, union, and government.

1 FOCUS

The Civil War was fought entirely on American soil—on roads, in towns, and in farm fields throughout the country. Antietam is an example of a battle that was fought in and near a small town. **Ask:** *If a nation is involved in a war, how is the cost of fighting the war different when the war is fought on its own soil, instead of being fought elsewhere? (Students should conclude that, although there would be military casualties in both cases, the cost would be higher for a nation that fights a war on its own soil. The costs would include many civilian casualties and the destruction of roads, railroads, factories, homes, and crops.)*

2 TEACH

Reading a Map Have students use the map to describe how soldiers for both sides used the area around Sharpsburg to prepare for battle. *(Accept all answers that describe the deployment of troops on the map, including the following: local roads were used to transport people and equipment; soldiers lined up for battle along roads, tree lines, and ridges; soldiers assembled in pastures and farm fields.)* **L2**, **ELL**

492

EXTENDING THE CONTENT

Battlefield Illumination Each year, on the first Saturday in December, the Antietam National Battlefield in Sharpsburg, Maryland, is illuminated. To honor the Confederate and Union soldiers who were casualties of the Battle of Antietam, one candle for each casualty is lit. The candles are placed in paper bags weighted with sand, and are lighted and placed on the battlefield by more than 800 volunteers. The battlefield can then be toured by car in total darkness except for the light of approximately 23,000 candles.

ANTIETAM: THE BLOODIEST DAY

FOUGHT ON SEPTEMBER 17, 1862, the Battle of Antietam, or Sharpsburg, was the bloodiest day in American history, with over 23,000 soldiers killed or wounded. Antietam changed the course of the Civil War. McClellan's Union forces stopped Lee's invasion of the North and forced him on the defensive. This strategic victory encouraged Lincoln to issue the Emancipation Proclamation.

MORNING

The battle began at dawn when Union artillery fired on Stonewall Jackson's forces in Miller Cornfield north of town. Union troops attacked the Confederates north of Dunker Church. For three hours, the battle lines swept back and forth along the West and East Woods, the Cornfield, and along Hagerstown Pike.

MIDDAY

Union soldiers emerged from the East Woods and were turned back by the Confederates in the West Woods. Later, the Yankees advanced toward "Bloody Lane," a sunken farm road held by the Confederates just south of Dunker Church. The Confederates held their line until midday, when the fighting stopped briefly.

AFTERNOON

After much fighting, the Union troops crossed Antietam Creek and slowly drove the Confederate forces back toward Sharpsburg. Just when all hope seemed lost, Confederate forces arrived from Harpers Ferry and stopped the Union advance. The day ended in a standoff that halted Lee's march northward. The next day, Lee began his retreat along the Potomac River.

LEARNING from GEOGRAPHY

1. **How do you think Bloody Lane got its name?**

2. **Why do you think Lee retreated after the Battle of Antietam?**

493

3 ASSESS

Have students answer the **Learning from Geography** questions.

4 CLOSE

Have students create a flowchart that shows the main sequence of events in the Battle of Antietam.

NGS ONLINE

Access National Geographic's Web site for current events, atlas updates, activities, links, interactive features, and archives at www.nationalgeographic.com

Did you know?

The Battle of Antietam was the bloodiest single day in American military history, resulting in approximately 23,000 soldiers dead or mortally wounded.

Answers to Learning from Geography

1. Students should conclude that some of the fiercest fighting occurred in that area. Because of this, it was called Bloody Lane.

2. Students should conclude that Lee retreated because he lost a large number of men, and many others were wounded. He may also have been short on ammunition and other supplies.

GLENCOE
TECHNOLOGY

MindJogger Videoquiz
Use **MindJogger Videoquiz** to review the Chapter 16 content.

Available in VHS

Reviewing Key Terms

1. The Union set up a **blockade** of Southern ports and the Confederacy went on the **offensive** by invading the North.

2. To challenge the Union blockade, **blockade runners** brought goods to Southern ports, while the **ironclad** *Merrimack* fought the Union's *Monitor*.

3. The **Union** needed to prevent the secession of the **border states** because of their strategic locations.

4. Strong opposition to the **draft** forced both Lincoln and Davis to suspend **habeas corpus,** which guarantees the accused the right to a hearing before being jailed.

Reviewing Key Facts

5. 1861–1865

6. strong support of the white population, fighting a defensive war, strong military leadership

7. Abraham Lincoln; Jefferson Davis

8. delivered supplies and comforted the wounded

9. to cut off Southern trade and prevent supplies from reaching the Confederacy

10. Union forces turned back Lee's troops.

11. It stated that all enslaved people within the Confederacy were free.

12. served as soldiers; worked behind the lines; worked to support the South's economy

13. destroyed farms and factories; destroyed rail system; caused shortages of food and other goods; caused inflation

14. Confederate soldiers had to lay down their arms, but were free to return home.

494

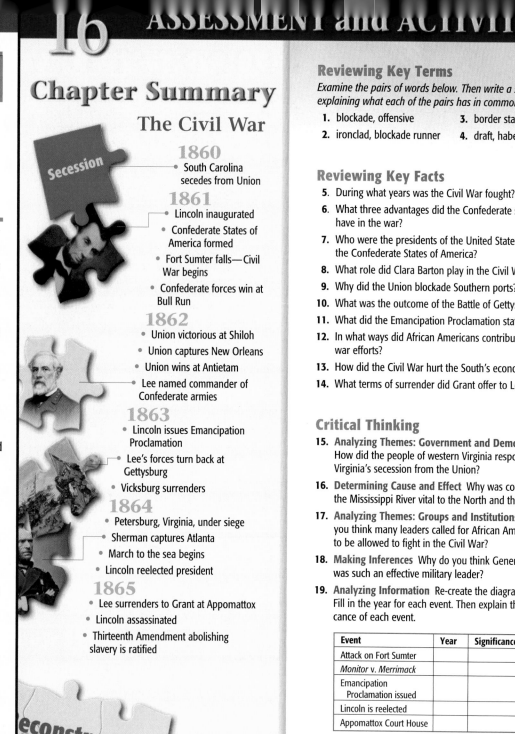

Chapter Summary
The Civil War

Secession

1860
- South Carolina secedes from Union

1861
- Lincoln inaugurated
- Confederate States of America formed
- Fort Sumter falls—Civil War begins
- Confederate forces win at Bull Run

1862
- Union victorious at Shiloh
- Union captures New Orleans
- Union wins at Antietam
- Lee named commander of Confederate armies

1863
- Lincoln issues Emancipation Proclamation
- Lee's forces turn back at Gettysburg
- Vicksburg surrenders

1864
- Petersburg, Virginia, under siege
- Sherman captures Atlanta
- March to the sea begins
- Lincoln reelected president

1865
- Lee surrenders to Grant at Appomattox
- Lincoln assassinated
- Thirteenth Amendment abolishing slavery is ratified

Reconstruction

494

Critical Thinking

15. They seceded and formed the new state of West Virginia.

16. It was a main transportation route.

17. Answers may include: provided additional troops in a war in which as many men as possible were needed to fight; their service would convince many Americans to accept equal rights.

18. He implemented bold plans, made good strategic moves, and had the respect of his men.

Reviewing Key Terms

Examine the pairs of words below. Then write a sentence explaining what each of the pairs has in common.

1. blockade, offensive
2. ironclad, blockade runner
3. border state, Union
4. draft, habeas corpus

Reviewing Key Facts

5. During what years was the Civil War fought?

6. What three advantages did the Confederate states have in the war?

7. Who were the presidents of the United States and of the Confederate States of America?

8. What role did Clara Barton play in the Civil War?

9. Why did the Union blockade Southern ports?

10. What was the outcome of the Battle of Gettysburg?

11. What did the Emancipation Proclamation state?

12. In what ways did African Americans contribute to the war efforts?

13. How did the Civil War hurt the South's economy?

14. What terms of surrender did Grant offer to Lee?

Critical Thinking

15. **Analyzing Themes: Government and Democracy** How did the people of western Virginia respond to Virginia's secession from the Union?

16. **Determining Cause and Effect** Why was controlling the Mississippi River vital to the North and the South?

17. **Analyzing Themes: Groups and Institutions** Why do you think many leaders called for African Americans to be allowed to fight in the Civil War?

18. **Making Inferences** Why do you think General Lee was such an effective military leader?

19. **Analyzing Information** Re-create the diagram below. Fill in the year for each event. Then explain the significance of each event.

Event	Year	Significance
Attack on Fort Sumter		
Monitor v. *Merrimack*		
Emancipation Proclamation issued		
Lincoln is reelected		
Appomattox Court House		

19. Attack on Fort Sumter: 1861, Civil War begins; *Monitor* v. *Merrimack*: 1862, first battle between two metal-covered ships; Emancipation Proclamation issued: 1863, freed all enslaved African Americans in the South; Lincoln is reelected: 1864, peace and a united nation were in sight; Appomattox Court House: 1865, Lee surrendered to Grant, ending the Civil War

Geography and History Activity

Study the map below and answer the questions.

20. Along what ridge were the Union troops positioned?

21. Who led forces across Rock Creek?

22. What five Confederate commanders are shown?

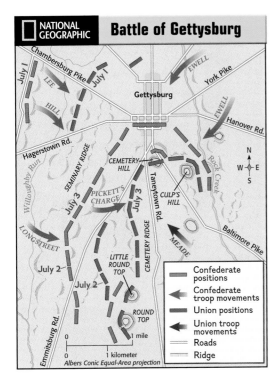

NATIONAL GEOGRAPHIC **Battle of Gettysburg**

Confederate positions

Confederate troop movements

Union positions

Union troop movements

Roads

Ridge

0   1 mile
0   1 kilometer
Albers Conic Equal-Area projection

Practicing Skills

23. Taking Notes Review the guidelines for taking notes on page 484. Then reread Section 5 about the last years of the Civil War. Create a time line showing the dates of battles and other important events discussed in the section.

 ## Technology Activity

24. Using the Internet Search the Internet for museums that specialize in Civil War artifacts and photo collections. Make a map showing the names and locations of these museums.

Self-Check Quiz
Visit tarvol1.glencoe.com and click on **Chapter 16—Self-Check Quizzes** to prepare for the chapter test.

Citizenship Cooperative Activity

25. Debating Issues A writ of habeas corpus is a court order that guarantees a person who is arrested the right to appear before a judge in a court of law. During the Civil War, President Lincoln suspended habeas corpus. Do you think that action was justified? Debate the issue as a group, with one side supporting and one side criticizing Lincoln's actions.

Economics Activity

26. Economic differences had always existed between the North and the South. From your reading of Chapter 16, would you say that the North or the South was better equipped economically for war? Explain your reasoning.

 ## Alternative Assessment

27. Portfolio Writing Activity To explain his reelection, Lincoln stated, "it is not best to swap horses while crossing the river." Write a paragraph that explains Lincoln's quotation and how it applied to him. Save your work for your portfolio.

Standardized Test Practice

Directions: Choose the *best* answer to the following question.

By gaining control of the Mississippi and Tennessee rivers, the Union was able to

A capture Fort Sumter.

B force the Confederacy to surrender.

C split the Confederacy.

D defeat the Confederate forces at Gettysburg.

Test-Taking Tip:

Eliminate answers that don't make sense. For example, Confederate forces, not Union forces, captured Fort Sumter. Therefore, choice **A** is incorrect.

Economics Activity

26. The North had more factories, a better developed rail system, and more ships and people.

 ## Alternative Assessment

27. Paragraphs should express the idea that it would have been disruptive to the war effort to change leadership.

 HISTORY *Online*

Have students visit the Web site at tarvol1.glencoe.com to review Chapter 16 and take the Self-Check Quiz.

Standardized Test Practice

Answer: C

Question Type: Geography

Answer Explanation: Information on page 487 explains how the Union control of those rivers cut off Texas, Louisiana, and Arkansas from the rest of the Confederacy.

Bonus Question ❓

Ask: How was Jefferson Davis taken to prison? *(in a horse-drawn ambulance)*

 ## Geography and History Activity

20. Cemetery Ridge

21. Ewell

22. Ewell, Hill, Lee, Longstreet, Pickett

Practicing Skills

23. Students should reread the activity on page 484 and create a time line with events from Section 5.

 ## Technology Activity

24. Maps should include the names and locations of museums that house Civil War collections.

Citizenship Cooperative Activity

25. Some students will think it was justified because of the necessities of war, while others will think it was an infringement on the rights of citizens.

THINKING CRITICALLY
You Decide

1 FOCUS

Tell students to look at the quilt pictured on page 496. Ask them to identify different patterns, images, or themes they see on the quilt. **Ask:** What types of patterns, images, or themes might you find on a memorial quilt made today? *(Answers will vary, but students may suggest that a quilt might contain more modern geometric patterns and images and themes about technology, patriotism, and war.)*

CURRICULUM CONNECTION

Music Army of the Potomac chief of staff General Daniel Butterfield composed the notes for the bugle call "Taps" early in July 1862. He wrote the piece to be played at lights-out and at funerals.

Quilting History

Quilts were not just used for comfort and protection during the Civil War. They also served as patriotic symbols, and they helped raise money for war materials. Northern quilts often reflected abolition themes. Patterns were created that were named "North Star" and "Underground Railroad." In the South, enslaved people made most of the quilts and designed them using colors and patterns inspired by African traditions.

Analyzing the Issue

In this activity, your group will be making a memorial quilt about the Civil War.

The group must decide how large of a quilt to make. Each panel—or square—in the quilt will have a different design, so the group must decide what they want to represent on the quilt. The panels should reflect your interests in the Civil War or how you feel about it. Keep in mind the experiences of all Americans during the war, such as soldiers, women, enslaved persons, and politicians.

Believe It or Not!

When the Civil War was over, fabric was hard to find, especially in the South. Quilts were made from uniforms of dead or returning soldiers. Family members inscribed on the quilts the dates and names of the battles fought by the soldiers.

Civil War quilt

EXTENDING THE CONTENT

Gunboat Quilts Some quilts were made to raise money for the war effort. The South, in need of gunboats, received donations to help build them from the sale of "gunboat quilts." Gunboat quilts consisted of floral arrangements made from floral prints. The flowers were cut out and applied to solid fabrics.

What To Do

After you have organized into groups, decide what role each member will play and what materials to use. Suggested materials are sheets of paper, drawing tools, and yarn.

1. As a group, select topics to be depicted on your Civil War memorial quilt panels. You can re-create whatever setting you choose—a battle scene, a scene at home, or any event that took place during the war.

2. Use colored pencils or markers to draw the scenes on pieces of construction paper. If possible, and with teacher supervision, laminate your drawing using a laminating machine.

3. When the panels are finished, make a quilt. Take a paper puncher and place holes at the four corners of each piece of paper.

4. String the yarn loosely through the holes so that each drawing is connected to the ones around it. Pull out the slack and tie the loose ends.

5. Hang your completed Civil War memorial quilt in your classroom.

Presentation

6. Once all of the quilts are finished, have one person per quilt group give a report of what their quilt represents. The group can also discuss how certain panels contribute to the overall meaning.

Go a Step Further

During the Civil War, Americans had to be very careful with any money that they did have. That is why they recycled old clothing to make quilts and made their food supplies last as long as possible. The cost of food rose dramatically in 1864. For example, the following costs were common: a dozen eggs, $6.00; a pound of butter, $6.25; a quart of milk, $10.00; and a pound of coffee, $12.00. Prepare a bar graph that compares those prices with prices today. Summarize what conclusions you can draw from your graph.

497

2 TEACH

Identifying Themes Before students begin, have them brainstorm a list of Civil War events, battles, or people that they would like to incorporate into their quilts. Students should then sketch the event, battle, or person they have chosen on a sheet of paper.

Once students have finished their sketches, they should review them as a group. Have groups think about how they will organize the pictures into a quilt. **Ask: Is there an overall theme to your sketches?** (*Students may create quilts with an overall theme such as "Women Spies" or "A Soldier's Life."*) Once students have identified a theme, they may begin to create their quilts. **L2**

3 ASSESS

Have students complete the **Presentation** activity on page 497.

4 CLOSE

Have students research Amish culture to understand the purpose of quilting in that community.

Answers

Groups should discuss how the different panels reflect an overall theme. For the **Go a Step Further** activity, have students visit several local food stores to check on prices, establish an average price for each of the items, and list those prices on the chalkboard. Have students make their bar graphs using that list. Students will realize that prices for these items were much higher in 1864 than today. Remind students that $1.00 in the 1860s was not worth the same as $1.00 today.

Timesaving Tools

TeacherWorks™ All-In-One Planner and Resource Center

- **Interactive Teacher Edition** Access your Teacher Wraparound Edition and your classroom resources with a few easy clicks.
- **Interactive Lesson Planner** Planning has never been easier! Organize your week, month, semester, or year with all the lesson helps you need to make teaching creative, timely, and relevant.

Use Glencoe's **Presentation Plus!** multimedia teacher tool to easily present dynamic lessons that visually excite your students. Using Microsoft PowerPoint® you can customize the presentations to create your own personalized lessons.

TEACHING TRANSPARENCIES

Graphic Organizer 3 L2

Why It Matters Chapter Transparency 17 L2

REVIEW AND REINFORCEMENT

Workbook Activity 17 L1

Time Line Activity 17 L2

Vocabulary Activity 17 L1

REVIEW AND REINFORCEMENT

Critical Thinking Skills Activity 17 L2

Take-Home Review Activity 17 L1

ENRICHMENT

Linking Past and Present Activity 17 L2

Primary Source Reading 17 L2

GEOGRAPHY

Geography and History Activity 17 L2

Meeting NCSS Standards

The following standards are highlighted in Chapter 17:

Section 1 | V | Individuals, Groups, & Institutions: A, B, C, D, E, F, G
Section 2 | X | Civic Ideals & Practices: A, B, C, F, G, H, I, J
Section 3 | II | Time, Continuity, & Change: A, B, C, E
Section 4 | II | Time, Continuity, & Change: A, B, C, D, E, F

FOLDABLES™

Study Organizer

Dinah Zike's Foldables are three-dimensional, interactive graphic organizers that help students practice basic writing skills, review key vocabulary terms, and identify main ideas. Additional chapter activities can be found in the **Reading and Study Skills Foldables** booklet.

ASSESSMENT AND EVALUATION

GLENCOE'S
ASSESSMENT
ADVANTAGE

Chapter 17 Test Form A L2

Chapter 17 Test Form B L2

Standardized Test Practice Workbook Activity 17 L2

Performance Assessment Activity 17 L1, ELL

ExamView® Pro Testmaker CD-ROM

MULTIMEDIA

- ⊙ Vocabulary PuzzleMaker CD-ROM
- ⊙ Interactive Tutor Self-Assessment CD-ROM
- ⊙ ExamView® Pro Testmaker CD-ROM
- ⊛ Audio Program
- ⊙ American History Primary Source Document Library CD-ROM
- ▭ MindJogger Videoquiz
- ⊙ Presentation Plus! CD-ROM
- ⊙ TeacherWorks CD-ROM
- ⊙ Interactive Student Edition CD-ROM
- ⊙ Glencoe Skillbuilder Interactive Workbook CD-ROM, Level 1
- ▭ ⊙ The American Republic to 1877 Video Program
- ♫ American Music: Hits Through History

SPANISH RESOURCES

The following Spanish language materials are available in the Spanish Resources Binder:

- • Spanish Guided Reading Activities
- • Spanish Reteaching Activities
- • Spanish Quizzes and Tests
- • Spanish Vocabulary Activity
- • Spanish Take-Home Review Activity
- • Spanish Summaries
- • The Declaration of Independence and United States Constitution Spanish Translation

THE HISTORY CHANNEL®

The following videotape programs are available from Glencoe as supplements to Chapter 17:

- • **The Lincoln Assassination Set** (ISBN 1-56501-568-1)*
- • **John Wilkes Booth** (ISBN 1-56501-715-3)

To order, call Glencoe at 1-800-334-7344. To find classroom resources to accompany many of these videos, check the following home pages:
A&E Television: www.aande.com
The History Channel: www.historychannel.com

*Available individually or in *The American Republic to 1877 Video Library.*

HISTORY Online

Use our Web site for additional resources. All essential content is covered in the Student Edition.

You and your students can visit tarvol1.glencoe.com, the Web site companion to **The American Republic to 1877.** This innovative integration of electronic and print media offers your students a wealth of opportunities. The student text directs students to the Web site for the following options:

- • **Chapter Overviews**
- • **Self-Check Quizzes**
- • **Student Web Activities**
- • **Textbook Updates**

Answers to the student Web activities are provided for you in the **Web Activity Lesson Plans.** Additional Web resources and Interactive Tutor Puzzles are also available.

Chapter 17 Resources

SECTION RESOURCES

Daily Objectives	Reproducible Resources	Multimedia Resources
SECTION 1 **Reconstruction Plans** 1. Compare Lincoln's plan for Reconstruction and the plan of the Radical Republicans. 2. Explain Andrew Johnson's proposal for handling Reconstruction.	Reproducible Lesson Plan 17–1 Daily Lecture and Discussion Notes 17–1 Guided Reading Activity 17–1* Section Quiz 17–1* Reteaching Activity 17–1* Reading Essentials and Study Guide 17–1* Enrichment Activity 17–1	Daily Focus Skills Transparency 17–1 Interactive Tutor Self-Assessment CD-ROM ExamView® Pro Testmaker CD-ROM Presentation Plus! CD-ROM
SECTION 2 **Radicals in Control** 1. Identify what some Southerners did to deprive freed people of their rights, and explain how Congress responded. 2. Cite the main features of Radical Reconstruction.	Reproducible Lesson Plan 17–2 Daily Lecture and Discussion Notes 17–2 Guided Reading Activity 17–2* Section Quiz 17–2* Reteaching Activity 17–2* Reading Essentials and Study Guide 17–2* Enrichment Activity 17–2	Daily Focus Skills Transparency 17–2 American Music: Hits Through History Interactive Tutor Self-Assessment CD-ROM ExamView® Pro Testmaker CD-ROM Presentation Plus! CD-ROM
SECTION 3 **The South During Reconstruction** 1. Identify what groups participated in the South's Reconstruction. 2. Explain how Southern life changed during Reconstruction.	Reproducible Lesson Plan 17–3 Daily Lecture and Discussion Notes 17–3 Guided Reading Activity 17–3* Section Quiz 17–3* Reteaching Activity 17–3* Reading Essentials and Study Guide 17–3* Enrichment Activity 17–3	Daily Focus Skills Transparency 17–3 Interactive Tutor Self-Assessment CD-ROM ExamView® Pro Testmaker CD-ROM Presentation Plus! CD-ROM
SECTION 4 **Change in the South** 1. Cite the changes that occurred in the South during the last years of Reconstruction. 2. Describe how African Americans were denied their rights.	Reproducible Lesson Plan 17–4 Daily Lecture and Discussion Notes 17–4 Guided Reading Activity 17–4* Section Quiz 17–4* Reteaching Activity 17–4* Reading Essentials and Study Guide 17–4* Enrichment Activity 17–4	Daily Focus Skills Transparency 17–4 Vocabulary PuzzleMaker CD-ROM Interactive Tutor Self-Assessment CD-ROM ExamView® Pro Testmaker CD-ROM Presentation Plus! CD-ROM

0:00 OUT OF TIME?
Assign the Chapter 17 **Reading Essentials and Study Guide.**

*Also Available in Spanish

 Blackline Master   Transparency   CD-ROM   DVD

Poster   Music Program   Audio Program   Videocassette

KEY TO ABILITY LEVELS

Teaching strategies have been coded.

L1 BASIC activities for all students
L2 AVERAGE activities for average to above-average students
L3 CHALLENGING activities for above-average students
ELL ENGLISH LANGUAGE LEARNER activities

NATIONAL GEOGRAPHIC Teacher's Corner

ADDITIONAL NATIONAL GEOGRAPHIC SOCIETY PRODUCTS

To order the following, call National Geographic at 1-800-368-2728:

- *GeoKit: The Civil War* (Kit)
- *GeoKit: Immigration* (Kit)
- *United States/Territorial Growth* (Map)
- *National Geographic Desk Reference* (Book)

NGS ONLINE

Access National Geographic's Web site for current events, atlas updates, activities, links, interactive features, and archives.

www.nationalgeographic.com

MEETING SPECIAL NEEDS

In addition to the Differentiated Instruction strategies found in each section, the following resources are also suitable for your special needs students:

- *ExamView® Pro Testmaker CD-ROM* allows teachers to tailor tests by reducing answer choices.

- The *Audio Program* includes the entire narrative of the student edition so that less-proficient readers can listen to the words as they read them.

- The *Reading Essentials and Study Guide* provides the same content as the student edition but is written two grade levels below the textbook.

- *Guided Reading Activities* give less-proficient readers point-by-point instructions to increase comprehension as they read each textbook section.

- *Enrichment Activities* includes a stimulating collection of readings and activities for gifted and talented students.

From the Classroom of...

Phil Trotter
San Diego School District
San Diego, CA

A State of the Union Address on the Fourteenth Amendment—Then and Now

Organize the class into an equal number of groups. Have half of the groups research the legal rights of people—particularly African Americans—just prior to the passage of the Fourteenth Amendment. The other half of the class should research how the amendment protects African Americans and other minorities today. Using as many specific examples as they can find, have each group write a State of the Union Address for either "then" or "now." Before having groups present their addresses to the class, ask all students to find articles in newspapers and magazines that deal with the rights and freedoms covered by the Fourteenth Amendment. These articles can be shared during class discussion after each group's State of the Union presentation.

ADDITIONAL RESOURCES FROM GLENCOE

- American Music: Cultural Traditions
- American Art and Architecture
- Outline Map Resource Book
- U.S. Desk Map
- Building Geography Skills for Life
- Inclusion for the Middle School Social Studies Classroom Strategies and Activities
- Teaching Strategies for the American History Classroom (Including Block Scheduling Pacing Guides)
- American Crafts Hands-On Activities
- American Games Hands-On Activities
- American History Flash Cards

Block Schedule

Activities that are suited to use within the block scheduling framework are identified by:

✔ Performance Assessment

Refer to Activity 17 in the Performance Assessment Activities and Rubrics booklet.

Why It Matters Activity

Ask students to think about how a civil war affects a country's economy, government, and population. As students read the chapter, have them identify the problems that the United States encountered after the Civil War. Discuss how the United States government tried to solve these problems and have students evaluate the effectiveness of the solutions.

GLENCOE TECHNOLOGY

The American Republic to 1877 Video Program

To learn about Reconstruction from the perspective of writers and artists of the period, have students view the Chapter 17 video "Life After the War" from **The American Republic to 1877 Video Program.**

 Available in DVD and VHS

MindJogger Videoquiz

Use **MindJogger Videoquiz** to preview the Chapter 17 content.

 Available in VHS

CHAPTER 17 Reconstruction and Its Aftermath

1865–1896

Why It Matters

We had survived our worst war, but the end of the Civil War left Americans to deal with a set of pressing issues. The status of some 3.5 million former enslaved people had yet to be decided. Nor had the terms by which the former Confederate states would rejoin the union been decided. How Americans would handle these issues would shape the future of our country.

The Impact Today

Debate over the rightful power of the federal government and the states continues to this day. Americans continue to wrestle with the problem of providing civil rights and equal opportunity to all citizens.

 The American Republic to 1877 Video *The chapter 17 video, "Life After the War," tells the story of Reconstruction through the eyes of writers and artists of the period.*

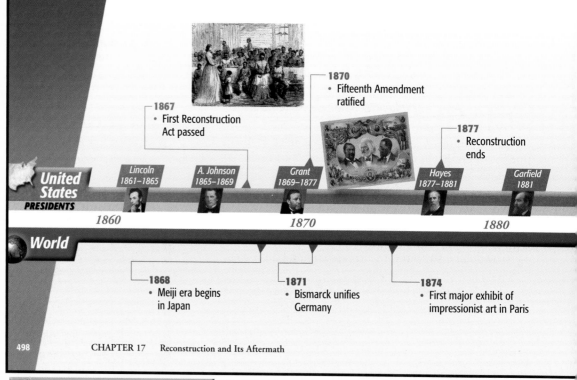

1867
• First Reconstruction Act passed

1870
• Fifteenth Amendment ratified

1877
• Reconstruction ends

United States PRESIDENTS

Lincoln 1861–1865

A. Johnson 1865–1869

Grant 1869–1877

Hayes 1877–1881

Garfield 1881

1860   1870   1880

World

1868
• Meiji era begins in Japan

1871
• Bismarck unifies Germany

1874
• First major exhibit of impressionist art in Paris

Reading Strategy   PURPOSE FOR READING

Anticipation guides are a useful strategy to test students' background knowledge and focus their reading. Begin by saying: "During the Civil War, large parts of the country were destroyed. After the war, political leaders faced the challenge of creating one nation again from the Union and Confederacy." On the board or an overhead, list students' responses to: *What policies need to be put into place to reunite the nation?* Have students copy five policies from the list that they think are the most important and decide whether they *agree* or *disagree* with each policy. As they read the chapter, have them correct any misconceptions. **L1**

Ruins of the North Eastern Depot, Charleston, South Carolina Southerners faced the task of rebuilding cities, industries, and farms devastated by war.

Introducing
CHAPTER 17

FOLDABLES ™
Study Organizer

Comparison Study Foldable Make this foldable to help you compare and contrast Reconstruction in the Northern and Southern states.

Step 1 Mark the midpoint of the side edge of a sheet of paper.

> Draw a mark at the midpoint.

Step 2 Turn the paper and fold the edges in to touch at the midpoint.

Step 3 Turn and label your foldable as shown.

> North
> Reconstruction
> South

Reading and Writing As you read the chapter, write facts that show how Reconstruction differed and was the same in the Northern states and Southern states. Write the facts in the appropriate places inside your foldable.

FOLDABLES ™
Study Organizer
Dinah Zike's Foldables

Purpose Students make and use a compare-contrast foldable to collect and organize information about Reconstruction in the Northern and Southern states. Students will compare and contrast facts that show how Reconstruction differed and was the same in the Northern and Southern states by using the foldable.

➤ Have students complete *Reading and Study Skills Foldables* Activity 11. **L1**

HISTORY
Online

Introduce students to chapter content and key terms by having them access **Chapter Overview 17** at tarvol1.glencoe.com

1890
• Poll taxes and literacy test initiated in Mississippi

1896
• *Plessy* v. *Ferguson* rules segregation constitutional

Arthur
1881–1885

Cleveland
1885–1889

B. Harrison
1889–1893

Cleveland
1893–1897

1890   *1900*

1882
• Beginning of British occupation of Egypt

1896
• Ethiopia defeats invading Italians

HISTORY
Online

Chapter Overview
Visit tarvol1.glencoe.com and click on **Chapter 17— Chapter Overviews** to preview chapter information.

TIME LINE
ACTIVITY

Have students review the time line on pages 498–499 as they read the chapter. Have students identify presidents that served in office during the course of Reconstruction.

More About the Photo

Sherman's march through South Carolina began in February 1865. At least a dozen towns were either partially or totally burned. Countless homes and farms were destroyed, as well as significant portions of the state's railroads. Sherman's army finally left the state in March 1865. Have students discuss this photograph of a demolished railroad depot. Ask them what details show the aftermath of war and the need for Reconstruction.

1 FOCUS

Section Overview

This section describes the competing plans for bringing the Southern states back into the Union.

Reading Preview

Answers to Graphic: Ten Percent Plan: 10 percent swear loyalty, ban slavery; **Wade-Davis Plan:** 50 percent swear loyalty, ban slavery, no Confederates could hold office; **Restoration:** most Southerners could swear loyalty for amnesty, officials and landowners apply to president, denounce secession, and ratify Thirteenth Amendment

Preteaching Vocabulary
Have students give examples of how the term *radical* can be used as an adjective or a noun.

Main Idea
Differences over how Reconstruction should be carried out divided the government.

Key Terms
Reconstruction, amnesty, radical, freedmen

Reading Strategy
Taking Notes As you read the section, re-create the diagram below and describe each of the Reconstruction plans.

Plan	Description
Ten Percent Plan	
Wade-Davis Plan	
Restoration	

Read to Learn
- how the Reconstruction plans of Lincoln and the Radical Republicans differed.
- what President Johnson's Reconstruction plans were.

Section Theme
Groups and Institutions The South worked to rebuild its economy and its institutions.

Preview of Events

♦1864		♦1865		♦1866

July 1864 Congress passes Wade-Davis Bill

March 1865 Freedmen's Bureau is established

April 9, 1865 Lee surrenders

April 14, 1865 President Lincoln is assassinated

Lincoln's second Inaugural Address

AN American Story

About a month after President Lincoln began his second term of office, the Civil War ended and the soldiers returned to their homes. One Illinois veteran wrote upon reaching the family farm, "The morning after my arrival, September 29th, I [took off] my uniform of first lieutenant, put on some of my father's old clothes, and proceeded to wage war on the standing corn. The feeling I had while engaged in this work was sort of [odd]. It almost seemed, sometimes, as if I had been away only a day or two, and had just taken up the farm work where I had left off."

Reconstruction Debate

The Civil War saved the Union but shook the nation to its roots. As Americans attempted to reunite their shattered nation, they faced many difficult questions. For example, should the slaveholding Southerners be punished or forgiven? What rights should be granted to the freed African Americans? How could the war-torn nation be brought back together?

500 CHAPTER 17 Reconstruction and Its Aftermath

SECTION RESOURCES

📁 Reproducible Masters
- Reproducible Lesson Plan 17–1
- Daily Lecture and Discussion Notes 17–1
- Guided Reading Activity 17–1
- Section Quiz 17–1
- Reteaching Activity 17–1
- Reading Essentials and Study Guide 17–1
- Enrichment Activity 17–1

🖥 Transparencies
- Daily Focus Skills Transparency 17–1

Multimedia
- 💿 Interactive Tutor Self-Assessment CD-ROM
- 💿 ExamView® Pro Testmaker CD-ROM
- 💿 Presentation Plus! CD-ROM

The war had left the South with enormous problems. Most of the major fighting had taken place in the South. Towns and cities were in ruin, plantations had been burned, and roads, bridges, and railroads destroyed.

More than 258,000 Confederate soldiers had died in the war, and illness and wounds weakened thousands more. Many Southern families faced the task of rebuilding their lives with few resources and without the help of adult males.

People in all parts of the nation agreed that the devastated Southern economy and society needed rebuilding. They disagreed bitterly, however, over how to accomplish this. This period of rebuilding is called Reconstruction. This term also refers to the various plans for accomplishing the rebuilding.

Lincoln's Plan

President Lincoln offered the first plan for accepting the Southern states back into the Union. In December 1863, during the Civil War, the president announced what came to be known as the **Ten Percent Plan.** When 10 percent of the voters of a state took an oath of loyalty to the Union, the state could form a new government and adopt a new constitution—a constitution banning slavery.

Lincoln wanted to encourage Southerners who supported the Union to take charge of the state governments. He believed that punishing the South would serve no useful purpose and would only delay healing the torn nation.

The president offered amnesty—a pardon—to all white Southerners, except Confederate leaders, who were willing to swear loyalty to the Union. Lincoln also supported granting the right to vote to African Americans who were educated or had served in the Union army. However, he would not force the Southern states to give rights held by white Americans to African Americans.

In 1864 three states that the Union army occupied—Louisiana, Arkansas, and Tennessee—established governments under Lincoln's plan. These states then became caught in a struggle between the president and Congress when Congress refused to seat the states' representatives.

A Rival Plan

A group of Republicans in Congress considered Lincoln's plan too mild. They argued that Congress, not the president, should control Reconstruction policy. Because these Republicans favored a tougher and more radical, or extreme, approach to Reconstruction, they were called **Radical Republicans.** A leading Radical Republican, **Thaddeus Stevens,** declared that Southern institutions "must be broken up and relaid, or all our blood and treasure have been spent in vain."

Controlled by the Radical Republicans, Congress voted to deny seats to representatives from any state reconstructed under Lincoln's plan. Then Congress began to create its own plan.

The Wade-Davis Bill

In July 1864, Congress passed the **Wade-Davis Bill.** The bill offered a plan much harsher than Lincoln's. First, a majority of white males in a state had to swear loyalty to the Union. Second, a state constitutional convention could be held,

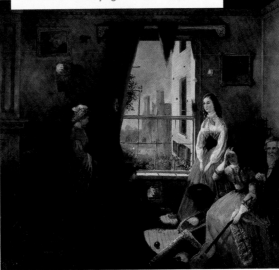

History *Through Art*

The Return to Fredericksburg After the Battle by David English Henderson A Virginia family returns to its home in war-shattered Fredericksburg. **Why do you think the painting shows no men of military age?**

2 *TEACH*

Reading Strategy

Debating Viewpoints Have students skim the section to find the opposing viewpoints on Reconstruction. Have them choose between the Radical Republicans' and Lincoln's plans for Reconstruction. Organize the class into two groups to debate the advantages and disadvantages of each plan. **L2**

History *Through Art*

The Battle of Fredericksburg was fought in and near Fredericksburg, Virginia, December 13–15, 1862. The Union Army of the Potomac under the command of Ambrose Everett Burnside had 122,000 troops and 312 guns. The Confederate Army of Northern Virginia under the command of Robert E. Lee consisted of about 79,000 men and 270 guns. About 1,300 Union soldiers and 600 Confederate soldiers were killed during this battle. An additional 16,000 soldiers were reported wounded or missing.

Answer: because they were likely killed during the Civil War

Reading Strategy   **READING THE TEXT**

Comparing and Contrasting Organize students into groups of four. Have each group brainstorm what might have taken place during a debate in Congress between supporters of President Lincoln's approach to Reconstruction and the Radical Republican's approach. Ask each group to create a list of arguments that each side might have used. **L2**

Guided Reading Activity 17-1

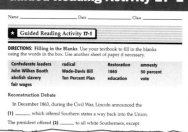

Name _____ Date _____ Class _____

★ Guided Reading Activity 17-1

DIRECTIONS: Filling in the Blanks Use your textbook to fill in the blanks using the words in the box. Use another sheet of paper if necessary.

Confederate leaders	radical	Restoration	amnesty
John Wilkes Booth	Wade-Davis Bill	1865	50 percent
abolish slavery	Ten Percent Plan	education	vote
fair wages			

Reconstruction Debate

In December 1863, during the Civil War, Lincoln announced the

(1) _____, which offered Southern states a way back into the Union.

The president offered (2) _____ to all white Southerners, except

---

Picturing History

Answer: Union troops tracked Booth down and, on April 26, cornered him in a barn near Port Royal, Virginia. When Booth refused to surrender, he was shot to death.

✓ Reading Check

Answer: He wanted to restore order quickly.

---

3 ASSESS

Assign Section 1 Assessment as homework or as an in-class activity.

🖲 Have students use **Interactive Tutor Self-Assessment CD-ROM.**

L2

Section Quiz 17-1

Name _____ Date _____ Class _____

★ Chapter 17   Score ____

Section Quiz 17-1

DIRECTIONS: Matching Match the items in Column A with the items in Column B. Write the correct letters in the blanks. *(10 points each)*

Column A	Column B
____ 1. amnesty	A. John Wilkes Booth
____ 2. radical	B. Restoration
____ 3. assassinated President Abraham Lincoln	C. extreme
____ 4. leading Radical Republican	D. a pardon
____ 5. Andrew Johnson's Reconstruction plan	E. Thaddeus Stevens

DIRECTIONS: Multiple Choice In the blank at the left, write the letter of the

---

but only white males who swore they had never taken up arms against the Union could vote for delegates to this convention. Former Confederates were also denied the right to hold public office. Finally, the convention had to adopt a new state constitution that abolished slavery. Only then could a state be readmitted to the Union.

Lincoln refused to sign the bill into law. He wanted to encourage the formation of new state governments so that order could be restored quickly. Lincoln realized that he would have to compromise with the Radical Republicans.

The Freedmen's Bureau

More progress was made on the other great issue of Reconstruction—helping African Americans freed from slavery. In March 1865, during the final weeks of the war, Congress and the president established a new government agency to help former enslaved persons, or freedmen. Called the **Freedmen's Bureau,** this agency was actually part of the war department.

In the years following the war, the Freedmen's Bureau played an important role in helping African Americans make the transition to freedom. The agency distributed food and clothing, and also provided medical services that lowered the death rate among freed men and women.

The Freedmen's Bureau achieved one of its greatest successes in the area of education. The bureau established schools, staffed mostly by teachers from the North. It also gave aid to new African American institutions of higher learning, such as Atlanta University, Howard University, and Fisk University.

The bureau helped freed people acquire land that had been abandoned by owners or seized by Union armies. It offered African Americans free transportation to the countryside where laborers were needed, and it helped them obtain fair wages. Although its main goal was to aid African Americans, the bureau also helped Southerners who had supported the Union.

✓ Reading Check **Examining** Why did Lincoln offer his plan for Reconstruction before the Civil War was over?

502   CHAPTER 17   Reconstruction and Its Aftermath

Picturing History

Actor John Wilkes Booth used this pistol to shoot Lincoln at Ford's Theater. The "wanted" poster promises a large reward for help in capturing Booth. **How was Booth finally captured?**

Lincoln Assassinated!

A terrible event soon threw the debates over Reconstruction into confusion. On the evening of April 14, 1865, President and Mrs. Lincoln attended the play *Our American Cousin* at Ford's Theater in **Washington, D.C.** It was just five days after the surrender of Lee's army and four years to the day after the fall of Fort Sumter.

As the Lincolns watched the play from a private box in the balcony, **John Wilkes Booth,** an actor and Confederate sympathizer, entered the box without anyone seeing him. Booth shot the president in the back of the head, then leaped to the stage and escaped during the chaos that followed the shooting. Aides carried the wounded president to the nearby house of William Petersen, a tailor. Lincoln died there a few hours later, without ever regaining consciousness.

After escaping from Ford's Theater, Booth fled on horseback to Virginia. Union troops tracked him down and on April 26 cornered him in a barn near Port Royal, Virginia. When Booth refused to surrender, he was shot to death.

Booth was part of a small group that plotted to kill high officials of the United States government. A military court convicted eight people of taking part in the plot. Four were hanged and the others imprisoned for life.

DIFFERENTIATED INSTRUCTION

Reading Support President Andrew Johnson had no formal schooling and remained unable to read well or write until he was almost 20 years old. Have students work in pairs to analyze President Johnson's background and write a personality profile that reflects how his life of struggle was reflected in his plans for Reconstruction. **L2**

📁 Refer to *Inclusion for the Middle School Social Studies Classroom Strategies and Activities* in the TCR.

News of Lincoln's assassination shocked the nation. African Americans mourned the death of the man who had helped them win their freedom. Northern whites grieved for the leader who had saved the Union.

A New President

When Lincoln died, Vice President **Andrew Johnson** became president. Formerly a Democratic senator from Tennessee, Johnson had been the only Southern senator to support the Union during the Civil War.

Soon after taking office, President Johnson revealed his plan for Reconstruction. He resented the slaveholders who had dominated the South and wished to punish them. As a result Radicals thought Johnson would create a harsh plan they could accept. Johnson, however, believed in giving the states control over many decisions, and he had no desire to help African Americans.

"Restoration"

Johnson announced his plan, which he preferred to call "Restoration," in May of 1865. Under his plan, most Southerners would be granted amnesty once they swore an oath of loyalty to the Union. High-ranking Confederate officials and wealthy landowners, however, could be pardoned only by applying personally to the president. This provision was Johnson's attack on the wealthy leaders who he believed had tricked the people of the South into seceding.

Johnson also appointed governors to Southern states and required them to hold elections for state constitutional conventions. Only whites who had sworn their loyalty and been pardoned would be allowed to vote. Johnson opposed granting all freed African Americans equal rights or letting them vote. He believed that each Southern state should decide what to do about freed people, saying, "White men alone must manage the South."

Before a state could reenter the Union, its constitutional convention had to denounce secession and abolish slavery. States also had to ratify the **Thirteenth Amendment** to the Constitution, which Congress had passed in January 1865. This amendment abolished slavery in all parts of the United States. By the end of 1865, all the former Confederate states except Texas had formed new governments and were ready to rejoin the Union. President Johnson declared that "Restoration" was almost complete.

✔**Reading Check** **Comparing** How did President Johnson's plan for Reconstruction differ from that of the Radical Republicans?

✔**Reading Check**

Answer: Johnson's plan gave the states control over many decisions, and it did not offer help to African Americans.

L1

Reteaching Activity 17–1

L1, ELL

Reading Essentials and Study Guide 17–1

L3

Enrichment Activity 17–1

4 CLOSE

Have students summarize the major Reconstruction plans described in this section.

SECTION 1 ASSESSMENT

Check for Understanding

1. **Key Terms** Use each of these terms in a sentence that will help explain its meaning: Reconstruction, amnesty, radical, freedmen.

2. **Reviewing Facts** What did the Thirteenth Amendment provide?

Reviewing Themes

3. **Groups and Institutions** Why do you think both Lincoln and the Radical Republicans excluded former Confederate officers from their Reconstruction plans?

Critical Thinking

4. **Drawing Conclusions** Do you think President Johnson's early ties to the South influenced his treatment of African Americans in his Reconstruction plans? Explain your answer.

5. **Comparing** Re-create the diagram below and compare Lincoln's Ten Percent Plan to the Radical Republicans' Wade-Davis Bill.

Reconstruction Plans	
Ten Percent Plan	Wade-Davis Bill

Analyzing Visuals

6. **Picturing History** Study the painting on page 501. What words would you use to describe the mood of the people?

Interdisciplinary Activity

Math Use the *Statistical Abstract of the United States* or another reference book to find information on the percentages of African American students enrolled in schools in 1860, 1870, and 1880. Use this information to create a bar graph.

SECTION 1 ASSESSMENT ANSWERS

1. Student work should reflect correct use of terms.

2. freedom from slavery throughout the United States

3. They wanted to punish former Confederates as traitors.

4. Answers will vary, but may note that his attitudes reflected views of some Southerners.

5. Ten Percent Plan: required 10 percent of voters in state to pledge loyalty to Union and accept a constitution banning slavery; Wade-Davis Bill: required 50 percent of white males to swear loyalty to Union, Confederates could not hold public office, new constitutions had to abolish slavery

6. Answers may include: sad, dejected, hopeless, gloomy, depressed.

Interdisciplinary Activity Students should create accurate graphs reflecting student enrollment.

1 FOCUS

Section Overview

This section explains how the control of Congress by Radical Republicans shaped Reconstruction.

BELLRINGER
Skillbuilder Activity

 Project transparency and have students answer the question.

Daily Focus Skills Transparency 17–2

Reading Preview

Answers to Graphic: What is it: the formal charging of wrongdoing; **Who was impeached:** President Andrew Johnson; **Outcome of the trial:** the Senate vote was one short of the two-thirds majority required to remove Johnson from office

Preteaching Vocabulary
Ask students to read the definition of *impeach* on page 507. Explain that to impeach is to bring charges against. After a formal charge is made, then, according to the Constitution, the impeachment trial takes place in the Senate.

SECTION 2 Radicals in Control

Guide to Reading

Main Idea
Radical Republicans were able to put their version of Reconstruction into action.

Key Terms
black codes, override, impeach

Reading Strategy
Organizing Information As you read the section, re-create the diagram below and provide information about impeachment.

Impeachment	
What is it?	
Who was impeached?	
Outcome of the trial?	

Read to Learn
- what some Southerners did to deprive freed people of their rights, and how Congress responded.
- what the main features of Radical Reconstruction were.

Section Theme
Civic Rights and Responsibilities
Southern states created new governments and elected new representatives.

Preview of Events

♦1865	♦1867	♦1869	♦1871

1865
First black codes passed

March 1867
Radical Reconstruction begins

November 1868
Ulysses S. Grant elected president

February 1870
Fifteenth Amendment extends voting rights

Ku Klux Klan flag

★★★★★★★★
AN
American Story

For three days in May 1866, white mobs in Memphis, Tennessee, burned African American churches, schools, and homes. Close to fifty people, nearly all of them African American, were killed in the rioting. Many Northerners saw the rampage as an attempt by whites to terrorize African Americans and keep them from exercising their new freedoms. This incident and similar riots in other Southern cities helped convince Radical Republicans that President Johnson's Reconstruction plans were not strong enough.

African Americans' Rights

During the fall of 1865, the Southern states created new governments that met the rules President Johnson laid down, and Southern voters elected new representatives to Congress. More than one dozen of these representatives had been high-ranking officials in the Confederacy—including the Confederacy's vice president, Alexander H. Stephens. When the newly elected Southern

504   CHAPTER 17   Reconstruction and Its Aftermath

SECTION RESOURCES

📁 **Reproducible Masters**
- Reproducible Lesson Plan 17–2
- Daily Lecture and Discussion Notes 17–2
- Guided Reading Activity 17–2
- Section Quiz 17–2
- Reteaching Activity 17–2
- Reading Essentials and Study Guide 17–2
- Enrichment Activity 17–2

🎬 **Transparencies**
- Daily Focus Skills Transparency 17–2

Multimedia
- American Music: Hits Through History
- Interactive Tutor Self-Assessment CD-ROM
- ExamView® Pro Testmaker CD-ROM
- Presentation Plus! CD-ROM

representatives arrived in Washington, D.C., Congress refused to seat them. Many Republicans refused to readmit the Southern states on such easy terms and rejected Johnson's claim that Reconstruction was complete.

To many in the North, it seemed that Johnson's plan for Reconstruction was robbing the Union of its hard-won victory. In addition Northerners realized that the treatment of African Americans in Southern states was not improving.

Black Codes

In 1865 and early 1866, the new Southern state legislatures passed a series of laws called black codes. Key parts of these laws aimed to control freed men and women and to enable plantation owners to exploit African American workers.

Modeled on laws that had regulated free African Americans before the Civil War, the black codes of each Southern state trampled the rights of African Americans. Some laws allowed local officials to arrest and fine unemployed African Americans and make them work for white employers to pay off their fines. Other laws banned African Americans from owning or renting farms. One law allowed whites to take orphaned African American children as unpaid apprentices. To freed men and women and many Northerners, the black codes reestablished slavery in disguise.

Challenging the Black Codes

In early 1866 Congress extended the life of the Freedmen's Bureau and granted it new powers. The Freedmen's Bureau now had authority to set up special courts to prosecute individuals charged with violating the rights of African Americans. These courts provided African Americans with a form of justice where they could serve on juries.

Congress also passed the **Civil Rights Act of 1866.** This act granted full citizenship to African Americans and gave the federal government the power to intervene in state affairs to protect their rights. The law overturned the black codes. It also contradicted the 1857 *Dred Scott* decision of the Supreme Court, which had ruled that African Americans were not citizens.

President Johnson vetoed both the Freedmen's Bureau bill and the Civil Rights Act, arguing that the federal government was overstepping its proper authority. He also said that the laws were unconstitutional because they were passed by a Congress that did not include representatives from all the states. By raising the issue of representation, Johnson indirectly threatened to veto any law passed by this Congress.

Republicans in Congress had enough votes to override, or defeat, both vetoes, and the bills became law. As the split between Congress and the president grew, the possibility of their working together faded. The Radical Republicans abandoned the idea of compromise and drafted a new Reconstruction plan—one led by Congress.

🔲 Citizenship
The Fourteenth Amendment

Congress wanted to ensure that African Americans would not lose the rights that the Civil Rights Act granted. Fearing it might be

🖌 History *Through Art*

His First Vote by Thomas Waterman Wood
Wood's oil painting emphasized the importance of the ballot to African American voters. **How did African American males gain the right to vote?**

CHAPTER 17   Reconstruction and Its Aftermath   505

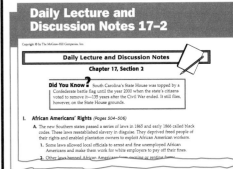
Creating a Time Line Ask students to work in small groups to create a time line of Reconstruction. Encourage them to include important events, acts, people, and amendments and to use graphics for illustration. Ask a volunteer from each group to present the time line to the class. You may wish to create a class time line on the bulletin board incorporating all events from students' time lines. **L1**

🖌 History *Through Art*

The Fifteenth Amendment is the last of three Reconstruction amendments. The Thirteenth and Fifteenth Amendments were meant to guard the people against the misuse of state power. **Answer:** The passage of the Fifteenth Amendment gave African American males the right to vote.

📖 Reading Strategy   READING THE TEXT

Using Graphic Organizers Discuss with students the different viewpoints of major groups affected by Reconstruction. Organize students into groups of four to choose from the following roles: Radical Republican, freed African American, white Southerner, and white Northerner. Each student should make a list of Reconstruction needs from that person's point of view and create a graphic organizer illustrating the most important needs. Then have each group discuss the needs shown on the organizer and cooperatively develop a plan for Reconstruction that incorporates these needs. Have each group create a large graphic organizer that illustrates this cooperative Reconstruction plan.
    🗂 **L2**

L1, ELL

Guided Reading Activity 17-2

Name _____ Date _____ Class _____

★ **Guided Reading Activity 17-2**

DIRECTIONS: Recalling the Facts Use the information in your textbook to answer the questions. Use another sheet of paper if necessary.

1. What series of laws did the new Southern state legislatures pass in 1865 and early 1866? _____

2. What did key parts of these laws aim to do? _____

3. What authority did Congress give to the Freedmen's Bureau in early 1866? _____

4. What did Congress pass in 1866 that granted full citizenship to African Americans? _____

5. What did this law overturn and contradict? _____

6. Why did President Andrew Johnson veto the Freedmen's Bureau Bill and the Civil Rights Act? _____

7. How did Congress respond to Johnson's vetoes? _____

8. What did Congress do to avoid having the Civil Rights Act overturned? _____

9. Which was the only Southern state to ratify the Fourteenth Amendment? _____

10. What signal did Republican victories in the elections of 1866 send to Congress? _____

11. How did the First Reconstruction Act divide the 10 Southern states? _____

12. What did this act guarantee African American males? _____

13. What law did Congress pass in March 1867 to limit the president's power? _____

14. How did President Johnson violate this act? _____

15. What did the House of Representatives do in response? _____

16. When did African American men win the right to vote? _____

✓ Reading Check

Answer: The Fourteenth Amendment provided full citizenship to all people born in the United States. It also states that no state could take away a citizen's life, liberty, and property without due process of the law and that every citizen was entitled to equal protection of the laws.

History *and the* Humanities

🎵 American Music: Hits Through History, "Kiowa Hymn II"

challenged and overturned in court, Congress in June 1866 passed a new amendment to the Constitution.

The **Fourteenth Amendment** granted full citizenship to all individuals born in the United States. Because most African Americans in the United States had been born there, they became full citizens. The amendment also stated that no state could take away a citizen's life, liberty, and property "without due process of law," and that every citizen was entitled to "equal protection of the laws." States that prevented any adult male citizen from voting could lose part of their representation in Congress. 📖 (*See pages 247–248 for the entire text of the Fourteenth Amendment.*)

The amendment barred prominent former Confederates from holding national or state office unless pardoned by a vote of two-thirds of Congress. The Fourteenth Amendment was interpreted as not including members of the Native American tribes. Not until 1924 did Congress make all Native Americans citizens of the United States.

Congress declared that Southern states had to ratify the amendment to be readmitted to the Union. Of the 11 Southern states, only Tennessee ratified the Fourteenth Amendment. The refusal of the other states to ratify the amendment delayed its adoption until 1868.

Republican Victory

The Fourteenth Amendment became a major issue in the congressional elections of 1866. Johnson urged Northern and Southern state legislatures to reject it. He also campaigned vigorously against Republican candidates. Many Northerners were disturbed by the nastiness of Johnson's campaign. They also worried about violent clashes between whites and African Americans, such as the riots that erupted in Memphis, Tennessee, and New Orleans, Louisiana.

The Republicans won a decisive victory, increasing their majorities in both houses of Congress. The Republicans also gained control of the governments in every Northern state. The election gave Congress the signal to take Reconstruction into its own hands.

✓ Reading Check **Describing** What does the Fourteenth Amendment provide?

Radical Reconstruction

The Republicans in Congress quickly took charge of Reconstruction. Most Radicals agreed with Congressman James Garfield of Ohio that

❝we must compel obedience to the Union, and demand protection for its humblest citizen.❞

President Johnson could do little to stop them because Congress could easily override his vetoes. Thus began a period known as Radical Reconstruction.

Reconstruction Act of 1867

On March 2, 1867, Congress passed the **First Reconstruction Act.** The act called for the creation of new governments in the 10 Southern states that had not ratified the Fourteenth Amendment. Tennessee, which had ratified the amendment, kept its government, and the state was quickly readmitted to the Union.

The act divided the 10 Southern states into five military districts and placed each under the authority of a military commander until new governments were formed. The act also guaranteed African American males the right to vote in state elections, and it prevented former Confederate leaders from holding political office.

To gain readmission to the Union, the states had to ratify the Fourteenth Amendment and submit their new state constitutions to Congress for approval. A **Second Reconstruction Act,** passed a few weeks later, required the military commanders to begin registering voters and to prepare for new state constitutional conventions.

Readmission of States

Many white Southerners refused to take part in the elections for constitutional conventions and state governments. Thousands of newly registered African American voters did use their right to vote. In the elections, Republicans gained control of Southern state governments. By 1868, seven Southern states—Alabama, Arkansas, Florida, Georgia, Louisiana, North Carolina, and South Carolina—had established new governments and met the conditions for readmission to the Union. By 1870, Mississippi, Virginia, and Texas were restored to the Union.

DIFFERENTIATED INSTRUCTION

At-Risk Students Have students skim this section to list the laws, acts, and amendments. Organize students into pairs to create a mnemonic device that can be used to memorize each law, act, or amendment. Ask volunteers to share a mnemonic device with the class without revealing what it stands for and have other students guess which law, act, or amendment it represents. **L1**

📁 Refer to *Inclusion for the Middle School Social Studies Classroom Strategies and Activities* in the TCR.

Military Reconstruction Districts, 1867

- Military district boundary
- ⭐ Union general in command

1st District
⭐ John Schofield

VA.

Tennessee rejoined the Union in 1866.

TENN.

N.C.

4th District
⭐ Edward Ord

ARK.

S.C.

MISS. ALA. GA.

2nd District
⭐ Daniel Sickles

TEXAS

LA.

MEXICO

0   250 miles
0   250 kilometers
Lambert Equal-Area projection

5th District
⭐ Philip Sheridan

Gulf of Mexico

3rd District
⭐ John Pope

FLA.

ATLANTIC OCEAN

30°N

Geography *Skills*

After taking control of Reconstruction, Congress divided the South into five districts under the command of military officers.
1. **Region** Which two states made up the largest district?
2. **Analyzing Information** Why did no Union troops occupy Tennessee?

Geography *Skills*

Answers:
1. Texas and Louisiana
2. because Tennessee had rejoined the Union in 1866, before Radical Reconstruction began

Geography Skills Practice
Ask: Which district did John Pope command? *(third)*

3 ASSESS

Assign Section 2 Assessment as homework or as an in-class activity.

⊙ Have students use **Interactive Tutor Self-Assessment CD-ROM.**

L2

Challenge to Johnson

Strongly opposed to Radical Reconstruction, President Johnson had the power as commander in chief of the army to direct the actions of the military governors. For this reason Congress passed several laws to limit the president's power.

One of these laws, the **Tenure of Office Act** of March 1867, was a deliberate challenge. It prohibited the president from removing government officials, including members of his own cabinet, without the Senate's approval. The act violated the tradition that presidents controlled their cabinets, and it threatened presidential power.

Impeaching the President

The conflict between Johnson and the Radicals grew more intense. In August 1867—when Congress was not in session—Johnson suspended Secretary of War **Edwin Stanton** without the Senate's approval. When the Senate met

again and refused to approve the suspension, Johnson removed Stanton from office—a deliberate violation of the Tenure of Office Act. Johnson angered the Republicans further by appointing some generals the Radicals opposed as commanders of Southern military districts.

Outraged by Johnson's actions, the House of Representatives voted to impeach—formally charge with wrongdoing—the president. The House accused Johnson of misconduct and sent the case to the Senate for trial.

The trial began in March 1868 and lasted almost three months. Johnson's defenders claimed that the president was exercising his right to challenge laws he considered unconstitutional. The impeachment, they argued, was politically motivated and thus contrary to the

INTERDISCIPLINARY CONNECTIONS ACTIVITY

Music Newly freed African Americans used songs to express their feelings about the difficulties they endured under the black codes. The Civil Rights Act of 1866 outlawed the black codes. Have students consider the circumstances and feelings of a freed person living in 1866 after the passage of the Civil Rights Act. Ask students to write the words to a song to express the feelings of freed men and women about the act and its elimination of the black codes. Have volunteers share their completed songs with the class. **L2**

✓ Reading Check

Answer: The Senate was one vote short of the number needed to convict Johnson and remove him from office.

L1

Reteaching Activity 17–2

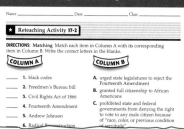

L1, ELL

Reading Essentials and Study Guide 17–2

L3

Enrichment Activity 17–2

4 CLOSE

Discuss the Thirteenth, Fourteenth, and Fifteenth Amendments. Include the difficulties in implementing these amendments.

508

---

spirit of the Constitution. Samuel J. Tilden, a Democrat from New York, claimed that Congress was trying to remove the president from office without accusing him of a crime "or anything more than a mere difference of opinion."

Johnson's accusers argued that Congress should retain the supreme power to make the laws. Senator Charles Sumner of Massachusetts declared that Johnson had turned

> ❝the veto power conferred by the Constitution as a remedy for ill-considered legislation . . . into a weapon of offense against Congress.❞

In May the senators cast two votes. In both instances the result was 35 to 19 votes to convict the president—one vote short of the two-thirds majority required by the Constitution for conviction. Several moderate Republicans voted for a verdict of not guilty because they did not believe a president should be removed from office for political differences. As a result, Johnson stayed in office until the end of his term in March 1869.

Election of 1868

By the presidential election of 1868, most Southern states had rejoined the Union. Many Americans hoped that conflicts over Reconstruction and sectional divisions were behind them.

Abandoning Johnson, the Republicans chose General **Ulysses S. Grant,** the Civil War hero, as their presidential candidate. The Democrats nominated Horatio Seymour, a former governor of New York.

Grant won the election, gaining 214 of 294 electoral votes. He also received most of the votes of African Americans in the South. The 1868 election was a vote on Reconstruction, and the voters supported the Republican approach to the issue.

The Fifteenth Amendment

After the election Republicans developed their last major piece of Reconstruction legislation. In February 1869, Congress passed the **Fifteenth Amendment.** It prohibited the state and federal governments from denying the right to vote to any male citizen because of "race, color, or previous condition of servitude."

African American men won the right to vote when the Fifteenth Amendment was ratified and became law in February 1870. Republicans thought that the power of the ballot would enable African Americans to protect themselves. That belief, it turned out, was too optimistic.

📖 *(See page 248 for the entire text of the Fifteenth Amendment.)*

✓ Reading Check **Explaining** What was the outcome of the impeachment trial of President Johnson?

SECTION 2 ASSESSMENT

Checking for Understanding

1. **Key Terms** Write a short paragraph in which you use these key terms: black codes, override, impeach.
2. **Reviewing Facts** Discuss two ways Southerners violated Lincoln's plan for Reconstruction.

Reviewing Themes

3. **Civic Rights and Responsibilities** How did Congress challenge the black codes set up by Southern states?

Critical Thinking

4. **Drawing Conclusions** If you had been a member of the Senate, would you have voted for or against convicting President Johnson? Why?
5. **Summarizing Information** Re-create the diagram below and answer the questions about these amendments.

	Date ratified	Impact on life
Fourteenth Amendment		
Fifteenth Amendment		

Analyzing Visuals

6. **Geography Skills** Examine the map that appears on page 507; then answer these questions. What are the geographic divisions of the South shown on the map? Which military district was composed of only one state? Which states made up the Third District?

Interdisciplinary Activity

Expository Writing Write a one-page essay in which you argue for or argue against the Radical Republicans' plan for Reconstruction.

SECTION 2 ASSESSMENT ANSWERS

1. Student work should reflect correct use of terms.
2. Former Confederate officials were chosen for Congress, and treatment of African Americans did not improve.
3. It granted power to the Freedmen's Bureau to prosecute those who violated rights of African Americans; it passed Civil Rights Act of 1866.
4. Students should have reasons for their choice.
5. Fourteenth Amendment: July 1868, most African Americans became full U.S. citizens; Fifteenth Amendment: February 1870, any male citizen could not be denied the vote
6. the five Southern districts controlled by the military during Reconstruction; Virginia; Florida, Georgia, Alabama

Interdisciplinary Activity Essays should demonstrate knowledge of the Reconstruction plan of the Radical Republicans.

SECTION 3 The South During Reconstruction

Guide to Reading

Main Idea
After the Civil War the South had to rebuild not only its farms and roads, but its social and political structures as well.

Key Terms
scalawag, carpetbagger, corruption, integrate, sharecropping

Reading Strategy
Organizing Information As you read the section, re-create the diagram below and describe improvements in the South in the field of education.

Improvements in education

Read to Learn
• what groups participated in Reconstruction in the South.
• how Southern life changed during Reconstruction.

Section Theme
Continuity and Change The Republican Party dominated Southern politics during Reconstruction.

Preview of Events

◆1865	◆1867	◆1869	◆1871

1865
Freedmen's Bank is established

1866
Ku Klux Klan is formed

1869
African Americans serve in House of Representatives

1870
First African American is elected to the Senate

Mississippi Senator Hiram Revels

AN American Story

"The dust of our fathers mingles with yours in the same graveyards. . . . This is your country, but it is ours too." So spoke an emancipated African American after the Civil War. Most formerly enslaved people did not seek revenge or power over whites, only respect and equality. The petition of an African American convention in 1865 stated: "We simply ask that we shall be recognized as *men;* . . . that the same laws which govern *white men* shall govern *black men;* . . . that, in short, we be dealt with as others are—in equity and justice."

New Groups Take Charge

During Reconstruction the Republican Party came to dominate Southern politics. Support for the Republican Party came mainly from three groups. One group was African Americans who were overwhelmingly Republican. Support also came from white Southerners who supported Republican policies, and white settlers from the North. These groups dominated the state constitutional conventions and state governments.

CHAPTER 17   Reconstruction and Its Aftermath   **509**

1 FOCUS

Section Overview
This section examines the political struggle in the post-Civil War South over the progress of Reconstruction.

BELLRINGER
Skillbuilder Activity

 Project transparency and have students answer the question.

Daily Focus Skills Transparency 17–3

Reading Preview

Answers to Graphic: New public schools were created for white children and African American children; several schools offering advanced education to African Americans were opened.

Preteaching Vocabulary
Have students read the subsection "Scalawags and Carpetbaggers" on page 510. Ask them to draw a cartoon illustrating the origins of one of these words.

SECTION RESOURCES

🗂 Reproducible Masters
• Reproducible Lesson Plan 17–3
• Daily Lecture and Discussion Notes 17–3
• Guided Reading Activity 17–3
• Section Quiz 17–3
• Reteaching Activity 17–3
• Reading Essentials and Study Guide 17–3
• Enrichment Activity 17–3

📄 Transparencies
• Daily Focus Skills Transparency 17–3

Multimedia
🖲 Interactive Tutor Self-Assessment CD-ROM
🖲 ExamView® Pro Testmaker CD-ROM
🖲 Presentation Plus! CD-ROM

2 TEACH

Daily Lecture and Discussion Notes 17–3

Making a Chart Have students skim the section to create a two-column chart. One column should list how the South changed during Reconstruction, and the other should list how it stayed the same. **L1**

Objectives and answers to the student activity can be found in the **Web Activity Lesson Plan** feature at tarvol1.glencoe.com

L1, ELL

Guided Reading Activity 17–3

African Americans in Government

African Americans played an important role in Reconstruction politics both as voters and as elected officials. In states where African American voters were the majority, they contributed heavily to Republican victories.

African Americans did not control the government of any state, although they briefly held a majority in the lower house of the South Carolina legislature. In other Southern states they held important positions, but never in proportion to their numbers.

At the national level, 16 African Americans served in the House of Representatives and 2 in the Senate between 1869 and 1880. **Hiram Revels,** one of the African American senators, was an ordained minister. During the Civil War he had recruited African Americans for the Union army, started a school for freed African Americans in St. Louis, Missouri, and served as chaplain of an African American regiment in Mississippi. Revels remained in Mississippi after the war and was elected to the Senate in 1870. He served a year in the Senate, where he declared he received "fair treatment."

Blanche K. Bruce, the other African American senator, also came from Mississippi. A former runaway slave, Bruce had taught in a school for African Americans in Missouri when the war began. In 1869 he went to Mississippi, entered politics, and became a superintendent of schools. He was elected to the Senate in 1874, serving there for six years.

Scalawags and Carpetbaggers

Some Southern whites supported Republican policy throughout Reconstruction. Many were nonslaveholding farmers or business leaders who had opposed secession in the first place. Former Confederates despised them for siding with the Republicans and called them scalawags, a term meaning "scoundrel" or "worthless rascal."

Many Northern whites who moved to the South after the war also supported the Republicans and served as Republican leaders during Reconstruction. Critics called these Northerners carpetbaggers because they arrived with all their belongings in cheap suitcases made of carpet fabric. Although some of the carpetbaggers were greedy and took advantage of the situation in the South, most did not. Many carpetbaggers were former Union army soldiers or members of the Freedmen's Bureau who liked the South and wanted to settle there. Others were reformers from the North—including lawyers, doctors, and teachers—who wanted to help reshape Southern society.

Many Southerners ridiculed the Reconstruction governments and accused them of corruption—dishonest or illegal actions—and financial mismanagement. While some officials made money illegally, the practice was hardly widespread. Indeed, there was probably less corruption in the South than in the North.

Resistance to Reconstruction

Most white Southerners opposed efforts to expand African Americans' rights. Carl Schurz, a Republican from Missouri who toured the South right after the war, reported:

❝Wherever I go—the street, the shop, the house, the hotel, or the steamboat—I hear the people talk in such a way as to indicate that they are yet unable to conceive of the Negro as possessing any rights at all.❞

Plantation owners tried to maintain control over freed people in any way they could. Many told African Americans they could not leave the plantations. Most white land owners refused to rent land to freedmen.

Other white Southerners also made life difficult for African Americans. Store owners refused them credit, and employers refused to give them work. Some whites also used fear and force to keep freedmen in line.

The Ku Klux Klan

Violence against African Americans and their white supporters became commonplace during Reconstruction. Much of this violence

Student Web Activity
Visit tarvol1.glencoe.com and click on **Chapter 17— Student Web Activities** for an activity on the first African American members of Congress.

510   CHAPTER 17   Reconstruction and Its Aftermath

COOPERATIVE LEARNING ACTIVITY

Making a Collage Organize students into groups of three to create a collage illustrating the changes that took place in the South during Reconstruction. Have students choose one of the following areas to be covered on the collage: educational changes, agricultural changes, and industrial changes. Have groups use poster board divided into three equal sections to create the collage. Students should use drawings, words, photographs, and so on to show the changes on the designated section of the collage. As a group, have students decide which items to use for each section and assemble the collage. Encourage groups to title their collage and display it in the classroom. Ask volunteers to explain their collages to the rest of the class. **L1, ELL**

People In History

Frederick Douglass 1817–1895

Frederick Douglass escaped slavery in 1838 and quickly emerged as a leader of the movement for liberty for African Americans. During the Civil War, he urged President Lincoln to free the enslaved people, and he helped organize African American troops to fight for freedom.

After Lincoln was assassinated, Douglass opposed President Johnson's Reconstruction program. Instead he supported the Radical Republican plan. A skilled and powerful speaker, Douglass traveled throughout the nation insisting on full equality for African Americans. He was particularly outspoken in support of the Fifteenth Amendment, guaranteeing African American men the right to vote. To Douglass, the vote meant that African Americans would not only be full citizens but would also have a weapon to protect their rights.

People In History

Frederick Douglass moved to Washington, D.C., in the 1870s and became a stalwart Republican. He was appointed marshal (1877–1881) and recorder of deeds (1881–1886) for the District of Columbia, *chargé d'affaires* for Santo Domingo, and minister to Haiti (1889–1891). **Ask:** **Which Amendment gave African American men the right to vote?** *(the Fifteenth Amendment)*

✔ Reading Check

Answer: Most white Southerners refused to testify in court against those who attacked African Americans.

3 ASSESS

Assign Section 3 Assessment as homework or as an in-class activity.

🌐 Have students use **Interactive Tutor Self-Assessment CD-ROM.**

L2

Section Quiz 17–3

---

was committed by secret societies organized to prevent freed men and women from exercising their rights and to help whites regain power.

The most terrifying of these societies, the **Ku Klux Klan,** was formed in 1866. Wearing white sheets and hoods, members of the Klan launched "midnight rides" against African Americans, burning their homes, churches, and schools. The Klan killed as well. In Jackson County, Florida, the Klan murdered more than 150 people over a three-year period. Klan violence often increased before elections, as the group tried to scare African Americans to keep them from voting. The Klan also attacked white supporters of Reconstruction.

The tactics of the Klan and other violent groups had the support of many Southerners, especially planters and Democrats. These Southerners, who had the most to gain from the reestablishment of white supremacy, saw violence as a defense against Republican rule.

Taking Action Against Violence

Southerners opposed to terrorism appealed to the federal government to do something. In 1870 and 1871, Congress passed several laws to try to stop the growing violence of the Klan. These laws had limited success. Most white Southerners refused to testify against those who attacked African Americans and their white supporters. Still, enough arrests were made to restore order for the 1872 presidential election.

✔ **Reading Check** **Explaining** Why did laws to control the Ku Klux Klan have little effect?

Some Improvements

Despite the violence, Reconstruction brought important changes throughout the South. This was especially true in education.

Education improved for both African Americans and whites. African Americans saw education as an important step to a better life. In many regions they created their own schools, contributing both labor and money to build the schools.

The Freedmen's Bureau and private charities played a major role in spreading education. Northern women and free African Americans came South to teach in these schools. By 1870 about 4,000 schools had been established, with 200,000 students. More than half the teachers in these schools were African American.

CHAPTER 17 Reconstruction and Its Aftermath **511**

DIFFERENTIATED INSTRUCTION

Reading Support Many families separated by slavery sought to reunite after their emancipation and the war's end. African Americans used a family record to keep track of births, deaths, and marriages after emancipation. Ask students to create their own family record with the following information: Name, Born, Married, Died. Discuss the difficulties in trying to recreate this information from memory. **L1**

📂 Refer to *Inclusion for the Middle School Social Studies Classroom Strategies and Activities* in the TCR.

✓ **Reading Check**

Answer: They rented a plot from landowners.

L1

Reteaching Activity 17–3

L1, ELL

Reading Essentials and Study Guide 17–3

L3

Enrichment Activity 17–3

4 CLOSE

Have students review the charts they made in the "TEACH" activity. Ask them to add another column to the chart to list the changes they would have made in the South during Reconstruction.

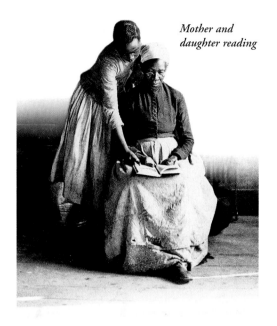

Mother and daughter reading

Public Schools

In the 1870s Reconstruction governments began creating public school systems for both races, which had not existed in the South before the war. Within a few years, more than 50 percent of the white children and about 40 percent of African American children in the South were enrolled in public schools. Northern missionary societies also established academies offering advanced education for African Americans. Some academies developed into colleges and universities, such as Morehouse College and Atlanta University.

Generally, African American and white students attended different schools. Only Louisiana, South Carolina, and Florida required that schools be integrated—include both whites and African Americans—but the laws were not enforced.

Farming the Land

Along with education, most freed people wanted land. Some African Americans were able to buy land with the assistance of the Freedmen's Bank, established in 1865. Most, however, failed to get their own land.

The most common form of farmwork for freed individuals was sharecropping. In this system a landowner rented a plot of land to a sharecropper, or farmer, along with a crude shack, some seeds and tools, and perhaps a mule. In return sharecroppers shared a percentage of their crop with the landowner.

After paying the landowners, sharecroppers often had little left to sell. Sometimes there was barely enough to feed their families. For many, sharecropping was little better than slavery.

✓ **Reading Check** **Explaining** How did sharecroppers get land to farm?

SECTION 3 ASSESSMENT

Checking for Understanding

1. **Key Terms** Define each term using a complete sentence: scalawag, carpetbagger, corruption, integrate, sharecropping.

2. **Reviewing Facts** How did some Southerners try to maintain control over freed people?

Reviewing Themes

3. **Continuity and Change** How did the state governments under Reconstruction reform education?

Critical Thinking

4. **Drawing Conclusions** Why was voting and owning land so important to newly freed African Americans?

5. **Organizing Information** Re-create the diagram below and identify the three groups that made up the Southern Republican Party.

Analyzing Visuals

6. **Picturing History** Study the picture above. Write a paragraph that explains who the people are and why reading is important to them.

Interdisciplinary Activity

Reading Bring newspapers to class and search for stories that show groups of people struggling for their rights throughout the world. After reading the articles aloud in class, post the items on the bulletin board with the heading "Let Freedom Ring."

SECTION 3 ASSESSMENT ANSWERS

1. Student work should reflect correct use of terms.
2. Some told freed slaves they could not leave their plantations; many refused to rent land to African Americans or give them work; stores refused credit; some whites resorted to violence and intimidation.
3. They created public school systems for both races.
4. Voting gave them a voice in government and made them fully participating citizens; owning land gave them economic independence.
5. African Americans, white Southerners who supported Republican policies, white settlers from the North
6. Answers should accurately describe the picture.

Interdisciplinary Activity Students should bring in current newspapers and select articles about groups struggling for their rights.

SECTION 4 Change in the South

Guide to Reading

Main Idea
Democrats steadily regained control of Southern governments as support for Radical Reconstruction policies decreased.

Key Terms
reconciliation, commission, cash crop, poll tax, literacy test, grand-father clause, segregation, lynching

Preview of Events

♦1870	♦1885	♦1900
1877 Hayes wins presidency; Reconstruction ends	**1890** Poll taxes and literacy tests begin in Mississippi	**1896** *Plessy* v. *Ferguson* rules segregation constitutional

Reading Strategy
Comparing As you read the section, re-create the diagram below and list the advantages and disadvantages of an agricultural economy.

Agricultural Economy

Advantages	Disadvantages

Read to Learn
• what changes occurred in the South during the last years of Reconstruction.
• how African Americans were denied their rights.

Section Theme
Continuity and Change The Democratic Party began to regain control of Southern politics.

AN
American Story

In 1875 the carpetbag governor of Mississippi faced growing violence between whites and African Americans in his state. He appealed to President Grant for troops to restore order. The president's attorney general responded: "The whole public are tired out with these . . . outbreaks in the South, and the great majority are now ready to condemn any interference on the part of the government. . . . Preserve the peace by the forces in your own state. . . ." Sharp in tone, the attorney general's letter reflected the government's desire to end Reconstruction.

Struggle for the Speaker's chair in a Southern statehouse, 1875

Reconstruction Declines

During the Grant administration, Northerners began losing interest in Reconstruction. Many believed it was time for the South to solve its own problems. By 1876 Southern Democrats were regaining political and economic control in the South. Some freed men and women went back to work for landholders because they had no other way to make a living.

CHAPTER 17   Reconstruction and Its Aftermath   **513**

---

2 TEACH

Writing an Essay Have students write essays outlining the successes of the Democrats and the failures of the Republicans that led to increased popularity of the Democratic Party. Have students volunteer information from their essays. **L1**

🎩 **Analyzing** *Political Cartoons*

Answer: Answers will vary but may include that the woman represents Lady Liberty and she is turning away in shame or disappointment because of the scandals in the Grant administration.

Reconstruction declined for other reasons. The old Radical leaders began to disappear from the political scene. Thaddeus Stevens died in 1868, and others retired or lost elections.

Another factor that weakened enthusiasm for Reconstruction was racial prejudice in the North. This prejudice was exploited by opponents of Reconstruction. They argued that only Southerners really knew how to deal with African Americans and that the fate of the freed people should be left to the South.

Southerners protested what they called "bayonet rule"—the use of federal troops to support Reconstruction governments. President Grant had sent federal troops to the South to stop violence or to enforce the law only when absolutely necessary. Generally, though, he tried to avoid any clashes with the South.

Republican Revolt

In the early 1870s, reports of corruption in Grant's administration and in Reconstruction governments spread throughout the nation. Some Republicans split with the party over the issue of corruption. Another group of Republicans broke with the party over Reconstruction, proposing peaceful **reconciliation**—coming together again—with Southern whites. Calling themselves Liberal Republicans, these two groups nominated **Horace Greeley,** a newspaper editor from New York, to run against Grant in the 1872 presidential election.

The Democrats also supported Greeley for president because he offered a chance to defeat the Republicans. Despite the division in the Republican ranks, however, Grant was reelected.

The Amnesty Act

During the 1872 election campaign, Liberal Republicans called for expanded amnesty for white Southerners. In May 1872, Congress passed the **Amnesty Act,** which pardoned most former Confederates. Nearly all white Southerners could vote and hold office again. The amnesty changed the political balance in the South by restoring full rights to people who supported the Democratic Party.

Democrats Regain Power

In Southern states such as Virginia and North Carolina, where a majority of voters were white, Democrats soon regained control of state governments. In states where African Americans held a majority or where white and African American populations were nearly equal, the Ku Klux Klan and other violent groups helped the Democrats take power by terrorizing Republican voters.

In an election in Mississippi in 1875, Democrats won by a 30,000 majority, although the Republicans had held a 30,000 majority in the previous election. The Democrats used threats to pressure white Republicans to become Democrats. As one Republican put it:

❝No white man can live in the South in the future and act with any other than the Democratic Party unless he is willing and prepared to live a life of social isolation.❞

🎩 **Analyzing** *Political Cartoons*

Problems in the Grant administration hurt the Republican Party. **Who does the woman at the far right represent? Why is she turning away?**

COOPERATIVE LEARNING ACTIVITY

Illustrating the End of Reconstruction Organize the class into groups of three to look through the section for dates, events, and people that played a significant role in the end of Reconstruction. Have each group choose a type of graphic organizer to display this information. Then ask group members to choose one of the following to illustrate on the graphic organizer: events, dates, people. Encourage students to draw their own illustrations or use pictures, drawings, clip art, and so on. Have groups create and assemble their graphic organizers. 📦 **L1, ELL**

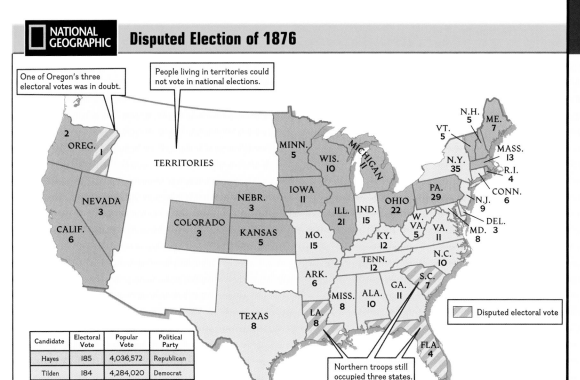

Disputed Election of 1876

One of Oregon's three electoral votes was in doubt.

People living in territories could not vote in national elections.

TERRITORIES

OREG. 2, 1

NEVADA 3

CALIF. 6

COLORADO 3

NEBR. 3

KANSAS 5

MINN. 5

WIS. 10

IOWA 11

MICHIGAN 11

ILL. 21

IND. 15

MO. 15

ARK. 6

TEXAS 8

LA. 8

MISS. 8

ALA. 10

TENN. 12

KY. 12

OHIO 22

W. VA. 5

VA. 11

N.C. 10

S.C. 7

GA. 11

FLA. 4

MD. 3

DEL.

N.J. 9

PA. 29

N.Y. 35

CONN. 6

R.I. 4

MASS. 13

VT. 5

N.H. 5

ME. 7

Disputed electoral vote

Northern troops still occupied three states.

Candidate	Electoral Vote	Popular Vote	Political Party
Hayes	185	4,036,572	Republican
Tilden	184	4,284,020	Democrat

The Democrats also used violence to persuade African Americans not to vote. By 1876 Republicans held a majority in Congress in only three Southern states—Florida, South Carolina, and Louisiana.

During these years the Republicans had other problems they could not blame on the Democrats. In 1873 a series of political scandals came to light. Investigations uncovered top government officials making unfair business deals, scheming to withhold public tax money, and accepting bribes. One scandal involved the vice president, and another the secretary of war. These scandals further damaged the Grant administration and the Republicans. At the same time, the nation suffered an economic depression. Blame for the hard times fell on the Republicans.

By the time of the congressional elections in 1874, charges of corruption and economic mismanagement had badly weakened the Republican Party. Democrats gained seats in the Senate and won control of the House. For the first time since the Civil War, the Democratic Party controlled

 Geography *Skills*

Because of some conflicting results, a committee of 15 members from Congress and the Supreme Court decided the final count in the 1876 election.
1. **Location** Which Southern states sent in election returns that were disputed?
2. **Analyzing Information** By how many electoral votes did Hayes finally win?

a part of the federal government. This situation further weakened Congress's commitment to Reconstruction and protecting the rights of newly freed African Americans.

 Reading Check **Identifying** Who was reelected president in 1872?

The End of Reconstruction

President Grant considered running for a third term in 1876. Most Republican leaders preferred a new candidate—one who could win back the Liberal Republicans and unite the party.

CHAPTER 17   Reconstruction and Its Aftermath   **515**

Geography *Skills*

Answers:
1. Louisiana, Florida, South Carolina
2. one

Geography Skills Practice
Ask: In what region was there the most support for the Democratic Party in the 1876 election? *(in the South)*

✓ **Reading Check**

Answer: President Grant

DIFFERENTIATED INSTRUCTION

Reading Support Have students research the final results of the 2000 presidential election. Ask students to create a chart that shows how George W. Bush lost the popular vote to Al Gore, Jr., but won the Electoral College vote to become president. Remind students that candidates need a majority of the Electoral College votes to win the presidency. **L1**

📂 Refer to *Inclusion for the Middle School Social Studies Classroom Strategies and Activities* in the TCR.

Did you know?

Republicans held a private swearing in for Hayes on the evening before the official inauguration ceremony.

Who?What?Where?When?

Horace Greeley Greeley was a prominent nineteenth-century writer and newspaper editor whose editorials against the spread of slavery into the Western territories before the war helped shape antislavery public opinion in the North. Greeley is known as the founder of *The New Yorker* magazine and as the person who popularized the expression, "Go west, young man." He died one month after the 1872 election, in which he unsuccessfully challenged Ulysses S. Grant's bid for a second term as president.

The Election of 1876

The Republicans nominated **Rutherford B. Hayes,** governor of Ohio, for president. A champion of political reform, Hayes had a reputation for honesty, and he held moderate views on Reconstruction. The Democrats nominated New York governor **Samuel Tilden.** Tilden had gained national fame for fighting political corruption in New York City.

After the election, Tilden appeared to be the winner, receiving almost 250,000 more votes than Hayes. However, disputed returns from Florida, Louisiana, South Carolina, and Oregon—representing 20 electoral votes—kept the outcome in doubt. Tilden had 184 electoral votes, only one short of what he needed to win. Yet if Hayes received all 20 of the disputed votes, he would have the 185 electoral votes required for victory.

In January Congress created a special commission, or group, of seven Republicans, seven Democrats, and one independent to review the election results. But the independent resigned, and a Republican took his place. After examining the reports of state review boards, the commission voted 8 to 7 to award all 20 disputed votes, and the election, to Hayes. The vote followed party lines.

Democrats in Congress threatened to fight the verdict. Republican and Southern Democratic leaders met secretly to work out an agreement that would allow the Democrats to accept Hayes as president. On March 2, 1877—almost four months after the election—Congress confirmed the verdict of the commission and declared Hayes the winner. He was inaugurated president two days later.

Compromise of 1877

The deal congressional leaders made to settle the election dispute, the **Compromise of 1877,** included various favors to the South. The new government would give more aid to the region

What If...

Lincoln Had Survived?

Lincoln's main goal had been to preserve the Union. In his second Inaugural Address, he indicated that he would deal compassionately with the South after the war ended:

> 66With malice toward none; with charity for all, with firmness in the right as God gives us to see the right, let us strive on to finish the work we are in, to bind up the nation's wounds, to care for him who shall have borne the battle and for his widow and his orphan. . . .99

—Abraham Lincoln, Second Inaugural Address, March 1865

President Lincoln did not live to carry out his plan. On April 14, 1865, just five days after Lee's surrender, he was assassinated.

Andrew Johnson, who succeeded to the presidency, attempted to carry out Lincoln's Reconstruction policies. He was hampered in this effort because as an unelected president he had little popular following. In addition, as a former Democrat, he could not command the support of the Republican majority in Congress. As a Tennessean and former slaveholder, he offended the Radicals. If these handicaps were not enough, his critics viewed Johnson as self-righteous, hot-tempered, stubborn, and crude.

In March 1868 the House adopted 11 articles of impeachment against Johnson. Although Johnson was acquitted and served out his term, any influence he might have had on Reconstruction was lost.

Ticket to Johnson's impeachment trial

U. S. SENATE
Impeachment *of the* President
ADMIT THE BEARER
MARCH 13. 1868
Geo. T. Brown
Sergeant-at-Arms.

INTERDISCIPLINARY CONNECTIONS ACTIVITY

Economics Have students use the section to create a chart showing the changes in the economy of the New South. Have them first list the major cities of the New South. In another column have them describe the major economic bases of the New South. Have students skim this and other sections of this chapter to describe in a third column the economic bases of the South before the Civil War. Finally, have students research the present economic bases of some major cities in the South and list this information in a fourth column. **L3**

and withdraw all remaining troops from Southern states. The Democrats, in turn, promised to maintain African Americans' rights.

In his Inaugural Address, Hayes declared that what the South needed most was the restoration of "wise, honest, and peaceful local self-government." During a goodwill trip to the South, Hayes announced his intention of letting Southerners handle racial issues. In Atlanta he told an African American audience:

❝. . . your rights and interests would be safer if this great mass of intelligent white men were left alone by the general government.❞

Hayes's message was clear. The federal government would no longer attempt to reshape Southern society or help Southern African Americans. Reconstruction was over.

✓ **Reading Check** **Summarizing** What effect did the Compromise of 1877 have on Reconstruction?

Lincoln's funeral carriage

What might have happened?

1. How did Lincoln and Johnson differ in qualities of leadership? In personality? Do you think these qualities made a difference in the way political leaders responded to the two presidents?

2. Would Reconstruction have taken a different course if Lincoln had not been assassinated? Explain.

Change in the South

❝I am treated not as an American citizen, but as a brute. . . . [A]nd for what? Not that I am unable to or unwilling to pay my way; not that I am obnoxious in my personal appearance or disrespectful in my conduct; but simply because I happen to be of a darker complexion.❞

John Lynch, a member of Congress who had once been enslaved, spoke these words. At the end of Reconstruction, many African Americans faced lives of poverty, indignity, and despair.

A New Ruling Party

Many Southern whites hated Republicans because of their role in the Civil War and in Reconstruction. When Reconstruction ended, political power in the South shifted from the Republicans to the Democrats.

In some regions, the ruling Democrats were the large landowners and other groups that had held power before the Civil War. In most areas, however, a new ruling class took charge. Among their ranks were merchants, bankers, industrialists, and other business leaders who supported economic development and opposed Northern interference. These Democrats called themselves **"Redeemers"** because they had "redeemed," or saved, the South from Republican rule.

The Redeemers adopted conservative policies such as lower taxes, less public spending, and reduced government services. They drastically cut, or even eliminated, many social services started during Reconstruction, including public education. Their one-party rule and conservative policies dominated Southern politics well into the 1900s.

Rise of the "New South"

By the 1880s forward-looking Southerners were convinced that their region must develop a strong industrial economy. They argued that the South had lost the Civil War because its industry and manufacturing did not match the North's. **Henry Grady,** editor of the *Atlanta Constitution,* headed a group that urged Southerners to "out-

CHAPTER 17 Reconstruction and Its Aftermath **517**

✓**Reading Check**

Answer: It effectively ended Reconstruction because President Hayes promised that the federal government would no longer try to reshape the South or intervene to protect the rights of Southern African Americans.

Where?When?Who?What?

Mississippi Although the official returns for the 1876 election were disputed in several states, there were voting irregularities in other states as well, such as Mississippi. Mississippi's electoral votes went to the Democratic candidate, Tilden. But there is evidence that Republican voters, many who were African American, were threatened and assaulted as they tried to vote. Because a majority of the people in Mississippi were African Americans and Republicans, the suppression of the African American vote could have changed the results of the election in that state.

Reading Strategy READING THE TEXT

Comparing and Contrasting Review with students the fact that it is possible to win the popular vote in a presidential election but still lose the presidency. Explain that this is because when Americans vote in presidential elections, they are not voting directly for a presidential candidate. They are voting for that candidate's electors. The votes of 270 electors are needed to win the presidency. Ask students to research to find out why American presidents are elected this way, and ask them to identify the pros and cons of this system. Then organize students into two panels to compare and contrast election by electoral vote with election by direct vote. **L2**

✓ Reading Check

Answer: Prices were forced down.

Did you know?

Today, the South still leads the nation in the production of cotton and tobacco. But the Southern region also leads the United States in the production of foods such as chickens, hogs, turkeys, shrimp, peanuts, pecans, sweet potatoes, and peaches.

you don't say...

Jim Crow Jim Crow comes from the song "Jim Crow" by Thomas D. Rice popularized in the mid-1830s. The song portrayed African Americans as happy-go-lucky, childlike people who wanted nothing more from life than something good to eat and a chance to sing and dance.

Yankee the Yankees" and build a "New South." This New South would have industries based on coal, iron, tobacco, cotton, lumber, and the region's other abundant resources. Southerners would create this new economy by embracing a spirit of hard work and regional pride. In 1886 Grady told a Boston audience that industrial development would allow the New South to match the North in a peaceful competition.

Southern Industries

Industry in the South made dramatic gains after Reconstruction. Some of the strongest advances were in the textile industry. Before the Civil War, Southern planters had shipped cotton to textile mills in the North or in Europe. In the 1880s textile mills sprang up throughout the South. Many Northern mills would later close as companies built new plants in the South.

Other important industries were lumbering and tobacco processing. The tobacco industry was developed largely through the efforts of **James Duke** of North Carolina. Duke's American Tobacco Company eventually controlled almost all tobacco manufacturing in the nation.

The iron and steel industry also grew rapidly. In the mid-1800s William Kelly, an American ironworker, and Henry Bessemer, a British engineer, had developed methods—called the **Bessemer process**—to inexpensively produce steel from iron. Steel answered industry's need for a sturdy, workable metal. By 1890 Southern mills produced nearly 20 percent of the nation's iron and steel. Much of the industry was in Alabama near deposits of iron ore.

Fact · Fiction · Folklore

Presidential Elections

Hayes was the only president to win the electoral vote, but lose the popular vote. Actually, three other times in American history—in the elections of John Quincy Adams in 1824, Benjamin Harrison in 1888, and George W. Bush in 2000—the candidate who lost the popular vote won the election.

Factors in Growth

A cheap and reliable workforce helped Southern industry grow. Most factory workers put in long hours for low wages. Sometimes whole families, including children, worked in factories. African Americans got few opportunities in industry except in the lowest-paying jobs.

A railroad-building boom also aided industrial development. By 1870 the Southern railroad system, which had been destroyed during the war, was largely rebuilt. The miles of track more than doubled between 1880 and 1890.

Still, the South did not develop an industrial economy as strong as the North's. The North was still industrializing more rapidly. The South remained primarily agricultural.

Economics
Rural Economy

Supporters of the New South hoped to change Southern agriculture as well as industry. They pictured small, profitable farms raising a variety of crops rather than large plantations devoted to growing cotton.

A different economy emerged, however. Some plantations were broken up, but many large landowners kept control of their property. When estates were divided, much of the land went to sharecropping and tenant farming, neither of which was profitable.

Debt caused problems as well. Poor farmers had to buy on credit to get the food and supplies they needed. The merchants who sold on credit charged high prices for their goods, increasing the farmers' debt. The quickest way for farmers to repay that debt, they thought, was to grow cash crops—crops that could be sold for money. As in the past, the biggest cash crop was cotton. An oversupply of cotton forced prices down, however. The farmers then had to grow even more cotton to try to recover their losses.

Sharecropping and reliance on a single cash crop hampered the development of a more modern agricultural economy. Instead, the rural South sank deeper into poverty and debt.

✓ Reading Check **Describing** What happened to prices when more cotton was produced than could be sold?

EXTENDING THE CONTENT

Growth of Southern Industry The South maintained its agricultural roots in the aftermath of the Civil War and used agriculture as a basis for industrialization. The region's forests supported a growing furniture industry, with 44 furniture factories producing products in the South by the turn of the century. By that time the South was also using its tobacco crop to manufacture nearly all of the nation's cigarettes. Textile production increased, with the number of Southern textile mills growing from 161 in 1880 to 400 in 1900. The region also used its natural resources to become the nation's leading producer of building materials such as bricks, precut lumber, windows and doors, and roofing shingles.

A Divided Society

As Reconstruction ended, African Americans' dreams for justice faded. In the last 20 years of the 1800s, racism became firmly entrenched, and individuals took steps to keep African Americans separated from whites and to deny them basic rights.

Voting Restrictions

The Fifteenth Amendment prohibited any state from denying an individual the right to vote because of race. Southern leaders, however, found ways to get around the amendment and prevent African Americans from voting.

Many Southern states required a poll tax, a fee that people had to pay before voting. Because many African Americans could not afford the tax, they could not vote. The tax also prevented many poor whites from voting. Another approach was to make prospective voters take a literacy test in which they had to read and explain difficult parts of state constitutions or the federal Constitution. Because most African Americans had little education, literacy tests prevented many from voting.

Literacy tests could also keep some whites from voting. For this reason some states passed grandfather clauses. These laws allowed individuals who did not pass the literacy test to vote if their fathers or grandfathers had voted before Reconstruction. Because African Americans could not vote until 1867, they were excluded. Georgia enacted a poll tax and other limits as early as 1870. Such laws, however, did not become widespread until after 1889. African Americans continued to vote in some states until the end of the 1800s. Then, voting laws and the constant threat of violence caused African American voting to drastically decline.

Jim Crow Laws

Another set of laws hurt African Americans. By the 1890s segregation, or the separation of the races, was a prominent feature of life in the South.

The Southern states formed a segregated society by passing so-called **Jim Crow laws.** Taking their name from a character in a song, Jim Crow

laws required African Americans and whites to be separated in almost every public place where they might come in contact with each other.

In 1896 the Supreme Court upheld Jim Crow laws and segregation in *Plessy v. Ferguson.* The case involved a Louisiana law requiring separate sections on trains for African Americans. The Court ruled that segregation was legal as long as African Americans had access to public facilities or accommodations equal to those of whites. 📖
(See page 626 of the Appendix for a summary of Plessy v. Ferguson.)

The problem, however, was that the facilities were separate but in no way equal. Southern states spent much more money on schools and other facilities for whites than on those for African Americans. This "separate but equal" doctrine provided a legal foundation for segregation in the South that lasted for more than 50 years.

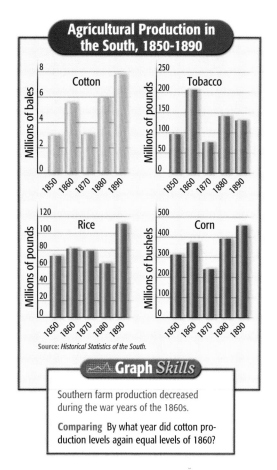

Agricultural Production in the South, 1850-1890

Cotton — Millions of bales (1850–1890)

Tobacco — Millions of pounds (1850–1890)

Rice — Millions of pounds (1850–1890)

Corn — Millions of bushels (1850–1890)

Source: *Historical Statistics of the South.*

Graph Skills

Southern farm production decreased during the war years of the 1860s.

Comparing By what year did cotton production levels again equal levels of 1860?

Graph Skills

Answer: 1880

Graph Skills Practice
Ask: About how many bushels of corn were produced in 1890? *(about 450 million)*

3 ASSESS

Assign Section 4 Assessment as homework or as an in-class activity.

Have students use **Interactive Tutor Self-Assessment CD-ROM.**

L2

Section Quiz 17–4

Name _____ Date _____ Class _____

⭐ Chapter 17   Score

Section Quiz 17-4

DIRECTIONS: Matching Match the items in Column A with the items in Column B. Write the correct letters in the blanks. *(10 points each)*

Column A	Column B
_____ 1. coming together again	A. Ulysses S. Grant
_____ 2. African American civil rights leader	B. Ku Klux Klan
_____ 3. Horace Greeley's opponent	C. W.E.B. DuBois
_____ 4. terrorized Republican voters	D. segregation
_____ 5. separation of the races	E. reconciliation

L1

Reteaching Activity 17–4

Name _____ Date _____ Class _____

⭐ **Reteaching Activity 17-4**

DIRECTIONS: Crossword Puzzle Complete the crossword puzzle by writing the term that matches each clue.

Amnesty Act	New South	Horace	industry
agricultural	cotton	sharecropping	poll tax
literacy test	textile	Jim Crow laws	W.E.B. Du Bois
James Duke			

Across
1. African American writer and civil rights leader
5. Prospective voters had to read and explain diffic...

EXTENDING THE CONTENT

African American Sharecroppers Although the end of slavery released African Americans from working on plantations, they often remained tied to wealthy landowners through sharecropping, debt, and local laws that limited their ability to choose their employer. Anti-enticement laws kept African American farmers from getting work offers from any landowner except the one for whom they worked, tying them to that landowner throughout their working lives. Anti-vagrancy laws prevented African Americans from traveling around the region freely to look for work, forcing them to remain in one local area.

Reading Check

Answer: the separation of the races

Analyzing *Political Cartoons*

Answer: The African American man represents the right to vote; the group of men represents the opposition to African Americans voting.

L1, ELL

Reading Essentials and Study Guide 17–4

L3

Enrichment Activity 17–4

4 CLOSE

Ask students to interpret the statement, "Reconstruction was both a success and a failure."

Analyzing *Political Cartoons*

African Americans were often barred from voting. **What do the people in the cartoon represent?**

Violence Against African Americans

Along with restrictions on voting rights and laws passed to segregate society, white violence against African Americans increased. This violence took many terrible forms, including lynching, in which an angry mob killed a person by hanging. African Americans were lynched because they were suspected of committing crimes—or because they did not behave as whites thought they should.

Reconstruction's Impact

Reconstruction was both a success and a failure. It helped the South recover from the war and begin rebuilding its economy. Yet economic recovery was far from complete. Although Southern agriculture took a new form, the South was still a rural economy, and that economy was still very poor.

Under Reconstruction African Americans gained greater equality and began creating their own institutions. They joined with whites in new governments, fairer and more democratic than the South had ever seen. This improvement for African Americans did not last long, however. In the words of African American writer and civil rights leader **W.E.B. Du Bois,**

> ❝The slave went free; stood a brief moment in the sun; then moved back again toward slavery.❞

The biggest disappointment of Reconstruction was that it did not make good on the promise of true freedom for freed African Americans. The South soon created a segregated society.

Reading Check **Describing** What is segregation?

SECTION 4 ASSESSMENT

Checking for Understanding

1. **Key Terms** Define the following terms: reconciliation, commission, cash crop, poll tax, literacy test, grandfather clause, segregation, lynching.
2. **Reviewing Facts** How did the Bessemer process affect Southern industry?

Reviewing Themes

3. **Continuity and Change** In what industries did the South make great gains after Reconstruction?

Critical Thinking

4. **Determining Cause and Effect** Explain how the Amnesty Act helped the Democratic Party regain its strength.
5. **Organizing Information** Re-create the diagram below and describe how the poll tax and literacy tests restricted voting rights.

Analyzing Visuals

6. Study the election map on page 515. Which candidate received the greater number of popular votes? Who won the election?

Interdisciplinary Activity

Government Research to find out how many African Americans hold seats in Congress today. Make a list of their names and states of residence. Be sure to include members of both the House of Representatives and the Senate.

520　CHAPTER 17　Reconstruction and Its Aftermath

SECTION 4 ASSESSMENT ANSWERS

1. Student work should reflect correct use of terms.
2. The Bessemer process allowed Southern mills to produce steel inexpensively from iron. By 1890 20 percent of U.S. iron and steel was produced by Southern mills.
3. textiles, lumbering, tobacco processing, iron, steel
4. It allowed nearly all white Southerners to vote and hold office again; Southern Democrats gradually began to regain control of the state governments.
5. Poll tax: because many African Americans and poor whites could not afford the tax, they could not vote; Literacy tests: because most

African Americans had little education and could not read, these tests kept them from voting
6. Tilden; Hayes

Interdisciplinary Activity Students' lists should contain current information.

Identifying the Main Idea

Why Learn This Skill?

Historical details, such as names, dates, and events, are easier to remember when they are connected to a main idea. Understanding the main idea allows you to grasp the whole picture or story.

Learning the Skill

Follow these steps to identify a main idea:
- Before you read the material, find out the setting of the article or document: the time, the place, and who the writer is.
- Read the material and ask, "What is the purpose of this information?"
- Identify supporting details.
- Identify the main idea or central issue.

Practicing the Skill

In the passage below, W.E.B. Du Bois, an African American scholar, describes the attitudes of people in Charleston, South Carolina, just after the Civil War. Read the passage and answer the questions that follow.

The economic loss which came through war was great, but not nearly as influential as the psychological change, the change in habit and thought….

The hatred of the Yankees was increased. The defeated Southern leaders were popular heroes. Numbers of Southerners planned to leave the country and go to South America or Mexico….

The labor situation, the prospect of free Negroes, caused great apprehension. It was accepted as absolutely true by most planters that the Negro could not work without a white master.**99**

A plantation owner meets her former slaves following emancipation.

1. Du Bois begins by naming two kinds of losses from the war. What are they? Which does he say was greater?

2. What is the main idea of the passage?

3. What details support the main idea?

4. Does the painting support or negate Du Bois's main idea?

Applying the Skill

Identifying the Main Idea Bring a news article about a current event to class. Identify the main idea and supporting details in the article.

 Glencoe's **Skillbuilder Interactive Workbook CD-ROM, Level 1,** provides instruction and practice in key social studies skills.

521

TEACH

Identifying the Main Idea This skill demonstrates how to read and find the main idea. By reading a quote from W.E.B. Du Bois, students will practice how to find the main idea using a primary source.

Have students work in pairs to apply the steps on this page to identify the main idea of "Change in the South" on pages 517–518. The main idea of the section is that the South's economy became more industrialized beginning in the 1880s.

Additional Practice

L2

Chapter Skills Activity 17

Name _____ Date _____ Class _____

★ Chapter Skills Activity **17**

Identifying the Main Idea

Identifying main ideas as you read will help you understand and remember historical events. To identify the main idea of a passage, figure out the purpose of the passage. What picture is the author presenting? Look for important details and try to determine how they are related to each other.

DIRECTIONS: Radical Reconstructionist Thaddeus Stevens made this proposal to Congress in 1867. Read the passage. Then answer the questions on a separate sheet of paper.

Four million persons have just been freed from a condition of dependence. These are people who, through no fault of their own, have no knowledge of business and do not even have the simplest elements of education. Few of

GLENCOE
TECHNOLOGY

CD-ROM
Glencoe Skillbuilder Interactive Workbook CD-ROM, Level 1

This interactive CD-ROM reinforces student mastery of essential social studies skills.

ANSWERS TO PRACTICING THE SKILL

1. economic and psychological; psychological

2. Psychological changes had the greatest impact on the South after the Civil War.

3. hatred of Yankees increased, defeated Southern leaders were heroes, many Southerners planned to leave the country, the African American labor situation caused apprehension

4. Answers will vary but may include the idea that the painting supports Du Bois's opinion that freed people were apprehensive after the Civil War.

Applying the Skill Students should identify the main idea and supporting details in a news article.

Reviewing Key Terms

1. Some Southerners received **amnesty,** or a pardon, after the war for swearing allegiance to the Union and renouncing secession.

2. **Black codes** were laws passed by Southern states to control freed African Americans and allow plantation owners to exploit African American workers.

3. The **poll tax,** a fee charged by many Southern states at the polls, kept poor African Americans and whites from voting.

4. Enslaved African Americans who had gained their freedom were sometimes called **freedmen.** A Freedmen's Bureau was set up to help them make the transition from slavery to full citizenship.

5. The Congress voted to **impeach,** or lodge a set of charges for wrongdoing against, President Johnson.

6. **Segregation,** or the separation of the races, was common in the South after the Civil War.

Reviewing Key Facts

7. It distributed food and clothing, provided medical services, established schools, helped people acquire land, provided transportation to jobs, and helped workers obtain fair wages.

8. Andrew Johnson

9. by granting full citizenship to all individuals born in the United States and prohibiting states from denying citizens constitutional privileges without "due process of law"

10. It did not have the votes to convict him and remove him from office. He was found not guilty.

Chapter Summary

Reconstruction and Its Aftermath

Reconstruction Plans
• Ten Percent Plan
• Wade-Davis Bill
• "Restoration"

Radicals in Control
• Civil Rights Act of 1866
• The Fourteenth Amendment
• President Johnson is impeached
• The Fifteenth Amendment

End of Reconstruction
• Interest in Reconstruction declines
• Amnesty Act
• Election of 1876
• Compromise of 1877

Change in the South
• Southern industry grows
• Economy remains agricultural
• Many white and African American farmers turn to sharecropping
• Jim Crow laws promote segregation

522

11. the right to vote for African Americans

12. They voted and served as elected officials in some Southern states.

13. It terrorized African Americans and other Republican voters to keep them from casting their votes.

14. because the ballots from three states were disputed

15. *Plessy* v. *Ferguson*

Reviewing Key Terms

Explain why each of these terms is used in a chapter about Reconstruction.

1. amnesty
2. black codes
3. poll tax
4. freedmen
5. impeach
6. segregation

Reviewing Key Facts

7. What services did the Freedmen's Bureau provide?
8. Who succeeded Lincoln as president?
9. How was the Fourteenth Amendment supposed to help African Americans?
10. What verdict did the Senate reach in the trial of President Johnson?
11. What right does the Fifteenth Amendment protect?
12. What role did African Americans play in early Reconstruction politics in the South?
13. What tactic did the Ku Klux Klan use to influence elections in the South?
14. Why was a special commission needed to decide the presidential election of 1876?
15. What Supreme Court decision upheld the legality of segregation so long as "separate but equal" facilities were provided?

Critical Thinking

16. **Analyzing Themes: Civic Rights and Responsibilities** How did the black codes deny rights?

17. **Analyzing Primary Sources** Explain the following quote as it applies to Reconstruction: "The slave went free; stood a brief moment in the sun; then moved back again toward slavery."

18. **Analyzing Themes: Economic Factors** Why did growing cotton after the Civil War send many Southern farmers into debt?

19. **Organizing Information** Re-create the diagram below and explain two important concessions that were made in the Compromise of 1877.

Compromise of 1877

Critical Thinking

16. They restricted the rights of freedmen and allowed plantation owners to continue to exploit African American laborers.

17. African Americans were freed from slavery and enjoyed some rights in the South during Reconstruction. But when local and state leaders in the South assumed control again, they passed laws and participated in actions to deny African Americans their rights.

Practicing Skills

The excerpt below was written by Charlotte Forten, one of many African American teachers who went South to teach freed individuals during the period of Reconstruction. Read the excerpt, which describes her first days of teaching school. Then answer the questions that follow.

 . . . I never before saw children so eager to learn, although I had had several years' experience in New England schools. Coming to school is a constant delight and recreation to them. They come here as other children go to play. The older ones, during the summer, work in the fields from early morning until eleven or twelve o'clock, and then come to school, after their hard toil in the hot sun, as bright and as anxious to learn as ever.

20. What is the main idea of this passage?
21. What details support the main idea of this passage?

Citizenship Cooperative Activity

22. **Registering to Vote** Laws about voter registration vary from place to place. Working with a partner, contact your local election board to find out what the requirements for voter registration are in your community. Then design a brochure that encourages citizens to register to vote.

Economics Activity

23. What happened to the price of cotton when an oversupply of cotton was on the market? How do you think prices would change if the demand for cotton were greater than the supply? Explain.

 ## Geography and History Activity

Turn to the map on page 515 to answer the following questions.

24. **Location** Electoral votes are based on population. What were the six most populous states in 1876?
25. **Region** Which political party gained the most votes in the western states?
26. **Place** How many electoral votes were in dispute?

Self-Check Quiz
Visit tarvol1.glencoe.com and click on **Chapter 17— Self-Check Quizzes** to prepare for the chapter test.

 ## Alternative Assessment

27. **Portfolio Writing Activity** Review the chapter to make a list of specific ways that Southern states tried to deny equal rights to African Americans after the war. Then decide which amendment(s)—Thirteenth, Fourteenth, or Fifteenth—should have prevented each action. Put this information in an essay using standard grammar and spelling.

Standardized Test Practice

Directions: Read the passage below. It is an excerpt from the Fifteenth Amendment to the Constitution. Then answer the question that follows.

The right of citizens of the United States to vote shall not be denied or abridged by the United States or any State on account of race, color, or previous condition of servitude.

The Congress shall have power to enforce this article by appropriate legislation.

The main idea of the Fifteenth Amendment is that

A enslaved people convicted of crimes had the right to a fair trial.

B slavery was made illegal in every state of the Union.

C the government was not allowed to deny a person's right to vote on the basis of race.

D Congress had the right to set voting restrictions in whatever state it chose.

Test-Taking Tip

This question asks for the *main idea* of the passage—in this case, of the Fifteenth Amendment. Read through all the answer choices before choosing the best one. Make sure you look for information in the passage to support your answer.

Economics Activity

23. The price of cotton decreased. Prices would increase because the need for more cotton would drive the prices up.

 ## Geography and History Activity

24. New York, Pennsylvania, Ohio, Illinois, Missouri, Indiana
25. Republican
26. 20

Alternative Assessment

27. Students' essays should include the actions taken in Southern states to limit African Americans' freedoms and should note whether the Thirteenth, Fourteenth, or Fifteenth Amendment was passed to prevent these types of actions.

Have students visit the Web site at tarvol1.glencoe.com to review Chapter 17 and take the Self-Check Quiz.

Standardized Test Practice

Answer: C
Question Type: Civics
Answer Explanation: An explanation of the Fifteenth Amendment can be found on page 508.

Bonus Question ?

Ask: Which president mentioned in this chapter served as an indentured servant to a tailor?
(Andrew Johnson)

---

18. Farmers bought food and supplies on credit. Farmers grew more cotton as a cash crop, which forced prices down and plunged farmers deeper into debt.

19. The federal government would give more aid to the South and withdraw remaining federal troops from Southern states.

Practicing Skills

20. African Americans had a great hunger for knowledge and wanted to learn.

21. The children want to go to school instead of playing. They go to school eager to learn after working hard all morning.

Citizenship Cooperative Activity

22. Students should use information acquired from the board of elections to design a brochure that encourages citizens to register to vote.

Unit 7 Resources

SUGGESTED PACING CHART

Unit 7 (1 Day)	Chapter 18 (6 Days)	Chapter 19 (6 Days)	Unit 7 (2 Days)
Day 1 Introduction	**Day 1** Chapter 18 Intro, Section 1	**Day 1** Chapter 19 Intro, Section 1	**Day 1** Wrap-Up/Project **Day 2** Unit 7 Assessment
	Day 2 Section 2	**Day 2** Section 2	
	Day 3 Section 3	**Day 3** Section 3	
	Day 4 Section 4	**Day 4** Section 4	
	Day 5 Chapter 18 Review	**Day 5** Chapter 19 Review	
	Day 6 Chapter 18 Assessment	**Day 6** Chapter 19 Assessment	

Use the following tools to easily assess student learning in a variety of ways:

- Performance Assessment Activities and Rubrics
- Chapter and Unit Tests
- Section Quizzes
- Standardized Test Practice Workbook

- www.tarvol1.glencoe.com
- Interactive Tutor Self-Assessment CD-ROM
- MindJogger Videoquiz
- ExamView® Pro Testmaker CD-ROM

TEACHING TRANSPARENCIES

Unit 7 Map Overlay Transparencies
L2

Cause-and-Effect Transparency 7
L2

READING SUPPORT FROM
JAMESTOWN ⚓ EDUCATION

- *Timed Readings Plus in Social Studies* help students increase their reading rate and fluency while maintaining comprehension. The 400-word passages are similar to those found on state and national assessments.

- *Reading in the Content Area: Social Studies* concentrates on six essential reading skills that help students better comprehend what they read. The book includes 75 high-interest nonfiction passages written at increasing levels of difficulty.

- *Reading Fluency* helps students read smoothly, accurately, and expressively.

- *Jamestown's Reading Improvement,* by renowned reading expert Edward Fry, focuses on helping build your students' comprehension, vocabulary, and skimming and scanning skills.

- *Critical Reading Series* provides high-interest books, each written at three reading levels.

For more information about these products, see the Jamestown Education materials in the Classroom Solutions in the front of this Teacher Wraparound Edition. To order these products, call Glencoe at 1-800-334-7344.

Unit 7 Resources

ASSESSMENT

Unit 7 Pretests L2

Unit 7 Posttests L2

INTERDISCIPLINARY ACTIVITIES

American Literature Reading 7 L2

Interdisciplinary Connection 7 L2

Economics and History Activity 7 L2

APPLICATION AND ENRICHMENT

Cooperative Learning Activity 7 L1, **ELL**

Citizenship Activity 7 L1

HANDS-ON ACTIVITIES

Hands-On History Activity 7 L1

History Simulations and Problem Solving 7 L1

Reading List Generator CD-ROM

GLENCOE BOOKLINK

The Glencoe BookLink CD-ROM is a database that allows you to search more than 15,000 titles to create a customized reading list for your students.

- Reading lists can be organized by students' reading level, author, genre, theme, or area of interest.

- The database provides Degrees of Reading Power™ (DRP) and Lexile™ readability scores for all selections.

- A brief summary of each selection is included.

Leveled reading suggestions for this unit:

For Students at a Grade 6 Reading Level:
- *If Your Name Was Changed at Ellis Island,* by Ellen Levine

For Students at a Grade 7 Reading Level:
- *Forward into Light: The Struggle for Women's Suffrage,* by Madeleine Meyers

For Students at a Grade 8 Reading Level:
- *Freedom Rides: Journey for Justice,* by James Haskins

Extending the Content

Readings for the Teacher
- *Bury My Heart at Wounded Knee: An Indian History of the American West, Thirtieth Anniversary Edition,* by Henry Holt & Company, Inc., 2001.
- *Ellis Island Interviews,* by Checkmark Books, 1998.

Multimedia Links
- *Adventures of the Old West: Cowboys & Trail Drives.* DVD. Madacy Records, 2000.

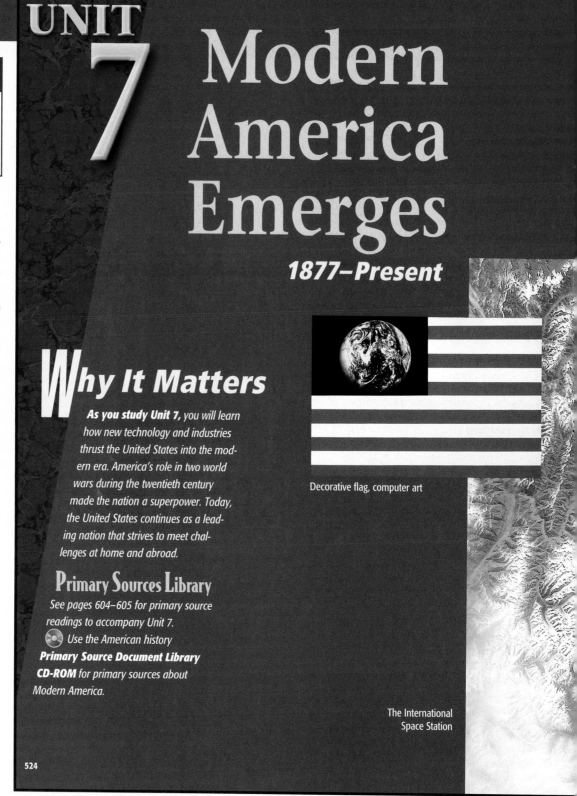

`0:00` **Out of Time?**

If time does not permit teaching each chapter in this unit, you may want to use the **Reading Essentials and Study Guide** summaries.

Unit Overview

Unit 7 describes the growth that took place that propelled the United States into the modern era. It shows how two world wars transformed the United States into a superpower. **Chapter 18** describes the continuing growth and expansion during the latter part of the nineteenth century. **Chapter 19** focuses on the emergence of modern America through the twentieth century.

Unit Objectives

After studying this unit, students will be able to:
1. Discuss the development of the United States from 1877 to the present.
2. Explain how inventions and technology influenced the development of modern America.
3. Describe the impact of immigration, city growth, and developments in education from 1877 to the present.
4. Identify key events and turning points in the evolution of United States foreign policy.

Why It Matters Activity

Have students think about how technology influences their everyday lives. Ask students to predict what advancements might be made to improve people's lives in the twenty-first century.

UNIT 7 Modern America Emerges

1877–Present

Why It Matters

As you study Unit 7, you will learn how new technology and industries thrust the United States into the modern era. America's role in two world wars during the twentieth century made the nation a superpower. Today, the United States continues as a leading nation that strives to meet challenges at home and abroad.

Decorative flag, computer art

Primary Sources Library

See pages 604–605 for primary source readings to accompany Unit 7.
Use the American history
Primary Source Document Library CD-ROM for primary sources about Modern America.

The International Space Station

TEAM TEACHING ACTIVITY

Language Arts Ask a Language Arts teacher to help students collect and read a series of poems or song lyrics written about America or various American cities from 1877 to the present. Encourage students to collect poems from different decades and regions of the country. Have them discuss how the poems reveal changes over time. **L1**

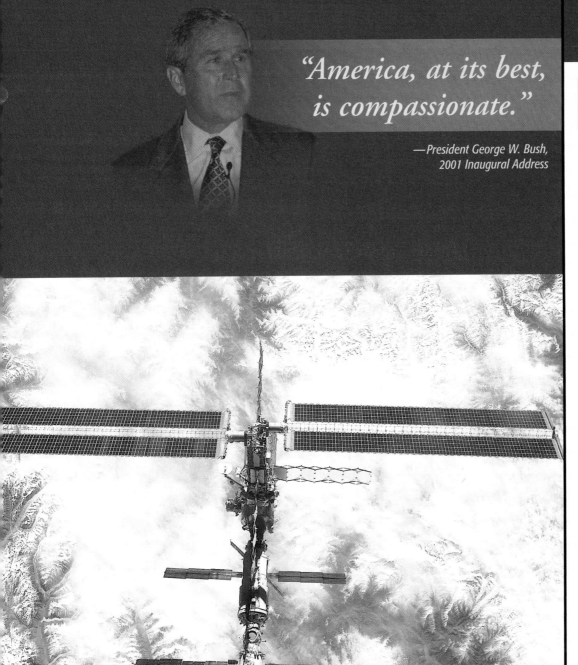

"*America, at its best, is compassionate.*"

—*President George W. Bush, 2001 Inaugural Address*

GLENCOE
TECHNOLOGY

 CD-ROM
American History Primary Source Document Library CD-ROM
Use the **American History Primary Source Document Library CD-ROM** to access primary source documents related to the emergence of Modern America.

More About the Photo

The United States National Aeronautics and Space Administration (NASA) announced a new program in 1984. Its goal was to establish a permanent space station as the next step forward after the space shuttle entered service in April 1981. The station was to create jobs, benefit space research, and increase foreign policy prestige for the United States. In 1994 NASA combined its project with a Russian project to produce the International Space Station (ISS). Other countries were also involved with the project, including Japan, Canada, Brazil, and the Western European countries of the European Space Agency. The estimated date for completion of the space station is 2006, though the first crew exchange took place in March 2001.

 Glencoe Literature Library

As students study the unit, have them read *Letters from Rifka* by Karen Hesse from the **Glencoe Literature Library.** The Glencoe Literature Library consists of novels and other readings for middle school students, along with study guides that offer instructional support and student activities.

SERVICE-LEARNING PROJECT

Encourage students to work in groups and research the services available in your area to help victims of disasters in the United States and around the world. In particular, have them seek out organizations that try to fill needs that are not addressed by other relief efforts. Ask what kind of help or donations the organizations need. For example, do they need funds, food, clothing, or volunteers? Have students choose a need and create a project to fill that need. Once they choose a specific project, help the group work toward its objectives. Students should divide tasks according to interest and abilities. **L1,** ELL

Refer to **Building Bridges: Connecting Classroom and Community through Service-Learning in Social Studies** from the National Council for the Social Studies for information about service-learning.

Chapter 18 Resources

Timesaving Tools

TeacherWorks™ All-In-One Planner and Resource Center

- **Interactive Teacher Edition** Access your Teacher Wraparound Edition and your classroom resources with a few easy clicks.
- **Interactive Lesson Planner** Planning has never been easier! Organize your week, month, semester, or year with all the lesson helps you need to make teaching creative, timely, and relevant.

Use Glencoe's **Presentation Plus!** multimedia teacher tool to easily present dynamic lessons that visually excite your students. Using Microsoft PowerPoint® you can customize the presentations to create your own personalized lessons.

TEACHING TRANSPARENCIES

Graphic Organizer 2 L2

Why It Matters Chapter Transparency 18 L2

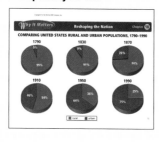

REVIEW AND REINFORCEMENT

Workbook Activity 18 L1

Time Line Activity 18 L2

Vocabulary Activity 18 L1

REVIEW AND REINFORCEMENT

Critical Thinking Skills Activity 18 L2

Take-Home Review Activity 18 L1

ENRICHMENT

Linking Past and Present Activity 18 L2

Primary Source Reading 18 L2

GEOGRAPHY

Geography and History Activity 18 L2

Meeting NCSS Standards

The following standards are highlighted in Chapter 18:

Section 1 III People, Places, & Environments: A, B, D, E, H, I, K
Section 2 VIII Science, Technology, & Society: A, B, C, D
Section 3 V Individuals, Groups, & Institutions: A, B, C, D, E, F, G
Section 4 IX Global Connections: B, F, G

FOLDABLES™ Study Organizer

Dinah Zike's Foldables are three-dimensional, interactive graphic organizers that help students practice basic writing skills, review key vocabulary terms, and identify main ideas. Additional chapter activities can be found in the *Reading and Study Skills Foldables* booklet.

Chapter 18 Resources

ASSESSMENT AND EVALUATION

**Chapter 18 Test
Form A** L2

**Chapter 18 Test
Form B** L2

**Standardized Test Practice
Workbook Activity 18** L2

**Performance Assessment
Activity 18** L1, ELL

**ExamView® Pro
Testmaker CD-ROM**

MULTIMEDIA

- Vocabulary PuzzleMaker CD-ROM
- Interactive Tutor Self-Assessment CD-ROM
- ExamView® Pro Testmaker CD-ROM
- Audio Program
- American History Primary Source Document Library CD-ROM
- MindJogger Videoquiz
- Presentation Plus! CD-ROM
- TeacherWorks CD-ROM
- Interactive Student Edition CD-ROM
- Glencoe Skillbuilder Interactive Workbook CD-ROM, Level 1
- The American Republic to 1877 Video Program
- American Music: Hits Through History

SPANISH RESOURCES

The following Spanish language materials are available in the Spanish Resources Binder:

- Spanish Guided Reading Activities
- Spanish Reteaching Activities
- Spanish Quizzes and Tests
- Spanish Vocabulary Activity
- Spanish Take-Home Review Activity
- Spanish Summaries
- The Declaration of Independence and United States Constitution Spanish Translation

THE HISTORY CHANNEL®

The following videotape programs are available from Glencoe as supplements to Chapter 18:

- **The Railroads That Tamed the West** (ISBN 0-7670-0033-1)
- **Ellis Island** (3 pack) (ISBN 0-7670-0005-6)
- **The White House-Great American Monuments** (ISBN 1-56501-643-2)

To order, call Glencoe at 1-800-334-7344. To find classroom resources to accompany many of these videos, check the following home pages:
A&E Television: www.aande.com
The History Channel: www.historychannel.com

Use our Web site for additional resources. All essential content is covered in the Student Edition.

You and your students can visit tarvol1.glencoe.com, the Web site companion to **The American Republic to 1877.** This innovative integration of electronic and print media offers your students a wealth of opportunities. The student text directs students to the Web site for the following options:

- **Chapter Overviews**
- **Student Web Activities**
- **Self-Check Quizzes**
- **Textbook Updates**

Answers to the student Web activities are provided for you in the **Web Activity Lesson Plans.** Additional Web resources and Interactive Tutor Puzzles are also available.

Chapter 18 Resources

SECTION RESOURCES

Daily Objectives	Reproducible Resources	Multimedia Resources
SECTION 1 **The Western Frontier** 1. Explain why settlers moved west. 2. Discuss the reasons why settlers came into conflict with Native Americans.	Reproducible Lesson Plan 18–1 Daily Lecture and Discussion Notes 18–1 Guided Reading Activity 18–1* Section Quiz 18–1* Reteaching Activity 18–1* Reading Essentials and Study Guide 18–1* Enrichment Activity 18–1	Daily Focus Skills Transparency 18–1 Interactive Tutor Self-Assessment CD-ROM ExamView® Pro Testmaker CD-ROM Presentation Plus! CD-ROM
SECTION 2 **Invention and Industry** 1. Analyze how American cities and industries changed at the turn of the century. 2. Describe the challenges immigrants to the United States faced.	Reproducible Lesson Plan 18–2 Daily Lecture and Discussion Notes 18–2 Guided Reading Activity 18–2* Section Quiz 18–2* Reteaching Activity 18–2* Reading Essentials and Study Guide 18–2* Enrichment Activity 18–2	Daily Focus Skills Transparency 18–2 Interactive Tutor Self-Assessment CD-ROM ExamView® Pro Testmaker CD-ROM Presentation Plus! CD-ROM
SECTION 3 **Reform at Home, Expansion Abroad** 1. Examine the ways in which the Progressive movement changed America. 2. Review the reasons the United States sought to expand overseas.	Reproducible Lesson Plan 18–3 Daily Lecture and Discussion Notes 18–3 Guided Reading Activity 18–3* Section Quiz 18–3* Reteaching Activity 18–3* Reading Essentials and Study Guide 18–3* Enrichment Activity 18–3	Daily Focus Skills Transparency 18–3 Interactive Tutor Self-Assessment CD-ROM ExamView® Pro Testmaker CD-ROM Presentation Plus! CD-ROM
SECTION 4 **World War I and Its Aftermath** 1. Understand what role the United States played in World War I. 2. Summarize how the nation changed during the 1920s.	Reproducible Lesson Plan 18–4 Daily Lecture and Discussion Notes 18–4 Guided Reading Activity 18–4* Section Quiz 18–4* Reteaching Activity 18–4* Reading Essentials and Study Guide 18–4* Enrichment Activity 18–4	Daily Focus Skills Transparency 18–4 Vocabulary PuzzleMaker CD-ROM Interactive Tutor Self-Assessment CD-ROM ExamView® Pro Testmaker CD-ROM Presentation Plus! CD-ROM

0:00 OUT OF TIME?
Assign the Chapter 18 **Reading Essentials and Study Guide.**

*Also Available in Spanish

 Blackline Master   Transparency   CD-ROM   DVD

Poster   Music Program   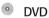 Audio Program   Videocassette

KEY TO ABILITY LEVELS

Teaching strategies have been coded.

- **L1** BASIC activities for all students
- **L2** AVERAGE activities for average to above-average students
- **L3** CHALLENGING activities for above-average students
- **ELL** ENGLISH LANGUAGE LEARNER activities

NATIONAL GEOGRAPHIC Teacher's Corner

INDEX TO NATIONAL GEOGRAPHIC MAGAZINE

The following articles relate to this chapter.
- "Federal Lands," by Richard Conniff, February 1994.
- "The Way West," by John G. Mitchell, September 2000.
- "The American Prairie: Roots of the Sky," by Douglas H. Chadwick, October 1993.
- "New Life for Ellis Island," by Alice J. Hall, September 1990.
- "Central Park: Oasis in the City," by Joel L. Swerdlow, May 1993.
- "The Bolshevik Revolution," by Dusko Doder, October 1992.
- "The Okies—Beyond the Dust Bowl," by William Howarth, September 1994.

ADDITIONAL NATIONAL GEOGRAPHIC SOCIETY PRODUCTS

To order the following, call National Geographic at 1-800-368-2728:
- *GeoKit: Eyewitness to the 20th Century* (Book)
- *National Geographic Desk Reference* (Book)
- *Full Steam Ahead: The Race to Build a Transcontinental Railroad* (Book)
- *American Indians: A Brief History* (Video)
- *Immigration: The Triumph of Hope* (Video)
- *1914–1918: World War I* (Video)

NGS ONLINE

Access National Geographic's Web site for current events, atlas updates, activities, links, interactive features, and archives.
www.nationalgeographic.com

MEETING SPECIAL NEEDS

In addition to the Differentiated Instruction strategies found in each section, the following resources are also suitable for your special needs students:

- *ExamView® Pro Testmaker CD-ROM* allows teachers to tailor tests by reducing answer choices.

- The *Audio Program* includes the entire narrative of the student edition so that less-proficient readers can listen to the words as they read them.

- The *Reading Essentials and Study Guide* provides the same content as the student edition but is written two grade levels below the textbook.

From the Classroom of...

Debbie Dumler
Lyons Middle School
Sterling, KS

A Classroom Industry

Set up a small in-class industry. First, have students select a simple product to produce, for example, spirit ribbons to support an athletic team (students can wear these or put them on their lockers before a big game or tournament) or bookmarks. Next, help students organize the class into divisions of labor. There will need to be managers, production workers, and a sales force (if you would like to distribute your product throughout the school). You can also sell shares in the company to acquire working capital. Students should set up their industry based on information in the chapter and what they already know about companies and how they work. If you have a school newsletter or newspaper, some students could act as an advertising team, designing ads. Posters and flyers could also be used as advertising materials. Any profits could go toward a classroom party or be given to a local charity.

ADDITIONAL RESOURCES FROM GLENCOE

- American Music: Cultural Traditions
- American Art and Architecture
- Outline Map Resource Book
- U.S. Desk Map
- Building Geography Skills for Life
- Inclusion for the Middle School Social Studies Classroom Strategies and Activities
- Teaching Strategies for the American History Classroom (Including Block Scheduling Pacing Guides)
- American Crafts Hands-On Activities
- American Games Hands-On Activities
- American History Flash Cards

Block Schedule

Activities that are suited to use within the block scheduling framework are identified by:

✔ **Performance Assessment**

Refer to Activity 18 in the Performance Assessment Activities and Rubrics booklet.

W*hy It Matters Activity*

Have students brainstorm a list of issues that a country might encounter as it expands, such as the need for better roads and means of transportation. As students read the chapter, they should identify how the United States government tried to resolve expansion issues and evaluate the effectiveness of the resolutions.

GLENCOE
TECHNOLOGY

The American Republic to 1877 Video Program

To learn more about immigrant railroad workers, have students view the Chapter 18 video, "The Builders of Our Railroads" from **The American Republic to 1877 Video Program.**

 Available in DVD and VHS

MindJogger Videoquiz

Use **MindJogger Videoquiz** to preview the Chapter 18 content.

Available in VHS

CHAPTER 18 Reshaping the Nation

1877–1929

Why It Matters

Growth has been a constant part of the American experience. Beginning as a small cluster of colonies on the Atlantic coast, the nation expanded beyond the Mississippi River to the Pacific Ocean. As it became powerful, the United States moved beyond its territorial limits in search of new markets and colonies. The United States also began to take a major role in shaping world affairs.

The Impact Today

The nation's responsibilities as an international power demand open attitudes to new ideas. Americans adjust to these ideas in ways that assure the future of a free and democratic society.

 The American Republic to 1877 *Video* The chapter 18 video, "The Builders of Our Railroads," examines the life and hardships that immigrants faced as workers on the railroads.

1869
• First transcontinental railroad completed

1886
• Statue of Liberty dedicated

1879
• Edison invents electric light

1898
• U.S. goes to war with Spain

United States PRESIDENTS

Grant 1869–1877 | Hayes 1877–1881 | Garfield 1881 | Arthur 1881–1885 | Cleveland 1885–1889 | B. Harrison 1889–1893 | Cleveland 1893–1897 | McKinley 1897–1901

1870   *1885*   *1900*

World

1866
• Transatlantic telegraph line successfully completed

1869
• Suez Canal opens

1895
• José Martí leads revolt in Cuba

526   CHAPTER 18   Reshaping the Nation

Reading Strategy ◣ PURPOSE FOR READING

Graphic organizers can help students organize the information in this chapter. Point out to students: "Native Americans were relocated to reservations on the Great Plains and in the Southwest. Settlers arrived from Eastern states and foreign countries that had very different environments." Draw a graphic organizer on the chalkboard. List three headings: the East, the Great Plains, and the West. Generate a class discussion about the differences in the environments of these regions. Have the class complete the organizer. Conclude by asking students to select one of the environments and complete the following one sentence summary: *Relocation to a new environment such as the _____ will affect me as a settler _____.* **L1**

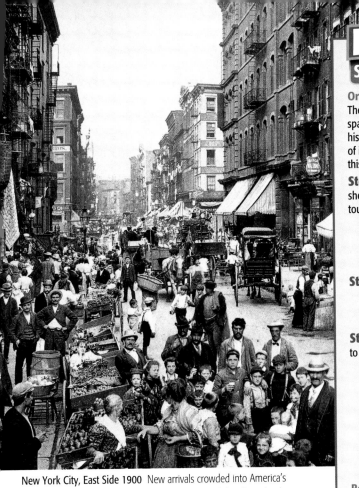

New York City, East Side 1900 New arrivals crowded into America's cities and brought with them the cultural heritage of their homelands.

FOLDABLES™
Study Organizer

Organizing Information Study Foldable
The content of Chapter 18 covers a large time span and many important events in American history. To help you understand a large amount of information, you must first organize it. Make this foldable to help you.

Step 1 Mark the midpoint of a side edge of one sheet of paper. Then fold the outside edges in to touch at the midpoint.

Step 2 Fold in half from side to side.

Step 3 Open and cut along the inside fold lines to form four tabs. Label your foldable as shown.

Cut along the fold lines on both sides.

Reading and Writing As you read the chapter, write down key ideas under each appropriate tab.

FOLDABLES™
Study Organizer — Dinah Zike's Foldables

Purpose This foldable will help students organize the large amount of information in Chapter 18 by requiring students to categorize that information under four main groupings. As students create and complete this foldable, they must first determine the relevant facts in the chapter text, and then group that information under the appropriate category.

📁 Have students complete **Reading and Study Skills Foldables** Activity 11. **L1**

HISTORY *Online*

Introduce students to chapter content and key terms by having them access **Chapter Overview 18** at tarvol1.glencoe.com

TIME LINE ACTIVITY

As students read the chapter, have them review the time line on pages 526–527. Ask students to identify events on the time line that contributed to improved communication and transportation.

1901
• President McKinley assassinated

1917
• U.S. enters World War I

1920
• Nineteenth Amendment grants woman suffrage

1927
• Charles Lindbergh flies across Atlantic

T. Roosevelt 1901–1909 | Taft 1909–1913 | Wilson 1913–1921 | Harding 1921–1923 | Coolidge 1923–1929

1915   *1930*

1905
• Albert Einstein announces theory of relativity

1914
• World War I begins

1919
• Treaty of Versailles signed

1928
• Alexander Fleming discovers penicillin

HISTORY *Online*

Chapter Overview
Visit tarvol1.glencoe.com and click on **Chapter 18— Chapter Overviews** to preview chapter information.

CHAPTER 18   Reshaping the Nation   **527**

More About the Photo

Many immigrants settled in New York City's Lower East Side during the wave of immigration that occurred during the late 1800s and early 1900s. Italian, Chinese, Irish, Russian, and Jewish neighborhoods maintained an ethnic character. Immigrants were drawn to areas where cheap tenement houses were plentiful and a familiar culture could be found. One such tenement house was built by German-born Lukas Glockner at 97 Orchard Street in 1863. Over the next 70 years, Glockner's tenement house would be home to 7,000 immigrants from 20 different countries.

1 FOCUS

Section Overview

This section describes how white settlers and Native Americans came into conflict with each other during westward expansion.

BELLRINGER
Skillbuilder Activity

Project transparency and have students answer the question.

Daily Focus Skills Transparency 18–1

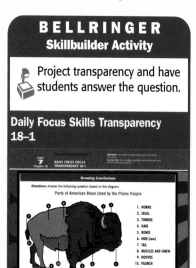

Reading Preview

Answers to Graphic: Promontory Point: site in Utah where builders completed the first transcontinental railroad line in 1869; **Homestead Act:** passed in 1862 providing free land to settlers; **Farmers' Alliance:** self-help group for farmers, members established the Populist Party

Preteaching Vocabulary
Have students look up unfamiliar words listed under **Key Terms** and then use each term in a sentence. Tell students the Latin prefix *trans-* means "across." Have them speculate on the meaning of the term *transcontinental*.

SECTION 1 The Western Frontier

Guide to Reading

Main Idea
Following the Civil War, settlers began to move west, which led to conflict with Native Americans.

Key Terms
boomtown, transcontinental, vaqueros, reservation

Reading Strategy
Organizing Information As you read the section, re-create the diagram below and describe the significance of each of the following.

	Significance
Promontory Point	
Homestead Act	
Farmers' Alliance	

Read to Learn
- why settlers moved west.
- why settlers came into conflict with Native Americans.

Section Theme
Geography and History Railroads led the way west and opened the Great Plains to settlement.

Preview of Events

♦1870	♦1880	♦1890	♦1900
1869 First transcontinental railroad completed	**1876** Battle of Little Bighorn	**1890** Populist Party organized	**1896** McKinley elected president

Gold nuggets

AN American Story

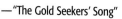

"We'll cross the bold Missouri, and we'll steer for the West,
And we'll take the road we think is the shortest and the best,
We'll travel over plains where the wind is blowing bleak,
And the sandy wastes shall echo with—Hurrah for Pikes Peak."
—"The Gold Seekers' Song"

Miners sang this hopeful song in 1859 as they headed for Pikes Peak, Colorado, where gold had been discovered.

There remained one last frontier for Americans to settle—the Trans-Mississippi West. This area lay between the Mississippi River and the Sierra Nevada Mountains and included the Great Plains, the Rocky Mountains, and the Great Basin. The first white settlers were fur traders who had started moving into the West in the early 1800s. By the time of the Civil War, however, mineral discoveries had drawn another type of pioneer to the West—the miner. Soon, the whole region was a mining frontier.

528   CHAPTER 18   Reshaping the Nation

SECTION RESOURCES

📂 Reproducible Masters
- Reproducible Lesson Plan 18–1
- Daily Lecture and Discussion Notes 18–1
- Guided Reading Activity 18–1
- Section Quiz 18–1
- Reteaching Activity 18–1
- Reading Essentials and Study Guide 18–1
- Enrichment Activity 18–1

📄 Transparencies
- Daily Focus Skills Transparency 18–1

Multimedia
- 🖥 Interactive Tutor Self-Assessment CD-ROM
- 🖥 ExamView® Pro Testmaker CD-ROM
- 🖥 Presentation Plus! CD-ROM

Settling the West

Miners, ranchers, and farmers settled on the Great Plains, despite resistance from Native Americans. With the closing of this last frontier, the United States fulfilled the dream of Manifest Destiny.

The Mining Boom

In 1858, prospectors found gold in Colorado and Nevada. The gold strikes created boomtowns—towns that grew up almost overnight near mining sites—as thousands of prospectors headed to the region. The miners soon found other metals as well, including copper, lead, and zinc.

The discovery of valuable minerals helped bring the railroads west. Gold, silver, and other ore had little value unless it could be shipped east to factories. Miners also needed food and supplies. Wagons and stagecoaches could not move goods fast enough, but railroads could.

Railroad construction was often supported by large government subsidies—loans and land grants from the government. The first task facing the railroads was to build a transcontinental rail line—one that would span the continent and connect the Atlantic and Pacific coasts. The Union Pacific Company began laying track westward from Nebraska, while the Central Pacific worked eastward from California. On May 10, 1869, the two sets of tracks met at **Promontory Point,** Utah. The railroads brought a wave of new settlers to the West—ranchers and farmers.

The Cattle Kingdom

When the Spanish settled the Southwest, they brought with them a breed of cattle called **longhorns** that gradually spread across Texas. At the same time, the Civil War had caused a shortage of beef in the east, driving prices up. To get the cattle to market, the Texas ranchers organized cattle drives—herding hundreds of thousands of cattle north to the railroad.

The sudden increase in the longhorns' value set off what became known as the **Long Drive**—the herding of cattle 1,000 miles or more to meet the railroads. In the late 1860s, the **Chisholm**

Trail extended from San Antonio, Texas, to Abilene, Kansas. The **Goodnight-Loving Trail,** named for ranchers Charlie Goodnight and Oliver Loving, swung west through New Mexico Territory and then turned north. During the peak years of the "Cattle Kingdom," from the late 1860s to the mid-1880s, the trails carried millions of cattle north:

> 66At the end of the trail, cattle crowded the stockyards. Railroad cities—Omaha, Abilene, Kansas City, Chicago—flourished during the 20-year heyday of cattle driving.99

Life on the Trail

Cattle driving was hard work. Cowhands rode in the saddle up to 15 hours every day, in driving rain, dust storms, and blazing sun. The life was lonely, too. Cowhands saw few outsiders.

Many cowhands were veterans of the Confederate army. Some, like **Nat Love,** were African Americans who moved west in search of a better life after the Civil War. Others were Hispanics. In fact, the tradition of cattle herding began with Hispanic ranch hands in the Spanish Southwest. These vaqueros developed many of the skills—riding, roping, and branding—that cowhands used on the drives.

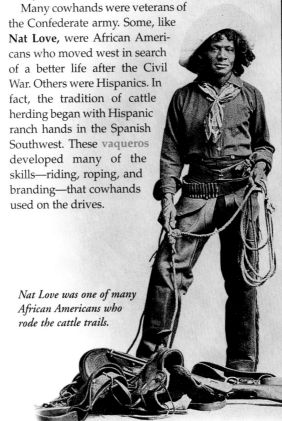

Nat Love was one of many African Americans who rode the cattle trails.

CHAPTER 18   Reshaping the Nation   **529**

2 TEACH

Daily Lecture and Discussion Notes 18–1

Outlining Work with students to create an outline of the section. Use the main heads for Roman numerals I to III, and have students provide details to fill in the subheads. **L1**

CURRICULUM CONNECTION

Science Many prospectors mistook pyrite, fool's gold, for the real thing. Cautious miners could perform simple experiments to test the malleability, durability, tarnish resistance, and density that identified gold. Gold does not break when it is hammered, and gold placed on a shovel and thrust into a campfire will not melt. In addition, low temperature and acid will not affect gold.

Reading Strategy   READING THE TEXT

Monitoring Comprehension As students read the section, they might encounter text or information that they do not understand, and they should adjust their reading strategies to clarify the ideas. Model how this is done by reading the section aloud. As you read, say things such as "What do I think is the main reason that mining drew so many people?" (predicting); "Why were most of the mines located in the west?" (evaluating); "What have I heard about ghost towns and is it correct based on the information described here?" (activating prior knowledge). Modeling how you read helps students think about strategies they can use as they read independently. **L1**

Guided Reading Activity 18-1

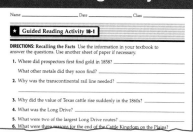

★ **Guided Reading Activity 18-1**

DIRECTIONS: Recalling the Facts Use the information in your textbook to answer the questions. Use another sheet of paper if necessary.

1. Where did prospectors first find gold in 1858? _____
   What other metals did they soon find? _____
2. Why was the transcontinental rail line needed? _____
3. Why did the value of Texas cattle rise suddenly in the 1860s? _____
4. What was the Long Drive? _____
5. What were two of the largest Long Drive routes? _____
6. What were three reasons for the end of the Cattle Kingdom on the Plains? _____

 Reading Check

Answer: to move cattle to railroad towns for transport east

CURRICULUM CONNECTION

Technology The first public railroad in the world opened in Great Britain in 1825 and ran for 20 miles (32 km). The first public railroad in the United States began operating in 1830. Known as the Baltimore and Ohio Railroad, it ran on 13 miles (21 km) of track in Maryland. The first transcontinental line was finished in 1869. Railroads remained the nation's chief form of long-distance transportation until passenger airplanes took over in the late twentieth century.

you don't say...

Dogie At roundup time there were usually some motherless calves, who were called "dough-guts," which later became "dogie." Because the calves were prematurely weaned, their stomachs could not digest grass and swelled as a result.

✛Geography

The Cattle Kingdom Ends

The open-range cattle industry collapsed even more quickly than it had risen. Too many animals on open ranges resulted in overgrazing, depriving both livestock and wild animals of food. Overproduction drove prices down, and sheepherders and farmers competed with ranchers for land. Finally, two severe winters in the mid- and late-1880s killed thousands of animals. The cattle industry survived, but the day of large herds on the open range ended. From then on, ranchers raised herds on fenced-in ranches. With the end of the Cattle Kingdom, another group of settlers arrived on the Plains—the farmers.

Farmers Settle the Plains

The early pioneers who reached the Great Plains did not believe they could farm the dry, treeless area. In the late 1860s, however, farmers began settling there and planting crops. In a short time, the Plains changed from "wilderness" to farmland. In 1872 a Nebraska settler wrote,

> ❝One year ago this was a vast houseless, uninhabitable prairie. . . . Today I can see more than thirty dwellings from my door.❞

Several factors brought settlers to the Plains. The railroads made the journey west easier and cheaper. Above-average rainfall made the Plains better suited to farming. New laws offered free land.

In 1862 Congress passed the **Homestead Act,** which gave 160 free acres of land to any settler who paid a filing fee and lived on the land for 5 years.

Homesteading lured thousands of new settlers to the Great Plains. Some were immigrants who had begun the process of becoming American citizens and were eligible to file for land. Others were women. Although married women could not claim land, single women and widows had the same rights as men—and they took advantage of the Homestead Act to acquire property.

To survive on the Plains, the farmers—known as **sodbusters**—had to find new ways of doing things. Lacking wood, they cut sod into bricks to build houses. They used windmills to pump water and barbed wire to fence in their property.

The Oklahoma Land Rush

The last part of the Plains to be settled was the Oklahoma Territory, which Congress had designated as "Indian Territory" in the 1830s. After years of pressure from land dealers and white settlers, the federal government opened Oklahoma to homesteaders in 1889. Settlement had changed the Plains dramatically. No one felt these changes more keenly than the Native Americans who had lived on the Plains for centuries.

 Reading Check **Explaining** What was the purpose of the Long Drive?

On the Great Plains *Living on the Plains meant settlers had to build houses that did not require lumber on this treeless land. A Plains family's first home was usually made of sod.*

530

DIFFERENTIATED INSTRUCTION

Reading Support Have students make a bar graph showing the approximate miles of railroad track in the United States from 1860 to 1900. Give them the following figures: 1860—31,000 miles; 1870—53,000 miles; 1880—93,000 miles; 1890—167,000 miles; 1900—193,000 miles. Have students each write three math problems based on their graphs, then exchange papers with a partner to solve each other's problems. **L2**

📂 Refer to **Inclusion for the Middle School Social Studies Classroom Strategies and Activities** in the TCR.

NATIONAL GEOGRAPHIC

Western Native American Lands, 1860–1890

Sitting Bull's and Crazy Horse's warriors defeated Custer and 200 U.S. troops at Little Bighorn.

The massacre of the buffalo changed the lives of the Plains Indians.

Sioux warriors ambush U.S. troops on December 21, 1866.

About 200 Sioux and 25 soldiers were killed at Wounded Knee.

Indian reservations in 1890

Battle

Geography *Skills*

During the late 1800s, Native Americans and the United States Army fought many battles over land.
1. **Location** In what present-day state was the Battle of Little Bighorn fought?
2. **Analyzing Information** Which Native American nations resettled in or near the Oklahoma Territory?

Native American Struggles

Many Native American groups lived on the Plains. The buffalo that roamed there provided most of the essentials the Plains peoples needed for daily living. As railroads, miners, ranchers, and farmers spread west, however, vast numbers of buffalo were slaughtered.

The federal government recommended moving the Native Americans to reservations. Reservations were tracts of land set aside for Native Americans. Many refused to accept the reserva-

tion policy. Some clashed with settlers. Soon, fighting began between the United States Army and various Native American groups.

Little Bighorn

The Sioux received lands in the Black Hills of South Dakota. Yet soon crews and settlers discovered gold in the Black Hills, and miners swarmed onto the reservation.

The government reduced the size of most reservations or moved the Native Americans to lands less desirable. The Sioux decided they should not have to honor government policy when whites did not. **Sitting Bull** and **Crazy Horse** led their people off the reservation. Near the Little Bighorn River in southern Montana Territory, they joined forces with several thousand other Sioux and Cheyenne.

CHAPTER 18   Reshaping the Nation   **531**

Geography *Skills*

Answers:
1. Montana
2. Arapaho, Cherokee, Creek, Choctaw, Chickasaw, Comanche

What?Where?When?Who?

Native American Schools Schools off the reservation were an important part of the federal government's efforts to assimilate Native Americans into white society in the late 1800s. Many Native American parents were reluctant to send their children away from home. One mother of a 10-year-old girl insisted that she be allowed to accompany her daughter to school. Education, the mother explained, would make the child regard her mother as a savage. In the end, the woman was allowed to be with her daughter.

Did you know?

For generations the nomadic peoples of the Plains had only dogs to haul their possessions as they traveled from one hunting area to another. Then in the 1600s, horses—either traded or stolen from Spanish settlers in the Southwest—changed the Plains peoples' way of life. By the mid-1700s, almost every Plains group rode on horseback.

INTERDISCIPLINARY CONNECTIONS ACTIVITY

Civics The American Indian Movement, an activist group, was established in 1968 to promote Native American civil rights. Members of the group briefly occupied the Bureau of Indian Affairs offices in 1972, then led 200 Sioux in a 71-day takeover of Wounded Knee. The takeover was an effort to demand a review of 300 treaties with the United States government. Have students research the activities of this group and other Native American efforts to gain an equal footing in the American political structure. Have students present their findings in a written report. **L2**

3 ASSESS

Assign Section 1 Assessment as homework or as an in-class activity.

🕮 Have students use **Interactive Tutor Self-Assessment CD-ROM.**

L2

Section Quiz 18–1

L1

Reteaching Activity 18–1

In June 1876 Lieutenant Colonel **George Custer** and more than 200 troops sent to round up the Sioux faced an unexpected group of several thousand. In the battle, the Native Americans killed Custer and all of his troops. The Sioux and Cheyenne won the battle, but within months government soldiers had forced them to surrender.

The Nez Perce and the Apache

In the 1870s other Native American people beside the Sioux and Cheyenne resisted the move to reservations. One of these was the Nez Perce of eastern Oregon. In 1877 the government ordered the Nez Perce to move to a smaller reservation in Idaho. The Nez Perce attempted to flee, led by **Chief Joseph.** They evaded capture for nearly two months before surrendering to United States troops just 40 miles from the Canadian border. In advising his people to give up, Chief Joseph said:

> 66....I am tired. My heart is sick and sad. From where the sun now stands, I will fight no more forever.99

The government forced the Nez Perce onto an Oklahoma reservation instead of resettling them

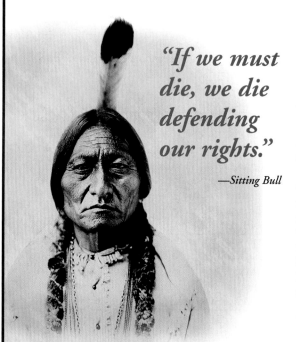

"If we must die, we die defending our rights."

—*Sitting Bull*

in their native Northwest. Unused to the climate and terrain, many of them died.

A group of Apache, led by **Geronimo,** became the last Native American nation to resist. By the time the Americans captured Geronimo in 1886, American troops had confined every Native American nation to reservations.

Wounded Knee

One final episode of Native American resistance took place in the Dakota Territory. In December 1890 United States soldiers tried to disarm a large band of Plains Native Americans gathered at **Wounded Knee** on the Pine Ridge Reservation in South Dakota. The result was a massacre in which more than 200 Native Americans and 25 soldiers lost their lives. Wounded Knee marked the end of armed conflict between the United States government and Native Americans.

New Policies

During the 1880s the plight of Native Americans led to calls for more humane policies. Sentiment for reform grew with the publication of Helen Hunt Jackson's book, *A Century of Dishonor.* Jackson wrote about the broken treaties and mistreatment Native Americans endured at the hands of the government and settlers.

Congress changed government policy in the Dawes Act in 1887. The act proposed to break up the reservations and to end individual identification with a tribal group. Each Native American would receive a plot of reservation land. The goal was to encourage the Native American people to become farmers. Eventually, they would become American citizens. Native American children would be sent to white-run boarding schools. Some of the reservation lands would be sold to support this schooling.

Over the next 50 years, the government divided up the reservations. Speculators acquired most of the valuable land. With Native American resistance at an end, nothing remained to stop white settlers. In 1890 the census report stated that the Trans-Mississippi West was so broken up by acres of settlement that a frontier line could no longer be identified. The last frontier, and with it the Old West, had disappeared.

✓ **Reading Check** **Identifying** Who led the Nez Perce on their journey of escape?

CRITICAL THINKING ACTIVITY

Analyzing Information In 1879 Chief Joseph of the Nez Perce, in an appeal to President Rutherford B. Hayes, said: "Let me be a freeman—free to travel, free to stop, free to work, free to trade where I choose, free to choose my own teachers, free to follow the religion of my fathers, free to think and talk and act for myself—and I will obey every law or submit to the penalty." Ask students which of these requests are guaranteed by the Bill of Rights. *(all)* Also ask them to tell how these rights were denied to Native Americans. *(They were forced to live on reservations.)* **L1**

Farmers in Protest

After the Civil War, farming expanded in the West and South. The supply of crops grew faster than the demand for them, however, and prices fell steadily. At the same time, farmers' expenses—for transporting their goods, for seed, and for equipment—remained high.

Organizing

Farmers blamed their troubles on the high shipping rates of the railroads. To solve their problems, farmers formed self-help groups, such as the **Farmers' Alliance.** In 1890, members of the Alliance established the **Populist Party.**

The Party urged the federal government to help keep prices for farmers' crops high. It also called on government to nationalize, or take over, public transportation and communication. Populists hoped that nationalization would finally end the railroads' high rates.

Most important, the Populists demanded that the government expand the money supply by permitting silver to become, along with gold, the basis for money. America maintained the gold standard in which each paper dollar was redeemable in gold. To make sure it had enough gold, the government limited the amount of paper money. This limited the amount of money available. Meanwhile, the population increased. As each dollar gained in value, farmers earned less as prices dropped and the value of their debts increased.

Poster celebrating the farmer, 1876

I FEED YOU ALL!

Election of 1896

In the presidential election of 1896, the major issue was whether the government should accept silver for making coins. The Democrats nominated **William Jennings Bryan,** a strong supporter of silver. The Republicans nominated **William McKinley,** a strong supporter of gold. The Populists also endorsed Bryan, but the Democrat lost. Big business backed the Republican McKinley, as did factory workers. Urban America now had more political strength than rural America. America was changing from a farming nation to an industrial nation.

✓**Reading Check** **Describing** What actions did the Populist Party want government to take regarding the railroad industry?

✓**Reading Check**

Answer: to nationalize, or take over the railroads
L1, ELL

Reading Essentials and Study Guide 18–1

Study Guide
Chapter 18, Section 1
For use with textbook pages 528–533
THE WESTERN FRONTIER

KEY TERMS	
boomtown	Towns built rapidly near mining sites (page 529)
transcontinental	Crossing the continent, connecting the Atlantic and Pacific coasts (page 529)
vaqueros	Hispanic ranch hands in the Spanish Southwest (page 529)
reservation	Land set aside for Native Americans (page 531)

DRAWING FROM EXPERIENCE
Have you and your friends ever had trouble getting along with other people in your school? What caused the conflict? Were you able to settle your differences? How?
This section focuses on how railroads paved the way for the settlement of the Great Plains.

ORGANIZING YOUR THOUGHTS
Use the chart below to help you take notes as you read the summaries that follow. Think about the conflicts that arose between settlers moving west and the Native Americans already living there. After reading the sections, explain how each of the following Native Americans encouraged others to resist the United States government and white settlers.

Conflict Between Settlers and Native Americans	
Sitting Bull and Crazy Horse	
Chief Joseph	
Geronimo	

L3

Enrichment Activity 18–1

Name _____ Date _____ Class _____

★ Enrichment Activity 18-1

Building a House
When Easterners moved west to live on the Great Plains, they left many things behind, including styles of building homes that did not work on the almost treeless prairie. Because they lacked lumber to build homes, the pioneers built houses of sod—the most abundant material on the Plains. Some carved dugouts into the sides of hills and covered the dugouts with brick-like rectangles made of packed soil and grass roots.

4 CLOSE

Ask: If gold was discovered in a remote part of North America, would you leave your home and family to try to search for it? Why?

SECTION 1 ASSESSMENT

Checking for Understanding

1. **Key Terms** Use each of these terms in a sentence that will help explain its meaning: boomtown, transcontinental, vaquero, reservation.

2. **Reviewing Facts** Who was Chief Joseph?

Reviewing Themes

3. **Geography and History** What was the transcontinental railroad? How did it influence settlement?

Critical Thinking

4. **Drawing Conclusions** In what ways did the government reservation policy ignore the needs of Native Americans?

5. **Organizing Information** Re-create the diagram below and list new ways farmers adapted to life on the Plains.

Farming on the Plains

Analyzing Visuals

6. **Geography Skills** Study the map of Western Native American Lands on page 531. When did the Battle of Wounded Knee occur? Where were the Shoshone reservations located?

Interdisciplinary Activity

Art Create a poster that the United States government might have used to encourage farmers to move west. Display your posters in class.

SECTION 1 ASSESSMENT ANSWERS

1. Student work should reflect correct use of terms.

2. Nez Perce leader who tried to help his people flee from forced relocation to a reservation.

3. railway built in 1869 connecting Atlantic and Pacific coasts; brought new wave of ranchers and farmers to the West

4. Answers may include: railroad crews and miners continued to enter the reservations; the size of the reservations was reduced; undesirable land was given to Native Americans; and the reservation's climate and terrain were unfamiliar.

5. used sod to build houses, windmills to pump water, and barbed wire for fencing

6. 1890; Oregon and Wyoming

Interdisciplinary Activity Posters should give vivid descriptions and encourage people to move west.

SECTION 2 Invention and Industry

1 FOCUS

Section Overview

This section describes the industrial growth the United States experienced during the late 1800s.

BELLRINGER
Skillbuilder Activity

Project transparency and have students answer the question.

Daily Focus Skills Transparency 18–2

Reading Preview

Answers to Graphic: Thomas Edison: developed electrical power sources; Samuel Gompers: led the American Federation of Labor to secure workers' rights; Jane Addams: founded Hull House to provide education and medical care to the poor

Preteaching Vocabulary
Point out that the word *trust* has several meanings. Ask students to name some of them and then explain how the word is used in the section.

Guide to Reading

Main Idea
During the late 1800s, the United States experienced tremendous industrial growth.

Key Terms
horizontal integration, trust, monopoly, vertical integration, collective bargaining, settlement house

Reading Strategy
Organizing Information As you read the section, re-create the diagram below and explain the importance of these individuals.

	Importance
Thomas Edison	
Samuel Gompers	
Jane Addams	

Read to Learn
- how American cities and industries had changed at the turn of the century.
- what challenges immigrants to the United States faced.

Section Theme
Science and Technology New inventions promoted economic growth.

Preview of Events

♦1880	♦1890	♦1900	♦1910

—1879
Thomas Edison develops first practical lightbulb

—1886
American Federation of Labor forms

—1889
Jane Addams founds Hull House

—1903
Wright brothers fly at Kitty Hawk

Train song sheet

AN American Story

Rugged construction gangs labored on the Union Pacific and other railways during the transportation boom of the late 1800s. A favorite song was:

Well, every morning at seven o'clock
There were 20 tarriers [drillers] a-workin' at the rock,
And the boss comes round and he says "Kape still!"
And come down heavy on the cast iron drill,

And drill, ye tarriers, drill!"
Drill, ye tarriers, drill!
For it's work all day for sugar in your tay,
Down behind of the railway and,
Drill, ye tarriers, drill!
And blast!
And fire!

Even as settlers moved west to farm the last American frontier, farmers in other parts of the country moved to the cities. They took jobs in the new urban industries that recent inventions made possible. The United States was changing from a rural nation into a modern, industrial nation.

SECTION RESOURCES

📁 Reproducible Masters
- Reproducible Lesson Plan 18–2
- Daily Lecture and Discussion Notes 18–2
- Guided Reading Activity 18–2
- Section Quiz 18–2
- Reteaching Activity 18–2
- Reading Essentials and Study Guide 18–2
- Enrichment Activity 18–2

🖱 Transparencies
- Daily Focus Skills Transparency 18–2

Multimedia
- 💿 Interactive Tutor Self-Assessment CD-ROM
- 💿 ExamView® Pro Testmaker CD-ROM
- 💿 Presentation Plus! CD-ROM

The Growth of Industry

The nation's rich farmlands, great forests, and mighty rivers helped the early colonists develop a strong agricultural economy. As the nation grew, Americans developed resources of a different kind. In addition to talented inventors, they had eager investors, willing workers, and a pro-business government. These new resources made the expansion of American industry possible.

★ Geography

Rich Natural Resources

The United States also possessed other necessary ingredients for industry—plenty of natural resources. Large deposits of coal lay in western Pennsylvania, the Mississippi Valley, and Appalachia. The shores of Lake Superior held major supplies of iron ore. Mines in western states contained gold, silver, lead, zinc, and copper.

These minerals formed the base of heavy industry in the United States. A heavy industry produces materials such as iron or steel. Out of these materials, Americans built railroads, bridges, skyscrapers, and machinery for the factories that transformed the nation. By the late 1800s, the United States had become the world's number one manufacturing nation.

Railroads Lead the Way

During the Civil War, trains carried troops, weapons, and supplies to the front. After the war, railroads became a driving force behind America's economic growth. Railroad construction increased the demand for iron, steel, coal, timber, and other goods, which created thousands of new jobs for Americans.

The railroads allowed American industry to expand into the West. They moved rural people to the cities and brought homesteaders to the Plains. They united the nation's regions and helped bring American society together.

American Inventions

During the late 1800s, an invention boom spurred the growth of industry. The government granted many **patents**—licenses protecting people's rights to make, sell, or use their inventions.

Two discoveries revolutionized the iron and steel industries. The first was the use of coke (soft coal with the impurities removed). Coke was an excellent fuel for iron-smelting blast furnaces. The second was the Bessemer Process, discovered independently by William Kelly and Henry Bessemer. The process used blasts of cold air to burn off impurities from heated iron. Because steel could now be made cheaply, steel production soared.

Cheap, durable steel then became the basis for other industrial advances. Train rails made of steel lasted much longer than iron rails. Steel beams supported bigger, heavier bridges and buildings. Steel was used for making new machinery and many other products.

Americans also developed new sources of power. Thomas Alva Edison led others in building the first large power plant to furnish elec-

Their first flight at Kitty Hawk, North Carolina, encouraged the Wright brothers to continue their experiments. Soon, they would have a practical aircraft and the world would have a new form of transportation.

Reading Strategy — READING THE TEXT

Brainstorming Organize the class into three groups. Have each group choose one of the new technologies mentioned in this section. Ask groups to determine the target audience for the technology and brainstorm ways in which to market that technology to its audience. **L1**

2 TEACH

Daily Lecture and Discussion Notes 18–2

Copyright © The McGraw-Hill Companies, Inc.

Daily Lecture and Discussion Notes

Chapter 18, Section 2

Did You Know? George Curtis filed a suit against Orville and Wilbur Wright for patent rights to their airplane. A court ruled in favor of the Wright brothers.

I. The Growth of Industry (Pages 535–537)

A. Talented inventors, eager investors, willing workers, and a pro-business government made the expansion of United States industry possible.

  1. Rich natural resources such as coal, iron, gold, silver, lead, zinc, and copper helped form the base for heavy industry in the United States.

  2. Railroads, bridges, skyscrapers, and machinery for factories were built from the materials produced by heavy industry.

  3. The United States became the world's leading manufacturing nation by the late 1800s.

B. Railroads became the powerhouse behind the United States's economic growth. American industry expanded in the West as a result of the railroads, creating thousands of new jobs for Americans. The regions of the United States were connected by the railroads, and American society was brought together.

C. Patents, protecting people's right to make, sell, or use their own invention, were granted during the invention boom of the late 1800s.

  1. The discoveries of coke, soft coal with the impurities removed, and the Bessemer Process, a process that used blasts of cold air to burn off impurities from heated iron, allowed steel to be made cheaply.

  2. The production of steel soared and was used to make new machinery and many other products.

  3. New sources of power were developed. Thomas Edison led others in building the first large power plant to supply electricity to entire cities.

  4. By 1900 electric power was used in homes and offices, and ran streetcars, elevators, and factories.

D. Advancements also took place in the communications industry.

  1. Cyrus Field laid a transatlantic telegraph cable in 1866. Messages sent to Europe arrived in minutes rather than in weeks.

  2. Alexander Graham Bell developed the telephone in 1876, which led to the establishment of the American Bell Telephone Company.

  3. By 1902 Italian inventor Guglielmo Marconi transmitted radio messages as far away as 2,000 miles.

turn

Making a Graphic Organizer

Work with students to create a graphic organizer that reflects how advancements in technology, communication, and transportation encouraged the growth of industry. **L1**

Who?What?Where?When?

The Wright Brothers The flight of the Wright brothers in 1903 marked the beginning of modern aviation. History was made in 1909 when the U.S. military purchased a Wright-designed airplane for $30,000, which became the world's first military plane. Soon after, the Wright brothers began their first manufacturing firm, the Wright Company, in Dayton, Ohio. Firms such as the Wright Company and others were able to produce 15,000 planes by the end of World War I.

Did you know?

On October 21, 1929, the 50-year anniversary of the invention of the electric light, Henry Ford moved Edison's original lab in Menlo Park to Greenfield Village, a large museum site in Dearborn, Michigan. Then 82, Edison recreated his original experiment that resulted in the invention of the first electric light.

Who? What? Where? When?

Thomas Edison Thomas Edison, the youngest of seven children, was born in Milan, Ohio. Edison's first financially successful invention was an improved stock ticker designed to send the price of gold to investors. His later improved ticker netted Edison $40,000, an astounding amount for the sale of a patent at the time. The money allowed Edison to open his first workshop in Newark, New Jersey.

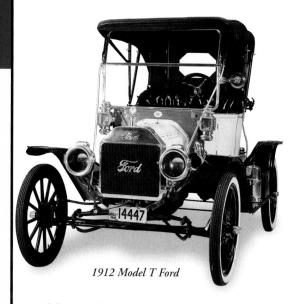

1912 Model T Ford

tricity to entire cities. By the turn of the century, electric power lit homes and offices and ran streetcars, elevators, and factories.

Communications

Important inventions appeared in communications. The telegraph had already brought rapid changes before the Civil War. Then in 1866, **Cyrus Field** laid a transatlantic telegraph cable. Now a message sent to someone in Europe arrived in minutes instead of weeks. The telephone was developed by **Alexander Graham Bell,** a young teacher of the deaf, who filed for a patent in 1876. A few years later, the American Bell Telephone Company was established.

Experiments were beginning in radio communication as well. In 1895 Italian inventor **Guglielmo Marconi** transmitted the first messages, and, by 1902, radio messages were being sent for thousands of miles.

Transportation

Two other inventions began a transportation revolution in the United States—the automobile and the airplane. In the early 1900s, **Henry Ford** developed a gasoline-powered automobile that could be built cheaply using an assembly line. In 1903, **Orville** and **Wilbur Wright** built and tested the first successful engine-powered aircraft at **Kitty Hawk, North Carolina.** Their success marked the beginning of the modern aircraft industry.

536   CHAPTER 18   Reshaping the Nation

$ Economics

An Age of Big Business

With the economy growing, many railroads and other businesses looked for ways to expand. To do so, they needed to raise **capital,** or money, to buy equipment and hire workers. One way a company could raise capital was by becoming a **corporation**—a company that sold shares, or stock, of its business.

One major industry that grew rapidly during this era was the oil industry. In 1870, **John D. Rockefeller** organized the Standard Oil Company. To build Standard Oil, Rockefeller used horizontal integration—the combining of competing companies into one corporation. Rockefeller also increased his control of the oil industry by forming a trust—a group of companies managed by the same board of directors. Using a trust enabled Rockefeller to create a monopoly—almost total control of an industry by one company.

The steel industry also became a huge business in the late 1800s. The leading figure in the early steel industry was **Andrew Carnegie.** His company became powerful through vertical integration—acquiring companies that provided the materials he needed. Carnegie bought coal and iron mines, warehouses, ships, and railroads to gain control of all parts of the steel-making process.

Industrial Workers

Industrial growth in the late 1800s created new jobs and raised the standard of living for many workers. Laborers, however, worked 10 to 12 hours a day, six days a week. Factories and mines were often noisy, polluted, and unsafe.

Dissatisfied workers organized into groups, called labor unions, to demand better pay and working conditions. In 1869, America's first large industrial union, called the **Knights of Labor,** was organized and grew to more than 700,000 members. After some of its members were accused of using violence, the Knights lost members and influence in the 1890s.

In 1886, a group of unions joined together to form the **American Federation of Labor** (AFL). The AFL represented skilled workers. Its first leader was **Samuel Gompers.** The AFL pushed

---

DIFFERENTIATED INSTRUCTION

At-Risk Students Have each student make a list of all the electrical equipment in his or her home (refrigerator, TV, computer, radio, washing machine, and so forth). Then have students ask a parent or other adult to check off the ones that were in their homes when they were growing up. Finally, have students ask their grandparents or older friends to do the same. **Ask: What do the lists tell you about the explosion of inventions in the recent past?** Discuss students' answers. **L1**

📁 Refer to *Inclusion for the Middle School Social Studies Classroom Strategies and Activities* in the TCR.

for higher wages, better working conditions, and the right to bargain collectively. In collective bargaining, unions represent workers in bargaining with management.

Many workers used strikes to achieve their goals. They refused to do their jobs until their employers agreed to certain demands. In 1877 a national railroad strike became the first of many violent confrontations between workers and employers. Few strikes succeed between 1865 and 1900, however. Employers usually hired other workers or waited until the strikers ran out of money and returned to work. Most Americans viewed labor unions in a negative manner and government authorities usually sided with employers against strikers.

By the end of the 1800s most workers found themselves with less political power and control of the workplace. Meanwhile, the big businesses managed to protect their interests and wealth.

✓ **Reading Check** **Identifying** Who developed the telephone?

Immigrant children learned American ways in the classroom.

The Growing Cities

As people moved to the cities to take factory jobs, they transformed America from a rural country into an urban nation. The cities also grew because of the arrival of new immigrants.

The New Immigrants

After the Civil War, many immigrants arrived from southern and eastern Europe. Others came from China, Japan, and Mexico. When they arrived they were processed at government reception centers. The two most famous were **Ellis Island** in New York Harbor, and **Angel Island** in San Francisco Bay.

Most immigrants settled in cities and looked for factory work. People of the same **ethnic group**—with the same language and customs—tended to form communities. Neighborhoods of Jewish, Italian, Polish, Chinese, and other groups developed in large cities.

HISTORY Online

Student Web Activity
Visit tarvol1.glencoe.com and click on **Chapter 18—Student Web Activities** for an activity on immigrant life.

✓ **Reading Check**

Answer: Alexander Graham Bell

HISTORY Online

Objectives and answers to the student activity can be found in the **Web Activity Lesson Plan** feature at tarvol1.glencoe.com

Did you know?

Fewer than 10 percent of immigrants to America in the late nineteenth and early twentieth centuries had trades or specific work skills. These immigrants provided much of the physical labor that built America. One immigrant upon arriving in America wrote, ". . . the streets were not paved with gold; . . . the streets were not paved at all; [immigrant workers] were expected to pave them."

CURRICULUM CONNECTION

Health By 1830 about 1,000 ships carried cotton from the United States to England annually. Merchants tried to find cargo to fill the empty ships returning to the United States and stumbled on an unusual cargo of people. These ships were unsanitary and poorly ventilated and were a breeding ground for diseases such as trachoma and malignant typhus, dubbed *ship fever.*

CHAPTER 18   Reshaping the Nation   **537**

INTERDISCIPLINARY CONNECTIONS ACTIVITY

Art Explain to students that immigrants sought to re-create the cultural heritage they left behind by establishing family traditions. Ask students to choose one of their family's traditions to illustrate on a poster. Have them portray the following on their posters: description of the tradition, how the tradition reflects and preserves cultural heritage, and how the tradition has changed through the years. Encourage students to include photographs, illustrations, essays, poems, and so on. **L2,** ELL

3 ASSESS

Assign Section 2 Assessment as homework or as an in-class activity.

🖲 Have students use **Interactive Tutor Self-Assessment CD-ROM.**

L2

L1

Immigrants Face Discrimination

Not all Americans welcomed newcomers to their country. The immigrants' languages and customs seemed strange to some Americans and aroused distrust and discrimination.

Many Americans wondered if immigrants could ever be assimilated into American life. Some people, especially workers, blamed immigrants for low wages. Employers found that immigrants would accept lower wages than native Americans. Others resented the different cultures and religions of the many immigrants.

In the late 1800s hostility grew toward many of the new racial and ethnic groups coming into the country. Immigrants became easy targets of hostility for Americans disturbed by the rapid social changes.

Life in the Cities

Cities were exciting places that offered jobs, stores, and entertainment. However, there was also substandard housing and desperate poverty. The gap between the rich and the poor was staggering.

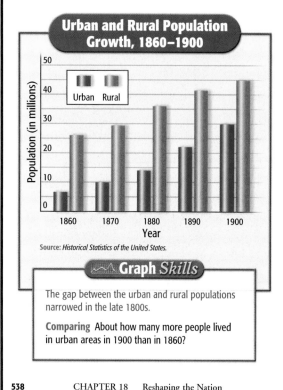

Urban and Rural Population Growth, 1860–1900

Source: *Historical Statistics of the United States.*

Graph Skills

The gap between the urban and rural populations narrowed in the late 1800s.

Comparing About how many more people lived in urban areas in 1900 than in 1860?

Tenement Life

People poured into the cities faster than housing could be built. The poor often lived in **tenements**—huge apartment buildings—with as many as four people living in each of the small, dark rooms. The rapid growth of cities produced other serious problems as well, including disease, crime, and poor sanitation.

The Middle Class and the Upper Class

The cities also had a growing middle class. The middle class included the families of professional people such as doctors, lawyers, and ministers. An increasing number of managers and salaried office clerks also became part of the middle class.

The middle class enjoyed a comfortable life. Many families began moving from cities to the suburbs, residential areas that sprang up outside of city centers.

At the top of the economic and social ladder stood the very rich. Wealthy people lived very differently than did most Americans. They built enormous mansions in the cities and huge estates in the country. The term **"Gilded Age"** —'gilded' refers to something covered with a thin layer of gold—became associated with America of the late 1800s. The Gilded Age suggested both the extravagant wealth of the time and the terrible poverty that lay underneath.

Cities in Crisis

The rapid growth of the cities produced serious problems. Terrible overcrowding in tenement districts created sanitation and health problems. Garbage accumulated in city streets. Filth created a breeding ground for disease.

The poverty in the cities also led to crime. Orphans and homeless children sometimes resorted to picking pockets and other crimes. Gangs roaming the poor neighborhoods committed more serious crimes.

Seeking Solutions

Religious groups, such as the Salvation Army, set up soup kitchens to feed the hungry and opened shelters for the homeless. The poor also received help from settlement houses.

CRITICAL THINKING ACTIVITY

Making Generalizations Explain the origin of the term *melting pot*, which comes from Israel Zangwill's 1908 play *The Melting Pot*. The play coined the term to describe America's mixture of nationalities and ethnic groups. Describe *melting pot* as a theory in which immigrants of various nationalities are assimilated into one culture. Also explain that many sociologists disagree with this theory. James Banks, a noted multicultural author, describes America as a patchwork quilt in which ethnic groups maintain their cultural identity while forming a part of the main culture. Discuss the underlying assumptions that form the basis of these two theories. Challenge students to choose which theory they think accurately describes America and describe why. **L3**

These houses provided education, medical care, playgrounds, nurseries, and libraries to the poor. One famous settlement house was **Hull House** in Chicago, founded by **Jane Addams** in 1889. Addams explained:

Jane Addams

66We were ready to perform the humblest neighborhood services. We were asked to wash the newborn babies, and to prepare the dead for burial, to nurse the sick, and to 'mind the children.' 99

A Danish immigrant named Jacob Riis shocked many Americans with his photographs of the horrible living conditions in New York. He challenged his readers to renew the face of the cities.

During the 1880s and 1890s, many reformers accepted Riis's challenge. They campaigned for clean water and better sewage systems. They demanded better ventilation, plumbing in all new buildings, and mandatory vaccinations. These improvements meant that fewer people died of diseases like typhoid and smallpox.

Education

Most Americans in 1865 had attended school for an average of only four years. Government and business leaders and reformers believed that for the nation to progress, the people needed more schooling. Toward the end of the 1800s, education became more widely available to Americans.

By 1914 nearly every state required children to have at least some schooling. More than 80 percent of all children between the ages of 5 and 17 were enrolled in elementary and secondary schools.

A Changing American Culture

Many Americans began to enjoy increasing amounts of leisure time. The large crowds in the cities increased the popularity of spectator sports—including baseball, football, basketball, and boxing. People also flocked to nickelodeon theaters, which charged 5 cents to see a movie.

New types of music and literature developed at the turn of the century. Band music, jazz, and ragtime became popular. Writers such as Mark Twain, Stephen Crane, and Jack London produced stories that described the real lives of people at the time. More and more people began to read newspapers and magazines.

✓**Reading Check** **Describing** What did settlement houses provide?

4 CLOSE

Organize students into small groups to create a three-column table illustrating social problems, solutions, and alternatives. Ask groups to identify in the first column the social problems described in this section. In the second column, students should describe the solutions that were used. Students should explain their alternative solutions in the third column.

SECTION 2 ASSESSMENT

Checking for Understanding

1. **Key Terms** Write a paragraph about American corporations. Use the following terms: horizontal integration, vertical integration, trust.

2. **Reviewing Facts** Where is Ellis Island? What purpose did it serve?

Reviewing Themes

3. **Science and Technology** Which of the inventions in Section 2 do you think is the most valuable to today's world? Explain.

Critical Thinking

4. **Making Comparisons** Explain how the Knights of Labor and the American Federation of Labor were alike and how they were different.

5. **Organizing Information** Re-create the diagram below and write three ways in which cities were changing at the turn of the century.

Changing Cities

Analyzing Visuals

6. **Graph Skills** According to the graph on page 538, about how many more people lived in rural than in urban areas in 1860? What conclusion can you draw about total population between 1860 and 1900?

Interdisciplinary Activity

Art Create a collage illustrating the origins of immigrants who came to the United States in the late 1800s and early 1900s.

CHAPTER 18 Reshaping the Nation **539**

SECTION 2 ASSESSMENT ANSWERS

1. Student work should reflect correct use of terms.

2. in New York Harbor; served as a government reception center for immigrants

3. Answers will vary, but students should support their choices with valid reasons.

4. Both were labor unions that worked to improve working conditions. The Knights was an industrial union that lost influence in the 1890s. The AFL represented skilled workers and supported collective bargaining.

5. Answers will vary but may include: increased immigration to cities, formation of ethnic neighborhoods, rise of tenements, overcrowding, increase of disease, crime, and sanitation problems.

6. about 18–20 million more; total population grew steadily

Interdisciplinary Activity Collages should reflect the origins of different immigrant groups.

SECTION 3 Reform at Home, Expansion Abroad

1 FOCUS

Section Overview

This section describes progressive reforms and role of the United States in international affairs.

BELLRINGER
Skillbuilder Activity

Project transparency and have students answer the question.

Daily Focus Skills Transparency 18–3

Reading Preview

Answers to Graphic: Seventeenth Amendment: direct election of senators; Nineteenth Amendment: gave women the right to vote; Sherman Antitrust Act: made it illegal for companies to limit competition

Preteaching Vocabulary
Call on volunteers to explain how two of the **Key Terms** relate to the reforming spirit that marked the Progressive movement.

Guide to Reading

Main Idea
Progressive reform affected many areas of life and the United States took a more active role in international affairs.

Key Terms
muckraker, suffragist, imperialism, yellow journalism

Reading Strategy
Organizing Information As you read the section, re-create the diagram below and describe these amendments and laws.

	Contributions
Seventeenth Amendment	
Nineteenth Amendment	
Sherman Antitrust Act	

Read to Learn
- how the Progressive movement changed America.
- why the United States sought to expand overseas.

Section Theme
Groups and Institutions Progressive reformers worked to extend voting rights, improve working conditions, and promote temperance.

Preview of Events

♦1890   ♦1900   ♦1910   ♦1920

1890
Sherman Antitrust Act passed

1909
W.E.B. Du Bois helps found the NAACP

1920
Nineteenth Amendment gives women the right to vote

AN American Story

Jacob Riis

Newspaper reporter Jacob Riis shocked Americans in 1890 with his book *How the Other Half Lives*. With words and powerful photographs, Riis vividly portrayed immigrant life in New York City's crowded tenements. Said Riis: "We used to go in the small hours of the morning into the worst tenements to count noses and see if the law against overcrowding was violated and the sights I saw gripped my heart until I felt that I must tell of them, or burst."

The reform spirit gained strength during the late 1800s and flourished during the early 1900s. Some reformers believed that rapid social and economic change had resulted in a disordered and corrupt society. These reformers, called **progressives,** believed that the efforts of individuals and government could make society better and more fair. As progressive leaders reached positions of power in government, they passed laws affecting government employees, business practices and public health. These progressive laws form the basis for modern ideas of the role of government.

SECTION RESOURCES

📁 Reproducible Masters
- Reproducible Lesson Plan 18–3
- Daily Lecture and Discussion Notes 18–3
- Guided Reading Activity 18–3
- Section Quiz 18–3
- Reteaching Activity 18–3
- Reading Essentials and Study Guide 18–3
- Enrichment Activity 18–3

📖 Transparencies
- Daily Focus Skills Transparency 18–3

Multimedia
- Interactive Tutor Self-Assessment CD-ROM
- ExamView® Pro Testmaker CD-ROM
- Presentation Plus! CD-ROM

The Progressive Movement

Progressives believed that urban problems were caused by corruption. **Political machines**—powerful organizations linked to political parties—controlled many cities. Political bosses gained votes for their parties by doing favors for people. Although some did help people, many bosses were dishonest. To break the power of political bosses, reformers founded groups that worked to make city governments more honest and efficient.

Cities troubled by poor management or corruption tried new forms of government. After the tidal wave of a hurricane devastated Galveston, Texas, in 1900, the task of rebuilding the city overwhelmed the mayor and city council. Galveston's citizens persuaded the state legislature to approve a new charter that placed the city government in the hands of five commissioners. The new commission efficiently rebuilt the city. By 1917 commissions governed nearly 400 cities.

Controlling Business

Progressives also believed that government had to keep large combinations of companies from becoming too powerful. In 1890, Congress passed the **Sherman Antitrust Act,** making it illegal for companies to limit competition. During the 1890s, the government rarely used the Sherman Act to curb business. Instead, it applied the act against labor unions, claiming that union strikes interfered with trade. Not until the early 1900s did the government win cases against trusts with the Sherman Act.

Reformers also called for regulations on railroad rates. In 1887 Congress passed the Interstate Commerce Act, which required railroads to charge "reasonable and just" rates. The act also created the **Interstate Commerce Commission** (ICC) to supervise the railroad industry and, later, the trucking industry.

The New Reformers

Some journalists, nicknamed muckrakers, helped progressives by exposing injustices. Magazine writer **Lincoln Steffens** was one of the most effective muckrakers. Steffens exposed corrupt political machines in New York, Chicago, and other cities. His articles strengthened the demand for urban reform.

Another writer, **Ida Tarbell,** described the unfair practices of the oil trust. Her articles led to public pressure for more government control over big business.

In his novel *The Jungle* (1906), **Upton Sinclair** described the horrors of the meatpacking industry. His shocking descriptions of unhealthful practices in meatpacking spurred Congress to pass the Meat Inspection Act and the Pure Food and Drug Act.

✓ **Reading Check** **Identifying** What are trusts?

Expanding Democracy

In the early 1900s, progressives backed a number of reforms to expand the people's direct control of the government. Oregon took the lead in giving voters more power. The reforms included a direct primary election, and the initiative, the referendum, and the recall.

The **initiative** allowed citizens to place a measure or issue on the ballot in a state election. The **referendum** gave voters the opportunity to accept or reject measures that the state legislature enacted. The **recall** enabled voters to remove

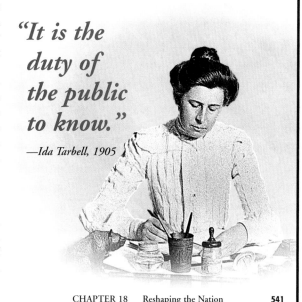

"It is the duty of the public to know."

—Ida Tarbell, 1905

CHAPTER 18   Reshaping the Nation   **541**

2 TEACH

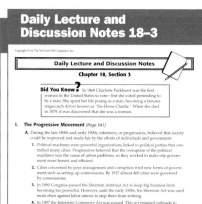

Daily Lecture and Discussion Notes 18–3

Copyright © by The McGraw-Hill Companies, Inc.

Daily Lecture and Discussion Notes

Chapter 18, Section 3

Did You Know ? In 1868 Charlotte Parkhurst was the first woman in the United States to vote—but she voted pretending to be a man. She spent her life posing as a man, becoming a famous stagecoach driver known as "Six-Horse Charlie." When she died in 1879, it was discovered that she was a woman.

I. The Progressive Movement (Page 541)

A. During the late 1800s and early 1900s, reformers, or progressives, believed that society could be improved and made fair by the efforts of individuals and government.

1. Political machines were powerful organizations linked to political parties that controlled many cities. Progressives believed that the corruption of the political machines was the cause of urban problems, so they worked to make city government more honest and efficient.

2. Cities concerned by poor management and corruption tried new forms of government such as setting up commissions. By 1917 almost 400 cities were governed by commissions.

3. In 1890 Congress passed the Sherman Antitrust Act to keep big business from becoming too powerful. However, until the early 1900s, the Sherman Act was used most often against labor unions to stop them from striking.

4. In 1887 the Interstate Commerce Act was passed. This act required railroads to charge "reasonable and just rates," and it created the Interstate Commerce Commission to supervise the railroad industry and later the trucking industry.

B. Some journalists, called muckrakers, helped the Progressive movement by exposing injustices.

1. Lincoln Steffens was an effective muckraker who wrote articles that uncovered corrupt political machines. His articles strengthened the cause of the reformers and helped build up the demand for urban reform.

2. Ida Tarbell wrote about the unfair practices of the oil trust. Her articles led to public pressure for more control over big business.

3. The horrors of the meat-packing industry were shockingly described in Upton Sinclair's novel *The Jungle* in 1906. Congress was urged into passing the Meat Inspection Act and the Pure Food and Drug Act.

turn

Recognizing Issues Ask students to complete this statement: *The first step in solving a problem is _____ . (recognizing a problem exists)* Then have students list the problems that progressives tried to address. **L2**

✓ **Reading Check**

Answer: large combinations of companies

L1, ELL

Guided Reading Activity 18–3

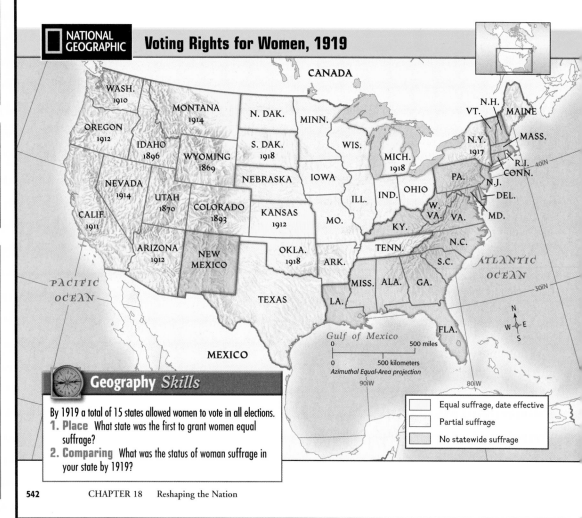

unsatisfactory elected officials from their jobs. These reforms were called the Oregon system. Other western states soon adopted the reforms.

Progressives also changed the way United States senators are elected. The Constitution had given state legislatures the responsibility, but party bosses and business interests often controlled the process. The **Seventeenth Amendment** provided for the direct election of senators. Ratified in 1913, the amendment gave the people a voice in selecting their representatives.

🏛Citizenship
The Fight for Suffrage

Women at the Seneca Falls Convention in 1848 had called for the right to vote. After the Civil War, Congress passed the Fifteenth Amendment, giving voting rights to freed men—but not to women. Some leading abolitionists became **suffragists**—men and women who fought for woman suffrage, or women's right to vote.

Suffragists won their first victories in the West. Wyoming led the nation in giving women the vote. Between 1910 and 1913, five other states adopted woman suffrage. In the meantime suffragists continued their struggle to win the vote everywhere.

In 1919 the Senate voted in favor of the **Nineteenth Amendment,** which allowed woman suffrage. The amendment was ratified in 1920, in time for women to vote in that year's presidential election. For the first time, American women were able to participate in the election of their national leaders.

🧭 Geography *Skills*

Answers:
1. Wyoming
2. Answers should be correct for your state.

Who?What?Where?When?

Jacob Riis Theodore Roosevelt called Jacob Riis the "best American I ever knew." In his book *How the Other Half Lives*, Riis wrote passionately of the squalid living conditions, the lack of ventilation and light, and the poor sanitation experienced by the tenant dwellers on New York's Lower East Side. His muckraking articles brought about such changes as a window for each apartment, a stairway airshaft for each tenant building, and limits on the number of families occupying the available apartments.

NATIONAL GEOGRAPHIC Voting Rights for Women, 1919

🧭 Geography *Skills*

By 1919 a total of 15 states allowed women to vote in all elections.
1. **Place** What state was the first to grant women equal suffrage?
2. **Comparing** What was the status of woman suffrage in your state by 1919?

☐ Equal suffrage, date effective
☐ Partial suffrage
☐ No statewide suffrage

542   CHAPTER 18   Reshaping the Nation

DIFFERENTIATED INSTRUCTION

Reading Support Bring a game of Monopoly to class. Display the board and, if necessary, outline the basic rules of the game. Then have volunteers, working individually or with partners, present a lesson based upon the game. For example, they might demonstrate the acquisition of houses or buying up of railroads to explain what trusts were, how they operated in this era, and how President Theodore Roosevelt tried to "bust" them. **L2**

📂 Refer to *Inclusion for the Middle School Social Studies Classroom Strategies and Activities* in the TCR.

A Progressive in the White House

The wave of progressive reform that began to sweep across the United States eventually reached the level of presidential politics. The first progressive president was Republican **Theodore Roosevelt,** who took office after President McKinley was assassinated. Beginning in 1902, Roosevelt began to take action against companies that had violated the Sherman Antitrust Act. His administration sued trusts in the railroad, beef, tobacco, and oil industries. Roosevelt also believed strongly in the need for **conservation**—the protection and preservation of natural resources.

Reform Continues

Roosevelt's successor, **William Howard Taft,** continued many of Roosevelt's policies. **Woodrow Wilson,** who became president after Taft, introduced his own progressive reforms. He convinced Congress to create the **Federal Reserve**—a system of 12 regional banks supported by a central board based in Washington. Wilson also established the **Federal Trade Commission** to investigate corporations for unfair trade practices.

Prejudice and Discrimination

Despite progressive reforms, many Americans still faced **discrimination**—unequal treatment because of their race, religion, ethnic background, or place of birth.

Some Americans faced discrimination because of their religion. Many Americans feared that Catholic immigrants threatened the American way of life.

Many Jewish immigrants came to America to escape prejudice in their homelands. Some found the same anti-Semitic attitudes in the United States. Landlords, employers, and schools discriminated against Jews.

Discrimination was also based on race. In California and other western states, Asians struggled against prejudice and resentment. White Americans claimed that Chinese immigrants, who worked for lower wages, were taking away jobs. Legislation limited the rights of immigrants from Japan as well as China.

"Is there no redress, no peace, no justice in this land for us? Tell the world the facts."

—Ida B. Wells

African Americans Seek Justice

African Americans faced discrimination in both the North and the South. Although officially free, African Americans were denied basic rights and restricted to second-class citizenship. In 1896, the Supreme Court, in *Plessy* v. *Ferguson,* legalized segregation, which recognized the legality of "separate but equal" facilities.

African Americans rose to the challenge of achieving equality. **Booker T. Washington** founded the Tuskegee Institute to teach African Americans technical skills to help them escape poverty. **Ida B. Wells,** editor of an African American newspaper, began a crusade to end lynching.

W.E.B. Du Bois was one of the most important African American leaders of the time. Du Bois urged African Americans to fight for civil rights. Under no circumstances, he said, should they accept segregation. Du Bois helped found the **National Association for the Advancement of Colored People** (NAACP) in 1909. This interracial group has remained at the forefront of efforts to gain legal and economic equality for African Americans.

Mexican Americans Work Together

Immigrants from Mexico had long come to the United States as laborers, especially in the West and Southwest. Between 1900 and 1914,

CHAPTER 18   Reshaping the Nation   **543**

Who?What?Where?When?

Western Women In addition to being allowed to own and run their own ranches and farms, Western women were the first to win the right to vote. The first seven states to grant woman suffrage were in the West, beginning with Wyoming, while still a territory, in 1869.

Did you know?

The National Park System is one of the best symbols of Theodore Roosevelt's conservation philosophy. The National Park System includes approximately 83.3 million acres of land. The largest area is Wrangell-St. Elias National Park and Preserve in Alaska at 13,200,000 acres, or 16.3 percent of the entire system. The smallest unit in the system is Thaddeus Kosciuszko National Memorial in Pennsylvania at 0.02 of an acre.

INTERDISCIPLINARY CONNECTIONS ACTIVITY

Language Arts Through education, work opportunities, technology, and social involvement, the appearance of the "new woman" meant changes in American life. Have students explore how these changes were perceived by writing two letters for a newspaper's editorial page. The first letter should be from a "new woman" who describes how her everyday life has improved in recent years. The second letter should be from the perspective of a man or woman who resents the changes in daily life that have occurred as more women enter the workplace and classroom. Both letters should cite specific examples to support their main ideas. L3

Geography Skills

Answers:
1. the Caribbean
2. Cuba and Puerto Rico

✓ **Reading Check**

Answer: The people, rather than the state legislatures, were given the power to elect senators directly.

3 ASSESS

Assign Section 3 Assessment as homework or as an in-class activity.

🔊 Have students use **Interactive Tutor Self-Assessment CD-ROM.**

L2

Section Quiz 18–3

L1

Reteaching Activity 18–3

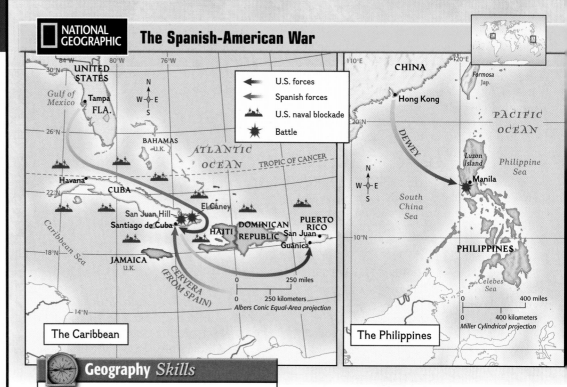

NATIONAL GEOGRAPHIC   The Spanish-American War

U.S. forces
Spanish forces
U.S. naval blockade
Battle

The Caribbean

The Philippines

Geography Skills

American troops sailed from Tampa, Florida, to the south coast of Cuba in June 1898. Admiral Dewey had already sailed from Hong Kong to Manila.
1. **Movement** According to the two maps, in which area did more of the fighting take place?
2. **Analyzing Information** On what two Caribbean islands did United States forces land?

---

the Mexican American population grew dramatically as people crossed the border to escape revolution and economic troubles in Mexico.

Like other immigrant groups, Mexican Americans encountered discrimination and violence. Relying on themselves to solve their problems, they formed self-defense associations to raise money for insurance and legal help. In labor camps and Mexican neighborhoods, they organized self-help groups to deal with overcrowding, poor sanitation, and inadequate public services.

✓ **Reading Check** **Describing** How did the Seventeenth Amendment extend the people's role in the democratic process?

Overseas Expansion

By 1890, the United States spanned the continent from the Atlantic to the Pacific. Americans now began to look west across the Pacific for new frontiers. They wanted to expand America's trade and power.

Expanding Horizons

Americans knew that they faced competition from other nations overseas. The late 1800s and early 1900s were an age of imperialism—a time when powerful European nations, as well as Japan, created large empires. The search for markets and raw materials in Asia and Africa drove imperialism.

Imperialism convinced many Americans that if the United States wanted to keep its economy growing, it too had to expand its power overseas. Some Americans also had a sense of mission. They wanted to share Christianity and Western civilization with the people of Asia.

Many American settlers in Hawaii set up sugarcane plantations and began selling sugar to the United States. In the early 1890s, they

544   CHAPTER 18   Reshaping the Nation

CRITICAL THINKING ACTIVITY

Predicting Consequences During the latter half of the nineteenth century and the first part of the twentieth century, the reach of the United States expanded into the Caribbean islands and Central America, and thousands of miles across the Pacific. Have students consider the consequences of this overseas expansion in terms of the growth of American military and economic power. Then have each student write a short paragraph predicting how the United States would have been different today if the nation had not pursued expansionist and imperialist policies at that time in its history; had maintained neutrality in world conflicts; and had remained within the boundaries of the North American continent. Have students share their views of an alternative United States development in class. **L3**

decided that Hawaii should join the United States so that they would not have to pay tariffs on their exports. In 1893, the sugar planters overthrew the Hawaiian queen, and five years later the United States annexed Hawaii.

The Spanish-American War

The people of Cuba had lived under Spanish rule for centuries. In 1895, Cubans, led by **José Martí,** began a war of independence against Spain. Many Americans sympathized with the Cubans. American support was intensified by yellow journalism—sensational, biased, and often false reporting by many of the nation's leading newspapers.

In early 1898, President McKinley sent the battleship *Maine* to protect Americans living in Cuba. On February 15, 1898, the *Maine* exploded, killing 266 people. American papers blamed the Spanish. On April 25, 1898, Congress declared war on Spain.

The opening of the Spanish-American War found the United States unprepared to fight. In 1898 the U.S. Army had only 28,000 soldiers. To correct the situation, Congress approved the addition of over 30,000 soldiers to the regular, or permanent, army and authorized a large volunteer force. Among the volunteers was a cavalry unit called the "Rough Riders," led by Colonel Leonard Wood and his second in command, Lieutenant Theodore Roosevelt.

The first battle of the Spanish-American War happened thousands of miles away in the Spanish colony of the **Philippines.** In May 1898 shortly after war was declared, Commodore George Dewey sailed his fleet into Manila. With his command, "You may fire when ready, Mr. Gridley," the onslaught began. When the firing was over, the Spanish fleet was destroyed. Not a single American vessel was lost.

At the time Dewey did not have the support needed for a land attack. He decided to block Manila until help arrived. In July support troops arrived in the Philippines. American forces, backed by Filipino rebels under General Emilio Aguinaldo, captured Manila in August.

Meanwhile, the rest of the Spanish fleet was blockaded in Santiago Harbor in the Caribbean. By the end of June, Americans forces, including the Rough Riders, had landed in Cuba and were pushing toward the city of Santiago. After fierce fighting, American troops won at El Caney and San Juan Hill. The Spanish surrendered.

✓ **Reading Check** **Describing** What happened to the *Maine?*

✓ **Reading Check**

Answer: The battleship exploded, killing 266 people.

L1, ELL

Reading Essentials and Study Guide 18–3

Study Guide

Chapter 18, Section 3

For use with textbook pages 540-545

REFORM AT HOME, EXPANSION ABROAD

KEY TERMS

muckraker	Journalists who exposed injustices (page 541)
suffragist	A person who fought for women's right to vote (page 542)
imperialism	The creation of large empires (page 544)
yellow journalism	Sensational, biased, and often false reporting by journalists (page 545)

DRAWING FROM EXPERIENCE

Have you ever been treated unjustly because of your gender, race, religion, ethnic background, or place of birth? If so, how did it make you feel? If not, how do you think you might feel? This section focuses on how Progressive reformers worked to make society better and more fair.

L3

Enrichment Activity 18–3

Name _____ Date _____ Class _____

★ **Enrichment Activity 18-3** ★

March on Washington

This news article appeared in a Baltimore newspaper on March 3, 1913.

8,000 WOMEN MARCH IN WASHINGTON, D.C.

Eight thousand women, marching in the woman suffrage pageant today, practically fought their way foot by foot up Pennsylvania Avenue, through a surging throng that completely defied Washington police, swamped the marchers, and broke their procession into little companies. The women, trudging stoutly along under great difficulties, were able to complete their march only when troops of cavalry from Fort Myers were rushed into Washington to take charge of Pennsylvania Avenue. No inauguration has ever produced such scenes, which in many instances amounted to nothing less than riots.

SOURCE: Stevens, Doris. *Jailed for Freedom, American Women Win the Vote.* NewSage Press.

DIRECTIONS: Classifying Information Newspaper articles often provide information to answer the questions *Who?, What?, When?, Where?,* and *Why?* Based on this article and what you know, complete the information below with as much detail as you can about the incident.

Who? _____
What? _____
When? _____
Where? _____
Why? _____

Activity **DIRECTIONS: Creating a Sign** Many women in the march carried signs with slogans. On a separate sheet of paper, design a sign that the writer of the article might have held while viewing the march. Be ready to explain your slogan. Did the writer of the original news story support woman suffrage, the right to peaceful marches, or the crowd's actions? How can you tell?

4 CLOSE

Review the political and business reforms discussed in this section. Have students name and defend the reform that they consider the most important in each category.

SECTION 3 ASSESSMENT

Checking for Understanding

1. **Key Terms** Define: muckraker, suffragist, imperialism, yellow journalism.

2. **Reviewing Facts** Name five groups who were the targets of discrimination in the late 1800s and early 1900s.

Reviewing Themes

3. **Groups and Institutions** Who were suffragists? What right does the Nineteenth Amendment provide?

Critical Thinking

4. **Identifying Assumptions** Some who favored American expansion believed it was the nation's mission to "civilize" the "uncivilized" people of the world. What do you think they meant by *uncivilized*?

5. **Organizing Information** Re-create the diagram below and list two reasons for American expansion overseas.

Reasons for expansion

Analyzing Visuals

6. **Geography Skills** Examine the map on page 542. Why do you think the percentage of states allowing woman suffrage was so much higher in the West than in the East?

Interdisciplinary Activity

Expository Writing Find a newspaper article that deals with the role of women today. Rewrite the article to reflect how this information might have been presented in the late 1800s and early 1900s.

CHAPTER 18   Reshaping the Nation   **545**

SECTION 3 ASSESSMENT ANSWERS

1. Student work should reflect correct use of terms.

2. Catholics, Jews, Asians, African Americans, and Mexican Americans faced discrimination.

3. supporters for women's right to vote; gave women the right to vote

4. Answers may include: not conforming to the American way of life or not practicing an "acceptable" religion (that is, in the Judeo-Christian tradition).

5. to keep the economy growing; to promote Christianity and Western civilization

6. Students may suggest that on the frontier, where women shared the hardships and dangers equally with men, support for woman suffrage was more widespread.

Interdisciplinary Activity Students' articles should reveal their knowledge of the role of women in the late 1800s and early 1900s.

1 FOCUS

Section Overview
This section explains how the entry of the United States into World War I led to Germany's surrender.

BELLRINGER
Skillbuilder Activity

Project transparency and have students answer the question.

Daily Focus Skills Transparency 18–4

Reading Preview

Answers to Graphic: German U-boats torpedo American merchant ships; Germans sink *Lusitania*; Germans resume U-boat attacks without warning.

Preteaching Vocabulary
Use the **Vocabulary PuzzleMaker CD-ROM** to create crossword and word search puzzles.

SECTION 4 World War I and Its Aftermath

Guide to Reading

Main Idea
The United States entered World War I and helped the Allies win.

Key Terms
nationalism, propaganda, reparations, Prohibition

Reading Strategy
Organizing Information As you read the section, re-create the diagram below and list events that prompted the United States to enter the war.

Read to Learn
• what role the United States played in World War I.
• how the nation changed during the 1920s.

Section Theme
Global Connections The entry of the United States into the war eventually led to Germany's surrender.

Preview of Events

♦1910	♦1915	♦1920
1914 World War I begins	**1917** United States enters war	**1920** Prohibition begins

Jeannette Rankin

★★★★★★★
AN
American Story

The swift chain of events that led to war in Europe in 1914 stunned Americans. Most agreed with Jeannette Rankin—the first woman to serve in the U.S. Congress, at a time when women could not even vote in most states—that "You can no more win a war than you can win an earthquake." Most Americans wanted the country to stay out of other countries' affairs. They saw no good reason to get involved in a conflict that they believed grew out of national pride and greed. As time went on, however, the United States found it more and more difficult to remain neutral.

The people of the time called the conflict the World War, or the Great War, because they believed that never again would there be another like it. The conflict, which began in Europe, soon spread. Although the United States tried to remain neutral, it was drawn into the conflict. Over the next few years, nearly 30 nations were at war. The main campaigns were fought in Europe, but armies also fought in the Middle East, Africa, and China, and navies clashed worldwide.

546   CHAPTER 18   Reshaping the Nation

SECTION RESOURCES

📁 **Reproducible Masters**
• Reproducible Lesson Plan 18–4
• Daily Lecture and Discussion Notes 18–4
• Guided Reading Activity 18–4
• Section Quiz 18–4
• Reteaching Activity 18–4
• Reading Essentials and Study Guide 18–4
• Enrichment Activity 18–4

📖 **Transparencies**
• Daily Focus Skills Transparency 18–4

Multimedia
Vocabulary PuzzleMaker CD-ROM
Interactive Tutor Self-Assessment CD-ROM
ExamView® Pro Testmaker CD-ROM
Presentation Plus! CD-ROM

World War

The tensions that led to World War I went back many years. The conflicts grew as European nations pursued dreams of empire, built up their armies, and formed alliances.

War Erupts in Europe

Nationalism—a feeling of intense loyalty to one's country or group—caused much of the tension in Europe. Because of nationalism, Britain and Germany raced to build the largest navy. To protect themselves, European nations began to form **alliances**—defense agreements among nations.

In June 1914, a Serbian terrorist named Gavrilo Princip assassinated Archduke Franz Ferdinand, heir to the throne of the Austro-Hungarian Empire. Austria-Hungary blamed Serbia's government for the attack, and declared war on Serbia.

At this point, the alliance system brought about a world war. Russia decided to help Serbia, which caused Austria-Hungary's ally Germany to declare war on Russia as well as on Russia's ally France. Germany then invaded Belgium, so Britain, which had promised to protect Belgium, declared war on Germany.

The "Great War" had begun. On the one side were the **Allied Powers**—Great Britain, France, and Russia. On the other side were the **Central Powers**—Germany, Austria-Hungary, and the Ottoman (Turkish) Empire. Japan and Italy joined the Allies as well.

The British and French stopped the German attack on France at the **Battle of the Marne.** For the next three years, the two sides faced each other across an elaborate network of trenches. The war had reached a stalemate.

America Enters the War

When World War I began, President Wilson declared the United States to be neutral. To gain the support of Americans, both the Allies and the Central Powers used propaganda—information designed to influence opinion. As the war went on, Americans began to side with the Allies. At the same time, American trade with the Allies soared.

To stop the American assistance to the Allies, Germany began using submarines, known as U-boats, to sink cargo ships headed to Britain. In May 1915, a U-boat sank the passenger ship *Lusitania,* killing more than 1,000 people, including 128 Americans. After Wilson denounced the attack, Germany promised to warn neutral ships before attacking.

Picturing **History**

The *Lusitania* left New York for England on May 1, 1915. Germany had placed a warning notice in American newspapers, but few people took it seriously. How did the United States respond to German U-boat attacks?

Lusitania
May 7 1915
Have been
torpedoed
send help.

NOTICE!
TRAVELLERS intending to embark on the Atlantic voyage are reminded that a state of war exists between Germany and her allies and GreatBritain and her allies; that the zone of war includes the waters adjacent to the British Isles; that, in accordance with formal notice given by the Imperial German Government, vessels flying the flag of Great Britian or of any of her allies, are liable to destruction in those waters and that travellers sailing in the war zone on ships of Great Britian or her allies do so at their own risk.
IMPERIAL GERMAN EMBASSY,
WASHINGTON, D. C., APRIL 22, 1915.

2 TEACH

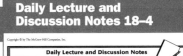

Daily Lecture and Discussion Notes 18–4

Copyright © by The McGraw-Hill Companies, Inc.

Daily Lecture and Discussion Notes

Chapter 18, Section 4

Did You Know ? During World War I, Herbert Hoover called for "Meatless Mondays" and "Wheatless Wednesdays," asking Americans to conserve food for the war effort.

I. **World War** (Pages 547–549)

  A. The world changed with World War I. The United States was unwillingly pulled into the conflict, and the war affected all aspects of American life.

    1. In Europe, nationalism, an intense loyalty to one's country or group, led Great Britain and Germany to race to build the largest navy. European alliances, or defense agreements among nations, were formed to protect European nations.

    2. The assassination of Archduke Franz Ferdinand, heir to the throne of the Austro-Hungarian Empire, by a Serbian terrorist in 1914 led to a declaration of war on Serbia by Austria-Hungary.

> **Reading Strategy**

Reviewing Facts Ask students to recall the statements in the text about America's involvement with the Allies before its entry into the war. **Ask:** How was the United States already helping the Allies before it entered the war? *(by trading with them)* Use that answer to introduce and discuss the additional help that came with America's official entry into the war. **L1**

Picturing **History**

William Jennings Bryan, Wilson's first secretary of state, strongly supported neutrality. After the sinking of the *Lusitania*, it was with great reluctance that he signed Wilson's first note of protest to Germany. When Wilson prepared a second and stronger protest, Bryan refused to sign it. Instead, he quit his cabinet position.
Answer: Congress declared war on Germany.

> **Reading Strategy**   **READING THE TEXT**

Preparing a Front Page Have students discuss how the outbreak of war in Europe, or United States entry into the war, might have been covered on the front page of a newspaper. Tell them to create such a front page, conducting research as needed. Articles and features may include: headlines and lead articles about the assassination in Sarajevo; background information about the rise of European nationalism; maps to review the European alliances; events that led to or triggered United States entry into the war; and comments from American politicians and European diplomats. Various roles to be assigned include layout editor, illustrators, researchers, and writers. Students may want to use desktop publishing software to prepare their front pages. **L2**

L1, ELL

Guided Reading Activity 18-4

Name _____ Date _____ Class _____

★ Guided Reading Activity 18-4

DIRECTIONS: Recalling the Facts Use the information in your textbook to answer the questions. Use another sheet of paper if necessary.

1. What is nationalism?
2. Why did European nations feel the need to form alliances prior to World War I?
3. What countries made up the Allied Powers? _____
4. What countries made up the Central Powers? _____
5. Why did the United States declare war on Germany in 1917? _____
6. What was the purpose of the Selective Service Act? _____
7. Who were the Bolsheviks? _____
8. What is an armistice? _____
9. What was the name of the treaty signed to end World War I? _____
10. Why didn't the United States join the League of Nations? _____
11. What caused many workers to go on strike during the 1920s? _____
12. What was the Red Scare? _____
13. Why were many Americans worried about immigration after the war?
14. Which Amendment repealed Prohibition? _____
15. What product changed American society in the 1920s? _____

you don't say...

Stalemate The term *stalemate* comes from the game of chess. It describes a situation in which one player cannot make any move without putting his or her king in a position to be captured (and, as a result, losing the game). It is an apt term for the draw that took place along the Western Front during World War I.

In 1917, Germany broke its promise and ordered its U-boats to attack without warning. In mid-March, U-boats sank three American ships. President Wilson asked Congress to declare war on Germany on April 2, 1917.

Americans Join the Allies

Shortly after declaring war, Congress passed the **Selective Service Act,** establishing a military draft. By the end of the war, about 3 million American men had been drafted, and another 2 million had volunteered. More than 300,000 African Americans joined the military.

As America prepared to enter the war, Russia withdrew. In November 1917, the **Bolsheviks**—a group of Communists led by Vladimir Lenin—overthrew Russia's government. In March 1918, they signed a treaty ending the war with Germany. Shortly afterward, the Germans launched a massive offensive in France. Their goal was to smash the British and the French armies before the Americans could fully mass their strength. As a result, shortly after the Americans were assigned their first divisional area north of Paris at Cantigny, the German army was about 40 miles from Paris.

American Troops in Battle

At Cantigny about 4,000 soldiers of the First Division made the first American offensive action of the war. After a bitter battle, these troops won the first victory ever by Americans fighting in Europe.

In June 1918, American divisions were ordered to the Marne River. The objective was to recapture **Belleau Wood.** For 24 hours a day for the next two weeks, U.S. marines fought their way through the forest. The Americans finally took the forest—but at a cost of thousands of casualties.

The Germans launched a massive offensive at **Château-Thierry** along the Marne in July. Together the Americans and the French fought back the Germans, breaking their offensive strength, and for the first time, the Allies held the upper hand.

In late September, the United States First Army under the command of General **John J. Pershing,** attacked German military forces along the Meuse River and Argonne Forest in northeastern France. Victory at the battle of **Meuse-Argonne,** after 47 days of heavy fighting, caused the German lines to crumble.

Much of World War I was fought from trenches where soldiers spent weeks at a time.

548

DIFFERENTIATED INSTRUCTION

Reading Support Have students brainstorm sounds that they associate with patriotism (for example, melodies of specific patriotic songs, a trumpet fanfare, or a 21-gun salute). Ask students which sounds might provide an effective setting for a patriotic song about the Allied cause in World War I or for a brief speech by an American politician. Interested students might extend this activity by writing and presenting a song or promotional speech based upon their choice of setting. **L1**

☞ Refer to *Inclusion for the Middle School Social Studies Classroom Strategies and Activities* in the TCR.

With their troops in retreat, German military leaders realized they had little chance of winning the war. On October 4, 1918, the German government appealed for an **armistice.** An armistice is an agreement to end the fighting. On November 11, 1918, an armistice based on Allied demands was signed by both sides. The fighting was over, and plans began to build a lasting peace.

Searching for Peace

In January 1919, President Wilson and other world leaders met in Paris to negotiate a treaty ending the war. The **Treaty of Versailles,** as it was known, set up the **League of Nations**—an international organization to preserve the peace. It required Germany to make reparations—or payments—for the damage it had caused. The treaty also created new nations including Czechoslovakia, Yugoslavia, and Poland.

When Wilson presented the Treaty of Versailles to the Senate for ratification, Republicans argued that the League of Nations would limit America's independence. The Senate rejected the treaty. The United States never did join the League of Nations.

✓Reading Check **Describing** What happened in April 1917?

The 1920s

Tired of war and world responsibilities, Americans were ready to seek enjoyment. It was a time of new pastimes and new heroes. Crossword puzzles and the Chinese game of Mah Jongg became national obsessions. Athletes like base-

Europe After World War I

New Nations

0   300 miles
0   300 kilometers
Azimuthal Equidistant projection

Geography *Skills*

1. **Region** What new nations bordered Germany?
2. **Analyzing Information** Which new nations did not have any coastline along a sea or an ocean?

ball's **Babe Ruth** and golf's **Bobby Jones** became larger-than-life heroes. Americans gloried in the feat of **Charles Lindbergh,** who completed the first nonstop solo flight across the Atlantic.

A Time of Turmoil

Labor and management had put aside their differences during the war years. A sense of patriotism, high wages, and wartime laws helped keep conflict to a minimum. Once the war was over, conflict flared anew. The war-stimulated economy cooled down, and veterans

✓Reading Check

Answer: The United States entered the war.

Geography *Skills*

Answers:
1. Lithuania, Poland, Czechoslovakia, and Austria
2. Czechoslovakia, Austria, and Hungary

3 ASSESS

Assign Section 4 Assessment as homework or as an in-class activity.

🔵 Have students use **Interactive Tutor Self-Assessment CD-ROM.**

L2

Section Quiz 18–4

Name _____ Date _____ Class _____

★ Chapter 18   Score ____

Section Quiz 18-4

DIRECTIONS: Matching Match the items in Column A with the items in Column B. Write the correct letters in the blanks. *(10 points each)*

Column A	Column B
____ 1. defense agreement among nations	**A.** nativism
____ 2. anti-immigrant feelings	**B.** armistice
____ 3. a group of Communists	**C.** alliance
____ 4. agreement to end fighting	**D.** U-boat
____ 5. destroyed the *Lusitania*	**E.** Bolsheviks

DIRECTIONS: Multiple Choice In the blank at the left, write the letter of the

L1

Reteaching Activity 18–4

Name _____ Date _____ Class _____

★ Reteaching Activity 18-4

DIRECTIONS: Sequencing Events Number the events in the order in which they occurred.

____ **A.** Congress passes the Selective Service Act.

____ **B.** The Allied and Central Powers are formed.

____ **C.** The United States declares war on Germany.

____ **D.** A German U-boat sinks the *Lusitania*.

____ **E.** American soldiers take their first offensive action of the war.

____ **F.** The League of Nations is formed.

____ **G.** The Bolsheviks overthrow Russia's government.

INTERDISCIPLINARY CONNECTIONS ACTIVITY

Music Few things stir feelings of nationalism as does the sound of one's national anthem. Have students learn the words to one of the following: our national anthem, the national anthem of a country of their ancestry, the national anthem of the country in which they were born (if other than the United States), or the national anthem of one of the countries mentioned in Section 4. As students share the national anthems, ask them to comment on how pride in one's country, expressed positively in national anthems, could eventually lead to war. **L1**

L1, ELL

Reading Essentials and Study Guide 18–4

Study Guide
Chapter 18, Section 4

For use with textbook pages 546–550

WORLD WAR I AND ITS AFTERMATH

KEY TERMS	
nationalism	A feeling of intense loyalty to one's country or group *(page 547)*
propaganda	Information designed to influence opinion *(page 547)*
reparations	Payments *(page 549)*
Prohibition	A total ban on the manufacture, sale, and transportation of alcohol *(page 550)*

DRAWING FROM EXPERIENCE

Have you ever found yourself arguing with someone, even though you had tried to avoid the argument? Do you sometimes find it easier to stay out of other people's problems?
This section focuses on how the United States was pulled into World War I, how the war was

L3

Enrichment Activity 18–4

Name _____ Date _____ Class _____

★ **Enrichment Activity 18-4** ★

You Have a Choice

Once the United States became involved in World War I, the country worked quickly to prepare for fighting. The nation's industry expanded to supply weapons. Women and minorities replaced men who had left their jobs in industry to join the armed forces. The government worked to resolve labor disputes, and workers agreed not to strike so production of vital war materials would not be interrupted. In order to supply food for the Allied war refugees, the government encouraged farmers to produce more food and the public to eat less. The Committee on Public Information hired speakers, writers, artists, and actors to build support for the war by convincing Americans that the war represented a battle for democracy and freedom. The political cartoon to the right, appeared in 1917.

SOURCE: Bailey, Thomas A. and David M. Kennedy. The American Pageant. A History of the Republic: Stanford University

DIRECTIONS: Analyzing the Cartoon
The cartoon presents a clear message about what was expected of Americans. List the symbols and words that the cartoonist used to persuade Americans to support the war. Tell the meaning of each.

Symbol/Words	Meaning
_____	_____
_____	_____
_____	_____

Activity **DIRECTIONS: Drawing a Political Cartoon** On a separate sheet of paper, draw your own political cartoon supporting a current issue of importance. Use an approach similar to the one in the 1917 cartoon.

4 CLOSE

Have students name ways in which the American entry into the war and participation in the peace negotiations made a decisive difference.

---

found they had to compete for a declining number of jobs. Workers in general wanted to preserve and, if possible, hike the wages paid during the war. When management refused to cooperate many workers resorted to their chief bargaining tool—the strike. Although strikes had been in use in America since the 1870s, those which took place after World War I were numerous and violent. In 1919 alone there were more than 3,600 strikes involving millions of workers.

The Red Scare

Many Americans believed there was a strong tie between union activism and radicalism. The belief helped fuel a movement to fight radicalism in the United States. Known as the **Red Scare,** the movement began with a general concern with communism. **Communism** is a theory that advocates the elimination of private property. It is also a totalitarian system of government in which a single party controls the citizens.

The fears many Americans felt also led to an increase in **nativism**—or anti-immigrant feelings. World War I had dramatically slowed the huge flow of immigration that had begun in the 1880s. After the war ended, heavy immigration resumed. Many Americans saw the newcomers as a threat to their jobs and their security.

Prohibition

In 1920, Prohibition began. This was a total ban on the manufacture, sale, and transportation of alcohol. People began making and selling alcohol illegally, however. Prohibition also contributed to the rise of organized crime. Prohibition was finally repealed in 1933 with the passage of the **Twenty-first Amendment.**

A Booming Economy

With the end of World War I and the start of the 1920s came another industrial revolution. As energy poured into industry, goods poured out. Among the products that gained popularity in the 1920s were telephones, vacuum cleaners, refrigerators, and canned goods. While these items and others like them made it possible for Americans to spend less time on household chores and more time on recreation another product had an even greater impact. The product was the automobile.

The automobile industry revolutionized American society. The industry used so much steel, glass, wood, gas, and rubber that it provided jobs for millions of workers. It transformed American buying habits, making installment buying a way of life. It promoted highway construction and travel.

✓ **Reading Check** **Identifying** What is Prohibition? When did it go into effect?

SECTION 4 ASSESSMENT

Checking for Understanding

1. **Key Terms** Write headlines for events during World War I using each of the following terms: nationalism, propaganda, reparations.

2. **Reviewing Facts** What did the Selective Service Act do?

Reviewing Themes

3. **Global Connections** What was the Treaty of Versailles? Why did the U.S. Senate reject it?

Critical Thinking

4. **Analyzing Information** Why did the United States experience an economic boom in the early 1920s?

5. **Organizing Information** Re-create the diagram below and describe how nationalism led to war.

Analyzing Visuals

6. **Geography Skills** Examine the map showing European borders following World War I on page 549. Which of the following was not a new nation—Poland, Latvia, or Bulgaria?

Interdisciplinary Activity

Descriptive Writing Make a list of three to five adjectives that you think describe the mood of the nation during World War I. Draw or paint these adjectives on poster board in a way that expresses the words' meanings.

SECTION 4 ASSESSMENT ANSWERS

1. Student work should reflect correct use of terms.

2. It established a military draft.

3. treaty ending the war; It established the League of Nations to preserve world peace; opponents argued it would limit America's independence.

4. Popular appliances were produced, and the new automobile industry stimulated other industries that supported it.

5. Answers may include any two of the following: nationalism resulted in navy buildup; formation of alliances; assassination; Serbia blamed for assassination; countries of one alliance declared war against opposition.

6. Bulgaria

Interdisciplinary Activity Drawings and paintings should express the words' meanings.

Building a Database

McKinley-Roosevelt campaign item, 1900

Why Learn This Skill?

Have you ever collected baseball cards or catalogued the CDs in your collection? Have you ever kept a list of the names and addresses of your friends and relatives? If you have collected information and kept some sort of list or file, then you have created a database.

Learning the Skill

An electronic database is a collection of facts that are stored in files on the computer. The information is organized in fields.

A database can be organized and reorganized in any way that is useful to you. By using a database management system (DBMS)—special software developed for record keeping—you can easily add, delete, change, or update information. You give commands to the computer telling it what to do with the information and it follows your commands. When you want to retrieve information, the computer searches through the files, finds the information, and displays it on the screen.

Practicing the Skill

Theodore Roosevelt is one of the presidents discussed in this chapter. Follow these steps to build a database of the political and cultural events that took place during his presidency.

Theodore Roosevelt was the nation's twenty-sixth president.

❶ Find information about the events during this period from encyclopedias, histories, and the Internet. Determine what facts you want to include in your database.

❷ Follow instructions in the DBMS you are using to set up fields. Then enter each item of data into its assigned field.

❸ Determine how you want to organize the facts in the database—chronologically by the date of the event, or alphabetically by the name of the event.

❹ Follow the instructions in your computer program to place the information in order of importance.

❺ Check that the information in your database is all correct. If necessary, add, delete, or change information or fields.

Applying the Skill

Building a Database Bring current newspapers to class. Using the steps just described, build a database of political figures mentioned in the newspapers. For example, you may wish to build a database of national leaders or government officials in your community. Explain to a partner why the database is organized the way it is and how it might be used in this class.

ANSWERS TO PRACTICING THE SKILL

If students work at school computers, spot-check their progress, offering advice as requested. Invite students to share information about their completed databases. Identify the fields that are used most often, as well as ideas that are original and practical.

Applying the Skill Students may prefer to build their databases in pairs. Again, have students share information about the organization and use of their databases. Point out notable similarities and differences.

TEACH

Building a Database Students who know how to construct and use a database may save themselves time in locating specific facts and identifying relationships among facts. Begin discussion of this page by taking a class survey to find out if any students have done computer database searches. (Students who have used a computerized card catalog at the library have used a database.)

In discussing the construction of a database, give some examples of fields, such as the year that an event takes place, the name of the event, or people connected with the event. Then explain that all of the data fields related to the same subject make up a record, and that a collection of records is a data file.

Additional Practice

L2

Chapter Skills Activity 18

Name _____ Date _____ Class _____

★ **Chapter Skills Activity 18**

Building a Database

An electronic database is a collection of facts that are stored in files on a computer. The information is organized in fields. Once the database is created, you can specify the information you need, and the computer searches the files to display the information.

DIRECTIONS: From 1892 through 1924, approximately 22 million people immigrated to the United States by passing through Ellis Island in New York. This was one of the main processing centers for immigrants. Many people are interested today in learning more about their ancestors. To make this process easier, a database has been created to organize all of the information about those 22 million people. This database allows you to search for a specific person by name, age, or other category. Using the chart below, copy each item given into the appropriate database field. Then answer the questions.

GLENCOE TECHNOLOGY

MindJogger Videoquiz
Use **MindJogger Videoquiz** to review the Chapter 18 content.

📼 Available in VHS

Reviewing Key Terms

1. the state of spanning North America, connecting the Atlantic and Pacific coasts

2. tracts of land set aside for Native Americans

3. the practice whereby unions represent workers in bargaining with management

4. a man or a woman who fought for women's right to vote

5. the time during the late 1800s and early 1900s when powerful European nations, as well as Japan, created large empires

6. a feeling of intense loyalty to one's country or group

7. information designed to influence opinion

8. the total ban, beginning in 1920, on the manufacture, sale, and transportation of alcohol

Reviewing Key Facts

9. towns that grew up almost overnight near gold strikes

10. May 10, 1869

11. take ownership of railroads and promote use of silver as well as gold for money

12. to raise money to buy equipment and hire workers

13. the steel industry; through vertical integration, acquiring companies that provided the materials his steel company needed

14. political party organizations that influenced or controlled many cities

15. to provide African Americans with technical skills to help them escape poverty

Chapter Summary
Reshaping the Nation

1869
- First transcontinental railroad completed

1870
- Rockefeller organizes Standard Oil Company

1876
- Sioux defeat Custer's forces at Little Bighorn

1886
- Trade unions form AFL

1886
- Statue of Liberty is dedicated

1890
- Massacre at Wounded Knee

1892
- Populist Party formed

1901
- Theodore Roosevelt becomes president after assassination of McKinley

1903
- Wright Brothers fly motorized airplane

1908
- Ford introduces the Model T

1909
- NAACP is formed

1914
- World War I begins

1917
- U.S. enters World War I

1919
- Eighteenth Amendment prohibits alcohol

1920
- Nineteenth Amendment grants woman suffrage

1927
- Lindbergh flies across the Atlantic

552

Reviewing Key Terms
On a sheet of paper, define the following terms.

1. transcontinental
2. reservation
3. collective bargaining
4. suffragist
5. imperialism
6. nationalism
7. propaganda
8. Prohibition

Reviewing Key Facts

9. What are boomtowns?

10. When was the transcontinental rail line completed?

11. What did the Populist Party call for government to do?

12. Why does a corporation sell shares of its business?

13. What industry did Andrew Carnegie lead? How did his company become so powerful?

14. What are political machines?

15. Why did Booker T. Washington start the Tuskegee Institute?

16. Where was the Spanish-American War fought?

17. When did the United States enter World War I?

18. What amendment to the Constitution granted women the right to vote?

Critical Thinking

19. **Making Inferences** Another name for the Populist Party was the People's Party. Why do you think the Populists considered themselves to be a party of the people?

20. **Evaluating** Which of the inventions described in the chapter do you think brought about the most dramatic change in people's lives? Explain.

21. **Drawing Conclusions** Why do you think the right to vote was important to women?

22. **Analyzing Themes: Culture and Traditions** Re-create the diagram below and describe two ways you think immigrants try to preserve their cultural heritage.

> **Preserving their heritage**
> ◯   ◯

16. in the Philippines and the Caribbean

17. April 1917

18. the Nineteenth Amendment

Critical Thinking

19. Answers may include: promoted the needs of people over the needs of private business and government; called for reforms to improve people's lives.

20. Answers will vary but should be well supported.

21. Without the vote, women had little influence over the laws that were made and the people who were elected.

22. Answers may include preserving religion, language, and customs.

Geography and History Activity

Reading a Thematic Map *Study the thematic map below; then answer the questions that follow.*

NATIONAL GEOGRAPHIC
The Cattle Kingdom

Legend:
- Goodnight-Loving Trail
- Western Trail
- Chisholm Trail
- Sedalia Trail
- Railroad
- Cattle ranch

0   100 miles
0   100 kilometers
Albers Conic Equal-Area projection

23. What geographic region is shown?
24. In what part of Texas were most of the large cattle ranches located?
25. What did the towns where the trails ended have in common? Why was this important?

Practicing Skills

Making Inferences

26. Many Americans wanted the United States to remain neutral during World War I. Why do you think many Americans feared war?
27. How might economic interests get in the way of the nation remaining neutral?

HISTORY *Online*

Self-Check Quiz
Visit tarvol1.glencoe.com and click on **Chapter 18— Self-Check Quizzes** to prepare for the chapter test.

Citizenship Cooperative Activity

28. **Community Service** Working in groups of three, interview one of your community's officials to learn how you can begin taking an active role in the community. Members of your group may wish to volunteer for some sort of community service, then perform the service and report your experiences to your classmates.

Economics Activity

29. **History and Economics** Today many Native Americans still live on reservations. Some reservations have developed their own businesses and industries to help make them more self-sufficient. With a partner, research to find information about a reservation in the United States today. Write a report describing one of the major businesses on that reservation.

 Alternative Assessment Activity

30. **Portfolio Writing Activity** Research the life of one of the men or women from the chapter. Prepare a one-page biography of that person and share it with the class.

Standardized Test Practice

Directions: Choose the *best* answer to the following question.

People in the late 1800s took advantage of the open grasslands of the West to develop which of these industries?

A	Banking	C	Ranching
B	Manufacturing	D	Mining

Test-Taking Tip

The important words in this question are *open grasslands.* Banking and manufacturing do not need open grasslands, so you can easily eliminate answers **A** and **B**.

Citizenship Cooperative Activity

28. Have students obtain a list of community officials from the Internet or take them to the library to obtain a list. If students volunteer for community service, allow time for them to report their experiences to the class.

Economics Activity

29. Students' reports should describe a reservation in the United States and its major businesses.

 Alternative Assessment

30. Biographies should contain significant information about the person chosen.

HISTORY *Online*

Have students visit the Web site at tarvol1.glencoe.com to review Chapter 18 and take the Self-Check Quiz.

Standardized Test Practice

Answer: C
Question Type: Economics
Answer Explanation: According to page 529, ranchers traveled along trails, herding cattle north to meet the railroads.

Bonus Question ?

Ask: By what nickname were the members of the American forces known? *(doughboys)*

Geography and History Activity

23. Students' answers should include the American Southwest.
24. the northern part near New Mexico Territory and Indian Territory (the Panhandle)
25. near rail lines; to simplify transportation

Practicing Skills

26. Answers may include: loss of life, fear of fighting on United States soil, and fear that the government would be threatened if the United States was defeated.
27. The Allies' demand for supplies boosted industry in the United States. The United States also had an interest in protecting its international trade.

553

Timesaving Tools

TeacherWorks™ All-In-One Planner and Resource Center

- **Interactive Teacher Edition** Access your Teacher Wraparound Edition and your classroom resources with a few easy clicks.
- **Interactive Lesson Planner** Planning has never been easier! Organize your week, month, semester, or year with all the lesson helps you need to make teaching creative, timely, and relevant.

Use Glencoe's **Presentation Plus!** multimedia teacher tool to easily present dynamic lessons that visually excite your students. Using Microsoft PowerPoint® you can customize the presentations to create your own personalized lessons.

TEACHING TRANSPARENCIES

Graphic Organizer 7 L2

Why It Matters Chapter Transparency 19 L2

REVIEW AND REINFORCEMENT

Workbook Activity 19 L1

Time Line Activity 19 L2

Vocabulary Activity 19 L1

REVIEW AND REINFORCEMENT

Critical Thinking Skills Activity 19 L2

Take-Home Review Activity 19 L1

ENRICHMENT

Linking Past and Present Activity 19 L2

Primary Source Reading 19 L2

GEOGRAPHY

Geography and History Activity 19 L2

Meeting NCSS Standards

The following standards are highlighted in Chapter 19:

Section 1	IX	Global Connections: B, C, D, E, G
Section 2	X	Civic Ideals & Practices: A, B, C, E, F, G, H, I
Section 3	VI	Power, Authority, & Governance: B, C, D, F, H, I
Section 4	IX	Global Connections: A, B, C, D, E, G

FOLDABLES™

Study Organizer Dinah Zike's **Foldables** are three-dimensional, interactive graphic organizers that help students practice basic writing skills, review key vocabulary terms, and identify main ideas. Additional chapter activities can be found in the **Reading and Study Skills Foldables** booklet.

Chapter 19 Resources

ASSESSMENT AND EVALUATION

Chapter 19 Test Form A L2

Chapter 19 Test Form B L2

Standardized Test Practice Workbook Activity 19 L2

Performance Assessment Activity 19 L1, ELL

ExamView® Pro Testmaker CD-ROM

MULTIMEDIA

- Vocabulary PuzzleMaker CD-ROM
- Interactive Tutor Self-Assessment CD-ROM
- ExamView® Pro Testmaker CD-ROM
- Audio Program
- American History Primary Source Documents Library CD-ROM
- MindJogger Videoquiz
- Presentation Plus! CD-ROM
- TeacherWorks CD-ROM
- Interactive Student Edition CD-ROM
- Glencoe Skillbuilder Interactive Workbook CD-ROM, Level 1
- The American Republic to 1877 Video Program
- American Music: Hits Through History

SPANISH RESOURCES

The following Spanish language materials are available in the Spanish Resources Binder:

- Spanish Guided Reading Activities
- Spanish Reteaching Activities
- Spanish Quizzes and Tests
- Spanish Vocabulary Activity
- Spanish Take-Home Review Activity
- Spanish Summaries
- The Declaration of Independence and United States Constitution Spanish Translation

The following videotape programs are available from Glencoe as supplements to Chapter 19:

- **The Stock Exchange** (ISBN 0-7670-0562-7)
- **Drive for the American Dream** (ISBN 1-56501-221-6)
- **Ronald Reagan: The Many Lives** (ISBN 1-56501-099-X)

To order, call Glencoe at 1-800-334-7344. To find classroom resources to accompany many of these videos, check the following home pages:
A&E Television: www.aande.com
The History Channel: www.historychannel.com

Use our Web site for additional resources. All essential content is covered in the Student Edition.

You and your students can visit tarvol1.glencoe.com, the Web site companion to **The American Republic to 1877.** This innovative integration of electronic and print media offers your students a wealth of opportunities. The student text directs students to the Web site for the following options:

- **Chapter Overviews**
- **Student Web Activities**
- **Self-Check Quizzes**
- **Textbook Updates**

Answers to the student Web activities are provided for you in the **Web Activity Lesson Plans.** Additional Web resources and Interactive Tutor Puzzles are also available.

Chapter 19 Resources

SECTION RESOURCES

Daily Objectives	Reproducible Resources	Multimedia Resources
SECTION 1 **Depression and a Second World War** 1. Explain how President Roosevelt responded to the Great Depression. 2. Understand the actions that led to the outbreak of World War II.	Reproducible Lesson Plan 19–1 Daily Lecture and Discussion Notes 19–1 Guided Reading Activity 19–1* Section Quiz 19–1* Reteaching Activity 19–1* Reading Essentials and Study Guide 19–1* Enrichment Activity 19–1	Daily Focus Skills Transparency 19–1 Interactive Tutor Self-Assessment CD-ROM ExamView® Pro Testmaker CD-ROM Presentation Plus! CD-ROM
SECTION 2 **Turning Points** 1. Examine the ways the United States attempted to stop the spread of communism. 2. Review the actions African Americans took to secure their rights.	Reproducible Lesson Plan 19–2 Daily Lecture and Discussion Notes 19–2 Guided Reading Activity 19–2* Section Quiz 19–2* Reteaching Activity 19–2* Reading Essentials and Study Guide 19–2* Enrichment Activity 19–2	Daily Focus Skills Transparency 19–2 Interactive Tutor Self-Assessment CD-ROM ExamView® Pro Testmaker CD-ROM Presentation Plus! CD-ROM
SECTION 3 **Modern America** 1. Analyze the ways in which the Watergate scandal affected the nation. 2. Summarize how the Cold War ended.	Reproducible Lesson Plan 19–3 Daily Lecture and Discussion Notes 19–3 Guided Reading Activity 19–3* Section Quiz 19–3* Reteaching Activity 19–3* Reading Essentials and Study Guide 19–3* Enrichment Activity 19–3	Daily Focus Skills Transparency 19–3 Interactive Tutor Self-Assessment CD-ROM ExamView® Pro Testmaker CD-ROM Presentation Plus! CD-ROM
SECTION 4 **The War on Terrorism** 1. Describe how Americans responded to terrorism. 2. Discuss the actions the government took to fight terrorism.	Reproducible Lesson Plan 19–4 Daily Lecture and Discussion Notes 19–4 Guided Reading Activity 19–4* Section Quiz 19–4* Reteaching Activity 19–4* Reading Essentials and Study Guide 19–4* Enrichment Activity 19–4	Daily Focus Skills Transparency 19–4 Vocabulary PuzzleMaker CD-ROM Interactive Tutor Self-Assessment CD-ROM ExamView® Pro Testmaker CD-ROM Presentation Plus! CD-ROM

0:00 OUT OF TIME?
Assign the Chapter 19 **Reading Essentials and Study Guide.**

*Also Available in Spanish

 Blackline Master   Transparency   CD-ROM   DVD

Poster   Music Program   Audio Program   Videocassette

KEY TO ABILITY LEVELS

Teaching strategies have been coded.

L1 BASIC activities for all students
L2 AVERAGE activities for average to above-average students
L3 CHALLENGING activities for above-average students
ELL ENGLISH LANGUAGE LEARNER activities

NATIONAL GEOGRAPHIC — Teacher's Corner

INDEX TO NATIONAL GEOGRAPHIC MAGAZINE

The following articles relate to this chapter.

- "Hiroshima," by Ted Gup, August 1995.
- "Pearl Harbor: A Return to the Day of Infamy," by Thomas B. Allen, December 1991.
- "National Trail to Recall Civil Rights Marches," Geographica, March 1994.
- *Vietnam: The Hard Road to Peace*, (A Special Edition), November 1989.
- "Reinventing Berlin," by Peter Ross Range, December 1996.
- "Inside the Kremlin," by Jon Thompson, January 1990.

ADDITIONAL NATIONAL GEOGRAPHIC SOCIETY PRODUCTS

To order the following, call National Geographic at 1-800-368-2728:

- *GeoKit: 20th Century: 1910–1945* (Kit)
- *GeoKit: Eyewitness to the 20th Century* (Book)
- *National Geographic Desk Reference* (Book)
- *1929–1941: The Great Depression* (Video)
- *Capitalism, Communism, Socialism Series* (Video)
- *Branches of Government Series* (Video)

NGS ONLINE

Access National Geographic's Web site for current events, atlas updates, activities, links, interactive features, and archives.

www.nationalgeographic.com

MEETING SPECIAL NEEDS

In addition to the Differentiated Instruction strategies found in each section, the following resources are also suitable for your special needs students:

- *ExamView® Pro Testmaker CD-ROM* allows teachers to tailor tests by reducing answer choices.
- The *Audio Program* includes the entire narrative of the student edition so that less-proficient readers can listen to the words as they read them.
- The *Reading Essentials and Study Guide* provides the same content as the student edition but is written two grade levels below the textbook.
- *Guided Reading Activities* give less-proficient readers point-by-point instructions to increase comprehension as they read each textbook section.

From the Classroom of...

Cheryl Smith-Fountain
Sidney Lanier School
Montgomery, AL

A Civil Rights Tour

Explain to students that Montgomery, Alabama, is considered by some historians to be the birthplace of the modern civil rights movement. Supply students with a Montgomery city map. (This map can be obtained from reference material at the local library, or there are several map resources on the Internet that can easily be printed out.) Have pairs of students research the Chapter 19 contents and other reference materials to find sites in Montgomery that have historical connections with the civil rights movement, such as the Parsonage and the state capitol. After each pair has a list of sites, have students write a description of a tour through the city, giving brief histories of their sites. Each group can present its tour to the class, using maps to show how to travel from one site to the next and explaining the significance of each site.

ADDITIONAL RESOURCES FROM GLENCOE

- American Music: Cultural Traditions
- American Art and Architecture
- Outline Map Resource Book
- U.S. Desk Map
- Building Geography Skills for Life
- Inclusion for the Middle School Social Studies Classroom Strategies and Activities
- Teaching Strategies for the American History Classroom (Including Block Scheduling Pacing Guides)
- American Crafts Hands-On Activities
- American Games Hands-On Activities
- American History Flash Cards

 Block Schedule

Activities that are suited to use within the block scheduling framework are identified by:

Performance Assessment

Refer to Activity 19 in the Performance Assessment Activities and Rubrics booklet.

Why It Matters Activity

Although terrorist attacks have taken place in other parts of the world, terrorist attacks within the United States have been rare. On September 11, 2001, the United States suffered devastating terrorist attacks in New York City and Washington, D.C. **Ask: How do you think the government should deal with terrorism?**

GLENCOE
TECHNOLOGY

The American Republic to 1877 Video Program

To learn more how Americans reacted to the terrorist attacks on September 11, have students view the Chapter 19 video "America Responds to Terrorism" from **The American Republic to 1877 Video Program.**

 Available in DVD and VHS

MindJogger Videoquiz

Use **MindJogger Videoquiz** to preview the Chapter 19 content.

 Available in VHS

CHAPTER
19
The Making of Modern America

1929–Present

Why It Matters

During the twentieth century, Americans suffered through wars and economic and political unrest. The end of the Cold War brought about communism's fall in many parts of the world and the triumph of democracy. A new world was at hand—or so it seemed. Long-hidden national and ethnic rivalries flared into violence in various parts of the world. The threats to peace included acts of terrorism.

Its Impact Today

In the twenty-first century, the world faces great challenges. Acts of terrorism present a threat to freedom and security. Although most nations condemn such acts, terrorism is likely to remain a global concern.

The American Republic to 1877 Video The chapter 19 video, "America Responds to Terrorism," focuses on how Americans united after the events of September 11, 2001.

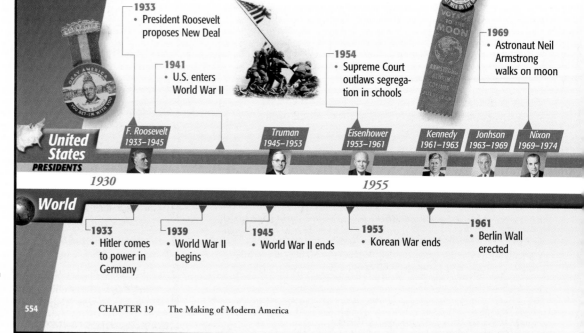

United States PRESIDENTS

- **1933** • President Roosevelt proposes New Deal
- **1941** • U.S. enters World War II
- **1954** • Supreme Court outlaws segregation in schools
- **1969** • Astronaut Neil Armstrong walks on moon

F. Roosevelt 1933–1945 | Truman 1945–1953 | Eisenhower 1953–1961 | Kennedy 1961–1963 | Jonhson 1963–1969 | Nixon 1969–1974

1930 — *1955*

World

- **1933** • Hitler comes to power in Germany
- **1939** • World War II begins
- **1945** • World War II ends
- **1953** • Korean War ends
- **1961** • Berlin Wall erected

554   CHAPTER 19   The Making of Modern America

Reading Strategy   PURPOSE FOR READING

Quick free write is a good way to help students organize their thoughts about the topic of technology. Begin by saying: "The inventions of the late 1800s changed the social and economic landscape of the nation. The industrial growth that followed transformed American business." Have students write for a few minutes on the following: *How would new technology or an invention affect you socially and economically?* **L1**

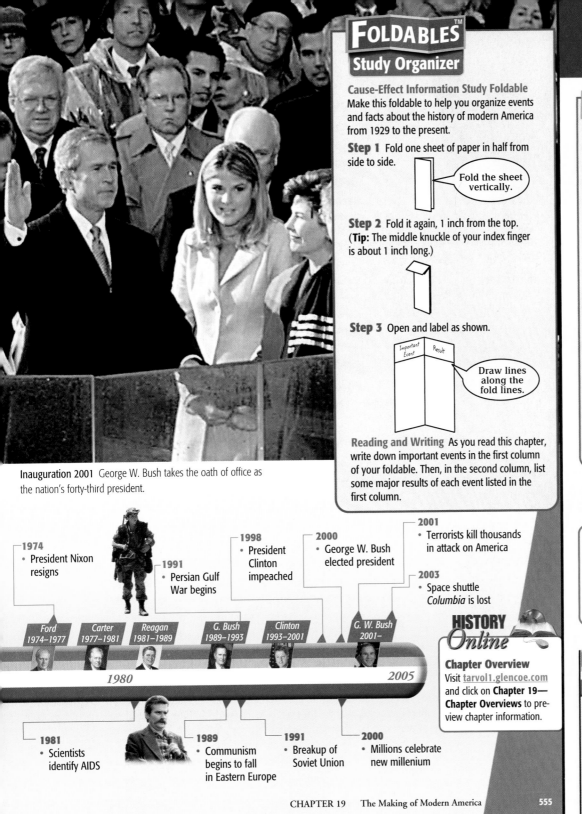

Inauguration 2001 George W. Bush takes the oath of office as the nation's forty-third president.

FOLDABLES™
Study Organizer

Cause-Effect Information Study Foldable
Make this foldable to help you organize events and facts about the history of modern America from 1929 to the present.

Step 1 Fold one sheet of paper in half from side to side.

Fold the sheet vertically.

Step 2 Fold it again, 1 inch from the top. (**Tip:** The middle knuckle of your index finger is about 1 inch long.)

Step 3 Open and label as shown.

Important Event *Result*

Draw lines along the fold lines.

Reading and Writing As you read this chapter, write down important events in the first column of your foldable. Then, in the second column, list some major results of each event listed in the first column.

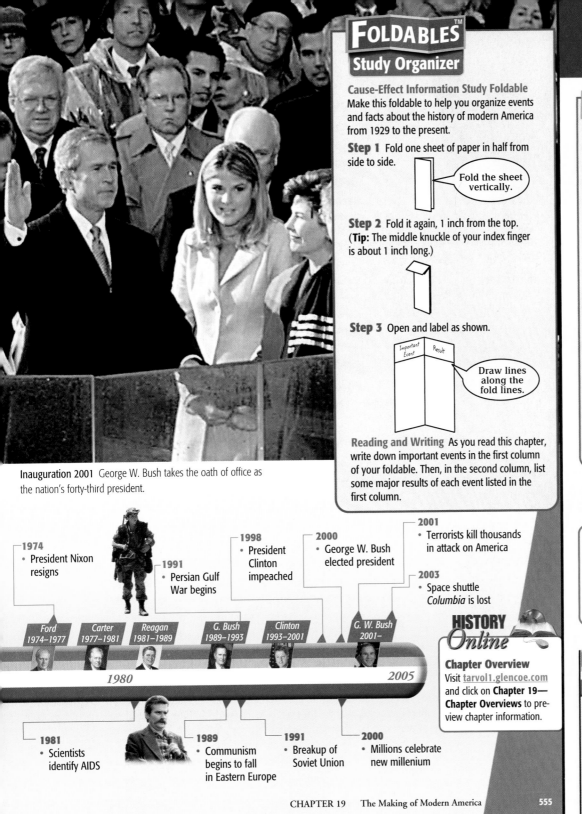

1974
• President Nixon resigns

1991
• Persian Gulf War begins

1998
• President Clinton impeached

2000
• George W. Bush elected president

2001
• Terrorists kill thousands in attack on America

2003
• Space shuttle *Columbia* is lost

Ford 1974–1977

Carter 1977–1981

Reagan 1981–1989

G. Bush 1989–1993

Clinton 1993–2001

G. W. Bush 2001–

1980 *2005*

1981
• Scientists identify AIDS

1989
• Communism begins to fall in Eastern Europe

1991
• Breakup of Soviet Union

2000
• Millions celebrate new millenium

HISTORY Online
Chapter Overview
Visit tarvol1.glencoe.com and click on **Chapter 19— Chapter Overviews** to preview chapter information.

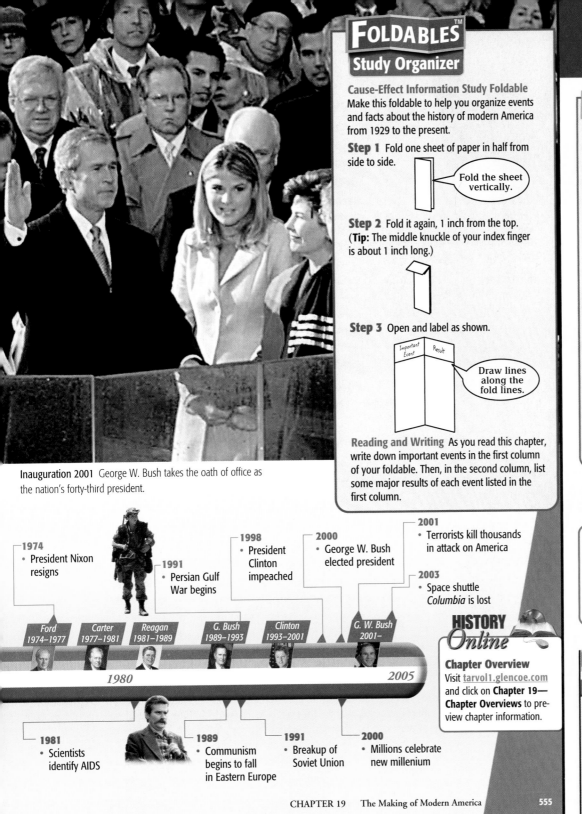

CHAPTER 19 The Making of Modern America **555**

FOLDABLES™
Study Organizer
Dinah Zike's Foldables

Purpose This activity requires students to create a table and organize information from the chapter on it. As students read the chapter, they must select important events, writing them in the first column of the foldable. Then students must determine the results, or effects, of those events, placing that information in the second column of the foldable. Students may include different events on their foldables, but they should be able to explain why they think those events are important in American history.

Have students complete **Reading and Study Skills Foldables** Activity 11. **L1**

HISTORY Online

Introduce students to chapter content and key terms by having them access **Chapter Overview 19** at tarvol1.glencoe.com

TIME LINE
ACTIVITY

As students read the chapter, have them review the time line on pages 554–555. Ask them how events in 1945, 1991, and 2001 may have resulted in major shifts in the focus of United States foreign policy.

More About the Photo

George W. Bush took office after a great deal of controversy over the 2000 presidential election. Although Bush won the electoral vote, he received fewer popular votes than his Democratic opponent, Al Gore, Jr. When George W. Bush was inaugurated, he and his father, George H.W. Bush, became only the second father and son in American history to both serve as president. The other father and son presidents were John Adams and John Quincy Adams.

1 FOCUS

Section Overview

This section describes how President Roosevelt responded to the Great Depression and how the United States joined with allied nations to fight a world war.

BELLRINGER
Skillbuilder Activity

Project transparency and have students answer the question.

Daily Focus Skills Transparency 19–1

Reading Preview

Answers to Graphic: Answers may include: formation of alliances; fear and anger after World War I and the Great Depression; dictators seizing power; and invasions.

Preteaching Vocabulary
Have students use three **Key Terms** in a sentence that describes Germany during World War II.

Depression and a Second World War

Guide to Reading

Main Idea
The United States maintained its free enterprise system during the Great Depression and won victory in a global conflict at great cost.

Key Terms
dictator, genocide, Holocaust, island hopping

Reading Strategy
Organizing Information Re-create the diagram below to identify three causes of World War II.

Causes

→
→ World War II
→

Read to Learn
• how President Roosevelt responded to the Great Depression.
• what actions led to the outbreak of World War II.

Section Theme
Global Connections The United States joined with allied nations to fight a world war to protect rights and freedoms.

Preview of Events

♦1925   ♦1935   ♦1945

1929
Stock market crashes, triggering Great Depression

1939
World War II begins in Europe

1941
Japanese attack Pearl Harbor; U.S. enters the war

1945
World War II ends

AN American Story

Unemployed man seeking work

During the early years of the Great Depression, the number of homeless people in the United States skyrocketed. One woman described her amazement when she first saw how people had to live outside one Midwestern city: "Here were all these people living in old, rusted-out car bodies. There were people living in shacks made of orange crates. . . . This wasn't just a little section, this was maybe ten miles wide and ten miles long. People living in what ever they could junk together."

The Great Depression

The severe economic crisis of the 1930s was called the **Great Depression.** It marked the longest, deepest, and most devastating economic depression ever experienced by the United States.

The bubble of American prosperity burst when the New York stock market collapsed in October 1929. Thousands of investors lost all their savings. Wall Street—the nation's financial center—was in a state of shock. In the booming

---

SECTION RESOURCES

📁 **Reproducible Masters**
• Reproducible Lesson Plan 19–1
• Daily Lecture and Discussion Notes 19–1
• Guided Reading Activity 19–1
• Section Quiz 19–1
• Reteaching Activity 19–1
• Reading Essentials and Study Guide 19–1
• Enrichment Activity 19–1

📄 **Transparencies**
• Daily Focus Skills Transparency 19–1

Multimedia
🔵 Interactive Tutor Self-Assessment CD-ROM
🔵 ExamView® Pro Testmaker CD-ROM
🔵 Presentation Plus! CD-ROM

economy of the 1920s, many people invested money in the stock market. As the value of stocks rose, people began borrowing to buy stocks.

In October 1929, stock prices fell dramatically. Investors panicked and began selling their stocks. Many could not pay back their loans, which weakened the banks. Millions of people lost their savings and their jobs.

The Economy Crumbles

The stock market crash shook people's confidence in the economy. Other factors, working together, sent the economy into a long tailspin.

Farm income shrank. For many farmers, years of dry weather made the situation even worse. In parts of the Great Plains a long drought turned fertile land into a **Dust Bowl.** Many farmers had to give up their land. Many industries declined. In the months before the stock market crash, the automobile and construction industries suffered from lagging orders. As a result, employers cut wages and laid off workers. With their incomes slashed, many Americans could no longer afford the consumer goods that the nation's industries had been churning out.

Borrowed money had fueled much of the economy in the 1920s. Farmers, plagued by low prices since the end of World War I, bought land, equipment, and supplies on credit. Consumers used credit to buy cars. Investors borrowed to buy stocks. Many small banks suffered when consumers defaulted, or failed to meet loan payments. Large banks, which had bought stocks as an investment, suffered huge losses in the stock market crash. These losses forced thousands of banks across the nation to close between 1930 and 1933, and many depositors lost their money.

Weaknesses also sapped the strengths of foreign economies. During the late 1920s, bank funds for loans dried up. International trade slowed down because, without American loans, other nations had less money to spend.

Joblessness and Poverty

As the Depression tightened its grip on the United States, millions lost their jobs. In 1932, about one out of every four workers were out of work. The unemployed felt devastated. One out-of-work man wrote about developing:

> 66a feeling of worthlessness—and loneliness; I began to think of myself as a freak and misfit.99

Long lines of hungry people snaked through the streets of cities, waiting for hours to receive a slice of bread or a bowl of soup donated by local government or charities.

Those who had lost their homes built shelters out of old boxes and other debris. Some referred to these shantytowns as **Hoovervilles** after President Hoover. As the Depression dragged on, many Americans lost faith in their government. They blamed President Hoover for their hard times because none of his policies eased the suffering of massive unemployment.

Roosevelt's New Deal

During the 1932 presidential election, Franklin Delano Roosevelt promised a "new deal for the American people." With the nation's economy crumbling, the American people elected Democrat **Franklin Delano Roosevelt** as president. Roosevelt sent Congress proposals to fight the Depression that collectively became known as the **New Deal**.

Dorothea Lange photographed a homeless Oklahoma family during Dust Bowl days.

Daily Lecture and Discussion Notes 19–1

Creating a Graphic Organizer
Ask students to scan the section to identify the problems that fueled the Great Depression and the New Deal programs that were created to solve them. Then have students create a graphic organizer illustrating these problems and resolutions. **L1**

L1, ELL

Guided Reading Activity 19–1

Reading Strategy — READING THE TEXT

Monitoring Comprehension As students read the section, they might encounter text or information that they do not understand, and they should adjust their reading strategies to clarify the ideas. Model how this is done by reading the section aloud. As you read, say things such as "How far away were most of the battles in the Pacific compared to Japan?" (visualizing); and "What have I heard about the atomic bomb and is it correct based on the information described here?" (activating prior knowledge). Modeling how you read helps students think about strategies they can use as they read independently. **L1**

Answer: Roosevelt's proposals to fight the Depression

What?Where?When?Who?

Civilian Conservation Corps From its start in 1933 until World War II, about 3 million young men worked in the CCC. It provided clothes, shelter, and employment. A CCC worker made $30 a month, $25 of which was sent back home to his family. Other workers became part of the Tennessee Valley Authority, one of the nation's largest and cheapest suppliers of power. Through the work of the TVA, electricity was brought to many rural areas.

Did you know?

One New Deal agency, the National Recovery Administration, encouraged businesses to set a minimum wage and abolish child labor. The owner of Philadelphia's professional football team showed his patriotic spirit in 1933 by naming his club the Eagles, after the symbol of the National Recovery Administration.

you don't say...

Bulls and Bears When the stock market rises, it is called a bull market. If prices drop, it is called a bear market. These terms may come from the way the two animals attack. A bull throws its victims up in the air, and a bear knocks its victims down.

The New Deal created the **Civilian Conservation Corps** (CCC). The CCC put about 3 million young men to work on projects such as planting trees and building levees to prevent floods. It also established the **Public Works Administration** (PWA). The PWA provided jobs by building huge public works, such as roads, hospitals, and schools. The New Deal's **Agricultural Adjustment Administration** (AAA) raised farm prices and controlled farm production.

Roosevelt then asked Congress to pass the **Social Security Act.** This created a tax paid by all employers and workers that was used to pay pensions to retired people. Another tax funded **unemployment insurance**—payments to people who lost their jobs.

Americans seemed better off in 1936 than they had been when Roosevelt took office in 1933. Even so, when FDR began his second term, the Great Depression had not ended. He continued to push for more reform. In 1937 business slowed and another recession hit the nation.

This time Americans blamed Roosevelt and the New Deal. When FDR proposed numerous programs after this, Congress would not cooperate with the President.

Although reform under Roosevelt ended, the New Deal produced lasting effects. It greatly increased the power of the presidency and the size of the federal government. It also established the idea that the federal government is responsible for the welfare of needy Americans. By the late 1930s, the economy had almost recovered. Just as the domestic problems seemed to be ending, however, World War II began.

✓ **Reading Check** **Explaining** What was the New Deal?

World War II

Less than 25 years after World War I, the United States found itself at war again. This war, though, was different from World War I. It was a

The plight of flood victims standing in a relief line contrasts sharply with the family shown on the billboard.

WORLD'S HIGHEST STANDARD OF LIVING

There's no way like the American Way

DIFFERENTIATED INSTRUCTION

Gifted and Talented Have students use the Internet or library resources to compare World War I with World War II. The comparison should include the number of nations participating and their names, the number of soldiers mobilized, the number of lives lost, and the amount of money spent. Students might present their information as an oral report. Charts and graphs illustrating the statistics should accompany the report. **L3**

📂 Refer to *Inclusion for the Middle School Social Studies Classroom Strategies and Activities* in the TCR.

fight for survival, and, before it was over, it involved almost every country in the world. By the end of 1941, 22 countries had already declared their support for the **Allies**—the United States, Great Britain, France, China, and the Soviet Union. The **Axis** Powers—Germany, Italy, and Japan—were also supported by Romania, Bulgaria, and Hungary.

The Road to War

The events leading to World War II began in the 1920s. Several dictators—leaders who control their nations by force—seized power by playing on the fear and anger people felt after World War I and during the Great Depression.

The first dictator to take power was **Benito Mussolini** in Italy. In Germany, many people rallied around **Adolf Hitler**—leader of the National Socialist Worker's Party, or Nazi Party. The Depression also brought military leaders to power in Japan. In 1940, Germany, Italy, and Japan signed a pact and became allies.

In September 1939, Hitler sent his armies into Poland. Two days later, Britain and France declared war on Germany. World War II had begun. Germany's armed forces quickly overran Poland. The following spring, Hitler's troops invaded France, which surrendered a few weeks later. Then, in June 1941, Hitler ordered a massive attack on the Soviet Union.

Japan Attacks Pearl Harbor

Americans watched the war in Europe with concern, but did not want to become involved. Roosevelt promised to stay neutral. He asked Congress to pass the **Lend-Lease Act,** allowing America to sell, lease, or lend weapons to nations whose security was vital to America's defense. Britain and the Soviet Union began receiving lend-lease aid.

While Roosevelt tried to help Britain, Japanese troops seized France's colony of Indochina and threatened nearby British colonies. The United States tried to stop Japan by applying economic pressure. Desperate for resources and confident of Japan's military might, the Japanese government began planning an attack on the United States.

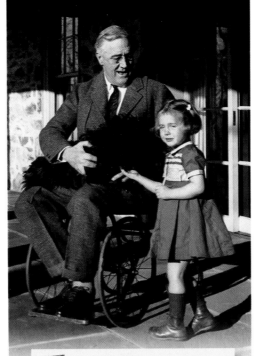

Picturing **History**

Franklin D. Roosevelt, who was paralyzed by polio as a young man, is shown with Ruth Bie, the daughter of the caretaker at FDR's estate. **Through what two of the nation's great crises did Roosevelt serve as president?**

On December 7, 1941, Japanese warplanes attacked the American naval base at **Pearl Harbor,** Hawaii. The attack enraged Americans. The next day, Roosevelt went before Congress. Calling December 7 "a day which will live in infamy," he asked for a declaration of war on Japan. On December 11, Germany and Italy declared war on the United States. The United States then joined the Allies—Great Britain, France, and the Soviet Union—against the Axis powers.

On the Home Front

By the time the United States entered the war, the fighting had already been going on for more than two years, and it was to continue for almost four more. The war years had a deep effect on Americans and on the nation as a whole. Out of the war came new technology, a new prosperity, and a new sense of power and strength.

CHAPTER 19   The Making of Modern America   **559**

Did you know

The Great Depression put once affluent individuals in unemployment lines alongside factory workers and actors. Breadlines over a block long became a symbol of the times. Many people placed newspapers under their clothes to stay warm in the winter or stuffed cardboard into their shoes to hide the holes.

CURRICULUM CONNECTION

Economics Because of a surplus of apples, the International Shippers Association set up a system for unemployed people to sell apples. A person could get credit for $1.75 to buy 100 to 120 apples. The person would then sell each apple for 5 cents, making a small profit.

INTERDISCIPLINARY CONNECTIONS ACTIVITY

Civics Each state has a state department charged with helping individuals and families in need, such as identifying individuals in need of financial assistance, maintaining the welfare of children, and assisting individuals with disabilities. Invite an official from your local Department of Human Services to speak to your class. Have the class prepare a set of questions to ask the official. Have the official discuss programs available to those in need. Ask students to write a one-page essay summarizing what they learned. **L2**

Geography *Skills*

Answers:
1. the northern coast of France (Normandy)
2. July 10, 1943

Geography Skills Practice
Ask: Where did the British defeat the German tank division in 1942?
(El Alamein, Egypt)

Who?What?Where?When?

Jeannette Rankin Jeannette Rankin, the first woman elected to Congress, was the only member of the House to cast a dissenting vote against American entry into both World War I and World War II. A statue of Rankin now stands in the Capitol in Washington, D.C., bearing the motto: "I cannot vote for war."

Did you know?

After Germany turned its attention from Britain to an invasion of the Soviet Union, Roosevelt extended aid to the Russians under Lend-Lease. No terms were ever established after World War II, however, for the return of the billions of dollars worth of goods transferred to the Soviet Union under Lend-Lease. But in 1993, Russia agreed to pay the World War II Lend-Lease debt of the former Soviet Union and started making payments in 1994.

NATIONAL GEOGRAPHIC **World War II in Europe and Africa**

Allied Forces
Major Axis powers
Greatest extent of Axis control
Allied or Ally-controlled
Neutral nations

D-Day June 6, 1944
FINAL SOVIET DRIVE July-Aug., 1944
Aug. 15, 1944
Nov. 8, 1942
July 10, 1943
1942 - The British defeat the German tank division at El Alamein.

Geography *Skills*

1. **Place** Where did the Allied forces land on D-Day?
2. **Analyzing Information** When did Allied forces invade Sicily?

After Pearl Harbor, millions of Americans rushed to enlist in the armed forces. Those who remained at home had to provide food, shelter, training, and medical care for all those in uniform.

During the war, industry expanded rapidly. Incomes rose and unemployment fell. For the first time, a large number of women—about 350,000—served in the military. At the same time, far more women than ever before entered the work force.

The war also created new opportunities for African Americans—in the armed forces and in the nation's war factories. Although many minority groups made gains during the war, Japanese Americans experienced discrimination after the attack on Pearl Harbor. Worried about their loyalty, the government forced Japanese Americans on the West Coast to relocate to **internment camps.**

The War in Europe and the Mediterranean

Until late in 1942, the Axis held the upper hand in Eastern and Western Europe and in North Africa. In November, British and American

CRITICAL THINKING ACTIVITY

Predicting Consequences The United States had maintained a position of neutrality during World War II until the Japanese attacked Pearl Harbor. Ask students to write short essays describing how such neutrality could have affected the outcome of the war and the shape of the world today. Have several students with different points of view read their essays in class. Use the views stated in the essays as the basis for a class discussion. **L2**

troops landed in North Africa, which was then under German control. After driving the Germans out of North Africa, the British and Americans made plans to invade southern Europe. The Axis also suffered severe defeat in Eastern Europe in early 1943. Soviet forces freed the Russian city of Leningrad and forced the German army at **Stalingrad,** exhausted by months of heavy fighting, to surrender.

Italian Campaign

In the summer of 1943 the Allies took control of the island of Sicily and landed on the Italian mainland in September. As the Allies advanced, the Italians overthrew dictator Benito Mussolini and surrendered. However, German forces in Italy continued to fight.

The Allies encountered bitter resistance at **Monte Cassino** in central Italy and at **Anzio,** a seaport near Rome. German forces kept the Allies pinned down on the beaches at Anzio for four months. The Allies finally broke through the German lines and liberated Rome in June 1944.

Audie Murphy, most decorated soldier of WWII

Air War Over Germany

While fighting raged in North Africa and Italy, the Allies launched an air war against Germany. The bombing caused massive destruction in many German cities and killed thousands of German civilians. Yet the attacks failed to crack Germany's determination to win the war.

D-Day

As the Soviets pushed toward Germany from the east, the Allies were planning a massive invasion of France from the west. General **Dwight Eisenhower,** the commander of Allied forces in Europe, directed this invasion, known as Operation Overlord.

On June 6, 1944—**D-Day**—Allied ships landed thousands of troops on the coast of Normandy. After wading ashore the troops faced land mines

and fierce fire from the Germans. From Normandy, the Allies pushed across France. On August 25, French and American soldiers marched through joyful crowds and liberated Paris.

Victory in Europe

Germany fought for survival on two fronts. In the east the Soviets pushed the Germans out of eastern Europe. In the west the British and Americans approached the German border.

In December 1944, the Germans mounted a last desperate offensive. In the **Battle of the Bulge** the Germans at first drove troops and artillery deep into a bulge in the Allied lines. After several weeks the Allies pushed the Germans back. The battle, resulting in at least 100,000 casualties, marked the end of serious German resistance.

By April 1945, Soviet troops had reached Berlin, and British and American forces were sweeping across western Germany. On April 30, 1945, Adolf Hitler committed suicide. One week later, Germany surrendered.

President Roosevelt did not share in the Allied victory celebration. Less than four weeks earlier, he had died. His vice president, **Harry S Truman,** succeeded him.

The Holocaust

As the Allies liberated Germany and other parts of Europe, they found horrifying evidence of Nazi brutality. The Nazis hated Jews and committed genocide—the killing of an entire group of people. They built death camps where they killed thousands of Jews every day in gas chambers. As many as 6 million Jews died in what became known as the Holocaust.

War in the Pacific

Soon after the attack on Pearl Harbor, Japanese forces landed in the Philippines. Filipino and American troops commanded by General **Douglas MacArthur** were forced to retreat to the rugged Bataan Peninsula west of Manila and the small island of Corregidor. After months of

HISTORY.
Online
Student Web Activity
Visit tarvol1.glencoe.com and click on **Chapter 19 —Student Web Activities** for an activity on World War II.

HISTORY
Online

Objectives and answers to the student activity can be found in the **Web Activity Lesson Plan** feature at tarvol1.glencoe.com

Who?What?Where?When?

Charles Drew Charles Drew, an African American, was the first medical director of the American Red Cross Blood Bank. He received the NAACP's Spingarn Medal for his research in both American and British blood plasma projects. Through his research a dry plasma method of storage was developed, allowing for extended use of plasma on the battlefields of World War II and the saving of many lives.

you don't say...

WASPs Although women were not allowed to serve in combat, they were pilots. Members of the Women's Airforce Service Pilots (WASPs) flew warplanes to the places where they were needed, freeing men for combat duty. The obstacles women faced were enormous. Resentful males often refused to fly with them, and in one case a male pilot may have sabotaged a plane, killing a female pilot. WASPs flew more than 60 million miles in all types of planes, and 38 WASPs died while on duty.

EXTENDING THE CONTENT

Dust Bowl The Dust Bowl emerged from 300,000 square miles of Great Plains territory that had been stripped of its protective buffalo grass. The first of the great dust storms began on November 11, 1933. "Black blizzards" swept the region, carrying off much-needed topsoil. One "blizzard" blew away 300 million tons of topsoil. The dust storms continued on and off for 10 years. The westerly winds carried the dust and deposited it on ships as far as 300 miles away on the Atlantic Ocean.

Geography Skills

Answers:

1. Manchuria, a large part of the northeast, and the coast
2. Hiroshima, Nagasaki

3 ASSESS

Assign Section 1 Assessment as homework or as an in-class activity.

Have students use **Interactive Tutor Self-Assessment CD-ROM.**

L2

Section Quiz 19–1

L1

Reteaching Activity 19–1

fierce fighting, the exhausted Allied troops there surrendered. The Japanese forced their Bataan prisoners—many sick and near starvation—to march to a prison camp more than 60 miles away. Many died on the way.

With Japan's string of quick victories, American morale was low. In May 1942 American and Japanese fleets clashed in the Coral Sea northeast of Australia. American ships were heavily damaged, but the Japanese suffered crippling losses. The **Battle of the Coral Sea** halted the Japanese advance on Australia.

An even greater victory followed in June. In the **Battle of Midway,** northwest of Hawaii, the American navy destroyed four Japanese aircraft carriers and hundreds of airplanes. This was the first major Japanese defeat.

The United States then adopted a strategy known as island hopping—seizing an island and using it as a base to attack the next island.

Between August 1942 and February 1943, American forces engaged in one of the most fierce campaigns of war for control of **Guadalcanal,** one of the Solomon Islands. With superior air and naval power, the Americans finally secured the island.

Taken in June 1944, Guam and other nearby islands provided a base for launching bombing strikes on Japan. In October, American ships destroyed most of the Japanese fleet at the **Battle of Leyte Gulf** in the Philippines.

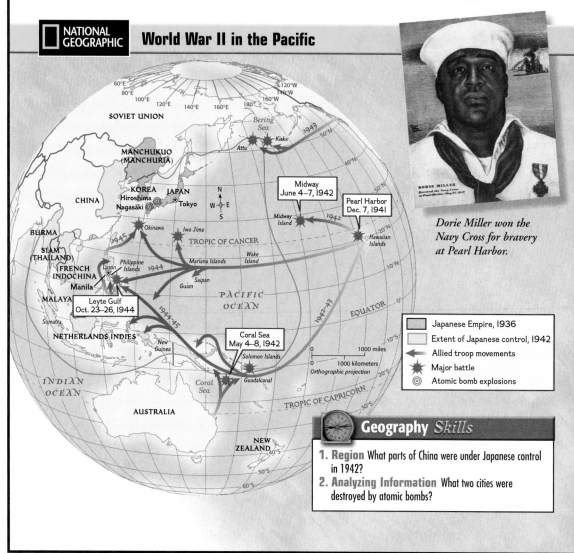

NATIONAL GEOGRAPHIC World War II in the Pacific

Dorie Miller won the Navy Cross for bravery at Pearl Harbor.

Geography Skills

1. **Region** What parts of China were under Japanese control in 1942?
2. **Analyzing Information** What two cities were destroyed by atomic bombs?

EXTENDING THE CONTENT

Dorie Miller During World War II, Doris "Dorie" Miller enlisted in the United States Navy as Mess Attendant at a time when African Americans could only serve in the steward's branch. Eventually, he was promoted to Ship's Cook, Third Class. During the attack on Pearl Harbor on December 7, 1941, Miller took over a machine gun aboard the battleship *West Virginia*, and fired upon attacking Japanese planes. He manned the gun without assistance until it ran out of ammunition, after which he was ordered to abandon ship. On May 27, 1942, honored as one of the first heroes of World War II, Miller received the Navy Cross.

American forces now closed in on Japan itself. In March 1945 they seized the island of **Iwo Jima** and in June the island of **Okinawa,** the last stop before invading Japan itself. Before the invasion took place, however, the United States decided to use a new weapon—the atomic bomb.

At the urging of Albert Einstein, President Roosevelt had begun the **Manhattan Project,** a top-secret attempt to build an atomic bomb. After the bomb was ready, President Truman demanded that Japan surrender. When Japan refused, Truman ordered the use of the bomb.

The United States dropped two atomic bombs in August 1945. The first destroyed the city of Hiroshima. The second destroyed the city of Nagasaki. After the bombings, Japan agreed to surrender. August 15—**V-J Day,** for "Victory over Japan"—marked the end of World War II.

After the War

World War II was the costliest and most destructive war ever. At least 50 million soldiers and civilians died—more than during any other war. The war devastated billions of dollars worth of property. Life in some countries would not return to normal for many years.

Hitler had appealed to national pride and racial hatred in Germany, using force to silence all opposition. Hitler's Nazi party blamed Ger-

Raising the flag at Iwo Jima

many's economic problems on its Jewish population and killed nearly 6 million Jews and millions of other people in concentration camps.

People from all over the world looked for ways to prevent such a terrible conflict from happening again. Many believed that an international organization dedicated to freedom and cooperation could ensure peace. The American people looked forward to a future in which peace would be preserved. However, they would soon be disappointed.

✓ **Reading Check** **Identifying** What event occurred on December 7, 1941? What did this event lead to?

SECTION 1 ASSESSMENT

Checking for Understanding

1. **Key Terms** Write a short paragraph in which you use all of the following key terms: dictator, genocide, Holocaust.
2. **Reviewing Facts** Who was president of the United States when World War II began? Who was president when it ended?

Reviewing Themes

3. **Global Connections** What did the Lend-Lease Act, supported by Roosevelt, provide?

Critical Thinking

4. **Determining Cause and Effect** How did the role of government in American democracy change as a result of the Depression and the New Deal?
5. **Organizing Information** Create a diagram like the one shown here and identify three causes of the Great Depression.

Great Depression

Analyzing Visuals

6. **Geography Skills** Examine the maps on page 560 and page 562. What are the topics of the maps? Did Japanese control in 1942 include the Philippine Islands? The Hawaiian Islands? Was Finland under Axis control at one time or another? Was France? How can you tell?

Interdisciplinary Activity

Language Arts Write newspaper headlines about three important events covered in Section 1.

SECTION 1 ASSESSMENT ANSWERS

1. Student work should reflect correct use of terms.
2. Franklin Roosevelt; Harry Truman
3. It allowed the U.S. to sell, lease, or lend weapons to nations whose security was vital to America's defense.
4. more government intervention; work relief and assistance

programs; social security benefits; regulation of banking and business
5. Answers may include any three of the following: buying on credit, stock market crash, industries slowed, lagging orders, international trade slumps.
6. World War II in Europe and Africa; World War II in the Pacific; yes;

no; yes; yes; by looking at the key, which shows the greatest extent of Axis control

Interdisciplinary Activity Headlines should announce three important events covered in Section 1.

✓ **Reading Check**

Answer: Japanese attack on Pearl Harbor; United States entry into World War II

L1, ELL

Reading Essentials and Study Guide 19–1

Study Guide

Chapter 19, Section 1

For use with textbook pages 556–563

Depression and a Second World War

KEY TERMS	
dictator	A leader who controls a country by force *(page 559)*
genocide	The killing of an entire group of people *(page 561)*
Holocaust	The killing of about six million Jews by the Germans during World War II *(page 561)*
island hopping	Seizing an island and using it as a base to attack the next island *(page 562)*

DRAWING FROM EXPERIENCE

What do you know about the Holocaust? Have you read any books or watched any movies about the Holocaust?
This section focuses on how the United States and other Allied nations fought to protect rights and freedoms during World War II.

ORGANIZING YOUR THOUGHTS

Use the chart below to help you take notes as you read the summaries that follow. Think about how Americans were affected by the Great Depression and World War II.

President Roosevelt's New Deal

L3

Enrichment Activity 19–1

Name _____ Date _____ Class _____

★ **Enrichment Activity 19-1** ★

The Four Freedoms Speech

In 1941 President Franklin D. Roosevelt made this speech:

In the future days which we seek to make secure, we look forward to a world founded upon four essential human freedoms.

The first is freedom of speech and expression—everywhere in the world.

The second is freedom of every person to worship God in his own way—everywhere in the world.

The third is freedom from want—which translated into world terms, means economic understandings which will secure to every nation a

4 CLOSE

Have students work in pairs. One partner is to list the causes of the Depression, and the other of World War II. Then the partners should agree that the lists are complete or modify them.

1 FOCUS

Section Overview

This section describes how communism and civil rights affected United States foreign and domestic policies.

Reading Preview

Answers to Graphic: 1948: formation of West Germany; 1953: cease-fire ends Korean conflict; 1954: *Brown* v. *Board of Education* ends segregation; 1964: Congress passes Civil Rights Act; 1973: United States troops leave South Vietnam

Preteaching Vocabulary
Ask volunteers to define the terms *civil* and *disobedience*. Based on the definitions given, have students discuss possible meanings of the term *civil disobedience*.

SECTION 2 Turning Points

Guide to Reading

Main Idea
During the second half of the twentieth century, Americans struggled with communism abroad and civil rights at home.

Key Terms
stalemate, affluence, segregation, civil disobedience, feminist

Reading Strategy
Sequencing Information Create a time line like the one below and identify key events in the postwar world.

1948   1953   1954   1964   1973

Read to Learn
- how the United States attempted to stop the spread of communism.
- what actions African Americans took to secure their rights.

Section Theme
Civic Rights and Responsibilities
American minorities and women intensified their efforts to secure their full rights as citizens.

Preview of Events

◆1945   ◆1955   ◆1965   ◆1975

1950 Korean War begins
1959 Fidel Castro takes over Cuba
1963 President Kennedy is assassinated
1973 U.S. ends role in Vietnam

AN American Story

The three most powerful men in the world met around a conference table in Yalta to discuss the fate of the postwar world. President Roosevelt hoped to promote his vision of postwar cooperation. Prime Minister Churchill spoke elegantly and forcefully. Soviet leader Stalin remained stubbornly opposed to much of what was proposed. Stalin said to his aides: "They want to force us to accept their plans on Europe and the world. Well, that's not going to happen." As the Allies discovered, Stalin had his own plans.

Big Three at Yalta

The Cold War Era

As World War II ended, a bitter rivalry developed between the United States and the Soviet Union. It was known as the **Cold War.** The problems leading to the Cold War began when Stalin refused to allow promised free elections in Eastern Europe. Instead, the Soviets set up communist governments. In response, the new American president, Harry S Truman, announced a new policy in 1947. The **Truman Doctrine** was a commitment to help nations resist communism.

In June 1948, the United States, Great Britain, and France united the zones of Germany they controlled to form a new nation, which became West Germany. To protest this decision, the Soviet Union sealed off Berlin, which was in the East

---

SECTION RESOURCES

📁 **Reproducible Masters**
- Reproducible Lesson Plan 19–2
- Daily Lecture and Discussion Notes 19–2
- Guided Reading Activity 19–2
- Section Quiz 19–2
- Reteaching Activity 19–2
- Reading Essentials and Study Guide 19–2
- Enrichment Activity 19–2

🖨 **Transparencies**
- Daily Focus Skills Transparency 19–2

Multimedia
- 💿 Interactive Tutor Self-Assessment CD-ROM
- 💿 ExamView® Pro Testmaker CD-ROM
- 💿 Presentation Plus! CD-ROM

German sector. President Truman responded with an airlift to bring food, fuel, and other supplies to Berlin. In April 1949, the United States, Canada, and the countries of Western Europe created the **North Atlantic Treaty Organization** (NATO)—a mutual defense pact.

The Korean War

The Cold War was not limited to Europe. In 1949, **Mao Zedong** formed a new communist government in China. Shortly afterward, American troops found themselves fighting Mao's forces in Korea.

Korean Service Medal

In June 1950, the communist nation of North Korea invaded South Korea. American and United Nations (UN) forces came to South Korea's defense. As they pushed the North Koreans back, China intervened. Huge numbers of Chinese troops drove the UN troops back into South Korea.

The UN forces eventually stopped the Chinese, then pushed them back to the border between North and South Korea. The war then became a stalemate—a situation in which neither side could win. A cease-fire agreement was finally reached in July 1953. After years of fighting, Korea remained divided. By fighting in Korea, the United States showed that it would willingly fight to halt communist expansion.

Eisenhower's Administration

Although international relations between the United States and the Soviet Union remained tense in the 1950s, the American economy generated a new level of prosperity.

In 1952, Republican Dwight D. Eisenhower won the presidential election. Eisenhower wanted to make the federal government smaller, but he believed that the government should protect the basic welfare of all Americans. He expanded Social Security and approved greater funding for public housing for poor people.

The Nation Expands

The greatest domestic program of the Eisenhower presidency involved building a network of interstate highways. In June 1956 Congress passed the Federal Highway Act to provide easy transportation for military forces in case of an attack. The law funded the construction of more than 40,000 miles of highways that tied the nation together.

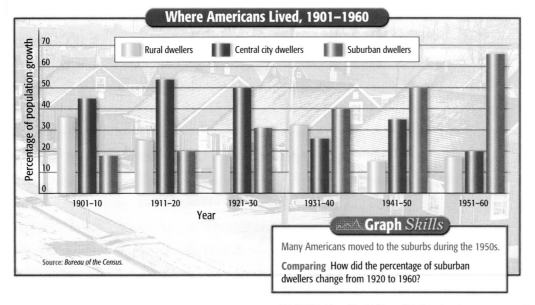

Where Americans Lived, 1901–1960

Rural dwellers | Central city dwellers | Suburban dwellers

Percentage of population growth (y-axis: 0, 10, 20, 30, 40, 50, 60, 70)

Year (x-axis: 1901–10, 1911–20, 1921–30, 1931–40, 1941–50, 1951–60)

Source: *Bureau of the Census.*

Graph Skills

Many Americans moved to the suburbs during the 1950s.

Comparing How did the percentage of suburban dwellers change from 1920 to 1960?

2 TEACH

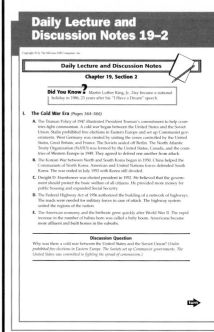

Daily Lecture and Discussion Notes 19–2

Copyright © by The McGraw-Hill Companies, Inc.

Daily Lecture and Discussion Notes

Chapter 19, Section 2

Did You Know? Martin Luther King, Jr., Day became a national holiday in 1986, 23 years after his "I Have a Dream" speech.

I. The Cold War Era *(Pages 564–566)*

A. The Truman Policy of 1947 illustrated President Truman's commitment to help countries fight communism. A cold war began between the United States and the Soviet Union. Stalin prohibited free elections in Eastern Europe and set up Communist governments. West Germany was created by uniting the zones controlled by the United States, Great Britain, and France. The Soviets sealed off Berlin. The North Atlantic Treaty Organization (NATO) was formed by the United States, Canada, and the countries of Western Europe in 1949. They agreed to defend one another from attack.

B. The Korean War between North and South Korea began in 1950. China helped the Communists of North Korea. American and United Nations forces defended South Korea. The war ended in July 1953 with Korea still divided.

C. Dwight D. Eisenhower was elected president in 1952. He believed that the government should protect the basic welfare of all citizens. He provided more money for public housing and expanded Social Security.

D. The Federal Highway Act of 1956 authorized the building of a network of highways. The roads were needed for military forces in case of attack. The highway system united the regions of the nation.

E. The American economy and the birthrate grew quickly after World War II. The rapid increase in the number of babies born was called a baby boom. Americans became more affluent and built homes in the suburbs.

Discussion Question

Why was there a cold war between the United States and the Soviet Union? *(Stalin prohibited free elections in Eastern Europe. The Soviets set up Communist governments. The United States was committed to fighting the spread of communism.)*

Responding to a Quote Share with students this statement from President Truman: "History will remember my term of office as the years when the cold war began to overshadow our lives." Discuss the effectiveness of his words in describing the United States's postwar concerns about the Soviet Union. **L1**

Graph Skills

Answer: It increased by approximately 45 percent.

Reading Strategy   READING THE TEXT

Identifying the Main Idea Students should identify main ideas as they read. Text features, such as headings, subheadings, boldfaced terms, and graphics, are good indicators of main or key ideas. As students read the section, have them make a list of ideas by creating an outline or drawing a graphic organizer. **L1**

Guided Reading Activity 19–2

Name _____ Date _____ Class _____

★ Guided Reading Activity **19-2**

DIRECTIONS: Recalling the Facts Use the information in your textbook to answer the questions. Use another sheet of paper if necessary.

1. What was the Truman Doctrine? _____
2. Who won the 1952 presidential election? _____
3. Where did American troops fight Mao Zedong's forces? _____
4. What was the goal of the Federal Highway Act? _____
5. When did Alaska and Hawaii enter the Union? _____
6. What was the ruling of the Supreme Court in *Brown v. Board of Education*?
_____
7. What civil rights law did President Lyndon B. Johnson persuade Congress to pass?
_____
8. Who was assassinated on April 4, 1968? _____
9. What groups found inspiration in the struggle of African Americans for equal rights? _____
10. Who organized thousands of Hispanic migrant farm workers into the United Farm Workers? _____
11. When did Congress pass the Indian Civil Rights Act? _____
12. Who seized power in Cuba in 1959? _____
13. What did the Berlin Wall symbolize? _____
14. How many American troops were in Vietnam by the end of 1968? _____
15. What was President Nixon's plan to achieve "peace with honor" called? _____
16. What reaction did the Cambodian invasion spark? _____
17. How many Vietnamese died between 1965 and 1975 due to the Vietnam War? _____

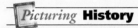

Picturing **History**

Answer: *Brown* v. *Board of Education*

✔ **Reading Check**

Answer: North Atlantic Treaty Organization; members pledge to defend one another in case of attack

Did you know?

Because Congress never declared war, the United States involvement in the Korean struggle has never been officially called a "war," but rather a "conflict."

The nation itself also grew during Eisenhower's presidency. In 1959 Alaska and Hawaii entered the Union, bringing the number of states to 50.

1950s Prosperity

After World War II, the American economy began to grow very rapidly. This rapid growth increased Americans' affluence, or wealth, and also led to the baby boom—a dramatic increase in the nation's birthrate.

During the 1950s, many new homes were built in the suburbs. Usually located on the fringes of major cities, suburban housing developments appealed to many Americans. In addition to affordable homes, they offered privacy, space, and a sense of belonging to a community.

✔ **Reading Check** **Identifying** What does NATO stand for? What is its purpose?

The Civil Rights Era

After World War II, many African Americans began to fight for equal opportunity in jobs, housing, and education, and for an end to segregation—the separation of people of different races.

The Civil Rights Movement

The modern civil rights movement began in the early 1950s. **Thurgood Marshall,** an African American lawyer, brought a case to the Supreme Court challenging segregation in schools. In 1954, in the case of *Brown v. Board of Education,* the Supreme Court ruled that segregation in schools was unconstitutional.

In December 1955, a woman named **Rosa Parks** was arrested in Montgomery, Alabama, for refusing to leave a section of a bus reserved for white people. Shortly afterward, African Americans in Montgomery began to **boycott**— to refuse to use—the city's buses. Finally, in 1956, the Supreme Court ruled that all segregated buses were unconstitutional.

At the meeting to organize the boycott, a young minister named **Dr. Martin Luther King, Jr.,** emerged as one of the leaders of the civil rights movement. King believed that African Americans should use nonviolent protests and civil disobedience, or the refusal to obey laws that are considered unjust.

Kennedy and Johnson

As the civil rights movement grew, Americans prepared for the 1960 presidential election. The Republicans nominated Vice President **Richard Nixon,** the Democrats Senator **John F. Kennedy.** The election was close, but Kennedy won.

Picturing **History**

The Supreme Court ruled that it was unconstitutional to separate schoolchildren by race, but African American students faced difficulties trying to attend previously all-white schools. **What Court ruling said that segregated schools were against the law?**

Dr. Martin Luther King, Jr.

DIFFERENTIATED INSTRUCTION

At-Risk Students According to the domino theory, if one country fell to communism, its neighboring countries might also follow. Ask students to demonstrate the domino theory by first labeling real dominoes with names of countries in Asia, Europe, and Africa. Students should then set up a display of the dominoes in the order that American leaders thought communism would take hold. Knock over one domino that will topple them all. Encourage students to explain the meaning of the domino theory in their own words. **L1**

Refer to *Inclusion for the Middle School Social Studies Classroom Strategies and Activities* in the TCR.

Kennedy proposed more government spending on education and a program to help poor people get jobs. Congress refused to pass most of Kennedy's proposals, believing they cost too much money. On November 22, 1963, during a visit to Dallas, Texas, President Kennedy was shot and killed. Vice President **Lyndon Johnson** became president.

Lyndon Johnson outlined a set of programs called the **"Great Society."** Perhaps the most important laws passed as part of the Great Society were those establishing **Medicare** and **Medicaid.** Medicare helped pay for medical care for senior citizens. Medicaid helped poor people pay for their hospital bills.

The Struggle Continues

During Kennedy's and Johnson's administrations, the civil rights movement continued to grow. In February 1960, four African American students refused to leave a lunch counter in Greensboro, North Carolina, that was reserved for white people. This was the beginning of the **sit-in** movement. Protestors would show up where they were excluded and refuse to leave.

In 1963, Dr. Martin Luther King, Jr., led a march in Birmingham, Alabama. After police attacked the marchers, President Kennedy sent a civil rights bill to Congress to outlaw segregation. To rally support for the bill, many civil rights organizations organized a march on Washington, D.C., in August 1963. Late in the afternoon, King spoke to the crowd in ringing words of his desire to see America transformed:

> ❝I have a dream that one day this nation will rise up and live out the true meaning of its creed: 'We hold these truths to be self-evident; that all men are created equal.'...❞

Southern Democrats blocked Kennedy's civil rights bill. Johnson eventually persuaded Congress to pass the **Civil Rights Act of 1964,** which outlawed discrimination in hiring and banned segregation. The next year, African Americans organized a march in Selma, Alabama, to demand the right to vote. Police again attacked the marchers, and President Johnson asked Congress to pass the **Voting Rights Act of 1965.**

Other Voices

By the mid-1960s the civil rights movement had won many victories. Yet a growing number of African Americans grew tired of the slow pace of change.

Malcolm X, a leader in the Nation of Islam (or Black Muslims), emerged as an important new voice. He criticized integration, declaring that the best way to achieve justice was for African Americans to separate themselves from whites. Later, instead of racial separation, Malcolm X called for "a society in which there could exist honest white-black brotherhood." He was shot and killed in February 1965.

Riots broke out in many major cities during the mid-1960s. In the summer of 1965 violent conflict broke out in the Watts section of Los Angeles. In a week of rioting 34 people died and much of Watts burned to the ground. Between 1965 and 1967 riots broke out in many American cities, including San Francisco and Chicago. In July 1967 urban riots devastated neighborhoods and buildings in Newark, New Jersey, and Detroit, Michigan.

On April 4, 1968, racial tension took another tragic turn. An assassin shot and killed Dr. Martin Luther King, Jr. King's assassination set off angry rioting in more than 100 cities.

Other Groups Seek Rights

Women, Hispanics, and Native Americans found inspiration in the struggle of African Americans for equal rights. In 1966, feminists—activists for women's rights—formed the National Organization for Women. NOW fought for equal rights for women in all aspects of life. They campaigned for an **Equal Rights Amendment** (ERA) to the Constitution, but were unable to get the states to ratify it.

Despite the defeat of the ERA, women did make progress. In 1972 the federal government outlawed discrimination against women in educational programs receiving federal funds.

In the 1960s the rapidly growing Hispanic population sought equal rights. The term Hispanic American refers to those Americans who have come, or are descended from others who have come, to the United States from the nations

What?Where?When?Who?

Professional Sports In 1947 Jackie Robinson became the first African American to play major-league baseball. Other professional sports integrated at different times. Professional football, for example, had its first African American player (Charles W. Follis) in 1904, and African American prize fighters and jockeys had been successful before that. It was not until 1950 that an African American, Charles "Chuck" Cooper, was signed to play on a National Basketball Association team.

Did you know?

Edward Teller, the chief developer of the hydrogen bomb, advocated more testing of such weapons. He said, "It won't be until the bombs get so big that they can annihilate everything that people will really become terrified and begin to take a reasonable line in politics."

INTERDISCIPLINARY CONNECTIONS ACTIVITY

Civics Ask students if they believe discrimination (racial or otherwise) still exists in the United States. Have students support an answer to this question by providing an illustration or a photo. If students believe that discrimination continues today, their illustration or photo should demonstrate evidence of it. Students who believe that discrimination does not exist should show an everyday example of cooperation between people with obvious differences. Work with students to prepare a display of the visuals, and follow up with a class discussion. **L1**

CURRICULUM CONNECTION

Civics Increased Native American activism led to several important court decisions. In one, the Pueblo people of Taos, New Mexico, regained Blue Lake, a place sacred to their religious life. In 1975 a federal court declared that the Passamaquoddy and Penobscot nations had a valid claim to more than half the state of Maine—and to $81.5 million in damages and unpaid rents.

Did you know?

Some college students showed their unhappiness over the Vietnam War by staging teach-ins, or all-night sessions in which students, faculty, and guest speakers denounced the war. Other students occupied college administration buildings, held school officials captive, and then used the media attention to state their cases.

of Latin America and Spain. In the early 1960s, migrant workers formed unions to fight for better wages and working conditions. Their leader, **César Chávez,** organized thousands of farmworkers into the United Farm Workers (UFW). The efforts of Chávez called attention to the migrant workers' cause. Others besides Chávez worked to secure equal rights for Hispanic Americans. Hispanic men and women organized to fight discrimination and to elect Hispanics to government posts. The League of United Latin American Citizens won suits in federal court to guarantee Hispanic Americans the right to serve on juries and to send their children to unsegregated schools.

The Americans with Disabilities Act of 1990 requires institutions to provide disabled people with easier access to public transportation.

Native Americans

In the 1960s Native Americans demanded political power. In 1968 Congress passed the Indian Civil Rights Act, which formally protected the constitutional rights of all Native Americans. At the same time, the new law recognized the right of Native American nations to make laws on their own reservations.

Believing the process of change too slow, some Native Americans began taking stronger action. In February 1973 members of the **American Indian Movement** (AIM) seized Wounded Knee, South Dakota, the site of the 1890 massacre of the Sioux by federal troops. Wounded Knee was part of a large Sioux reservation. The people there suffered from terrible poverty and ill health. After several months, the siege ended, but it focused national attention on the terrible living conditions of many Native Americans.

Americans With Disabilities

People with disabilities also sought equal treatment in the 1960s and 1970s. Congress responded by passing a number of laws. One law concerned the removal of barriers that prevented some people from gaining access to public facilities. Another law required employers to offer more opportunities for disabled people in the workplace. Yet another asserted the right of children with disabilities to equal educational opportunities.

✔ **Reading Check** **Analyzing** What did the Supreme Court rule in *Brown* v. *Board of Education*?

The Vietnam Era

Even as the civil rights movement tried to remake American society at home, the United States continued to struggle against communism abroad, particularly in Vietnam.

Kennedy's Foreign Policy

In 1959, **Fidel Castro** seized power in Cuba. The following year, Castro allied with the Soviet Union. In April 1961, President Kennedy allowed approximately 1,500 Cubans, trained by the Central Intelligence Agency, to land in Cuba

---

CRITICAL THINKING ACTIVITY

Making Generalizations To review the Vietnam War and the events associated with it, ask students to make a list of generalizations about the war. The following generalizations might stir student thinking: the Vietnam War grew out of political repression in South Vietnam; the United States did not utilize the extent of its resources during the conflict; not only the American people but their leaders were divided over the proper course of action in Vietnam. When their lists are completed, have students choose various generalizations and try to find facts in the chapter that support or expand upon them. **L2**

at the **Bay of Pigs.** Their mission to overthrow Castro's government failed.

Two months later, Soviet leader **Nikita Khrushchev** told Kennedy that the West must get out of Berlin. Kennedy refused. Shortly afterward, the East German government, with Soviet support, built a wall dividing East Berlin from West Berlin. The **Berlin Wall** became a symbol of communist repression.

In October 1962, Kennedy decided to **blockade**—or close off—Cuba, until the Soviets removed the nuclear missiles they were installing there. As Soviet ships headed toward the blockade, the world waited to see if nuclear war would break out. Abruptly, the Soviet ships turned back. After days of negotiations, the Soviets agreed to pull their missiles out of Cuba.

War in Vietnam

In the late 1950s, President Eisenhower had sent military supplies and advisers to South Vietnam. President Kennedy continued this policy. Despite American aid, the **Vietcong**—the communist forces in South Vietnam—grew stronger. The Vietcong received weapons and supplies from North Vietnam.

The War Escalates

In August 1964, North Vietnam allegedly attacked American ships in the Gulf of Tonkin. In response, Congress authorized the president to use force to defend Americans against attack. Gradually, the American troops shifted from defending their bases to trying to find and destroy the Vietcong. In mid-February 1965, Johnson ordered sustained bombing of North Vietnam. Then, on March 8, the first United States combat troops landed in Vietnam. Next, in April Johnson decided to increase American forces in South Vietnam and to use combat troops for offensive actions.

As the war escalated, North Vietnam increased its support of the Vietcong. To meet the situation, American commander General William Westmoreland asked for additional troops and a commitment to a land war. By the end of 1965, there were more than 180,000 American troops in Vietnam. By the end of 1968, the total had increased to more than 500,000.

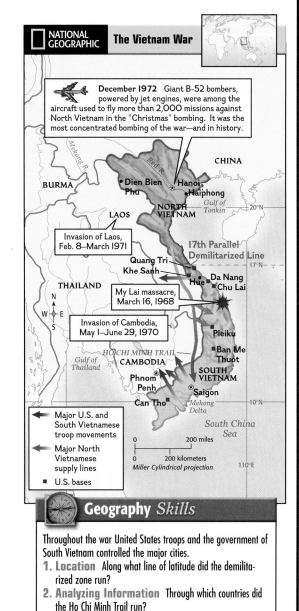

December 1972 Giant B-52 bombers, powered by jet engines, were among the aircraft used to fly more than 2,000 missions against North Vietnam in the "Christmas" bombing. It was the most concentrated bombing of the war—and in history.

CHINA

BURMA

Mekong R.

Red R.

• Dien Bien Phu

• Hanoi
• Haiphong

Gulf of Tonkin

NORTH VIETNAM

LAOS

Invasion of Laos, Feb. 8–March 1971

17th Parallel Demilitarized Line

Quang Tri
Khe Sanh

17°N

THAILAND

Hue • Da Nang
• Chu Lai

My Lai massacre, March 16, 1968

Invasion of Cambodia, May 1–June 29, 1970

• Pleiku

• Ban Me Thuot

HO CHI MINH TRAIL

Gulf of Thailand

CAMBODIA

SOUTH VIETNAM

Phnom Penh

• Saigon

Can Tho

Mekong Delta

10°N

South China Sea

Major U.S. and South Vietnamese troop movements

Major North Vietnamese supply lines

U.S. bases

0   200 miles

0   200 kilometers
Miller Cylindrical projection

110°E

Geography Skills

Throughout the war United States troops and the government of South Vietnam controlled the major cities.

1. **Location** Along what line of latitude did the demilitarized zone run?

2. **Analyzing Information** Through which countries did the Ho Chi Minh Trail run?

Opposition to the War

The American people disagreed sharply over the Vietnam War. Many young people opposed the war, especially the draft. However, opposition to the war was not limited to the young. Members of Congress and the news media became critical of Johnson's policies, too.

Geography Skills

Answers:
1. 17°N latitude line
2. North Vietnam, Laos, Cambodia, South Vietnam

3 ASSESS

Assign Section 2 Assessment as homework or as an in-class activity.

⟐ Have students use **Interactive Tutor Self-Assessment CD-ROM.**

L2

Section Quiz 19–2

Name _____ Date _____ Class _____

★ Chapter 19   Score ▢

Section Quiz 19-2

DIRECTIONS: Matching Match the items in Column A with the items in Column B. Write the correct letters in the blanks. (10 points each)

Column A   **Column B**

___ 1. African American lawyer   A. Nikita Khrushchev
___ 2. seized power in Cuba   B. Thurgood Marshall
___ 3. organized United Farm Workers   C. Lyndon Johnson
___ 4. Soviet leader   D. César Chávez
___ 5. outlined "Great Society" programs E. Fidel Castro

DIRECTIONS: Multiple Choice. In the blank at the left, write the letter of the ...

L1

Reteaching Activity 19–2

Name _____ Date _____ Class _____

★ Reteaching Activity 19-2

DIRECTIONS: Completing an Outline Fill in the outline below by writing the letters of the items that belong under each topic.

Turning Points After World War II

I. American Growth and Prosperity   IV. Kennedy's Foreign Policy

II. Demands for Change   V. War in Vietnam

III. Increased Equality

★ FACT BANK

A. Martin Luther King, Jr. led a march in Alabama in 1963.
B. On February 13, 1965, Johnson ordered sustained bombing of North Vietnam.
C. Alaska and Hawaii entered the Union.
D. Congress passed a law requiring employers to offer more opportunities for disabled people.
E. General William Westmoreland asked for additional troops.
F. New homes were built in the suburbs.
G. In 1968 Congress passed the Indian Civil Rights Act.
H. The sit-in movement began in Greensboro, North Carolina.
I. In October 1962, Kennedy decided to blockade Cuba.
J. The construction of more than 40,000 miles of highways tied the nation together.
K. César Chávez organized thousands of farm workers.
L. Many young people opposed the war.
M. In the spring of 1970, Nixon announced the invasion of Cambodia.
N. Congress passed the Civil Rights Act of 1964.
O. The National Organization for Women campaigned for an Equal Rights Amendment.
P. In February 1973, members of the American Indian Movement seized Wounded Knee, South Dakota.
Q. Kennedy refused to have the West leave Berlin.

EXTENDING THE CONTENT

Khrushchev and Nixon During a visit to the United States, an exchange between Khrushchev and Nixon became heated before television cameras. A casual conversation quickly escalated to the possibility of war over the situation in Berlin. Khrushchev complained, "You don't know anything about communism except fear of it." Nixon cautioned the Soviet leader that "if war comes, we both lose."

✓ Reading Check

Answer: Richard Nixon

L1, ELL

Reading Essentials and Study Guide 19–2

Study Guide

Chapter 19, Section 2

For use with textbook pages 564–570

TURNING POINTS

KEY TERMS	
stalemate	A situation in which neither side can win *(page 565)*
affluence	Wealth *(page 566)*
segregation	The separation of people of different races *(page 566)*
civil disobedience	The refusal to obey laws that are unjust *(page 566)*
feminist	An activist for women's rights *(page 567)*

DRAWING FROM EXPERIENCE

Have you ever experienced any kind of discrimination in your life? Were you ever excluded from a group or an activity for any reason? How does it feel to be treated unfairly?

L3

Enrichment Activity 19–2

★ Enrichment Activity 19-2 ★

Response to the Red Scare

Technology advanced during the years between 1945 and 1954. The Red Scare resulted in a rapid increase in the development of technologies that could be used for defense. Study the time line below.

Some Advances in Technology, 1945–1954

DIRECTIONS: Interpreting a Time Line Use the time line to answer the following questions.

1. In what year did the United States first explode an atomic bomb? _____
2. How many years passed before the Soviet Union tested its first atomic bomb? _____
3. What developments occurred in 1946? _____
4. How many years passed between the explosion of a hydrogen bomb by the United States and by the Soviet Union? _____
5. What happened in the same year that a United States aircraft reached supersonic speeds? _____

Activity **DIRECTIONS: Writing a Memo** Which of the technological changes shown on the time line could have been used for defense? You are an FBI agent in charge of maintaining security on the technologies. Write a memo to the other agents in your office in which you explain how the technologies could be used and how you recommend that security be maintained.

4 CLOSE

Have students brainstorm a list of ways in which the United States and its people prospered during the 1950s, the groups that were left out of the prosperity or denied rights, and what was done to try to address their needs.

As the 1968 election approached, President Johnson announced he would not run for reelection. The violence of the 1960s led many Americans to support candidates who promised to restore order. The Republican Party nominated Richard Nixon, Eisenhower's vice president. Nixon narrowly defeated Democrat Hubert Humphrey. Nixon promised to find a way to end the Vietnam War, pledging America would have "peace with honor."

Nixon and Vietnam

President Nixon's plan to achieve "peace with honor" was called Vietnamization. As American troops were withdrawn, the United States would step up efforts to train and equip South Vietnamese forces. In time these forces would take over total responsibility for the war.

Nixon's hope was that ultimately the North Vietnamese would grow tired of the war and negotiate peace. To hasten that end, Nixon secretly ordered the bombing of Cambodia because the Vietcong and North Vietnamese were using sanctuaries—safe places—there as springboards for offensives into South Vietnam. Then in the spring of 1970 Nixon announced the invasion of Cambodia.

The Cambodian invasion sparked demonstrations on college campuses throughout the nation. Many demonstrations were accompanied by violence. Four students were killed at Kent State University in Ohio and two were killed at Jackson State College in Mississippi. Antiwar protests increased.

The End of American Involvement

Previous attempts at negotiations had stalled. Then in late 1972 a breakthrough came. The final agreement was reached in January 1973. The last American troops pulled out of South Vietnam. Despite the peace agreement, North Vietnam's army launched a full-scale invasion of South Vietnam in early 1975. By May 1975, South Vietnam had fallen. Vietnam was united into one country, under the control of a communist government. America's longest war was over.

The Vietnam War took a staggering toll of lives and caused great suffering. More than 58,000 Americans were dead. Over 1 million Vietnamese—civilians as well as soldiers on one side or the other—died between 1965 and 1975. The relatives of the American soldiers who had been classified as missing in action, or as **MIAs,** continued to demand that the government press the Vietnamese for information. As the years passed, however, the likelihood of finding anyone alive faded.

✓ **Reading Check** **Identifying** Who succeeded Lyndon Johnson to the presidency?

SECTION 2 ASSESSMENT

Checking for Understanding

1. **Key Terms** Define: stalemate, affluence, segregation, civil disobedience, feminist
2. **Reviewing Facts** What role did Rosa Parks play in the struggle for civil rights?

Reviewing Themes

3. **Civic Rights and Responsibilities** Describe the various actions taken by African Americans to secure civil rights at this time.

Critical Thinking

4. **Drawing Inferences** Do you think President Nixon succeeded in attaining "peace with honor?" Explain.
5. **Organizing Information** Re-create the chart shown here, and describe each.

	Description
Truman Doctrine	
NATO	
Brown v. *Board of Education*	
Great Society	

Analyzing Visuals

6. **Geography Skills** Study the map of the Vietnam War on page 569. Where did most of the United States bases lie? Why do you think those sites were chosen?

Interdisciplinary Activity

Citizenship Create a time line of the civil rights movement. Research and clip pictures from magazines and newspapers of historic and present-day civil rights events and issues. Add captions.

570 CHAPTER 19 The Making of Modern America

SECTION 2 ASSESSMENT ANSWERS

1. Student work should reflect correct use of terms.
2. Her refusal to give up her bus seat started the Montgomery bus boycott. In 1956 the Supreme Court ruled that all segregated buses were unconstitutional.
3. Answers may include boycotts and marches.
4. Answers will vary.
5. Truman Doctrine: commitment to help nations resist communism; NATO: United States-European mutual defense pact; *Brown* v. *Board of Education:* outlawed segregation in schools; Great Society:

President Johnson's set of social programs

6. along the coast of South Vietnam; easier access for transporting troops and supplies

Interdisciplinary Activity Time lines should depict civil rights issues.

Critical Thinking SKILLBUILDER

Problem Solving

Why Learn This Skill?

Imagine you got a poor grade on a math test. You wonder why, since you always take notes and study for the tests. To improve your grades, you need to identify your specific problem and then take actions to solve it.

Learning the Skill

There are six key steps you should follow that will help you through the process of problem solving.

- Identify the problem. In the example in the first paragraph, you know that you are not doing well on math tests.
- Gather information. You know that you always take notes and study. You work on math problems every day for an hour. You also know that you sometimes forget details about math formulas.
- List and consider possible solutions. Instead of working on the math problems by yourself, you might try working with a friend or a group.
- Consider the advantages and disadvantages of each solution.

A wounded American soldier reaches for a fallen comrade.

- Now that you have considered the possible options, you need to choose the best solution to your problem then carry it out.
- Evaluate the effectiveness of the solution. This will help you determine if you have solved the problem. If you earn better grades on the next few math tests, you will know.

Practicing the Skill

Reread the material in Section 2 about the Vietnam War. Use that information and the steps above to answer the following questions.

1. What problems did the United States face in the Vietnam War?

2. What options were available to President Johnson? To President Nixon? What were the advantages and disadvantages?

3. Explain the solution President Nixon implemented.

4. Evaluate the effectiveness of Nixon's solution. Was it successful? How do you determine this?

Applying the Skill

Problem Solving President Roosevelt implemented a set of programs called the New Deal. Identify the problem that the New Deal was designed to deal with. List other possible solutions and their advantages and disadvantages. Then, write a short evaluation of the chosen solution.

 Glencoe's **Skillbuilder Interactive Workbook CD-ROM, Level 1,** provides instruction and practice in key social studies skills.

571

ANSWERS TO PRACTICING THE SKILL

1. Answers may include: North Vietnam increased its support of the Vietcong; Vietcong and North Vietnamese were using sanctuaries in Cambodia.

2. Answers will vary, but students should list at least two realistic options for each president and the probable advantages and disadvantages of each.

3. Nixon withdrew American troops but continued to provide training and equipment to South Vietnam.

4. Answers will vary, but students should support their answers with evidence from the text.

Applying the Skill Students' written evaluations should identify the problem and list advantages and disadvantages of all proposed solutions.

1 FOCUS

Section Overview

This section explains how the end of the Cold War affected the United States.

Reading Preview

Answers to Graphic: Watergate: Nixon–forced to resign presidency; Operation Desert Storm: George H.W. Bush–United States led military action after Iraq invaded Kuwait; Impeachment trial: Clinton–the Senate held a trial and acquitted the president; Students should explain the significance of each event.

Preteaching Vocabulary
Have pairs of students look up the **Key Terms** in the Glossary. Then have them restate each definition in their own words.

Modern America

Guide to Reading

Main Idea
The end of the Cold War brought new challenges to the United States—both at home and abroad.

Key Terms
embargo, human rights, federal debt, perjury, Internet, ozone, global warming, terrorism

Reading Strategy
Organizing Information Re-create the chart below. For each event, identify the president who was involved. Then summarize the significance of each event.

Event	Summary
Watergate	
Operation Desert Storm	
Impeachment trial	

Read to Learn
- how the Watergate scandal affected the nation.
- how the Cold War was ended.

Section Theme
Government and Democracy Presidential scandals tested the American political system, but the constitutional system of checks and balances provided safeguards against the abuse of power.

Preview of Events

◆1970	◆1980	◆1990	◆2000
└1974 President Nixon resigns from office	└1989 Communist governments in Eastern Europe collapse	└1991 Allies launch Operation Desert Storm	└1998 Bill Clinton is impeached

Nixon button

AN
American Story

To improve relations with the Communist world, President Richard Nixon made a historic visit to China in February 1972. Nixon later described how he felt upon his arrival in Beijing, the Chinese capital: ". . . 'The Star Spangled Banner' had never sounded so stirring to me as on that windswept runway in the heart of Communist China. . . . As we left the airport, [Chinese leader Chou En-lai] said, 'Your handshake came over the vastest ocean in the world—twenty-five years of no communication.'"

Crisis of Confidence

Even while the Vietnam war raged on, President Nixon attempted to improve American relations with the Communist world. Nixon's efforts were one step along the way to ending the Cold War. President Nixon came to the White House with the hope of bringing America together. However, illegal activity in the administration forced him to resign. While still reeling from the scandal, Americans elected Jimmy Carter to the presidency in 1976. President Carter had some success in foreign affairs. The administration lost the American people's confidence because of its inability to pull the nation out of an economic slump and failure to secure the release of hostages in Iran.

SECTION RESOURCES

Nixon's Administration

When President Nixon took office in 1969, he hoped to build a more stable world. The People's Republic of China played a key role in Nixon's plan. If the United States opened relations with China, it might make the Soviet Union more cooperative. The United States resumed trade with China in 1971.

America's improved relations with China convinced the Soviet Union to improve relations with the United States as well. The Soviets invited Nixon to Moscow. They agreed to sign an arms control treaty limiting the number of nuclear missiles both sides could have.

During the 1970s, the United States also became involved in the Middle East. Angry at America's support for Israel, the Arab states with oil imposed an embargo—a ban on shipments—of oil. This caused gasoline prices to skyrocket. The oil crisis ended when Secretary of State **Henry Kissinger** negotiated an agreement between Arab and Israeli leaders.

Nixon tried to reduce the federal government's role in people's lives. To give state governments more influence, he introduced **revenue sharing**—a plan for giving federal taxes back to the states. Although he reduced the federal government's role, Nixon did create the Environmental Protection Agency (EPA).

Nixon's policies were popular with the American people. As a result, he was reelected in a landslide in 1972. Shortly afterward, however, a scandal disrupted his presidency.

Watergate

During the election campaign, burglars were caught trying to break into the Democratic Party offices at the Watergate apartment complex. Nixon denied that his staff had ordered the break-in. After a Senate committee uncovered his staff's involvement, Nixon denied ordering a cover-up.

The House of Representatives began proceedings to **impeach,** or formally accuse, the president of abusing his power. On August 9, 1974, Richard Nixon resigned as president. His vice president, **Gerald Ford,** succeeded him.

Gerald Ford's administration faced growing economic problems, caused in part by the oil embargo. This, plus the Watergate scandal,

President Nixon leaves the White House.

2 *TEACH*

Daily Lecture and Discussion Notes 19–3

Copyright © by The McGraw-Hill Companies, Inc.

Daily Lecture and Discussion Notes

Chapter 19, Section 3

Did You Know? Bill Clinton earned $200,000 per year as president. He received $150,000 to pay for expenses, travel, and official entertainment. Presidents are provided with housing, health care, and transportation during their terms in office. President Clinton will receive a lifetime pension of $97,500 per year.

I. **Crisis of Confidence** *(Pages 572–574)*

A. Richard Nixon took office in 1969. He hoped to help build a more stable world.

1. President Nixon reopened United States relations with China. Trade with China reopened in 1971, and President Nixon visited China in 1972.

2. United States relations with the Soviets also improved. The United States and the Soviets agreed to an arms control treaty, limiting the number of nuclear missiles each could have.

3. During the 1970s, the United States supported Israel, which upset many Arab nations. These nations staged an oil embargo, banning oil shipments to the United States. Secretary of State Henry Kissinger negotiated an agreement between Israeli and Arab leaders. The agreement ended the oil crisis.

4. President Nixon gave federal taxes back to the states. He created the Environmental Protection Agency (EPA).

B. President Nixon was reelected in 1972. But during the election campaign, President Nixon's staff had spies break into the Democratic party offices in the Watergate apartment complex in Washington. When this break-in became public, President Nixon denied his staff's involvement and also denied ordering a cover-up.

1. The House of Representatives began impeachment proceedings against President Nixon. They formally accused the president of abusing his power. President Nixon resigned from office in August 1974.

2. Vice President Gerald Ford then became president. He lost the 1976 election to Democratic candidate Jimmy Carter.

C. President Carter tried to fix the economy, deal with foreign policy issues, and fight for human rights around the world.

1. President Carter arranged negotiations that led to the first peace treaty between Israel and an Arab nation.

2. President Carter withdrew economic and military aid from nations that violated human rights, such as Argentina, South Africa, and Iran.

Reading Strategy

Outlining Instruct students to use the heads and subheads to outline the section. Discuss how the end of the Cold War influenced domestic and foreign policies during the late 1980s to the present. **L2**

What?Where?When?Who?

Earth Day By the early 1970s, 70 percent of Americans ranked the environment as the nation's most pressing domestic problem. This concern was apparent in Americans' support for the first Earth Day held on April 22, 1970. An estimated 20 million Americans participated in this ecological rally to improve the environment. More than 14,000 schools, colleges, and community groups held workshops and other events across the country.

Reading Strategy   READING THE TEXT

Using Possible Sentences Choose five vocabulary words and write them on the board. Write sentences using the words either correctly or incorrectly. Then ask students to comment on whether the sentences are "possible." As students encounter the key vocabulary during the reading, they note each term's usage in the selection's context. After reading, students should reread the sentences. Revise the sentences using the students' suggestions. **L1**

✔ Reading Check

Answer: August 9, 1974; Gerald Ford

CURRICULUM CONNECTION

Civics After Gerald Ford assumed the presidency, he pardoned Richard Nixon. Immediately, the stock market plunged and Ford's popularity rating dropped from 71 percent to 50 percent.

---

turned many people against Ford. In 1976, voters elected the Democratic candidate, **Jimmy Carter,** to the presidency.

The Carter Presidency

When Jimmy Carter took office, his first priority was to fix the economy. He tried to speed economic growth by cutting taxes and increasing government spending, but his policies did little to improve the economy.

Carter spent much of his time dealing with foreign policy problems. He arranged for new negotiations between Israeli and Egyptian leaders at Camp David. These negotiations eventually led to opening Egyptian-Israeli economic and diplomatic relations. It marked the first time that an Arab nation recognized Israel's right to exist.

Carter based much of his foreign policy on human rights—a concern that governments around the world grant more freedom to their people. He withdrew economic and military aid from some of the worst offenders, including Argentina, South Africa, and Iran. In November 1979, Iranian students with the support of fundamentalists in the government seized the American embassy in Tehran. They then held 52 Americans hostage.

The hostage crisis and the nation's ongoing economic problems damaged President Carter politically. In the 1980 election, the Republican candidate, **Ronald Reagan,** easily defeated Carter. Shortly afterward, Iran released the American hostages.

✔**Reading Check** **Identifying** When did President Richard Nixon resign? Who succeeded him?

New Challenges

The 1980s and 1990s saw great changes. By the end of the 1980s, communism in Europe had collapsed. At the same time, America's economy began to rapidly expand.

(Clockwise from lower left) Leaders of Egypt, United States, and Israel celebrate 1979 peace treaty; Americans held hostage in Iran, 1979; President Reagan and Soviet leader Gorbachev meet at 1988 summit in Moscow.

574 CHAPTER 19 The Making of Modern America

DIFFERENTIATED INSTRUCTION

Reading Support Ask students to work in small groups to create a database—using a computer or paper-and-pencil—of the presidents in this chapter. Instruct groups to create the following four fields: president, action, characteristic, and strengths/weaknesses. Instruct groups to determine which president has the most strengths and to reveal the results to the class. Discuss the discrepancies in each group's results and whether data can truly be unbiased. **L2**

📂 Refer to *Inclusion for the Middle School Social Studies Classroom Strategies and Activities* in the TCR.

The Reagan Presidency

Ronald Reagan had promised to reduce the role of the government in people's lives. He slashed taxes, eliminated many government regulations, and cut back many government programs. His policies seemed to work. After a brief recession in 1982, the economy began to grow rapidly, and the stock market boomed.

Reagan also began a rapid buildup of American military forces. By cutting taxes while increasing military spending, Reagan greatly increased the federal debt—the amount of money the government had to borrow to pay for its programs. His policies were popular with the American people. Reagan easily won reelection in 1984. Shortly after his second term began, **Mikhail Gorbachev** became the new leader of the Soviet Union.

The Soviet economy was on the edge of collapse. The American military buildup had forced the Soviet Union to respond, and it simply could not afford to keep up. Gorbachev saw that the time had come to reform the communist system.

Reagan began negotiations with Gorbachev to reduce the number of nuclear missiles under their control. Gorbachev's reforms, and Reagan's willingness to improve relations, began to change the Soviet Union.

The Bush Presidency

Ronald Reagan's popularity enabled his vice president, **George Bush,** to win the Republican nomination and defeat the Democratic nominee, Michael Dukakis, in the 1988 presidential election. Once in office, Bush continued negotiations with the Soviet Union.

(Clockwise from lower right) Celebrating the fall of the Berlin wall, 1989; Reading about the allied air strike in Iraq, 1991; President Clinton prepares to address nation after his impeachment, 1998.

What?Where?When?Who?

The Fall of the Berlin Wall On November 9, 1989, after more than 28 years, the Berlin Wall was torn down and ceased to act as an impenetrable barrier between communist East Germany and democratic West Germany. This event paved the way for the reunification of Germany and the dismantling of the Soviet Union, both of which occurred within the following two years. Though George Bush was president at the time the wall came down, Ronald Reagan is often credited with shaping events that led to the fall of the wall, such as signing the Intermediate-Range Nuclear Forces Treaty with Mikhail Gorbachev in 1987.

Did you know?

Before undergoing a cancer-related surgery during which he would be under an anesthetic, President Ronald Reagan transferred the powers of the presidential office to Vice President George Bush. This marked the first transfer of power of this kind. (Following the attempt made on Reagan's life on March 30, 1981, Bush assumed some presidential responsibilities, but no formal transfer of power was made.) On the morning of July 13, 1985, George Bush became acting president. Later that same day, following his surgery, Reagan again assumed the powers of his office.

INTERDISCIPLINARY CONNECTIONS ACTIVITY

Civics Some of the issues addressed in Section 3 unite the world because they create common concerns, goals, and needs. Tell students that they will be involved in the search for solutions to these issues in their adult years. Hold a roundtable discussion on an issue selected by the class. Then organize the class into a number of committees to investigate various aspects of the issue. Have groups report their findings to the class. Ask students to suggest ways in which they as adults would attempt to resolve the issue. **L3**

Saddam Iraqi leader Saddam Hussein liked to be called by his first name. When pronounced correctly, with the emphasis on the second syllable, *Saddam* means "leader," "learned one," or "he who confronts. " President Bush insisted on pronouncing the name with the emphasis on the first syllable, however. When spoken this way, *Saddam* means "a boy who fixes or cleans shoes," a grave insult in many Arab countries.

Who?What?Where?When?

Madeleine Albright President Clinton named Madeleine K. Albright secretary of state. She was the first woman to serve in that post and the highest-ranking woman ever to serve in the federal government. Previously, Albright served as United Nations ambassador for the United States.

In late 1989, demonstrators filled the streets of Eastern Europe demanding more democracy. Within weeks, most of the communist governments in Eastern Europe collapsed. The Berlin Wall was torn down, and the following year East Germany and West Germany reunited. By the end of 1991, the Communist Party had been outlawed in Russia, and the Soviet Union had broken up into 15 separate republics.

While communism collapsed in Europe, a serious crisis developed in the Middle East. In 1990, Iraq invaded Kuwait. President Bush persuaded European and Arab nations to join the United States in an effort to free Kuwait. Bush then launched **Operation Desert Storm**—a massive attack on Iraqi forces that freed Kuwait and destroyed much of Iraq's army.

The Clinton Presidency

George Bush's popularity soared after the war against Iraq. But the onset of an economic recession left many Americans dissatisfied. The Democrats nominated **Bill Clinton,** governor of Arkansas, to run against Bush in 1992. Many Americans decided to vote for a third party candidate—businessman Ross Perot. Perot's candidacy split the vote three ways, enabling Clinton to win the election with only 43 percent of the popular vote.

After assuming office, Clinton cut government spending to reduce the deficit. He also convinced Congress to pass the Family Medical Leave Act. In 1993, he helped reach an agreement giving Palestinians the right to their own government in Israeli territory.

Another foreign policy issue involved change in trade policy. The **North American Free Trade Agreement** (NAFTA), which took effect in 1994, called for the gradual removal of tariffs and other trade barriers on most goods produced and sold in North America.

After Clinton won reelection in 1996, the economy continued to grow rapidly. For the first time in many years, the government balanced the budget and ran a **surplus**—it took in more money than it spent. With the Cold War over, Clinton's foreign policy focused on resolving regional conflicts.

As Clinton struggled with foreign policy problems, a scandal emerged involving a personal relationship between the president and a White House intern. Some evidence suggested that the president had obstructed justice and committed perjury, or lied under oath, to conceal the relationship. The House of Representatives voted to impeach President Clinton. The Senate then held a trial and acquitted the president.

The Election of 2000

The impeachment scandal left the country divided. For the 2000 election, the Democrats nominated Vice President **Al Gore.** The Republicans nominated Governor **George W. Bush** of Texas, son of former President Bush.

The 2000 election was one of the closest in history. Gore led in the popular vote, but the results in Florida were disputed and on election night no one knew who won. Without Florida's 25 electoral votes, neither Bush nor Gore had the 270 electoral votes needed to win. As the Florida ballots were being recounted, Bush and Gore went to court to challenge the recount process. The dispute was finally resolved by the Supreme Court. On January 20, 2001, George W. Bush became the 43rd president of the United States.

A New Bush Administration

The new president quickly established his administration. One of his first responsibilities was to name cabinet members. Bush named retired General of the Army **Colin Powell** to be secretary of state. He chose **Donald Rumsfeld** to serve as secretary of defense.

Bush continued the practice of expanding the number of women in high-level positions in his administration. Included were **Gale Norton** as Secretary of Interior and **Christine Todd Whitman** as head of the Environmental Protection Agency. The new Secretary of Labor, **Elaine Chao,** was the first Asian American woman appointed to a president's cabinet. National Security Adviser, **Condoleezza Rice,** was the first African American woman to hold that post.

During the election campaign, Bush promised a tax cut and he soon presented his tax plan to Congress. The plan generated much debate.

CRITICAL THINKING ACTIVITY

Defending a Point of View Have students choose one of the domestic and foreign policies of one president covered in this section. Tell them to state whether they agree or disagree with it and explain why. Have them support their answers with facts from the text or their personal knowledge. **L2**

People In History

Colin Powell 1937–

During the Persian Gulf War, the highest-ranking military officer serving was Colin Powell, the chairman of the Joint Chiefs of Staff. He was the youngest person and the first African American to hold that position. A four-star general, Powell had a very distinguished military career for thirty-five years, serving twice in Vietnam and working for four presidents.

Born to Jamaican immigrants, Powell was raised in Harlem and the South Bronx of New York City. He attended public school and the City College of New York, where he studied geology and began military training.

After the Gulf War, Powell wrote an autobiography and established a charitable organization, America's Promise—the Alliance for Youth, that helps children.

In 2001, Powell went to work for his fifth president, George W. Bush, as the first African American secretary of state.

CHAPTER 19
Section 3, 572–578

Supporters argued that it was the people's money and that they deserved it back. They also claimed that the tax cut would help the economy. Opponents argued that the money could be used more responsibly elsewhere, such as for Social Security or for paying off the national debt. In June 2001 President Bush signed into law the largest reduction in federal taxes since 1981.

As the president's top military advisor, Colin Powell laid out a blueprint for intervention in international conflict. The Powell Doctrine called for using American troops only when a vital interest is at stake and there is a clear and realistic goal.

✓ **Reading Check** Determining Cause and Effect
What event sparked Operation Desert Storm?

Looking to the Future

As Americans entered a new century, they faced many uncertainties—and opportunities. New technologies and a changing society had begun to transform America in new ways.

President Bush said one of his major aims was to stimulate global economic growth:

❝We know that nations that open their economies to the benefits of trade are more successful in climbing out of poverty. . . . [F]ree trade encourages the habits of liberty. . . .❞

Since 1995 the World Trade Organization (WTO) has administered trade practices between many nations. The WTO has more than 146 members.

Growth of technology boosted economic growth. Personal computers were being used in homes, schools, and businesses in greater numbers than ever before. Through the Internet, a worldwide linking of computer networks, American students could communicate with students in other countries.

A Changing Society

Because Americans were living longer than in the past, elderly people formed an increasing portion of the population. The Census Bureau reported that more than 12 percent of the population was over 65 years of age in the year 2000.

CHAPTER 19   The Making of Modern America   **577**

EXTENDING THE CONTENT

Condoleezza Rice Supported by parents who stressed the importance of education, Condoleezza Rice entered the University of Denver when she was only 15 years old. At age 19 she graduated with honors and went on to earn a Master's degree from the University of Notre Dame. After receiving a doctorate in political science from the University of Denver, Rice became a foreign policy analyst and worked in the Reagan administration as adviser to the Joint Chiefs of Staff.

✓ Reading Check

Answer: Students may note the population increases of the elderly, Asian Americans, and Hispanic Americans.

L1

Reteaching Activity 19–3

L1, ELL

Reading Essentials and Study Guide 19–3

L3

Enrichment Activity 19–3

4 CLOSE

Have students create two- or three-sentence summaries for each of the major parts of this section.

An important issue facing the nation was reform of Medicare. Medicare is the federal health care program for the elderly. By the summer of 2002, both the House and the Senate had passed bills that added a benefit for prescription drugs.

Congress also reacted to an increase in corporate scandals. For example, at one large energy trading company, Enron, corporate leaders cost investors and employees billions of dollars before the company went bankrupt. The federal government tightened accounting regulations and toughened penalties for dishonest executives.

By 2002, more than 10 percent of the population was foreign-born. Asian Americans made up about 4 percent of the population; Hispanic Americans more than 12 percent. The Hispanic community is now the nation's largest minority community.

Environmental Challenges

For years, scientists noted that the earth's atmosphere was losing ozone. This layer of gas protects life on Earth from cancer-causing rays of the sun. In 1987, the United States and 24 other nations agreed to stop making chemicals that might be weakening the ozone layer.

Scientists continued to debate the effects of global warming. They warned that the steady increase in average world temperatures could bring about major changes in weather patterns, the environment, and crop production.

Threats to Peace and Security

Preserving peace remains the most pressing global issue. In the late 1900s and early 2000s, acts of terrorism multiplied.

Terrorism—the use of violence by groups against civilians to achieve a political goal—threatened the security of the nation. On April 19, 1995, a massive bomb exploded at the Murrah Federal Building in downtown Oklahoma City, leaving 168 dead. The tragedy focused national attention on the violent anti-government feelings of private American militia groups. In January 1998, Theodore Kaczynski pleaded guilty to a string of mail bombings, dating from 1978 to 1995, which killed 3 and injured 29 others. Kaczynski hoped to inspire a rebellion against modern industrial society. These are examples of **domestic terrorism.** People engage in domestic terrorism when they attack people in their own country.

In addition to concern about domestic terrorism, the United States also faced **international terrorism.** As the world's most powerful nation, the United States frequently served as a target for terrorists—either those acting independently or with the support of a hostile government. The attack on the World Trade Center and the Pentagon on September 11, 2001, was an example of international terrorism.

✓ Reading Check **Explaining** Describe one way in which the nation's population is changing.

SECTION 3 ASSESSMENT

Checking for Understanding

1. **Key Terms** Define: embargo, human rights, federal debt, perjury, terrorism
2. **Reviewing Facts** When did Iranian students take Americans hostage?

Section Theme

3. **Government and Democracy** What is impeachment? Was President Nixon impeached? Was President Clinton?

Critical Thinking

4. **Drawing Conclusions** Do you think President Reagan's actions proved he was committed to reducing the role of government in the lives of Americans? Explain.
5. **Sequencing** Re-create the time line below and identify important events for each of the dates.

1971	1979	1991	2000

Analyzing Visuals

6. **Picturing History** Select one of the news photographs that appears on pages 574–575. Write one paragraph about the photo. Identify the people and describe what is happening.

Interdisciplinary Activity

Geography Illustrate a world map showing the cities and regions discussed in the section.

SECTION 3 ASSESSMENT ANSWERS

1. Student work should reflect correct use of terms.
2. November 1979
3. to formally accuse; no, Nixon resigned before he could be impeached; yes, but later the Senate held a trial and acquitted Clinton
4. Students may note that Reagan cut taxes, eliminated many regulations, and cut back many government programs.
5. 1971: U.S. trade begins with China; 1979: American hostages held in Iran; 1991: breakup of Soviet Union; 2000: George W. Bush elected president
6. Students' paragraphs should identify the people and describe the events that are pictured.

Interdisciplinary Activity Illustrations on the world map should show the cities and regions discussed in the section.

SECTION 4 The War on Terrorism

Guide to Reading

Main Idea
After suffering the worst terrorist attack in its history, the United States launched an effort to fight international terrorism.

Key Terms
counter-terrorism

Reading Strategy
Organizing Information As you read about America's war on terrorism, complete a diagram like the one below to explain how Americans responded to the events of September 11, 2001.

September 11, 2001

Read to Learn
• how Americans responded to terrorism.
• what actions the government took to fight terrorism.

Section Theme
Global Connections The United States called for a worldwide coalition to fight against terrorism.

Preview of Events

| ◆1975 | ◆1985 | ◆1995 | ◆2005 |

1979
Soviet Union invades Afghanistan

1988
Al-Qaeda is organized

1998
Bombs explode at U.S. embassies in Kenya and Tanzania

2001
Attack on the Pentagon and World Trade Center

Rescue workers carry out an injured man at the World Trade Center.

AN American Story

The first airliner hit the World Trade Center's north tower in New York City at about 8:45 in the morning. Eighteen minutes later, a second plane hit the south tower. Those who died on the airplanes were the first victims. Fire and falling wreckage from the twin towers of the World Trade Center killed thousands more, and hundreds of rescuers—fire fighters, police officers, and volunteers—themselves became victims. "The smoke was so bad, I was suffocating. When the buildings toppled, it was like a volcano," one survivor noted. "We have a lot of heroes," said one firefighter, "and we lost a lot of good people."

The crash of two passenger airplanes into the World Trade Center was not an accident. Early on the morning of September 11, 2001, terrorist hijackers had seized control of the planes, then deliberately flew them into the buildings. Terrorists took control of a third plane and crashed into the Pentagon, the headquarters of the nation's Department of Defense. Hijackers also seized a fourth airplane, but passengers heroically attacked the hijackers, causing that plane to crash in Pennsylvania. In all, thousands died.

CHAPTER 19   The Making of Modern America   **579**

---

1 FOCUS

Section Overview
This section describes the terrorist attacks that occurred in the United States on September 11, 2001, the reasons for the attacks, and the nation's response to them.

BELLRINGER
Skillbuilder Activity

Project transparency and have students answer the question.

Daily Focus Skills Transparency 19–4

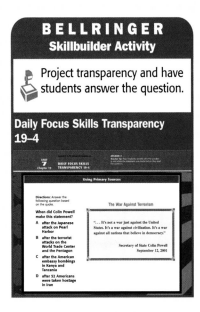

Reading Preview

Answers to Graphic: donated blood; raised money and collected food and other supplies for victims and rescue workers; firefighters and medical workers from other parts of the country traveled to New York to help

Preteaching Vocabulary
🔹 Use the **Vocabulary PuzzleMaker CD-ROM** to create crossword and word search puzzles.

SECTION RESOURCES

📁 **Reproducible Masters**
• Reproducible Lesson Plan 19–4
• Daily Lecture and Discussion Notes 19–4
• Guided Reading Activity 19–4
• Section Quiz 19–4
• Reteaching Activity 19–4
• Reading Essentials and Study Guide 19–4
• Enrichment Activity 19–4

🖨 **Transparencies**
• Daily Focus Skills Transparency 19–4

Multimedia
🔹 Vocabulary PuzzleMaker CD-ROM
🔹 Interactive Tutor Self-Assessment CD-ROM
🔹 ExamView® Pro Testmaker CD-ROM
🔹 Presentation Plus! CD-ROM

2 TEACH

Daily Lecture and Discussion Notes 19–4

Copyright © by The McGraw-Hill Companies, Inc.

Daily Lecture and Discussion Notes

Chapter 19, Section 4

Did You Know? The large, well-connected Federal Bureau of Investigation (FBI) has played a key role in identifying the terrorists involved in the September 11, 2001, attacks. However, in 1908 the FBI started out small, with only 34 investigators. Through the years, it has become a powerful force. Today the FBI employs more than 12,000 agents.

I. The Terrorist Threat *(Pages 580–581)*

A. Terrorism is a major concern for all countries in the twenty-first century. Terrorism is the use of violence by groups against civilians to achieve a political goal. Some recent attacks can be linked to Afghanistan.

1. The Soviet Union invaded Afghanistan in 1979. The Soviet Union supported the pro-communist government. Muslims from other Arab nations helped Afghanistan fight the Communists. A Saudi Arabian Muslim named Osama bin Laden used his family's wealth to help the Afghanistan resistance.

2. Bin Laden started a group called al-Qaeda in 1988. The group's name means "the Base." The groups recruited Muslims to fight the Soviets and bought weapons for resistance fighters in Afghanistan. The Afghan fighters also received technical assistance and training from the United States, Pakistan, Saudi Arabia, and other countries. Afghanistan is one of the most rugged and mountainous countries in the world. The Soviets found it very hard to move troops and supplies on this terrain. Soviet troops pulled out of Afghanistan in 1989, and bin Laden became a hero to many Muslim fundamentalists.

3. Bin Laden first operated from Sudan and then from Afghanistan. A militant Muslim fundamentalist group, called the Taliban, began to control Afghanistan. Bin Laden led al-Qaeda to drive Americans and other non-Muslims out of the Middle East. He believed that western ideas conflicted with those of the Muslim culture.

4. Bin Laden called on militant Muslims to kill Americans anywhere in the world. Truck bombs in Tanzania and Kenya were set off at the American embassies, killing more than 200 people, including 12 Americans, and injuring about 4,500 others.

5. In response to the attacks on the embassies, President Clinton ordered that cruise missiles be launched at terrorist camps in Afghanistan. The camps were destroyed, but bin Laden survived and continued to target Americans.

Determining Attitudes Have students brainstorm words and images that they associate with the Middle East. List the words and images on the chalkboard, then have students categorize each of them as either positive or negative. Discuss the origin of these images with students. **L1**

Did you know?

Rescue dogs, trained to search through disaster ruins, may receive years of training prior to working on recovery missions. The dogs must be trained to remain calm and focused in the face of loud noises; to move in a specific way when rubble shifts beneath them; and to negotiate confined spaces.

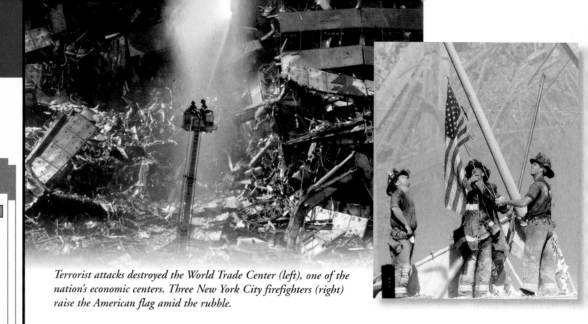

Terrorist attacks destroyed the World Trade Center (left), one of the nation's economic centers. Three New York City firefighters (right) raise the American flag amid the rubble.

Many New York City rescue workers who went to help also lost their lives when the towers collapsed. Hundreds of firefighters, police officers, and volunteers gave their lives in the line of duty trying to save others. Among those who died were Fire Department chaplain Mychal Judge and first deputy commissioner William Feehan, a 42-year veteran of the fire department. The largest number of New York City firefighters to have died in a single disaster before the terrorist attack was 12.

The Terrorist Threat

The attacks on the World Trade Center and the Pentagon were acts of terrorism. Terrorism is the use of violence by groups against civilians to achieve a political goal.

Who Was Responsible?

Intelligence sources and FBI investigators quickly identified **Osama bin Laden** as the prime suspect. Like most people in the Middle East, bin Laden is a **Muslim**—someone who believes in and practices the religion of Islam. Although the vast majority of the 1 billion Muslims worldwide believe Islam rejects terrorism, militant **fundamentalists** like bin Laden do not. They believe that any action is justified to drive American influence out of the Arab world.

Bin Laden believed that Western ideas had harmed Muslim society. His experience in Afghanistan convinced him that superpowers could be beaten.

War in Afghanistan

In 1979 the Soviet Union had invaded the nation of **Afghanistan,** in Southwest Asia, to support that nation's pro-communist government. Muslims from across the Middle East went to Afghanistan to fight against the Soviets. Among them was bin Laden, who came from one of Saudi Arabia's wealthiest families. In 1988, he founded an organization called **al-Qaeda** (al KY-duh), or "the Base." Al-Qaeda recruited Muslims to fight against the Soviets and bought arms for the Afghanistan soldiers. After Soviet forces withdrew from Afghanistan, bin Laden became a hero to many fundamentalists.

Terrorist Acts

Operating first from Sudan and then from Afghanistan—which was then under the control of Muslim fundamentalists known as the **Taliban**—bin Laden led al-Qaeda on a mission to drive Americans and other non-Muslims out of the Middle East. In 1998, terrorist truck bombs exploded at the American embassies in the African countries of **Kenya** and **Tanzania.** The bombs killed more than 200 people, includ-

580   CHAPTER 19   The Making of Modern America

Reading Strategy   READING THE TEXT

Monitoring Comprehension One of the most important reading strategies a student can learn is that he or she must monitor his or her reading comprehension. As students read, they should be aware of when they have missed something. They can monitor comprehension by questioning themselves as they read. If they do not understand an important idea, they need to reread, review, or read on to clarify what is unclear. **L1**

ing 12 Americans, and injured over 4,500. In late 1999, terrorists linked to al-Qaeda were arrested trying to smuggle explosives into the United States in an attempt to bomb targets in Seattle, Washington. In October 2000, terrorists backed by al-Qaeda crashed a boat loaded with explosives into the **USS** *Cole,* an American warship, while it was refueling in Yemen.

✓**Reading Check** **Describing** How did Osama bin Laden become so influential in Afghanistan?

A New War Begins

Then on September 11, 2001, terrorists struck on an even greater scale. The shock was felt across the nation, and thousands of people sought a way to help.

The Spirit of America

From coast to coast, thousands attended prayer services and vigils. Across the nation, Americans lined up to donate blood. Others raised money and collected food, blankets, and other supplies for the victims and rescue workers. Firefighters and medical workers from many cities headed to New York to help.

Using a combination of imagination and hard work, young people throughout the nation volunteered to help. Students in Western Springs, a village near Chicago, Illinois, encouraged their entire community to take part in a toys, books, and games garage sale to raise money. Students at a school in Cedar Rapids, Iowa, started a project called Working for America. The students worked by doing chores for family and neighbors and donated money they earned to the Red Cross. The South Bronx Job Corps Center put

NATIONAL GEOGRAPHIC **Terrorism Against Americans, 1970–2002**

1	1970 Terrorists hijack airplanes to Jordan
2	1979 Fifty-two Americans held hostage in Iran for more than a year
3	1983 Bombing of U.S. Marine barracks in Beirut, Lebanon, kills 241
4	1985 TWA flight 847 hijacked; hostages held for 17 days in Beirut, Lebanon
5	1986 Bombing at West Berlin dance club; kills 3, injures 150
6	1988 Bomb on Pan Am flight 103 kills 270 in Lockerbie, Scotland
7	1993 Bomb at World Trade Center kills 6
8	1995 Truck bomb destroys a federal building in Oklahoma City; kills 168, injures more than 500
9	1996 Bomb at U.S. complex in Dhahran, Saudi Arabia, kills 19 American soldiers
10	1998 Bombings at U.S. embassies in Kenya and Tanzania kill more than 200
11	2000 Bomb kills 17 American sailors and injures 39 aboard USS *Cole*
12	2001 Hijacked airliners crash into the World Trade Center, the Pentagon, and a field in Pennsylvania, killing thousands
13	2002 Bombs in Indonesia kill over 200

CHAPTER 19   The Making of Modern America   **581**

L1, ELL

Guided Reading Activity 19-4

Name _____ Date _____ Class _____

★ **Guided Reading Activity 19-4**

DIRECTIONS: Recalling the Facts Use the information in your textbook to answer the questions. Use another sheet of paper if necessary.

1. When did terrorists crash airplanes into the World Trade Center and the Pentagon? _____
2. What religion do most people in the Middle East follow? _____
3. When did the Soviet Union invade Afghanistan? _____
4. Who founded an organization called al-Qaeda in 1988? _____
5. Who did al-Qaeda recruit to fight the Soviets? _____
6. Where did terrorist truck bombs kill more than 200 people? _____
7. What did President Clinton do shortly after the embassy bombings? _____
8. What did Osama bin Laden hope to accomplish through acts of terrorism? _____
9. How did people throughout the nation help after the terrorist attacks in New York City, Washington, D.C., and Somerset, Pennsylvania? _____
10. Why did President Bush visit the Islamic Center in Washington? _____
11. Who was appointed to the new cabinet-level post, Homeland Security? _____
12. What did the USA Patriot Act of 2001 do? _____
13. How did world leaders respond to the death and devastation in America? _____
14. What ethnic groups make up the Northern Alliance? _____
15. What did Bush demand that the Taliban do? _____

✓**Reading Check**

Answer: Osama bin Laden recruited and organized Muslims to fight against the Soviet Union and supplied them with weapons.

Who?What?Where?When?

Fighting Terrorism The Joint Terrorism Task Force (JTTF) was established in 1979 to address the problems concerning terrorist investigations. The JTTF is comprised of members from numerous agencies, including the FBI, the U.S. Marshals Service, the Immigration and Naturalization Service, the New York State Police, and the U.S. Secret Service. The integration of the many agencies, each bringing its own unique skills and investigative specialties to the task force, makes this unit formidable in combating terrorism.

DIFFERENTIATED INSTRUCTION

Reading Support Have students discuss where they were when the terrorist attacks occurred on September 11, 2001, how they first heard about the attacks, and what their initial reaction was. Then have students create an audio scrapbook of these memories by composing one-minute messages expressing their feelings or relating their experiences of that day. When everyone has contributed to the audiotape, play the entire tape in class and use it as a springboard to discuss how these acts of terrorism have affected their lives. **L1**

📁 Refer to *Inclusion for the Middle School Social Studies Classroom Strategies and Activities* in the TCR.

AMERICA'S HEROES

New York City Fire Department Chaplain Mychal Judge, shown here in prayer, was killed while administering last rites to a firefighter.

New York City firefighter Tony James salutes during a funeral service.

Jessica Malone, who comes from a large family of firefighters, went to New York City to help.

together canine care packages for search and rescue dogs at the World Trade Center site.

Fair Treatment

Realizing that many people might turn their anger against Muslims in the United States, President Bush visited the Islamic Center in Washington, D.C. There he issued a statement explaining that Islam is a peaceful religion. He urged all Americans to uphold the nation's values and treat Muslim Americans fairly.

President Bush created a special fund to help the children of Afghanistan. Many of the children in Afghanistan are orphans and do not have enough to eat. The president asked the children of the United States to send $1—or whatever they could—to America's Fund for Afghan Children.

New Threats

Concern over the use of biological and chemical weapons grew in the wake of the September 11 tragedy. Letters containing deadly anthrax spores were mailed to several political leaders and the news media. Anthrax is an animal disease that has existed for tens of thousands of years.

Law enforcement investigated to determine the identity and the motives of the attackers, but so far, no suspects have been identified. Officials do not think al-Qaeda sent the anthrax.

Protecting America

President Bush and his advisers began planning a response to the terrorist attacks. The president placed the armed forces on high alert. Fighter aircraft began patrolling the skies over major

> *In the face of all this evil, we remain strong and united, "one nation under God."* —President George W. Bush

INTERDISCIPLINARY CONNECTIONS ACTIVITY

Civics Some global issues, such as terrorism, unite people by creating common concerns, goals, and needs. Ask students to research various examples of how recent acts of terrorism have united people. Tell students to list possible advantages of such unification and ways in which it might lead to resolutions for problems of terrorism. Have students share their lists in a class discussion about what group measures might be taken in the future to combat or help prevent terrorism. **L3**

cities. Security at airports was increased, and the FBI began a massive investigation. The president created a new federal agency called the Office of **Homeland Security,** to coordinate counter-terrorism efforts. Counter-terrorism involves military or political activities intended to combat terrorism. He named Pennsylvania governor Tom Ridge to head the agency. 📖 *(See pages 604–605 of the Appendix for President Bush's address to Congress after the attacks.)*

The Office of Homeland Security had trouble coordinating counter-terrorism efforts. In June 2002, President Bush asked Congress to combine all of the agencies responsible for the public's safety into a new department to be called the Department of Homeland Security.

In late October 2001, Congress passed and the president signed into law new measures to combat terrorism. The **USA Patriot Act of 2001** gave federal prosecutors and FBI agents new powers to investigate those who plot or carry out acts of terrorism. The law expanded the power of federal agents to tap telephones and track Internet usage in the hunt for terrorists. It also permits agents to conduct secret searches of a suspect's home or office without giving prior notice to the owner of the property.

Attorney General **John Ashcroft** promised that government agents would waste no time putting the new tools to use in the hunt for terrorists. Although both houses of Congress passed the bill overwhelmingly, some critics expressed concern that measures could be used not only against suspected terrorists, but people and organizations engaged in lawful activity. To make sure civil liberties were not compromised by the new law, many of its powers will expire in late 2005, unless extended by Congress.

Building a Coalition

The death and devastation caused by terrorism affected not only Americans, but also people around the world. World leaders responded with statements of sympathy and outrage. NATO members promised to support the United States as did other nations including India, Pakistan, Turkey, and Israel. Some Muslim nations, including Saudi Arabia and Egypt, offered more limited support because they feared widespread protests from their people.

On the Trail of Terrorism

The war against terrorism first concentrated on Afghanistan where bin Laden was reported to be in hiding. The Taliban controlled most of Afghanistan and imposed their religious views on the Afghan people. Taliban leaders had come under criticism for discriminating against women and being intolerant of other religions. Since 1996, when the Taliban captured the Afghan capital, **Kabul,** the main opposition force, the **Northern Alliance,** had battled the Taliban but had made little headway.

President Bush demanded that the Taliban in Afghanistan turn over bin Laden and his supporters. After the Taliban refused, on October 7 the U.S. military attacked Taliban and al-Qaeda forces. Cargo jets also dropped food, medicine, and supplies to the Afghan people.

The air strikes by U.S. warplanes allowed the Northern Alliance to quickly take control of the country. After the Taliban fell from power, the United States and its allies worked with Afghan leaders to create a new government to run the country. Nations around the world pledged more than four billion dollars to help Afghanistan. Thousands of American and allied troops began arriving in Afghanistan to act as peacekeepers and to hunt for al-Qaeda terrorists. Afghan leaders selected Hamid Karzai to serve as Afghanistan's new president.

Although the war in Afghanistan was going well, terrorist attacks in South Asia and the Middle East created new problems. In December 2001, terrorists from Kashmir—a region in northern India—attacked India's parliament. India has fought many wars with Pakistan over Kashmir. India's leaders blamed Pakistan for the attack on the parliament, and began mobilizing India's army.

By June 2002, the two nations were ready to go to war. The situation was very dangerous because both sides had nuclear weapons. Although India and Pakistan eventually stepped back from the threat of nuclear war, neither side showed signs of setting aside their arms.

South Asia was not the only region where terrorism created problems. In the Middle East, Palestinian terrorists sent suicide bombers into Israel. These bombers concealed explosives under their clothing. They detonated the bombs

Did you know?

Many ironworkers from Local 40, whose members built the World Trade Center's Twin Towers in the early 1970s, returned to the site to volunteer their time. Working up to 12 hours at a time, the ironworkers cut steel with torches and pulled away remnants and debris with cranes, allowing rescue workers to search deeper into the rubble.

What?Where?When?Who?

Homeland Security The Department of Homeland Security brings together 22 agencies and 170,000 employees. This marks the biggest federal reorganization since the National Security Act was passed in 1947. At that time, President Truman and Congress agreed to combine the War Department and the Department of the Navy into what is now called the Department of Defense.

CRITICAL THINKING ACTIVITY

Analyzing Information Have students work with partners to research and write a report about biological warfare, focusing on anthrax. Ask them to answer the following questions in their reports: What are the various ways of contracting anthrax? What protective measures can be taken to help prevent contracting anthrax? What are possible long-term affects of using anthrax as a biological weapon in warfare? How does biological warfare differ from other acts of terrorism? Have students share their reports with the rest of the class. **L1**

3 ASSESS

Assign Section 4 Assessment as homework or as an in-class activity.

Ⓢ Have students use **Interactive Tutor Self-Assessment CD-ROM.**

L2

Section Quiz 19–4

L1

Reteaching Activity 19–4

Americans gathered at parks, churches, and fire stations across the nation to express not only their grief but their patriotism.

in Israeli restaurants, shops, and buses, killing dozens of other people. After several suicide bombings took place in Israel, the Israeli army invaded several Palestinian cities where they believed the terrorist groups were based.

In response to the violence in the Middle East, President Bush outlined a plan for ending the Israeli-Palestinian conflict. He announced his support for the creation of a Palestinian state living in peace beside Israel. He asked Israel to stop raiding Palestinian cities. At the same time, he demanded Palestinian leaders stop terrorist attacks and reform their government to make it more democratic and less corrupt.

Continuing the War on Terrorism

President Bush made it clear that while the war on terrorism would start by targeting al-Qaeda, it would not end there. "It will not end," the president announced, "until every terrorist group of global reach has been found, stopped, and defeated." He also warned that the United States would regard "any nation that continues to harbor or support terrorism" as an enemy.

The war against terrorism, President Bush warned Americans, would not end quickly, but it was a war the people of the United States were now called to fight:

> 66 Great harm has been done to us. We have suffered great loss. And in our grief and anger we have found our mission and our moment.... We will not tire, we will not falter, and we will not fail. 99

Widening the War on Terror

The attacks of September 11, 2001, raised fears that al-Qaeda and other terrorist groups might acquire nuclear, chemical, or biological weapons. These **weapons of mass destruction** could kill tens of thousands of people all at once.

In his 2002 State of the Union address, President Bush said his goal was "to prevent regimes that sponsor terror from threatening America or our friends with weapons of mass destruction." He singled out Iraq, Iran, and North Korea, claiming these states "and their terrorist allies constitute an axis of evil arming to threaten the peace of the world."

584   CHAPTER 19   The Making of Modern America

EXTENDING THE CONTENT

The Northern Alliance and the Taliban At the time of the September 11, 2001, terrorist attacks on the United States, the Northern Alliance was an Afghanistan Islamic rebel faction opposed to Afghanistan's militant Islamic Taliban regime. The alliance was composed of Afghanistan's minorities—Tajiks, Uzbeks, and other groups—while the Taliban primarily consisted of the Pashtun, the country's largest ethnic group. The Taliban took control of Afghanistan's capital, Kabul, in 1996, after which it took control of most of the country. As of September 11, 2001, the alliance had successfully resisted the Taliban's rule, though alliance members controlled less than 10 percent of the country.

In October 2002, North Korea announced that it had restarted its nuclear weapons program. The Bush administration used diplomatic pressure to persuade the North Koreans to stop. However, North Korea warned the U.S. that it would continue to build its nuclear power.

Confronting Iraq

Iraq's dictator Saddam Hussein had already ordered the use of chemical weapons twice, once in Iraq's war against Iran in the 1980s and again against the Kurds, an ethnic minority in northern Iraq who had rebelled against Hussein. After the Gulf War in 1991, UN inspectors found evidence that Iraq had developed biological weapons and was working on a nuclear bomb.

In the summer of 2002, President Bush increased pressure on Iraq. On September 12, he asked the UN to pass a new resolution demanding that Iraq give up its weapons of mass destruction. The president made it clear that the United States would act with or without UN support.

In mid-October, Congress voted to authorize the use of force against Iraq. Then, in early November, the United Nations set a deadline for Iraq to readmit weapons inspectors. It required Iraq to declare all of its weapons of mass destruction, to stop supporting terrorism, and to stop oppressing its people. The resolution threatened Iraq with "serious consequences" if it did not cooperate.

Iraq agreed to allow UN inspectors into the country, but questions arose over whether Iraqi officials were cooperating as they had promised. President Bush argued that the Iraqis were still hiding weapons of mass destruction. The Bush administration asked the UN Security Council to pass a resolution calling for the use of force in Iraq. When Council members France and Russia said they would veto a resolution, the United States prepared for war.

On March 20, the American military, aided by soldiers from Great Britain, attacked. Over the next six weeks, much of Iraq's army fell into disarray. American troops quickly seized control of the country. On May 1, President Bush declared the end of major combat operations. About 140 Americans, and several thousand Iraqis, had died.

The controversy over Iraq and the fighting, though, continued. While many Iraqis welcomed the fall of Saddam Hussein's regime, others did not. U.S. and British troops faced continued attacks. By the fall of 2003, more Americans had died after May 1 than had died in the six weeks of major combat. As American deaths and expenses mounted, President Bush began to seek support from the UN and other countries to rebuild Iraq. Despite the capture of Saddam Hussein in December 2003, the path toward a free and stable Iraq appeared to be long and difficult.

✓ **Reading Check** **Analyzing** Why did President Bush call for military action against Saddam Hussein's regime?

✓ **Reading Check**

Answer: The president called for Iraq to stop its weapons program and to stop oppressing its people.

L1, ELL

Reading Essentials and Study Guide 19–4

L3

Enrichment Activity 19–4

4 CLOSE

Have students list some of the various acts of terrorism mentioned in this section. Ask them to discuss why different responses, solutions, or counter-terrorist measures might be necessary for each case of terrorism.

SECTION 4 ASSESSMENT

Checking for Understanding

1. **Key Terms** Define: counter-terrorism.
2. **Reviewing Facts** What happened to the USS Cole when it was refueling in Yemen?

Reviewing Themes

3. **Global Connections** Do you think the dangers of terrorism require global cooperation? Explain and support your point of view with reasons.

Critical Thinking

4. **Drawing Conclusions** Why do you think President Bush specifically chose to visit the Islamic Center in Washington, D.C.?
5. **Organizing Information** Use a diagram like the one below to identify what you think are the three major effects of terrorism on Americans.

Effects of terrorism

Analyzing Visuals

6. **Geography Skills** Examine the map on terrorism on page 581. How many Americans were taken hostage in Iran? What events on the map took place in the 1990s?

Interdisciplinary Activity

Expository Writing How will world events affect your future? Write an essay entitled "The World's Future and My Own" identifying important issues and explaining how events could affect your life.

SECTION 4 ASSESSMENT ANSWERS

1. Student work should reflect correct use of terms.
2. Terrorists backed by al-Qaeda crashed a boat loaded with explosives into the USS Cole.
3. Answers will vary, but students should cite the benefits of cooperative efforts.

4. to prevent all Muslims from being blamed for the attacks
5. Answers will vary but may include: made Americans more fearful of traveling by airplane; made Americans more patriotic; made Americans more accepting of domestic security measures to combat terrorism.

6. 52; Students should identify the four bombings that occurred in the 1990s.

Interdisciplinary Activity Essays should demonstrate students' understanding of recent world events and how those events could affect their lives.

MindJogger Videoquiz
Use **MindJogger Videoquiz** to review the Chapter 19 content.

Available in VHS

Reviewing Key Terms

1.–8. Students' paragraphs should include factual information from the chapter, reflecting correct use of terms.

Reviewing Key Facts

9. to provide security for retired people

10. Allied forces landed in Normandy, France, and began the invasion of Europe.

11. It provided a base for an invasion of Japan.

12. Alaska and Hawaii

13. Her refusal to leave a section of a bus reserved for white people started the Montgomery bus boycott. The Supreme Court ruled that segregated buses were unconstitutional.

14. Hispanic American who organized farmworkers in the United Farm Workers union, which called attention to conditions of migrant workers

15. to force the removal of Soviet missiles from the island

16. President Nixon; to expand South Vietnam's military role in the war while reducing the United States's role

17. Jimmy Carter

18. to free Kuwait from an Iraqi takeover

19. Hijackers seized control of American airplanes and deliberately crashed them into the World Trade Center towers and the Pentagon. The war on terrorism began.

20. The department coordinates counter-terrorism efforts.

Chapter Summary

The Making of Modern America

Depression and World War

• A severe economic depression affects much of the world during the 1930s.

• Aid to the Allies and the Japanese attack on Pearl Harbor pull the United States into World War II.

• The surrender of Germany and Japan in 1945 ends the war.

The Cold War

• The desire to contain communism leads the United States to assume an active role in world affairs.

• The cold war rivalry leads to conflict in Korea and confrontation in Cuba.

The Civil Rights Era

• In the 1950s African Americans renew their struggle for full equality.

• Women and minority groups begin to work for change in their own right.

The Vietnam Era

• Unable to end the war quickly, the United States finds itself increasingly drawn into the Vietnam War.

• Illegal activities by government officials result in the Watergate scandal and the resignation of President Nixon.

Search for Solutions

• President Ronald Reagan acts quickly to limit the size of the federal government and build the nation's military.

• The United States and allies liberate Kuwait after Iraqi invasion.

New Challenges

• During the 1990s, the nation enjoys prosperous economic times, but the government is shaken by scandal and the impeachment trial of President Clinton.

• America seeks to meet the challenges of terrorism both at home and abroad.

• Saddam Hussein is deposed as Iraqi leader.

586

Reviewing Key Terms

On a sheet of paper, use all of the following terms to write several short, historically accurate paragraphs relating to the information in the chapter. Try to use more than one term in a sentence.

1. Holocaust
2. stalemate
3. segregation
4. civil disobedience
5. embargo
6. federal debt
7. terrorism
8. counter-terrorism

Reviewing Key Facts

9. What was the purpose of the Social Security Act?

10. What happened on D-Day?

11. Why was Okinawa a strategic site during World War II?

12. What states joined the nation in 1959?

13. Describe Rosa Parks's role in the struggle for civil rights.

14. Who was César Chávez?

15. Why did President Kennedy call for a blockade of Cuba in 1962?

16. Who proposed the policy of Vietnamization? What was its goal?

17. Who won the presidential election in 1976?

18. What was the purpose of Operation Desert Storm?

19. What is significant about September 11, 2001?

20. What is the Department of Homeland Security?

Critical Thinking

21. Drawing Conclusions Do you think the expansion of the federal government during Franklin Roosevelt's presidency was necessary? Why or why not?

22. Explaining What does the term "Cold War" mean and how did it apply to the post-World War II era?

23. Organizing Information Re-create the chart shown here and list three steps taken during Nixon's presidency to end United States involvement in Vietnam.

24. Analyze What are the two major challenges Americans face today? Explain why you made your choices.

Critical Thinking

21. Answers should reflect students' understanding of Roosevelt's New Deal programs.

22. It describes the rivalry between the United States and the Soviet Union. The Soviets tried to expand; the United States tried to contain expansion.

23. withdrawal of United States troops; bombing of communist-controlled areas; pursuing peace negotiations with the North Vietnamese

24. Answers may include: equal rights, environmental concerns, economic concerns, and terrorism.

Geography and History

Study the map below. Then read the statements that follow. Identify whether each statement is true or not true and explain your answer.

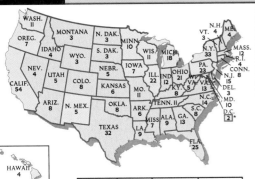

NATIONAL GEOGRAPHIC **Election of 2000**

Candidate	Electoral Vote	Popular Vote	Political Party
Bush	271	50,456,002	Republican
Gore	266	50,999,897	Democrat

* 1 elector from Washington, D.C., abstained.

25. A total of 438 electoral votes were cast.

26. Gore received more popular votes than Bush.

27. Gore received strong support from the southeastern states.

Practicing Skills

28. **Problem Solving** Describe a decision that you might face today or in the near future, such as the choice to go to college or to get a job after high school. List the steps of the problem-solving process. Write the questions and information you would consider at each step and what your answers might be. Evaluate what you think would be your best option.

 Technology Activity

29. **Using the Internet** Use the Internet to research the life of one of the men or women discussed in Chapter 19. Prepare a list of 10 key facts about that person. Share your list with the class.

Self-Check Quiz
Visit **tarvol1.glencoe.com** and click on **Chapter 19— Self-Check Quizzes** to prepare for the chapter test.

Citizenship Cooperative Activity

30. **Serving on a Jury** With a partner, think about what happens if you receive a jury notice in the mail. Write a description of what you would do next and what you would expect to happen. Then note what you plan to tell the judge about your understanding of a juror's responsibilities. Share your writing with the class.

Economics Activity

31. Research for information, then summarize your findings in a short report that answers these questions. What field or career area interests you? What education and skills are required to enter it? What attitudes, work habits, and other qualities does it take to succeed on the job?

 Alternative Assessment

32. **Portfolio Writing Activity** Choose an event that you think has had a great impact on everyday life in the United States. Write a column for a newspaper describing how that change has affected your life.

Standardized Test Practice

The cold war between the United States and the former Soviet Union was a rivalry between what two forms of government?

F communism and socialism

G communism and dictatorships

H communism and democracy

J democracy and monarchy

Test-Taking Tip

When you are studying for an exam, use a dictionary to look up important terms. Communism, dictatorship, socialism, democracy, and monarchy are words describing different types of government. Which choices contain words that describe the U.S. government?

Citizenship Cooperative Activity

30. Answers will vary. Students might point out that a prospective juror becomes part of a pool from which jurors are chosen. During the selection process, a person may be questioned by the judge and by attorneys for each side. Prospective jurors should answer each question honestly.

Economics Activity

31. Summaries should answer all questions about the chosen career.

 Alternative Assessment

32. Suggest that students consider the following questions as they write their newspaper articles: Has the effect on my life been positive or negative? Why?

HISTORY *Online*

Have students visit the Web site at tarvol1.glencoe.com to review Chapter 19 and take the Self-Check Quiz.

Standardized Test Practice

Answer: H
Question Type: History
Answer Explanation: According to page 564, one of the events leading to the Cold War was Stalin's refusal to allow free elections in Eastern Europe.

Bonus Question ?

Ask: In 1989 Virginia elected the nation's first African American governor since Reconstruction. Who was he? *(L. Douglas Wilder)*

 Geography and History

Students' explanations should reflect data from the map and the electoral totals.

25. not true

26. true

27. not true

Practicing Skills

28. Students should use the steps described on page 571. They should describe each step of the process and write why they think the decision they made is the best option.

 Technology Activity

29. Lists should contain significant information about the person chosen.

Appendix

Using an Appendix Explain to students that an Appendix is additional material found at the end of a book. Have students look at the table of contents on page 588. Ask students to identify the materials found in the Appendix.

Review the descriptions of each Appendix item from the information on page 589. After students have read the descriptions of each item, have them turn to the page where this item is found, using the page number references from the table of contents. Ask students to describe what information is found on the pages and how it can help them as they read their textbooks.

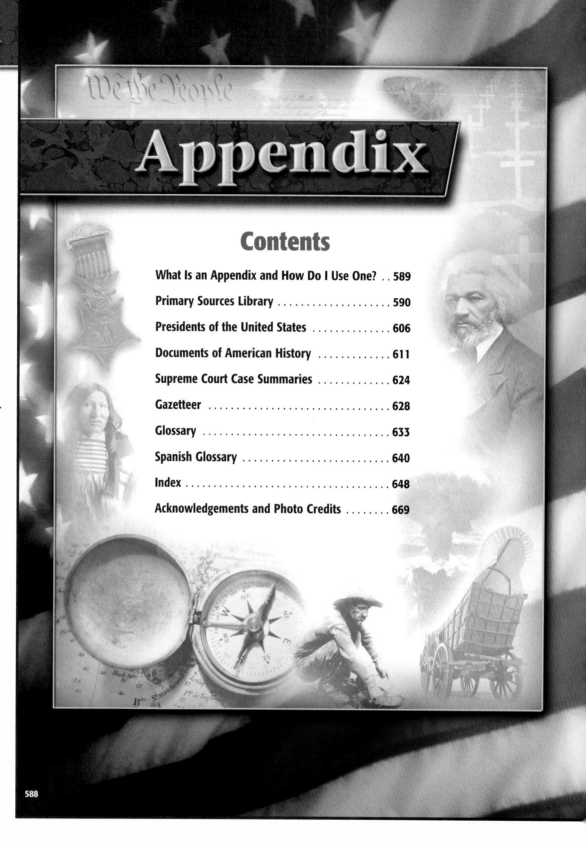

Appendix

Contents

What Is an Appendix and How Do I Use One?

An appendix is the additional material you often find at the end of books. The following information will help you learn how to use the appendix in **The American Republic to 1877.**

Primary Sources Library

The **Primary Sources Library** provides additional first-person accounts of historical events. Primary sources are often narratives by a person who actually experienced what is being described.

Presidents of the United States

The **presidents** have served as our nation's leaders. In this resource you will find information of interest on each of the nation's presidents, including their term in office, political affiliation, and their occupations before they became president.

Documents of American History

This is a collection of some of the most important writings in American history. Each **document** begins with an introduction describing the author and placing the selection within its historical context.

Supreme Court Case Summaries

The **Supreme Court Case Summaries** provide readable discussions of important Supreme Court cases. The summaries are listed in alphabetical order and include a summary of the facts of the case and its impact.

Gazetteer

A **gazetteer** (GA•zuh•TIHR) is a geographical dictionary. It lists some of the largest countries, cities, and several important geographic features. Each entry also includes a page number telling where this place can be found in your textbook.

Glossary

A **glossary** is a list of important or difficult terms found in a textbook. Since words sometimes have other meanings, you may wish to consult a dictionary to find other uses for the term. The glossary gives a definition of each term as it is used in the book. The glossary also includes page numbers telling you where in the textbook the term is used.

Spanish Glossary

A **Spanish glossary** contains everything that an English glossary does, but it is written in Spanish. A Spanish glossary is especially important to bilingual students, or those Spanish-speaking students who are learning the English language.

Index

An **index** is an alphabetical listing that includes the subjects of the book and the page numbers where those subjects can be found. The index in this book also lets you know that certain pages contain maps, graphs, photos, or paintings about the subject.

Acknowledgements and Photo Credits

This section lists photo credits and/or literary credits for the book. You can look at this section to find out where the publisher obtained the permission to use a photograph or to use excerpts from other books.

Test Yourself

Find the answers to these questions by using the Appendix on the following pages.

1. What does ironclad mean?
2. Who was the sixth president of the United States?
3. On what page can I find out about Anne Hutchinson?
4. Where exactly is Roanoke located?
5. What was the Supreme Court's decision in *Marbury v. Madison?*

Appendix Contents   **589**

Have students complete the **Test Yourself** questions on page 589. As students answer the questions, have them identify where in the Appendix they found the answers.

Have students write five questions on a sheet of paper similar to those on page 589, with the answers written on the back of the paper. Have students exchange their questions with another student. Students should answer the questions using the Appendix and identify where they found each answer.

Have students review different books to see what other types of information can be placed in an Appendix. Have students use the Appendix throughout the study of the textbook.

Answers to Test Yourself

1. An ironclad is an armored naval vessel.
2. John Quincy Adams was the sixth president of the United States.
3. Information about Anne Hutchinson can be found on page 79.
4. Roanoke is an island off the coast of present-day North Carolina located at 35° N/76° W.
5. The Supreme Court ruled that it has the final say on what the Constitution means and the Court defined its right to determine whether a law violated the Constitution.

Introduction

Have students complete the activities that follow to familiarize themselves with the types of primary sources.

Printed Publications

To help students analyze printed publications, instruct students to read the first two paragraphs under "Declaration of Natural Rights" in the Declaration of Independence (page 154). Discuss this passage in class, using such questions as: Is this a primary or secondary source? What is the main idea of the passage? What do you think this passage means?

Oral Histories

Work together with an English or Language Arts teacher to help students complete the following oral history activity. Interview a relative or friend who is much older than you to see how their life was different from yours when he or she was a teenager. Create a list of interview questions such as: What regular chores did you have to do? What did you and your friends talk about? What were your classes like in school?

Ask students to provide a transcript, or written record, of the interview and discuss their findings with the class.

Working With Primary Sources

Suppose that you have been asked to write a report on changes in your community over the past 25 years. Where would you get the information you need to begin writing? You would draw upon two types of information—primary sources and secondary sources.

Definitions

Primary sources are often first-person accounts by someone who actually saw or lived through what is being described. In other words, if you see a fire or live through a great storm and then write about your experiences, you are creating a primary source. Diaries, journals, photographs, and eyewitness reports are examples of primary sources. **Secondary sources** are secondhand accounts. For instance, if your friend experiences the fire or storm and tells you about it, or if you read about the fire or storm in the newspaper, and then you write about it, you are creating a secondary source. Textbooks, biographies, and histories are secondary sources.

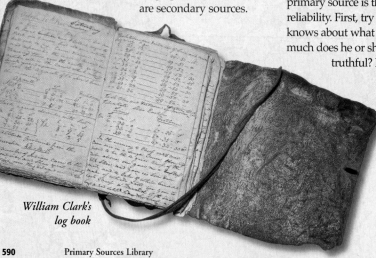

William Clark's log book

Checking Your Sources

When you read primary or secondary sources, you should analyze them to figure out if they are dependable or reliable. Historians usually prefer primary sources to secondary sources, but both can be reliable or unreliable, depending on the following factors.

Time Span

With primary sources, it is important to consider how long after the event occurred the primary source was written. Chances are the longer the time span between the event and the account, the less reliable the account is. As time passes, people often forget details and fill in gaps with events that never took place. Although we like to think we remember things exactly as they happened, the fact is we often remember them as we wanted them to occur.

Reliability

Another factor to consider when evaluating a primary source is the writer's background and reliability. First, try to determine how this person knows about what he or she is writing. How much does he or she know? Is the writer being truthful? Is the account convincing?

Opinions

When evaluating a primary source, you should also decide whether the account has been influenced by emotion, opinion, or exaggeration. Writers can have reasons to distort the truth to suit

Teacher Notes

After studying the introduction to the Primary Sources Library, students should be able to meet the following objectives:

- explain the difference between primary sources and secondary sources.
- identify the different types of primary sources.
- understand that primary sources offer a unique view of people and events in a particular era.

their personal purposes. Ask yourself: Why did the person write the account? Do any key words or expressions reveal the author's emotions or opinions? You may wish to compare the account with one written by another witness to the event. If the two accounts differ, ask yourself why they differ and which is more accurate.

Interpreting Primary Sources

To help you analyze a primary source, use the following steps:

- **Examine the origins of the document.**
  You need to determine if it is a primary source.
- **Find the main ideas.**
  Read the document and summarize the main ideas in your own words. These ideas may be fairly easy to identify in newspapers and journals, for example, but are much more difficult to find in poetry.

- **Reread the document.**
  Difficult ideas are not always easily understood on the first reading.
- **Use a variety of resources.**
  Form the habit of using the dictionary, the encyclopedia, and maps. These resources are tools to help you discover new ideas and knowledge and check the validity of sources.

George Washington's compass

 Songs & Poems

Ask students to write a poem about a happy event in their life. Suggest that the poem be in a standard form such as a limerick, haiku, or sonnet.

Personal Records

Ask students to describe what it might be like to witness an important public event. Provide the following guidelines: Write a journal entry describing the event. Begin by giving an overview of the event, including some objective facts. Then make the event personal by focusing on your own opinions or feelings.

Visual Materials

Help students create a poster showing how your community or state has changed during the twentieth century. Students may use photographs or original drawings.

 Artifacts

To help students analyze artifacts, provide the following instructions: Find a primary source from your past such as a photograph, a report card, or a letter. Bring this source to class and explain what it shows about the time from which it comes.

Classifying Primary Sources

Primary sources fall into different categories:

 Printed Publications

Printed publications include books such as autobiographies. Printed publications also include newspapers and magazines.

 Songs & Poems

Songs and poems include works that express the personal thoughts and feelings, or political or religious beliefs, of the writer, often using rhyming and rhythmic language.

 Visual Materials

Visual materials include a wide range of forms: original paintings, drawings, sculptures, photographs, film, and maps.

Oral Histories

Oral history collects spoken memories and personal observations through recorded interviews. By contrast, oral tradition involves stories that people have passed along by word of mouth from generation to generation.

Personal Records

Personal records are accounts of events kept by an individual who is a participant in, or witness to, these events. Personal records include diaries, journals, and letters.

 Artifacts

Artifacts are objects such as tools or ornaments. Artifacts present information about a particular culture or a stage of technological development.

Primary Sources Library **591**

Teacher Notes

Through the study of the selections in the Primary Sources Library and their accompanying questions, students should be able to:

- find main ideas in the selections.
- analyze information in a variety of written texts in order to make inferences and generalizations.
- provide an interpretation of the material in their own words.

Unit Link

Use the primary source selections on pages 592–593 to accompany study of Unit 1, "Different Worlds Meet."

Reinforcing Vocabulary

Review the **Reader's Dictionary** with students on page 592 to be sure they understand any unfamiliar terms. Write *prophecy* on the chalkboard. Ask students to use the term in a sentence.

Background Information

Oral Tradition Ancient people handed down their culture, traditions, and histories through the oral tradition. Through storytelling, they passed on their literary heritage from one generation to the next. Explain that family histories are often shared in the oral tradition. Ask volunteers to share family stories. Then ask how the stories provide insight into certain time periods.

For use with Unit 1

Different Worlds Meet

Until the arrival of Christopher Columbus, the lifestyle and culture of Native Americans had endured for centuries. They told stories, sang songs, and recited tales that recounted their past and their close relationship with the natural world. These stories and songs survived through oral tradition. This means that each generation passed down its stories and songs to its young people by word of mouth. As you read, think about how oral history, folklore, and tradition connect us to the past.

Reader's Dictionary

Lakota: a member of the Sioux people of central and eastern North America

prophecy: a prediction about the future

Black Hills: mountains in the western Dakotas and northeast Wyoming

elder: a person who is honored for his or her age and experience

Pinta: one of the three ships under Columbus's command during his first trip to the Americas

White Buffalo Calf Woman Brings the First Pipe

Joseph Chasing Horse of the Lakota people tells the story of the White Buffalo Calf Woman.

We **Lakota** people have a **prophecy** about the white buffalo calf. How that prophecy originated was that we have a sacred bundle, a sacred pipe, that was brought to us about 2,000 years ago by what we know as the White Buffalo Calf Woman.

The story goes that she appeared to two warriors at that time. These two warriors were out hunting buffalo . . . in the sacred **Black Hills** of South Dakota, and they saw a big body coming toward them. And they saw that it was a white buffalo calf. As it came closer to them, it turned into a beautiful young Indian girl.

[At] that time one of the warriors [had bad thoughts] and so the young girl told him to step forward. And when he did step forward, a black cloud came over his body, and when the black cloud disappeared, the warrior who had bad thoughts was left with no flesh or blood on his bones. The other warrior kneeled and began to pray.

And when he prayed, the white buffalo calf, who was now an Indian girl told him to go back to his people and warn them that in four days she was going to bring a sacred bundle.

So the warrior did as he was told. He went back to his people, and he gathered all the **elders,** and all the

Kiowa animal hide calendar

EXTENDING THE CONTENT

Dakota Groups The Lakota were originally part of a larger group, the Dakota, who lived in the northern woodlands. Within the Dakota were three closely related language groups: the Dakota-speakers, the Nakota-speakers, and the Lakota-speakers. They lived in forests, harvested wild rice, and made maple sugar. Invasions by the French and battles with other Native American peoples forced many Nakota and Lakota to break from the larger Dakota group and move westward, where they developed distinctive Plains cultures.

leaders, and all the people in a circle and told them what she had instructed him to do. And sure enough, just as she said she would, on the fourth day, she came.

Astrolabe

They say a cloud came down from the sky, and off of the cloud stepped the white buffalo calf. As it rolled onto the earth, the calf stood up and became this beautiful young woman who was carrying the sacred bundle in her hand.

As she entered into the circle of the nation, she sang a sacred song and took the sacred bundle to the people who were there to take [it from] her.

. . . And she instructed our people that as long as we performed these ceremonies we would always remain caretakers and guardians of sacred land. She told us that as long as we took care of it and respected it that our people would never die and would always live.

The sacred bundle is known as the White Buffalo Calf Pipe because it was brought by the White Buffalo Calf Woman. . . .

When White Buffalo Calf Woman promised to return again, she made some prophecies at that time. One of those prophecies was that the birth of a white buffalo calf would be a sign that it would be near the time when she would return again to purify the world. What she meant by that was that she would bring back [spiritual] harmony. . . .

Columbus Crosses the Atlantic

 Personal Records

Christopher Columbus reached the new world on October 12, 1492. At sea for over two months, his sailors worried that they would not find land before their food and water ran out. Columbus's entries in his logs show the mood of his crew, and their impressions of the natives.

October 11:

The crew of the **Pinta** spotted some . . . reeds and some other plants; they also saw what looked like a small board or plank. A stick was recovered that looks manmade, perhaps carved with an iron tool . . . but even these few [things] made the crew breathe easier; in fact the men have even become cheerful.

October 12:

The islanders came to the ships' boats, swimming and bringing us parrots and balls of cotton thread . . . which they exchanged for . . . glass beads and hawk bells . . . they took and gave of what they had very willingly, but it seemed to me that they were poor in every way. They bore no weapons, nor were they acquainted with them, because when I showed them swords they seized them by the edge and so cut themselves from ignorance.

Analyzing Primary Sources

1. What did the Indian girl tell the Lakota warriors?
2. What prophecy did the White Buffalo Calf Woman make to the people?
3. What does the use of the animal hide tell you about the people who made the calendar?
4. Why were the members of Columbus's crew cheerful when they spied the objects at sea?

Primary Sources Library

 History *and the* Humanities

American Music: Hits Through History, "Iroquois Round Dance"

Alternative Assessment

Inform students that according to a United Nations report, maize and potatoes are among the food staples around the world. Point out that Native Americans cultivated maize and potatoes. Have students research the history of one of these two crops. Then have students write a newspaper article that discusses the crop. Articles should include information about where and when the crop was first cultivated and the importance of the crop today.

GLENCOE TECHNOLOGY

CD-ROM
American History Primary Source Document Library CD-ROM

Use the **American History Primary Source Document Library CD-ROM** to access other primary source documents related to Native Americans and Columbus's voyage.

Analyzing Primary Sources

1. to go back to the Lakota and warn them that in four days she would bring them a sacred bundle
2. that the birth of a white buffalo calf would signal the time when she would return to purify the world
3. Answers will vary. Students may suggest that the Lakota had many uses for hides, and that hides symbolize a connection with or a respect for nature. The calendar is significant because the Lakota believed it was important to keep track of the seasons and important events.
4. The objects looked humanmade, so they thought that land must be nearby.

593

Unit Link

Use the primary source selections on pages 594–595 to accompany study of Unit 2, "Colonial Settlement."

Reinforcing Vocabulary

Review the **Reader's Dictionary** with students on page 594 to be sure they understand any unfamiliar terms. Write *habitations* on the chalkboard. Ask students to use the term in a sentence.

Background Information

The Literary Letter Explain to students that, unlike Franklin's letter, which Franklin hoped would remain private, Crevecoeur's was a literary letter, addressed to a particular person, but actually intended for a large audience. Tell them that the full text of Crevecoeur's letter shows that it was addressed to a "Mr. F.B.," but Crevecoeur published the letter for a wide audience in a collection of his literary letters. Have students discuss books they have read in which a narrative is told or a topic is treated in a series of letters.

For use with Unit 2

Colonial Settlement

Early America was a nation of people unafraid to experiment. Because colonists often had to learn new ways of obtaining food and shelter in a primitive country, they grew to appreciate ingenuity. Because of the need to cooperate—for companionship, and even for survival—they overlooked the differences in cultures that separated them in the old country. As you read these primary source selections, think about how the necessity to adapt affected the way the colonists approached everyday situations.

Reader's Dictionary

enlightened: informed

haughty: proud, vain

indigence: poverty

habitation: home

phial: small bottle

blunder: mistake

tolerable: satisfactory

What is an American?

Printed Publications

J. Hector St. John Crevecoeur of France traveled widely in the American colonies and farmed in New York. His Letters from an American Farmer *was published in 1782.*

I wish I could be acquainted with the feelings and thoughts which must . . . present themselves to the mind of an **enlightened** Englishman, when he first lands on the continent. . . . If he travels through our rural districts he views not the hostile castle, and the **haughty** mansion, contrasted with the clay-built hut and miserable cabin, where cattle and men help to keep each other warm, and dwell in meanness, smoke, and **indigence.** A pleasing uniformity of decent competence appears throughout our **habitations.** The meanest of our log-houses is dry and comfortable. . . . What then is the American, this new man? He is either a European, or the descendant of a European, hence that strange mixture of blood, which you will find in no other country. I could point out to you a family whose grandfather was an Englishman, whose wife was Dutch, and whose son married a French woman, and whose present four sons have now four wives of different nations. . . . There is room for everybody in America; has he particular talent, or industry? He exerts it in order to produce a livelihood, and it succeeds. . . .

Butter churn

EXTENDING THE CONTENT

Franklin's Experiments In 1747, Franklin began his electrical experiments. He supported the hypothesis that lightning is an electrical phenomenon, and proposed an effective method of demonstrating the truth of it. Franklin was not the first person to perform his celebrated experiment with the kite. Because details of his plan were published in London, others in England and France carried out his experiment before Franklin himself did.

Ben Franklin

Personal Records

We often think of Benjamin Franklin as a successful diplomat and inventor. In 1750, Franklin wrote to a friend about an experiment that did not go as well as he had planned.

I have lately made an experiment in electricity, that I desire never to repeat. Two nights ago, being about to kill a turkey by the shock from two large glass jars, containing as much electrical fire as forty common **phials,** I . . . took the whole [charge] through my own arms and body, by receiving the fire from the united top wires with one hand, while the other held a chain connected with the outsides of both jars. The company present (whose talking to me, and to one another, I supposed occasioned my inattention to what I was about) say, that the flash was very great, and the crack as loud as a pistol; yet, my senses being instantly gone, I neither saw the one nor heard the other. . . . Nothing remains now of this shock, but a soreness in my breast-bone, which feels as if it had been bruised. I did not fall, but suppose I should have been knocked down, if I had received the stroke in my head. The whole was over in less than a minute.

You may communicate this to Mr. Bowdoin, as a caution to him, but do not make it more public, for I am ashamed to have been guilty of so notorious a **blunder;.** . . . I am yours . . .

B. Franklin

P.S. The jars hold six gallons each.

Penn's Colony

Personal Records

In a letter written in 1683, William Penn describes the growth of his colony.

Our capital town is advanced to about 150 very **tolerable** houses for wooden ones; they are chiefly on both the navigable rivers that bound the ends or sides of the town. The farmers have got their winter corn in the ground. I suppose we may be 500 farmers strong. I settle them in villages, dividing 5,000 acres among ten, fifteen, or twenty families, as their ability is to plant it. . . .

Hornbook from colonial school

Analyzing Primary Sources

1. How does de Crevecoeur describe the typical home in the colonies in the late 1700s?
2. What do you think Franklin was trying to learn with his experiment?
3. During what season of the year did Penn write this letter? How can you tell?

History *and the* Humanities

American Art and Architecture, Transparency 6, *Penn's Treaty with the Indians*

Alternative Assessment

Have students research and report on an early settlement established in the Americas by the Spanish, the French, the Dutch, or the Swedish. Provide a focus for research by suggesting that students answer the following questions: When was the settlement established? Why did they settle there? What were some of the cultural differences that existed after it was settled? Have them write a brief report summarizing their findings.

GLENCOE TECHNOLOGY

CD-ROM
American History Primary Source Document Library CD-ROM

Use the **American History Primary Source Document Library CD-ROM** to access other primary source documents related to colonial settlement.

Analyzing Primary Sources

1. Homes are dry and comfortable.
2. Answers will vary, but he may have been assessing the effect of electricity on animals.
3. It is probably autumn because Penn mentions that the farmers recently planted their winter corn.

Creating a Nation

In settling North America, the colonists developed a sense that they were taking part in the birth of a new society, where people had the opportunity to better themselves. As you read these primary source selections, think about the reasons the colonists began to find fault with Great Britain. What words would you use to describe the American "spirit" that made them determined to fight for independence?

Reader's Dictionary

sovereign: king or leader

destitute: lacking

procure: gain or obtain

gall: to become sore by rubbing

Powderhorn

Block Schedule

Team Teaching These selections may be implemented in a team-teaching context, in conjunction with English/Language Arts.

Unit Link

Use the primary source selections on pages 596–597 to accompany study of Unit 3, "Creating a Nation."

Reinforcing Vocabulary

Review the **Reader's Dictionary** with students on page 596 to be sure they understand any unfamiliar terms. Ask students to use each term in a sentence. Have them compare the meaning of the term *sovereign* with *king*.

Background Information

Persuasion Point out that persuasive writing attempts to sway the reader to think or act in a particular way. Ask students to identify the course of action promoted in each of the selections. Then ask: Which selection is the most persuasive? Why?

Common Sense

Printed Publications

In Common Sense, *written in January 1776, patriot Thomas Paine called upon the colonists to break away from Great Britain.*

Every thing that is right begs for separation from [Great] Britain. The Americans who have been killed seem to say, 'TIS TIME TO PART. England and America are located a great distance apart. That is itself strong and natural proof that God never expected one to rule over the other.

The Bold Americans

Songs & Poems

Broadside ballads—emotionally-charged story poems printed on a single sheet of paper—were distributed widely and helped fuel colonists' passion for freedom.

Come all you bold young Bostonians, come
   listen unto me:
I will sing you a song concerning liberty.
Concerning liberty, my boys, the truth I will
   unfold,
Of the bold Americans, who scorn to be
   controlled.
We'll honor George, our **sovereign,** on any
   reasonable terms,
But if he don't grant us liberty, we'll all lay down
   our arms.
      But if he will grant us liberty, so plainly
         shall you see,
      We are the boys that fear no noise!
         Success to liberty!

596   Primary Sources Library

EXTENDING THE CONTENT

Thomas Paine After gaining popularity by writing about freedom and human rights, Thomas Paine alienated readers and ruined his reputation at the time with his book *The Age of Reason*. His criticism of churches was perceived as a message of atheism. In fact Paine objected only to organized religion, not worship of God.

Surviving at Valley Forge

Personal Records

Below are excerpts from the personal records of two different people who served at Valley Forge. The first selection is by Albigence Waldo, a surgeon who tended the sick and injured.

I am sick—discontented . . . Poor food—hard lodging—cold weather—fatigue—nasty cloathes—nasty cookery. . . . I can't endure it—Why are we sent here to starve and freeze? . . .

In this selection, soldier Joseph Plumb Martin, age 16 at the time, remembers the hardships on the way to Valley Forge.

The army was not only starved but naked. The greatest part were not only shirtless and barefoot, but **destitute** of all other clothing, especially blankets. I **procured** a small piece of rawhide and made myself a pair of moccasins, which

Military drum of the American Revolution

kept my feet (while they lasted) from the frozen ground, although, as I well remember, the hard edges so **galled** my ankles, while on a march, that it was with much difficulty and pain that I could wear them afterwards; but the only alternative I had was to endure this inconvenience or to go barefoot, as hundreds of my companions had to, till they might be tracked by their bloods upon the rough frozen ground.

Immigrant Life in America

Personal Records

A German immigrant wrote this account of his experiences.

But during the voyage there is on board these ships terrible misery, stench, fumes, horror, vomiting, many kinds of sea-sickness, fever . . . all of which comes from old and sharply salted food and meat, also from very bad and foul water, so that many die miserably. . . .

Many parents must sell and trade away their children like so many head of cattle. . . . [I]t often happens that such parents and children, after leaving the ship, do not see each other again for many years, perhaps no more in all their lives.

Analyzing Primary Sources

1. What is the main point that Thomas Paine makes in the excerpt from *Common Sense*?
2. What do the bold Americans scorn?
3. What might have kept the soldiers from leaving Valley Forge, under such horrible conditions?

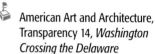
Primary Sources Library

History *and the* Humanities

- American Music: Hits Through History, "The World Turned Upside Down"
- American Art and Architecture, Transparency 14, *Washington Crossing the Delaware*

Alternative Assessment

Call on a volunteer to define the term *boycott*. Point out that the boycott has served as an effective form of political and economic protest throughout our country's history. Have students write an editorial that might have appeared in a colonial newspaper. Tell them to write an editorial that encourages colonists to stop buying British goods.

GLENCOE TECHNOLOGY

CD-ROM
American History Primary Source Document Library CD-ROM

Use the **American History Primary Source Document Library CD-ROM** to access other primary source documents related to the American independence movement.

Analyzing Primary Sources

1. that it makes sense for the American colonies to be politically separate from Great Britain
2. being controlled
3. Answers will vary. Some students may know that many soldiers did leave.

Discipline, penalties for desertion, a sense of honor, or commitment to the Revolution may have kept them, as well as the grim prospect of traveling alone through the wilderness without provisions.

597

For use with Unit 4

Block Schedule

Team Teaching These selections may be implemented in a team-teaching context, in conjunction with English/Language Arts.

Unit Link

Use the primary source selections on pages 598–599 to accompany study of Unit 4, "The New Republic."

Reinforcing Vocabulary

Review the **Reader's Dictionary** with students on page 598 to be sure they understand any unfamiliar terms. Ask students to use each term in a sentence. Ask students why someone about to give an important speech to a large audience might seem *agitated*.

Background Information

The Journal Review with students that a journal is a daily record of events kept by an individual who participates in or witnesses these events. Journals are often valuable historical documents. Ask students: What might be the advantages of writing down ideas and impressions in a journal day by day, as the events take place? What are the limitations of this method?

The New Republic

The Constitution established a completely new framework of government that was meant to be flexible and lasting. Along with the excitement of starting a new nation came challenges and growing pains. Many people, both American-born and foreign-born, wondered: Can this new kind of government last? As you read these primary source selections, think about how well the government served the people as the nation grew.

Reader's Dictionary

gallery: outdoor balcony

proclamation: announcement

agitated: upset and nervous

ungainly: awkward, clumsy

plainest manner: in a simple way

discord: disagreement, conflict

rapture: joy

marsh: soft, wet land

corduroy-road: a road made of logs laid side by side

Washington's First Inaugural

Personal Records

Pennsylvania Senator William Maclay was one of the many witnesses to the nation's first presidential inauguration.

The President was conducted out of the middle window into the **gallery** [overlooking Wall Street], and the oath was administered by the Chancellor [the highest judicial officer in the state of New York]. Notice that the business done was communicated to the crowd by **proclamation** . . . who gave three cheers, and repeated it on the President's bowing to them.

As the company returned into the Senate chamber, the President took the chair and the Senators and Representatives their seats. He rose, and all arose also, and [he] addressed them. This great man was **agitated** and embarrassed more than ever he was by the leveled cannon or pointed musket. He trembled, and several times could scarce make out to read, though it must be supposed he had often read it before. . . . When he came to the words *all the world,* he made a flourish with his right hand, which left rather an **ungainly** impression. I sincerely, for my part, wished all set ceremony in the hands of the dancing-masters, and that this first of men had read off his address in the **plainest manner,** without ever taking his eyes from the paper, for I felt hurt that he was not first in everything.

Copy of letter written by President Washington

EXTENDING THE CONTENT

What's That Name? When George Washington became the nation's first president, no one knew how to address him. John Adams suggested "His Highness, the President of the United States and Protector of the Rights of the Same." The House of Representatives finally settled on "President of the United States."

Song of Liberty

Songs & Poems

The following song is one of the hundreds of anonymous patriotic songs written, printed, and distributed in little song books during the early 1800s.

The fruits of our country, our flocks and
   our fleeces,
What treasures immense, in our mountains
   that lie,
While **discord** is tearing Old Europe to
   pieces,
Shall amply the wants of the people
   supply;
New roads and canals, on their bosoms
   conveying,
Refinement and wealth through our forests
   shall roam,
And millions of freemen, with **rapture**
   surveying,
Shall shout out "O Liberty! this is thy home!"

Flag flown at Fort McHenry during War of 1812

On the Road

Printed Publications

David Stevenson described a journey by stagecoach along a typical route of the time.

Sometimes our way lay for miles through extensive **marshes,** which we crossed by **corduroy-roads.** . . . At others the coach stuck fast in mud, from which it could be [moved] only by the combined efforts of the coachman and passengers; at one place we traveled . . . through a forest flooded with water, which stood to a height of several feet. . . . The distance of the route from Pittsburgh to Erie is 128 miles, which was accomplished in forty-six hours . . . although the [stagecoach] by which I traveled carried the mail, and stopped only for breakfast, dinner and tea, but there was considerable delay by the coach being once upset and several times "mired."

A woman named Elizabeth Smith Geer wrote about winter travel in her diary:

My children gave out with cold and fatigue and could not travel, and the boys had to unhitch the oxen and bring them and carry the children on to camp. It was so cold and numb I could not tell by feeling that I had any feet at all. . . . I have not told you half we suffered.

Analyzing Primary Sources

1. What was it about Washington's public speaking manner that Maclay criticized?
2. In the song, what does the phrase "treasures immense" mean?
3. How did roads of the early 1800s differ from roads that we travel on today?

History *and the* Humanities

⚑ American Music: Hits Through History, "College Hornpipe/ Belle Catherine"

Alternative Assessment

Have students read the definition of *cabinet.* Ask students to think about President Washington choosing his first cabinet. Have them write a help-wanted ad for one of these official positions: secretary of war, secretary of the treasury, or secretary of state.

GLENCOE TECHNOLOGY

CD-ROM
American History Primary Source Document Library CD-ROM

Use the **American History Primary Source Document Library CD-ROM** to access other primary source documents related to the new Republic.

Analyzing Primary Sources

1. Washington appeared embarrassed; he fumbled during his speech; his motions seemed stiff and awkward.
2. Students should note that the reference is to the nation's natural resources.
3. Rather than being paved, well kept, and easy to travel, the early roads went through mud and marshes. Water mired the coach or blocked its path.

Primary Sources Library

Block Schedule

Team Teaching These selections may be implemented in a team-teaching context, in conjunction with English/Language Arts.

Unit Link

Use the primary source selections on pages 600–601 to accompany study of Unit 5, "The Growing Nation."

Reinforcing Vocabulary

Review the **Reader's Dictionary** with students on page 600 to be sure they understand any unfamiliar terms. Write *inclemency* on the chalkboard. Ask students to give examples of inclemency in the weather.

Background Information

Oral Histories By word of mouth, people have passed on their histories from one generation to the next. Explain that family histories are often shared in the oral tradition. Ask volunteers to share family stories. Then ask how the stories provide insight into certain periods of time.

The Growing Nation

In the early 1800s, the United States had a firmly established democracy, but the freedoms it guaranteed did not extend to everyone. Native Americans were forced from their lands, while African Americans were enslaved—torn from their homelands and often separated from their families. As you read these primary source selections, think about how long these conditions existed before ideas of reform began to take hold.

Reader's Dictionary

detachment: group or body of people

inclemency: harsh conditions

auction block: site where enslaved people were bought and sold

piteous: sad, distressed

vociferously: loudly

battery: a grouping of weapons

rent: opened or parted

Trail of Tears

Printed Publications

Although recognized as a separate nation by several U.S. treaties, the Cherokee people were forced to leave their lands because white people wanted it for farming. Thousands died before they reached Indian Territory, the present-day state of Oklahoma. This forced journey came to be called the Trail of Tears. A newspaper published this account.

On Tuesday evening we fell in with a **detachment** of the poor Cherokee Indians . . . about eleven hundred Indians—sixty wagons—six hundred horses, and perhaps forty pairs of oxen. We found them in the forest camped for the night by the road side . . . under a severe fall of rain accompanied by heavy wind. With their canvas for a shield from the **inclemency** of the weather, and the cold wet ground for a resting place, after the fatigue of the day, they spent the night . . . many of the aged Indians were suffering extremely from the fatigue of the journey, and the ill health consequent upon it . . . several were then quite ill, and one aged man we were informed was then in the last struggles of death.

Map of Georgia in 1826 showing Cherokee land (left) and seal of Cherokee Nation (right)

EXTENDING THE CONTENT

The Cherokee In 1791 a treaty ceded part of Cherokee territory to the United States and established the permanent rights of the tribe to the remaining territory. Between 1790 and 1819, several thousand Cherokee migrated west of the Mississippi. There they become known as the Western Band. In 1820 the Cherokee established a system modeled on the United States government. They elected a principal chief, a senate, and a house of representatives. The Cherokee were designated among the Five Civilized Tribes because of this system.

Delicia Patterson

 Oral Histories

Delicia Patterson provided this look at life under slavery. She was 92 years old when she was interviewed.

I was born in Boonville, Missouri, January 2, 1845. Mother had five children but raised only two of us. I was owned by Charles Mitchell until I was fifteen years old. They were fairly nice to all of their slaves. . . .

When I was fifteen years old, I was brought to the courthouse, put up on the **auction block** to be sold. Old Judge Miller from my county was there. I knew him well because he was one of the wealthiest slave owners in the county, and the meanest one. He was so cruel all the slaves and many owners hated him because of it. He saw me on the block for sale, and he knew I was a good worker. So, when he bid for me, I spoke right out on the auction block and told him:

Anti-slavery banner

"Old Judge Miller, don't you bid for me, 'cause if you do, I would not live on your plantation. I will take a knife and cut my own throat from ear to ear before I would be owned by you. . . ."

So he stepped back and let someone else bid for me. . . . So I was sold to a Southern Englishman named Thomas Steele for fifteen hundred dollars. . . .

Religious Camp Meeting

 Personal Records

The desire for self-improvement was closely connected to a renewed interest in religion. By the 1830s, the Second Great Awakening, the second great period of religious revival in the United States, was in full swing. The camp meeting was especially important to isolated frontier families. One preacher, James Finley, described a revival meeting:

The noise was like the roar of Niagara. . . . Some of the people were singing, others praying, some crying for mercy in the most **piteous** accents, while others were shouting most **vociferously**. . . . At one time I saw at least five hundred swept down in a moment, as if a **battery** of a thousand guns had been opened upon them, and then immediately followed shrieks and shouts that **rent** the very heavens.

Analyzing Primary Sources

1. Do you think the writer of the newspaper article feels sympathy toward the Cherokee?
2. Why did Delicia, the formerly enslaved woman, not want to serve on Judge Miller's plantation?
3. What scene is James Finley describing?

 History *and the* Humanities

American Art and Architecture, Transparency 11, *The Buffalo Chase, Mouth of the Yellowstone*

Alternative Assessment

Have students research recent government policies toward Native Americans. Ask students to create a graphic organizer comparing and contrasting these policies with those of the Jackson administration. How do they differ? How are they similar?

GLENCOE TECHNOLOGY

 CD-ROM
American History Primary Source Document Library CD-ROM

Use the **American History Primary Source Document Library CD-ROM** to access other primary source documents related to the nation's development and growth.

Analyzing Primary Sources

1. The writer shows empathy for the exiles through choice of words and expressions.
2. He was a cruel person.
3. a camp revival meeting

Primary Sources Library

Team Teaching These selections may be implemented in a team-teaching context, in conjunction with English/Language Arts.

Unit Link

Use the primary source selections on pages 602–603 to accompany study of Unit 6, "Civil War and Reconstruction."

Reinforcing Vocabulary

Review the **Reader's Dictionary** with students on page 602 to be sure they understand any unfamiliar terms. Write *suffrage* on the chalkboard. Ask students who is entitled to suffrage today.

Background Information

The Spiritual Point out that the lyrics of spirituals, or religious folk songs, alluded to stories from the Bible. The spirituals often reflected the connection that enslaved African Americans felt to enslaved people in the Bible. Spirituals provided a way to create unity and also to protest. Passed down through the oral tradition, spirituals helped to form African American culture. Spirituals inspired later musical forms, most notably the blues.

For use with Unit 6

Civil War and Reconstruction

The American Civil War, or the War Between the States, was a major turning point for the American people. When the fighting ended, 600,000 Americans had lost their lives, slavery had been abolished, and most of the South lay in ruin. Leaders argued over how to reunite the shattered nation. And even though slavery had been abolished, African Americans quickly discovered that freedom did not mean equality. As you read these selections, think about the changes that took place during this era.

Reader's Dictionary

exterminating: destructive
bondage: slavery
suffrage: the right to vote
musket: soldier's rifle

Swing Low, Sweet Chariot

Songs & Poems

Spirituals—songs of salvation—provided the enslaved African Americans who wrote and sang them with not only a measure of comfort in bleak times but with a means for communicating secretly among themselves.

Swing low, sweet chariot,
Coming for to carry me home,
Swing low, sweet chariot,
Coming for to carry me home.

I looked over Jordan and what
   did I see
Coming for to carry me home,
A band of angels coming after me.
Coming for to carry me home.

If you get there before I do,
Coming for to carry me home,
Tell all my friends I'm coming too,
Coming for to carry me home.

I'm sometimes up and sometimes down,
Coming for to carry me home,
But still my soul feels heavenly bound,
Coming for to carry me home.

The Fisk Jubilee Singers

EXTENDING THE CONTENT

Black Codes During Reconstruction the newly structured Southern states passed a series of acts that became known as black codes. These laws sharply restricted the rights of newly freed African Americans. While varying from state to state, they usually included vagrancy laws that allowed unemployed African Americans to be hired out as forced labor; apprenticing laws, which allowed children to be bound out to white employers if the courts determined them to be without proper care; and limitations on African American occupations and property rights.

On the Plight of African Americans

 Personal Records

In 1867 Frederick Douglass appealed eloquently to Congress on behalf of African Americans.

. . . Yet the Negroes have marvelously survived all the **exterminating** forces of slavery, and have emerged at the end of 250 years of **bondage,** not [sad and hateful], but cheerful, hopeful, and forgiving. They now stand before Congress and the country, not complaining of the past, but simply asking for a better future.

. . . It is true that a strong plea for equal **suffrage** might be addressed to the national sense of honor. Something, too, might be said of national gratitude. A nation might well hesitate before the temptation to betray its allies. There is something . . . mean, to say nothing of the cruelty, in placing the loyal Negroes of the South under the political power of their rebel masters. . . . We asked the Negroes to [support] our cause, to be our friends, to fight for us and against their masters; and now, after they have done all that we asked them to do . . . it is proposed in some quarters to turn them over to the political control of the common enemy of the government and of the Negro. . . .

What, then, is the work before Congress? . . . In a word, it must [allow African Americans to vote], and by means of the loyal Negroes and the loyal white men of the South build up a national party there, and in time bridge the [gap] between North and South, so that our country may have a common liberty and a common civilization. . . .

The Fire of Battle

 Personal Records

Union soldier George Sargent served in the area west of Washington, D.C., throughout the Shenandoah Valley. He wrote his impressions of how soldiers react in battle.

Can you imagine a fellow's feelings about that time, to have to face thousands of **muskets** with a prospect of having a bullet put through you? If you can, all right; I can't describe it. I've heard some say that they were not scared going into a fight, but I think it's all nonsense. I don't believe there was ever a man who went into battle but was scared, more or less. Some will turn pale as a sheet, look wild and ferocious, some will be so excited that they don't know what they are about while others will be as cool and collected as on other occasions.

Analyzing Primary Sources

1. What does "Swing Low, Sweet Chariot" show about the condition and faith of the people who sang it?
2. What did Frederick Douglass urge Congress to do?
3. What does George Sargent say happens to all soldiers in battle?

History *and the* Humanities

- American Art and Architecture, Transparency 15, *A Rainy Day in Camp*
- American Music: Hits Through History, "Johnny Comes Marching Home"
- American Art and Music, Mathew Brady

Alternative Assessment

Have students read the Fourteenth Amendment on pages 247–248. Then ask them to write and illustrate a picture book for new voters, explaining the rights the amendment guarantees.

GLENCOE TECHNOLOGY

 CD-ROM
American History Primary Source Document Library CD-ROM

Use the **American History Primary Source Document Library CD-ROM** to access other primary source documents related to the Civil War and Reconstruction.

Analyzing Primary Sources

1. Answers will vary. Students might mention the hard life and deep faith of enslaved people, the hatred of slavery, and their longing for freedom.
2. Students should note that Douglass is asking Congress to allow African Americans to vote and participate in the democratic process.
3. Sargent believes that all soldiers in battle feel fear.

603

Block Schedule

Team Teaching These selections may be implemented in a team-teaching context, in conjunction with English/Language Arts.

Unit Link

Use the primary source selections on pages 604–605 to accompany study of Unit 7, "Modern America."

Reinforcing Vocabulary

Review the **Reader's Dictionary** with students on page 604 to be sure they understand any unfamiliar terms. Write *tolerance* on the chalkboard. Have students brainstorm a list of words to define its meaning.

Background Information

Purpose Explain that *purpose* is the intent to explain, persuade, or inform. An author may have more than one purpose. Have students read President Bush's address to Congress after the attacks on New York City and Washington, D.C. **Ask: What do you think was the purpose of President Bush's address?** *(Students may note that he was trying to justify why the United States and other countries should fight terrorism.)*

For use with Unit 7

Modern America Emerges

In the years following the Civil War modern American was born. The United States became an urban industrial nation. Millions of immigrants came to the United States following the promise of freedom and economic opportunity. As its society became more diverse, Americans struggled to end discrimination at home and to preserve freedom overseas. In the twenty-first century, Americans faced the challenge of fighting terrorism to preserve freedom. As you examine these selections, think of the challenges and opportunities facing the United States today.

Reader's Dictionary

extremism: the holding of unreasonable views

humanitarian: committed to improving the lives of other people

pluralism: society with different ethnic and religious groups

tolerance: acceptance of and fairness toward people who hold different views

Proud to Be an American

"God Bless the USA," by singer Lee Greenwood, topped the country music charts in the 1980s. It was adopted as a theme song for President Reagan's 1984 reelection campaign.

I'm proud to be an American
where at least I know I'm free,
And I won't forget the men who died
who gave that right to me,
And I gladly stand up next to you
and defend her still today,
'Cause there ain't no doubt I love this land
God Bless the U.S.A.

Address to Congress

On September 20, 2001, President George W. Bush addressed Congress, nine days after New York City and Washington, D.C., were shaken by suicide aircraft attacks.

On September the eleventh, enemies of freedom committed an act of war against our country. Americans have known wars—but for the past 136 years, they have been wars on foreign soil, except for one Sunday in 1941 [the attack on Pearl Harbor]. Americans have known the casualties of war—but not at the center of a great city on a peaceful morning. Americans have known surprise attacks—but never before on thousands of civilians. All of this was brought upon us in a single day—and night fell on a different world, a world where freedom itself is under attack. . . .

EXTENDING THE CONTENT

Search Dogs As rescue workers were organized to search for survivors in the aftermath of the collapse of the World Trade Center towers, search dogs and their handlers traveled to New York City to help recover victims. Over 300 dogs were a part of the rescue effort. Working 12-hour shifts, dogs and their handlers searched in teams of 4 after beams and large pieces of concrete were removed from the disaster area. When a dog ended its shift, it underwent a health check at a mobile veterinary clinic, which contained four operating stations and x-ray facilities. Common injuries suffered by the search dogs included eye irritations due to dust and wounded paws caused by shattered glass and concrete.

The terrorists [who carried out the attack] practice a fringe form of Islamic **extremism** that has been rejected by Muslim scholars and the vast majority of Muslim clerics—a fringe movement that perverts the peaceful teachings of Islam. . . .

This group [al-Qaeda] and its leader, a person named Osama bin Laden, are linked to many other organizations in different countries. . . . The leadership of al-Qaeda has great influence in Afghanistan and supports the Taliban regime in controlling most of that country. . . .

The United States respects the people of Afghanistan—after all, we are currently its largest source of **humanitarian** aid—but we condemn the Taliban regime.

[The terrorists] hate what we see right here in this chamber—a democratically elected government. Their leaders are self-appointed. They hate our freedoms—our freedom of religion, our freedom of speech, our freedom to vote and assemble and disagree with each other. . . .

This is not, however, just America's fight. And what is at stake is not just America's freedom. This is the world's fight. This is civilization's fight. This is the fight of all who believe in progress and **pluralism, tolerance,** and freedom. . . .

The civilized world is rallying to America's side. They understand that if this terror goes unpunished, their own cities, their own citizens may be next. Terror, unanswered, can not

President Bush thanks rescue workers

only bring down buildings, it can threaten the stability of legitimate governments. And we will not allow it. . . .

I ask you to uphold the values of America, and remember why so many have come here. We are in a fight for our principles, and our first responsibility is to live by them. No one should be singled out for unfair treatment or unkind words because of their ethnic background or religious faith. . . .

Great harm has been done to us. We have suffered great loss. And in our grief and anger we have found our mission and our moment. Freedom and fear are at war. The advance of human freedom—the great achievement of our time, and the great hope of every time—now depends on us. Our Nation—this generation—will lift a dark threat of violence from our people and our future. We will rally the world to this cause, by our efforts and by our courage. We will not tire, we will not falter, and we will not fail.

Analyzing Primary Sources

1. What themes does Lee Greenwood express in his song?
2. To what other tragic event does President Bush compare the events of September 11, 2001?
3. Why does the president believe other nations should help in the fight against terrorism?

History *and the* Humanities

- American Music: Hits Through History, "Rhythm is Gonna Get You"
- American Art and Architecture, Transparency 39, *Still Life with Red Car 1986*

Alternative Assessment

Have students create posters that address themes found in the unit. Students may use photos and quotations found in newspapers and magazines that focus on themes such as human rights, technology, or terrorism. Display the posters around the classroom.

GLENCOE TECHNOLOGY

CD-ROM
American History Primary Source Document Library CD-ROM

Use the **American History Primary Source Document Library CD-ROM** to access other primary source documents related to modern America.

Analyzing Primary Sources

1. Students may suggest that themes of pride, patriotism, honor, comradery, love, and loss are expressed in Greenwood's song.
2. the Japanese attack on Pearl Harbor on December 7, 1941
3. President Bush argued that if other countries do not fight terrorism, their own citizens and cities may be the next to be attacked. He also stated that terrorism threatens the stability of legitimate governments.

Presidents of the United States

In this resource you will find portraits of the individuals who served as presidents of the United States, along with their occupations, political party affiliations, and other interesting facts.

**The Republican Party during this period developed into today's Democratic Party. Today's Republican Party originated in 1854.

1 George Washington

Presidential term: 1789–1797
Lived: 1732–1799
Born in: Virginia
Elected from: Virginia
Occupations: Soldier, Planter
Party: None
Vice President: John Adams

2 John Adams

Presidential term: 1797–1801
Lived: 1735–1826
Born in: Massachusetts
Elected from: Massachusetts
Occupations: Teacher, Lawyer
Party: Federalist
Vice President: Thomas Jefferson

3 Thomas Jefferson

Presidential term: 1801–1809
Lived: 1743–1826
Born in: Virginia
Elected from: Virginia
Occupations: Planter, Lawyer
Party: Republican**
Vice Presidents: Aaron Burr, George Clinton

4 James Madison

Presidential term: 1809–1817
Lived: 1751–1836
Born in: Virginia
Elected from: Virginia
Occupation: Planter
Party: Republican**
Vice Presidents: George Clinton, Elbridge Gerry

5 James Monroe

Presidential term: 1817–1825
Lived: 1758–1831
Born in: Virginia
Elected from: Virginia
Occupation: Lawyer
Party: Republican**
Vice President: Daniel D. Tompkins

6 John Quincy Adams

Presidential term: 1825–1829
Lived: 1767–1848
Born in: Massachusetts
Elected from: Massachusetts
Occupation: Lawyer
Party: Republican**
Vice President: John C. Calhoun

7 Andrew Jackson

Presidential term: 1829–1837
Lived: 1767–1845
Born in: South Carolina
Elected from: Tennessee
Occupations: Lawyer, Soldier
Party: Democratic
Vice Presidents: John C. Calhoun, Martin Van Buren

8 Martin Van Buren

Presidential term: 1837–1841
Lived: 1782–1862
Born in: New York
Elected from: New York
Occupation: Lawyer
Party: Democratic
Vice President: Richard M.
  Johnson

9 William H. Harrison

Presidential term: 1841
Lived: 1773–1841
Born in: Virginia
Elected from: Ohio
Occupations: Soldier, Planter
Party: Whig
Vice President: John Tyler

10 John Tyler

Presidential term: 1841–1845
Lived: 1790–1862
Born in: Virginia
Elected as V.P. from: Virginia
Succeeded Harrison
Occupation: Lawyer
Party: Whig
Vice President: None

11 James K. Polk

Presidential term: 1845–1849
Lived: 1795–1849
Born in: North Carolina
Elected from: Tennessee
Occupation: Lawyer
Party: Democratic
Vice President: George M.
  Dallas

12 Zachary Taylor

Presidential term: 1849–1850
Lived: 1784–1850
Born in: Virginia
Elected from: Louisiana
Occupation: Soldier
Party: Whig
Vice President: Millard
  Fillmore

13 Millard Fillmore

Presidential term: 1850–1853
Lived: 1800–1874
Born in: New York
Elected as V.P. from: New York
Succeeded Taylor
Occupation: Lawyer
Party: Whig
Vice President: None

14 Franklin Pierce

Presidential term: 1853–1857
Lived: 1804–1869
Born in: New Hampshire
Elected from: New Hampshire
Occupation: Lawyer
Party: Democratic
Vice President: William R. King

15 James Buchanan

Presidential term: 1857–1861
Lived: 1791–1868
Born in: Pennsylvania
Elected from: Pennsylvania
Occupation: Lawyer
Party: Democratic
Vice President: John C.
  Breckinridge

16 Abraham Lincoln

Presidential term: 1861–1865
Lived: 1809–1865
Born in: Kentucky
Elected from: Illinois
Occupation: Lawyer
Party: Republican
Vice Presidents: Hannibal
  Hamlin, Andrew Johnson

17 Andrew Johnson

Presidential term: 1865–1869
Lived: 1808–1875
Born in: North Carolina
Elected as V.P. from: Tennessee
Succeeded Lincoln
Occupation: Tailor
Party: Republican
Vice President: None

18 Ulysses S. Grant

Presidential term: 1869–1877
Lived: 1822–1885
Born in: Ohio
Elected from: Illinois
Occupations: Farmer, Soldier
Party: Republican
Vice Presidents: Schuyler Colfax,
Henry Wilson

19 Rutherford B. Hayes

Presidential term: 1877–1881
Lived: 1822–1893
Born in: Ohio
Elected from: Ohio
Occupation: Lawyer
Party: Republican
Vice President: William A.
Wheeler

20 James A. Garfield

Presidential term: 1881
Lived: 1831–1881
Born in: Ohio
Elected from: Ohio
Occupations: Laborer, Professor
Party: Republican
Vice President: Chester A.
Arthur

21 Chester A. Arthur

Presidential term: 1881–1885
Lived: 1830–1886
Born in: Vermont
Elected as V.P. from: New York
Succeeded Garfield
Occupations: Teacher, Lawyer
Party: Republican
Vice President: None

22 Grover Cleveland

Presidential term: 1885–1889
Lived: 1837–1908
Born in: New Jersey
Elected from: New York
Occupation: Lawyer
Party: Democratic
Vice President: Thomas A.
Hendricks

23 Benjamin Harrison

Presidential term: 1889–1893
Lived: 1833–1901
Born in: Ohio
Elected from: Indiana
Occupation: Lawyer
Party: Republican
Vice President: Levi P. Morton

24 Grover Cleveland

Presidential term: 1893–1897
Lived: 1837–1908
Born in: New Jersey
Elected from: New York
Occupation: Lawyer
Party: Democratic
Vice President: Adlai E.
Stevenson

25 William McKinley

Presidential term: 1897–1901
Lived: 1843–1901
Born in: Ohio
Elected from: Ohio
Occupations: Teacher, Lawyer
Party: Republican
Vice Presidents: Garret Hobart,
Theodore Roosevelt

26 Theodore Roosevelt

Presidential term: 1901–1909
Lived: 1858–1919
Born in: New York
Elected as V.P. from: New York
Succeeded McKinley
Occupations: Historian, Rancher
Party: Republican
Vice President: Charles W.
Fairbanks

27 William H. Taft

Presidential term: 1909–1913
Lived: 1857–1930
Born in: Ohio
Elected from: Ohio
Occupation: Lawyer
Party: Republican
Vice President: James S.
Sherman

28 Woodrow Wilson

Presidential term: 1913–1921
Lived: 1856–1924
Born in: Virginia
Elected from: New Jersey
Occupation: College Professor
Party: Democratic
Vice President: Thomas R.
Marshall

29 Warren G. Harding

Presidential term: 1921–1923
Lived: 1865–1923
Born in: Ohio
Elected from: Ohio
Occupations: Newspaper Editor,
Publisher
Party: Republican
Vice President: Calvin Coolidge

30 Calvin Coolidge

Presidential term: 1923–1929
Lived: 1872–1933
Born in: Vermont
Elected as V.P. from:
Massachusetts
Succeeded Harding
Occupation: Lawyer
Party: Republican
Vice President: Charles G. Dawes

31 Herbert C. Hoover

Presidential term: 1929–1933
Lived: 1874–1964
Born in: Iowa
Elected from: California
Occupation: Engineer
Party: Republican
Vice President: Charles Curtis

32 Franklin D. Roosevelt

Presidential term: 1933–1945
Lived: 1882–1945
Born in: New York
Elected from: New York
Occupation: Lawyer
Party: Democratic
Vice Presidents: John N. Garner,
Henry A. Wallace, Harry S
Truman

33 Harry S Truman

Presidential term: 1945–1953
Lived: 1884–1972
Born in: Missouri
Elected as V.P. from: Missouri
Succeeded Roosevelt
Occupations: Clerk, Farmer
Party: Democratic
Vice President: Alben W.
Barkley

34 Dwight D. Eisenhower

Presidential term: 1953–1961
Lived: 1890–1969
Born in: Texas
Elected from: New York
Occupation: Soldier
Party: Republican
Vice President: Richard M.
Nixon

35 John F. Kennedy

Presidential term: 1961–1963
Lived: 1917–1963
Born in: Massachusetts
Elected from: Massachusetts
Occupations: Author, Reporter
Party: Democratic
Vice President: Lyndon B. Johnson

36 Lyndon B. Johnson

Presidential term: 1963–1969
Lived: 1908–1973
Born in: Texas
Elected as V.P. from: Texas
Succeeded Kennedy
Occupation: Teacher
Party: Democratic
Vice President: Hubert H. Humphrey

37 Richard M. Nixon

Presidential term: 1969–1974
Lived: 1913–1994
Born in: California
Elected from: New York
Occupation: Lawyer
Party: Republican
Vice Presidents: Spiro T. Agnew, Gerald R. Ford

38 Gerald R. Ford

Presidential term: 1974–1977
Lived: 1913–
Born in: Nebraska
Appointed as V.P. upon Agnew's resignation; succeeded Nixon
Occupation: Lawyer
Party: Republican
Vice President: Nelson A. Rockefeller

39 James E. Carter, Jr.

Presidential term: 1977–1981
Lived: 1924–
Born in: Georgia
Elected from: Georgia
Occupations: Business, Farmer
Party: Democratic
Vice President: Walter F. Mondale

40 Ronald W. Reagan

Presidential term: 1981–1989
Lived: 1911–2004
Born in: Illinois
Elected from: California
Occupations: Actor, Lecturer
Party: Republican
Vice President: George H.W. Bush

41 George H.W. Bush

Presidential term: 1989–1993
Lived: 1924–
Born in: Massachusetts
Elected from: Texas
Occupation: Business
Party: Republican
Vice President: J. Danforth Quayle

42 William J. Clinton

Presidential term: 1993–2001
Lived: 1946–
Born in: Arkansas
Elected from: Arkansas
Occupation: Lawyer
Party: Democratic
Vice President: Albert Gore, Jr.

43 George W. Bush

Presidential term: 2001–
Lived: 1946–
Born in: Connecticut
Elected from: Texas
Occupation: Business
Party: Republican
Vice President: Richard B. Cheney

The Magna Carta

The Magna Carta, signed by King John in 1215, marked a decisive step forward in the development of constitutional government in England. Later, it became a model for colonists who carried the Magna Carta's guarantees of legal and political rights to America.

1. . . . [T]hat the English Church shall be free, and shall have its rights entire, and its liberties unimpaired. . . . we have also granted for us and our heirs forever, all the liberties written out below, to have and to keep for them and their heirs, of us and our heirs:

39. No free man shall be seized or imprisoned, or stripped of his rights or possessions, or outlawed or exiled, or deprived of his standing in any other way, nor will we proceed with force against him, or send others to do so, except by the lawful judgment of his equals, or by the law of the land.

40. To no one will we sell, to no one deny or delay right or justice.

41. All merchants may enter or leave England unharmed and without fear, and may stay or travel within it, by land or water, for purposes of trade, free from all illegal exactions, in accordance with ancient and lawful customs. This, however, does not apply in time of war to merchants from a country that is at war with us. . . .

42. In future it shall be lawful for any man to leave and return to our kingdom unharmed and without fear, by land or water, preserving his allegiance to us, except in time of war, for some short period, for the common benefit of the realm. . . .

60. All these customs and liberties that we have granted shall be observed in our kingdom in so far as concerns our own relations with our subjects. Let all men of our kingdom, whether clergy or laymen, observe them similarly in their relations with their own men. . . .

63. . . . Both we and the barons have sworn that all this shall be observed in good faith and without deceit. Witness the abovementioned people and many others. Given by our hand in the meadow that is called Runnymede, between Windsor and Staines, on the fifteenth day of June in the seventeenth year of our reign.

Illuminated manuscript, Middle Ages

The Mayflower Compact

On November 21, 1620, 41 colonists aboard the Mayflower drafted this agreement. The Mayflower Compact was the first plan of self-government ever put in force in the English colonies.

In the Name of God, Amen. We, whose names are underwritten, the Loyal Subjects of our dread Sovereign Lord King James, by the Grace of God, of Great Britain, France, and Ireland, King, Defender of the Faith, etc. Having undertaken for the Glory of God, and Advancement of the Christian Faith, and the Honour of our King and Country, a Voyage to plant the first Colony in the northern Parts of Virginia; Do by these Presents, solemnly and mutually, in the Presence of God and one another, covenant and combine ourselves together into a civil Body Politick, for our better Ordering and Preservation, and Furtherance of the Ends aforesaid: And by Virtue hereof do enact, constitute, and frame, such just and equal Laws, Ordinances, Acts, Constitutions, and Officers, from time to time, as shall be thought most meet and convenient for the general Good of the Colony; unto which we promise all due Submission and Obedience. In Witness whereof we have hereunto subscribed our names at Cape-Cod the eleventh of November, in the Reign of our Sovereign Lord King James, of England, France, and Ireland, the eighteenth, and of Scotland, the fifty-fourth, Anno Domini, 1620.

The Fundamental Orders of Connecticut

In January 1639, settlers in Connecticut, led by Thomas Hooker, drew up the Fundamental Orders of Connecticut—America's first written Constitution. It is essentially a compact among the settlers and a body of laws.

Forasmuch as it has pleased the Almighty God by the wise disposition of His Divine Providence so to order and dispose of things that we, the inhabitants and residents of Windsor, Hartford, and Wethersfield are now cohabiting and dwelling in and upon the river of Conectecotte and the lands thereunto adjoining; and well knowing where a people are gathered together the Word of God requires that, to maintain the peace and union of such a people, there should be an orderly and decent government established according to God, . . . do therefore associate and conjoin ourselves to be as one public state or commonwealth. . . .

1. It is ordered . . . . that there shall be yearly two general assemblies or courts; . . . The first shall be called the Court of Election, wherein shall be yearly chosen . . . so many magistrates and other public officers as shall be found requisite. Whereof one to be chosen governor . . . and no other magistrate to be chosen for more than one year; provided always there be six chosen besides the governor . . . by all that are admitted freemen and have taken the oath of fidelity, and do cohabit within this jurisdiction. . . .

Documents

The English Bill of Rights

In 1689 William of Orange and his wife, Mary, became joint rulers of England after accepting what became known as the Bill of Rights. This document assured the people of certain basic civil rights.

. . . And thereupon the said lords spiritual and temporal and commons . . . do . . . declare That the pretended power of suspending of laws or the execution of laws by regal authority without consent of parliment is illegal. . . .

That levying money for or to the use of the crown . . . without grant of parliament for longer time or in other manner than the same is or shall be granted is illegal.

That it is the right of the subjects to petition the king and all commitments and prosecutions for such petitioning are illegal.

That the raising or keeping a standing army within the kingdom in time of peace unless it be with consent of parliament is against law. . . .

That election of members of parliament ought to be free. . . .

Seal of William and Mary

That excessive bail ought not to be required nor excessive fines imposed nor cruel and unusual punishments inflicted. . . .

The Articles of Confederation

The Continental Congress attempted to establish a federal union by drawing up the Articles of Confederation in 1777. The Articles did not go into effect until 1781, however, because some states delayed approval of the new plan of government.

Articles of Confederation and Perpetual Union Between the States of New Hampshire, Massachusetts Bay, Rhode Island and Providence Plantations, Connecticut, New York, New Jersey, Pennsylvania, Delaware, Maryland, Virginia, North Carolina, South Carolina, and Georgia.

ARTICLE I.

The style of this confederacy shall be "The United States of America."

ARTICLE II.

Each state retains its sovereignty, freedom, and independence, and every power, juris-

diction, and right which is not by this confederation expressly delegated to the United States in Congress assembled.

ARTICLE III.

The said states hereby severally enter into a firm league of friendship with each other, for their common defense, the security of their liberties, and their mutual and general welfare, binding themselves to assist each other against all force offered to, or attacks made upon them, or any of them, on account of religion, sovereignty, trade, or any other pretense whatever.

ARTICLE IV.

[T]he free inhabitants of each of these states . . . shall be entitled to all privileges and immunities of free citizens in the several states. . . .

The Federalist, No. 10

James Madison wrote several articles supporting ratification of the Constitution for a New York newspaper. In the excerpt below, Madison argues for the idea of a federal republic.

By a faction, I understand a number of citizens . . . who are united and actuated by some common impulse . . . adverse to the rights of other citizens. . . .

The inference to which we are brought is that the causes of faction cannot be removed and that relief is only to be sought in the means of controlling its *effects*. . . .

James Madison

A republic, by which I mean a government in which the scheme of representation takes place . . . promises the cure for which we are seeking. . . .

The two great points of difference between a democracy and a republic are: first, the delegation of the government, in the latter, to a small number of citizens elected by the rest; secondly, the greater number of citizens, and greater sphere of country, over which the latter may be extended.

The effect of the first difference is . . . to refine and enlarge the public views, by passing them through the medium of a chosen body of citizens, whose wisdom may best discern the true interest of their country, and whose patriotism and love of justice will be least likely to sacrifice it to temporary or partial considerations. . . .

The Federalist, No. 51

In the first of these two excerpts, the writer, either Madison or Alexander Hamilton, discusses the nature of society and government. In the second excerpt, the writer reveals his thoughts about protecting individuals and groups against the will of the majority.

If men were angels, no government would be necessary. If angels were to govern men, neither external nor internal controls on government would be necessary. In framing a government which is to be administered by men over men, the great difficulty lies in this: you must first enable the government to control the governed; and in the next place oblige it to control itself. A dependence on the people is, no doubt, the primary control on the government. . . .

It is of great importance in a republic not only to guard the society against the oppression of its rulers, but to guard one part of the society against the injustice of the other part. Different interests necessarily exist in different classes of citizens. If a majority be united by a common interest, the rights of the minority will be insecure. . . . [I]n the federal republic of the United States . . . the society itself will be broken into so many parts, interests, and classes of citizens, that the rights of individuals, or of the minority, will be in little danger from interested combinations of the majority. In a free government the security for civil rights must be the same as that for religious rights. It consists in the one case in the multiplicity of interests, and in the other in the multiplicity of sects. . . .

The Federalist, No. 59

In this federalist paper, Alexander Hamilton explains why Congress, and not the states, should have the final say in how federal elections are conducted.

The natural order of the subject leads us to consider . . . that provision of the Constitution which authorizes the national legislature to regulate, in the last resort, the election of its own members. . . . Its propriety rests upon the evidence of this plain proposition, that every government ought to contain in itself the means of its own preservation. . . . Nothing can be more evident, than that an exclusive power of regulating elections for the national government, in the hands of the state legislatures, would leave the existence of the union entirely at their mercy. They could at any moment annihilate it, by neglecting to provide for the choice of persons to administer its affairs. . . .

It is certainly true that the state legislatures, by forbearing the appointment of senators, may destroy the national government. But it will not follow that, because they have a power to do this in one instance, they ought to have it in every other. . . . it is an evil; but it is an evil which could not have been avoided without excluding the states . . . from a place in the organization of the national government. If this had been done, it would doubtless have been interpreted into an entire dereliction of the federal principle; and would certainly have deprived the state governments of that absolute safeguard which they will enjoy under this provision. . . .

Washington's Farewell Address

At the end of his second term as president, George Washington spoke of the dangers facing the young nation. He warned against the dangers of political parties and sectionalism, and he advised the nation against permanent alliances with other nations.

. . . Citizens by birth or choice of a common country, that country has a right to concentrate your affections. The name of American, which belongs to you in your national capacity, must always exalt the just pride of patriotism more than any appellation derived from local discriminations. With slight shades of difference, you have the same religion, manners, habits, and political principles. You have in a common cause fought and triumphed together. . . .

In contemplating the causes which may disturb our union it occurs as matter of serious concern that any ground should have been furnished for characterizing parties by *geographical* discriminations. . . .

No alliances, however strict, between the parts can be an adequate substitute. They must inevitably experience the infractions and interruptions which all alliances in all times have experienced. . . .

The great rule of conduct for us in regard to foreign nations is, in extending our commercial relations to have with them as little *political* connection as possible. . . .

The Star-Spangled Banner

During the British bombardment of Fort McHenry during the War of 1812, a young Baltimore lawyer named Francis Scott Key was inspired to write the words to "The Star-Spangled Banner." In 1931 Congress officially declared "The Star-Spangled Banner" as our national anthem. Below are the first and fourth verses.

O! say can you see by the dawn's early light,
What so proudly we hailed at the twilight's last gleaming,
Whose broad stripes and bright stars through the perilous fight,
O'er the ramparts we watch'd, were so gallantly streaming?
And the Rockets' red glare, the Bombs bursting in air,
Gave proof through the night that our Flag was still there;

O! say does that star-spangled Banner yet wave,
O'er the Land of the free, and the home of the brave!

O! thus be it ever when freemen shall stand,
Between their lov'd home, and the war's desolation,
Blest with vict'ry and peace, may the Heav'n rescued land,
Praise the Power that hath made and preserv'd us a nation!
Then conquer we must, when our cause it is just,
And this be our motto— "In God is our Trust;"
And the star-spangled Banner in triumph shall wave,
O'er the Land of the Free, and the Home of the Brave.

The Monroe Doctrine

In 1823 President James Monroe proclaimed the Monroe Doctrine. Designed to end European influence in the Western Hemisphere, it became a cornerstone of United States foreign policy.

. . . With the existing colonies or dependencies of any European power we have not interfered and shall not interfere. But with the Governments who have declared their independence and maintained it, and whose independence we have, on great consideration and on just principles, acknowledged, we could not view any interposition for the purpose of oppressing them, or controlling in any other manner their destiny, by any European power in any other light than as the manifestation of any unfriendly disposition toward the United States. . . .

Our policy in regard to Europe, which was adopted at an early stage of the wars which have so long agitated that quarter of the globe, nevertheless remains the same, which is, not to interfere in the internal concerns of any of its powers; to consider the government *de facto* as the legitimate government for us; to cultivate friendly relations with it, and to preserve those relations by a frank, firm, and manly policy, meeting in all instances the just claims of every power, submitting to injuries from none. . . .

Documents

The Seneca Falls Declaration

One of the first documents to express the desire for equal rights for women is the Declaration of Sentiments and Resolutions, issued in 1848 at the Seneca Falls Convention in Seneca Falls, New York. Led by Elizabeth Cady Stanton, the delegates adopted a set of resolutions modeled on the Declaration of Independence.

Elizabeth Cady Stanton

When, in the course of human events, it becomes necessary for one portion of the family of man to assume among the people of the earth a position different from that which they have hitherto occupied, but one to which the laws of nature and of nature's God entitle them, a decent respect to the opinions of mankind requires that they should declare the causes that impel them to such a course.

We hold these truths to be self-evident: that all men and women are created equal; that they are endowed by their Creator with certain inalienable rights; that among these are life, liberty, and the pursuit of happiness; that to secure these rights governments are instituted, deriving their just powers from the consent of the governed. Whenever any form of government becomes destructive of these ends, it is the right of those who suffer from it to refuse allegiance to it, and to insist upon the institution of a new government, laying its foundation on such principles, and organizing its powers in such form as to them shall seem most likely to effect their safety and happiness.

The Emancipation Proclamation

On January 1, 1863, President Abraham Lincoln issued the Emancipation Proclamation, which freed all enslaved people in states under Confederate control. The Proclamation was a step toward the Thirteenth Amendment (1865), which ended slavery in all of the United States.

... That on the 1st day of January, in the year of our Lord 1863, all persons held as slaves within any state or designated part of a state, the people whereof shall then be in rebellion against the United States, shall be then, thenceforward, and forever free; and the Executive Government of the United States, including the military and naval authority thereof, will recognize and maintain the freedom of such persons, and will do no act or acts to repress such persons, or any of them, in any efforts they may make for their actual freedom. . . .

And I further declare and make known that such persons, of suitable condition, will be received into the armed service of the United States. . . .

And upon this act, sincerely believed to be an act of justice, warranted by the Constitution upon military necessity, I invoke the considerate judgement of man-kind and the gracious favor of Almighty God. . . .

The Gettysburg Address

On November 19, 1863, President Abraham Lincoln gave a short speech at the dedication of a national cemetery on the battlefield of Gettysburg. His simple yet eloquent words expressed his hopes for a nation divided by civil war.

Four score and seven years ago our fathers brought forth on this continent a new nation, conceived in liberty, and dedicated to the proposition that all men are created equal.

Now we are engaged in a great civil war, testing whether that nation, or any nation so conceived and so dedicated, can long endure. We are met on a great battlefield of that war. We have come to dedicate a portion of that field as a final resting place for those who here gave their lives that that nation might live. It is altogether fitting and proper that we should do this.

But, in a larger sense, we can not dedicate—we can not consecrate—we can not hallow—this ground.

The brave men, living and dead, who struggled here, have consecrated it far above our poor power to add or detract. The world will little note nor long remember what we say here, but it can never forget what they did here. It is for us, the living, rather, to be dedicated here to the unfinished work which they who fought here have thus far so nobly advanced. It is rather for us to be here dedicated to the great task remaining before us—that from these honored dead we take increased devotion to that cause for which they gave the last full measure of devotion; that we here highly resolve that these dead shall not have died in vain; that this nation, under God, shall have a new birth of freedom; and that government of the people, by the people, for the people, shall not perish from the earth.

Soldier's kit, Civil War

Gettysburg Memorial

I Will Fight No More

Shield made of buffalo hide

In 1877 the Nez Perce fought the government's attempt to move them to a smaller reservation. After a remarkable attempt to escape to Canada, Chief Joseph realized that resistance was hopeless and advised his people to surrender.

Tell General Howard I know his heart. What he told me before I have in my heart. I am tired of fighting. . . . The old men are all dead. It is the young men who say yes or no. He who led the young men is dead. It is cold and we have no blankets. The little children are freezing to death. My people, some of them have run away to the hills, and have no blankets, no food; no one knows where they are—perhaps freezing to death. I want to have time to look for my children and see how many of them I can find. Maybe I shall find them among the dead. Hear me, my chiefs. I am tired; my heart is sick and sad. From where the sun now stands I will fight no more forever.

The Pledge of Allegiance

In 1892 the nation celebrated the 400th anniversary of Columbus's landing in America. In connection with this celebration, Francis Bellamy, a magazine editor, wrote and published the Pledge of Allegiance. The words "under God" were added by Congress in 1954 at the urging of President Dwight D. Eisenhower.

I pledge allegiance to the Flag of the United States of America and to the Republic for which it stands, one Nation under God, indivisible, with liberty and justice for all.

Students in a New York City school recite the Pledge of Allegiance

The American's Creed

William Tyler Page of Friendship Heights, Maryland, wrote The American's Creed. This statement of political faith summarizes the true meaning of freedom available to all Americans. The U.S. House of Representatives adopted the creed on behalf of the American people on April 3, 1918.

I believe in the United States of America as a Government of the people, by the people, for the people; whose just powers are derived from the consent of the governed; a democracy in a republic; a sovereign Nation of many sovereign States; a perfect union, one and inseparable; established upon those principles of freedom, equality, justice, and humanity for which American patriots sacrificed their lives and fortunes.

I therefore believe it is my duty to my Country to love it; to support its Constitution; to obey its laws; to respect its flag, and to defend it against all enemies.

The Fourteen Points

On January 8, 1918, President Woodrow Wilson went before Congress to offer a statement of aims called the Fourteen Points. Wilson's plan called for freedom of the seas in peace and war, an end to secret alliances, and equal trading rights for all countries. The excerpt that follows is taken from the President's message.

. . . We entered this war because violations of right had occurred which touched us to the quick and made the life of our own people impossible unless they were corrected and the world secured once for all against their recurrence. What we demand in this war, therefore, is nothing peculiar to ourselves. It is that the world be made fit and safe to live in; and particularly that it be made safe for every peace-loving nation which, like our own, wishes to live its own life, determine its own institutions, be assured of justice and fair dealing by the other peoples of the world as against force and selfish aggression. All the peoples of the world are in effect partners in this interest, and for our own part we see very clearly that unless justice be done to others it will not be done to us. The program of the world's peace, therefore, is our program; and that program, the only possible program, as we see it, is this:

I. Open covenants of peace, openly arrived at, after which there shall be no private international understandings of any kind but diplomacy shall proceed always frankly and in the public view.

II. Absolute freedom of navigation upon the seas, outside territorial waters, alike in peace and in war, except as the seas may be closed in whole or in part by international action for the enforcement of international covenants.

XIV. A general association of nations must be formed under specific covenants for the purpose of affording mutual guarantees of political independence and territorial integrity to great and small states alike. . . .

Brown v. Board of Education

On May 17, 1954, the Supreme Court ruled in **Brown** *v.* **Board of Education of Topeka, Kansas** *that racial segregation in public schools was unconstitutional. This decision provided the legal basis for court challenges to segregation in every aspect of American life.*

. . . The plaintiffs contend that segregated public schools are not "equal" and cannot be made "equal" and that hence they are deprived of the equal protection of the laws. Because of the obvious importance of the question presented, the Court took jurisdiction. . . .

Our decision, therefore, cannot turn on merely a comparison of these tangible factors in the Negro and white schools involved in each of the cases. We must look instead to the effect of segregation itself on public education.

In approaching this problem, we cannot turn the clock back to 1868 when the Amendment was adopted, or even to 1896 when *Plessy* v. *Ferguson* was written. We must consider public education in the light of its full development and its present place in American life throughout the Nation. Only in this way can it be determined if segregation in public schools deprives these plaintiffs of the equal protection of the laws.

Today, education is perhaps the most important function of state and local governments. Compulsory school attendance laws and the great expenditures for education both demonstrate our recognition of the importance of education to our democratic society. . . . In these days, it is doubtful that any child may reasonably be expected to succeed in life if he is denied the opportunity of an education. Such an opportunity, where the state has undertaken to provide it, is a right which must be made available to all on equal terms.

We come then to the question presented: Does segregation of children in public schools solely on the basis of race, even though the physical facilities and other "tangible" factors may be equal, deprive the children of the minority group of equal educational opportunities? We believe that it does.

. . . We conclude that in the field of public education the doctrine of "separate but equal" has no place. Separate educational facilities are inherently unequal. Therefore, we hold that the plaintiffs and others similarly situated for whom the actions have been brought are, by reason of the segregation complained of, deprived of the equal protection of the laws guaranteed by the Fourteenth Amendment. . . .

Troops escort students to newly integrated school

John F. Kennedy's Inaugural Address

President Kennedy's Inaugural Address on January 20, 1961, set the tone for his administration. In his address Kennedy stirred the nation by calling for "a grand and global alliance" to fight tyranny, poverty, disease, and war.

We observe today not a victory of party but a celebration of freedom—symbolizing an end as well as a beginning—signifying renewal as well as change. For I have sworn before you and Almighty God the same solemn oath our forebears prescribed nearly a century and three-quarters ago.

The world is very different now. For man holds in his mortal hands the power to abolish all forms of human poverty and all forms of human life. And yet the same revolutionary beliefs for which our forebears fought are still at issue around the globe—the belief that the rights of man come not from the generosity of the state but from the hand of God.

We dare not forget today that we are the heirs of that first revolution. Let the word go forth from this time and place, to friend and foe alike, that the torch has been passed to a new generation of Americans—born in this century, tempered by war, disciplined by a hard and bitter peace, proud of our ancient heritage—and unwilling to witness or permit the slow undoing of those human rights to which this nation has always been committed, and to which we are committed today at home and around the world.

Let every nation know, whether it wishes us well or ill, that we shall pay any price, bear any burden, meet any hardship, support any friend, oppose any foe to assure the survival and the success of liberty.

This much we pledge—and more.

To those old allies whose cultural and spiritual origins we share, we pledge the loyalty of faithful friends. United, there is little we cannot do in a host of cooperative ventures. Divided, there is little we can do. . . .

Let us never negotiate out of fear. But let us never fear to negotiate.

Let both sides explore what problems unite us instead of belaboring those problems which divide us. . . .

Let both sides seek to invoke the wonders of science instead of its terrors. Together let us explore the stars, conquer the deserts, eradicate disease, tap the ocean depths, and encourage the arts and commerce. . . .

And so, my fellow Americans: ask not what your country can do for you—ask what you can do for your country.

My fellow citizens of the world: ask not what America will do for you, but what together we can do for the freedom of man. . . .

President Kennedy speaking at his inauguration

I Have a Dream

Dr. Martin Luther King, Jr.

On August 28, 1963, while Congress debated wide-ranging civil rights legislation, Dr. Martin Luther King, Jr., led more than 200,000 people in a march on Washington, D.C. On the steps of the Lincoln Memorial he gave a stirring speech in which he eloquently spoke of his dreams for African Americans and for the United States. Excerpts of the speech follow.

. . . There are those who are asking the devotees of civil rights, "When will you be satisfied?"

We can never be satisfied as long as the Negro is the victim of the unspeakable horrors of police brutality. . . .

We cannot be satisfied as long as the Negro's basic mobility is from a smaller ghetto to a larger one.

We can never be satisfied as long as a Negro in Mississippi cannot vote and a Negro in New York believes he has nothing for which to vote. . . .

I say to you today, my friends, that in spite of the difficulties and frustrations of the moment I still have a dream. It is a dream deeply rooted in the American dream. I have a dream that one day this nation will rise up and live out the true meaning of its creed: "We hold these truths to be self-evident, that all men are created equal."

I have a dream that one day on the red hills of Georgia the sons of former slaves and the sons of former slaveowners will be able to sit down together at the table of brotherhood.

I have a dream that one day even the state of Mississippi, a desert state sweltering with the heat of injustice and oppression, will be transformed into an oasis of freedom and justice.

I have a dream that my four little children will one day live in a nation where they will not be judged by the color of their skin but by the content of their character. . . .

. . . When we let freedom ring, when we let it ring from every village and every hamlet, from every state and every city, we will be able to speed up that day when all of God's children, black men and white men, Jews and Gentiles, Protestants and Catholics, will be able to join hands and sing in the words of the old Negro spiritual: "Free at last! Free at last! Thank God Almighty, we are free at last!"

The March on Washington

Supreme Court Case Summaries

The following summaries give details about important Supreme Court cases.

Brown v. Board of Education (1954)

In *Brown* v. *Board of Education of Topeka, Kansas* the Supreme Court overruled *Plessy* v. *Ferguson* (1896) [see p. 626] making the separate-but-equal doctrine in public schools unconstitutional. The Supreme Court rejected the idea that truly equal but separate schools for African American and white students would be constitutional. The Court explained that the Fourteenth Amendment's requirement that all persons be guaranteed equal protection of the law is not met simply by ensuring that African American and white schools "have been equalized…with respect to buildings, curricula, qualifications and salaries, and other tangible factors."

The Court then ruled that racial segregation in public schools violates the Equal Protection Clause of the Constitution because it is inherently unequal. In other words, nothing can make racially segregated public schools equal under the Constitution because the very fact of separation marks the separated race as inferior. In practical terms, the Court's decision in this case has been extended beyond public education to virtually all public accommodations and activities.

Dred Scott v. Sandford (1857)

Dred Scott was taken by slaveholder John Sandford to the free state of Illinois and to the Wisconsin Territory, which had also banned slavery. Later they returned to Missouri, a slave state. Several years later, Scott sued for his freedom under the Missouri legal principle of "once free, always free." In other words, under Missouri law enslaved people were entitled to freedom if they had lived in a free state at any time. Missouri courts ruled against Scott, but he appealed the case all the way to the United States Supreme Court.

Dred Scott

The Supreme Court decided this case before the Fourteenth Amendment was added to the Constitution. (The Fourteenth Amendment provides that anyone born or naturalized in the United States is a citizen of the nation and of his or her state of residence.) The court held that enslaved African Americans were property, not citizens, and thus had no rights under the Constitution. The decision also declared that it was unconstitutional to prohibit slavery in the territories. Many people in the North were outraged by the decision, which moved the nation closer to civil war.

Furman v. Georgia (1972)

This decision put a halt to the application of the death penalty under state laws then in effect. For the first time, the Supreme Court ruled that the death penalty amounted to cruel and unusual punishment, which is outlawed in the Constitution. The Court explained that existing death penalty laws did not give juries enough guidance in deciding whether or not to impose the death penalty. As a result, the death penalty in many cases was imposed arbitrarily, that is, without a reasonable basis in the facts and circumstances of the offender or the crime.

The Furman decision halted all executions in the 39 states that had death penalty laws at that time. Since the decision, 38 states have rewritten death penalty laws to meet the requirements established in the Furman case.

Gibbons v. Ogden (1824)

Thomas Gibbons had a federal license to operate a steamboat along the coast, but he did not have a license from the state of New York to travel on New York waters. He wanted to run a steamboat line between Manhattan and New Jersey that would compete with Aaron Ogden's company. Ogden had a New York license. Gibbons sued for the freedom to use his federal license to compete against Ogden on New York waters.

Gibbons won the case. The Supreme Court made it clear that the authority of Congress to regulate interstate commerce (among states) includes the authority to regulate intrastate commerce (within a single state) that bears on, or relates to, interstate commerce.

Before this decision, it was thought that the Constitution would permit a state to close its borders to interstate commercial activity—which, in effect, would stop such activity in its tracks. This case says that a state can regulate purely internal commercial activity, but only Congress can regulate commercial activity that has both intrastate and interstate dimensions.

Gideon v. Wainwright (1963)

After being accused of robbery, Clarence Gideon defended himself in a Florida court because the judge in the case refused to appoint a free lawyer. The jury found Gideon guilty. Eventually, Gideon appealed his conviction to the United States Supreme Court, claiming that by failing to appoint a lawyer the lower court had violated his rights under the Sixth and Fourteenth Amendments.

The Supreme Court agreed with Gideon. In *Gideon v. Wainwright* the Supreme Court held for the first time that poor defendants in criminal cases have the right to a state-paid attorney under the Sixth Amendment. The rule announced in this case has been refined to apply whenever the defendant, if convicted, can be sentenced to more than six months in jail or prison.

Korematsu v. United States (1944)

After the Japanese bombing of Pearl Harbor in 1941, thousands of Japanese Americans on the West Coast were forced to abandon their homes and businesses, and they were moved to internment camps in

In 1983 Fred Korematsu (center) won a reversal of his conviction.

California, Idaho, Utah, Arizona, Wyoming, Colorado, and Arkansas. The prison-like camps offered poor food and cramped quarters.

The Supreme Court's decision in *Korematsu v. United States* upheld the authority of the federal government to move Japanese Americans, many of whom were citizens, from designated military areas that included almost the entire West Coast. The government defended the so-called exclusion orders as a necessary response to Japan's attack on Pearl Harbor. Only after his reelection in 1944 did President Franklin Roosevelt rescind the evacuation orders, and by the end of 1945 the camps were closed.

Marbury v. Madison (1803)

During his last days in office, President John Adams commissioned William Marbury and several other men as judges. This action by Federalist president Adams angered the incoming Democratic-Republican president Thomas Jefferson. Jefferson then ordered James Madison, his secretary of state, not to deliver the commissions, thus blocking the appointments. William Marbury sued, asking the Supreme Court to order Madison to deliver the commission that would make him a judge.

The Court ruled against Marbury, but more importantly, the decision in this case established one of the most significant principles of American constitutional law. The Supreme Court held that it is the Court itself that has the final say on what the Constitution means. This is known as judicial review. It is also the Supreme Court that has the final say in whether or not an act of government—legislative or executive at the federal, state, or local level—violates the Constitution.

McCulloch v. Maryland (1819)

Following the War of 1812, the United States experienced years of high inflation and general economic turmoil. In an attempt to stabilize the economy, the United States Congress chartered a Second Bank of the United States in 1816. Maryland and several other states, however, opposed the competition that the new national bank created and passed laws taxing its branches. In 1818, James McCulloch, head of the Baltimore branch of the Second Bank of the United States, refused to pay the tax to the state of Maryland. The case worked its way through the Maryland state courts all the way to the United States Supreme Court.

The Supreme Court declared the Maryland tax unconstitutional and void. More importantly, the decision established the foundation for expanded Congressional authority. The Court held that the necessary and proper clause of the Constitution allows Congress to do more than the Constitution expressly authorizes it to do. The decision allows Congress to enact nearly any law that will help it achieve any of its duties as set forth in the Constitution. For example, Congress has the express authority to regulate interstate commerce. The necessary and proper clause permits Congress to do so in ways not actually specified in the Constitution.

Miranda v. Arizona (1966)

In 1963, police in Arizona arrested Ernesto Miranda for kidnapping. The court found Miranda guilty on the basis of a signed confession. The police admitted that neither before nor during the questioning had Miranda been advised of his right to consult with an attorney before answering any questions or of his right to have an attorney present during the interrogation. Miranda appealed his conviction, claiming that police had violated his right against self-incrimination under the Fifth Amendment by not informing him of his legal rights during questioning.

Miranda won the case. The Supreme Court held that a person in police custody cannot be questioned unless told that he or she has: 1) the right to remain silent, 2) the right to an attorney (at government expense if the accused is unable to pay), and 3) that anything the person says after stating that he or she understands these rights can be used as evidence of guilt at trial. These rights have come to be called the Miranda warning. They are intended to ensure that an accused person in custody will not unknowingly give up the Fifth Amendment's protection against self-incrimination.

In 1963, the arrest of Ernesto Miranda (left) led to a landmark decision.

New York Times Company v. United States (1971)

In June 1971, the *New York Times* published its first installment of the "Pentagon Papers," a classified document about government actions in the Vietnam War era. The secret document had been leaked to the *Times* by antiwar activist Daniel Ellsberg, who had previously worked in national security for the government. President Richard Nixon went to court to block further publication of the Pentagon Papers. The *New York Times* appealed to the Supreme Court to allow it to continue publishing without government interference.

The Supreme Court's ruling in this case upheld earlier decisions that established the doctrine of prior restraint. This doctrine protects the press (broadly defined to include newspapers, television and radio, filmmakers and distributors, etc.) from government attempts to block publication. Except in extraordinary circumstances, the press must be allowed to publish.

Plessy v. Ferguson (1896)

In the late 1800s railroad companies in Louisiana were required by state law to provide "separate-but-equal" cars for white and African American passengers. In 1890 a group of citizens in New Orleans selected Homer Plessy to challenge that law. In 1892, Plessy boarded a whites-only car and refused to move. He was arrested. Plessy appealed to the Supreme Court, arguing that the Louisiana separate-but-equal law violated his right to equal protection under the Fourteenth Amendment.

Homer Plessy lost the case. The Plessy decision upheld the separate-but-equal doctrine used by Southern states to perpetuate segregation following the Civil War. The court ruled that the Fourteenth Amendment's equal protection clause required only equal public facilities for the two races, not equal access to the same facilities. This decision was overruled in 1954 by *Brown* v. *Board of Education of Topeka, Kansas* (discussed previously).

Roe v. Wade (1973)

Roe v. *Wade* challenged restrictive abortion laws in both Texas and Georgia. The suit was brought in the name of Jane Roe, an alias used to protect the privacy of the plaintiff.

In this decision, the Supreme Court ruled that females have a constitutional right under various provisions of the Constitution—most notably, the due process clause—to decide whether or not to terminate a pregnancy. The Supreme Court's decision in this case was the most significant in a long line of decisions over a period of 50 years that recognized a constitutional right of privacy, even though the word *privacy* is not found in the Constitution.

Tinker v. Des Moines School District (1969)

During the Vietnam War, some students in Des Moines, Iowa, wore black armbands to school to protest American involvement in the conflict. Two days earlier, school officials had adopted a policy banning the wearing of armbands to school. When the students arrived at school wearing armbands, they were suspended and sent home. The students argued that school officials violated their First Amendment right to free speech.

The Supreme Court sided with the students. In a now-famous statement the court said that "it can hardly be argued that either students or teachers shed their constitutional rights of freedom of speech or expression at the schoolhouse gate." The Supreme Court went on to rule that a public school could not suspend students who wore black armbands to school to symbolize their opposition to the Vietnam War. In so holding, the Court likened the students' conduct to pure speech and decided it on that basis.

United States v. Nixon (1974)

In the early 1970s, President Nixon was named an unindicted co-conspirator in the criminal investigation that arose in the aftermath of a break-in at the offices of the Democratic Party in Washington, D.C. A federal judge had ordered President Nixon to turn over tapes of conversations he had with his advisers about the break-in. Nixon resisted the order, claiming that the conversations were entitled to absolute confidentiality by Article II of the Constitution.

The decision in this case made it clear that the president is not above the law. The Supreme Court held that only those presidential conversations and communications that relate to performing the duties of the office of president are confidential and protected from a judicial order of disclosure. The Court ordered Nixon to give up the tapes, which revealed evidence linking the president to the conspiracy to obstruct justice. He resigned from office shortly thereafter.

Worcester v. Georgia (1832)

State officials in Georgia wanted to remove the Cherokees from land that had been guaranteed to them in earlier treaties. Samuel Worcester was a Congregational missionary who worked with the Cherokee people. He was arrested for failure to have a license that the state required to live in Cherokee country and for refusing to obey an order from the Georgia militia to leave Cherokee lands. Worcester then sued the state of Georgia. He claimed that Georgia had no legal authority on Cherokee land because the United States government recognized the Cherokee in Georgia as a separate nation.

The Supreme Court agreed with Worcester by a vote of 5 to 1. Chief Justice John Marshall wrote the majority opinion which said that Native American nations were a distinct people with the right to have independent political communities and that only the federal government had authority over matters that involved the Cherokee.

President Andrew Jackson supported Georgia's efforts to remove the Cherokee to Indian Territory and refused to enforce the court's ruling. After the ruling Jackson remarked, "John Marshall has made his decision. Now let him enforce it."

Supreme Court Cases

The gazetteer is a geographical dictionary that lists political divisions, natural features, and other places and locations. Following each entry is a description, its latitude and longitude, and a page reference that indicates where each entry may be found in this text.

A

Afghanistan country in southwestern Asia (33°N/63°E) RA13, 580

Africa continent of the Eastern Hemisphere south of the Mediterranean Sea and adjoining Asia on its northeastern border (10°N/22°E) RA15, 41

Alabama state in the southeastern United States; 22nd state to enter the Union (33°N/87°W) RA3, 319

Alamo Texas mission captured by Mexican forces in 1836 (29°N/98°W) 365

Alaska state in the United States, located in northwestern North America (64°N/150°W) RA2

Albany capital of New York State located in the Hudson Valley; site where Albany Congress proposed first formal plan to unite the 13 colonies (42°N/74°W) 119

Allegheny River river in western Pennsylvania uniting with the Monongahela River at Pittsburgh to form the Ohio River (41°N/79°W) RA5, 123

Andes mountain system extending along western coast of South America (13°S/75°W) 18

Antietam Civil War battle site in western Maryland (40°N/77°W) 472

Appalachian Mountains chief mountain system in eastern North America extending from Quebec and New Brunswick to central Alabama (37°N/82°W) RA5, 60

Appomattox Court House site in central Virginia where Confederate forces surrendered, ending the Civil War (37°N/78°W) 491

Arizona state in the southwestern United States; 48th state to enter the Union (34°N/113°W) RA2, 28

Arkansas state in the south central U.S.; acquired as part of Louisiana Purchase (35°N/94°W) RA3, 310

Asia continent of the Eastern Hemisphere forming a single landmass with Europe (50°N/100°E) RA15, 17

Atlanta capital of Georgia located in the northwest central part of the state (34°N/84°W) 423

Atlantic Ocean ocean separating North and South America from Europe and Africa (5°S/25°W) RA14, 16

Australia continent and country southeast of Asia (25°S/125°E) RA15, 42

Austria-Hungary former monarchy in central Europe (47°N/12°E) 547

B

Baltimore city on the Chesapeake Bay in central Maryland (39°N/77°W) 87

Barbary Coast north coast of Africa between Morocco and Tunisia (35°N/3°E) 289

Bay of Pigs site of 1961 invasion of Cuba by U.S.-trained Cuban exiles (22°N/79°W) 568

Beijing capital of China located in the northeastern part of the country (40°N/116°E) 572

Belgium country in northwest Europe (51°N/3°E) RA15, 668

Bering Strait waterway between North America and Asia where a land bridge once existed (65°N/170°W) 17

Beringia land bridge that linked Asia and North America during the last Ice Age (65°N/170°W) 17

Berlin city in east central Germany; former capital divided into sectors after World War II (53°N/13°E) 564

Birmingham city in north central Alabama; scene of several civil rights protests (33°N/86°W) 567

Black Hills mountains in southwestern South Dakota; site of conflict between the Sioux and white settlers during 1870s (44°N/104°W) 535

Boston capital of Massachusetts located in the eastern part of the state; founded by English Puritans in 1630 (42°N/71°W) 78

Brazil country in eastern South America (9°S/53°W) RA14, 55

Breed's Hill site near Boston where the Battle of Bunker Hill took place (42°N/71°W) 145

Buffalo industrial city and rail center in New York State (43°N/79°W) 315

Bull Run site of two Civil War battles in northern Virginia; also called Manassas (39°N/77°W) 466

C

Cahokia largest settlement of the Mound Builders, built in Illinois after A.D. 900 (39°N/90°W) 30

California state in the western United States; attracted thousands of miners during gold rush of 1849 (38°N/121°W) RA2, 371

Cambodia country in Southeastern Asia bordering Gulf of Siam; official name Democratic Kampuchea (12°N/105°E) RA15

Canada country in northern North America (50°N/100°W) RA14, 17

Cape of Good Hope southern tip of Africa (34°S/18°E) 44

Caribbean Sea tropical sea in the Western Hemisphere (15°N/75°W) RA9, 19

Central America area of North America between Mexico and South America (11°N/86°W) RA8, 17

Chancellorsville Virginia site of 1863 Confederate victory (38°N/78°W) 486

Charleston city in South Carolina on the Atlantic coast; original name Charles Town (33°N/80°W) 89

Chesapeake Bay inlet of the Atlantic Ocean in Virginia and Maryland (38°N/76°W) 72

Chicago largest city in Illinois; located in northeastern part of the state along Lake Michigan (42°N/88°W) 318

Chile South American country (35°S/72°W) RA14

China country in eastern Asia; mainland (People's Republic of China) under communist control since 1949 (37°N/93°E) RA15, 565

Chisholm Trail pioneer cattle trail from Texas to Kansas (34°N/98°W) 529

Cincinnati city in southern Ohio on the Ohio River; grew as a result of increasing steamship traffic during the mid-1800s (39°N/84°W) 265

Cleveland city in northern Ohio on Lake Erie (41°N/82°W) 423

Colombia country in South America (4°N/73°W) RA14, 26

Colorado state in the western United States (39°N/107°W) RA3, 29

Colorado River river that flows from the Colorado Rockies to the Gulf of California (36°N/113°W) RA4, 284

Columbia River river flowing through southwest Canada and northwestern United States into the Pacific Ocean (46°N/120°W) 357

Concord village northwest of Boston, Massachusetts; site of early battle of the American Revolution (42°N/71°W) 143

Connecticut state in the northeastern United States; one of the original 13 states (42°N/73°W) RA3, 79

Cuba country in the West Indies, North America (22°N/79°W) RA9, 52

Czechoslovakia former country in central Europe; now two countries, the Czech Republic and Slovakia (49°N/16°E) RA15

Dallas a leading city in Texas (33°N/97°W) 567

Delaware state in the northeastern United States; one of the original 13 states (39°N/75°W) RA3, 84

Detroit city in southeastern Michigan; site of significant battles during the French and Indian War and the War of 1812; center of automobile industry (42°N/83°W) 125

Dodge City Kansas cattle town during the 19th century (37°N/100°W) 535

Dominican Republic country in the West Indies on the eastern part of Hispaniola Island (19°N/71°W) RA9, 47

East Germany country in central Europe; reunified with West Germany in 1990 (52°N/12°E) 569

Egypt country in northeastern Africa (27°N/27°E) RA12, 574

England division of the United Kingdom of Great Britain and Northern Ireland (52°N/2°W) 40

Erie Canal the waterway connecting the Hudson River with Lake Erie through New York State (43°N/76°W) 318

Ethiopia country in eastern Africa, north of Somalia and Kenya (8°N/38°E) RA15

Europe continent of the northern part of the Eastern Hemisphere between Asia and the Atlantic Ocean (50°N/15°E) RA15, 38

Florida state in the southeastern United States (30°N/85°W) RA3, 93

Fort McHenry fort in Baltimore harbor; inspired poem that later became "The Star-Spangled Banner" (39°N/76°W) 299

Fort Necessity Pennsylvania fort built by George Washington's troops in 1754 (40°N/80°W) 118

Fort Sumter Union fort during the Civil War located on island near Charleston, South Carolina; site of first military engagement of Civil War (33°N/80°W) 453

Fort Ticonderoga British fort on Lake Champlain (44°N/73°W) 144

France country in western Europe (50°N/1°E) RA15, 40

Fredericksburg city and Civil War battle site in northeast Virginia (38°N/77°W) 486

Freeport city in northern Illinois; site of 1858 Lincoln-Douglas campaign debate (42°N/89°W) 448

Gadsden Purchase portion of present-day Arizona and New Mexico; area purchased from Mexico in 1853 (32°N/111°W) 374

Galveston city on the Gulf of Mexico coast in Texas; created nation's first commission form of city government (29°N/95°W) 541

Gaza Strip narrow coastal strip along the Mediterranean (31°N/34°E) RA12

Georgia state in the southeastern United States (33°N/84°W) RA3, 90

Germany country in central Europe; divided after World War II into East Germany and West Germany; unified in 1990 (50°N/10°E) RA15, 547

Gettysburg city and Civil War battle site in south central Pennsylvania; site where Lincoln delivered the Gettysburg Address (40°N/77°W) 486

Great Britain commonwealth comprising England, Scotland, and Wales (56°N/2°W) 559

Great Lakes chain of five lakes, Superior, Erie, Michigan, Ontario, and Huron, in central North America (45°N/87°W) RA5, 60

Great Plains flat grassland in the central United States (45°N/104°W) RA4, 390

Great Salt Lake lake in northern Utah with no outlet and strongly saline waters (41°N/113°W) RA3, 378

Greece country in southeastern Europe (39°N/21°E) RA15

Grenada country in the Caribbean (12°N/61°W) RA9

Guadalcanal island in the Solomons east of Australia (10°S/159°E) 562

Guam U.S. possession in the western Pacific Ocean (14°N/143°E) 562

Guatemala country in Central America, south of Mexico (16°N/92°W) RA8, 23

Gulf of Mexico gulf on the southeast coast of North America (25°N/94°W) RA5, 92

Gulf of Tonkin gulf in South China Sea east of northern Vietnam (20°N/108°E) 569

Haiti country on Hispaniola Island in the West Indies (19°N/72°W) RA9, 47

Harpers Ferry town in northern West Virginia on the Potomac River (39°N/78°W) 448

Hartford capital of Connecticut located along the Connecticut River (42°N/73°W) 79

Hawaii state in the United States located in the Pacific Ocean (20°N/157°W) RA2

Hiroshima city in southern Japan; site of first military use of atomic bomb, August 6, 1945 (34°N/132°E) 563

Hispaniola island in the West Indies in North America (17°N/73°W) RA9, 47

Horseshoe Bend Alabama site where Creek-U.S. battled in 1814 (33°N/86°W) 298

Hudson Bay large bay in northern Canada (60°N/86°W) RA14, 61

Hudson River river flowing through New York State (53°N/74°W) 316

Hungary country in central Europe (47°N/20°E) RA15

Idaho state in the northwestern U.S.; ranks among top states in silver production (44°N/115°W) RA2, 541

Illinois state in the north central United States; one of the states formed in the Northwest Territory (40°N/91°W) RA3, 195

Indian Territory land reserved by the United States government for Native Americans, now the state of Oklahoma (36°N/98°W) 342

Indiana state in the north central United States; one of the states formed in the

Gazetteer

Northwest Territory (40°N/ 87°W) RA3, 195

Indochina region in Southeast Asia (17°N/105°E) 559

Iowa state in the north central U.S. acquired as part of the Louisiana Purchase (42°N/94°W) RA3, 541

Iran country in southwestern Asia (31°N/53°E) RA13, 574

Iraq country in southwestern Asia (32°N/42°E) RA13, 576

Ireland island west of England, occupied by the Republic of Ireland and by Northern Ireland (54°N/8°W) RA14

Israel country of the Middle East in southwestern Asia along the Mediterranean Sea (33°N/34°E) RA12, 574

Italy country in southern Europe along the Mediterranean (44°N/11°E) RA15, 39

Jamestown first permanent English settlement in North America; located in southeastern Virginia (37°N/77°W) 72

Japan island country in eastern Asia (36°N/133°E) RA15, 544

Kansas state in the central United States; fighting over slavery issue in 1850s gave territory the name "Bleeding Kansas" (38°N/99°W) RA3, 442

Kentucky state in the south central United States; border state that sided with the Union during the Civil War (37°N/87°W) RA3, 282

Korea peninsula in eastern Asia between China, Russia, and the Sea of Japan, on which are located the countries North Korea and South Korea (38°N/127°E) RA15, 565

Kuwait country of the Middle East in southwestern Asia between Iraq and Saudi Arabia (29°N/49°E) RA13, 576

Lake Erie one of the five Great Lakes between Canada and the U.S. (42°N/81°W) RA5, 61

Lake Huron one of the five Great Lakes between Canada and the U.S. (45°N/83°W) RA5, 61

Lake Michigan one of the five Great Lakes between Canada and the U.S. (43°N/87°W) RA5, 61

Lake Ontario the smallest of the five Great Lakes (43°N/79°W) RA5, 61

Lake Superior the largest of the five Great Lakes (48°N/89°W) RA5, 61

Laos southeast Asian country, south of China and west of Vietnam (20°N/102°E) RA15

Latin America Central and South America; settled by Spain and Portugal (14°N/90°W) RA14

Lexington Revolutionary War battle site in eastern Massachusetts; site of first clash between colonists and British, April 19, 1775 (42°N/71°W) 143

Leyte island of the east central Philippines, north of Mindanao (10°N/125°E) 562

Little Rock capital of Arkansas located in the center of the state; site of 1957 conflict over public school integration (35°N/92°W) 423

London capital of United Kingdom located in the southeastern part of England (51°N/0°) 73

Louisiana state in the south central United States (31°N/93°W) RA3, 298

Louisiana Territory region of west central United States between the Mississippi River and the Rocky Mountains purchased from France in 1803 (40°N/95°W) 124

Lowell city in Massachusetts (43°N/83°W) 391

Maine state in the northeastern United States; 23rd state to enter the Union (45°N/70°W) RA3, 324

Mali country in Western Africa (16°N/0°) RA14, 41

Manila capital and largest city of the Philippines located on southwest Luzon Island and Manila Bay (14°N/121°E) RA15, 562

Maryland state in the eastern United States; one of the original 13 states (39°N/76°W) RA3, 87

Massachusetts state in the northeastern United States; one of the original 13 states (42°N/72°W) RA3, 79

Massachusetts Bay Colony Pilgrim settlements along the Charles River (42°N/71°W) 78

Mediterranean Sea sea between Europe and Africa (36°N/13°E) RA14–15, 39

Memphis Tennessee city on the Mississippi River near the Mississippi border (35°N/90°W) 403

Mexican Cession territory gained by the United States after war with Mexico in 1848 (37°N/111°W) 374

Mexico country in North America south of the United States (24°N/104°W) RA8, 19

Mexico City capital and most populous city of Mexico (19°N/99°W) 24

Michigan state in the north central United States; one of the states formed in the Northwest Territory (45°N/85°W) RA3, 195

Midway Islands U.S. possession in the central Pacific Ocean (28°N/179°W) 562

Minnesota state in the north central United States; fur trade, good soil, and lumber attracted early settlers (46°N/96°W) RA3

Mississippi state in the southeastern United States; became English territory after French and Indian War (32°N/90°W) RA3, 319

Mississippi River river flowing through the United States from Minnesota to the Gulf of Mexico; explored by French in 1600s (29°N/ 89°W) RA5, 30

Missouri state in the south central U.S.; petition for statehood resulted in sectional conflict and the Missouri Compromise (41°N/93°W) RA3, 324

Missouri River river flowing through the United States from the Rocky Mountains to the Mississippi River near St. Louis (39°N/90°W) RA5

Montana state in the northwestern United States; cattle industry grew during 1850s (47°N/112°W) RA3, 503

Montgomery capital of Alabama located in the central part of the state; site of 1955 bus boycott to protest segregation (32°N/86°W) 566

Montreal city along the St. Lawrence River in southern Quebec, Canada (45°N/73°W) 60

Moscow capital of former Soviet Union and capital of Russia (56°N/37°E) 573

Nagasaki Japanese city; site of the second atom-bombing in 1945, ending World War II (32°N/130°E) 563

Nashville capital of Tennessee located in the north central part of the state (36°N/87°W) 423

Natchez city in western Mississippi along the Mississippi River (32°N/ 91°W) 316

National Road road from Baltimore, Maryland, to Vandalia, Illinois (40°N/81°W) 315

Gazetteer

Nebraska state in the central United States (42°N/101°W) RA3, 442

Netherlands country in northwestern Europe (53°N/4°E) RA15, 77

Nevada state in the western United States (39°N/117°W) RA2, 510

New Amsterdam town founded on Manhattan Island by Dutch settlers in 1625; renamed New York by British settlers (41°N/74°W) 83

New England region in northeastern United States (42°N/72°W) 76

New France French land claims stretching from Quebec to Louisiana (39°N/85°W) 92

New Hampshire state in the northeastern United States; one of the original 13 states (44°N/72°W) RA3, 80

New Jersey state in the northeastern United States; one of the original 13 states (40°N/75°W) RA3, 84

New Mexico state in the southwestern United States; ceded to the United States by Mexico in 1848 (34°N/107°W) RA2, 369

New Netherland Dutch Hudson River colony (42°N/72°W) 83

New Orleans city in Louisiana in the Mississippi Delta (30°N/90°W) 92

New Spain part of Spain's empire in the Western Hemisphere (35°N/110°W) 92

New York state in the northeastern United States; one of the original 13 states (43°N/78°W) RA3, 83

New York City city in southeastern New York State at the mouth of the Hudson River; first capital of nation (41°N/74°W) 84

Newfoundland province in eastern Canada (48°N/56°W) RA14, 46

Nicaragua country in Central America (13°N/86°W) RA9

Normandy region along French coast and site of D-Day invasion, June 6, 1944 (48°N/2°W) 561

North America continent in the northern part of the Western Hemisphere between the Atlantic and Pacific oceans (45°N/100°W) RA14, 16

North Carolina state in the southeastern United States; one of the original 13 states (36°N/81°W) RA3, 89

North Dakota state in the north central U.S.; Congress created Dakota Territory in 1861 (47°N/102°W) RA3, 531

North Korea Asian country on the northern Korean Peninsula (40°N/127°E) RA15, 565

North Vietnam communist nation in Southeast Asia; unified with South Vietnam in 1976 to form Vietnam (21°N/106°E) RA15, 569

Northwest Territory territory north of the Ohio River and east of the Mississippi River (47°N/87°W) 196

Ohio state in the north central United States; first state in the Northwest Territory (40°N/83°W) RA3, 195

Ohio River river flowing from Allegheny and Monongahela rivers in western Pennsylvania into the Mississippi River (37°N/85°W) RA5, 28

Oklahoma state in the south central United States; Five Civilized Tribes moved to territory in the period 1830–1842 (36°N/98°W) RA3, 530

Oregon state in the northwestern United States; adopted woman suffrage in 1912 (44°N/124°W) RA2, 356

Oregon Trail pioneer trail from Independence, Missouri, to the Oregon Territory (42°N/110°W) 358

Pacific Ocean world's largest ocean, located between Asia and the Americas (0°/175°W) RA14–15, 43

Panama country in the southern part of Central America, occupying the Isthmus of Panama (8°N/81°W) RA9

Pearl Harbor naval base at Honolulu, Hawaii; site of 1941 Japanese attack, leading to United States entry into World War II (21°N/158°W) 559

Pennsylvania state in the northeastern United States (41°N/78°W) RA3, 85

Persian Gulf gulf in southwestern Asia between Iran and the Arabian Peninsula (28°N/50°E) RA13

Peru country in South America, south of Ecuador and Colombia (10°S/75°W) RA14, 26

Philadelphia city in eastern Pennsylvania on the Delaware River; Declaration of Independence and the Constitution both adopted in city's Independence Hall (40°N/75°W) 85

Philippines island country in southeast Asia (14°N/125°E) RA15, 545

Pikes Peak mountain in Rocky Mountains in central Colorado (38°N/105°W) 285

Pittsburgh city in western Pennsylvania; one of the great steelmaking centers of the world (40°N/80°W) 423

Plymouth town in eastern Massachusetts, first successful English colony in New England (42°N/71°W) 77

Poland country on the Baltic Sea in Eastern Europe (52°N/18°E) RA15, 549

Portugal country in southwestern Europe (38°N/8°W) RA14, 44

Potomac River river flowing from West Virginia into Chesapeake Bay (38°N/77°W) RA5, 87

Providence capital of Rhode Island; site of first English settlement in Rhode Island (42°N/71°W) RA3

Puerto Rico United States commonwealth in the West Indies (18°N/67°W) RA9

Quebec city in Canada, capital of Quebec Province, on the St. Lawrence River; first settlement in New France (47°N/71°W) 62

Rhode Island state in the northeastern United States; one of the original 13 states (41°N/72°W) RA3, 80

Richmond capital of Virginia located in the central part of the state; capital of the Confederacy during the Civil War (37°N/77°W) 388

Rio Grande river between the United States and Mexico in North America; forms the boundary between Texas and Mexico (26°N/97°W) RA4, 372

Roanoke island off the coast of present-day North Carolina that was site of early British colonizing efforts (35°N/76°W) 71

Rocky Mountains mountain range in western United States and Canada in North America (50°N/114°W) RA4, 32

Russia name of republic; former empire of eastern Europe and northern Asia-coinciding with Soviet Union (60°N/64°E) RA15, 549

Sacramento capital of California located in the north central part of the state (38°N/121°W) 372

Salt Lake City capital of Utah located in the northern part of the state; founded by Mormons in 1847 (41°N/112°W) 361

San Antonio city in south central Texas (29°N/98°W) 365

San Diego city in southern California (33°N/117°W) 93

Gazetteer

San Francisco city in northern California on the Pacific coast (38°N/122°W) 372

Santa Fe capital of New Mexico located in the north central part of the state (36°N/106°W) 92

Santa Fe Trail cattle trail from Independence, Missouri, to Santa Fe, New Mexico (36°N/106°W) 370

Saratoga Revolutionary War battle site in the Hudson Valley of eastern New York State (43°N/74°W) 168

Savannah city in far eastern Georgia (32°N/81°W) 90

Seattle Washington city bordered by Puget Sound and Lake Washington (47°N/122°W) RA2

Seneca Falls town in New York State; site of women's rights convention in 1848 (43°N/77°W) 426

Shiloh site of 1862 Union victory in Tennessee (35°N/88°W) 469

Sicily Italian island in the Mediterranean (37°N/13°E) 561

Sierra Nevada mountain range in eastern California (39°N/120°W) RA4, 32

South America continent in the southern part of the Western Hemisphere lying between the Atlantic and Pacific oceans (15°S/60°W) RA14, 16

South Carolina state in the southeastern United States; one of the original 13 states (34°N/81°W) RA3, 89

South Dakota state in the north central United States; acquired through the Louisiana Purchase (44°N/102°W) RA3, 531

South Korea country in Asia on the Korean Peninsula (36°N/128°E) RA15, 565

South Vietnam country in Southeast Asia united in 1976 with North Vietnam to form Vietnam (11°N/107°E) RA15, 569

Soviet Union former country in northern Europe and Asia (60°N/64°E) 559

Spain country in southwestern Europe (40°N/4°W) RA14, 46

St. Augustine city in northeastern Florida on the Atlantic coast; oldest permanent existing European settlement in North America, founded in 1565 (30°N/81°W) 53

St. Lawrence River river flowing from Lake Ontario, between Canada and the United States, through parts of Canada to the Atlantic Ocean (48°N/69°W) 60

Stalingrad city in the former Soviet Union on the Volga River; present name Volgograd (49°N/42°E) 561

Switzerland European country in the Alps (47°N/8°E) RA15

Taiwan island country off the southeast coast of China; seat of the Chinese Nationalist government (24°N/122°E) RA15

Tehran capital of Iran (36°N/52°E) RA13, 574

Tennessee state in the south central United States; first state readmitted to the Union after the Civil War (36°N/88°W) RA3, 319

Tenochtitlán Aztec capital at the site of present-day Mexico City (19°N/99°W) 24

Texas state in the south central United States; Mexican colony that became a republic before joining the United States (31°N/101°W) RA3, 363

Tokyo capital of Japan located on the eastern coast of Honshu Island (36°N/140°E) 562

Toronto city in Canada on Lake Ontario; capital of the province of Ontario (44°N/79°W) RA14

Trenton capital of New Jersey located on the Delaware River in the central part of the state; site of Revolutionary War battle in December 1776 (40°N/75°W) 167

Union of Soviet Socialist Republics See Soviet Union.

United Kingdom country in northwestern Europe made up of England, Scotland, Wales, and Northern Ireland (56°N/2°W) RA14

United States country in central North America; fourth largest country in the world in both area and population (38°N/110°W) RA2–3, RA14

Utah state in the western United States; settled by Mormons in 1840s (39°N/113°W) RA2, 378

Valley Forge Revolutionary War winter camp northwest of Philadelphia (40°N/75°W) 173

Venezuela South American country on the Caribbean Sea (8°N/65°W) RA14

Vermont state in the northeastern United States; 14th state to enter the Union (44°N/73°W) RA3, 144

Vicksburg city and Civil War battle site in western Mississippi on the Mississippi River (42°N/85°W) 486

Vietnam country in southeastern Asia (16°N/108°E) RA15, 568

Virginia state in the eastern United States; colony of first permanent English settlement in the Americas (37°N/80°W) RA3, 72

Washington state in the northwestern United States; territory reached by Lewis and Clark in 1805 (47°N/121°W) RA2, 261

Washington, D.C. capital of the United States located on the Potomac River at its confluence with the Anacostia River, between Maryland and Virginia coinciding with the District of Columbia (39°N/77°W) RA3, 262

West Indies islands in the Caribbean Sea, between North America and South America (19°N/79°W) RA9, 47

West Virginia state in the east central United States (39°N/81°W) RA3, 462

Willamette Valley valley of the Willamette River in western Oregon (45°N/123°W) 359

Wisconsin state in the north central United States; passed first state unemployment compensation act, 1932 (44°N/91°W) RA3, 195

Wounded Knee site of massacre of Native Americans by soldiers in southern South Dakota in 1890 and of American Indian Movement protest in 1973 (43°N/102°W) 532

Wyoming state in the western United States; territory provided women the right to vote, 1869 (43°N/108°W) RA3, 531

Yorktown town in southeastern Virginia and site of final battle of Revolutionary War (37°N/76°W) 185

Yugoslavia country in southeast Europe, on the Adriatic Sea (44°N/20°E) RA15, 549

Gazetteer

Glossary

A

abolitionist a person who strongly favors doing away with slavery (p. 418)

abstain to not take part in some activity, such as voting (p. 439)

adobe a sun-dried mud brick used to build the homes of some Native Americans (p. 32)

affluence the state of having much wealth (p. 566)

alien an immigrant living in a country in which he or she is not a citizen (p. 271)

alliance a close association of nations or other groups, formed to advance common interests or causes (pp. 122, 547)

ambush a surprise attack (p. 187)

amendment an addition to a formal document such as the Constitution (pp. 213, 221)

American System policies devised by Henry Clay to stimulate the growth of industry (p. 324)

amnesty the granting of pardon to a large number of persons; protection from prosecution for an illegal act (p. 501)

annex to add a territory to one's own territory (p. 367)

Antifederalists individuals who opposed ratification of the Constitution (p. 212)

apprentice assistant who is assigned to learn the trade of a skilled craftsman (p. 112)

appropriate to set something aside for a particular purpose, especially funds (p. 223)

archaeology the study of ancient peoples (p. 17)

arsenal a storage place for weapons and ammunition (p. 448)

article a part of a document, such as the Constitution, that deals with a single subject (p. 209)

artifact an item left behind by early people that represents their culture (p. 17)

astrolabe an instrument used by sailors to observe positions of stars (p. 40)

B

backcountry a region of hills and forests west of the Tidewater (p. 105)

bicameral consisting of two houses, or chambers, especially in a legislature (p. 193)

black codes laws passed in the South just after the Civil War aimed at controlling freedmen and enabling plantation owners to exploit African American workers (p. 505)

blockade cut off an area by means of troops or warships to stop supplies or people from coming in or going out; to close off a country's ports (pp. 179, 463)

blockade runner ship that sails into and out of a blockaded area (p. 468)

bond a note issued by the government, which promises to pay off a loan with interest (p. 261)

boomtown a community experiencing a sudden growth in business or population (pp. 376, 529)

border ruffians Missourians who traveled in armed groups to vote in Kansas's election during the mid-1850s (p. 443)

border states the states between the North and the South that were divided over whether to stay in the Union or join the Confederacy (p. 461)

bounty money given as a reward, such as to encourage enlistment in the army (p. 482)

boycott to refuse to buy items from a particular country (p. 134)

bureaucracy system in which nonelected officials carry out laws and policies (p. 337)

burgesses elected representatives to an assembly (p. 73)

C

cabinet a group of advisers to the president (p. 259)

Californios Mexicans who lived in California (p. 373)

canal an artificial waterway (p. 318)

capital money for investment (pp. 308, 399, 536)

capitalism an economic system based on private property and free enterprise (p. 308)

caravel small, fast ship with a broad bow (p. 40)

carbon dating a scientific method used to determine the age of an artifact (p. 19)

carpetbaggers name given to Northern whites who moved South after the Civil War and supported the Republicans (p. 510)

cash crop farm crop raised to be sold for money (pp. 103, 518)

casualty a military person killed, wounded, or captured (p. 469)

caucus a meeting held by a political party to choose their party's candidate for president or decide policy (pp. 269, 337)

cede to give up by treaty (p. 374)

census official count of a population (p. 314)

charter a document that gives the holder the right to organize settlements in an area (p. 71)

charter colony colony established by a group of settlers who had been given a formal document allowing them to settle (p. 110)

checks and balances the system in which each branch of government has a check on the other two branches so that no one branch becomes too powerful (p. 210)

circumnavigate to sail around the world (p. 49)

citizen a person who owes loyalty to and is entitled to the protection of a state or nation (p. 229)

civil disobedience refusal to obey laws that are considered unjust as a nonviolent way to press for changes (p. 566)

civil war conflict between opposing groups of citizens of the same country (p. 444)

civilization a highly developed culture, usually with organized religions and laws (p. 22)

classical relating to ancient Greece and Rome (p. 39)

clipper ship a fast sailing ship with slender lines, tall masts, and large square sails (p. 387)

coeducation the teaching of male and female students together (p. 427)

collective bargaining discussion between an employer and union representatives of workers over wages, hours, and working conditions (p. 537)

Columbian Exchange exchange of goods, ideas, and people between Europe and the Americas (p. 60)

commission a group of persons directed to perform some duty (p. 516)

committee of correspondence an organization that used meetings, letters, and pamphlets to spread political ideas through the colonies (p. 137)

compromise agreement between two or more sides in which each side gives up some of what it wants (p. 204)

concurrent powers powers shared by the states and the federal government (p. 219)

Conestoga wagon sturdy vehicle topped with white canvas and used by pioneers to move west (p. 283)

conquistador Spanish explorer in the Americas in the 1500s (p. 51)

constituents people that members of Congress represent (p. 223)

constitution a formal plan of government (pp. 89, 193)

corruption dishonest or illegal actions (p. 510)

cotton gin a machine that removed seeds from cotton fiber (pp. 308, 398)

counter-terrorism military or political activities intended to combat terrorism (p. 583)

coureur de bois French trapper living among Native Americans (p. 62)

court-martial to try by a military court (p. 326)

credit a form of loan; ability to buy goods based on future payment (p. 403)

culture a way of life of a group of people who share similar beliefs and customs (p. 19)

customs duties taxes on foreign imported goods (p. 280)

debtor person or country that owes money (p. 90)

decree an order or decision given by one in authority (p. 364)

demilitarize to remove armed forces from an area (p. 326)

depreciate to fall in value (p. 197)

depression a period of low economic activity and widespread unemployment (pp. 199, 350)

desert to leave without permission (p. 173)

dictator a leader who rules with total authority, often in a cruel or brutal manner (p. 559)

disarmament removal of weapons (p. 326)

discrimination unfair treatment of a group; unequal treatment because of a person's race, religion, ethnic background, or place of birth (pp. 392, 543)

dissent disagreement with or opposition to an opinion (p. 76)

diversity variety or difference (p. 104)

domestic tranquility maintaining peace within the nation (p. 217)

draft the selection of persons for required military service (p. 481)

drought a long period of time with little rainfall (p. 29)

due process of law idea that the government must follow procedures established by law and guaranteed by the Constitution (p. 228)

effigy rag figure representing an unpopular individual (p. 134)

Electoral College a special group of voters selected by their state's voters to vote for the president and vice president (p. 210)

emancipate to free from slavery (p. 475)

Glossary

embargo an order prohibiting trade with another country (pp. 290, 573)

emigrant a person who leaves a country or region to live elsewhere (p. 358)

empresario a person who arranged for the settlement of land in Texas during the 1800s (p. 363)

encomienda system of rewarding conquistadors with tracts of land and the right to tax and demand labor from Native Americans who lived on the land (p. 55)

Enlightenment movement during the 1700s that spread the idea that knowledge, reason, and science could improve society (p. 208)

entrenched occupying a strong defensive position (p. 486)

enumerated powers powers belonging only to the federal government (p. 219)

executive branch the branch of government, headed by the president, that carries out the nation's laws and policies (p. 210)

export to sell goods abroad (p. 109)

factory system system bringing manufacturing steps together in one place to increase efficiency (p. 309)

famine an extreme shortage of food (p. 393)

favorite son candidate that receives the backing of his home state rather than of the national party (p. 335)

federal debt the amount of money owed by the government (p. 575)

federalism the sharing of power between federal and state governments (pp. 208, 219)

Federalists supporters of the Constitution (p. 211)

federation a type of government that links different groups together (p. 33)

feminist a person who advocates or is active in promoting women's rights (p. 567)

fixed costs regular expenses such as housing or maintaining equipment that remain about the same year after year (p. 403)

forty-niners people who went to California during the gold rush of 1849 (p. 375)

free enterprise the freedom of private businesses to operate competitively for profit with minimal government regulation (p. 308)

freedman a person freed from slavery (p. 502)

frigate warship (p. 297)

fugitive runaway or trying to run away (p. 438)

genocide the deliberate destruction of a racial, political, or cultural group (p. 561)

global warming a steady increase in average world temperatures (p. 578)

grandfather clause a clause that allowed individuals who did not pass the literacy test to vote if their fathers or grandfathers had voted before Reconstruction began; an exception to a law based on preexisting circumstances (p. 519)

greenback a piece of U.S. paper money first issued by the North during the Civil War (p. 483)

guerrilla tactics referring to surprise attacks or raids rather than organized warfare (p. 344)

guerrilla warfare a hit-and-run technique used in fighting a war; fighting by small bands of warriors using tactics such as sudden ambushes (p. 180)

habeas corpus a legal order for an inquiry to determine whether a person has been lawfully imprisoned (p. 481)

hieroglyphics an ancient form of writing using symbols and pictures to represent words, sounds, and concepts (p. 24)

Holocaust the name given to the mass slaughter of Jews and other groups by the Nazis during World War II (p. 561)

horizontal integration the combining of competing firms into one corporation (p. 536)

human rights rights regarded as belonging to all persons, such as freedom from unlawful imprisonment, torture, and execution (p. 574)

Ice Age a period of extremely cold temperatures when part of the planet's surface was covered with massive ice sheets (p. 17)

impeach to formally charge a public official with misconduct in office (pp. 223, 507, 573)

imperialism the actions used by one nation to exercise political or economic control over smaller or weaker nations (p. 544)

implied powers powers not specifically mentioned in the Constitution (pp. 221, 268)

import to buy goods from foreign markets (p. 109)

Glossary

impressment forcing people into service, as in the navy (pp. 265, 290)

indentured servant laborer who agreed to work without pay for a certain period of time in exchange for passage to America (p. 87)

Industrial Revolution the change from an agrarian society to one based on industry which began in Great Britain and spread to the United States around 1800 (p. 307)

inflation a continuous rise in the price of goods and services (pp. 175, 483)

integrate to end separation of different races and bring into equal membership in society (p. 512)

interchangeable parts uniform pieces that can be made in large quantities to replace other identical pieces (p. 309)

internal improvements federal projects, such as canals and roads, to develop the nation's transportation system (p. 322)

Internet a worldwide linking of computer networks (p. 577)

ironclad armored naval vessel (p. 468)

Iroquois Confederacy a powerful group of Native Americans in the eastern part of the United States made up of five nations: the Mohawk, Seneca, Cayuga, Onondaga, and Oneida (p. 117)

island hopping a strategy used during World War II that called for attacking and capturing certain key islands and using these islands as bases to leapfrog to others (p. 562)

joint occupation the possession and settling of an area shared by two or more countries (p. 357)

joint-stock company a company in which investors buy stock in the company in return for a share of its future profits (p. 71)

judicial branch the branch of government, including the federal court system, that interprets the nation's laws (p. 210)

judicial review the right of the Supreme Court to determine if a law violates the Constitution (pp. 222, 281)

laissez-faire policy that government should interfere as little as possible in the nation's economy (pp. 279, 350)

landslide an overwhelming victory (p. 336)

legislative branch the branch of government that makes the nation's laws (p. 209)

line of demarcation an imaginary line running down the middle of the Atlantic Ocean from the North Pole to the South Pole dividing the Americas between Spain and Portugal (p. 47)

literacy the ability to read and write (p. 113)

literacy test a method used to prevent African Americans from voting by requiring prospective voters to read and write at a specified level (p. 519)

lock in a canal, an enclosure with gates at each end used in raising or lowering boats as they pass from level to level (p. 318)

log cabin campaign name given to William Henry Harrison's campaign for the presidency in 1840, from the Whigs' use of a log cabin as their symbol (p. 351)

Loyalists American colonists who remained loyal to Britain and opposed the war for independence (p. 145)

lynching putting to death a person by the illegal action of a mob (p. 520)

maize an early form of corn grown by Native Americans (p. 19)

majority more than half (p. 335)

Manifest Destiny the idea popular in the United States during the 1800s that the country must expand its boundaries to the Pacific (p. 360)

manumission the freeing of some enslaved persons (p. 201)

martyr a person who sacrifices his or her life for a principle or cause (p. 448)

Mayflower Compact a formal document, written in 1620, that provided law and order to the Plymouth colony (p. 77)

mercantilism the theory that a state's or nation's power depended on its wealth (pp. 59, 109)

mercenary paid soldier who serves in the army of a foreign country (p. 164)

migration a movement of a large number of people into a new homeland (p. 17)

militia a group of civilians trained to fight in emergencies (pp. 118, 142)

minutemen companies of civilian soldiers who boasted that they were ready to fight on a minute's notice (p. 142)

mission religious settlement (pp. 54, 92)

monopoly total control of an industry by one company (p. 536)

Morse code a system for transmitting messages that uses a series of dots and dashes to represent the letters of the alphabet, numbers, and punctuation (p. 389)

mosque a Muslim house of worship (p. 42)

mountain man a frontiersman living in the wilderness, as in the Rocky Mountains (p. 357)

muckraker a journalist who uncovers abuses and corruption in a society (p. 541)

mudslinging attempt to ruin an opponent's reputation with insults (p. 336)

national debt the amount of money a national government owes to other governments or its people (p. 260)

nationalism loyalty to a nation and promotion of its interests above all others (pp. 293, 547)

nativist a person who favors those born in his country and is opposed to immigrants (p. 395)

naturalization to grant full citizenship to a foreigner (p. 229)

neutral taking no side in a conflict (p. 163)

neutral rights the right to sail the seas and not take sides in a war (p. 290)

neutrality a position of not taking sides in a conflict (p. 265)

nomads people who move from place to place, usually in search of food or grazing land (p. 17)

nominating convention system in which delegates from the states selected the party's presidential candidate (p. 337)

nonimportation the act of not importing or using certain goods (p. 134)

normal school a two-year school for training high school graduates as teachers (p. 413)

Northwest Passage water route to Asia through North America sought by European explorers (p. 60)

nullify to cancel or make ineffective (pp. 271, 338)

offensive position of attacking or the attack itself (p. 463)

ordinance a law or regulation (p. 196)

override to overturn or defeat, as a bill proposed in Congress (p. 505)

overseer person who supervises a large operation or its workers (pp. 106, 403)

ozone the layer of gas composed of a form of oxygen that protects the earth and its people from cancer-causing sun rays (p. 578)

pacifist person opposed to the use of war or violence to settle disputes (p. 85)

partisan favoring one side of an issue (p. 268)

patent a document that gives an inventor the sole legal right to an invention for a period of time (pp. 308, 535)

Patriots American colonists who were determined to fight the British until American independence was won (p. 145)

patroon landowner in the Dutch colonies who ruled like a king over large areas of land (p. 83)

perjury lying when one has sworn an oath to tell the truth (p. 576)

persecute to treat someone harshly because of that person's beliefs or practices (p. 76)

petition a formal request (pp. 148, 196)

pilgrimage a journey to a holy place (p. 42)

Pilgrims Separatists who journeyed to the colonies during the 1600s for a religious purpose (p. 77)

plantation a large estate run by an owner or manager and farmed by laborers who lived there (p. 55)

plurality largest single share (p. 335)

poll tax a tax of a fixed amount per person that had to be paid before the person could vote (p. 519)

popular sovereignty political theory that government is subject to the will of the people (p. 218); before the Civil War, the idea that people living in a territory had the right to decide by voting if slavery would be allowed there (p. 442)

preamble the introduction to a formal document, especially the Constitution (pp. 151, 217)

precedent a tradition (p. 259)

prejudice an unfair opinion not based on facts (p. 392)

presidio Spanish fort in the Americas built to protect mission settlements (p. 54)

privateer armed private ship (pp. 179, 297)

Prohibition the nationwide ban on the manufacture, sale, and transportation of liquor in the United States that went into effect when the Eighteenth Amendment was ratified in 1919 (p. 550)

Glossary

propaganda ideas or information designed and spread to influence opinion (pp. 137, 547)

proportional to be the same as or corresponding to (p. 203)

proprietary colony colony run by individuals or groups to whom land was granted (pp. 83, 111)

pueblo home or community of homes built by Native Americans (pp. 29, 54)

Puritans Protestants who, during the 1600s, wanted to reform the Anglican Church (p. 77)

R

radical extreme (p. 501)

ranchero Mexican ranch owner (p. 371)

rancho huge properties for raising livestock set up by Mexican settlers in California (p. 371)

ratify to give official approval to (pp. 185, 211, 476)

Rebel Confederate soldier, so called because of opposition to the established government (p. 464)

reconciliation settling by agreement or coming together again (p. 514)

Reconstruction the reorganization and rebuilding of the former Confederate states after the Civil War (p. 501)

recruit to enlist soldiers in the army (p. 165)

relocate to force a person or group of people to move (p. 342)

Renaissance a period of intellectual and artistic creativity, c. 1300–1600 (p. 39)

rendezvous a meeting (p. 357)

reparations payment by the losing country in a war to the winner for the damages caused by the war (p. 549)

repeal to cancel an act or law (p. 134)

republic a government in which citizens rule through elected representatives (p. 193)

republicanism favoring a republic, or representative democracy, as the best form of government (p. 218)

reservation an area of public lands set aside for Native Americans (p. 531)

reserved powers powers retained by the states (p. 219)

resolution a formal expression of opinion (p. 134)

revenue incoming money (p. 133)

revival a series of meetings conducted by a preacher to arouse religious emotions (p. 413)

royal colony colony run by a governor and a council appointed by the king or queen (p. 111)

S

scalawags name given by former Confederates to Southern whites who supported Republican Reconstruction of the South (p. 510)

secede to leave or withdraw (pp. 285, 338, 438)

secession withdrawal from the Union (p. 451)

sectionalism loyalty to a region (pp. 322, 437)

sedition activities aimed at weakening established government (p. 271)

segregation the separation or isolation of a race, class, or group (p. 519, 566)

Separatists Protestants who, during the 1600s, wanted to leave the Anglican Church in order to found their own churches (p. 77)

settlement house institution located in a poor neighborhood that provided numerous community services such as medical care, child care, libraries, and classes in English (p. 538)

sharecropping system of farming in which a farmer works land for an owner who provides equipment and seeds and receives a share of the crop (p. 512)

slave code the laws passed in the Southern states that controlled and restricted enslaved people (p. 405)

smuggling trading illegally with other nations (p. 109)

speculator person who risks money in order to make a large profit (pp. 125, 261)

spiritual an African American religious folk song (p. 405)

spoils system practice of handing out government jobs to supporters; replacing government employees with the winning candidate's supporters (p. 337)

stalemate a situation during a conflict when action stops because both sides are equally powerful and neither will give in (p. 565)

states' rights rights and powers independent of the federal government that are reserved for the states by the Constitution; the belief that states' rights supersede federal rights and law (pp. 271, 451)

strait a narrow passageway connecting two larger bodies of water (p. 49)

strike a stopping of work by workers to force an employer to meet demands (p. 392)

subsistence farming farming in which only enough food to feed one's family is produced (p. 101)

suffrage the right to vote (pp. 336, 426)

suffragist a man or woman who fought for a woman's right to vote (p. 542)

tariff a tax on imports or exports (pp. 262, 338)

technology the application of scientific discoveries to practical use (pp. 40, 308)

Tejano a Mexican who claims Texas as his home (p. 363)

telegraph a device or system that uses electric signals to transmit messages by a code over wires (p. 389)

temperance the use of little or no alcoholic drink (p. 413)

tenant farmer farmer who works land owned by another and pays rent either in cash or crops (pp. 92, 402)

terrace a raised piece of land with the top leveled off to promote farming (p. 26)

terrorism the use of violence by groups against civilians to achieve a political goal (p. 578)

theocracy a form of government in which the society is ruled by religious leaders (p. 23)

Tidewater a region of flat, low-lying plains along the seacoast (p. 105)

toleration the acceptance of different beliefs (p. 79)

total war war on all aspects of the enemy's life (p. 490)

trade union organization of workers with the same trade or skill (p. 392)

Transcendentalist any of a group of New England writers who stressed the relationship between human beings and nature, spiritual things over material things, and the importance of the individual conscience (p. 415)

transcontinental extending across a continent (p. 529)

triangular trade a trade route that exchanged goods between the West Indies, the American colonies, and West Africa (p. 102)

tribute money paid for protection (pp. 52, 289)

trust a combination of firms or corporations formed by a legal agreement, especially to reduce competition (p. 536)

turnpike a road that one must pay to use; the money is used to pay for the road (p. 315)

unalienable right a right that cannot be surrendered (p. 154)

unconstitutional not agreeing or consistent with the Constitution (p. 262)

Underground Railroad a system that helped enslaved African Americans follow a network of escape routes out of the South to freedom in the North (p. 422)

utopia community based on a vision of a perfect society sought by reformers (p. 412)

vaquero Hispanic ranch hand (p. 529)

vertical integration the combining of companies that supply equipment and services needed for a particular industry (p. 536)

veto to reject a bill and prevent it from becoming a law (p. 349)

vigilantes people who take the law into their own hands (p. 377)

War Hawks Republicans during Madison's presidency who pressed for war with Britain (p. 293)

writ of assistance legal document that enabled officers to search homes and warehouses for goods that might be smuggled (p. 133)

Yankee Union soldier (p. 464)

yellow journalism a type of sensational, biased, and often false reporting (p. 545)

yeoman Southern owner of a small farm who did not have enslaved people (p. 402)

Glossary

A

abolitionist/abolicionista una persona que favorece firmemente suprimir la esclavitud (p. 418)

abstain/abstenerse no tomar parte de una actividad, como de votar (p. 439)

adobe/adobe un ladrillo de lodo, seco al sol, usado para construir las casas de los Nativos Americanos (p. 32)

affluence/afluencia la condición de tener mucha riqueza (p. 566)

alien/extranjero una persona inmigrante que vive en un país en el cual no es ciudadano (p. 271)

alliance/alianza una asociación íntima entre naciones u otros grupos formada para avanzar intereses o causas que llevan en común (pp. 122, 547)

ambush/emboscada un ataque por sorpresa (p. 187)

amendment/enmienda una adición a un documento formal tal como la Constitución (pp. 213, 221)

American System/Sistema Americano políticas ideadas por Henry Clay para estimular el crecimiento de la industria (p. 324)

amnesty/amnistía el otorgar perdón a un número grande de personas; la protección del proceso a causa de una acción ilegal (p. 501)

annex/anexar añadir un territorio a su propio territorio (p. 367)

Antifederalists/antifederalistas personas que estaban en contra de que se ratificara la Constitución (p. 212)

apprentice/aprendiz asistente asignado para aprender el oficio de un artesano experto (p. 112)

appropriate/destinar apartar para un propósito en particular, dicho especialmente de fondos (p. 223)

archaeology/arqueología el estudio de pueblos antiguos (p. 17)

arsenal/arsenal un lugar para el almacenaje de armas y municiones (p. 448)

article/artículo una parte de un documento tal como la Constitución que trata de un solo tema (p. 209)

artifact/artefacto un artículo dejado por pueblos antiguos que representa su cultura (p. 17)

astrolabe/astrolabio un instrumento usado por los marineros para observar las posiciones de las estrellas (p. 40)

B

backcountry/monte una región de colinas y bosques al oeste de la orilla del mar (p. 105)

bicameral/bicameral que consiste de dos cámaras, especialmente dicho en una legislatura (p. 193)

black codes/códigos negros leyes establecidas en el Sur al terminar la Guerra Civil para controlar a los libertos y permitir a los dueños de plantaciones la explotación de los trabajadores afroamericanos (p. 505)

blockade/bloqueo el cerrar un área por medio de tropas o de buques de guerra para prohibir el entrar y el salir de abastos y de personas; cerrar los puertos de un país (pp. 179, 463)

blockade runner/forzador de bloqueo un buque que navega adentro y afuera de un área bloqueada (p. 468)

bond/bono una obligación hecha por el gobierno la cual promete pagar un préstamo con interés (p. 261)

boomtown/pueblo en bonanza una comunidad experimentando un auge repentino de comercio o población (p. 376, 529)

border ruffians/rufianes fronterizos hombres de Missouri que viajaban en grupos armados a votar en la elección de Kansas a mediados de los años 1850 (p. 443)

border states/estados fronterizos los estados entre el Norte y el Sur que fueron divididos sobre el problema de quedarse en la Unión o de unirse a la Confederación (p. 461)

bounty/gratificación dinero dado como recompensa, como para animar el alistamiento en el ejército (p. 482)

boycott/boicotear rehusar comprar artículos de un país en particular (p. 134)

bureaucracy/burocracia sistema en el cual oficiales no elegidos administran las leyes y políticas (p. 337)

burgesses/burgueses representantes elegidos para una asamblea (p. 73)

C

cabinet/gabinete un grupo de consejeros al presidente (p. 259)

Californios/californios mexicanos que vivían en California (p. 373)

canal/canal vía artificial de agua (p. 318)

capital/capital dinero para inversión (pp. 308, 399, 536)

capitalism/capitalismo un sistema económico basado en la propiedad particular y la empresa libre (pp. 308, 701)

caravel/carabela un buque pequeño y veloz con una proa ancha (p. 40)

carbon dating/datar con carbón un método científico usado para determinar la edad de un artefacto (p. 19)

carpetbaggers/*carpetbaggers* nombre dado a los blancos norteños que se trasladaban al Sur después de la guerra y apoyaban a los republicanos (p. 510)

cash crop/cultivo comercial cosecha cultivada para vender por dinero (pp. 103, 518)

casualty/baja un miliciano muerto, herido, o capturado (p. 469)

caucus/junta electoral una reunión llevada a cabo por un partido político para escoger el candidato a la presidencia de su partido o para decidir políticas (pp. 269, 337)

cede/ceder abandonar por tratado (p. 374)

census/censo registro oficial de una población (p. 314)

charter/carta de privilegio un documento que otorga los derechos de organizar establecimientos en una área (p. 71)

charter colony/colonia a carta colonia establecida por un grupo de colonizadores a quienes se les había dado un documento formal permitiéndoles colonizar (p. 110)

checks and balances/inspecciones y balances el sistema en el cual cada rama de gobierno refrena las otras dos ramas para que ninguna rama vuelva a ser demasiado poderosa (p. 210)

circumnavigate/circunnavegar navegar alrededor del mundo (p. 49)

citizen/ciudadano una persona que debe ser leal y tiene derecho a la protección de un estado o nación (p. 229)

civil disobedience/desobediencia civil el rehusar obedecer las leyes que uno considera injustas como una manera pacífica para inisistir en cambios (p. 566)

civil war/guerra civil conflicto entre grupos opuestos de ciudadanos del mismo país (p. 444)

civilization/civilización una cultura sumamente desarrollada, generalmente con religiones y leyes organizadas (p. 22)

classical/clásico relacionado a Grecia y Roma antigua (p. 39)

clipper ship/buque clíper un buque veloz con líneas delgadas, mástiles altos, y grandes velas cuadradas (p. 387)

coeducation/coeducación la enseñanza conjunta de estudiantes hombres y mujeres (p. 427)

collective bargaining/negociaciones colectivas discusión entre el empresario y los representantes sindicales de los trabajadores sobre salario, horas, y condiciones del taller (p. 537)

Columbian Exchange/Cambio Colombiano el cambio de productos, ideas, y personas entre Europa y las Américas (p. 60)

commission/comisión un grupo de personas dirigidas a hacer algún deber (p. 516)

committee of correspondence/comité de correspondencia una organización que usaba reuniones, cartas, y panfletos para propagar ideas políticas para las colonias (p. 137)

compromise/compromiso un acuerdo entre dos o más partidos en el cual cada partido abandona algo de lo que quiere (p. 204)

concurrent powers/poderes concurrentes poderes compartidos por los estados y el gobierno federal (p. 219)

Conestoga wagon/conestoga vehículo firme cubierto de lona blanca usado por los pioneros para moverse hacia el oeste (p. 283)

conquistador/conquistador explorador español en las Américas en los años 1500 (p. 51)

constituents/constituyentes personas representadas por miembros del Congreso (p. 223)

constitution/constitución un plan formal de gobierno (pp. 89, 193)

corruption/corrupción acciones deshonestas o ilegales (p. 510)

cotton gin/despepitadora de algodón una máquina que sacaba las semillas de las fibras de algodón (pp. 308, 398)

counter-terrorism/contraterrorismo actividades militares o políticos con el fin de combatir el terrorismo (p. 583)

coureur de bois/*coureur de bois* cazador de pieles francés viviendo entre los Nativos Americanos (p. 62)

court-martial/consejo de guerra someter a juicio por un tribunal militar (p. 326)

credit/crédito una forma de préstamo; la capacidad de comprar productos basada en pagos futuros (p. 403)

culture/cultura la manera de vivir de un grupo de personas que tienen en común sus creencias y costumbres (p. 19)

customs duties/derechos de aduana impuestos sobre productos importados del extranjero (p. 280)

debtor/deudor persona o país que debe dinero (p. 90)

decree/decreto una orden o decisión dada por alguién de autoridad (p. 364)

demilitarize/desmilitarizar quitar fuerzas armadas de un área (p. 326)

depreciate/depreciar caer en valor (p. 197)

depression/depresión un período de poca actividad económica y de desempleo extenso (pp. 199, 350)

desert/desertar salir sin permiso (p. 173)

dictator/dictador un líder que manda con plena autoridad, a menudo de una manera cruel o brutal (p. 559)

disarmament/desarme el quitar armas (pp. 326)

discrimination/discriminación trato injusto de un grupo; trato parcial a causa de la raza, la religión, los antecedentes étnicos, o lugar de nacimiento de alguién (pp. 392, 543)

dissent/dissension desacuerdo con u oposición a una opinion (p. 76)

diversity/diversidad variedad o diferencia (p. 104)

domestic tranquility/tranquilidad doméstica mantener la paz dentro de la nación (p. 217)

draft/reclutamiento la selección de personas a servicio militar requirido (p. 481)

drought/sequía un largo período con poca lluvia (p. 29)

due process of law/proceso justo de ley idea de que el gobierno debe de seguir los procesos establecidos por ley y garantizados por la Constitución (p. 228)

E

effigy/efigie una figura rellenada de trapos que representa una persona impopular (p. 134)

Electoral College/Colegio Electoral un grupo especial de votantes escogidos por los votantes de sus estados para elegir al presidente y al vicepresidente (p. 210)

emancipate/emancipar liberar de la esclavitud (p. 475)

embargo/embargo una orden que prohibe el comercio con otro país (pp. 290, 573)

emigrant/emigrante una persona que sale de un país o una región para vivir en otras partes (p. 358)

empresario/empresario una persona que arregló la colonización de tierra en Texas durante los años 1800 (p. 363)

encomienda/encomienda sistema de recompensar a los conquistadores con extensiones de tierra y el derecho de recaudar impuestos y exigir mano de obra a los Nativos Americanos que vivían en la tierra (p. 55)

Enlightenment/Siglo de las Luces movimiento durante los años 1700 que propagaba la idea de que el conocimiento, la razón, y la ciencia podrían mejorar la sociedad (p. 208)

entrenched/atrincherado que ocupa una fuerte posición defensiva (p. 486)

enumerated powers/poderes enumerados poderes que pertenecen solamente al gobierno federal (p. 219)

executive branch/rama ejecutiva la rama de gobierno, dirigida por el presidente, que administra las leyes y la política de una nación (p. 210)

export/exportar vender bienes en el extranjero (p. 109)

F

factory system/sistema de fábrica sistema que junta en un solo lugar las categorías de fabricación para aumentar la eficiencia (p. 309)

famine/hambre una escasez extrema de comida (p. 393)

favorite son/hijo favorito candidato que recibe el apoyo de su estado natal en lugar del partido nacional (p. 335)

federal debt/deuda federal la cantidad de dinero debido por el gobierno (p. 575)

federalism/federalismo el compartir el poder entre el gobierno federal y los gobiernos estatales (pp. 208, 219)

Federalists/federalistas apoyadores de la Constitución (p. 211)

federation/federación una forma de gobierno que une grupos diferentes (p. 33)

feminist/feminista una persona que aboga por o está activa en promulgar los derechos de la mujer (p. 567)

fixed costs/costos fijos gastos regulares tal como de vivienda o mantenimiento de equipo que se quedan casi iguales año tras año (p. 403)

forty-niners/forty-niners personas que fueron a California durante la fiebre del oro en 1849 (p. 375)

free enterprise/libre comercio la libertad de empresas privadas para operarse competetivamente para ganancias con la mínima regulación gubernamental (p. 308)

freedman/liberto una persona liberada de la esclavitud (p. 502)

frigate/fragata buque de guerra (p. 297)

fugitive/fugitivo evadido que trata de huir (p. 438)

G

genocide/genocidio el eradicar un grupo racial, político, o cultural (p. 561)

global warming/calentamiento mundial un aumento contínuo del promedio de temperaturas mundiales (p. 578)

grandfather clause/cláusula de abuelo una cláusula que permitía votar a las personas que no aprobaron el examen de alfabetismo si sus padres o sus abuelos habían votado antes de que empezó la Reconstrucción; una excepción a una ley basada en circunstancias preexistentes (p. 519)

greenback/billete de dorso verde un billete de la moneda de EE.UU. expedido primeramente por el Norte durante la Guerra Civil (p. 483)

guerrilla tactics/tácticas de guerrilla referente a ataques sorpresas o incursiones en lugar de la guerra organizada (p. 344)

guerrilla warfare/contienda a guerrilleros una técnica de tirar y darse a la huída usada en combates de guerra (p. 180)

H

habeas corpus/hábeas corpus una orden legal para una encuesta para determinar si una persona ha sido encarcelada legalmente (p. 481)

hieroglyphics/jeroglíficos una forma antigua de escribir usando símbolos y dibujos para representar palabras, sonidos, y conceptos (p. 24)

Holocaust/Holocausto el nombre dado a la matanza extensa de judíos y otros grupos por los nazis durante la Segunda Guerra Mundial (p. 561)

horizontal integration/integración horizontal la asociación de firmas competitivas en una sociedad anónima (p. 536)

human rights/derechos humanos derechos, tal como la libertad de encarcelamiento ilegal, tortura, y ejecución, considerados como pertenecientes a todas las personas (p. 574)

I

Ice Age/Época Glacial un período de temperaturas extremadamente frías cuando parte de la superficie del planeta estaba cubierta de extensiones masivas de hielo (p. 17)

impeach/acusar acusación formal a un oficial público de mala conducta en la oficina (pp. 223, 507, 573)

imperialism/imperialismo las acciones usadas por una nación para ejercer control político o económico sobre naciones más pequeñas y débiles (p. 544)

implied powers/poderes implícitos poderes no mencionados específicamente en la Constitución (pp. 221, 268)

import/importar comprar bienes de mercados extranjeros (p. 109)

impressment/requisición captura de marineros para forzarlos a servir en una marina extranjera (pp. 265, 290)

indentured servant/sirviente contratado trabajador que consiente trabajar sin pago durante un cierto período de tiempo a cambio del pasaje a América (p. 87)

Industrial Revolution/Revolución Industrial el cambio de una sociedad agraria en una basada en la industria que empezó en la Gran Bretaña y se promulgó a los Estados Unidos alrededor del año 1800 (p. 307)

inflation/inflación aumento contínuo del precio de productos y servicios (pp. 175, 483)

integrate/integrar suprimir la segregación de las razas diferentes e introducir a membrecía igual y común en la sociedad (p. 512)

interchangeable parts/partes intercambiables piezas uniformes que pueden ser hechas en grandes cantidades para reemplazar otras piezas idénticas (p. 309)

internal improvements/mejoramientos internos proyectos federales, tal como canales y carreteras, para desarrollar el sistema de transportación de una nación (p. 322)

Internet/Internet enlace a través de todo el mundo de redes de computadoras (p. 577)

ironclad/acorazado buque armado (p. 468)

Iroquois Confederacy/Confederación Iroquesa un grupo poderoso de Nativos Americanos de la región oriental de los Estados Unidos compuesto de cinco naciones: los pueblos mohawk, séneca, cayuga, onondaga y oneida (p. 117)

island hopping/saltar islas una estrategia usada durante la Segunda Guerra Mundial que demandó el atacar y capturar ciertas islas importantes para usarlas como bases para saltar por encima de otras (p. 562)

J

joint occupation/ocupación en común la posesión y colonización de un área como esfuerzo compartido por dos o más países (p. 357)

joint-stock company/compañía por acciones una compañía en la cual los inversionistas compran acciones de la compañia a cambio de una porción de las ganancias en el futuro (p. 71)

judicial branch/rama judicial la rama de gobierno, incluyendo el sistema de tribunales federales, que interpreta las leyes de una nación (p. 210)

judicial review/repaso judicial el derecho del Tribunal Supremo para determinar si una ley viola la Constitución (pp. 222, 281)

L

laissez-faire/*laissez-faire* la creencia de que el gobierno no debe de involucrarse en los asuntos comerciales y económicos del país (pp. 279, 350)

landslide/victoria arrolladora una victoria abrumadora (p. 336)

legislative branch/rama legislativa la rama de gobierno que redacta las leyes de una nación (p. 209)

line of demarcation/línea de demarcación una línea imaginaria a lo largo del medio del Océano Atlántico desde el Polo Norte hasta el Polo Sur para dividir las Américas entre España y Portugal (p. 47)

literacy/alfabetismo la capacidad de leer y escribir (p. 113)

literacy test/examen de alfabetismo un método usado para prohibir a los afroamericanos a votar por requerir a presuntos votantes que pudieran leer y escribir a niveles especificados (p. 519)

lock/esclusa en un canal un recinto con puertas en cada extremo y usado para levantar y bajar los buques mientras pasan de un nivel al otro (p. 318)

log cabin campaign/campaña de cabaña rústica el nombre dado a la campaña para la presidencia de William Henry Harrison en 1840, debido al uso de una cabaña rústica de troncos como su símbolo por los whigs (p. 351)

Loyalists/lealistas colonizadores americanos que quedaron leales a la Bretaña y se opusieron a la guerra para la independencia (p. 145)

lynching/linchamiento matar a una persona a través de la acción ilegal de una muchedumbre airada (p. 520)

maize/maíz una forma antigua de elote cultivado por los Nativos Americanos (p. 19)

majority/mayoría más de la mitad (p. 335)

Manifest Destiny/Destino Manifiesto la idea popular en los Estados Unidos durante los años 1800 de que el país debería de extender sus fronteras hasta el Pacífico (p. 360)

manumission/manumisión el liberar a unas personas esclavizadas (p. 201)

martyr/mártir una persona que sacrifica su vida por un principio o una causa (p. 448)

Mayflower Compact/Convenio del Mayflower un documento formal escrito en 1620 que proporcionó leyes para el mantenimiento del orden público en la colonia de Plymouth (p. 77)

mercantilism/mercantilismo idea de que el poder de una nación dependía de ampliar su comercio y aumentar sus reservas de oro (pp. 59, 109)

mercenary/mercenario soldado remunerado para servir en el ejército de un país extranjero (p. 164)

migration/migración el movimiento de un gran número de personas hacia una nueva patria (p. 17)

militia/milicia un grupo de civiles entrenados para luchar durante emergencias (pp. 118, 142)

minutemen/*minutemen* compañías de soldados civiles que se jactaban de que podrían estar listos para tomar armas en sólo un minuto (p. 142)

mission/misión una comunidad religiosa (pp. 54, 92)

monopoly/monopolio control total de una industria por una persona o una compañía (p. 536)

Morse code/código Morse un sistema para transmitir mensajes que usa una serie de puntos y rayas para representar las letras del abecedario, los números, y la puntuación (p. 389)

mosque/mezquita una casa de alabanza musulmana (p. 42)

mountain man/hombre montañés colonizador que vivía en el monte, como en las Montañas Rocosas (p. 357)

muckraker/expositor de corrupción periodista que descubre abusos y corrupción en una sociedad (p. 541)

mudslinging/detractar intentar arruinar la reputación de un adversario con insultos (p. 336)

national debt/deuda nacional la cantidad de dinero que un gobierno debe a otros gobiernos o a su pueblo (p. 260)

nationalism/nacionalismo lealtad a una nación y promoción de sus intereses sobre todos los demás (pp. 293, 547)

nativist/nativista una persona que favorece a los nacidos en su patria y se opone a los inmigrantes (p. 395)

naturalization/naturalización el otorgar la plena ciudadanía a un extranjero (p. 229)

neutral/neutral que no toma partido a ninguna persona ni a ningún país en un conflicto (p. 163)

neutral rights/derechos neutrales el derecho para navegar en el mar sin tomar partido en una guerra (p. 290)

neutrality/neutralidad una posición de no tomar partido en un conflicto (p. 265)

nomads/nómadas personas que se mueven de lugar a lugar, generalmente en busca de comida o de tierras para pastar (p. 17)

nominating convention/convención nominadora sistema en el cual los diputados estatales escogieron al candidato para la presidencia de su partido (p. 337)

nonimportation/no importación la acción de evitar la importación o uso de ciertos productos (p. 134)

normal school/escuela normal una escuela con programa de dos años para entrenar a los graduados de preparatoria para ser maestros (p. 413)

Northwest Passage/Paso Noroeste ruta acuática para Asia por América del Norte buscada por exploradores europeos (p. 60)

nullify/anular cancelar o hacer sin efecto (pp. 271, 338)

O

offensive/ofensiva la posición de atacar o el mismo ataque (p. 463)

ordinance/ordenanza una ley o regulación (p. 196)

override/vencer rechazar o derrotar, como un proyecto de ley propuesto en el Congreso (p. 505)

overseer/capataz persona que supervisa una operación grande o a sus trabajadores (pp. 106, 403)

ozone/ozono el estrato de gas compuesto de una forma de oxígeno que protege la tierra y a su gente de los rayos del sol que causan el cáncer (p. 578)

P

pacifist/pacifista persona opuesta al uso de guerra o violencia para arreglar disputas (pp. 85)

partisan/partidario a favor de una parte de un asunto (p. 268)

patent/patente un documento que da al inventor el derecho exclusivo legal de una invención durante un período de tiempo (p. 308, 535)

Patriots/patriotas colonizadores americanos que estaban determinados para luchar en contra de los británicos hasta que se ganara la independencia americana (p. 145)

patroon/*patroon* terrateniente de las colonias holandesas que gobernaba áreas grandes de tierra como un rey (p. 83)

perjury/perjurio el mentir después de haber jurado decir la verdad (p. 576)

persecute/perseguir tratar cruelmente a alguién a causa de sus creencias o prácticas (p. 76)

petition/petición una solicitud formal (pp. 148, 196)

pilgrimage/peregrinación un viaje a un sitio sagrado (p. 42)

Pilgrims/peregrinos separatistas que viajaron a las colonias durante los años 1600 por un propósito religioso (p. 77)

plantation/plantación una finca grande manejada por el dueño o un gerente y cultivada por trabajadores que vivían allí (p. 55)

plurality/pluralidad el mayor número de individuos (p. 335)

poll tax/impuesto de capitación un impuesto de una cantidad fija por cada persona que tenía que ser pagada antes de que pudiera votar la persona (p. 519)

popular sovereignty/soberanía popular la teoría política de que el gobierno está sujeto a la voluntad del pueblo (p. 218); antes de la Guerra Civil, la idea de que la gente que vivía en un territorio tenía el derecho de decidir por votar si allí sería permitida la esclavitud (p. 442)

preamble/preámbulo la introducción de un documento formal, especialmente la Constitución (pp. 151, 217)

precedent/precedente una tradición (p. 259)

prejudice/prejuicio una opinión injusta no basada en los hechos (p. 392)

presidio/presidio un fuerte español en las Américas construido para proteger las colonias misioneras (p. 54)

privateer/buque corsario buque armado privado (pp. 179, 297)

Prohibition/Prohibición entredicho contra la fabricación, transportación, y venta de bebidas alcohólicas por todo los Estados Unidos (p. 550)

propaganda/propaganda ideas o información diseñadas para influenciar la opinión (pp. 137, 547)

proportional/proporcional que son iguales o que corresponden (p. 203)

proprietary colony/colonia propietaria colonia dirigida por personas o grupos a quienes se les había otorgado la tierra (pp. 83, 111)

pueblo/pueblo una casa o una comunidad de casas construidas por Nativos Americanos (pp. 29, 54)

Puritans/puritanos protestantes que, durante los años 1600, querían reformar la iglesia anglicana (p. 77)

R

radical/radical extremo (p. 501)

ranchero/ranchero dueño de rancho mexicano (p. 371)

rancho/rancho propiedades grandísimas para producir ganado establecidas por colonizadores mexicanos en California (p. 371)

ratify/ratificar dar aprobación oficial para (pp. 185, 211, 476)

Rebel/rebelde soldado confederado, así nombrado a causa de su oposición al gobierno establecido (p. 464)

reconciliation/reconciliación arreglar por acuerdo o por reunirse de nuevo (p. 514)

Reconstruction/Reconstrucción la reorganización y la reconstrucción de los anteriores estados confederados después de la Guerra Civil (p. 501)

recruit/reclutar enlistar a soldados para el ejército (p. 165)

relocate/reubicar forzar a una persona o a un grupo de personas a trasladarse (p. 342)

Renaissance/Renacimiento un período de creatividad intelectual y artística, alrededor de los años 1300–1600 (p. 39)

rendezvous/*rendezvous* una reunión (p. 357)

reparations/reparaciones pago por el país que pierde una guerra al país que gana por los daños causados por la guerra (p. 549)

repeal/revocar cancelar un decreto o ley (p. 134)

republic/república un gobierno en el cual ciudadanos gobiernan por medio de representantes elegidos (p. 193)

republicanism/republicanismo que favorece una república, o sea una democracia representativa, como la mejor forma de gobierno (p. 218)

reservation/reservación un área de tierra pública apartada para los Nativos Americanos (p. 531)

reserved powers/poderes reservados poderes retenidos por los estados (p. 219)

resolution/resolución una expresión formal de opinión (p. 134)

revenue/ingresos entrada de dinero (p. 133)

revival/renacimiento religioso una serie de reuniones dirigidas por un predicador para animar emociones religiosas (p. 413)

royal colony/colonia real colonia administrada por un gobernador y un consejo nombrados por el rey o reina (p. 111)

scalawags/*scalawags* nombre dado por los confederados anteriores a los blancos sureños que apoyaban la Reconstrucción republicana del Sur (p. 510)

secede/separarse abandonar o retirar (pp. 285, 338, 438)

secession/secesión retiro de la Unión (p. 451)

sectionalism/regionalismo lealtad a una región (pp. 322, 437)

sedition/sedición actividades con el propósito de debilitar un gobierno establecido (p. 271)

segregation/segregación la separación o aislamiento de una raza, una clase, o un grupo (pp. 519, 566)

Separatists/separatistas protestantes que, durante los años 1600, querían dejar la iglesia anglicana para fundar sus propias iglesias (p. 77)

settlement house/casa de beneficencia institución colocada en una vecindad pobre que proveía numerosos servicios a la comunidad tal como cuidado médico, cuidado de niños, bibliotecas, y clases de inglés (p. 538)

sharecropping/aparcería sistema de agricultura en el cual un granjero labra la tierra para un dueño que provee equipo y semillas y recibe una porción de la cosecha (p. 512)

slave code/código de esclavos las leyes aprobadas en los estados sureños que controlaban y restringían a la gente esclavizada (p. 405)

smuggling/contrabandear cambiar ilegalmente con otras naciones (p. 109)

speculator/especulador persona que arriesga dinero para hacer una ganancia grande (pp. 125, 261)

spiritual/espiritual una canción popular religiosa afroamericana (p. 405)

spoils system/sistema de despojos la práctica de dar puestos gubernamentales a los partidarios; reemplazar a los empleados del gobierno con los partidarios del candidato victorioso (p. 337)

stalemate/estancamiento una situación durante un conflicto cuando la acción se para debido a que ambos partidos son igualmente poderosos y ningún de los dos lo abandonará (p. 565)

states' rights/derechos estatales derechos y poderes independientes del gobierno federal que son reservados a los estados por la Constitución (pp. 271, 451)

strait/estrecho un paso angosto que conecta dos extensiones más grandes de agua (p. 49)

strike/huelga un paro de trabajo por los trabajadores para forzar al empresario a satisfacer demandas (p. 392)

subsistence farming/agricultura para subsistencia labranza que produce solamente la comida que se necesita para dar de comer a la familia del trabajador (p. 101)

suffrage/sufragio el derecho al voto (pp. 336, 426)

suffragist/sufragista un hombre o mujer que luchaba para el derecho al voto de la mujer (p. 542)

tariff/tarifa impuesto sobre productos importados o exportados (pp. 262, 338)

technology/tecnología el uso de conocimientos científicos para propósitos prácticos (pp. 40, 308)

Tejano/tejano un mexicano que reclama Texas como su patria (p. 363)

telegraph/telégrafo un aparato o sistema que usa señales eléctricas para transmitir mensajes a códigos a través de alambres (p. 389)

temperance/templanza el uso de poca o de ninguna bebida alcohólica (p. 413)

tenant farmer/granjero arrendatario un granjero que labra la tierra de otro dueño y paga renta ya sea con la cosecha o al contado (pp. 92, 402)

terrace/terraza una parcela de tierra elevada y allanada para fomentar la agricultura (p. 26)

terrorism/terrorismo el uso de la violencia contra ciudadanos para lograr un gol político (p. 578)

theocracy/teocracia una forma de gobierno en la cual la sociedad está gobernada por líderes religiosos (p. 23)

Tidewater/Orilla del Mar una región de llanuras planas y bajas alrededor de la costa del mar (p. 105)

Spanish Glossary

toleration/tolerancia el aceptar creencias diferentes (p. 79)

total war/guerra total la guerra en todo aspecto de la vida del enemigo (p. 490)

trade union/gremio una organización de artesanos con el mismo oficio o destreza (pp. 392)

Transcendentalist/transcendentalista uno de un grupo de escritores de Nueva Inglaterra que acentuaban la relación entre los seres humanos y la naturaleza, asuntos espirituales sobre asuntos materiales, y la importancia de la conciencia particular (p. 415)

transcontinental/*transcontinental* que se extiende a través del continente (p. 529)

triangular trade/trato triangular una ruta de comercio para cambiar productos entre las Antillas, las colonias americanas, y África del Oeste (p. 102)

tribute/tributo dinero pagado para protección (pp. 52, 289)

trust/cártel una combinación de firmas o sociedades anónimas formada por un acuerdo legal, especialmente para reducir la competición (pp. 536)

turnpike/autopista una carretera que uno debe de pagar para usar; el dinero se usa para pagar el costo de la carretera (p. 315)

unalienable right/derecho inalienable un derecho al que no se puede renunciar (p. 154)

unconstitutional/anticonstitucional no de acuerdo ni consistente con la Constitución (p. 262)

Underground Railroad/Ferrocarril Subterráneo un sistema que ayudó a los afroamericanos esclavizados a seguir una red de rutas de escape afuera del Sur hacia la libertad del Norte (p. 422)

utopia/utopía una comunidad basada en una visión de la sociedad perfecta buscada por los reformistas (p. 412)

vaquero/vaquero trabajador ranchero hispánico (p. 529)

vertical integration/integración vertical la asociación de compañías que abastecen con equipo y servicios necesarios para una industria particular (p. 536)

veto/vetar rechazar un proyecto de ley y prevenir que vuelva a ser una ley (p. 349)

vigilantes/vigilantes gente que toman la ley en sus propias manos (pp. 377)

War Hawks/halcones de guerra republicanos durante la presidencia de Madison que insistían en la guerra con la Bretaña (p. 293)

writ of assistance/escrito de asistencia documento legal que permitía a los oficiales que exploraran las casas y bodegas en busca de productos que tal vez pudieran ser de contrabandeado (p. 133)

Yankee/yanqui soldado de la Unión (p. 464)

yellow journalism/periodismo amarillista una clase de reportaje sensacional, prejuzgado, y a menudo falso (p. 545)

yeoman/terrateniente menor dueño sureño de una granja pequeña que no tenía esclavos (p. 402)

Spanish Glossary

Index

Italicized page numbers refer to illustrations. The following abbreviations are used in the index:
m = map, c = chart, p = photograph or picture, g = graph, crt = cartoon, ptg = painting, q = quote

Index

Index

Index

Index

Index

Index

Index

Index

Acknowledgements and Photo Credits

Acknowledgements

50 From *Morning Girl* by Michael Dorris. Text © 1992 by Michael Dorris. Reprinted with permission from Hyperion Books for Children.

107 From *The Kidnapped Prince* by Olaudah Equiano. Adapted by Ann Cameron. Copyright © 1995 by Ann Cameron. Reprinted by permission of Alfred A. Knopf, Inc.

140 Excerpt from *Johnny Tremain* by Esther Forbes. Copyright © 1943 by Esther Forbes Hoskins, © renewed 1971 by Linwood M. Erskine, Jr., Executor of the Estate of Esther Forbes Hoskins. Reprinted by permission of Houghton Mifflin Co. All rights reserved.

295 From *Night Flying Woman: An Ojibway Narrative* by Ignatia Broker. Copyright © 1983 by the Minnesota Historical Society. Reprinted by permission.

567, 623 Reprinted by arrangement with the Heirs to the Estate of Martin Luther King, Jr., c/o Writers House, Inc. as agent for the proprietor. Copyright © 1963 by Martin Luther King, Jr., copyright renewed 1991 by Coretta Scott King.

604 "God Bless the USA," words and music by Lee Greenwood. Copyright © 1984 Songs of Universal Inc. and Universal Songs of Polygram International Inc. (BMI) International Copyright Secured. All Rights Reserved.

Glencoe would like to acknowledge the artists and agencies who participated in illustrating this program: Morgan Cain & Associates; Ortelius Design, Inc.; QA Digital.

Photo Credits

COVER (tl)Corbis, (tc)PhotoDisc, (tr)Chicago Historical Society, (bl)Massachusetts Historical Society; (br)Mongerson-Wunderlich Gallery, Chicago, (flag) PhotoDisc, (background)Library of Congress; **iv** (t)file photo, (b)Peabody Museum of Salem; **ix** Stock Montage; **v** (t)Grant Heilman Photography, (tc)Mark Burnett, (b)PhotoDisc, (bc)Superstock; **vi** Michael Freeman; **vii** Kari Haavisto; **x** Field Museum of Natural History; **xi** Chester County Historical Society, West Chester, PA; **xiv** Corbis; **xv** (t)courtesy Ford Motor Company, (b)PhotoDisc; **xvii** Collection of Michael Barson; **xviii** Larry Kunkel/FPG **RA16, RA17** PhotoDisc; **2** (t)Robert W. Madden/National Geographic Society, (b)Rich Buzzelli/Tom Stack & Associates; **4** (t)David M. Dennis, (b)Walter Meayers Edwards/National Geographic Society; **5** Private Collection; **6** (t)Museum of Ethnology, (t)Johnny Johnson (bl)Jerry Jacks/courtesy Arizona State Museum, University of Arizona, (l)Eliot Cohen; **7** Jeremy Horner/Stone; **9** Richard Alexander Cooke III, Scala/Art Resource, NY; **12** Scala/Art Resource, NY; **12-13** Brown Brothers; **14** (l)Bridgeman/Art Resource, NY; (r)Addison Doty/Morning Star Gallery, **15** (t)Ed Simpson/Stone, (bl)Michel Zabe'/Museo Templo Major; (br)Heye Foundation, National Museum of The American Indian/Smithsonian Institution; **16** file photo; **17** Heye Foundation, National Museum of The American Indian/Smithsonian Institutute; **22** Boltin Picture Library; **23** (l)Richard Alexander Cooke III, (r)David Hiser/Stone; **25** (t)DDB Stock Photo, (bl)Michel Zabe', (background)USDA, (br)N. Carter/North Wind Picture Archive, (br)Inga Spence/DDB Stock Photo; **27** Museum of Ethnology; **28** Jerry Jacka/courtesy Arizona State Museum, Arizona University; **29** David Muench; **34** (t)file photo, (b)Addison Doty/Morning Star Gallery; **36** U.S. Architect of the Capitol, (b)National Museum of African Art/Jeffrey Ploskonka, (l)Archivio Fotografico del Museo Preistorico Etnografico L. Pigorini, Roma; **37** ©Architect of the United States, (t)The Library of Congress, (b)file photo, ©National Portrait Gallery, Smithsonian Institution/Art Resource, NY; **38** Brown Brothers; **40** (l)NASA, (r)National Maritime Museum; **43** Peabody Museum of Salem; **44** Giraudon/Art Resource, NY; **45** Doug Martin; **46** Giraudon/Art Resource, NY; **47** Culver Pictures; **50** (t)Louise Erdrich, (b)Musee de L'Homme, Palais de Chateau, Paris; **51** courtesy The Oakland Museum; **52** Collection of Colonel Stuart S. Corning/Rob Huntley/Lightstream; **54** Museo de Historia, Chapultepec/Bob Schalkwijk; **56** Walter Edwards; **57** (t)Chas W. Polzer, (c)Greg Edwards, (b)Edwardo Fuss; **58** SuperStock; **59** "Kateri Tekakwitha" by Father Claude Chauchetiere, S.J., around 1690, photo by Bob Peters, St. Francis Xavier Mission, Kahnawake, Quebec; **60** Corbis; **61** courtesy The Oakland Museum; **63** Maritime Museum, Seville/Artephot/Oronoz; **64** (t)University Museum of National Antiquities, Oslo, Norway, (c)U.S. Architect of the Capitol, (b)courtresy The Oakland Museum; **66** Plimoth Plantation; **66-67** Corbis; **67** Brown Brothers; **68** (t)Hulton/Archive, (b)file photo; **69** (t)New York Historical Society, (bl)Courtesy Haffenreffer Museum of Anthropology, Brown University, (br)Courtesy The Oakland Museum; **70-71** Jamestown-Yorktown Foundation; **72** National Portrait Gallery, Smithsonian Institution/Art Resource, NY; **74** Richard T. Nowitz/National Geographic Society; **75** (t)Jamestown Foundation, (c)file photo, (b)Bob Pratt/ National Geographic Society; **76** Plimoth Plantation; **78** courtesy Pilgrim Society, Plymouth, MA; **79** Brown Brothers; **82** courtesy Winterthur Museum; **84** Glencoe file photo; **86** British Museum; **88** Corbis; **89** Courtesy of APVA Preservation Virginia; **90** Culver Pictures; **91** (t)Larry Stevens/Nawrocki Stock Photo, (b)Nawrocki Stock Photo; **92** Gibbes Museum of Art; **93** Historical Picture Collection/Stock Montage; **94** (t)National Portrait Gallery, Smith-

sonian Institution/Art Resource, NY, (tc)Private Collection, (bc)courtesy Haffenreffer Museum of Anthropology, Brown University, (b)Historical Picture Collection/Stock Montage; **96** (t)Smithsonian Institution, (b)Peabody Museum of Salem; **97** Timothy Fuller; **98** (l)Chicago Historical Society, (r)courtesy Historic Deerfield Inc./Amanda Merullo **99** (t)courtesy Old John Street United Methodist Church, (bl)Blue Ridge Institute & Museums/Ferrum College, (br)Yale University Art Gallery, **100** Colonial Williamsburg; **101** (l)Lee Snider/Corbis, (r)Bruce M. Wellman/Stock Boston; **102** Peabody Essex Museum/Mark Sexton, **104** courtesy American Antiquarian Society; **105** Colonial Williamsburg; **107** Royal Albert Memorial Museum, Exeter, England; **108** Yale University Art Gallery; **109-110** Yale University Art Gallery; **111** National Portrait Gallery, London/SuperStock; **111-112** PhotoDisc; **112** The Ohio Historical Village, Columbus, Ohio, Photo by Doug Martin; **116** courtesy American Antiquarian Society; **118** Culver Pictures; **120** file photo; **121** Musee de L'Homme/M. Delaplanche; **122** State Historical Society of Wisconsin Museum Collection; **124** Amanita Pictures; **126** (t)Colonial Williamsburg, (tc)courtesy American Antiquarian Society, (bc)Musee de L'Homme/M. Delaplanche (b)Library of Congress; **128** David A. Schorsch; **128-129** Corbis; **129** file photo; **130** (tl)Archive Photos, (tr)courtesy Peabody & Essex Museum, Salem, MA, (b)Stock Montage; **131** (t)Painting by Don Troianni, www.historicalartprints.com (cr)DAR Museum on loan from Boston Tea Party Chapter, (cl)courtesy American Antiquarian Society, (r)Massachusetts Historical Society; **132** Crown copyright. Historic Royal Palaces. Photograph David Chalmess; **134** Massachusetts Historical Society; **135** Patrick Henry Before the Virginia House of Burgesses (1851) by Peter F. Rothermel. Red Hill, The Patrick Henry National Memorial, Brookneal, VA; **136** file photo; **138** (tr)Corbis-Bettmann, (br)courtesy American Antiquarian Society, (c)DAR Museum on loan from Boston Tea Party Chapter, (tc)The Royal Collection, Her Majesty Queen Elizabeth II (l)Stock Montage; **140** Culver Pictures/SuperStock; **141-142** North Wind Picture Archives; **144** Concord Museum, Concord, MA; **146** Private Collection; **147** White House Historical Association; **148** Historical Society of Pennsylvania; **149** Stock Montage; **150** Virginia Historical Society, All Rights Reserved; **152** Painting by Don Troiani, www.historicalartprints.com; **155** Corbis; **157** Deposited by the City of Boston, courtesy Museum of Fine Arts, Boston; **160** (l)Virginia Historical Society, (r)Giraudon/Art Resource; **160-161** Frances Tavern Museum, New York City; **161** file; **162** West Point Museum; **163** North Wind Picture Archive; **164** (l)Corbis-Bettmann, (r)UPI/Corbis-Bettmann; **166** Brown Brothers; **172** Chicago Historical Society; **173** The Valley Forge Historical Society; **174** Corbis; **175** Eric P. Newman Numismatic Education Society; **176** file photo; **177** William T. Ranney, MARION CROSSING THE PEDEE, 1850, 1983.125; Amon Carter Museum, Fort Worth, Texas; **178-179** (background)Library of Congress; **179** (inset)Massachusettes Historical Society; **180** Stock Montage; **182** Archives Division, Texas State Library; **183** Chicago Historical Society; **184** Lafayette College Art Collection, Easton, PA. Gift of Mrs. John Hubbard; **185** Trumball Collection, Yale University Art Gallery; **186** Courtesy J. Quintus Massie on behalf of descendants; **188** Painting by Don Troiani, www.historicalartprints.com (bl)Virginia Historical Society, (tr)The Metropolitan Museum of Art, Gift of John S. Kennedy, 1897. (97.34); **190** Picture Research Consultants; **190-191** Corbis; **191**(bl)Corbis Bettmann, (c) White House Historical Association, (br)New York Historical Society; **192** North Wind Picture Archive; **193** Picture Research Consultants; **194** file photo; **196** (background)PhotoDisc; **197** (r)Independence National Historic Park, (l)Chicago Historical Society; **199** Independence National Historical Park; **200** Corbis-Bettmann; **201** (r)Delaware Art Museum, Wilmington. Gift of Absalom Jones School, Wilmington, (l)Moorland Spingarn Research Center, Howard University; **202** SuperStock; **203** Library of Congress; **204** Independence National Historic Park; **207** Independence National Historical Park; **208** National Portrait Gallery; **209** Fred Maroon/Smithsonian Institution; **210** Supreme Court Historical Society; **211** file photo; **212** Bequest of Winslow Warren, courtesy Museum of Fine Arts, Boston; **213** file photo; **214** (t)Library of Congress, (c)Bettmann/Corbis, (b)Fraunces Tavern Museum; **215** Independence National Historic Park; **216** Picture Research Consultants; **220** Massachusetts Historical Society; **221** SuperStock; **224** White House/Liaison Agency; **226** Bob Daemmrich/Stone; **228** Sylvain Grandadam/Stone; **230** Mark Burnett; **244** Boltin Picture Library; **249** Cobalt Productions; **251** Paul Conklin; **252** Museum of American Textile History; **254** (inset)Smithsonian Institution; **254** Smithsonian Institution; **254-255** (t)Independence National Historic Park/Joseph Painter, **256** (t) file photo, (c) White House Historical Association, (b)Erich Lessing/Art Resource, NY; **257** (t)Boston Naval Library & Institute Collection, (bl)Yale University Art Gallery, (c)White House Historical Association, (br)Collection of David J. & Janice L. Frent; **258** Frank & Marie-Therese Wood Print Collection, Alexandria, VA; **260** Aaron Haupt; **261** David R. Frazier; **263** Atwater Kent Museum; **265** Chicago Historical Society; **268** courtesy Winterthur Museum; **269** Stock Montage; **271** Archive Photo; **272** Stock Montage; **274** Library of Congress; **276** (tl)Duke University

Archives, (tr)Royal Ontario Museum, Toronto/National Geographic Society, (c)White House Historical Association, (b)Eric Lessing/Art Resources, NY; 276-277 Don Troianni, www.historicalartprints.com, 277(t)file photo, (c)White House Historical Association, (b)North Wind Picture Archives; 278 The White House Historical Association; 279 North Wind Picture Archive; 280 (r)The Huntington - San Marino, CA/SuperStock, (l)Corbis; 282 West Virginia State Museum; 288 North Wind Picture Archives; 289 Corbis; 292 Field Museum of Natural History; 293 Brown Brothers; 295 (l)Darlene Pfister/Minneapolis Star Tribune, (r)Minnesota Historical Society; 296 Princeton University Library; 297 Library of Congress; 299 Stock Montage; 301 Missouri Historical Society; 302 (t)White House Historical Association, (background)Kendall Cross, (cl)White House Historical Association, (cr)Library of Congress, (b)New York State Historical Association, Cooperstown; 304 ((l)Smithsonian Institution, Burstein Collection/Corbis, (r)Bob Mullenix; 304-305 (t)Corbis, (presidential gallery) White House Historical Association; 305 (l,r)New York Historical Society; 306 Corbis; 307 Aaron Haupt; 309 (tl)Baker Library, Harvard University, (tr)Lowell National Historical Park, (bl)file photo, (br)File photo, (background)file photo; 314 Corbis; 315 Stock Montage; 316 (tl)Michael G. Buettner, Lincoln Highway Association, (br)Douglas Kirkland/Corbis; 317 (tr)SuperStock, (l)David G. Houser/Corbis, (br)Henry Diltz/Corbis; 324 (t)Boot Hill Museum/Henry Groskinsky, (b)Peter Menzel; 325 (l)Library of Congress, (r)Collection of the Boston Public Library, Print Division, 326 file photo; 328 (t)Smithsonian Institution, (b)New York Historical Society, (r)Anthony Richardson, (bc)James Monroe Museum & Memorial Library, (l)Craig McDougal, (tc)The Metropolitan Museum of Art, Rogers Fund, 1942. (42.95.11); 328-329 St. Louis Art Museum, Eliza McMillan Fund; 329 courtesy Charleston Museum; 331 Library of Congress; 333 Boatmen's National Bank of St. Louis; 334 Collection of David J. & Janice L. Frent; 335 New York Historical Society; 337 Library Company of Philadelphia; 338 North Wind Picture Archive; 340 Archives & Manuscripts Division of the Oklahoma Historical Society; 340-341 Kevin C. Chadwick/National Geographic Society; 341 (l)White House Historical Association, (r)Archives & Manuscripts Division of the Oklahoma Historical Society; 343 SuperStock; 344 National Museum of American Art, Smithsonian Institution. Gift of Mrs. Joseph Harrison, JR/Art Resource, NY; 349 New York Historical Society; 350 (l)National Portrait Gallery, Smithsonian Institution/Art Resource, NY, (r)Smithsonian Institution; 354 (l)Stock Montage, (r)Collection of David J. & Janet L. Frent; 354-355 (t)The Manoogian Foundation, on loan to the National Gallery of Art, Washington. Photo by Lyle Peterzell, (presidential gallery) White House Historical Association; 355 (l)Collection Mrs. J. Maxwell Moran, (r)Collection of David J. & Janice L. Frent; 356 Nikki Pahl; 357 Archive Photo; 359 Henry Groskinsky; 362 Archives Division, Texas State Library; 363 Institute of Texas Culture; 364 Friends of the Governor's Mansion, Austin; 366 Archives Division, Texas State Library; 369 Panhandle Plains Historical Museum; 370 Thomas Gilcrease Institute of American Art, Tulsa, OK; 371 file photo; 373 California State Library; 375 courtesy The Oakland Museum; 376 (l)White House Historical Association, (c)Doug Martin, (l)Levi Strauss & Company; 377 Denver Public Library, Western History Collection; 378 Bettmann/Corbis; 379 (l)Corbis-Bettmann, (r)Wenham Museum; 380 courtesy Denver Public Library Western History Department; 382 American Museum, Bath,England/Bridgeman Collection/SuperStock, Inc.; 383 Timothy Fuller; 384 (t)Smithsonian Institution, (c,b)file photo; 384-385 (t)SuperStock, (presidential gallery) White House Historical Association; 385 (l)North Wind Picture Archive, (r)National Portrait Gallery, Smithsonian Institution; 386 Smithsonian Institution/Charles Phillips; 391 Jack Naylor; 392 Museum of Fine Arts, Boston, M. & M. Karolik Collection; 394 (l)Museum of the City of New York, (r)Bostonian Society/Mark Sexton; 397 Grant Heilman Photography; 399 (l)Bettmann/Corbis, (r)Smithsonian Institution; 401 John Deere Museum; 402 (l)The J. Paul Getty Museum, (r)Bettmann/Corbis; 404 (cr)Adam Woolfitt/Corbis (br)Valentine Museum, (bl)courtesy Charleston Museum, (background)New York Historical Society; 406 Stock Montage; 408 (t)John Deere Museum, (tr)Smithsonian Institution/Charles Phillips, (c)file photo (b)T.W. Wood Art Gallery, Montpelier, VT; 410 (t)The American Antiquarian Society, (br)FPG, (b)file photo, 410-411 (t)SuperStock, (presidential gallery) White House Historical Association; 411 (l)Chicago Historical Society, (r)from Fletcher's History of Oberlin College, courtesy Oberlin College; 412 National Portrait Gallery, Smithsonian Institution, Washington DC; 414 (t)City Art Museum of St. Louis/SuperStock, (bc)Brown Brothers, (bl)Museum of American Textile History; 418 Peabody Essex Museum/Mark Sexton; 419 Library of Congress; 420 Collection of William Gladstone; 422 Bettmann/Corbis; 425 Mount Holyoke College Art Museum, South Hadley, Massachusetts; 426 (l)Chicago Historical Society, (r)Meserve Collection; 427 (tr)Maria Mitchell Association, (bc)National Archives of Canada, (br)Corbis, (l)Nebraska State Historical Society, (tc)Hulton Archive; 430 (t)New York Historical Society, (c)Peabody Essex Museum/Mark Sexton, (b)Library of Congress; 432 Mark Burnett; 432-433 Painting by Don Troiani, www.historicalartprints.com; 433 PhotoDisc; 434-435 (t) Corbis, (presidential gallery) White House Historical Association; 435 (t)Medford Historical Society, courtesy Robert M. Hicklin, Jr., (bl)Missouri State Historical Society, (br)Photo Network; 436 Frank & Marie-Therese Wood Print Collection, Alexandria, VA; 437 Collection of David J. & Janice L. Frent; 438 New York Historical Society;

440 Corbis; 441 Library of Congress; 442 Schlesinger Library, Radcliffe College; 444 H. Armstrong Roberts; 445 North Wind Picture Archive; 446 (l)Corbis, (r)Missouri State Historical Society, (l)Jim Gensheimer; 446 447 Kevin C. Chadwick/National Geographic Society; 447 courtesy Illinois State Historical Library; 449 Chicago Historical Society; 450 (t)courtesy Chicago Historical Society, (b)Library of Congress; 456 (tc)Missouri State Historical Society, (bc)courtesy Chicago Historical Society, (t)NorthWind Picture Archive; 458 (l) Museum of the Confederacy, (r)Corbis; 458-459 Painting by Don Troiani, www.historicalartprints.com, (presidential gallery) White House Historical Association; 459 (l)Time-Life Books Inc. from the series "Civil War"/Edward Owen, National Archives, (r)Illinois State Historical Library; 460 PhotoDisc; 461 Seventh Regiment Fund, New York City; 463 PhotoDisc 464 National Archives; 465 (r)File photo, (l)Corbis-Bettmann; 466 Manassas National Battlefield Park/Larry Sherer; 467 National Archives; 468 PhotoDisc; 471 Medford Historical Society Collection/Corbis; 473 McLellan Lincoln Collection, The John Hay Library, Brown University/John Miller; 474-475 PhotoDisc; 476 Glencoe file photo; 478 Collection of Larry Williford; 479 (l)Museum of the Confederacy, (r)PhotoDisc 480 FPG; 481 National Archives; 482 (l)Brown Brothers, (r)Corbis; 484 MAK I; 485 Picture Research Consultants; 486 Michigan Capitol Committee, photography by Peter Glendinning; 490 (l)Matt Meadows, (r)Glencoe file photo; 491 (l)Brown Brothers, (r)Corbis; 494 (t)McLellan Lincoln Collection, The John Hay Library, Brown University/John Miller, (bc)Painting by Don Troiani, www.historicalartprints.com, (tc)Corbis, (b)National Archives; 496 ©Shelburne Museum, Shelburne, Vermont; 497 Aaron Haupt; 498 (l)North Wind Picture Archive, (r)file photo; 498-499 (t)Corbis, (presidential gallery) White House Historical Association; 499 Museum of American Political Life; 500 National Museum of American History/Smithsonian Institution; 501 Gettysburg National Military Park; 504 Chicago Historical Society; 505 Tennessee Botanical Gardens & Museum of Art, Nashville; 509 Corbis; 511 Chester County Historical Society, West Chester, PA; 512 National Museum of American History, Smithsonian Institution/Rudolf Eickmeyer; 513 North Wind Picture Archive; 514 Stock Montage; 516 file photo, Corbis; 517 Bettmann/Corbis; 520 (t)Morning Star Gallery, Addison Doty photo, Museum of American Political Life, (b)Bob Mullenix; 520-521 Collection of Mr. & Mrs. Paul Mellon, Board of Trustees, National Gallery of Art; 521 National Park Service Collection; 522 file photo, National Portrait Gallery, Smithsonian Institution/Art Resource, NY, Collection of David J. & Janice L. Frent, (b)Corcoran Gallery of Art; 523 National Museum of American Art, Washington, DC/Art Resource, NY; 524 John Sohm/Chromosohn/Stock Boston; 524-525 NASA; 525 John Sohm/Chromosohn/Corbis; 526, (l)Stanford University Museum of Art; (r)Rudi von Briel; 526-527 (t)Lisa Ades, (b)The White House Historical Association; 527 (tc)Bettmann Archive, (b)Collection of Colonel Stuart S. Corning/Rob Huntley/ Lightstream, 528 (l)courtesy The Oakland Museum; 529 Duke University; 530 (l) Nebraska State Historical Society, Lincoln, (r)Montana Historical Society, Helena; 532 Denver Public Library, Western History Collection; 533 New York Historical Society; 534 Picture Research Consultants; 535 National Air and Space Museum; 536 courtesy Ford Motor Company; 537 Jacob A. Riis Collection, Museum of the City of New York; 539 University of Illinois at Chicago, Jane Addams Memorial Collection; 540 Archive Photo; 541 Pelletier Library/Alleghany College; 543 Oscar B. Willis/The Schomburg Center for Research in Black Culture, New York Public Library; 546 Corbis; 547, (l)Corbis-Bettmann, (c)Corbis, (r)Larry O. Nighswander/National Geographic Society Image Collection; 548 Brown Brothers; 552 (b)Bettmann Archive, (t)Stanford University Museum of Art, (tc)Rudi von Briel, (bc)Collection of Colonel Stuart S. Corning/Rob Huntley/Lightstream; 554 (l, r)collection of David J. & Janice L. Frent, (c)PhotoDisc; 554-555 (t)Corbis, (b)The White House Historical Association; 555 (t)Bettmann/Corbis, (b)Peter Marlow/Magnum Photos; 556 W.H. Clark/H. Armstrong Roberts; 557 Library of Congress; 558 Margaret Bourke-White, Life Magazine, Time, Inc; 559, 561 Corbis; 562, 563 Library of Congress; 564 US Army; 565 Superstock; 566 (l)Flip Schulke/Black Star, (r)Corbis; 568 file photo; 571 Larry Burrows/Time, Inc; 572 Collection of David J. & Janice L. Frent; 573 Alex Webb/Magnum Photos; 574 (l)Liaison Agency, (r)David Burnett/Contact Press Images, (b)Dirck Halstead/Gamma Liaison; 575 (t)Greg Gibson/AP/Wide World Photos; (b)Black Star; 576, 577, 578, 579 Corbis; 580 (l) Corbis, (r)Thomas E. Franklin/Bergen Record/SABA/ Corbis; 582 (l)Corbis, (c)Joe Raedle/Getty News, (r)Sygma/Corbis, (background)AFP/Corbis; 583 Library of Congress; 584 (t)Steve Liss/Time; 586 Reuters/Timepix; 588 (tr, lc)file photo, (bc)Brown Brothers, (others, background)PhotoDisc; 590 (t) PhotoDisc, (b)Missouri Historical Society; 591 Chicago Historical Society; 592 National Anthropological Archives, Smithsonian Institution; 593 National Maritime Museum; 594 W. Saunders/TimePix; 595, 596 Brown Brothers; 597 file photo; 598 Corbis; 599 Smithsonian Institution; 600 Corbis; 601 Massachusetts Historical Society, Boston; 602 courtesy Fisk University, Nashville, TN; 605 Reuters/TimePix; 606-610 The White House Historical Society; 610 (bc, br)Corbis; 611 North Wind Picture Archives; 613 courtesy Winterthur Museum; 614 Corbis; 614-615 Corbis; 617 National Portrait Gallery/ Smithsonian Institution; 618 (l)file photo, (r)Mark Burnett; 619 (t)Denver Art Museum, (b)Corbis; 621, 622 Corbis; 623 Flip Schulke/Black Star; 624 Missouri State Historical Society; 625, 626 Corbis.

Photo Credits

CLASSROOM ELECTION SPECIAL

TIME

PRESIDENT
GEORGE W. BUSH

NOVEMBER 3, 2004

FOUR MORE YEARS

ELECTION ★ NOTEBOOK

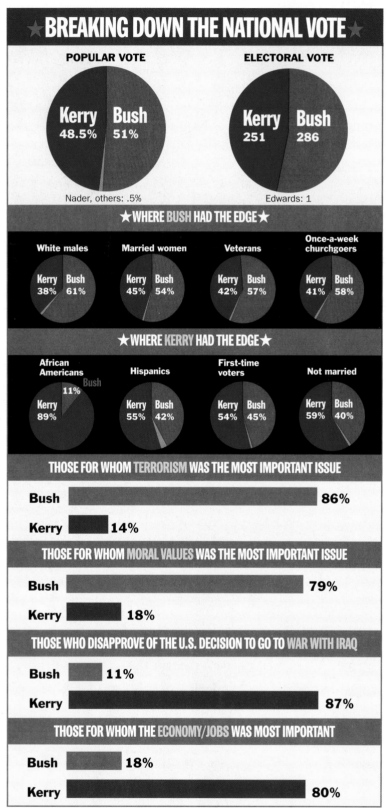

★ BREAKING DOWN THE NATIONAL VOTE ★

POPULAR VOTE

Kerry 48.5% **Bush** 51%

Nader, others: .5%

ELECTORAL VOTE

Kerry 251 **Bush** 286

Edwards: 1

★ WHERE BUSH HAD THE EDGE ★

White males
Kerry 38% Bush 61%

Married women
Kerry 45% Bush 54%

Veterans
Kerry 42% Bush 57%

Once-a-week churchgoers
Kerry 41% Bush 58%

★ WHERE KERRY HAD THE EDGE ★

African Americans
Bush 11%
Kerry 89%

Hispanics
Kerry 55% Bush 42%

First-time voters
Kerry 54% Bush 45%

Not married
Kerry 59% Bush 40%

THOSE FOR WHOM TERRORISM WAS THE MOST IMPORTANT ISSUE

Bush — 86%
Kerry — 14%

THOSE FOR WHOM MORAL VALUES WAS THE MOST IMPORTANT ISSUE

Bush — 79%
Kerry — 18%

THOSE WHO DISAPPROVE OF THE U.S. DECISION TO GO TO WAR WITH IRAQ

Bush — 11%
Kerry — 87%

THOSE FOR WHOM THE ECONOMY/JOBS WAS MOST IMPORTANT

Bush — 18%
Kerry — 80%

Source: National Election Pool exit poll conducted by Edison/Mitofsky. Margin of error is ±3 percentage points for national data and ±4 percentage points for state data.

★ NUMBERS ★

34 Number of states visited by George W. Bush during the presidential campaign

41 Number of states visited by Senator John Kerry

36 Number of visits made by Kerry to Ohio, the most by any candidate to one state

630,000 Total number of TV campaign commercials aired this election season

5,480 Number of campaign ads aired in Florida's Miami-Fort Lauderdale market during October

$1.45 billion Total spent at all levels on campaign advertising this year

$140 million Amount raised during the campaign by liberal 527 groups (non-profit organizations whose goal is to influence elections)

$75 million Amount raised by conservative 527 groups

2,256 Number of lawyers the Democrats sent to Ohio to monitor voting

8 Number of U.N. electoral assistance workers in Iraq

Samantha Appleton/Aurora

ELECTION ★ NOTEBOOK

★ VERBATIM ★

"My fellow Americans, this is the most important election of our lifetime."

JOHN KERRY,
Massachusetts Senator, accepting the Democratic nomination for President

"Trying to challenge the two-party dictatorship is like trying to climb a cliff with a slippery rope."

RALPH NADER,
independent candidate, who won less than 1% of national vote

"Jenna and I aren't very political, but we love our Dad too much to watch from the sidelines."

BARBARA BUSH,
23, on why she and her twin sister decided to campaign

"We promised ... that every vote would count and that every vote would be counted."

JOHN EDWARDS,
Democratic vice-presidential candidate, at 2:30 a.m. on Nov. 3, 2004, on why Kerry was holding back his concession

"I'll reach out to everyone who shares our goals."

GEORGE W. BUSH,
at his first post-election press conference, Nov. 5, 2004

★ A LOOK AT VOTER TURNOUT ★

More Americans voted for—and against—George W. Bush than for any other presidential candidate in U.S. history, and turnout was higher than in any election since 1968. Among 18- to 24-year-olds, turnout rose by 5.8 percentage points, with nearly 2 million more members of this age group voting than in 2000.

Turnout of Young Voters in Presidential Elections, 1972–2004

	1972	1976	1980	1984	1988	1992
% of 18- to 24-year-olds who voted	52%	45%	43%	44%	39%	46%
% of adults 25 and over who voted	68%	66%	66%	67%	64%	67%

	1996	2000	2004
% of 18- to 24-year-olds who voted	36%	36.5%	42.3%
% of adults 25 and over who voted	61%	64%	70%

Source: The Center for Information and Research on Civic Learning and Engagement; 2004 figures are preliminary estimates based on exit polls

★ WHAT HAPPENED IN THE SWING STATES ★

Three of the most intense battles between Kerry and Bush came in Pennsylvania, Ohio, and Florida, key swing states with a total of 68 electoral votes among them. While Kerry won in Pennsylvania, Bush carried Florida and Ohio. A Kerry win in either Florida or Ohio would have given him the White House.

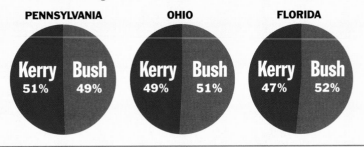

PENNSYLVANIA — Kerry 51% / Bush 49%
OHIO — Kerry 49% / Bush 51%
FLORIDA — Kerry 47% / Bush 52%

FOUR MORE YEARS

How the Bush team orchestrated its nail-biting win
By **NANCY GIBBS**

IN THE END, AN ELECTION that was supposed to be about all the ways the country is divided at least brought Americans together at 193,000 polling places in democracy's messy leap of faith. Turnout was huge even in states where the result was assured. In Ohio the polls closed at 7:30, but the lines were so long that people were still voting at midnight. Some people admitted they just did not want to face their neighbors or their children at the end of the day and say they had not bothered to show up. Others said if you don't vote, you can't complain and did not want to be silent at a time like this.

About 120 million Americans voted, 15 million more than in 2000. When the electoral votes were tallied, Republican George W. Bush had won 286 to Democrat John Kerry's 251. Of the three most hotly contested swing states, Kerry took Pennsylvania, while

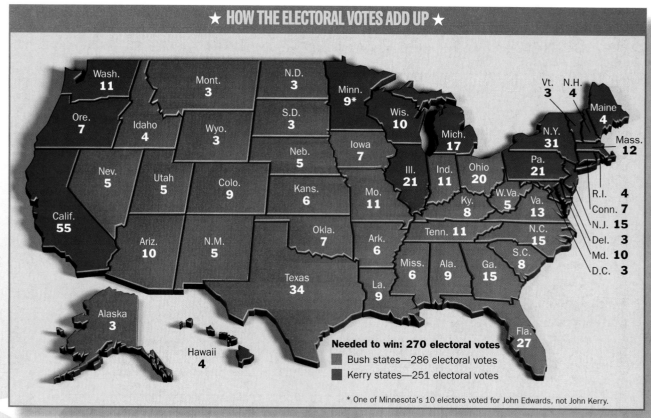

★ HOW THE ELECTORAL VOTES ADD UP ★

Wash. 11 · Mont. 3 · N.D. 3 · Minn. 9* · Vt. 3 · N.H. 4 · Maine 4
Ore. 7 · Idaho 4 · Wyo. 3 · S.D. 3 · Wis. 10 · Mich. 17 · N.Y. 31 · Mass. 12
Nev. 5 · Utah 5 · Colo. 9 · Neb. 5 · Iowa 7 · Ill. 21 · Ind. 11 · Ohio 20 · Pa. 21
Calif. 55 · Ariz. 10 · N.M. 5 · Kans. 6 · Mo. 11 · Ky. 8 · W.Va. 5 · Va. 13 · R.I. 4 · Conn. 7
Okla. 7 · Ark. 6 · Tenn. 11 · N.C. 15 · N.J. 15 · Del. 3 · Md. 10 · D.C. 3
Texas 34 · La. 9 · Miss. 6 · Ala. 9 · Ga. 15 · S.C. 8
Alaska 3 · Hawaii 4 · Fla. 27

Needed to win: 270 electoral votes
■ Bush states—286 electoral votes
■ Kerry states—251 electoral votes

* One of Minnesota's 10 electors voted for John Edwards, not John Kerry.

Bush snagged Florida and Ohio. Bush also became the first president since 1988 to win a majority of the popular vote, with about 51% to 48.5% for Kerry.

So consider the obstacles Bush overcame to win the hotly contested election. Since the country previously

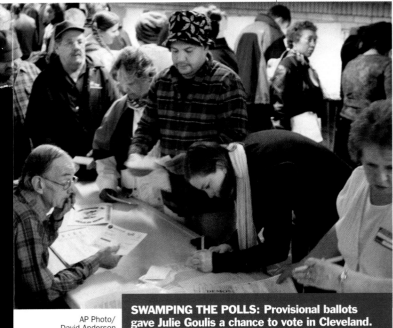

AP Photo/
David Anderson

SWAMPING THE POLLS: Provisional ballots gave Julie Goulis a chance to vote in Cleveland.

met at the polls, voters have encountered a record deficit, job losses, airport shoe searches, rising bankruptcies, and bruising battles over stem-cell research and the definition of marriage. On the eve of Election Day, fully 55% of voters said the country was moving in the wrong direction. Only 49% approved of the job the president was doing, and anything below 50% is supposed to be fatal to an incumbent. A war that Bush promised would cost no more than $50 billion a year

is running at nearly three times that. His character and values were attacked by well-organized detractors throughout the campaign. And he faced an opponent with a long record of public service, decorations from his service during the Vietnam War, and a Democratic base that had never been so united.

Bush says the war on terrorism is not a clash of civilizations, but this campaign was, by his careful design. He never really pretended to have much to say to Democrats beyond I will keep you safe. He relied largely instead on inspiring those who agreed with him already, who want to protect marriage as an institution, think stem-cell research has been oversold, and believe abortion is a sin. Even Republicans who disagreed with him on one or more issues—like the civil libertarians who would like the Patriot Act changed or the fiscal conservatives who worry about the massive national debt—are still willing to side with him.

His 97% approval rate within his party surpassed even Ronald Reagan's. Bush plainly understood that his best weapon against Kerry was less what Bush did than who he was. You may disagree with me, he said at every stop, but you know where I stand.

Overall, Bush succeeded in making Kerry appear an elitist defending moderation at a time when nothing less than passion would do. In Boston at their convention, the Democrats held a somber remembrance of 9/11. A month later in New York City, the Republicans unleashed a battle cry, and the contrast was plain: the party of victims vs. the party of warriors.

For Kerry supporters, there is some consolation that Bush will have to take responsibility for finishing what he started in Iraq. For Bush supporters, there is an obligation to recognize that the intense effort of the other side was as much an expression of love of country as any pledge, hymn, or flag. For people on both sides, there is relief that the day affirmed the sustaining virtue of American democracy. However fierce the battle and however high the stakes, on Election Day citizens go to the polls, close a curtain, and cast their vote—and then go home to honor the outcome because we have only one president at a time.

REPUBLICANS EXTEND CONTROL OF CONGRESS

G.O.P. Strengthens Its Decade-Long Grip on the House, Adds Senate Seats

REPUBLICANS PICKED up seats in both chambers of Congress on Election Day, leaving Speaker Dennis Hastert (R-IL) and Majority Leader Tom DeLay (R-TX) in charge of the House and toppling Tom Daschle (D-SD) from his post as Senate Minority Leader. The key to strengthening G.O.P. control of the House lay in Texas, where four incumbent Democrats lost

their seats as a result of a controversial redistricting plan backed by DeLay. This is the sixth consecutive election since 1994 in which Republicans have held a majority in the House.

Democrats had hoped to regain control of the Senate this year but wound up losing ground. They were defeated in several pivotal races, including those in Georgia, South Carolina, North Carolina, Alaska, and

Florida. Despite these losses, Senate Democrats will retain enough votes to make it hard for Republicans to pass legislation without opposition. That's because it takes 60 votes to end debate on a bill.

Given the makeup of the new Congress, Republicans say they'll push for approval of measures that have been stalled—including oil exploration in the Arctic National Wildlife Refuge and limits on lawsuits.

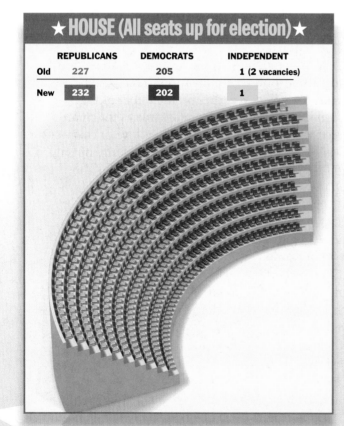

★ HOUSE (All seats up for election) ★

	REPUBLICANS	DEMOCRATS	INDEPENDENT
Old	227	205	1 (2 vacancies)
New	232	202	1

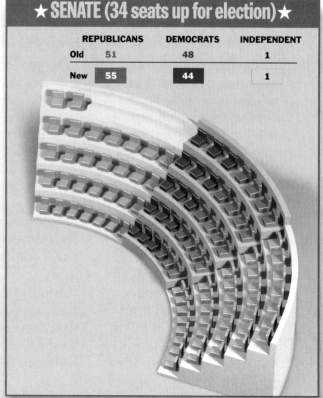

★ SENATE (34 seats up for election) ★

	REPUBLICANS	DEMOCRATS	INDEPENDENT
Old	51	48	1
New	55	44	1

Faces to watch in the 109th Congress

AP Photo/Doug Dreyer

★ SENATOR
JOHN THUNE (R-SD)

The Giant Killer

Elections are not just about votes. They're also about symbols. And for Senate Republicans, minority leader Tom Daschle has long been Moby Dick. Here was a Democrat from a solidly Republican state, South Dakota, who not only couldn't be defeated but also seemed to emerge from each electoral and legislative battle bigger and more powerful. So when John Thune arrives in Washington, he will not be just another freshman senator. He will be a conquering hero—the man who fulfilled the G.O.P.'s 18-year quest to unseat Daschle.

Thune, a former congressman, ran a profoundly focused race, taking every opportunity to remind voters that Daschle's positions on gun control and abortion set him at odds with "South Dakota values." But he did not bag his big game alone. Majority leader Bill Frist broke with Senate etiquette by visiting South Dakota to campaign for Daschle's ouster. In fact, the last time a Senate leader visited his opposite's state to rail against him was in 1900.

★ SENATOR
BARACK OBAMA (D-IL)

"We're All Connected"

In the past year, Barack Obama, 43, has been compared, in all seriousness, to Abraham Lincoln, Martin Luther King Jr., and Bill Clinton. Democrats debate whether he should run for President in 2012 or 2016. Following a landslide victory on Election Day, Obama became the only African American in the U.S. Senate— and just the third in the past 100 years.

AP Photo/Stephan Savoia

The turning point in Obama's career came in Boston on July 27, 2004, when he delivered one of the best speeches ever heard at a political convention. Facing thousands of Democrats, he spoke of a country not pockmarked by racism or fear— a place in which an African immigrant could marry a Midwestern white woman and their middle-class son could go to Harvard Law School. And he told the cheering crowd that "we're all connected as one people. If there is a child on the South Side of Chicago who can't read, that matters to me . . . If there's an Arab American family being rounded up without benefit of an attorney or due process, that threatens my civil liberties."

★ SENATOR
MEL MARTINEZ (R-FL)

The Tough-Talking Cuban

When Cuban parents launched Operation Pedro Pan in 1960, they were trying to get their children safely out of Cuba and into the U.S. Nobody knew then that one of those children—Mel Martinez— would go on to become the first Cuban American elected to the U.S. Senate. Martinez, now 58, served as Secretary of Housing and Urban Development from 2001 to 2003 and received strong support from the White House and Florida Governor Jeb Bush.

AP Photo/Chris Omeara

★ REPRESENTATIVE
ALLYSON SCHWARTZ (D-PA)

An Advocate for Children

As a state senator, Allyson Schwartz was called the "Mother of Pennsylvania Children's Health Insurance" for devising an insurance plan that many states later copied. Now she hopes to pass similar legislation on the federal level. Schwartz is one of 65 women who will serve in the House—a gain of five from the 108th Congress. Among the new faces are Melissa Bean (D-IL), who unseated Philip Crane, the longest-serving Republican in the House; and Gwen Moore (D-WI), the first African American to represent Wisconsin.

Courtesy Allyson Schwartz